Language, Eros, Being

ELLIOT R. WOLFSON

Language, Eros, Being

Kabbalistic Hermeneutics and Poetic Imagination

FORDHAM UNIVERSITY PRESS
New York / 2005

Library of Congress Cataloging-in-Publication Data

Wolfson, Elliot R.
Language, eros, being : kabbalistic hermeneutics and poetic imagination / Elliot R. Wolfson.—1st ed.
p. cm.
Includes bibliographical references and index.
ISBN 0-8232-2418-X (hardcover) — ISBN 0-8232-2419-8 (pbk.)
1. Cabala—History. 2. Masculinity of God. 3. Femininity of God. 4. Poetics. 5. Imagination—Religious aspects—Judaism. 6. Hermeneutics—Religious aspects—Judaism. I. Title.
BM526.W644 2004
296.1′6—dc22 2004022169

Printed in the United States of America
07 06 05 6 5 4 3 2 1
First edition

Making a book could mean exchanging the *void of writing* for *writing the void.*

—Edmond Jabès, *The Book of Margins*

Writing unfolds like a game that invariably goes beyond its own rules and transgresses its limits. In writing, the point is not to manifest or exalt the act of writing, nor is it to pin a subject within language; it is rather a question of creating a space into which the writing subject constantly disappears.

—Michel Foucault, "What Is an Author?"

Charles Mopsik
in memoriam

Oublions d'espérer. Discrète et contenue,
Que l'âme de chacun de nous deux continue
Ce calme et cette mort sereine du soleil.

—Paul Verlaine, *Circonspection*

Contents

	Preface	xi
	Prologue: Timeswerve/Hermeneutic Reversibility	xv
1	Showing the Saying: Laying Interpretative Ground	1
2	Differentiating (In)Difference: Heresy, Gender, and Kabbalah Study	46
3	Phallomorphic Exposure: Concealing Soteric Esotericism	111
4	Male Androgyne: Engendering E/Masculation	142
5	Flesh Become Word: Textual Embodiment and Poetic Incarnation	190
6	Envisioning Eros: Poiesis and Heeding Silence	261
7	Eunuchs Who Keep Sabbath: Erotic Asceticism / Ascetic Eroticism	296
8	Coming-to-Head, Returning-to-Womb: (E)Soteric Gnosis and Overcoming Gender Dimorphism	333
	Epilogue	372
	Notes	391
	Bibliography	599
	Index of Names and Book Titles	715
	Index of Subjects and Terms	729

Preface

In taking the poets as testimony for things unknown,
they are citing authorities that cannot be trusted.

—Heraclitus

In the conclusion of his remarks upon receiving the 1977 Bialik Prize, Gershom Scholem commented:

> The discovery of the tremendous poetic potential within Kabbalah, in its own language no less than in its poetry proper, which has also come down to us with great richness—all these constitute a realm which has hardly been examined and which holds the promise of great discoveries. . . . the tools have not yet been created for understanding the lyric plane within language of the Kabbalists and the Hasidim. Without creating these tools, this question cannot be fully encompassed. My own secret longing to do so has not been fulfilled and remains unsatisfied. Thus, at the conclusion of my remarks, allow me to express the wish that we may look forward to someone who will remove the dust hiding the true face of such books as *Sefer ha-Temunah*, *Berit Menuḥah*, or *Ḥemdat Yamim*, to reveal the poetic depths in their imagery and that of many similar books.[1]

When I happened upon the study of Jewish mysticism over two decades ago, of course, I could not have had any idea that the words of Scholem would serve as the guideword on my path, an evocation at the beginning, challenging and leading me on the way to crafting a poetics of kabbalah. It is futile to wonder if Scholem would have approved my attempts to heed the poetic assonance reverberating in the intricate imaginary worlds described in kabbalistic lore, but that matters little in accepting the responsibility of relating my work to him and expressing thereby gratitude of the highest order for a scholar, the thanking of thinking in the footsteps of the other.[2]

My first major gesture in this direction was *Through a Speculum That Shines: Vision and Imagination in Medieval Judaism*, published in 1994. In that work, I set out to lay the groundwork for theorizing a poetics of kabbalah by investigating the phenomenological contours of the contemplative envisioning of the divine in the history of Jewish mysticism, highlighting especially the configuration of God's luminous forms in the shape of an anthropos within the imagination. In consonance with the teachings of mystic visionaries in various traditions, kabbalists assent to the view that the primary task of the imaginative faculty is to depict imaginally what is without image, to embody that which is not a body, to give form to the formless.[3] The imagination is not, as Hobbes put it, a "*decaying sense*,"[4] but it is, rather, in Henry Corbin's telling phrase, the "psychospiritual" faculty, usually identified in medieval sources as the heart, the "intermediate plane" of the "Imaginative Presence," the *coincidentia oppositorum* of the hidden and manifest.[5]

A terse but far-reaching articulation of the phenomenological import of prophetic visualization may be detected in *3 Enoch*, the *Hebrew Apocalypse of Enoch*, also transmitted as *Sefer Heikhalot* or *Pirqei Rabbi Yishma'el*, a text whose date and provenance is uncertain though it is has been conservatively traced to the fifth or sixth centuries.[6] A reliable *terminus a quo* is difficult to determine for, as Philip S. Alexander judiciously put it, the work is "not the total product of a single author at a particular point in time, but the deposit of a 'school tradition' which incorporates elements from widely different periods."[7] A reasonable *terminus ad quem*, however, can be established in the tenth century, since at this historical juncture the influence of the text is discernible. The traditions preserved within the contours of this textual accretion indicate a conflation of Palestinian and Babylonian sources. The historiographical qualms notwithstanding, what is crucial for my philosophical standpoint is the technical expression that appears near the beginning of the text to denote the contemplative vision. Metatron, whose identity as Enoch has not yet been revealed, beckons the ascending R. Ishmael, "Come in peace into the presence of the high and exalted King to behold the likeness of the chariot."[8] R. Ishmael will achieve the climax of the otherworldly journey when he enters in peace before the divine glory—the *yeridah la-merkavah* according to my interpretation[9]—in order to behold the likeness of the chariot, *lehistakkel bi-demut ha-merkavah*. I would render this richly nuanced idiom "to envision the image of the chariot," that is, to conjure through contemplation the enthronement of the celestial king, the glorification of the divine—the mythopoeic underpinning of the figurative representation in anthropomorphic form—envisioned in gender terms as the masculine glory uniting with the feminine throne. The predicate *lehistakkel* is literally to gaze, but in this context it has the more specific connotation to contemplate by forming a mental image. *Demut*, similarly, is an expression with deep poetic assonance, and particularly important is the appearance of this term in Ezekiel's vision of the chariot in conjunction with various entities that constitute the architecture of the imaginal realm of the *merkavah*. We would do well, therefore, to render *demut* as verbal image, word-picture in the Wittgensteinian sense, a term that bespeaks the convergence of showing and saying, a theme that will be exposed in chapter one. To contemplate the image of the chariot is to envision the glory on the throne, a gazing that is possible only to the extent that the one gazing is circumscribed within the field of what is gazed upon; the conventional epistemological distinction between subject and object no longer pertains, as the seeing of the image of the chariot presupposes that one has been incorporated into the very image that is seen.

In the aforementioned monograph, I identified as a principal, if not exclusive, textual basis for the phenomenological affirmation of absence and presence with respect to God the prophecy of Ezekiel, the exiled priest who had visions of God's glory within the spatial boundaries of Babylonia. It is difficult to offer a definition of mysticism that would adequately cover all of the phases and stages of Jewish history, but a recurrent theme in Jewish mystical texts has been the desire to experience what prophets of yore experienced, envisioning the presence, the glory of the Lord, *kevod yhwh*, in forms forbidden for priests and other Israelites to worship iconically, though seemingly permissible for poets to depict imaginally. That is, ancient Israelite culture was distinguished from its neighboring societies by the explicit injunction against worshipping an idol of God—even though both textual and archaeological evidence indicate that the deuteronomistic-priestly sanction was not always observed by the populace—but this did not stop poetic souls, whose words are preserved in works of prophecy, from depicting God in very graphic form.

Like the prophets of old, albeit in fundamentally different historical circumstances, medieval kabbalists cultivated simultaneously a rich iconography and a vigorous iconoclasm—an unyielding and aggressive rejection of the physical representation of God, on the one hand, and an amplification of bold mythical imagery to depict God, on the other.[10] It is precisely the aniconism—the prohibition of representing God in pictorial forms—that fostered a remarkable imaginative representation of the nonrepresentable in ancient Israelite/Judean prophecy and its mystical aftermath through the centuries, where specific meditational practices were cultivated for the stated aim of attaining a vision of the invisible. The locus of that gnosis was typically situated in the heart/imagination of the visionary, the site where the routine division between inside and outside is dissolved in the theophanic play of double mirroring, the heart mirroring the image that mirrors the image of the heart. From that vantage point we can speak accurately of kabbalah as *speculative* theosophy, that is, a wisdom of God that is discerned in the mirror (*speculum*) of the enlightened mind/heart that reflects the immanence of the divine light refracted in the world of discriminate beings as well as the transcendent power of the true divine being, which is without form or image.[11]

A distinctive feature of the kabbalist visionary tradition, based on older sources, revolves about the specular entwining of anthropomorphism and theomorphism: envisioning the divine as human mirrors envisioning the human as divine. The mirror imaging is expressed even more precisely in Jewish esoteric gnosis in terms of the correlation of anthropomorphic imagery and letter symbolism. The human form by which the divine is visually contemplated is equated with the letters of the name, an idea expressed by the numerical equivalence of *adam* and the letters of the Tetragrammaton when spelled out in full, *ywd he waw he*. To see the glorious light is to contemplate the name, which is identified, moreover, as Torah, the root word whence the other letters of the Hebrew alphabet, the matrix language of creation, sprout forth. By confronting the imaginary configuration of the divine, we took the initial step on the way to articulating philosophically the poiesis propelling the elaborate symbol-making in the physiognomy of kabbalah.

With this volume, *Language, Eros, Being: Kabbalistic Hermeneutics and Poetic Imagination*, I offer a second attempt to disentangle the threads of the inaugurating vision with an eye to elucidating the ascetic underpinnings of the imaginal inscription of the divine body/name in overtly erotic terms. As I assume there is no form—sentient or imagined—that is not embodied, even the form of the formless, and there is no embodiment that is not engendered, even the invisible astral body, *corpus sidereum*, it is incumbent on me to delve deeper into the question of gender signification in the symbolic lifeworld of kabbalah. Building on previous studies, I make a case once more for the monolithic nature of gender symbolism in kabbalistic literature, showing how the feminine has been viewed as ontically derivative of the masculine, an idea, I hasten to add, hardly unique to the androcentrism of traditional kabbalah.[12] The emphasis on the ascetic turn of the erotic imagination will, I hope, bring my earlier work on phallomorphism and homoeroticism into clearer focus.

Let me conclude these prefatory remarks by noting that I am mindful, all too diminutively, that there is no one definitive way to illumine the theme of this analysis. Ultimately, as Heidegger reminded us with respect to Hölderin's poetry, every way is errant.[13] The undertaking of this book, accordingly, may swirl its way to being undermined, as it will inevitably lead, if faithful to the trace of its own calling, to speaking what cannot be spoken in unspeaking what has been spoken. In that reticence radiates the epiphany of not-showing encountered repeatedly in and on the course of reading.

Prologue: Timeswerve/Hermeneutic Reversibility

Ring them bells, ye heathen
From the city that dreams,
Ring them bells from the sanctuaries
Cross the valleys and streams,
For they're deep and they're wide
And the world's on its side
And time is running backwards
And so is the bride.

—Bob Dylan, "Ring Them Bells"

The figures I shall discuss in chapter one are philosophers who for years have accompanied me on the path of an often relentless attempt to elucidate hermeneutical assumptions in the hope of illumining the mystery of the imaginative faculty and *ars poetica*. The field of my vision, so to speak, has been leveled, to the degree that is possible, by a focus on kabbalistic sources ranging from the twelfth to the twenty-first centuries, a large temporal swath by anyone's account. The use of German and French philosophers primarily from the nineteenth and twentieth centuries to interpret texts of traditional kabbalah, whose ideas may be ancient but whose incipient articulation in a Hebrew idiom is to be traced to a rich creative period from the twelfth to fourteenth century, demands a defense against the obvious charge of anachronism.

Telling of Time in Time of Telling

I begin by stating unequivocally that I seek not to validate my account on historical grounds. Whether or not any of the thinkers to be discussed in chapter one has had direct or indirect connection with kabbalah is not a necessary condition to justify the employment of their insights in decoding this singularly complex expression of the Jewish religious imagination. Nonetheless, one cannot by any means rule out such links. On this score, it is of interest to ponder the possibility that Western esoteric speculation, which is greatly indebted to kabbalistic tradition, has had an impact on the history of linguistics, especially evident in the period of Romanticism and its aftermath, including Heidegger, well versed in the theosophy of Böhme[1] and its reverberations in the idealist philosophy of Schelling.[2]

Let me reiterate that in spite of the possibility and even likelihood of textual influence, my argument rests on a different foundation. Without ignoring or even rejecting the tacit assumption of classical philology that the competent scholar can reconstruct historical-literary settings, I am not certain this approach should be granted hegemony in the pursuit of hermeneutic discernment. To discredit philology would be to discard one of the most important tools in the effort to discern authorial intent, but this is not the only matter relevant to the construal of meaning and truth. To think otherwise would be to lapse uncritically into the lair of positivism. The issue is expressed with unusual clarity by Dan Lusthaus in the preface to his impressive phenomenological study of the Yogācāra tradition of Buddhism in India and China:

> The move from philology to philosophy does not entail a rejection of philology. On the contrary, philology is one of the necessary foundations on which philosophical investigations into systems remote in time and language stand. Without carefully establishing realistic and judicious limits through meticulous philological and historical work on the range of hermeneutic possibilities offered by a bare text, philosophical speculation can easily lead itself astray. Nonetheless, it is also necessary to eventually go beyond merely doing philology, in order to explore what a text *means* rather than merely collating it with materials related to it, or assigning it an historical spot, or detailing its social significance and context.[3]

As a methodological axiom, therefore, it is valid to assert that hermeneutical beliefs cannot to be separated from suppositions regarding temporality.[4] In Heideggerian terms, the historiographical project, the writing of history, is bolstered by a chronological conjecture with respect to speaking/thinking of time; but to speak or to think of time is to be caught in an extenuating circularity: my telling of time cannot be disentangled from my time of telling. It is important to note here a shift from the Husserlian project of dissociating time from the inner sense of internal time-consciousness to the project of thinking *chronos*, the "spacing of time,"[5] not, however, in the sense that Bergson criticized—calculating the stream of time in measurable points on a chronometer—but in the poeticized manner of being open to being that is open, cracking the time line at its seam, as it were, to expand the horizon beyond the limit of limitlessness that perforce limits the limitlessness of limit.[6] For most, I suppose, chronology—and the historical narrative we construct on its basis—extends orderly, even if impenetrably, from beginning to end, but for some doubtless it proceeds from end to beginning, and for still others, probably fewer, it rebounds like a boomerang from middle to middle, starting and finishing always in between.

The philologist's privileging of historical proximity in determining lexicography is predicated on the assumption regarding the linear character of time—the quadrant of the circle is partitioned by imaginary time lines—just as the cartographer assumes a linear grid in charting spatial dimensions even though scientific evidence indicates that the geometric character of space is cylindrical. The sequential model, however, is only one possible explanation—reinforced by a pervasive pragmatism that presumes the forward motion of time's arrow and the chain of causal efficiency that serves as foundation for our sense of predictable patterns of behavior in nature—but it is by no means the view uniformly affirmed by physicists, astrologists, cosmologists, mathematicians, or philosophers of science. Without delving into the thicket of theoretic grappling that this subject demands, I pose the rhetorical question: What would be the consequences if a historian were to take seriously the conclusion reached on the basis of Einstein's General Theory of Relativity that spacetime—the "mathematical structure" that "serves as a unifying causal background for phenomena"[7]—is to be regarded as a curve?[8] Does this does not at least entail the possibility that the past is as much determined by the present as the present by the past?

Spacetime and the Looping of the Line

The theoretical implications of Einstein's insights relative to the issue at hand were drawn explicitly by Hermann Weyl, who noted that in a spacetime with a specific gravitational arrangement, a person's "world line"—that is, one's trajectory in the fourth dimension—might loop back and intersect with itself. The possibility of future connecting with past, of time moving backwards, "arises because a gravitational field implies that spacetime is curved, and the curvature might be great enough and extended enough to join a spacetime to itself in novel ways."[9] In the temporal continuum, which presents itself in intuition as "a fluid whole rather than a set of discrete elements,"[10] the individual time-point exists only as a "transition point."[11] When the movement is considered mathematically, "the continuum of path-points *spreads over* the continuum of time-points in a continuous monotone manner."[12] From an alternative perspective, however, the continuous flow of phenomenal time exemplifies a "connectivity arising from the non-independence of the individual points,"[13] and hence it follows that the trajectory of the curve, "the *path* of a moving point," which is "spread out over both space and time,"[14] makes possible the return to the point of departure and departure from the point of arrival, a closed loop figuratively depicting the object/subject becoming its own past. Time reversal, therefore, does not, theoretically, imply a mechanical retracing of previous moments but circumambulating the curve, going back to the future and arriving at the past.[15] Alternatively expressed, to posit the legitimate possibility of time reversal rests on the presumption regarding the relativity of simultaneity, which in turn renders the distinction between past, present, and future, as Einstein put it when receiving news of the death of his friend Michele Besso, "a stubbornly persistent illusion."[16]

In order to prevent potential misinterpretation on the part of my readers, let me state unequivocally that the reversibility of time that I wish to affirm is not a reiteration of the myth of cosmic reversal articulated by Plato, a version of the doctrine of the eternal recurrence of the same predicated on the assumption that as the cosmos rotates in one direction due to the agency of the transcendent cause, it stores up the energy to revolve in the opposite direction of its own accord,[17] a notion that can be properly criticized on grounds that it denies the indeterminacy of future eventualities. Here it is apposite to recall Alfred North Whitehead's claim that time exhibits the quality of "irreversibility." In a move intending to escape binary oppositions, Whitehead insists that this irreversibility is dependent on the "cumulative character of time,"[18] which arises, in turn, from the "concrescence" of "actual entities" or "actual occasions"[19] through a process of prehension that affects the "passage of the cause into the effect" such that the "past has an objective existence in the present which lies in the future beyond itself. . . . Cut away the future, and the present collapses, emptied of its proper content. Immediate existence requires the insertion of the future in the crannies of the present."[20] Reversibility, on this account, entails the presentational immediacy of a temporal atomicity,[21] the novel recurrence and spontaneous reenactment of a moment that has never been, and consequently the past is no more determinate of the future than the future is of the past, both living on and through the indeterminate present.[22]

Moreover, the link I discern between the curvature of time and the symbolic imagination does not depend, as it does in the case of Corbin's phenomenology of the *mundus imaginalis*, on discarding "causal historical filiation" in favor of the "continuity of 'hierophanic time,' "[23] "a discontinuous, qualitative, pure, psychic time" that is distinguished categorically from "quantitative physical time . . . measured according to homogeneous, uniform units of time and chronology regulated by the movements of the stars."[24] I agree with Corbin that a deeper temporal experience entails an intensity that measures time "in which the past remains present to the future, in which the future is already present to the past, just as the notes of a musical phrase, though played successively, nevertheless persist all together in the present and thus form a phrase." Yet I cannot accept the binary opposition he draws (in part indebted to Eliade's dichotomy of the sacred/eternal and profane/historical) by ascribing cyclical time to a "transhistoric truth" and linear time to "material historic truth."[25] My argument rests on taking seriously an alternative understanding of time as a reversible swerve, a scientific perspective that conflicts with the commonsensical view of time's irreversible linearity.

Let me refer briefly to a learned summation of the subject by the philosopher Barry Dainton in the elucidation of the phenomenon of "time in reverse." Dainton proposes a thought experiment that rests on the hypothesis that we live in a "Gold universe," so named after the physicist Thomas Gold, who raised the profile of the model of a symmetrical universe in the 1960s, that is, a universe whose time line is extended proportionately between two end points.[26] The symmetry of the imaginary termini is explicable on the hypothesis that if there is enough mass in the universe, then at some point in the future, gravitational forces will cause the universe to fall back on itself—even if we assume, as current astrophysicists suggest on the basis of examining telescopic images from the outermost reaches of intergalactic space, that the universe is expanding and hence exhibits a negative energy, an energy that would challenge the intractability of the laws of gravitation, an antigravity, as it is commonly called. If the end point we call the "beginning" is envisioned as the "big bang," the end point that is the end relative to that beginning will be the "big crunch."

There are, however, two ways to explain the symmetry. According to one, entropy is low at the beginning and progressively expands until the end; and according to the other, entropy increases until the contraction sets in and then it begins to diminish. The logical projectile of the second possibility leads to positing a perfectly symmetrical universe balanced by a "singularity" at either end of the space-time spectrum—a "dimensionless point of infinite density." If we assume this to be the case, it follows that the sequence of events would run a parallel but inverse course from each singularity to the midpoint. Contrary to the widespread conviction of the irreversibility of time, Dainton reminds the reader that there are many scientists who "believe that the laws of fundamental physics are time-reversible, in which case any physical process can run in reverse. But in addition we must take care not to assume that *our* way of looking at things is in any way privileged."[27]

To be sure, as Dainton also notes, not all interpreters of quantum theory accept the proposition that the laws of nature are fully time-reversible, arguing that there is an asymmetry between past and future—past and present may be fixed, but future is indeterminate.[28] For the purpose of this discussion, I will ignore the latter and consider only the implications of the former for the very prospect that nature's laws—the laws by which we impute a nature to the coalescence of imagined realities, even when we lapse and say there is no nature—exhibit this quality of time reversibility, the temporal swerve. This possibility pushes the hermeneutical issue in question to the surface. Imagining reversibility undermines absolute certainty in ascribing the term "beginning" to one end point and "end" to the other, since there is no way of falsifying the claim that what appears as end to us might appear as beginning to an observer surveying the sequence in reverse order.[29] In a perfectly symmetrical universe, we cannot dispose of the possibility of a sentient being seeing straightforwardly what we see invertedly. If this is so, and seemingly there is no reason to doubt that it is so, then what we imagine as the end must logically be the beginning for one looking from the other end of a particular curve. On the grander, cosmological scale, if from our vantage point the cosmos manifests "inflationary expansion," for one on the other end that property would be regarded as "gravitational implosion."

Time's Other: *Coincidentia Oppositorum*

I would propose that the scientific premise briefly outlined above confirms a hermeneutical criterion of truth that has been often associated with mystical consciousness, an archaic logic—decidedly non-Aristotelian—that paradoxically affirms the identity of opposites in virtue of their difference, an orientation that gained special prominence through the promulgation of the doctrine of *coincidentia oppositorum* by Nicholas Cusanus in fifteenth-century Italy.[30] According to Aristotle's excluded middle, the structure of grammatical syntax leads one necessarily to the logically sanctioned subject that bears opposite qualities—simultaneously, however, and not concurrently—that is, for instance, the face is black or white, black then white, or white then black, but not white and black at the same time and in the same relation. Cusanus, by contrast, posits that both polarities subsist at the same moment, thus leading to his signature notion of a coincidence of opposites. The validity of this surmise can be gainsaid by the simple observation that if what we consider to be "first" can be considered at the same time "last"—a conclusion discussed above—then the thing so considered must be both first and last at the same time and in the same relation, itself and its other.

From this thought experiment we can deduce that there is no necessary correlation between causal sequence and the direction of time, the "causal arrow" and "world arrow," since we can reasonably imagine—and the epistemic criterion here is simply to be able to imagine, for the hypothetical is sufficient to make the theoretical point whose validity is not dependent on empirical verification[31]—time-reversed counterparts existing in a situation where the world arrow would point in the opposite direction to the causal arrow. Even more perplexing is the realization that there is no final certainty about the directional vicissitude of our own standpoint, our angle of vision. If we start from the premise that laws of physics (according to mechanics and electrodynamics) are time-symmetrical, a reasonable if not demonstrable premise, there is no way out of the logical conundrum that what appears to us as cause may itself be effect or, perhaps better expressed, is both cause and effect contemporaneously. The time line, accordingly, would have to be measured independently of empirical patterns of change and variation, and, properly speaking, this computation would undermine any claim to ultimate, exclusive, or even privileged validity of the so-called "transmission model of causality"[32] and its implicit linear and hierarchical structuring of experience.[33]

The critique of time as absolute simultaneity sets into sharp relief a genetic fallacy of historical positivism and opens the way to brood over the reversibility of the temporal flow; the past may not, after all, extend monodirectionally into the present, which was its future, but rather may swerve its way curvilinearly, future awaiting its past, past becoming its future. We could, then, think of time's motion as comprising two movements—procession and return—following exactly the same pattern of development in different directions.[34] Would the relativization of knowledge implied by the historicist premise not have to be adjusted, or the very least defended, by a more careful taxonomy if one were to accept (not just on poetic grounds but scientifically) that the way forward is the way back; the way back, the way forward?[35]

One might respond that a distinction is still in order between the microscopic and macroscopic perspectives, and since the former is more germane to our empirical reality, the claim that time unfolds linearly is methodologically cogent to yield knowledge of the past about which we feel confident enough to judge regarding its accuracy, legitimacy, and veracity.[36] I would counter that this distinction is valid to a point, but beyond that point to continue to affirm it would be to beg the question. If it is acknowledged that at the macrolevel, time ideationally displays the trait of reversibility, one cannot rest easy with the conclusion that at the microlevel, time is irreversible. Utilizing basic geometric principles, which in some measure still prevail as providing the framework within which quantitative analyses of physical occurrences are proffered, we would say that micro and macro can be related in one of three ways: as skewed, intersecting, or parallel.[37] If the first option, then the two would have to be considered utterly distinct, as the very term "skewed" technically denotes lying on different and unrelated planes, but, if that is the case, then the two time axes would have to be interpreted anisotropically, that is, one would have to assume the possibility that events on the two planes transpire in distinct temporal directions, presumably exemplifying random sequences in relation to one another, a proposition that would make it impossible to determine the direction of the time flow in either one of the planes, since the prospective alternative frame of reference (what we may call the hyperplane) has been rendered irrelevant;[38] if the second option, then at some axial point the two crisscross; and if the third option, then the two spheres are to be conceived as coplanar lines that at every point on the axis would have to demonstrate symmetry demanded by the mathematical requirement that at every point two parallel lines are equidistant from one another.[39] From this it follows, if not empirically then at least theoretically, that the apparent irreversibility of time in the intersubjective sphere must be squared away with the reversibility of time manifest in the plane of "irreality" where explanatory models evolve and hit the "ground" running, so to speak, in accord with a calibration that may not readily suit the calculating conquest of time to which we seem so beholden.

Time Reversibility/Telescopically Envisioned

A similar appeal to the reversibility of time and the implicit objection to a principle of successive causality—the serial constitution in and through a threefold continuum measured by the retentional, impressional, and protentional nodes of consciousness—can be elicited from an entirely different intellectual base, the ontological phenomenology of Merleau-Ponty, a sphere of thinking more congruent with my own philosophic disposition and training.[40] In comparison with the scientific account explored above, I shall labor a bit more on the pathways of Merleau-Ponty's thinking, as in his thought I find an affinity with the understanding I have derived from the study of kabbalistic literature and consequently feel it is legitimate to use his jargon to formulate hermeneutical and phenomenological suppositions in reading these sources. In spite of the incongruity between my treatment of Merleau-Ponty and quantum physics, it is significant that the engagement with the former has been set in dialogue with the latter. Methodologically, the appeal is to apply a natural scientific model of time to the humanist effort to understand historical experience.

As a way into the topic in Merleau-Ponty's writings, we might say that the phenomenon of time reversibility, for him, is contemplated from within the frame of the reversibility of seeing/being seen, that is, a doubling of vision—the inherent reflexivity of the perceptual—that maintains identity of difference in difference of identity.[41] Reversibility, in short, is a basic feature of time and perception, two poles of Merleau-Ponty's ontology of alterity.[42] Time and perception, in turn, are entwisted in the tangle of language, the bridge that (dis)joins world and consciousness, a theme that I will explore in more depth in the following chapter.

Particularly relevant to the discussion here is Merleau-Ponty's response to Saussure's distinction between "synchronic linguistics of speech," *une linguistique synchronique de la parole*, and "diachronic linguistics of a language," *une linguistique diachronique de la langue.*[43] In Merleau-Ponty's opinion, we are to conceive synchrony and diachrony as enveloping rather than opposing one another. By undercutting this polarity, one can entertain the possibility that a linguistic system "never exists wholly in act but always involves latent or incubating changes. It is never composed of absolutely univocal meanings which can be made completely explicit beneath the gaze of transparent constituting consciousness."[44] Language is uncertain—of this we can be certain; words are not blocks cemented in place but rather stones drifting this way, floating that way, synchronically, diachronically, two equal measures of time, returning forward, advancing backward.

We have already, perhaps too abruptly, put our finger on the thread that ties together language and time in Merleau-Ponty's thinking (a theme that will be especially relevant in the ensuing analyses)—the quality of openness, indeterminacy, or, in technical philosophical parlance, transcendence. The resistance to ontological finality and the polyvalence implied thereby lies at the heart of Merleau-Ponty's *philosophie de l'ambiguïté.*[45] Hence, in the context of remarking on the "sexual atmosphere" of intersubjective interplay in *Phénoménologie de la perception*, Merleau-Ponty noted that "ambiguity is of the essence of human existence, and everything we live or think has always several meanings."[46] The insistence on ambiguity has to be seen as a response to the "structuralist attitude," which he tellingly describes as the "intent to circumscribe the act of speaking where it is *formed* . . . the intent to return to the originating, to the *Ursprung* . . . the intent to grasp the cohesion of the synchronic-diachronic whole within speech, the *monumental* speech, therefore, mythical, if one likes." This concise but incisive account of structuralism is immediately followed by what may be one of Merleau-Ponty's most profound, albeit cryptic, articulations of the hermeneutical basis of his phenomenological ontology: "Ambiguity of the constitutive act of science: the exclusive attention to the verbal chain, to phonics and semantics *intertwined*, is: 1st, the exigency to grasp the *Ursprung Entdeckung* of the *Ursprung*. 2d, the reduction to the *Gegenstand*, i.e. *Verdeckung* of the *Ursprung*."[47]

In this comment, if we are attentively attuned, we may discern the ground in which Merleau-Ponty's affirmation of temporal reversibility is anchored, a ground that will serve as my own springboard. To articulate a synchronic-diachronic whole within speech—that would surely constitute "monumental," even "mythical," speech, as Merleau-Ponty suggests. Attaining such a whole, however, is not possible from our perceptual standpoint. Relying on the opinion of the linguists of his day, Merleau-Ponty contends that:

> univocal signification is but one part of the signification of the word, that beyond it there is always a halo of signification that manifests itself in new and unexpected modes of use, that there is an operation of language upon language which, even without other incitements, would launch language back into a new history, and makes of the word-meaning itself an enigma. Far from harboring the secret of the being of the world, language is itself a world, itself a being—a world and a being to the second power, since it does not speak in a vacuum, since it speaks *of* being and *of* the world and therefore redoubles their enigma instead of dissipating it.[48]

Indeed, as Merleau-Ponty insists, the dynamics of perception and the syntax of language are both chiasmic; just as no word can render meaning so transparent that the need for interpretation is eradicated, so the gap that abides between seer and seen assures one that what one is seeing will never be the whole of it.[49] In line with Nietzsche's perspectivism, Merleau-Ponty remarks that the sensible thing "is not really *observable*: there is always a skipping over in every observation, one is never at the thing itself."[50] Merleau-Ponty concurs with those who would argue that to see is to have "something" (*etwas*), but that something is always subject to "infinite analysis,"[51] and hence one can never say that "something" has been seen. Rejecting the identification of substance as a "spatio-temporally individuated this," an idea well entrenched in Western philosophy and science, Merleau-Ponty wrote, *il n'y a que des rayonnements d'essences (verbales), il n'y pas d'insécables spatio-temporels. La chose sensible elle-même est portée par une transcendance* ("there are only radiations of (verbal) essences, there are no spatio-temporal indivisibles. The sensible thing itself is borne by a transcendency").[52] Sensible beings, or what we perceive to be such, are "radiations of verbal essences"—a notion that resonates with a central imaginal modality of Jewish esotericism, as will be discussed on many occasions in this monograph.

In a passage penned near the end of his "working notes," which extended from January 1959 to March 1961, Merleau-Ponty remarked, somewhat playfully, "vision is tele-vision, transcendence, crystallization of the impossible."[53] Insofar as visible objects can never be seen in their entirety, all vision must be considered "tele-vision," literally, seeing-afar, the very impossibility that renders vision possible. That which I see, I see because what I see cannot be seen but as that which is not seen, transcendency, the nothing it is perceived (not) to be. I shall return to the confluence of the visible and invisible in Merleau-Ponty's phenomenology later in my analysis, but what is worthy to add at this juncture is that the imperceptibility of perception results from what Merleau-Ponty calls the "reconquest of the *Lebenswelt*," that is, the "reconquest of a *dimension*, in which the objectifications of science themselves retain a meaning and are to be understood as true . . . the pre-scientific is only an invitation to comprehend the meta-scientific and this last is not non-science."[54] The metascientific, as the prescientific, is not to be confused with nonscience, for it does not necessitate the dissolution of scientific objectification and mathematical calculation. Yet it is clearly beyond the scientific, for the *Lebenswelt*, in Merleau-Ponty's judgment, is the "universal Being" that is "non-thematized."[55] In the reconquest of the lifeworld, we thus discern the mutuality of ostensibly conflicting impulses: the urge to uncover, on the one hand, and the discovery that every uncovering is a covering over, on the other. As it happens, in English, the word "recover" uncovers the paradox, for it means both "to expose" and "to conceal."

For Merleau-Ponty, synchrony and diachrony are harnessed together in a "specular image" seen through the double mirror of body and world in the "perceptual lived experience" (*vécu perceptif*)[56] of the *Lebenswelt*,[57] but he questioned the assumption that they form a coherent whole; on the contrary, the pairing of the two suggests fragmentation, breaking open the verbal/visual chain to a link beyond the phonic and optic, "to the absolute, to the transcendental field, to the wild and 'vertical' being" (*lêtre sauvage et "vertical"*), the passage to which is "by definition progressive, incomplete."[58] If we are to use the language of totality, *Gestalt*, it is precisely in the sense of positing "transcendence, being at a distance . . . inflated with non-being or with the possible, that it is not only *what it is* (*gonflé de non-être ou de possible, qu'il n'est pas ce qu'il est seulement*). . . . It is openness (*Elle est ouverture*)."[59]

Perception presupposes a *Gestalt*, yet the latter does not entail "imposition of an essence, a *vor-stellen*,"[60] but rather "openness," the "non-explicated horizon,"[61] "wild or brute Being" (*l'Être sauvage ou brut*),[62] the "common tissue of which we are made."[63] The intricate connection of time, language, and perception is made explicit in the following passage:

> Understand that the *Gestalt* is already transcendence: it makes me understand that a line is a vector, that a point is a center of forces—There are neither absolute lines nor points nor colors in the things. . . . We have to pass from the thing (spatial or temporal) as identity, to the thing (spatial or temporal) as difference, i.e. as transcendence, i.e. as always "behind," beyond, far-off . . . the present itself is not an absolute coincidence without transcendence . . . the present, also, is ungraspable from close-up, in the forceps of attention, it is an encompassing.[64]

The unraveling of this complex philosophical matter requires a sustained reflection on time consciousness and historical intentionality, a task that clearly lies beyond the scope of this prologue.[65] Suffice it to say, however, that if linearity is not the determinative characteristic of time, common sense and pragmatic concern notwithstanding, then there is no compelling reason to privilege a hermeneutical approach based on a serialized conception of history as the only or even the best way to narrate the historical account. On the contrary, as Merleau-Ponty counseled the reader, "we must recognize that the present diffuses into the past to the extent that the past has been present. History is the history of successive synchronies, and the contingency of the linguistic past invades even the synchronic system."[66]

The plausibility of past invading the present rests on the ascription of reversibility to the timeline. Charted geometrically, time is a serial of three points, past, present, and future, but beyond them there is a fourth dimension, in Merleau-Ponty's language, the specter of transcendence that cannot be reified as an idealized essence or even as the "primal impression" of transcendental subjectivity, which Husserl envisioned as the "source-point" in consciousness whence temporal objects endure. The fourth dimension is the element of time that escapes the purview of reflective intentionality, a dimension beheld singularly by the double take, turning back to see ahead, the visibility of the invisible rendered invisible in its visibility, the moment that endures as what passes and passes as what endures—*le temps du désir*[67]—perpetually retrieving an irretrievable perpetuity[68] in the extenuated point encircling the past that is not yet the future that is no more than the present expecting the past and recollecting the future.[69]

For Merleau-Ponty, time embraces an inescapable contradiction, for on the one hand it "must *constitute itself*," but on the other, it must "be always seen from the point of view of someone who *is of it*." Time is at all times configured from the vantage point of one already situated in the time to be configured. The contradiction can be "lifted" but "only if the new present is itself a transcendent," a term that implies that "it is not there, that it was just there," that is, this "new present" is the moment with which one never coincides inasmuch as it recurringly returns as what has never been.[70] We must say of the "new present"—I would prefer avoiding the term "present" as it might conjure images of presence and thus suggest the possibility of representation—that it is "not a segment of time with defined contours that would come and set itself in place," but a "cycle defined by a central and dominant region and with indecisive contours—a swelling or bulb of time (*un gonflement ou une ampoule du temps*)."[71] Time "must be understood as a system that embraces everything—Although it is graspable only for him who is there, is at a present."

Time's panorama is scoped microscopically from the opening of the moment, the "impressional consciousness" of the present, the *Urerlebnis*, primal experience, "in reality not a term *effectively* untraversable (temporal knob), but a transcendent, an optimum, an *etwas*. . . . And the 'to be conscious' of this *Urerlebnis* is not coincidence, fusion with . . . it is separation (*écart*) . . . which is the foundation of space and of time."[72] The now of time, which cannot be separated from the here of space, though it be neither temporal nor spatial, in Merleau-Ponty's phenomenological architectonic[73] points the way to the transcendence embodied in the triadic immanence of being, temporality, and subjectivity.[74] It is here that I have found a compelling argument to respond to the alleged challenge of anachronism, a notion of transcendence that opens the time line not by appeal to either an eternity beyond time or an "eternal now" (*nunc stans*), the timelessness of the fullness of time,[75] but rather by heeding the moment that enduringly abides in passing away.[76]

Perceptual Faith and the Paradox of Temporal Beholding

Given the significance of this point to the hermeneutical enterprise in general and to the path I am undertaking in particular, I think it worthwhile to dwell a bit longer on Merleau-Ponty's account of time, keeping our focus on disclosing the intertwining of temporalities in the field of reversible traction, an ontophenomenological assumption that poses a serious challenge to the serial conception of time. To make sense of this assertion, it will be helpful to recall that in the chapter on temporality in *Phénoménologie de la perception*, Merleau-Ponty begins by opposing the widespread metaphorical depiction of time as that which passes or flows by, that which runs its "course," images that imply a sequence with each point determined by a dual causal connectedness, stretching bidirectionally. "If time is similar to a river, it flows from the past towards the present and the future. The present is the consequence of the past, and the future of the present."[77] Merleau-Ponty argues that this proposition involves an inherent inconsistency—in a sense, a reiteration of Xeno's paradox—for to conceive time as a flowing "succession of instances of *now* . . . destroys the very notion of 'now,' and that of succession."[78] If "now," by definition, is that which comes to be in passing, for in passing it comes to be, it cannot be the same "now" that passes in coming to be, but if "now" does not persist as that which passes in coming to be, it cannot be the same "now" that comes to be in passing. How, then, are we to speak of succession?

On the basis of this calculation, Merleau-Ponty concludes that we are obliged to distinguish the "ideal nature of time" (*l'idéalité du temps*) and the mundane conception of "constituted time" (*le temps qu'elle constitue*).[79] The distinction is implied in his quip *Le temps suppose une vue sur le temps*, "Time presupposes a view of time."[80] What in the nature of time would lead one to imagine a view of time presupposed by time? How can we avoid treating such a statement as anything but a rhetorical redundancy that may strike the ear with poetic intrigue but little, if any, philosophical merit? It is, however, precisely by attending the superfluity of a time before time that we will begin to grasp Merleau-Ponty's insights regarding the reversibility of time and the temporal nature of embodied subjectivity.

The dual facet of time, "time" and "time before time"—the phenomenological binary that replaces the metaphysical antinomy of eternity and time—is further explained in the literary depiction of temporal events as "shapes cut out[81] by a finite observer from the spatio-temporal totality of the objective world." Merleau-Ponty locates temporality, which is inseparably linked with spatiality, in the "objective world" whence events are cut like slabs of material by finite observers. Elsewhere, in a tone that strikes me as mystical, Merleau-Ponty writes, "if I consider the world itself, there is simply one indivisible and changeless being in it," *il n'y a qu'un seul être indivisible et qui ne change pas*.[82] This ontological supposition is the eidetic premise for the imperceptible, epistemological foundation that Merleau-Ponty calls "perceptual faith" (*foi perceptive*), the belief that "includes everything that is given to the natural man in the original in an experience-source, with the force of what is inaugural and present in person, according to a view that for him is ultimate and could not conceivably be more perfect or closer."[83]

The presence of which he speaks is not to be construed as Husserl's depiction of the *Präsenfeld* as "immanent consciousness" in opposition to "transcendent consciousness," that is, "being at a distance" (*être à distance*). Merleau-Ponty insists that temporality—which he identifies further as "time of the body, taximeter time of the corporeal schema" (*temps du corps, temps-taximètre du schema corporel*)—discloses the essential properties of subject and object in one gesture without reducing one to the other.[84] Body and consciousness are compounded, therefore, by the grammar of the perceptual faith that is both spatial and temporal.

Temporal Chiasm/Crossing Field of Presence

In this time before time, there is no "event" of which to speak, no occasion to mark, because there is no change, and in the absence of change there can be no variation in perspective and consequently, no possibility that something eventful might eventuate. In the uneventfulness of time, sequential causality and the implied inferential logic have no ultimate standing.[85] To chart the fluidity of time as a "series of possible relations before and after," that is, as a chronological sequence with defined vectors of action-reaction, is *simpatico* with the temporal sensibility that haunts our ego-centered narratives. In a manner reminiscent of Bergson,[86] Merleau-Ponty writes that we can think of "time that is constituted" as the "ultimate recording of time, the result of its *passage*, which objective thinking always presupposes yet never manages to fasten on to." The spatialization of the temporal implied thereby is not, however, illustrative of ideal time, what we may call "pre-noetic time,"[87] "the other time that is true" (*un autre temps, le vrai*), whence one can truly discern the "nature of flux and transience itself" (*le passage ou le transit lui-même*).[88] In contrast to Husserl's *prä-phenomenal Zeitlichkeit*, the immanent sense of "pre-phenomenal temporality,"[89] Merleau-Ponty locates time in the chasm (*écart*) that separates and unites subject and object, "the point where the passage from the self into the world and into the other is affected, at the crossing of the avenues."[90] "Being's *écart* is the coming to be of temporality and it is here we find the sense and possibility of subjectivity."[91] Time, on this account, is at once the partition that bridges and the bridge that partitions.

Merleau-Ponty confidently proclaims, against common wisdom, that time is "not like a river, not a flowing substance."[92] If, however, "real time" is not like a river, what metaphor is better suited to capture the transience of time consciousness? Faithful to his phenomenological roots, Merleau-Ponty affirms that the experience of time entails continuity and interruption, durability and interlude. Temporal cohesion issues from an intentional synthesis of three recurrent modalities, but the distinctive feature of that synthesis is that it "must always be undertaken afresh," for "any supposition that it can be anywhere brought to completion involves the negation of time."[93]

To attribute a fixed quality to time is to negate it—the logic here is reminiscent of the apophaticism of negative theology: affirmation is negation when the affirmation is attributed to the one that transcends all affirmation even the affirmation of being one[94]—since the property that best qualifies time is indeterminacy, "openness upon being" (*ouverture à l'être*).[95] This is the intent of Merleau-Ponty's provocative allegation that the "objective world is too much of a plenum for there to be time."[96] Time is continuously in the making; hence at no time can time be circumscribed in a self-enclosed body; the "objective world" is a product of human construction, an orderly and effective edifice, to be sure, but one that can always be destabilized by the chiasmic texture of time's interruptive flow—the temporality of the event instantiates the event of temporality in the disruption of familiar patterns that are remembered and/or anticipated.[97] The eruption of time, its eventuality, leads to the "experience of dis-illusion, wherein precisely we learn to know the fragility of the 'real' . . . and that the meaning of the 'real' is not reduced to that of the 'probable,' but on the contrary the 'probable' evokes a definitive experience of the 'real' whose accomplishment is only deferred."[98] In the final analysis, Merleau-Ponty does not escape the shadow of Cartesian skepticism.[99] "The mistrust with regard to lived experience is philosophical—one postulates that the consciousness deceives us about ourselves and about language and one is right: this is the only way to *see* them."[100] Perhaps there is no aspect of human experience that underscores this mistrust more faithfully than the domain of time. In its essential inessentiality, the being of time is perpetually on the way to becoming the time of being.

Yet if there were naught but unbounded openness, there would be no time, or, put differently, if the openness were completely open-ended, there would be no end to open and consequently no open to end. The confluence of permanence and change, the experience of time as genuine novelty—the circularity that implies "everything that is said at each 'level' anticipates and will be taken up again,"[101] the paradoxical return of that which is continually new, Nietzsche's eternal recurrence, in Derrida's term, "iterability"[102]—is captured in the metaphorical depiction of time as the "field of presence" (*champ de présence*). What is characteristic of a field is that it exhibits enclosure and openness, a piece of land hedged in as what spreads forth. Structurally, the field is the open enclosure of the enclosed opening; at the horizon of that field is the timeless measure of measureless time, an abidingly discontinuous stream held within the banks of its flow. Accordingly, the field is a more suitable metaphor than the image of the stream to characterize the "living present" of spacetime, the site of the instant shaped by the immanent coexistence and succession of temporalized appearances.[103] In Merleau-Ponty's poetic description:

> Everything, therefore, causes me to revert to the field of presence as the primary experience in which time and its dimensions make their appearance unalloyed. . . . It is here we see a future sliding into the present and on into the past. Nor are these three dimensions given to us through discrete acts. . . . Ahead of what I see and perceive, there is, it is true, nothing more actually visible, but my world is carried forward by lines of intentionality which trace out in advance a least the style of what is to come. . . . The present itself, in a narrow sense, is not posited. . . . Husserl uses the terms protentions and retentions for the intentionalities which anchor me to an environment. They do not run from a central *I*, but from my perceptual field itself, so to speak, which draws along in its wake its own horizon of retentions, and bites into the future with its protentions.[104]

Merleau-Ponty betrays the influence of Husserl's later thinking about internal time consciousness with the significant qualification that he does not locate the source of temporalization in the transcendentally phenomenologizing I, but in the being that is shared by subject and object, what he would later refer to as the "flesh of the world" and the "flesh of the body." In fairness to Husserl, however, it must be said that in the most developed expression of his thought, the prototemporalization of the living present is the locus of the bodiliness of both the constituting subjectivity of transcendental consciousness and the constituted present of immanent temporal objects.[105] Be that as it may, for Merleau-Ponty, as for numerous others, the movement of time revolves about the persistently ephemeral axis of the present: "Past and future exist only too unmistakably in the world, they exist in the present, and what being itself lacks in order to be of the temporal order, is the not-being of elsewhere, formerly and tomorrow."[106]

The texture of the moment is thickened by the interplay of perception, memory, and expectation, a phenomenological insight that bends the time line extending from past to future through the present. The "course of time" consists not only of the "passing of present to past, but also that of the future to the present. If it can be said that all prospection is anticipatory retrospection, it can equally well be said that all retrospection is remembered prospection."[107] This passage of time is thus not to be construed as a linear procession but rather as a circular reversion marked by the simultaneous motion by which "it moves throughout its whole length."[108] The three temporal modes cohere in the present not as a "multiplicity of phenomena" but as

> one single phenomenon of running-off. Time is the one single movement appropriate to itself in all its parts, as a gesture includes all the muscular contractions necessary for its execution. . . . Hence time, in our primordial experience of it, is not for us a system of objective positions, through which we pass, but a mobile setting which moves away from us, like the landscape seen through a railway carriage window.[109]

In time, being and passing are synonymous, for to be in time is to be destined to pass from time.

Temporal Ecstasy and the Doubling of Horizon

Temporalization consists not of a succession of now points but of their coherence as centrifugal movements in the ecstasy of the present, the "zone in which being and consciousness coincide."[110] "It is the essence of time to be not only actual time, or time which flows, but also time which is aware of itself, for the explosion or dehiscence of the present towards a future is the archetype of the *relationship of self to self*, and it traces out an interiority or ipseity."[111] The consequence of the ecstatic orientation is drawn explicitly in a comment from Heidegger's *Sein und Zeit* cited by Merleau-Ponty: "The future is not posterior to the past, or the past anterior to the present. Temporality temporalizes itself as future-which-lapses-into-the-past-by-coming-into-the-present."[112] If we emphasize the confluence of past, present, and future in the moment that passes in coming to be the moment that comes to be in passing, we can use the metaphor of "river" to refer to time, but not because it flows endlessly, as is commonly held.[113]

The ecstasy of the moment, therefore, "reveals the dimensions of time not as conflicting, but as inseparable: to be now is to be from always and for ever."[114] If we are to speak of a synthesis of retention, impression, and protention in the present, it is a "transition-synthesis," which bespeaks the "action of a life which unfolds . . . time bears itself on and launches itself afresh. Time as an indivisible thrust and transition can alone make possible time as successive multiplicity, and what we place at the origin of intratemporality is a constituting time."[115] Alternatively expressed, time in its ideality is to be envisioned from the openness of the horizon, an openness that is open on account of its enclosure, the limitlessness of limit, no-being that is more than less of being-no. From the center of time's margin, we behold the margin of time's center.

The pivotal function of the horizon—one of several technical terms that Merleau-Ponty appropriated from Husserl's transcendental phenomenology—conveys the curvature of the timeline.[116] "It is not the past that pushes the present, nor the present that pushes the future, into being . . . it is a brooding presence moving to meet him,[117] like a storm on the horizon."[118] The matter is clarified from another passage in *Phénoménologie de la perception*, where the author elaborates on the role of the "object-horizon structure," identified as the medium through which objects are "distinguished from each other" as well as "disclosed."[119] The horizon is always double in nature, constituted by a "presumptive synthesis" (*synthèse présomptive*) of memories and expectations, held together concurrently and not sequentially.[120] The flow of duration, therefore, is a present that comprises immediacy of past and imminence of future, but not in predictable, fixed measures; the movement of time cannot be played like a musical score. Put differently, the twofold horizon, looking back/looking ahead, guarantees that past is not and never is past if it is simply the past that it has been, nor is future the future if it is simply the future that it is to be. An essential link, it seems, joins together openness of horizon and indeterminacy of time. Merleau-Ponty returned to this correlation in the unfinished working notes penned in March 1959, thinking the matter through the phenomenological prism of Husserl and Heidegger:

> It is the very structure of a horizon—but it is evident that this structure means nothing in the in itself [*en soi*]—that it has meaning only in the *Umwelt* of a carnal subject [*sujet charnel*], as *Offenheit*, as *Verborgenheit* of Being. . . . the ontological milieu is not thought of as an order of "human representation" [*représentation humaine*] in contrast with an order of the in itself—It is a matter of understanding that truth itself has no meaning outside of the relation of transcendence, outside the *Ueberstieg* toward the horizon—that the "subjectivity" and the "object" are one sole whole, that the subjective "lived experiences" [*"vécus" subjectifs*] count in the world, are part of the *Weltlichkeit* of the "mind," are entered in the "register" which is Being. . . . It is not we who perceive, it is the thing that perceives itself yonder—it is not we who speak, it is truth that speaks itself at the depths of speech—Becoming-nature of man which is the becoming-man of nature—The world is a field, and as such is always open. Resolve similarly the problem of the unicity or plurality of times (Einstein): by return to the idea of horizon.[121]

How does returning to the idea of the horizon help one resolve the problem of unicity and plurality with respect to the texture of time? "Through that horizon—already language has tripped me—we come to grasp that it is not we who perceive but the thing yonder that perceives itself" (*Ce n'est pas nous qui percevons, c'est la chose qui se perçoit là-bas*). Merleau-Ponty insists that time is "not a real process" or an "actual succession" that one can record; it is rather that which "arises from *my* relation to things,"[122] a "dimension of our being" rather than an "object of our knowledge."[123] The relational ontology—a sense of being that is not reified as an immutable or circumscribable essence—mitigates against speaking of time in the Kantian sense as a "datum of consciousness"; it is more precise to say, following Husserl, that "consciousness unfolds or constitutes time. Through the ideal nature of time, it ceases to be imprisoned in the present."[124] If time is conceived as the "immanent object of a consciousness," then time is "brought down to one uniform level,"[125] that is, the discrete point that comes to be and passes away incessantly without any connective tissue tying it to past or future and, consequently, in no time at all. The "fabric of experience" is constituted by the "flesh of time," which is not a string of temporally individual now-points sequentially displacing one another, but a "simultaneity," "cohesion," or "intertwining" (*entrelacs*) of discrete now-points mediated by a horizon of other now-points that are always present as past or future.[126] The presence of the present yields the present of the presence remembering the past that is future and anticipating the future that is past, a presence, that is, enfolded in a double absence that renders the timeline irreversibly reversible. From that standpoint we set out on the path to uncover what may be recovered.

Language, Eros, Being

CHAPTER ONE

Showing the Saying: Laying Interpretative Ground

For every philosophical work, if it is a philosophical work, drives philosophy beyond the standpoint taken in the work. The meaning of a philosophical work lies precisely in opening a new realm, setting new beginnings and impulses by means of which the work's own means and paths are shown to be overcome and insufficient.

—Martin Heidegger, *Schelling's Treatise on the Essence of Human Freedom*

Genealogical Mis/givings

In this book I set out once again to expose the veil of poetic imagination woven within the fabric of the Jewish esoteric tradition, demarcated generically by scholar and adept as "kabbalah." The semantic range of the term encompasses practice and theory, in Western philosophical jargon, or, in rabbinic locution, *ma'aseh* and *talmud*, a way of doing and a way of thinking. To speak of one is not to exclude the other, a perspective that has been enhanced by a critique of the so-called Scholemian school for focusing more on the speculative dimensions of kabbalah to the detriment of the existential, an orientation that has been traced to the influence of Christian kabbalah, and in particular the work of Johannes Reuchlin, on Scholem.[1] Leaving aside both the accuracy of this charge against Scholem and the validity of characterizing the ruminations of Renaissance Christian kabbalists as nontheurgical,[2] the main point to emphasize here is that I do not accept the conceptual split between the practical and theoretical, and thus when I speak of a theosophic structure, the performative gesture is implied, and conversely, when I speak of a performative gesture, the theosophic structure is implied. Indeed, the redemptive nature of kabbalistic esotericism ensues from the inextricable reciprocity of doing and knowing: mystical knowledge is a corollary of contemplative practice, contemplative practice a corollary of mystical knowledge.[3] In the balance of this chapter, I will offer some preliminary observations regarding hermeneutical assumptions that undergird the path and regarding the methodological steps necessary to walk the path, as these will help orient the reader to the twists and turns that will be encountered in the effort to undo the interpretative lattice of language, eros, and being, a threefold chord enfolded in the wisdom of kabbalah.

First, a word about the term "kabbalah." It is not my concern or interest at the moment to discuss the long and diverse philological history of the term, though surely it is reasonable to assume that attunement to philology is a critical tool in historiographical reconstruction.[4] Even when focusing more finely on the limited semantic role of this term to denote esoteric gnosis, it must be acknowledged that "kabbalah" linguistically is multivalent and perhaps even—at the root—unstable, indeterminate, rootless.

How does one classify a historical phenomenon as multifaceted as kabbalah? Scholem remarked in the first of his ten "unhistorical aphorisms" on kabbalah, published in 1958, that a genuine esoteric tradition could not be divulged by the historian or philologist seeking to present the "mystical discipline of kabbalah" for, ironically, if it were divulged, it would not be the esoteric tradition it purported to be.[5] Those familiar with my work know full well that Scholem's ironic understanding of secrecy has served as a springboard for my own incursions into the hermeneutical duplicity of secrecy: to be a secret, the secret cannot be disclosed as the secret it purports to be, but if the secret is not disclosed as the secret it secretly cannot be, it cannot be the secret it exposes itself not to be.[6] The caution Scholem offers regarding the possibility of an adequate scholarly presentation of kabbalistic esotericism seems well placed.

Even if one were not convinced by the double bind of secrecy, intricacies of kabbalah, ideational and practical, would preclude the possibility of proffering an adequate taxonomy, let alone an acceptable account of origins. These limitations notwithstanding, the duty of the scholar is to provide explanatory models that may be applied to texts morphologically. By "texts" I have in mind manifold cultural markings, ranging from literary artifacts to bodily gestures, but something still distinctively human in the domain of sentient animal beings. The matter of morphology is derived from the science of linguistics, the study of verbal forms that are likened to branches one pursues in search of the root, though coming to root does not mean one comes to rock bottom but rather to a ground that sways.

In Foucauldian terms, scholars are faced with the constrictive function of controlling discourses through ordering systems of classification. All such systems are subject to their own dismantling, as any appropriate method of interpretation must be attentive to discontinuities and irregularities that interrupt and constrain the production of a particular archaeology of knowledge seeking to explain the past. The corpus of material studied under the rubric of kabbalah is no exception. Indeed, the quest for "origins" of kabbalah, paradoxically, obfuscates the possibility of comprehending the historical emergence of the phenomenon, as the notion of "origin" logically entails the proposition that every moment is a homogeneous totality, manifesting a unique confluence of events the significance of which is charted in predominantly spatial and temporal terms, but at the same time the moment evolves in an uninterrupted flow that allows one to identify something as cause engendering effect in temporal succession and spatial extension. The search for origins accordingly masks both the discontinuity and continuity necessary to (mis)apprehend beginnings.

We would do better to replace the modernist notion of origin with the idea of genealogy articulated by Foucault, a tracing of lineage that recognizes ruptures and divergences in the process of extending the line, an orientation that disturbs what was considered stable, fragmenting what was thought unified, picturing heterogeneity in what was imagined hegemonic.[7] Utilizing the genealogical approach we may chart an "effective history," in contrast to the more traditional history of ideas, which demarcates the inception of a phenomenon, always a "singular event" destabilizing taxonomy and defying thematization in a manner comparable to Heidegger's deconstruction of the ontotheological tradition by affirming ontological difference (the forerunner of Derrida's *différance*),[8] as a merging of multiple forces rather than a discrete entity emerging at a particular time and place.[9] Genealogy is a pursuit of beginnings without assuming an origin to be found; there is no/*thing* in the beginning but a commingling of events that will be interpreted anew repeatedly in variable historical and cultural contexts, a sequence of enfolding resisting the attempt to unfold the beginning, a complex image of simplicity. "Where the soul pretends unification or the self fabricates a coherent identity, the genealogist sets out to study the beginning—numberless beginnings whose faint traces and hints of color are readily seen by an historical eye. The analysis of descent permits the dissociation of the self, its recognition and displacement as an empty synthesis, in liberating a profusion of lost events."[10]

Having this goal in mind, we can say that a major current of Jewish esotericism—in the accepted but questionable taxonomy of contemporary scholarship, "theosophic" in contrast to "ecstatic" kabbalah—is focused principally on the imaginary envisioning of ten luminous emanations that reveal the light that must remain hidden if it is to be revealed.[11] A variety of terms are used to name these emanations, but the one that became most emblematic was *sefirot*, an idiom initially employed in the first section of an older, multilayered anthology of cosmological speculation, *Sefer Yeṣirah*, the "Book of Formation."[12] In the course of generations, allegedly new and more intricate images have been deployed by kabbalists in the poetic envisioning, but these have been in great measure based on principles already at work in earlier sources, albeit reticently, such as the idea that each of the *sefirot* reflects all the others, or the even more arcane notion that there is a decade of potencies either above or within the first of the *sefirot* that parallel the ten regular gradations, a philosophical idea imaged mythically as the primal human form perched above a second human form, perhaps the symbolic locus of the secret of the androgyne, to be discussed in more detail in the following chapters.[13]

In spite of the evolving complexity of kabbalistic theosophy, the *sefirot* remained structurally at the core of the contemplative visualization that characterizes the way of wisdom, the life experience, transmitted by masters of tradition. Solomon Rubin, a nineteenth-century scholar whose works have unfortunately been summarily dismissed or completely ignored in contemporary scholarship, offered an impressive delineation of the semantic range of this term.[14] In his *Heidenthum und Kabbala*, published in 1893, Rubin specified (in German and what he proposed as its Hebrew equivalent) eight connotations of the term *sefirot*: divine essence (*Götter; aṣmut*), heavenly spheres (*Gestirne; galgalim*), mysterious circles (*geheimnissvolle Zirkel; agulim*), beams of light (*Lichtstrahlen; orot*), mystical colors (*Farben-Mystik; livnat ha-sappir*), numbers (*Zahlen; misparim*), primal ideas or ten utterances (*Urideen oder zehneiniger Logos; ma'amarot*), and pious-ethical attributes (*göttlich-ethische Attribute; middot*).[15]

To do justice to Rubin's insights we would need to discourse lengthily about each of the items on his list, but that undertaking clearly would take us too far off course. Suffice it to note that implicit in Rubin's account is a recognition of what Scholem himself later identified as the two main "symbolic structures" by which the process of the "manifestation of God, his stepping outside" was understood, the "symbolism of light and the symbolism of language."[16] With all the textual and theoretical advances in the field of kabbalah studies—and they have been considerable—there has not been much progress on this point. That is, Scholem's observation that *sefirot* are viewed primarily under the symbolic guise of light and language is a generalization that has stood the test of time and is still a credible explanatory paradigm. In the kabbalist's imaginal representation of the infinite "stepping out" of its boundlessness, an image that pushes against the limit of understanding,[17] emanation of light coincides with revelation of name. Consequently, as we shall uncover on this path of recovery, seeing and hearing are intertwined in mystical envisioning—to behold the invisible is to heed the ineffable.[18]

Ars Poetica and the Symbolic Imagination

In line with the insight of the Russian linguist, Roman Jakobson, I presume that for traditional kabbalists the "poetic function" of language, which is described as the promotion of the "palpability of signs" that "deepens the fundamental dichotomy of signs and objects," cannot be confined to poetry but it is characteristic of discourse more generally.[19] Poetry, according to Jakobson, is the "most formalized manifestation of language" insofar as the "poetic function dominates over the strictly cognitive function" and "the linguistic fiction of the substantivized and hence hypostatized process grows into a metonymic image of life as such."[20] Jakobson affirms the priority of poetry by noting that the "poeticity of the verbal act makes it very clear that communication is not of prime importance," an assumption that is linked to the surmise that "every verbal act in a certain sense stylizes and transforms the event it depicts."[21]

The roots of the conception of poetry as a mode of viewing the world that is transformative rather than imitative (à la Aristotelian poetics) lie in eighteenth-century German aesthetics.[22] Especially important is the reverberation of this critical shift in Wilhelm Dilthey's characterization of "poetic technique" as a "transformation of the content of lived experience into an illusory whole existing merely in the reader's or listener's representations."[23] The "substratum" of all poetry may be the "lived or living experience" (*Erlebnis, lebendige Erfahrung*), and consequently "[e]very image of the external world can indirectly become the material for the creativity of the poet,"[24] but "poetic form," the production of which is the "*achievement of the poetic genius*," "arises only through a transformation of representation of life into aesthetic constituents and relations."[25] As Dilthey articulated the matter in fragments from 1907 and 1908 that were to be used for a revised *Poetics*, "A lived experience is a distinctive and characteristic mode in which reality is there-for-me. A lived experience does not confront me as something perceived or represented; it is not given to me, but the reality of lived experience is there-for-me because I have a reflexive awareness of it, because I possess it immediately as belonging to me in some sense."[26]

The reflexivity to which Dilthey refers, which is the distinguishing mark of the lived experience, is constituted by a "qualitatively determined reality" that "runs its course in time; it is experienced as a sequence that elapses; its temporal relations can be apprehended. But in the structural nexus of this temporal course, that which, although past, endures as a force in the present receives a peculiar character of *presence*. . . . But this presence, this character of a dynamic unity, even this consciousness of it, is after all only the consequence of a property of the structural nexus which constitutes lived experience."[27] Lived experience is determined by this sense of presence, the fulfillment of time, that imparts meaning to the qualitatively determined reality in its totality. In the dynamic unity of the structural mesh, all modes of time converge. "Therefore lived experience is not merely something present, but already contains past and future within its consciousness of the present. . . . Lived experiences are related to each other like motifs in the andante of a symphony: they are unfolded (explication) and what has been unfolded is then recapitulated or taken together (implication). Here music expresses the form of a rich lived experience."[28] Through the musicality of lyrical time, the poet gives verbal utterance to the unfolding of an ineffable present wherein past is recollected as future and future anticipated as past.[29]

In my attempt to engage the poetics of kabbalistic lore, I embrace the expansive understanding of language as poetic gesture that goes beyond representation and communication, a stance that has had a decisive impact on a variety of contemporary philosophical studies,[30] but the further presumption that there is necessarily a dichotomy between sign and object is more objectionable. I do not think it anachronistic to say that kabbalists were aware of the plight of human consciousness that has been documented in a particularly poignant way by modern philosophers pondering nature from a post-Kantian constructivist perspective: All knowledge is mediated, and hence nothing can be known without the intermediary of a sign; there is no escape from the snare of metaphoricity, as it were, for even what is presumed, either on a commonsensical or a more scientific basis, to be a direct, immediate experience is, upon reflection, a complex lattice of semiotic signs informing the mind having the experience. To be sure, kabbalists, like poets, posit an indissoluble link between words and things, an "ontocentricity of language,"[31] and hence we cannot ascribe to them the view, expressed in the linguistic model of Ferdinand de Saussure, that the bond between signifier and signified is arbitrary.[32] On the contrary, as any number of scholars have duly noted, it is axiomatic for kabbalists to assume that language, and particularly Hebrew, presumed to be the language of creation, is essential; cosmology cannot be separated from semiotics, as the cosmological event is decipherable as a sign that must be interpreted. Nevertheless, the matter is complicated by the fact that kabbalists must (following the reason of their own mythologic) assume that the things to which words refer, the signified of the signifier, are themselves signs, since the ineffability of ultimate reality can never be known except through the prism of language. If we are to suppose a genuine confluence of the ontic and linguistic, then there would be no way out of the further assumption that what is real is a sign that points beyond itself to another sign in an *infinite semiosis*, a seemingly endless play of representation.[33]

Particularly relevant for understanding the kabbalistic perspective is the application of Kantian epistemology by Ernst Cassirer to the realm of symbols. According to Cassirer, every form of existence becomes visible to the human mind only through the spectacle of the symbol. One cannot confront reality immediately; the universe is symbolic in its nature. "Instead of dealing with the things themselves," writes Cassirer in *An Essay on Man*, a condensed and somewhat more accessible presentation of his *Die Philosophie der Symbolischen Formen*, "man is in a sense constantly conversing with himself. He has so enveloped himself in linguistic forms, in artistic images, in mythical symbols or religious rites that he cannot see or know anything except by interposition of this artificial medium."[34] In *Sprache und Mythos*, Cassirer expresses the matter: "For all mental processes fail to grasp reality itself, and in order to represent it, to hold it at all, they are driven to the use of symbols. But all symbolism harbors the curse of mediacy: it is bound to obscure what it seeks to reveal."[35]

The basic mode of apprehension is the symbol, but the symbol is at best a form of appearance, albeit the form of appearance that gives shape to the reality it mirrors. In substance, Cassirer's view accords with the transcendental orientation of Husserlian phenomenology according to which it is nonsensical to distinguish an external "world" from world-representation (*Weltvorstellung*). The phenomenological reduction, the *epoché*, places the question of the "objectivity" of the world vis-à-vis the "subjectivity" of the mind in brackets, thereby neutralizing any epistemic priority given to fact over fiction. As Heidegger reminds the reader in *Sein und Zeit*, transmitting the teaching of Husserl, the methodology of phenomenology is captured in the maxim "To the things themselves!" (*Zu den Sachen selbst!*), which means "to let what shows itself be seen from itself, just as it shows itself from itself" (*so wie es sich von ihm selbst her zeigt, von ihm selbst her sehen lassen*).[36] This does not imply a return to naïve realism or an uncritical acceptance of the natural standpoint of empirical sciences; on the contrary, what distinguishes phenomenology, in the words of Don Ihde, is the "use of reflective indirectness" typified by "*the metaphor of the mirror*."[37] Worldhood is hence conceived as a unity-pole constituted in the intentional structure of consciousness, an act of sense-bestowing (*Sinngebung*) that renders it impossible to separate "within" and "without" decisively.[38] If we begin from an epistemological perspective that does away with the clear-cut distinction between representation and reality, image and phenomenon,[39] then the question raised by Jakobson regarding "reality" independent of symbolic forms becomes irrelevant.

Following in the footsteps of Cassirer, which in a significant way lead back to Schelling,[40] we maintain that for traditional kabbalists the symbol is a "structural form" that articulates experience but in such a manner that casts doubt upon the virtue of differentiating truth from appearance.[41] It serves no end to suppose that the symbolic form points to an external world set in opposition to internal consciousness any more than it does to suppose the opposite to be so, nor is there any compelling reason to associate myth with the former and symbol with the latter.[42] On the contrary, the symbol signifies linguistically what is experienced imaginally as myth. As Cassirer at one point put it:

> In this, its basic function, language does not stand alone; it is closely connected from the outset with another potency of the mind. The attainment of objectivity takes place not only through the power to give names, but through the formation of images as well. . . . Here, too, as with language, the act of determination moves from inside to outside, not from outside to inside. To put it more precisely, there is never, of course, any such opposition in itself; rather, we introduce it by bringing in a false way of looking at things when we consider the unitary process of determining objects. This determining is always and necessarily two-sided; it is a revelation enacted from the inside on the outside and from outside on the inside.[43]

The price of solving one problem is leaving another unattended. That is, the "curse of mediacy" to which Cassirer referred is in no way alleviated; quite the opposite, it is intensified, for every form of existence becomes visible or comprehensible only through the symbol. If this is the case, however, what is imagined is itself an image of something else that will be imagined as image, an apparently infinite regress that leads to Cassirer's insight that the symbol inevitably obscures the reality it seeks to reveal. In a similar vein, albeit in a different terminological register, Husserl critiqued the representative role assigned to images on grounds that the "imaginality of the image is not manifest in the image itself," and hence it is more accurate to speak of the image as "essentially concealing its character as image."[44] Analogously, in the mind of kabbalists all things in the universe are viewed symbolically as images of the sefirotic potencies, but the latter are themselves symbolic screens upon and through which the boundless and indeterminate light is projected and refracted, a light that cannot be delimited as light without ceasing to be the light that is to be delimited, a light that comprehends darkness not as its antinomy, nor as a reflection of the same, but as the identically different that is differently identical.

Linguistic Veiling/Revisioning Imagelessness

The approach of kabbalists resonates with the theory of correspondence expressed at the beginning of *Tabula Smaragdina*, the "Emerald Tablet," a series of gnomic utterances attributed to the legendary Hermes Trimegistus,[45] "I speak not fictitious things, but that which is certain and true. What is below is like that which is above, and what is above is like that which is below, to accomplish the miracles of one thing."[46] As Gilles Quispel has noted, the opening principle resonates with the belief that the material world is a replica of the spiritual world of ideal archetypes, as is propounded, for instance, in the Middle Platonism of Eudorus, who flourished in Alexandria in the first century BC. The influence of Eudorus is discernible in the Hermetic writings, and hence there is a textual-historical basis to assume an affinity between the ancient esoteric lore and the *Emerald Tablet*.[47] The merging of Hermetic theurgy and Platonic idealism proved to be an especially important catalyst in the evolution of medieval Christian, Islamic, and Jewish esotericism.

The point that is particularly germane for the study of kabbalistic lore is the formulation of cosmic isotropy in the guise of the doctrine of signatures. That is, the cosmos is a semantic field wherein everything is a sign pointing beyond itself to an interior reality that is itself a sign pointing to what can only (im)properly be termed insignificant, that is, unknowable, unnameable, beyond the reach of conceptual and/or verbal signification. As Philo of Alexandria put it, commenting on Jacob's naming the site of his dream-vision of the ladder that extended from earth to sky, the "abode of God" and the "gateway to heaven" (Gen. 28:17):

> For neither indeed is it possible to get an idea of any other incorporeal thing among existences except by making material objects our starting-point. . . . Correspondingly, then, the conception of the intelligible world was gained from the one which our senses perceive: it is therefore a kind of gate into the former. For as those who desire to see our cities go in through gates, so all who wish to apprehend the unseen world are introduced to it by receiving the impression of the visible world.[48]

Many centuries later, Jacob Böhme (1575–1624), the German cobbler-theosophist, expressed the occult wisdom in language even more germane to kabbalistic tradition: "Therefore the greatest understanding lies in the signature, wherein man . . . may not only learn to know himself, but therein also he may learn to know the essence of all essences; for by the external form of all creatures, by their instigation, inclination and desire, also by their sound, voice, and speech which they utter, the hidden spirit is known; for nature has given to everything its language according to its essence and form."[49] From that vantage point, which calls to my mind Spinoza's metaphysical formula, *deus sive natura*, we can speak hyperliterally of the cosmos as the book of nature, that is, nature is the palimpsest on which the erasure of the ineffable is erased in the inscripted traces of what appears, apparently, as real.

The ontological implication of the symbolic approach was well drawn by Scholem, who observed, "nature, Kabbalistically seen, is nothing but a shadow of the divine name."[50] To speak more precisely, even the name YHWH is shadow, not light, or, in language more endemic to kabbalists, a garment, since it too reveals the one true reality by concealing it. Utilizing the metaphor of Goethe, *der Gottheit lebendiges Kleid*, "the living garment of the deity," to explain the theosophic conception cultivated by the circle in Gerona but which we can liberally apply to many kabbalistic authors, Scholem notes that the sefirotic garments "are not of the kind that could be removed from the deity; they are the forms of its manifestation." These emanations, moreover, represent "the name or names of God. . . . Creation can subsist only to the extent that the name of God is engraved in it."[51] As the matter is expressed in one zoharic passage, the *sefirot* are "ten holy crowns of the holy name" (*asarah kitrin qaddishin di-shema qaddisha*).[52] In a second zoharic passage, from the *Idra Zuṭa* stratum, the sefirotic emanations are depicted as the multiple lights that collectively are the name of God, revealing the infinite radiance that cannot be revealed:

Thus I have seen sparks that glisten from the supernal spark, hidden of the hidden [*ṭemira de-khol ṭemirin*]. . . . and in the light of each and every gradation is revealed what is revealed [*itggalyya mah de-itggalyya*], and all the lights are united . . . and one is not separated from the other. Each and every light of all the sparks, which are called arrayments of the king [*tiqqunei malka*] and crowns of the king [*kitrei malka*], radiates and is united with that innermost light that is within [*nehora dilego lego*] and is not separated from without, and thus everything rises to one gradation and everything is crowned in one matter, and one is not separated from the other, he and his name are one. The light that is revealed [*nehora de-itggalyya*] is called the garment of the king [*levusha de-malka*], the innermost light that is within [*nehora dilego lego*] is the concealed light [*nehora satim*], and within it dwells the one that is not separate and is not revealed [*u-veih sharya ha-hu de-lo itpperash we-lo itggalyya*], and all of these sparks and all of these lights radiate from the holy ancient One [*atiqa qaddisha*], concealed of all concealed [*setima de-khol setimin*], the supernal spark [*boṣina ila'ah*]. When all the lights that have emanated are contemplated, nothing is found but the supernal spark that is hidden and not revealed [*we-khad misttakkelan kullehu nehorin de-itppashsheṭan lo ishttekhaḥ bar boṣina ila'ah de-aṭmar we-lo itggalyya*].[53]

The name, which comprises the sefirotic gradations, the "glorious garments" (*levushin diqar*), "veritable garments" (*levushin qeshot*), "true arrayments" (*tiqqunei qeshot*), and "true sparks" (*boṣinei qeshot*) that reveal the hidden light of the infinite, the "supernal spark" (*boṣina ila'ah*), is configured in the imagination in potentially manifold semiotic deflections and ocular displacements, although the principal form by which it is imaged is an anthropos, the primal Adam in whose image the lower Adam was created.[54] "It has been taught: "When all the holy crowns of the king [*kitrin qaddishin de-malka*] are arrayed in their arrayments, they are called *adam*, the image [*diyoqna*] that contains everything."[55] The continuous chain of being that emanates from the divine pleroma is but an image of this image, a "mere appearance of mere appearance."[56] In another essay, Scholem described the dialectic in terms that inevitably call to mind the notion of an inaccessible primordial language, the *Ursprache*, proffered by Walter Benjamin, to which we shall return below: "One could say that all of creation is only a language, a symbolic expression of that level which cannot be apprehended by thought, and that this level serves as a basis for every structure which is subject to apprehension through thought. The entire world is thus a symbolic body, within whose concrete reality there is reflected a divine secret."[57] Symbols, writes Scholem, are born "of the memory of ecstatic moments of an inexpressible content."[58] To say, then, that the entire world is a "symbolic body" reflecting the "divine secret" implies that nature is a mirror of (dis)semblance, a veil unveiling the unveiling of the veil veiling the (un)veiling of the veil.[59]

The symbolic orientation of kabbalah can be expressed as this doubling of vision—what appears is always image, but image can be seen only as image. Can the mind extricate itself from this entanglement? True, it is misguided to argue, as some postmodern readers have, that traditional kabbalists eschewed ontology,[60] for even though they posit an excess of being beyond affirmation and negation[61] (what Jean-Luc Marion has called the "third way" of mystical theology based on the conjecture that the *hyperousios*, in the lexicon of Dionysius the Areopagite, is a "saturated phenomenon," *le phénomène saturé*, the surplus of the given that does not present itself as a visible spectacle and hence cannot be an object of predication or denial)[62] as the source whence all beings arise and whither they shall return, this being-that-is-more-than-being, the otherwise-than-being, is being nonetheless, "being-no," we might say, as opposed to "no-being," the manifest (un)seen in the splintering of the four-letter name through the filter of ten *sefirot*.

From the kabbalistic standpoint, as I have already noted, the process of emanation is envisioned concurrently as vocalization of the name that is ineffable and manifestation of the image that is invisible, an ontic coincidence of the optic and verbal that renders comprehensible the phenomenon of synesthesia on the experiential level. Moreover, inasmuch as the name comprises the twenty-two letters of the Hebrew alphabet, semiotic folds of boundless light-energy, as it were, the substance—as much wave as particle—of everything that exists in all realms of being, we can say that kabbalists viewed the array-ment of the divine image as the unfolding of language and the flowering of light; to put on a garment is to render visible the invisible, to inscript erasure, to don the nameless in the book that is entirely the name.[63] This book is the *meqor ḥayyim* (*fons vitae*), the fount whence the life force incessantly issues forth. Emanation of the divine potencies is thus imagined simultaneously through three different prisms: radiation of light, flowing of water, calling forth of the name.[64] The three images figuratively convey the sense that the emanative process is the weaving of a veil through which the veil of weaving is unveiled, a theme that reverberates with contemporary notions of poiesis as setting foot on an initiatory path, that is, a path that winds its way to the inception that is yet to come, the "proto-coming/bringing-about-as-temporal,"[65] an idea particularly prominent in the thinking poetics of Heidegger's later work[66] but affirmed in other influential philosophical reflections of the twentieth century, including Franz Rosenzweig's new thinking[67] and Hans-Georg Gadamer's critical hermeneutics.[68]

If, however, language is the veil through which the veil must be unveiled, then the unveiling itself is a form of veiling that will be veiled in the unveiling. In a separate study, I have argued that the hermeneutical position adopted in zoharic literature (and in my opinion this may be extended to a plethora of other kabbalistic texts) is that there is no naked truth to be disrobed, for truth that is truly naked—divested of all appearance—is mere simulation that cannot be seen. Apparent truth, truly apparent, is disclosed through the concealment of its disclosure.[69]

Primordial Language/Semiosis of Being

We begin with the assumption that the most important feature of human imagination is language, for the images through which we braid the strands of reality in our lived bodily experience are linguistic in nature.[70] In some measure, this sentiment has been the warp and woof of the philosophical sensibility from antiquity, a point well captured in the statement in the *Metalogicon* of John of Salisbury (c. 1115–1180), *grammatica est totius philosophicae cunabulum*, "grammar is the cradle of all philosophy."[71] The hermeneutical circle in which we seem to be inextricably caught—or, in the vernacular of the day, the invariable hard-wiring of the human brain—is such that being is thought primarily from the perspective of language, and hence ontological categories are inseparable from grammatical assumptions. In Husserl's formulation, the objects that "pure logic" seeks to examine are "given to it in grammatical clothing. Or, more precisely, they come before us embedded in concrete mental states which further function either as the *meaning-intention* or *meaning-fulfillment* of certain verbal expressions—in the latter case intuitively illustrating, or intuitively providing evidence for, our meaning—and forming a *phenomenological unity* with such expressions."[72]

This insight, referred to as the Copernican revolution in the philosophical thought of our time,[73] is encapsulated in Benjamin's remark in his essay "On Language as Such and On the Language of Man," written in 1916 but unpublished in the author's lifetime:[74] "Language communicates the linguistic being of things. The clearest manifestation of this being, however, is language itself."[75] The basic premise of linguistic theory—the "situation of language"—rests on the proposition that "*the linguistic being of all things is their language.*"[76] Benjamin insists that the "understanding of linguistic theory depends on giving this proposition a clarity that annihilates even the appearance of tautology. This proposition is untautological, for it means: that which in a mental entity is communicable *is* its language."[77] Prima facie, Benjamin's insistence seems absurd, for can the assertion that language is the linguistic being of all things be anything but tautological? The import of his comment, however, is that words are not to be identified with the essence of things. Indeed, Benjamin casts aside this theoretical possibility as the mistaken claim of a "mystical linguistic theory": "For according to mystical theory the word is simply the essence of the thing. That is incorrect, because the thing in itself has no word, being created from God's word and known in its name by a human word."[78]

For Benjamin, the theological belief that everything was created by the "word of God" is to be grasped by taking to heart that all existing things have the potential to be named by human speech and thereby communicated, not that their substance is language: "In the word creation took place, and God's linguistic being is the word. All human language is only reflection of the word in name."[79] Homiletically combining the two accounts of Adam's creation in the opening chapters of Genesis, Benjamin remarks that the divine image with which Adam was created is the mind, which expresses itself through humanity's distinctive aptitude to assign names to material objects.[80] Our charge is to convert the "unspoken nameless language of things" into sounds.[81] Naming, then, is sign-making, the core activity of representation, which, as Benjamin reminds the reader in the prologue to his work on the origin of the literary genre of German tragedy (*Trauerspiel*, literally, mourning play), is shared by artist and philosopher.[82] Benjamin goes so far as to say that it is the mission of the philosopher "to restore, by representation, the primacy of the symbolic character of the word, in which the idea is given self-consciousness, and that is the opposite of all outwardly-directed communication."[83] What is at the heart of philosophical contemplation, then, is representation through the symbolic as opposed to the communicative aspect of language. In line with this understanding, Benjamin identifies Adam, and not Plato, as the "father of philosophy," for his naming things was "so far removed from play or caprice" that there was "as yet no need to struggle with the communicative significance of words."[84] Naming, symbol-making, representation of a noncommunicative sort—these are the qualities of language appropriate to the paradisiacal state.

It is particularly the verbal gesture of representing by name that allows us to speak of the linguistic nature of reality, for in the process of naming, language itself is communicated as potentiality for communication.[85] By affixing names upon things of nature, humans have the potential to translate the "nameless, unspoken language, the residue of the creative word of God" into communicable form. Benjamin's reading of the archaic narrative-myth of the Tower of Babel and the confounding of the one language, *safah aḥat*, that all the world as one people, *am eḥad*, shared (Gen. 11:1–9) yields the notion of a "metaphysics of language" whereby "pure language" (*reine Sprache*), unlimited and infinite in its vagueness, is transformed into multiple languages of lexical signification, always limited and finite in its lucidity.[86] The latter is the basis for analytical knowledge, but in addition to the "communicating function," signs of "human language" have a "symbolic function" that is related to the incommunicability of "language as such." As Benjamin puts it, "language is in every case not only communication of the communicable but also, at the same time, a symbol of the noncommunicable,"[87] a formulation that had a profound impact on Scholem's understanding of the symbolic nature of language attested in the linguistic theory of medieval kabbalism, as noted above.[88]

At this juncture, what is critical for our discussion is to mark the equation of name and thing in Benjamin's metaphysics of language and the implied linguistic construction of reality. By "construction of reality" I do not intend to impose on Benjamin an idealist epistemology that would reduce nature to consciousness. My intent, rather, is an explanation, perhaps more difficult to label, that does away with the dichotomy between reality and language in affirming the externality of the internal and the internality of the external, the way of the poet for whom the saying is in the showing and the showing in the saying, a distinctly Heideggerian turn of phrase that will lead us on our path.[89] To speak of the linguistic nature of the tree is not to say that the tree is nothing outside the name I give it, but that the tree (un)masks itself, variously and variably, in the names by which it is called.

Along similar philosophical lines, Gadamer wrote that the "linguistic interpretation of the world" implies the "experience of the world that is linguistically sedimented in the lived-world," for language provides the "schematization of our access to the world."[90] In this sense, we speak of language disclosing the nature of beings, not, however, in the form of a mimetic theory of truth and the presumed correspondence between substance and reason (*veritas est adaequatio rei et intellectus*), the accordance of declamation and matter, but as a constitutive factor in shaping reality as it appears, the real appearance of the apparently real.[91] Needless to say, Gadamer's view evolves from the thought of Heidegger,[92] well expressed in the comment, "At the same time it becomes manifest that being, as the presencing of what is present, is already in itself truth, provided we think the essence of truth as the gathering that clears and shelters; provided we dissociate ourselves from the modern prejudice of metaphysics . . . that truth is a property of beings or Being."[93] The particularly linguistic turn is made clear in Heidegger's assertion, "In thinking Being comes to language. Language is the house of being. In its home man dwells."[94] In *Einführung in die Metaphysik*, delivered as a lecture course in 1935 but not published until 1953, Heidegger wrote "we seek to win back intact the naming force of language and words [*Nennkraft der Sprache und Worte*]; for words and language are not just shells into which things are packed for spoken and written intercourse. In the word, in language, things first come to be and are" (*Im Wort, in der Sprache werden und sind erst die Dinge*).[95] In *Beiträge zur Philosophie (Vom Ereignis)*, written between 1936 and 1938 though published only posthumously in 1989, Heidegger put the matter in the following way: "Be-ing and the origin of language. . . . Language and *man*. Is language given along with man or man along with language? Or does one become and be, through the other, not at all two different things? And why? Because both *belong* equally *to* be-ing. Why [is] man 'essential' for determining what is ownmost to language—man as? [As] guardian of the truth of being."[96]

The human being is the "guardian of the truth of being," *Wächter der Wahrheit des Syns*, for what belongs essentially to the human comportment in the world, "the ownmost of being-there" (*das Wesen des Da-seins*), is "the grounding of the truth of be-ing" (*der Gründung der Wahrheit des Seyns*), "the en-thinking of be-ing" (*das Er-denken des Seyns*), through "the naming of its essential sway" (*die Nennung seines Wesens*).[97] The en-owning (*das Ereignis*) of being from this perspective—to be reappropriated by philosophy—is to think being from the origin of language, *der Ursprung der Sprache*.[98] The full intent of this claim can only be appreciated if we recall that, for Heidegger, "origin," *Ursprung*, is decoded hyperliterally as *Ur-sprung*, the "originary leap," "an attaining-the-ground-by-leaping" (*das Sich-den-Grund-erspringen*).[99] In contrast to the "beginning" (*Beginn*), the starting point of a temporal process that runs its course from a commencement subject to commemoration to an end subject to anticipation, the "guiding attunement" (*Leitstimmung*) to the origin (*Ursprung*) requires "inceptual thinking" (*anfängliche Denken*) through which "the truth of the projecting-open" (*der Wahrheit des Entwurfs*) is grasped;[100] that is, the thinking that springs from the grounding of the sway, the "opening as clearing" that "brings the self-sheltering-concealing to pass" (*die Eröffnung als Lichtung das Sichverbergen zum Geschehen bringen*),[101] the initiation of an historical epoch through the "playing-forth" (*das Zuspiel*) of presence and absence[102]—not to be construed as antithetical polarities rendered identical in the homogeneity of conjunction but as opposites correlated in the heterogeneity of their disjuncture.[103] The intimate proximity of origin and language suggests that the latter is the (un)veiling that allows beings to appear in the veil of their unveiling.

The special task of the thinker, shared inimitably by the poet, is related to the propensity of language, and particularly to the act of saying,[104] to name the opening that must remain open if it is the opening that is (un)named, the "originary retrieval" (*ursprünglichere Wiederholung*) of the "first beginning" (*ersten Anfangs*), the "essential swaying of being itself" (*die Wesung des Seins selbst*), the "origin that is always withdrawing as it grasps far ahead" (*betriebene Ursprung, der sich immer entziehend am weitesten vorausgreift*),[105] the "hidden reign of the origin of the truth of beings as such" (*die verborgene Herrschaft des Ursprungs der Wahrheit des Seienden als solchen*).[106] But how does one recover the ground engrounded in the disswaying of the sway? How does one return to the "unsurpassable" beginning that "can never be comprehended as the same, because it reaches ahead and thus each time reaches beyond what is begun through it and determines accordingly its own retrieval?"[107] The way of reclamation is through the "knowing awareness that speaks by first keeping silent in Dasein's sustaining inabiding" (*in jenem Wissen, das spricht, indem es zuvor aus der ausstehenden Inständigkeit im Da-sein schweigt*).[108] In speaking by keeping silent, the concept (*Begriff*) of Being portends what cannot be grasped but as the "in-grasping" (*In-begriff*), enopening of open in withdrawal of withdrawal, dissembling the semblance of truth apparently inapparent.[109]

Verbal Imaging/Word Disclosure

To grasp this dimension of Heidegger's thought, we must bear in mind that for him the essence of language is not in speaking (*sprechen*) but in saying (*sagen*),[110] that is, in the "showing" (*zeigen*) of what is pledged (*Zusage*) in the promise of what has been said (*das Gesagte*), an encircling of the same in the identity of difference.[111] "The essential being of language is Saying as Showing [*Das Wesende der Sprache ist die Sage als die Zeige*]. Its showing character is not based on signs of any kind; rather, all signs arise from a showing within whose realm and for whose purposes they can be signs."[112] As the poet would envision it, the essence of thinking, which arises in thinking about essence, is captured in Heidegger's own poetic declamation, *Das Wesen der Sprache: Die Sprache des Wesens*, "the being of language: the language of being,"[113] the "guideword" (*Leitwort*) that beckons one away from the conventional understanding of language as sign-affixing to the experience of language as a saying that is a showing.[114] In the saying-showing are the "primal tidings" (*Ur-Kunde*) imparting to us the "being of language" in the "language of being."[115] Elsewhere, Heidegger depicts the transition from propositional statement to poetic saying in the following way:

> A *word* is *not* a relationship. A word discloses [*erschliesst*]. It opens up. The decisive moment in language is significance [*Bedeutung*]. Sounds also belong to language, but they are not the fundamental [characteristics]. I can understand the same meaning in different languages. The essential character of language is the "saying," that a word says something, not that it sounds. A word shows something. Saying means showing, Language is the showing [of something].[116]

I digress momentarily from the main path to bring to the surface the challenge to the dichotomy of image and word implicit in the correlation of showing and saying. Heidegger's affirming the former as the demarcating characteristic of the latter is related to a larger phenomenological claim embraced by him, in a measure due to the influence of Nietzsche's aesthetic judgment that the artist embodies the "primordial desire for mere appearance"[117] since in the artist's mind the semblance (*Schein*) or form that appears constitutes reality.[118] I will cite two passages from the published volume based on the notes for the 1936-to-1937 lecture course "Nietzsche: Will to Power as Art" that are especially relevant to the topic. In the first, in a section that bears the title *Der Rausch als formschaffende Kraft*, "Rapture as Form-Engendering Force," Heidegger comments on Nietzsche's statement that the artist "accords no value to anything that cannot become form":[119]

> But by way of a commentary on Nietzsche's definition let us say only this: form, *forma*, corresponds to the Greek *morphē*. It is the enclosing limit and boundary [*umschließende Grenze und Begrenzung*], what brings and stations a being into that which it is, so that it stands in itself: its configuration [*die Gestalt*]. Whatever stands in this way is what the particular being shows itself to be, its outward appearance [*sein Aussehen*], *eidos*, through which and in which it emerges, stations itself there as publicly present, scintillates, and achieves pure radiance.[120]

Attunement to Nietzsche's depiction of the "aesthetic state," as Heidegger calls it, gives way to the conclusion that "artistic relation to form is love of form for its own sake, for what it is."[121] The logical implication of this assertion, however, is that truth resides in the form of appearance. In a second passage, Heidegger cites a remark of Nietzsche that makes this very point, " 'Semblance' as I understand it is the actual and sole reality of things," and then comments, "That should be understood to mean not that reality is something apparent, but that being-real is in itself perspectival, a bringing forward into appearance, a letting radiate; that is in itself a shining. Reality is radiance."[122] Heidegger well understood that a consequence of Nietzsche's hermeneutical perspectivism is an epistemic challenge to the distinction between semblance and reality, mimesis and meaning, imaginality and objectivity.[123] Heidegger cites Nietzsche's own words relating to this issue, "Hence I do not posit 'semblance' in opposition to 'reality,' but on the contrary take semblance to be the reality which resists transformation into an imaginative 'world of truth.' A particular name for that reality would be 'will to power,' designated of course intrinsically and not on the basis of its ungraspable, fluid, Protean nature."[124] With poetic aplomb, Heidegger entwines his way along Nietzsche's path:

> Reality, Being, is *Schein* in the sense of perspectival letting-shine. But proper to that reality at the same time is the multiplicity of perspectives, and thus the possibility of illusion and of its being made fast, which means the possibility of truth as a kind of *Schein* in the sense of "mere" appearance. If truth is taken to be semblance, that is, as mere appearance and error, the implication is that truth is the fixed semblance which is necessarily inherent in perspectival shining—it is illusion.[125]

There is much to mine from Nietzsche's thought transmitted in the voice of Heidegger's interpretation. Viewing the matter more limitedly, Nietzsche supposes that for the artist, the image, what appears, is what is real. The errand of the creator is to destroy the illusion of reality in order to create "new names and valuations and appearances of truth."[126] Heidegger enunciates the phenomenological implications of this insight. To say that semblance is reality is to imply that being is determined as "perspectival letting-shine," that is, what is shows itself in the multiple perspectives by which it is named. The "phantasmata solipsism" and "epistemic parasitism"[127] articulated as part of the critique of representationalism bring to mind Wittgenstein's assertion that phenomenology is the "grammar of the description of those facts on which physics builds its theories."[128] For Wittgenstein, life-forms (*Lebensformen*) of experience are reducible to language games (*Sprachspiele*), that is, propositional statements whose meaning is determined by grammatical rules that are socially constructed. This accords well with the Heideggerian perspective on the linguistic and hermeneutical turn in philosophy, which on the one hand denies the factuality of metaphysical realities beyond the play of language but, on the other, acknowledges the inherent limitations of language to disclose fully what shows itself in the saying, since what shows itself does so in the concealment of its showing.[129] To maintain this, one must accept that truth does not yield a standard by which real appearance is distinguished from the apparently real, an illusion, a lie. We shall return to the intermingling of truth and deception rooted in the interplay of presence and absence, the veritable deception of esotericism that is the invariable consequence of our epistemological suspicion and nature's relentless withdrawal, its love to hide,[130] but for now we assent to the aesthetic judgment that for the artist, being is letting-appear.[131]

Of the various art forms, poesy is privileged as the paradigmatic art, for it is thought to manifest what is disclosed most fully in uncovering the showing of the saying.[132] All other artistic forms are pervaded by the hermeneutic function of language to open the opening of saying, the circumscription of naming. Hence, in his rumination on Hölderin's hymn *Der Ister*, Heidegger links the uniqueness of the poetic undertaking to the act of "naming," "to call to its essence that which is named in the word of poetizing, and to ground this essence as poetic word. Here, 'naming' is the name for poetic telling."[133] To heed the dimension of the word as "verbal icon,"[134] we must dwell poetically,[135] for only such dwelling occasions the "poetic experience with the word" (*einer dichterischen Erfahrung mit dem Wort*) in the "country"[136] where "thinking encounters its neighborhood with poetry" (*In dieser Gegend trifft das Denken auf die Nachbarschaft zur Dichtung*).[137]

The byword "the being of language; the language of being" illumines the last line of Stefan George's poem *Das Wort: Kein Ding sei wo das Wort gebricht*, "Where word breaks off no thing may be," the "statement" (*Aussage*) or "theorem" (*Lehrsatz*)[138] to which Heidegger repeatedly returns—like a mantra—in the lecture *Das Wesen der Sprache* in an effort to bring to light the belonging-together (*Zueinandergehören*) of language and being. In the "poet's renunciation" (*der Verzicht des Dichters*), a curious phrase whose meaning is still to be decoded, the "relation between thing and word comes to light . . . the word is what first brings that given thing, as the being that it is, into this 'is': that the word is what holds the thing there and relates it and so to speak provides its maintenance with which to be a thing."[139]

> The word's rule springs to light as that which makes the thing be a thing. The word begins to shine as the gathering which first brings what presences to its presence. The oldest word for the rule of the word thus thought, for Saying, is *logos*: Saying which, in showing, lets beings appear in their "it is."
>
> The same word *logos*, however, the word for Saying [*Sagen*], is also the word for Being [*Sein*], that is, for the presencing of beings [*das Anwesen des Anwesenden*]. Saying and Being, word and thing, belong to each other in a veiled way [*gehören in einer*

verhüllten], a way which has hardly been thought and is not to be thought out to the end.[140]

The human being is uniquely endowed with the word that unveils the veil of being, for "man is man only because he is granted the promise of language, because he is needful to language, that he may speak it."[141] The circularity of Heidegger's hermeneutic is discernible in Paul Ricoeur's comment that interpretation, which cannot be separated from language, must arrive at being-in-the-world, but it is precisely being-in-the-world that is presupposed by interpretation. "First there is being-in-the-world, then understanding, then interpreting, then saying. . . . It is indeed true that it is from the heart of language that we say all this; but language is so made that it is able to designate the ground of existence from which it proceeds and to recognize itself as a mode of the being of which it speaks." The symbolic function of language is located in the "circularity between *I speak* and *I am* . . . the living circle of expression and of the being-expressed."[142] From within this circle we can discern the belonging-together of language and being.

Epiphany of Not-Showing/Occluded Occlusion

The way that language and being belong together, however, is veiled, not because the matter is presently concealed and will eventually be revealed, but, in a more enduring sense, because not-showing is intrinsic to the showing that is the saying: "To say means to show, to make appear, the lighting-concealing-releasing offer of world."[143] With this, we arrive at a facet of Heidegger's thinking that resonates deeply with the dialectic of esotericism at play in kabbalistic theosophy: every act of revealing is a concealing, for the truth cannot be revealed unless it is concealed. Disclosure is thus a form of occlusion, letting-go a holding-in.[144] In Heidegger's own words, "Retaining belongs to concealment. The mystery [of being] is concealment, which is [at the same time] unconcealing itself as such."[145] To comprehend the intertwining of concealment and unconcealment, which Heidegger speaks of in the context of illumining the way of remembrance and forgetfulness, we must take hold of the fact that, for him, to think the "essence of language from the essence of Being" is to think the "essence of language expressly as logos, as the Laying that gathers!"[146] Etymologically, the word *logos*, which conventionally denotes both inward thought and external statement, is derived from *legein*, related to the Latin *legere*, to lay out, to lay down, to lay before.[147] Staying attuned to the philological assonance facilitates our understanding of the performative gesture of saying—and, it must emphasized, it is precisely in the performativity of saying as the bringing forth of being rather than in the propositional ascription of semantic meaning to the beings of which one speaks that we must seek the singularity of Heidegger's contribution to the path of poetic thinking[148]—as a letting-lie of what lies before us, the laying-down that gathers up itself and others.[149] "Laying . . . speaks without a sound: there is. To lay and to tell relate in the same mode to the same, in the mode of letting-appear. Telling turns out to be a laying, and it is called λέγειν."[150]

At its foundation, language is the laying-that-gathers, the letting-appear of what remains hidden, exhibiting what persists in its abandon, speaking the root word of being, "there is," without making a sound, the "presently present lingering in unconcealment as in the open expanse" (*Das gegenwärtig in der Unverborgenheit Anwesende weilt in ihr als der offenen Gegend*), proceeding "from unconcealment toward concealment," the "transition from coming to going" wherein what is present "comes to presence out of absence,"[151] the "transitional arrival in departure" (*die übergängliche Ankunft in den Weggang*) of the "twofold absence" (*zwiefältigen Ab-wesen*) of the "presencing of all that lingers" (*das Anwesen alles Weiligen*) "between approach and withdrawal" (*zwischen Hervorkommen und Hinweggehen*),[152] the "disjunction" (*Un-Fuge*) that endures in the "jointure of the while" (*die Fuge der Weile*).[153] Language as the "gathering letting-lie-before of what is present in presencing"[154] takes place within the confines of the "lighting/clearing" (*Lichtung*),[155] the "open place" (*offene Stelle*), that holds back in extending forward, concealing the revealing of concealing in revealing the concealing of revealing:

> That which is can only be, as a being, if it stands within and stands out within what is lighted in the clearing. Only this clearing grants and guarantees to us human beings a passage to those beings that we ourselves are not, and access to that being that we ourselves are. Thanks to this clearing, beings are unconcealed in certain changing degrees. And yet a being can be *concealed*, too, only within the sphere of what is lighted. Each being we encounter and which encounters us keeps to this curious opposition of presence [*Gegnerschaft des Anwesens*] in that it always withholds itself at the same time in a concealedness [*indem es sich zugleich immer in eine Verborgenheit zurückhält*]. The clearing in which beings stand is in itself at the same time concealment [*Die Lichtung, in die das Seiende hereinsteht, ist in sich zugleich Verbergung*].[156]

Lichtung is the saying-showing of language that makes manifest the "thinging" of things[157] or the "worlding" of world,[158] the advent of the event (*Ereignis*) that comes forth in the withdrawal of its coming,[159] a withholding-eruption that yields the mythic-poetic measure[160] of worldhood. Language in general, and poetic language in particular, display the interplay of presence and absence,[161] for the showing-saying is always a seeing of "what comes to presence in unconcealment,"[162] but what comes to presence cannot be represented except from the vantage point of what is absent, an ontological presumption that underscores the distinctively temporal comportment of the present as the recurring site of being's veiled disclosure: "Even what is absent is something present, for as absent from the expanse, it presents itself in unconcealment. . . . All things present and absent are gathered and preserved in *one* presencing for the seer."[163]

The poet poetizes the "poetically true word" that "names that which poetically is," the "poetic truth" that must be poetized (*das Zu-Dichtende*), a naming that is not merely a linguistic declaration of what has been formed verbally in the imagination but rather the "poetic saying" that is itself "the poetizing" in accordance with the essence of what is to be poetized. However, that which is to be poetized essentially and necessarily "lies concealed in something that can never be identified or found anywhere or anytime or in any way as something actual that is, something among actual beings." Poetizing is thus a "pure seeking that does not restrict itself to beings," a "telling finding of being" through which "what is to be found" (*das Zu-findende*) "remains entirely concealed." Yet this finding is considered supreme "because it is that which is always already revealed for human beings and is the nearest of all that is near."[164] What prevails as that which is to be poetized is not a being but Being, that which is "always already revealed" but yet "remains entirely concealed." The poem is an "unveiling of concealment,"[165] which is not to say that the concealment is removed by the disclosure of unveiling; on the contrary, what is unveiled is the concealment and thus the secret of the unspoken persists in the saying of the poet. Indeed, in the case of every great poet, it is the unspoken that constitutes the "single poetic statement" that is spoken in every poem.[166] The poetic word, therefore, is the sign that "shows—and in showing, it makes manifest, yet in such a way that it simultaneously conceals."[167]

Saying the Unsaid/Laying Bare Full Exposure

A consequence of the dual function of the sign to reveal and to hide is that truth doubles itself as the enclosed opening of open enclosure.[168] Thus the revealing/concealing of *Lichtung*,[169] the "gathering which clears and shelters,"[170] is a "double concealment" (*dieses zwiefache Verbergen*), the clearing that "is pervaded by a constant concealment in the double form of refusal and dissembling" (*ein ständiges Verbergen in der Doppelgestalt des Versagens und des Verstellens*).[171] In the concealment that "conceals and dissembles itself,"[172] truth is revealed as untruth.[173] "The nature of truth, that is, of unconcealedness, is dominated throughout by a denial. . . . This denial, in the form of a double concealment, belongs to the nature of truth as unconcealedness [*Zum Wesen der Wahrheit als der Unverborgenheit gehört dieses Verweigern in der Weise des zwiefachen Verbergens*]. Truth, in its nature, is untruth."[174] On the one hand, disclosure of concealment is what makes the showing of truth possible, for if concealment would not be concealed, nothing would be revealed. On the other hand, for truth to show itself, concealment must be disclosed in the doubling of its concealedness. Hermeneutically, in the re/covery of what has been un/covered, untruth belongs inextricably to truth: "Truth is un-truth, insofar as there belongs to it the reservoir of the not-yet uncovered, the un-uncovered, in the sense of concealment. In unconcealedness, as truth, there occurs also the other 'un-' of a double restraint or refusal. Truth occurs as such in the opposition of clearing and double concealing."[175]

The truthfulness of truth, which, for Heidegger, resounds most fully in the etymology of the Greek *aletheia*, is determined by the belonging-together of concealed and unconcealed. "Belonging-together," *Zueinandergehören*, in Heidegger's later writings is a technical term that denotes a "gathering by way of difference," that is, the grouping of entities that are considered the same, though not identical or equal, for their pairing is predicated on preserving the presence of difference rather than cultivating the absence of indifference.[176] It follows that what is disclosed is revealed from what is hidden, and what is hidden from what is disclosed. In Heidegger's near-mystical clamor, he writes of the "remaining concealed/remaining unconcealed" that holds sway as "that which really has no need to bring itself expressly to language, since this language itself arises from it."[177]

For Heidegger, the unsaid—as opposed to the unsayable[178]—belongs essentially to what is said; indeed, the latter derives from and constantly abides within the framing of the former. It is in the way of language that it speaks itself as language most conspicuously "when we cannot find the right word for something that concerns us, carries us away, oppresses or encourages us. Then we leave unspoken what we have in mind and, without rightly giving it thought, undergo moments in which language itself has distantly and fleetingly touched us with its essential being."[179] When there is no word to speak, there the stillness of language (re)verberates. What better way to articulate the inadequacy of words but with words written to articulate the inadequacy of words? "There is some evidence that the essential nature of language flatly refuses to express itself in words—in the language, that is, in which we make statements about language. If language everywhere withholds its nature in this sense, then such withholding is in the very nature of language."[180]

> Everything spoken stems in a variety of ways from the unspoken,[181] whether this be something not yet spoken, or whether it be what must remain unspoken in the sense that it is beyond the reach of speaking. Thus, that which is spoken in various ways begins to appear as if it were cut off from speaking and the speakers, and did not belong to them, while in fact it alone offers to speaking and to the speakers whatever it is they attend to, no matter in what way they stay within what is spoken of the unspoken.[182]

In the conclusion of the lecture "The Nature of Language," Heidegger relates the intersection of language and the unspoken to the image of the breaking of the word in the last line of George's *Das Wort: Kein Ding sei wo das Wort gebricht*, "Where word breaks off no thing may be." Having thought "within the neighborhood[183] of the poetic word" (*der Nachbarschaft zum dichterischen Wort*), Heidegger offers a conjecture (*vermutend sagen*), a kind of midrashic gloss,[184] I would say, on the verse, "An 'is' arises where the word breaks up," *Ein "ist" ergibt sich, wo das Wort zerbricht.*[185] Explicating his own gloss, Heidegger continues, "To break up here means that the sounding word returns into soundlessness, back to whence it was granted: into the ringing of stillness which, as Saying, moves the regions of the world's fourfold into their nearness. This breaking of the word is the true step back on the way of thinking."[186] The breaking up of the word, the turnabout on the path of thinking, comes by way of returning the sounded word to the soundlessness whence it came forth, a ringing stillness that resounds with the saying that draws together the fourfold (*Geviert*)—earth, sky, divinities, and mortals—elements that precede everything that is present, the beginning of the gathering-dispersal, space-time continuum, now-point whence what is to come comes before it has come as what is to come, time's triadic wedge swirling in the space of its temporal emplacement.[187]

The fracture of the word thus serves as a catalyst to draw together the four elements in the "simple onefold of their self-unified fourfold" (*der Einfalt ihres aus sich her einigen Gevierts*).[188] Through the eruption of rupture we uncover what remains rooted, mystery of origin, beckoning remembrance (*Andenken*) of what is yet to come in thinking of (*Denken an*) what has been,[189] a "thoughtful remembrance" that "does not mean merely thinking of that which has been . . . but simultaneously thinking ahead 'to' what is coming, giving thought to the locality of the homely and the ground that is to be founded," a showing that will "let appear that which is said only because it has before this already been shone upon by that which thus appears as what is to be poetized."[190] Thinking commemoratively commits the poet to an "enigmatic unfaithfulness," for "thoughtful remembrance proper" (*das eigentliche Andenken*) is linked to the fact that memory is retained in the form of vanishing, "an inconspicuous passing away into what is coming, into a decisive belonging to whatever is coming."[191] Recollection, which is summoned by poetic utterance, is like a river that is "underway into what has been" at the same time that "it proceeds into what is coming," a double movement that marks the rhythm of temporality (as opposed to clock time), which imparts the destiny of historicity to humankind—running ahead to the past as the authentic and singular future of one's own being.[192] The "inner recollection" is not exhausted in "merely returning to something bygone and remaining there, becoming ossified in such remaining with whatever is bygone. . . . Genuine inner recollection is a turning toward what is undisclosed and turned inward into what has been. Genuine inner recollection is intimation."[193] By recollecting inwardly, the way is opened back to the fourfold, the source whence what has been proceeds in the form of what is to come and what is to come in the form of what has been.

Significantly, in another context, Heidegger referred to the enfolding of the fourfold in their mutual belonging as the "gift of the outpouring" that "stays the onefold of the fourfold of the four. . . . What is gathered in the gift gathers itself in appropriatively staying the fourfold . . . giving gathering of the onefold fourfold into a single time-space, a single stay."[194] The staying of the fourfold in the gifting of the gift accounts for the gathering of the elements into the single time-space that provides the framework (*Gestell*) of what is held together (*Verhältnis*) in the unifying dispersal of what we experience visibly as world.[195] In Heidegger's mythopoeic ontology, earth, sky, divinities, and mortals "belong together by way of the simpleness of the united fourfold. Each of the four mirrors in its own way the presence of the others."[196] In the "mirror-play of the fourfold,"[197] the event of world occurs, an episode impelled by the outbreak of word in the outpouring of gift. The breaking-through of holding-in, the "insurrection" (*Aufstand*) that grounds "sheer endurance" (*bloße Andauern*),[198] imparts to one who is properly attuned knowledge of the way of language as sending forth the withheld, laying out the gathered-in. In this breach, the originary evocation takes hold, a splintering of word visibly audible in the restoration of saying to silence.[199]

Thinking Poetically/Sheltering-Opening

For Heidegger, the correlation of language and being is thought from the standpoint of the saying, the "neighborhood" within which both poetry and thinking move, indeed the place of philosophical aporia wherein it cannot be decided "whether poetry is really a kind of thinking, or thinking really a kind of poetry."[200] The two modalities "belong to each other even before they ever could set out to come face to face one to the other."[201] As I noted above, belonging-together is a *terminus technicus* in Heidegger's writings, a turn of phrase that is intended to demarcate sameness without obliterating difference. Thus, Heidegger concludes, "Poetry and thinking meet each other in one and the same only when . . . they remain distinctly in the distinctness of their nature" (*Das Dichten und das Denken begegnen sich nur dann . . . als sie entschieden in der Verschiedenheit ihres Wesens bleiben*).[202] Precisely on account of disparity we can speak of semblance in the province of poetic thought, thinking poetically, that ensues from "letting language, *from within* language, speak to us, in language, of itself, saying its nature."[203] Similar to Jakobson, albeit in a different terminological register, Heidegger accepts that the poetic informs us about the nature of language more generally: "Projective saying is poetry. . . . Poetry is the saying of the unconcealedness of what is. . . . Language itself is poetry in the essential sense. . . . Language is not poetry because it is the primal poesy; rather, poesy takes place in language because language preserves the primal nature of poetry."[204]

But what is it about poetry that leads Heidegger to conclude that language is poetry in the essential sense? The clue is offered in the following statement regarding the nature of language and the role of the poet:

> But when does language speak itself as language? Curiously enough, when we cannot find the right word for something that concerns us, carries us away, oppresses or encourages us. Then we leave unspoken what we have in mind and, without rightly giving it thought, undergo moments in which language itself has distantly and fleetingly touched us with its essential being. But when the issue is to put into language something which has never yet been spoken, then everything depends on whether language gives or withholds the appropriate word. Such is the case of the poet. Indeed, a poet might even come to the point where he is compelled—in his own way, that is, poetically—to put into language the experience he undergoes with language.[205]

Language speaks most essentially in poetic diction, for of all forms of discourse the poem most acutely opens a cleft between sign and object, thereby making possible the saying of the unsayable.[206] To presume, however, that every form of language partakes of the poetic implies that language is essential to the way of not being by being not that of which it partakes. Alternatively expressed, the verbal sign marks both the limit and limitlessness of human experience,[207] "a saying not-saying," *sagendes Nichtsagen*, according to Heidegger's telling locution,[208] the unsaying of the said in the saying of the unsaid. As he puts it in "The Thinker as Poet," "Thinking's saying would be stilled in its being only by becoming unable to say that which must remain unspoken. . . . What is spoken is never, and in no language, what is said."[209] Beyond the world of signifiers lies the realm of silence, the horizon of sound, which is not to be construed as the unrepresentable fullness of being (in classical and medieval Neoplatonic ontology) but the bare negativity that circumscribes the possibility of speech in its divergent significations, a bare negativity disclosed in the showing of the saying, the deconstructive tendency in language to undermine itself and the illusory duality of self and world proposed in its wake.[210] By heeding the saying of the showing, the word resounds with the incipient silence of not-saying.[211] To quote Heidegger again:

> The word fails, not as an occasional event—in which an accomplishable speech or expression does not take place, where only the assertion and the repetition of something already said and sayable does not get accomplished—but originarily. The word does not even come to word, even though it is precisely when the word escapes one that the word begins to take its first leap. The word's escaping one is enowning as the hint and onset of be-ing. The word's escaping is the inceptual condition for the self-unfolding possibility of an originary-poetic-naming of be-ing.[212] All saying has to let the ability to hear arise within it. Both must have the same origin. . . . Reticence in silence stems from the saying origin of language itself. . . . Saying grounds as reticence in silencing. Its word is not somehow only a sign for something totally other. What it names is what it means. But "meaning" is owned up to only as *Da-sein* and that means in thinking-questioning.[213]

Reticence in silence grounds the saying of language, for the saying, as the shibboleth of thought, is a word that questions and thereby embraces truth as disclosive opening, the open that opens, the questioning of being on the path of thought, the transporting into the unique word of the poet or thinker that compels us to enown that word as if it were being heard for the first time repeatedly.[214] The questioning brings one to the horizon of ontological understanding, that is, the horizon from which beings come to be understood from the ground of being, that which "reveals itself as the ground that gives ground and accounts for itself . . . the gathering of beings and letting them be."[215] Meaning, it should be recalled, is already defined by Heidegger in *Sein und Zeit* as *das Woraufhin des Entwurfs, aus dem her etwas verständlich wird*, "the upon-which of the project in terms of which something becomes intelligible as something."[216] The hermeneutical path meanders to the point of the pointless, the abyss, *Abgrund*, which denotes the "complete absence of ground,"[217] the upon-which of the pro/ject, which grounds by gathering the beings it lets go in the letting-be of what is to be.

The question of meaning is intricately connected to the ontological horizon, the medium upon which being is projected and from which it is understood. The space of the horizon, the "projecting-open,"[218] however, cannot be imagined without time, for the determination of being from the perspective of human subjectivity is the finitude of temporality, which is linked essentially to imagination[219] as the site wherein beings are brought to openness in the unconcealment of being as the letting-presence of the absence that prevails in the presencing of what is not yet present, the future that anticipates the past recollecting the future.[220] The imaginative faculty opens the ontological horizon as time-space, the "clearing of self-sheltering-concealing," the gifting of beings withholding disclosure.[221] For Heidegger, the poet incarnates the clearing-concealing as the poet is gifted with the ability to shelter the other in the enclosed opening of open enclosure. Poetic language exhibits the quality of bringing forth into manifestness (*Hervorbringen in die Offenbarkeit*) the silence hidden in the instantiation of the word.[222]

Enveloping Silence/Chiasmic Wordfold

Language is, in the telling phrase of Merleau-Ponty, the "double of being" (*la doublure de l'être*) since "we cannot conceive of an object or idea that comes into the world without words."[223] Although we presume that the linguistic gesticulation (*gesticulation linguistique*) is dependent on an "awareness of truth," it is in fact the "vehicle of truth," and hence language "leads us to the things themselves to the precise extent that it *is* signification before *having* a signification [*avant d'avoir une signification, il est signification*] . . . language before language [*le langage avant le langage*]."[224] The intent of Merleau-Ponty may be gauged from another passage where he mentions (in the name of Humboldt) the "inner speech-form" (*innere Sprachform*) or (in a figure of speech more reflective of his own time) "word concept" (*Wortbegriff*), identified further as "linguistic gesture," that is, the prereflective, immediate consciousness of body that facilitates the determination of one's spatial-temporal bearings to worldly things without thematically representing or objectifying them. The significations, expressive of the "corporeal intentionality" that demarcate the contours of a lived body's phenomenal landscape, inflect the written/spoken word "without ever changing them into words or breaking the silence of consciousness." The word that is written/spoken is "pregnant with a meaning which can be read in the very texture of the linguistic gesture . . . and yet it is never contained in that gesture, every expression always appearing to me as a trace, no idea being given to me except in transparency, and every attempt to close our hand on the thought which dwells in the spoken world leaving only a bit of verbal material in our fingers."[225] Prior to the division into antinomies, subject and object, interior and exterior, mind and body, embodiment bespeaks the correlation of a "prereflective zone of the openness upon Being" (*la zone préréflexive de l'ouverture à l'Être*) to a "Being-subject" (*l'Être-sujet*), a subject that is emptied of all representation, ideas, images, thoughts, even the designation "mind" or "ego," mindfulness empty of mind.[226] Alluding to this "perceived life" (*vie perçue*), Merleau-Ponty notes that "at the level of the human body" he will describe a "pre-knowing [*pré-savoir*]; a pre-meaning [*pré-sens*], a silent knowing [*savoir silencieux*]."[227]

The venture is to establish a "more muted relationship with the world," a relationship that is designated "openness upon the world" (*ouverture au monde*), a prelinguistic, preconceptual, presentient release that cannot be grasped by the reflective modalities of intervention through which mundane commerce is mediated.[228] Merleau-Ponty insists that the only way that access to things in the world is ensured is to purify the notion of subjectivity to the point that there is no "subjectivity" or "Ego," to become "consciousness [that] is without inhabitant," to discover the "nothing" (*le rien*) or the "void" (*le vide*), the "capacity for the plentitude of the world, or rather which needs it to bear its own emptiness" (*qui est capable de la plenitude du monde ou plutôt qui en a besoin pour porter son inanité*).[229] The metaphysical isolation of the idealist position, epitomized by the self-reflexivity of the Cartesian *cogito*, is challenged by the notion of things gazing at the consciousness that gazes upon them, a twofold mirroring whereby the egological and ontological are absorbed in a field of perceptual reciprocity, worldliness of mind and mindfulness of world: "It is not we who perceive, it is the thing that perceives itself yonder—it is not we who speak, it is truth that speaks itself at the depths of speech—Becoming nature of man which is the becoming-man of nature."[230] Implied in this utterance, it seems, is the assumption that consciousness—which is always embodied—is the emptiness that is full, and world, the fullness that is empty. Perceptual awareness, being open to the presence that is "neither being-object nor being-subject, neither essence nor existence,"[231] is speech without syllabic enunciation. In this din of unsaying, one may unearth the meeting point of intercorporeality,[232] the phenomenological ground zero where subject is not subject to being other than object, nor object to being other than subject.

Building on Heidegger's rejection of the conventional epistemic binary, consciousness/world, Merleau-Ponty locates the precategorical ground that transcends the antonym of subjectivity and objectivity in the lived body. In this nondual, prepredicative state, if a state it be at all, language (*la langue*), which is based on differentiating one thing from another, is not appropriate, but we can speak of "speech" (*la parole*), a form of embodied communication, the gestured speaking of the speaking gesture,[233] that does not disturb the "intertwining" (*l'entrelacs*) of subject and object in the "chiasm" (*le chiasme*) where neither subject nor object loom.[234] However, even the emergence of particular languages does not compromise the interdependence of consciousness and world; the reciprocity of vision is maintained in the shared texture of the "flesh" (*la chair*), Merleau-Ponty's designation for the rudimentary element of being, the openness of the body-subject enfolded in the openness of being.[235] "The flesh of the world . . . is indivision of this sensible Being that I am and all the rest which feels itself [*se sent*] in me, pleasure-reality indivision—The flesh *is a mirror phenomenon* and the mirror is an extension of my relation with my body."[236] Body and word are held together in the flesh/mirror of "non-difference" (*non-différence*), the chiasm, wherein opposites are equally indifferent in virtue of being indifferently equal.[237] The convergence cannot be denied without ipso facto being affirmed; the linguistic nature of being and the ontic nature of language find their ontological foundation in this ever-changing ground arising from the "world of silence . . . where there are non-language significations."[238] In the final analysis, "language realizes, by breaking the silence [*le langage réalise en brisant le silence*], what the silence wished and did not obtain. Silence continues to envelop language; the silence of the absolute language [*langage absolu*], of the thinking language [*langage pensant*]."[239] Rejecting the possibility of a "direct ontology," Merleau-Ponty designates his "indirect" method, which entails "being in the beings" (*l'être dans les étants*), "negative philosophy," for, in the pattern of "negative theology," ultimate knowledge consists of a silence that "envelops" speech, but this silence is complimentary to rather than the "contrary of language."[240]

Inscripting the Invisible/Envisioning the Ineffable

Plainly stated, my contention is that applying the poetics I have delineated, in great measure informed by Heidegger, may enhance the study of kabbalistic hermeneutics and poetic imagination.[241] Attested in the intricate symbolic world of medieval kabbalah is a nexus of language, imagination, and world-making that is indicative of a poetic orientation to being in the world; the emphasis of this study, then, is not restricted to the literary form of poetry—indeed, the vast majority of the texts with which I will be engaged are not, strictly speaking, poems—but to an ontic sensibility whereby things of the world are envisioned as word-images infused with the vibrancy of visual verbalization.[242] For the kabbalist, as the poet, language, the multivalent vocalizations of the unspeakable name, informs us about the duplicitous nature of truth as the concealed disclosure of the disclosed concealment, the plentitude diminished in its overflowing, the absence brimful in its withholding; all that exists is a symbolic in/articulation of the ineffable name, the word that is not a sign but a showing that manifests the facade of reality in its inexhaustible linguistic potentiality.[243] Scholem remarked that the one link that masters of kabbalah, in contrast to other mystics (a distinction to which I do not subscribe),[244] have with poets "is their belief in language as an absolute, which is as if constantly flung open by dialectics. It is their belief in the mystery of language which has become audible."[245] The dialectics to which Scholem referred is the paradoxical understanding of the symbol (an understanding that he shared with Benjamin) as communication of the incommunicable. A consequence of identifying YHWH as the root word, the primal language, is that ineffability assumes the posture of the measure of what is spoken. It follows, moreover, that the positive value that kabbalists bestow on language does not mean they oppose in principle the restraint and limitation of speech that are often associated with mystical experience.[246] The affirmation of language as inherently symbolic implies that language inevitably exceeds its own boundary; the mystic, as poet, grasps that truth of speech as a saying of what cannot be spoken but in speaking the unspoken.[247]

For the kabbalist, divine autogenesis reflects this process, envisioned as the word breaking out in the outbreaking of silence. The emanation of the *sefirot* by which the nameless dons the attire of the name is experienced in the withdrawal/bestowing, a pattern that well suits the nature of language, epitomized by the poetic, as speaking the inaudible, inscripting the invisible.[248] The boldest application of this dialectic—not to be construed in the Hegelian sense as the identity of identity and nonidentity but rather in postmodern logic, whereby identity and nonidentity are identical precisely because they are not identical[249]—is found in the Lurianic kabbalah that began to circulate in various versions in the sixteenth and seventeenth centuries, though I consider the mythologoumenon to be much older, traceable to different strata of zoharic literature. The myth of catharsis underlying the notion of *ṣimṣum*, the contraction of the infinite into itself to create a space, an opening, the clearing in which God will be present by being absent, relates to the topos of divine suffering.[250] The manifestation of what is hidden, the creation of an other for that which has no other since it comprehends everything within itself, is a rupture of the primal, nondifferentiated one, the articulation of the name by which the nameless is to be called. The process of delimitation can be viewed in textual terms as the constriction of the limitless within the boundaries of Torah, which is identified symbolically with the ineffable name.[251] The Lurianic teaching discloses a basic tenet of the poiesis of kabbalistic contemplation at play at a much earlier historical moment: the primary linguistic gesture on the part of the kabbalist—reading the word that is inscripted—liberates God from his originary suffering in scripting the word that is spoken, the showing of the saying of the nameless name, a feat that marks the ontological limit where being is nothing in the nothing of being and nothing being in the being of nothing,[252] the "insubstantial Substance of all things, who transcends all substance,"[253] the ontic perimeter of the semiotic horizon.

To savor the mystical intuition of the divine as the coincidence of being and nothing—what may be considered for the kabbalist, as his counterpart in medieval Islamic and Christian mystical speculation, the primary ontological binary that comprises other binary constructions, the binary of binaries, we might say—one must reclaim the middle excluded by the logic of the excluded middle, for it is only by positioning oneself in that middle between extremes that one can appreciate the identity of opposites in the opposition of their identity: that a thing is not only both itself and its opposite, but neither itself nor its opposite.[254] Even nondiscrimination must not be treated as the antinomy of discrimination; true insight into the oneness of everything requires that one transcend all distinctions, even the distinction of distinctiveness and indistinctiveness, unconditional unity and conditional multiplicity.[255] From a phenomenological standpoint, the path of the inclusive middle engendered by the ontological coincidence of opposites is discerned experientially in knowing that the invisible (the use of the definite article is unfortunate as it has the potential of conveying a sense of being qua substance; what is marked semiotically as "invisible" can be seen only as not seen if it is not seen as seen) is rendered visible by the cloaking of invisibility, the secret exposed in the obfuscation of secrecy. In kabbalistic lore, there is symmetry between emanation and esoteric hermeneutics: the one as the other entails a process of uncovering preexistent roots by laying bare the complex simplicity of the simple complexity of Ein Sof.[256]

In the context of discussing the philosophical quandary of eternity versus creation, Abraham Abulafia elegantly expressed the matter of hermeneutic dissembling: "My intention is to hide and to reveal, to reveal and to hide, for the truth is deep for the enlightened and how much more so for the ignorant!"[257] This orientation, which I consider basic to the esoteric texture of kabbalah from its inception, is enunciated explicitly by sixteenth-century kabbalists in Safed, utilizing a maxim that can be traced to the Muslim philosopher Avicenna: "disclosure is the cause of concealment and concealment the cause of disclosure."[258] That which is without limit can be revealed only when concealed, for if not concealed, it could not be revealed as the concealed being it appears (not) to be.[259] All that exists, therefore, is simultaneously a manifestation and occlusion of the divine essence; in language utilized by many Sufi masters, the world of separation (*farq*), which is known by human beings through sentient and rational forms, is a veil (*ḥijāb*) that hides the divine light by rendering it visible, the self-disclosure (*tajallī*) of the true reality (*al-ḥaqq*) that is without form and consequently beyond representation.[260]

That this matter was considered occult wisdom that should not be readily divulged is attested by a remark of Averroës (1126–1198), the Spanish-Muslim philosopher credited with an elaborate defense of Aristotelianism. In a passage in his *Tahāfut al-Tahāfut* (*The Incoherence of the Incoherence*), a refutation of al-Ghazālī's attack on the philosophers, *Tahāfut al-Falāsifa*, Averroës relates the philosophical view that God is the totality and agent of all existent beings to the dictum "there is no reality besides Him," which is ascribed to the "chief of the Sufis." Averroës insists that this is "knowledge of those who are steadfast in their knowledge, and this must not be written down and it must not be made an obligation of faith, and therefore is not taught by the Divine Law. And one who mentions this truth where it should not be mentioned sins, and one who withholds it from those to whom it should be told sins too."[261] Several points are notable. First, Averroës sees no conflict between the philosophical and mystical perspectives; on the contrary, they are identical insofar as both affirm a metaphysical monism positing one ultimate reality for all that exists. Indeed, the view expressed by Averroës accords with the doctrine regarding divine unity (*tawḥīd*) promulgated by al-Ghazālī, aptly described as "Semitic monotheism seen through the prism of Neoplatonism,"[262] that is, the thesis that the universe has no independent existence, for the only thing that is real is God and all things proceed by way of emanation from the one true source. Second, this gnosis is esoteric and hence should not be committed to writing—a view ironically transmitted in a written text—nor is it an essential part of one's religious obligations. Third, it is equally transgressive to reveal the truth to one unworthy of receiving it and to conceal it from one worthy of receiving it. What is crucial from my perspective to reiterate is that even Averroës affirmed the occult wisdom promulgated by the Sufi doctrine to be philosophically viable.

It would be useful to recall the distinction between "exoteric monotheism" and "esoteric and gnostic theomonism" introduced by Corbin to explain the paradox of unity and multiplicity in Islamic theosophy, expressed in a particularly poignant way in the thought of Muḥyīddīn Ibn al-ʿArabī (1165–1240) and his school.[263] By "theomonism" Corbin intends "no more than the philosophical expression of the interdependence of Creator and created—interdependence, that is, on the level of theophany."[264] The oneness of being (*waḥdat al-wujūd*),[265] the essence (*māhiyya*) of the one true reality (*al-ḥaqq*), is manifest in the multiplicity of divine names and attributes (*asmāʾ wa-ṣifāt*) enclothed in the created beings (*al-khalq*) of the material universe. In *al-Futūḥāt al-Makkiya* (*Meccan Revelations*), Ibn ʿArabī describes the world as "God's mirror," for "the knowers see nothing in it but God's form."[266] Shortly after making this point, however, Ibn ʿArabī recoils somewhat by noting the bewildering nature of the paradoxical identification and nonidentification of the identity and nonidentity of God and world, a paradox even for those who possess esoteric gnosis (*maʿrifa*):

> The knowers try to separate (*faṣl*) Him from the world, but they are unable to do so; they try to make Him identical with the world (*ʿayn al-ʿālam*), but that does not become verified for them, so they remain impotent. Their understandings become wearied and their intellects bewildered. Their tongues speak about Him in contradictory expressions. At one time they say "He," at another, "Not He," and at still another, "He/not He" [*huwa lā huwa*].[267]

In Corbin's own words, "The world of phenomena is the theophanic world; in no way is it an illusion—its existence is real, since it is actually the theophany, the other self of the absolute."[268] To speak of the cosmos as the epiphany of the one true being is tenable only if one presumes that disclosure is concealment, for the ipseity of this being is revealed through "seventy veils of light and darkness," in the language of the oft-cited prophetic dictum (*ḥadīth*); indeed, there can be no "other self of the absolute" since the latter is by definition the being that comprehends all being and thus allows for no alterity, in the formulation of Azriel of Gerona, the thirteenth-century kabbalist, applied to the infinite (identified by him as either Ein Sof or *Keter*, the first emanation), *ein huṣ mimmennu*, "there is nothing outside it."[269] The very notion of the "other self of the absolute" is nothing but a veil veiling the fact that there is no other self of the absolute; by this account the cosmos is the epiphany of the unity of the one (*aḥadiyyat al-aḥad*) unveiled through the veils of the unity of the many (*aḥadiyyat al-kathra*).[270] The thirteenth-century Persian mystic, ʿAzīz ibn-Muḥammad-i Nasafī, put it this way:

> Everything taken together is God's being; for there is only one being as such, since within being neither a duality nor a multiplicity with regard to being is possible. Since God alone and nothing else has being, everything that is must necessarily be God. He is the first, He is the last, He is the outer and also the inner, He is the knowing and likewise He is the known.[271]

Nasafī draws the paradoxical implication of the esoteric monism by noting that the "true being," which is the being of the divine, "is a being that appears as nonbeing [*nēst-numāy*], but imaginary being, the being of the world, is a nonbeing that appears as being [*hastnumāy*]. The world *is* through God, God *appears* through the world. God is the reality of the world, the world is the form of God."[272]

Reiterating this perspective in slightly different terminology, Corbin notes that "each creature has a twofold dimension: the Creator-creature typifies the *coincidentia oppositorum*. From the first this *coincidentia* is present to Creation, because Creation is not *ex nihilo* but a theophany. As such, it is Imagination."[273] The world of differentiation is a coincidence of opposites, exemplifying the temporal contingency of created beings and the eternal necessity of the uncreated being. God is the one infinite being that contains all finite beings, and hence each of the finite beings must be considered a part of the one infinite being, but none of these finite beings, either alone or collectively, manifests the full power of the one infinite being, and hence each of the finite beings must be considered apart from the one infinite being. As Corbin summed up the matter, the "Creative Imagination is a theophanic imagination, and the Creator is one with the imagining Creature because each Creative Imagination is a theophany, a recurrence of the Creation. Psychology is indistinguishable from cosmology; the theophanic Imagination joins them into a psycho-cosmology."[274] Within the spectrum of the imaginal topography, God, world, and mind converge so that revelation, creation, and redemption are three prisms through which the mystical paradox of seeing all things in the one and the one in all things is apprehended.[275]

Following in the footsteps of Corbin, Toshihiko Izutsu explicates the theophanic insight that the phenomenal world is a "*coincidentia oppositorum* of Unity and Multiplicity."[276] Commenting on the remark in the *Gulshan-e Rāz* of Maḥmūd Shabastarī, "bright night amidst the dark daylight" (*shab-e roushan miyān-e rūz-e tārik*), Izutsu suggests that "bright night" refers to the "peculiar structure of Reality as it discloses itself at the stage of the subjective and objective *fanā'* in which one witnesses the annihilation of all outward manifestations of Reality." Night thus signifies the effacement of phenomenal difference in the "darkness of the original indiscrimination." The state wherein "nothing is discernible" is also described as "bright" because "absolute Reality in itself—that is, apart from all considerations of the limitations set by the very structure of our relative consciousness—is essentially luminous, illuminating its own self as well as all others." The second part of Shabastarī's remark, "amidst the dark daylight," denotes that the "absolute Unity is revealing itself in the very midst of Multiplicity, in the form of determined, relative things." In the "phenomenal daylight," the "absolute Reality is clearly visible in the external world." Yet this daylight is dark because the "things that appear in it are in themselves of the nature of darkness and non-existence."[277] The night of the infinite in which the variegated sentient forms are no longer discernible is bright, whereas the daylight of the phenomenal world of appearances is dark. Material objects are veils through which the invisible is revealed and concealed.

It is noteworthy that Corbin and Izutsu formulate the axiom of Islamic esotericism in the celebrated language of Nicholas of Cusa, a thinker from a later date and a different cultural context. The use of the term *coincidentia oppositorum* is fortuitous as it affords us an opportunity to consider Cusanus's thinking in some more detail—the dialectic metalogic that underlies metaphysical panenhenism (based on the Greek *pan en hen*, all-in-one),[278] the mystical insight that the one contains all things and yet remains distinct. Needless to say, it is beyond the scope of this chapter to present an adequate, let alone comprehensive, account of the intricate speculative meditations of Cusanus, as much poetic as philosophic, but for our immediate purposes I shall mention some salient themes in the hopes of elucidating the panenhenic orientation that I ascribe to kabbalists.

In *De docta ignorantia*, Nicholas argues that we can distinguish between God as *maximum absolutum* and the universe as *maximum contractum*, respectively the subject matter of books one and two, but in the knowledge of faith, the "learned ignorance," the spiritual vision of the "absolute seeing power" (*virtute visiva absoluta*) that exceeds reason, we confront the axiom—adduced dialectically through paradox rather than discursively through demonstration—underlying the mystery of incarnation, the *coincidentia oppositorum* of the limited and unlimited, captured in the maxim that is the theme of book three, *maximum simul contractum et absolutum*.[279] Insofar as God is the "absolute form of all formable things, He enfolds in Himself the forms of all things" (*Deus autem, cum sit ratio absoluta omnium formabilium rationum, in se omnium rationes complicat*),[280] we can speak of the divine, the absolute maximum, as the limitless delimitation of all beings,[281] and the universe, the contracted maximum, as a mirror through which the invisible is rendered visible. To behold this paradox is to perceive the matter from the vantage point of "absolute sight" (*visus absolutus*) or "absolute vision" (*visio absoluta*) that "encompasses all modes of seeing." As one would expect, this applies most precisely to God—a point that Cusanus links etymologically to the word *theos*, to which he refers as the "great name"[282]—the pure seeing in which there is no distinction between seer and seen. Cusanus tests the limits of language in an attempt to articulate the paradox of the compresence of infinite finitude and finite infinity in the vision that transcends the polarity of subject and object:

"For in Absolute Sight every contracted mode of seeing is present uncontractedly. For all contraction of sight is present in Absolute Sight, because Absolute Sight is the Contraction of contractions [*contractio contractionum*]. For it is Uncontractible Contradiction [*Contractio enim est incontrahibilis*]."[283] To see with absolute sight is to envision the totality from the divine perspective, that is, to see the one in all things and all things in the one, to see that the one is everything but no thing, a possibility fully actualized in Jesus, who, as the word incarnate, was the maximum human being. Cusanus explains the matter by the metaphor of the seed and branch: the truth of the seed is the truth of the branch, and thus the branch is depicted as a manifestation of the power of the seed. Analogously, "in God, the Son is—in accordance with His absolute omnipotence and infinite light—the true disclosing of the Father. But every creature is a disclosing of the Father and participates diversely and contractedly in the Son's disclosing [of Him]. Some creatures disclose Him more dimly, others more clearly—in accordance with a diversity of theophanies, or manifestations of God."[284]

From this standpoint, creation can be conceived technically as theophany. Cusanus is careful to emphasize, however, that the cosmic mirror is not a perfect reflection of the infinite divine essence; between the absolute infinity of God and the infinity of the created world there always remains an infinite distance, the unknowable and unnameable essence of the Absolute Maximum.[285] The fact that everything derives from God precludes the possibility that God be limited to any particular thing; expressed syllogistically, if God is all things, God can be no thing, for if God were not no thing, God would be some thing and hence not all things.[286] The "essence of all essences," writes Cusanus, "is each essence in such a way that it is all of them together and none of them in particular."[287] The paradoxical identity of transcendence and immanence rests on a more primary (conceptually and not chronologically) paradox that every disclosure of the infinite is perforce concealment. In his own words, "Who could understand the following: how all things are the image of that one, infinite Form and are different contingently—as if a created thing were a god manqué, just as an accident is a substance manqué, and a woman is a man manqué? For the infinite Form is received only finitely, so that every created this is, as it were, a finite infinity or a created god, so that it exists in the way in which this can best occur."[288] From this vantage point we can, nay must, conclude that God both is and is not identical with the world, identical precisely because different, different precisely because identical.[289]

When the matter of the mystical vision is seen through this prism, it is no longer necessary to posit an unbridgeable chasm separating symbol (whether understood as word or image) and symbolized, a rift maintained by the presumption of a transcendental reality set over and against all appearances that are immanent. On the contrary, the symbolized can be ascertained only through the symbol, and the symbol through the symbolized. In a memorable formulation of one zoharic passage, based on terminology utilized in an older talmudic legend,[290] the mystery of traversing ontic boundaries—the descent of the divine potencies into this world in the form of embodied Jewish souls and the ascent of the latter back to the former—is characterized in the following way: "Verily the world is inverted [*alma be-hippukha ihu mammash*], the supernal ones below and the lower ones above."[291] One will discern in the turn of phrase *alma be-hippukha* an echo of the archaic occult wisdom discussed previously in this chapter, the homology between heaven and earth, but beyond the image of mirror reflection, the zoharic text affirms an actual crossing of lines; the world is on its head because what is above is below and what is below is above.[292]

This double mirroring at the base of the kabbalists' construction of the identity of God, self, and world can also be expressed through a post-Romantic understanding that would eliminate the dichotomy between appearance and reality in assuming that reality is naught but appearance, a view that I briefly mentioned in conjunction with Heidegger's reading of Nietzsche.[293] At the heart of what I will call poetic envisioning is the imaginary configuration of that which has no image through the semblance of what it appears not to be. Sensory entities are symbolic of the divine names and attributes, the *sefirot*, but the latter themselves are paradigmatic images—*specula*—of what cannot be represented imagistically. Kabbalistic poetics militates against positing an ontic distinction between internal reality and external appearance, as the image is both the reality of the divine potency and the forms of its appearance within human imagination. From this standpoint, one can speak of the natural world as a sign of the spiritual reality, but a sign that depends not on the analogical rift between worlds but on blurring the celestial-terrestrial opposition,[294] a "confluence of the two seas."[295] As Baḥya ben Asher formulated the principle widely confirmed in medieval literature, art, music, and other cultural manifestations, "From the sensible and what is perceptible to the eye we can attest to what is not perceptible."[296]

Here we come upon one of the most significant differences between kabbalists and their coreligionists whose epistemology and ontology were informed by the principle that Aristotle affirmed in the beginning of *De interpretatione*: spoken words are symbols of mental experience, and written words are symbols of spoken words. Philosophical sages at the time that kabbalah began to flourish combined this maxim with another basic tenet of Aristotelian thought: human reason ascertains knowledge by abstracting an essence from the sense data stored and combined in the imagination; the name assigned to that entity, which issues from the mouth, is an image of the idea, and the name that is written is a graphic image of the verbal image.[297] For the kabbalist, the inherent identity of God, human (which denotes more particularly the male Jew),[298] and world precludes the possibility of affirming a realism that accords with Aristotelian epistemology. I am unaware of any kabbalist who would contest the assumption that there is a single essence shared by all three, whence follow the corollaries that knowledge of God is equivalent to self-knowledge, and self-knowledge to knowledge of the cosmos.[299] The consubstantiality of self and God in kabbalistic literature—concomitantly the basis for the ecstatic experience of conjunction (*devequt*) and the theurgic efficacy accorded ritual action integral to the theosophic speculation promulgated by kabbalists[300]—is coupled with the correspondence of the macrocosm and microcosm, the depiction of the world as a "large human" (*adam gadol*) and the human as a "small world" (*olam qaṭan*).[301] God, world, and human are intertwined in a reciprocal mirroring,[302] and hence the kabbalistic perspective may be termed "cosmotheandric,"[303] an adjective that conveys the ultimate indistinguishability of the three correlative elements, the triadic signpost, as it were, God-human-world. To comprehend this properly, one must bear in mind that for kabbalists, the mirror is a medium that renders appearance real and reality apparent, and hence the likeness between image and what is imaged is a matter of ontic resemblance and not simply optic reflexivity.

The point is illustrated by a brief comment by Jacob ben Sheshet: "Since Jacob our patriarch, peace be upon him, was truthful, the attribute of truth was bestowed upon him to arouse the paradigm upon him as the verse says 'Your name shall no longer be Jacob etc.' (Gen. 32:29)."[304] The attribute of truth (*middat ha-emet*) is the sefirotic archetype or paradigm (*dugma*)[305] that is conferred upon Jacob; significantly, the author emphasizes that Jacob was worthy of receiving this attribute because he was truthful and thereby already exemplified it in his demeanor—to receive the gift, one must already possess what is to be gifted, but one cannot possess what is to be gifted if one has not received the gift. The arousal of the divine gradation is transformative, a contention confirmed by the citation of the verse that marks the metamorphosis of Jacob into Israel.

Though not stated explicitly, it is probable that Jacob ben Sheshet had in mind a much older exegetical tradition that understood the change in name as the onomastic demarcation of the angelification/divinization of the earthly Jacob.[306] Be that as it may, what is crucial to elicit from these words is an understanding of paradigm as ontic similitude and not merely as rhetorical trope. The epistemological underpinning of this point is the Empedoclean principle of "like knowing like"[307]—in the language used by the zoharic author, "every type loves its own type, and it proceeds and goes after its own type" (*kol zina raḥim leih le-zineih we-itmeshikh we-azil zina batar zineih*),[308] or, in the parallel formulation of Moses de León, "all matters proceed in perpetuity, each thing after its own kind" (*kol ha-inyyanim nimshakhim le^colam min be-mino*).[309] If we presume that a thing is known only by something of a kindred nature, it must follow that to know God, the self must be of the same substance as God, and to know the world, the self must be of the same substance as the world. In the ultimate metaphysical sense, therefore, there is no possibility of a nondivine reality, and thus it is implausible to speak of a mental idea as an image of an independently existing essence, let alone to envisage the spoken word as a copy of this image and the written word as a copy of the copy.

The use of the mirror metaphor should not mislead one into thinking in binary terms; on the contrary, in kabbalistic discourse, to speak of *x* mirroring *y* means that *x* and *y* are of the same substance and hence ontically indistinguishable.[310] To put the matter in technical scholastic terminology, the cosmology proffered by kabbalists is concurrently exemplarist and analogical. Consider the formulation of Ezra ben Solomon of Gerona, one of the main disciples of Isaac the Blind: "It is known that the emanation [*ha-aṣilut*] of the two worlds was as one, and they are in the pattern of one another [*zeh dugmat zeh*], one corresponding to the other [*zeh le^cumat zeh*]."[311] We find no credible evidence for a distinction between emanation and creation, a distinction known from religious philosophers who sought to harmonize the Neoplatonic approach and scriptural account (interpreted doctrinally as the volitional creation).[312] Ezra uses one word, *aṣilut*, "emanation," to denote both worlds concurrently, "as one." The upper world is identified as the rabbinic *olam ha-ba*, the world to come, which is linked to the "seven extremities" (*sheva qeṣawwot*), divided into six extremities (*shesh qeṣawwot*) and the seventh, which is called the "holy" (*qodesh*), in the center, and these, in turn, are divided into the seventy nations—based on the kabbalistic axiom that each of the ten *sefirot* comprised all the others. The six extremities yield twelve on account of a second kabbalistic axiom—each attribute comprises its opposite—and thus six must be doubled. The seventy and twelve allude to the mystery of the "seventy names standing amidst the twelve tentacles of the world" (*shivʿim shemot omdim be-tokh sheteim esreh zeroʿot olam*).[313] The lower world, designated by the rabbinic idiom, *olam ha-zeh*, "this world," the world of nature, parallels the *sefirot*, and hence Ezra speaks of the "sevenfold" *zayin*[314] connected to this world, which divides into seventy nations who stand amid these twelve diagonal boundaries; and the median line, the holy, corresponds to Zion.

In the language of one zoharic passage, "The holy One, blessed be he, made everything so that this world would be in the likeness [*ke-gawna*] of that which is above and the one would be conjoined [*leitdabbeqa*] to the other so that his glory would be above and below."[315] The juxtaposition of the words *ke-gawna* and *leitdabbeqa* to describe the relation of the lower to the upper worlds underscores that the images of mirroring and merging are not in opposition. According to the formulation of a parallel zoharic text, God "made the lower world in the likeness of the upper world, and the one stands parallel to the other, so that all will be unified in one unity."[316] And in a third passage, another key technical term is introduced: "The holy One, blessed be he, produced in the earth according to the likeness [*ke-gawna*] of heaven, and everything alludes [*remiza*] to what is above."[317] Articulating a worldview that resonates with the distinction made explicitly by Proclus between two modes of representation, the secretive hinting of the symbol—which implies a concomitant disclosure and concealment—and the mimetic portrayal of the icon, the kabbalist would affirm that all that exists in the material universe, which comprises the celestial and terrestrial realms, symbolically alludes to and iconically represents the supernal world of divine emanations.[318] Nevertheless, the relationship between upper and lower is to be viewed reciprocally, as "the upper world depends on the lower and the lower on the upper."[319]

In *Shushan Edut*, de León affirms a similar point, emphasizing the ontological dependence of all existence on the divine emanations comprised in the Tetragrammaton:

> The secret of the worlds is that all of them exist in the subsistence of the ten *sefirot* that are dependent on that-which-is-without being[320] [*be-qiyyum ha-eser sefirot ha-teluyyot bi-velimah*], and all of them exist in gradations, one atop the other . . . until they all ascend to the secret of the awesome faces [*ha-panim ha-noraʾim*] whence the light emerges. . . . Thus, you must know that the awesome faces, illuminating and glistening, are ten *sefirot belimah*, the principle of everything [*kelal ha-kol*], in the secret of his name, blessed be he.[321]

In a second passage, de León reiterates the view, but from an anthropocentric perspective, interpreting the biblical injunction to cleave to God as a mandate to exist in the pattern of the supernal archetype.

> Indeed, in accordance with the existence of everything [*qiyyum ha-kol*], man must be in the pattern of above [*dugma shel maʿalah*] as it is said "cleave to him" (Deut. 10:20) and it is written, "walk in his ways" (ibid., 28:9), in that very image [*be-oto dugma mammash*]. Contemplate [*hitbonen*] the matter of what Solomon said in his wisdom, as all his words were inward [*kol devaraw penimiyyim*] and all of them were balanced on the holy scale [*we-khullam be-sheqel ha-qodesh shequlim*].[322] Understand that he saw that the gradations [*maʿalot*] and worlds [*olamot*] were all clasped together [*neʾeḥazim*], one within the other, and there is one pattern [*dugma*] for them, and he said in the secret of what is written "For God is in heaven and you are on earth; that is why your words should be few" (Eccles. 5:1). . . . All worlds are a pattern within a pattern [*dugma be-tokh dugma*] from the first element to the last element so that he, blessed be he, will be one without division. Adam was created in the image of God, an entity prepared in his pattern to correspond to what is above. . . . Therefore "your words should be few," that is, your words, your affairs, and the needs of your body should be modest since you must be in one pattern like him.[323]

This passage lends support to Scholem's assertion that in zoharic kabbalah, theogony and cosmogony "represent not two different acts of creation, but two aspects of the same. On every plane . . . creation mirrors the inner movement of the divine life. . . . Everywhere there is the same rhythm, the same motion of the waves."[324] Furthermore, de León's remark attests that this mirroring, the correspondence between upper and lower, is not a matter of mimetic reflection but rather an affirmation of metaphysical panenhenism, which is predicated on ontological participation in the ceaseless flux of the many issuing from and returning to the infinite spring of the one.[325] It is reasonable, conceptually and historically, to express the relation of God-and-world in kabbalistic thought by the Neoplatonic model of *complicatio-explicatio*, the dialectic of the enfolding and unfolding of all things in and from God. A key semiotic marker that articulates this idea is the twofold connotation of the term *dugma*, and its cognate *ke-gawna*, referring to the model and its copy. When de León, for instance, speaks of the patriarchs and matriarchs respectively as *dugma elyonit* or *dugma elyonah*, the "supernal pattern,"[326] what he intends to say is that the sign itself is the signified, creating a seemingly endless mirror-play of nonrepresentational representation, the mirror mirroring the mirrored mirroring the mirror.

By attending properly to the import of these words, one is in a better position to understand the reciprocal reciprocity that bridges the imaginal and real, the metaphorical and literal, a doubling of the double that yields the structure of the fourfold. In this fourfold, ecstatic and theurgic cannot be separated: mystical conjunction (*devequt*) is precisely what facilitates the unification of God in all things. The import of the scriptural axiom that Adam is endowed with the image of God is that the Jewish male must diminish his engagement with the physical so that he can prepare his being to be in the pattern of the supernal archetype, *adam qadmon*, the form of primal Adam configured in the imagination, and thereby transform the world at large into a pattern of that supernal archetype. The construction of the imaginal body is critical to establishing the unity of the one in all things. In this respect, the human is accorded a distinguished ontic status even though all things are infused with and therefore can be said to mirror the divine reality. As de León puts it in *Sefer ha-Rimmon*:

> The image of the lower world is from the upper world, and all the gradations concatenate in one chain so that his glory extends in all of them and his unity evolves in all worlds. Indeed, the blessed one brings forth Adam to rule in this world in the supernal pattern [*dugma elyonit*] . . . so that he will discern and know him and so that he will be a proper creature . . . and through him the world will be aligned, and he is the pattern of what is above insofar as he makes an effort to worship and to know him.[327]

The point is reiterated in *Sefer ha-Mishqal*:

> Man [*adam*] is in the secret of the true supernal pattern [*be-sod dugma elyonah amitit*] over all other beings below, for he is unique [*oleh bifnei aṣmo*], and thus he is called a microcosm [*olam qaṭan*]. . . . You must know and comprehend that the secret of the supernal soul [*sod ha-neshamah ha-elyonah*] is in the pattern of the Creator [*dugmat ha-bore*] just as the son is in the pattern of the father, for he is his edifice verily [*binyyano mammash*]. Similarly, the supernal soul is the edifice of the pattern of the Creator [*binyan dugmat bore*], and this is the "divine image" [*ṣelem elohim*], the image of the pattern of the Creator, for the body is not in the image of the Creator, blessed be he.[328]

I shall return to the hermeneutical implications of the fourfold mirror-play in chapter five; suffice it here to note that my interpretation provides a response to what I consider two erroneous dichotomies that have plagued the understanding of symbol and metaphor in contemporary kabbalah scholarship. The first is Scholem's distinction between the "symbolic aspect" of the kabbalistic view, which affirms the continuous chain of being arising from the assumption concerning the presence of the infinite—a presence of what is perforce absent—in all things so that everything in the various levels of being or worlds mirrors the sefirotic paradigms, and the "magical aspect," which is predicated on the theurgical notion that there is reciprocal action and reaction between the divine and mundane.[329] I do not think it necessary to separate these two aspects, as the very possibility of the latter is dependent on the former, and the former on the latter; the discernment that all things are one facilitates the appreciation that actions below affect what is above, and actions above, what is below; alternatively, appreciation that actions below affect what is above, and above, what is below facilitates the discernment that the multiplicity of discrete beings are substantively one. In the morphology of medieval kabbalah, the symbolic and magical cannot be separated.

The second binary that can be shown to be mistaken is proffered by Yehuda Liebes. Although Liebes is to be commended for correcting Scholem's dichotomization of the symbolic and theurgic by pointing out that the word *dugma* in zoharic literature "means symbol, one which not only represents but influences the upper worlds,"[330] his presentation suffers from introducing another false dichotomy between the "symbolic" and "mythic," the former denoting an imaginary state, and the latter something actual. In my judgment, there is no philosophical basis for making such a distinction, as the zoharic landscape defies any hard-and-fast line dividing imagined and real. To meander in the imaginal time-space fashioned by the kabbalists of the *Zohar* is to find oneself always in the middle, along the path, betwixt and between, conceiving the imagined as real and the real as imagined. The symbol is a sign and as such it is a bridge that leads from one shore to another, but when one comes upon the latter, one discerns that it itself is naught but a bridge that leads to another shore, and so on in a seemingly endless crossing of bridges, an orientation that Umberto Eco has astutely called "pansemioticism";[331] the inherent proliferation of the symbolic sign is captured in the poetic trope of de León, *dugma be-tokh dugma*, exemplar within exemplar. But how does one account for the veracity of the exemplar when the exemplum is itself an exemplar? In this web of dissimulation, image within image, can one credibly distinguish symbolic as imaginary and mythic as real?

Let us take a closer look at the passages in *Zohar* that Liebes comments on to establish his taxonomy. The first affirms the necessity of the companions, the rabbinic members of the contrived mystical fraternity, the *ḥavrayya*, to follow the paradigm (*dugma*) of the patriarchs who loved and embraced one another in a bond of fidelity.[332] Following the prevalent theosophic symbolism, already attested in one bahiric pericope,[333] Abraham, Isaac, and Jacob stand symbolically in the sublunar sphere of human history for *Ḥesed*, *Gevurah*, and *Raḥamim*, the three central *sefirot*, the right, left, and median balance. Needless to say, the rabbis who belong to the fellowship, the disciple-colleagues of Simeon ben Yoḥai, are the product of the literary imagination of the anonymous kabbalists, the self-effaced authors responsible for the bulk of the homilies anthologized as *Sefer ha-Zohar.* To determine what is real and what is imagined in zoharic narratives, to even entertain the possibility of such a distinction, one must first take hold of the fact that there are four levels of identity that must be considered, though the last is only implied: divine emanations, biblical personae, rabbinic figures, and unnamed kabbalists—every thing/word can potentially be ascribed to some reality on each of these planes of being, computed, it stands to reason, always from a human vantage point. To unpack the previous sentence properly, it would be necessary to focus on the intricate relationship of time and narrativity in these four planes, in the language of traditional kabbalah, the four garments through which the formless light is adorned to be (un)seen in its manifest concealment, but of necessity I must be brief and concentrate even more restrictively on the core of the counterposition I shall occupy in opposition to Liebes.[334]

At play in zoharic *derashot* are four temporal modalities corresponding to the four identities. The full significance of this correlation demands an independent investigation, but for my immediate purposes it is sufficient to note that the four modalities can be grouped under two types of temporality: the first, which stands by itself, comprises the genus of eternal time, that is, time eternal, the unfolding of divine darkness in multiple folds of light that constitute the eternality of time and the temporality of eternity; and the remaining three constitute the genus of temporal time, the time of temporality measured by human technology and recorded as the annals of historical epochs. The movement through these four levels is presented at times as an exegetical journey of a linear sort, passing, presumably hierarchically, from the mundane to the divine, the lower to the upper, the corporeal to the spiritual, but the journey is anything but linear. The line, for the kabbalists, is always to be considered in conjunction with the circle, two geometric prisms through which time and space are configured in human imagination.[335] To be attuned to this linear circularity,[336] which, in my way of thinking, constitutes the measure of space, time, and imagination, is to experience the traversing of temporal identities, the past is the present as future, the present, the future as past, the future, past as present. In this mesh of mirroring, there is no sense of immutable identity and consequently no fixed boundary, no cast-iron fence, that justifies the rigid distinction between mythic and symbolic.

The problematic nature of the attempt to contrast the two is even more pronounced in the zoharic text that Liebes cites in the accompanying note.[337] In that passage (which appears in the section made up of the discourses attributed to the *yanuqa*,[338] the precocious son of Rav Hamnuna Sava,[339] the zoharic version of the topos of the wunderkind), the vision of *Shekhinah* as it appeared initially to Moses is contrasted with the vision of Jacob: Moses saw the divine presence in the garb of an angel, Jacob saw only an image (*le-moshe kad itḥazei leih be-qadmita iqrei mal᾿akh le-ya῾aqov lo itḥazei hakhi ela be-dugma*). Liebes renders the end of the passage "Jacob could do this only in a symbolic way."[340] Support for translating *be-dugma* as "symbolic" may be gathered from the proof-text cited in and exegetically glossed in the continuation of the zoharic homily, *we-raḥel ba᾿ah da diyoqna de-raḥel aḥra*, "'And Rachel came' (Gen. 29:9), this is the image of the other Rachel." The zoharic author hands the reader the hermeneutical tool necessary to decipher the scriptural verse: Rachel is linked symbolically to *Shekhinah*, the "other Rachel." A fundamental axiom of kabbalistic hermeneutics is the belief that earthly figures correspond to sefirotic archetypes.[341] As de León formulates the matter, "The matriarchs are the secret of the image above [*sod dugma shel ma῾lah*] just as the patriarchs are the supernal image [*dugma elyonit*]. . . . Indeed, the secret of this matter is a hidden and wondrous secret in the secret of his divinity."[342]

Up to this point I concur with Liebes. The difficulty, however, is in using the word "mythic" to refer to the angelic vision of Moses that is set in contrast to the symbolic experience of Jacob. The word "symbolic," it seems to me, should encompass the former as well. The words *dugma* and *diyoqna* are used to denote the physical manifestation of the spiritual reality in the mundane world, whereas *mal᾿akh* signifies an incarnational form of a more reified sort, the subtle or ethereal body, a theme to which I shall return in chapter five. The challenge I would offer to Liebes is brought into sharper relief when we consider another zoharic passage that he alludes to in his explication of the aforecited text, wherein the conjunction of Moses and *Shekhinah* is contrasted with that of Jacob: the former was conjoined *be-gufa*, literally, "in the body," and the latter *be-ruaḥ*, "in the spirit."[343] According to Liebes, this nomenclature indicates that the coupling of Moses was "physical," that is, "it actually took place" and thus he had to separate from his wife, whereas that of Jacob was "spiritual," that is, "it was carried out symbolically through his coupling with his wife Rachel." One cannot deny that the zoharic author wants to establish a distinction between the two biblical figures and their respective relationships to *Shekhinah*, but I do not see the merit of not using the word "symbolic" to demarcate the conjunction of Moses and the divine presence. In my opinion, such a move is rooted in a misconception about the nature of symbol as distinct from reality. The examples he adduces of the symbolic also embrace an ontic reality, actualized in the imagination, that would justify the use of the term "mythic," just as the examples of the mythic still entail the bridging of the ostensibly distinct ontological realms, the spiritual and corporeal, the invisible and visible, that would justify the use of the term "symbolic."

What has not been sufficiently appreciated in previous scholarship is the relevance of this monistic orientation in assessing the role of the particular language that kabbalists exploit in the mapping of the divine physiognomy. The repeated employment of anthropomorphic and erotic metaphors characterizes the essential commission of poiesis as the construction of the narrative form[344] wherein anthropomorphism and theomorphism converge, the forging of a nonrepresentational language that points to the paradoxical imaging of God in human terms and the human in divine terms.[345] In seeing God, one sees oneself, for in seeing oneself, one sees God. The mythic import of kabbalistic symbolism secures the representation of the nonrepresentable by creating an imaginal body,[346] a body whose ontic status is that of a "real" if not "actual" entity.[347] The symbol, therefore, is diaphanous, for it speaks the unspeakable and thereby allows the invisible to be seen, a paradox that yields the hermeneutic conclusion that every act of representation is a mode of interpretation.

No kabbalist from the late Middle Ages to the present would argue with the assumption that the God of Judaism is incorporeal. However, kabbalists well understood that the vibrancy of religious experience in a theistic tradition is predicated on the possibility of imaging the divine anthropomorphically, of picturing God's invisibility, rendering the forbidden image in such a way that on the one hand, iconoclasm was not compromised,[348] and on the other, they did not succumb to what Corbin referred to as "metaphysical idolatry,"[349] that is, the danger of rejecting multiple theophanic forms of the divine and thereby reifying the one God in anthropomorphic terms to preserve the efficacy of ritual worship. The imaginal forms of the sefirotic potencies are neither literal facts nor figurative truths. Rather, they are symbols constructed in the imagination through which the suprasensible reality is experienced (not merely described) in sensual terms. In the moment of ecstatic experience, the breach between image and reality is bridged, as that which is most abstract, merely a figure of speech, is fully embodied.[350]

An interesting application of this phenomenon, and one that has particular relevance to the discussion at hand, is found in a comment of Jacob ben Sheshet that occurs in the context of his distinguishing between the status of one who is conjoined to the sixth emanation, *Tif'eret*, the "throne," and the tenth emanation, *Shekhinah*, the "footstool":

> The one conjoined [*ha-daveq*] to his throne in a unified conjunction without pause [*devequt aḥadi beli hefseq*] is called "throne," and the one conjoined to his glory and his presence is called "footstool," and similarly the throne and footstool are called by their names. This is the principle [*kelal*]: That which is conjoined is called by the

> name of the thing to which it is conjoined and the thing by the name of that which is conjoined to it.[351]

The principle, it should be clear, is a version of the teaching of Empedocles mentioned above. From the perspective of the medieval kabbalist epitomized by Jacob ben Sheshet, the sharing of the name is indicative of a convergence of identity, perhaps bordering on the doctrine of *homoousios*. What is even more pertinent is that in the continuation of his argument, Jacob utilizes this principle to explain anthropomorphic expressions in the scriptural and rabbinic corpora:

> All this is proof that what is conjoined to a thing is called by its name and similarly the thing by the name of that which is conjoined to it. Do not forget this matter in every place that you find "the hand of the Lord," "the face of the Lord," "the ears of the Lord," "the eyes of the Lord," for even though I have written this matter from my heart, know that, in truth, it is a received and great matter [*davar mequbbal we-gadol*], and the philosophers cannot contradict it, all the more so the masters of the true tradition [*ba῾alei ha-qabbalah ha-amitit*]. And this is a great tenet [*iqqar*] by which to comprehend several hidden things and to explain several verses such as "The hand of the Lord was upon me" (Ezek. 37:1), "The eyes of the Lord ranging over the whole earth" (Zech. 4:10), "On that day, he will set his feet on the Mount of Olives" (ibid., 14:4), and many other verses like these, and to comprehend the essence of the intent of several matters in the words of our rabbis, peace be upon them.[352]

In obvious contradistinction to the allegorical explanation proffered by the "philosophers," Jacob maintains that anthropomorphic representations of God allude to a secret that is illumined by the principle "what is conjoined to a thing is called by its name and similarly the thing by the name of that which is conjoined to it." For the kabbalist, therefore, one can speak of the incarnation of the word, albeit not in the Christological sense of the materialization of the divine in the person of Jesus[353] but, rather, in the convergence of the semiotic and somatic, the word-become-image configured symbolically in imagination, a convergence that is transmitted in the esoteric gnosis as the identity of the name and human form, the divine body that is the sacred writ.[354] In chapter five, I will discuss in more detail the philosophical underpinnings and implications of the incarnational motif in kabbalistic literature, focusing primarily on the thirteenth century. For my immediate purposes, I will cite an exemplary articulation of the theme from the zoharic anthology, a passage wherein the structural and functional homology between human, world, and Torah is affirmed on the basis of elaborating the rabbinic notion that the world exists on account of Torah, an idea that imparted cosmic significance to traditional observance on the part of Jews:

> Come and see: He who is occupied with Torah upholds the world . . . and there is no limb in the human being [*bar nash*] that does not have a creature in the world corresponding to it, for just as the human being is divided into limbs, and they are arranged as gradations upon gradations, arrayed one atop the other, but they are all

> one body, so too with respect to the world, all of the created beings are limbs, and they exist one atop the other, and when they are arrayed they are all verily one body. Everything is in the pattern of Torah, for Torah is composed of limbs and parts that exist one atop the other, and when they are arrayed they all make up one body.[355]

The human body corresponds to the cosmic body, which in turn corresponds to the textual body of Torah. The physical entities of the world, the limbs of human anatomy, and the letters of Torah are all signs that point beyond themselves to the unmanifest font of all being. The extent to which the kabbalistic idea embraces an incarnational perspective is made clear in the comment of the fifteenth-century kabbalist Meir Ibn Gabbai, based on older sources:

> Just as the supernal Torah, which is the secret of the Written Torah . . . is the secret of the unique name [*sod shem ha-meyuḥad*], and it is called *torah* for it instructs [*morah*] about and discloses the existence and unity of the one Lord . . . so this concrete [*murgeshet*] Torah that Moses placed before the children of Israel instructs about the place whence it was hewn, which is the supernal, spiritual Torah, the secret of *Tif'eret Yisra'el*, the unique name, and it is the secret of the Tree of Life.[356]

The imaginal shape of the human form assumed by Torah relates specifically to the ideal politic of Israel or, to be more exact, to the community of readers who mystically envision the secrets embedded in the text through inspired exegetical practice and thereby represent the whole of the nation in thought and practice, contemplation and ritual. Through the textual mediation of the kabbalistic fraternity, the imaginal body, the supernal Torah, Tree of Life, the *sefirah* of *Tif'eret Yisra'el*, the "splendor of Israel," is garbed in twenty-two letters contained in the name YHWH, the archetypal pattern for the Torah that Moses transmitted to Israel in the sublunar realm. The homologous relation between Torah and Israel is expressed in the correspondence of the number of letters of the scroll and the number of adult male Israelites above the age of twenty who left Egypt (Exod. 12:37; Num. 11:21), an idea encoded acrostically in the letters of the word *yisra'el-yesh shishim ribbo otiyyot la-torah*, "There are 600,000 letters in Torah,"[357] the 600,000 corresponding to the six lower *sefirot* from *Ḥesed* to *Yesod*, which are comprised in *Tif'eret*, symbolically represented by the letter *waw* (the numerical value of which is six) of the Tetragrammaton.[358]

The poetic impulse stimulating the kabbalist's attempt to visualize the word as the simulacrum through which the imageless is imaged coincides well with the following account of Baudelaire's notion of poetry:

> Poetic language aspires to be a world, to be the word which will create a world. Poetry and the poem as object—an assemblage of words—are proclaimed as the key to the enigma of the world. . . . Poetry proclaims the primacy of language, its possible perfection, its self-sufficiency. It is in and through creative (poetic) language that duality, division and disjunction will be resolved. The ideal and the real, the abstract and the concrete will be reunited. At last the word will become flesh, at last the

> word will be palpable—palpable flesh become the living word. It is the word as magic, as alchemy. . . . Language alone produces the construct and the sought-for transformation, Language *is*. Alone.[359]

In the formation of the poetic symbol, there is a coincidence of language and embodiment that provides the means by which kabbalists have erotically encountered transcendence, the wholly other garbed in the garment of the other, a garbing that opens the enclosure of infinity to the finitude of extension.[360] From this perspective, kabbalistic poiesis may be considered a form of abyssal thinking, for it thinks that which lays the foundation by extending the horizon of what may be thought,[361] commending one to attend the silence of the clamor in the clamor of the silence.[362] As one contemporary writer has astutely put it:

> To think the poetic place means remembering that the silence marking that place has its own contours; it also means knowing that such silence is not to be confused with mere quiet, but needs to be heard as the unvocalized voice of the poem. . . . A voice estranged from language, rendering the effort to listen to language in the poem rare, demanding, and painful at once. More than any other feature of the poem this demand that silence be heard is the peculiar difficulty of reading the poem.[363]

In line with poets, kabbalists speak of the unspeakable, desiring, in Michel de Certeau's telling formulation, to "disappear into what they disclose, like a Turner landscape dissolved in air and light. An ab-solute (un-bound), in the mode of pain, pleasure, and a 'letting-be' attitude (Meister Eckhart's *Geläzenheit*), inhabits the torture, ecstasy, or sacrifice of language that can *say* the ab-solute, endlessly only by erasing itself."[364] To speak the unspeakable, to envision the invisible,[365] is the burden the poet bears, to break language by abnegating self to the other in the imaginal representation of what persists as unrepresentable, to see with the blindness that blinds the eye that sees, to hear with the deafness that deafens the ear that hears, to speak with the silence that silences the tongue that speaks.[366] According to the credo of kabbalistic piety, the sacrifice of language, uttering/envisioning the ineffable, is consequent to the harnessing of carnal desire: The ascetic negation of the physical body allows for the ocular apprehension of God's imaginal body: only the heart that is pure from carnal desire can mirror images of the invisible.[367] In a manner consonant with Eckhart, the kabbalistic ideal of visual contemplation rested on a paradoxical inversion: purging the mind of images of the sensory world through a regimen of abstinence facilitated envisioning the divine in images of an erotic intimacy and intensity.[368] It is of interest to recall the observation of Harold Bloom that kabbalah "proposes to give suffering a meaning, by way of an interpretation of Scripture that depends overtly upon an audacious figuration, the *Sefirot*."[369] Bloom links the desire to give suffering meaning with the ascetic ideal articulated by Nietzsche, the "vicious circle of mastery,"[370] which entails a change in the process of willing rather than the abolition of the will to live, as we find, for instance, in the philosophy of Schopenhauer reflecting both Buddhist tradition and Christian Platonism.[371]

The ascetic penchant, especially as it is manifest in the desire of the artist to be different and to be elsewhere, does not embrace a "will to nothingness" or "revulsion from life." On the contrary, renunciation can cloak desire even more consuming than overt affirmation.[372] The poet finds joy in the actual, embracing the innocence of becoming through the affirmation of *amor fati* and eternal return of the same, saying yes to all that is no rather than saying no to all that is yes, a posture more typical for Platonic-Christian asceticism, the metaphysical and moral suppositions of which Nietzsche rejected. One would do well to recall the remark of Schelling that "actual power lies more in delimitation than expansion and that to withdraw oneself has more to do with might than to give oneself,"[373] the philosophical basis for his idea, perhaps reflective in part of the influence of kabbalah, that contraction, and not extension, is the beginning of everything, the temporal enfolding of the eternal unfolding.[374] Nietzsche obviously would have rebuffed the kenotic dimensions of Schelling's insight, but the logic underlying his own thinking on the power of denial is not dissimilar: to be the hammer one must first be the flute.[375]

For Nietzsche, asceticism is affirmative of life in the extreme—indeed, the "'motor' of reactive forces"[376]—when it is expressive of the desire to transform being not by fleeing into the atemporal, supersensible, noumenal world but by inserting oneself ever more deeply into the crevices of time and fissures in space. "Becoming must be explained without recourse to final intentions; becoming must appear justified at every moment (or incapable of being evaluated, which amounts to the same thing); the present must absolutely not be justified by reference to a future, nor the past by reference to the present. . . . More strictly: one must admit nothing that has being—because then becoming would lose its value and actually appear meaningless and superfluous."[377] The poet has the chore of bestowing form upon chaos by producing images that display the permanence of flux in the perpetuity of its becoming.[378] The images fashioned poetically belie the metaphysical distinction between appearance and truth,[379] for what is true is what appears in the truth of its appearance. "All that is intransitory that is but an image! And the poets lie too much. But the best images and parables should speak of time and becoming: they should be a eulogy and a justification of all transitoriness."[380] Nietzsche's words call to mind Rilke's description of the media of poetic reflection as mirrors replete with sieve holes that are like "interstices of time" (*Zwischenräume der Zeit*).[381] The poem, however, is not a sieve that can catch the image, but the mirror of temporal spaces and spatial intervals in and through which the image transpires.

Poiesis is emblematic of artistic creation more generally, which Nietzsche evocatively characterized as making images in time. Hence, in a comment penned in 1872, he wrote, "But where does artistic power make its appearance? In the crystal certainly. The formation of shape" (*Die Bildung der Gestalt*).[382] The production of forms requires the artist to be finely attuned to the patterns of change, the rhythms of becoming, for perceiving shape in space and time ensues from measuring the fluctuation of the individual interval of sound in light of a standard of measurement;[383] poetic truth is expressed in images that always emerge from a concrete set of embodied circumstances.[384] A constant motif in Nietzsche's writing concerns the duplicitous role accorded rhythm as the measure of musicality that models our aesthetic, that is, the perception (from the Greek *aiesthesis*) of time and language.[385] Particularly noteworthy is Nietzsche's observation that rhythm is "*an attempt at individuation.* For rhythm to exist, there must be multiplicity and becoming. . . . Rhythm is the form of becoming, [and] generally the *form of the world of appearances.*"[386] For Nietzsche, rhythmic shape, temporal form, and linguistic gesture coalesce in the formative power of the artist to fashion images out of the capricious tempo of becoming. The images preserve "complex forms of relative life-duration within the flux of becoming,"[387] and thereby facilitate the artist's overcoming of time, an overcoming that is itself overcome by the constant need to undergo the overcoming, a lifting of the veil to expose the dissemblance of all phenomena, an uncovering so painful that it may inflict suffering on others,[388] a removal of the mask that reveals that masking is without truth beyond the (un)masking of the mask,[389] a "veiling dissimulation"[390] that leads Nietzsche to associate the untruth of truth with the figure—or, to speak more accurately, the nonfigure, the simulacrum—of woman,[391] the "veiled enigma" of "remote proximity."[392]

In the preface to the second edition of *Die fröhliche Wissenschaft*, published in 1887, Nietzsche wrote, "We no longer believe that truth remains truth when one pulls off the veils; we have lived too much to believe this. . . . Perhaps truth is a woman who has grounds for not showing her grounds?"[393] The only truth to behold is truth that is manifest in the dissimilitude of not-showing. It is in this sense that truth is depicted parabolically as a woman, the embodiment of deceit, the veil that reveals by concealing and conceals by revealing. But this is precisely the role assigned to the artist in general and to the poet in particular. "The poet," Nietzsche remarks in another passage from this composition, "sees in the liar a foster brother [*Milchbruder*] whose milk he has drunk up; that is why the latter has remained stunted and miserable and has not even got as far as having a good conscience."[394] As Nietzsche put it in an aphorism from *Der Wille zur Macht*, first published in 1901, "The world with which we are concerned is false, i.e., is not a fact but a fable and approximation on the basis of a meager sum of observations; it is 'in flux,' as something in a state of becoming; as a falsehood always changing but never getting near the truth: for there is no 'truth.'"[395] The force of dissemblance, which the poet enacts in the use of symbols to express the "native malady of language,"[396] is identified as the will to power, the greatest expression being the self-overcoming of the artist, a process that arises from the aesthetic ability to confront the eternal recurrence of the same without positing final meaning or ultimate aim.[397]

Nietzsche refers cryptically to this process in another aphorism from the aforementioned collection: "'Thinking' in primitive conditions (pre-organic) is the crystallization of forms, as in the case of crystal.—In *our* thought, the essential feature is fitting new material into old schemas . . . *making* equal what is new."[398] The crystallization of forms associated with thinking (*denken*) is reminiscent of the aforecited depiction of artistic power as the shaping of images. In particular, poetic fabrication (*Erdichten*) signifies the role of imagination in the construction of reality.[399] Artistic self-overcoming—the becoming of what one is[400]—is to be sought in the poeticizing that precedes thought, Nietzsche's mythical notion of the transhuman,[401] for in the invention of poetic images the transitory is imaged as interminable, the concrete envisioned as surpassing the limit imposed by the abstract classification through which the concrete is known.[402] "To impose upon becoming the character of being—that is the supreme will to power. . . . That *everything recurs* is the closest *approximation of a world of becoming to a world of being*:—high point of the meditation."[403] Redemption consists of the higher soul's ability to will the fate of the past as if it were a product of one's own freedom, and it is the poet in particular, the "reader of riddles," who assumes the mantle of "redeemer of chance" by teaching others to create the future and thereby unfetter the causal chain of the past.[404]

Bloom aptly draws the conclusion that for Nietzsche, the artistic wish can be posed as "a superb definition of the motive for metaphor, for the life-affirming deep motive of all poetry." Kabbalah, he goes on to say, is unique insofar as it is "simply, already poetry, scarcely needing translation into the realms of the aesthetic. Beyond its direct portrayal of the mind-in-creation, Kabbalah offers both a model for the processes of poetic influence, and maps for the problematic pathways of interpretation."[405] The texture of eros that has informed the worldview of kabbalists through the generations is determined by the merging of body and word in the symbolic imagination of one who has gained mastery over the physical body through an ascetic lifestyle. The path of our inquiry, our be/musement, sets out from and returns to this point.

CHAPTER TWO

Differentiating (In)Difference: Heresy, Gender, and Kabbalah Study

There is a crack in everything
That's how the light gets in.

—Leonard Cohen

To the extent that thinking poetically is embodied thinking, and it does not seem possible to conceive of human embodiment that is not gendered—even the construct of an immaterial body that has figured prominently in many theological mythologems is engendered—it is necessary to delve into the matter of gender construction in kabbalistic lore before we proceed to an exposition of the erotic nature of poiesis through the prism of the poetic nature of eros. The preliminary discussion will span two chapters, the first on the larger question of gender and the study of kabbalah, itself cast into something of a broader conceptual framework, and the second on the more specific phallomorphic dimension of kabbalistic esotericism, focused in particular on the rite of circumcision as the paradigmatic expression of the indispensable link between secrecy and sexuality.

Imprinting Difference/Baptismal Erasure, Phallic Inscription

In recent years, many have sought the voice of the feminine in the spiritual depths of Judaism. Some have naturally turned to the rich legacy of medieval Jewish mysticism, known generically as kabbalah, as an authoritative source in which to anchor the feminine envisioning of the divine. Prima facie, there is plausibility to this approach insofar as one of the distinctive features of the esoteric tradition is the characterization of the divine as masculine and feminine. In search of a traditional corpus in which to ground female images of the Jewish God, this has been a logical avenue of (re)constructive theology, with particular emphasis placed on the kabbalistic symbol of *Shekhinah*, the divine presence imaginally configured in overtly feminine language.

One observer (predictably a man) hyperbolically proclaimed that kabbalah embodies the "secret feminine side" of Judaism.[1] It is hard to know for certain what was intended by this endorsement, but to my ear, it brings to mind the sentiment that kabbalistic spirituality is the mythopoeic corrective to the legalistic androcentricism of rabbinic Judaism. It will be recalled that Scholem set in contrast—or, according to some passages in his oeuvre, opposition—the idealized halakhic community of male-dominated talmudic culture to the mythic-symbolic poiesis of kabbalists.[2] He did not, however, focus on the possible gender dimension of this distinction. On the contrary, the few pronouncements he made—and especially the oft-cited remark in the introduction to *Major Trends in Jewish Mysticism* (to be discussed briefly below) regarding the lack of women in this chapter of the religious history of Judaism—leave one with the impression that he would not have assented to a feminine characterization of the poetic-imaginal dimensions of kabbalah. It seems, at least, that our eager reader had something of this sort in mind when he proclaimed passionately and fervently that kabbalah is the "secret feminine side" of Judaism.

Perhaps it would be best to let such comments slide, as they may be viewed as relatively harmless exhortative exclamations meant to inspire newfound expressions of ancient Jewish pietism. This may be so, but exaggerated and misinformed claims of this sort can also be motivated by an ambition to avow moral supremacy for the tradition. Thus, for example, in the opinion of one scholar, the "Jewish outlook" toward the feminine expressed in kabbalah is to be contrasted with the "Christian-Islamic tradition" that depicts woman as the "embodiment of 'original sin' and the cause of misery and death." The presumed Jewish perspective, which is aligned with alchemy, Hinduism, and Buddhism, is to view woman (rendered respectively in the relevant theological mythologies in the guise of *Shekhinah*, Shakti, and Prajna) as the "Fount of life, love, and transcendental ecstasies; the bestower of energy and of awareness."[3]

A sustained engagement with kabbalistic sources for two decades has led me to question these and similar characterizations of traditional kabbalah. Through arduous textual study I have discerned a consistent and recurrent pattern—and by "pattern" I do not mean an immutable essence or structure; pattern connotes, rather, the old that recurrently appears as novel, the invisible (to be distinguished from "not visible") that casts its shadow from the perimeter of the visual field to the opening of the center that is naught but the center of the opening. To state the thesis boldly: the earliest literary documents studied in the search for "origins of kabbalah," texts that can be dated to the twelfth and thirteenth centuries (though I readily acknowledge that some of these textual artifacts preserve older fragments of tradition, transmitted either orally or in writing), reify androcentric propensities in what has come to be known as the formative period of talmudic culture. Medieval kabbalah intensifies the nascent phallomorphism of the rabbinic imaginary.[4]

To substantiate my view I will adduce a statement in *Sefer ha-Zohar*, the "Book of Splendor," the major anthology of kabbalistic lore; the beginnings of its literary production are traceable to Castile in the thirteenth and fourteenth centuries, though gestation of its textual fragments may involve pushing the date considerably back to late antiquity and redaction into the form of a book extending the date considerably forward to at least the sixteenth century.[5] Before considering the passage, let me say something briefly about the composition of this work, which has received much attention from academic kabbalah scholarship.[6] In my earliest studies on *Zohar* I assumed, reflective of the more general consensus, a unified textual whole (excluding, of course, *Raʿaya Meheimna* and *Tiqqunei Zohar*, following Scholem's suggestion), as if there were a literary consistency that justified referring to it and its author in the singular; in studies from what I now deem to be my middle period I assumed, in accordance with the pioneering study of Liebes, that the body of *Zohar* is a work produced by a fraternity of kabbalists; in the third and present stage, I still think the zoharic anthology preserves multiple voices, including ideas that are either absent from or contradictory to treatises of Moses de León, but I nevertheless maintain on hermeneutical grounds that it is possible to continue to speak of a unifying factor that allows for difference; the weave of the textual fabric does not disrupt the possibility of iteration that renews itself indefinitely, a point to which I shall return below. On this score, scholars of *Zohar* can benefit from the wisdom and experience of biblicists who do not deny the form-critical approach but who nevertheless discern repeating thought patterns. The position I wish to affirm is well expressed in the following summation offered by Seth Daniel Kumin regarding the implications for biblical study of his structuralist analysis of the "logic of incest" in ancient Hebraic mythology:

> Various schools of source and textual criticism primarily use fragmentary analysis, seeking to determine the origin (and authorship) of individual fragments. Structuralist theory suggests that, when fragments are edited and redacted, their structure and perhaps narrative elements would be transformed to fit the structure of the editor, thus all fragments would betray identical structure. This is supported by the ethnographic evidence presented here. The analysis reveals that all four strata include the same mythemes and are thus structurally and culturally indistinguishable. This supports the use of holistic analysis of text found in the literary school of biblical study.[7]

To be perfectly clear, let me state emphatically and unequivocally that I do not think the holistic-structuralist approach should ignore or efface difference; on the contrary, what I am suggesting is that it is precisely this approach that illumines difference vis-à-vis sameness, novelty vis-à-vis repetition. It is thus justifiable, in my opinion, to continue to speak of "zoharic kabbalah," as a taxonomy of this sort does not level the composite text to a monolithic and univocal system.

To return to the zoharic text:

> Why is it written, "Thereupon Hezekiah turned his face to the wall [and prayed to the Lord]" (Isa. 38:2)? He set his face to be aligned opposite *Shekhinah* for he had sinned with respect to this place. Inasmuch as all the women of the world exist in the mystery of *Shekhinah*, she dwells on the man who has a woman, but not on the man who has no woman. Therefore, he aligned himself to be arrayed in relation to her, and he accepted upon himself to get married, and afterwards he "prayed to the Lord."[8]

Ostensibly, one might surmise that the zoharic passage lends support to the exuberant depiction of kabbalah as a recovery of the "secret feminine side" of Judaism, since their being located in the mystery of *Shekhinah* elevates the status of women. Close scrutiny of the text, however, suggests otherwise, for the value assigned to the female—that is, the ethical worth imparted the feminine gender in accord with the cultural canons that shaped the sociopolitical comportment of communities to which kabbalists belonged—is determined exclusively from the male perspective.[9] The adulation of the feminine belies a masculine desire to amass power in the hierarchical setting of boundaries. Hence the connection established between earthly women and *Shekhinah* serves the purpose of validating the instrumentalist view of marriage as the means by which Jewish men can be conjoined to the divine.[10] As we discern from the case of Hezekiah, revisioned through the exegetical lens of the medieval Spanish kabbalist, one cannot turn wholeheartedly to God in prayer if one is single. It follows that no intrinsic worth is accorded the feminine in the assertion that the last of the *sefirot* is the ontic source of all women; quite the contrary, this parallel reifies on symbolic grounds the subordination of the feminine, marking the value of a woman strictly in terms of her husband.

Although kabbalistic writings well document both the aspiration to discover the underlying oneness of reality and techniques necessary to achieve it, the quest for "ontological monomorphism"[11] did not serve as a catalyst for medieval kabbalists to break down social divisions between men and women within the Jewish community, let alone ethnic boundaries separating Jew and non-Jew in society at large.[12] Nowhere in traditional kabbalistic literature, as far as I am aware, do we hear of a tendency to harmonize or equalize the roles of men and women.[13] To be sure, kabbalists portray ritual, with a special focus on liturgical practices, in terms of gender transformations that render fluid the distinction between male and female—Jewish men are feminized so that the divine female may be masculinized and the antediluvian androgyny restored[14]—but there is no mechanism by which gender difference in the historical arena is to be transcended. Indeed, as I have argued in previous publications and as I elaborate in different parts of this work, especially the final chapter, the eschatological ideal of overcoming gender dimorphism and the related claim that the infinite cannot be described as either male or female when understood (inter)contextually may express covert forms of the androcentric denigration of women.

To cast my point in sharp relief, I would like to mull over the implications of kabbalistic symbolism against the backdrop of the baptismal formula of some early Christian churches retrievable from Paul's description of those who are baptized in Christ: "There is neither Jew nor Greek, there is neither slave nor free man, there is neither male nor female; for you are all one in Christ Jesus" (Gal. 3:28).[15] The mode of argumentation here is not driven by any presumption, explicit or implicit, regarding historical or even textual connections linking Paul and medieval kabbalists. To be sure, these possibilities cannot be ruled out by the canons of critical scholarship, but neither can they be proven beyond any shadow of doubt. My path of thinking, rather, as I enunciated in the Prologue, goes forth from discerning shared structures of thought in different historical junctures, a phenomenon I explain not by appeal to transhistorical archetypes (à la Jung, Eliade, or Corbin) but on the basis of a scientifically defensible conception of time as a reversible swerve.

An echo of the sacramental formulation is discernible in Colossians 3:9–11, technically considered deutero-Pauline[16] but consistent with a sentiment expressed by Paul:[17] those who believe in Christ are said to take off the "old human" (*palaios anthropos*), the spirit controlled by carnal lusts, and put on the "new human" (*kainos anthropos*), the spirit renewed in knowledge and created in the image of God,[18] an anthropological demarcation that transcends the distinctions between "Greek and Jew, circumcised and uncircumcised, barbarian and Scythian."[19] In a third and genuinely Pauline passage, the image of the somatic body is summoned to convey the overcoming of difference in the unity of spirit enacted through baptism: Just as the "body is one and has many members . . . so it is with Christ. For by one Spirit we were all baptized into one body—Jews or Greeks, slaves or free—and all were made to drink of one Spirit" (1 Cor. 12:12–13).[20]

From Paul's perspective, the baptismal slogan of "putting on" Christ as a garment (Gal. 3:27) alludes to being reborn in Christ, that is, participating in the unified body of Christ, a "new creation" (Gal. 6:15; 2 Cor. 5:17)[21] that will no longer be classified by the ethnic opposition of the "other without," circumcised and uncircumcised (cf. Gal. 5:6; Rom. 3:29–30, 10:12–13), or by gender polarity, the "other within," male and female.[22] In a section of Acts, the Pauline vision is reiterated in the narrative setting of a debate between some members of the Pharisee party and Paul, Barnabas, and others colleagues who had gone up to Jerusalem to inquire of the apostles and elders of the validity of challenging the Jewish insistence that only one circumcised by the custom of Moses could be saved. Predictably, the Pharisees retort that it is necessary to uphold this practice, as it is only by way of circumcision and obedience to Torah that one is delivered (15:1–4). In the words ascribed to Peter we find the blurring of boundaries. The dissemination of the gospel accords an opportunity for the Gentile to hear the word and have faith in the heart, a receiving of the "holy spirit" that renders the outsider an insider and consequently effaces a rigid distinction between inside and outside (15:7–9).[23]

The theme is reiterated in logion 22 of the *Gospel of Thomas*, in the rejoinder of Jesus to the question of his disciples, which is instigated by his own remark, whether they would enter the kingdom as children:

> When you make the two one, and when you make the inside like the outside and the outside like the inside, and the above like the below, and when you make the male and the female one and the same, so that the male not be male nor the female female; and you fashion eyes in place of an eye, and a hand in place of a hand, and a foot in place of a foot, and a likeness in place of a likeness; then will you enter [the kingdom].[24]

A similar statement attributed to Jesus is cited and interpreted in the ancient text of unknown provenance and date, the so-called *Second Epistle of Clement to the Corinthians* 12.2: "For when the Lord himself was asked by someone when his kingdom would come, he said: 'When the two shall be one, and the outside as the inside, and the male with the female neither male nor female.'"[25] A third version of this saying occurs in the *Martyrdom of Peter*, considered by some scholars to have been originally part of the *Acts of*

Peter. The relevant dictum occurs in a section of the text where Peter requests of the Roman executioners that he be crucified "head downwards," explaining that the upside-down posture reveals the "mystery of all nature, the beginning of all things," that is, this was the posture of Adam when he was cast down from heaven to earth. Peter must hang invertedly to manifest the likeness of the first man who

> established the whole of this cosmic system, being hung up as an image of the calling, in which he showed what is on the right hand as on the left, and those on the left as on the right, and changed all the signs of their nature, so as to consider fair those things that were not fair, and take those that were really evil to be good. Concerning this the Lord says in a mystery, "Unless you make what is on the right hand as what is on the left and what is on the left hand as what is on the right and what is above as what is below and what is behind as what is before, you will not recognize the Kingdom."[26]

The posture adopted by Peter in his crucifixion is intended to be a visual representation of Adam, who signifies the mystery of turning one thing into its opposite, destabilizing the binary difference such that above is below, below above, right left, left right, good evil, evil good, and, we may suppose, male is female, and female male.

On the face of it, then, these parallel statements in early Christian literature suggest that the baptismal ideal did indeed imply an erasure of gender difference, perhaps even a challenge to the hierarchy promoted by the conventions of patriarchal marriage.[27] Although for the most part this construal did not greatly influence matters on the ground, so to speak, it would appear that the presumed overcoming of sexual difference in the body of Christ did impact medieval theological debates regarding the possibility of God having assumed the form of a woman,[28] a possibility reflected as well in artistic portrayals of Jesus as feminine and in textual sources penned by women insisting that the body, aligned with the feminine, and not reason, aligned with the masculine, is the true image of Christ's humanity.[29] This line of interpretation has been resurrected by a number of feminist scholars who have sought to anchor textually the contemporary appeal for women's equality and ordination in a scriptural foundation.[30] However, to assess properly the possibility for anchoring the call to overcome gender bifurcation in this manner, one must chart the contours of gender construction in line with the topography of a particular cultural context.

Let us consider, for instance, what appears to be Paul's own parenthetical qualification to the overtly sexist hierarchy he established on the basis of the account of creation of woman from man in the second chapter of Genesis. According to Paul, women must wear veils whereas men are to be bareheaded, since the head of man is Christ and the head of a woman is her husband—the rationale for this opinion is elicited from the scriptural account whereby woman was made from man but not man from woman (1 Cor. 11:3–10). The text is interrupted at this juncture with the observation that "in the Lord woman is not independent of man nor man of woman; for as woman was made from man, so man is now born of woman. And all things are from God" (ibid., 11:11–12). Whether or not these words are authentically Pauline, we can accept that they reflect a genuine struggle on the part of someone between the leveling of sexual difference suggested by the baptismal ideal, on one hand, and the gender imbalance of social reality supported textually by the narrative of the second chapter of Genesis, on the other.[31]

Notwithstanding the validity of this claim, the chauvinistic bias sheds light on the fact that the "egalitarian" promise of spiritual androgyny rests on the restoration of the woman to the man whence she was taken; the man, not the woman, is identified as the head of the body, which is the Church (Coloss. 1:18).[32] The point I am raising comes into sharper focus in the response of Jesus to Salome's query about the time of salvation in a fragment of the apocryphal *Gospel according to the Egyptians* preserved in a citation of Julius Cassianus as reported by Clement of Alexandria: "When you trample underfoot the integument of shame, and when the two become one and the male is one with the female, and there is no more male and female."[33] This remark includes an additional element that is useful in ascertaining whether or not the archaic baptismal tradition endorsed genuine gender complementarity or reification of the androcentric bias by promoting incorporation of the female in the male. If we assume, as seems eminently warranted, that the "integument of shame" is the corruptible body, which is engendered as female, then this dictum implies that the overcoming of gender binarism comes by way of abrogating fleshly desire. The reconstituted androgyne, therefore, would not imply an egalitarian leveling of difference; on the contrary, the ideal is expressive of and further substantiates the hierarchical ontology of gender difference. It is thus likely that the baptismal proclamation that there is no more male or female alludes to a state wherein the female has been restored to the male, forming thereby the perfect Adam who bears the divine image, symbolized by Christ (Coloss. 1:15),[34] the primal androgyny that is the progenitor of the sexually dimorphic humanity.[35]

The point is substantiated by other references made by Clement of Alexandria to selections from this text. In the context of discrediting heretics who misuse scriptural verses to legitimate an encratic rejection of sexuality and procreation, Clement offers the following interpretation of a passage from the aforementioned gospel: "When Salome asked, 'How long will death maintain its power?' the Lord said, 'As long as you women bear children.'" Clement contends that the dictum of Jesus does not support the view of "life as evil and the creation as rotten"; rather his intent is to be explained by the pedagogical assumption that he instructed in accord with the "normal course of nature," wherein death follows on the heels of birth.[36] While Clement's strategy to undermine the encratic exegesis is understandable in light of his belief that marriage and childbearing are no more sinful than continence, it seems fairly obvious that the interpretation he proposes as wrong is in fact quite accurate. The logic of the soteriological teaching attributed to Jesus is transparently clear: since death is an inevitable correlation to birth, the only way to be rid of the former is to eradicate the latter. The strategy recommended to achieve that goal is to adopt a life of celibacy, for, if followed religiously, the latter is a foolproof form of birth control.

In another passage, Clement again refers to words of Jesus spoken to Salome: "They maintain that the Savior personally said, 'I am come to destroy the works of the female.' 'Female' refers to sexual desire, and its works are birth and decay."[37] In the minds of the extreme Christian ascetics opposed by Clement, salvation can come only when carnal lust is annihilated. This is the intent of the aforecited comment that death has power "as long as women give birth," that is, "as long as sexual desire is still at work."[38] In a third passage, Clement discredits the unfettered celibate practice on the basis of what he considered to be Paul's claim that since it was the woman (the author of the pastoral epistle refers to her by the proper name "Eve" in the preceding verse when noting that Adam was created first and then followed Eve, an obvious exegetical gloss on Genesis 2:21–24) who was deceived by the serpent and thus brought transgression to the world,[39] she can be saved by childbearing, *dia tes teknogonias* (1 Tim. 2:14–15).[40] Setting aside whether or not Clement's exegesis of the Pauline[41] passage is accurate—though I note that other church fathers, for example, Gregory of Nyssa, used the same verse to justify the ideal of virginity[42]—what is suggestive is that salvation for a woman is linked to bringing children into the world, an activity that, needless to say, could not be fulfilled (at least according to the ancient understanding of reproduction) if both partners categorically renounced engaging in physical sex.

To be sure, as the continuation of the verse makes clear, the promise that woman will be saved through giving birth is only valid if she "continues in faith, love, and holiness, with modesty," that is, if she embraces the virtues demanded of all who wish to participate in the Christian community. Notwithstanding the validity of this comment, I think it reasonable to argue that the redemption of woman is related primarily to her biological capacity to conceive, gestate, and give birth—to be, as the name "Eve," *ḥawwah*, is explicated midrashically in Genesis 3:20, *em kol ḥai*, the "mother of all living"; the agent responsible for human mortality is enjoined to rectify the situation by bearing progeny, for the rearing of children extends the chain of engenderment and thereby serves as a partial antidote to the punishment of death.[43]

On the surface this may seem to be a positive evaluation of the feminine—the woman, after all, is accorded a critical role in the drama of salvation—but when the matter is scrutinized more circumspectly, it becomes clear that underlying this portrayal is a stereotypical sexist view of woman; indeed, the misogyny is enhanced by the fact that the instrumentalist conception of woman is combined with the theological belief that Eve was most responsible for original sin and the consequent condemnation of human nature. Along similar lines, I would argue that the personification of eros as female cannot be explained simply as a linguistic contingency, nor is it reasonable to advocate a distinction between the natural equality of male and female sanctioned by God (and presumably enacted through the baptismal rite) and societal subordination fortified in the customs of marriage determined by human convention and law;[44] the patriarchal stereotype of female sexual insatiability, though surely linked to the biological fact that women, as opposed to men, can experience multiple orgasms in rapid succession,[45] is fostered by a cultural bias that has had adverse ramifications socially, politically, and economically.

It is likely that a comparable androcentric implication is at work in logion 22 from *Gospel of Thomas* with which we began this excursus. This manner of reading would explain in part the ostensible contradiction between this saying and logion 114 at the conclusion of the work, where Jesus, in response to Simon Peter's request that Mary

Magdalene leave the presence of the disciples "for women are not worthy of life," preaches that "every woman who will make herself male will enter the kingdom of heaven."[46] The reply of Jesus to some extent destabilizes the fixed gender categories presupposed by Peter, for women are not confined to remaining women, as they exhibit the potentiality to become male, a response that ultimately reinscribes the sexism of Peter based on the symbolic correlation of the feminine with bodiliness and sensuality and the masculine with mindfulness and spirituality.[47]

A similar stance is made more explicitly in the *Dialogue of the Savior*, an eschatological treatise composed in all likelihood in the second century and preserved in a very fragmentary condition in one of the Nag Hammadi codices. The affinity of this text in content and style to *Gospel of Thomas* has been noted by scholars, and hence it is especially relevant to assess the attitude to femininity proffered in this source.[48] One of the first references to Mary, the only woman included with the disciples, is a seemingly positive affirmation of the feminine, for she is said to have uttered a particular truth "as a woman who had understood completely" (139:13).[49] The words no doubt are meant to catch the reader's attention, as one would have expected (given the cultural assumptions contemporary with the time of composition of the treatise) that women are not naturally predisposed to present truth coherently and persuasively. In a subsequent exchange between the Savior and Mary, the underlying issue becomes more apparent on the surface. After the Savior reportedly says, "Whatever is born of truth does not die. Whatever is born of woman dies"—a statement that degrades the feminine by categorically contrasting what is *born of truth*, the eternal-spiritual, and what is *born of woman*, the ephemeral-somatic—Mary inquires of the master, "Tell me, Lord, why I have come to this place to profit or to forfeit?" The Savior responds, "You make clear the abundance of the revealer!" (140:14–18).[50]

This dialogic exchange reaffirms the notion that a woman, stereotypically associated with materiality and sexuality, is capable of revealing the pneumatic truth, a theme alluded to in the Gospel narratives (Luke 24:10–11; John 20:18) and attested in other early Christian works, most prominently the *Gospel of Mary*.[51] In another passage, the capability of women apprehending truth is validated in the remark attributed to Mary, "I want to understand all things" (141:13–14).[52] It seems, however, from the following comment that the underlying assumption that accounts for the reversal of gender stereotypes according to the author of this treatise is that Mary has divested herself of her bodily, that is to say, womanly nature: "[Mary] said, 'There is but one saying I will [speak] to the Lord concerning the mystery of truth: In this have we taken our stand, and to the cosmic are we transparent" (143:6–10).[53] The "mystery of truth" is linked to becoming "transparent" to the cosmic, which I propose signifies overcoming the corporeality of the mundane.

Support for this conjecture may be gathered from the continuation of the text, wherein Judas inquires of Matthew about the garments in which those who depart from the decay of the flesh will be clothed (143:11–15). The implicit misogyny becomes most explicit in the response of the Savior and the explication of Matthew to the query of

Judas about how one should pray (144:14–15): "The Lord said, 'Pray in the place where there is no woman.' Matthew said, 'Pray in the place where there is [no woman],' he tells us, meaning, 'Destroy the works of womanhood,' not because there is any other [manner of birth], but because they will cease [giving birth]'" (144:16–21). The *sine qua non* for prayer is annihilation of womanhood, the capacity for giving birth, for the spiritual act of worship is most effective when physical existence is completely obliterated. Mary offers an intriguing retort, "They will never be obliterated," but unfortunately the counterresponse of the Savior is too badly damaged to be reconstructed (144:22–145:1).[54] Nevertheless, from what is decipherable it may be concluded that according to this source, spiritual procreation, in contrast to physical reproduction, is rendered symbolically as a male trait, and thus the ascetic renunciation implied in the abrogation of womanhood entails masculinization of the feminine.

In a similar vein, the intent of abolishing the polarity of male and female in logion 22 of the *Gospel of Thomas* corresponds to the mandate to transform the female into male affirmed in saying 114,[55] since the redemptive gesture consists of reconstituting the original androgynous state wherein the female was contained in the male, a reconstitution that amounts to realizing the light of the divine image hidden within everyone.[56] It follows, then, that "making the two one" is equivalent to "making the female male."[57] The androcentric underpinnings are brought into clearer focus in logion 79. In response to a woman's blessing the womb of Mary that bore Jesus and her breasts that nourished him, Jesus instructs her about the days to come when she will utter, "Blessed are the womb which has not conceived and the breasts which have not given milk."[58] That is to say, exalting the womb and breasts not for their respective generative and nurturing functions but for cessation from the same intonates the final beatitude—the womb worthy of adulation is the virginal womb not tarnished by pregnancy, and the breasts worthy of esteem are the breasts not stimulated by the labor of birth to give suck. The ultimate felicity, therefore, is one wherein the woman stops carrying out the physiological roles distinctive to being a woman.

In line with other expressions of encratic asceticism on the part of women in early Christian communities,[59] the import of this dictum is that by means of adopting the life of renunciation the female becomes male, and consequently the bisexualism of the exilic state gives way to the eschatological reconstitution of one gender, a re/pairing of the split of the primal androgyne into two sexes.[60] However one is to construe the relationship of the *Gospel of Thomas* to other Gnostic treatises,[61] on this issue there is a basic similarity in approach: the spiritual quest demands that one must, as the author of the tractate *Zostrianos* put it, "flee from the madness and bondage of femaleness."[62] Salvific knowledge requires that one part from "somatic darkness," "psychic chaos," and "feminine desire,"[63] and only on the basis of such a purification can one be baptized in the waters of eternal light to receive the image of the glory and to be transformed into an "angel of the male race."[64] We may conclude, therefore, that the ideal of spiritual transvestism in these late-antique sources derives from and reinforces the patriarchal construction of gender identity and the discursive modes of cultural representation generated thereby.[65]

Neither Male nor Female/Androcentric (Ef)Facing Difference

It would be beneficial here to recall the observation of Rita Gross on the passage from the fourteenth chapter of the Mahāyāna Buddhist text, *The Sūtra of Sagara, the Naga King*, in which Jewel Brocade, the daughter of the king, confronts Mahakasyapa:

> You have said: "One cannot attain Buddhahood with a woman's body." Then, one cannot attain it with a man's body either. What is the reason? Because the thought of enlightenment is neither male nor female. The Buddha has said: "The one who perceives through the eyes is neither male nor female nor are [the perceptions of] the ears, nose, mouth, body, and mind male or female." What is the reason? Because only the virtuous have eyes of Emptiness. The one who perceives through Emptiness is neither male nor female. . . . The one who perceives through enlightenment has the Dharma which is neither male nor female.[66]

As Gross rightly notes, the "androcentric expectations" that a Buddha must be male are undermined by the "sex-neutral" line of reasoning that leads one to the realization that the state of wakefulness or enlightenment consists of perceiving through "eyes of emptiness" (*sunyātā*),[67] that is, seeing all things as nondifferentiated, and hence coming to the insight that the dharma can be neither male nor female. Transcending gender dimorphism is related, therefore, to the larger epistemological task of discerning the ontological emptiness of all phenomena, going beyond all distinction, even the distinction between distinction and nondistinction, to the point of realizing that formlessness itself is a form that must be eradicated. However, Gross offers an important cautionary proviso: "Nevertheless, to some extent the context remains androcentric, in that discriminations against women, *not discriminations against men*, are the problem to be overcome by sex-neutral understandings."[68]

That Gross, whose project is to offer a revalorization of Buddhism, which entails critiquing the misogyny from within the tradition by demonstrating that its principles render the androcentric bias unacceptable intellectually and morally, nonetheless makes the point that expressions of sexual neutrality may themselves be a type of androcentrism is all the more significant. To be sure, it is her wish, as she states explicitly, that feminists get beyond the choice between androcentric and sex-neutral models so that they may salvage the usable past, the ethical mandate that is the ultimate purpose of the feminist agenda. The crucial point from my perspective, however, is her hesitation to jump into the fray, so to speak, by uncritically ascribing feminist value to dicta that seemingly efface gender difference. As Gross correctly notes, the denial of androcentrism and misogyny underlying the ostensible claims of sex-neutrality, which are analogous to the language of the female becoming male in the Christian sources cited above,[69] "is a more destructive and dangerous form of opposition to gender equality than outright opposition to egalitarian reforms."[70]

Interestingly, Gross returned to the passage from *The Sūtra of Sagara* in her introduction to feminism and religion, but there her tone is even more critical, as she reminds the reader:

> [T]hese statements about the irrelevance and emptiness of gender were made in an androcentric context, which has limited their historical impact and effectiveness, just as parallel statements from Christian scriptures have not been translated into Christian institutional forms. Like many other feminists, I do not believe that sex-neutral statements, by themselves, are ever sufficient to overcome androcentrism because sex-neutral ideals do not affirm femaleness and are often covertly male.[71]

Indeed, it is important to recall that statements that depict enlightenment as the erasing of gender difference at the level of ultimate reality must be evaluated in light of other statements (on occasion from the same literary source) that insist on the need for the female to become male by divesting herself of her femaleness, which is stereotypically associated, as it is in Western thought, with the body, sensuality, passions, irrationality, and taking on the form of the man, related to the realm of intellect and the spiritual overcoming of carnal enticement. One example here will suffice; the teaching of the Buddha as recorded in a text appropriately called *The Sūtra on Changing the Female Sex* (*Fo shuo chüan nü shen ching*):

> If women can accomplish one thing [dharma], they will be freed of the female body and become sons. What is that one thing? The profound state of mind which seeks enlightenment. Why? If women awaken to the thought of enlightenment, then they will have the great and good person's state of mind, a man's state of mind, a sage's state of mind. . . . If women awaken to the thought of enlightenment, then they will not be bound to the limitation of a woman's state of mind. Because they will not be limited, they will forever separate from the female sex and become sons.[72]

It should come as no surprise that in a second passage from this work, Buddha gives the following misogynist account of and advice to women: "The female's defects—greed, hate, and delusion and other defilements—are greater than the male's. . . . You should have such an intention. . . . Because I wish to be freed from the impurities of the woman's body. I will acquire the beautiful and fresh body of a man."[73]

On the basis of these citations and others that could have been cited, I submit that any fair-minded reader, one not burdened by an apologetic need to whitewash the ideational stains and moral shortcomings of a tradition, would conclude that the gender transformation is asymmetrical—never do we hear of the male having to become female in order to attain *bodhi* consciousness; the demand is placed always on women to become men in order to enter the Buddha-land of pure virtue, a realm that is described as exclusively male, that is, divested of all carnal desire. I thus concur with Lucinda Joy Peach, who noted that the "gender transformation into a male reinforces the belief that it is in fact necessary for females to take on a male form in order to become Enlightened. The gender shift, although signifying the insubstantiality and ephemerality of sex, also reinforces the image that women are incapable of attaining Enlightenment in female form."[74]

The teaching on *sunyātā* provides the logic necessary to carry one over to the other shore, so to speak, but the androcentric, and on some occasions misogynist, elements in these sources cannot be overlooked, as Gross and Peach have amply reminded us. In my judgment, the insights of these scholars can be applied without qualification to similar expressions of overcoming gender dimorphism in traditional kabbalistic sources. The place accorded the feminine in the mythic representation of God on the part of kabbalists in no way secured the release of women from rigidly prescribed roles in society.[75] Quite the contrary, the mythicized theosophic orientation of kabbalah has exemplified a tendency to radicalize sexual difference in the social arena and consequently to foster an even greater inflexibility in ascribing a subordinate role to women.[76] One might argue that the use of gender imagery to depict the divine nature and the human relationship thereto is merely symbolic or metaphorical since this ideal state of being is beyond all discrimination and difference. It is nevertheless true that symbolic portrayals of the feminine in negative terms reinforce stereotypes in the social arena, and this does not bode well for using the tradition reconstructively (in an uncritical manner) to substantiate an egalitarian, feminist perspective. The conclusion of Peach with regard to Buddhist texts should serve as a warning to scholars of kabbalah: "the symbolic value of gender operates to denigrate females as more worldly, while elevating males as more spiritual. These associations, even if only symbolic, can hardly be positive for 'real women'!"[77]

To illustrate the point, I cite here another passage from *Zohar.* After having paraphrased the rabbinic dictum that the Israelites, in contrast to the heathen nations, were purified at Sinai from the filth with which the serpent had inseminated Eve,[78] the medieval kabbalist adds:

> Come and see: The Torah was only given to males, as it is written, "This is the Torah that Moses placed before the sons of Israel" (Deut. 4:44), and women are exempt from the directives of Torah. Moreover, all of them revert to their impurity as it was in the beginning after they sinned, and it is harder for the woman to divest herself of pollution than it is for the man, and thus you find more women involved in sorcery and pollution than men, for women derive from the left side and they cleave to harsh judgment.[79]

The author of the zoharic passage extends the external distinction between Israel and the nations to an internal distinction between Jewish men and women. Assuming a position that must be judged extreme even in its historical context, the medieval kabbalist asserts that Jewish women are exempt entirely from the commandments prescribed in the Torah.[80] No attempt is made here to qualify the matter in line with the talmudic conception that distinguishes between negative commands, which apply equally to men and women, and positive commands, which can be further distinguished with regard to those precepts dependent on and those independent of time, the former applicable only to men, the latter to men and women.[81] The rabbinic tendency—by which I mean *Weltanschauung*, a worldview by and through which identity, communal and individual, civic and domestic, is constructed—is to correlate responsibility and subjecthood; one who occupies a lower rung on the anthropological scale, one of diminished social power when judged from within the axiological framework of rabbinic law (*halakhah*, from the root *hlkh*, to go, as in the way of the path), is tagged legally as one having a reduced sense of responsibility and therefore as less of a person. This perspective is expanded to its extreme in the aforecited zoharic text: if women are relieved from the duty to fulfill any commandment, we must assume that they are not considered embodied human subjects at all; technically, they do not fall under the taxon *adam*, that is, humanity in the fullest sense, except through the matrimonial bond and carrying out the task of childbearing, which, ironically enough, is a positive commandment incumbent on the Jewish male.[82] It is critical to underscore that the zoharic view is not the one typically expressed by scholars of talmudic jurisprudence in medieval centers of rabbinic learning.

Beyond the strictly nomian explanation, the author of the zoharic passage offers an ontological reason to account for the total exemption of women: Torah is given exclusively to men because women are marked, somatically and psychically, with a stain of impurity. Thus, utilizing a motif expressed in archaic sources,[83] the serpentine nature of women is summoned to explain why they are prone to the lure of magic, the spiritual force that disseminates from the left bank of judgment, the side of the evil inclination.[84] The point is pronounced previously in this section of *Zohar*, offered as a response by R. Isaac to the query of R. Joseph, "Why is it that all kinds of magic and sorcery are only found in women?" "We have learned that when the serpent came upon Eve he cast the filth into her, into her he cast it, and not upon her husband."[85] The zoharic reply is presented as an exegesis of an aggadic teaching, a homiletic technique well attested in kabbalistic literature from its historical inception, based on the belief that esoteric wisdom was encoded in rabbinic dicta. This particular saying intimates that women are the prime recipients of the impure seed, the filth (*zuhamah*), discharged by the serpent;[86] hence the discrepancy between sexes with regard to bodily purity.

Red/White Rose: Feminine Duplicity

Far from glorifying the feminine, kabbalistic gender stereotypes have fostered harsher views regarding the ineffectiveness and potential destructiveness of women's participation in traditional rituals.[87] The hardening of the attitude toward women is linked to the symbolic affinity drawn between femininity and the demonic, a point that Scholem made more generally in his explanation for the lack of women participants in the history of kabbalism.[88] I concur with several scholars who have challenged Scholem's assumption that the exclusion of women from Jewish mystical groups is tied exclusively or even primarily to this symbolic correlation.[89] That the latter has nevertheless played a role in the profiling of women in kabbalistic literature cannot be denied.[90]

In the mind of many kabbalists, including the anonymous voices preserved in the composite zoharic text, Jewish women are Janus-faced, bearing the likeness of *Shekhinah* and Lilith. In great measure, the two female figures, or to speak more precisely, the two configurations of the feminine physiognomy, are shaped in the poetic imagination by the contrast that crystallized in the postexilic sapiential tradition: enduring beauty of Lady Wisdom on one hand, and ephemeral allure of estranged woman on the other.[91] Needless to say, vilification and veneration of the feminine are not contradictory or clashing perspectives; on the contrary, they are both expressive of the androcentric marginalization of women,[92] as we find, for example, in the attribution of both excess and justice to the feminine in ancient Greece.[93] The duplicitous nature of the female in the imaginal representations of kabbalists, which in all likelihood tap into much older demonic portrayals, is related in an especially poignant way to the menstrual cycle of the Jewish woman, part of the month deemed pure and permitted to her husband and in another part impure and forbidden.[94] The dual portrait of the female body reflected in laws and customs pertaining to menstruation instantiates a mystical secret of ontological significance: just as the same woman fluctuates from one state to its opposite, *Shekhinah* and Lilith are two facets of one being rather than two distinct beings.[95]

In the poetic image that appears in the beginning of the introduction in the Mantua edition of *Zohar* (1558), and all subsequent editions based thereon,[96] *Shekhinah*, referred to as *kenesset yisra'el*, "Community of Israel," is portrayed in the scriptural image, *shoshannah ben ha-ḥohim* ("rose amongst the thorns"; Song 2:2), for just as the rose "is red and white, so the Community of Israel has judgment and mercy."[97] Why is *Shekhinah* singled out in this way? Surely, the author of this passage would have assented to the view articulated by kabbalists prior to the zoharic period: *kol middah u-middah kelulah be-ḥevratah* ("each and every attribute is found in the one in proximity to it"), that is, its opposite,[98] and thus we must acknowledge that any of the *sefirot* could have been characterized in the terms applied to *Shekhinah*. As Jacob ben Sheshet expressed the matter in *Sefer ha-Emunah we-ha-Biṭṭaḥon*, explaining why the divine names can be both masculine and feminine:

> The names at times are in the masculine and at other times feminine, and there is no doubt about this because it is the truth. . . . And the reason for this matter is that even though with respect to the names there is a difference between the attribute of judgment and the attribute of mercy, whatever is in the one is in the other [*kol mah she-yesh ba-zeh yesh ba-zeh*], and on account of this the attribute of judgment changes [*mithappekhet*] into the attribute of mercy and the attribute of mercy into the attribute of judgment . . . for if the attributes were not all contained one within the other [*kullan kolelot zo et zo*] it would be impossible for one to change into the other.[99]

Utilizing contemporary jargon, we might say the *sefirot* manifest a "gender hybridity"; attributes aligned with the masculine possess the potential for judgment and attributes aligned with the feminine possess the potential for mercy.[100] One might protest, accordingly, that the binary opposition pertains equally to male and female, and thus logically it would have been tenable to speak of the two faces of the male, Samael and *Tif'eret*, the sinister force of darkness and the holy force of light. However, as the opening comment in the Mantua recension of the zoharic text attests, the author of the homily focused exclusively on the twin nature of the female conveyed by the scriptural image of the rose perched atop its thorns. Fluctuation of *Shekhinah*, or as Scholem put it, the "ambivalence" manifest in the "alternating phases" of judgment and mercy,[101] is measured by the fact that it is one and the same energy force that may be divine or demonic, the red/white rose.

The dual prism through which *Shekhinah* is imaged reflects and is reflected by the attitude of kabbalists toward Jewish women in the mundane sphere, who likewise oscillate between holiness and contamination. This assertion rests on the larger metaphysical assumption regarding the correspondence of above and below, a principle affirmed by kabbalists uniformly, to the best of my knowledge. As I mentioned briefly in the first chapter, this principle, an axiom of occult philosophy, is expressed in the beginning of *The Emerald Tablet*. The origin of the document is clouded in mystery, though it is surmised that it began to circulate in Arabic and Latin in the thirteenth century. What is important for my purpose is that the maxim that appears therein, "as above, so below"—which for good reason may be considered archaic—resonates with the theosophic perspective adopted by kabbalists at roughly this time. In the rabbinic idiom, appropriated by kabbalists to express the hermetic wisdom epigrammatically, "earthly dominion is like the heavenly dominion," *malkhuta de-arʿa ke-ein malkhuta di-reqiʿa*.[102] One would be foolhardy to think this symbolic homology did not inform the orientation of kabbalists in the lived world, including, most relevantly, their attitudes and behavior toward women, ascribing to them the function of being specula to reflect the male splendor, vessels to receive the seminal discharge.

The extent to which androcentrism is operative in both the divine and human spheres is underscored in an especially poignant way in the following comment by Isaac of Acre, a kabbalist active in the early part of the fourteenth century, on the biblical narrative of the Garden of Eden. Isaac explains the mechanics of the first sin in terms of Eve's desire to be equal in stature to Adam, an act that he links exegetically to the aggadic motif of the yearning of the moon to shine with the same brilliance as the sun, which some rabbis had compared metaphorically to two kings who wished to wear one crown:[103]

> You already know, as I have written, that the two countenances were equal, the light of the one as the light of the other, in the six days of creation. Thus, *Tifʾeret* and *Aṭarah* correspond to the first and second days, *Ḥesed* and *Paḥad* to the third and fourth days . . . *Neṣaḥ* and *Hod* to the fifth and six days, *Yesod Olam* is the Sabbath, and he has no counterpart, but *Kenesset Yisraʾel* is his counterpart.[104] She complained and sought benefit for herself, and similarly the moon with respect to the sun, and Eve with respect to Adam, for it is all one matter, but this is the sprit of God, sanctified and blessed, and the others were created corporeally. The intention of Eve vis-à-vis Adam her husband when she ate the fruit was to rise above Adam and to rule over him so that he would be in need of her power. When she saw that the eating harmed her and that she was punished on account of it, she said, "I will also feed my husband so that he, too, will be punished, and his stature will not be greater than my stature." On account of this intention she was punished and the matter was reversed, and she was in need of the power of her husband, and her desire[105] was directed to him all day to receive the overflow and the progression from him. Thus, when *Aṭarah* complained that two kings could not make use of one crown, she was demanding on behalf of herself, and her light was diminished, and she became the speculum that does not shine . . . . Contemplate how primal

Adam was created two-faced, neck opposite neck, equal in power and one in actuality. Afterwards "he took one of his ribs" (Gen. 2:21) from his side, that is, one of his parts . . . and from one two were made, and even though they are two, they are one, as it says, "and they will be one flesh" (ibid., 24). His attention is constantly directed to her and her attention is constantly directed to him, and his wife is as himself [*ishto ke-gufo*], "for this one was taken from the man" (ibid., 23), understand this.[106]

Ontically, woman is derived from man and thus she must be subservient—a sexist orientation pervasive in the thinking of medieval kabbalists; I have yet to find one traditional kabbalistic source that proves to be an exception. In chapter four I shall return to this point, but what is especially important to note here is that according to Isaac of Acre, the intent of the primordial disobedience, which serves as the paradigm for transgression in general, was that woman wanted to usurp power, to gain the upper hand over man and thereby change the natural order. The punishment, consequently, entailed a reversal of her subversive intention: the female was made to occupy an inferior position. As a result of the defiance, primordial Adam, characterized by a state wherein male and female were "equal in power and one in actuality," was severed into a gender binary of disproportionate corollaries. Isaac of Acre, in line with other kabbalists in his generation, expresses the ancillary position of the feminine by the rabbinic phrase *ishto ke-gufo*.

Lest there be any misunderstanding, it behooves me to say that in the older sources, as well as in medieval ritual codes and talmudic commentaries that preserve the philological resonance of the idiom intact, the expression *ishto ke-gufo* has a pragmatic connotation exclusively, that is, the husband is responsible for the wife's well-being, a legal truism stemming from the fact that, rabbinically conceived, the wife is judged to be the husband's economic property[107]—not a desirable or condoning situation, to be sure, but one that falls short of making an ontological claim regarding the inherently contingent rank of the female vis-à-vis the male.[108] According to one dictum transmitted by the anonymous *tanu rabbanan* ("our rabbis taught"), the halakhic view gave way to—or perhaps was shaped by—the ethical maxim that a husband must love his wife as himself but honor her even more, *ha-ohev et ishto ke-gufo we-ha-mekhabbedah yoter mi-gufo*.[109] There is no indication that talmudically the economic equation of a man's wife and himself was meant to be taken ontologically,[110] yet this is precisely how the phrase is understood by kabbalists who presume on the basis of the scriptural account that woman is of the same substance as man, bone of his bones, flesh of his flesh,[111] and hence the primal unity is attained when she is restored to him to be/come "one flesh."[112] The realm below reflects the pattern above: the light of the feminine potency was diminished—the "lesser light," a speculum that does not shine—on account of her complaining that two kings could not make use of one crown. The weakened position of Eve in the terrestrial realm corresponds to the muted status of *Shekhinah* in the divine.

The enduring hold of this analogical asymmetry may be gauged from the fact that even the efforts of the seventeenth-century messianic figure Sabbatai Ṣevi to reform the status of women, important as such efforts are for social, political, or even cultural history, did not produce significant changes in the symbolic treatment of the feminine.[113] When one casts a glance at the textual panorama of traditional kabbalah from its literary beginnings to the present, cluttered as it is with so many disparate formulations, the uniformity on this issue is astonishing.[114] In spite of occasional references to the study of kabbalistic texts or participation in specific rituals with mystical intent by women at certain historical junctures, as well as credible evidence for women's visionary experiences,[115] traditional circles of Jewish mystics (including Eastern European Hasidic groups of the eighteenth and nineteenth centuries and kabbalistic fraternities from other geographical and cultural settings)[116] have been exclusively male even to this very day. So powerful were the stereotypes promoted by kabbalists that even in the one celebrated case when select Ashkenazi women of the seventeenth century were more intimately involved in study and practice, due in part to the composition of works in Yiddish that rendered esoteric teachings more accessible, the key figures portrayed their own spirituality in images of a distinctively masculine patrimony.[117]

Androgyny and the Dialectics of Masculinity

We must plumb deeper into the zoharic image of the rose, as this image in particular can afford us the opportunity to ascertain the mysterious nature of eros and the erotic nature of mystery. The first thing to note is that the image of the rose enthroned on its thorns portends that mercy and judgment are entwined on one stem. The two-faced character of *Shekhinah* is expressive of an ontological principle embraced by practitioners of kabbalah from its inception as a literary-historical phenomenon: androgyny is applicable to each of the divine attributes; that is, not only is it the case that the divine anthropos in its totality comprises masculine and feminine, but every aspect of the anthropomorphic configuration (with the possible exception of *Keter*, the first of the *sefirot*, in the writings of some kabbalists)[118] displays the power to overflow and the will to receive. In support of this claim, I cite a striking illustration from Joseph Gikatilla, the Castilian kabbalist likely to have been part of the circle responsible for the composition/redaction of zoharic literature in its embryonic stage:[119]

> All the grades [*maʿalot*][120] receive potency and actuality from the tip of the *yod*[121] of the name YHWH, blessed be he, and thus each grade from all of the grades of YHWH, blessed be he, has two aspects: One aspect—it receives from what is above it, and the other aspect—that through which it bestows goodness on what is beneath it. . . . Thus each and every level has two elements: the potency of reception [*koaḥ qibbul*], to receive the influx from the one that is above it, and the potency of bestowal [*koaḥ ha-shefa*], to bestow goodness on that which is beneath it. In this way, the chariots are called "androgynous," from the perspective of receiving [*meqabbel*] and overflowing [*mashpiʿa*], and this is a great secret of the mysteries of faith [*sitrei emunah*]. The one who comprehends this will comprehend the secret of the cherubim, the secret of the structure of the chariot made by King Solomon in the Temple.[122]

The *sefirot* as a whole, and each one separately, beginning with *Ḥokhmah*[123] (in Gikatilla's theosophic compositions, *Keter* is not distinguished terminologically or ontically from

Ein Sof[124] and thus is ostensibly above gender differentiation),[125] exemplify the dual quality of overflowing and restricting—a "great secret" of the "mysteries of faith," the secret of the cherubim, the structure of the chariot, which were male and female (according to the tradition transmitted in the name of Rav Qatina).[126] An interesting attempt at formulating this idea is offered by Joseph ben Shalom Ashkenazi, a kabbalist active in the first half of the fourteenth century, who is to be given credit for articulating the dual character of *sefirot* in a manner that does not blatantly contradict the principle of contradiction. Thus, according to this kabbalist, the "covenant of the one set in the middle" (*berit yaḥid mekhuwwenet ba-emṣa*) mentioned in *Sefer Yeṣirah* 1:3

> alludes to the fact that all the *sefirot* are mixed from *alef mem shin* and their natures, and therefore at times mercy changes to judgment and at times judgment to mercy, and there is no absolute simplicity [*pashuṭ gamur*] in all the *sefirot* except for the supernal *Keter*,[127] for if mercy were only in the nature of water, it could not be transformed into the attribute of judgment, and similarly if the attribute of strength were limited to fire alone, it could not be transformed into the attribute of mercy, for water is the opposite of fire, and the nature of opposites is that they are two attributes that in reality are at a decisive distance, each one on the opposite extreme from the other, unable to be in the same subject at the same moment. Hence, it was necessary that in the potency of fire there is the potency of water and in the potency of water the potency of fire.

In the continuation of this passage, Joseph ben Shalom remarks that the image of the covenant of unity (*berit yaḥid*, or, according to a widely attested variant, *berit yiḥud*) set in the middle underscores that "two contraries are united in one potency" (*shetei temurot mityaḥdot be-khoaḥ eḥad*), as we find in the case of *Tif'eret*, positioned between *Ḥesed* on the right and *Din* on the left, rather than positing mercy and judgment as two independent opposites. The author distinguishes between "contraries" (*temurot*), and "opposites" (*hafakhim*); the former, in contrast to the latter, cohere in one substratum, maintaining the difference of their identity in lieu of the identity of their difference. "Thus the tongue [*lashon*] mediates forever between the upper world and lower world, which are not two opposites, since the tongue receives and overflows, and similarly *Yesod* mediates between *Neṣaḥ* and *Hod* to indicate that they are not opposites."[128]

The principle of mediation—configured imaginally as the tongue above and as the phallus below, an image unanimously affirmed in kabbalistic writings and derived textually from the depiction of the *berit yaḥid* and the anthropomorphic form of the ten *sefirot* in *Sefer Yeṣirah* 1:3[129]—renders opposites contrary, which is to say, the opposites interact with and are transformed into one another, balanced by the mediating principle, like the median bar, the "tongue," of the scales. The polarity of contraries, right and left, mercy and judgment, masculine and feminine, are unified in the simple force, *koaḥ ha-pashuṭ*, the supernal source of all being, the nondifferentiated one wherein opposites are disclosed as being the same in virtue of their difference and different in virtue of their being the same.[130] Androgyny in the sefirotic realm thus conveys the notion of one nature that has two manifestations (*temurot*) rather than a unity that comprehends genuine opposites (*hafakhim*). Philosophically, it is possible to transpose the mythopoeic idiom of the kabbalists into the principle of causality attested in the following words of Proclus, the fifth-century Neoplatonist, in his commentary on Plato's *Parmenides*:

> Everywhere what is imperfect joins itself to the perfect through its fitness for such gifts, just as the perfect joins itself to the imperfect because of its perfecting power. These are the two intermediaries between the imperfect and the perfect, between what participates and what is participated—eagerness for perfection on the part of the imperfect, and on the part of the higher powers capacity to confer it. Thus the imperfect being undergoes perfecting and what participates acquires in a secondary degree the characters possessed primarily by that in which it participates.[131]

The distinction Proclus makes between the "imperfect" and "perfect," "what participates" and "what is participated," the two main forms wherein the activity of the One manifests itself,[132] corresponds to the kabbalistic interpretation of the rabbinic attributes of judgment and mercy, the nature of the former being identified as the capacity to receive and the latter as the potency to bestow. If this contention is granted, and I see no credible reason to deny it, then the relevance of the citation to explicate the orientation of medieval kabbalists should be obvious: just as Proclus affirmed the interaction of the imperfect and perfect to the point that the imperfect is perfected by receiving the "gift" of the perfect and the perfect participates in the imperfect through the act of bestowing upon the imperfect, so the kabbalists emphasized that mercy and judgment interact and are contained in one another, at times mercy donning the garb of judgment, and at other times judgment, the garb of mercy. The kabbalists, moreover, would have concurred with the view of Proclus that

> contrariety is an imitation of the two principles that come after the One; and just as Limit and the Unlimited are united with one another, so also, by participation in them, the contraries in the Ideas imitate their transcendent unity. For this reason contraries everywhere depend from a single summit (*Phaedo* 60b); just as the Dyad there springs from the One and has being about it. The better of two contraries is an imitation of Limit, while the inferior imitates the Unlimited, which is the reason why the physicists say that the worse of two contraries is a deprivation of Limit.[133]

In the undifferentiated One, contraries are not distinguishable as oppositional; on the contrary, "all is in all and all divine entities are united with one another in a such a way that all things are in each and each is in all, and they are connected by divine amity" (θείας φιλίας).[134] Notwithstanding the seeming dissolution of contrariety in the indifference of the One, the Hellenic cultural bias was such that Proclus could not sever himself from demarcating the limited as superior and the unlimited as inferior.[135] The underlying gender bias is brought to light in a second passage from the *Timaeus* commentary, wherein Proclus explicates the ostensibly egalitarian remark of Socrates that the "natures of women should be formed to the same harmonious blend of qualities as those of men; and they should all be given a share in men's employments of every sort, in war as well as in their general mode of life" (18c, 1–4):[136]

> Plato rationally established the belief that the virtues of men and women are the same, since he is of the opinion that there is only one human form and not two different forms, one for the male and one for the female. . . . Others, however, concur that there is a difference of a formal nature between man and woman, refusing to admit that their virtues are the same even though Plato has shown this is possible and advantageous. . . . Yet, to admire further Plato's thought, it is necessary to elevate ourselves to the All and the order of the All: we can ascertain an admirable conformity [σύμπνοιαν] between the male and female. With regard to the gods the two sexes are so strongly intertwined that the same divinity may be called male and female, as Hélios, Hermès, and certain other gods.[137] And even when the sexes are separate, the works of male and female, which are of the same order, are common. The works are realized without doubt primarily by the male, and in an inferior degree by the female—this is what is found as well in the case of mortal beings, nature illustrates that the female is weaker in everything than the male—nevertheless, all that is accomplished by the male is accomplished also by the female in an inferior degree.[138]

I shall return momentarily to the obvious disparity between the two genders articulated by Proclus, but for now it is necessary to emphasize the identity of difference that is posited in the hyperessential unity beyond the dimorphic division into male and female. Indeed, in another passage from the *Parmenides* commentary, Proclus delineates the status of contraries on four levels of being—the sublunar corporeal cosmos, the heavens, the soul, and the intellect:

> In sum, the contraries in Matter flee one another; those in heavens co-exist, but by accident of the fact that their common subject is receptive of both; the contraries in souls exist with one another as such, for their essences are in contact; and those in intellect even participate in one another. That is, the procession of the contraries begins with participation, moves through contact and coexistence in the same subject, and ends in mutual avoidance.[139]

Participation (μέθέξις), a technical term introduced by Plato to account for the relationship of the one ideal form to its multiple manifestations (*Sophist* 251–259; *Parmenides* 132c–d; *Republic* 585b–c), is utilized by Proclus to describe how each level of being participates in the one above it, the chain leading back to the First Principle (πρῶτον παντελῶς), the supraexistential unity (ὑπερούσιον), the ineffable (ἄρρητόν) and unknowable (ἄγνωστον) source whence all beings emanate and whither they return,[140] the unity splintering into the dyadic relation of cause and effect, participant (μετέχον) and that which is participated in (μετεχηόμενον).[141]

The key difference between the kabbalistic teaching and the view of Proclus relates to the imagistic representation of metaphysical truth—a turn of phrase that does not entail for me a binary distinction between mythos and logos. For kabbalists, embellishing the rabbinic tradition, the weaker party of the dyad is the limited, represented figuratively as the attribute of judgment and engendered as feminine, and the stronger is the unlimited, the attribute of love, engendered as masculine. Although all of the *sefirot* are characterized by this dual potentiality, the documents produced by kabbalists from an early period attest that the principle of androgyny was applied to *Shekhinah* in a distinctive manner. It is worthwhile dwelling on this matter as it will shed light on the construction of gender more generally, but prior to delving into the primary textual evidence, I think it beneficial to bring to the reader's attention an observation of Erich Neumann regarding the "original hermaphroditic form of uroboros," which he ascribes to the archetype of the Great Mother:

> Androgyny is a primitive characteristic, and, so too, is the combination of virginity and fertility in goddesses, and of fertility and castration in gods. The masculine traits of the female still coexist side by side with the feminine traits of the male. If the goddess holds the lily, the feminine symbol, in one hand and the snake, the masculine symbol, in the other, this is entirely in keeping with the fact that the eunuchs who serve her are male prostitutes, dancers, and priests.[142]

My appeal to Neumann does not mean that I personally accept the truth of Jungian archetypes nor that I believe this is the only or even the best theoretical template to explicate the worldview of medieval kabbalists. I would contend, however, that if we bracket the specific location of the symbol in the hypothetical collective unconscious, the Jungian orientation is congenial to the kabbalistic outlook: Just as in Jung's theory the symbol is perceived to be the "manifest visibility of the archetype, corresponding to its latent invisibility,"[143] in the epistemology of kabbalists, *sefirot* are the manifest visibility of the invisible Ein Sof. According to Neumann, symbolic images, which are delineated as the "projections of the formative side of human nature that creates order and assigns meaning" in the construction of what we consider to be the "objective world,"[144] refer to an indeterminate "spiritual reality," the invisible presence, the "archetype *an sich*," in Jung's adaptation of the Kantian locution,[145] that can never be stripped of symbolic embellishment; every symbol, therefore, must be interpreted in terms of another symbol, forming thereby a "symbol group" or "symbol canon,"[146] a cluster of symbols embodied in the variegated cultural forms of myth, art, religion, and language.[147] In this psychic state, which is relived in and through the images, symbols, and projections of interior processes that constitute the world of dreams

> inside and outside are not discriminated from one another. The feeling of oneness with the universe, the ability of all contents to change shape and place, in accordance with the laws of similarity and symbolic affinity, the symbolic character of the world, and the symbolic meaning of all spatial dimensions—high and low, left and right, etc.—the significance of colors, and so forth, all this the world shares with the dawn period of mankind. Here as there, spiritual things take on "material" form, becoming symbols and objects.[148]

The symbolic mentality is designated by Neumann as "uroboric" and "pleromatic," the former "because it is dominated by the symbol of the circular snake, standing for total nondifferentiation, everything issuing from everything and again entering into everything, depending on everything, and connecting with everything," and the latter "because the ego germ still dwells in the pleroma, in the 'fullness' of the unformed God."[149]

Neumann observes, moreover, that androgyny applies to the Great Mother, the archetypical archetype, as it were, in the binary form of virginity and fertility, both aspects of the feminine potency; within the matriarchal context, we can, indeed must, speak of a female androgyne, the female comprising both female and male.[150] Neumann offers the following poetic account:

> Thus the Great Mother is uroboric: terrible and devouring, beneficent and creative; a helper, but also alluring and destructive; a maddening enchantress, yet a bringer of wisdom; bestial and divine, voluptuous harlot and inviolable virgin, immemorially old and eternally young. This original bivalence of the archetype with its juxtaposed opposites is torn asunder when consciousness separates the World Parents. To the left, there is ranged a negative series of symbols—Deadly Mother, Great Whore of Babylon, Witch, Dragon, Moloch; to the right, a positive series in which we find the Good Mother who is Sophia or Virgin, brings forth and nourishes, and leads the way to rebirth and salvation. Here Lilith, there Mary; here the toad, there the goddess; here a morass of blood, there the Eternal Feminine. . . . The power of the primordial Great Mother archetype rests on the original state where everything is intermingled and undifferentiated. Not to be grasped because ever in flux.[151]

There is, of course, a major difference between traditional kabbalistic symbolism and the perspective proffered by Neumann: the latter assumes a matriarchal framework, whereas the former is incontestably patriarchal.[152] Hence the Primal Being envisioned by medieval kabbalists to which we may apply the description of an "original hermaphroditic form of uroboros" is the male androgyne of the hyphenated reality Ein Sof–*sefirot*, and not the female androgyne of the Great Mother.[153] This shift bespeaks that, for kabbalists, the bivalency of gender is to be construed from the vantage point of the male and, more specifically, from the perch of the phallus, and this applies equally to the divine and human anthropomorphic figures. According to Neumann, the negative attributes on the left and the positive ones on the right are "two modes" of the "matriarchal consciousness," the initiative and receptive, formative and transformative, masculine and feminine,[154] that are integrated in the archetype of the Great Mother, characterized as "flux" rather than "substance," the "original state where everything is intermingled and undifferentiated." I shall return at a later stage in this chapter to the philosophical implications of nondifferentiated unity, but suffice it here to underscore that in kabbalistic lore the uroboric quality is also associated in a distinctive way with the feminine and particularly with the imaginal symbol of *Shekhinah*, but in this context the matter must be seen from an androcentric perspective; the positive aspects of femininity are valenced as masculine and the negative as feminine.

Let us recall the observation of Scholem that "while the *Shekhinah* is predominantly described in feminine symbols, it is not entirely without active, masculine aspects." The "female character" of *Shekhinah* is thus linked with "restrictive and dangerous features.

The restraint of the flow of life, a quality intrinsic to the activity of judgment (*Din*), frequently entails destructive consequences for the world. But when the *Shekhinah* functions as a medium for the downward flow of life-giving energies, it is understood in male symbols, the most prominent of which is the divine name *Adonai* (Lord)."[155] Scholem elucidates the point by interpreting a zoharic passage wherein the image of the redeeming angel, *ha-mal'akh ha-go'el* (Gen. 48:16), is applied to *Shekhinah*, "the angel[156] that is sometimes male and sometimes female. When it bestows blessings on the world, it is male, and it is called 'male,' like a male that bestows blessings on a female, but when it stands in judgment on the world, then it is called female like a female that is pregnant."[157] The text is exemplary of the kabbalistic outlook: masculinity is aligned with the attribute of mercy, the act of bestowing, and femininity with the attribute of judgment, the act of constricting.[158] In the execution of judgment, *Shekhinah* restrains the effluence pouring forth from above, and she is thus compared to a pregnant woman who holds the fetus within the womb where gestation takes place. By contrast, in disseminating blessing to the worlds below, *Shekhinah* assumes a masculine persona, for she is like the man that fills the woman with seminal discharge.[159]

The point is confirmed in another zoharic homily focused on the exegetical application of the image of the redeeming angel to *Shekhinah*. In the previous chapter, I had the opportunity to mention a different part of this text, which is one of the discourses of the *yanuqa*, the child prodigy. I will translate and comment upon the section of the homily whence we may elicit a deeper appreciation of angelhood and divine providence:

> He opened and said "The angel that has redeemed me from all evil—bless [the lads; in them may my name be recalled, and the names of my fathers Abraham and Isaac, and may they be teeming multitudes upon the earth]" (Gen. 48:16). Jacob uttered that verse through the holy spirit [*ruaḥ qudsha*], and if it was uttered through the holy spirit, there must be mystery of wisdom [*raza de-ḥokhmata*] within it. "The angel"—he calls [*Shekhinah*] angel [*mal'akh*] and he calls it by other names. Why is it called *mal'akh* here? This refers to when she[160] was sent from above and she receives the splendor from the speculum above, for then the father and mother bless her. They say to her "Go, my daughter, and keep after your house, watch your house, thus you will do for your house: go and feed them. Go, for the world below awaits you, the members of your household are expecting food from you. You have all that is necessary to provide for them." Then she is an angel. You might say that there are several places where she is called "angel" and she does not come to feed the world, and, moreover, that she does not feed the worlds with this name but rather through the name YHWH. Thus it surely is: When sent from the father and mother, she is called angel, but when resting on the place of the two cherubim, she is called YHWH.[161]

Shekhinah assumes the role of angel (*mal'akh*) when she is sent on her mission, receiving the overflow of blessing from the "father" and "mother," *Ḥokhmah* and *Binah*, by way of the "speculum above," *Tif'eret*. The purpose of the angelic calling is to provide sustenance to her household, the worlds below the divine emanations. Yet, as the author of the passage makes clear, *Shekhinah* does not fulfill the task of feeding the worlds through the agency of the title *mal'akh*, but rather by means of the Tetragrammaton, the name that designates the masculine potency of mercy. *Shekhinah* is endowed with the name when she assumes the posture of dwelling upon the cherubim. I submit that encoded here is a cryptic allusion to the transposition of *Shekhinah* from feminine to masculine, from vessel to channel, from throne to enthroned. As the matter is delineated elsewhere in *Zohar*:

> R. Simeon said: When the holy One, blessed be he, is crowned in his crowns, he is crowned from above and below. From above—from the place of the depth of all. By what is he crowned below? By means of the souls of the righteous. Consequently, life is augmented from above and below, and the place of the sanctuary is encompassed from all sides, the well is filled, the sea is completed, and then it gives to everything. It is written "Drink water from your cistern, running water from your well" (Prov. 5:15)—initially "your cistern" [*borekha*] and afterward "your well" [*be'erekha*], for the word "cistern" [*bor*] denotes only that which is vacuous and does not flow, and "well" [*be'er*], the flowing waters, but it is all one place. The place to which the impoverished are attached is called "cistern," for it has nothing of its own, but only that which is placed within it. And what is it? *Dalet*. Afterward it becomes a well [*be'er*] that flows and is filled from all sides. And what is it? *He*. It is filled from above and flows from below. It is filled from above, as we said, and it flows from below, from the souls of the righteous.[162]

The central gradation of the sefirotic pleroma, which is designated by the traditional honorific title for God, the holy One, blessed be, is crowned from the "depth of everything" above, that is, the great womb of all being, or *Binah*, and from the "souls of the righteous" below, the offspring of the seed implanted in *Shekhinah* by *Yesod*. As a consequence of the seminal implantation, *Shekhinah* is transposed from a cistern (*bor*), the empty vessel to which the impoverished take hold, to a well (*be'er*) overflowing with water, a transposition that is demarcated semiotically as the metamorphosis from *dalet*, the letter that signifies poverty (*dal*), to *he*, the letter that signifies surplus. The agency that transforms the vacuous pit into a living well consists of the aforementioned souls of the righteous, referred to as the "impoverished," a term that, in my judgment, signifies "spiritual" as opposed to "material" poverty, that is, the righteous void themselves of want and desire and thus are seemingly meager in the ways of the corporeal world.

In chapter seven, I shall elaborate on the phallic empowerment of ascetic renunciation, the erotic excess of sensual lack, but suffice it here to note the transformation of *Shekhinah* from *dalet* to *he*, from a receptacle devoid of all content to the ever-gushing stream that continuously irrigates the world below. Although not stated explicitly, it is abundantly clear to ears well attuned to zoharic forms of symbolic figuration that the two facets of *Shekhinah*, cistern (*bor*) and well (*be'er*), refer respectively to the feminine and masculine characteristics, the former marking the receptivity *Shekhinah* exemplifies vis-à-vis the sefirotic world of unity, and the latter, the largesse *Shekhinah* demonstrates vis-à-vis the natural world of differentiation.

In another zoharic passage not mentioned by Scholem but perhaps at the back of his mind, the ascription to *Shekhinah* of the name "Adonai," the epithet by which the Tetragrammaton is pronounced, and the designation that signifies providence and governance of the physical universe, is explained as a consequence of her being illumined from the phallic potency of the covenant:

> It is written "Behold the ark of the covenant, sovereign of all the earth" (Josh. 3:11), "the ark" [*aron*] is the speculum that does not shine, "the covenant" [*berit*] the speculum that shines . . . the sun that illumines her and she is a covenant together with him. "The ark of the covenant" [*aron ha-berit*]—precisely. "Sovereign of all the earth" [*adon kol ha-areṣ*], the covenant is the sovereign of all the earth, and this ark is sovereign because the sun illumines her and illumines the entire world. Thus she is called, and from him she receives the name, and this ark is called sovereign [*adon*] in the mystery of *alef dalet nun yod* [*adonai*]. As we say, the righteous one [*ṣaddiq*] and righteousness [*ṣedeq*], similarly sovereign [*adon*] and my lord [*adonai*], one dependent on the other.[163]

The epithet *adonai* denotes the providential role of *Shekhinah*, which she takes on when she receives the overflow from the masculine potency *Yesod*, designated *adon*. In virtue of receiving the illumination from *Yesod*, also referred to as the sun, *Shekhinah*, the female vessel, is transposed into part of the "covenant." This is the esoteric meaning of the expression *aron ha-berit, Shekhinah* is the ark (*aron*) that shelters the phallic potency (*berit*) and thereby inherits the name *adon* from it in the form of *adonai*. As the reader is told at the end of the passage, the relationship of *adon* to *adonai* is precisely like that between *ṣaddiq* and *ṣedeq*, terms that are applied respectively in zoharic literature and other kabbalistic texts to *Yesod* and *Shekhinah*. We may conclude, therefore, that sovereignty, or governance over this world, is not indicative of the feminine prowess of *Shekhinah* à la the figure "mother earth" or "mother nature," as some have maintained, but rather it marks her capacity to contain the phallus and be transformed thereby into the "lower wisdom," the "great sea" that sustains all beings in the differentiated world of cosmic space and time.[164] It is correct to speak of *Shekhinah* as the ruler and source of life of all worlds below the sefirotic pleroma, but it is not accurate to attribute this quality to the female aspect of the divine potency.[165] On the contrary, the interpretation of Joshua 3:11, whereby the two expressions, *aron ha-berit* and *adon kol ha-areṣ*, are rendered equivalent, signifies the transformation of the feminine by the masculine whence the former is entrusted with the task of sustaining all existence by channeling the divine overflow from above. Moses de León makes the point in symbolic language that underscores even more poignantly the phallic dimension of this transmutation:

> The lower *Shekhinah*. We have already spoken and broached the secret of the upper *Shekhinah* . . . and the one below is in the pattern of the upper *Shekhinah*.[166] In the pattern of all the matters that are ascribed to the upper *Shekhinah*, all the names and all the matters that she dispenses to the supernal channels, in that very pattern [*dugma mammash*] she overflows to the lower beings in order to bestow upon them

> the efflux and to sustain them. And thus she is called "a woman of valor, crown of her husband" (Prov. 12:14), that is, "glorious crown" (Isa. 62:3; Prov. 4:9). Since *Shekhinah* dwells with the lower beings, she pours out to them, giving them power and strength, satisfying all their needs, as it says, "She rises while it is still night, and supplies provisions for her household, the daily fare of her maidens" (Prov. 31:15), for she is assuredly a "woman of valor" [*eshet ḥayil*], and she is "Esther the daughter of Abihail" (Esther 2:15).[167]

Malkhut, the last of the *sefirot*, the lower *Shekhinah*, is in the pattern of *Binah*, the third *sefirah*, the upper *Shekhinah*, and thus just as *Binah* sustains the *sefirot* that emanate from her, so *Malkhut* sustains the world of differentiated beings. However, and this is the critical point, *Malkhut* assumes this comportment (marked by the expression "woman of valor" [*eshet ḥayil*], and the figure of Esther whose father was Abihail, which can be decoded hyperliterally as *avi ḥayil* ["father of valor"]) in virtue of what she receives from her male consort, *Tif'eret*, the sixth *sefirah*; when the Matrona is united with the King, she is elevated to the status of *aṭeret baʿlah*, "crown of her husband," and *aṭeret tif'eret*, "glorious crown," or, to render it more precisely in this context, the "crown of *Tif'eret*." The elevation of *Malkhut* to the rank of crown is one of the key symbolic representations of the gender metamorphosis of the female; her incorporation and restitution to the male, whence she was taken according to the engendering myth of the second chapter of Genesis accepted and embellished by kabbalists, a restoration that is fully realized in the eschatological future.

The positive depictions of *Shekhinah* as the matrix of being invariably relate to her transposition into a male, a critical point unfortunately missed by scholars who imprudently present traditional kabbalah as proffering an affirmative view of the feminine as an autonomous force completing the masculine, the "goddess of the kabbala," in Raphael Patai's felicitous but misleading formulation.[168] I do not deny and never have denied in my work the obvious truism that medieval kabbalah is saturated with imaginal representations of the divine in gendered terms, mental icons set primarily in the cast of the king and his consort, *malka* and *maṭronita*, according to the locution that occurs frequently in zoharic homilies. Many of my critics have charged that my analyses of gender have failed to take this rudimentary point into account, blinded as I am presumed to be from the obvious adulation of the feminine in kabbalistic symbolism. Nothing could be further from the truth. The task for me, however, has not been simply to collect and regurgitate the litany of images of the feminine constructed in the male imaginary of traditional kabbalists, to wit, bride, heavenly Jerusalem, throne, temple, tabernacle, moon, sea, earth, and so on, but to evaluate and determine the gender valence of these depictions within a larger hermeneutical scheme.

The position that may be elicited from the zoharic passage describing *Shekhinah* as the androgynous angel is reiterated in parallel language several times by Joseph of Hamadan, another kabbalist who apparently had intimate links to the zoharic circle.[169] Given the importance of this theme for ascertaining the gender traits applied to *Shekhinah* and the widespread misapprehension on this score advanced by kabbalah scholars, I will cite a passage from *Sefer Tashaq,* one of Joseph's principal compositions:[170] "It is written afterward 'the radiance surrounding it' (Ezek. 1:4), this alludes to Matrona, for she is the mystery of the androgyne, male and female, at times she is called masculine and other times feminine."[171] *Shekhinah* is identified as the "mystery of the androgyne," *raza de-androginos,* for it is manifest at times as male and other times as female. In other passages, the intent of the designation is made more explicitly: in relation to the potencies above her, whence she receives the overflow, the divine presence is female, but in relation to the worlds below, upon which she bestows the overflow, she is male.[172]

Another feature of the androgynous nature of *Shekhinah* is disclosed in the aforecited text in the image of *nogah,* "radiance," the word used in Ezekiel's chariot vision to describe the "appearance of the image of the glory of the Lord" (1:28). In the writings of Joseph of Hamadan, as in zoharic literature and other kabbalistic texts influenced thereby, *nogah* refers symbolically to the crown that encircles the glory. Thus, to offer one illustration:

> "The radiance surrounding it," a great light encompassed that cloud, and this is the light created on the first day, and the righteous are sustained by that light . . . and thus [the sages], blessed be their memory, said the light hidden for the righteous is the light created on the first day,[173] which surrounds the holy chariot . . . and this is the diadem [*aṭarah*] that crowns the righteous, as [the sages], blessed be their memory, said, the holy One, blessed be he, in the future will be a crown on the head of each and every righteous man,[174] and this is "the radiance surrounding it."[175]

No explicit mention is made here of *aṭeret berit,* but I would suggest, based on other passages penned by this kabbalist, that the halo of the radiance, which is assimilated into the crown donned by the righteous, the resplendent aura encircling the head, is linked symbolically to the corona of the phallus.[176] One text in particular is noteworthy, as it supports my surmise:

> When the righteous are crowned in this letter *zayin,* the Matrona encompasses and covers them and they are below . . . the mystery of the crown of the holy One, blessed be he, and the crown that crowns the righteous who sit in the Garden of Eden . . . . Thus, just as the letter *zayin* has a crown, so the day of Sabbath is the crown and diadem of all the days the holy One, blessed be he, created. Thus you find a crown above and *waw* below, for it is a crown of the six days in which God, blessed be he, made heaven and earth . . . the crown of the six days is the day of Sabbath, which surrounds everything . . . and the day of Sabbath, which corresponds to the letter *zayin,* is from the word *mazona,* the sustenance [*mazon*] of the day of Sabbath, sustenance for everything, and therefore Sabbath is called "covenant" [*berit*], for it is the covenant of the holy One, blessed be he . . . the ninth emanation, which is called the attribute of the righteous one [*middat ṣaddiq*], the holy covenant [*berita qaddisha*] that pours fine oil upon the Matrona . . . and the head of *zayin* is in the image of *yod,* the crown atop the covenant, which is called the corona of the phallus [*aṭarah di-verita*].[177]

I will refrain from unpacking this passage in the detailed manner it merits, but the points most pertinent to our discussion are patently clear and worthy of demarcation. The first thing to note is the movement from ecstatic experience to theosophic structure, two sides of one coin rather than discrete typological grids, the specular image wherein mirror and mirrored are welded in causal reciprocity; the object seen is the cause of reflection on the surface, for in the absence of the object there is no reflection, and yet reflection is also the cause of object seen, for in the absence of reflection there is no object seen. Both aspects of the speculative are explicated in terms of the orthography of *zayin*, broken into a *yod* atop *waw*. The older apocalyptic motif preserved and transmitted in rabbinic literature, of the righteous sitting in the Garden of Eden with crowns on their heads, is interpreted kabbalistically as a reference to *Shekhinah* enveloping the righteous to whom she is conjoined just as the crown sits on top of *waw* to make the shape of the letter *zayin*.[178] Reflected therein is the "mystery of the crown of the holy One, blessed be he" (*raza de-taga de-qadosh barukh hu*) the mystery of Sabbath, the seventh day that crowns the six days of creation, the covenant (*berit*) of the divine. Although not stated explicitly, it is plausible to assume that this covenant is androgynous in nature—a basic tenet of medieval kabbalistic symbolism—a point substantiated by both the presumed orthography and etymology of *zayin*.

Let me begin with the latter: The author threads together *zayin* and *mazon* (sustenance)—the latter is from the root *zwn*, to sustain, to make provisions, to give food—and on that basis another layer of the connection between *zayin* and Sabbath appears; the Sabbath is the divine potency that is the source of sustenance in the world, the covenant, *berit* (or *berita*), which is identified further as the ninth emanation, *Ṣaddiq*, the channel through which the oil, the sefirotic efflux, overflows to *Shekhinah*. In this matter, the androgyny is aligned hierarchically in the form of the male on top of the female, the preferred sexual posture according to the rabbinic sexual ethos. But there is another dimension to the androgyny, one that overturns the tables, so to speak: the female rising to the head of the male, or, in the prophetic idiom, the female surrounding the male (Jer. 31:21). This, too, is symbolized by the letter *zayin*, which can be broken orthographically into *yod* atop *waw*, the *yod* standing for the corona (*aṭarah di-verita*) and the *waw* for the shaft (*guf*) of the penis.[179] In the concluding section of chapter eight, I shall discuss the symbol of the crown and the process of coronation in greater detail as they pertain to the eschatological overcoming of gender dimorphism, but what I have written will suffice to carry us forward on the path at this juncture.

Scholem well grasped the androgynous status of *Shekhinah*, but he did not take into account the androcentric bias of this symbolism and assuredly he did not disclose the phallocentrism of the kabbalistic tradition.[180] On the contrary, Scholem wrote of the "dialectics of femininity" in his account of symbolic depictions of *Shekhinah* in kabbalistic literature, which includes the "element of giving."[181] "Dialectics" signifies the twofold character of which we have been speaking, but for Scholem, and for most other established scholars of kabbalah, the active and passive traits of *Shekhinah* are assigned to the "feminine." In another passage, Scholem describes the "principle of femininity" manifest in the "upper *Shekhinah*," the *sefirah* of *Binah*, as the "full expression of ceaseless creative power—it is receptive, to be sure, but is spontaneously and incessantly transformed into an element that gives birth, as the stream of eternally flowing divine life enters into it."[182] In my estimation, it would have been more exacting to refer to the "dialectics of masculinity," for both elements, active bestowal and passive reception, are features of the male. Note that Scholem himself remarked that the feminine is "receptive," but she can be "spontaneously and incessantly transformed" into an active force that gives birth "as the stream of eternally flowing divine life" enters into her.

Needless to say, the ontological foundation of the zoharic symbolism, the belief that the female derives from the male, is far from Scholem's purview. I would contend, nevertheless, that latent in his remarks is recognition of the phallocentric deportment. The female is valenced as a source of life and blessing only when she receives the stream of life transmitted through the phallic channel. The subtle point, which has been either missed or rejected by most scholars of kabbalah, is made with compelling simplicity by Moses de León:

> Thus, from this you can know what is said "Let the earth bring forth every kind of living creature" (Gen. 1:24), for there is a living creature above the living creature, and "the living creature that is beneath the God of Israel" (Ezek. 10:20) is the living creature that is known, which rules in the night, and she comprises the appropriate overflow from the "river that comes forth from Eden" (Gen. 2:10). She "brings forth the living creature," precisely, by means of the emanation of the living creature that is above.[183]

We can speak of *Shekhinah* in procreative terms, as the earth that yields the living creature (*nefesh ḥayyah*) of every kind, on account of the efflux that the feminine, the lower living creature, receives from the masculine potency, the upper living creature,[184] through the phallic medium of the river that comes forth from Eden to irrigate the garden. Both genders are thus envisioned from the perspective of the phallus, the wellspring of divine creativity in the symbology of traditional Jewish esotericism.[185]

In one of his voluminous compositions, Moses Ḥayyim Luzzatto, the eighteenth-century kabbalist, poet, playwright, scholar, grammarian, and moralist, offers a succinct articulation of the kabbalistic doctrine of the dual nature of *nuqba*, the technical term of the feminine potency:

> I will explain to you the matter of "he established the earth" (Prov. 3:19). The feminine has two aspects, the aspect of the vessel that is in her, as they said "A woman does not cut a covenant except with regard to one who makes her into a vessel,"[186] and also the existence of the feminine from the side of *Yesod*, for the corona of the phallus is the beginning of the existence of the feminine [*aṭeret ha-yesod hi re'shit meṣi'ut ha-nuqba*], understand this well. The first intercourse is in the mystery of the potencies [*sod ha-gevurot*], and she is constructed through them to receive afterward the male waters, and she is called "sea" [*yam*] in this aspect. Afterward, in the mystery of the male waters, she becomes the earth [*ereṣ*] that is sown and yields produce.[187]

As is his wont, Luzzatto lucidly enunciates the status accorded the feminine in the kabbalistic construction of gender.[188] There are two aspects to *Shekhinah*: one that is, properly speaking, engendered as feminine, and another that is masculine. With regard to the former, *nuqba* assumes the role of a vessel that receives the seminal discharge (designated by the technical term *mayyin dukhrin* [male waters], which stand in contrast to *mayyin nuqvin* [female waters])[189] and thus she is portrayed symbolically as the sea. In virtue of her will to receive, the feminine assumes a covenantal status (the kabbalistic rendering of the talmudic idiom having obvious phallic implications).[190] Additionally, *nuqba* has a second aspect that is engendered as masculine, an aspect that is identified as the corona of the phallus (*aṭeret ha-yesod*) the site that Luzzatto designates the "beginning of the existence of the feminine" (*re'shit meṣi'ut ha-nuqba*). Implied in this remark is an idea that, in my judgment, can be traced to kabbalistic sources from a relatively early period but which assumes a more prominent stance in the esoteric teaching transmitted in the name of Luria: the uppermost aspect of the divine is engendered as purely masculine, a right without a separate left standing over and against it, a right that encompasses the left as an aspect of itself, a male configuration with no female other; the ontic root of the latter is located, more specifically, in the corona of the phallus.[191] From this we may glean that the term *aṭarah* when applied to *Shekhinah* denotes the state wherein the feminine surrounds the male in the manner that the corona is the encircling part of the phallus,[192] a state that was at the beginning and that will be restored at the end, a state imaginally depicted as *keter malkhut*.[193] In virtue of this quality, we can speak of the earth that yields its produce, an activity that denotes propagation. As I noted above, in relationship to worlds beneath her, *Shekhinah* assumes the disposition of effluent male, a property captured mythopoeically in the image of *aṭarah*. Crown of kingship, *keter malkhut*, resting on the king's head is symbolically interchangeable with the image of the phallic corona, *aṭeret berit*.

I would be remiss if I did not note that in the continuation of the passage, Luzzatto emphasizes that the fecundity of *nuqba* is the "secret of mercy" that stems from the feminine aspect itself, an aspect that is hidden in the "membrane of the ether of the supernal, hidden wisdom" (*qeruma de-avveira de-ḥokhmata illa'ah setima'ah*), which is lodged in the "cavity of the skull" (*ḥallala de-gulgalta*) of *Arikh Anpin*, the primal manifestation of the hidden infinite,[194] also referred to as "ancient of the ancient" (*atiqa de-atiqin*) and "concealed of the concealed" (*ṭemira di-ṭemirin*), images culled from the complex theosophic ruminations of *Idra Rabba*, the section of zoharic literature upon which he is commenting.[195] Without entering into the intricacy of this symbolism, let me simply remark that in Luzzatto's formulation, the membrane signifies the "matter of separation" (*inyan ha-havdalah*), for "all the lights above this membrane are the secret of the supernal waters, and that which is within this membrane is the secret of the lower waters." From this Luzzatto concludes that "all of the emanation is from the aspect of the supernal waters, but there is also the secret of the lower waters given only to *nuqba*, and this is the secret of 'By wisdom the Lord established the earth,' *yhwh be-ḥokhmah yasad areṣ* (Prov. 3:19)."[196] The principle of femininity relates to the quality of division, separation, distinction, a principle that is represented imagistically as the membrane of the ether of the supernal wisdom that is hidden within the skull of the uppermost configuration of the divine anthropos.[197]

In the continuation, which is the section I translated above, Luzzatto explicitly links the membrane surrounding the skull to the corona of the phallus (*aṭeret ha-yesod*). There is no penis here, only the phallic potency wedged in the head,[198] a potency that includes the potential for division, for the mythopoeic logic demands that if there is a desire to project, there must be the will to receive.[199] Reading the cosmogonic myth in the beginning of the scriptural account hyperliterally, the separation of upper and lower waters, portrayed respectively as male and female, is greatly embellished in the drama of divine autogenesis. There is much to say about Luzzatto's interpretation and even more about the zoharic text itself, but suffice it here to note that emission of fluids on the part of the female is engendered as masculine. Conceptually, this is a consequence of locating the ontic source of the female in *aṭeret yesod*. As a philological aside, it is of significance to mark that in the jargon formulated by Luria's interpreters, *yesod* is the term that also denotes female genitalia, womb, or uterus; the crown of that foundation, which would correspond to *aṭeret berit*, seems to be associated with the clitoris.[200]

Phallic Mother and the Masculine Imaginary

The scholar of kabbalah in its embryonic stages must reconstruct cultural context principally from the use of metaphorical systems of signification both open and tacit; indeed, the latter may prove to be more significant in ascertaining the semantic application of symbols and their instantiation within social communities whose very existence revolved about the transmission of secret teachings and occult practices.[201] It is certainly reasonable to assume that representations of the feminine in any given setting may be profitably examined in terms of the treatment of women in the sphere of intersubjective commerce.[202] Considerable progress has been made in the academic study of medieval Jewish history, with far greater attention being paid to retrieving something of the proverbial silent voice of women's lives from rabbinic and lay documents, including letters found in the Cairo Geniza written by women.[203] It is important to note, however, that ideologies of gender do not always reflect the respective socioeconomic status of men and women,[204] nor is it necessarily the case that literary representations are to be decoded as accurate depictions of historical facticity.[205] The conclusion reached by Penny Schine Gold after surveying the proliferation of iconographic depictions of Mary in Europe in the twelfth and thirteenth centuries is instructive:

> The artistic (and theological) images of the Virgin were, like the images of women in secular literature, the creations of men, and can be understood as fulfilling the emotional needs of the monks and clerics who created them. The Virgin serves as a perfect embodiment of the conflicting ideals of virginity and motherhood that men believed in for women, and celibate men might feel particularly attached to such female imagery exactly because of their isolation from real women. . . . As in literature, we see in art that the proliferation of female images is not in itself neces-

> sarily a sign of "improvement" in attitudes toward women; we must look past the quantity of images to the content of the images.[206]

The materialist bias, moreover, may blind one to the fact that even if we can make a case that in a given society women occupy a fairly important place in the commodity of exchange, this does not preclude the endurance of male anxieties that endorse negative cultural stereotypes about women. Gender analysis in much of the academic study of Jewish history has been driven by this impulse: If one can document a more active role of women in a particular society, then one makes a case for a corrective to the dominant patriarchal androcentricity.[207]

I am surely sympathetic to broadening the scope of sources that one uses in studying the past and believe in the obligation of higher institutions of learning worldwide to promote and patronize the pursuit of such knowledge, yet I remain doubtful that this approach will do much to counter the persistent sexism evident in medieval rabbinic depictions of women as morally, intellectually, and physically inferior to men. For the most part, kabbalists belonged to the rabbinic intelligentsia, some serving as communal leaders and others occupying positions in close proximity to the seats of power and influence. From this perspective the exclusion of women from the literary kabbalistic fraternities should come as no surprise. As Tova Rosen commented in her recently published monograph on gender construction and medieval Hebrew poetry, given the scarcity of medieval Jewish women writers, the feminist project of "gynocritics" is impracticable: "The path left for the medievalist feminist is thus approaching the issues of women and gender via male-authored texts."[208] This conclusion is surely apposite for the study of kabbalah. It is worthwhile citing Rosen's general description of the cultural context whence medieval Jewish male writers emerged:

> The textual institutions were men's sanctuaries from which women were banished. The study of Scriptures and rabbinical literature, mysticism, and philosophy and even the practicing of liturgy had all been the exclusive domains of male creativity. In medieval Judaism, even more than in its hosting cultures, writing was considered an exclusively male—and essentially virile—competence. . . . The pen (and pen-*man*-ship)—metonymic of writing, and of the writer himself—often stands for men's productivity and prowess, authorship and authority.[209]

In spite of the persistent claim on the part of kabbalists to the oral nature of esoteric lore and practice—a claim made always in written documents—at least as far as historians are concerned there is little question that kabbalah as a historical phenomenon evolved in highly literate circles wherein writing was viewed as the principal channel for transmission and embellishment of the traditions.[210] In a separate study I have explored at length the phallocentric dimensions of the writing of God's body and the construction of gender in kabbalistic myth.[211] In this matter, kabbalists were perfectly attuned to the stereotype that prevailed from the classical to the medieval period and beyond: Writing in general, and the writing of mystical secrets in particular, is an activity valorized exclusively as masculine. The position adopted uniformly by kabbalists is well summarized in a pithy statement that appears in a document considered genuinely to have been penned by Isaac Luria, *Perush Sifra di-Ṣeniʿuta* (Commentary on the Book of Concealment): "The matter of this inscription [*gilluf*] is that [the letters] are engraved so that the lower becomes a receptacle for the supernal in the likeness of male and female, so that the one will receive the overflow from the other, and consequently the one will be within the other and the one will be above the other."[212]

From the kabbalists' perspective, only one with a circumcised phallus, which corresponds to the writing tool, is worthy of inscribing the esoteric matters, a theurgical activity that assumes the soteriological significance of unifying female and male and thereby restoring the former to the latter. Instead of promoting egalitarianism, kabbalah actually had the effect of reifying the androcentric hegemony. Those who have challenged my work on gender by recording the litany of feminine images elicited from kabbalistic treatises have forgotten (or perhaps, in some cases, have never become acquainted with) the warning of Toril Moi that studying images of women represented in texts authored by men is "equivalent to studying false images of women."[213] The stereotypical images of women are another and maybe even more insidious form of erasure on the part of men.

How ideology and social realities intermingle is unquestionably an important matter, but one that requires a different sort of inquiry from what is embraced in this book. In principle, I concur with the observation of the French sociologist Pierre Bourdieu that the

> symbolic revolution called for by the feminist movement cannot be reduced to a simple conversion of consciousnesses and wills. Because the foundation of symbolic violence lies not in mystified consciousnesses that only need to be enlightened but in dispositions attuned to the structure of domination of which they are the product, the relation of complicity that the victims of symbolic domination grant to the dominant can only be broken through a radical transformation of the social conditions of production of the dispositions that lead the dominated to take the point of view of the dominant on the dominant and on themselves.[214]

To effect a real symbolic shift there must be genuine changes in the sociopolitical arena and specifically in the conditions and institutions that control economic production and the distributions of goods and services, for in the end, the social world "constructs the body as a sexually defined reality and as the depository of sexually defining principles of vision and division."[215] Yet those changes, as vital as they are, do not guarantee that the transformation in a cultural symbolic will take root, as it is possible—and I believe empirically verifiable—that androcentric prejudices endure even in ostensibly more egalitarian societies.

On this score, it is worthwhile to draw the reader's attention to the research of Leslie C. Orr on temple ritual in medieval Tamil Nadu. After noting the correlation of an increase in feminine symbolism in the mythopoeic domain and a decline in women's agency and control over their social situations, she concludes:

> Although the relationships between the power and freedom of human women, on the one hand, and "the feminine" in ritual and symbol, on the other, are complex

> and various, it seems to me quite certain that the identification of the last several centuries of temple women as the "wives of God" or as representatives of divine feminine forces has not empowered them in any effective, pragmatic sense.[216]

This is an extremely subtle point with major import in the study of the imaginal representations of the feminine and the cultural value accorded women in existing societies, though I readily acknowledge that it is imperative for a scholar tackling this issue to be mindful of the specific characteristics that are manifest in different sociopolitical settings.

What significance, then, can be accorded kabbalah in the contemporary effort to modify and transform patriarchal symbolism, to locate a site for the "feminine imaginary," in Irigaray's terms, in the traditional landscape? A variety of feminist scholars themselves have noted that it is not sufficient to lift descriptions of the masculine and feminine out of the particular milieu that served to produce them, as the issue of gender (and body more generally) cannot be so isolated.[217] This critique may be leveled against a number of prominent scholars who have discussed the role of gender in the theosophic symbolism of medieval kabbalah. Little attention has been paid on their part to the philosophical meaning of embodiment in kabbalistic literature, and in the absence of such an understanding, it is implausible to expect that one would have the intellectual wherewithal to unravel the subtleties and nuances of gender symbols.[218]

Previous scholarship has tended to take the use of gender for granted without analyzing the way that it functions within a larger hermeneutical environment. The failure is based first and foremost on the lack of distinction between gender as cultural marker and sex as biological specification. Let me note here a relatively simple example that sheds much light on the methodological issue at hand. Ḥayyim Vital reports that he heard from his teacher, Luria, that the five aspects of soul—*yeḥidah, ḥayyah, neshamah, nefesh*, and *ruaḥ*—correspond respectively to Enoch, Adam, Eve, Abel, and Cain. Why, then, does Cain emerge before Abel? "Since Adam sinned and the shells [*qelippot*] that come forth from the powers of judgment [*gevurot*] were augmented, the attribute of the feminine [*beḥinat ha-nuqba*], which is Cain, is revealed first, in the secret of 'a women of valor is a crown for her husband' (Prov. 12:4)."[219]

Obviously, attributing the quality of femininity to Cain cannot be understood in a biological manner; the mark of the feminine is culturally determined and hence identified as the aspect of judgment, which is embodied in the figure of Cain, the "woman of valor" (*eshet ḥayyil*) who is a "crown for her husband" (*aṭeret baʿlah*). On account of Adam's transgression, divine judgment is augmented in the world, and consequently Cain came into being prior to Abel, who embodies the attribute of loving-kindness. Following Foucault's description of the body as an "empirical-transcendental double,"[220] we may treat "cultural" and "biological" as two aspects of human embodiment. Symbols of engenderment in kabbalistic sources may be fruitfully contemplated through the prism of this distinction, though it seems likely, as Anne Fausto-Sterling has argued, that beliefs about gender are themselves determinative of scientific assumptions regarding sexual identity, and thus any sharp line separating physical and social bodies, the "real" and "constructed," is subject to erosion.[221] In an attempt to "cut through the Gordian knot of dualistic thought," sexuality should be analyzed as a "somatic fact *created* by a cultural effect."[222] The sexualized body of human deportment may be viewed tactically as a socially constructed "inscriptive surface" whence one can decipher indelible cultural markings.[223]

As an illustration of the interpretative implications of upholding the distinction between gender and sex, I will focus on the symbol of the mother, which has been unequivocally and uncritically interpreted by contemporary kabbalah scholars as signifying the feminine aspect of the divine.[224] I have chosen this particular example because it fits into a pattern discernible in the study of other religious cultures wherein maternal images of the divine are emphasized in an effort to redress gender imbalance in theological language.[225] For the purposes of this discussion I will mention one relatively recent case in point. In response to the claim of Scholem (mentioned above) that women were exempt from kabbalistic fraternities on account of the correlation of the feminine and demonic, Moshe Idel has written:

> In opposition to this, the feminine emanation with which kabbalists have been greatly engaged and have attributed to her important functions—the emanation of *Binah*—is not considered (in most cases) to be a source of the forces of evil.[226] The position of this emanation as the "mother of the world" [*em ha-olam*]—that is, mother of the lower seven emanations, which are called the "world," or "mother of the children" [*em ha-banim*] or the "great mother" [*ha-em ha-gedollah*], instructs about a decidedly positive valuation.[227]

I note parenthetically that on a number of occasions in his writings Scholem discusses the symbol of mother in kabbalistic theosophy and on at least one occasion he commented on the complex gender metamorphosis implied thereby.[228] Leaving aside the fairness of the critique of Scholem on this score, what is crucial for my purposes is that Idel's claim—and, to repeat, I do not suggest that his stance is exceptional in the academic study of kabbalah[229]—rests on at least two faulty assumptions: first, that the symbolic image of motherhood in kabbalistic theosophy implies a positive attitude to actual mothers in Jewish society, and second, that the imaginal symbol of mother is to be discerned biologically and not culturally. With regard to the first assumption, let us recall the sober warning of Caroline Walker Bynum on the status of women in Christian Europe: "There is little evidence that the popularity of feminine and maternal imagery in the high Middle Ages reflects an increased respect for actual women by men. . . . Those same authors who equate motherhood or the Virgin Mary with compassion and nurture also use woman as a symbol of physical or spiritual weakness, of the flesh, of sin, of inability to bear burdens or resist temptation."[230]

There is little doubt in my mind that this observation can be applied to kabbalists as well. The utilization of feminine imagery, even the maternal symbol, is found in the very texts that reaffirm negative stereotypes of women promoted by the clerical ideology of medieval theology with the valorization of soul/reason over body/emotion, a dualism that was often an articulation and rationalization for misogyny. With regard to the second assumption, this is a perfect illustration of the covert androcentrism to which I alluded above, for while it is an incontestable physiological fact (hardly altered by time or place) that women naturally give birth, in a given cultural setting the role of motherhood, understood semiotically, can be masculinized, an archaic mythical insight that has been especially appreciated in psychoanalytic theory.[231] In my assessment, this is precisely what we find in traditional kabbalistic literature.

The symbol of mother as employed by kabbalists in no way celebrated the feminine or even challenged the devaluation of the female and the corporeal as some scholars have argued, for instance, with respect to Julian of Norwich's concept of Jesus as generative mother;[232] quite the contrary, when the images of motherhood utilized by medieval kabbalists are considered culturally as opposed to anatomically, it becomes clear that they relate to the masculine aspect of the feminine, the quality of the female that is linked to overflowing, breaking through boundaries, scaling the wall, so to speak, which is precisely why the catalyst for transgression is typically associated with what Scholem aptly designated the "hypertrophy" of the feminine power,[233] that is, the urge of judgment to extend limitation beyond its limits and thereby emulate the phallic potency of the male to bestow on the other. Thus, in the zoharic corpus and related Hebrew theosophic works of de León, *Binah* is designated the "world of the masculine" (*alma di-dekhura*; *olam ha-zakhar*) in contrast to *Malkhut*, the "world of the feminine" (*alma de-nuqba; olam ha-neqevah*).[234] In this context, I will cite a zoharic passage that addresses the issue of the ostensible conflict between the characterization of *Binah* as feminine and the designation "world of the masculine."

> It has been said that the supernal world is a world of the masculine. When the matter rises from the Community of Israel and above, all is masculine. Whence do you know? From the burnt offering [*olah*]. Why is it called *olah?* Because it rises[235] above the feminine, and thus [it is written] "he shall make his offering a male without blemish" (Lev. 1:10). . . . What is the meaning of "without blemish" [*tamim*]? Rather, as it is written [with respect to Abraham], "Walk before me and be perfect" (Gen. 17:1). When was he perfect [*tamim*]? In the moment he was circumcised, for the masculine does not exist and is not known except in that place that is called *tamim*.[236] And what is it? The sign of the covenant through which the masculine is distinguished from the feminine[237] . . . and from that place and above everything is masculine, and from the feminine and below everything is feminine. . . . You might say that there is also a feminine above. However, the terminus of the body illustrates about the whole body, which is masculine. The head of the body is female until the terminus is reached, and when the terminus is manifest, the whole becomes male. But here the beginning and end is female, for the arrayment of the body [*tiqqun gufa*] is completely female.[238]

Preserved in the above passage is an illustration of the gender dynamics at work in the theosophic doctrine embraced by the zoharic fraternity: *Binah* commences as a female configuration, but the body as a whole is demarcated as male, since the end of it, *Yesod*, the phallic potency, is unambiguously masculine;[239] hence the suitability of the designation *alma di-dekhura*. By contrast, *Malkhut* is depicted as a body whose beginning and end is female, and hence the name *alma de-nuqba* is affixed to her. What is most significant for our immediate purposes is the view that *Binah* manifests the feminine trait primarily in her role as womb that receives the seminal fluid from *Ḥokhmah* and the masculine trait in opening the womb to bear the fruit of the seed implanted in the ground of the mother. The gestation of the fetus and unbolting of the womb, therefore, denote two stages in the transposition of *Binah* from vessel that contains to spring that overflows, from feminine constriction to masculine effulgence.[240] It is with regard to both properties, which I have elsewhere dubbed "phallic womb,"[241] that *Binah* assumes the task of motherhood. The point is substantiated textually in the following zoharic passage, which describes both *imma ila'ah*, the "supernal mother," *Binah*, and *imma tata'ah*, the "lower mother," *Malkhut*:

> Come and see: When a man is in his house,[242] the essence of the house is his wife [*iqqara de-veita devittehu*],[243] for *Shekhinah* is not removed from the house on account of his wife, as we have learnt, it is written "Isaac then brought her into the tent of his mother Sarah" (Gen. 24:67), for the candle was lit.[244] For what reason? Because *Shekhinah* came to the house. The mystery of the matter: The supernal mother is not found in relation to the male except when the house is arrayed [*be-zimna de-ittatteqena beita*] and male and female are joined together. Then the supernal mother casts her blessings to bless them. In this manner, the lower mother is not found in relation to the male except when the house is arrayed and the male comes to his woman and they are joined as one. Then the lower mother casts her blessings to bless them. Thus a male is crowned by two women in his house in the pattern of what is above . . . the supernal woman to array, crown, and bless him, the lower woman to unite with him and to be sustained by him. In this manner it is below when a man marries . . . and he is crowned by two women, one above and one below.[245]

The woman is accorded a distinctive role in the theurgic drama insofar as her presence in the spatial habitation secures the presence of *Shekhinah* therein. On the surface one might be tempted (as some modern scholars have) to elicit from this feature of kabbalah a feminist sensibility based on the supposedly active role assigned to Jewish women. However, when one takes hold of the knife of critical feminist theory and scratches beneath the textual surface, it becomes abundantly obvious that the zoharic author is promoting a purely instrumentalist view of the woman as the one who provides the space—and hence the symbolic significance of referring to a wife as the "essence of the house"—in which the male can cohabit, discharge his seminal overflow, and thereby unite with *Shekhinah*. This is precisely what is affirmed in the conclusion of the passage: just as above the male potency, *Tif'eret*, is positioned between *Binah* and *Malkhut*, respectively the upper and lower woman, receiving from the former and bestowing upon the latter, so below, when the man gets married, he is situated between *Malkhut* and his earthly wife.[246]

The dynamic comportment of the gender composition should be obvious from the fact that vis-à-vis the imaginal world of emanation, *Malkhut* is female, receiving the blessing from above, whereas vis-à-vis the mundane world of differentiation, she assumes male characteristics, bestowing blessing on the man below.[247] The latter is precisely the valence of "motherhood" when applied to *Malkhut* (as well as, indeed in emulation of, *Binah*), that is, maternity signifies bestowing and nourishing, qualities that are gendered as masculine.

The inadequacy of simplistically decoding references to *Binah* as mother as positive valorization of the feminine is underscored by the juxtaposition of the maternal symbol with the depiction of *Binah* as king. To cite one glaring example from Moses de León's *Shushan Edut*: " 'The mother of the children is joyous' (Ps. 113:9) whence come forth all beings . . . the world that is concealed in its being, it is not heard on the outside in its gazing, for it is the king that stands within his chamber."[248] To comprehend the function of the symbol of mother in kabbalistic theosophy, one must take stock of the transformation of gender imagined by the medieval male kabbalists, that is, in the role of mothering, the female body is engendered as masculine, it assumes the characteristics that would justify speaking of her as him.[249] With this insight we can explain why *Shekhinah*, in addition to being linked symbolically to the matriarchs, is sometimes described as embodied in the figure of David or, expressed somewhat differently, why *Shekhinah* occupies the place of David in the world of emanation:[250] when *Shekhinah* receives the efflux of light from the supernal *sefirot*, she is symbolized as female, but when she overflows to sustain the natural world, she is male.[251]

The attribution of the title *Malkhut*, "kingship" or "dominion," to *Shekhinah* similarly denotes the providential role the last of the attributes in the world of unity assumes vis-à-vis the realities below in the world of division. Just as the upper mother, *Binah*, is depicted as king in relation to the seven lower emanations (*sefirot ha-binyan*), so the lower mother, *Shekhinah*, also portrayed as daughter, dons the demiurgical cloak of *Binah* and stands as king in relation to the created world.[252] The demiurgical character of *Shekhinah* vis-à-vis the mundane is illumined in a zoharic passage depicting the emanation of the *sefirot* and the consequent creation of the physical universe: "When the holy One, blessed be he, wanted to create worlds, he emitted one concealed light [*nehora setima'ah*] . . . and it is the supernal world [*alma ila'ah*]. Furthermore, that supernal light spread forth and produced a craftsman [*umana*], the light that does not shine (*nehora de-lo nahir*), and it produced the lower world (*alma tata'ah*)."[253]

Decoding the text theosophically, the concealed light, which is the supernal world, is *Binah*, which produces the light that does not shine, *Malkhut*, the craftsman of the lower world. In the continuation of the text, the reader is informed of the process by which the demiurgic status is appropriated by *Malkhut*: "Insofar as this light does not shine, it must be bound above and bound below, and through the lower bond it is bound to be illumined in the supernal bond, and through the supernal bond that light that does not shine brings forth all the forces and the many types of camps."[254] In the aspect of kingly mother, *Malkhut* is masculinized and she is thus configured in the countenance of David, the fourth leg of the chariot that joins the three patriarchs to complete the supernal throne of glory.[255] The fourfold unity is expressed in the word *shabbat*, the *shin* symbolizing the three patriarchs and the *beit* and *taw*, which spell *bat*, the daughter. From a symbolic standpoint, the mystical significance of Sabbath relates to the unification of the fourfold through the elevation of *Shekhinah* as crown on the head of the patriarchs, a coronation that proleptically anticipates the eschatological restoration of the feminine to the masculine.[256]

In line with one of the trends of contemporary feminist theory, I assume that gender types are sociocultural constructs expressed in but not reducible to biological terms.[257] As any number of feminist theorists have taught us, gender and sex should not be identified in an absolute manner; biological facticity is not always determinative of gender identity.[258] Joan Scott, building on the work of Foucault, remarked that gender relates to the knowledge about sexual difference that provides human beings with a mechanism for ordering the social world. "It follows then that gender is the social organization of sexual difference. But this does not mean that gender reflects or implements fixed and natural physical differences between women and men; rather gender is the knowledge that establishes meanings for bodily differences."[259] When the discussion is cast in this light, it will be seen how precarious would be an attempt to base current feminist theology in Judaism on the symbolic representation of the feminine in medieval kabbalistic treatises. The revisioning will not rest securely on this textual foundation.

To avoid misunderstanding, let me be clear that in my judgment the project of a constructive feminist theology of Judaism can succeed without this presumption, for the refracting of these texts through the contemporary lens may well render feminine images of God in accord with present concerns.[260] This, it seems, coincides with the midrashic process so basic to the constitution of tradition in the religious history of Judaism: textual expansion and hermeneutical reinscription of older tropes in an effort to delineate the parameters of the worldview in which a given reader is situated, the pouring of old wine into new wineskins.[261] From that perspective we can say that within the tradition are the seeds of discourse necessary to bear fruit of a different color, texture, odor, and taste; we may even be justified in saying that the implicit axiology of the traditional symbolism exceeds its own social limitations.[262] The rich legacy of kabbalah, therefore, may serve as a repository of images that feminist theologians can reinterpret and extrapolate through creative (mis)reading, reflecting a genuinely feminist perspective rather than merely expropriating "feminized patriarchal images" in "transvestite masquerade,"[263] which, when properly fathomed, serve only to reinforce the androcentric subservience of women.[264] As an early advocate for a feminist revival of Jewish theology, Judith Plaskow, put the matter:

> There are obvious advantages to having a feminine element in God that is a firmly established aspect of the tradition. Yet when the tradition is a male one—both with regard to Judaism in general and Kabbalism in particular—female images are apt to come with certain limitations. . . . The *Shekhinah* is a usable image for feminists only if it is partly wrenched free from its original context, so that the tradition becomes a starting point for an imaginative process that moves beyond and transforms it.[265]

More recently, Melissa Raphael reacts to contemporary Jewish feminists who "have repudiated patriarchal Judaism and celebrate the ancient Near Eastern goddess once worshipped by syncretistic Israelites and the goddesses that have emerged in the Jewish mystical and esoteric traditions" by observing that that "in patriarchal Hasidism and Kabbalah, *Shekhinah* and the feminine *sefirot* are always subservient to male divine attributes."[266] In a second note, responding more specifically to Alix Pirani's attempt to utilize Jewish mystical sources to construct a paganized Judaism based on retrieval of the goddess image, Raphael responsibly reminds the reader again that personifications of the feminine in traditional kabbalistic lore are "always subordinated to masculine elements of deity."[267] The author is correct to point out the disjuncture between the Jewish feminist project based on according "equal homage" to the masculine and feminine and the kabbalistic doctrine itself in which the latter is subsidiary to the former.

If we were to apply the approach adopted by Irigaray to medieval kabbalah, we would have to "go back through the masculine imaginary to interpret the way it has reduced [women] to silence, to muteness or mimicry," and "from that starting point and at the same time, to (re)discover a possible space for the feminine imaginary."[268] The engendering of God in terms of current needs and cultural assumptions regarding the status of women and men is an ethical task of the highest priority.[269] The work of critical hermeneutics, re/covering structures of thought as they appear from within philological concealedness,[270] can be seen as contributing in a helpful way to the therapy of a culture's collective soul.[271] But, as we are aware, the therapeutic process can be blocked when perceptions of the past are obscured or skewed on account of present concerns and future desires.

In previous studies, I have endorsed the need to consider construction of gender in the rich and complex world of kabbalistic symbolism from this cultural perspective. In the present work, I shall expand the quest to retrace the "masculine imaginary" by painting the picture upon a larger canvas, focusing my lens on the ascetic eroticism of kabbalistic contemplation and the erotic asceticism entailed thereby.[272] Because I am a Jewish male, there has been an inclination on the part of some readers to assume that I am reinscribing the androcentric stereotypes uncovered in the material. To these readers, it seems, my critical sensibility has masked itself as a recapitulation of negative views of the feminine prevalent in kabbalistic ritual and myth.[273] To some extent the enterprise of critique, whether undertaken by women or men, enmeshes the scholar in bolstering what is criticized, implicating one in erasure and inscription simultaneously.[274] The reader should bear in mind, however, that my aim has been and remains one of deconstructing and destabilizing the gender categories that have dominated the worldview espoused by transmitters of the chain of kabbalah.[275] To deconstruct a text entails cracking its binding,[276] taking apart, clearing away; but to clear away, one must take hold. How does one take hold of what must be cleared away? By letting go, withholding the appropriating, appropriating the withholding.[277] Hence the deconstructive hermeneutic, according to the neologism of Simon Critchey, is a *clôtural* reading, that is, a reading that radically questions the principles it presupposes,[278] an ongoing engaging of the text in a play of *différance* and presence that "arises only in relation to a specific and completed historical configuration which it ceaselessly seeks to repeat and interrupt."[279]

I sympathize with the contemporary tendency to seek multiple voices in the reading of texts, and I applaud the attempt (in great measure inspired by feminist criticism)[280] to avoid a singular and hegemonic hermeneutic. The point has been articulated, for instance, by Irigaray, who argues that the

> architectonics of the text, or texts, confounds the linearity of an outline, the teleology of discourse, within which there is no possible place for the "feminine," except in the traditional place of the repressed, the censured. . . . For what is important is to disconcert the staging of representation according to the *exclusively* "masculine" parameters, that is, according to a phallocratic order. It is not a matter of toppling that order so as to replace it—that amounts to the same thing in the end—but of disrupting and modifying it, starting from an "outside" that is exempt, in part, from phallocratic law.[281]

One way to (re)open the "figures of philosophical discourse," therefore, is "to interrogate *the conditions under which systematicity itself is possible*: what the coherence of the discursive utterance conceals of the conditions under which it is produced, whatever it may say about these conditions in discourse."[282] The appeal to hermeneutical diversity is emphasized as well by Hélène Cixous, who argued, betraying the influence of the Derridean notion of writing (*écriture*) as *différance*, that feminine texts should "strive in the direction of difference, struggle to undermine the dominant phallogocentric logic, split open the closure of the binary opposition and revel in the pleasures of open-ended textuality."[283]

Surely one of the most important contributions of feminist theory to the hermeneutical enterprise in the historical reconstruction of the past has been the undermining of the dominance of patriarchal language and the implied challenge to essentialist claims to truth and meaning.[284] This enterprise has found support in the shift in ascertaining the meaning of a text from the "original" intent of the author to the polyvalence of multiple readers. As Elizabeth Grosz has noted, this change in focus has had "liberating effects for feminist theory" by opening up a "whole history of patriarchal discourses to feminist appropriations and recontextualizations. Any text, however patriarchal it may have been at its outset and in its author's intentions, can be read from a feminist point of view . . . that is, from the point view that brings out a text's alignment with, participation in, and subversion of patriarchal norms."[285]

In line with this insight, my insistence on the phallocentrism of medieval kabbalah should be seen as a feminist reading. However, I must say with regret that the portrayal of gender in kabbalistic sources themselves does not supply evidence for multivocality or even a fissure in the edifice that would support this slant. Assuredly, none of the relevant texts were written by women and thus they do not convey the perspective of feminine experience, but they also do not self-consciously challenge the dominant patriarchy of rabbinic culture.[286] On the contrary, they exemplify a remarkable degree of homogeneity; surprisingly, changes in time and place have had virtually no effect on the phallocentric disposition. The monotony can be explained in part by the fact that the conditions of production and consumption of kabbalistic ideas and practices have been so severely limited through the ages, restricted as they were to men with rabbinic training, that there is little change with regard to the major themes that engaged their imagination. One may surmise that had these conditions been more diverse, the range of attitudes reflected in the sources would have been wider, as is attested, indeed, by the current situation in which a more diverse population is reading and engaging kabbalistic texts even though traditional kabbalists preserve older structures intact through genuine acts of repetition.

Dynamism and Stasis in Kabbalistic Symbolism

To avoid potential misunderstanding and opening the door for others to ascribe to me an essentialist phenomenology, let me state unequivocally that my assumption regarding repetition of structure does not presuppose an ontological condition of presence that imposes sameness and precludes difference. On the contrary, in my mind, the history of kabbalism as a religious phenomenon illustrates that the presumed immutability of system occasions novel interpretation. In the wisdom of the tradition, if it is old, it is because it is new, but it is new because it is old.[287]

I offer here one textual example from Abraham Abulafia to illustrate the larger hermeneutical point. In *Sitrei Torah*, one of his commentaries on the *Guide of the Perplexed* of Maimonides, Abulafia attempts to uphold the veracity of both the traditional belief that the world was created anew (*ḥadash*) and the philosophically sanctioned view that it is eternally old (*qadmon*)—the former conveyed by the literal sense of Scripture and the latter by the allegorical—blatantly acknowledging that this possibility, affirmed by the prophetic tradition, is a challenge to the law of contradiction:

> Know concerning the image [*ṣiyyur*] of the world either being created alone or eternal and created together, even though it appears that the two matters are opposites and they would not be found in the same subject at the same time, that is to say, one thing being eternal and created together, this is a matter that the human intellect is prevented from comprehending. Even so, we know that the prophet comprehends his truth by way of the narrative [*haggadah*] and story [*sippur*] that the Lord, blessed be he, dictates to him in the prophetic kabbalah that he transmits to him.[288]

The theological debate of creation versus eternity can be taken as paradigmatic for the dialectical confluence of innovation and conservation in the exegetical imagination. Just as creation and eternity are both to be affirmed as veritable options, so the simultaneity of truth as novel and erstwhile is to be maintained, a fundamental axiom of interpretation—linked to an underlying conception of time as the instant of novel reiteration, the repetition of the same as different in the renewal of the different as same—legitimated not by reason but by prophetic experience whence disseminated the oral tradition in a presumed unbroken chain (*qabbalah mi-peh el peh*). System, therefore, is precisely what accounts for interruption of order by chaos, the intervention of the moment that renders time continuously discontinuous and discontinuously continuous.

One is here reminded of Rosenzweig's remark in a letter to Rudolf Ehrenburg (dated 12 December 1917): "System ist *nicht Architektur*, wo die Steine das Gebäude zusammensetzen und um des Gebäudes willen da sind (und sonst aus keinem Grund); sondern

System bedeutet, daß jedes Einzelne den Trieb und Willen zur *Beziehung* auf alle andern Einzelnen hat; das 'Ganze' liegt jenseits bewußten Gesichtskreises, es sieht nur das Chaos der Einzelheiten in das es seine Fühlfäden ausstreckt."[289] Rosenzweig expresses his wish to preserve a viable notion of system that will not be subject to his own criticism of the totalizing and essentializing tendencies inherent in Idealist philosophy. System, therefore, does not denote an architectural structure that is formed by assembling individual stones whose meaning is determined only by the sense of the whole, but rather a striving on the part of all individual entities qua individual for relationship and interconnectivity; the viability of system is thus related to affirming a unity perpetually in the making, a sense of the whole that is not order but chaos, a totality that must always lie "beyond a conscious horizon" (*jenseits bewußten Gesichtskreises*).

In the continuation of the letter, Rosenzweig notes that in the Hegelian system, each individual position is anchored only in the whole (*jede einzelne Position nur im Ganzen verankert*) and is thus linked exclusively to two others, the one that immediately precedes it and the one that immediately succeeds it. In the system affirmed by Rosenzweig, the genuine novelty of each temporal moment is not determined by its perpetual occupying a median position in a linear sequence between what came before and what comes after. On the contrary, to the extent that the moment is authentically novel, it is experienced as the constant resumption of what is always yet to be, the return of what has never been, the vertical intervention that opens the horizontal timeline to the spherical fullness of eternity.

In a more modern idiom, the matter can be expressed in terms of Jakobson's insight that "the concepts of a system and its changes are not only compatible but indissolubly tied."[290] The context where this comment appears is a criticism of the antimony set up by Saussure between stasis/synchrony and dynamism/diachrony. According to Jakobson, our linguistic experience indicates that synchrony embraces the dynamic, and diachrony, the static. Consequently, coexistence and modification are not mutually exclusive opposites; they reflect the concurrent dimensions of time, simultaneity and succession. Just as simultaneity cannot be experienced without succession nor succession without simultaneity, so permanence cannot be discerned without change nor change without permanence. It is precisely on account of structural similarity that we can speak of thematic variation. Confirmation of this insight can be sought in contemporary neuroscience: on the one hand, a dominant tendency is assigned to each hemisphere of the brain—syncretic processing to the right and diacritic processing to the left—but on the other hand, it is presumed that the actual tasks of convergence and divergence require bihemispheric interaction. Jacques Chevalier, a pioneer in the field of neurosemiotics, expresses the point when he writes that

> brain and sign activity involves a bimodal reticulation of similarities and differences. Sign activity following a syncretic pattern contains elements of diacritic processing; things can be said to resemble one another provided that they are perceived as being different in some respect (Christ viewed as a Lamb *is not* a lamb). Likewise, diacritic events can take place provided the brain apprehends a common terrain within

which oppositions can play themselves out (as between the Beast and the Lamb slain in Revelation, both of whom are animal representations of invisible spirits).[291]

The convergence of sameness and difference can be thought as well in conjunction with Derrida's notion of iterability. We would do well to begin by noting that for Derrida,

> [A text] is not a finished corpus of writing, some content enclosed in a book or its margins, but a differential network, a fabric of traces referring endlessly to something other than itself, to other differential traces. Thus the text overruns all the limits assigned to it so far (not submerging or drowning them in an undifferentiated homogeneity, but rather making them more complex, dividing and multiplying strokes and lines).[292]

To impose limits on a text in the hope of recognizing its "legitimacy" and "relative specificity" is a "kind of discontinuity prompted by resistance and protectionism." In fact, textual beginning is marked by citation "in the creases [*faux plis*] of a certain veil, a certain mirrorlike screen. . . . The mirror of a mirror."[293] Nothing in the text is self-contained, limited by the boundary of its own skin; each word overflows its articulation. It is in this sense that Derrida is willing to employ the Husserlian notion of transcendence to describe the "literary intentionality" in writing and reading. That is, the text may be construed as an "intentional object" whose meaning derives from the noematic structure of a particular nonempirical subjectivity linked to an intersubjective and transcendental community. The transcendent is the textual overflow that exceeds any particular intention on the part of the author or interpretation on the part of the reader, and hence it (if we are even permitted to use the word "it" in describing the space of this transcendence) cannot be thematized as an ontological essence or metaphysical truth—there is no self-identity of the literary thing as such—for it is inscribed in a "play of foldings," the crease that bespeaks difference, complexity, instability, novelty.[294] In response to the claim that literary theorists associated with deconstruction resist the "transcendental reading," Derrida remarked:

> I believe no text resists it absolutely. Absolute resistance to such a reading would purely and simply destroy the trace of the text. I'd say rather that a text is poetico-literary when, through a sort of original negotiation, without annulling either meaning or reference, it does something with this resistance, something that we'd have a lot of trouble defining. . . . For such a definition would require not only that we take into account multiple, subtle and stratified conventional and intentional modifications, but also at a certain point the questioning of the values of intention and convention which, with the textuality of the text in general and literature in particular, are put to the test of their limits. If every literary text plays and negotiates the suspension of referential naivety, of *thetic* referentiality (not reference or the intentional relation in general), each text does so differently, singularly.[295]

I have cited this passage in full as it stands as extremely important evidence that Derrida has not unqualifyingly rejected the notion of transcendental meaning in a text. Quite the contrary, he states explicitly that if a reading exemplifies absolute resistance of this sort, it destroys the trace of the text, and consequently the play of interpretation would be compromised. Derrida even employs Husserl's technical term *epoché* to designate the "irony of detachment with regard to metaphysical belief or thesis," a suspension of transcendence that is "irreducible in poetic or literary experience."[296] The deferral must occur singularly with each text, for every composition resists taxonomy in a distinctive way. What is shared is the trace in the surplus of meaning, the gifting of indeterminacy that fosters seemingly endless determinations.[297] Inability to comprehend a text once-and-for-all is what endows it with future resonance.

Derrida speaks accordingly of writing with a "desire not to be understood . . . because if such a transparency of intelligibility were ensured it would destroy the text, it would show that the text has no future [*avenir*], that it does not overflow the present, that it is consumed immediately."[298] To have a future requires that there is a past, but if there is a past, there must have been a beginning. The beginning, however, is marked by a paradox: to be the beginning, the beginning must have begun, but if the beginning has already begun, it cannot be the beginning it must begin to be. There is thus duplicity in/at the beginning: what appears to be new must have already been, the beginning that subsequently began beforehand to begin. To this Derrida refers when he observes that every act of writing leaves one with the "impression of making a beginning—but in fact that which is the same in texture is ceaselessly exposed to a singularity which is that of the other (another text, someone else, another word of the language). Everything appears *anew*: which means newness and repetition together."[299]

From this we may conclude that the porous nature of textual borders does not rule out, as some interpreters of deconstruction have assumed, the mandate to read a text in context. On the contrary, what is at stake for Derrida is discerning context by attending to contradictory meanings that highlight ambiguities in texts, an interpretative gesture that opens the gap between author and reader. The point is adroitly articulated by Christina Howells:

> The so-called "play" of interpretation, which Derrida refers to as "dissemination," is a play in the linguistic mechanism perhaps, but it is not the "free play" beloved of some of Derrida's less rigorous followers. It is rather the demonstration of textual self-contradiction which is the essence of the deconstructive project. It differs from the standard philosophical technique of finding flaws in the logic of an opponent's argument in that the contradictions uncovered reveal an underlying incompatibility between what the writer believes him- or herself to be arguing and what the text itself actually says. This gap between authorial intention and textual meaning is a key focus of deconstruction.[300]

No reading is entirely novel; insofar as "all writing is historicized," that is, occurs within a specific historical setting, it follows that every act of reading is a re/calling, a re/tracing. It is in this sense that Derrida considers himself "very much a historian" and the task of deconstruction "very historicist" even though one must "be suspicious of the metaphysical concept of history."[301] Derrida, the leading exponent of a hermeneutic that challenges claims to the integrity of text and reader as subsisting entities, has nonetheless affirmed the paradox of "newness and repetition" in his understanding of the texture of literary experience. Thus he describes his own writing: "I'm well aware of the fact that at bottom it all unfolds according to the same law that commands these always different things."[302] And in another context, Derrida similarly portrays his compositions in terms of an amalgam of ancient and novel: "What I write resembles, by my account, a dotted outline of a book to be written, in what I call—at least for me—the 'old new language,' the most archaic and the newest, unheard of, and thereby at present unreadable."[303]

It lies beyond the scope of this chapter to engage all the intricacies of Derrida's comment; suffice it to say that his notion of reading and writing as the constant renewal of the same that is different in the sameness of its difference is predicated on an assumption regarding the nature of time determined by the singularity of each moment that is to come, the future that as future is indeterminate, unpredictable, the "now" that cannot be "present" since it is not a presence that may be represented.[304] I note en passant that this depiction of the future and of temporality more generally is at the base of Derrida's utilization of messianic and eschatological modes of expression to convey a notion of justice that is beyond the law or, as he himself occasionally puts it, using Kafka's locution, before the law.[305] The very nature of "messianicity," which is "older than all religion, more originary than all messianism,"[306] is predicated on the presumption that no repetition can exhaust the novelty of what is to come, but to suppose the singularity of every new moment as the wholly other, we must posit that each moment is identical in its otherness. The technical term Derrida employs to refer to this phenomenon is "iterability," which is characterized by the "twin aspects of repetition of the same and affirmation of the new." For Derrida, the paradox of the "altering-altered repetition" is most poignantly captured in the verbal gesture of naming, for each time I address an other with a proper name, the name is both shared by others and distinctive to the person being addressed. "The very possibility of the name is iterability: the possibility of repeating the same, but each time to name an other or to name the same otherwise. It is with the same word that I designate the same in a new way each time."[307]

Reading is thus troped as "repetition with difference," the "genetic code of translation,"[308] but this can be facilitated only by one who has requisite philological aptitude to study a text in its contextuality. Derrida is unambiguous: "This is my starting point: no meaning can be determined out of context, but no context permits saturation. What I am referring to here is not richness of substance, semantic fertility, but rather structure: the structure of the remnant of iteration."[309] As Derrida has put it in another place:

> Deconstruction is not a method for discovering that which resists the system; it consists, rather, in remarking, in the reading and interpretation of texts, that what has made it possible for philosophers to effect a system is nothing other than a certain dysfunction of "disadjustment," a certain incapacity to close the system. . . . Basically, deconstruction as I see it is an attempt to train the beam of analysis onto this disjointing link.[310]

The dysfunction of thought, which accounts for a thinker's desire for system, is a form of dislocation that limits totalization but at the same time renders clear the framework within which the impulse for totality takes shape. Derrida depicts his own hermeneutical strategy as "a gesture that is philosophical and, at the same time, in excess of the philosophical."[311] The task is to be more than philosophical while still remaining philosophical. If that which exceeds the limit shows itself only within the boundary of the limit, then the surplus of textual meaning will be determined by the delimiting of meaning in the text.

The issue, then, is not denying context but determining its parameters, demarcating borderlines of a text without reifying its fluidity. Methodologically, I presume that it is possible to derive meaning from a text by comparing it to contemporaneous works that originated in a similar sociological context. I assume, moreover, that we can deduce from the ideas recorded in texts something of the life experiences of the people who wrote them. As banal as this observation seems, it appears necessary to assert that interpretation requires philological competence, as textual polysemeity cannot be appreciated if the reader is unaware of the language in which a text has been written and from which it must be translated in each reading.[312] Minimally, I take for granted that the task of deconstruction cannot be carried out from a state of linguistic incompetence, nor is it justified to deem all readings equally viable. As Derrida himself has noted, any theme he discusses cannot be "detached or dissociated from its linguistic embodiment, its lexical and above all nominal embodiment, or as others would be quick to say from its nominal representation."[313] Even more telling is Derrida's recent confession that the philological discipline by which he was trained has continued to inspire in him an ineradicable respect:

> Those models of philological, micrological, I'd say even grammatico-logical demands, for me have never lost their irrecusable authority. . . . Even when I give the impression of transgressing, putting into question, displacing, it is always under their authority, with a sense of responsibility in the face of a certain philological morality, before a certain ethics of reading or writing. In short: before the law.[314]

One will obviously recognize the celebrated locution of Kafka, previously mentioned, which, for Derrida, signifies that deconstruction must always be carried out under the weight of the philological meaning that it seeks to problematize.[315] "A transgression," Derrida astutely observes, "should always know what it transgresses, which always makes the transgression impure, and compromised with what it transgresses."[316] Those who assume that deconstruction may be performed on a text without any philological ability to read that text in its own language transgress against the very notion of transgression as preservation of bond from which one is emancipated. The method I have adopted accords with the strategy of reading suggested by deconstructionism. The place of the text "carries within itself the law of its displacement, of its internal heterogeneity," and thus philosophy is characterized by the "double bind" of being "at home with itself . . . in not being at home with itself."[317]

That I assume structures of thought may be recovered philologically, structures influenced but not causally determined by historical factors, does not subject kabbalistic texts to a standard of rigid uniformity;[318] on the contrary, structure accounts for heterogeneity, system for unpredictability.[319] A genuinely "variegated phenomenology" of kabbalah, which is based on attending to the "spiritual polymorphism in Jewish mysticism," should not be set in polar opposition to a "monochromatic phenomenology," for it is precisely when one sees the recurring pattern that the changes become most visible.[320] In the hermeneutical praxis of scholar and adept alike, innovation and repetition are not mutually exclusive but well forth from the spot where the novel is recurringly ancient and the ancient interminably novel.

Gender Fluidity/Structural Inflexibility

To return to the topic of gender: surely gender symbolism in traditional kabbalistic literature is dynamic, presupposing as it does crossing of boundaries and intermingling of identity, male in female and female in male, one containing the other within which the other is contained. The breakdown of opposition takes root, according to the formulation of the sixteenth-century Moroccan kabbalist, Simeon Lavi, in the depiction of the origin prior to the beginning as a nondual state wherein "the force of overflowing [*mashpiʿa*] and that of receiving [*mushpa*] were in one unity [*aḥdut eḥad*] in the depths of the Nothing."[321] Messianic rectification (*tiqqun*) is analogously depicted as transcending the expected gender hierarchy, overturning the table such that the force that overflows (*mashpiʿa*) and the capacity to receive (*meqabbel*) exchange positions,[322] the vessel (*keli*), the bride (*kallah*), that receives the seminal discharge is transformed into the crown (*kelil*) that encircles the head of the king.[323] This particular insight corroborates the general observation of Scholem: "In kabbalistic terms, the place where Creation began as a process within God Himself is identical with the site of redemption and atonement."[324] What Scholem did not point out is that from the kabbalist's vantage point, origin and destiny both exhibit the transposability of masculine and feminine qualities and the consequent overcoming of gender dimorphism, a theme that I have discussed in previous publications and that I will discuss again at greater length in chapter eight.

What is critical to note here is that medieval kabbalistic texts allocate one gender, the masculine, which comprises within itself female/male. Once the male androgyne splinters into binary opposition, we can speak—functionally and not ontically, correlatively and not substantially—of two disparate genders to which fixed characteristics are attributed. Consider the remark of Vital in explaining how there can be gender differentiation in the divine realm: "The supernal light emanates and extends below, and when it reaches a point that its power is weakened, it is called 'feminine' [*neqevah*], but when it is still above it is called 'masculine' [*zakhar*], for the female properties derive from the brain of the male [*moaḥ ha-zakhar*]."[325] In spite of the flexibility of gender transformation attested in kabbalistic lore, the process is determined by this inflexible structure, and hence while one may legitimately speak of variability in kabbalistic gender symbolism, it is not helpful to introduce the notion of ambiguity.[326] To state the matter bluntly, kabbalistic interpretation of ritual involves the male donning the female form and the female the male, but it would be utterly meaningless to posit that this implies the possibility of a "womanly man" or "manly woman."[327]

I have yet to find a traditional kabbalistic text that deviates from the following principle articulated by Luria, explaining the zoharic image of the "book weighed on the balance" (*sifra de-shaqil be-matqela*), which describes the "book of concealment" (*sifra di-ṣeniʿuta*):[328] "The emanator must be arrayed in masculine and feminine so that all of the emanation will unfold in this manner, and the judgments will be sweetened in mercy, for the male is mercy and the female judgment as is known."[329] In similar but somewhat more expansive language, Luzzatto articulates the kabbalistic principle of gender construction under the rubric of "the matter of copulation and the male and female waters" (*inyan ha-ziwwug u-mayyin dukhrin we-nuqvin*):

> The right and the left must act harmoniously and thus copulation is necessary to join them. The order of their union is as follows: The masculine is the secret of mercy, and it is the root of created beings from this aspect. The feminine is the secret of judgment, and it is the root of created beings from this aspect. Both of them must sustain their branches, but this sustenance cannot come about except by means of the power of renewal that they receive from the emanator. The arousal must ascend from below to above and, accordingly, the feminine must be aroused initially so that it will appear to be ready to receive the efflux of the masculine, and then the masculine can have an influence upon her.[330]

As complex as kabbalistic symbolism can be, the issue of gender is surprisingly simple: Male and female are correlated consistently with the activity of projection and the passivity of restriction. To be sure, we must be on guard against reifying these as polar opposites, for the relevant sources attest that passivity can be an expression of activity and activity an expression of passivity.[331] This provision notwithstanding, the kabbalistic orientation is translucent in its mythopoeic simplicity: the potency to overflow is masculine, the capacity to withhold is feminine. Adopting an earlier rabbinic tradition, kabbalists link the male and female potencies respectively with the attributes of mercy and judgment and their designated names YHWH and Elohim. The religious obligation imposed traditionally on the Jewish man to unify the God of Israel is interpreted as the harnessing of male and female, a pairing of right and left, the will to bestow and the desire to contain.

Beyond the theurgical task of re/pairing the masculine and feminine potencies, the traditional duty to proclaim the oneness of God was understood by kabbalists as providing the occasion to restore the unified differentiation of the manifold to the nondifferentiated oneness of Ein Sof. This task was signaled out as the mystical rationale for prayer, the true *kawwanah*, intentionality, that the *maskil*, the enlightened sage, had to cultivate. As Ezra of Gerona, writing in the first half of the thirteenth century, put it: "Thus must a man know how to unify God [*ṣarikh adam ladaʿat ki leyyaḥed shem*], he is one and he has no second, as it says, 'besides him there is no other' (Deut. 4:35), and to unify him through the ten emanations in the infinite [*leyyaḥdo be-eser sefirot be-ein sof*]."[332] The intent of the concluding phrase, the directive to unify the many in the one, the limited in the limitless that is limited by no limit but the limit of limitlessness, is made clearer by Ezra in a passage from another composition: "a man must be on guard and unify everything to the infinite [*ṣarikh adam lehizaher u-leyyaḥed ha-kol ad ein sof*] to show that he is cause of everything and everything is from him."[333]

In slightly different but essentially comparable terms, Ezra's younger colleague, Azriel ben Menaḥem, admonishes his reader to know that "the worshipper must remove from himself every obstacle and hindrance, to return a thing to its nothingness."[334] To comprehend the meaning of the concluding phrase *lehashiv davar el afisato*, "to return a thing to its nothingness," one must be apprised of the fact that, according to Azriel, obviously indebted to technical philosophical discourse, the "foundation of created beings" (*yesod ha-nivra'im*) consists of three elements, nothingness (*efes*), matter (*ḥomer*), and form (*ṣurah*). It should come as no surprise that nothingness can be demarcated only as that which cannot be demarcated and persists in being the nothing that it is; Azriel thus describes nothingness in terms of the quality to change: the matter that is renewed, *inyan she-nitḥaddesh*, is called *efes*. Curiously, it is allied with the attribute of judgment, *middat ha-din*.[335] We may surmise that this identification is based on the premise that judgment facilitates constriction, and without the latter nothing discrete would be discernible in the process of creation, a basic tenet of kabbalah that resonates with Spinoza's dictum *omnis determinatio est negatio*. The same idea is expressed in slightly different terminology by Azriel describing the flux of emanation: "the surge that issues from the source of *Ḥokhmah* is called 'blessing' [*berakhah*], for the diminution increases progressively and 'he makes his nothing something' "[336] (*she-ha-mi'uṭ mitrabbeh we-holekh we-asah eino yeshno)*.[337]

The nothing, then, is not a discriminate presence, sensible or intelligible, nor is it the absence of such a presence, a present absence absently present, an absent presence presently absent, but rather the potency of all that is or will be in the panoply of possible beings, the what-it-is-to-be that is itself beyond the polarity of being and nonbeing, the potentiality that is fully actual as the actuality that is fully potential. Azriel's characterization of the infinite as *efes* calls to mind Nicholas of Cusa's depiction of God in his *De apice theoriae* as *posse ipsum*, "potency as such," that is, the potency that comprises all potencies, absolute contingency, the potency that there will necessarily be accidental beings, the potency of infinite possibilities but itself not any one of them; indeed, *posse* does not demarcate an essence but an event, a verb, not a noun, not a condition but the precondition for conditionality, the "possibility-to-be" (*posse esse*) of all that may come to be, the "actualized possibility" (*possest*), that is, the actualization of all possibilities, which are potentially infinite in number. God's unlimited being is marked by Cusanus as "negative infinity," the enfolding of all possibilities that may unfold in the universe;[338] in the absolute, therefore, there is no distinction between potentiality (*posse*) and actuality (*esse*).[339]

Insofar as this is the case, the attribution of an essence to the divine should not be viewed as a gesture of essentializing, since the essence of this being consists precisely in the fact that it has no essence and thus cannot be delimited by any one being. Alternatively expressed, *posse* is a verb, the infinitive, rather than a substantive; God is neither *esse* nor *non-esse*, being or nonbeing; in the dialectic logic of *coincidentia oppositorum*, "not-being is maximum being, just as the Minimum is the Maximum."[340] To apprehend this secret, sight must replace knowledge, but a seeing by which the mind ascends to the vision of the incomprehensible, ineffable, and invisible, that is, a vision that is seeing-all, which is seeing no-thing, vision that is blindness, beholding nothing becoming, becoming nothing, to be comprehended, named, or seen, the plentitude of nothing that is the capability of all that is capable (*posse omnis posse*).[341]

For Azriel, the term *efes* designates precisely this omnipotent potency that is no thing or state, the indeterminate determinacy that is manifest in the concealment of determinate indeterminacy. By contrast, matter, aligned with the attribute of mercy (*middat raḥamim*), is the aspect that does not change and hence it allows for change, the principle described as that which "stands in itself" (*ha-omed be-aṣmo*), the immutable that makes mutability possible. Azriel links this conception of matter to the word *ṭuvo* (his goodness) in the liturgical blessing *ha-meḥaddesh be-ṭuvo be-khol yom maʿaseh bereʾshit*: "Every day he renews the act of creation [*meḥaddesh maʿaseh bereʾshit*] like the waters of a river that do not cease and they are renewed each moment and each hour." Note the implicit paradox: the waters that never cease are renewed continuously; from the vantage point of the logic of the excluded middle, if the waters never cease, why must and how could they be renewed continuously? Precisely because they never are not do they always come to be.

What accords this quality to matter is form, which Azriel demarcates as the "potentiality in matter" (*koaḥ she-yesh ba-ḥomer*). More specifically, form endows the material substratum with the capacity to configure forms, *she-hu meṣṣayer ṣurotaw we-noten bo koaḥ ṣiyyur leṣayyer ṣurot*. The quality of form to bestow form, to in/form the other by way of re/forming the same, is captured in Azriel's poetic characterization of it as "the source of the spring whence the pool emanates" (*maqor ha-maʿayan she-ha-bereikhah mitpasheṭet mimmenu*).[342]

The term *efes* thus technically demarcates the space suspended betwixt matter and form. To restore everything to this de/ontological state is the task of worship when the latter is conceived mystically as a contemplative practice that extends the measure to the immeasurable, elevating the word to silence. It seems reasonable to suggest that *efes* is correlated with *Keter*, the will that is without limit, the will that expands infinitely to the font in which all things submerge in nondifferentiated oneness, the *ayin* that is no-thing because it is everything, the *coincidentia oppositorum*, the fullness of being beyond the polarity of being and nonbeing.[343] Azriel alludes to this point when he situates unity (*ha-yiḥud*) at the moment of transition "when the light disappears and darkness comes or when darkness disappears and the light sparkles, to attest that the Lord is unified in all the opposites" (*she-ha-adon yaḥid le-khol ha-temurot*).[344]

In Azriel's language, there is nothing outside the infinite, no "other" that is not to be considered part of the nothing that is the superessentiality of everything that is,[345] or, in the Dionysian formulation, which the Spanish kabbalist, I think, would have accepted as a credible characterization of Ein Sof, "The cause of all . . . rejects all doubleness in an excess of simplicity [κατὰ μίαν ἁπλότητος ὑπερβολὴν πᾶσαν διπλόην ἀπαναινομένη] . . . it encompasses all in its unlimitedness beyond simplicity."[346] Inasmuch as this is the case, we must presume a collapse of polarity in the unlimited and indifferent one; to take hold of that collapse, however, one must hold fast to the opposites that are collapsed. Thus, in his commentary on the daily liturgy, Azriel explains that the concluding word of the standing prayer of eighteen benedictions is *ba-shalom*, "in peace," for "it completes all the deficiencies [*mashlim ha-ḥisronot*], as we say 'There is no vessel in the world that holds blessing like peace,'[347] for peace makes opposites equal [*mashweh bein ha-hafakhim*] since it is from the root of indifference [*me-iqqar shaweh*] concerning which there is nothing outside it, and hence all the attributes are sealed within it."[348] Language here seems decidedly inadequate: opposites remain opposite only if they are identical in their opposition, but if they are identical in their opposition, they cease being oppositional; alternatively one might say—indeed, one must say—opposites are identical only if they are opposite in their identification, but if opposites are opposite in their identification, they cease being identical.

As to the ultimate metaphysical question about sameness and difference, we can distinguish two main approaches in kabbalistic literature. Let me hasten to add that by two approaches I do not mean to suggest distinct camps rigidly separated by impenetrable ideological fences; on the contrary, the two, which are sometimes attested in a single author, are equally plausible ways to explain the coincidence of opposites in the infinite; on the one hand, identity of difference whereby otherness is effaced in sameness, and on the other, difference of identity whereby otherness is faced in sameness. Alternatively expressed, according to the first paradigm the infinite is beyond predication and negation and hence it is neither x nor not-x, whereas the second paradigm affirms that the infinite simultaneously is both x and not-x.

It may be useful to recall an observation made by Heidegger in the context of elucidating the belonging-together of poetry and thinking. I had the opportunity to discuss this matter in chapter one; suffice it here to reiterate briefly that in Heidegger's mind, sameness is to be contrasted with "equality," for the "same never coincides with the equal" (*das Selbe deckt sich nie mit dem Gleichen*), whereas the equal "always moves toward the absence of difference [*Unterschiedlose*], so that everything may be reduced to a common denominator."[349] Employing this language, we can say that kabbalistic masters vacillated between depicting Ein Sof as wavering betwixt identity of opposition, that is, an equality that effaces all difference, and as opposition of identity, that is, a sameness that upholds difference.[350]

To illustrate the point, let us consider in more detail some of Azriel's depictions of Ein Sof. In one passage, Azriel describes Ein Sof plainly and simply as the "complete indifference in the perfect unity in which there is no variation" (*ha-hashwa'ah gemurah be-aḥdut ha-sheleimah she-ein bah shinnuy*).[351] The notion of *hashwa'ah*, which I have rendered "indifference," holds the key to explaining the ultimate theological paradox that emerges from the attempt to explain how a multiplicity of powers can be said to emanate from God without negating the fundamental axiom of monotheism as it was commonly understood by the rabbinic elite in the late Middle Ages;[352] the clarification of this issue, moreover, has direct bearing on the setting of theoretical parameters through which to view the intricacies of gender construction. In his commentary on the portrayal of *sefirot* as depths (*omaqim*) in *Sefer Yeṣirah* 1:7, Azriel remarks that "all the depths are equal in one indifference [*shawim be-hashwa'ah aḥat*] even though each one of them is differentiated according to its way, all of them are identical in their terminus [*shawim be-sofam*]."[353] From this remark, it would seem that the indifferent one is a unity that subsumes difference.

In a second passage from the commentary, Azriel writes that the title *adon yaḥid* (unique master) is "an allusion to the infinite [*ein sof*], master of the unique name [*adon shem ha-meyuḥad*], for he is equivalent to everything [*shaweh la-kol*] and everything is unified in his non-differentiatedness" (*ha-kol mit'aḥed be-hashwwa'ato*). The text of *Sefer Yeṣirah* 1:6 accentuates that "and he has no second" (*we-ein lo sheni*) to indicate that "even though the potentiality for duality [*koaḥ sheniyyut*] is from him, he has no second, for everything is undifferentiated within him" (*ha-kol shaweh bo*). Indeed, the poetic image used in this passage of *Sefer Yeṣirah* to demarcate the unity of ten *sefirot*—"their end is fixed in their beginning and their beginning is fixed in their end"—conveys, according to Azriel, that "everything is unified like a flame of fire unified in its colors, and all of them are identical in one root" (*we-khulan shawim be-iqqar eḥad*).[354] The term *hashwa'ah* thus denotes the indistinct oneness—what the authors of the Iyyun circle referred to, perhaps due to the influence of Azriel, as *aḥdut ha-shaweh*, the "equanimous one"[355]—the one wherein differences are rendered identical in the identity of their difference. As Azriel tersely expresses the monistic ideal elsewhere, "all is conjoined and unified to the infinite" (*ha-kol davaq u-meyuḥad ad ein sof*).[356] Finally, in a brief treatise on the nature of faith and heresy, *derekh ha-emunah we-derekh ha-kefirah*, Azriel lists as erroneous the view of a person who acknowledges that God's being supersedes all other beings (*yeter al ha-kol*), contains everything indifferently (*shaweh la-kol*), and is lacking nothing (*ein huṣ mimmenu*), but who nonetheless maintains that opposites (Azriel uses the words *hafakhim* and *temurot* interchangeably) are separated in the "secrecy of their root" (*seter iqqaram*) just as they are distinct in the visible realm.[357] From this we may conclude that the right view consists of discerning that opposites are indifferently the same in the concealed origin, the "secrecy of their root." A similar view, albeit in different terminology, is affirmed by Azriel's colleague, Jacob ben Sheshet, in explaining why the first letter of the Decalogue is *alef* in the word *anokhi* (Exod. 20:2):

> He began with *alef*, for one [*eḥad*] is its root, "Their king marches before them, the Lord at their head" (Micah 2:13),[358] and it corresponds to the inner and hidden essence [*hawayah penimit we-nisteret*], shut tight [*sogeret u-mesuggeret*],[359] ascending way above *Ḥokhmah*, and there is none amongst us who knows whereto it is unified without end or limit[360] . . . and it is called "will" [*raṣon*], for the Creator does not change when he alters every matter, from construction to destruction and from destruction to construction, and he acts according to his will, his nothing is his something and his something his nothing . . . and opposites are balanced in his will [*ha-hafakhim yesharim bi-reṣono*].[361]

Absolute (In)Difference/Engendering Alterity

In the infinite, opposites simultaneously face one another and turn their back on one another; indeed, though this may be quite difficult to envision, facing each other occurs precisely as a consequence of their backs being turned on one another just as their backs being turned on one another occurs as a consequence of their facing each other. The spatial image is meant to express the ontological axiom of absolute indifference, a metalogic of textual reasoning that moves beyond the dialectical identity of identity and nonidentity, a mode of thinking that affirms the identity of the nonidentical by discerning the nonidentity of the identical. Plotinus had this maxim in mind when he wrote: "For the true being is never not being, or being otherwise; and this is being always the same; and this is being without any difference. So it does not have any 'this and that'; nor, therefore, will you be able to separate it out or unroll it or prolong it or stretch it; nor, then, can you apprehend anything of it as before or after."[362] Not-being (μὴ εἶναι) cannot be ascribed to the true being (ἀληθῶς εἶναί), the One, inasmuch as in the true being there is no difference, no basis to distinguish between being and not-being. Nicholas of Cusa, to whom I have referred on several occasions, summoned a similar paradoxical truth to illumine the Christological mystery of the trinity:

> For in the case of God we must, as far as possible, precede contradictories and embrace them in a simple concept. For example, in God we must not conceive of distinction and indistinction as two contradictories but [must conceive of] them as antecedently present in their own most simple Beginning, where distinction is not anything other than indistinction; and then we will conceive more clearly that the trinity and the oneness are the same thing. For where distinction is indistinction, trinity is oneness; and, conversely, where indistinction is distinction, oneness is trinity.[363]

The paradox can also be formulated geometrically: "For the identity in an infinite circle is so great that it precedes all oppositions—even relative oppositions. For in an infinite circle other and different are not opposed to identity."[364] God is the "Absolute Form in which all otherness is oneness and all diversity is identity,"[365] and thus he is called by Cusanus "not-other" (*non aliud*), for all that is other is contained in the "essence of essences" (*essentiarum essentiam*), the "inessential" essence, and therefore cannot be considered as genuinely *other* except as not-other that "is not other than Not-other."[366]

To clarify the matter, we would do well to ponder the depiction of the Absolute in the idealist philosophy of Schelling. The affinity of Schelling's thought to kabbalah and its possible dependence thereon has been noted by a number of scholars.[367] My contribution here is to suggest that the attitude of kabbalists regarding the ontic status of opposites can be beneficially examined in conjunction with the portrayal of the *Ungrund* in Schelling's thought, which, in a comparable manner, posits an opposition of coincidence in opposition to the coincidence of opposition. In *Philosophische Untersuchungen über das Wesen der menschlichen Freiheit und die damit zusammenhängenden Gegenstände* (1809), the "original ground" is said to be "*before* all ground and before all existence, thus before any duality at all. . . . Since it precedes all opposites, these cannot be differentiated within it or be in any way present in it. Thus it cannot be designated as the identity of opposites, but only as their absolute *indifference*." In the abyss, the ground that is before all ground, that is, the ground that has no ground and is therefore, properly speaking, groundless, "all opposites are broken, which is nothing other than their very non-being, and which therefore has no predicate except predicatelessness, without therefore being a nothing or an absurdity."[368] The "indifference" of the unground precludes the possibility of positing a resolution of antinomical forces in the absolute: "Let the following commentary be made on what was just said: real and ideal, darkness and light, or however else we wish to designate the two principles, can never be predicated of the unground *as opposites*. But nothing hinders their being predicated of it as non-opposites, i.e., in disjunction and each *for itself*; whereby, however, this very duality (the actual twofoldness of the principles) is posited."[369]

Schelling's view can be seen as a response to the Hegelian logic of the identity of difference, which is summed up in the *Phänomenologie des Geistes* (1807) in the statement that the "opposite is not merely *one of two*—if it were, it would simply *be*, without being an opposite—but it is the opposite of an opposite, or the other is itself immediately present in it." For Hegel, opposites are dialectically resolved in the unity that comprises a thing and its opposite: "Only thus is it difference as *inner* difference, or difference *in its own self*, or difference as *infinity*."[370] From Schelling's perspective this inner difference is no difference at all, since the difference is part of a self-identical essence. As Hegel himself admits:

> But through the Notion of inner difference, these unlike and indifferent moments . . . are a *difference* which is no *difference*, or only a difference of what is *selfsame*, and its essence is unity. As positive and negative they stimulate each other into activity, and their being is rather to posit themselves as not-being and to suspend themselves in the unity. The two distinguished moments both subsist; they are implicit and are opposites in themselves, i.e. each is the opposite of itself; each has its "other" within and they are only one unity.[371]

In the section on *Logik*, the first part of *Encyklopädie der philosophischen Wissenschaften im Grundrisse* (1830), Hegel reiterates this perspective when he writes in section 116 that "Essence is mere Identity and reflection in itself only as it is self-relating negativity, and in that way self-repulsion. It contains therefore essentially the characteristic of **Difference.**"[372] Hegel begins from the supposition that if we assume that identity and difference are equally independent such that identity must be viewed as irreducibly different from difference—the very position adopted by Schelling—then all we have is difference and hence no basis to demonstrate or discourse about difference. Accordingly, identity itself is defined as a "negative self-relation," that is, "it draws a distinction between it and itself,"[373] and consequently, difference is comprised within identity as its other. Indeed, the task of thinking, fulfilled most perfectly in the science of mathematics, is "to reduce existing differences to Identity."[374] Philosophy in general (and speculative logic in particular) recognizes variety as "determinate or specific difference," but "it also undoubtedly urges its disciples not to rest at mere diversity, but to ascertain the inner unity of all existence."[375]

"Essential difference" is cast in terms of the ostensible antithesis between the positive as the "identical self-relation" and the negative as the "different by itself." It would seem, therefore, that "either has an existence of its own in proportion as it is not the other." Yet the "one is made visible in the other, and is only insofar as that other is." From this we must conclude that essential difference is opposition "according to which the different is not confronted by *any* other but by *its* other," that is, each contrary in the antithesis of positive and negative "is stamped with a characteristic of its own only in its relation to the other: the one is only reflected into itself as it is reflected into the other. . . . Either in this way is the other's *own* other."[376] The positive as "identical self-relation" contains the negative as the "difference of difference within its own self," and thus the contraries, which are "supposed to express an absolute difference," are "at bottom the same: the name of either might be transferred to the other."[377] The ground, therefore, is the "unity of identity and difference . . . the reflection-into-self, which is equally reflection-into-an-other, and vice versa. It is essence put explicitly as a totality."[378]

To be sure, Hegel asserts that the ground is not only unity but also the "difference of identity and difference," but in the final analysis, this is not a genuine difference insofar as the other is part of the same. Schelling's perspective, by contrast, is to maintain a bona fide sense of difference by affirming the unity of identity and indifference,[379] that is, a unity that embraces the disjunction of opposites coexisting as nonopposites. In Schelling's post–Identity Philosophy, God is the "nonground" (*Ungrund*) as the "absence of ground" (*Abgrund*), a state that is prior to all opposition and even beyond the overcoming of opposition; it is this quality that merits the term "absolute indifference," the *indifference of différance* in Derridean terms.[380]

Expanding this way of thinking in the third version of *Die Weltalter* (1815), Schelling writes that duality is found "in the primordial beginnings of nature," and hence the

> ground of the antithesis is as old as, nay, is even older than, the world . . . just as in everything living, so already in that which is primordially living, there is a doubling that has come down, through many stages, to that which has determined itself as what appears to us as light and darkness, masculine and feminine, spiritual and corporeal. Therefore, the oldest teachings straightforwardly represented the first nature as a being with two conflicting modes of activity.[381]

From the beginning there is the doubling (*die Doppelheit*) of the infinite that renders the "first principle," with regard to itself, in contradiction; indeed, the latter is of the very nature of the primordial being.[382] "Therefore, two principles are already in what is necessary of God: the outpouring, outstretching, self-giving being, and an equivalently eternal force of selfhood, of retreat into itself, of Being in itself. That being and this force are both already God itself, without God's assistance."[383] In the philosophical terms that Schelling imputes to the theosophic symbolism, the affirmative will to overflow is identified as egoity (*die Egoität*) and the negative propensity to withdraw as selfhood (*die Selbstheit*). The principle of the "eternal antithesis," which is characteristic of the nature of the primordial being, entails the assumption that "each, by nature, is equally originary an equally essential, each also has the same claim to be that which has being. Both hold their own weight and neither yields to the other. . . . Hence, it only follows from that necessity that the one unity decomposes into two unities, the simple antithesis (that we may designate as A and B) intensifies itself into that which has been doubled."[384] Schelling explicitly rejects the Hegelian dialectic whereby the antithesis would be overcome. He insists to the contrary:

> [W]hat has been set against each other has the same essentiality and originality. The force with which the being closes itself off, denies itself, is actual in its kind as the opposite principle. Each has its own root and neither can be deduced from the other. If this were so, then the antithesis would again immediately come to an end. But it is impossible *per se* that an exact opposite would derive from its exact opposite.[385]

If the two primordial forces were fully apart, without reciprocal contact, there would be no unity and we would be forced to posit two Godheads in the vein of ancient Persian Zoroastrianism: "The antithesis rests on this, that each of the two conflicting powers is a being for itself, a real *principle*. The antithesis is only as such if the two conflicting principles conduct themselves as actually independent and separate from each other."[386] In another passage, Schelling offers a formulaic presentation of what Heidegger later called his Ontotheology, the primordial theo-logy of Being, which is to say, the questioning of beings as a whole:[387]

> The pure Godhead [*lautere Gottheit*] is indivisibly the eternal Yes [*ewiges Ja*] and the eternal No [*ewiges Nein*] and the free unity [*freie Einheit*] of both. From this it automatically follows that the Godhead can be the eternal No = B only insofar as the Godhead is, as such, at the same time the ground of Itself as the eternal Yes. Then from this the reverse also necessarily follows. As B or the eternal No, it is the Godhead only insofar as it is at the same time A, that is, that it posits Itself as the eternal Yes.[388]

To say of the divine essence that it is simultaneously negative and positive is not to conflate the two to the point that difference is effaced but rather to embrace the nonduality of oppositional forces, the indifference—a state of "nondivorce" (*Ungeschiedenheit*), which is not free from all difference but negates it (*nicht eine von aller Differenz freie, sondern eine sie verneinende*)[389]—through which difference is preserved.[390] "For since God is not the cause of the Other through a special volition but through God's mere essence, the Other is certainly not the essence of God, but it belongs to God's essence, indeed, in a natural and inseparable way. It therefore follows that if the pure Godhead = A, and that the Other = B, then the full concept of the living Godhead which has being is not merely A, but is A + B."[391]

It may very well be that the rubric "oldest teachings" mentioned by Schelling as straightforwardly representing the first nature as a being with two conflicting modes of activity refers to the secret gnosis of kabbalah, even though the primary conduit of this doctrine would have likely been Böhme's depiction of the *Ungrund*, the self-enfolding God, as both *Nichts* (nothing) and *Alles* (everything), the single will in which all creation lies, the eternal one beyond the polarities of love and anger, light and darkness.[392] The evidence seems to point to the likelihood that Schelling drew from the wellsprings of Jewish esoteric lore—either directly from a compilation of material translated by Christian Knorr von Rosenroth in *Kabbala Denudata* (Sulzbach 1677–1684)[393] or through secondary channels such as Friedrich Christoph Oetinger[394]—to formulate his logic of identity and indifference, the absolute unity that arises from the belonging-together (*Zusammengehörigkeit*) of two oppositional forces in a third that sustains rather than obliterates dichotomy.[395] The interrelationship of two discrete qualities yields the indifference that facilitates difference of identity (A + B) as opposed to identity of difference (A = B).

In the theosophic symbolism adopted by kabbalists, God is depicted as balancing two major attributes, the outpouring of right-sided mercy and the constricting of left-handed judgment, masculine impulse to overflow and feminine capacity to receive. God's becoming, and the nature of being that may be adduced therefrom are measured by this balance, a harmony that preserves opposites in their opposition. From the thirteenth century, kabbalists employed the terms *hashwa'ah*, which, as Scholem noted, corresponds to the Latin *indistinctio* or *aequalitas*, and *hashwa'at ha-aḥdut*, the "equanimous one," to describe the lack of differentiation—or what we might call the indifference of opposites—either in Ein Sof or in the will that is coeternal with it.[396] Analogously, Schelling describes the unity of the first being not through the resolution or overcoming of opposites, but rather in maintaining the antithesis as "one and the same, that is the affirmation and the negation, that which pours out and that which holds on. . . . Precisely that which is set in opposition can only be essentially and, so to speak, personally, 'one,' insofar as it is only the individual nature of the person that is able to unite that which is in conflict."[397] The absolute can be encoded as "one and the same = x" insofar as it is the case that "A = x" and "B = x" whence follows "A and B are one and the same," that is, "both are x." To say that "both are x," however, does not entail that there is no difference between the "x" that A is and the "x" that B is; it signifies rather that A and B are both "x" to the extent that the "something = x, that B is" is not identical to the "something = x, that A is." The kabbalistic influence is conspicuous in Schelling's surmise that "it is certainly possible that one and the same = x is both Yes and No, Love and Wrath, Leniency and Strictness."[398] Schelling proffers a distinctive approach to unity predicated on the assumption that "something is one and the same and also the exact opposite of itself."[399]

We may conclude, therefore, that "God itself is of two different kinds; first the negating force (B) that represses the affirmative being (A), positing it as the inwardly passive or as what is hidden; second, the outstretching, self-communicating being that in clear contrast holds down the negating power in itself and does not let it come outwardly into effect."[400] Each of the two conflicting powers and the unity of both are independent real principles. "The true meaning of this unity that has been asserted in the beginning is therefore this: 'one and the same = x' is as much the unity as it is the antithesis. Or both of the opposed potencies, the eternally negating and the eternally affirming potency, and the unity of both make up the one, inseparable, primordial being."[401] Comparably, according to the thinking of some kabbalists, there is a resolution of opposites in Ein Sof in the manner suggested by Hegel, but according to others, convergence of opposites does not entail denial of difference. An illustration of the complexity of this issue may be elicited from a zoharic passage wherein a distinction is made between Ein Sof and *Ayin*, the infinite and the nothing:

All attachment, unity, and perfection is hidden in that hiddenness that cannot be understood or known, and the will of all wills is contained in it. Ein Sof cannot be known, and it does not produce end [*sof*] or beginning [*re'shit*] like the primordial *Ayin* that brings forth beginning and end. What is the beginning? The supernal point that is the beginning of everything, the concealment that exists within Thought. And it produces an end, which is call the "end of the matter" (Eccles. 12:13). But there are no wills, lights, or sparks in that Ein Sof. All these sparks and lights depend on it to exist, but they do not comprehend. The one who knows but does not know is none other than the supernal will, the concealed of all concealed, *Ayin*.[402]

The indifference of Ein Sof is described in the above passage by the contrast drawn between it and *Ayin*, the first of the sefirotic gradations. This indifference is related not only to the claim that Ein Sof is incomprehensible but also to the fact that it does not generate beginning or end, that is, the infinite is beyond temporal emplacement. By contrast, the first *sefirah*, even though it is nothing, is delimited by the emanation of the lower nine *sefirot* bound by the beginning, which is the supernal point or *Ḥokhmah*, and the end of the matter, *sof davar*, which is the final point or *Malkhut*. There are, however, other zoharic texts wherein Ein Sof or even *Keter* is described as pure mercy with no admixture of judgment, a realm of being wherein the negative is utterly contained in the positive, the left completely incorporated in the right, the feminine fully enfolded in the masculine.[403] We may, following Neumann, refer to the "inchoate" Ein Sof as an illustration of the unity of the "World Father" and "World Mother" joined in "uroboric union," a "state of existence transcendent and divine . . . a state of union beyond the opposites."[404] The transcendence of opposites, however, is expressive of the containment of the female in the male rather than the erasure of both male and female.

Transposition of Gender/Transvaluation of Values

Refocusing our gaze on the texts of Luria and Luzzatto, we observe that in kabbalistic lore, masculinity is valorized as mercy, the right side of beneficence, and femininity as judgment, the left side of limitation. From that perspective we might be inclined to apply the logic of Schelling and speak of a unity comprised of two separate qualities. Repeatedly, the esoteric tradition in Judaism affirms the alchemical emphasis placed on the sacred union of male and female in the divine and earthly realms;[405] hence the supreme theurgic meaning accorded sexual intercourse between husband and wife, with an appropriate role assigned to each gender in the coital mating.[406] The union of the two, however, results in the amelioration of judgment by mercy, the reabsorption of the feminine into the masculine. Obviously, the pairing of male and female will have an impact on both parties, and the possibility of interaction and intermingling rests on the inclusion of each in the other,[407] but the ultimate purpose of heterosexual bonding is the reintegration of the part into the whole whence it was severed, a restoration that signals a gender transposition of the female.[408] The difference between male and female is thus no difference at all, as the latter is incorporated ontically in the former, and the coincidence of opposites is fully realized with the obliteration of difference in the identity of the same.

I will cite as an illustration of this motif a lengthy passage from Nathan of Nemirov (1780–1845), the disciple of Naḥman of Bratslav. The language of Nathan rhetorically reflects Naḥman's distinctive teaching; however, the substance of his remarks is not at all remarkable, as they reiterate a perspective ubiquitously affirmed in kabbalistic sources:

> On the basis of the scriptural verse "They shall attain joy and gladness, whole sorrow and sighing flee" (Isa. 35:10), in the second part of *Liqquṭei* [*MoHaRaN*],[409] the principle [is established] that a man must be constantly happy and to be so overcome with joy that he captures the sorrow and sighing, which are melancholy[410] and sadness; he should capture them and enter them into happiness against their will until the sorrow and sighing will be transformed into happiness. . . . This is the aspect of the commandment to procreate for it is known that the essence of the grip of sadness and melancholy is in the aspect of the woman, for she is the side of the feminine, which is the side of harsh judgment, and the essence of the grip of sadness, which is the strength of judgment, is there, and this is the aspect of what is said with respect to the side of the feminine "her feet descend unto death" (Prov. 5:5), for sadness is the aspect of the side of death. . . . The essence of happiness and joy is in the aspect of the masculine in the aspect of "strength and joy are in his place" (1 Chron. 16:27), which is said with regard to the consecration of the phallus for strength is in it and it is the joy of the Matrona. This is the aspect of the commandment to procreate that a man must fulfill this commandment verily in holiness and purity, and by means of this commandment he merits to capture the melancholy, sorrow, and sighing within happiness. . . . This is the aspect of the need for a man to gladden his wife through the matter of this commandment . . . for the essence of the sanctity of intercourse is by means of happiness, which is the consecration of the phallus, for this is the essence of the aspect of the unity and intercourse that is commanded through which man and woman are conjoined. Consequently, the aspect of sorrow and sighing, which is sadness, the strength of judgment that latches on to the woman, is ameliorated and abrogated. By means of the holiness of this commandment the sorrow and sighing are annulled and they are transformed into happiness, which is the essence of the sanctity of intercourse, the aspect of the consecration of the phallus. . . . This is the aspect of the happiness of the wedding . . . for the essence of the consecration of the phallus is happiness . . . and the essence is to transform sorrow and sighing, the aspect of the side of the feminine, to happiness . . . for this is the essence of the perfection of happiness when sorrow and sighing are transformed into happiness, which is the aspect of the unification of the wedding.[411]

The text, as the saying goes, speaks for itself—though, I must add, a text can speak for itself only if there are ears of a reader to take heed. The sanctioned union between husband and wife is viewed primarily as the means by which the Jewish adult male fulfills the religious obligation to procreate. When viewed from the halakhic frame of reference, the virtue of domestic sex is that it extends the line of engenderment biologically through the mother, but culturally, given the patriarchal dominance, the line is thought to extend the legacy of the father exclusively or at least primarily, even though the identity of the offspring is determined by the mother and not the father. From a symbolic standpoint, however, the ultimate goal of the coupling is not the elongation of the ontic chain but the amelioration of judgment by mercy. The cohabiting of husband and wife facilitates the repair of the severance of the androgyne above, and thus the sanctity (*qedushshshah*) of the sexual act is invariably linked by kabbalists to the intentionality of thought that transforms carnal eros into a spiritual eros, a point that I shall elaborate in chapter seven. At this juncture it is important to underline that the repair results in the restoration of the feminine into the masculine, the transformation of the capacity to contain into the power to overflow, the vessel sprouting forth as a spring. Transposition of gender occasions a transvaluation of values.

Running the risk of redundancy, let me again emphasize that I am not denying that according to kabbalistic lore, traversing of gender boundaries applies to both female and male. My point is, rather, that there is invariability in the change, a rigidity that fosters the fluency: when male becomes female, he constricts, when female becomes male, she overflows. To comprehend this point—indeed to enter at all into the garden of gender speculation tended by kabbalists—it is necessary to bear in mind that the symbolic circumlocutions mythically convey the metaphysical dialectic of bestowing and receiving. Commenting on the anthropomorphic depiction of the *sefirot*, the anonymous author of *Sefer ha-Peli'ah* formulated the matter axiomatically: "Do not consider in your mind that there is a human or an image of a human, God forbid, but everything is for the sake of making the ear understand, for they called him a man [*adam*] on account of the fact that they receive an influx and a blessing from him. He overflows and because he overflows he is called 'male' and the one that receives is called 'female,' but, God forbid, that there is there a male or female."[412] The erotic play of implanting seed articulates in poetic garb the dual ontological principle of releasing and retaining.

Underlying the somatic imagery of the theosophic myth is an archaic notion of cosmological causality based on the inter/polarity of active agent and passive recipient, engendered as male and female.[413] I will mention briefly two interesting attestations from ostensibly disparate cultural contexts to illustrate the antiquity of this orientation. The first example is the Pythagorean view recorded in Aristotle, *Metaphysics* 985b, according to which the ten primary numbers, which are the principles of being, are arranged in two antinomical columns, "limited and unlimited, odd and even, one and plurality, right and left, male and female, rest and movement, straight and curved, light and darkness, good and evil, square and oblong."[414] This view is reaffirmed in a single, fragmentary line of Pythagoras concerning embryology cited by Galen, "On the right boys, on the left girls."[415]

The second example is from the *Tao-te Ching*, the ancient Chinese wisdom sayings of Laozi, the "old master," traditionally attributed to Lao-tzu: the universal principle of being, the way of nature whence we discern the nature of the way, is manifest through the interface of positive and negative, active-outward masculine (*hsiung*) and passive-inward feminine (*tz'u*).[416] All beings "support *yin*," the shadowy-lunar female, and "embrace *yang*," the luminous-solar male,[417] an idea that evolved in later Taoism into the axiom of the primal cosmic force manifest through an interplay of complementary and oscillating forces, "an energy of creative generosity and an inflexibility of order,"[418] the balance of the inner alchemy of the heavenly breath descending from the brain or heart, and the earthly breath ascending from the kidneys.[419]

The evidence I have marshaled is admittedly meager but it is enough to show that the suggestion that kabbalists arbitrarily linked masculinity with the active-right and femininity with the passive-left cannot be upheld.[420] These associations were obviously much older, as the passages of the *Tao-te Ching*, Aristotle, and Galen plainly indicate. Medieval kabbalists did not fabricate these associations; their view that they are transmitting an ancient esoteric wisdom has support in external sources. From the kabbalist's vantage point, which resonates with the alchemical wisdom shared and expressed in similar terms of heterosexual conjunction in Eastern and Western sources,[421] the creative process requires a balance of both poles or, better, the momentum to swing from one pole to its opposite, but it would be brushing against the grain of being if a female were to overflow and remain female or if a male were to constrict and remain male. A female overflowing is masculine, a male constricting feminine; the creative process entails the balance of projecting and contracting, breathing out and breathing in. Only through contraction is the formless light expanded into form both ontically and imaginally. Alternatively expressed, the feminine is the primal garment that enfolds the infinitely extending light, the line that encompasses the point in which it is encompassed. Gender valence is not affected by this qualification, as the female is still valued in relation to the male as the vessel that delimitedly contains the limitlessly overflowing potency.

Consider a second passage from *Sefer ha-Peli'ah*, which occurs in the context of a sustained homiletical explication of the biblical account of the creation of woman from the rib or side of man in Genesis 2:22. In this exposition, the author divulges the gender implication of the sexual dynamic as it applies to both divine and human spheres:

> Concerning the emanation of *Shekhinah*, the verse states "I planted you with noble vines, all with choicest seed" [*we-anokhi netaʿtikha shoreq kullo zera emet*] (Jer. 2:21), *kullo* is written without a *waw* to indicate that it alludes to the bride that is comprised of the All [*kallah ha-kelulah min ha-kol*], which is the true seed [*zera emet*]. From here, my son, you can understand and contemplate the secret of the bridegroom and bride, and the commandment to procreate. Know, in truth, my son, that all the essences [*hawwayot*] are "like the nakedness of a man with spirals" [*ke-maʿar ish we-loyot*] (1 Kings 7:36), like a man wrapped in his ornament [*ke-ish ha-meʿureh be-livyah shelo*]. My son, see the hidden matters, and now I will mention to you true words concerning which you cannot dispute, diverge, or question, for they are taken from the mouth of the angel of God, verily an angel. Know that this world is a shadow of the supernal world. . . . See and understand that everything is in the supernal pattern, and there is procreation in the upper gradation, for on Sabbath the King unites face to face with the Queen by way of the window,[422] which is *Yesod*, and then the body becomes one and all of the world is blessed and standing in peace,

happiness, and quiet. Listen, my son, to what the sages have alluded in their words "Honor your wives"[423] and you will be enriched in the manner of "From the north the gold will emerge" (Job 37:22). It is like what the rabbis, blessed be their memory, said "Those who are bringing the incense anew should come and cast a lot."[424] The intention is that since a woman is in the pattern of *Shekhinah* the rabbis, blessed be their memory, said "Honor your wives." Now, my son, listen to what one tanna alluded to when he said "He who nullifies the commandment to procreate is considered as if he commits murder and diminishes the likeness,"[425] and the intention is he causes a diminution of mercy from the woman and consequently she receives from [the attribute of] Fear, and he diminishes the likeness [*demut*] from the image [*ṣelem*], which is *Tif'eret*, so that there is only half a person.[426]

Enunciated in this passage is a theme repeatedly affirmed by kabbalists: Theurgical efficacy is imparted to carnal sexuality as an action that enhances the unity of male and female in the realm of divine potencies. The ontological assumption is stated explicitly as an indisputable matter that was revealed to the author orally through the agency of an angel, even though it is attested in a plethora of earlier written sources: The terrestrial world is a "shadow" (*ṣel*) of the world of emanation, and hence everything in the latter is the "supernal pattern" (*dugma elyonah*) of what is found in the former. Obviously, inasmuch as the medium to enhance the union above is the heterosexual mating of husband and wife, a theurgic role will be assigned to both genders. In and of itself, however, this is hardly a challenge to the androcentric bent of traditional kabbalistic symbolism.[427] On the contrary, the androcentrism becomes even more evident when one considers the nature of the particular task assigned to the woman, which consists primarily of being the proper vessel to receive the seminal flow from her husband.[428] Moreover, as a consequence of sexual union, the female receives the attribute of mercy from the male, but in its absence she is judgmental and dreadful. When feminine is joined with masculine—union of the "likeness" (*demut*) and "image" (*ṣelem*) with which primal Adam was created—she receives the "true seed" (*zera emet*) from *Yesod* and is thus transformed into a creative potency.

In the texts I have mentioned, and countless others that could have been added, is articulated a principle that has uniformly influenced kabbalists throughout history: the constitutive instability of gender stabilizes the phallocentricism,[429] for the feminized male exemplifies delimiting, and the masculinized female, extending. Even the reversal of gender underlying the eschatological symbol of the elevation of *Malkhut* to *Keter*, the tenth power being restored to the crown encompassing the head of the male, preserves the structure intact. I have examined this symbolism previously in some of my studies and I will explore it in detail again in the final chapter of this book, but suffice it here to note that just as the beginning is marked by the splintering of the indivisible unity of the androgynous male—the "gendered sex-before-gender"[430]—into the polarity of male and female, a splintering patterned after the model of the "unnatural" and patriarchal account of the creation of man and woman, *ish* and *ishshah*, in the second chapter of Genesis,[431] the woman being constructed out of the male, the end, analogously, is marked by the restoration of the female to the male whence she was taken.[432] In this state, opposite sexes are fully integrated, for the human being is whole, of one piece, *shalem*, and the female is reincorporated into the male in the image of the encircling crown, an idea often linked by kabbalists to the scriptural expression *neqevah tesovev gaver* (Jer. 31:21), the "female encompasses the male."[433] The kabbalistic orientation bears a striking resemblance to a view expressed in some of the ancient gnostic texts. Consider the following summation offered by Anne McGuire:

> Even while idealizing the union of male-female pairs, the gendered metaphors of Irenaeus' account point neither to a gender balance nor to an equalizing of male and female. Rather, they provide graphic depiction of the calamitous consequences of independent female activity and the benefits of restoring the rebellious female to her proper place. At almost every crucial redemptive moment, the mythic narrative reinforces ancient Mediterranean ideologies of gender relations by idealizing redemption and marriage alike as coming about through the hierarchical union of a superior, perfect, and dominant male and an inferior, imperfect, and subordinate female. In the end, the independent and rebellious Sophia-Achamoth is redeemed and restored precisely by returning to her proper place as subordinate female bride.[434]

Although kabbalists have not emphasized the rebellious nature of the feminine potency in a manner that is commensurate with the theologoumenon articulated by Gnostics in late antiquity, the depiction of redemption as the restoration of the feminine to the masculine in gnostic soteriology resonates with kabbalistic eschatology. The reversal of sexual positioning signified by the prophetic formulation of the female surrounding the male signals not the empowerment of the female, which one might interpret as a rupture in the androcentric fabric, but her absorption and reintegration into the body of the male. In the *Endzeit*, as in the *Urzeit*, there is one gender, for the feminine is restored to the masculine, and the image of God is reconstituted in its pristine form.[435] We are thus justified in speaking about the male androgyne as the engendering symbol of kabbalistic theosophy. Rather than making room for the feminine as a genuine other, the myth of androgyny reifies the androcentric hierarchy by demarcating the feminine as other in relation to and contained within the masculine.[436]

CHAPTER THREE

Phallomorphic Exposure: Concealing Soteric Esotericism

Unfolded out of the folds of the woman man comes unfolded,
and is always to come unfolded. . . .

—Walt Whitman

Re/Covering the Un/Covered: Taking Hold of Letting-Go

As I intimated in the preceding chapter, the project of reshaping the feminine in contemporary liturgical discourse—and thereby destabilizing the male-centered symbolic that has dominated Judaism—can proceed without relying on philological and historical research, but the re/envisioning is proportionately impoverished to the degree that it neglects or obfuscates the tradition it purports to reflect. I am not so naïve as to ignore the fact that shared existential circumstances impact the reader's interpretative stance. On the contrary, I readily acknowledge that the reader is prejudiced by hermeneutical assumptions that mirror a complex web of factors ranging from the socioeconomic to the neurobiological. At the same time, each moment of reading is idiosyncratic, novel, unique. Precisely because our vision is so splintered do we have so many possibilities to retrieve. There is always more to say, especially, it seems, when there appears less to say.

I presume that philology enables one to take hold of the text's meaning, an appropriation facilitated by being entrusted to words preserved in the text, preserved as that which calls forth other words, re/sounding, tracing, interpretation. In this matter, I follow Heidegger: "When something is understood but still veiled, it becomes unveiled by an act of appropriation and this is always done under the guidance of a perspective which fixes that with regard to which what has been understood is to be interpreted." On the basis of this hermeneutical claim, Heidegger concludes: "interpretation is grounded in a *fore-sight* that 'approaches' what has been taken in fore-having with a definite interpretation in view. What is held in the fore-having and understood in a 'fore-seeing' view becomes comprehensible through the interpretation." That interpretation is grounded in fore-having, fore-sight, and fore-conception implies that it "is never a presuppositionless grasping of something previously given."[1]

To appropriate the meaning of a text, one must render it from one's own interpretative perspective, but the latter is shaped by presuppositions that are shared with others in a particular cultural context. Appropriation cannot be severed from disappropriation; taking hold depends on letting go. Articulating the fundamental paradox of understanding as interpretation, Heidegger notes, "When the particular concretion of the interpretation in the sense of exact text interpretation likes to appeal to what 'is there,' what is initially 'there' is nothing else than the self-evident, undisputed prejudice of the interpreter, which is necessarily there in each point of departure of the interpretation as what is already 'posited' with interpretation as such, that is, pre-given with fore-having, fore-sight, fore-conception."[2] In slightly different terminology, Gadamer identified the "central problem of hermeneutics" as the "problem of application that exists in all understanding,"[3] by which he meant the ability of a reader to apply his or her own self in eliciting meaning from a text without negating or obfuscating the alterity of either text or reader. To place oneself in the text is to become aware of the otherness of the text, but to become aware of the otherness of the text demands that one persist on one's own. Gadamer refers to this process as the "real fusing of horizons," which takes place "in the process of understanding," a fusion that entails the simultaneous projection and removal of the historical horizon by means of which the reader accomplishes the task of "effective-historical consciousness."[4] Situating himself in this continuum of philosophical hermeneutics, Ricoeur remarked that the "oscillation between Same and Other" overcome by the "fusion of horizons" might be upheld as the "ideal type of reading":

> Beyond the alternatives of confusion and alienation, the convergence of writing and reading tends to establish, between the expectations created by the text and those contributed by reading, an analogizing relation, not without resemblance to that in which the relation of standing-for the historical past culminates. . . . The twofold status of reading makes the confrontation between the world of the text and the world of the reader at once a stasis and an impetus. The ideal type of reading, figured by the fusion but not confusion of the horizons of expectation of the text and those of the reader, unites these two moments of refiguration in the fragile unity of stasis and impetus.[5]

The path of hermeneutics, the hermeneutical path, leads us to the spot whence interpretative uncovering recovers the text, a paradox that relates to the circular structure of understanding, to go back in every forward motion, to go forward in every turning back, never the same, always different. The hermeneutic circle of which I speak is associated with the temporality of there-being, which is to be distinguished from linear temporality of ordinary world-time; the nonsuccessive, recurring present eternally will be what it is not until it is professed not to be what it is.[6] Reader and text are wed together in this circular dance, the interpretative embrace, the task of translation—indeed, interpretation is always translation—for to translate one must hear again what has yet to be said, to interpret the re/utterance in retrospective anticipation of setting foot on new shores.[7] As

Gadamer put it, "The example of the translator, who has to bridge the gulf between languages, shows clearly the reciprocal relationship that exists between interpreter and text, corresponding to the mutuality of understanding in conversation. For every translator is an interpreter. . . . The translator's task of re-creation differs only in degree, not qualitatively, from the general hermeneutical task presented by any text."[8]

The interpretative nature of reading as translation summons one hermeneutically (a viewpoint brought to literary fruition by Derrida) to replace the closed book with an open text. What is written is not finished, for each event of reading is a reinscription of the superfluity of meaning limitlessly delimited in a seemingly endless chain of interpretation. To cite Gadamer again, "Writing is more than a repetition in print of something spoken. To be sure, everything that is fixed in writing refers back to what was originally said, but it must equally as much look forward for all that is said is always already directed toward understanding and includes the other in itself."[9] I would not subscribe to the priority given here to the oral over the written, a repetition of a bias that can be traced to antiquity in several cultural settings determined by contemporary anthropological taxonomies.[10] I wish to bracket this aspect of Gadamer's thinking to salvage what seems to me poetically sound: the text does not record a final word, as what is written will be read, and thus new things will be said that are as much part of the text as what was written/spoken at the inception. That the other voices of interpretation cannot be predicted is integral to the indeterminacy/spontaneity that marks the way of the path. Here we touch upon the nexus of time and reading, the sense in which reading embraces the flow of temporality in its bringing to light what has been laid away, the superfluity of meaning, determinate in its unpredictability and predictable in its indeterminacy, an implication of Derrida's manner of reading[11] but an idea implied already in Rosenzweig's *Sprachdenken*, the dialogical basis for his "new thinking," which served as an important inspiration for Levinas.[12]

Reading thus may be construed as (re)writing. The mutual openness of text and reader fosters an erotic bond predicated on the yearning of the one to be contained in and thereby encompass the other. The point was articulated by Roland Barthes in his analysis of the "pleasure of the text" (*le plaisir du texte*):

> *Text* means *Tissue*; but whereas hitherto we have always taken this tissue as a product, a ready-made veil, behind which lies, more or less hidden, meaning (truth), we are now emphasizing, in the tissue, the generative idea that the text is made, is worked out in a perpetual interweaving; lost in this tissue—this texture—the subject unmakes himself, like a spider dissolving in the constructive secretions of its web.[13]

Maurice Blanchot, too, has expressed this motif, "The writer writes a book, but the book is not yet the work. There is a work only when, through it, and with the violence of a beginning which is proper to it, the word *being* is pronounced. This event occurs when the work becomes the intimacy between someone who writes it and someone who reads it."[14] From the reader's perspective, each reading occurs in a different moment, demanding an interpretation, and hence the text itself in the profoundest way is never the same. Borges poetically captured this dimension of reading in his interpretation of Emerson's statement that "a library is a magic chamber in which there are many enchanted spirits":

> When the book lies unopened, it is literally, geometrically, a volume, a thing among things. When we open it, when the book surrenders itself to its reader, the aesthetic event occurs. And even for the same reader the same book changes, for we change; we are the river of Heraclitus, who said that the man of yesterday is not the man of today, who will not be the man of tomorrow. We change incessantly, and each reading of a book, each rereading, each memory of that rereading, reinvents the text. The text too is the changing river of Heraclitus.[15]

Neither text nor reader is complete; texts always require readers and readers texts, both changing continually in the flux of time, the otherness of one in relation to the otherness of the other, interpretation arising in between. In this between, we can discern the erotic texture of reading, extending to display the other as same from the perspective of the same as other and the same as other from the perspective of the other as same.[16] Hermeneutics, it has been argued, is a "nihilistic vocation,"[17] for it rests on the assumption that truth is a matter of interpretation rather than fact. Nietzsche already noted the threat of nihilism arising from this notion of truth: "There are many kinds of eyes . . . and consequently there are many kinds of 'truths,' and consequently there is no truth."[18] Even the proposition that there is only interpretation cannot be taken for granted as a principle of truth; at best, it is a marking of conditions that make interpretation possible. The search for truth is always deferred, for one is caught in a network of contextually bound and generated interpretations.[19] If the truth is that there is no truth, then this truth is true only if it is false, but it is false only if it is true. There does not appear to be a logical way out of this paradox.

Nihilistic implications of hermeneutical circularity notwithstanding, one can on good philosophical grounds still maintain that there is truth to be appropriated in the event of reading. This truth, however, is best conceived as meaning that appears through questioning the text. In the felicitous formulation of Gadamer:

> The hermeneutical task becomes automatically a questioning of things and is always in part determined by this. . . . If a person is trying to understand something, he will not be able to rely from the start on his own chance previous ideas. . . . Rather, a person trying to understand a text is prepared for it to tell him something. That is why a hermeneutically trained mind must be, from the start, sensitive to the text's quality of newness. But this kind of sensitivity involves neither "neutrality" in the matter of the object nor the extinction of one's self, but the conscious assimilation of one's own fore-meanings and prejudices. The important thing is to be aware of one's own bias, so that the text may present itself in all its newness and thus be able to assert its own truth against one's own fore-meanings.[20]

Emilo Betti expresses the matter in an idiom that may resonate better with a postmodernist discourse:

> The fact that the hermeneutical task can never be completed entails that the meaning contained within texts, monuments, and fragments is constantly reborn through life and is forever transformed in a chain of rebirths; but this does not exclude the fact that the objectivated meaning-content still remains an objectivation of the creative force of an Other, to which the interpreter should seek access, not in an arbitrary way, but with the help of controllable guidelines.[21]

The complex and subtle relationship of text and reader requires the recognition of the mutuality and reciprocity between the two that precludes complete identification or diametric opposition. The text is not simply what the reader says, nor is the reader merely reflecting what the text says. Interpretation arises from the confrontation of text and reader, which results in the concomitant bestowal and elicitation of meaning.

In his study, *The Ascetic Imperative in Culture and Criticism*, Geoffrey Harpham refers to the same phenomenon as resistance, a term he derives from his interpretation of asceticism: "The distinctive feature of resistance is that it suspends two apparently antagonistic terms . . . in a relationship of interdependence so that both opposition and relation are maintained. Text and reader, we could say, exist neither in opposition to each other nor are they one and the same. They exist only in a condition of mutual resistance."[22] In my opinion, Harpham provides a model that allows us to avoid choosing between the mutually exclusive opposites mentioned above. The reader engages the text in a way that the text interacts with but resists the reader just as the reader interacts with but resists the text. From the perspective of mutual resistance, resisting the resisting, hermeneutics may be viewed as an ascetic discipline. William Elford Rogers, to whom I am indebted for this formulation, explains the nexus between asceticism and textual interpretation in the following semiotic terms particularly indebted to Peirce:

> But one way of describing what goes on in interpreting a text is to say that the interpreter tries, so far as possible, to become totally absorbed in the signs of the text, such that the interpreter purges from consciousness purely private feelings and awareness of the separate "I" of the "I think." That is, the interpreter aims at a pure consciousness of the representative function of the signs woven together to make the text. . . . The interpreter who practices interpretation as an ascetic discipline is oriented toward the representative function of the text for the virtual, indefinitely future community that gives signs their reality. To be totally absorbed in the text means to have nothing in one's own reading that is not potentially real.[23]

The ascetic discipline thus provides a model of reading that bridges the difference of reader and text without effacing difference, as the reader will always remain foreign to the text and the text to the reader, a strangeness that strangely enough only increases with the intimacy of absorption. "Reading takes place in the space of inescapable difference and tension between the authority of the author/text to impose meaning and the freedom of the obtrusive reader to make meaning. If we recognize the complexities of textuality, it cannot be any other way."[24]

Radical Hermeneutics/Timely Thinking from the Root

In my analysis of the gender implications of kabbalistic symbolism, I have availed myself of contemporary feminist critique to expose tendencies of thought that have fashioned the traditional perspective, but in so doing, I have implicated myself in the structures I seek to subvert. A proper understanding of my project and the site that I wish to occupy in the history of Jewish textual interpretation requires the reader to grasp that the verbal reification that ensues from the critical enterprise is itself an expression of intellectual insurrection.[25] The possibility of affirming ostensibly antithetical positions is buttressed by my assumption (shared by other scholars as well) that tradition in Judaism is by its nature an ongoing process of critique and reflection that is based on effective misreading and creative refashioning. The scholarly enterprise of contextual reading—that is, situating the text in historical/philological context—is part of the continuous enterprise of cultural formation.[26] This enterprise can profitably be seen as a form of radical thinking that is concurrently innovative and conservative, rooted but revolutionary. To think radically means to think from the root, which embraces the paradox of articulating again what is yet to be articulated. Radical hermeneutics thinks from the ground and hence calls into question everything given on the pathway of thought.[27]

The hermeneutical insight can be expressed as well in the image of marginalia inscribed in books, which shifts the focal point of the reader and undermines the hierarchy of meaning by marginalizing the center and centering the margin:

> The writing in the margin . . . is, in every case, an attack on the integrity of the text in whose margin it takes place. Whether it expands, changes, explains, or criticizes the text, the marginal note always has an unavoidable impact on it. By intruding upon the text, it tears it up, opening it toward the outside, and disturbs the truce between intratextual relations. The marginal text ignores the margin of the text. It begins where the text stops and blurs the text's borders.[28]

By opening the text to the outside, marginal notations extricate the boundaries of the text even as they provide the frame that helps give it shape. This is the import of the observation that the "marginal text ignores the margin of the text." How do we apply this to the matter of tradition? Tradition is expanded by the very forces that keep it constricted. The margins constitute the center, but there is no center that is not marginal. Traditionally, claims to traditional authority have been predicated on affirming the new as old by appropriating the old as new. This is part of a more rudimentary quality of the epistemic process that involves the imaginary conjuring of the hackneyed as novel. As Derrida put it, "The fact is, production of the new—and imagination—are only productions: by analogical connection and repetition, they bring to light what, without being there, *will have been* there."[29] Massimo Cacciari has related the (un)masking of the old as new to the cultural task of inscribing the contours of tradition:

> Tradition is the writing of continuous displacements, of the interminable exodus, which Moses initiated. It registers the traces, the fragments of this dispersion. In it every part is retracted into another one, each sign refers to another one, thus reveal-

ing the Origin. One belongs to the history of this *Entstellung* only by renouncing the unveiling of the "first time"; belonging and renunciation occupy the same space. One belongs to the writing of the tradition only by inscribing oneself in the *loss* that it witnesses; the exodus is the perennial re-creation of the loss, a presence that perennially vanishes. Tradition *wants* such a loss.[30]

The calling into question of the contemporary project on a textual basis is thus itself part of the constructivist task, the interpretative stance that lays the ground by clearing the way. The emphasis placed on commentary as the means of approaching the text entails, in George Steiner's perceptive language, a "hermeneutical unendingness" that betrays a profound dialectical movement:

> On the one hand, there is a sense in which all commentary is itself an act of exile. All exegesis and gloss transports the text into some measure of distance and banishment. . . . On the other hand, the commentary underwrites—a key idiom—the continued authority and survival of the primary discourse. It liberates the life of meaning from that of historical-geographical contingency. In dispersion, the text is homeland.[31]

The text of boundary is determined from within the boundary of text. Reading recurringly reshapes the contours of this delimitation, resulting in the ongoing destabilization of the dichotomy between inside and outside. If text is indeed homeland, the line separating indigenous and alien in the mapping of cultural identity must be subject to constant alteration. Through the radical hermeneutics that I have adopted in my study of gender in Jewish mysticism, I have set out to accomplish the othering of the other, identifying difference by differentiating identity, a task that paradoxically succeeds to the extent that it fails and fails to the extent that it succeeds.

Ontology of Eros/Language of Being

A further assumption underlying my own textual reasoning[32] on the matter of gender is that the prevailing attitudes toward masculinity and femininity that emerge from the symbolic language employed by traditional male kabbalists can be gathered only as a result of a sustained analysis of the ontology of eros presumed in these sources. In line with a proclivity well attested by the study of diverse religious cultures, kabbalists affirm an intricate connection between sexuality and religion; indeed, from their perspective, erotic symbolism is the most appropriate language in which the life of mystical piety can be expressed. The perspective is formulated eloquently by Annemarie Schimmel: "The mystical poet, translating purely spiritual matters into the sphere of sensuality, certainly tries to form out of the formless ocean of the Godhead something which may represent at least a small 'image' of the Reality."[33] This chapter continues my examination of the assorted ways in which gender is imaged from the vantage point of the erotic impulse expressed within the symbolic parameters of the visionary gnosis cultivated and explicated by kabbalists.

In kabbalistic sources, eros, which is inseparable from but not identical to the libidinal drive,[34] demarcates the striving of all being for ontic unity and completeness. This characterization of eros is especially obvious in the literary strata of zoharic literature, the principle anthology of theosophic lore and ecstatic hermeneutics, which was redacted over a long period of time beginning in the later part of the thirteenth century and continuing well into the sixteenth century, and in the complex corpus that evolved from the multiple explications of the teachings of Luria in the sixteenth and seventeenth centuries, a major part of which can be seen as an interpretative expansion of zoharic kabbalah fostered by revelatory exegesis. Moreover, inasmuch as kabbalists do not separate ontology from language, and particularly the language of creation, which is identified as Hebrew[35]—an idea rooted in a much older assumption attested in biblical and postbiblical literature and anchored philologically in the dual meaning of the Hebrew *davar* as "thing" and "word"[36]—it follows that everything may be decoded as a semiotic encoding of the erotic impulse; all that takes place is to be viewed as a symbolic allusion to the linguistic energy that pulsates beneath the manifold masks of God's manifest camouflage. The convergence of eros and language in kabbalistic sources resonates with the following remarks of Steiner:

> Eros and language mesh at every point. Intercourse and discourse, copula and copulation, are sub-classes of the dominant fact of communication. . . . Sex is a profoundly semantic act. . . . To speak and to make love is to enact a distinctive twofold universality: both forms of communication are universals of human physiology as well as social evolution. It is likely that human sexuality and speech developed in close-knit reciprocity. . . . The seminal and the semantic functions determine the genetic and social structure of human experience. Together they construe the grammar of being.[37]

Steiner's account, as he himself was well aware,[38] is an entirely apt depiction of the kabbalistic understanding of language as expressive of the eros of being. For kabbalists, contemplative envisioning of God ensues from the intersection of the sexual and semantic.[39] The portrayal of the erotic in verbal discourse, the language of eroticism, which encompasses both oral and written forms, articulates the flesh, the bodily sign, reverberating with the eroticism of language.[40] As Gregory Woods insightfully put it, "Eros pitches his house in the human body. It is here that all declarations of love, poetic or otherwise, have their origin; and it is hither that, even after the dizziest flights of spirituality, they must return. The verbal flourish of erotic candour . . . is an echo of the body's signs, an articulation of the flesh."[41] The symbology of theosophic kabbalah, however, exemplifies a larger ontological assumption that has impacted various esoteric currents of Judaism: the body in its true essence is identified with the letter, and thus the thinner the material flesh, the more erotic the nature of the textual body.[42] As will become clearer to one who stays the course of this book, precisely at this juncture the lines of asceticism and eroticism crisscross.

The convergence of anthropomorphic and letter symbolism provides the conceptual rationale for the unreserved utilization of sexual language on the part of kabbalists to characterize both the imaginal body of God and the mystical experience of erotic embodiment.[43] The kabbalistic ideal of detachment from desire rests not on the removal of all images of God from the human psyche but on the paradoxical imaging of the image of what has no image, an envisioning rooted in the noetic interplay of the apophatic and kataphatic.[44] Here it is helpful to recall the link between sexual renunciation and prohibition on images suggested by Freud in *Moses and Monotheism*.[45] In striking contrast, kabbalistic literature yields the idea that repudiation of the sexual instinct fosters the production of images, that is, ascetic control of the body cleanses the imaginative faculty, the medium for contemplative envisioning of the incorporeal as a body engaged in blatantly sexual activities.[46] Just as the specular image in the mirror is not identical to the object of which it is an image, so the image of God in the imagination is not identical to God, the being of whom there is no image.[47] The ascription of an imaginal body to God occupies a median position between the extremes of naïve realism (God is literally a body) and allegorical reductionism (in no way can we meaningfully attribute corporeality to God).[48]

Mystical Envisioning/Imaginal Representation

Scholem, apparently reflecting both the influence of the narrative philosophy of Schelling with renewed emphasis on mythology[49] and the thinking-in-images (*Bilddenken*) of Benjamin,[50] remarked that there is an inescapable conflict between "conceptual thinking" and "symbolic thinking" based on concrete mythical images. In the history of kabbalah, one can find evidence of both modes of thought, although, according to Scholem, there is no question that the primary and dominant phenomenon is the latter. In his own words: "The discursive thinking of the Kabbalists is a kind of asymptotic process: the conceptual formulations are an attempt to provide an approximate philosophical interpretation of inexhaustible symbolic images, to interpret these images as abbreviations for conceptual series. The obvious failure of such attempts shows that images and symbols are nothing of the sort."[51] In another context, Scholem similarly speaks of two basic tendencies in kabbalah, the "mystical direction expressed in images and symbols whose inner proximity to the realm of myth is often very striking," and the "speculative" attempt to assign "ideational meaning to the symbols." Regarding the latter, Scholem writes:

> The speculative expositions of kabbalistic teaching largely depended on the ideas of neoplatonic and Aristotelian philosophy, as they were known in the Middle Ages, and were couched in the terminology customary to these fields. Hence the cosmology of the Kabbalah is borrowed from them and is not at all original, being expressed in the common medieval doctrine of the separate intellects and the spheres. Its real originality lies in the problems that transcend this cosmology.[52]

Bracketing the validity of Scholem's attempt to differentiate medieval Jewish philosophy and kabbalah on these grounds,[53] it is instructive that here, in contrast to other places in his work,[54] he suggested that images are privileged in the kabbalistic worldview. In my own scholarly writings, and especially in my monograph on the visionary experience of God in medieval Jewish mysticism, I have expanded this approach by arguing that, by and large, kabbalists have considered imagination the divine element of the soul that enables one to gain access to the realm of incorporeality by transmuting sensory data and/or rational concepts into symbols. The primary function of imagination, therefore, may be viewed as hermeneutical. Through images in the heart, the divine, whose essence is incompatible with all form, is manifest in the formlessness of the imaginal presence. An early articulation of the visionary nature of the kabbalistic theosophy is found in the exposition attributed to Isaac the Blind of the mandate in *Sefer Yeṣirah* (1:4) to "investigate" (*ḥaqor*) the *sefirot*: "Construct an edifice that is comprehended through the sense faculty [*ha-binyan ha-mussag be-herggesh*] and imagine it [*we-shaʿer oto*] in the attributes of the causes that emanate from them and that are built from them [*be-middot ha-sibbot ha-neʾeṣalot mehem we-ha-benuyyot ba-hem*]."[55] The configuration of the divine emanations, the edifice, is constructed in the imagination on the basis of what is apprehended from sense experience. The image, therefore, renders the imageless phenomenologically accessible without undermining its nonphenomenalizability.

The paradox that the hidden God appears to human beings in multiple forms, including, most significantly, that of an anthropos, is the enduring legacy of the revelatory tradition that has influenced and challenged Judaism throughout the ages. Ironically, the iconoclastic constraint against the use of images in worshipping God has fostered some of the most daring imaginative representations of the divine in the history of religions. Indeed, the role of the imaginal construct to serve as a symbolic intermediary allowing for the imaging of the imageless God is attested in prophetic, apocalyptic, aggadic, and poetic texts, although it is developed and articulated most fully in medieval mystical literature, including the esoteric works of the Rhineland Jewish Pietists, the theosophic kabbalah, exemplified by the various strata of zoharic literature, and in the prophetic kabbalah elaborated in the compositions of Abraham Abulafia and his disciples.

In this context, I shall illustrate my point from the depiction of the phenomenological contours of *kawwanah*, the *terminus technicus* in rabbinic literature for ritual intentionality, offered by Ḥayyim Vital, preeminent disciple of Luria. The reappropriation of corporeal images as part of the mystical understanding of *kawwanah*, which I will render as proper mental focusing, is poignantly conveyed in a passage from the fourth part of Vital's *Shaʿarei Qedushshah*.[56] Vital characterizes the "secret of communion and the perfect intention" (*sod ha-hitdabbequt we-ha-kawwanah ha-shelemah*) as a state in which one must constantly see oneself as "a soul without any body" (*nefesh beli guf kelal*). The one who attains this disembodiment, which is related by Vital to the spiritual exercise of *hitbodedut*, is able to draw upon himself the "holiness of the holy spirit" (*lehamshikh alav qedushshat ruaḥ ha-qodesh*) when he prays or recites psalms.[57]

The pietistic path described by Vital actually involves five stages of attainment: the secret of conjunction (*sod ha-hitdabbequt*), the secret of equanimity (*sod ha-hishtawwut*), the secret of meditation (*sod ha-hitbodedut*), the comprehension of the holy spirit (*ruaḥ ha-qodesh*), and the experience of prophecy (*nevuʾah*).[58] If one has the requisite moral and religious virtues, then one can embark upon this fivefold spiritual path that leads ultimately to prophecy. Consistent with other sixteenth-century kabbalists, who in turn based their views on older meditation manuals, Vital considers subjugation of the body (achieved through specific acts of asceticism) as the necessary precondition for the mystical experience of contemplation, which is described primarily as visionary communion with the divine. To receive supernal illumination, the soul must be completely separated from the body, emptied of all material sensations and corporeal desires.[59]

What is remarkable, however, is that immediately after Vital finishes the characterization of *hitbodedut* as the radical stripping away of all things corporeal,[60] he cites a passage from the anonymous kabbalistic treatise, *Maʿarekhet ha-Elohut*, in all probability composed in the first decades of the fourteenth century in the school of Solomon Ibn Adret, the disciple of Moses ben Naḥman, which deals with the esoteric gnosis of *Shiʿur Qomah*, a cluster of older texts in which explicit dimensions are attributed to the limbs of the Creator, thereby reinscribing and expanding the anthropomorphic nature implied by the scriptural account of prophetic visions.[61] The ultimate secret of the prophetic experience is the imaginative representation of the divine as an anthropos. Only one who transforms the physical body into something spiritual—a transformation that is presented in the relevant texts as angelification of the mystic—is capable of imaging the divine form in bodily images.[62] The point is expounded in a remark of Judah Ḥayyat in his fifteenth-century commentary on *Maʿarekhet ha-Elohut*, which Vital himself cites in this context:[63]

> The lower anthropos is a throne for the supernal anthropos, for the physical limbs that are in him allude to the spiritual limbs above, which are the divine potencies, and not for naught does it say "Let us make Adam in our image" (Gen. 1:26). Inasmuch as this image is the image of the spiritual, supernal anthropos, and the prophet is the physical man who, in the moment of prophecy, is almost transformed into a spiritual entity, and his external senses almost depart from him, thus he sees the image of an anthropos, just as he sees his image in a glass mirror.[64]

The distinguishing feature of prophecy, according to Vital, is the conjunction of the soul to its ontic root in the realm of the *sefirot*, an experience that is predicated on the purification rather than the nullification of the body. Thus, Vital characterizes the "matter of prophecy" (*inyan ha-nevuʾah*) in the third part of *Shaʿarei Qedushshah*:

> When a person is in pure matter without any of the filth of the evil inclination and without any of the faculties of the elemental soul, and he has no sin that blemishes some root in the roots of his soul, and he prepares himself to be conjoined to his supernal root, then he can be conjoined to it. Even though he is worthy of this, he must remove his soul entirely and separate it from all corporeal matters, and then he can be conjoined to his spiritual root.[65]

In another passage from this section of the text, Vital goes so far as to compare this separation to a simulated death: "He should close his eyes and separate his thought from all matters of this world as if his soul departed from him like one who has died who feels nothing at all."[66] This deathlike separation, however, does not entail the complete abrogation of corporeal images from prophetic vision, a wiping clean of the mirror of consciousness; on the contrary, as Vital describes at great length, a consequence of the soul's separation from the body is the imaginative ascent to the divine realm that culminates in the spiritual entities assuming corporeal form within the imagination.[67]

The task that Vital assigns to the prophet conforms to what he defines in other passages as the more general mission of the life of piety. The purpose of the conjunction of the soul and God is the spiritual vision of the latter accorded the former.[68] This vision is depicted in terms of the *Shiʿur Qomah*, that is, the *sefirot* are configured as an anthropos in the human mind. The sinful soul is compared to a copper mirror so full of stains and rust that nothing can be seen in it; by contrast, the pure soul is like a clear and bright mirror in which the "supernal, holy things take shape."[69] That the visualization of the divine form is the ultimate goal of *devequt* and the true intent of *kawwanah* may be deduced from Vital's admonition to the reader that "he should place the name [of God] before his eyes, as it is written, 'I am ever mindful of the Lord's presence' (Ps. 16:8), and he should intend to conjoin his thought to it, and he should not cease even for a moment; this is the secret of 'to cleave to him' (Deut. 11:22), 'and to him shall you cleave' (ibid., 10:20)."[70]

Kawwanah, rendered kabbalistically, is predicated on a visual image of the letters of the Tetragrammaton, in which are contained the ten *sefirot* that are configured in the shape of an anthropos. The experience of *devequt*, moreover, is realized only to the extent that one cleaves to the form of God that one has visualized in one's imagination. From that vantage point the imagination, which is frequently designated in mystical sources as the heart, is the throne upon which *Shekhinah* dwells.[71] The critical aspect of *kawwanah* in kabbalistic piety, therefore, is not union (or communion) with God per se, but the anthropomorphic representation and visual apprehension of God that ensues from the state of conjunction. To avoid potential misunderstanding, let me emphasize that I am not denying that unitive experiences were cultivated by theosophic kabbalists betraying Aristotelian and Neoplatonic influences. My point is, rather, that these experiences of union serve the ultimate goal of inducing mystical consciousness, which is the immediate and direct presence of God visually comprehended as an imaginal body.[72]

The enduring quest to attain a vision of the image of the imageless God may be termed the impulse for idolatry that stubbornly lingers in the heart of any theism, especially pertinent in the domain of liturgical practice.[73] To be sure, this impulse is mitigated by the ultimate paradox that if the God seen is not the invisible God, then it is not God who has not been (un)seen.[74] Nonetheless, from the kabbalistic perspective, the yearning to image what has no image lies deep in the poetic sensibility of the Jewish soul, with its unique propensity for prophecy. Every image of God conjured in the imagination, and that would include, most poignantly, the theosophic symbols crafted by kabbalists themselves, may be considered an "icon of the invisible God."[75]

The ideal of mystical contemplation to be elicited from kabbalistic sources does not culminate in the imageless vision of God as inaccessible light, light beyond light, a prominent idea in the eastern and western branches of Christian mysticism due in great measure to the influence of the anonymous monk who published his works under the name of Dionysius the Areopagite.[76] To be sure, as I noted in chapter one, from a relatively early stage kabbalists embraced the Neoplatonic mode of discourse to communicate the idea that the ladder of contemplation experientially culminates in the paradoxical positing of thought that can be thought only as what cannot be thought, darkness illumined as darkness, immeasurability measured as immeasurable. From this vantage point we may wish to characterize contemplation in kabbalistic sources in apophatic terms as unknowing, unseeing, unsaying, fostering, as it were, "imageless prayer"[77] as the mystical form of worship, which supersedes the conventional, sanctioned mode of liturgy. The cogency of this argument notwithstanding, kabbalists have repeatedly emphasized that there is no way to visualize the formless except by means of form, just as the ineffable name cannot be pronounced except through its epithet.[78]

In his study, "*Shiʿur Komah*: The Mystical Shape of the Godhead," Scholem noted the insight that he considered "crucial for the metaphysics of the Kabbalah." Insofar as the "formless substance" (*die gestaltlose Substanz*) of Ein Sof is "immediately present, in its full reality, in all stages of emanation and creation," it follows that "there is no thoroughly shaped image that can completely detach itself from the depths of the formless" (*Untergrund des Gestaltlosen*). The immanence of the formless in every form yields the fundamental paradox of the kabbalistic worldview: "The truer the form, the more powerful the life of the formless within it. To delve into the abyss of formlessness [*den Abgrund des Gestaltlosen*] is no less absurd an undertaking for the Kabbalists than to ascend to the form itself; the mystical nihilism [*der mystische Nihilismus*] that destroys any shape dwells hand in hand with the prudent moderation [*die Besonnenheit*] struggling to comprehend that shape."[79] Reflected here is a basic tenet in Scholem's approach to mysticism, informed by a long-standing orientation in the German theosophic tradition: the mystical experience is an encounter with the absolute or infinite, the "shapeless abyss" (*der gestaltlose Abgrund*), and thus that experience is potentially nihilistic inasmuch as its formlessness threatens to undermine the forms transmitted by texts and rituals of traditional authority.[80]

What is most important to underscore in this context is Scholem's insight regarding the dialectic entwining of the formless and form: the latter emerges from and returns to the former. Significantly, Scholem concluded this essay by noting that not only did kabbalists display a courage in employing "daring and, often enough, grotesque images" to represent the divine, but "they were also inspired by the certainty with which, in the course of comparing the theory of emanation with the mystical linguistic theory of the name of God,[81] they grasped the imagelessness which, as a great modern thinker put it, is the refuge of all images."[82] The modern thinker to whom Scholem referred is Benjamin, who wrote in a short piece first published in *Neue schweizer Rundschau* in November 1929 of the "blissful yearning that has already crossed the threshold of image and possession, and knows only the power of the name—the power from which the loved one lives, is transformed, ages, rejuvenates itself, and, imageless, is the refuge of all images."[83]

Leaving aside the appropriateness of utilizing Benjamin's comment to elucidate a matter in the kabbalistic tradition, what is critical for our purposes is the fact that Scholem gave expression to the dialectical relationship that pertains between the imageless and the image, the nameless and the named, the hidden and the revealed.[84] In an exegesis of the biblical narrative about the journey of Jacob from Beersheba to Ḥaran included in the stratum of the zoharic compilation designated *Sitrei Torah*,[85] we find the following description of the relationship of the "concealed secret" (*sitra setimaʾah*) and the "splendor of the speculum that shines" (*zohar aspaqalaryya de-nahara*), the central emanation, *Tifʾeret*:

> In that splendor dwells the one that dwells, it is a name for the concealed one that is not known at all [*leha-hu de-satim de-lo yediʿa kelal*]. It is called the "voice of Jacob" [*qol yaʿaqov*], in it is seen the faith of everything [*be-hai itḥazei meheimanuta de-khola*]. The one that is concealed and not known at all dwells in this one, YHWH, perfection of all aspects [*shelimu de-khol sitrin*]; he is above and below.[86]

I am here bracketing discussion of the main theme in this passage, the departure of Jacob from Beersheba and his entry to Ḥaran, which is mapped onto the topography of imaginal space as the descent from the realm of the holy to the other side of impurity, as I wish to concentrate only on the articulation of the philosophic notion noted above, the garbing of the hidden, unknowable, nameless one in the four-letter name, YHWH. Through the name the nameless itself is named, albeit as the name of the nameless.

The wisdom excavated from the *Sitrei Torah* text accords in a striking way with the following account of the ineffable character of the One in Dionysius the Areopagite:

> Seeing this, the theologians celebrate it as nameless and in accordance with all names. Thus, they call it nameless when the godhead itself, in one of the mystical sights of the symbolic manifestation of God, rebukes him who says "What is the name?" by saying "To what end do you ask my name, for it is the most wondrous of all?" (Judg. 13:17–18) and leads him away from a knowledge of the divine names. For is not this truly the most wondrous name: the nameless beyond all names, which is placed beyond "every name which is named either in this age or in the future?" (Eph. 1:21).[87]

To refer to the "nameless beyond all names" as the "most wondrous of names" embraces the same paradox that the medieval kabbalist responsible for the aforecited zoharic text affirmed in the attempt to account for the relation of the nameless to the name: only through the name can one apprehend the nameless beyond all names, and thus the nameless itself may be designated the greatest of names.

The theme is expressed in a singular way in the mystical diary *Oṣar Ḥayyim*, composed in the early part of the fourteenth century by Isaac of Acre. Isaac reports that the method of contemplation that he received from the master of his generation[88] consisted of setting the image of the ten *sefirot* in one's mind, a process linked exegetically to the verse "I set YHWH before me always" (Ps. 16:8).[89] The psalmist's insistence that one have the letters YHWH in mind is interpreted kabbalistically as the necessity to conjure an image of the sefirotic potencies in the imagination, for the *sefirot* are contained within the name. The nature of that image is depicted, moreover, in anthropomorphic terms, for the presumption is that the name, which is the esoteric essence of Torah, may be configured as an anthropos, an idea anchored exegetically in the numerical equivalence of the word *adam* and the full spelling of the letters of the name, *yod-he-waw-he* (both equal 45).

To be sure, as Isaac of Acre notes, the objective of the contemplative path is to be conjoined to Ein Sof, the boundless source of all that exists beyond all names, but the only way to attain that end is through the demarcated letters of the name. In Isaac's own words, "As long as I contemplate this ladder, which is the name of the holy One, blessed be he, I see my soul cleaving to Ein Sof."[90] The name is the ladder that connects the kabbalist to that which is beyond the name, but there is no way to get beyond the name except through the name. This is the intent of Isaac's remark that he could visualize himself cleaving to Ein Sof, the otherwise-than-being that lies beyond all names,[91] only as long as he was contemplating the four-letter name, which assumes the form of an anthropos in the imagination of one who contemplates.

Consider as well Isaac's account of the meditation practice connected to vocalizing the names in the heart in his biblical commentary *Me'irat Einayim*:

> After having intended their vocalization, one should intend in his heart that the ten *sefirot* are unified in him and all is unified in Ein Sof. . . . Moreover, I will include an intention regarding the unique name [*shem ha-meyuḥad*] together with the intention of the vocalizations that were mentioned, and it is that I intend when I see in my heart the crown of the *yod* of the unique name, which is the tip of the *yod*, mentioned in the words of the rabbis, blessed be their memory, with respect to *Keter*, and the *yod* itself to *Ḥokhmah*, the *he* to *Teshuvah*, the *waw* to *Tif'eret* together with the six extremities, for it is their foundation, and the final *he* to *Aṭarah*, until Ein Sof.[92]

Building on the contemplative visualization technique attested in earlier kabbalistic sources whereby the vocalization of the name, whose enunciation is prohibited, is envisioned in the heart, which I assume refers to the imagination,[93] Isaac articulates the *kawwanah* associated with imagining the ten *sefirot* comprised in the letters of YHWH. However, the last words of the *Me'irat Einayim* passage concur with the aforecited remark in *Oṣar Ḥayyim*, as in both texts the author asserts that the name, which is visualized in the heart as an anthropos, is the way to the nameless, the infinite and boundless. Since every human body is experienced in a particular gendered embodiment, the imaginal body of God will similarly display gender characteristics. Indeed, as I already remarked, the depiction of God in overtly sexual images is a recurring and salient feature of kabbalistic poiesis.

Phallocentric Representation of Transcendence

Here it is appropriate for me to respond to a recurring misinterpretation of my understanding of sexual symbolism in kabbalistic sources, which I have argued stems from a phallocentric propensity. Several of my critics have contested that my approach smacks of psychoanalytic reductionism.[94] In the first instance, I would counter with the obvious and somewhat banal observation that matters germane to the study of religions (from a variety of methodological perspectives) cannot be treated in isolation from the psychological. Max Horkheimer astutely observed long ago: "Religion acquires all its content from the psychological processing of worldly events, but in the process it gains its own shape, a shape that acts in turn upon psychical capability and human destiny to form a unique factor that influences social development as a whole."[95] More recently, James Hillman has articulated a similar point from a slightly different perspective: "Psychology and theology need their inherent link, else theology loses soul and psychology forgets the Gods. . . . We may not divide psychology from theology any more than we may divide soul from spirit."[96]

Insofar as I, too, embrace the impossibility of such a division and thus affirm the intrinsic correlation of these two modules of consciousness, seeing them as complementary filters through which the thought rays of human imagination may be refracted, it follows that it is incorrect to apply the term "reductionist" to my thinking. On the contrary, I would contend that the perspective I articulate is expansionist in the extreme, as it extends the understanding of the erotic beyond the limited domain of psychosexual biography, which is focused typically on genital sexuality or any of its symbolic and somatic displacements.[97] It is apposite to evoke a comment of Freud offering a defense of his own use of the term "libido" to refer to the basic instinctual impulse expressed in various forms of love:

> By coming to this decision, psycho-analysis has let loose a storm of indignation, as though it had been guilty of an act of outrageous innovation. Yet it has done nothing original in taking love in this "wider" sense. In its origin, function, and relation to sexual love, the "Eros" of the philosopher Plato coincides exactly with the love-force, the libido of psycho-analysis . . . and when the apostle Paul, in his famous epistle to the Corinthians, praises love above all else, he certainly understands it in the same "wider" sense. But this only shows that men do not always take their great thinkers seriously, even when they profess most to admire them.[98]

It lies beyond the scope of this chapter to analyze properly Freud's assertion that the eros of Plato and Paul corresponds to the libido of psychoanalytic theory.[99] What is noteworthy, however, is that Freud genuinely believed that the libidinal instinct of which he spoke embraced a far wider range of meaning. My own appropriation of psychoanalytic categories is based similarly on an expansive rather than a restricted understanding of the relevant terminology.[100] In order to elucidate my position, I will refer once more[101] to a comment by Neumann relating to the use of overt sexual images in ancient Egyptian mythology: "To call such images 'obscene' is to be guilty of a profound misunderstanding. Actually . . . the sexual symbolism that appears in primitive cult and ritual has a sacral and transpersonal import, as everywhere in mythology. It symbolizes the creative element, not personal genitality. It is only personalistic misunderstanding that makes these sacral contents 'obscene.'"[102]

Neumann illustrates the point by noting that the "personal incarnation" of the Great Mother in the "particular woman" with whom the ritual copulation transpires, "is of no consequence. For the man she is a *kedesha*, a holy one (*kadosh* = holy),[103] the goddess who stirs up the deeper layers of his being in sexuality. Yoni and lingam, female and male, are two principles which come together beyond the person, in holiness, where the personal is shed away and remains insignificant."[104] In my judgment, Neumann's approach can be applied without distortion to the repeated use of sexual symbolism on the part of kabbalists, irrespective of the question of the ultimate truth value that one might assign to his analytic notion of individual consciousness passing through stages of archetypal development.[105] Implicit and explicit references to the divine genitals, and especially to the phallus, do not convey the attribution of a coarse body to God. To assume that to be the case reflects a modernist sensibility regarding the inappropriateness of using phallic or more generally erotic imagery to characterize spiritual matters.[106] George Ryley Scott expresses the point raised by Neumann in somewhat more direct terms:

> Much of the alleged obscenity associated with phallic worship has been, and is, due to the failure to consider the subject in relation to the moral and mental concepts actuating those who originated it. Almost without exception the modern critic views phallicism strictly in relation to twentieth-century moralistic and ethical ideals. In consequence, he promptly labels as an expression of obscenity every form which phallic worship assumed in the past.[107]

To assess erotic symbolism in classical kabbalistic sources, which I contend are overwhelmingly phallocentric, it is necessary to assimilate more fully my discussion of symbol as the primary means through which the form of divine embodiment inheres in human imagination. As I have labored long in previous studies to articulate, kabbalists by and large presume that images produced by the imagination are symbolic representations through which the invisible becomes visible and the inaudible audible. The imaginal figuration of God in human consciousness is always embodied, and consequently the content of the symbol is experienced (and not merely described postexperientially) in terms of the body. The symbol is a fusion of "opposite equals" (in Whitman's telling phrase)[108] held together in the sensible experience of transcendence that the symbol elicits.[109] The experience of transcendence irrupts ecstatically at the limit of the temporal horizon and is thus accessible only through a web of symbolic deflections; by nature, therefore, the symbol reveals and conceals concurrently.[110] What is envisioned in mystical enlightenment is experienced and interpreted in symbols drawn from our shared phenomenological sensibilities, but what we experience in the everyday world alludes semiotically to the imaginal world of poetic prisms.[111] The philosophic point has been well expressed by Aziz Esmail in a manner that relates precisely to the theme of this volume:

> When it is read without preconceptions, mystical literature often gives the impression of a fundamental ambiguity of meaning. This is especially true with regard to its erotic content. It is a commonplace that mystical poetry is often intensely sensual. This is usually explained by its exegetes and commentators—apologists, in fact—as a symbolic device. Because spiritual love, it is said, is impossible to put into words, the categories of human love are the best available means in which to depict the higher relationship. But this explanation is open to several objections. To begin with, there is no experience, other than a simple sensation, which is not mediated through language. . . . Moreover, symbolism cannot be reduced to a verbal artifice. . . . In this perspective, it is not only the sacred which is perceived in terms of the world; the world too is perceived, thanks to the power of metaphor, in terms of the

sacred. In regard to the conception of love in mystical literature, then, what this suggests is a simultaneous, indivisible perception of both worldly and spiritual eros.[112]

The form envisioned in contemplative practice is the primal Adam configured as the name YHWH, the mystical essence of Torah and hence of Hebrew language more generally.[113] That the root word is ineffable, the proper name *par excellence,* indicates that the matrix of all language—the originary word of poiesis—transcends language, but the spiritual reality contemplated in mystical enlightenment is nonetheless constructed symbolically through language; in the world of traditional kabbalists, there is no way beyond the word, for even that which is beyond the word is marked by the word that demarcates (no)thing beyond the word, the Tetragrammaton, the din of divine creativity, heard silently, the pure phoneme-grapheme signifying nothing but the intention to signify.[114]

Circumcision, Secrecy, Re/Veiling the Veil

As one might expect from a mystical path that emerges within a patriarchal culture that views the rite of circumcision as the supreme mark of ethnic identity,[115] an intricate connection between the male organ and secrecy would naturally arise.[116] In the case of traditional kabbalistic lore, hardly altered by changes in time or place and still promoted in some orthodox circles today, the phallic nature of esotericism is expressed in the elevation of the *membrum virile* to the focal point of the contemplative's visualizing the form of God's body, a theosophic point that found support in the widely held physiognomic assumption that the penis comprises the virility of the whole body.[117] However, given the kabbalistic understanding of the imaginal body as the incarnate form of YHWH, and, by extension, the correlation between the site of circumcision and the name,[118] it is more appropriate to speak of "phallus," a semiotic ascription, rather than "penis," a biological organ. By identifying the phallus as the veiled object of mystical vision, I have in mind the attribute of God, and its corresponding part in the body of the male Jew, that functions as the ultimate mark of signification. I am obviously indebted to the Lacanian notion of the phallus as signifier without a signified, although I have taken the liberty to reformulate it in terms of the symbolism embraced by kabbalists.[119]

The word "phallus" refers to an imaginary symbol, the "signifier of desire," rather than the physical organ.[120] This is not to suggest that there is no relationship whatsoever between the symbolic phallus and the biological penis in either Lacanian psychoanalytic theory or kabbalistic theosophy. The point is, rather, that the fascination with and emphasis placed on the *membrum virile* in both systems of thought (albeit in an obviously varied terminological register) lies in the fact that this organ serves as the semiotic marker that gives meaning to the other in the construction of the identity of the same, a position expressive of a "linguistic idealism" that makes it impossible to escape to a prelinguistic or extralinguistic dimension of existence that is not mediated by the necessarily linguistic interpretation of the subject.[121] In Lacan's own words: "For the phallus is . . . the signifier intended to designate as a whole the effects of the signified, in that the signifier conditions them by its presence as a signifier. . . . The phallus is the privileged signifier of that mark in which the role of the logos is joined with the advent of desire."[122] Addressing why one is to speak of the phallus and not the penis, Lacan remarked:

> Because the phallus is not a question of a form, or of an image, or of a phantasy, but rather of a signifier, the signifier of desire. In Greek antiquity the phallus is not represented by an organ but as an insignia; it is the ultimate significative object, which appears when all the veils are lifted. Everything related to it is an object of amputations and interdictions. . . . The phallus represents the intrusion of vital thrusting or growth as such, as what cannot enter the domain of the signifier without being *bared* from it, that is to say, covered over by castration.[123]

A succinct account of Lacan's notion of the phallus in contrast to the penis is given by Anika Lemaire: "The term 'Phallus,' as used by Lacan, is not to be confused with the real, biological sex, with what is called the penis. It is an abstract signifier, which, like any symbol, goes beyond its materiality and beyond what it represents."[124] Similarly, Ellie Ragland-Sullivan has written: "By 'phallic signifier' or Phallus, Lacan means the symbolic or representational agent of separation, and not the male sex organ per se. There is only an equivalence when gender identification is confused in language with the Oedipal drama. Language then attempts to describe the indescribable in reductionist terms of biology, archetypal myth, and the like."[125]

Let us heed Lacan's own words in the aforecited passage, "In Greek antiquity the phallus is not represented by an organ but as an insignia; it is the ultimate significative object, which appears when all the veils are lifted." But when all the veils are lifted, what does one see? Not the organ but an insignia, a sign to re/present the unrepresentable, an aesthetic judgment that is culturally determined, as Lacan's dependence on Greek antiquity clearly demonstrates. Unrepresentability itself must always be conditioned by representational forms configured in specific cultural contexts.[126]

The deployment of the notion of the phallic signifier to articulate the kabbalistic viewpoint regarding the object of visionary contemplation is also enhanced by the Lacanian assumption that the phallus can fulfill its function as signifier only when it is veiled. Lacan designates this veiling by the Hegelian term (mediated through Freud) *Aufhebung*,[127] that is, "uplifting," which denotes the dialectical raising-up and passing-over, preserving what is annulled and annulling what is preserved.[128] Lacan concludes, accordingly, that the phallus "can play its role only when veiled, that is to say, as itself a sign of the latency with which any signifiable is struck, when it is raised (*aufgehoben*) to the function of signifier. The phallus is the signifier of this *Aufhebung* itself, which it inaugurates (initiates) by its disappearance."[129] The uplifting of the veiling indicates that the phallus cannot signify the Other unless it were in the place of the Other, but to be in the place of the Other, it cannot be the Other except as Other to what it cannot be. The phallus is the "dimension that founds and mediates alterity,"[130] the "differential mark of sexual identification"[131]—maleness determined by possession and femininity by lack thereof[132]—and thus it is only through the phallus that the subject comes to recognize desire for the Other.

The narcissistic character of this phallocentrism (to be discussed more fully below) is expressed by the fact that desire for the Other is located in the subject who discerns that he is "divided by the signifying *Spaltung*,"[133] that is, the splitting of the phallus/signifier in constituting the identity of sexual difference. The phallocentric implications are unabashedly affirmed by Lacan when he notes that "in order to be the phallus, that is to say, the signifier of the desire of the Other . . . a woman will reject an essential part of femininity, namely, all her attributes in the masquerade. It is for that which she is not that she wishes to be desired as well as loved."[134] In another essay, Lacan offers a semiotic demarcation of the phallocentric pattern in his account of the (il)legitimacy of inscripting the expression *la femme*:

> The woman can only be written with *The* crossed through. There is no such thing as *The* woman, where the definite article stands for the universal. There is no such thing as *The* woman since of her essence . . . she is not all.[135] . . . There is woman only as excluded by the nature of things which is the nature of words. . . . It none the less remains that if she is excluded by the nature of things, it is precisely that in being not all, she has, in relation to what the phallic function designates of *jouissance*, a supplementary *jouissance*.[136]

Various exponents of Lacanian theory have noted that *jouissance* is correlated with the feminine side of the sexualized body, denoting the surplus of desire that cannot be circumscribed within the confines of phallomorphic signification, a "something more," the "supplement," that is related to the phenomenon of "mystical ejaculations."[137] As Slavoj Žižek put it, the "feminine resistance to symbolic identification" in Lacanian thought is not due to the "effect of a preexistent feminine substance opposing symbolization." The re/marking of woman as "not-all," the refusal of the feminine to be integrated into the symbolic order of the phallic signifier, ascribes to the female the status of the "nonexistent 'nothing' which nonetheless makes the existing elements 'not-all.'" The "not-all" is the Limit that introduces "a gap into the fullness of being" and thus assumes "logical priority" to the All: "From this perspective, the seemingly misogynist definition of woman as truncated man actually asserts her ontological priority: her 'place' is that of a gap, of an abyss rendered invisible the moment 'man' fills it out." Woman is defined as negativity or lack, but this is a positive classification implying that "she is the Limit, the abyss, retroactively filled out by the mirage of soul," which is associated with man who is thought to possess the noumenal soul beyond his phenomenal, bodily existence. The "masculine" denotes "the universal network of causes and effects founded in an exception," whereas the "feminine" denotes "the universe of boundless dispersion and divisibility which, for that very reason, can never be rounded off into a universal Whole."[138] In a reversal of traditional metaphysics, the nonsubstantial void, that which has no positive ontological consistency of its own, the imperfect female, is the cause of the reified substance, thematized as *res cogitans*, the "thinking substance" beyond the material substratum of the extended body, the perfect male.

Others have argued, however, that, in spite of ascribing to the feminine the quality of "not-all," the mystical experience of the boundless espoused by Lacan is a form of "phallic monism"[139] that excludes women on grounds that psychosexual identity, inseparably entwined with the dynamic of gender, is still defined from the standpoint of (dis)possessing the phallus.[140] Here again we must underscore that phallus denotes symbolic signifier and not bodily penis. Bearing that in mind, the exclusion of women must itself be viewed as linguistic in nature; that is, the phallic definition of gender poses woman as the taxonomic exception, the "not" that she is vis-à-vis the male. To be sure, the linguistic turn imparts a degree of indeterminacy, inasmuch as one's gender is not determined solely by anatomical facticity.[141] This sense of indeterminacy notwithstanding, for Lacan the phallus remains the axis of desire and consequently the locus of the dyad whence the fundamental splitting of subjectivity ensues, a structure of thought that I find quite compatible with the engendering myth of the androgynous phallus in the kabbalistic tradition, which I will discuss in detail in the following chapter. The nonphallic enjoyment, therefore, must be seen as an integral feature of phallic signification. Just as the ultimate signifier, the "signifier that represents the subject for all other signifiers," is the "signifier of the lack of the signifier," so the phallus symbolically is a sign that coincides with its own impossibility inasmuch as it embodies the representation of the nonrepresentational. Accordingly, the phallus signifies the signification of the feminine lacking signifier. In this respect, we can speak of the contours of a masculine, mystical subjectivity along the lines affirmed by Lacan.[142]

There is another aspect of Lacan's thought that manifests a striking similarity to, or at the very least can be helpful in articulating, a key feature of the phallic symbolism that has dominated the kabbalistic landscape. To uncover this dimension, we must attend Lacan's insistence that the sexuation of the subject is based primarily on the absence of the (phallic) signifier occasioned in theory by the child's fear of castration, a fear that is linked originarily with the phallus that the mother lacks, the imaginary object of desire whose symbolic valence ensues from the recognition that desire so construed cannot be satisfied.[143] We have already remarked that the phallus assumes its signifying function precisely when it disappears, that is, the signifier that demarcates presence must itself be absent.[144] The ultimate expression of this occlusion is castration. As Lacan puts it, "man is but a signifier because where he comes into play as a signifier, he comes in only *quoad castrationem*, in other words, insofar as he has a relation to phallic *jouissance*."[145] In an astonishing dialectical twist, phallic *jouissance* is linked to symbolic castration, which is the precondition for man's assuming his role as the signifier that marks the boundary of self and other. I assume this is what Lacan intends when he writes that "short of castration, that is, short of something which says no to the phallic function, man has no chance of enjoying the body of the woman, in other words, of making love."[146] Reversing what one would expect, heterosexual lovemaking, which Lacan identifies as a form of poetry,[147] is made dependent on castration, the abnegation of phallic potency.

It follows, then, that the phallus is a "symbolic organ defined by negation" since "we first become aware of it through the sense of castration. . . . The phallus, a presence that cannot exist without implying absence, is invisible in its fully realized state."[148] For Lacan, castration is related to the "signifying hole" or the "hole of the signifier," which is the "radiating center," the delineation of sexual difference determined by the "presence/absence of the penis."[149] Simply put, the phallus is the de/cisive signifier that cannot be specularized; hence it is most adequately represented by the minus sign, a marker of the absence that is present in the presence of its absence.[150] Inasmuch as the phallus is the signification that marks "empty space," it "transforms the organ of pleasure into a sign of a lack" and thereby embodies the law that "forces renunciation."[151] As Žižek reminds the reader, "When Lacan speaks of 'phallic *jouissance*,' we should always bear in mind that the phallus is the signifier of castration—phallic *jouissance* is therefore *jouissance* under the condition of symbolic castration that opens up and sustains the space of desire."[152]

Remarkably, a similar confluence of themes is found in the complex symbolism repeated often in kabbalistic literature. The focal point of mystical seeing is the sign that must be kept out of sight, the ninth emanation in the divine pleroma that corresponds to the phallic potency, in the words of Vital, the "aspect of *Yesod*, which is a hidden and concealed place."[153] Numerous texts could be cited in support of the idea that the gradation of the divine that corresponds most precisely to secrecy is *Yesod*, but here I shall limit myself to a few examples. In one zoharic passage, which is part of the *yanuqa* stratum, the matter is expressed in an exposition of Jacob's blessings bestowed on Ephraim and Menasseh, sons of Joseph, before his demise (Gen. 48:8–20):

> What is written above? "He blessed Joseph and said" (Gen. 48:15), yet we do not find blessings to him here, for only afterwards does he bless him, as it is written, "Joseph is a fruitful bough" (Gen. 49:22). Rather, when he blessed these two lads, he blessed Joseph, for they could not be blessed except through Joseph, but since he is occluded and he is not phenomenalizable, it is written surreptitiously [*mi-go de-ihu vi-ṭemiru we-lo itḥazei le᾽itggalla᾽ah khetiv bi-ṭemiru*], "In them may my name be recalled, and the names of my fathers" (Gen. 48:16). From the fathers they were placed, and from no other place. "In the midst of the earth"—this is the covering [*kissuya*] to cover what is necessary.[154]

There is much to mine from this passage, but I will focus on the issue at hand, the locus of secrecy in the phallic potency of the divine and its reverberations for understanding the workings of the fraternity dedicated to the exposure and concealment of secrets. Joseph, known as the righteous one, corresponds symbolically to *Yesod*, the place that is "occluded" and "not phenomenalizable." Concealment is linked in a special way to this attribute. We learn more of this occlusion in the interpretation of "in the midst of the earth" in the conclusion of the citation: the moment of blessing proceeds from the union of male and female when the phallus is sheltered in and veiled by the female receptacle in which it is implanted.

In another zoharic passage, we read, "The holy One, blessed be he, is concealed and revealed; the revealed is the house of judgment below and the concealed is the place whence all blessings disseminate."[155] The "house of judgment below" refers to *Shekhinah* and the "place whence all blessings disseminate," to *Yesod*. The aspect of disclosure is thus linked symbolically with the feminine, and that of secrecy with the masculine. In the continuation of the passage, a moral maxim is derived from the ontological correspondence: blessings rest upon the one whose words are secretive (*bi-setimu*), since concealment is linked to the wellspring of blessing, whereas the evil eye is cast upon one who is not discrete, since disclosure is linked to the place of judgment. Here one may detect an allusion to the method adopted by the *maskilim* of the zoharic fraternity: to reveal by way of concealing, to maintain the secrecy so that the secret is hidden in the secret that is exposed.

Secrecy is tied, first and foremost, to the interpretative gesture that is associated with the phallic potency; the mystery relates to and is revealed through the holy seal inscripted on the flesh, the covenant of circumcision.[156] The point is enunciated succinctly in *Tiqqunei Zohar*, a section that belongs to the later strata of zoharic literature: "The upper waters are the Written Torah, the lower waters the Oral Torah, and the thread that is between them is *Yesod*, which is the mystery of Torah" (*raza de-orayyta*).[157] Utilizing an older cosmological motif preserved in rabbinic literature,[158] the author of this comment correlates the Written Torah and Oral Torah respectively with the upper and lower waters, which are gendered as masculine and feminine,[159] and the thread that connects them is *Yesod*, the phallic potency, which is the site of mystery; the secret, therefore, is the hermeneutic bridge that binds text and interpretation.

To be more precise, the dimension of God that is, paradoxically, present in its absence is the corona of the phallus (*aṭeret yesod*). So prevalent is this idea, what I would call a ground concept of the tradition, that I could easily fill a chapter citing pertinent passages that illustrate the point, but the immediate concerns of this chapter call for self-restraint, so I will adduce as proof a second passage from Vital: "*Yesod* is the aspect that is appropriate to hide and to conceal, and on account of his glory, blessed be he, they did not publicize it but only explained its place, which is beneath his feet.[160] *Yesod* itself is composed of male and female in the secret of the phallus [*yesod*] and the corona [*aṭarah*] that is in him."[161] *Yesod* thus exemplifies a dual nature: it is disclosed as the locus of concealment, a disclosure, perforce, that preserves the concealment of what is disclosed.

The phallic gradation of the divine embodies what I have termed "hermeneutical duplicity"—for the secret to be secretive, it must be hidden in its exposure, exposed in its being hidden. The duplicity is engendered by kabbalists in a hierarchical way that we would expect from an androcentric and at times misogynist culture: hiddenness, the more inward and consequently more valuable, is rendered as masculine, and exposure, the more outward and consequently less valuable, as feminine. But how is the phallus engendered as both male and female? The male is the shaft of the penis (*yesod*) and the female the corona (*aṭarah*). As Isaac of Acre articulates the matter, "You already know that the secret of circumcision [*sod ha-milah*] alludes to *Ṣaddiq* . . . and the corona that is revealed through the excision of the foreskin alludes to *Aṭarah*."[162] The identification of the corona—what I have steadfastly referred to as the feminine element of the androgynous phallus[163]—as the locus of contemplative envisioning can be well expressed by the Lacanian dialectic of the signifier that is veiled in the unveiling of the veil,[164] that is, the object of mystical vision is the phallic sign manifest in the exposure of its hiddenness.

Here it is incumbent to note that in kabbalistic lore the genitals of a woman are also portrayed as hidden, an idea that is linked to the pietistic virtue of modesty promulgated in classical rabbinic literature, which demands of women that they conceal themselves from the phallic gaze,[165] an attitude informed by a long-standing exegetical association of the feminine and interiority, which in turn fostered the symbolic representation of women in tropes that denote sheltering as well as the disproportional allocation of domestic responsibilities to the mother of a household.[166] This metaphorical depiction underlies the zoharic idiom of "fixing the house" applied to the woman when she prepares herself to be the abode to receive the seminal fluid of the male donor.[167] The vagina is thus referred to figuratively as the "holy of holies," the most interior space of the Temple complex wherein the ineffable name was pronounced by the high priest on Yom Kippur, the most solemn day on the Jewish calendar. On account of the kabbalists' belief in the natural propensity of the female to be seductive, women are bridled with the virtue of modesty and implored to stay inside, to prepare the house for the entry of the man, and not to flaunt a public display of sensuality or erotic enticement. The moral standard is affirmed by the zoharic author: "Come and see: In every place, the man chases after the woman and he arouses love in relation to her . . . and the way of the world is such that it is not praiseworthy for a woman to chase after the man."[168]

Without ignoring or downplaying the intertextual links that connect the kabbalists to their rabbinic ancestors, it is worthwhile considering that the approach of kabbalists in this matter accords well with the stance toward the female body propagated in medieval society, based on tropes that stretch back to antiquity, and especially the connection that is drawn between chastity and the occlusion or enclosure of the woman in a domicile setting.[169] The theme of secrecy associated with female genitalia in zoharic and other kabbalistic literature should be seen against the background of the accentuated gynecological use of the concept of secret to refer to women's private parts and diseases related thereto beginning in Europe in the twelfth century.[170] Monica Green, who has studied this phenomenon in detail, astutely notes that this semantic shift may have been due in part to the fact that men were "presumed to constitute the principal audience for gynecological literature . . . and it is therefore men's perspective on women's bodies that renders the topic 'secret.'"[171] I submit that one can apply these words without qualification to the symbolic representations of the secrecy of women, especially in the portrayal of the genitals, in kabbalistic literature, informed, as it was, by contemporary philosophic, scientific, and medical discourse. In the last analysis, it is a matter of men's perspective on women and the anatomical generalities they presumed to be in order that is reflected in their construction of femininity, a construction that bolstered misogynist structures of traditional authority that empowered men and impaired women.

The eidetic structure of the cloaked phallus as the object of contemplative vision is based, therefore, on a presumption regarding the dissimilitude of esotericism: What is revealed is disclosed in its concealment, for what is concealed is hidden in its disclosure. The hermeneutical disposition is conveyed in an especially poignant way by the ritual of circumcision, for the sign of this covenant is made by way of a cut, the marking imprinted by removing the foreskin.[172] In language that is remarkably suitable to the symbolism of traditional kabbalah, Irigaray observed that circumcision, which she calls the "Jewish operation" in contrast to castration,[173] "lies in the realm of the sign. What is cut away is only cut away in order to make a sign. . . . But almost the reverse of castrating, this excision is what marks the body's entry into the world of signs."[174]

Given the centrality of the covenant of circumcision as the primary marker of ethnic identity in rabbinic Judaism (based in great measure on the priestly precedent), it should come as no surprise that kabbalists would interpret this ceremonial *rite de passage* as the paradigm for an esoteric hermeneutic, that is, a hermeneutic based on the unmasking of the mystery that is concealed. Significantly, we recall that in one midrashic context, circumcision is referred to as the secret (*sod*) or mystery (*mistorin*) that God revealed exclusively to Israel, an idea related exegetically to "The secret of the Lord is for those who fear him; to them he makes his covenant known" (Ps. 25:14).[175] The intricate correlation between circumcision and the enigmatic elaborated by kabbalists unquestionably derived in part from this earlier source.

Beyond this association, however, the link between circumcision, secrecy, and concealment in kabbalistic tradition can be viewed as an embellishment of the rabbinic emphasis on the need to conceal the circumcised penis, an aspect of the etiquette of modesty (*ṣeniᶜut*) required of the Jewish male.[176] Symbolically, for kabbalists, circumcision embodies the hermeneutical play of secrecy, which rests on the presumption that the wisdom that encompasses a hidden mystery (*ṣeniᶜuta*) will be disclosed exclusively to the humble (*ṣenuᶜin*), for they know the art of concealing the concealment in disclosing the disclosure.[177] This art is linked uniquely to circumcision, the sacrament through which the Jew enacts the role of dissimulation by cutting away the foreskin to create the sign, the presence that is re/presented through its own absence.[178] The nexus between contemplative envisioning and circumcision,[179] which is an intricate elaboration of a theme expressed in rabbinic sources in conjunction with attempts to explain the change effected in Abraham's visionary status as a result of being circumcised,[180] underscores the extent to which the ocular desire on the part of medieval kabbalists, in line with the prophetic call of ancient Israel, entailed a "rhetoric of obscuration," the "juxtaposition of revelation and concealment," that allows one access to the "inaccessible dimension" whereby the other's presence is experienced as the other that is absent.[181]

The paradox is fully expressed in the insistence on the part of kabbalists that it is forbidden to gaze on the phallus (or, more precisely, the corona) that is laid bare.[182] In the disclosure is the concealment, for the inscripting of the sign occasions the erasure of the name that cannot be written.[183] Moreover, the cut of circumcision relates symbolically to the ascetic abrogation of sexual desire,[184] which is understood by kabbalists as an expression of phallic *jouissance*, the yearning to project, to overflow, to come to rest in the shelter of the feminine other. Expressed in psychoanalytic terms, the adaptation of sexual asceticism on the part of kabbalists is a feature of the construction of self rooted in or reflective of the primal narcissistic impulse to extend phallically into space, to be contained in and encircled by the veil of absence.[185] The psychological drive may be viewed as an application of the structure of theosophic myth or, alternatively, the structure of theosophic myth may be viewed as an application of the psychological drive. From my perspective the psychological and theosophic are distinguishable but not detachable. The prominent part accorded the ascetic denial of sensual pleasure is thus related dialectically to the phallomorphism that has informed the mythical theosophy adopted by kabbalists: abstaining from carnal sexuality strengthens male virility.[186] As Lacan himself noted, the yearning not to ejaculate, which is linked thematically to the wish not to think, should be understood as the desire not to want to desire.

> Who does not know from experience that it is possible not to want to ejaculate? Who does not know from experience, knowing the recoil imposed on everyone, in so far as it involves terrible promises, by the approach of *jouissance* as such? Who does not know that one may not wish to think?—the entire universal college of professors is there as evidence.
> But what does *not wanting to desire* mean? The whole of analytic experience—which merely gives form to what is for each individual at the very root of his experience—shows us that not to want to desire and to desire are the same thing.[187]

Lacan's analysis of *jouissance* as the renunciation that is beyond phallic desire but is nonetheless an expression of it can be applied heuristically to explain the complex nexus of asceticism and eroticism in kabbalistic wisdom. In particular, the image of the eunuch (to be discussed in greater detail in chapter seven) is utilized by kabbalists as a self-referential term to demarcate the phallic empowerment of ascetic abjuration, an empowerment that supplants immediate gratification of physical pleasure with deferral of psychic *jouissance*, a castration of the penis to erect the phallus.[188] Mary Daly's comment that Christian sublimation of sensuality has been a "phallic flight from lust into lustful asceticism"[189] applies equally well to the sexual renunciation that is part and parcel of the meditation discipline preached by kabbalists. Adopting the felicitous expression of Margaret Miles, we may associate asceticism in kabbalistic tradition with the "pleasure of no pleasure,"[190] provided we bear in mind the phallic measure of this pleasure.

Naturally, when I write of the phallocentric nature of the visionary gaze in Jewish mysticism, I do not intend to say, as one critic crudely put it, that these mystics desired to partake in a "cosmic sex show."[191] A grosser misrepresentation of my position is hardly imaginable. The same critic has protested against my thesis by arguing that "one could easily make a case that the goal of Jewish mysticism was to achieve Divine enlightenment and that visualizing the Divine Face would promote this end," but "it is not at all clear what is served by imaging the Divine phallus."[192] Leaving aside for the moment the distinct possibility (indeed, I would contend, likelihood) that the face itself can and does function in these very texts as a euphemism or symbolic displacement for the phallus,[193] one could counter that the opposition implied in this remark between enlightenment that comes by way of seeing the face, on the one hand, and vision of the phallus, on the other, reflects a complete lack of understanding on the part of this reader of my use of erotic symbolism to characterize the nature of mystical experience fostered by study of the traditions transmitted by kabbalists. As I noted above, the term "phallus" in my presentation of kabbalistic gnosis represents the imaginary signifier, which cannot be reduced to the biological organ, although I would not sever entirely the relationship between the symbolic and the somatic. The use of pornographic language to characterize my thesis reflects a basic confusion of phallus and penis that results in imparting to me a reductionist stance. In my understanding of the tradition, to behold the phallus is to take hold of the name. There is no embodiment to speak of that is not semiotic.

My insistence that the corona of the phallus (*aṭeret berit*) is the object of vision rests on the assumption that the primary site of mystical enlightenment (*haskalah*) is the crowning visage of the anatomical part that represents the creative potency of God.[194] Support for this conjecture is attested in countless sources, but for our immediate concern I will cite one especially vivid passage from Jacob Ṣemaḥ, disciple of Vital:

> When the sign of the covenant [*ot ha-berit*], the foundation and governance of the worlds [*qiyyum we-hanhagat ha-olamot*], is garbed in the shells [*qelippot*], this instructs about governance firm in its judgments [*ha-hanhagah ha-qashah be-dineiha*] . . . when he is garbed in the holy gradations, that is, the secret of the feminine [*sod ha-neqevah*], then is the rectification of the world [*tiqqun ha-olam*], and his opening to overflow [*petiḥato lehashpiʿa*]. . . . There are two shells that garb, the foreskin [*orlah*] and pulling back the membrane [*periʿah*]. . . . Samael and Lilith, that is, the other gods [*elohim aḥerim*], and the face of *Shekhinah* is the sign of the covenant [*ot berit*], the *yod* of governance [*ha-hanhagah*]. With regard to this it says, "You should have no other gods before me" (Exod. 20:3), that is, the shells that cover the covenant.[195]

To see the face of *Shekhinah* is to gaze on the sign of the covenant, the *yod* inscribed on the phallus in the act of circumcision, also identified as the corona exposed when the coverings are removed like the rainbow in the sky.[196] I note in passing that this text confirms the analysis I offered in chapter two regarding the gender valence of divine providence in this world; the name *malkhut*, which is applied to *Shekhinah*, denotes her capacity to overflow and sustain the beings of the cosmos, an attribute that is linked to the sign of the covenant, the *yod*, which is the corona of the phallus (*aṭeret berit*). As I have argued at length in previous studies, zoharic kabbalah in particular imparts central importance to this eidetic structure.[197] Hence the key verse that informed the experiential framework of the circle of kabbalists whence this literature disseminated, "And the enlightened will shine with the splendor of the sky" (*we-ha-maskilim yazhiru ke-zohar ha-raqiʿa*; Dan. 12:3), is interpreted in decisively phallomorphic terms.

The ecstatic experience of imaginary symbol-making, which in turn intensifies the ecstasy, is depicted particularly as the luminosity of the splendor (*zohar*), which refers either to the aspect of the head that corresponds functionally to what we may legitimately call the supernal phallus (designated by the technical locution *boṣina de-qardinuta*, which I translate as "hardened spark") or to the aspect that occupies the position of the phallus in the midsection of the body, the ninth of the ten emanations, *Yesod*, the foundational spring that gathers the energy of the body as a whole.[198] In either case, the attribute of God that is contemplated and visualized is the phallic potency in its upper or lower manifestation, a potency that encompasses within itself the totality of the imaginal body of the divine, the anthropomorphic configuration of the power of the name YHWH. Thus only one who is circumcised can study Torah, for Torah is the name, and the circumcised male Jew alone possesses the sign to cleave to the name.[199]

The contextualization of sefirotic illumination in the phallic gradation is well captured in the following remark of Gikatilla, commenting on the attribution of the biblical expression *sekhel ṭov*, "good insight" (Ps. 111:10), to *Yesod*, designated by the divine name *el ḥai*, the "living God" (derived from Ps. 42:3):

> On occasion this attribute is called *sekhel ṭov*, for from this attribute a person enters the speculum that shines, and by means of the attribute *el ḥai* a person contemplates [*yaskil*] a way to enter, to know, to comprehend, and to become wise in the truth of the Lord, blessed be he. And this attribute, which is called *sekhel ṭov*, stands with the person when he fulfills the Torah and the commandments. The sign [of the matter]: "The beginning of wisdom is the fear of the Lord, good insight to those who practice it" [*re'shit ḥokhmah yir'at yhwh sekhel ṭov le-khol oseihem*] (Ps. 111:10). The great secret is: "The one who contemplates a matter will find success" [*maskil al davar yimṣa ṭov*] (Prov. 16:20). Since David, may peace be upon him, was conjoined to this attribute, he would say, "with respect to David there was contemplation" [*le-dawid maskil*][200] (Ps. 32:1), for every expression [related to] *maskil* is dependent on this place. . . . Know that there is a difference between the one who contemplates [*maskil*] and the one who understands [*mevin*], for the secret of the one who understands is from the emanation of the source of understanding [*hamshakhat meqor binah*] and the one who contemplates is from the emanation of the good [*hamshakhat ha-ṭov*], the beginning and the end.[201]

The phallic gradation of the divine is here called *sekhel ṭov* for it is the locus of contemplation. The kabbalist who contemplates the imaginal form of God through the prism of the sefirotic emanations is conjoined to this particular attribute in the manner of the figure of David who stands symbolically for *Shekhinah*, the tenth attribute, which is the feminine complement of *Yesod*. That is, just as *Shekhinah* (symbolically incarnate in David) is enlightened by means of being conjoined to *Yesod*, so the kabbalist visionary is illumined through cleaving to this potency. Moreover, contemplation is contrasted with understanding, the former linked to *Yesod*, the ninth gradation, and the latter to *Binah*, the third gradation. The one who understands has access to the beginning of the overflow of divine beneficence in the womb of the great mother, the attribute of *Binah*, whereas the one who contemplates is focused on the end of the overflow, the head of the spout, which is located in *Yesod*, the foundation.

Much like the authors of the *Zohar*, but without utilizing technical theosophical imagery, Gikatilla assumes that the aspect that corresponds to the phallus relates to the creative energy of the divine, the garbing of the imageless in the image of the name YHWH, the Torah in its mystical essence. Basic to Gikatilla's kabbalah is the identification of Torah and God, which he expressed in the image of Torah as a text woven from the names of God, which all derive from the Tetragrammaton, the trunk of the tree that encompasses the totality of sefirotic potencies.[202] So complete is this identity of God and Torah that Gikatilla speaks of the infinity of the one as parallel to the infinity of the other.[203]

Appropriating further the symbolic identification of Torah and covenant, which is implied in any number of classical rabbinic sources,[204] Gikatilla locates the source of the former in the latter. Thus, in one passage,[205] he distinguishes three kinds of covenant and their corresponding gradations in the divine pleroma: (a) The covenant of *Binah* described as the covenant of the mouth, the covenant of the tongue, and the covenant of the lips (*berit ha-peh u-verit ha-lashon u-verit ha-sefatayim*); (b) the covenant of the living God (*berit el ḥai*), the attribute of *Yesod*, linked to the covenant of circumcision (*berit milah*), which is also identified as the covenant of peace (*berit shalom*), the covenant of the rainbow (*berit ha-qeshet*) and the covenant of Sabbath (*berit shabbat*); and (c) the covenant of the master (*berit adonai*), the tenth gradation, *Shekhinah* or *Malkhut*, which is the covenant of Torah (*berit ha-torah*). Gikatilla relates to the androgynous nature of the latter by emphasizing that the covenant of Torah mediates between *Yesod* and *Malkhut*, male and female. This element is at play as well in Gikatilla's remark that the covenant of Torah comprises the dual Torah of rabbinic thought: the masculine potency is linked to Written Torah and the feminine to Oral Torah, an idea already attested in *Sefer ha-Bahir.*[206]

In chapter four, I shall have the opportunity to reflect in more detail on the understanding of androgyny displayed by kabbalistic authors. At the moment it is sufficient to note that the notion of androgyny operative here is predicated on the androcentric presumption regarding the ontological derivation of the female from the male organ. Hence in the continuation of the passage, Gikatilla notes that when *Malkhut* is conjoined to *Yesod* and *Binah*, she is referred to by the expressions derived from *Sefer Yeṣirah*, "covenant of the foreskin" (*berit ha-maʿor*) and "covenant of the tongue" (*berit ha-lashon*). The latter is identified more precisely as the "secret of Torah that derives from *Binah*,"[207] but since the Israelite males would not have received the Torah had they not been circumcised, the covenant of the tongue is intertwined with the covenant of the foreskin. Alternatively, the covenant of the tongue is interpreted phallically, which is predicated on the further assumption that the covenant of the foreskin is interpreted semiotically. What is real about the phallus points upward to the tongue, and what is real about the tongue points downward to the phallus, for revelation of Torah is justified by circumcision of the flesh and circumcision of the flesh by revelation of Torah. As Gikatilla's mentor, Abraham Abulafia, put the matter in *Oṣar Eden Ganuz*:

> Therefore, you must strive to discern the matter of the secret of the covenant of circumcision and the secret of the covenant of the tongue, which are two matters. The covenant of circumcision instructs about the human being who was uncircumcised at birth and by all accounts he must be circumcised. The covenant of the tongue also alludes to the fact that he was uncircumcised and he had to be circumcised. Thus these two covenants comprise Abraham and Moses. The father who brings into being the body is Abraham, from the organ, and the master that produces speech is Moses and this is the name. Accordingly, Abraham our patriarch and Moses our master were both pillars of the world. Analogously, the organ brings us to this world and the tongue will bring us to life in the world-to-come.[208]

Abraham and Moses correspond respectively to the two covenants delineated in *Sefer Yeṣirah*, the covenant of the phallus and the covenant of the tongue, for the letters of *avraham* can be transposed into *meha-ever* (from the organ), which refers to the penis, and the letters of *mosheh* can be transposed into *ha-shem* (the name),[209] which is YHWH.[210] The covenant of the tongue, which is the name, that is, the root word that comprises all twenty-two letters of the Hebrew alphabet or the Torah in its mystical essence, is transmitted only to one circumcised in the flesh:[211]

> Thus it was appropriate to decree for us the covenant of circumcision [*berit milah*] whose secret is the four beasts [*arba ḥayyot*], for our essence is from them, and the covenant is decreed in the form of the warp and woof [*sheti wa-erev*]. The law is to cut this physical penis [*ha-berit ha-gufanit*] and to cleave to the spiritual [*ruḥanit*] from it, which is knowledge of the name [*yediʿat ha-shem*], for it is not possible for the name to be revealed until they appropriate his ways in the warp and woof, and this is "they made the covenant" [*berit asu*], that is, if a man does not know the act of God, he does not know him. How does one know him? Through the covenant of the sacred language.[212]

On the basis of these texts and countless others that could have been cited, one can speak legitimately of the phallomorphic nature of the covenant of Torah, for the latter is localized ontically in the phallic gradation. This principle, based on the unequivocal language of *Sefer Yeṣirah*, is seemingly shared by all traditional kabbalists. What is especially worthy of our attention is the fact that the phallus is depicted as the site of androgyny in the divine anthropos. Gikatilla reiterates this view when he sets out to explain the androgynous nature of the covenant of circumcision, which is the secret of Sabbath:

> Know that the covenant of circumcision is the secret of Sabbath, in the secret of cutting [the foreskin] [*milah*] and exposing [the corona] [*periʿah*], in the secret of "Remember [*zakhor*] the day of Sabbath" (Exod. 20:8) and "Guard [*shamor*] [the day of Sabbath]" (Deut. 5:12), "remember" for the day and "guard" for the night, corresponding to El Ḥai and Adonai. Since the covenant of circumcision comprises the covenant of these two *sefirot*, Scripture said, "Had it not been for my covenant day and night, I would not have established the laws of heaven and earth" (Jer. 33:25). . . . Know that the covenant, which is called day and night, is the secret of *milah* and *periʿah, zakhor* and *shamor*, El Ḥai and Adonai, the Written Torah and the Oral Torah, for they are the laws of heaven and earth, the one corresponding to the other. This is the secret of "Meditate on his Torah day and night" (Ps. 1:2), the day is the Written Torah, the secret of El Ḥai, the secret of *zakhor*, the secret of *milah*, and night is the secret of the Oral Torah, the secret of Adonai, the secret of *shamor*, the secret of *periʿah*. Therefore, the Torah is transmitted only to one who received the covenant of the flesh [*berit basar*], for through the covenant of the flesh one enters the covenant of the tongue [*berit ha-lashon*], which is the reading of the Torah.[213]

In the continuation of the passage, Gikatilla completes his train of thought by elaborating on the connection between the Tetragrammaton, the covenant of the tongue (Torah), and the covenant of the foreskin (circumcision). Through the sealing of the name on the flesh as a consequence of the rite of circumcision, the body is worthy of receiving the words of the covenant of the mouth and tongue. "All is contained in the covenant of circumcision,"[214] writes Gikatilla, for it is the locus of the male and female, Written and

Oral Torah. The phallus, therefore, is a symbol that not only depicts most emphatically the potency of God in biological terms but is the signifier whose absent presence (which may be expressed phenomenally as the veiled disclosure) makes all other significations possible within the linguistic matrix of a particular cultural formation.

To put the matter in the psychoanalytic terms of Neumann, discussed above, the application of phallic images to the divine in Jewish mysticism, especially conspicuous in medieval kabbalistic sources, is meant to convey the creative aspect of God in a transpersonal way, which he presumed to be characteristic of the mythological consciousness more generally. As Neumann reminds us in another context, the "primordial image," which he also identifies as the "archetype," refers "not to any concrete image existing in space and time, but to an inward image at work in the human psyche."[215]

To be sure, Neumann's terminology, "inward image," bespeaks the dualist perspective typically assumed by referentialist representationalism, which is characteristic of logocentric epistemologies that have labored under the weight of the metaphysics of presence: the subject, it is presumed, stands over and against objective reality represented in the reflective gaze.[216] My appropriation of Neumann's term is predicated on the qualification that the notion of inwardness is not taken in the representationalist vein to imply an external form that is the objective correlate to the subjective image, which is the mental picture or idea. On the contrary, the notion of symbolic form that I have employed to interpret the kabbalistic sources seeks to overcome the epistemic binaries reified by the rational discourse of modernism: real versus imagined, somatic versus psychic, external versus internal, experienced versus interpreted.

I assume that the construction of myth in the guise of the imaginal symbol is a unitary consciousness that transcends the dualism of inside and outside, subjective and objective. Representation, therefore, is not simply the mimetic reflection of the object in the mirror of consciousness; it entails rather a performative act that brings forth that which was not given and thereby facilitates the reciprocal configuration of self in the world and of world in the self.[217] In line with current trends of epistemological inquiry, therefore, I embrace the move from a reflexive to a constitutive understanding of knowledge and the formation of human experience. With that qualification in place, we can appropriate Neumann's language in the effort to account for the phallocentricism ubiquitously attested in kabbalistic sources. For kabbalists, this inclination is encapsulated most comprehensively in the sacrament of circumcision, the enforced incision of the covenantal inscription. The traditional rite thus serves as a symbol for the mystical experience par excellence insofar as it embodies the dialectic of concealment and disclosure as well as the paradoxical affirmation of phallic desire through its abnegation.

CHAPTER FOUR

Male Androgyne: Engendering E/Masculation

There is no time for any thing but the torments of love & desire
The Feminine & Masculine Shadows soft, mild & ever varying
In beauty: are Shadows now no more, but Rocks in Horeb
Then all the Males combined into One Male & every one
Became a ravening eating Cancer growing in the Female
A Polypus of Roots of Reasoning Doubt Despair & Death.

—William Blake, "Jerusalem"

Engendering God in Ancient-Throne Mysticism

As a number of biblicists and historians of religion have noted, the monotheistic ideal that evolved in ancient Israel was inextricably bound to the patriarchal rejection of the female element within the divine. Raphael Pattai observed in the introduction to his monographic study on the *Hebrew Goddess*, "In view of the general human, psychologically determined predisposition to believe in and worship goddesses, it would be strange if the Hebrew-Jewish religion, which flourished for centuries in a region of intensive goddess cults, had remained immune to them. Yet this precisely is the picture one gets when one views Hebrew religion through the polarizing prisms of Mosaic legislation and prophetic teaching."[1] Pattai goes on to qualify this perception by noting that adoration of the feminine continued to play an important role in the history of Judaism in spite of the official stance restricting cultic worship to the one God of Israel portrayed in exclusively masculine terms.

Even if one were to quibble with Pattai's psychological orientation, one would be hard-pressed to deny that monotheism as it evolved in ancient Israel is not a full-scale rejection of polytheism but a modification of its mythological force by eliminating the consort of the male deity from the pantheon, a strategy that continued to inform the religious imagination of sages, prophets, and poets in a variety of postbiblical Judaisms.[2] This is not to deny that traces of the polytheistic veneration of goddesses are attested in both literary and material remains from ancient Israel.[3] Select biblical passages yield evidence that in spite of the official priestly policy, Israelites continued to worship a female counterpart to Yahweh, reflecting the Canaanite Asherah, companion of Baal (1 Kings 18:19; 2 Kings 21:7), or Astarte (1 Sam. 7:4), and the somewhat ambiguous figure designated Queen of Heaven (Jer. 44:17). A later echo of this older polytheism is discernible in the representations of the feminine figure of Wisdom (Prov. 1–9).[4]

The female images of a divine figure notwithstanding, the textual and material data from ancient Israel support the view that the evolution of Judaism as a religious culture sanctioned dislodging the female from the imaginary theological landscape and the consequent privileging of the masculine form of God. The history of Jewish mysticism fits well into this pattern. Hence the central visionary image, informed by priestly and prophetic strands of the tradition, is the divine king sitting on his throne.[5] The form of the glory envisioned repeatedly by the authors of texts classified as *merkavah* mysticism—and in using the term "authors," I do not distinguish in a hard and fast way between compositional and redactional phases of the process of text production—is masculine. In some of the pertinent passages, especially in the textual aggregate transmitted as *Heikhalot Rabbati*, the throne assumes a feminine character vis-à-vis the masculine glory, the bride that is the precious vessel to receive the king. The moment of enthronement, accordingly, is portrayed as sacred union.[6]

It is necessary to recall that this textual unit also preserves the provocative motif of the glory bending down, hugging, caressing, and kissing the icon of Jacob engraved on the throne at the time when Israel utters the doxology below (Isa. 6:3). That Jacob's countenance is associated with the feminized throne should come as no surprise, as one would adduce from the logic of the mythologic that the weaker entity in a hierarchical relation would be personified as female and the stronger as male. Hence the glorious king is configured as bridegroom, and Jacob, the secondary divine/angelic power, as the bride-throne into which he is assimilated. In this poetic image are contained the seeds that sprouted into the symbol of the androgynous divine anthropos more fully exposed and embellished in various currents of medieval Jewish esotericism.

The imaginal role assumed by the throne and the drama that surrounds it is analogous to the imaging of Torah in rabbinic material as the feminine playmate who engages the attention of God's musing prior to creation, an idea rooted in the still older female portrayal of wisdom from the late Second Temple period, itself an interesting blending of an archaic Israelite sensibility and the Hellenic philosophical spirit. I think it reasonable to assume that the aggadic tradition regarding the female depiction of Torah, attested equally in midrashic sources and in early liturgical poetry, points to a mythical conception of a feminine hypostasis in the heavenly realm that complements the male glory.[7] God is not portrayed as sitting on Torah, of course, as that would be an absurd scenario to imagine. But there are other images that convey something of the same message, the eros that links and separates the divine glory and Torah, for instance, the nearly reverse image of Torah sitting in the lap of the holy One, or the holy One strapping Torah onto his arm as a phylactery. In kabbalistic texts, we find the interpretative merging of these disparate images into a unifying theme.

In the more elaborately anthropomorphic texts classified under the rubric of *Shiʿur Qomah*, it is again obvious that the visible, measurable, and nameable form of the divine is male in nature; indeed, explicit reference is made in some literary fragments of this genre to God's penis, even though its exact measure is not given, at least not in the texts that have been uncovered hitherto.[8] In another strand of ancient Jewish esotericism preserved in the medieval compilation *Sefer Yeṣirah*,[9] reference is also made to the divine anthropos, depicted in terms of ten *sefirot* corresponding to ten fingers, five against five, with the covenant of oneness (*berit yiḥud*) set in the middle of the body in the covenant of the tongue and mouth (*milat lashon wa-feh*) and the covenant of the foreskin (*milat ha-maʿor*).[10] The phallus itself is thus singled out as one of two foci of divine unity.

More important, perhaps, is the anatomical parallel drawn between the tongue and phallus, word of mouth and covenant of circumcision. In one of my earlier essays, I examined the reverberation of this motif in the correlation of Torah study and circumcision, a theme firmly rooted in the soil of rabbinic culture and greatly expanded by the kabbalistic imagination.[11] What is critical to point out here is that the theoretical foundation for the phallomorphic sensibility that overwhelmed traditional kabbalah is established textually in the portrayal of the twofold covenant of unity in the first part of *Sefer Yeṣirah*. In the course of many years of study, I have yet to discover a kabbalistic source that would reject or contest my formulation, and this is so as much for those who would be classified as theosophic kabbalists as it is for those who would be classified as ecstatic kabbalists.[12] It is appropriate to conclude, therefore, that phallomorphism is a quality shared by the different strands of Jewish esotericism.

Medieval Reverberations/From Nuts to Bolts

Allusions to the secret doctrine regarding the divine androgyne are found in the writings of the Rhineland Jewish Pietists. As recent scholarship has shown, the esoteric theosophy cultivated by the German Pietists, particularly those who belonged to the Kalonymide family, bears a striking resemblance to Provençal and Spanish kabbalists. The attribution of gender to the divine realm is clearly one of the more significant similarities worthy of consideration.

The androgynous character of God is portrayed in several different symbolic ways. One of the earliest formulations of this idea in Pietistic sources is in a cluster of texts dealing with *sod ha-egoz*, the "secret of the nut." According to these texts, the nut, an image applied to the chariot/throne probably on the basis of Song 6:11, is characterized as hermaphrodite, with part of it corresponding to the penis and another part to the vagina.[13] Moreover, as I argued in a study written sometime ago, the older aggadic motif of the image of Jacob engraved on the throne occupies a central position in the esoteric theosophy expounded by Kalonymide German Pietism, expressed most fully in the works of Eleazar of Worms.[14] Homiletically expanding earlier sources, the Pietists utilized this image to formulate a secret doctrine of an acutely erotic texture. The mythic depiction of God's embracing, caressing, and kissing the icon of Jacob (in what appears to be the earliest textual accretion, the word *iqonin* is explicitly utilized)[15] is a symbolic representation of the sacred union in the realm of the chariot, an act that is theurgically set into motion by the liturgical utterance of the *sanctus* by the community of Israel below. At the core of my argument is the conjecture that the identity of Jacob's image is blurred with the throne, which is the lower, feminine glory in relation to the upper, masculine glory. Accordingly, enthronement portends the sacred union in the divine realm. This represents a central element in the Pietistic understanding of the divine nature, a theosophical premise that imparts theurgical and mystical significance to liturgical worship.[16]

The slippage between Jacob's image engraved on the throne and Jacob (or Israel) as the glorious form seated upon the throne relates to a conceptual indeterminacy that is not uncommon in esoteric symbolism.[17] The quality of indeterminacy does not, in my mind, connote a lack of pattern or structure nor does it imply that the scholarly account is not subject to critical inquiry; it simply underscores that the esoteric symbol rests on the paradoxical affirmation of ostensibly conflicting viewpoints. In this particular case, the image of Jacob bespeaks the double vision that is the mystery of reflection. This, it seems, is the main epistemic point of the tradition regarding the iconic representation of Jacob: the image inscribed on the throne mirrors the glory that sits upon the throne.[18] The face of the glory, in other words, is envisioned through the mask of Jacob's visage, the smooth-skinned one, according to the biblical idiom (Gen. 27:11). To speak of reflection in this instance implicates one in a thought pattern that defies linear logic, for Jacob's countenance, which is engraved on and hence is part of the throne, is a representation of the face of the anthropomorphic form seated on the throne, a form that itself coheres only in the imaginal configuration of the throne. In the gaze of imagination, the divide between glorious throne and enthroned glory, the image and what is imaged, is transcended.

One of the themes basic to kabbalists who adopted and elaborated a theosophic conception of God is that of the divine androgyne, referred to by the technical locution *du-parṣufim*, a corruption of the Greek term *dyprosopon* (literally, two-faced) employed in the rabbinic aggadah to characterize the nature of Adam at creation.[19] In kabbalistic parlance, this term denotes the idea that God is simultaneously male and female, that is, that there is a masculine and feminine aspect to the divine, the anthropomorphic enclothing of the metaphysical principles of bestowal and receptivity. Bracketing for the moment the question of the possible antiquity of this idea (or related images) in the history of Judaism, it is beyond question, as various scholars have duly noted, that the notion of a divine syzygy lies at the core of the theosophic speculation that marks the distinguishing composition of the mythic imagination of kabbalists.

Consider, for example, the following testimony of the thirteenth-century Castilian kabbalist, Todros ben Joseph Abulafia, regarding the aggadic motif of *du-parṣufim*: "Know that all the elements of the proper tradition [*ha-qabbalah ha-nekhonah*], in their principles and details, are all built upon this foundation, and they revolve around this point. It is a deep secret upon which are hanging very high mountains."[20] Abulafia's words are not hyperbole; the theosophic tradition is encapsulated in the symbol of the divine androgyne. In a similar vein, the zoharic authorship thus reflects on the biblical verses, "This is the record of Adam's line. When God created Adam, he made him in the likeness of

God; male and female he created them. And when they were created, he blessed them and called them Adam" (Gen. 5:1–2):

> R. Simeon said: Supernal secrets have been revealed in these two verses. "Male and female he created them," so that one may know the supernal glory, the mystery of faith, for by means of this mystery Adam was created. . . . From here [we learn that] every image in which male and female are not found is not a supernal image as is appropriate, and this has been established in the secret of the Mishnah.[21] Come and see: The holy One, blessed be he, will not place his dwelling in the place wherein male and female are not found. Blessings are not found except in the place where male and female are found as one,[22] as it is written, "And when they were created, he blessed them and called them Adam." It is not written, "he blessed him and called him Adam," for he is not called Adam except when male and female are one.[23]

Numerous other texts could have been cited to illustrate the point, but the two examples that I have noted are sufficient to underscore the central place occupied by the image of androgyny in kabbalistic thought. This is a commonplace in scholarly literature, and the purpose of this chapter is not to traverse a path already well trodden but to illuminate aspects of the kabbalistic myth that have not been sufficiently appreciated. In particular, as I made clear in chapter two, I am interested in uncovering the presuppositions regarding the cultural construction of gender. Toward that end, in this chapter I shall investigate again the androcentric underpinnings of the engendering symbol that I have termed the "male androgyne" in an effort to articulate that both masculinity and femininity are contained ontically in the male; from the kabbalist's vantage point, there is one gender with two sexuated instantiations.

Moreover, as I explored in detail in chapter three, inasmuch as traditional kabbalistic symbolism locates the ontological root of both masculinity and femininity in the phallic potency, it is appropriate to speak of an "androgynous phallus." There is thus justification in labeling the androgyne myth in the esotericism of medieval kabbalah as phallocentric. This does not mean, as some of my critics have mistakenly presumed, that I ignore images of the feminine in the writings of kabbalists.[24] What it does suggest is my contention that even these images must be understood as expressive of a prevailing phallocentric worldview. The following words of Elizabeth Grosz succinctly capture the point I have tried to raise: "Phallocentrism is explicitly *not* the refusal of an identity for women (on the contrary, there seems to be a proliferation of identities—wife, mother, nun, secretary, etc.), but rather, the containment of that identity by other definitions and identities."[25]

Gifting of the Feminine: Divine Syzygy and Illicit Sexuality

I begin my analysis of the myth of the androgyne in kabbalistic symbology with an in-depth discussion of *Sefer ha-Bahir*, an anthology of diverse theosophic traditions long thought to be one of the first and most influential works of early kabbalah, which surfaced in the twelfth and thirteenth centuries, most likely in Provence, and was then transported to Catalonia and Castile, perhaps originating in part from Babylonia or even Palestine.[26] Whatever the provenance of the discrete textual threads woven together and redacted into a discrete composition, the *Bahir* may be considered one of the foundational documents that provided mythical symbols and poetic images elaborated upon in subsequent kabbalistic texts, especially in the various strata of *Sefer ha-Zohar*, arguably the main repository of medieval kabbalah. As my discussion of the relevant bahiric passages will illustrate, in this document the ontological structures that informed the kabbalists' understanding of gender construction are already evident, although couched in complex and often obscure parabolic language.

In *Sefer ha-Bahir*, the idea of the divine syzygy is contextualized in terms of the primordial anthropos.[27] Indeed, in a manner allegedly jarring for the medieval rabbinic circles within which the text circulated, several passages in the *Bahir* attest that the divine image (*ṣelem elohim*) by means of which Adam was created relates to the correspondence between human and divine limbs.[28] Thus in one instance the divine image is linked to the following seven limbs:[29] two hands, head, body, two thighs, and the male and female sex organs, which are considered as one (*berit milah we-zugo ḥashvinan ḥad*).[30] In another passage wherein the ten *ma'amarot*—divine "utterances" or "sayings" by means of which the world was created, according to an older interpretative disclosure—are explicated, the eighth stands symbolically for the "eight that are naught but seven" (*shemonah hem einam ela sheva*), the eight extremities (*shemonah qeṣawwot*) in the body of man: the right and left hands, the right and left feet, the head, the torso of the body, the phallus that is balanced in the middle (*berit makhri*ʿ*a*), and the female who is the counterpart (*zug*) to the male.[31] Unlike the former passage, wherein the female was considered one entity with the male, in this selection the female complements the male and is enumerated as an autonomous force. Hence the delineation of the eight potencies in this passage concludes with the midrashic flourish, "as it written 'and he will cleave to his wife to be one flesh' (Gen. 2:24), thus there are eight, and corresponding to these are the eight days of circumcision, and these eight are merely seven for the torso and phallus are one" (*de-guf u-verit ḥad hu*).[32]

Just as the divine anthropos is characterized in these androgynous terms, so the human below must emulate this state of harmony by man cleaving to his wife and becoming one flesh, according to the locution of Genesis 2:24, which is cited in the second bahiric context mentioned above. In yet another passage, we read of seven holy forms[33] of God that correspond to seven limbs in the human being: two thighs, two hands, head, the body of the phallus,[34] and the woman who complements the man.[35] The female potency of the divine is thus considered part of the male in the way that the woman was part of man according to the second creation myth in Genesis.[36] Thus, after delineating the six limbs, one of the authorial/redactional voices incorporated in the bahiric text comments: "You said there were seven! The seventh is his wife, as it is written, '[Hence a man leaves his father and mother and clings to his wife] so that they become one flesh' (Gen. 2:24). Thus she was taken from his rib, as it is written, 'He took one of his ribs.' "[37]

Implied in this passage is an ontological explanation of heterosexual intercourse, obviously from an androcentric perspective; the psychic need of man to unite with woman is related to the fact (according to the biblical account) that she is constructed from a part taken from him. It is noteworthy that in this bahiric passage sexual union is presented as the means by which the male reclaims the component of himself severed in the construction of his feminine partner, a central theme of kabbalistic eroticism.[38] Empirically, vaginal coitus facilitates the containment of the male (or, at least, a prominent appendage of the male anatomy) in the female, but the kabbalistic symbolism is predicated on the assumption that this containment is expressive of the ontic dependence of the female on the male—the vessel is valorized in terms of what it contains and thus itself becomes what is contained. The decidedly androcentric explanation of coitus, which is anchored exegetically in the biblical description of man and woman cleaving together to form one flesh, is applied in the kabbalistic source to the feminine potency of the divine, which is depicted as the seventh limb that completes the supernal form. The intent of this bahiric passage is made explicit in an anonymous text extant in manuscript with the heading *ṭaʿam ha-ziwwug* (the rationale for sexual union):

> It is written in *Sefer ha-Bahir* that the holy One, blessed be he, created seven forms in man, and they are divided as the hands, the feet, the head, and the phallus.[39] The six are masculine and the seventh is feminine for she completes the seven forms. When the holy One, blessed be he, created Adam, he joined all the forms together, and afterwards he blessed and separated one of them, which is the female, the seventh form that completes [the other forms], for man is not complete without her, as it is written, "It is not good for man to be alone; I will make a fitting helper for him" (Gen. 2:18), and it is written, "[Thus a man should take leave of his father and his mother, and cleave to his wife] so that they become one flesh" (ibid., 24).[40]

The erotic impulse of the male is understood in psychological terms as a desire to restore the part that was separated in the original creation. From this vantage point, heteroeroticism must be viewed as covertly homoerotic, for if the other is naught but a manifestation of the same, love of other is in truth an expression of love for the same. Here it would be apposite to recall the remark of Lacan that "there is no access to the opposite sex as Other except via the so-called partial drives wherein the subject seeks an object to take the place of the loss of life he has sustained due to the fact that he is sexuated."[41] Repeatedly in kabbalistic literature, coitus is presented in this way, merging the psychological and ontological, that is, the psychological basis of man's desire for a woman is the ontological quest for overcoming the deficiency that ensues from the separation of the male androgyne into distinct sexualized beings. The restoration of the female to the male, the repair of the fissure of the primal androgyny, what later kabbalists, including the zoharic authorship, refer to as *tiqqun*, is the mystical rationale for sexual intercourse, as the woman receives the man's seed and can thus become the fruit-producing tree extending the line of progeny—the body of engenderment, in Mopsik's felicitous locution.

In a symbolic reversal to which I have already alluded, the somatic act of the female containing the male is transformed into the property of the female being contained by the male. The textual reasoning can be traced to the scriptural justification for man's yearning to cohabit the space of a woman: Since woman (*ishshah*) was constructed out of man (*ish*), a husband must cleave carnally to his wife to become one flesh (Gen. 2:22–25).[42] Heterosexual intercourse, which is to transpire ideally within a monogamous scenario,[43] is the means by which the male androgyne is rectified. There is no question that the woman is accorded a critical, albeit instrumentalist, role in this drama as the vessel to receive the seminal fluid whence the new being will be engendered, but—and here is the crucial point for a proper gender analysis—as a result of the male-female bonding, the one that contains is transformed into the one that is contained, and the one that is contained into the one that contains. This may be upheld by some scholars as the "active" dimension of the feminine, but one could not make such a claim unless one were willing to mark receiving as active rather than passive. Even if one were willing to commit logically to such a position, it is not an accurate account of what is textually attested in traditional kabbalistic literature.

The androgynous nature of the divine is derived as well from another verse cited in the *Bahir*: "in the image of God he created him, male and female he created them" (Gen. 1:27). According to the understanding of the *Bahir*, reiterated recurrently in subsequent kabbalistic literature, the divine image in which Adam was created comprises male and female, yet the latter is contained in the former, and not vice versa. Simply put, kabbalists, informed by earlier rabbinic authorities, understood the notion of androgyny suggested in the account of the creation of Adam in the first chapter of Genesis in light of the myth of the construction of woman out of man articulated in the second chapter.[44] The merging of the two scriptural narratives yielded an androcentric understanding of heterosexual intercourse as a means to reestablish the original male androgyne.[45] To cite one of countless texts that illustrate the point, Gikatilla thus commented in *Sod ha-Ḥashmal*:

> In every place that you see "likeness" [*demut*] it is the secret of the forms that take shape in *Malkhut* . . . and in every place that you see "image" [*ṣelem*] it is the secret of all the forms that take shape by means of *Yesod*, and this is the secret of "Let us make Adam in our image and in our likeness" (Gen. 1:26), and the secret of the saying that the male soul [*nishmat zakhar*] does not come out without the female soul [*nishmat neqevah*], which is his spouse [*bat zugo*] . . . and this is the secret of "he took one of his ribs" (ibid., 2:21), and the secret of "and he brought her to the man" (ibid., 22), and the secret of "This one at last is bone of my bones etc." (ibid., 23), and the secret of "and he shall cling to his wife so that they become one flesh" (ibid., 24).[46]

The gender construction is alluded to in the bahiric parable of the king's seven sons, which introduces the aforementioned delineation. These sons, aligned atop one another, are the seven holy forms that are compared to seven limbs, which include either the full form of a woman or the female genitals that complement the phallus. The parabolic image pictorially expresses the philosophic principle of the ontological containment of the feminine in the masculine, a motif that is articulated more explicitly by later kabbalists.

The primordial androgyny is further illustrated by a second parable in the same context: "To what may this be compared? To a king who decided to plant in his garden nine male trees, and all of them were to be palm trees. He said, 'If all of them will be of the same species, they will not be able to exist.' What did he do? He planted a citron tree [*etrog*] amongst them, and it is one of the nine that arose in his mind to be male, but the citron is female."[47] The imagery employed in this parable is derived from the ritual of the four species (based on Lev. 23:40) that each male Jew, according to rabbinic tradition, is obligated to take on the festival of Tabernacles. The two central species are the palm branch (*lulav*) and the citron (*etrog*), which correspond symbolically to the masculine and feminine attributes of the divine. The fact that the tree that is female was initially one of the males symbolizes that the female aspect of the divine pleroma (represented by the image of the garden)[48] is itself part of the masculine.[49]

The point is emphasized once again in the continuation of the *Bahir* where the citron is associated symbolically with the beloved described in Song 6:10; already encoded in this passing reference is the symbolic reading of the Song as the dramatic portrayal of the relationship between masculine and feminine personae of the divine:[50]

> What is the splendor [*hadar*]? That is, the splendor of the All [*hadar ha-kol*], and that is the splendor of the Song of Songs concerning which it says, "Who is it that shines through like the dawn, beautiful as the moon, radiant as the sun, awesome as bannered hosts" (Song 6:10). This refers to the feminine and on account of her the female was taken from Adam, for the upper and lower worlds could not exist without the female.[51]

Significantly, the feminine potency is designated in the aforecited passage by the expression "splendor of the All" (*hadar ha-kol*). Beyond the obvious connection to the biblical idiom *peri eṣ hadar* (Lev. 23:40), interpreted in targumic and classical rabbinic literature as a reference to the citron,[52] this phrase intimates that the feminine is the glory or majesty (*hadar*) of the masculine, which is designated by the term *kol*, the All,[53] a term that may denote the fullness in its totality (pleroma, *male*) or the phallic aspect that comprises the power of the whole. Just as the penis was considered the part of the male anatomy that gathered in all the body's energies, so this attribute of the divine anthropos was thought to comprise the totality of God's creative might; the expression *hadar ha-kol* alludes to the splendor of the phallus, for the potency of the latter is manifest through the agency/mirror of the feminine/other. Moreover, just as the female was constructed from the body of the male, so the citron (*etrog*) is taken from the tree of splendor (*eṣ hadar*); both images convey the ontically derivative state of the female.[54]

The kabbalistic symbol as I have interpreted it accords with a view expressed in any number of mythologoumena wherein the image of the feminine is associated with creation and the natural world, the boundaries of measurable space and the rhythms of calibrated time. The female is the threshold that marks the passage from the imaginal realm of symbol to the material sphere of metaphor, the womb and ground of being, what we call "nature." Already attested in the *Bahir* is an allusion to the nexus between the feminine potency and the demiurgical role of creation, a theme exploited in later kabbalistic sources, as I partially explore below. What needs to be emphasized at this moment is that from the vantage point of a gender semiotic, the yielding of produce—an activity associated with the matrix principle—phallically transforms the female. The nascent kabbalistic symbolism betrays a typical androcentric strategy whereby the life-bestowing activities of the female are culturally appropriated as masculine traits.[55] The point is reiterated in the following passage:

> Why was she called *tamar* and not by other names? For she was a female. You think because she was a female? Rather she comprised male and female, for all palm trees comprise male and female.[56] How is this? The palm branch is masculine, and the fruit from the outside is masculine, but from the inside it is feminine. How is this? The nucleus of the date is split like a [vagina of a] woman, and corresponding to her is the power of the moon above. The holy One, blessed be he, created Adam male and female, as it says, "He created them male and female" (Gen. 1:27).[57]

According to this tradition-complex, which is found as well in several other bahiric passages, the nature of androgyny is determined from the standpoint that woman is derived ontically from and hence is ontologically dependent on man—the esoteric significance of the narrative about the creation of Adam as male and female. The branch of the palm tree is masculine, but its fruit is masculine from the outside and feminine from the inside. This is the symbolic import of the name *tamar.* The nucleus of the date is linked symbolically to the vagina, which in turn is associated with the power of the moon.[58]

One of the boldest images utilized by medieval kabbalists to express the ontological dependence of the female on the male is what I have dubbed the androgynous phallus, a subject discussed at some length in chapter three. It will be recalled that I utilize Lacanian jargon to explicate the kabbalistic symbolism, noting especially the assumption that both masculinity and femininity are constructed from the perspective of the male organ.[59] This idea is expressed in several bahiric passages, including most conspicuously in the following explanation of the letter *ṣaddi*: "[Just as] this *ṣaddi* is *yod nun*, so too the mate [*zug*] is *yod nun*. Thus it is written, 'Righteous, foundation of the world' [*ṣaddiq yesod olam*] (Prov. 10:25)."[60] The letter *ṣaddi*, which represents *ṣaddiq*, the "righteous one," the divine gradation anatomically correlated with the phallus, can be orthographically broken into *yod* on top of *nun*, the male (*yod* is the sign of the covenant of circumcision) over the female (*nun* metonymically stands for *neqevah*). Contained within the one letter, therefore, is the duality of male and female.

The ontological contextualization of the feminine in the phallus is made in another bahiric context as well, wherein the palm branch (*lulav*) is identified as the trunk of the tree (*guf ha-illan*) and the citron (*etrog*) as the heart: "What is the palm branch? [The word *lulav*] is written *lo lev* for the heart is given to him. And what is the heart? This refers to the thirty-two mysterious paths of wisdom."[61] The secret of the containment of feminine in the masculine is alluded to in the name of the male potency, *lulav*, the palm branch (an obvious phallic symbol), which is decoded as *lo lev*, literally, "to him the heart belongs." The feminine potency is portrayed as the heart (*lev*) because it comprises the thirty-two paths of wisdom (according to the opening passage of *Sefer Yeṣirah*, the means by which the world was created)—thirty-two is written in Hebrew as *lamed-beit*, the consonants of *lev*. The meaning of *lo lev*, therefore, is that the feminine (*lev*) belongs to him (*lo*).[62] The esoteric significance of *lulav*, when kabbalistically decoded, intones the axiom of which I have been writing, the ontological dependence of the female on the male.

The paradoxical status of the feminine as attached to yet separate from the male is reiterated in terms of the symbol of the citron and palm branch in another passage: "What is the holy? This is the citron, which is the splendor of the All [*hadar ha-kol*]. Why is its name called *hadar*? Do not read *hadar* but rather *ha-dar*.[63] This is the citron that is separated from the bond of the palm branch. But the ritual of the palm branch is not fulfilled except through it, and it too is joined with the All, for it is one with the All and it is united with everything."[64] The status of the feminine vis-à-vis the masculine is here portrayed by an astute interpretation of the halakhic praxis. That is, three of the four species, the palm branch, the myrtle, and the willow, are all bound as one entity, whereas the fourth, the citron, is separate. The ritual, however, is not fulfilled unless the fourth is united with the other three to form one integral unit. An allusion to the status of the fourth is given in the playful gloss of *hadar* as *ha-dar*, the "one who dwells." The ritualistic joining of the citron to the palm branch reenacts the integration of the feminine in the masculine.

The same idea is imparted in an altogether different symbolic register in the one section of the bahiric text where the term *sefirot* appears.[65] The homiletic context to which I refer is an interpretation of the gesture of Aaron's lifting his hands to bless the people of Israel (Lev. 9:22). The ten fingers are said to be a symbolic allusion (*remez*) to the "ten *sefirot* by means of which heaven and earth were sealed," an embellishment of one of the descriptions of the *sefirot* in the first section of *Sefer Yeṣirah*. In the *Bahir*, the term *sefirot* is linked exegetically to the verse "The heavens declare the glory of God" (Ps. 19:2), which indicates that the term has a twofold connotation, narration (*sippur*) and illumination (*sappir*), for the heavens declare (*mesapperim*) the divine glory through their radiance. In response to the question "What are they?" we are told that they are classified in three groups, three forces (*ḥayyalot*), three dominions (*memshalot*), and three sanctifications (*qedushshot*). The three triads equal the sum of nine, leading to the obvious question "Why are there three sanctifications and not four? Because the sanctifications above are threefold."[66]

At this juncture the critical passage appears: "What is the meaning of 'holy holy holy' followed by 'the Lord of hosts' (Isa. 6:3)? The first 'holy' is the supernal crown [*keter elyon*], the second 'holy' is the root of the tree [*shoresh ha-illan*], the third 'holy' is that which adheres and is united in all of them [*daveq u-meyuḥad be-khullan*], 'the Lord of hosts, his glory fills all the earth.' "[67] I propose that reflected in this text is an attempt to harmonize the archaic theologoumenon based on portraying the divine as a composite of three potencies and the alternative scheme based on ten *sefirot*. The three occurrences of the word *qadosh* are semiotic signposts that point to the three potencies that comprise the whole pleroma, the triune identity of the primordial ground. The author of this passage, however, assumes that the third *qadosh* has two aspects signified by the expression *daveq u-meyuḥad*, for it is both attached to and separate from the pleroma.[68] The dual character is elucidated in the continuation of the bahiric text, which is worthy of full citation:

What is the meaning of "his glory fills all the earth" (Isa. 6:3)? The earth that was created on the first day, which is above, corresponding to the land of Israel, was filled from the glory of the Lord. And what is it? Wisdom, as it is written, "The wise shall inherit glory" (Prov. 3:25), and it says, "Blessed be the glory of the Lord from his place" (Ezek. 3:12).

What is the divine glory? To what may this be compared? To a king who had the matrona in his chamber, and all of his troops delighted in her,[69] and she had sons who come every day to see the face of the king and to bless him. They said to him: Our mother, where is she? He said to them: You cannot see her now. And they said: Blessed is she in whatever place she is."

Why is it written "from his place?" Because there is no one who knows his place.[70] To what may this be compared? To a princess who came from afar and no one knew whence she came, until they saw that she is a woman of valor,[71] pleasing and commendable in all her deeds. They said: This one was certainly taken from the side of light, for her deeds illumine the world. They asked her: From where are you? She said: From my place. They said: If so, the men of your place are great. Blessed are you and blessed is your place.

Is not this glory of the Lord one of his hosts? Is it not inferior? Why, then, do they bless it? To what may this be compared? To a man who has a beautiful garden, and outside the garden and close to it there is a beautiful field.[72] . . . Initially, he irrigated his garden and the water went all over the garden but not upon the field that is not connected, even though everything is one. Therefore he opened a place for it and irrigated it separately.[73]

In this string of parables there are many motifs that evolved into foundational themes in kabbalistic theosophy, but for my immediate purposes I shall limit my focus to the liminal status of the feminine, the last of the three potencies, situated between the world of light and the physical universe. The liminality is accentuated by the analogical drift of the initial comment that the earth filled by the glory is the supernal land created on the first day, which corresponds to the terrestrial land of Israel. The Sophianic potency is thus identified as the *imago terrae*, that is, the archetypal image of earthliness embodied in the divine presence that dwells within the boundaries of the holy land, metonymically representing the cosmos at large.[74]

Even if one is not prepared to accept Scholem's surmise that preserved in the *Bahir* is a trace of the ancient Gnostic myth of the fallen Sophia,[75] there is little room to doubt that in the kabbalistic context, as in the older Gnosticism, the female figure, which is identified as both the glory (*kavod*) and wisdom (*ḥokhmah*), assumes the dual role of being rooted in and displaced from the pleroma. This is the force of the expression *daveq u-meyuḥad*, conjoined yet distinct, the former expressed scripturally in the verse "Blessed be the glory from his place" (Ezek. 3:12), that is, the remote place that is inaccessible and unknown, and the latter by the verse "Lord of hosts, his glory fills all the earth" (Isa. 6:3), that is, the immanence of *Shekhinah* permeating the physical universe.

Interestingly, the danger of reifying the feminine as an independent potency is connected especially to the liturgical gesture—how can the glory be blessed when it is but one of many potencies, indeed, an inferior one? This remark anticipates the concern of later kabbalists who perceived the separation of the feminine from the masculine as the paradigm for transgression; worship of the female as autonomous is tantamount to idolatry. I shall return to this motif at a later point in this chapter, but what is crucial to note here is that in response to the question, another parable is introduced to drive home the duplicitous nature of the feminine. Just as the field that is unified with yet separate from the garden must be irrigated independently, so the feminine potency that is attached to yet distinct from the other (masculine) potencies must be blessed separately.

The doubling of the daughter, the third member of the threefold pleroma, gives way to a quaternity, the twin image of mother and daughter, the upper and lower *Shekhinah*, complementing the father and son, an occult truth encoded semiotically in the Tetragrammaton, the four-letter name that is actually composed of three letters, *yod*, *he*, and *waw*, the fourth letter consisting of the duplication of the *he*. In the words of Jacob ben Sheshet: "Thus the name is from three letters, 'built from encircling hills' (Song 4:4), and they are four when they are joined together, 'so that they will be one Tabernacle' (Exod. 26:6)."[76] One is here reminded of Jung's assessment of the role of the quaternity in Western alchemy and its relationship to the structure of the triad:

> The number three is not a natural expression of wholeness, since four represents the minimum number of determinants in a whole judgment. It must nevertheless be stressed that side by side with the distinct leanings of alchemy (and of the unconscious) towards quaternity there is always a vacillation between three and four which comes out over and over again. . . . In alchemy there are three as well as four *regimina* or procedures, three as well as four colours. There are always four elements, but often three of them are grouped together, with the fourth in a special position—sometimes earth, sometimes fire. Mercurius is of course *quadratus*, but he is also a three-headed snake or simply a triunity. This uncertainty has a duplex character—in other words, the central ideas are ternary as well as quaternary. . . . Four signifies the feminine, motherly, physical; three the masculine, fatherly, spiritual. Thus the uncertainty as to three or four amounts to a wavering between the spiritual and the physical—a striking example of how every human truth is a last truth but one.[77]

In another passage, Jung himself (citing the Latin translation of Abraham Herrera Cohen's *Porta Coelorum* included in *Kabbala Denudata*)[78] relates the alchemical process of transformation encapsulated in the axiom of Maria the Prophetess, also known as Maria Hebraea, that is, Maria the Jewess, first referred to by Zosimus the Panopolitan in Hellenistic Egypt around the beginning of the fourth century,[79] "One becomes two, two becomes three, and out of the Third comes the One as the Fourth," to the kabbalistic doctrine of Adam Qadmon, the pleroma of the ten sefirotic potencies symbolically encoded in the Tetragrammaton, the divine name that is made up of three different letters, *yod, he*, and *waw*, and the repetition of the *he*. "In the Hebrew word YHVH . . . *he* is the feminine and is assigned as a wife to *yod* and to *vau*. As a result *yod* and *vau* are masculine, and the feminine *he*, though doubled, is identical and therefore a single unit.

To that extent the essential Name is a triad. But since *he* is doubled, the Name is also a tetrad or quaternity—a perplexity which coincides most strangely with the Axiom of Maria."[80]

The ontologically derivative status of the feminine underlies the various figurative representations in the *Bahir* that describe the bestowing of wisdom (*ḥokhmah*) upon Solomon. That is, the wisdom granted to Solomon is, parabolically conceived, the daughter given in matrimony by the king to his son.[81] The conjugal imagery—glaring in its ostensible challenge to the accepted sexual mores of the tradition—conveys the notion that the female is originally part of the male, and hence the bestowal of the daughter to the son signifies the restoration of an aspect of the male that has been severed in the splitting of the primordial male androgyne. In line with classical rabbinic texts, the bahiric author identifies Torah and wisdom, which he further associates with *Shekhinah*, the feminine presence of the divine pleroma, also characterized as the wellspring (*berekhah*) of God's blessing (*berakhah*), an image that conveys her demiurgical role as angel of the world.[82]

As I have argued previously, the structure underlying this myth is an older archaic theologoumenon preserved in *Bahir* based on the symbolic triad of father, daughter, and son (in some passages the latter is identified as Solomon).[83] Even though this mythic teaching is conflated in some bahiric passages with the system of ten potencies, and surely this is the way the kabbalists who first utilized the *Bahir* interpreted the matter, it is possible to reconstruct an independently existing tradition that configures the divine as three and not ten potencies. In a primeval state, the daughter is integrated fully in the father, together constituting the androgynous form of divine wisdom—indeed in this state it is not even appropriate to conceive of father and daughter as distinct hypostases—but in a secondary stage, the daughter splits off from the father, and she is given to the son so that the original balance of gender will be restored. In order to restore that balance, the daughter had to be given to the son for she could no longer pair with the father.[84] The dynamic of the mythic structure is particularly transparent in the following passage:

> There is no beginning [*re'shit*] except for wisdom [*ḥokhmah*], as it says, "The beginning of wisdom is the fear of the Lord" (Ps. 111:10), and there is no wisdom except for blessing, as it says,[85] the Lord blessed Solomon, and it is written, "The Lord had given wisdom to Solomon" (1 Kings 5:26). This may be compared to a king who gave his daughter in marriage to his son, and he gave her to him as a gift,[86] and he said to him, "Do with her as you wish."[87]

Implied in the bahiric passage is the distinction between upper and lower wisdom, a motif that Scholem related thematically, if not textually, to the double doctrine of Sophia in Valentinian Gnosticism.[88] I would like to draw attention to one particular Nag Hammadi composition that presents an even more tantalizing affinity with the tradition-complex I have reconstructed from the bahiric anthology. I refer to the *Expository Treatise on the Soul*, also known as *Exegesis on the Soul*, a text that is presumed to have been composed in the third century. The citing and interpreting of passages from biblical and Homeric scripture, as well as echoes and traces of themes discussed in Hermetic and philosophical sources, suggest a syncretistic milieu like that of Alexandria, where Hebraic and Hellenistic elements were easily combined.[89] For the purposes of this chapter I will focus on the engendering myth operative in the treatise with a special eye to ascertaining the affinities and differences between it and the mythopoeic teaching preserved in the *Bahir.*

The tract begins with the assertion that "wise men of old" gave the soul a "feminine name," but it is "female in her nature as well." When the soul was alone with the father, "she was virgin and in form androgynous."[90] The literary setting of the text, however, is written from the vantage point of the soul being displaced from the pleroma. We learn from the soul's appeal to the father, which follows the initial narrative section, that she "abandoned" her house and "fled" from the "maiden's quarters."[91] A reason is not offered to explain why the soul deserted her original setting to sojourn in the "domain of the flesh and the perceptible realm," rendered imagistically by the scriptural symbol of the land of Egypt.[92] In the fallen state, the soul is defiled by promiscuous behavior, giving herself freely and repeatedly to "wanton, unfaithful adulterers," "copulating with whomever she meets."[93] Suffering affliction, shame, and humiliation, the widowed soul[94] repents of her involvement with prostitution, turning to the father with weeping, entreating him to restore her to the home she vacated. The father expresses his mercy on the soul and will make "her womb turn from the external domain and will turn it again inward, so that the soul will gain her proper character. . . . For the womb of the body is inside the body like the other internal organs, but the womb of the soul is around the outside like the male genitalia, which are external."[95]

This passage is quite extraordinary, predicated, as it is, on the distinction between the womb of the body and the womb of the soul. The former is inside the body, whereas the latter is external, the comparison to the male genitals suggesting that the womb of the soul assumes a masculine valence. Be that as it may, the turning inward of the womb of the soul is presented as a cleansing of the external pollution, the baptismal renewal of the soul, a rejuvenation and regeneration that occasions ascent to the father, restoration to the "place where originally she had been," the re/turn that is identified symbolically as repentance and as resurrection of the dead, the "beginning of salvation."[96]

In response to the soul's petition, the father sends down the bridegroom, who is the soul's brother, the "firstborn," an image that calls to mind the scriptural designation of the collective entity of the people of Israel (Exod. 4:22), which was appropriated and applied to Jesus (Mark 1:11; Matt. 3:17; Luke 3:22; John 1:34).[97] The son descends from the heavenly abode, and the soul is renewed by purifying herself of all her transgressions in the bridal chamber,[98] where she sits and awaits the arrival of the bridegroom, contrasted with her licentious roving about in search of satisfying her sensual appetite. The asexual character of the spiritual marriage of son and daughter in the bridal chamber is contrasted with the sexual intercourse of carnal marriage; the purpose of the pneumatic bonding is to reconstitute the primary syzygy, the androgynous form wherein the female is contained in the male and the one gender is re-enacted. The precise language of the text is worth citing:

> But [once] they unite [with one another], they become a single life. Wherefore the prophet said (Gen. 2:24) concerning the first man and the first woman, They will

> become a single flesh. For they were originally joined to one another when they were with the father before they led astray the man, who is her brother. This marriage has brought them back together again and the soul has been joined to her true love, her real master, as it is written (cf. Gen. 3:16; 1 Cor. 11:1; Eph. 5:23), For the master of the woman is her husband.[99]

In an astonishing resemblance to the tradition-complex preserved in the *Bahir,* the mythologoumenon in the *Expository Treatise on the Soul* affirms the triadic structure of the divine pleroma, the father, son, and daughter, and not the more typical trinity of father-mother-son, an archaic mythic structure that is attested in other gnostic works such as *Trimorphic Protennoia,* Apocryphon of John, and *Allogenes.* I note, in passing, a precise parallel in another Nag Hammadi text, *Eugnostos the Blessed*:

> The First who appeared before the universe in infinity is Self-grown, Self-constructed Father, and is full of shining, ineffable light.[100] In the beginning, he decided to have his likeness become a great power. Immediately, the principle (*or* beginning)[101] of that light appeared as Immortal Androgynous Man. His male name is "[Begotten,] Perfect [Mind]." And his female name (is) "All-wise Begettress Sophia. It is also said that she resembles her brother and her consort. She is uncontested truth; for here below error, which exists with truth, contests it.[102]

The continuation of the document tells of how the pairing of son and daughter, the Savior and Sophia, or Pistis Sophia, as she is also called, produced six androgynous spiritual beings in the pattern of the first androgynous man. The twelve powers, six male and six female, beget seventy-two powers, the totality of the six contained in each of the twelve, and each one of the seventy-two powers reveals five powers, to yield a sum of 360 powers, the union of which is called the "will."[103] What is most important for our purposes is the depiction of the pleroma in terms of three potencies: father, son, and daughter. Moreover, in the *Expository Treatise,* as in the bahiric fragments, the father wills that the son and daughter unite as bridegroom and bride, a gesture that is described in both literary contexts as the giving of a gift on the part of the father.[104] The logic of the mythos in the gnostic and bahiric contexts affirms a union that is illicit when judged from the perspective of human society—son and daughter are joined in holy matrimony. In both settings, the primary engendering myth dispenses with the figure of the mother as the goddess-consort of the father; the maternal image does appear in some passages in the *Bahir,* most significantly in polemical dialogue with the Christological symbol of the Virgin Mary,[105] but it does not figure as an inherent component of the primary triad.[106]

In both texts, the androgynous condition is described as a state wherein the female is ontically subservient to the male. Heterosexual intercourse is a form of unity that preserves the separation of male and female, whereas spiritual marriage overcomes that separation by restoring the female back to the male whence she was taken. A crucial difference, however, is that in the *Expository Treatise on the Soul* there is no reference, explicit or implicit, to the identification of the feminine soul, or the firstborn son for that matter, as divine wisdom. In the bahiric passages, by contrast, the theme of the daughter is expressed distinctively in the image of wisdom, which is compared parabolically to a gift bestowed by the king upon his son.

The juxtaposition of the image of the gift and matrimonial language is prima facie jarring, inasmuch as the act of taking a wife, according to rabbinic law, is a contractual, legal transaction and not a present. What in the nature of this bestowal necessitates its being characterized as a giving of a gift? The clue is provided in the concluding remark, "Do with her as you wish." To appreciate the intent of this comment, it would be useful to recall Derrida's reflection on the nature of the gift as that which opens the circle of economy, the circular exchange of goods, so as to defy reciprocity or symmetry:[107]

> [T]he *given* of the gift (*that which* one gives, *that which* is given, the gift as given thing or as act of donation) must not come back to the giving (let us not already say to the subject, to the donor). It must not circulate, it must not be exchanged, it must not in any case be exhausted, as a gift, by the process of exchange, by the movement of circulation of the circle in the form of return to the point of departure. . . . It is perhaps in this sense that the gift is the impossible.[108]

Elsewhere Derrida draws a more specific connection between language and textuality and the dynamic of giving and taking that is associated with the gift:

> The definition of language, of a language, as well as of the text in general, cannot be formed without a certain relation to the gift, to giving-taking. . . . Reduced to its barest formality, the structural principle . . . is that all semantic ambivalence and the syntactico-semantic problem of giving-taking are not situated only within language, the words of language or the elements of a textual system. Language is also an example of it as is any textual determination. In short, one must not only ask oneself . . . how is it possible that to give and/or to take are said this way or that way *in* a language, but one must also remember first of all that language is as well a phenomenon of gift-countergift, of giving-taking—and of exchange. . . . Everything said in language and everything written about giving-taking in general *a priori would fold back on* language and writing as giving-taking. Giving *would come back, come down* to taking and taking to giving, but this would come back to fold itself over not only on language or writing but toward the text in general, beyond its linguistic or logocentric closure, beyond its narrow or common meaning.[109]

The bahiric parable can be profitably read through the lens of Derrida's account of the economy of the gift and particularly its link to the temporalization of language in the dynamic of giving and taking, opening and closing. That the prince is given the princess as a gift by the king signifies that the act of giving is not a symmetrical relation; nothing the son does can reciprocate the action of the father, for there is no exchange of commodities, no mutual give and take. Moreover, the son who receives the daughter as gift cannot bestow this gift unto another; the daughter belongs exclusively to the son to whom she has been given as a gift. Finally, in the absence of reciprocity, the recipient of the gift assumes complete control and mastery over that which is given; in the act of giving, the donor relinquishes all claims of ownership and possession with respect to the gift.

In the bahiric passage, the power of entitlement is of a decidedly sexual nature—hence the prince is instructed by his father to do as he pleases with the princess.[110] The symbolic import of the parable blatantly contradicts the normative strictures of biblical law, for the taboo of siblings mating (Lev. 18:9) is undermined by the relationship that is described between the son and daughter of the king. The secret alluded to here, which later kabbalists relate to the mystery of illicit sexual relations (*sitrei arayot*) mentioned in the Babylonian Talmud (Ḥagigah 11b), is that the sexual prohibitions necessary to preserve the fabric of human society must be transgressed in a symbolic manner in the divine realm.[111] In that respect, the gift of wisdom is truly the impossible, that which defies the limits of temporal possibility, as the only time of the gift is the present, the paradoxical instant that is an effraction in the circularity of time, the repetitious pattern of the cycle of nature.[112]

The transgressive element, that which breaks through and defies the dialectic of presence and absence by persisting as that which cannot be present, discloses the essential nexus of the gift and secrecy. Again Derrida's language is helpful, for he notes that the paradox of the gift (revealed in the thought of Jan Patocka) is that it is always "the gift of something that remains inaccessible, unpresentable, and as a consequence secret. . . . The gift is the secret itself, if the secret *itself* can be told. Secrecy is the last word of the gift which is the last word of the secret."[113] The gift is marked by

> structural paradoxes, the stigmata of the impossibility. . . . So as not to take over the other, the overtaking by surprise of the pure gift should have the generosity to give nothing that surprises and appears *as* gift, *nothing that presents itself as present, nothing that is*; it should therefore be surprising enough and so thoroughly made up of a surprise that it is not even a question of getting over it, thus of a surprise surprising enough to let itself be forgotten without delay. . . . The secret of that about which one cannot speak, but which one can no longer silence.[114]

To heed the resonance of the gifting of the gift, we must plumb more deeply into the depths of secrecy. In what sense is the secret associated with the gift? Just as the disclosure of the secret undermines its claim to being a secret, so the gifting of the gift is annulled in the giving of the gift. The "unconditional respect" of the secret, Derrida tells us, is that the "secret is not phenomenalizable. Neither phenomenal nor noumenal."[115] The secret is not something that can be unveiled, since it "remains inviolable even when one thinks one has revealed it."[116] The secret is "nonprovisional, heterogeneous to all manifestation. This secret is not a reserve of potential knowing, a potential manifestation. And the language of ab-negation . . . *necessitates* doing the impossible, necessitates going there where one cannot go."[117] To be a secret the secret must persist as secret, mute and impassive, and thus one can speak of the secret *ad infinitum* without disrupting its secrecy. The ineffability of the secret, paradoxically, generates a seemingly endless chain of verbal attempts to articulate the secret.[118] It is in this sense that we can speak of the secret as the "non-thematizable, non-objectifiable, non-sharable" absolute, that is, the *ab-solutum*, the condition of any bond that is itself cut off from any bond, the unconditional that resists the "daylight of phenomenality" but which nevertheless facilitates the thematization, objectification, and communication of all that is shared in language, the utter singularity of the word that interminably defies any attempt to determine it.[119]

In one context, Derrida relates the duplicity of the secret as the saying of what cannot be said, the hermeneutical condition of *différance*, to the biblical narrative of the *aqedah*, Abraham's attempted sacrifice of Isaac (Gen. 22:1–19). Elaborating on Kierkegaard's observation that Abraham both speaks and does not speak, Derrida notes that he "speaks in order not to say anything about the essential thing he must keep secret. Speaking in order not to say anything is always the best technique for keeping a secret."[120] Only by speaking what cannot be spoken can the secret be preserved.

The secret necessarily exemplifies this double bind, for the secret can be a secret only to the extent that it is hidden, but the secret can be hidden only to the extent that it is revealed. To be veiled the secret must be unveiled, to be unveiled it must be veiled.[121] As Derrida expresses the matter elsewhere, the secret is "the thing to be dissimulated, a thing that is neither shown nor said, signified perhaps but that cannot or *must* not first be delivered up to self-evidence."[122] The secret is thus linked to a process that Derrida refers to as *dénégation*;[123] that is, the secret of necessity is the negation that negates itself. Through negating the negation, the secret both is and is not what it is, a dissimulation that dissimulates in the concealment of disclosure: "There is a secret of denial and a denial of the secret. The secret as such, as *secret*, separates and already institutes negativity; it is a negation that denies itself. It de-negates itself. This denegation does not happen to it by accident; it is essential and originary."[124]

The paradoxical nature of secrecy entails that the secret exceed the dichotomy of veiling and unveiling, dissimulation and revelation. Precisely with respect to the overcoming of dichotomies and occupying the space between does the condition of giving the gift illumine the nature of the secret. The secret can be safeguarded only if the secret has been divulged and thus is no longer a secret, and similarly the gift can be given only if it has been exposed as a gift and thus is no longer a gift. From another perspective, however, the pure secret can never be transmitted if it is to remain a secret, nor can the pure gift be given if it is to remain a gift.[125] In the telling of the secret, the secret is told because it is not told; in the giving of the gift, the gift can be given to the extent that it is not given.[126]

To apply this insight to the specific context of the bahiric parable, the giving of the daughter to the son as a gift on the part of the father is the secret of the emanation of divine wisdom. The transgressive nature of the gift precludes the disclosure of the secret. Mystical gnosis, therefore, is predicated on the mythopoeic attribution of an incestuous relationship to God. The endogamous tendency, the realization of which is forbidden in the human domain, alone can symbolically express the truth of the *hieros gamos* in the divine: if there is only one true reality, the manifold are branches that stem from but must be returned to the root, at least according to the mythologic of medieval kabbalah.[127] In the familial structure, incest is, in the words of René Girard, an "extreme form of violence" that "plays in consequence an extreme role in the destruction of differences."[128] For this very reason incest is an appropriate figuration to depict the abolition of difference that is characteristic of divine unity.

That the giving of the gift entails an intentional transgression of a sexual norm is implied as well in the following passage:

> They asked him, "What is 'With that he took him to the lookout point' (Num. 23:14). What is the lookout point [*sedeh ṣofim*]? As it is written, 'Come, my beloved, let us go out to the field' (Song 7:12). What is 'let us go out to the field' [*neṣe ha-sadeh*]? Do not read 'field' [*sadeh*] but carriage [*shiddah*]. His heart said to the holy One, blessed be he, 'Come, my beloved, and let us go stroll and I will not sit constantly in one place.'"
>
> What is his heart [*libbo*]? He said to him: "If Ben Zoma is on the outside,[129] then you are with him! The heart [*lev*] refers to the thirty-two[130] and they are hidden, and by means of them the world was created."[131]
>
> What are the thirty-two? He said to him: "The thirty-two paths. This may be compared to a king who was in the innermost of his chambers. The number of chambers was thirty-two and each chamber had a path. Is it fitting for this king to gather everything into his chambers by way of his paths? You would say 'No!' Is it fitting for him to reveal his pearls, treasures, precious things, and gems? You would say 'No!' What did he do? He touched the princess and comprised all the paths in her and in her garments. The one who wants to enter should look here. She was married to the king and she was also given to him as a gift. On account of his love for her, he sometimes calls her 'my sister,' for they are from one place, and sometimes he calls her 'my daughter,' for she is his daughter, and sometimes he calls her 'my mother.'"[132]

The heart of God, associated in other bahiric passages with the feminine,[133] is related specifically to the thirty-two paths of wisdom mentioned at the beginning of *Sefer Yeṣirah*. What is most significant to note in this text is the intricate use of gender symbols to convey the process of emanation of the feminine potency from the masculine. Again, we see that, in open contradiction to the normative sexual taboo, the king "touches" his own daughter, an obvious euphemism for sexual intercourse, and thereby comprises the thirty-two paths within her.[134] The incestuous relationship is conveyed as well by the image of the daughter being given to the king as a gift, which is contrasted with the image of her being married to him.

It is likely, moreover, that the paths contained within the feminine potency are related to the phallus.[135] Ontologically, the being of the female is constituted by the phallic energies derived from the male; indeed, the female comprises within herself the thirty-two paths of the masculine wisdom.[136] Finally, based on an earlier midrashic pericope, the love relationship between king and princess is construed in terms of three feminine images: sister, daughter, and mother.[137] The image of sister, the reader is explicitly told, indicates that the two derive from the same source, and the image of daughter suggests that the female comes from the male. The image of mother at first blush would seem to signify that in some sense the male comes from or is sustained by the female. Upon closer examination, however, it becomes clear that even the image of the mother does not challenge the ontological dependency of the female on the male, for in fact the three feminine images depict different kinds of love that the king has for the princess, a point that may be deduced from the midrashic tradition that served as the basis for this remark. The original parable, linked exegetically to the verse "O maidens of Zion, go forth and gaze upon King Solomon wearing the crown that his mother gave him on his wedding day, on his day of bliss" (Song 3:11), is offered as a way of delineating three levels of God's love for Israel, the highest one being that of the love of the son for the mother. Clearly, the intent here is not to imply that Israel is the mother of God, but only that God can love Israel even as a son loves his mother. The same explanation should be applied to the bahiric text, although the referents in that context are the king and the princess.[138]

The imagery of incest between father and daughter is employed explicitly in another passage. In this context, the divine attributes of mercy and judgment are referred to respectively as silver (*kesef*) and gold (*zahav*), based on the verse, "Silver is mine and gold is mine—says the Lord of Hosts" (Ḥaggai 2:8). With the focus on the word *zahav*, the reader is told that the attribute of judgment is called by this name because it is said to comprise three attributes signified by the three letters that make up the word *zahav*, the masculine (*zakhar*) symbolized by the *zayin*, the feminine or the soul (*neshamah*) symbolized by the letter *he* (since there are five names for the soul[139] and the letter *he* has the numerical value of five), and the foundation (*qiyyum*) of the other two designated by the *beit* (since the numerical value of this letter is two and the foundation is the attribute that unites male and female).[140] The function of the *beit* is further elucidated by the following parable:

> This may be compared to a king who had a good, pleasant, beautiful, and perfect daughter, and he married her to a prince. He clothed her, crowned her, adorned her, and gave her to him for a lot of money. Is it possible for the king to sit outside his house? You would say: No! Is it possible for him to sit all day with her constantly? You would say: No! What does he do? He places a window between himself and her, and whenever the daughter needs her father or the father the daughter, they join together through the window, as it is written, "The royal princess, her dress embroidered with golden mountings, is led inside to the king" (Ps. 45:14).[141]

It would appear from this tradition-complex as well that the basic myth involved the division of an androgynous male into a male (*zayin*) and a female (*he*) connected in turn by their foundation (*beit*). It is likely that the word "foundation," *qiyyum*, has a phallic connotation.[142] The implication of the mythic structure is disclosed by the parable: the king gives his daughter to a prince, but he continues to unite with her indirectly by way of the window. Despite the separation necessitated by the unfolding of the cosmic process, the father and daughter must have a mechanism to unite; these unifications reflect the fact that father and daughter are ontically of the same nature. The father-daughter incest, therefore, functions as a symbol to denote the sacred union above, which entails the reintegration of the lower and upper wisdom, by way of the phallic potency, designated here by the image of the window on account of the dual role of opening and closing.[143]

That the giving of the gift is in defiance of the natural order and social convention is substantiated by another passage in which the mythical conception of wisdom is placed by the redactor of the text in a somewhat different context:

> There is no judgment if there is no wisdom, for it says, "The Lord had given wisdom to Solomon" (1 Kings 5:26), and afterwards he judged the case [of the two mothers and the one infant] correctly, as it says, "When all Israel heard the decision that the king had rendered, they stood in awe of the king; for they saw that he possessed divine wisdom to execute justice" (1 Kings 3:28).
> What is the wisdom that the holy One, blessed be he, gave to Solomon? Solomon bears the name of the holy One, blessed be he, as it says,[144] "every Solomon mentioned in the Song of Songs is holy except for one." The holy One, blessed be he, said: "Since your name is like the name of my glory, I will marry you to my daughter." Was she given [to him] in matrimony? Let us say that she was bestowed upon him as a gift, as it is written, "The Lord had given wisdom to Solomon." [The nature of that wisdom] is not explained. Where, then, is it explained? In the continuation when it is written, "they saw that he possessed divine wisdom to execute justice." This refers to the very wisdom that God had given him,[145] which is with him in his chamber and in his midst to execute justice. What is [the meaning of] "to execute justice?" Whenever a person executes justice, the wisdom of God is in his midst, to assist him and to draw him near. If not, it keeps him at a distance and even punishes him, as it is written, "I, for my part, will discipline you" (Lev. 26:28).[146]

The nature of the gift is explicated in this passage by the contrast that is made between betrothal and the giving of the gift. Wisdom, which is identified as the hypostatic daughter of God, is already married, but she still can be given as a gift to Solomon. Reflecting on this remark, Scholem surmised that since wisdom is already married in the upper spheres, she was offered as a gift to Solomon in the terrestrial world.[147] I would add that this bestowal can take place because of the ontological resemblance between Solomon and God, a resemblance that is depicted in terms of the image of Solomon bearing the name of God. The meaning of this remark can be decoded only in light of two talmudic traditions: First, that the name of God is "peace" (*shalom*),[148] and, second, that the etymology of Solomon (*shelomo*) is *melekh she-ha-shalom shelo*, "the king to whom peace belongs."[149] The more specific theosophic connotation is related to the fact that in a number of bahiric passages the word *shalom* functions as a technical term to designate the attribute of God that corresponds to the phallic potency in the divine anatomy.[150] This is certainly the import of the statement that the name of Solomon is like the name of the glory. We may deduce from this passage that the technical term for the divine glory, *kavod*, itself has a phallic connotation.[151] Now we can better understand the comment that *ḥokhmah* was already married and given to Solomon as a gift. This does not imply, as Scholem explained, that *ḥokhmah* is married to the divine potency in the upper sphere and therefore must be given to Solomon as a gift in the terrestrial realm. On the contrary, the feminine wisdom is given as a gift to Solomon because this is the proper name of the masculine potency of the divine.[152]

While other passages dealing with the syzygy could be cited, it is sufficient from the texts discussed above to draw the following conclusions: just as the human below comprises male and female, so too the divine image above, and just as below the female is comprised within the male, so too above the female aspect is part of the male. The same symbolic structure is expressed in different imagery in another bahiric passage: "The students [of R. Amora] asked him, What is the *dalet*? He said to them, To what may this be compared? To ten kings who were in one place and all of them were wealthy. One of them was wealthy but not like the rest of them. Even though his wealth was great, he is called poor [*dal*] in relation to the wealthy ones."[153]

By an obvious play on the words *dalet* and *dal*, the fourth letter of the Hebrew alphabet symbolizes the divine gradation that is impoverished. In this context, the impoverished gradation is not distinguished in terms of gender from the other potencies that are depicted parabolically as kings. However, in subsequent kabbalistic literature, in some cases based on this very passage, the impoverished one, symbolized by the *dalet*, is associated more explicitly with the feminine *Shekhinah*, the state of poverty linked essentially to the character of femininity as that which has nothing of its own but only what it receives from the beneficent male.[154] The feminine quality of *dalet* is implicit in the *Bahir* itself,[155] for there is something distinctive about the potency symbolized by that letter inasmuch as it is both wealthy like the other potencies and poor in relation to them. Structurally, this parallels the image of the field that is connected to, yet separate from, the garden. The ontological condition of the feminine is that she is a weakened or inferior male.[156]

It may be concluded that, according to the myth proffered in the bahiric text, the upper wisdom is valorized as male and the lower wisdom as female, but even the latter is ultimately masculine. The point is epitomized in the parable, already alluded to above, of the seven sons of the king:

> He sat and expounded for them, there is *Shekhinah* below as there is *Shekhinah* above.[157] And what is this *Shekhinah*? I would say that it is the light that emanates from the first light, which is wisdom. This one, too, encompasses everything [*mesovev ha-kol*],[158] as it says, "all the earth is filled with his glory" (Isa. 6:3). What is its function here? To what may be this compared? To a king who has seven sons and he placed each and every one in his place. He said to them, Sit one atop the other! The lowest one said, I will not sit below and I will not be far from you! He said to them, Behold, I will rotate and I will see you all day, and this is the meaning of "all the earth is filled with his glory." Why is he amongst them? In order to establish and to sustain them.[159]

As we have seen, the lower *Shekhinah*, the light that emanates from the first light or wisdom, the upper *Shekhinah*, is elsewhere described in strikingly feminine images. Here, however, she is treated parabolically as one of the seven sons of the king. The ontological containment of the feminine in the masculine is reinforced in the continuation of this passage. The seven sons are related to the "seven holy forms," which are the seven limbs that make up the divine image with which Adam was created. The limbs are delineated as follows: two thighs, two hands, the phallus, and the head. The seventh is found in the woman who was constructed from the side (or rib) of the man.[160]

The ultimate religious task of the pious Jew—and the final goal of the historical process itself—is to achieve a state wherein the female is reintegrated into the male. In one section of the *Bahir*, a reworking of the aggadic interpretation of the word *yinnon* in Psalms 72:17 as a reference to the proper name of the Messiah,[161] the anonymous author reflects, "[The word *yinnon*] has a double *nun*, the bent *nun* and the straight *nun*, for [the redemption] must happen through the masculine and the feminine."[162] Commenting on this, Scholem noted, "This is Jewish gnosis, in pronounced contrast to antinomian and encratist tendencies."[163] Scholem goes on to contrast the idea of redemption implied in the bahiric text with the gender transformation enunciated in an apocryphal remark attributed to Jesus in the *Gospel of Thomas*. I have already had the occasion to mention this passage in chapter two, but it is worth repeating here. In response to the request of Simon Peter to ask Mary to leave the presence of the community of initiates since "women are not worthy of life," Jesus retorted: "I myself shall lead her to make her male, so that she too may become a living spirit resembling you males. For every woman who will make herself male will enter the kingdom of heaven."[164] This, according to Scholem, signifies a "triumph over the masculine and feminine . . . that reestablishes their original unity, but says nothing of redemption itself resulting from the union of the masculine and feminine. The conjunction of the two principles is certainly not the same as overcoming them in the reestablishment of an original androgynous state."[165]

Scholem's attempt to contrast the Christian gnosis and the Jewish on this score cannot be upheld. The Jewish gnosis as expressed in the *Bahir* and developed further in subsequent works of kabbalah is predicated on a notion of redemption that signifies a return to an original unity in the divine pleroma. In this unity, sexual differentiation is transcended, but only as a result of the feminine being absorbed into the masculine, and not because gender difference is completely obliterated so that there is neither male nor female, in the famous locution of Paul.[166] Heterosexual bonding is the mark of partial and temporary redemption in an unredeemed world; in the moment that redemption is consummated, however, the female is so totally contained in the male that there is no longer the need for the union of two distinct entities. The fragmentation of exile and the alienation of self are overcome not by hierogamy—the "continual coupling of the masculine and feminine potencies"[167]—but by "ritual androgynization"[168]—the ontological assimilation of the feminine in the masculine and the consequent reconfiguration of the male androgyne. Redemption signifies not the eradication of gender[169] but the restoration of the female to the male so that the female is contained in the male and the male in the female.

The kabbalistic perspective, in my judgment, accords with the position articulated in the ancient Valentinian gnostic *Gospel of Philip* (68:22–25), a work whose affinity to medieval kabbalah has been noted by various scholars:[170] "When Eve was still in Adam, death did not exist. When she was separated from him death came into being. If he enters again and attains his former self, death will be no more."[171] In a second passage from this work (70:10–20), it is again emphasized that the cause of death in the world was the separation of female from male, a remarkable rendering of the scriptural narrative of the sin of the first couple in the Garden of Eden. The task of Christ, accordingly, is "to repair the separation which was from the beginning" by joining together male and female in the bridal chamber.[172] Following the critical passage in Genesis 2:24 that speaks of the pairing of man and woman as the means by which the primordial condition of "one flesh" is attained, reinforced by the citation of this passage and its application to the "great mystery" of the relationship between Christ and the Church by Paul in the letter to the Ephesians (5:32), the author of the gnostic gospel presents spiritual marriage as the way that the original androgynous state is reconstituted.[173]

This union, which is enacted sacramentally within the bridal chamber, cannot be severed: "But the woman is united to her husband in the bridal chamber. Indeed those who have united in the bridal chamber will no longer be separated. Thus Eve separated from Adam because it was not in the bridal chamber that she united with him" (70:17–21).[174] Though the author of this text speaks of two forms of union, "marriage of defilement" and "undefiled marriage" (82:5), the latter is qualitatively different from the former; in an analogous manner to the *Expository Treatise on the Soul* discussed above, the bonding of man and woman in the corporeal world is (hetero)sexual in nature in contrast to the bonding in the "world of mystery," a spiritual pairing of will and not desire (82:8), which occasions the restoration of the female to the male and the consequent reconfiguration of the primordial state of androgyny wherein gender difference is eradicated. This is the intent of the following passage: "Whereas in this world the union is one of husband with wife—a case of strength complemented by weakness—in the eternal realm (aeon) the form of union is different, although we refer to them by the same names" (76:6–9).[175]

This, I surmise, is the message of the bahiric interpretation of the messianic name Yinnon. To be sure, as Scholem already observed, this text indicates that the messianic redemption involves both the masculine and feminine elements of the divine. Yet a close inspection of this redactional setting, as well as other texts in the *Bahir*, suggests that the feminine is itself part of the masculine. Hence immediately preceding the bahiric reflection on the name Yinnon, it is emphasized that the orthographic form of the straight *nun* appears at the end of a word to instruct that the "straight *nun* comprises the bent and the straight, but the bent is the foundation." The bent *nun*, which symbolically represents the anatomical connection of the brain and spinal cord, is considered to be the essence of the body. Yet the straight *nun* represents the state of androgyny, as it says explicitly in the conclusion of the passage, *nun arukhah kelulah mi-zakhar u-neqevah* (the elongated *nun* is comprised of masculine and feminine),[176] the very containment signified by the messianic name Yinnon.

The gender construction symbolized by the two forms of the letter entails not the polarity of male and female but the male, on the one hand, and the androgynous unity of male and female, on the other. The same point is made in the next textual unit of the *Bahir*, which deals with the open and closed *mem*, corresponding respectively to the masculine and feminine:

> Why is the open *mem* comprised of masculine and feminine and the closed [*mem*] masculine? To teach you that the essence of the *mem* is masculine. The opening [of

the *mem*] is added for the sake of the feminine. Just as the male does not give birth through the opening so the closed *mem* is not open, and just as the female gives birth and is open so the *mem* is closed and opened. Why did you include an opened and closed *mem*? For it is said, "Do not read *mem* but rather *mayyim*." The woman is cold and thus needs to be warmed by the male.[177]

According to this passage, the closed *mem* symbolizes the sterile male depicted as well as the barren womb. By contrast, the open *mem* comprises male and female and thus symbolizes the womb that gives birth. The open *mem* is a sign of fertility and virility because it contains both male and female. The fertile womb is represented by the open *mem*, which is linked essentially to the masculine, *iqqar ha-mem hu ha-zakhar*; indeed, the latter term may signify more specifically the *membrum virile*.[178] Hence the male organ is compared to the womb that gives birth, and the masculine is feminized. Alternatively, the gender transformation may be expressed as the masculinization of the feminine, that is, the womb that gives birth is valorized as a phallus, a motif that recurs in subsequent kabbalistic literature.[179]

It is possible, moreover, as I have suggested in another context, that the intricate gender symbolism in this text is an historical allusion to Christianity, insofar as Jesus was typically portrayed as the son that issued from the womb of the virgin, that is, the closed *mem*. Leaving aside this possibility, it can be concluded that in the *Bahir* the emphasis on the androgynous aspect of the Messiah, reflected in the double *nun* of the name Yinnon, is related to the presumption, borne out by the redactional setting wherein the aforementioned name is mentioned, that the female is part of the male. The kabbalistic mythos, attested in *Bahir* and subsequent texts, is essentially a deep reading of the Priestly version (Gen. 1:26–27) of the creation of man and woman (especially as mediated through the rabbinic conception of the primordial androgyne) in light of the Yahwist version (Gen. 2:21–24). That is, in the engendering myth of kabbalistic theosophy, there is no appreciable difference in orientation between the two creation accounts. On the contrary, the secondary status accorded the woman in the Yahwist version is used to interpret the ostensibly more egalitarian approach of the Priestly version.[180]

Splintering the Androgyne and Gender Im/Balance

The symbolic structure that I have claimed is operative in various strata of the bahiric text is confirmed, in my opinion, in one of the few kabbalistic texts that may have been authored by Abraham ben David of Posquiéres (known by the acronym Rabad), presented in the chain of tradition preserved by a number of kabbalists at a somewhat later date as one of the progenitors of esoteric lore.[181] Various scholars have commented on this passage, a sustained reflection on the rabbinic legend that Adam was created androgynous (*du-parṣufim*).[182] However, given the central importance and foundational aspect of this text, it would be prudent to cite it in full:

The Rabad explained that the reason for the creation [of Adam] as androgynous [*du-parṣufin*] was so that the woman would obey her husband for her life depends

> on him, and they should not each go his or her own way, but rather there should be a closeness and friendship between them without separation. Then there will be peace between them and harmony in their abode. Thus one finds with respect to the "agents of truth, whose action is truth."[183] The reason for the androgyny indicates two things. First, it is known that two opposites were emanated, one of pure judgment [*din gamur*] and the other of pure mercy [*raḥamim gemurim*]. If they had not been emanated as androgynous, each of them would act in accordance with its own attribute. It would then appear as if they were two [separate] powers, and each one would act without any connection to the other and without its assistance. But now that they were created androgynous, all their actions take place together, in an evenly balanced manner and perfect unity, without any separation. Moreover, if they had not been created androgynous, no perfect unity could emerge from them, the attribute of judgment could not rise to that of mercy, nor that of mercy to judgment. Now that they have been created androgynous, each of them draws close and unites with the other, and yearns and desires to be joined to the other, so that the tabernacle will be one. You find proof of this in the fact that each of the [divine] names refers to the other.[184] Thus you find that YHWH [the attribute of mercy] indicates the attribute of judgment, and Elohim [the attribute of judgment] the attribute of mercy, as in "the Lord rained upon Sodom and Gomorrah sulfurous fire" (Gen. 19:24). He passed from one attribute to the other.[185]

The two attributes of God, expressed in more or less standard rabbinic terminology, are correlated with the masculine and feminine aspects of the divine, which correspond to the earthly man and woman. The author of this text emphasizes that the attributes should not act independently but rather in concert, for to separate the attributes of judgment and mercy would be akin to creating a division in the Godhead between male and female or, in traditional terms, positing two divine powers.[186] The conjunction of the two attributes enables one to pass into the other so that acts of judgment can be ascribed to the name associated with mercy (YHWH) and acts of mercy to the name associated with judgment (Elohim). The unity of male and female is related, moreover, to the harmony that reigns between sun and moon, which are described in the liturgical blessing of the moon as "agents of truth, whose action is truth." This state stands in contrast to that which is described in the talmudic legend of the diminishing of the light of the moon, wherein the moon and sun are at odds with one another.[187] The scriptural account of the androgynous nature of the original human creation bespeaks the balance of male and female, sun and moon, the mystery of the image of two kings sharing one crown.

The same meaning is implied in the following passage in a commentary on the account of creation (*maʿaseh bereʾshit*) attributed to Isaac the Blind: "'When the Lord God made earth and heaven' (Gen. 2:4)—the name was not complete until Adam was created in the image of God and the seal was complete."[188] We may presume that, following an older midrashic tradition,[189] Isaac relates the complete name, which consists of YHWH and Elohim, to the attributes of mercy and judgment. In the symbolic purview of the kabbalist, as we have seen, these attributes correspond respectively to the masculine power to overflow and the feminine capacity to receive. Isaac (or an anonymous kabbalist whose view has been transmitted in his name) connects the complete name, which signifies divine androgyny, to the creation of Adam, who is said to have been made in God's image, *ṣelem elohim*. Through the manifestation of the image that is androgynous, the seal (*ḥotam*), which is the name of creation, YHWH Elohim (linked exegetically to Gen. 2:4), was completed. The implicit meaning of the text is rendered explicit in the following remark of Ezra of Gerona: "It says, 'May the glory of the Lord endure forever' (Ps. 104:31), for the name was not complete until Adam was created in the image of God, and the seal was complete. Thus the prophet said to the king of Tyre, 'You were the seal of perfection,' [*atah ḥotem tokhnit*] (Ezek. 28:12), that is to say, he was on the level of the first Adam who completed the ten *sefirot*."[190]

In what sense, however, does Adam complete the sefirotic pleroma? Ezra's point seems to be that the creation of Adam as male and female signifies the androgynous nature of the divine potencies, overflowing and receiving. But for Ezra, as for other kabbalists, including those responsible for the composition and/or redaction of the *Bahir*, the locus of androgyny is the phallus. The point is made artfully by Ezra in his commentary on the verse "a king bound in the tresses," *melekh asur ba-rehatim* (Song 7:6): "The drawing close of the glory to the glory and its unification [*qirvat ha-kavod ba-kavod we-hitaḥdutah*], and it compared the stature [*qomah*] to a palm tree [*tamar*], the tree that is male and female, one trunk and two branches [*we-ha-guf eḥad we-ha-anafim shenayyim*]."[191] In astonishingly simple terms, Ezra expresses the complex engendering myth adopted and elaborated by medieval kabbalists. The image of the king being bound in the tresses signifies the *hieros gamos* of the male and female glories, the sixth and tenth *sefirot*. However, the implicit heterosexual imagery of the reference to the two glories is immediately qualified by Ezra's interpretation of the words "Your stately form is like the palm," *zo'̓t qomatekh damtah le-tamar* (Song 7:8). On the face of it, the literal sense of the text suggests that the female persona is being described. Yet for Ezra, the palm tree alerts us to the fact that this is an androgynous being, as this type of tree, according to older sources, was believed to comprise both male and female traits.[192] The comparison of the body of the divine—the word *qomatekh* calls to mind the technical esoteric idiom *shi'ur qomah* (the "measure of the stature")[193]—to the palm tree alludes to the mystery of the androgynous phallus, "one trunk" with "two branches," that is, one gender with two sexuated manifestations, male and female.

The wisdom contained in this text, an ancient thread woven in the fabric of medieval kabbalah, is well expressed in a zoharic passage wherein the realization of the "holy unity" (*yiḥuda qaddisha*) of the divine is made dependent on the discernment that judgment is mercy and mercy judgment, an insight that is presented as the theosophical intent of the biblical injunction to know that the Lord is God, *lada'at ki yhwh hu ha-elohim* (Deut. 4:35). To apprehend the secret of worship, one must harness the two hearts, the evil and good inclinations,[194] by containing left in right, female in male.[195] But one cannot fathom the bond of faith unless one differentiates the opposites that are identical in their differentiation. And when the opposites are so differentiated, the hierarchical relationship comes into clear view: male takes priority over female.[196] The tone is set at the very beginning of the aggadic commentary attributed to Rabad: "The reason for the creation [of Adam] as androgynous was so that the woman would obey her husband for her life depends on him, and they should not each go his or her own way, but rather there should be a closeness and friendship between them without separation."

The anthropological perspective reflects the theosophic; to argue that the former is merely contingent on specific historical factors while the latter is an atemporal metaphysical truth may be dismissed as an apologetic argument. The orientation of the kabbalists precludes the tenability of separating the two spheres, for the assumption is that there is a reciprocal mirroring of the mundane and divine. The social dominance of woman by man in the earthly realm reflects the ontically inferior status of the feminine vis-à-vis the masculine within the Godhead. Just as in the anthropological sphere, woman must be subservient to man, so in the divine realm, judgment must be conjoined to mercy so that there will be no separation above. Divine unity depends ultimately on the containment of judgment in mercy, the union of female and male, which is marked by the onomastic conjunction YHWH Elohim.[197]

The perspective affirmed in this kabbalistic text, which expresses a symbolic theme reiterated in a plethora of sources, is typical of the medieval rabbinic attitude toward women as subordinate to men, an engendering that is rooted exegetically in the myth of the creation of woman from man in the second chapter of Genesis. Consider the formulation of Abraham ben David in his *Baʿalei ha-Nefesh*:

> Initially, the Creator, may his name be elevated and blessed, created his world in six days, and on the sixth he created cattle, creeping beings, and wild beasts, and at the end he created man, like someone who is making a banquet and he prepares all the needs of the meal, and afterwards he brings his guests. In an analogous manner, the Creator, may he be elevated, acted, for after he created the heavens and the constellations, and the earth and all of its produce, the seas and all that comes forth from them, he created man and positioned him over all the lower beings, as it is written, "You have made him master over your handiwork, laying everything beneath his feet" (Ps. 8:7). You also bestowed the supernal beings to serve him, as it is written, "They shall serve as lights in the expanse of the sky to shine upon earth" (Gen. 1:15). . . . How wondrous are the acts of the Creator, and who can comprehend their secret? For all the creatures were created male and female, but man was created as one, and afterward from him he created for him a "fitting helper" (ibid., 2:18). Who can stand on the depth of his wonders to reach the limit of the wisdom of his actions? . . .
>
> I will say in the simplicity of my mind that for the welfare of man and for his pleasure God created him as one, for had they been created male and female from the earth as the rest of the creatures were created, the woman would have been in relation to the man like the female beast in relation to the male, for she does not accept the sovereignty of the male and she does not stand with him in order to serve him . . . and they also do not unite one with another since originally this one was created

> by itself and that one was created by itself. Therefore, the Creator saw the need of man and his pleasure, and he created him alone, and he took one of his ribs and constructed the woman from it, and he brought her to man to be his wife, and to be a helpmate and support to him for she is considered by him as one of his limbs that was created to serve him. Thus, man rules over her like he rules over his limbs, and she desires him as his limbs desire the pleasure of his body. . . .
> Thus [the verse says] "I will make a fitting helper for him" (ibid.), I will create her in the manner that she will be a helpmate opposite him [*ezer kenegddo*], a "helpmate" [*ezer*] so that she will serve him in all his needs, "opposite him" [*kenegddo*] so that she will constantly stand with him. Therefore, when the man saw her he knew that she was taken from him, he said, "Hence a man leaves his father and mother and he cleaves to his wife, so that they become one flesh" (ibid., 2:24), that is, "it is appropriate for this one to be with me constantly and I will be with her, and we will be one flesh." Thus, it is appropriate for a man to love his wife like himself, to honor her, to have compassion over her, and to protect her as he would protect one of his limbs. Similarly, she is obligated to serve him, to honor him, and to love him as herself for she was taken from him.[198]

Consistent with earlier rabbinic sources, Abraham ben David emphasizes that the Jewish man is obligated to express through his actions and words the love of his wife, but it cannot be denied that on the whole this passage presents an androcentric perspective. Focusing exclusively on the second biblical account of the creation of the female from one of the ribs taken from the male, the latter is accorded a position of supremacy and dominion over the former. Indeed, in this matter, the human being is distinguished from all other sentient beings: only Adam is created initially as a male so that he could rule over the female constructed from one of the limbs of his body. This anthropological conception underlies the theosophic position expressed in the mystery of the androgyne attributed to the same author. The unity of male and female in the divine realm is predicated on the subordination of the latter to become a vessel to receive the luminous/seminal discharge of the former. The cooperation of these two attributes, the making of balances, is made possible because Adam was created androgynous, but the nature of androgyny is decidedly masculine, for the left was contained in the right; on account of that containment one attribute can be refracted, enclothed, and merged in its opposite.

Any rupture in the divine is detrimental, but the severance of female from male and the consequent adulation of her as an autonomous power are treated by kabbalists as far more problematic. Note, for instance, that repeatedly in kabbalistic texts one finds the admonition against reifying the female and worshipping her exclusively, a theme already attested, as I noted above in passing, in a bahiric fragment. Consider, for example, the zoharic gloss on the interpretation of the "heave offering," *terumah*, as "two of one hundred," *terei mi-me'ah*:

> Come and see: All the holy gradations of the mystery of faith [*darggin qaddishin di be-raza di-meheimanuta*] through which the holy One, blessed be he, is revealed are the ten gradations . . . and the ten amount to one hundred. When it is incumbent

> to elevate the lower point, it is forbidden to take her by herself, but rather her and her consort, and these are the two from the hundred . . . for it is necessary not to separate them at all but to unite her and her consort.[199]

Reification of the feminine potency is portrayed as the theological root for idolatry,[200] referred to as "heresy" (*harisah*) in the anonymous *Maʿarekhet ha-Elohut*,[201] but we do not find any corresponding warning about worshipping the male exclusively. On the contrary, just the opposite is true, as is attested, for instance, by another passage in the zoharic corpus,[202] an exegetical reflection on the scriptural account of the night of deliverance of the Israelites from Egyptian servitude, "this night is the Lord's vigil," *hu ha-laylah ha-zeh la-yhwh shimmurim* (Exod. 12:42).[203] Encoded here is the kabbalistic teaching that redemption comes by way of the union of male and female, a secret contained in the plural form of *shimmurim* as well as in the expression *ha-laylah ha-zeh*, for the noun *laylah* is feminine and the pronoun *zeh* masculine. The unification of the two notwithstanding, the masculine is privileged. Thus, we read in the continuation of the zoharic text, "In the place that male and female are found there is praise only for the male. Hence, in their praises, the Israelites praised the male and not the female, as it is written, 'this [*zeh*] is my God and I will glorify him' (ibid., 15:2), for there is no praise in a place where male and female are found except for the male."[204] That worship of the female constitutes idolatry, whereas worship of the male (especially in the place of union of male and female) is pious devotion, is an application of the larger axiological assumption that feminine judgment ideally must be contained in masculine mercy, the crowning point that is the foundation stone.

The unity of male and female within the pleroma is predicated on the subordination or passivity of the female. The theosophical structure reflects and reifies the social dynamic. The point is made in slightly different terms by the grandson of Rabad, Asher ben David, who comments thus on the symbolic significance of the Tetragrammaton:

> The three letters of the explicit name [*shem ha-meforash*] are called "his great name" [*shemo ha-gadol*], and they are *yod he waw* . . . and they are the name of the one concealed [*neʿelam*] who engraves them through wisdom, but the final *he* is repeated and it alludes to the glory of God, and it is called in the Torah *kevod YHWH*, and it is called in the language of the rabbis, blessed be their memory, *Shekhinah*, and it is the attribute of judgment that joins the attribute of mercy.[205]

The Tetragrammaton is made up of three letters, *yod he waw*, which represent the masculine potency of the divine, and the last letter, *he*, which is a repetition of the second letter, symbolizes the feminine glory that must be conjoined to the masculine. The joining of judgment with mercy results in the amelioration of the former by the latter, which signifies the dependence of the feminine on the masculine. Woman is thus categorically accorded the role of serving the man, for ontically she draws her life force from him.[206]

Many texts could have been cited to illustrate the prominence of this androcentric perspective in the discourse of the kabbalists, but one source that is particularly illuminating and bold in its formulation is the treatise, *Maʿarekhet ha-Elohut*. Elaborating on the aggadic motif that God had to combine the attributes of judgment and mercy in order to create the world, the anonymous kabbalist writes:

> The beginning of thought [*teḥillat ha-maḥshavah*] is for the sake of the completion of what is necessitated by the end of the action [*sof ha-maʿaseh*].[207] At the beginning of this thought [the attribute of judgment] was joined together with mercy, that is to say, the attribute of judgment was contained in mercy potentially but not in actuality. This is the reason that the man rules in his house,[208] and "all the honor of the princess is inward" (Ps. 45:14). From here the enlightened will be aroused regarding what will be made comprehensible below with respect to what they said regarding the creation of Adam and his wife. Initially there arose in thought [the idea] to create two, but in the end only one was created. By means of this concatenation Adam and Eve were created below androgynous, that is, even though it arose in thought that they would actually be two, if they had been originally created as two the one would turn in one direction and the other in another direction in the way of animals, and the man would not have been able to extract his desire from the woman and to be assisted by her in the preservation of the species and in the worship of his Creator. However, insofar as they were originally androgynous, even when they are separated they are one flesh and they are attached to one another with youthful love. The man whose wife has died has already been compared to someone who has lost something.[209]

The conjunction of male and female, so central to the occult wisdom and praxis of kabbalah, is predicated on the reestablishment of the original androgynous state wherein the female aspect of judgment is contained in the male aspect of mercy. According to a zoharic gloss, the word *ishshah*, "woman," can be decoded as "*esh he*, bound as one,"[210] that is, the three consonants of *ishshah, alef shin he*, can be broken into *esh*, which means "fire," and the remaining letter *he*, a scribal circumlocution for the Tetragrammaton; hence in the name *ishshah* is encoded an allusion to the mystery of the amelioration of judgment by mercy, the incorporation of the feminine in the masculine. The nature of the male androgyne is highlighted in the following anonymous text, apparently representing an early Geronese tradition, that affirms the morphological correspondence of the divine anthropos and the limbs of the human body purportedly implied by the verse "Let us make Adam in our image and in our likeness" (Gen. 1:26):

> The head of man corresponds to *Keter Elyon*, which is the splendor and glory of the whole body. Concerning this the prophet said, "His head is finest gold" (Song 5:11). The brain and the palate of man correspond to *Ḥokhmah*, which is the inwardness of all the intermediaries, as it is written, "his palate is delicious" (ibid., 5:16). His tongue corresponds to *Binah* to bring to light all the forces. This is the meaning of the verse "and all of him is delightful" (ibid.), for just as the tongue is the essence of all one's speech, so *Binah* emits all the forces by means of the flux that comes forth from her. The extension of the body corresponds to *Tif'eret*, for it is the force and strength of the whole body. Concerning this attribute Moses our

teacher, peace be upon him, said, "O God, the God of the spirits of all flesh" [*el elohei ha-ruḥot le-khol basar*] (Num. 16:22). The arms correspond to *Ḥesed* and *Gevurah*, *Ḥesed* is the right and *Gevurah* the left, *Ḥesed* is mercy and *Gevurah* judgment. His feet correspond to *Neṣaḥ* and *Hod, Neṣaḥ* on the right and *Hod* on the left. *Yesod* corresponds to the phallus that is set in the middle. This is the form that we have explained . . . and it corresponds to the human body, for the nine *sefirot* are portrayed as an anthropos.

A person should not err when he does not see the tenth *sefirah*, for when *Tif'eret* was mentioned there was enough [of an allusion], and the intelligent one will understand. When Aḥer saw the completion of the [sefirotic] edifice and he saw as well *Malkhut*, the tenth attribute, he cut the shoots and said, "Heaven forbid, perhaps there are two powers."[211] He did not consider in his heart that the wife of a man is set aside and prepared for him all the time, in a perfect union without any separation, like the heart of a man who is prepared. Concerning it the verse said, "And the Lord spoke to his heart" (Gen. 8:21). She is also called soul [*neshamah*] . . . the soul [*nefesh*] is the tenth attribute, that is, the will [*raṣon*], for by means of her the supernal will [*raṣon ha-elyon*] is revealed and is actualized. She is also called the house of God [*beit el*], for she is a house for beauty [*beit le-tif'eret*]. She is also called *beit tif'eret*, "and I will add glory to my glorious house" (Isa. 60:7). She is also called *kol*, as it says, "I the Lord do all these things" (ibid., 45:7). She is the celestial Jerusalem and the celestial daughter of Zion.[212]

This text, which graphically illustrates the point that I was making above regarding the masculine nature of the divine androgyny, is apparently one of the earliest attempts on the part of a kabbalist to depict the correspondence of divine and human limbs. One is immediately struck by the fact that the divine image is principally a male form. To be sure, the feminine aspect of the divine, the tenth attribute or *Malkhut*, is treated as the spouse of the sixth emanation, *Tif'eret*, but this image does not imply ontological autonomy; on the contrary, it is emphasized that the wife is united with her husband like the heart is united with the rest of the body, an image that doubtless conveys ontological dependence. Other names of the tenth emanation are given at the end of the passage, but they are not related directly to the image of the anthropos, even though some of them attest to an instrumentalist characterization of the female; thus *Shekhinah*, the "celestial Jerusalem" or the "celestial daughter of Zion," is identified as the will by means of which the supernal will is made known,[213] the house of God or, more specifically, the house of *Tif'eret*, that is, the vessel that contains the masculine potency.[214] The critical point is that the anthropomorphic image is primarily masculine, for the feminine element is comprised within the male.

Overcoming Gender Dimorphism and the *Coincidentia Oppositorum*

The implications of the kabbalistic principle of androgyny articulated in the text attributed to the Rabad are drawn out explicitly in many passages scattered in the landscape of what has been preserved as zoharic literature, *sifrut ha-zohar,* which is not a single composition but an anthology of disparate textual units that cohere together philologically and ideationally. For example, in one passage, we find the following description of primordial Adam: "When the holy One, blessed be he, created man he created him perfect, as it says, 'God made man straight' [*asher asah elohim et ha-adam yashar*] (Eccles. 7:29). 'Man' [*et ha-adam*]: male and female, and the female was contained in the male; thus it is written straight."[215] The perfect human form is one wherein the female is comprised in the male. In one zoharic homily, the theme is linked exegetically to God's partitioning light and darkness (Gen. 1:4): "If you say there was an actual separation [*havdalah mammash*], it is not so. Rather, day comes from the side of light, which is the right, and night comes from the side of darkness, which is the left, and when they emerged as one he separated them. The separation was from his side, to gaze face-to-face, and to cleave one to the other, so that all would be one."[216]

Obviously influenced by the language of the creation of woman from the rib or side of man (Gen. 2:21–24), the above interpretation of the creation of light and dark, which facilitated the demarcation of the first day and night, is interpreted theosophically as the emanation of the male and female potencies from the primordial androgyne. The remark that the "separation was from his side" reminds the reader that this androgyne was gendered as the male that comprises the female within itself, a very precise reading of the biblical text. The purpose of the separation is to provide the ontic condition that makes possible the union that is troped in the ocularcentric term of gazing face-to-face (*le'istakkela anppin be-anppin*), a spectral state that presupposes the existence of an other; that alterity, however, is short-lived, as the ultimate purpose of the conjunction of male and female is to restore the latter to the former so that the original androgyne will be reestablished, "to cleave one to the other, so that all would be one" (*le'itddabbeqa da be-da lemehewei kola ḥad*).

The reintegration of the feminine in the masculine as a consequence of heterosexual union is depicted as well as the containment of left in the right, judgment in mercy. To cite two pertinent examples, both of which deal with the hierogamy in the divine pleroma:

> When the Matrona sits with the King and they are joined face-to-face, who will come between them? Who will come close to them? When they are joined the one is sweetened[217] by the other. . . . Therefore the judgments are sweetened, one in the other, and the upper and lower beings are perfected.[218]

> The feminine emanates in her side and cleaves to the side of the masculine until she is separated from his side and comes to join with him face-to-face. When they are joined they appear indeed as one body. From here it is learnt that the male alone appears as half-a-body [*pelag gufa*], all merciful, and so it is with the female,[219] but when they are joined as one everything appears indeed as one body. And thus it is. So too when a male unites with a female everything is one body, and all the worlds are joyous, for everything is blessed from the complete body. This is the mystery of "Therefore the Lord blessed the Sabbath day and hallowed it" (Exod. 20:11), for

> everything was found as one complete body. The Matrona cleaves to the King and thus there is one body. Therefore blessings are found on that day. From here [it can be deduced] the one who is not found as male and female is called half-a-body.[220]

Without a mate of the opposite sex, neither man nor woman would be complete. Yet true equality—signified by the oxymoron "same but other"—between male and female may be envisioned only when the sexual duality is finally overcome, for in that situation the negative aspect of the feminine is neutralized or ameliorated by her containment in the masculine. Hence the alterity of the feminine in relation to the masculine is not an irreducible otherness; on the contrary, the conception articulated in *Zohar* is predicated on the possibility of effacing the feminine by enfolding her back into the masculine, an idea that patently runs counter to our biological facticity.[221] As I noted in chapter two, prior to the division of divine unity into a gendered binary of male and female represented by the double-faced Adam, the latter was contained in the former. The notion of containment here implies that in the preemanative stage male and female are not distinguishable as distinct forces, but this does not imply a complete transcendence of gender, since this state is one in which the female is ontically contained in the male.

According to the idiomatic expression of one zoharic passage, the ostensible equalization of gender difference is described as a state wherein "everything rises on one scale and in one root everything is united" (*we-khola be-ḥad matqela salqa u-min shorsha ḥad khol itḥabar*).[222] The image of the scale with its two weights connotes the binary of male and female. To speak of one scale is to imply that there is balance between the two, an idea further substantiated by the claim that everything is united in one root, that is, in the one source there is no sexual differentiation inasmuch as the feminine is enfolded back into the masculine whence it derived. As I have noted several times, androgyny in kabbalistic theosophy is primarily and essentially male, the female being a secondary entity with a lower ontological and axiological status.

The philosophical import of the myth of the androgyne is enunciated in a passage in *Ketem Paz*, the zoharic commentary by Simeon Lavi:[223]

> Now, my son, open the eye of your intellect to understand the root of this secret from its essence, for it is amongst the secrets that are concealed in the matter of creation. Bless the Lord who has advised me regarding this secret. You already know that wisdom necessitates that in the mystery of the world of unity [*be-sod olam ha-aḥdut*] the androgyne was created in one body [*livro du parṣufin be-guf eḥad*], for the primal Adam and his counterpart were created androgynously, to instruct about the unity of emanation. This was not the case with respect to the creation of all other animate beings, for the male was created alone and the female alone. However, in the case of primal Adam and his counterpart, who are the image and likeness [*ṣelem u-demut*], they were created androgynous [*du-parṣufin*] in one body, to instruct about the supernal Adam in whose image Adam was created, for the powers of bestowing and receiving were in complete unity [*aḥdut aḥat*] in the depths of the Nothing [*omqei ha-ayin*].
>
> When his wisdom decreed to emanate and to reveal his glory, the emanation

extended from here to there until it stood in the place that it stood, as his wisdom, blessed be he, necessitated. It was necessary for the light that was extending to return back and to be hidden, as we have said on many occasions.[224] The face of the moon turned to the face of the sun, face-to-face, and thus day was distinguished from night, for they made use of one crown, and the moon was diminished in order to receive light from the sun. In this manner, in the beginning of creation, primal Adam was androgynous. Afterward the holy One, blessed be he, divided him, and they turned face-to-face in the pattern of the celestial lights. From here you can understand the indictment of the moon against the sun, which is alluded to in their words, may peace be upon them: The moon said before the blessed one, "Can two kings make use of one crown?" The complaint of the earth was against heaven, in the secret of "and the earth was formless and void" [*tohu va-vohu*] (Gen. 1:2), flabbergasted and dumbfounded [*toheh u-voheh*].[225] They compared this parabolically to a king who acquired two servants. On the one he decreed [that he be sustained from the depository and on the other he decreed that he toil and eat].[226]
The principle that arises from all this is that when a boundary was given to each one and it was appointed over its labor, regarding the one that rules during the day that it rule during the day and regarding the one that rules during the night that its rule be at night, as it is written, "the great light for the rule of day and the small light for the rule of night" (Gen. 1:16), peace arose in the world for the lesser one is subservient to the greater one, and they turned in the glance of love [*shavu be-mabaṭ ha-ahavah*].[227]

Fearful Asymmetry/One Eye and the World That Is Entirely Masculine

From a logical standpoint—at least the binary logic that has informed Western philosophical reasoning since antiquity—it is reasonable to assume that gender is meaningful to the degree that one posits correlative terms, that is, there can be masculine only if there is feminine and feminine only if there is masculine. The possibility of imagining one gender without the other seemingly makes as little sense as trying to imagine right without left, before without after, above without below, and so on; gender, simply put, is a function of difference, and in the absence of difference there can be no gender.[228] Yet the kabbalistic orientation has been shaped precisely by a *fearful asymmetry* of this sort. In one of his compositions, de León expresses the matter in straightforward and relatively simplistic terms that call to mind parallel formulations in zoharic literature: "The left is contained in the right, and the essence is in the right, which comprises the left. . . . And thus you can know that since the essence is in the right, in every place it is on top of the left . . . and this is the secret of what is said 'And Aaron lifted his hands toward the nation and blessed them' (Lev. 9:22), it is written 'his hand' [*yado*] to illustrate that the essence is in the right."[229]

It is possible to speak of the right being contained in the left but not in the same manner that the left is contained in the right, for the essence is in the right and not in the left; ontologically, there is one hand as the right comprises the left within itself. One might still argue that I would have to grant that the right itself is not conceivable without its opposite, even if I insist that, for kabbalists, the left has no autonomous ontic status. Since the language in which I think, converse, and write is reflective of this binary opposition, I must concede the validity of the point. However, the ontology promoted by kabbalists is not beholden to the differential logic; in the discourse of kabbalistic mythopoeisis, gender is not a function of correlation but of self-actualized singularity. As I have already remarked, in great measure this is due to the influence of the biblical notion—reflective of a parthenogenetic cosmogony—that woman is anatomically contained in and excised from man whence she was constructed into an independent being (*ezer kenegddo*), a helpmate facing/opposing him (Gen. 2:18).

Beneath this stone one may find the ontological principle par excellence that informed the worldview of medieval kabbalists, that being in its manifold aspects is colored by this asymmetry: the primal form of the formless, configured in the mirror of imagination, is the male that contains the female within itself as other. Thus we find explicit characterizations of the highest emanation of the divine, sometimes even of the infinite itself, as a world of pure masculinity prior to the dimorphic division into male and female. As Joseph of Hamadan put it:

> The *sefirah* of *Keter* is exclusively male for it does not receive, but the rest of the *sefirot* are androgynous . . . overflowing and receiving, overflowing from one side and receiving from one side, and thus they are called androgynous. The attributes that are called male are *Ḥokhmah, Tif'eret, Neṣaḥ,* and *Ṣaddiq*, they overflow and receive with the exception of the attribute of *Keter* whose gradation is greatly expanded, he sees and is not seen, and the attributes that restrain the overflow are called the attributes that receive, *Binah, Gevurah, Hod*, and *Malkhut*.[230]

In a similar vein, commenting on the words in *Sefer Yeṣirah* 1:6, "for the Lord is one and he has no second" (*she-adon yaḥid we-ein lo sheni*), Joseph ben Shalom Ashkenazi, elaborating upon the language of Azriel of Gerona in the latter's commentary to the same passage,[231] writes:

> [T]he Supernal Crown [*keter elyon*] is necessarily one on account of the force that is unified in it, and the Supernal Crown has no potentiality for duality [*koaḥ sheniyyut*] just as it is inappropriate to ascribe to the Cause of Causes [*illat ha-illot*][232] the numerical value of oneness [*mispar aḥdut*], multiplicity [*ribbuy*], existence [*meṣi'ut*], differentiation [*hefred*], place [*maqom*] or boundary [*gevul*], so it is with respect to the Supernal Crown, for between it and the power of its cause there is no distinction but that the one is cause and the other effect. Since the Supernal Crown is singular [*yaḥid*], one must be careful with respect to the bond of unity [*lehizaher be-qesher ha-yiḥud*], and "he has no second," duality [*sheniyyut*] is not appropriate to it at all.[233]

According to this kabbalist, between Ein Sof and *Keter*, the first emanation, there is no substantial difference other than the fact that one is the cause and the other the effect, a turn of phrase we find as well in David ben Yehudah he-Ḥasid.[234] The import of this locution can be appreciated only if one is mindful of the philosophical axiom widely affirmed by medieval thinkers that the effect always shares a nature with its cause, whether this is explained in Aristotelian terms, because the actuality of the cause must be similar to the actuality of the effect, or in Plotinian terms, because what participates in its cause cannot be wholly different from its source.[235] Needless to say, this one difference makes quite a difference, as may be seen from Joseph ben Shalom Ashkenazi's interpretation of the directive in *Sefer Yeṣirah* 1:4, "ten and not nine":

> This comes to warn you about the Supernal Crown [*keter elyon*], even though it is not comprehended, and thus it is called "nothing" [*ayin*], even so it contains in itself the reality of being for itself [*meṣi'ut yesh bo le-aṣmo*]. Therefore it says "ten and not nine," so you would not say that since the Supernal Crown is not comprehended just like the Cause of Causes, perhaps, God forbid, the Supernal Crown would not be included in the enumeration; thus is says "ten and not nine," so as not to remove the Supernal Crown from the *sefirot*.[236]

Keter, though it is nothing (*ayin*), is counted as the first emanation as it contains within itself some numerical distinction—it possesses the ontic status of *meṣi'ut yesh*, which I have rendered "reality of being." Ein Sof, by contrast, completely transcends all enumeration and demarcation even the ascription of (non)being; thus the reader is warned by Joseph ben Shalom Ashkenazi not to think it appropriate to attribute a "potency of life," *koaḥ nafshi*, to the *causa causarum*.[237] Still, the proximity of Ein Sof and *Keter* is such that the two cannot be ontically separated,[238] and hence just as all duality is to be removed from the former, so must all duality be removed from the latter; the one, as the other, may be characterized as a unity of nondifferentiation. "The secret is that the Cause of Causes necessitates from itself the Supernal Crown, the intellect in its uttermost simplicity [*sekhel pashuṭ be-takhlit ha-peshiṭut*] to the point that there is no difference between it and its cause except that the one is the cause and the other the effect."[239]

The exclusively masculine nature of God's highest manifestation is affirmed in the statement in *Idra Rabba*, "There is no left in this concealed Ancient One [*atiqa*], for everything is right."[240] Glossing this passage, Vital remarked, "It is known that in the Ancient One there is no left because it is entirely right . . . and the two faces are considered as one."[241] From this we see that, in the nonbinary logic that kabbalists apply to account for the highest aspect of the divine, it is possible, indeed necessary, to speak of maleness without complementary femaleness; there is only one side, a world that is entirely right without any corresponding left, a world of pure mercy without any admixture of judgment. In other passages from the *Idrot* strata of zoharic literature, the asymmetry is conveyed by the image of the open eye on the right that is not complemented by a corresponding eye on the left as we find in the lower configuration, *Ze'eir Anpin*, which comprises both mercy and judgment.[242] The zoharic symbolism impels us to contemplate a notion of masculinity before the division into female and male, right-sidedness prior to the distinction between left and right. Articulating the gender implications of the zoharic image, Moses Cordovero wrote:

> In the secret of the equilibrium below in *Zeᶜeir Anpin*, there is right and left and thus there are two eyes, the right eye and left eye, but *Keter* is entirely right . . . and just as below there are two eyes for the sake of the equilibrium between right and left, above they become one on account of the unity. . . . Below right and left are two, but above they are one, and verily everything is right. This matter relates to the secret that all ten *sefirot* are unified in the root of unity and their dissemination causes their diversification. . . . Hence when the *sefirot* ascend to *Keter* they do not exhibit right or left and branching out, but rather everything is right and one unity, and from the right the left comes forth. . . . Thus the existence that is prior to the emanation of the left is right, and hence *Keter* is mercy, for the existence that precedes every place of judgment is mercy and from mercy everything concatenates. Therefore, when the entities return to the single point in their source, they are all contained in mercy, for there is no left there as it did not yet emanate and everything is right and one reality. This is the principle for all existents: They are all rooted in *Keter* and they are all right and one aspect.[243]

In the fullness of the divine nothing, the luminous dark of *Keter*, the feminine is so completely incorporated in the masculine that there is no need to demarcate it as autonomous.[244] To be even more precise, according to the formulation adopted by many kabbalists, the incorporation of the female in the male in the primal androgyny wherein opposites coalesce is positioned in the phallic corona. Expressed geometrically, the female assumes the form of the encircling line that crowns the point.[245] I detect an allusion to this secret in the following passage included in the printed version of *Sifra di-Ṣeniᶜuta*:

> "God said, Let us make man" (Gen. 1:26). It does not say "the man" [*ha-adam*] but simply "man" [*adam*] to exclude the supernal man who was made through the complete name.[246] When the one was perfected, the other was perfected, male and female were perfected to perfect everything. YHWH—the aspect of the male, Elohim—the aspect of the female. The male emanated and he was arrayed in his arrayments like the measure of the mouth of the penis [*ke-amah de-fumeih de-amah*].[247] The kings that were destroyed exist here, the judgments of the male are strong in the beginning and at rest in the end, and it is the opposite for a female.[248]

The supernal Adam, the divine anthropos in whose image the earthly Adam was created, comprises male and female, a point signified biblically by the use of the full name YHWH Elohim in conjunction with the creation of this form. What, however, was the nature of the masculine and feminine in the highest level of the Godhead? "The male emanated and he was arrayed in his arrayments like the measure in the mouth of the penis." I suggest that embedded in this passage is the idea that the primordial anthropomorphic form was male, the female element being found in the image of the mouth of the penis, that is, the corona.[249] In this spot is the ontic root of the feminine in the male androgyne, and hence therein the unbalanced forces of judgment, the Edomite kings who perished, are found in a rectified state.[250] In what is apparently an exposition of this text in the *Idra Rabba* section of *Zohar*, we read:

> When this penis [*amah*] extends, the side of strength [*gevurah*] extends from those strengths of the feminine, and it is sunk in the feminine in a place that is marked in the genitals, the covering of the whole body of the feminine, and in that place it is called the nakedness of the bride, the place to hide the penis, which is called "mercy" [*ḥesed*], in order to ameliorate this strength that is comprised of five strengths in that mercy that is comprised of five mercies. The mercy is on the right and the strength on the left, the one is ameliorated by the other, and they are called *adam*, comprised of two sides.[251]

What is implicit in this older source is made explicit by later kabbalists, especially Luria and his disciples. I will cite several texts that illustrate the centrality of this theme in the symbolic hierarchy of Lurianic kabbalah. Vital writes in one passage:

> Our rabbis, blessed be their memory, have said that the soul has five names: *nefesh, ruaḥ, neshamah, ḥayyah, yeḥidah.*[252] *Yeḥidah* is from *Arikh Anpin*, and it is called *yeḥidah,* for from *Arikh* and below there is a female, but in *Arikh Anpin* there is no female but only male [*ein bo neqevah ki im dekhura*], and the reason is that from *Imma* and below there are judgments, and thus there is a female for the female is the aspect of judgments. . . . Concerning him Scripture says, "Behold the eye of the Lord is upon those who fear him" (Ps. 33:18). The explanation is that there are two eyes below, right and left, but he is mercy within mercy, and thus he is called "eye," for there is but one eye. Hence, it is called *yeḥidah*, for there is no female there but only male [*ki ein sham neqevah ki im zakhar*], [and thus it] is called singular [*yaḥid*].[253]

The gradation of soul that corresponds to *Arikh Anpin* is called *yeḥidah* because there is no other in relation to it, as it contains everything in a nondifferentiated unity. The matter is explicated in a second passage: "The great encompassing reality, which is *yeḥidah* in the aspect of *Arikh Anpin*, does not encompass from the perspective of parts but rather it encompasses everything in one equanimity . . . and therefore it is called *yeḥidah*, for in it there is only one aspect alone in a single equanimity."[254] In a discourse on the world of emanation, Vital described the relationship of *Keter* to Ein Sof in similar language:

> Initially, *Keter* was a single point comprised of ten. This point emanated and it garbed the entire light of Ein Sof. . . . Know that this light that is above *Keter*, even though it has some judgment, it is so ameliorated that it is not considered judgment at all, but when it enters *Keter*, which is already a vessel, it is considered judgment. But everything is one configuration [*parṣuf eḥad*] since the vessel is pure and refined. Thus, there is no feminine in it as there is below in *Abba* and *Imma, Zeʿeir* and *Nuqba*, but everything is comprised in one configuration, and concerning it is said the "eye of the Lord" (Ps. 33:18), and there are not two eyes, that is, *Ḥesed* and *Din*, for everything is one.[255]

In the light of Ein Sof, which is garbed in the point of *Keter*, the aspect of judgment is completely mitigated, and even in the vessel of *Keter*, which contains this light, judgment is dissolved entirely in mercy and is thus not discernible as a distinct quality. Since there is no polarity of mercy and judgment in the highest configuration, in contrast to what is found in the other configurations, the poetic image of one eye is applied to *Keter.* In another passage, the purely masculine nature of the divine in its ontologically originary state is expressed by Vital in the image of the "first copulation" (*ziwwug ri'shon*):

> Indeed, in the first time of the first copulation, the male was aroused by himself [*nit'orer ha-zakhar me-aṣmo*] without arousal of the feminine, and there arose in him the will and the desire to copulate [*raṣon we-ta'awah lehizdawweg*] even though as of yet there was no aspect of the female waters [*mayyin nuqvin*]. Therefore, this copulation is very hidden and it was not in the aspect of the intercourse of his genitalia[256] with her genitalia, for the feminine was still not created in the world. If this so, with who would there be copulation when the world was created? Therefore, this first copulation was in the supernal will, thought, the upper brain, in the secret of the supernal will that is entirely masculine and without any mark of the feminine, and understand this.[257]

In the uppermost aspect of the Godhead, the feminine is not yet separated from the masculine, and hence copulation cannot be understood in heterosexual terms; there is no female "other" to arouse the male through the feminine waters (the orgiastic fluids of the woman) and to receive his seed. The first copulation, therefore, entails the autoerotic arousal of the male, *nit'orer ha-zakhar me-aṣmo*, a theme that is expressed in other Lurianic texts by the image of *sha'ashu'a*, the delight that God experiences with himself before creation in the eros of self-contemplation.[258] The autoerotic/narcissistic motif is expressed, for instance, in Luria's commentary on *Sifra di-Ṣeni'uta*:

> This delight [*sha'ashu'a*] is for the sake of the copulation [*ziwwug*], to bring forth the masculine waters [*mayyin dukhrin*] from above to below, for just as there is delight in the souls of the righteous below in relation to the feminine waters [*mayyin nuqvin*], so there must be delight in which to take pleasure and to bring forth the masculine waters, in the secret of the wine that gladdens, and from our flesh we see[259] that joy [*simḥah*] and delight [*ta'anug*] increase desire [*ta'awah*].[260]

Insofar as the highest facet of the divine—even the infinite, according to the mythopoeic daring of the Lurianic teaching—is depicted as purely masculine,[261] it follows that the initial desire to copulate and thereby unite with another must arise from the autoerotic stimulation of the male (typical of the phallocentric imagination) that is expressive of the creative and self-generating power of the ultimate ground of being, the "self-rolling wheel."[262] Here we come upon one of the most sensitive and astonishing elements in the boldness of the theogonic/cosmogonic myth in strands of zoharic kabbalah that were developed later by Luria and his disciples: The first stirring of the infinite to create is expressed in the image of sexual autoexcitation, an act that is considered from the anthropocentric perspective one of the most deplorable transgressions[263] with the unfortunate outcome that the soul is deprived entry into the divine pleroma and a postmortem vision of *Shekhinah* is denied. In terms of the specific doctrine endorsed by Lurianic kabbalists, the initiating gesture on the part of Ein Sof mirrors the transgressive act on the part of Adam that is not ameliorated fully until the arrival of the Messiah.[264] What I said above with respect to incest must be applied as well to masturbation: societal norms and taboos are suspended in the imaginal realm, a suspension that is not a mandate for antinomian behavior but rather points to the fact that the logic of the myth requires a reversal of the mores that are considered to be the fabric of human civilization. As de León perceptively expressed the matter in one of his kabbalistic responsa, "The matters that appear reprehensible before one who does not know, they are concealed and hidden matters, and they are revealed before the one who spoke and the world came into being, and they are all in the secret of his name."[265]

The impetus for arousal in the male's desire to project is thus depicted in the overtly sexual image of "masculine waters," the seminal flow that issues from above to sustain the lower *sefirot* and the worlds below. This desire necessitates the othering of the one, a division of the male androgyne into the masculine potency to overflow and the feminine capacity to receive. Just as in the lower plane of being the righteous souls incite (and, according to some passages, even constitute) the feminine waters that arouse the male to unite with the female,[266] so in the upper plane there is sexual arousal in the form of masculine waters overflowing from above to below. In the supreme gradation of the divine, there is no feminine that stands apart from the masculine, but we still can, indeed must, speak of the feminine incorporated in the masculine.[267] As Vital puts it in one passage:

> The aspect of male and female does not signify the complete unity as when there is one male alone. Thus we find in the *Zohar*, in the *Idra* of *Naso* and of *Ha'azinu*,[268] that the aspect of the male and female is only from *Abba* and *Imma* and below, but above in *Atiq Yomin* and *Arikh Anpin* there is no aspect of male and female. . . . Therefore, within it there is no aspect of male and female as two completely distinct configurations [*parṣufin gemurim nifradim*]. Indeed, the masculine and feminine within it are contained in one configuration alone, for the aspect of the masculine, which is the Tetragrammaton in the numerical value of forty-five,[269] stands on the right side of *Arikh*, and the Tetragrammaton with the numerical value of fifty-two[270] that is within it is the aspect of the feminine that stands on the left. . . . The entire right side of *Arikh* is called masculine and the entire left side is called feminine. However, since everything is one configuration alone, it thus says in the book of *Zohar* that regarding *Keter* it is said "See, then, that I, I am he; there is no god beside me" (Deut. 32:39), for he is one without a second with him, and he has no feminine.[271]

In the ultimate source of all being above the configurations, *Atiq Yomin*, as well as in the first of the five configurations of the divine, *Arikh Anpin*, there is no division into distinct masculine and feminine personae.[272] Yet a key difference between the two must be noted: *Atiq Yomin* entirely transcends differentiation, even the rudimentary distinction between the two permutations of the Tetragrammaton, one that numerically equals forty-five and one that equals fifty-two, respectively the masculine and feminine potencies, which are present in *Arikh Anpin*, even though there is no autonomous female that stands over and against the male. The androcentric bias is expressed at the conclusion of the passage wherein Vital interprets the monotheistic proclamation "there is no god beside me" as a reference to the theosophic claim that *Keter*, the first of the *sefirot*, has no feminine other. Significantly, the lack of gender polarity is not expressed as the female that has no male but only as the male that has no female.[273] The point is driven home in another passage:

> Above only the masculine is discernible and the feminine is comprised in him [*lemaʿalah ein nikkar raq zakhar levad we-ha-nuqba kelulah bo*], and thus the facet of consciousness [*moaḥ*] of the masculine, [the name of] forty-five, is alone, and that of the feminine, [the name of] fifty-two, is alone, but with respect to *Abba* and *Imma* the masculine and feminine are completely distinct configurations, and each one must give of its portion to each of its progeny, to the son and to the daughter. . . . Hence, you see that there are five configurations, and in each one there are [the names of] forty-five and fifty-two, but only the first configuration is without a female, for in the case of the other four configurations, each one produced a female as a counterpart. . . . In *Arikh Anpin*, there are [the names of] forty-five and fifty-two, and he is one configuration that has no partner at all . . . and thus it is in *Atiq*, which is above the five configurations and is not included in their enumeration, as is known, for he is the root of everything.[274]

In a number of texts, the feminine quality of the highest manifestation of the divine, whose gender is unambiguously marked as masculine, is identified more specifically as the corona of the phallus, *aṭeret yesod*.[275] Thus, for example, Vital describes *malkhut de-arikh*, that is, the attribute of *Malkhut* in the configuration of *Arikh Anpin*, as the "aspect of the corona [*ha-aṭarah*] that is in the head of *Yesod* that is within him. Subsequently, from the aspect of *Malkhut* a complete configuration [*parṣuf shalem*] is produced, which is called *Malkhut*."[276] The sexual play by which the androgynous male deity amuses himself is linked explicitly to the corona. Thus, commenting on the expression "when it arose in his will to create the Torah,"[277] Joseph Ibn Ṭabul writes: "The explanation of 'it arose in his will' is that all the reality of the worlds were made by way of grace without female waters, and thus it says 'it arose in his will,' for his light emanates below, but when it returns and rises above to be contained in his source, it arouses him to overflow . . . for the light in his corona [*aṭarah*] becomes for him the female waters to arouse all the reality of the worlds."[278] In the absence of a discrete feminine persona to serve as the impetus for the male to ejaculate the seminal issue, it was necessary for the male to incite himself to overflow. In this uroboric state, the corona of the phallus functions as the feminine waters that stimulate the male in heterosexual foreplay. The arousal of the male to discharge seed in the emanation of light is the theosophic mystery of the traditional notion of thought arising in the will of God.[279]

The implication of the symbol of *aṭeret yesod* is that the *membrum virile* is the ontic source for both masculinity and femininity. The ontological problem of the feminine is resolved by locating the ultimate source for the female other in the phallic potency itself.[280] In one passage, Vital describes the origin of the feminine in the corona of the phallus and its subsequent development into an autonomous personification:

> With this you can understand that *Malkhut* is called by various names and they are all true, for *Malkhut* has several roots [*shorashim*] in accord with the change in time [*hishtannut ha-zeman*]. Thus do not wonder that *Malkhut* is the corona of the phallus [*aṭeret ha-yesod*] that is in man or how she is the female of a man [*ha-nuqba shel ha-adam*]. The matter is a great secret for with respect to every holiness the first root is not removed from there. Therefore the place of *Malkhut* was first in the root that is the corona of the phallus, and afterwards when she grew she was removed from there and she expanded bit by bit until she became a complete configuration [*parṣuf gamur*], and she was face-to-face with *Ze*ᶜ*eir Anpin*.[281]

Consider the following passage wherein Vital emphasizes the presumed biological underpinning of the mythologic symbolism related to *Ze*ᶜ*eir Anpin* and *Nuqba*, the son and daughter of the sefirotic pantheon who correspond to Adam and Eve in the sublunar sphere:

> Even though it is true that the crown of mercy [*iṭra de-ḥesed*] is male and the crown of strength [*iṭra di-gevurah*] is female, this is when the one disseminates into the body of *Ze*ᶜ*eir Anpin* and the other into the body of *Nuqba*, as is known. However, the whole time they are within *Ze*ᶜ*eir Anpin*, they are called completely masculine [*zekharim gemurim*], and, indeed, they disseminate into his body, as was mentioned above. In the time of copulation after the time that Adam sinned, he placed them in the foundation of his feminine [*yesod de-nuqbeih*] in the aspect of a drop of the masculine waters [*tippat mayyin dukhrin*], and hence they are completely masculine [*zekharim gemurim*]. . . . Therefore, when they were in *Ze*ᶜ*eir* they were called males and when they disseminate into the body of the feminine they are called females. Another explanation is that we certainly cannot say that every crown of strength is bestowed on his female and that there remains in him only the crown of mercies, for it is clear to us from the secret of what is written in the section of *Shelaḥ* in *Sefer ha-Zohar* [3:170a] that a woman's mind is weak [Babylonian Talmud, Pesaḥim 80b] because her mind includes only a half, which is the crown of strength, and if in the case of man his mind were from the crown of mercies alone, his mind, too, would be weak. Hence, it is necessary that the brain of the mind [*moaḥ ha-da*ᶜ*at*] of *Ze*ᶜ*eir Anpin* comprise the root of the crown of mercies and the root of the crown of strength. . . . Furthermore, the strengths [*gevurot*] that are in the male are called "woman of valor, a crown for her husband" [*eshet ḥayyil aṭeret ba*ᶜ*lah*] (Prov. 12:4), and there their level is higher than the mercies, for they are still in the vigor of their illumination, and they are higher than the illumination of the mercies. Understand well the secret of how the female is called "crown for her husband" [*aṭeret ba*ᶜ*lah*]. All the time that the force of her illumination is not weakened, and she is within the male, then she is greater than him, but when the strengths are bestowed on her and they spread forth in her body, and afterward they become the female waters [*mayyin nuqbin*] in her foundation [*bi-yesod shelah*], the souls that come out from there are the souls of female women [*neshamot ha-nashim ha-neqevot*], and they are

inferior [*geru'ot*] to the males for their illumination is weak. Remember this principle well, and do not forget it.[282]

The androcentricism of the traditional kabbalistic slant on gender is fully exposed in this passage. The female is accorded a positive value that even places her higher than the male, but only when she is contained in the male. This is the symbolic significance of the scriptural images "woman of valor" (*eshet ḥayyil*) and "crown of her husband" (*aṭeret baᶜlah*), two poetic tropes that demarcate the attributes of judgment (*din*) or strength (*gevurah*) contained in the man. Though it is not stated explicitly, I surmise that the image of the crown alludes to the phallic corona (*aṭeret berit*), which, as we have seen from a number of sources, is identified as the ontic source of the feminine in the masculine. However, when these forces of judgment separate from the male body of *Zeᶜeir Anpin* and coalesce to form the female body of *Nuqba*, they are localized in her womb, also called *yesod*, where they form the souls of "female women" (*nashim ha-neqevot*), souls that are described as being inferior to males. This process, which occurs on a lower level within the emanative scheme, parallels the status of gender in the inceptual conception within Ein Sof.

The productivity of the female depends on a masculine—and ultimately phallic—transformation. This is occasioned by the return of a trace of the light of Ein Sof into the space from which it vacated its light. This process results in the condensation of the midpoint, which must be decoded as the phallic element of the feminine out of which all worlds were to emerge. As Vital puts it in his brief sermon on creation, "The holy One, blessed be he, constricted himself in the creation of the world, for the world could not make use of the resplendent light, and he emanated from it a spark of one point, and the light thickened from the constrictions, and he arranged [*tiqqen*] the worlds, and they endured. In this point were contained the four worlds, for it is the *yod* of the name, and this world is called Ein Sof."[283] The symbolic depiction of the center point as the letter *yod* alludes to the process of phallicization to which I have referred, for that letter is the sign of the covenant incised on the circumcised flesh. The attribution of the phallic sign to the female potency underscores the gender transformation of the feminine, which may also be expressed as the transmutation of the signified into a signifier.

I will mention here a passage from the seventeenth-century Italian kabbalist, Menaḥem Azariah of Fano, that illustrates the symbolic intent of the image of the female surrounding the male, but it should be clear to the reader that there is nothing distinctively unique in this source. The particular context wherein the relevant remark occurs is a discussion about the unity of the first two emanations, *Keter* and *Ḥokhmah*, characterized respectively (following a much older tradition) as the will (*raṣon*) and thought (*maḥshavah*) of the boundless.

> One might consider it as if these were two activities but they are only one, naught but absolute concealment [*ha-heᶜelem ha-muḥlaṭ*]. Thus, it is expounded with respect to the Will, for the concealment is a bit diminished in terms of Thought. They are called Ein Sof since he must be garbed, the willful beginning [*hatḥalah reṣonit*] . . . and the positive affirmation will be justified also with respect to *Keter* . . . and all

> the more so in what comes after him, for he himself is verily the origin of the beginning [*re'shit hatḥalah mammash*], that is, the thought of the beginning [*maḥshevet ha-hatḥalah*] or the thoughtful beginning [*hatḥalah maḥshavit*]. . . . Concerning him it says in the *Tiqqunim*[284] "'I am first'—above to the infinite, and 'I am last'—below to no limit, 'and apart from me there was no god'—in the middle," for he is the God of gods, the inner vitality and soul of the *sefirot* and of all the worlds, the Lord of lords in the secret of the "feminine encompassing the male" (Jer. 31:21) "and Esther put on the royal garment" (Esther 5:1). One should not attribute the aspect of femininity in the elevated heights except in this manner.[285]

There is much import in the comment of Menaḥem Azariah, but suffice it to note that he has captured the critical element in the kabbalistic construction of gender, at the very least as it emerges from zoharic literature and its elaboration in Lurianic kabbalah. In the highest region of the divine, there is no rationale for speaking of an autonomous female standing over and against the male; at best, we can speak of the female enveloping the male, which converges symbolically with the image of the female being contained in the male, that is, encompassing is a form of integration, the feminine is the crowning part of the male. Lest one contend that the issue here is not the feminine per se but the attribution of gender more generally to the infinite will, it should be pointed out that the uppermost aspect of God, indeed even Ein Sof itself, is described by this kabbalist (based on earlier sources)[286] as "the world of masculinity" (*alma di-dekhura*) wherein *Malkhut*, the aspect of the femininity, is discernible only in the "secret of the crown that is included in *Yesod*," that is, the corona of the phallus.[287] The claim, then, is not that gender specification is inapplicable to *Keter*, but that it is problematic to posit an independent personification of the feminine. In the state of nondifferentiated unity, femininity denotes the quality of delimitation, which is portrayed (on the basis of Jer. 31:21 and Esther 5:1) as crown or garment.

In the final analysis, the ideal proffered in kabbalistic literature may be considered an elaborate mythotheosophic embellishment of the biblical conception. Althalya Brenner has thematized the view that dominated gender construction in biblical literature. As she points out, the conceptualization of masculine and feminine can be deduced from the "etymological derivation and semantic cognates" of the respective terms *zakhar* and *neqevah*, the root of the former (*zkhr*) denoting "to remember" and that of the latter (*nqb*) "to pierce," "to make a hole." Based on this philological attunement, Brenner concludes that the "'female' is sexed rather than gendered: she is an 'orifice'; orifices and holes require that they be filled. A 'male' is gendered: he is the carrier of memory, the one 'to be remembered,' thus a social agent."[288] In spite of the vast historical chasm separating the ancient Near Eastern context in which the texts of the Hebrew Bible were composed and the medieval setting that produced the kabbalistic compositions, the binary *zakhar/neqevah* yielded the same hierarchical discrepancy in the latter as in the former. Simply put, there is only one gender, masculinity, for the female is understood as receptacle to shelter the male and his seed. Jewish men are the sole agents of cultural remembrance since they alone bear the sign of covenantal identity on the flesh.[289]

In kabbalistic sources, the containment of the feminine in the masculine is repeatedly affirmed as the underlying ontic principle of gender constitution. Needless to say, I do not deny that the containment of the masculine in the feminine is equally attested. Human perfection is dependent on the union of the two sexes, for the one that projects requires the space in which to project and thereby be contained. Alternatively, the containment of male in female is poetically captured in a geometric image found in *Sefer ha-Bahir* and used subsequently by any number of kabbalists, "the circle that runs within the square."[290] The squared circle conveys gender balance, but from the androcentric perspective that lies at the core of kabbalistic symbolism, the insertion of the tridimensional phallic point (demarcated by the coordinates length, width, and depth) in the vaginal quadrangle, a union depicted semiotically as the containment of *yod* in the final *mem*.[291]

Erotic yearning is marked by the impulse of the masculine will to bestow and the feminine desire to receive. Coitus results in the insemination of the female by the male—the centering of the point in the middle of the square—that comes about through and sustains the containment of the male in the female. However, the latter results in the containment of the square in the circle. At the point in the middle, the midpoint, the locus of the phallus in the womb yields the phallic womb, the extending line of engenderment.[292] The latter image is signified as well by the mathematical sum of *yod* and *mem*, ten and forty, a number associated with the third of the ten emanations, *Binah*, on account of the rabbinic notion concerning the fifty gates of understanding, the last of which is withheld from human comprehension, even from Moses, the human being associated with the highest level of attainment.

At the point in the middle, the container is itself contained by that which is contained, that is, the female is restored to the male whence she was taken. The depiction of the male containing the female is obviously an androcentric inversion of the physiological fact that the male is contained in the female, in relation both to his mother at birth and to his partner in the act of intercourse. The formation of gender identity in kabbalistic theosophy is refracted through the speculum of this symbol, and hence it will appear inverted. The male's being contained in the female yields the female being contained in the male. Gender valuation is determined from the perspective of an erotic ontology that is thoroughly masculine in its orientation.

The repeated emphasis on heterosexual union as the appropriate symbol to depict divine unity is not predicated on a social awareness of sexual equality. On the contrary, a sustained reflection on kabbalistic symbolism suggests that the union of man and woman involves the masculinization of the female or, to put the matter in related but somewhat different terms, the restoration of the female to the male. In the succinct language of one zoharic passage, "Whenever male and female are united,[293] the two of them are called by the language of the male."[294] The ontological presupposition of the female having been constructed out of the male is balanced by the assumption that the elongation of the male requires the enclosure of the female. The symbolic formulations are never gender-neutral. What lies beyond gender figuration cannot be amplified in the imaginative faculty. For the symbol, which is the verbal prism through which the mythical form is visually refracted, to be apprehended, it must be instantiated as body, and no body is devoid of gender attribution. Along similar lines, we must understand that even the realm of spirit, the imaginal sphere between being and nonbeing, is gendered in somatic terms in kabbalistic lore. The sexual play of giving and taking in the *mundus imaginalis* is rendered in light of the scientific principle of form and matter, also expressed biologically as the masculine force of generation and the feminine force of gestation. Positive characteristics associated with images of women are predicated on the metamorphosis of the female into male, a transformation that rests on the patriarchal presumption that woman is ontologically part of man.[295]

CHAPTER FIVE

Flesh Become Word: Textual Embodiment and Poetic Incarnation

Principle 1st That the Poetic Genius is the true Man. and that the body or outward form of Man is derived from the Poetic Genius.

—William Blake, "All Religions are One"

For kabbalists in the late Middle Ages, in consonance with contemporaneous patterns of Christian and Islamic piety but especially the former, the body was a site of tension, the locus of sensual and erotic pleasure on the one hand, and the earthly pattern of God's image, the representation of what lies beyond representation, the mirror that renders visible the invisible, on the other. Given the intractable state of human consciousness as embodied—not to be understood, as I will elaborate below, along the lines of Cartesian dualism of mind/body but rather in Merleau-Ponty's phenomenological sense of the embodied mind/mindful body—it should come as no surprise that in spite of the negative portrayal of the body and repeated demands of preachers and homilists to escape from the clasp of carnality, in great measure due to the impact of Platonic psychology and metaphysics on the spiritual formation of the intellectual elite, the flesh continued to serve as the *prima materia* out of which ritual gestures, devotional symbols, and theological doctrines were fashioned.[1] There is, however, a critical difference that distinguishes Christianity from the various forms of mystical devotion that evolved historically in Judaism and Islam.

In the domain of the theological, which cannot be surgically extracted from other facets of medieval Christian societies, the dual role of body as "stigma of the fall" and "instrument of redemption" was mediated by the Eucharist, the central priestly rite that celebrated the mystery of transubstantiation through the miraculous consecration of bread and wine into body and blood, the sacrament believed to occasion liturgically the presence of Christ, a prolepsis of the Second Coming, advent of the appointed time, fostering the "paradoxical union of the body with the evanescence of the sacred."[2] As one might expect, Jews and Muslims provided alternative narratives to account for the commingling of the corporeal and transcendent, the visible and invisible, the literal and spiritual. Focusing on sources composed within rabbinic circles in places as diverse as Palestine,

Provence, Catalonia, Castile, the Rhineland, Italy, northern France, and England, just to name some of the geographic spots Jewish occultism can be detected in the twelfth and thirteenth centuries, we can identify a hermeneutic principle that explains the theomorphic representation of the human as divine and the anthropomorphic representation of the divine as human, the transfiguration of flesh into word, which I will pose alongside—not in binary opposition to—the more readily known Christological incarnation of the word into flesh.

To be sure, I think it artificial to distinguish these positions too sharply, for the hypothetical tenability of the word becoming flesh rests on the assumption that flesh is, in some sense, word, but flesh can be entertained as word only if and when word, in some form, becomes flesh. As it happens, in the history of medieval Latin Christendom, there is evidence of scribal inscriptions (including the words *Verbum caro factum est*) on the hearts of male and female saints—a hyperliteral reading of the figurative "book of the heart"—a gesture that effected the transformation of the written word into flesh and, conversely, the transformation of flesh into the written word.[3] Notwithstanding the compelling logic of this reversal and the empirical evidence to substantiate it, the distinction should still be upheld in an effort to account for the difference in the narratological framework of the two traditions, a difference that ensues from, though at the same time gives way to, an underlying sameness, sameness in the Heideggerian sense of belonging-together.[4]

If I were to translate my thinking into contemporary academic discourse, I would put it this way: Pitched in the heartland of Christian faith, one encounters the logocentric belief in the incarnation of the word in the flesh of the person Jesus, whereas in the textual panorama of medieval kabbalah, the site of the incarnational insight is the ontographic inscripting of flesh into word and the consequent conversion of the carnal body into the ethereal, luminous body, finally transposed into the literal body, the body that is the letter, hyperliterally, the name that is the Torah. Both narratives, therefore, presume a correlation of body and book but in an inverse manner: for Christians, the literal body is embodied in the book of the body; for Jews, the literal body is embodied in the body of the book.[5]

In the first chapter, we had the opportunity to mention briefly Merleau-Ponty's signature notion of the "flesh" expressed in the latter stages of his thinking. At this juncture, I shall revisit the transition from "phenomenology of body" to "ontology of flesh" that ensues from his thought in greater length,[6] as it provides a valuable theoretical introduction to the analysis of the phenomenon of textual embodiment and poetic incarnation in the religious philosophy cultivated by kabbalists.[7]

Intertext/Fleshword

As part of the effort to get beyond the epistemological and ontological binaries that have pervaded Western philosophy, Merleau-Ponty identifies "flesh" as the common dimension shared by subject and object: "It is already the flesh of things that speaks to us of our own flesh, and that speaks to us of the flesh of the other."[8] Merleau-Ponty begins from the standpoint that the "perceptual presence of the world" rests not on positive or negative judgments about the veracity of what is perceived in/by consciousness but on "our experience, prior to every opinion, of inhabiting the world by our body, of inhabiting the truth by our whole selves, without there being need to choose nor even to distinguish between the assurance of seeing and the assurance of seeing the true, because in principle they are one and the same thing—faith, therefore, and not knowledge, since the world is here not separated from our hold on it, since, rather than affirmed, it is taken for granted, rather than disclosed, it is non-dissimulated, non-refuted."[9]

The dichotomy between exterior and interior, largely informed by grammatical habit, is to be transcended in this faith, not in objectivity, not in subjectivity, but in that which is not disclosed, the nondissimulated, and hence the irrefutable, the present absence that haunts the visible as the desire for invisibility.[10] The philosophical effort to establish "intramundane" or "interobjective" relations linking body and world is misplaced, as it is given—the very opening that allows for the question—as the faith of being-in-the world.[11] Being (*l'Être*) or reality (*la réalité*)—terms that Merleau-Ponty uses as substitutes for the "in-itself" (*l'en soi*)—constitute the "common inner framework" (*membrure commune*) of the "macrophenomenon" and the "microphenomenon,"[12] two foci, or folds, of the perceptual field. Hence, as Merleau-Ponty remarks elsewhere, if we are to speak of the "meaning of being *In Itself*," "distance, divergence, transcendence, the flesh" will determine it.[13]

The "incarnate subjectivity"[14] of human perception can be described in optical terms as the double openness of body to world and world to body,[15] embodied consciousness of conscious embodiment, the reciprocity of "proximal vision" based on the presumed synergy between bodies. The "hard core" of this intercorporeality, therefore, the "thickness of flesh," is constituted by a "symbiotic interpenetration and interdependency" whereby "individual beings continuously mirror and reflect one another, setting in motion a process of reversibility in which sameness and difference turn into one another: the seer is seen; the seer sees herself being seen; the seer sees herself as seeing, as a seeing being. . . . It is in the medium of this reversibility, this interplay, that rudimentary forms of reciprocity first emerge."[16] Reflecting accurately the philosophic discourse of his time, Merleau-Ponty observed that philosophy had flattened the curve by moving to one or the other end of the spectrum, the "sole plane of ideality" or the "sole plane of existence." Avoiding the lure of the extremes of absolute objectivity and pure consciousness, one should seek a midpoint between "in-itself" and "for-itself," the midpoint of double vision—turning one way in turning the other—that looms in the center of the perceptual faith that Merleau-Ponty refers to as "the presence of the world" (*la présence du monde*): "the presence of its flesh to my flesh, that I 'am of the world,' and that I am not it, this is what is no sooner said than forgotten: metaphysics remains coincidence."[17] Expanding an insight of Husserlian phenomenology, Merleau-Ponty identifies the essence of corporeity as intentionality: human bodiliness thus is not determined by quantifiable extension or measurable sensoriality, the "objective body," but by kinesthetic sensations, hyletic materiality, impressionality, *Empfindnisse*, the "lived body," a complex field of intentional forms, physiological and psychological.[18]

In the imaginal domain here labeled "metaphysical," there is no difference to overcome, no opposites to coincide, but the coincidence of coincidence, the correlation by which the other without is perceived within the other without and the other within without the other within.[19] To be attuned to this coincidence/correlation is to comprehend something Merleau-Ponty designates as "primordial definition of sensibility," the "return of the visible upon itself, a carnal adherence of the sentient to the sensed and of the sensed to the sentient. For, as overlapping and fission, identity and difference, it brings to birth a ray of natural light that illuminates all flesh and not only my own."[20] Interflesh, correlation of body, subject, and word, the enfolding of flesh in the fold-between. Of this fold we can say it is not "an ontological void, a non-being," but the "hiatus . . . spanned by the total being of my body, and by that of the world; it is the zero of pressure between two solids that makes them adhere to one another."[21] Embodied consciousness of human subjectivity—a cumbersome but accurate formulation—is referred to as the "perceiving-perceived *Einfühlung,*" for the "reflexivity of body" (*la réflexivité du corps*) is constituted by the twofold intuition that presumes

> we are already in the being thus described, that we are of it, that between it and us there is *Einfühlung*. That means that my body is made of the same flesh as the world . . . and moreover that this flesh of my body is shared by the world, the world *reflects* it, encroaches upon it and it encroaches upon the world . . . they are in a relation of transgression or of overlapping—This also means: my body is not only one perceived among others, it is the measurant (*mesurant*) of all, *Nullpunkt* of all the dimensions of the world.[22]

It will be evident to the discerning ear that Merleau-Ponty aligns himself with an archaic perspective expressed in the history of early Greek philosophy—an idea, I might add in passing, for which there are impressive analogies in a number of ancient Eastern philosophical schools—regarding our inability to conceive being without language. For Merleau-Ponty, of course, the focus is cast on perception as the principal modality of experience, though in some manner the very contrast between perception and conception is rendered insignificant. What is novel is his relegating to language a secondary status vis-à-vis a more primary groping toward speech that (be)(speaks) the reciprocity of language and being:

> As my body, which is one of the visibles, sees itself also and thereby makes itself the natural light opening its own interior to the visible, in order for the visible there to become my own landscape, realizing (as it is said) the miraculous promotion of Being to "consciousness," or (as we prefer to say) the segregation of the "within" and the "without"; so also speech (*la parole*)—which is sustained by the thousands of ideal relations of the particular language (*le langage*), and which, therefore, in the eyes of science, is, as a constituted language, a certain region in the universe of significations—is also the organ and the resonator of all the other regions of signification and consequently coextensive with the thinkable. Like the flesh of the visible, speech is a total part of the significations, like it, speech is a relation to Being through a being, and, like it, it is narcissistic, eroticized, endowed with a natural

magic that attracts the other significations into its web, as the body feels the world in feeling itself.[23]

The relationship between being and speech (*la parole*), openly distinguished from language (*le langage*), is one of "solidarity" and "intertwining," rather than "parallel" or "analogy." If the function of language is to demarcate indifferent difference, speech is to intone different indifference, the "belongingness of the body to being and the corporeal relevance of every being." Reversing the Platonic legacy, Merleau-Ponty insists that we can no longer presume the existence of essences "above us, like positive objects, offered to a spiritual eye," but there is an essence "beneath us, a common nervure of the signifying and the signified, adherence in and reversibility of one another—as the visible things are the secret folds of our flesh, and yet our body is one of the visible things."[24] There is something beneath us, the invisible supposition of visible presence, the "nervure" (the word used in the original) that "bears the leaf from within, from the depths of its flesh, the ideas are the texture of experience, its style, first mute, then uttered."[25] Silence bears the speech as the "flesh" that demarcates and eradicates boundary in the joining-separating—"*that without which* there would be neither world nor language nor anything at all," the "essence" that "makes the world be a world," the "imperative grammar of Being," the "indecomposable nuclei of meaning, systems of inseparable properties."[26] The visible is thus "pregnant with the invisible," for the visible is always the other, but the other as such cannot be wholly visible and persist as other. The visible is the "flesh" in proximity that "ceases to be inaccessible" but nevertheless is subject to "infinite analysis."[27]

The word "flesh" does not denote facticity, whether material or spiritual, but a "*general thing*, midway between object and subject, a sort of incarnate principle that brings a style of being wherever there is a fragment of being."[28] "Fragments of being" are fleshed, as it were, from within the intertext of body and world, the "two circles," "two vortexes," "two concentric spheres,"[29] wheels within wheels, interweaving, crisscrossing, embodying language through/in language embodied, the word made flesh, the flesh made word. Merleau-Ponty demonstrates the circularity by appeal to the texture of sight and touch; both senses manifest, disclose, a "reflective redoubling"—to know what it is, one must be what one is yet to come to know; no touch without touching what is to be touched, no sight without seeing what is to be seen.[30] "Flesh," therefore, refers not to an empirical datum or "fact"; it is rather the basic "element" of being that nonetheless can be thought of as adhering to place and time, "to *location* and to the *now*."[31] Merleau-Ponty is emphatic on this point: "We must not think the flesh starting from substances, from body and spirit—for then it would be the union of contradictories—but we must think it, as we said, as an element, as the concrete emblem of a general manner of being."[32]

Merleau-Ponty's ontology, in some ways typically Cartesian, differs in one crucial respect from the rationalist psychology inspired by the meditations of Descartes on the nature of material being and mindfulness: no division between *cogito* and *cogitatum* has to be bridged, as the two never were and never can be separate; their opposition is the *raison d'être* of their being opposite. If we grasp the texture of flesh as the "coiling over of the visible upon the seeing body, of the tangible upon the touching body,"[33] then we would understand that there is no ontological difference to be made up, no epistemological need to explain what Pascal referred to as the inconceivable intermingling of matter and spirit.[34] The fleshliness of being, according to Merleau-Ponty, is not to be construed ontically as either material or mental substance, but as the *Horizonthaftigkeit*, the fold "surrounding the thin pellicle of the strict visible between two horizons,"[35] the "invisible," which is contrasted with the "non-visible." The latter refers to that which is visible but is not now in view, an absent presence, and the former to the "absence" that is " 'behind' the visible, imminent or eminent visibility," the "*Urpräsentiert* precisely as *Nichturpräsentierbar*, as another dimension," the "primeval(ly)-offered" that re/presents itself, doubling,[36] as the "non-primevally presentable,"[37] open enclosure, the focal point where secrecy and exposure exchange glances, the "lacuna that marks its place in one of the points of passage of the 'world.' It is this negative that makes possible the vertical world, the union of incompossibles, the being in transcendence, and the topological space and the time in joints and members, in dis-junction and dis-membering."[38]

In response to Kant's critique and, curiously, closer in spirit to the apophatic tradition, Merleau-Ponty was willing to continue to speak of metaphysics, but for him, the latter deals with the invisible, which is not "another visible," that is, a "positive" presence that is presently absent, but the negative absence as such that can only be absent as absently present:

> *Verborgenheit* by principle, i.e. invisible *of the visible*, *Offenheit* of the *Umwelt* and *Unendlichkeit*—*Unendlichkeit* is at bottom the *in itself*, the *ob-ject*—For me the infinity of Being that one can speak of is *operative*, militant finitude: the openness of the *Umwelt*—I am against finitude in the empirical sense, a factual existence that *has limits*, and this why I am for metaphysics. But it lies no more in infinity than in the factual finitude.[39]

There is no metaphysical object, no metaphysical subject; if there is a thematized metaphysical topos, it is *Vergorbenheit*, "concealment," by definition nonthematizable, demarcated, paradoxically, as the invisible of the visible, that is, the invisibility that makes visibility possible, nay, is the very sense of possibility, openness to being, the "environment." This openness is contrasted with the quality of *Unendlichkeit*, "limitlessness," the very property that makes feasible the "factual existence of that which has limits," and hence associated semantically with "in itself" and "ob-ject," the polarity of subjectivity withheld and objectivity projected, concealment of one in disclosure of other. Thus, in the continuation of the richly poetic meditation on the invisible, Merleau-Ponty associates it with "the possible as a claimant of existence (of which 'past' and 'future' are but partial expressions)—and the male-female relation (the two pieces of wood that children see fitting together of themselves, irresistibly, because each is the *possible of the other*)—and the 'divergence,' and the totality above the divergencies—and the thought-unthought relation (Heidegger)—and the relation of *Kopulation* where two intentions have one sole *Erfüllung*."[40]

The parallels to traditional kabbalistic symbolism are striking. The path winds its way to the unthought of thought, that is, the thought that is thought as unthought, an invisibility that renders visible the invisible presence by rendering invisible the visible absence, seeing within and without the metaphysical breach, open enclosure, divergence converging, convergence diverging, toward transcendence, difference in, identity indifferent, subject-object, gendered male female, duplicity singularly duplicitous.[41] Interestingly, Merleau-Ponty turns to the image of copulation to illumine the truth of duplicity; copulation—or at least of the sort the French philosophic poet generalized—presumes two intentions aiming at one target, the moment/place, here-now, of realization, fulfillment of will, *Erfüllung*.

Merleau-Ponty thus provides the contemporary ear a rhetoric to articulate anew the ancient kabbalistic hermeneutic of secrecy: The invisible is not an object of metaphysics—the transcendental other, ideal form, immaterial substance, or even astral body—nor is it to be identified as a metaphysical subject—the eye of mind/heart presumed to see what is beneath the veneer of appearance; it is, rather, the chasm between subject and object, the mark of divergence, noncoincidence, ontological in-difference, "a sort of straits between exterior horizons and interior horizons ever gaping open . . . a certain differentiation, an ephemeral modulation of this world."[42] For speech to capture this, it must come to and as silence:

> Speech does indeed have to enter the child as silence—break through to him through silence and as silence. . . . Silence = absence of the word due. It is this fecund negative that is instituted by the flesh, by its dehiscence—the negative, nothingness, is the doubled-up, the two leaves of my body, the inside and the outside articulated over one another—Nothingness is rather the difference between the identicals—.[43]

In the ensuing portrait of God's incorporate body elicited from select but sufficiently representative kabbalistic texts, I draw inspiration from Merleau-Ponty's notion of flesh as the "fecund negative," "dehiscence," the nothingness "doubled-up" as nothingness. In this "difference between identicals," the enfolded fold, inside is out and outside in, a place in thinking reminiscent of the account on the part of some kabbalists of the third *sefirah*, *Binah*, emblematic of the mother, the womb that bears the seed-thought of *Ḥokhmah*, the father, composed of the twenty-two letters of the Hebrew alphabet, which are comprised in YHWH; in the matrix of the womb, the letters take the form of *qol gadol*, the great voice that re/sounds as silence in the speaking forth of the seminal name. The voice/womb is inscripted with—circumscribed by—the second *ehyeh* in the name revealed to Moses, *ehyeh asher ehyeh*, "I will be as I will be" (Exod. 3:14), the name that signifies the temporal opening of ontological closure, the gesture mimicked in the prophetic expanse of interpretative constriction.

To apprehend the point, one must have in mind that the other occurrence of *ehyeh* is assigned to *Keter*, which is identified by some kabbalists as will and by others as thought, though proponents of both views agree that it is coterminous with infinity. The primary *sefirah*, the origin, signified by *alef*, paradoxically, cannot be the beginning, for the beginning bears the mystery of *beit*, the dyad, the second that is first.[44] The second is encoded semiotically—though decoded interpretatively—in *asher*, the word that links the two occurrences of *ehyeh*. A sign for this, a textual anchor, is implicit in the consonants of *asher*, for when rearranged they spell *ro'sh*, the "head," the beginning, *Ḥokhmah*, the bridge that connects *Keter* and *Binah*; inception and termination are both signified by *ehyeh*, "I will be," the resolute mark of time's curve, swerving from determinate indeterminacy at the inception to indeterminate determinacy at the termination. The temporal bend, so to speak, impels us to think the correlation of the unity of the three uppermost *sefirot* as the replication of nothing (*Keter*) (un)becoming everything (*Binah*) from the seed-word (*Ḥokhmah*) that comprises everything as nothing. From this spot we can begin to ponder the image-symbol of poetic incarnation in the mystical orchard of medieval kabbalah.

Hebrew and the Semiotics of Creation

A current that runs through the landscape of Jewish esotericism presumes that the microbe of being, the genome, as it were, is constituted by the letters that make up its name; in that respect, Hebrew, the sacred tongue, may be viewed as the cosmic language or, in the telling phrase of Böhme, *Natursprache*,[45] the single Adamic language that is purportedly the source to which all other languages may be traced.[46] The principle is enunciated in the following passage in *Sefer ha-Bahir*: "It is said that with regard to everything that the holy One, blessed be he, created in his world, he placed its name according to its matter, as it is written, 'and whatever Adam called each living creature, that would be its name' (Gen. 2:19), that is, its essence [*gufo*] was in this manner."[47]

The assertion that the name (*shem*) of an entity is its essence (*guf*)—when cast in the terminology of Western philosophy, the realist as opposed to nominalist orientation—presupposes an intrinsic connection between language and being[48] that rests in turn on the assumed correlation of letter and matter, a correlation likely springing from the mythopoeic sensibility expressed in detail in the second part of *Sefer Yeṣirah*,[49] where the line between religion, magic, and mysticism is not so easily drawn.[50] In the words of Jacob ben Sheshet, "The matter of the letters comprises the forms of all created beings, and you will not find a form that does not have an image in the letters or in the combination of two, three, or more of them. This is a principle alluded to in the order of the alphabet, and the matters are ancient, deep waters that have no limit."[51]

What exists in the world, examined subphenomenally, are the manifold permutations of the twenty-two Hebrew letters, themselves enfolded in the four-letter name YHWH; yet what is/appears phenomenally cannot be experienced but through the prismatic mosaic of "bodily language," the "corporeal intentionality," of the ecstatic and enstatic body,[52] that is, the body that stands without and is contiguous within an external world, the body that projects upon and receives from other projecting bodies;[53] whatever exists, ultimately, is nameable, even, or especially, the unnameable, the nameless that is un(named) in every (un)naming, the other of speech, the event—though in being so unnamed, it, too, slips from the abandon of namelessness—that is impossible to say, the unsaying that is heard repeatedly in the infinite speaking, speaking of the infinite, discourse—literally, that which "runs about" (*dis/currere*)—always extending beyond the grip of language.[54]

The kataphatic paradox is articulated in a brief observation in *Baddei ha-Aron u-Migdal Ḥananel*, an important but relatively neglected compendium of kabbalistic secrets on the nature of language composed in the fourteenth century by Shem Tov Ibn Gaon, disciple of Solomon Ibn Adret and Isaac ben Todros, disciples of Moses ben Naḥman, better known as Ramban or Naḥmanides, the thirteenth-century panoramic personality—halakhic authority, talmudic scholar, communal leader, biblical exegete, liturgical poet, and kabbalist. According to a passage in Shem Tov's treatise, the word *otiyyot* denotes that "letters" are "signposts" (*otot*) whose task it is to point the way leading from what is revealed to the concealed (*lirmoz al ha-nistarot min ha-niglot*).[55] Letters may be viewed as planks on a bridge connecting matters open and hidden. In medieval kabbalistic parlance, typified in the aforecited comment by Shem Tov, the terms *nistarot* and *niglot*, derived from Deuteronomy 29:28, refer respectively to the concealed world of emanation, the fullness of the divine potencies, and the revealed world of creation, the plethora of the material cosmos.

In the minds of kabbalists, the ontic division between upper and lower realms of existence, the world of unity (*olam ha-yiḥud*) and the world of separation (*olam ha-perud*), corresponds to the hermeneutical distinction between inner and outer layers of meaning in Scripture, an approach enhanced by the philosophically inspired reshaping of rabbinic exegesis in the Middle Ages, especially in the writings of Maimonides, which profoundly influenced kabbalists in the thirteenth century and beyond.[56] From the manifest we learn of the latent; letters, words, names, the name, language as such, serve as overt signs through which the in/significant is signified, signposts that allow us to imagine[57] a way across the chasm. As Azriel of Gerona put it succinctly, explaining the anthropomorphic language used to describe the *sefirot* in *Sefer Yeṣirah* (1:3): "Thus you must contemplate the hidden from the revealed" (*yesh lekha lehitbonen min ha-galuy al ha-nistar*).[58]

In a second passage, commenting on the characterization of the measure (*middah*) of the *sefirot* in the first part of *Sefer Yeṣirah* as *eser she-ein lahem sof*, "ten that are without limit" (1:6), Azriel elaborated the paradox of the merging of finitude and infinity in the sefirotic emanations presented as four links in an ontological chain—perhaps meant to convey the Neoplatonic hypostases leading invertedly from nature to the One[59]—disseminating from and leading back (through the contemplative gaze and practice of the enlightened kabbalist) to Ein Sof, *mehawweh*, the source of all being:[60]

> Everything is from the infinite [*ein sof*], and even though the matters [*devarim*] have a dimension [*shiʿur*] and measure [*middah*], and they are ten, the very measure that they have has no limit [*ein lah sof*], for the natural [*muṭba*] is from the sensible [*murgash*], and the sensible is from the intelligible [*muskal*], which is from the concealed height [*rom ha-neʿelam*], and the concealed is from the infinite. It follows that even the sensible, intelligible, and natural have no limit, and hence these attributes came to be, to contemplate through them to the infinite [*lehitbonen bahem be-ein sof*].[61]

The world of ten emanations—divided into four quarters, from bottom to top, the natural, sensible, intelligible, and the concealed height—occupies a median position between the boundlessness of Ein Sof and the boundedness of the material cosmos, a theme that Azriel captures in the seventh of the twelve hypothetical questions—presented in the form of a catechism[62]—with the evocative phrase *koaḥ bi-gevul mi-beli gevul* ("finite power that is unlimited").[63] The starting point for comprehending the paradox is to ponder philosophically that the infinite must produce that which is limited to illustrate that the limitlessness of its power must perforce include the capacity to produce a limit to that power:

> The infinite [*ein sof*] is perfection without deficiency [*sheleimut beli ḥissaron*] and it has finite power that is unlimited [*koaḥ bi-gevul mi-beli gevul*], and the boundary [*ha-gevul*] that emanates from him, which endows boundary on every existent [*ha-magbil le-khol maṣuy*], consists of the *sefirot* for they have the capacity to act perfectly or deficiently [*koaḥ lif ʿol be-hashlamah u-ve-ḥissaron*]. And if he did not create for them a boundary, we would not discern that he has the capacity to produce a boundary. Thus, to substantiate that there is nothing outside him [*ein huṣ mimmenu*], he produces a boundary by which things bounded are discerned in their boundedness [*ha-mugbalim nikkarim be-hagbalatam*]. Even though there is no boundary above, there is an allusion to the musing that comes from the infinite [*remez ha-hirhur me-ein sof*], which ascends and eludes extending in a boundary [*mitʿaleh u-mitʿalem me-hitpasheṭ bi-gevul*]. There is a boundary for everything grasped in the rumination of the heart and the allusion of thought [*yesh bi-gevul le-khol ha-nitpas be-hirhur ha-lev u-ve-remez ha-maḥshavah*] that extends below to be found in the word and to be seen by action [*ha-mitpasheṭ lemaṭah lehimaṣṣei be-dibbur u-le-harʾot lemaʿaseh*]. All that which comes under boundary has a measurement [*shiʿur*] and it has corporeality [*gashmut*], for every being that is grasped through rumination of the heart is called "body" [*guf*] even the spirit [*ha-ruaḥ*], and since the *sefirot* are the principle for everything bounded [*kelal le-khol mugbal*] they are the root [*shoresh*]. The philosophers [*ḥakhmei ha-meḥqar*] say that human intellect [*sekhel ha-adam*] has a limit, and from the way of custom [*mi-derekh ha-minhag*] we see that every thing has a boundary [*gevul*], measure [*shiʿur*], and dimension [*middah*].[64]

In his typical manner, Azriel offers a razor-sharp philosophical account (particularly indebted to Neoplatonic speculation) of Ein Sof assuming the form of the *sefirot*, which are ten in number. The paradox was alluded to in a cautionary manner by Azriel's master, Isaac the Blind, in his epistle to Naḥmanides and Jonah Gerondi in an attempt to respond to the charge that some "sages [*ḥakhamim*], wise men [*nevonim*], and pious individuals [*ḥasidim*]" in Spain were expounding kabbalistic secrets openly both in writing and orally and that they were guilty of the heresy of "cutting the shoots," that is, creating a division in the unity of God by positing a plurality of divine potencies: "The entities[65] are unified [*meyuḥadim*] 'like a flame bound to the coal, for the Lord is unique and there is no second, and before one what can you count?'[66] That is, 'before one' is the great name unified in all ten [*ha-shem ha-gadol ha-meyuḥad be-khol eser*], but I cannot elaborate in writing concerning what you asked."[67] Though Isaac was clearly alarmed at the public exposition of esoteric teaching on the part of kabbalists, perhaps his own disciples,[68] he could not allow the allegation concerning heresy to go unanswered. The response centers on the paradox of the one in ten, but Isaac holds back from elaborating in detail in writing, given the sensitive nature of the matter.

Azriel seeks to explicate the paradox by delineating the progression from the formless source, divested of all form, even the form of formlessness, to the finite form that is unlimited, the sefirotic potencies, which are the principle of everything that has a measure. Inasmuch as all things measurable are considered corporeal, it is possible, indeed necessary, to speak of the *sefirot* as the spiritual body that embodies the immeasurable infinite beyond all representation. Traversing the threshold of the imaginal to the imageless refocuses one's vision on the ultimate metaphysical puzzle, the mystery of the garment, in kabbalistic parlance, the nameless donning the garb of the name that is not spoken as written nor written as spoken, the delimiting of the limitless in the infinitely complex tenfold unicity, that is, one manifest in ten, configured as four letters of the name, which assume in the imagination the form of the primal anthropos, Israel, the firstborn son of the father.

Curiously but by no means uniquely, kabbalistic literature exemplifies an intersecting of two conceptual currents: on the one hand, the disparity between appearance that is truly apparent and truth that is apparently true, a metaphysical enigma that can be traced, at least in the history of Western philosophy, to the dualism of transcendence and corporeality that issues from the formalism of Platonic idealism,[69] and on the other, the creed of archaic Jewish wisdom, for lack of a better term, which views the world as having been created by means of Torah, the Hebrew letters through which vestments of the ineffable name are woven, semiotic ciphers that constitute the plentitude of being. The roots for this esoteric tenet may be sought in the cosmological belief that Hebrew is the "language of creation," according to the formulation of Jubilees 12:26, a treatise composed in all probability in the mid-second century B.C.E., presumably by a Jew in Palestine, perhaps of priestly lineage.[70] It is reasonable to assume that this conception is related to the older wisdom teaching, the contours of which may be culled from sections of Proverbs, Ecclesiastes, Job, Psalms, apocalyptic visions, apocryphal wisdom literature, Qumran fragments, passages in the Philonic corpus, and the dicta of Jesus preserved in canonical and gnostic gospels.[71] We are more concerned with the aftermath than the forehistory of this sapiential tradition, but an initial word, no matter how insufficient, about the latter can open the way to the former.

In one current of ancient Israelite tradition, with roots stretching back to ancient Mesopotamia,[72] wisdom was hypostasized or metaphorically depicted—there seems little sense in distinguishing sharply between these options when assessing the scriptural context—as the first of God's creations, the idealized woman of valor and glory, counterpoint to the degrading image of the whoring woman of sin and temptation. By the later part of the Second Temple period, as is attested in a number of sources (for example, Sirach 24:9–13 and Baruch 3:36–4:4), the image of the fullness of primordial wisdom[73] was identified by some as the Torah of Moses.[74] Philosophically, the symbolic identification must have engendered the thought that if God creates by means of wisdom, which is

Torah, then matters (*devarim*) created by the agency of the word (*dibbur*) would constitute and be constituted by the materiality of words (*devarim*).

Didactically, it may be useful to translate the ancient Jewish esoteric precept into contemporary scientific jargon. The letters would be viewed, accordingly, as elementary particles, waves of energy, cosmic strings, described by Paul Davies, a professor of natural philosophy, as "extremely narrow threadlike tubes of concentrated field energy." These tubes were possibly—astronomical searches have so far proved inclusive—produced after the big bang, when, it is further presumed, on account of the exceeding heat and density of the universe, the supraliminal, superluminal particles of stellar dust "tied themselves into knots and twists."[75] The undoing of these electromagnetic ripples of light-energy results in the coalescing of bodies, the objects of human scientific inquiry, philosophical wonder, and artistic inspiration, exemplifying motion and mass in an indecipherably linked manner. As we observed in the Prologue, from a theoretical standpoint it is imagined that the gravitational arrangement of spacetime is such that an individual trajectory betrays the characteristic of looping back. Consequently, the past may be as much drawn out of the future as the future is drawn out of the past, a reverting of temporal and spatial coordinates that disrupts the commonly held presumption regarding the linear sequence of cause preceding effect.

Utilizing this symbolic discourse, we might say that Hebrew letters for kabbalists are excitation nodes that generate visual and sonic aftershocks, producing semblance of light and resonance of sound expressive of infinity, looping round metric intervals of the fourth dimension, the space-time continuum, on the one hand, contracting gravity in restricting expansion, and on the other hand, attenuating antigravity in expanding restriction.[76] Matter, on this account, is a cloak, a veil, through which the luminous form-shadows of the Hebrew letters are concomitantly concealed and revealed. Scholem had in mind this foundational principle of kabbalistic cosmology when he wrote that the "worlds are nothing but names inscribed on the paper of the divine reality."[77] In spite of the diversity of opinions that properly characterizes the history of Jewish mysticism, the assumption that Hebrew is the "holy language" (*leshon ha-qodesh*) in the manner that I have just indicated binds together masters of Jewish esoteric lore across generations without any discernible rupture of time or space.[78]

The gnosis of the letters is worked out in intricate detail in the second part of *Sefer Yeṣirah*, although, interestingly enough, no explicit or even implicit reference to wisdom or Torah is discernible therein. As I have had the occasion to comment on this text in several of my previously published studies, I will not subject the work to a close textual scrutiny. In a sense, the particulars of this matter do not impinge on the argument I am advancing here, though, in general, I certainly acknowledge that particulars cannot be ignored if one is to determine the provenance and pedigree of a text. What is noteworthy for my purposes, however, is the principle of cosmic semiotics that one may elicit from the text, a taxonomy of embodiment: The materiality of body is constituted by the underlying letter permutations, subatomic linguistic structures—edifices constructed dynamically from the different combinations and vocalizations of the consonants—invisible to corporeal sight.

Textual confirmation for this idea can be sought in rabbinic literature of the formative period, as we find, for example, in the following dictum attributed to R. Simon: "Just as the Torah was given in the holy language, so the world was created by means of the holy language."[79] R. Simon's statement presumes an affinity, perhaps synchronicity, betwixt creation and revelation—just as the object of the latter consisted of Hebrew, the "holy tongue," so too the instrument of the former. The sentiment well attested in late antique Judaism that God created the world by gazing into the inscripted text of Torah in its primordial state can be viewed as an exegetical elaboration pieced together from several archaic theologoumena, including the demiurgical representation of divine wisdom, embracing, *inter alia*, the image of God's female playmate, visual figuration of the verbal icon of the will. The idea of a primordial text, the textualization of wisdom, resonates with a still older mythic notion of the heavenly tablets that bear the divine inscription whence the visionary sage learns the secrets of the cosmos, history, and time; the hypothetical green line, as it were, that circumscribes the symbolic tableau of the imagination.[80] If the instrument/blueprint of divine creativity, according to the mythologic of R. Simon or the teaching transmitted in his name, consists of letters, then objects of creation must be analogously constituted.

Book of Nature—Mirroring—Nature of Book

Whatever differences pertain to the rabbinic and occult perspectives, and surely such differences are essential to note, a shared view emerges with regard to the ascription of an ontic status to language and the consequent textual interpretation of reality; indeed, employing terminology that became fashionable in the speculative renaissance of the Latin West in the twelfth century, Torah can be identified as the "book of nature."[81] In the Jewish context, the metaphor is not to be understood metaphorically but hyperliterally, that is, Torah, the prototype of all books, the *hypertext*, if you will, informs us about the semantic character of nature; alternatively expressed, Torah was thought to impart cosmological and anthropological knowledge because the substance of the world and of the human self consists of the letters that constitute the building blocks of the revealed word. Medieval kabbalistic authors understood the rabbinic idealization of Torah in this manner, and there is at least enough ambiguity in dicta attributed to rabbis of the early period to entertain seriously the possibility that kabbalistic sources open a way to ascertain older forms of a mystical specularity predicated on the promotion of viewing the book as a speculum of nature and nature as a speculum of the book.[82] Franz Rosenzweig, a thinker who is on occasion critical of a mystical approach, correctly perceived that Jewish mysticism bridged the gap between God and Torah on precisely these grounds. Although no specific mention is made of the kabbalah, careful attention to Rosenzweig's words make it abundantly clear that he is formulating matters in accord with kabbalistic gnosis:

> The plain wording of the law conceals a hidden meaning which expresses nothing so much as the essence of the world. For the Jew, the book of the law can thus, as it were, replace the book of nature or even the starry heavens from which the men

of yore once thought they could interpret terrestrial matters by intelligible omens. That is the basic idea of countless legends with which Judaism expands the apparently constricted world of its law into the whole world, and on the other hand, precisely because it finds this world presaged in its law, already sees the world-to-come in it.[83]

Judah Halevi, the twelfth-century Andalusian poet and religious thinker with a discernible mystical propensity shaped in part by Sufi terminology,[84] provided a theoretical framework for this belief that was readily appropriated by kabbalists, given its resonance with semiotic notions expressed in older esoteric sources. In an extensive section from *Sefer ha-Kuzari* that deals with *Sefer Yeṣirah*, Halevi remarks that Hebrew is the "divine language" (*ha-lashon ha-elohit*) that God taught Adam and by which he assigned a name to every living creature (Gen. 2:19).[85] In an earlier part of the work, Halevi had already noted that according to tradition, Hebrew, the "noblest of languages," was spoken by God to Adam and Eve, as well as by Abraham, even though he came from Ur of the Chaldeans, where the indigenous language was Aramaic, which is the "mundane language" (*leshon ḥol*) in comparison to Hebrew, the "holy language" (*leshon ha-qodesh*).[86] To be sure, in that context Halevi acknowledges the semantic kinship between Hebrew, Aramaic, and Arabic, but he still argues that the former is superior to the others.[87] Hebrew is the "most perfect of all languages" because only in this language is there an intrinsic relationship between letters and the objects they signify. Hebrew is thus the "natural language," the original language spoken by God, angels,[88] and the first human couple, whereas all other languages are considered a matter of contrivance and convention.[89] Strictly speaking, the truth of this claim rests not in rational demonstration but in faith and commitment to tradition.[90] Just as there is, for Halevi, an ontic chasm separating angelic Israel and the rational human being, the special prophetic status of the Jews linked to the metarational divine matter (*amr ilāhī*; *inyan elohi*) that belongs uniquely to them, so there is an unbridgeable and inexplicable linguistic gap distinguishing Hebrew from other languages.

A similar outlook is affirmed by kabbalists in the second half of the thirteenth century (and countless others in the subsequent centuries who have added little substance to the early formulations), including, to name but a few salient examples, Joseph Gikatilla,[91] Joseph ben Shalom Ashkenazi,[92] and even Abraham Abulafia, whose views on language (not to mention many other topics) were largely dependent on Maimonides.[93] While it is true that Abulafia speaks about the containment of all seventy languages in Hebrew,[94] the linguistic assumption that justifies the use of other languages in the meditational practice, it is nonetheless clear from his writings that Hebrew is always singled out as the "natural" language, as opposed to other languages, which are conventional. A particular interesting formulation is offered by Abulafia in *Imrei Shefer*:

> The world in its entirety was created by means of our letters and our language, and the rest of the letters, languages, and nations are all of them set images [*dimyonot nisdarot*] to be comparable to us, just as an ape performs actions that he sees in the actions of man, in his desire to be like him, and just as the shadow-image [*ṣel*] of a

man appears to a man in a mirror that is in his hand, and he begins to do actions like him, neither adding nor subtracting. But these are without substance and everything is an act of reflection. Thus is the secret of all magic.[95]

I concur with Idel's observation that for Abulafia, the "holy language," which comprises all the other languages, "is not Hebrew in its semantic aspect but rather Hebrew in its more fundamental aspects, namely the consonants and vowels and the principle of the combination of letters, which is one of the major sources for the diversification of languages."[96] I cannot, however, accept the additional contention that "Abulafia emphasizes the natural dimension of human language not to prove that it was revealed by God but to underline that it is an integral part of human nature. It is because it is natural that it is also divine; the two concepts overlap in Abulafia's view." On this basis Idel concludes "the ecstatic kabbalist is much closer to the Aristotelian naturalistic position, a fact that clearly distinguishes this kind of Kabbalah from the two other kabbalistic models."[97] My own reading of kabbalistic sources renders such a distinction gratuitous. Abulafia and Moses de León, taken respectively as paradigmatic proponents of the two main types of kabbalah, prophetic-ecstatic and theosophic-theurgic,[98] would agree that Hebrew is the essential or natural language, the language by means of which the structure of natural entities may be decoded.[99] For both, moreover, the ontic character of the natural language is not to be sought in its semantic morphemes, that is, particular cultural configurations of the language, but in the phonemic and graphemic potentiality contained in Hebrew as a conceptual grid to chart the character of language more generally. Consider the following zoharic passage elucidating the immediately preceding assertion that Israel is distinguished among the Gentile nations (*goyim*) for only they can lay claim to possessing language that is veritable in its written and oral form (*ketav we-lashon*). "Through each letter they can envision the image [*diyoqna*] and form [*ṣiyyura*] as is appropriate. In the idolatrous nations, however, this mystery is not considered for they do not have a script [*ketav*] or speech [*lashon*]."[100] I propose that this comment can be interpreted in a manner that is perfectly consistent with Abulafia's understanding of Hebrew as the cosmic language.

The semantic essentialism, moreover, affords the Jew a distinctive opportunity to emulate God, for whom there is no schism between word and reality since the linguistic gesticulation (whether spoken or written) is an actualization of divine volition.[101] Halevi adduces the latter point from the opening paragraph of *Sefer Yeṣirah*, where mention is made of three books, *sefarim*, by which God created the world. The three books, which are delineated as *sefar*, *sippur*, and *sefer*, allude to the congruence of thought, speech, and writing. From the anthropocentric perspective, the three are experienced linearly as an evolution from the idea/image that is thought mentally without verbal expression, to words that are orally inflected, to the grapheme, the letter-marks, that are handwritten; whether thought, spoken, or inscripted, words at best are "signs" or "symbols" that point to the things they name but not to their essence. From a theocentric perspective, words in all three modalities constitute the essence of things they name, whence derives the creative potency of language. Yet Jews are distinguished linguistically from other ethnocultural identities because they possess the "holy language," the cant of prophecy that bestows upon them an angelic status and allows them to be guardians of the cosmic language.[102]

The kabbalistic ethnocentrism notwithstanding, a precise analogue to the perspective I have outlined in this section is found in Islamic mysticism; indeed, with respect to this matter, the notional proximity between Islam and Judaism is far more conspicuous than between Christianity and either Judaism or Islam. As with so much of Islamic occultism, the starting point is an expression in the Qur'ān in a section that delineates various signs (*āyāt*) of the divine in the world, which serve as part of the liturgical glorification of Allah in the evening and morning (30:17–27). The signs consist of the creation of man from dust and the creation of his spouse, the helpmate, with whom man can settle down and live harmoniously (20–22), the creation of the heavens and earth, and the diversity of ethnic and racial identities (22), the creation of patterns of human behavior and natural phenomena (23–24), and, finally, the fact that all things in the heavens and earth arise by the command, or will, of Allah (25). Everything that is in the cosmos, therefore, may be viewed as a sign marking the way to one that is both within and outside the cosmos.

These signs, we learn from another *sūrah*, should not be worshipped, for prayer is to be directed exclusively to Allah, the all-hearing and all-knowing (41:37–38). At the end of the *sūrah*, after a sustained chastisement of the "unbelievers," "Allah's enemies" (26–28), which unquestionably refers in this context to the Jews, who rejected the claims of the prophet and the authority of the Qur'ān, the new book of revelation, there appears the following remark: "We shall show them our signs in the distant regions and in their own souls, until it becomes clear to them that it is the Truth" (53). The Jews will be shown the signs in the "horizons," that is, the created universe, and in "human souls," until they finally discern the truth. The word "sign," *āya*, denotes the presence of the deity concealed in the manifestations of natural and psychological phenomena, *signa naturalia* and *signa data* in Augustinian terms.[103]

The significance of the sign is that it points beyond itself to the reality for which there is no sign; the plurality of signs reveal the transcendent one by veiling it in the multiplicity of forms by which it is revealed. Each letter of the revealed text is a sign—at once aurally and visually manifest—that comprises an infinity of meaning, inasmuch as the text is the incarnation of the divine form; hermeneutically, the matter of infinity is manifest in the potentially endless explications of the text elicited by countless readers, links in the cumulative chain of interpreters that stretches across the divide of time. Here it would be opportune to recall the contemporary notion of "infinite semiosis," as expressed in Robert Corrington's summation of Umberto Eco:[104] "All semiosis is prospectively infinite, because any given sign will have its own plentitude of dimensions and its own movement outward into uncountable radii of involvement."[105] From the standpoint of medieval Sufis and kabbalists, the innumerable transmutations of meaning stem from the fact that each sign/letter is a component of the textual corpus that constitutes the name of the nameless, the veil that renders the invisible visible and the visible invisible. Moreover, the occult wisdom in both traditions proffered a view of the cosmos in similar terms: Everything is a sign, a discrete indivisible, that guides one to the in/significant beyond the universe, devoid of all forms and images, the oneness of being (*waḥdat al-wujūd*) present in all things by virtue of being absent from all things. The world may accordingly be viewed as the book in which one discerns (de)scripted forms that lead from the visible to invisible or, better, from the visible invisibility to invisible visibility, from faces manifestly hidden to faces hiddenly manifest.[106]

The full implication of the Islamic notion of nature as the book in which the divine will is exposed and the paradoxes that pertain to the presumption that the natural and psychological phenomena are signs by which one discerns the unseen is drawn by the esoteric interpreters of the Qur'ān, the inscripted text of revelation, the "rolled-out parchment," whose words are considered to be signs of divine intention, linked especially to the eschatological day of judgment, comparable to entities in nature such as the mountain and the sea (Q 512:1–8). The esoteric reading elevates the book itself to a supreme position, embellishing the tradition that assigned the qur'ānic expression *umm al-kitāb*, literally, "mother of the book" (Q 3:7, 13:39, 43:4), to the Qur'ān itself, the "well-preserved tablet," *al-lawḥ al-maḥfūẓ* (Q 85:21–22), the *Urschrift*, fore/script, that comprises the forms of all that exists.

Read esoterically, the Arabic letters—bones, tissue, and sinews of the qur'ānic body—are signs that point to the unseen and thereby reveal the light by concealing it. The attitude of Sufis articulated by Annemarie Schimmel presents a perfect analogue to the perspective affirmed by kabbalists with respect to Hebrew: "Learning the Arabic letters is incumbent upon everybody who embraces Islam, for they are the vessels of revelation; the divine names and attributes can be expressed only by means of these letters—and yet, the letters constitute something different from God; they are a veil of otherness that the mystic must penetrate."[107] The metaphor of the veil is instructive, as the function of the veil is to disclose but at the same time to hide, indeed it discloses by hiding, hides by disclosing. In a similar vein, the letters of the matrix text, Torah for kabbalist, Qur'ān for Sufi, reveal and conceal the divine essence, the *face* beyond all veils, the pre/face, devoid of form, the pre/text, devoid of letter.[108] Kabbalist and Sufi would agree that if one remains bound to the letters of the scriptural text, then one is fettered by an idolatry of the book, mistaking the image for the imageless, the figurative for the prefigurative, but both would also insist that the way beyond letters (scripted and/or voiced) is by way of letters, visual-auditory signs, semiotic ciphers at once visible and audible—seen as heard, heard as seen—signs that communicate the incommunicable not through an equational model of symbolic logic but through an implicational model of poetic allusion.[109]

The proximity to the kabbalistic orientation becomes even more pronounced when we consider the embellishment of these motifs in the theosophic gnosis of Ibn ʿArabī, a teaching that has many affinities to kabbalistic wisdom. Just as the Qur'ān is the book that manifests the invisible deity through verbal images, so the cosmos is a book that unveils the divine presence through veils of phenomenal existence. In Ibn ʿArabī's own words, "God dictates to the hearts through inspiration everything that the cosmos inscribes in *wujūd*, for the cosmos is a divine book inscribed."[110] Two qur'ānic motifs are combined here: the identification of cosmic phenomena as signs pointing to the unicity of all being, and the idea of the heavenly book, primordial scripture, inscribed by the divine pen, *qalam* (Q 68:1).

In another passage, the hypostatic dimension is foregrounded as Ibn ʿArabī offers the Muslim corrective to the Christological trinity: "The Christians supposed that the Father was the Spirit (*al-Rúḥ*), the Mother Mary, and the Son Jesus; then they said 'God is the Third of Three,' not knowing that 'the Father' signifies the Name Allah, and that 'the Mother' signifies the *Ummu ʾl-Kitáb* . . . i.e., the ground of the Essence, and that 'the Son' signifies the Book, which is Absolute Being because it is a derivative and product of the aforesaid ground."[111] The common thread that ties together the triad of potencies is the belief in the ontological reality of the Arabic letters; the first manifestation, envisioned as father, is the most sacred of names, Allah; the second manifestation, envisioned as mother, corresponds to *umm al-kitāb*, the primordial text or the ground of the Essence; and finally, the third manifestation, envisioned as son, is the book, the absolute being that derives from the ground. There is much more to say about Ibn ʿArabī and the different layers of the Islamic esoteric tradition, but what is most critical for our purposes is to underscore the hypostatic personification of the qurʾānic text as the tablet that contains all cosmic forms that serve as the veils through which God is manifest and the concomitant figural representation of the cosmos as the book that comprises all semiotic signs that point to the truth that cannot be signified.

Envisioning YHWH/Eradicating Root Word

The unique contribution of medieval kabbalists—and on this point I do not see any appreciable difference between the two major trends according to the taxonomy that has dominated contemporary scholarship—centers around viewing YHWH, the most sacred of divine names, as comprising all the letters of the Hebrew alphabet, the one language considered natural and not conventional, essential and not contingent.[112] I cite here a representative formulation of this assumption from *Shaʿar ha-Niqqud*, a treatise on the meaning of the vowels composed by Gikatilla. The relevant remark weaves together the rabbinic tradition that the world-to-come and this world were created respectively by *yod* and *he*, the first two letters of the Tetragrammaton,[113] and the system laid out in the second part of *Sefer Yeṣirah* in which the letters are presented both as the means by which all things are created and their substance:

> All the worlds are dependent on the twenty-two letters, and the one who contemplates the secret of the permutation of the alphabet will comprehend the secret of the rotation of all entities in their ascent and descent by means of the secret of the property of the letters. The one who merits comprehending this will understand several mysteries and several levels that are hidden from the eyes of creatures, and he will comprehend and know the greatness of God, blessed be he, and how everything is made from the truth of his great name and how all is dependent on his name.[114]

In *Shaʿarei Orah*, a more extensive delineation of the different symbolic names associated with each of the ten emanations progressing from the bottom to the top, Gikatilla offers a succinct account of the linguistic theory that informed the thinking of kabbalists in his time and beyond to the present. The twenty-two letters are depicted as branches stemming from a tree whose trunk is inscribed with YHWH, the root word that is the origin of all language, the mystical essence of Torah.[115] Accordingly, all that exists may be perceived as a garment that both hides and reveals the name. Consider the formulation of this matter in the commentary on *Sefer Yeṣirah*, which records the teachings of Isaac the Blind, on the words "Thus every creature and every word goes forth in one name":[116]

> "In one name"[117]—their root is in one name, for the letters are branches that appear as flickering flames, within which there is movement, that are bound to the coal, and they are like twigs of a tree, its branches, and boughs, whose root is in the tree. Thus the weighing is from the hewing, the permutation from the weighing, and from the permutation is the form. All things [*devarim*] are made into a form, and all forms come forth from one name like a branch that comes forth from the root. It follows that everything is in the root, which is the one name, and thus it says at the end "one name."[118]

The "one name" from which all being comes forth is YHWH, the name that comprises within itself all letters of the Hebrew alphabet. From this vantage point, being is construed semiotically, that is, the letters constitute the nature of what is real, a point that is conveyed philologically by the expression *devarim*, which has the double connotation "things" and "words," though it is likely that in the above passage the term denotes more specifically the sefirotic entities, which are contained in the one name that comprises all the letters.[119] In the words of Azriel of Gerona:

> Thus the blessed holy One made everything inscribed [*rashum*], engraved [*ḥaquq*], hewn [*ḥaṣuv*], and sealed [*ḥatum*] in his name and its letters so that there will be in them the power to exist and to carry out their activities in his seal in which they are sealed, for they constantly receive from his well that is prepared to irrigate those in need. He and his name preceded it, and through his name he created everything, as it is written, "all that is called in my name" (Isa. 43:7), and he is the fount of life to sustain all living beings.[120]

That the human being plays a particularly important role in unifying the different realms through language is expressed in another passage from the commentary on *Sefer Yeṣirah* that preserves the teachings of R. Isaac:[121] "Man [*adam*] himself is constructed by the letters, and when that edifice was constructed the supernal spirit that guides him guides everything, and thus everything is joined together in the supernal and lower beings."[122] Just as the anthropomorphic shape above, primal Adam, is composed of the letters comprised in the name, so Adam below is made in the image of the name, the Torah in human garb, and thus the ideal body is composed of letters.[123] The linguistic conception of corporeality taken hyperliterally, that is, the letters constitute the material substance whence the body is constructed, is affirmed by Azriel in his commentary on the depiction of the covenant of the foreskin in *Sefer Yeṣirah*: "it produces an offspring that is formed by means of the twenty-two letters, and therefore one must contemplate from the revealed to the hidden."[124]

In the earliest kabbalistic documents, moreover, which remain the only tenable way for the contemporary scholar to uncover what the tradition may have been, even if it was, as kabbalists themselves insist, in part or whole transmitted orally, it is presumed that the potencies of God are correlated with the limbs of a human body, a theosophical claim linked exegetically to the anthropological assumption that Adam is created in the image and likeness of God (according to the account recorded by a priestly scribe) as well as the prophetic presumption (expressed perhaps most boldly by Ezekiel) that the divine glory appears in the likeness of a human form.[125] In subsequent generations, the anthropomorphism was embellished, or at least articulated more overtly,[126] but from its very inception, kabbalistic ontology rests on the supposition that the anthropos, to be identified more specifically as the circumcised Jewish male,[127] serves as the conduit connecting the divine and mundane realms.

The role of mediating agent is realized primarily through contemplative prayer and Torah study, as these ritual activities are dependent on the utilization and manipulation of the Hebrew alphabet, the constitutive element of all that exists. The goal for the kabbalist—indeed what justifies his being called a kabbalist[128]—is to receive the secret of the name, that is, to cleave to YHWH, the Deuteronomistic injunction interpreted in a manner very close to twelfth-century Neoplatonically influenced philosopher-poets, primarily of an Andalusian cultural background, as conjunction of thought (*devequt ha-maḥshavah*). Isaac and his disciples claim that this conjunction is the true mystical intent (*kawwanah*) of liturgical worship and study, an ideal achieved by few but with ramifications for all.[129]

In another crucial way, the ideal promulgated by kabbalists betrays affinity with the view enunciated in Islamic and Jewish philosophical sources. The kabbalists of the twelfth and thirteenth centuries, not to mention later generations, understood this conjunction, which comprised both an intellective and imaginal component, as an expression of prophecy, though in their case the contemplative ascent is more emphatically a personal experience of *unio mystica*, a more deeply expressed existential awareness that the fragmented soul can attain a sense of wholeness by being reincorporated into the Godhead.[130] Union with the divine name is occasioned by psychic transport—which is consequent to clearing mundane matters from the mind[131]—that in turn facilitates the theurgical unification of the divine potencies signified by letters of the name.

Though I have just spoken of the mystical conjunction facilitating the theurgical task, I think it better to imagine a core experience of ecstasy with two facets: reintegration of the soul in the divine, and fusion of the sefirotic potencies into harmonious unity.[132] Applying a linear logic, one might be tempted to treat these as two phases aligned in causal sequence, the former occasioning the latter. While there is cogency and heuristic value to this angle, it is not the only way the geometry of the matter may be diagrammed. When viewed morphologically as opposed to typologically, that is, under the semblance of form rather than type,[133] ecstasy and theurgy can be seen as two manifestations of the same phenomenon. The consonance of these two elements, which have been too sharply bifurcated by the prevailing slant in the critical study of Jewish mysticism, is necessitated by the ontological conviction regarding the divine/angelic status of the Jewish soul, an idea whose roots lie in the belief that the righteous or holy ones of Israel have been endowed with an angelomorphic nature, a conception that evolved in earnest in late–Second Temple Judaism, though likely based on a still older ancient near-Eastern mythological understanding of kingship.[134] In the intellectual milieu inhabited by medieval kabbalists, it is presumed that God and Israel are circumscribed within a monopsychic unity that levels out the ontic difference between cause and effect, and hence mystical union and theurgic unification are concurrent processes that have been artificially separated for extraneous taxonomic concerns by contemporary scholars of kabbalah.

A key text in which the contemplative ideal is laid out is the explanation of the vision of the *sefirot* mentioned in another passage from *Sefer Yeṣirah* 1:8: "Ten intangible *sefirot*: their vision [*ṣefiyyatan*] is like the appearance of lightning [*ke-mar'eh ha-bazaq*], and their limit [*takhlitan*] has no end, his speech is in them like that which flees, and they pursue his utterance like the storm, and before his throne they bow down." The "vision" (*ṣefiyyah*) is construed in the commentary attributed to Isaac as mystical comprehension designated on the basis of rabbinic elocution as "contemplation of one thing from another" (*hitbonenut davar mi-tokh davar*).[135] The phenomenological contours of this state are elucidated by the verse "And I wait to see what he will speak to me," *wa-aṣappeh lir'ot mah yedabber bi* (Hab. 2:1), which Isaac (or the anonymous hand allegedly recording his teaching for posterity) glosses as "for the word appeared to him" (*she-hayah ha-dibbur nir'eh elav*). From this one can deduce that contemplative visualization, which relates to the activity of both the emanations and the kabbalist, is a seeing of the word, an experience of synesthesia wherein image and sound, optic and verbal, coincide, to see what is spoken as the text coming to be written.[136]

But to what does the "word" (*dibbur*) precisely refer? And how is it seen? In the continuation of the commentary, the scope of the matter is further delineated through the image of the chain of being that extends from the lowest demarcation, *middah*, to the highest, *ne'elemet*, from the measurable and thus more fully exposed attribute to what is hidden, the secret beyond spatial demarcation even in the imaginal realm:

> The vision relates to the fact that each and every cause [*sibbah*] receives from the cause above it, for the attribute [*middah*] draws forth from the attribute that is hewn [*ḥaṣuvah*], and that which is hewn from the engraved [*ḥaquqah*], and that which is engraved from the marked [*reshumah*], and that which is marked from the hidden [*ha-ne'elemet*], everything is such that this is within that and that within this, everything is bound so that this is in that and that is in this.[137] How do they receive? The way of their receiving—something subtle and an essence [*davar daq we-hawayah*]. "Like the appearance" [*ke-mar'eh*], contemplation that has no substance [*hitbonenut she-ein bo mammash*], and "the appearance" is the pure and translucent splendor of the apprehension of one who receives [*zohar daqut zakkut hassagat ha-mitqabbel*]. "The appearance of lightning" [*ke-mar'eh ha-bazaq*], this is the purity and translucency of the apprehension of one who receives [*daqut zakkut hassagat ha-mitqabbel*]. "Their

> limit" [*takhlitan*] is not like their measure [*middatan*], for the measure [*ha-middah*] is a matter received by differentiated beings [*davar ha-mitqabbel la-nifradim*],[138] for the prophets saw the attributes [*middot*] in accord with their comprehension and by means of receiving their potencies they would expand their minds [*marḥivin maḥshavtan*] more than other human beings, and on account of this they had an expansion of soul to extend infinitely in the details [*raḥav ha-nefesh lehitpasheṭ bi-feratim be-ein sof*]. . . . "For the Lord is one," now the measure [*middah*] in the infinite alludes that is has no limit on any side. "From contemplating" the matters hidden from thought lest one get lost, for from what one comprehends one can discern what one cannot comprehend, and thus the measures [*middot*] arose, for language can comprehend only that which comes out from it, since a man cannot comprehend the measure of speech and the letters [*middat ha-dibbur we-ha-otiyyot*] but only the measure itself [*middatah be-aṣmah*], and there is no measure outside the letters. All the sublime measures are given to be meditated upon [*lehitbonen*], for each measure receives from the measure above it, and they are given to Israel to contemplate from the measure seen in the heart, to contemplate infinitely.[139]

On a previous occasion I had the opportunity to discuss some of the details of this richly nuanced and intricate account of the contemplative praxis. Here I will focus on the contribution this text makes to the theme of textual embodiment and poetic incarnation. The form contemplatively envisioned is the word of God as it is diffused through the chain of being that extends from what is concealed (*ha-neʿelemet*) to the exposed measure (*middah*). The hidden source is revealed in four links on the chain designated in descending order as "marked," "hewn," "engraved," and "measured," terms that relay the delimiting of the limitless light as it passes sequentially through the sefirotic filters. Significantly, the materialization of spirit is portrayed as the concretization of thought into letters whence speech—in both written and oral form[140]—is constructed, the articulation of the inaudible name in the constellation of the invisible image.[141]

The prophets, who are cast typologically as protokabbalists—the reinterpretation of classical prophecy is so basic to the kabbalistic worldview that ancient prophets are portrayed as having access to the secret wisdom of kabbalah and contemporary kabbalists, the "enlightened of Israel" (*maskilei yisraʾel*),[142] as having experiences of a prophetic nature—are distinguished by their capacity to expand their thought limitlessly beyond the limit of thought. By thought thinking what lies beyond the parameters of thought to think, the mind of the kabbalist envisions complex infinity from infinite complexity. The visualization is thus expressed as an ascent through various gradations, from the measurable attribute on the bottom to what is hidden on top, from the comprehensible to the incomprehensible. The spiritual elite of Israel are set apart by their capability of contemplating from the measure as it is seen in the heart to the infinite (*lehitbonen mi-tokh ha-middah ha-nirʾeit ba-lev lehitbonen ad ein sof*); hence the mystical state is referred to as "contemplation that has no substance" (*hitbonenut she-ein bo mammash*)—what is visualized contemplatively is "all that which the comprehension of thought comprehends to the infinite" (*kol mah she-hassagat ha-maḥshavah masseget ad ein sof*),[143] the trail of thought winding its way not to that which is not thought but to that which is thought as what cannot be thought, the unthought, beyond the polarity of being and not being.

Mystical illumination ensues from "contemplation that has no substance," that is, contemplation of what cannot be reified as an object of knowledge or subject of predication, the one that is lacking substance precisely because of the fullness of its insubstantiality. The "way of contemplation" (*derekh hitbonenut*) is thus compared figuratively to "sucking" (*yeniqah*) as opposed to "knowing" (*yediʿah*)[144] to convey the idea that meditation yields and is generated by an intimate and direct gnosis of divinity rather than discursive knowledge, a unified intuition of many in one rather than a composite inference of one from many.[145]

Seeing No-Thing: In/Sight Blinding Vision

To appreciate the phenomenological and ontological contours of the contemplative ideal, it would be beneficial to frame the discussion in light of certain assumptions in Neoplatonic literature and especially in Plotinus, who exerted in one way or another a profound influence on medieval philosophical and mystical accounts of psychic conjunction in the three monotheistic faiths. The limitations of space obviously prevent me from treating the Plotinian worldview adequately, let alone developments in Neoplatonic thought subsequent to Plotinus and particularly those that evolved in medieval Islamic centers of speculative learning in the tenth and eleventh centuries.

According to Plotinus, for the human mind to contemplate the first principle, the unknowable, nameless One,[146] a tenet traceable to Plato's description of the Good as that which is "beyond being,"[147] it must become like the One. The logic underlying this assumption rests on the ancient Hellenic wisdom espoused in the adage of Anaxagoras that things of similar nature are attracted to one another, or, in the related formulation of Empedocles, wisdom consists of "like by like," since it is "either identical with or closely akin to perception."[148] Even more pertinent for understanding Plotinus is his utilization of the Aristotelian formula, which is based on the aforementioned pre-Socratic principle, that the knower must be like the thing that is known.[149]

One passage in particular that is worthy of citation is from a relatively early treatise in the Plotinian corpus, indeed the one listed first in Porphyry's chronological order, in which Plotinus sets out to explain the "inner sight" by which one can apprehend the true form of the "inconceivable beauty," a way of seeing that is awakened when the eyes are shut.[150] If the mind is sufficiently purified of corporeal matters, then in turning inward, which is also depicted as an ascent to the intelligible realm[151]—a theme reiterated by many a mystic visionary, as Blake, for instance, put it in his epic poem *Jerusalem: The Emanation of the Great Albion*, "What is Above is Within, for every-thing in Eternity is translucent"[152]—it will see the "true light" that cannot be measured by metric dimensions; in the speculum of inner vision, the mind's eye sees what is without within and what is within without, and hence spectator and spectacle can no longer be differentiated: "For one must come to the sight with a seeing power made akin to and like what is seen. No eye ever saw the sun without becoming sun-like, nor can a soul see beauty without becoming beautiful. You must become first all godlike and all beautiful if you intend to see God and beauty."[153]

In the continuation of the passage, Plotinus distinguishes the vision of the Intellect, the place of forms or ideas, which are characterized as the intelligible beauty, and the vision of the Good, the "primary beauty," the origin that is beyond the "screen" of beauty.[154] If, however, the One is utterly unique, it can be like no other thing; in its absolute simplicity,[155] the One can have no form or substance, and hence the only way to become "like" the One is to be assimilated into the One. However, to be assimilated into what is "beyond being"—a designation, Plotinus reminds us, that makes no positive statement about the One but only implies that it is "not this," that is, it is not a particular something and thus cannot be compared to anything[156]—the mind must transcend the specificity of its own being by disposing the filters of intellection.

> [I]t would be absurd to seek to comprehend that boundless nature . . . but just as he who wishes to see the intelligible nature will contemplate what is beyond the perceptible if he has no mental image of the perceptible, so he who wishes to contemplate what is beyond the intelligible will contemplate it when he has let all the intelligible go. . . . But we in our travail do not know what we ought to say, and are speaking of what cannot be spoken, and give it a name because we want to indicate it to ourselves the best we can.[157]

An iconoclastic breaking of all form occasions contemplative envisioning of the formless.[158]

For Plotinus, there are three stages to the life of mind that correspond to the three hypostases, a correspondence that is predicated on the correlation of being and experience, the phenomenological and ontological, a critical feature of medieval kabbalah, as I have argued elsewhere:[159] what is real is real as experienced and what is experienced is experienced as real.[160] The ascent of mind can be seen as a progressive attempt to apprehend beauty,[161] to rise from discursive knowledge appropriate for the sensible world, that is, reasoning from premise to conclusion and transitioning from one object of thought to another, to an inner vision of intellect and the world of ideal forms wherein the distinction between subject and object is transcended, and finally to seeing the formless, the Good that is the source of ultimate beauty, radiant darkness beyond intellect and description.

Plotinus conceives the ascent in accord with a major impulse in the Platonic understanding of the philosophical life, as a way to attain knowledge of self, "to face death before we die."[162] But contained herein is a fundamental paradox, for the higher one ascends on the ladder of self-knowledge, climbing from the multiplicity of the sensible to the complexity of the intelligible and beyond to the simplicity of the One, the more one loses awareness of self, the more one gains knowledge of self;[163] at the summit of knowledge—the intellect contemplating naught but intellect, a mirror turned inward to mirror the mirror turned outward, the mirror mirroring the mirror mirrored in the mirror—is what Dionysius the Areopagite referred to as the source of all being, which is "before be-ing"[164] and hence neither is nor is not, known "through unknowing" (*agnosia*).[165] The path of contemplation is a process of purification, emptying the mind of images, concepts, and words,[166] but in the final stage, the return of the "alone" to the "Alone," the purging culminates in vision, albeit a seeing where the difference between seer and seen is no longer viable; the eye that sees is the eye that is seen as the eye that sees the eye that is seen.[167] This, Plotinus suggests, occurs when one is "possessed" by a god who

> brings his contemplation to a point of vision, and presents himself to his own mind and looks at a beautified image of himself; but then he dismisses the image, beautiful though it is, and comes to unity with himself, and, making no more separation, is one and all together with that god silently present, and is with him as much as he wants to be and can be. . . . While he is coming to know the god he must keep to an impression of him and form distinct ideas of him as he seeks him and discern what he is entering into; and when he has learnt with confidence that it is into the highest blessedness, he must give himself up to what is within and become, instead of one who sees, an object of vision to another who contemplates him shining out with thoughts of the kind which come from that world.[168]

In the meditative state—a noetic circle in which boundaries of thinking, thinker, and thought can no longer be discriminated—the mind stretches beyond the limits of mindfulness to be absorbed in the mindless but fully conscious source of all being.[169] Intellect is the most perfect image of the One, but even that image must be transcended if one is to see the imageless light about which we cannot speak adequately.[170] Concerning the One we must say that it is all things "by and in itself," since it contains all things in itself and they exist only by participation in it, but it is also none of them, since its being is in no way dependent on them.[171] Inasmuch as the One "is all things and not a single one of them,"[172] Plotinus insists that when we speak or think about it, we must dispense with every name; at best, we can "make signs [*sēmainein*] to ourselves about it"[173] in the manner of Egyptian hieroglyphs, a nondiscursive language based on ideogrammatic symbols rather than words and propositions:[174]

> When you have put away all things and left only himself, do not try to find what you can add, but if there is something you have not yet taken away from him in your mind. For even you can grasp something about which it is not possible any more to say or apprehend anything else; but it is something which has its place high above everything, this which alone is free in truth, because it is not enslaved to itself, but is only itself and really itself, while every other thing is itself and something else.[175]

Paradoxically, that which is known and named to be truly itself and nothing else cannot be known or named—as knowing and naming entail relating a thing to other things—but only experienced in the vision of that which is invisible, a seeing that sees nothing, not even not-seeing, the mind's eye gazing in the darkness of seeing light[176] wherein nothing is seen and nobody sees.[177] Even the term "one" is to be interpreted at best negatively, as denial of multiplicity, for if it were to be taken positively,

> it would be less clear than if we did not give it a name at all: for perhaps this name [One] was given it in order that the seeker, beginning from this which is completely indicative of simplicity, may finally negate this as well, because, though it was given as well as possible by its giver, not even this is worthy to manifest that nature; since that nature cannot be heard, nor may it be understood by one who hears, but, if at all, by one who sees. But if the seer tries to look at a form, he will not know even that.[178]

Not-seeing is previewed by abandoning all concepts and images, a seeing through the glass darkly.[179] From this vantage point, apophasis and mystical envisioning go hand in hand.[180]

Inscripting Ineffability/Enfolding Scroll

The Neoplatonic orientation, briefly outlined above, greatly informed the mystical speculation in the three monotheistic faiths and thereby transformed their respective theological sensibilities, based in great measure on the positive representations of the deity elicited from the canonical texts of ancient Israelite prophecy. In terminology used by historians of religion, the mystical element in the three monotheisms ensues from the juxtaposition of the kataphatic and apophatic, that is, a mysticism predicated on the possibility of envisioning the shape of God in conjunction with a mysticism that steadfastly denies the possibility of ascribing any form to the being beyond all configuration, indeed the being to whom we cannot even ascribe the attribute of being without denying the nature of that (non)being.

In mystical accounts gesticulated within the hermeneutical matrix of scriptural religious belief, the most important way the visionary and unitive experiences are mediated is through study of canonical texts. The experiences themselves may surpass the limits of language, but it is only through language that those limits are surpassed. The apophatic tendency to submerge all forms of sentient imaging in the formlessness of pure consciousness cannot be completely severed from the kataphatic insistence on the possibility of being in the presence of the divine. The juxtaposition of the kataphatic and apophatic has fostered the awareness on the part of the ones initiated in the secret gnosis that mystical utterance is an unsaying, which is not the same as the silence of not-speaking, but rather that which remains ineffable in being spoken, that which remains unknown in being known, that which remains unseen in being seen.

An important mystical theologian of the early Church in the fourth century who set out to expound the apophatic way was the Cappodocian father, Gregory of Nyssa, a man of letters who studied Scripture and Platonic writings as well as the treatises of Origen and Clement of Alexandria. In spite of Gregory's great admiration for Origen, in one crucial dimension their spiritual outlooks are incongruous.[181] For Origen, the soul pursues a path of light on the way to God, whereas for Gregory, the journey is from light to darkness, a darkness that is, to be sure, more fully light, indeed so luminous that it cannot be apprehended phenomenally except as dark.

In *De vita Moysis*, Gregory distinguishes three levels of vision of the invisible God that we may call the cosmological, anthropological, and theophanic. According to the first, the divine is seen in the contemplation of the potencies that act in the world, that is, vision by way of analogy, from the manifest to the hidden. According to the second, God is seen through the agency of the human being who is created in the divine image, that is, an internal seeing of the mind. The third is exemplified by the epiphany at the burning bush (Exod. 3:1–6): Moses divested himself of the earthly covering—depicted metaphorically by removing the sandals from his feet[182]—and beheld "the ineffable and mysterious illumination."[183] Moses was privileged to be instructed in the theophany (ἐν τῇ θεοφανεία παιδευθεὶς) because "he came to know that none of those things which are apprehended by sense perception and contemplated by the understanding really subsists, but that the transcendent essence and cause of the universe (ὑπερανεστώσης οὐσίας χαὶ αἰτίας τοῦ παντὸς), on which everything depends, alone subsists."[184] Just as Moses attained "knowledge of truth" (τῆς ἀληθείας γνῶσίς) through apprehension of the "truly real Being" (ἀληθῶς τὸ ὄντως ὄν),[185] "so now does everyone who, like him, divests himself of the earthly covering and looks to the light shining from the bramble bush, that is, to the Radiance which shines upon us through this thorny flesh and which is (as the Gospel says) the true light and the truth itself."[186]

The location of the vision in the bush is interpreted typologically by Gregory as a foreshadowing of "the mystery of the Lord's incarnation" (τὸ διὰ σαρχὸς παραδηλοῦσθαι τοῦ Κυρίου μυστήριον) whereby the hidden radiance of the one true being is manifest in the material body.[187] To apprehend the light of the invisible deity in the visible form of the "thorny flesh"—the incarnate body of Christ, the image of the infinite (τῇ εἰχόνι ἀοράτου)[188]—one must, like Moses, divest oneself of one's material corporeality; envisioning the body of what has no form is correlated with diminishing one's own bodiliness.

But what does it mean to see God? Gregory sheds further light on this enigma in a second passage in *De vita Moysis*, expounding the verse "So the people remained at a distance, Moses approached the thick cloud where God was" (Exod. 20:18). At the outset, Gregory remarks that this seems to contradict the theophany at the burning bush, "for then the Divine was beheld in light but now he is seen in Darkness."[189] Gregory is quick to point out, however, that the contradiction is only apparent: "Scripture teaches by this that religious knowledge comes at first to those who receive it as light. . . . But as the mind progresses and, through an ever greater and more perfect diligence, comes to apprehend reality, as it approaches more nearly to contemplation [θεωρία], it sees more clearly what of the divine nature [θείας φυσεως] is uncontemplated [ἀθεώρητον]."[190] By leaving behind all empirical data and conceptual categories, the mind penetrates deeper into the darkness:

> until by the intelligence's yearning for understanding it gains access to the invisible and the incomprehensible, and there it sees God. This is the true knowledge of

> what is sought: this is the seeing that consists in not seeing [τὸ ἰδεῖν ἐν τῶ μὴ ἰδεῖν], because that which is sought transcends all knowledge, being separated on all sides by incomprehensibility as by a kind of darkness.[191]

Inspired by Philo's interpretation of the scriptural locution of Moses entering into the dark cloud (*arafel*) as an allegorical depiction of his entry into the invisible and incorporeal realm, a view substantiated as well by God's response to Moses that he can behold the back but not the face of the glory (Exod. 33:23),[192] Gregory reads the verse as an expression of the view that contemplation is a progression to what cannot be contemplated; the pinnacle of the mind's ascent consists of beholding the "luminous darkness" (λαμπρῶ γνόφω), an oxymoron that resolves the exegetical problem with which Gregory began his exposition, the ostensible conflict between the theophany at the bush where God appears in the light and the later statement that Moses enters the cloud of darkness to encounter God is no clash at all, as the mystic vision is a seeing of *luminous darkness*, a vision of unseeing through the mirror of the infinite, the image of God mysteriously embodied in the person of Christ and to some degree in each human being,[193] that is, a seeing through which one comes to see that one cannot see, the blindness that is true insight.

The interweaving of affirmative and negative theology, anagogy and apophaticism, was expounded in more intricate philosophical detail by Dionysius the Areopagite.[194] Combining the rigor of logical analysis and the passion of poetic sensibility, Dionysius sought to articulate a mystical theology that was true to the kataphasis of scriptural faith and to the apophasis of philosophical contemplation. According to Dionysius's formulation in the *Divine Names* (588A–B):

> [W]e must not dare to resort to words or conceptions concerning the hidden divinity which transcends being, apart from what the sacred scriptures have divinely revealed. Since the unknowing of what is beyond is something above and beyond speech, mind, or being itself, one should ascribe to it an understanding beyond being. . . . Indeed the inscrutable One is out of the reach of every rational process. Nor can any words come up to the inexpressible Good, this One, this source of all unity, this supra-existent Being. Mind beyond mind, word beyond speech, it is gathered up by no discourse, by no intuition, by no name.[195]

God is hidden and transcendent and thus technically "surpasses all discourse and all knowledge" (593A);[196] the only positive attributions that are legitimately ascribed to God are the characteristics derived from the language of Scripture.

In this manner, Dionysius established a model employed subsequently by mystical exegetes in Judaism, Christianity, and Islam who sought to combine the apophatic and kataphatic, remaining faithful to the philosophical insight regarding the unknowability and ineffability of the One, on the one hand, and to the revealed word of God predicated on a plethora of affirmative statements about the divine nature, on the other. The juxtaposition of these distinct orientations to the texture of religious experience resulted in a paradox expressed by Dionysius and reiterated in one form or another by numerous mystic visionaries in the three faiths: "God is therefore known in all things and as distinct from all things. He is known through knowledge and through unknowing" (872A).[197] In more conventional terms, God is both transcendent and immanent, "the cause of everything" but not identical to any one thing, "since it transcends all things in a manner beyond being" (593C).[198] Insofar as there can be nothing outside God, God is "all things in all things," and thus it must be the case that God is known in all things. Yet God is "no thing among things (872A),"[199] for the one cannot be delimited or contained in any single entity and remain the one that is boundless, and hence God is apart from everything and is not known.

It is in this *unknowing* that God is most truly known, a matter that is considered to be a secret that should not be divulged to the uninitiated (597C). In his *Mystical Theology*, Dionysius follows Gregory of Nyssa and ascribes to Moses the status of having freed himself from "what sees and is seen," plunging

> into the truly mysterious darkness of unknowing. Here, renouncing all that the mind may conceive, wrapped entirely in the intangible and the invisible, he belongs completely to him who is beyond everything. Here, being neither oneself nor someone else, one is supremely united to the completely unknown by an inactivity of all knowledge, and knows beyond the mind by knowing nothing. (1001A)[200]

For Dionysius, the mystical agnosticism is attained in the last of the three stages of the mystical path: purgation, illumination, and union (*henosis*). The ideal of union is appropriated from Plotinus, but in Dionysius it should be rendered more precisely as divinization (*theosis*). The way that one rises to this state is by unknowing (*agnosia*), that is, by stripping the mind of all positive knowledge related to sense data and rational concepts, one is unified with the "intellectual light" (φῶς νοητὸν) (*Divine Names* 700D), which transcends all being and knowledge: "But again, the most divine knowledge of God, that which comes through unknowing, is achieved in a union far beyond mind, when mind turns away from all things, even from itself, and when it is made one with the dazzling rays, being then and there enlightened by the inscrutable depth of Wisdom" (872A–B).[201] The mandate of the contemplative life is to move beyond all images to the imageless. As Dionysius put it in the first of the letters to Gaius, "Someone beholding God and understanding what he saw has not actually seen God. . . . He is completely unknown and non-existent. He exists beyond being and he is known beyond the mind. And this quite positively complete unknowing is knowledge of him who is above everything that is known." The author leads his reader once again to the mystical paradox: "complete unknowing is knowledge of him who is above everything that is known" (1065A).[202]

With this ideational background we can better approach the nexus between negative theology and the mystical ideal of conjunction articulated in the history of kabbalah. In another passage from the commentary on *Sefer Yeṣirah* attributed to Isaac, the matter is presented in an appropriately enigmatic manner, centered on the doctrine of ten upper potencies that correspond to the lower ten *sefirot*:[203]

> Even though the word [*dibbur*] is in the infinite, there is nonetheless a subtle cause [*sibbah daqqah*] or subtle essence [*hawayah daqqah*] that thought comprehends

> through contemplation of the allusion from it [*masseget bah be-hitbonenut remez mimmenah*]; therefore, there is an emanation in thought [*sefirah ba-maḥshavah*], which is the subtle essence in which there is ten. The entities [*devarim*] have a measure and dimension but thought has no dimension, and thus they go ten in ten, from the subtle ones the inscribed [*min ha-daqqot ha-reshumot*], for from ten there are ten, subtle ones from the inwardness of the subtle ones [*daqqot mi-penimiyyut ha-daqqot*]. We discern from the potency of allusion of thought [*remez ha-maḥshavah*] what we can comprehend and what we must leave aside, for there is no comprehension of the thought of allusion [*hassagat maḥshevet ha-remez*] from there and beyond, since there is no power in the created being to comprehend the inwardness of the allusion of thought to comprehend the infinite [*penimiyyut remez ha-maḥshavah lehassig be-ein sof*]. . . . There is no capacity to contemplate the hidden essences that have no demarcation except through the thing that emanates from them. . . . From the demarcated essences there is contemplation of those that are not demarcated, and from the inwardness of the comprehension of their thought is there contemplation of their cause in the infinite [*mi-tokh penimiyyut hassagat maḥshavtam hitbonenut sibbotam be-ein sof*].[204]

The name can be viewed as the absolute language, a "mystical language of unsaying,"[205] lingering betwixt affirmation and negation, apophasis and kataphasis, speaking-away and speaking-with, a language that serves as the index of its own inability to be indexed, the computation of indeterminacy. If truth is truly beyond language, then silence alone is appropriate to truth, but silence is realized not in not-speaking but in unsaying, which is a saying nonetheless. If, however, not-speaking is the articulation of truth, then nothing is spoken, but if nothing is spoken, nothing is unspoken. To express the point more prosaically, images of negation are not the same as negation of images, for if the latter were faithfully heeded, the former would truly not be, as there would be nothing of which to (un)speak and hence there would be no data for either study, critical or devotional. Mystical claims of ineffability—to utter unutterable truths—utilize images that are negative but no less imagistic than the affirmative images they negate.[206]

This is precisely the point underscored in the contemplative mysticism propounded by Isaac and other kabbalists who considered him their master. The ultimate signifier is the Tetragrammaton, ultimate in the sense that it signifies what cannot be signified and thus itself resists signification. The name is a garment that reveals the nameless it conceals by concealing the revealing by which it reveals what it conceals. That the root word is ineffable, the proper name par excellence, indicates that the final (in a teleological and not a chronological sense) avowal of language transcends language, an insight conveyed in the technical designation of the uppermost gradation in the divine pleroma as *remez ha-maḥshavah* ("allusion of thought"), the aspect of thought grasped allusively, that which eludes thought, the "thought of allusion" (*maḥshevet ha-remez*), whence the incomprehensible is measured in the comprehension of the immeasurable.[207] Although not stated explicitly, this measure is the Torah, which is the name, envisioned in the heart of the kabbalist as the imaginal body of the macroanthropos.

Support for this surmise is found in an interpretation of the aggadic motif that God looked into Torah before creating the world, which Jacob ben Sheshet reports having heard in the name of Isaac the Blind: "This is similar to the explanation of 'he was contemplating Torah,' he saw the essences in himself, for they were essences from wisdom, and from within these essences, which are the essences of wisdom, he discerned that they would in the future be revealed."[208] In the continuation of the passage, Jacob ben Sheshet mentions the account of divine omniscience in the *Mishneh Torah* of Maimonides[209]—God knows all things by knowing himself, since his intellect contains the form of all things—as confirmation of the tradition attributed to Isaac, and he cites another passage from the *Guide* in which Maimonides discusses the mythopoeic theme that God takes counsel with his angelic retinue before acting in conjunction with the idea attributed to Plato that God contemplates the intelligible world.[210]

The attempt to harmonize the rabbinic, kabbalistic, and philosophic modes of discourse is noteworthy and demands fuller analysis, especially as it might shed light on the taxonomic distinctions that have dominated historiographical conceptions of medieval Jewish religious thought,[211] but for the purposes of this discussion I want only to emphasize that Jacob ben Sheshet preserves indisputable evidence that in the kabbalah of Isaac (or at least what is reported in his name), Torah is equated with the essences comprised in divine wisdom whence the sefirotic potencies emanate; to be even more precise, the emanations can be viewed as the disclosure of the hidden wisdom that is the primordial Torah.

An allusion to this may be discerned in the explanation of the expression *takhlitan* ("their limit") applied to the *sefirot* in *Sefer Yeṣirah*: "The limit of their comprehension, for each attribute has a limit and each limit has an end . . . but your commandment even though its beginning has a limit it extends and keeps going to the infinite, and if every thing that perishes has an end, no one can comprehend the limit of comprehension of your commandment, for a man only comprehends the chief attributes [*ro'shei middot*]."[212] The contrast between the limitless commandment and the limited *sefirot* underscores the fact that the former denotes the boundless aspect of the divine that unfurls within the boundary of the name.

Unsaying the Name/Naming the Unsaid

From the kabbalist's standpoint, the name is the paradigmatic symbol, the symbol of the paradigm, for it is expressive of the inexpressible. In the (un)saying of the name—apophasis as speaking-away, which entails not-speaking by speaking rather than speaking by not-speaking—divine potencies are concealed in the disclosure of their concealment. Inasmuch as the name is representative of language more generally, we can deduce from the prior statement that every speech-act (whether oral or written) is inherently analogical, comparing two ostensibly disparate things, a material entity and its spiritual counterpart. From a logical standpoint, however, the ontotheological schema of traditional kabbalah is informed by two ostensibly clashing claims: On the one hand, it is repeatedly emphasized that all language about God or the world of emanation is analogical, since

God is inherently incomparable to all other things, but on the other hand, it is presumed that an uninterrupted continuity permeates and connects all levels of existence from top to bottom, and thus there is a basic similarity of all things to the divine.[213]

In a sense, these two claims can be correlated with the description of the One in Plotinus (briefly mentioned above) as transcendent to and immanent in all things, a distinction that derives from Plato's account of the One in the *Parmenides*. If there is no rupture in the "chain of being," to use Lovejoy's memorable phrase—and as far as I can discern, no kabbalist from the late Middle Ages would tolerate such a rupture—why should analogy be the only means available to us to fashion theological discourse? To speak analogically is to use words equivocally as a bridge joining two incongruent things rendered the same by being different. Kabbalists would have surely assented to the view expressed by Ibn ʿArabī that one must concurrently affirm the transcendence of true reality vis-à-vis all beings and the immanence of that reality in all beings, the perspective, as we have seen in chapter one, that Corbin calls "theomonism" in contrast to monotheism, that is, the esoteric belief that the oneness of being (*waḥdat al-wujūd*) is manifest through the multiplicity of epiphanies (*tajalliyāt*) that constitute the different names of the ineffable, unnameable truth (*al-ḥaqq*) beyond all discrimination.[214]

The quintessential paradox of kabbalistic ontotheology can be expressed semiotically in the recognition that signifier discloses the nature of signified, and signified, the nature of signifier, precisely because the two are indifferently identical by being identically indifferent. The matter is expressed with rhetorical artistry in one zoharic passage wherein four different levels of meaning in Scripture are distinguished. The relevant comment occurs in the first part of the homily, where only two levels of meaning are mentioned: narratological and mystical, the garment and what is beneath it:

> Come and see: The supernal world and the lower world are balanced on one scale. Israel below and the supernal angels above. Concerning the supernal angels it is written, "He makes his angels into spirits" (Ps. 104:4). When they descend below they are garbed in the garment of this world, and if they were not garbed in the garment that is in the likeness of this world, they could not exist in this world and the world could not endure them. If this is so with respect to angels, how much more so with respect to Torah, which created them and all the worlds, and they exist on account of it, when it descends to this world, if it were not garbed in the garments of this world, the world could not endure. Thus the narrative of Torah is the garment of Torah. The one who thinks that the garment is the Torah itself, and not another matter, let his spirit deflate, and he will have no share in the world-to-come. Therefore, David said, "Open my eyes that I may perceive the wonders of your Torah" (Ps. 119:18), what is beneath the garment of Torah.[215]

In the continuation of the passage, the exegetical layering of Scripture is expanded from two to four levels, to wit, garment, body, soul, and soul of souls, which correspond respectively to the stories, laws, esoteric wisdom, and messianic secrets comprised within the text. In turn, the four levels of meaning are correlated ontically with the heavens and their angelic hosts, *Kenesset Yisraʾel*, *Tifʾeret Yisraʾel*, and *Atiqa Qaddisha*, that is, the tenth, sixth, and first of the sefirotic emanations.[216] What is essential for the present discussion is the initial contrast between the revealed and concealed. It is likely that the author of this unit was operating with the twofold distinction between soul and body, the latter configured as the visible garment that covers the invisible essence of the former, imagery (linked exegetically to Job 10:11) that is attested in zoharic literature and other kabbalistic treatises, including works of de León.[217]

The hermeneutical principle of dual meaning in the text, an orientation fairly widespread in the rabbinic elite from various geographical localities at the time *Zohar* began to crystallize into a discernible textual reality,[218] is based on the ontological parallelism between the supernal and mundane. The image of two worlds "balanced on one scale" (*be-ḥad matqela itqalu*) conveys similitude through difference.[219] Given the virtual identity of thing and word, there is no substantial difference whether we think of this weighing as a metaphysical gesture or a grammatical speech-act; to render dissimilar things equal in their incongruity is a claim about the nature of being as well as a claim about the nature of language.

In typical medieval fashion, kabbalists maintained that the spiritual is discerned through the physical, a cosmological principle that shaped their hermeneutic, as the hidden meaning of the text was thought to be discovered through its literal body, the body that is letter; mystical gnosis thus entails, according to the locution of one zoharic passage, a seeing of the secret "through the garment" (*mi-go levusha*) rather than by removing the garment,[220] a formulation that may be profitably compared to Ibn ʿArabī's insistence, reflecting the stance affirmed by a number of distinguished Sufi masters who preceded him, that the hidden, true reality—the face—cannot be seen except from behind a veil.[221] The veil renders the face spectacular, for in the effacement of the veil, the face is unveiled as that which is inherently not phenomenalizable.[222] In reverse emulation of the dissimilitude of Torah to conceal in the charade of revealing, the master of esoteric gnosis possesses the ability to reveal in the display of concealing. The capacity to divulge secrets, attributed in the zoharic passage to Simeon ben Yoḥai, is traced to the "skilled tongue," *leshon limmudim* (Isa. 50:4), which is identified as the "holy tongue," *leshon ha-qodesh*[223] or the "holy spirit," *ruaḥ ha-qodesh*, that is, the phallic potency of *Shekhinah,*[224] the lower wisdom (*ruaḥ*) that receives the overflow from the upper wisdom (*qodesh*) and is thereby transformed from passive female to active male.[225]

The intent of the aforecited zoharic passage is brought into sharper focus when discussed in conjunction with another text from this literary collage that appears in a dramatic section that chronicles the discourse of the elderly donkey driver focused on the mystery of conversion and the doctrine of metempsychosis.[226] The old man lures other members of the fraternity (and by implication, the reader) into his path by initially uttering three seemingly incomprehensible parables. In time, through the unfolding of the narrative, which is a staging of the hermeneutical dilemma of esotericism marked at each level of disclosure by the tension between the urge to reveal and the need to conceal, the donkey driver, outwardly foolish, discloses himself to be a true master.

It lies beyond the scope of this chapter to do justice to the literary complexity of this unit, but suffice it to note one critical point. The implicit hermeneutic principle in the narrative of the old man—the principle that shapes the mythologic of the story and that incites the exegetical moves of the kabbalist author—is that by plumbing the depths of the mystery of conversion of the Gentile, one shall be led to a mystical understanding of Torah. To grasp this one must bear in mind that the social-historical phenomenon of conversion suggested to the Castilian kabbalists a crossing of ontic boundaries that seemingly challenged the dualistic posture reiterated on numerous occasions in the zoharic text: Israel correlated with divine purity, and the nations of the world, with demonic impurity.

For our purposes it is necessary to ponder the part of the text that articulates the assumption regarding Torah and mystical secrets, an assumption that is at once ontological and hermeneutical—indeed, the two cannot be separated in the thinking of these kabbalists. The explanation of the garbing of a Jewish soul in a non-Jewish body, the key factor in understanding the mechanics of conversion, is interrupted, so it seems, by the observation of the old man that God hides secrets in the garments of Torah. Only the wise who are replete with eyes are capable of apprehending secrets, a vision designated as seeing through rather than discarding the garment, a crucial point to which I have already alluded. Shortly after the reader encounters this principle, the old man offers a parable of the beautiful maiden in a castle that recounts the erotic relationship that pertains between Torah and the "wise one of the heart" (*ḥakkima de-libba*).[227]

As in the zoharic homily that I have previously mentioned, four levels of meaning are delineated: *remiza* or *remizu* ("sign"); *derasha* ("homily"); *ḥiddah* ("allegory") or *haggadah* ("narrative"); and *razin setimin* ("hidden mysteries"). The four levels are presented sequentially as stages of ever-increasing disclosure, the first offered through the barrier of a wall, the second from behind a curtain, the third through a more subtle screen, and finally, the fourth, ostensibly clearing away all obstructions; the reader encounters the text face-to-face, which in zoharic idiom signifies union of the most intimate sort, the epitome of the erotic engagement.[228] When Torah exposes herself fully to her lover, he comes to realize that the secret was already present in the first stage when the initial hint was offered, and at that moment of enlightenment he understands that *peshaṭei di-qera*, the "literal" text—the text in its literal embodiment, the mien of letters—must be as it is, with no word added or subtracted. The linear progression from *peshaṭ* to *sod*, the exoteric to the esoteric, turns out, in fact, to be a circular excursion, as one learns that the mystical meaning disclosed at the end is the same as the literal sense revealed at the beginning.

To discern the mystery of the initial insinuation at the end confirms the hermeneutical point that the secret can be seen only through the garment of letters, the body of the text, unmasking the face in effacing the mask.[229] The uncovering of the innermost meaning at the culmination of the journey is thus a recovery of the overt sense disclosed allusively in the beginning. If it is true that every translation is interpretation, it is equally true that every interpretation is translation, literally "crossing over," by which one gives expression to the inward sense through the outward forms.[230] The somewhat unusual choice of the term *remiza* to denote *peshaṭ* in the initial delineation underscores that the mystical understanding—the illumination of the moment, momentarily momentous—of the revealed word, the light that manifests the name, and by extension of language more generally, rests on the presumption that the literal is metaphorical and the metaphorical literal.[231]

To be sure, on the face of it, the final disclosure—the fourth level—bears the intimacy of the face-to-face encounter, a showing that ostensibly does away with barriers and thus stands in sharp contrast to the intermediaries of the previous revelations: the wall, curtain, and screen; however, when one apprehends the truth that the secret exposed at the end was contained in the hint offered at the beginning, then it becomes apparent that even the "face" is a veil,[232] indeed the greatest of veils, since it can be unveiled only if it remains veiled as that which cannot be unveiled.[233] The polysemous and dissimulating nature of truth is such that when one lifts the veil, one does not uncover truth unveiled but yet another veil reveiling the invisible reality; seen everywhere, it is nowhere seen.

Unveiling the Veil/Veiling the Unveiled

Here it would serve us well to consider the image of the veil a bit more circumspectly, as the veil—distinctively it seems—manifests qualities typically engendered as feminine and associated with an esoteric hermeneutic, allusive, concealing, masking, beckoning, alluring, tempting one to imagine the face yet to be seen.[234] The preceding discussion illustrated the extent to which this dynamic is at play in the zoharic parable of the maiden without eyes. In chapter one, I had the occasion to comment briefly on the affinity between kabbalistic esotericism and the symbol of the veil in Sufism. It would be beneficial to expand on that discussion at this juncture as a way to open up further the boundaries of discourse regarding secrecy and its double arc of projecting and withholding in the zoharic text, which I take to be emblematic of a more ubiquitously held kabbalistic hermeneutic related to the duplicity of revealing and concealing, what I shall call analogical exemplarism, the mirror of mirroring.

By exploring this trajectory, moreover, we will be in a position to understand better the complex interface between the three Abrahamic faiths in the symbolic imaginary of the zoharic kabbalists, which had a profound impact on subsequent generations, including the ecumenism that achieves full theoretical flourish in the messianic heresies of Sabbatianism and Frankism of the seventeenth and eighteenth centuries whereby the borderlines separating Judaism, Christianity, and Islam, are eradicated even as they are preserved. Uprooting may be the operative word, as it conveys both the sense of uncovering and of ravaging the root. In terms of the specific theme of this discussion, the symbol of the veil seems to have been appropriated from an Islamic cultural orbit but applied in the service of the intricate polemical engagement with the Christological notion of incarnation of the Word.

Given the prominence of the veil in the dress code of Arabs before and after the rise of the prophet Muḥammad and the religion of Islam—originally, it seems, part of the attire for men as a sign of their being desert warriors and eventually transferred to women as an external mark of modesty, subservient social status, or self-effacing complicity through renunciation of sexual embodiment, in order to demarcate the boundary between believers and nonbelievers and thereby maintain the *umma* (the community of Muslims) and its symbolic order[235]—it should come as no surprise that the veil and the acts of veiling (*sitr*) and unveiling (*kashf, mukāshafah*) related to it would come to play a prominent role in Islamic esotericism in general and in Sufi epistemology in particular.[236] Needless to say, in this context, I can hardly do justice to the multifaceted texture of this symbol in the religious imagination of Muslims through the centuries. What I wish to emphasize particularly is the paradoxical nature of the veil as the site of concomitant disclosure and concealment, for it is with respect to this quality that we can discern a precise analogy to the image of the garment (*levush*, *malbush*) employed in kabbalistic literature to denote the medium that reveals by concealing and conceals by revealing.[237]

From a relatively early period, the image of lifting the veil was utilized by Sufis to convey mystical enlightenment or awakening, based on verses in the Qurʾān (50:22; 53:57–58; 82:1–6) where this activity is associated with the vision that will be manifest on the day of reckoning (*yawm ad-dīn*).[238] In general, it may be said that Sufis removed the image from its eschatological context and applied it to the inner journey of the seeker (*sālik*) to see the truth (*al-ḥaqq*) behind the veil, the visionary formulation of the mystical quest for union with the one. I do not mean to say that there is a categorical rejection of traditional eschatology on the part of Sufis, but only that their spiritual propensity for inwardness opened the way to a mystical interpretation that renders the eschaton more immediately present; in this sense, Sufis can be spoken of as having embraced an eschatology of and in the moment, mystical illumination in the present, the epiphany of the one true reality in the durationless instant (*ān* or *waqt*) that has no before or after, the interval that endures as that which elapses and elapses as that which endures.[239]

Al-Niffarī, active in the tenth century, expressed the matter laconically in words he attributes to God in his *Kitāb al-mawāqif* (*Book of Standings*): "My moment has come / The time has come for me to unveil my face and manifest my splendor."[240] The revelatory experience, the unveiling of the face (*wajh*), results in gnosis (*maʿrifa*), illumination (*ishrāq*), intuition (*dhawq*), knowledge by presence (*al-ʿilm al-ḥuḍūrī*), the momentous apprehension of the "oneness of existence" (*waḥdat al-wujūd*) in which the particularity of beings is annihilated like water dissolved in water, flame burst into flame.[241]

One of the earliest attestations of the prominence of the symbol of the veil in Sufism is associated with Rābiʿa of Basra (d. 801), the most celebrated woman in Sufi history. What is especially noteworthy is the manner in which Rābiʿa eroticized the image of the veil by describing the goal of the path as an unveiling of the beloved by the lover.[242] The gender implications of this representation are profound—the usual hierarchy on the face of it overturned by the image of the unveiling of the face of the beloved. The image of the veil in Islamic tradition, as I have already noted, is associated with the female, as the Muslim custom demands that women cover their faces in a display of sexual modesty. Recall the beginning of the account of Rābiʿa offered by the thirteenth-century Persian poet ʿAṭṭār: "Veiled with a special veil, veiled with the veil of sincerity, burned up in love and longing, enamored of proximity and immolation, lost in love-union, deputy of Maryam the pure, accepted among men."[243] Instead of the veil of modesty that one would expect to be associated with a Muslim woman, Rābiʿa is veiled in the "special veil," which is the "veil of sincerity." I assume this garb signifies her celibate renunciation, presented in Muslim hagiography as the prerequisite for her passionate and unmitigated yearning to unite with the one.[244] This would explain the designation of her as the "deputy of Maryam the pure," that is, the Virgin Mary.[245] Smith's rendering of the expression is even more striking, the "one accepted by men as a second spotless Mary."[246]

The veneration of Mary, mother of Jesus,[247] as the paragon of a chaste woman is anchored in several critical verses from both the Meccan (609–622 C.E.) and Medinan (622–632 C.E.) periods that uphold the Christological belief in the virginal conception (Q 3:35–47, 21:91; 66:12).[248] The acceptance of this tenet of orthodox Christianity is all the more striking given the unequivocal rejection of ascribing divine status to either Jesus (Q 4:171; 5:17, 75–76; 19:35–36; 43:57–59)[249] or Mary (Q 5:72–75, 116–120);[250] from the qur'ānic perspective, the conception of Jesus without a father is not taken as a proof of the incarnation but only as a mark of his unique prophetic status, his having come into being as an expression of God's direct creative fiat (Q 3:45, 4:171, 19:21), which places Jesus on a par with Adam (Q 3:59).[251]

Especially important for our discussion is the depiction of Mary in *Sūrat Maryam* (the only extended narrative from the Meccan period that deals with Jesus) as "screening herself away" from her people, the withdrawal that preceded the appearance of an angel (identified by later interpreters as Gabriel) in the form of a "well-shaped human being" (19:17). The scriptural linkage of the occlusion of Mary behind the curtain (*ḥijāb*) and the virginal conception (19:20–22) fostered a metaphorical interpretation on the part of Sufi exegetes focused on the ascetic renunciation required to traverse the spiritual path.[252] I suggest that *ḥijāb* in particular became a symbol of Mary's virginity, the denotation of the term as "curtain" giving way to the "veil." The adoration of Rābiʿa as a "second spotless Mary" is doubtless related to her own virginity and celibate lifestyle.[253] The "special veil" or the "veil of sincerity," it seems to me, may function as a symbolic denotation of Rābiʿa's celibacy, the overt sign of the gender transformation that facilitated her being accepted "among men," the "friends of God," on the way to unveiling the beloved.

Another critical dimension of the image of the veil is revealed in the following passage cited anonymously in the compendium of principles of Sufi piety, *Risāla al-qushayriyya*, by al-Qushayrī (d. 1074): "Certainty is unveiling, and unveiling takes place in three ways: by means of informing, by means of disclosure of the power [of God], and by means of the truths of faith." Explaining this dictum, al-Qushayrī advises the reader: "Know that in their way of speaking, unveiling consists of the revelation of something to the heart when it is possessed by remembrance of Him with no doubt remaining. Sometimes by unveiling they mean something similar to what is seen between waking and sleep. Many times they designate this state as steadfastness."[254]

By means of unveiling (*kashf*), the truth is manifest in the heart (*qalb*), the site that is repeatedly marked as the locus of spiritual vision in Sufi teaching, a manifestation that is all-encompassing, a point related in the above passage by another technical Sufi term, *dhikr*, the repetitive utterance of divine names that occasions the remembrance or recollection of the real, that is, the singular, meditative focus on the divine occasioned by repetition of divine epithets or qur'ānic phrases.[255] The unveiling designates a state of consciousness between wakefulness and sleep. We are not told more about this state, but I would surmise that al-Qushayrī chose this image to convey the idea that this mode of awareness is pure mobility, a state of wavering designated paradoxically as "steadfastness" (*baqā*ʾ), the Sufi expression that denotes persisting in the real.

To grasp the paradoxical identification of absolute motion and absolute stability implied in this depiction of unveiling, one must bear in mind that in technical Sufi terminology, which may be traced to al-Junayd (d. 910), *baqā*ʾ is dialectically tangled up with annihilation of *nafs*, the lower soul of the base instincts, the differentiated ego-self.[256] If one were to lay out the mystical path sequentially, *baqā*ʾ would be preceded by *fanā*ʾ ("passing away"), but from the enlightened perspective the two occur concurrently—the annihilation is the abiding and the abiding the annihilation,[257] an idea that is captured in the seemingly contradictory claim ascribed to al-Junayd in his account of the passing away of oneself from one's ecstasies (*mawājīd*) when one is overpowered by the real: "At that moment you both pass away and abide, and are found truly existent in your passing away; through the found existence (*wujūd*) of your other; upon the abiding of your trace in the disappearance of your name."[258]

True abiding, therefore, as al-Bisṭāmī, al-Junayd, and other Sufi masters put it, consists in the passing away of passing away (*fanā*ʾ *al-fanā*ʾ), the double negation that yields a positive predication.[259] Following the teaching of al-Junayd, al-Qushayrī spoke of the first passing away as the "passing away of the self and its attributes to endure through the attributes of the real," the second passing away as the "passing away from the attributes of the real through witnessing of the real," and the third and final passing away as "a person's passing away from witnessing his own passing away through his perishing in the ecstatic existentiality (*wujūd*) of the real."[260] When one takes hold of this insight, then one can appreciate al-Qushayrī's account of the unveiling as a state betwixt sleep and dream, a place of nonduality where to subsist one must subside and to subside one must subsist, the fullness of the moment (*waqt*) that abides in its passing and passes in its abiding.[261]

The essential point to draw from this text for the immediate concern of this discussion is that unveiling denotes the mystical awakening of the heart to the one true reality, a gnosis that is intricately connected to the secret of union. In one of the oldest and most celebrated Persian treatises on Sufism, *Kashf al-maḥjūb* (*The Unveiling of the Veiled*), al-Hujwīrī contrasts "absence" and "presence" by stating that the former "involves the sorrow of being veiled" and the latter "involves the joy of revelation."[262] In a second passage, he notes that the veils that obstruct one's knowledge of God are a result of ignorance; when ignorance is annihilated, veils vanish.[263] Apparently, this is the meaning of al-Hujwīrī's comment that "revelation [*mukāshafat*] implies the possibility of a veil [*ḥijāb*],"[264] that is, we can speak meaningfully of the revelation of truth only if it were previously veiled. Explicating a dictum of Abu ʾl-ʿAbbās al-Āmulī, al-Hujwīrī notes, "natural dispositions are the instruments and organs of the sensual part (*nafs*), which is the centre of 'veiling' (*ḥijāb*), whereas the spiritual part (*ḥaqīqat*) is the centre of revelation."[265]

In another passage, al-Hujwīrī uses a slightly different nomenclature to mark the two states of being, the inseparable manifestations of the ontological and psychological: "*Qabḍ* denotes the contraction of the heart in the state of being veiled (*ḥijāb*), and *basṭ* denotes the expansion of the heart in the state of revelation (*kashf*)."[266] Contraction of the heart is synonymous with the agitation of longing in a state of occultation (*ḥijāb*); expansion is the calm of contemplation in a state of revelation (*kashf*).[267] The master of esoteric gnosis, accordingly, is one who peers beyond the veil of the veil-keepers in the quest for a vision of the face.[268] By contrast, *majḥub* ("veiled") assumes the negative connotation of one who is not spiritually illumined and therefore does not perceive the divine light without the veils of sentient and rational forms.[269]

Veiling (*sitr*) and concealment (*istitār*) connote ignorance, whereas removing the veil (*kashf*) results in divine self-revelation (*tajallī*). The Sufi ideal is captured by the masterful pen of the Persian poet Rūmī (1207–1273) in his *Mathnawī*: "Beauty is from God, but the corporealist does not feel (the charm of) beauty without the veil (medium) of the garden. When the bodily medium is removed, (then) he (who is disembodied) perceives without (any) screen, like Moses,[270] the light of the Moon (shining) from (his own) bosom."[271] The depiction of Moses seeing the divine without any barrier is based, of course, on the biblical precedent that Moses was distinguished vis-à-vis all the other prophets insofar as he spoke directly with God ("mouth to mouth") and beheld the image of the Lord (Num. 12:8) and the later rabbinic notion that Moses saw the glory through a speculum that shines whereas the other prophets saw through a speculum that does not shine.[272]

Rūmī's exaltation of Moses along these lines is especially noteworthy in light of the exegesis of Exodus 33:18–23 in Sūra 7:143–144. According to the narrative in Exodus, the request of Moses to see the glory resulted in his seeing the back, not the front. In the qur'ānic reworking, Moses did not see God at all, for when the glory appeared on the mountain, the mountain turned into dust, thereby indicating that God's response to Moses that he should look upon the mountain and if it abides his demand would be answered positively was, in effect, a way of saying that seeing the unseen consists of (not)-seeing. Consider the commentary of Jaʿfar al-Ṣādiq: "You are not able to see me because you pass away. How can that which passes away find a way to that which abides? . . . The lord's face-to-face vision in respect to the servant is the annihilation of the servant. The servant's face-to-face vision of the lord and in the lord is enduring."[273]

In this text, we are introduced to the two key technical terms utilized in Sufi teaching to express the goal of mystical union, *fanā'* and *baqā'*, passing away and enduring. The scriptural foundation for these terms is Sūra 55:26, "All that dwells upon the earth is perishing [*fanin*], yet still abides [*fa-yabqa*], the face of your Lord, majestic, splendid." According to the mystical interpretation, by undoing the bonds that tie the soul to matters of the body, passing away from the impermanent self, the higher self abides with the beloved; significantly, persisting in that which abides is expressed as seeing the unseen, beholding the face that has no visible form to behold.

In spite of the unequivocal denial of the possibility of seeing God in Muslim faith, based firmly on the qur'ānic precedent of associating the word "unseen" (*ghayb*) with Allah (Q 11:31, 123; 13:9; 16:77; 35:18; 53:35), it is precisely the Sufi mandate, following the teaching of Muḥammad, to worship God "as if you see him."[274] This stands in contrast to Sūra 2:3, where belief in the unseen (*ghayb*) precedes the establishment of prayer (*ṣalāt*), one of the five fundamental pillars of Islam. On the other hand, the nexus between seeking God's face and prayer is attested in several verses (Q 6:52, 13;22, 18:28). Also relevant is the polemic in Sūra 4:153 against the children of Israel, referred to as the "people of the book,"[275] which, closely following the unfolding of the narrative plot in Exodus, links idolatry, exemplified in the worship of the golden calf,[276] to the desire to see God—in the qur'ānic version, the request is attributed to the Israelites as a whole, thus misreading the account in the Torah, where the petition to see the glory frontally (Exod. 33:12–16) is attributed to Moses alone, though, to be sure, the petition is intricately connected to the fate of the national collectivity. With respect to the emphasis placed on seeing the divine in a liturgical context, there is an important phenomenological affinity between Sufism and various forms of medieval Jewish mystical piety, revolving about the claim that prayer in a theistic tradition requires iconic representation of the divine within the imagination.[277]

In a second passage, Rūmī utilizes the erotic implication of unveiling to convey the difference between passing state (*ḥāl*) and permanent station (*maqām*): The former is compared to the "unveiling of that beauteous bride" and the latter to the king's "being alone with the bride." The bride "unveils before commons and nobles (alike)," but "in the bridal chamber the king is (alone) with the bride."[278] The unveiling is a state of attainment enjoyed by Sufis, but for the privileged among them it is followed by the more intimate rank of being exclusively with the bride, a unitive experience that is consequent to disrobing and unmasking. To attain visionary union, unitive vision, the heart of the seer must be purged of all images so that it may behold the invisible in its own reflection. "He whose clear breast has become devoid of (any) image (impression) has become a mirror for the impressions of the Invisible."[279]

The objective for one who walks the path is to rend the veil, to behold truth in its naked form. However, inasmuch as rending the veil reveals that which has no image, the unknowable essence that cannot be essentialized, the inaccessible presence that cannot be represented, it must be said that the veil conceals the face it reveals by revealing the face it conceals. Language is decidedly inadequate to mark the middle ground wherein concealing and revealing are identical in virtue of being different and different in virtue of being identical. Epistemologically the matter may be expressed in the following terms utilized by Ibn ʿArabī: The veil conveys both the incomparability (*tanzīh*) of the face and the image seen through the veil, for the image that is seen is an image and not the face, and the similarity (*tashbīh*) of the face and the image, for in the absence of an image the face could not be perceived.[280] In *Fuṣūṣ al-ḥikam*, Ibn ʿArabī notes that to become an imām and master of spiritual sciences, one must maintain both the incomparability and similarity of the ultimate reality in relation to all other existents in the chain of being, for to insist exclusively on either transcendence or immanence is to restrict that reality inappropriately.[281]

The mandate to lift the veils, therefore, does not result in discarding all possible veils; indeed, there can be no "final" veil to lift, as there must always be another veil through which the nonmanifest will be made manifest. In this respect, Sufi sensibility remained faithful to the qur'ānic declaration that it is not fitting for God to speak to a human "except by inspiration, from behind a veil, or by the sending of a messenger" (Q 42:51), that is, by way of an intermediary that renders the unseen (*ghayb*) visible. What is unveiled in the unveiling is not the face behind the veil but the veil before the face; that is, unveiling is the metaphorical depiction of removing the shells of ignorance that blind one from seeing the truth of the veil in the veil of the truth: God and world are identical in their difference.[282] The transcendence of God, the unity of the indiscriminate one (*aḥadiyyat al-aḥad*), renders all theological discourse at best analogical, since there is no way to speak directly about that which transcends all being, yet the divine is immanent in all things—indeed, mystically conceived, there is nothing but the single true reality that is all things, the unity of multiplicity (*aḥadiyyat al-kathra*).[283]

The Sufi accordingly knows that the light is too bright to be uncovered except through a covering.[284] In the last chapter of *Mishkāt al-anwār* (*The Niche of Lights*), which deals with the qur'ānic passage known in the tradition as the verse of light (Q 24:25), the eleventh-century Iranian mystic, al-Ghazālī, comments on the *ḥadīth* of the prophet briefly alluded to in chapter one: "God has seventy veils of light and darkness; were he to lift them, the august glories of his face would burn up everyone whose eyesight perceived him": "God discloses himself to his essence in his essence. Without doubt, the 'veil' is understood in relation to the thing that is veiled. The veiled among the creatures are of three kinds: those who are veiled by darkness alone, those who are veiled by sheer light, and those who are veiled by light along with darkness."[285] At the conclusion of these classifications there is a further specification of several subgroups of the ones "veiled by sheer lights," the highest being "those who have arrived":

> To them it has been disclosed that the one who is obeyed is described by an attribute that contradicts sheer oneness and utmost perfection. This belongs to the mystery which is beyond the capacity of this book to unveil . . . the relationship of this one who is obeyed is that of the sun among the lights. Therefore, they have turned their faces from the one who moves the heavens. . . . They have arrived at an existent thing that is incomparable with everything their sight has perceived. Hence, the august glories of his face—the first, the highest—burn up everything perceived by the sights and insights of the observers.[286]

Even at this level, where vision is blindness, and blindness, vision, there are different stages of attainment. For some the objects of vision alone are effaced, but for the "elect of the elect," perceived and perceiver are effaced in the supreme mystical state of *fanā'*, passing away, the annihilation of self as an entity ontically distinct from the One; the mimetic figuration gives way to the ecstatic vision in which the self vanishes; there is naught but vision, a seeing without seer or seen: "They become extinct from themselves, so that they cease observing themselves. Nothing remains save the One, the Real. . . . This is the ultimate end of those who have arrived."[287] For al-Ghazālī, the removal of the veil, the symbolic act that signifies the declaration of unity (*tawḥīd*), is the inner meaning of the qur'ānic verse "There is no god but he. Everything will perish except his own face" (Q 28:88). In the end, when the seventy veils of light and darkness are removed, there is pure light, the face without veil, the veil without face, invisibly visible, visibly invisible.

The self-manifestation of God, therefore, must be through the multitude of veils that make up the cosmos. The paradoxical nature of the veil to disclose what is occluded by way of occluding what is disclosed is evident in the tradition concerning the response of the archangel Gabriel to Muḥammad's query whether he had ever seen the Lord: "As it is, between me and Him there are seventy veils of light. If I ever came close to the one nearest to me I would get burnt."[288] If the highest of angels cannot approach the lowest of the veils separating him from the divine, how much more so must it apply to beings of the natural world. All that we consider real is veritably a veil; truth comes forth as unveiling the unveiling of the veil so that the unveiled is seen in the veil of the unveiled; disposing of the veil would result, by contrast, in veiling the veil and the consequent effacing of the face.

From a relatively early period al-Niffarī discerned that rending the veil—the ostensible goal of the mystical path—would result in an overpowering of light that would baffle the mind of created beings. "Knowings of the veil / cannot bear what appears / when the veil is torn."[289] To see the face behind the veil, one must be veiled from the unveiling; indeed, the one adroit in lifting the veils knows full well that throwing off the veil is itself a form of donning the veil. The paradox is articulated by al-Niffarī in a series of gnomic pronouncements:

> Once you have seen Me, unveiling and the veil will be equal.
> You will not stand in vision until you see My veil as vision and My vision as veil.
> There is a veil that is not unveiled, and an unveiling that is not veiled. The veil that is not unveiled is knowledge through me, and the unveiling that is not veiled is knowledge through me.
> No veil remains: Then I saw all the eyes gazing at his face, staring. They see him in everything through which he veils himself. He said to me: They see me, and I veil them through their vision of Me from Me.[290]

Several centuries later—precisely in the period when kabbalah began to flourish in southern France and northern Spain—Ibn ʿArabī elaborated the paradoxical mystery of the veil and its unveiling in a somewhat more technical philosophic tone commensurate with his speculative gnosis: "There is nothing in existence but veils hung down. Acts of perception attach themselves only to veils, which leave traces in the owner of the eye that perceives them."[291] Ephemeral contingencies are but veils hiding the eternal being, the necessary of existence, but it is through the concealment of these veils that the invisible is rendered visible: "Thus the Real becomes manifest by being veiled, so He is the Manifest / the Veiled. He is the Nonmanifest because of the veil, not because of you, and He is the Manifest because of you and the veil."[292] In another passage, Ibn ʿArabī expresses the matter as a commentary on the aforementioned *ḥadīth* that God possesses seventy veils of light and darkness:

> The dark and luminous veils through which the Real is veiled from the cosmos are only the light and the darkness by which the possible thing becomes qualified in its reality because it is a middle. . . . Were the veils to be lifted from the possible thing,

possibility would be lifted, and the Necessary and the impossible would be lifted through the lifting of possibility. So the veils will remain forever hung down and nothing else is possible. . . . The veils will not be lifted when there is vision of God. Hence vision is through the veil, and inescapably so.[293]

The veil came to signify the hermeneutic of secrecy basic to the esoteric gnosis of Sufism, envisioning the hidden secret revealed in the concealment of its revelation and concealed in the revelation of its concealment. Accordingly, the task is to discard the veils to reveal the truth, but if the veils were all discarded, there truly would be no truth to see. This is the import of the statement that the "veils will not be lifted when there is vision of God." If the unseen is to be seen, the vision manifestly must be "through the veil."[294] From that vantage point, all that exists is divine. Thus, commenting on the qurʾānic verse (mentioned above) "Everything will perish except his own face" (Q 28:88) in *Kitāb al-aḥadiyyah* (*A Treatise on the One Alone*), Ibn ʿArabī writes, "That which exists and is visible is He. There is nothing but He, so how could nothing cease to be?"[295] In this state of attainment, there is nothing but the One, and hence there is a cessation of cessation, the passing away of passing away (*fanāʾ al-fanāʾ*), which is the persistence (*baqāʾ*) of the manifold in the oneness of being: "Therefore, do not think anymore that you need to become nothing, that you need to annihilate yourself in Him. If you thought so, then you would be His veil, while a veil over Allah is other than He. How could you be a veil that hides Him? What hides Him is His being the One Alone."[296]

In accord with the long-standing Sufi tradition, Ibn ʿArabī affirms that when one passes away from passing away, all veils are abolished. It follows that if one could discard all need, even the need to discard all need, the desire not to desire the desire to desire not, then the last veil—the veil of thinking there is a last veil—would be removed. In the end of the passage, the reader is taken somewhat by surprise by the assertion "What hides Him is His being the One Alone." How can the attribute of oneness (*aḥadiyyah*) be a veil hiding the One? It can only be so if we grasp that veil and face are identical in their difference; to unveil the face, the veil must be faced, but the veil cannot be faced unless all veils are lifted and the very distinction between face and veil is eradicated; in discerning this truth, however, the visionary detects that he is the mirror/veil through which the face is seen as veil and the veil as face. In this unveiling, identity is realized through (not as) difference, and difference through (not as) identity. In *Futūḥāt al-makkiyya*, Ibn ʿArabī enunciates this very point:

> He who sees the Real plainly and openly
> sees Him only from behind a veil. . . .
> The form of the Seer has disclosed itself
> to him
> while he is the Seer—no, he is the veil.[297]

The mystical path is to train the mind so that one removes the veils in order to see truth unveiled, but the greatest of veils to remove is the belief that one can see truth without a veil. To unveil the veil, therefore, is to veil the unveiling, to see the unseeing as the manifestation of the concealment in the concealment of the manifestation, to behold the face of the veil veiling the veiling of the veil of the face.[298] The veil thus exhibits the structure of the esoteric hermeneutic basic to Sufism, the paradox that the visibility of the medium consists of its invisibility,[299] a supposition that fostered on the part of the adept an envisioning of the secret revealed in the concealment of its revelation and concealed in the revelation of its concealment.

At the peak of the visionary experience, the seer discerns, to paraphrase another celebrated Persian bard, Ḥāfiẓ (c. 1320–1389), that the only barrier (*ḥāyil*) separating the lover and the beloved is the selfhood of the lover;[300] the lover's heart is the site of the "synchronic coincidence of planes of vision" marked by a "continual flow back and forth between the heart of the poet and the primeval source from which he draws inspiration," the "perpetual oscillation between self-revelation of the Divine in its self-concealment, and the concealment of the Divine in its self-revelation; between a Beauty that attracts as it repels and a majesty that repels as it attracts."[301] To see the beauty reflected in the heart, the cup of cosmic vision,[302] the mirror of the invisible world, the heart must reveal the veil, an unveiling that imparts to the poet the epithet *lisān al-ghayb* (literally, "tongue of the unseen"), for his task consists of uttering the unutterable and thereby facilitating envisioning the invisible.[303] As the poet himself puts it, "I have made the journey into Nothing. / I have lit the lamp that / Needs no oil. . . . I have become the flame that needs / No fuel."[304] The visionary journey may thus be compared to crossing a bridge that is discerned not to be a bridge once crossed, that is, crossing the very bridge of crossing to the point that one can no longer speak of either bridge or crossing.

Rising Within: Dis/Placing Place in the Topography of the Imaginal

The blurring of the ontological distinction that ensues from crossing the bridge that in the end turns out not to have been a bridge, entering a gate that is no gate,[305] is the task of poetic metaphor. According to the enigmatic comment from a section in zoharic literature marked as belonging to the *Tosefta* stratum, "The bond of the pure bond [*quṭra de-quṭra dakhya*] ascends within and within [*saliq le-go le-go*] until the place [*atar*], the house of dwelling [*beit motva*], is not found. This place is no place [*ha-hu atar law atar*], it is not found above or below. It is negated with respect to everything, a state of annihilation [*mi-kola itʿavid avaddon hawwei*]."[306]

It is likely, as a number of traditional commentaries have noted, that there is an allusion in these words to the emanative process by means of which the hidden becomes manifest, the highest point being point/less, that is the point to which none can point, extending beyond extension, limitlessness delimiting limit delimiting limitlessness, in the language of the text, the "place that is no place" (*atar law atar*), the site where being is nothing and nothing is being, where concealed is revealed and revealed is concealed. I would add, however, that the dis/placement of place can also be read from an anthropocentric perspective, that is, the soul/mind is the "bond of the pure bond" that ascends within (*saliq le-go le-go*) until it reaches the highest of the emanations, *ayin*, no/thing, the threshold to infinity (*ein sof*), the place that is no-place. Yet it must be remembered that on the mystical path, contemplative ascent is at the same time turning inward.

This critical point is conveyed in the zoharic text by the equivocality of the term *saliq*, which can mean ascend, enter, and disappear; hence *saliq le-go* can be rendered as "rising within," an internal ascent, ascending to the chamber of the throne by entering the garden of the heart, entering the garden of the heart by ascending to the chamber of the throne,[307] to the point of the pointless, the no/thing that is everything, the state of annihilation (*avaddon*), wherein the heart/mind is stripped of all specificity so that it may behold everything in/as nothing, a state reminiscent of the Sufi *fanāʾ al-fanāʾ* (passing away of passing away), which constitutes *baqāʾ* (endurance, persistence). From this spot the poetic word ushers forth, enfolded in silence, disclosing being-as-mystery on the horizon where the imaginal representation of the nonrepresentable is made possible through disclosing the disclosure of what is openly hidden.

The paradoxical collapse of opposites—indeed the collapse of the collapse that still presupposes opposites to be collapsed—well captures the affair of language that has enchanted the poetic imagination of kabbalists in their effort to depict the mystery of the garment as the mirror that effectuates the overcoming of the inside/outside dichotomy. An affinity with Sufic terminology is especially evident in the author of *Shaʿarei Ṣedeq*. The final stages of the meditational practice of *derekh ha-shemot* ("way of the names") that leads to prophetic experience, which the author equates, following the appropriation of the Maimonidean ideal on the part of his teacher, Abraham Abulafia, with the disembodied state of intellectual conjunction (*devequt*), identified as well as worship of the heart (*avodah she-ba-lev*), which is predicated on knowledge of the name (*yediʿat ha-shem*), is described as follows:

> By drawing forth words from thought [*maḥshavah*] he will force himself to come out from under the rule of his natural intellect [*sikhlo ha-ṭivʿi*], for if he wants not to think he cannot, and he should be lead initially in the phases of writing [*ketav*] and speaking [*lashon*], and also through the mouth, which is the form [*ṣiyyur*]. When he is to come out from under its rule, another effort is necessary, which consists of drawing thought gradually forth from its source until reaching the level that will compel him not to speak and concerning which he has no ability to overcome. And if he has it in his power to prevail and to continue drawing forth, then he will go out from his inwardness, and it will take shape in his purified imaginative faculty [*koaḥ ha-dimyoni ha-zakh*] in the form of the translucent mirror [*marʾah zakkah*], and this is "the flame of the encircling sword" (Gen. 3:24), the back rotating and becoming the front. He discerns his inmost being [*mahut penimiyyuto*] as something outside himself. . . . For when a form is not perfect, it is detached from its essence until it is nullified and garbed in a purified imaginal form [*ṣurah dimyonit zakkah*] through which the letters are combined in a perfect, orderly, and adequate combination. It seems to me that this form is called by kabbalists "garment" [*malbush*].[308]

After having documented in graphic detail the arduous phases of the meditational practice of letter combination and the peculiar experiences ensuing therefrom, the author discloses the culminating state of contemplation whereby one passes beyond the threshold of thought and speech. The state of mindfulness devoid of concepts, images, and words leads experientially to the breakdown of the perceptual distinction between inside and outside, as the external form beheld by the adept is the radiance of the internal light, which in turn is a reflection of the external form.[309] The following description by Heinrich Zimmer of the Hindu form of Yoga known as *pūjā*, the veneration of the divine in one of its manifold aspects in the outer form of daily worship that calls forth through an inner image in the devotee, provides an interesting analogue:

> The actual goal is that the inner image of the deity and he who has conceived it should emerge from their duality and interpenetrate one another, that they should fuse into One (*samādhi*). The believer experiences the fact that the deity is not something different from himself—it does not dwell somewhere out in the world, it has not just come to visit him; it does not sit on a throne in some heaven beyond the heavens: out of his own formless inwardness he has built up every detail, and at the end of his devotions he lets it dissolve again in his formless inwardness, in the primordial waters of the unconscious, just as the Indian god unfolds the world and then, when it is ripe for dissolution, melts it down again into himself, the universal night, the primordial flood.[310]

To express the matter in a more contemporary phenomenological idiom, influenced particularly by Kantian epistemology, the noematic presence in consciousness inhering in some "objective" substance or substratum, the representation of an outer sense, is given to consciousness as an image of the noetic manifold of an inner sense projected outward as an object that stands over and against the mind (the German word *Gegenstand* is instructive), but that projection is itself predicated on the presumption that the noematic presence is a "subjective" projection of the noetic manifold.[311] At the moment of vision, through the force of the imagination that has been purified by ascetic practice and the purging of all discriminate forms, the heart of the mystic becomes a translucent mirror, the screen/veil through which the internal is externalized and the external internalized, the seeing of one's inward form projected outward as the outward image propelled inward, the vision in which the difference of identity between seer and seen is overcome in the identity of their difference[312]—the mind sees itself as the mirror reflecting the mind that mirrors, embracing thereby the paradox of visible invisibility of which we spoke above—and hence the imagination is referred to by the scriptural image of the "flame of the encircling sword," that is, the sword that revolves in such a way that the back becomes the front in confronting the front becoming the back.

In the polished mirror of imagination, the form detached from its essence, that is, the form that has no form, not even the form of formlessness, clothes itself in an "imaginal form." We are told, moreover, that through this form, "the letters are combined in a perfect, orderly, and adequate combination," which is identified with the kabbalistic notion of the garment (*malbush*).[313] I would suggest that the author is alluding here to the permutation of the Hebrew letters that constitute the Torah.[314] If this conjecture is correct, then the point of the passage is that Torah is the imaginal form through which the formless is envisioned.

It seems to me that Abulafia himself alludes to this secret in his treatises. For our purposes I shall cite and exegete a passage from *Oṣar Eden Ganuz*:

> How can a man comprehend the divine attribute [*middah elohit*] in his imagination [*be-dimyono*]? It is comprehended by him and not by us, for it cannot be comprehended. But we can comprehend what is appropriate for us to do in the ways of our attributes according to the narratives of the Torah and according to the commandments. The Torah was given to man and it speaks in the language of man.[315]

Abulafia begins by affirming an apophatic orientation well attested in philosophical and theological treatises composed by practitioners of the three monotheistic religions.[316] More specifically, it is related in his case (though the epistemological assumption he harbors is hardly unique) to the fact that human cognition is intractably dependent on the imaginative faculty (*koaḥ ha-medammeh*), and hence one cannot access the divine attribute (*middah elohit*) in and of itself, since it has no image. What we can apprehend positively are the stories and laws of Torah, which, according to the medieval philosophic interpretation of a talmudic dictum attributed to the school of R. Ishmael, adopted by Abulafia, most likely from Maimonides, are spoken in language comprehensible to a human being (*dibberah torah ke-lashon benei adam*). Even more significantly, according to the Maimonidean interpretation of this hermeneutical principle, the "human language," which is the rhetorical idiom of the revealed Scripture, is equated explicitly with the imaginative faculty of the multitude.[317]

That Abulafia speaks affirmatively of an inherently unknowable *middah elohit* is significant, for it underscores that the relation between the ontic and epistemic is asymmetrical; there is something that logically and metaphysically must be presumed to exist—indeed the ultimate being, designated by Abulafia by another technical philosophical term he borrowed from Maimonides, *meḥuyav ha-meṣi'ut* ("the necessary of existence"), that is, the being for whom existence and essence are not distinguishable insofar as the existence of this being is unconditionally necessary—that we cannot know. Abulafia is emphatic on this point for both the masses and the elite. Surely, in the case of the former, God's existence is not adduced on the basis of rational discernment (*hassagah*) but on tradition (*qabbalah*), but even in the case of the latter, Abulafia insists that the enlightened one (*ba'al sekhel*) whose "mind is essentially clear" (*eṣem moḥo zakh*) must receive this gnosis from a master who is accredited with being part of an unbroken chain of tradition.[318]

Wisdom about the name—referred to by various traditional idioms, to wit, "explicit name" (*shem ha-meforash*), "unique name" (*shem ha-meyuḥad*), and "glorious name" (*shem ha-nikhbad*), and also designated by the technical philosophical expression "essential name" (*shem ha-eṣem*)—culminates in a unitive experience attained by way of the meditational practice, which involves the ostensibly transgressive act of vocalization of the name, but even this knowledge is negative. In *Or ha-Sekhel*, Abulafia makes this point with reference to the divine name composed of *alef*, *he*, *waw*, *yod*, identified in medieval sources as "letters of concealment" (*otiyyot ha-haʿalamah*). To clarify the meaning of concealment, Abulafia cites the verse "This shall be my name forever, and this is my appellation from generation to generation," *zeh shemi le-olam we-zeh zikhri le-dor dor* (Exod. 3:15), and offers the following interpretation:

> It says in the tradition that it is written *leʿalem*, that is to say, it is appropriate to conceal, and thus its letters are the letters of concealment. This is what is understood by the masses, but the esoteric [*ha-neʿelam*] is not this, for *leʿalem* is an equivocal term [*dibbur meshutaf*], the first of its meanings is the matter of concealment [*ha-heʿelem*] and the second is the matter of elevation [*ha-maʿalah*]. It is appropriate to conceal [*leʿalem*] the letters of the name, that is, to elevate [*laʿaleh*] them . . . and proof for this is what is said immediately "this is my appellation" [*zeh zikhri*], which instructs that a man is obligated to mention it [*lehazkiro*]. And the secret of "from generation to generation" [*le-dor dor*] indicates that each generation and generation evolves through a name [*mitggalggel be-shem*].[319]

Abulafia's comment is a subtle subversion of a rabbinic tradition regarding the ineffability of YHWH sanctioned on the basis of the verse *zeh shemi le-olam we-zeh zikhri le-dor dor.* According to a reading of this verse preserved in two contexts in the Babylonian Talmud (Pesaḥim 50a, Qiddushin 71a), *zeh shemi le-olam* ("this is my name forever") is rendered (based on the Masoretic orthography) as *zeh shemi leʿalem* ("this is my name to conceal"). Thus, in a dictum transmitted in the name of R. Avina, the verse is interpreted as the scriptural basis for the custom not to pronounce the Tetragrammaton as it is written. Abulafia links the designation of the letters of the name, *otiyyot ha-haʿalamah* ("letters of concealment"), to the midrashic reading of *zeh shemi le-olam* as *zeh shemi leʿalem*, but he maintains that *leʿalem* is an equivocal term (*dibbur meshutaf*), one of its meanings being concealment (*heʿelem*) and the other, elevation (*ha-maʿalah*). The rabbinic gloss, *leʿalem otam*, to hide the letters of the name, is the reading appropriate for the masses, but for the select few the proper reading is *laʿaleh otam*, that is, to uplift the letters, which entails uttering the name in the manner that is apposite for each generation.

To grasp the full implication of this comment, one must bear in mind that Abulafia accepts the older esoteric equation of the name with Torah, and the further identification of the latter with *sekhel ha-poʿel*, the Active Intellect.[320] This equation fostered an audacious mystical application of the contemplative ideal of *devequt*. Alongside the language of philosophical thinkers, which, *pace* Scholem, I do not consider merely as "rationalizations" obscuring the true mystical intent of his teaching but rather as the speculative framework within which the latter was enveloped,[321] Abulafia construes intellectual conjunction as union with Torah.[322] Insofar as the latter is equated with the Tetragrammaton, the experience of conjunction thereto may be described as incorporation into the name, which, as Abulafia himself asserts in an evidently apophatic nod, denotes the essence that exceeds rational comprehension (*hassagat ha-sekhel*).[323] For Abulafia, as for Maimonides, the imaginative faculty is a vital component of the prophetic vision.

In *Ḥayyei Olam ha-Ba*, Abulafia frames the matter in a standard philosophical manner, beginning with an affirmation of the epistemological basis (traceable to the Platonic tradition) for the *via negativa* embraced by Maimonides as well: "His unity is too strong to be imagined by us in any image, for none of his creatures above or below can comprehend the truth of his unity, and *a fortiori* man cannot know the quiddity of his essence [*mahut aṣmo*], blessed be his name." Abulafia goes on to say that the limit of comprehension for prophets, sages, and philosophers alike is to remove all physical attributes from God, which arise on account of the imagination and thus obstruct one from attaining true knowledge. Abulafia concedes, in a manner that is consonant with Maimonides:

> It is not possible to imagine [*leṣayyer*] anything of the intelligible matters [*ha-devarim ha-muskkalim*] except by means of participation with comprehension of corporeal forms [*hassagat ṣurot gashmut*].[324] Thus even the prophet, in the moment that he comprehends the prophetic word [*ha-dibbur ha-nevu'i*] that emanates from God, blessed be he and blessed be his name, through the intermediary of the Active Intellect in man by means of the permutation of letters contemplated in the heart, it is not possible that he will not imagine [*yeṣayyer*] what he has comprehended in a corporeal form from one thing to another thing.[325]

In a critical way, however, Abulafia departs from his philosophical guide and reverts to an explanation of prophecy affirmed in Jewish Neoplatonic sources:[326]

> The prophet knows in truth that the body that he imagines in the moment of prophecy has no corporeal existence at all, but it is an intelligible entity that is entirely spiritual [*davar sikhli kullo ruḥani*], and it materializes [*hitggashshem*] in relation to him in the moment of his comprehension on account of the fact that the prophet is a body that envisions the truth in his spiritual intellect [*guf ha-maskil ha-emet be-sikhlo ha-ruḥani*] actualized in that moment.

The corporeal image of the incorporeal substance is configured in the imagination of the enlightened visionary (*maskil*), and it is identified further as the angel (*mal'akh*), a multivalent term that denotes in this context the imaginal form of the Active Intellect, incarnational presence that assumes the shape of an anthropos (the idealized Israel) in the imaginative faculty.[327]

Abulafia reiterates this mystery in slightly different terms in his discussion in *Sitrei Torah* of the Maimonidean conception of the name of the attribute of action (*shem ha-to'ar*), which is contrasted with the essential name (*shem ha-eṣem*), an "honorable secret that is appropriate for the select few" (*zeh ha-sod ha-nikhbad hu ra'uy la-yeḥidim*):

> Concerning this secret it is said "and in the hands of the prophets I will be imaged" [*u-ve-yad ha-nevi'im adammeh*] (Hos. 12:11), and when [the word *adammeh*] is transposed it spells *ha-adam*. And the secret of [the word] *u-ve-yad* refers to the holy name YHWA, and the secret of the name of the prophets [refers to] the wise [*sod shem ha-nevi'im ḥakhamim*], and they are the throne of glory [*kisse ha-kavod*], and this is the secret of the high priest [*kohen gadol*] who speaks to the prophets in the form of the prophetic anthropos [*ha-adam ha-navi*].[328]

Displaying his typically brilliant hermeneutical prowess, Abulafia employs linguistic and numerical exegetical devices to adduce the mystery of the prophetic experience from the biblical verse, which in turn is meant to illumine the mystery of the *shem ha-toʾar*, the name derived from God's providential action in the world. The expression *adammeh*, "I will be imaged," is composed of the same consonants as *ha-adam*, a transposition that alludes to Abulafia's contention that the form imagined in the prophetic vision is that of an anthropos. The imaginal form is related, moreover, to the divine name YHWA, the letters *yod he waw alef*, which are the "letters of concealment," *otiyyot ha-haʿalamah*, that I mentioned above; Abulafia deduces the name from the word *u-ve-yad*, for the latter is numerically equal to twenty-two (6 + 2 + 10 + 4), which is the same numerological value of YHWA (10 + 5 + 6 + 1).[329] It is reasonable to assume that this name is a cipher for the Torah, which is the Active Intellect, the objective correlate of the prophetic experience, inasmuch as the Torah is made up of the twenty-two letters. Confirmation of my explication is forthcoming from the final sequence of ideas that Abulafia threads together on the basis of numerical equivalencies, that is, each of the following equals 118: the prophets (*neviʾim*) are the sages (*ḥakhamim*), and they are the throne of glory (*kisse ha-kavod*), as they receive the word from the high priest (*kohen gadol*), that is, Metatron, who speaks to them in the image of the prophetic anthropos (*ha-adam ha-navʾi*).

I note in passing that the view espoused by Abulafia, which is affirmed by other kabbalists in the twelfth and thirteenth centuries who branded *Shekhinah*, angel of the presence (*malʾakh ha-panim*), the object of conjunction, bears a striking similarity to the Shīʿite belief in a revelatory encounter with the angel identified as the holy spirit (*rūḥ al-quds*) and Active Intellect (*ʿaql faʿʿāl*),[330] a theme that is especially prominent in the wisdom of illumination (*ḥikmat al-ishrāq*), the Oriental philosophy, cultivated by Avicenna, Suhrawardī, and Ibn ʿArabī, to name a few central figures. This wisdom entails, in the memorable formulation of Corbin, an "essential *theophanism*," which implies that "every theophany has the form of an angelophany, because it is determined by this correlation; and precisely in this essential determination, without which the divine being would remain unknown and inaccessible, lies the significance of the *Angel*."[331] The following account of the angelic epiphany proffered by Corbin could without distortion be applied to Abulafia's depiction of prophetic experience:[332]

> The figure of the Active Intelligence, which dominated all philosophy, reveals its proximity, its solicitude. The Angel *individuates himself* under the features of a definite person, whose annunciation corresponds to the degree of experience of the soul to which he announces himself: it is through the integration of all its powers that the soul opens itself to the transconscious and anticipates its own totality.[333]

The soul on the "way of return," which is the "way of gnosis" that leads one beyond the bondage of the physical cosmos, requires an angelic guide. Insofar as the "archetypal figure" is a mirror image of the soul, it follows that there will be "synchronism between the soul's awakening to itself and its visualization of the Guide."[334]

For Abulafia, the imaginal form of the *angelus interpres* is composed of the letters of Torah, which are comprised within the Tetragrammaton. The imagination thus serves not only as the prism through which the invisible is rendered visible and the ineffable declaimed as the name, but as the vehicle by which the soul merges with Torah in its mystical essence. To be conjoined to the name, therefore, is to be incorporated into the textual embodiment of the name, that is, the imaginal body constituted by the letters YHWH, which comprise all the letters of the Hebrew alphabet, the hylomorphic substance, as it were, of Torah, and, by extension, given the identification of Torah and *sekhel ha-poʿel*, of all that exists in the cosmos (the Active Intellect, according to the widespread cosmological view adopted by philosophical sages in each of the three monotheistic faiths in the High Middle Ages, believed to contain the forms of all existents in the sublunar sphere).

In the introduction to *Ḥayyei Olam ha-Ba*, Abulafia assigns to the seventy-two-letter name—that is, the name of seventy-two triplets derived exegetically from or anchored in the account of the angel of God (*mal'akh ha-elohim*) in Exodus 14:19–21, of which each verse contains seventy-two letters—the title *shem ha-divri*, the "name that is spoken," which comprises *divrei ha-shem*, the "words of the name," one of the standard rabbinic epithets for the divine presence. The secret is further unfurled when we recall that Abulafia adduces this name from the verse *mosheh yedabber we-ha-elohim yaʿanennu ve-qol*, "Moses spoke and God answered in a voice" (Exod. 19:19); the consonants of *mosheh yedabber* can be transposed into *shem ha-divri* and *divrei ha-shem*.[335] The key to understanding this comment is to bear in mind that in Abulafia's thinking, Moses alludes figuratively to Metatron—an identification related mnemonically to the fact that the letters of *mosheh*—*mem, shin, he*—can be decoded as an acrostic for *meṭaṭron sar ha-panim*—the anthropomorphic personification of the Active Intellect beheld by the visionary at the pinnacle of prophetic experience.[336]

Abulafia derives the designation of the Active Intellect as Metatron from Maimonides, but it takes on a special significance in his thinking. In the visionary encounter, occasioned by the technique of letter combination (*ḥokhmat ha-ṣeruf*), the holy spirit (*ruaḥ ha-qodesh*)—another traditional idiom adopted by Abulafia to speak of *sekhel ha-poʿel*—overflows onto the soul, "and it seems as if his entire body is anointed with the anointing oil, from his head to this feet, and he becomes the anointed one of the Lord and his messenger, and he is called angel of God, and his name will be called as the name of his master, which is Shaddai, by which Metatron, the angel of the face (*sar ha-panim*), is called."[337] The soul, unfettered from the knots of corporeality, is united with the Active Intellect and is thereby transposed into the body that is made up of the letters of Torah. The separation of the soul from the body, a form of simulated death that is true life, occasions the transposition of the body that restores the corporeal to its elemental form composed of the Hebrew letters. In *Sitrei Torah*, Abulafia formulates the matter succinctly:

> It is imagined [*meṣuyyar*] in your heart that through this form [*ṣurah*] is the separation of the soul [*peridat ha-nefesh*], which is a portion of the Lord that has 231 gates, and she is called "Assembly of Israel" [*kenesset yisra'el*], "there are 231" [*yesh r'al*], for she collects and gathers every speech beneath her intellective faculty [*koaḥ ha-sikhli*], which is called the "supernal Assembly of Israel" [*kenesset yisra'el ha-elyonah*], which is the mother of governance [*em ha-hashggaḥah*], that is, the cause of the governance

> [*sibbat ha-hashggaḥah*], and she is the intermediary between us and the Lord, and she is the Torah that emanates from the twenty-two holy letters. Know that all the limbs of your body are made of combinations of the form of the letters, this one with that one and that one with this one. And know, moreover, that just as you combine them all together and you divide the form of one letter from the form of another letter even though their matter is one, that is, the ink, and in one instant you may erase all of them from the tablet, so this angel will act with respect to all your moisture and to each and every one of your limbs until all of them will be restored to their first matter.[338]

The ecstatic experience is an encounter of the prophet with the Active Intellect, the form (*ṣurah*) that occasions the separation of the soul (*peridat ha-nefesh*) from its somatic confinement. The soul itself is ontically part of the Active Intellect, which is called the "supernal Assembly of Israel" (*kenesset yisra'el ha-elyonah*), a designation that signifies the linguistic nature of the intellect—the consonants of the term *yisra'el* are decoded as *yesh r'al*, "there are 231," a reference to the 231 gates, a cipher for all the possible letter permutations according to a passage in *Sefer Yeṣirah*.[339] The Active Intellect, moreover, is identified as Torah, for the body of the latter is constructed from the prime matter of the twenty-two Hebrew letters.

Utilizing another principle widespread in kabbalistic literature of his time, Abulafia affirms that the human body, that is, the corporeality stripped of its coarse materiality, is constituted by these very letters.[340] Just as all the letters can be reduced to the ink by means of which they were inscripted on a tablet, so the angelic presence of the Active Intellect, the intermediary between divine and human, the matrix of providence in the sublunar world, can decompose the corporeal body of the visionary and restore it to its "first matter." Inasmuch as Abulafia affirms the belief that angels are ontically composed of the twenty-two Hebrew letters, which are comprised within the Tetragrammaton,[341] the process of incorporation into Torah described in the above passage can also be referred to as "angelification." The mystical adept who follows the meditational path to its limit is transformed into the "anointed one of the Lord" (*meshiaḥ yhwh*),[342] the "angel of God" (*mal'akh ha-elohim*),[343] the "angel of the face" (*sar ha-panim*)[344]—all names of Metatron, the highest and most distinguished of the angelic figures, the one whose name is numerically equal to Shaddai, a numerical equivalence used by Abulafia and others before and after him to explain an older esoteric teaching applied to Metatron:[345] "his name is like the name of his master," *she-shemo ke-shem rabbo*, based on the scriptural characterization of the angel sent by God before the people of Israel, "My name is in him," *shemi be-qirbo* (Exod. 23:21).[346]

Metatron assumes the figure of Torah incarnate in the Active Intellect, the body that occupies an intermediary position between matter and form, the senses and reason. The meditational practice leads one to this state of mindfulness, conjunction with the Active Intellect, which translates into cleaving to the name, and being incorporated into the body of the text. I will cite another passage from *Oṣar Eden Ganuz* wherein the secret of prophecy as a progression from image (*ṣiyyur*) to speech (*dibbur*) to intellect (*sekhel*) is disclosed,[347] a sequence that articulates in another pitch the transformative experience implied in Abulafia's mystical ideal of intellectual conjunction and visionary ecstasy:

> Now I will disclose to you the wondrous secret that is hidden from the eyes of most of the sages of our generation, and I can almost say from the eyes of all of them . . . and it is that the imaginative faculty [*koaḥ ha-medammeh*] is the instrument for prophetic comprehension [*hassagat ha-nevu'ah*], and all of its comprehensions are images [*dimyonot*], parables [*meshalim*], and riddles [*ḥiddot*]. And it is one faculty found in most living beings [*baʿalei ḥayyim*] and everyone living that possesses a heart [*baʿal lev*], and its existence in man is as the existence of prophecy in a mirror [*mar'ah*] or in water [*mayyim*], and it is an imaginal form [*ṣiyyur dimmuy*]. As its name, so it is,[348] *dimyon medammeh*, and its secret is *daemon*, and he is the evil spirit and Satan. Yet, he is the *mediyun*, that is, the intermediary.[349] . . . The faculty of speech [*koaḥ ha-divri*] is the natural, human form [*ha-ṣurah ha-ṭivʿit ha-enoshit*] by which man is distinguished from the rest of the living beings. This faculty is wholly the natural speech that is in man [*kullo dibbur muṭba ba-adam*] in the seventy languages through the permutation [*ṣeruf*] of the twenty-two letters, and this is the faculty found potentially in every word [*dibbur*] and it emerges in its form [*ṣiyyuro*] from potentiality to actuality, moment after moment [*et aḥar et*]. This is what is alluded to in *Sefer Yeṣirah* when it says,[350] "Every word [*dibbur*] is found and every creation [*yiṣṣur*] comes forth from them, and thus every creation comes forth from one name [*shem eḥad*]." . . . It is thus revealed that the word [*dibbur*] instructs about the faculty of speech [*koaḥ ha-divri*], creation [*yiṣṣur*] instructs about the imaginative faculty, and the "one name" [*shem eḥad*], in which everything is, instructs about the rational faculty, and this rational faculty, the third, is superior to the other two, and it is the aim of the intention [*takhlit ha-kawwanah*].[351]

In this passage, Abulafia adduces from *Sefer Yeṣirah* a hierarchy of three potencies, *yiṣṣur* ("creation") refers to *koaḥ ha-medammeh* (the imaginative faculty), *dibbur* to *koaḥ ha-divri* (the faculty of speech), and *shem eḥad* ("one name") to *koaḥ ha-sikhli* (the rational faculty). Although not stated explicitly, it is reasonable to surmise that the latter is affixed to the Tetragrammaton, which is the Torah, the locus of the imaginary forms in and through which the imageless God is made accessible to the imagination of the prophet/mystic who envisions the invisible through the textual prism of narrative and law. In a manner consonant with the zoharic author, the prophetic kabbalist advocates a liberation of vision by means of vision—in beholding the veil of the text, the sage takes hold of the text of the veil and thereby discerns that the veil is neither real nor not-real.[352] In the garment-mirror, the name that is Torah, spirit is embodied and the embodied spiritualized.[353]

Poetic Incarnation and the Embodied Text of Textual Embodiment

What is revealed in the final hermeneutical disclosure is the veil of presuming there is an unveiling that results in a vision of the divine without the veil of the text, to apprehend the essence of God without the shibboleth of the name.[354] As the matter is expressed in another zoharic context, "The letters are inscribed in the supernal mysteries, for they all emerge from the mystery of the supernal Wisdom by way of the thirty-two paths that come forth from Wisdom. . . . All the letters are inscribed in a mystery and they are the bodies of Torah [*gufei torah*] for they exist to instruct and to notify about the supernal mysteries."[355] The author of this comment appropriates the rabbinic expression *gufei torah*, which denotes in the older sources the rudiments of law,[356] to formulate the idea of a mystical body of God, a body that is composed of letters that are at one and the same time linguistic signs and numeric ciphers of divine wisdom.[357]

From a literary standpoint, the hermeneutical maxim of God concealing esoteric matters in Scripture is contextualized in the middle of the discourse about the entrapment of the Jewish soul in a body of a Gentile—the "daughter of the priest," *bat kohen*, married to a "layman," *ish zar* (Lev. 22:12). As I remarked above, the full implication of this thematic juxtaposition is dependent on understanding that the sociohistorical phenomenon of conversion suggested to the Castilian kabbalists entailed a crossing of ontic boundaries that ostensibly contradicted the dualistic posture affirmed on numerous occasions in the zoharic text, Israel aligned with the holy right side of mercy, and the nations of the world, with the unholy left side of judgment.[358] Just as the existential situation of the convert necessitates a disjuncture between the non-Jewish body and the Jewish soul, the former demonic and the latter divine, so in the case of Torah there is a necessary difference that wedges a divide, a barrier, a veil, between the secret, the name that is the light, and the garb of letters. An analogous transgression of boundary, we are to presume, is realized by the enlightened exegete who can discern the absent presence of the present absence in the Torah. The identification of God and Torah has to be understood, at least according to the author of this homily, as a form of incarnation predicated on an ontic estrangement akin to the existential condition that makes conversion possible.

The surmise that the zoharic passage presents a counterincarnational doctrine to the standard Christian conviction that Jesus is the incarnation of the Word is enhanced by the description of the layman in whose body the priestly daughter is found. The author of the zoharic homily interprets the biblical expression *ish zar* as "alien man," that is, the one who comes from a foreign land, the other side, place of false worship, *avodah zarah*. Following the widespread belief in medieval rabbinic circles,[359] kabbalists in general, and those responsible for *Zohar* in particular, maintained halakhically that Christianity was idolatry, and hence we are justified in decoding the old man's discussion about conversion in more specific terms as the Christian entering into the covenant of Abraham. When viewed against this background one can appreciate better the import of the image of God hiding secrets in the body of Torah, that is, in the letters of the text that collectively constitute the material of the divine name YHWH. For zoharic kabbalists, it is appropriate to speak of a doctrine of incarnation—understood docetically—inasmuch as this name assumes the textual form of Torah, which is configured imaginally as the ideal anthropos or Israel.[360] Joseph of Hamadan, a somewhat enigmatic figure who may have been part of the fraternity responsible for the zoharic anthology, formulates the incarnational element of kabbalistic symbolism with daring precision:[361]

> Therefore the Torah is called as such for it instructs [*morah*] about the pattern of the holy One, blessed be he . . . the Torah, as it were, is the shadow of the holy One, blessed be he. . . . Praiseworthy is the portion of one who knows how to align limb corresponding to limb and form corresponding to form in the pure and holy chain, blessed be his name. Since the Torah is his form, blessed be he, he commanded us to study Torah so that we may know his pattern of the supernal form as some of the kabbalists[362] have said [with respect to the verse] "Cursed be the one who does not uphold the words of this Torah" (Deut. 27:26), "Is there a Torah that falls?" Rather this is a warning to the cantor to show the letters of the Torah scroll to the congregation so that they might see the pattern of the supernal form. How much more so [is it necessary] to study Torah so that he will see the supernal secrets and he will verily see the glory of the holy One, blessed be he, the whole time he studies Torah and he sits verily in the shade of the blessed One.[363]

In language that is quite bold, Torah is identified as the embodiment of the divine glory, the letters constituting the pattern of the supernal form, and thus the ritual of lifting the scroll affords the community of worshippers the opportunity to gaze upon the iconic manifestation of God.[364] The underlying anthropomorphic nature of this form is alluded to in the remark concerning the ability of the laudable person to align the limbs below and the limbs above. That is, the Torah, which is the name, is the divine form that assumes the shape of an anthropos.

Here it is of interest to recall an important but neglected suggestion made by Jeremy Zwelling in the introduction to his critical edition of *Sefer Tashaq*, one of the major treatises composed by Joseph of Hamadan. Contrary to Alexander Altmann, who proposed that the title should be decoded as an abbreviation for *terumah*, *shir ha-shirim*, and *yeḥezqel*, the three parts of Scripture interpreted in the composition, Zwelling submitted that *tashaq* is an acrostic for *temunat shem qodesh*, "image of the holy name." Zwelling supports his surmise by noting that a central theme in the work is an explication of the seventy-two names of God, but even more important, for Joseph of Hamadan, following the view expressed by kabbalists in the generations previous to him, each of the twenty-two Hebrew letters is to be considered the form and name of divinity. "These letters are images of the Divinity as he is expressed in the likeness of the human body. . . . Indeed the book presents us with numerous pictures of the Divine name, reflecting God's crystallization as a Chariot, the human body, the letters of the alphabet, the tetragrammaton, and the tabernacle, which is described as a body in which the soul of God dwells."[365]

I am inclined to agree with Zwelling's interpretation, though he leaves out the best proof for his position: The central locus of divine embodiment is the Torah, which is the name that comprises all the letters of the Hebrew alphabet, the "holy supernal chariot" (*merkavah elyonah qedoshah*) in whose pattern the tabernacle below was constructed. It is not coincidental that in one passage, immediately after affirming the depiction of Torah as the "pattern of an edifice" (*dugmat binyan*), Joseph of Hamadan describes the tabernacle (*mishkan*) as the body in which the soul of God's will is made tangible, that is, really imagined as imaginally real. Accordingly, Joseph of Hamadan renders the verse obligating every male Israelite to set aside an offering to God, *we-yiqḥu li terumah* (Exod. 25:2), as *yaʿaseh guf we-yaʿasu neshamah wa-ani etggashshem bo* ("make a body and soul and I will materialize therein"):[366]

> By way of wisdom you already know what I have alluded to that the entire Torah is wholly in the pattern of the holy and pure chain [*she-kol ha-torah hi kullah dugmat shalshelet ha-qedushshah we-ha-ṭehorah*], and therefore there is an open section and a closed section to allude to the pattern of the edifice [*dugmat ha-binyan*]. Everything was in heaven and afterward it materialized [*nitggashshem*] on earth.[367]

As I have already intimated, in the kabbalistic tradition, the anthropomorphic shape of God refers not to humanity in general but specifically to the Jew, a point often expressed in the relevant texts in terms of the rabbinic dictum (linked exegetically to Ezek. 34:31) that the title *adam* applies to Israel and not to the nations of the world.[368] In particular, the ethnocentric dimension of the incarnational myth, which has informed the kabbalistic orientation, is captured in the symbolic identification of God, Torah, and Israel implied in the zoharic comment "there are three gradations bound one to the other, the holy One, blessed be he, Torah, and Israel,"[369] an early formulation of the belief in a threefold unity that became axiomatic in later kabbalistic ontology and anthropology.[370] The full implication of this symbolism is brought to the surface in another passage from Joseph of Hamadan wherein he explicates the obligation incumbent upon every male Jew to write his own Torah scroll:[371]

> The reason for this commandment by way of kabbalah alludes to the fact that the Torah scroll is the holy of holies . . . for the entire Torah is the name of the holy One, blessed be he . . . and his Torah is within the holy One, blessed be he, and within him is his Torah, and this is what the kabbalists say the holy One, blessed be he, is in his name and his name is in him. "His name" is his Torah and the Torah is made through the pure and holy chain in the supernal image, and it is verily the shade of the holy One, blessed be he. . . . Therefore he commanded that each man should make a Torah scroll for himself to discern and to know that he cherishes the Torah and to allude to the unity and to demonstrate the pattern of the Creator, blessed be he. When the holy One, blessed be he, sees that each and every one in Israel has a Torah scroll that is precisely in the likeness of his pattern, blessed be he, the holy One, blessed be he, immediately causes his presence to dwell upon Israel, verily in his pattern, in the Torah scroll. Therefore God, blessed be he, commanded each and every man from Israel to make a Torah scroll for himself . . . this alludes to the fact that all of Israel is one form, as the sages, blessed be their memory, said all Israel is one body. . . . Since all of Israel is one supernal pattern, and each and every one from Israel is a limb of the chariot, each and every man from Israel must take a Torah scroll for himself so that the limb will cleave to the limb in the pure and holy chain.[372]

The incarnational theology that informs the kabbalistic standpoint is predicated on a distinctive understanding of corporeality. "Body" does not denote physical mass that is quantifiable and measurable but the phenomenological sense of the corporeal as lived presence. Medieval kabbalists, due to the influence of philosophical thinking that had informed the general cultural trends of European societies in the High Middle Ages, adopted a negative view towards the corporeal body (indeed, according to some passages in zoharic literature, the physicality of the human is linked to the demonic other side)[373] and thus considered the contemplative life as a way to escape the bonds of carnality. This explains the adoption of ascetic forms of piety on the part of kabbalists, with special emphasis placed on sexual abstinence.[374]

The positive valence accorded the body in kabbalistic symbolism, reflected in the repeated use of anthropomorphic images to depict God, images that on occasion embrace an intense erotic tone, is related to the textual nature of bodiliness, which, in turn, rests on an assumption regarding the bodily nature of textuality. The linguistic comportment of embodiment accounts as well for the theurgical underpinnings of the kabbalistic understanding of ritual epitomized in the saying "limb strengthens limb," that is, the performance of ceremonial acts by human limbs fortifies the divine attributes, which are imaginally envisioned as bodily limbs.[375] Alternatively expressed, insofar as Torah is the name YHWH, and the latter takes the form of an anthropos (an idea buttressed by the numerical equivalence of the four letters of the name written out in full and the word *adam*), it follows that each commandment can be represented as a limb of the divine body.[376]

Such a perspective reverses the generally assumed allegorical approach to scriptural anthropomorphisms promoted by medieval rabbinic exegetes, for instead of explaining anthropomorphic characterizations of God as a figurative way to accommodate human understanding,[377] the attribution of corporeal images to an incorporeal God indicates that the real body, the body in its most abstract tangibility, is the letter,[378] a premise that I shall call the principle of poetic incarnation.[379] When examined from the kabbalistic perspective, anthropomorphism in the canonical texts of Scripture indicates that human and divine corporeality are entwined in a mesh of double imaging through the mirror of the text that renders the divine body human and the human body divine.[380] Phenomenologically speaking, the lifeworld of kabbalists revolves about the axis of the embodied text of textual embodiment.

Embodying Ritual and Mystical Transfiguration

Beyond providing a radically different hermeneutical key to interpret Scripture, not to mention later rabbinic legends that ascribe corporeality to God, the understanding of textual embodiment advanced by kabbalists had practical implications in the mystical approach to ritual, which, in the final analysis, cannot be severed from the theurgical element described previously.[381] A hallmark of medieval kabbalists, both influenced by and reacting to philosophical explications of the commandments, was to view sacramental behavior as an instrument through which the physical body is conjoined to and transformed in light of the imaginal body of God manifest in the inscripted body of Torah. An early formulation of this theme can be found in Ezra of Gerona:

> The Torah and commandments, positive and negative, have been given to accustom man and to guide him in the good attributes, and so that the evil inclination will be drawn after the good inclination and it will be nullified in relation to it. . . . For this purpose are the commandments, devotional acts, prayers, and fasting, to subdue the evil inclination so that it will be compliant to the good inclination, and so that the body, whose foundation is dust and whose nature is evil and descends below, will be drawn after the soul whose foundation is life and whose nature is entirely good and ascends above.[382]

The performance of a ritual act requires a blessing that specifies the holiness with which God has sanctified the Jewish people:

> [F]ulfillment of a commandment is the light of life, and the one who accomplishes it below establishes and sustains its power . . . and in the separation of the soul from the body this light is like a magnet for the soul . . . for this light draws it . . . that is, the splendor of the soul is uplifted and stands in the place of the supernal beings and inwardly in the glory of the holy One, blessed be he.[383] . . . The intention in all of this is that man is comprised of all the spiritual matters [*devarim ruḥaniyyim*], and when a man walks in the good path the attribute of goodness, which is called the good angel, emanates on him, but when he walks in an evil path the attribute of evil, which is called the angel of death, emanates on him.[384]

The experience of being assimilated into the light as a consequence of fulfilling the ritual is predicated on the assumption that the action below stimulates the light above; since the commandments are part of Torah, and Torah is identical with God, ritualized gestures serve as the means by which the soul separates from the body and ascends to the light, augmenting the overflow of the divine efflux.[385] To cite a parallel passage from Ezra's commentary on talmudic aggadot:

> You must know that the commandment is light and the one who performs it below establishes and does something above. Therefore when a man is occupied with a commandment, the commandment itself is light, and thus it says, "for the commandment is a lamp and the teaching is a light" (Prov. 6:23), and he walks in the ways of light and he does not depart from it and it dwells in his midst. When the soul is separated from the body, this light is like a magnet for the soul, and[386] this is "his righteousness lasts forever" (Ps. 112:9), for this attribute[387] draws him. Thus, in the doing of the commandment, he takes the reward, for there is no reward above this . . . and concerning this the rabbis, blessed be their memory, said "the reward of a commandment is the commandment,"[388] that is, the speculum that shines.[389] And this is what Antigonus said to his disciples, "Do not be like servants who serve their master for the sake of receiving a reward."[390] Do not think that the performance of the commandment and the recompense are two things, it is not so.[391]

Utilizing earlier rabbinic dicta that affirm a deontological deportment based on recognizing the intrinsic value of fulfilling the law without any concern for reward, Ezra qualifies his own instrumentalist posture by positing that the rituals themselves are construed as textual instantiations of the divine essence: "the commandments are the attributes."[392] To equate the commandments and attributes implies that Torah, mystically conceived, is the name, whence it follows that ritual performance is the means by which the corporeal body is textualized and the textual body corporealized:

> The 248 positive commandments are to guide the limbs of man, which equal 248,[393] in a straight and good path, to purify him, to sanctify him, to cleanse him, to bless him, so that he may imitate his creator. The 365 negative commandments are to guide the sinews of man, which are 365, in a straight and good path and to protect him from an evil path and from a despicable quality. By means of this the soul and the body will be on one path and in harmony [*yihyu ha-guf we-ha-neshamah be-derekh eḥad u-ve-haskkamah aḥat*].[394] You must know that the pure Torah in its entirety was spoken from the mouth of God and there is no letter or dot in it that is not necessary for it is entirely a divine structure [*binyan elohim*][395] hewn from the name of the holy One, blessed be he.[396] . . . Since the commandments are the holy and pure body [*guf ha-ṭehorah we-ha-qedoshah*] the one engaged [in them] will be purified and sanctified.[397]

According to the perspective enunciated by Ezra, which is widely attested in kabbalistic literature, rituals not only purify the practitioner's body of its physicality but they transmute it into the luminous body composed of the letters comprised within the name, which is the Torah—at work here is the convergence of light and letter symbolism, a recurrent phenomenon in kabbalistic sources as scholars have duly noted.[398] That ritual acts may be considered limbs out of which the divine structure, *binyan elohi*, is assembled is predicated on this transformative mechanism. One should recall here that in a short treatise on the secret of the Tree of Knowledge, *Sod Eṣ ha-Daʿat*, Ezra comments that Adam, prior to his having eaten the forbidden fruit, was "completely spiritual" (*kullo ruḥani*) and "garbed angelically" (*lovesh malʾakhut*) like Enoch and Elijah. Hence he was permitted to eat of all the fruits of the Garden of Eden, which, Ezra is quick to point out, are "fruits of the soul," that is, just as in the corporeal realm food nourishes the body, in this antediluvian state these fruits were to sustain the life of the soul.[399]

The force of the expression *lovesh malʾakhut* is to convey the view that Adam's original body was angelic, that is, he wore—a locution that in medieval Hebrew texts denotes embodiment, since the soul was typically portrayed as being enclothed in the body—the angelic nature, a spiritual body (*guf ruḥani*)[400] that is sustained by the fruits of Eden, an idea doubtless influenced by the earlier rabbinic tradition that as a consequence of their transgression, the "garments of light" originally invested in Adam and Eve were changed into "garments of skin."[401] What is crucial for us to emphasize is that in Ezra's religious philosophy, the means by which the Jew, who is in the image of Adam and hence composed of the spiritual entities (*devarim ruḥaniyyim*), can be restored in part to this autochthonous state is through observing the commandments.

Implicit in the approach articulated by Ezra is an inextricable link between the referential and performative aspects of kabbalistic symbolism,[402] that is, insofar as rituals are ontologized as divine attributes and the latter are configured as limbs of an imaginal body correlated through ritual with the idealized body of the Jewish male, the envisioning of God on the part of the medieval kabbalist affords him an opportunity to act upon the reality to which he is ecstatically bound and within which he is ontically reincorporated. Moreover, given the semiological nature of that reality, the somatic performance may be viewed as a form of symbolic utterance. Just as the ontic identification of Torah and God effectively effaces the difference between commander and command and thus challenges a basic presupposition of biblical and rabbinic theism—an implication of the kabbalistic doctrine that has yet to be appreciated by critical scholarship—so the ontic identification of the Jewish soul and God effectively effaces the difference between commander and commanded.

The matter is made more explicit by Azriel of Gerona, who wrote that the "Torah is called 'name' [*shem*] . . . and God is his name and his name is he [*she-ha-shem hu shemo u-shemo hu*][403] . . . and by placing dust on [the scroll][404] the bodies of the sages trembled on account of the fear of the bodies of Torah [*gufei torah*], which is called 'name,' for they restore the soul[405] in the body, and since the Torah restores the soul in the body the bodies of the sages trembled."[406] What is especially noteworthy for our purposes is Azriel's appropriation of the idiom *gufei torah*, which, as I have already noted, is employed in the zoharic corpus as well in a hyperliteral sense to denote the textual body of God, which is the name. In the case of the Catalan kabbalist, however, *gufei torah* refer to the commandments, so-called because they restore the soul in the body of one who fulfills them.[407] A more mystical nuance intended by this expression, closer to the aforecited zoharic text, is offered in the continuation of the passage:

> Since the Torah is called "name" and it restores the soul, it has sections, chapters, and paragraphs, which are the open and closed sections, in the pattern of a complete structure [*binyan shalem*] just as a man has ligaments and joints in his hand and foot. And just as there are limbs upon which the soul is dependent and there are limbs upon which the soul is not dependent even though there is no gain or deficit to the health of the body, so there are sections and verses in the Torah that appear to one who does not know their explication as though they are worthy of being burnt, but the one who comprehends and knows their explanation sees that they are the bodies of Torah [*gufei torah*],[408] and the one who leaves out one letter or a single point from them is like one who diminishes a whole body. . . . All the commandments are called "truth" [*emet*] . . . and even though there are light and difficult commandments, the commandments are the glory. . . . Therefore, no one knows the reward for the commandments for all the commandments have a purpose, but their purpose has no limit. Whoever is occupied with the commandments the fear of the commandment should be upon him as if he were crowned and encircled in its glory.[409]

The ecstatic-theurgic nature of the commandments proffered by the Geronese disciples of Isaac the Blind is affirmed as well, albeit in a somewhat varied language, by Naḥmanides, who concluded that "a man is vanity and air, and he is nothing at all . . . for his eyes, his head, and all his limbs are nothing, but the commandments are his body, his limbs, and his soul."[410] In a manner consonant with Ezra and Azriel, Naḥmanides identifies the commandments as the tissue of the body as well as the fiber of the soul. Implicit in this comment is the mystical conception of Torah as body and the further identification of the latter with the sefirotic configuration of the divine in whose image the human body below, that is, the idealized body of the circumcised male Jew, is patterned. To mention one source here in support of this contention, Naḥmanides offers the following esoteric explanation of the injunction for the priests to wash their hands and feet before entering the Tent of Meeting (Exod. 30:19):

> By way of truth [*al derekh ha-emet*] this is on account of the fact that the top and bottom of man are the hands and feet, for the hands are higher than the rest of the body when one lifts them up and the feet are below, and they are in the form of man an allusion to the ten *sefirot* so that the entire body will be between them, as it says in *Sefer Yeṣirah*, "he decreed with him a covenant between the ten fingers of his hands and between the ten fingers of his feet, in the covenant of the tongue and the covenant of the foreskin."[411] Therefore, the servants of the supernal one were commanded to wash the hands and feet, and the washing is for the sake of holiness.[412]

Fulfillment of the commandments facilitates the transformation of the carnal body into the textual body of Torah, a state of psychosomatic equilibrium wherein the body becomes the perfect vehicle to execute the will of the soul and the soul becomes the perfect guide in directing the will of the body. The soul thus mirrors the embodiment of God's glory in Torah by donning the name that is envisioned in the form of an anthropos. As the incorporeal assumes the bodily contours of the scriptural text, the body of one who observes the commandments is transformed into a ritualized body composed of the very same letters.

Consider the following remark of Ezra on the expression *enhagkha*, "I would lead you" (Song 8:2): "the soul does not show its actions except through the body and the body has no action except through the soul, and thus the holy One, blessed be he, shows his wonders and signs by means of his attributes."[413] The word *enhagkha* is from the root *nhg*, "to lead" or "to guide," and one of its nominal conjugations is *hanhagah*, a technical term in medieval Hebrew for divine governance. Ezra's point, then, is that the mystery of providence entails the incorporeal God manifesting itself in the attributes in the same manner that the soul acts by means of the body. Insofar as the attributes are expressive of the divine name, and the name is the mystical essence of Torah, it follows that adhering to the commands affords one the opportunity to be incorporated into the "divine edifice," the "holy and pure body."

In a similar fashion, albeit in a different terminological register, Naḥmanides proffers an attenuated ascetic understanding of ritual, interpreting the overall rationale for the commandments as a harnessing of the body in the service of sacred matters. Accordingly, the priestly ideal of holiness (*qedushshah*) is understood by Naḥmanides as advocating a form of piety that exceeds the strict demands of law, an asceticism (*perishut*) that impels one to separate from hedonistic gratification even in areas permitted by halakhah.[414] The highest spiritual achievement, however, is for man to cleave in thought to God uninterruptedly and to love him constantly, so that even the most routine somatic act becomes an opportunity for worship.[415] In one passage, Naḥmanides makes it quite clear that in his opinion the pietistic ideal entails spiritualization rather than abrogation of the body:

> Those who are occupied with the commandments out of love according to the law and as it is appropriate together with matters of this world . . . will merit a good life in this world in accordance with the custom of the world and the life of the world-to-come where their recompense will be complete. Those who leave aside all matters of this world and do not pay attention to it as if they were not corporeal beings [*baʿalei guf*], and all their thoughts and intentions are toward their Creator alone, as in the case of Elijah, by the cleaving of their souls to the glorious name, they live forever in their bodies and in their souls, as it appears in Scripture in the case of Elijah and according to what is known of it from the kabbalah, and as it is in legends [*midrashim*] about Enoch and those belonging to the world-to-come who will rise in the time of the resurrection. Therefore scriptural verses say regarding the reward for the commandments "in order that your days will be lengthened" (Exod. 20:12), "in order that you may live" (Deut. 16:20), "in order that you may lengthen the days" (ibid., 22:7), for the language comprises all the types of life as is appropriate for each one.[416]

For those whose minds are completely focused on God—in technical terms, those who cleave to the glorious name (*shem ha-nikhbad*), which, for Naḥmanides, refers to *Shekhinah*, the object of conjunction[417]—it is as if they were incorporeal, without the impediment of the physical body, but in fact their reward is immortality of body and soul. Though not stated explicitly, the body that lives forever is not the natural body subject to generation and corruption, but the angelic body.

Support for this interpretation may be gathered from another passage in which Naḥmanides attempts to explain the aggadic tradition that Jacob did not die. According to Naḥmanides, the intent of the rabbinic claim is not to deny the demise of Jacob's physical body but to emphasize that consequent to that demise his soul, like the souls of all the righteous, was garbed in a "second garment" (*levushat ha-sheni*), that is, the ethereal body, by which he was bound to the "bundle of life," an eschatological expression (based on 1 Sam. 25:29) that signifies in this context the conjunction of the soul with and incorporation into the body of *Shekhinah*.[418] It is noteworthy that Menaḥem Recanati, an Italian exegete active in the early fourteenth century and influenced greatly by Spanish kabbalah, associates this second garment with the older eschatological motif of the "rabbinic garment" (*ḥaluqa de-rabbanan*), the garment/body donned by the soul and woven from one's deeds.[419] Naḥmanides does not make this association explicitly, but I think there is cogency in Recanati's suggestion.

I would infer, therefore, that the second garment does indeed refer to the *corpus astrale* the soul receives after being stripped of its fleshly encasement. Rendered kabbalistically, we can say the material of this body is the Hebrew letters, as the body is the garment woven from one's good deeds, and the substance of the latter derives from the words of the divine commands, words inscripted in the textual body of Torah, which, in the formulation of Naḥmanides himself, is composed entirely of the names of God.

In the primordial Torah, letters are not broken into discrete words and sentences, for the letters are the constituent elements—the particles—of the divine names. The Torah given to Moses had two aspects, the written text, which corresponds to the "way of our reading" (*derekh qeri'atenu*), which is also described as the "division according to the ritualistic reading" (*derekh ḥilluq qeri'at ha-miṣwah*), and the oral text, which is not a reference to the standard rabbinic Oral Torah but an occult reading by "way of the names" (*derekh ha-shemot*). There are two originary ways of reading Scripture—the term for the later is *miqra* from the root *qr'*, "to call out," "to invoke," "to read," whence the word *qeri'ah*, "recitation"—the mystical way of *shemot* transmitted orally and the ritual way of *torah* and *miṣwah* inscripted in written form; the textual ground of both is the primordial Torah, which as Naḥmanides describes, citing an ancient tradition (*qabbalah*), was written in black fire on white fire.[420]

Moreover, as I surmised in a study published in 1990, the theme of the second garment should be considered in conjunction with the "garment" (*malbush*) mentioned by Naḥmanides in his explanation of the epiphany of the divine glory to Abraham in the form of three men/angels (Gen. 18:1ff.). For Naḥmanides, expanding upon an earlier midrashic interpretation, the shift in identity of these characters from "men" to "angels" is to be explained as the mystery of the garbing of angels as men, the secret of the incarnation of the glory, which is seen exclusively by the "eyes of the flesh of the pure souls" (*einei basar be-zakkei ha-nefashot*), that is, a corporeal seeing that is possible for those who have achieved a state of spiritual perfection predicated on renunciation of physical pleasure and sensual gratification.[421] By linking the two exegetical excursuses, we can posit that for Naḥmanides, pious individuals have the capacity to experience what the soul of the righteous experiences when returning to Paradise after the death of the physical body, being attired in the more refined body. Commenting on the biblical injunction "and cleave to him" (Deut. 11:22), Naḥmanides affirms precisely such a possibility when he writes concerning the individuals whose love for God is so continual that they are conjoined to him even when involved in worldly affairs:

> It is possible for people of this level that their souls even in their lives are bound to the bundle of life, for they are themselves an abode [*ma'on*] for *Shekhinah* . . . their thoughts and actions are constantly with God. Thus Joshua warned them that even now in the land when the wondrous acts will withdraw from them, their thoughts should constantly cleave to the awesome and glorious name and their intention should not depart from God.[422]

In a passage in *Sha'ar ha-Gemul*, the section in *Torat ha-Adam* that deals at length with the subject of reward and punishment, Naḥmanides describes the world-to-come (*olam ha-ba*) as a state of being consequent to the resurrection of the dead (*teḥiyyat ha-metim*) wherein the deceased rise in body and soul (*anshei ha-teḥiyyah be-guf uve-nefesh*), rather than (as Maimonides argued) as a world of disembodied souls (*olam ha-neshamot*).[423] As to the nature of the body and soul in this state, Naḥmanides offers the following account:

> The existence of the soul [*qiyyum ha-nefesh*] in its unification with the supernal knowledge [*daʿat elyon*] is like the existence of the angels [*qiyyum ha-malʾakhim*], and the elevation of the soul over the body nullifies the corporeal faculties [*koḥot ha-gufiyyot*] . . . to the point that the body exists as the existence of the soul without eating or drinking . . . there is in this form deep secrets [*sodot amuqqim*] . . . for the existence of the body [*qiyyum ha-guf*] will be like the existence of the soul [*qiyyum ha-nefesh*], and the existence of the soul will be united with the supernal knowledge.[424]

The eschatological body will be like the original embodiment of Adam who, prior to the sin, was created to be immortal. The cleaving to the supernal knowledge, moreover, is depicted as an augmented luminosity of the face and as being garbed in the Holy Spirit, characteristics that are adduced from several biblical and rabbinic figures. We may conclude, therefore, that for Naḥmanides, the secret entails a somatic transformation that is in inverse relation to the mystery of incarnation, the glory assuming tangible shape when it appears in the world.

A striking example of the incarnational drift in the religious philosophy of Naḥmanides is found in his explanation of the manna consumed by the Israelites in their sojourn in the desert. Naḥmanides deduces the "great matter" (*inyan gadol*) of the manna from a talmudic debate concerning the verse "Each man ate bread of the mighty," *leḥem abirim akhal ish* (Ps. 78:25): According to Aqiva, *leḥem abirim* refers symbolically to the "bread that the ministering angels eat," whereas Ishmael maintains that angels do not eat and hence the verse must be interpreted literally as a reference to the "bread that is absorbed by the 248 limbs."[425] Naḥmanides writes:

> This matter of which R. Aqiva spoke is that the existence of the ministering angels is through the splendor of the presence [*ziw ha-shekhinah*] . . . and the manna is from the by-product of the supernal light that is materialized through the will of the Creator, may he be blessed [*ha-man hu mi-toledot ha-or ha-elyon she-nitggashshem be-raṣon borʾo yitbarakh*], and thus those who ate the manna and the ministering angels were sustained from one thing.[426]

Even though the ministering angels and the Israelites who ate the manna are both nourished by the "supernal light" of *Shekhinah*, the last of the sefirotic gradations, there is a critical difference between the two groups: the former derived their sustenance directly and the latter indirectly through an emanation of the light that assumes material form in compliance with the divine will. R. Ishmael, by contrast, as interpreted by Naḥmanides, emphasizes that the "bread of the mighty" cannot refer to manna eaten by angels, since they are sustained by the splendor itself and thus have no need for the lustrous substance that emanates therefrom. Without denying the biblical contention that the manna was physically consumed, Naḥmanides imparts spiritual significance to the eating by understanding it as an act that occasions (concretely and not figuratively) the unitive experience of the soul and the light that streams from *Shekhinah*.

Naḥmanides utilizes this contemplative ideal to explain the tradition that the Israelites were able to educe different tastes in the manna in accord with their desires, for "the soul by means of its thought is conjoined to the supernal beings." Partaking of the manna is a foretaste of the eschatological reward awaiting the righteous in the world-to-come, being conjoined to *Shekhinah*. Thus Naḥmanides interprets the dictum attributed to Rav that in the world-to-come there is no eating or drinking but only the righteous sitting with their crowns on their heads, sustained by the splendor of the presence,[427] in the following way:

> Those who belong to the world-to-come will be sustained in their pleasure by the splendor of the presence through their cleaving to the crown that is on their heads [*be-hidavqam bo ba-aṭarah she-be-ro'sham*], and the crown [*aṭarah*] is the attribute that is called in this way as the verse says "In that day, the Lord of Hosts shall become a crown of beauty" (Isa. 28:5), and it is said concerning her "wearing the crown that his mother gave him" (Song 3:11).[428]

The eschatological image of the righteous wearing the crown is rendered symbolically as conjunction with *Shekhinah*, the attribute that is designated *aṭarah* or *aṭeret ṣevi*, an idea well attested in other kabbalists from this period and beyond, as I have discussed in a number of my previous publications.[429] What is crucial to emphasize here is that for Naḥmanides, this image bespeaks a more reified form of bodily nourishment, being sustained by the splendor of the presence.

The spiritual spectrum, as it were, with eating manna on one end and cleaving directly to *Shekhinah* on the other, is reiterated by Naḥmanides in *Shaʿar ha-Gemul*. It is worth considering this reiteration, as the formulation is slightly different and affords the reader another vantage point. In the relevant passage, Naḥmanides begins by noting that with respect to the "pure of soul" (*zakkei ha-nefesh*), the same technical term he used in his remark concerning the ones worthy of seeing the garment, the incarnation of the glory in the anthropomorphic form of an angel, their "corporeal existence" (*qiyyum gufam*) is through "subtle things" (*devarim daqqim*), and the purest of them from things most subtle (*daqqim min ha-daqqim*). To illustrate the point Naḥmanides mentions that the Israelites who ate the manna

> were sustained by the manna absorbed in their limbs, for it is from the by-product of the supernal light that is materialized through the will of the Creator, blessed be he, and they were nourished from it in the desert from the time that their souls were elevated by what they apprehended of the miracles at the sea . . . but the soul of Moses, who was more elevated and unified than them in the knowledge of his Creator, had no need for this matter because his body was materialized and sustained through the splendor of the presence [*ziw ha-shekhinah*] and the supernal comprehension [*hassagah elyonah*].[430]

The manna, which is the by-product of the supernal light that materializes, is a higher and more sublime substance than the coarse food that nourishes the mortal body of tissues and blood; but the supernal light, the splendor of the presence, is even more subtle than the manna. Moses, in contrast to the Israelites who devoured the manna, was sustained by the splendor itself and hence had no need for an alternative manner of provision, an idea that Naḥmanides expounds on the basis of earlier rabbinic sources.[431] What is worthy of emphasis is the statement that the body of Moses was "materialized and sustained" through this splendor, a state, according to the opinion of R. Ishmael, characteristic of the angels. It is apposite to conclude, therefore, that the supreme body that Moses inhabited is the angelic body, the body that is constituted by the divine radiance.

On this basis we can draw the following parallel between language and body in the religious philosophy of Naḥmanides and the other Catalonian kabbalists previously discussed: Just as the way beyond language is through language, so the way beyond body is through body. This holds a key to understanding the role of asceticism in the formation of the mystical pietism affirmed by kabbalists of the period: Separation from sensual matters is not seen as a way to obliterate the body—commitment to rabbinic ritual precluded such an unmitigated renunciation of the natural world—but as a means for the metamorphosis of the mortal body into an angelic body, a body whose limbs are constituted by the letters of the name, the anthropomorphic configuration of Torah. Adorned in the apparel of this body, the soul is conjoined to the divine name.

Flesh Made Word / Specular Iconization of the Body as Text

While it was surely the opinion of kabbalists that the ideas I have mentioned were part of the ancient esoteric lore of Judaism, and indeed there is textual verification that at least in some measure their ideas were expansions of older doctrines, one cannot help but note the resemblance between the pertinent kabbalistic symbolism and several dogmas shared ubiquitously by orthodox Christians in the twelfth and thirteen centuries, a point not lost to some of the rabbinic figures (for example, Meir ben Simeon of Narbonne) who openly attacked kabbalists for espousing heretical views and promulgating blasphemous practices.[432] Specifically I have in mind the kabbalistic teaching regarding the incarnation of the name in the body of Torah, which implies as its corollary the materialization of Torah in the body of the name, and the even more striking affinity between the embodiment of the splendor of *Shekhinah* in tangible form and the consequent transformation of the corporeal body into a glorified body (*corpus glorificationis*) by partaking of that light, on the one hand, and representations of the divine flesh as the consecrated host in the medieval Christian imagination and the sacramental transubstantiation of the body into spirit, on the other.[433]

To be sure, the philosophical issue underlying these mythic formulations can be framed in metaphysical terms that would not necessarily be limited to a Christian context. That is to say, thinkers in different religious settings laboring under the impact of Neoplatonic theories of emanation, which, for all the diversity and complexity, uniformly posit a continuous chain of being, had to deal not only with the challenge of how the One becomes many, but also with how sensible substance arises from the intelligible, the corporeal from the incorporeal.[434] I would surely assent to this caution, but I am not persuaded of the wisdom of separating the Christological and Neoplatonic channels of influence in this matter. It is not even necessary to limit the former to textual sources, as there were other forms of communication, including especially the visual medium, that would have readily conveyed the symbolic power of the image of Christ's body in the formation of Christian piety.[435]

Notwithstanding the legitimacy of this rather obvious though regrettably neglected avenue to explain the transmission of Christian creed to masters of Jewish esoteric lore in European cities and towns, I would contend that the issue need not be restricted to historical influence, whether through text or image. Far more important is the logical inevitability that speculation of this sort will invariably yield a mythopoeic representation of the literal body, that is, the body that literally is literal, the body that is letter, an analogical literalism that accounts for the phenomenological resemblance between kabbalah and Christianity, a resemblance exploited—but not concocted—by Christian kabbalists in the Renaissance.

Assuredly, one must be on guard against making definitive claims regarding the origin of kabbalistic motifs, given the sophisticated exegetical prowess of kabbalists and the intricate ways they develop secret traditions either hinted at in older texts or transmitted orally, a belief in the antiquity of their traditions and practices that is persistently affirmed by practitioners of the occult wisdom; nevertheless, it behooves one to note the obvious affinity of the mythic understanding of Torah as the name and the related motif of shedding the somatic body and donning the luminous body, sometimes portrayed as being crowned by light, with Christological beliefs.[436] As I have already noted, there is no escaping the incarnational implications of the esoteric identification of Torah and the name, since the latter is the divine essence, a point made explicitly in several zoharic passages and confirmed by other kabbalists contemporary with the literary production of *Zohar*, for instance, Joseph Gikatilla, Menaḥem Recanati, Joseph of Hamadan, and the anonymous authors respectively of *Sefer ha-Yiḥud* and *Sefer ha-Temunah*.[437] Thus in one zoharic passage we read, "It has been taught that the holy One, blessed be he, is called Torah."[438] In a second passage, the matter is laid out in more detail based on the symbolic correspondence between the ten commandments revealed at Sinai, which contain the whole Torah, and the ten divine utterances, the emanations comprised within the Tetragrammaton:[439]

> The Torah is the name of the holy One, blessed be he. Just as the name of the holy One, blessed be he, is inscribed in ten utterances so Torah is inscribed in ten utterances; these ten utterances are the name of the holy One, blessed be he, and the Torah is entirely one name, verily the holy name of the holy One, blessed be he. . . . The one who is meritorious with respect to Torah is meritorious with respect to the holy name. R. Jose said that he is indeed meritorious with respect to the holy One, blessed be he, because he and his name are one.[440]

The Castilian kabbalists whose views are preserved in the zoharic homilies make even more explicit the assumption of their predecessors. The equation of Torah and the name implies that God is embodied in Torah, and consequently, engagement in study and fulfilling the commandments serve as the means by which one is conjoined to the divine. In the words of the *Zohar*: "He who is occupied with Torah it is as if he were occupied with the holy One, blessed be he, for Torah is entirely the name of the holy One, blessed be he."[441] But how can we speak of God being embodied in the text? Can light that is without limit be contained in letters that are limited by the shape of their very orthography? The mystery that is basic to zoharic kabbalah (though by no means unique to its fraternity) is that God is absent from the text in which God is present, since for God to be present in the text, God must be absent.

In spite of—or perhaps precisely on account of—the proximity of the gnosis promulgated by kabbalists and Christian faith, the incarnational thrust of the identification of Torah as the name and the name as divine body, especially as expressed in zoharic literature, has to be understood as a subtle polemical ploy vis-à-vis the Christological myth of incarnation of the Word. A poignant illustration of the point may be adduced in the following passage extracted from the *Zohar* in the opening homily on the verse "On the eighth day Moses called to Aaron, his sons, and the elders of Israel" (Lev. 9:1).

The homily begins by extolling the fortune of Israel for having received Torah, which is described as the "joy of the holy One, blessed be he," the object of his bemusement (*shaʿashuʿa*, a term derived from Prov. 8:30),[442] the place wherein he strolls, *aṭyyaluta*, apparently a zoharic coinage derived from the Hebrew *leṭayyel* ("to stroll"), a widespread euphemism in kabbalistic texts, attested already in *Sefer ha-Bahir*, for sexual intercourse,[443] the foot symbolizing the male (or, more precisely, the phallic) potency and the ground the female.[444] The older aggadic theme is embellished with the esoteric truism that the Torah is entirely the one holy name of God. The discussion circles around to the point that an explanation (attributed to R. Ḥiyya) is offered for why the first letter of Torah is *beit*, the second letter of the alphabet, a query that appears in classical rabbinic literature:[445] This letter signifies the dual Torah, oral and written, a doctrine that is also used in this context to explain the plural in "Let us make Adam in our image," that is, Adam was created by means of the Written and Oral Torah, reflected in the mentioning of image and likeness in tandem with his creation, the former correlated with the masculine and the latter with the feminine. According to R. Isaac, the orthographic structure of *beit* as the letter that is opened on one side and closed on three sides[446] is interpreted as a sign that Torah receives those who seek to be conjoined to her but she is closed from the other side in relation to those who close their eyes and turn away from her. It is at this point in the homily that the passage critical to my analysis appears:

> R. Judah said: *Beit* has two sides[447] and one that connects them. What do they come to teach? One for heaven, one for earth, and the holy One, blessed be he, connects and receives them. R. Eleazar said: These are the three holy, supernal lights bound as one, and they are the totality of Torah, and they open an opening to everything. They open an opening to faith and they are the abode of everything. Thus they are called *beit* for they make up the dwelling [*beita*]. And thus the beginning of Torah is *beit*, for it is the Torah, the remedy for the world. Therefore, whoever is occupied with Torah it is as if he were occupied with the holy name . . . for Torah is entirely the one supernal holy name. And since it is the holy name, it begins with *beit*, for it is the totality of the holy name in three knots of faith. Come and see: all those

occupied with Torah are conjoined to the holy One, blessed be he, and they are crowned in the crowns of Torah, and they are beloved above and below.[448]

The kabbalistic identification of Torah and the name is joined to an orthographic teaching regarding why the Torah begins with *beit*. According to the opinion attributed to R. Judah, *beit* refers to heaven, earth, and the divine being that unites the two.

I am not inclined to interpret this opinion theosophically; it seems rather that it is meant to be understood at face value: The three lines that make up the letter symbolize the heavenly and earthly realms and the divine being who unites them.[449] The theosophic explication is offered in the name of R. Eleazar. The three lines of *beit* refer to three holy, supernal lights that are bound as one, and they are the totality of Torah (*kelala de-oraita*). Insofar as the three potencies are the opening for faith, which may here denote the lower seven emanations, they are characterized as the abode (*beita*) of all that exists, and hence they are the three lines that make up *beit*, the letter that is the "totality of the holy name in three knots of faith" (*kelala di-shema qaddisha bi-telat qishrei meheimanuta*). All of Torah is the name and thus its first letter must encompass the totality of the name; the three lines—orthographic form of the letter—are knots of faith.

I would conjecture that the three knots of faith—faith is the fourth side, the opening created by three closed sides—may be decoded as the three letters contained in the Tetragrammaton, YHW, a name that is depicted pictorially by *beit*.[450] At the beginning is the second letter that is first; the letter made of three lines, which are three knots of faith, YHW.[451] Alternatively, the knots of faith may allude symbolically to *Ḥokhmah*, *Binah*, and *Tif'eret*, three configurations of the divine that are imaginally depicted in some zoharic passages as father, mother, son and are correlated respectively with YHW; the last letter of the name, the fourth party of the quaternity, the daughter, *Malkhut* or *Shekhinah*, is represented by the second *he*, the letter that has already appeared, a duplicate of the second, the element of faith, empty vessel, capacity to receive.

The beginning of Torah, therefore, is the letter that marks the mystery of the threefold unity, the totality of the name, the secret abode of faith. The Christological resonance in the zoharic locution *telat qishrei meheimanuta* has been noted.[452] Reinforcing this orientation, I would add that the author of the homily has combined the motif of Torah as the incarnation of the divine name and the trinitarian symbol of the three knots of faith. In this matter, as with regard to a number of crucial themes, the kabbalists whose ideas and interpretations are preserved in zoharic literature reflect a complex relationship to Christianity, which was viewed as the major competitor in the arena of salvation history, the perennial struggle between Synagogue and Church, Jacob and Esau, Israel/Adam and Gentile/Edom, not in binary opposition, but rather as attraction through repulsion, repulsion by attraction, a gesture that encompasses both at once, differently similar in virtue of being similarly different.

On the one hand, the kabbalists adopted a harsh stance and portrayed Christianity as the earthly instantiation of the demonic potency, Satan or Samael, long conceived to be the archon of Edom, progenitor of idolatry, *avodah zarah*, worship that leads one astray, the other that seduces the Jew (men seem to be especially vulnerable) both in the form of spiritual enticement (particularly in the guise of magic) and sexual temptation.[453] On the other hand, the very same kabbalists were duly impressed with and intrigued by aspects of this faith, including trinitarian and incarnational symbols, as well as Marian devotional imagery, and attempted to appropriate them as the authentic esoteric tradition,[454] perhaps even modeling the fraternity of Simeon ben Yoḥai and his comrades on the pattern of Jesus and his disciples.[455] In my judgment, the kabbalists hidden behind the personae of the zoharic fraternity sought to divest Christological symbols of their Catholic garb and redress them as the mystical truths of Judaism. The zoharic understanding of text as body, which provides the mechanism by which the body is understood as text, is a stunning illustration of this strategy.

I shall conclude with the citation and analysis of one final zoharic text that demonstrates the subtle and complex relationship between kabbalistic and Christological symbolism:

> "As for the tabernacle, make it of ten strips of cloth" (Exod. 26:1). Here is the mystery of unity, for the arrayment of the tabernacle was from several gradations, as it is written with respect to it, "and the tabernacle was one" (ibid., 26:6). This is to illustrate that all the parts of the body are all the mystery of one body. In a man, there are several upper and lower parts, the ones interior and the others revealed on the outside, and all of them are called one body, and the man is called one composition. So here, all the parts of the tabernacle are in the pattern of what is above and when all of them are joined as one, then it is written "and the tabernacle was one." The commandments of Torah are all parts and limbs in the mystery above, and when all of them are joined together, then all of them add up to one mystery. The mystery of the tabernacle, which consists of the parts and limbs, all compute to the mystery of Adam in the manner of the commandments of Torah, for the commandments of Torah are all of them the mystery of Adam, male and female. When they are joined together, they are one mystery of Adam.[456]

In this homily, the images of the tabernacle, the human body, the androgynous Adam, and the Torah are linked together like pearls in a necklace of symbolic equivalencies. The thread that ties the images together is the linguistic conception of embodiment, that is, what the four entities share in common is the assumption that they are constructed from letters of the Hebrew alphabet. In older rabbinic sources, one can find the notion that the tabernacle (*miqdash*), the earthly residence of the divine glory, microcosm of the universe, was built by means of the letters.[457] What the zoharic author adds is the depiction of the tabernacle in the shape of an anthropos. To grasp the hermeneutical move, we must bear in mind that in the above passage the tabernacle symbolically stands for the totality of the divine pleroma, a secret alluded to in the hyperliteral rendering of the verse that dictates the making of the tabernacle from ten strips of cloth, which correspond to the ten emanations from *Keter* to *Malkhut*. The mystery of the tabernacle's construction, therefore, imparts the wisdom that the multiplicity of divine powers cohere in a unified whole, that is, God's unity may be represented schismatically as a composite of discrete elements the infinity of which denies the possibility of fixed enumeration.

The organic unity of the tabernacle is illustrated further by comparing it to the human body. The anthropomorphic representation is illumined by a similar characterization of Torah, for the commandments are the limbs of the body of Torah, which is envisioned as the mystery of the androgynous Adam, the positive commandments engendered as masculine and the negative commandments as feminine. The conjunction of the two facilitates the constitution of the mystery of the divine anthropos, which is depicted both as the textualization of the tabernacle and the materialization of Torah—parallel processes in the hidden disclosure of the divine name. The secret of poetic incarnation imparted by masters of Jewish esoteric lore, beholding the luminous flesh from the word, may be seen as a countermyth to the image of the word/light made flesh in the Johannine prologue, a mythologoumenon that played an inestimable role in fashioning the hermeneutical aesthetic of medieval Christendom.

This is not to deny that in the history of Christian devotion the incarnational theme did express itself in terms of textual embodiment.[458] My point is, however, that the mythologic basis for this form of embodiment in Christianity is always the incarnation of the Word in the person of Jesus, whether this is understood veridically or docetically. As a consequence, medieval Christian piety was informed by the exegetical supposition that incarnation of the word in the flesh had the effect of removing the veil of the letter as expounded by Jews, who resolutely refused to accept the spiritual interpretation that the Christological understanding demanded; the literal meaning, intricately bound to the carnal law, thus killed the spirit by obstructing the true knowledge of the Last Things.[459] By contrast, in the kabbalistic wisdom that concretized in the course of the twelfth, thirteenth, and fourteenth centuries, incarnation of the flesh in the word preserved the letter of the veil, as the only credible means to apprehend the inner meaning of the law was thought to be through its outer covering, to behold mysteries of Torah from underneath the garment, to see the image of the imageless embodied iconically in the text that is the textual embodiment of the name.

CHAPTER SIX

Envisioning Eros: Poiesis and Heeding Silence

They turned their spotlights on the eroticism of the word,
but it was the eroticism of silence that dazzled.

—Edmond Jabès, *The Book of Margins*

Erotogenic Semiotic

As scholars have long noted, a salient feature of medieval kabbalah is the portrayal of religious experience in intensely charged erotic symbolism. Any attempt to separate the sexual and mystical threads in the tapestry of Jewish esotericism will prove to be futile.[1] From the kabbalists' vantage point, ecstatic experience—*ek-stasis*, standing out, which conveys metaphorically leaping to the ground in taking flight, turning inward by projecting outward[2]—facilitates knowing the secrecy of secrecy, the doubling of secret as secret, the eros of mystery wrapped in the exposé of the mystery of eros.

The specific qualities of erotic consciousness—a term that denotes both consciousness of eros and eros of consciousness—that may be elicited from kabbalistic teaching lends support to a more general insight: that matters pertaining to the spiritual have repeatedly been depicted in erotic images.[3] Years ago, George Ryley Scott characterized the eros of what he considered the religious impulse: "Eroticism . . . and religion, are emotional concepts betraying parallels and correlations. The one may easily prove to be a safety-valve for the other."[4] Mircea Eliade offers another formulation of this theme when he describes the confluence—or, in his precise locution, "coincidence of opposites"[5]—of the sexual and spiritual:

> In addition, one mustn't forget that sexuality, and especially sexual imagination and symbolics, have played a significant role throughout all of the *spiritual* history of humanity. I will give only one example of this, that of the ambiguity of sexual symbolism and vocabulary. All terms can be understood simultaneously in their concrete sense and in their spiritual, "mystical" sense. For certain Tantric schools, the

> Sahajiya, among others, the vocabulary, which is both paradoxical and enigmatic, aims to surprise and shock the noninitiated. Extremely arduous exercises of yoga meditation are presented in erotic terms: "coupling with an outcast prostitute," means in fact "a state of nirvanic joy" and "absolute liberty." For the initiates, this confusion in terms, permanent and omnipresent, aims to hasten the passing from a profane condition. The *coincidentia oppositorum* succeeds, on all levels, in revealing that ultimate and mysterious reality that is as inaccessible to understanding as is religious faith. It is quite obvious that there are circumstances in which, taking into account the disciple's level of preparation, the sexual techniques of yoga must be carried out concretely. Even in this case, the sexual experience finds itself in some way transfigured, and ceases to be of a uniquely physiological nature.[6]

I assume that some or perhaps many of the readers who may happen upon these pages would agree there is much with which to quibble in Eliade's account of the Sahajiya sect.[7] As I am no expert on Tantrism, I limit my reaction to the implication of his remarks for the understanding of religion more generally.[8] The "ultimate and mysterious reality" that is inaccessible to human understanding, is a theme well known to those familiar with the thought of Eliade, his taxonomic description of religious experience as *hierophany*, the appearance of the sacred, an appearance that is concurrently an occlusion, the sacred other in the *tremendum mysterion*, revealed only to the extent it is concealed from the one to whom it is revealed as concealed and concealed as revealed. In the above passage, Eliade makes the point that it is especially in the realm of sexual behavior that the mystery unfolds in its enfolding. Surely, if truth is a coincidence of opposites—coincidence and not identification—then it would follow that the mystery's re/veiling would conjure images of erotic yearning and that, inversely, fleshly thoughts of erotic yearning might convey—through gesture and word—the play of secrecy, duplicity, engendering possibility.

In these merging vectors, wheel within wheel, one re/covers truth uncovered in the enfolding of noetic poiesis unfolding poetic noesis. As I argued at length in the previous chapter, in kabbalistic lore, fully articulated in Castilian authors from the thirteenth and fourteenth centuries, the somatic points beyond itself as sign, for the body, or, perhaps more accurately, bodiliness, is to be construed as semiotic flesh, the flesh that is text, mirror, veil, wherein the image of the likeness is beheld in the likeness of the image. In language appropriate to this time, we can say that the erotic conveys a material and spiritual sense, not as separate semantic fields but as one meaning mirrored in the doubling of hermeneutic reflexivity. There is surely good reason to be suspicious about any assertion that makes a claim about "all of the *spiritual* history of humanity." The study of religion has progressed to a point that it is prudent to make assertions of a more limited and modest scope.[9] Indeed, even with respect to any particular religious culture, one must be wary of generalizations regarding the "dimensions of the sacred"[10] sweeping across time and place with no concern for the variegated and changing nature of sociopolitical and economic conditions.

The very notion of "religious experience" as a distinctive phenomenological category is a presumption that has been contested on grounds, largely staked by anthropologists and sociologists, that religion consists not of essential, ahistorical phenomena but of diverse and multifaceted social constructions.[11] Without denying the need to be circumspect in this manner, I would nonetheless submit that the description of Eliade is appropriate to what I call the traditional kabbalistic worldview that has evolved in sundry ways through the centuries. In spite of the polymorphous nature of kabbalah, with respect to the convergence of the spiritual and sexual in the interface of the erotic and esoteric—secrecy of eros laid bare in eros of secrecy—there is little alteration due to change in time or place. In kabbalistic teaching, it is a consequence of contemplative envisioning, which is realized through the imaginary transport to the imaginal realm, beholding the image of the text through the text that is image, that carnal sensuality is transformed into holy eroticism. With respect to this matter, I perceive no appreciable difference between theosophic and ecstatic kabbalah, to use the typological classification that has dominated contemporary scholarly discourse.

The ontic presupposition underlying the mechanics of this transformation relates to the principle of poetic incarnation explored in the previous chapter: All being is (un)veiled as a veil that unveils the veiling of the veil, the name that evokes the nameless, the name written one way and declaimed another. This knowledge is not merely theoretical; it is acquired—"received" would be the more appropriate term—as a consequence of devotional practice, though I would be equally comfortable saying that the devotional practice ensues from and is infused by this knowledge. According to a tradition transmitted in the name of Isaac the Blind, the "pious one" (*he-ḥasid*), by Ezra of Gerona:

> The essence of the worship of the enlightened [*maskilim*] and those who meditate on his name [*ḥoshvei shemo*] is "and cleave to him" (Deut. 13:5). This is the cardinal principle in Torah with respect to prayer and blessings, that one must harmonize his thought and his faith [*lehaskkim maḥshavto be-emunato*] as if it cleaved above, to unify [*leḥabber*] the name in its letters and to comprise within it the ten emanations [*sefirot*] like a flame bound to the coal, with his mouth he will mention it through its epithets, but in his heart he will combine it in its structure and as it is written. A sign for the matter is "Say to wisdom, you are my sister and call understanding a kinswoman" (Prov. 7:4).[12]

The task of the worshipper is to unite the two divine attributes "thought" (*maḥshavah*) and "faith" (*emunah*), to elevate the latter to the former, a restoration symbolically portrayed as the union of the diadem (*aṭarah*), the mark of kingship (*malkhut*), and the crown (*keter*), that is, the unification of the first and last of the ten *sefirot*, a theme already attested in the bahiric anthology based in part on an archaic mythopoeic motif of the fashioning of God's coronet from the prayers of Israel ascending heavenward.[13] As Ezra puts the matter in another context, commenting on the formulation of Moses regarding Israel's request to know when he would reveal the nature of God, "what is his name?" (*mah shemo*): "For this is the aim of intentionality and the secret of faith [*takhlit ha-kawwanah we-sod ha-emunah*]. This is [the meaning of] 'what is his name?,' the desire to know his cause and the connection of his name to the primal cause [*hitqqasher shemo be-ilah ha-ri'shonah*]."[14]

Knowledge of the name is linked to the "secret of faith," the mystery of the bond between the "primal cause" and the four-letter name, which comprises the ten *sefirot*. To know the name, therefore, is to possess the mystery, to envision God in the paradox of the one beyond number yielding ten without limit. Conjunction of human and divine, designated by the early kabbalists of Provence and Catalonia as *maḥshavah ha-deveqah*, "thought that cleaves," is occasioned by being conjoined to the letters YHWH, a state of mind—arising from meditative practice—depicted in decisively erotic language. For instance, Ezra, following the philosophical path epitomized by Maimonides,[15] relates the image of the kiss from the Song to the "pleasure of the conjunction of the soul to the source of life and the profusion of holy spirit" (*taʿanug devequt ha-neshamah bi-meqor ha-ḥayyim we-tosefet ruaḥ ha-qodesh*).[16]

I will offer a more extensive interpretation of this passage in the concluding chapter, but suffice it here to underscore that the kiss signifies the pleasure the soul experiences as it cleaves to the name, a pleasure linked to mystical enlightenment, a state that is elsewhere described by Ezra as "conjunction to nothing" (*devequt ba-ayin*), which parallels the expression found in the commentary on *Sefer Yeṣirah* attributed to Isaac the Blind, *hitbonenut she-ein bo mammash* (discussed in the previous chapter), contemplation of the insubstantial, a life so full it is identified with death.[17] Jacob ben Sheshet, a younger colleague of Ezra, affirms a similar position when he notes that "pleasure of the soul" (*oneg ha-nefesh*), in contrast to "pleasure of the body" (*oneg ha-guf*), is "wisdom and the good deed" (*ḥokhmah we-ha-maʿaseh ha-ṭov*).[18] The delight experienced by the soul is illumination of mystical gnosis that inspires virtuous behavior. In line with rabbinic pietism, itself textually inspired by the older wisdom tradition and reminiscent of Greek Stoicism, kabbalists were loath to separate wisdom from deed: the true sage is one whose sagacity is manifest in the mundane world of human commerce and social exchange.[19]

The cultural world of medieval kabbalists, as far as may be adduced from the extant literary remains, was intellectually elitist to the core. Typically, the kabbalist was well versed in classical rabbinic literature coupled with works of religious philosophy, both discursive and exegetical, indebted to ancient Greek wisdom.[20] In consort with their rabbinic and philosophic sources, kabbalists maintained that the life of mind, which is attained through mastery over the impulses, is gendered as masculine. One's manhood, accordingly, is proportionate to the restraint that one exemplifies in pursuit of wisdom.[21] The ideal of scholastic piety is epitomized in a statement attributed to Ben Zoma that defines virility as the conquering of one's desire, *ezehu gibbor ha-kovesh et yiṣro*.[22] For kabbalists as well, construction of masculinity is related to impulse control (especially sexual lust) and dedication to Torah study.[23]

One might argue on this basis that anthropological perfection is cast in the mold of an "effeminate" male, that is, a dominate portrait of the ideal man in talmudic culture is not the heroic warrior who masters others through physical prowess but rather the nonaggressive sage who masters himself and dedicates his energies to divine worship through prayer, study, and charitable deeds.[24] This portrait of the masculine is linked exegetically by rabbinic homilists to the statement of Isaac that may be referred to as the blessing before the blessing, that is, the verbal gesticulation that makes the act of blessing his sons possible, "the voice is the voice of Jacob but the hands are the hands of Esau" (Gen. 27:22), which, when decoded according to the dominant symbolic grid of the rabbis, denotes that the power of Israel derives from the voice (liturgical piety and textual study), whereas the power of Edom is from the hands (physical aptitude).[25]

The rabbinic ideal, therefore, might be seen as an inversion of the stereotypical Greco-Roman image of masculinity, a patriarchy that excluded women but construed its own sense of maleness in terms that would have been considered female by the prevailing external cultural frame of reference: mastery over a text as opposed to physical domination. Upon closer inspection, however, it becomes clear that the feminization of the male on the part of rabbinic teachers was itself a further substantiation of masculine hegemony through an androcentric co-opting and consequent subservience of the feminine. As I will explore in more depth in the next chapter, the matter reaches a head in kabbalistic symbolism (inspired by zoharic literature), in which the image of the eunuch, one of the self-referential terms adopted by kabbalists, signifies an amplified rather than diminished phallic potency.

Additionally, the kabbalistic orientation was enhanced by the Platonic heritage whereby matters of the intelligible realm are rendered in modes of erotic discourse.[26] Jewish mystics in the late Middle Ages, like pietists and visionaries of contemporary Christian and Muslim fraternities, were indebted to the Greek philosophical ideal of supremacy of the temperate soul over the excessive body.[27] They inherited as well the depiction of the activity of the rational soul in sexual images of the body.[28] Most importantly, the liaison between an individual's rational faculty and the supernal separate intellect, in some texts identified with God and in others differentiated, was imaged in erotic terms informed by the widespread androcentric claim that the inferior party assumes the characteristics of female, and the superior, those of the male, as we find, for example, in the standard depictions of matter in relation to form.[29] The patriarchal bias well ensconced in the Apollonian-Platonic and Jewish-Christian layers of Western consciousness is captured succinctly in the following declaration: "While the feminine is by nature unable to cast off materiality, the man becomes wholly removed from it and rises to the incorporeality of sunlight."[30]

By and large, medieval kabbalists appropriated the philosophical hostility toward sensuality and the consequent devaluation of the feminine, the conceptual basis for the ascetic lifestyle that facilitated the ascent of mind, engendered as male, to the ideal world of imaginal forms. To be sure, kabbalists were not at liberty to reject sexual behavior categorically, as procreation is the first commandment mentioned in Scripture; unmitigated celibacy as the highest spiritual ideal was not an option for kabbalists, no matter how adverse they were to the body and carnal passions. In accord with rabbinic ethos, kabbalists affirm human sexuality to the degree that it is the means to fulfill the injunction to procreate, to establish a "faithful household in Israel."[31] According to one rabbinic dictum, a Jewish man who willfully does not fulfill the obligation to procreate is guilty of diminishing the image of God. Kabbalists invested this ruling with metaphysical significance insofar as they identified the "image" more explicitly in theosophic terms; hence diminishing the image denotes weakening the imaginal configuration of the divine.

The zoharic authorship goes even further and portrays the man who dies childless as one who has castrated himself; since emasculation is associated with the demonic, such a person cleaves to the side of the unholy and is denied entrance before God when the soul separates from the corruptible body.[32] The failure to produce offspring is deemed by the zoharic circle to be a major offense, indeed the transgression for which the punishment of transmigration of the soul is prescribed.[33] There is an obvious tension at work here, for on the one hand, the affirmation of procreation seemingly advocates a life-affirming stance, whereas on the other hand, the particular weight accorded sensual pleasure in the sexual act belies a negative assessment of the physical. I do not think this is a tension that can be resolved; on the contrary, it is precisely its irresolution that is the most resolute feature of the mores of kabbalistic piety.

I wish to focus on one zoharic homily that conveys this crucial tension, or, to be more precise, in this homily one discerns the eschatological justification for an ascetic understanding of procreation. The passage to which I allude deals with the death of Nadab and Abihu, the sons of Aaron, who were consumed when they approached God and offered a "strange fire" (Lev. 10:1; Num. 3:4). Building on earlier rabbinic interpretation,[34] the author of the zoharic text maintains that the sin of Nadab and Abihu was that they entered the sanctuary while they were still single. The conviction that only a married priest should enter the sacred space rests on the assumption that the effluence of divine blessing is bestowed only where male and female are conjoined, since in that place alone will the masculine and feminine elements of the divine be united.[35] The "strange fire" that they offered is thus explicated in terms of their not unifying the letters of the name appropriately, thereby fortifying the rift in the divine nature.[36] Additionally, the bachelor status of Nadab and Abihu precluded the possibility of their fulfilling the obligation to procreate, which necessitated reincarnation.

Surprisingly, according to the zoharic exegesis, both sons come back in the person of Phineḥas, the grandson of Aaron, rather than in two separate men who would, as one might expect, rectify the transgression of dying childless by marrying and having children of their own. The mystical significance of the matter is revealed in the letters of Phineḥas: "It has been taught in the secret of the Mishnah:[37] Two, as a pair, *pen ḥas*, and thus it is said a small *yod* in the midst of the letters of Phineḥas, for the *yod* comprises two as one, and this is the secret of the matter."[38] The name "Phineḥas" is broken into two words, *pen* and *ḥas*, with the letter *yod* serving as the bridge connecting them. In the continuation of the passage, Eleazar inquires of his father, Simeon ben Yoḥai: Why did the sons come back as one person? He receives the following answer: "They were both half bodies [*palgei gufa*], for they were not married, and therefore they were comprised in one, as it is written, 'and she bore him Phineḥas; those are the heads etc.' (Exod. 6:25)."[39]

In several zoharic contexts, it is emphasized that only one who is married can be considered fully embodied.[40] By this standard, Nadab and Abihu must be considered "half bodies," since neither of them had a spouse. To make them whole, it was necessary for both to be reincarnated in the one person of Phineḥas. The two qualities embodied in Phineḥas are gendered respectively as female and male, *pen* corresponding to *Malkhut* and *ḥas*, to *Tif'eret*, even though there is no woman complementing the male. I propose that this figure symbolically instantiates the motif of the male androgyne, that is, the male that contains masculine and feminine. To be even more precise, I would conjecture that Phineḥas embodies the idea of the androgynous phallus. This seems to be the intent of the comment about the *yod* in name Phineḥas, which is between *pen* and *ḥas*, that is, the phallus that unites male and female, though in this case not in the sense of male cohabiting with female but in the sense of masculinity and femininity both deriving from this aspect of the human anatomy. Heterosexual mating and the having of offspring did not rectify the offense of dying childless; this was achieved, rather, by the reconstitution of androgyny in the divine represented by the letter *yod*, the sign of the covenant.[41] As the reincarnation of Nadab and Abihu, the priests who offered the "strange fire," Phineḥas possessed the zeal to avenge the sin committed against the covenant by Zimri, who cohabited with Cozbi the Midianite, the "strange woman" (Num. 25:6–8, 14–15). Phineḥas upholds the covenant by uniting the male and female attributes within the phallic potency, a gesture that imparts messianic significance to his fervor.

What is implied by this homily, and scores of other texts that I could have cited, is that the ultimate purpose of procreation is not the engenderment of the human body but the rectification of sexual desire, which has to be seen as part of the larger project of glorifying the body, which we discussed in the previous chapter and will discuss again in the succeeding chapter. For our purposes at this juncture, it is important to emphasize that kabbalists latched onto and amplified the rabbinic notion that sanctifying oneself in the act of coitus, which is linked exegetically to the verse "you shall sanctify yourselves and be holy" (Lev. 11:44),[42] is fulfilled by concentrating mentally on procreation as the singular rationale for engaging in sex. By focusing in this manner, one is attached to God and removed from the physical pleasure of intercourse, and as a consequence, the offspring that result from the union will be righteous and pure; by contrast, those who engage in sex for carnal gratification are endowed only with the animal soul, the lowest of the psychic grades, and their progeny are considered wicked.[43]

Beyond the procreative value of sexual behavior, however, kabbalists assigned a positive theurgic role to intercourse between husband and wife as the means to restore the female to the male whence she was taken. Sex, therefore, facilitates the ontic restoration of the prelapsarian androgynous state.[44] Notwithstanding this affirmative role, carnal eros is problematized fundamentally in medieval kabbalistic treatises. Indeed, the peak mystical experience of conjunction (*devequt*) is depicted repeatedly as a sublation of fleshy passion. Union between God and visionary, the male lover and female beloved, is troped as spiritual copulation (*ziwwug ruḥani*), a leitmotif linked especially to the Song of Songs.[45] Immortality was reinterpreted in terms of pleasure for the disembodied soul, a noetic pleasure that, paradoxically, is dependent on attaining desire beyond desire, which can be fulfilled only to the extent that it is unfulfilled.[46] Kabbalistic contemplation, I submit, is to be viewed in light of the gender transposition consistent with the philosophical ideal of intellectual eros.

Desire beyond Desire/Encircling Circularity

William Desmond has deftly formulated the erotics of contemplation that has informed Western metaphysics. In my judgment, his account of the impulse underlying the metaphysician's quest for unity may be profitably applied to kabbalists' descriptions of the ecstasy of contemplative envisioning:

> The eros of perplexity is driven to transcendence, troubled initially by a sense of lack. The thrust of mind's transcending seeks to overcome that lack, make determinate what is vague and indefinite, complete what is partial and unintegral. In other words, the eros of perplexity is impelled towards as complete a comprehension of the whole as is possible. It is a movement of transcendence wherein mind mediates progressively with being's otherness to make its enigmatic face available to determinate intelligibility. It is driven to the ideal of comprehensive intelligibility and knowing: knowing of the whole. Sometimes, too, it may define metaphysics as an absolutely autonomous thinking. The metaphysician then seeks approximation to the god of the philosophers: thought thinking itself.[47]
>
> The eros of perplexity appears as the energy of a process of determinate negation, which, through negation of what is now, constitutes a more fully intelligible determination. The process passes all the way to complete self-determining intelligibility. It completes itself in the overcoming of the negative, which is the complete internalizing of otherness and transcendence. Put otherwise, self-transcendence, in dialectical interplay with what is other, ultimately circles around itself on the way to absolute wholeness. Or, put otherwise again, the whole becomes an absolutely self-mediating circle of transcendence within which all otherness is sublated. Then the real result is that there is no between; there is no transcendence finally; there is the absolute as thought thinking itself in its other; but the other is thought again thinking itself, hence in the end there is no real otherness either. The excess of plentitude that gives the beginning, that sustains the between, and that outlives every completion in the middle and every closed circle of concepts is occluded.[48]

Lest one protest the wisdom of citing Desmond to illumine the study of medieval kabbalah, let me hasten to point out that the metaphysical tradition to which he refers (especially in Aristotelian and Neoplatonic sources that circulated in the High Middle Ages in Arabic, Hebrew, and Latin) had a major impact on the formation of kabbalistic symbolism. Whatever the soil wherein the conceptual roots of kabbalah might be uncovered, philosophical treatises played a significant role in providing kabbalists with discursive modes of discourse that informed both the experiences of mystical communion and the narrative recounting and/or contemplative envisioning connected to those experiences.[49] The correlation of eros and noesis, rooted in the Platonic notion of erotic reason, described by Desmond is entirely germane to a historical study of kabbalistic sources. In the latter, one discovers a similar linking of this correlation to the appropriation of Aristotle's characterization of divine activity (albeit transmitted through some channels as part of the Neoplatonic heritage) as self-intellection, *noesis noeseos*, "thought thinking thought," the self-enclosed circle of contemplation wherein thinking, thinker, and thought become indistinguishable.[50]

Pursuit of the contemplative ideal can be understood as the erotic desire to become other, to be incorporated into the other, which is part of the same. Longing to apprehend the other culminates in taking hold of the other, but taking hold of the other consists of being held by and/or in the other that was generated as part of the same. The totality of eros would be attained with the fulfillment of the striving for self-actualization by way of the other that is the same by being other, the same other, not other than the same.[51] I note parenthetically that this formulation brings us back to Lacan, who insisted (as noted briefly in chapter three) that the subject's desire is constituted as desire for the other, a desire that is marked, however, by the approach of *jouissance*, that is, the desire without an other, a desire expressed in the desire not to desire.[52]

More of this later, but suffice it here to note that the characterization of contemplation offered above is applicable to kabbalists who have affirmed the possibility of being absorbed in the boundless and nameless Ein Sof, the head-that-is-no-head, in accordance with the decapitating image of one zoharic passage.[53] Just as for the philosophically enlightened of the late Middle Ages, rejection of physical carnality gives way to the inculcation of rational desire, which comes to fruition in the reflexivity of consciousness thinking consciousness as the other thinking other as self, the mind, as it were, mirroring the mirror that mirrors the mirror,[54] so for the kabbalist, the spiritual eros of contemplative envisioning, the meditative ascent of human thought that culminates in its merging with the infinite, the hyperessence—that is, the essence beyond essence, the essence that cannot be essentialized except as inessential—thought as unthought, is predicated on the noetic transubstantiation of carnal sensuality.

The convergence of noetic and erotic is supported in kabbalistic symbology by the supposition that the generative force of the divine is related in the first instance to the mental process of contemplation, that is, that God germinates being through the elevation in thought of the phallic impulse to disseminate. The primeval truth is echoed in scriptural language, for the one who engages in sexual intercourse with his wife is said to "know" her.[55] Needless to say, this terminological usage sheds light not only on the conception of sexuality proffered in this literary setting but also on the notion of knowledge operative in the wider ancient Near Eastern cultural context.[56] Surely it is not wise to generalize based on a specific etymological point, and a lengthy discussion of this motif and its evolution through time, though surely warranted, lies beyond the purview of this chapter. I only wish to state here what seems to me to be the epistemological assumption resonating in many medieval kabbalistic texts based on the older philological practice: Intimate knowledge is at the core erotic. In the mystical symbolism embraced by kabbalists, eroticism of knowledge has a more specific esoteric application, for to know the secret, to know secretly, is to master by yielding, to yield by mastering—a dance that should be very familiar to those ensnared in the play of eros.

The link between eros and gnosis is enhanced by the kabbalists' adoption of the anatomic view traceable to Galen that locates the origin of semen in the brain. The importance of this notion, already attested in *Sefer ha-Bahir*,[57] for an appreciation of the utilization of erotic imagery on the part of kabbalists is well captured in the remark of Vital:

> It is known that all souls come forth from the mercies and strengths that are in the brain of consciousness [*moaḥ ha-daᶜat*], for the secret of copulation [*sod ha-ziwwug*] is dependent on there, as Scripture says "And Adam knew his wife Eve etc." (Gen. 4:1) and "no man knew her" (ibid., 24:16). Therefore, it is called knowledge [*daᶜat*] to show that from there derives the seminal drop of copulation [*tippat ha-ziwwug*], which is called "knowing" [*yediᶜah*].[58]

The original site of the phallic potency, designated by the technical term *yesod*, was in the brain (*moaḥ*), the fount of consciousness whence issues forth the spring of knowledge (*daᶜat*).[59] Within that brain are "mercies" (*ḥasadim*) and "strengths" (*gevurot*), that is, the ontic roots of mercy and judgment, respectively engendered as masculine and feminine, a necessary corollary of the proposition that the creative process, beginning in *olam aṣilut*, the world of emanation, is a balance of the two attributes. As Luria describes the process, when the two forms of consciousness (*moḥot*) from *Ḥokhmah* and *Binah*

> are expanded to enter into the head of *Zeᶜeir Anpin*, they too are engraved as male and female, and they are conjoined by the supernal knowledge [*daᶜat elyon*], which is in the pattern of the holy limb below [*dugmat ha-eiver ha-qadosh lemaṭṭah*], which is *Yesod*, and it enters the depth of the well [*omeq ha-beʾer*], which is the point of Zion below, like the womb of a woman . . . and this is the matter of the rupturing [*beqiᶜah*] on the part of the knowledge [*daᶜat*] to open the opening of the womb [*petaḥ ha-reḥem*], and this is "by his knowledge the depths burst apart" (Prov. 3:20). When they are united and contained one within the other, a third form of consciousness [*moaḥ*] is made that comprises the two of them and this is knowledge [*daᶜat*]."[60]

The symbolic correlation of the supernal knowledge or mind and the phallus is linked to the anatomical assumption that semen originates in the brain, which in turn provides the biological basis for the spiritual ideal of contemplation.

In a second passage, Vital transmits the matter in somewhat more technical terminology as a teaching he received directly from Luria:

> Another time I heard from my teacher, blessed be his memory, that *Zeᶜeir Anpin* unites with Leah through the aspect of the mind [*daᶜat*] that is within him, and it becomes the aspect of *yesod* through which he may be conjoined to Leah. And this is the secret of the verse "And Adam knew Eve his wife" (Gen. 4:1), for this supernal copulation [*ziwwug ha-zeh ha-elyon*], which is by means of the mind [*daᶜat*], is called knowledge [*yediᶜah*], and it is known that the copulation of the mind [*ziwwug ha-daᶜat*] is concealed and hidden [*bi-ṭemiru be-itkassya*].[61]

In a third, and perhaps most stimulating, passage, Vital attempts to explain the originary arousal within the infinite, an arousal that may be rendered in psychoanalytic terms as the (phallic) yearning to become other, to create difference of identity in the identity of difference. Vital calls the arousal the "first copulation" (*ziwwug ri'shon*), but since there is no gender polarity at this juncture, the female potency completely sealed within the male, this arousal must assume the character of masturbation—in Vital's own words *nit'orer ha-zakhar me-aṣmo*—by means of which the "will and desire to copulate" (*raṣon we-ta'awah lehizdawweq*) are actualized. Vital is quick to point out that this first copulation, which in fact is no copulation at all since there is as of yet no other and hence there is no need, strictly speaking, to be conjoined to another, is not ascribed to the region of the genitals, but to the "supernal will, thought, the upper brain, in the secret of the supernal will that is entirely masculine and without any mark of the feminine."[62]

We may conclude that the description of divine and human consciousness in Vital is decidedly orgasmic in nature. Needless to say, this notion is not the innovation of Vital but rather reflects a much older conception of the brain as the origin of seminal fluid embraced by kabbalists from early on, attested by its appearance in *Sefer ha-Bahir.* In the next chapter, I will explore this feature of kabbalistic lore in detail, particularly as it relates to the ascetic practice of retaining the discharge of semen from the corona of the penis (*aṭeret berit*) and elevating the sexual energy to the top of the head, whence it is transformed into the crown of royalty (*keter malkhut*), at once the crowning object of visualization, the subject who is crowned and thereby empowered to see, and the medium by which the former is envisioned and the latter envisions, an aspect of kabbalah that bears close phenomenological resemblance to Tantric practice. At this juncture, suffice it to note that Vital's characterization of the initial arousal of the infinite will as an autoerotic stimulation, resulting in the "first copulation" in the upper brain as opposed to the genitals, may be viewed as the mythopoeic underpinning of a kabbalistic ritual of withholding seminal discharge required of one who wished to behold the imaginal form in its unity and multiplicity, sameness and difference. The epistemological contour within which the lived experience of kabbalists has taken shape allows us to speak concomitantly of the noetic quality of eros and the erotic quality of noesis.[63] The confluence of these two marks the spot of poetic dwelling whence arise the symbols that have informed the kabbalists in their mandate to envision an invisible God, to speak of an inaudible name.

Jouissance / Toying Around

The philosophical notion of eros as the closed circle of thought thinking itself,[64] culminating in the ideal of solitary contemplation, coincides with the mythical symbol of the uroboros, the serpent eating its own tail, a hoary image that continued to be influential in the Middle Ages and beyond; we can assume this image was known to kabbalists[65] and linked exegetically to the depiction of the *sefirot* in *Sefer Yeṣirah* 1:6, "their end is fixed in their beginning and their beginning is fixed in their end."[66] The conceptual account of the autoerotic is offered in a poetically inspired manner by Dionysius the Areopagite, based, of course, on the older Platonic tradition. In this account, carnal eros is "an image of the true eros, a falling away from the true eros," which is identified as "a power of unifying, binding, and joining," characteristics associated with beauty and goodness.[67] In what strikes the attuned ear as ecstatic rapture, Dionysius demarcates the enrapt eruption of divine eros:

> An upward power to itself . . .
> A good procession of the separated unity,
> A simple, self moved, erotic motion—
> active of itself,
> Before be-ing, in the good,
> Flowing forth out of the good to beings,
> Returning again into the good;
> in this the divine eros is excellently
> manifested to be without beginning and
> without end.[68]

The symbolic representation has the advantage of making more explicit the inherently phallic-narcissistic dimension of the self-enclosed identity implied in the portrayal of divine eros as an "everlasting circle—moving around in unerring convolution . . . always abiding, proceeding, and returning, in the same, and according to the same."[69] It is advantageous to recall the following comment of Neumann: "The myth of Narcissus makes it quite clear that this is an attraction to one's own body. Especially characteristic of this adolescent stage is the narcissistic accentuation of the phallus as the epitome of the body and the narcissistic personality."[70] As I have already remarked in chapter three, I am not beholden to the archetypal symbolism underlying Neumann's comment, but I do think that what he said inadvertently applies well to the contemplative ideal that dominated Western metaphysics until the twentieth century. Perhaps, to be even more blunt, the mythopoeic presentation quite naturally results in gnostification of the epistemological and ontic monopsychism. The procession from and return of all things to the one is the ontic conception that provides the rationale for the drama of the redeemed redeemer, a drama of which it is presumed that the symbolic incarnation will be perceptible in history, leaving behind verbal tracings of imagination. A telling illustration of the phenomenon may be culled from the following account in the *Gospel of Truth* of the circularity inherent in the rudimentary guideline in the elitist and restrictive transmission of esoteric gnosis—the secret is to be exposed only to one willing to receive the teaching. "But those who are to receive teaching [are] the living who are inscribed in the book of the living. It is about themselves that they receive instruction, receiving it from the Father. . . . Since the perfection of the totality is in the Father, it is necessary for the totality to ascend to him."[71]

On the surface, it might appear that the contemplative goal proffered by kabbalists entails an emulation of a primal narcissism linked in some accounts to the mystical yearning for unity—the bonding with God expressive of the return of the pneumatic spirit to the womb whence it emerged.[72] In the balance of this chapter, I would like to apply this insight to the topic of divine (fore)thought and the phallic constitution of gender as it emerges from kabbalistic symbolism, especially as the matter evolves in zoharic and Lurianic sources, the two corpora discerned since the seventeenth century as major repositories. As a way of introducing this theme, I will examine briefly the mythic portrayal in prekabbalistic sources of God bemusing himself with Torah, which served as the textual basis for later developments. The path of our inquiry at this point requires reflection on the term *shaʿashuʿa*, for by listening attentively to philological resonances, we will be in a better position to apprehend the force of *jouissance* as the spiritual eros depicted in kabbalistic lore.

The term *shiʿasha* occurs in various conjugations in scriptural texts, a common denominator of which suggests a meaning of "to gladden," "to make joyous," "to amuse." Especially important for the tracks of the path I shall lay forth is the use of the term in the wisdom tradition attested in Proverbs and some of the Psalms. I begin with the depiction of wisdom in Proverbs 8:30: *wa-ehyeh eṣlo amon wa-ehyeh shaʿashuʿim yom yom mesaḥeqet lefanav be-khol et*, "I was with him as a confidant, and I was [his] daily delight, toying before him at every moment." In the next verse, wisdom is further described as *mesaḥeqet be-tevel arṣo we-shaʿashuʿai et benei adam*, "Rejoicing in his inhabited world, delighting humankind" (8:31). Wisdom thus occupies the interesting position of delighting the divine and humanity.

It is plausible to suggest that the connotation of *shaʿashuʿa* in this context is illumined by the depiction of Ephraim as *yeled shaʿashuʿim*, "a delightful child," in Jeremiah 31:20.[73] Particularly pertinent are the occurrences of the term in Psalms: *be-rov sarʿappai be-qirbi tanḥumekha yeshaʿasheʿu nafshi*, "When I am filled with worries, your consoling soothes my soul" (94:19); *be-ḥuqqotekha eshtaʿasha*, which can be rendered "I take delight in your laws," but may be better translated "I contemplate your laws" (119:16), which would parallel the expressions in the previous verse, *be-fiqqudekha asiḥah we-abbiṭah orḥotekha*, "I study your precepts and I regard your ways" (ibid., 15); *gam edotekha shaʿashuʿai*, "Your decrees, too, are objects of my contemplation" (ibid., 24), based on the expression in the preceding verse *avddekha yasiaḥ be-ḥuqqekha*, "Your servant studies your laws" (ibid., 23); *we-eshtaʿasha be-miṣwotekha*, "I contemplate your commandments" (ibid., 47), which parallels *ki fiqqudekha darashti*, "I have investigated your precepts" (ibid., 45); *toratkha shaʿashuʿai* ("Your teaching is my amusement" (ibid., 77, 92, 174), and similarly *miṣwotekha shaʿashuʿai*, "Your commandments are my delight" (ibid., 143).

From the different occurrences we can conclude that two main meanings, "to take delight" and "to contemplate," are conveyed in the word "bemuse," understood not in its more conventional connotation as "to bewilder" or "to stupefy," but rather, in accord with an archaic sense, "to be engrossed in thought," as a poet devoted to and taken with the Muse of inspiration. Both connotations seem to be preserved in a beautifully poetic utterance in one of the Qumran Thanksgiving Scrolls, *teshʿasha nafshi wa-efraḥah ke-[sho]shanah we-libbi niftaḥ le-maqor olam*, "My soul is delighted, and I bloom like a [li]ly, and my heart is opened to the eternal spring" (1QH^a xviii 31).

Turning to rabbinic literature, I begin with the aggadic statement attributed to Joshua ben Levi: Moses is portrayed as saying before God, "Master of the world, you possess a hidden treasure in which you take delight each day," *ḥemdah genuzah yesh lekha she-atah mishtaʿasheʿa bah bekhol yom*.[74] In an earlier study, I suggested that the expression *mishtaʿasheʿa bah*, which is derived from the description of wisdom in Proverbs 8:30, has a sexual connotation in the talmudic dictum.[75] The remark of Joshua ben Levi points to a mythic conception of female Torah with which God is erotically involved.[76] It is also likely that in this passage the term *mishtaʿasheʿa* connotes some form of mental activity on the part of the masculine God vis-à-vis the feminine Torah. This is certainly the case in the exegesis of Proverbs 8:30 connected to the first verse in Scripture recorded at the beginning of *Genesis Rabbah*: the wisdom that is the confidant with whom God delights is identified as Torah, the blueprint that God consults prior to the creation of the world: "Thus the holy One, blessed be he, looked into Torah and he created the world," *kakh hayah ha-qadosh barukh hu mabiṭ ba-torah u-vore ha-olam*.[77] The looking into Torah can be understood in a contemplative sense, the erotic nature of which is underscored by the exegetical link connecting the act of looking to the word *shaʿashuʿim*. We have an early attestation in this passage for a theme that evolves into a central tenet in later kabbalistic literature: the eroticism of the gaze.

Support for my reading is found in *Seder Avodah le-Yom ha-Kippurim*, composed by Yose ben Yose, a liturgical poet who lived in Palestine in the fourth or fifth centuries. The poem, which begins with the words *atah khonanta olam be-rov ḥesed*, describes God in the following way: *be-or dat shiʿashaʿta we-raglekha siḥeqah*, "You delighted in the light of Torah, which was frolicking before you."[78] What is the form of the delight? It can be shown from other parts of the poem that *shaʿashuʿa* relates to a cognitive process. For example, in one passage, the idiom *shaʿashuʿa midrash* parallels *hege kitvei qodesh*, indicating that midrashic exegesis is a counterpart to recitation of Scripture.[79] In another poem of Yose ben Yose, which begins *azkir gevurot eloha neʾddari*, we find the following description of God and the primordial Torah: *amon saḥaqo dat shaʿashuʿav hi hegyono ad amod segullah*.[80] The word *shaʿashuʿa* is here explicitly identified as contemplation or meditation (*higgayon*). According to an ancient mythic tradition that is reflected in both midrashic and poetic literary forms, the creative process ensues from God's thought, which is portrayed as his erotic engagement (*shaʿashuʿa*) with the feminine Torah. In the beginning, at the beginning, *bereʾshit*, God muses over Torah and thereby bemuses and amuses himself.

Prior to examining medieval esoteric texts in which the aggadic myth is expanded, I take note of sources that mention the notion of an originary act of God portrayed as toying with the letters of Torah. In his commentary on *Sefer Yeṣirah*, Sabbatai Donnolo recasts the statement from *Genesis Rabbah*: "We have learnt that two thousand years before the creation of the world the holy One, blessed be he, contemplated the twenty-two letters of Torah [*hayah ha-qadosh barukh hu meshaʿasheʿa et esrim u-shetayim otiyyot shel torah*]. He combined and rotated them and made from all of them one word. He rotated [the word] frontwards and backwards through all twenty-two letters."[81] Donnolo has joined the aggadic motif of *shaʿashuʿa* and the praxis of letter combination articulated in *Sefer Yeṣirah*. How does God amuse himself with the source of his musing? By combining letters of Torah through specified rotations, back to front, front to back. These rotations account for the creative process, the beginning that gives way to and ensues from *shaʿashuʿa*, the will-to-create, to hold in by issuing forth, temporal encircling of erotic trembling: what is was not and what was not is.

An important marker in charting the trajectory of the motif of *shaʿashuʿa* is found in the opening lines of an anonymous poem written in southern Italy in the ninth or tenth century around the same region and time as Donnolo: *adon keʿalah be-maḥshavto livro olamo hu levaddo khe-meʾaz bi-mekhon taʿaṣumo we-shaʿashuʿa lefanav ke-miqqedem ḥokhmat rishshumo.*[82] God is here described as being alone prior to the creation in the "dwelling of his strength" (*mekhon taʿaṣumo*), which I take to refer to the throne on the basis of the expressions *mekhon kisʾekha* (Ps. 89:15) and *mekhon kisʾo* (ibid., 97:2). In this primordial space, the "wisdom of his inscription," *ḥokhmat rishshumo*, i.e., Torah, was amusement (*shaʿashuʿa*) before him. Significantly, the aggadic trope is combined with the rabbinic idiom that denotes divine volition, "thus it arose in thought," *kakh alah ba-maḥshavah.*[83] The proximity of these ideas does not mean necessarily that for this poet the rising in divine thought is sexually nuanced. In later kabbalistic literature, however, the two ideas were indeed blended together, and the expression *alah ba-maḥshavah* was employed euphemistically to denote sexual arousal of a contemplative sort, the rising of phallic energy/light to the brain.[84] I will lay aside the fuller account of this matter until we come around to it again at a subsequent point in the discussion.

Another dimension of *shaʿashuʿa* that I think worthy of note is attested in the poems of Shelomo ha-Bavli, who lived in the tenth century, apparently in northern Italy. In one of his poems, he describes the Torah scroll as *sefer tanḥumekha marat nefesh shaʿashuʿim*, "book of your comforts, solace for the embittered soul."[85] The connection between *shaʿashuʿa* and divine compassion is fueled by the scriptural expression *tanḥumekha yeshaʿasheʿu nafshi*, "your consolations soothe my soul" (Ps. 94:14).[86] Shelomo ha-Bavli applies this image to Torah, which thus becomes the book of God's comforts. In a second poem, one finds the expression *shaʿen shaʿashuʿa tanḥum deveqekha ka-ezor*, "comfort-delight surrounds those who cling to you like loincloth."[87]

The image of loincloth and its association with *dbq*, "to cleave," is based on the prophetic description of God's relationship to Israel: "For as the loincloth clings close to the loins of a man, so I caused all of the house of Israel and all of the house of Judah to cleave to me [*hidbaqti elai*], thus says the Lord, that they will be my people, for the name, praise, and splendor [*ule-shem we-litehillah ule-tifʾaret*], but they did not hear" (Jer. 13:11). Leaving aside the thought-provoking depiction of Israel's cleaving to God by way of the three elements, name (*shem*), praise (*tehillah*), and splendor (*tifʾeret*),[88] the contextual meaning of which still needs to be illumined, I will simply note that Shelomo ha-Bavli appropriated the scriptural imagery to depict God's mercy, which he names *shaʿashuʿa tanḥum*, the comfort-delight that encircles those who cleave to him—the people of Israel—like the loincloth that surrounds the genitals of a man. *Shaʿashuʿa* conveys the intimacy of the (homo)erogenic zone in the special relationship that pertains between God and Israel, epitomized in the liturgical community of male Jews.

The application of *shaʿashuʿa* to God's special erotic relationship to Israel is discernible in a much older source, a poem of Yannai, who lived in Palestine in the early Byzantine period. In my judgment, the eroticism attested in his poetic utterance relates more specifically to the bond between the male God and male Jews. The *qerovah*, which is a poetic exegesis on the expression "and to Israel, his people" (Exod. 18:1), sets out to extol the distinctive virtues of the Jewish folk. In the course of the poem, it becomes clear that the biblical reference has been significantly delimited, as it applies specifically to Jewish males. Thus at one point, we read of God's relationship to Israel, *sam bahem ḥotamo / arev lo nitfei damo*, "He placed his seal in them / pledged to him are they who drip his blood."[89] Clearly, this image is exclusionary, as it pinpoints Jewish males—the circumcised who bear the divine seal[90]—as the correct object of the locution "Israel, his people." Following an idea attested in early rabbinic midrash, expressed especially in terms of the exegetical application of the words of God to Jerusalem—"When I passed by you and saw you wallowing in your blood, I said to you, 'By your blood, live'" (Ezek. 16:6)—to circumcision,[91] in the poem of Yannai the blood of this rite is viewed as the sign of the oath that binds Israel to God. That is, the divine impresses his seal upon the flesh of the Israelite males and through the covenantal cut they pledge their being to God, a pledge sealed in blood.

The poem concludes *shiᶜsheᶜam ke-omein be-shikhmo / tikkenam yesodei hadomo*. As the modern editor of the text has properly noted, the first part is indebted to the words attributed to Moses as he speaks to God: "Did I conceive all this people, did I bear them, that you should say to me, 'Carry them in your bosom as a nurse carries an infant [*ka'asher yissa ha-omen et ha-yoneq*] to the land that you have promised on oath to their fathers?'" (Num. 11:12).[92] However, two discrepancies between the verse and the poem of Yannai are noteworthy: First, the place of nursing is transferred from the bosom to the shoulder, and second, the verb *yissa* ("carry") is replaced by *shiᶜasha*.[93] How do we render the expression *shiᶜsheᶜam ke-omein be-shikhmo*? "Like a nurse, he comforted them upon his shoulder." How so? The continuation points the way, "he established for them the foundations of his footstool."[94] God's relation to circumcised Jewish males is depicted in the image of the nurse who carries the babe on his shoulders, an image that is re/veiled in the second image of God implanting the Jews in the land of Israel, the divine footstool on earth, the mundane place that corresponds imaginally to the heavenly throne.

The tradition attested in the tenth-century southern Italian material is reformulated in the thirteenth century by Eleazar of Worms, a leading figure of the Rhineland Jewish pietists, in his *Hilkhot ha-Kavod*: "The holy One, blessed be he, was occupied prior to the world, and two thousand years before Torah he was occupied with his expansive wisdom, and he combined the letters [*hayah oseq be-ḥokhmato ha-reḥavah we-ṣiref ha-otiyyot*]."[95] Although not stated explicitly, the notion of "expansive wisdom" in Eleazar's thought, reflected in other Pietistic sources, embraces the myth of God engaged in contemplative activity of an erotic nature expressed specifically in letter combination. Significantly, this praxis, which may be traced to the second part of *Sefer Yeṣirah*, is located mythopoeically in the two thousand years before God was occupied with Torah. What the rabbinic figures considered the first act, the beginning, is here demoted to second, but what is preserved from antiquity is the priority accorded language as the primary means of divine creativity and the characterization of the latter by a combination of the contemplative and erotic.

At this juncture we can turn to a critical passage in *Sefer ha-Bahir* that includes a parable that substantially expands the aggadic myth, an expansion that well serves to guide us to the imaginal topography of kabbalistic symbolism:

R. Amora sat and expounded, "Why is it written 'And the sea is full of the Lord's blessing, take possession on the west and south'? (Deut. 33:23). In every place *beit* is blessed, for it is the fullness [*ha-male*], as it says, 'And the sea is full of the Lord's blessing' [*u-male birkat yhwh*]. From there he gives drink to the needy and from the fullness he took counsel at the beginning."
To what may this be compared? To a king who wanted to build his palace with hard granite. He cut out rocks and carved stones, and there emerged for him a well of abundant living water. The king said, "Since I have flowing water, I will plant a garden and I will delight in it [*eshtaᶜasheᶜa bo*], the whole world and I, as it is written, 'I was with him as a confidant, a source of delight [*shaᶜashuᶜim*] every day'" (Prov. 8:30).
The Torah said, "For two thousand years I was delighting in his lap [*be-ḥeiqo shaᶜashuᶜim*], as it says, 'every day' [*yom yom*], and his day [*yomo*] is one thousand years, as it says, 'For in your sight a thousand years are like yesterday'" (Ps. 90:4).[96]
From here forward it is temporarily [*le-ittim*], as it says, "in every time" (Prov. 8:30), but the remainder [*ha-sheᶜar*] everlastingly [*le-olam*], as it says, "my glory I will hold in for you" (Isa. 48:9).
What is "my glory" [*tehillati*]? As it is written, "a praise [*tehillah*] of David, I will extol you" (Ps. 145:1).
What is the praise? For "I will extol you" [*aromimkha*]. And what is exaltation [*romemut*]? For "I will bless your name forever and ever" (ibid.).
And what is the blessing? To what may this be compared? To a king who planted trees in his garden, even though rain has fallen, the [garden] draws constantly and the ground is moist, he must irrigate [the trees] from the spring, as it says, "The beginning of wisdom is the fear of the Lord, a sound understanding for all who practice it" (ibid., 111:10). If you say she will be lacking something, thus it says, "Praise of him [*tehillato*] is everlasting" (ibid.).[97]

The aggadic reading of Proverbs 8:30 is reformulated here in an effort to describe the fullness of God, the *male*, symbolized by the letter *beit* and also identified as blessing, wisdom, the primordial Torah whence God took advice in the beginning. Torah/wisdom is depicted parabolically as the spring of living water that gushes forth—spontaneously according the narrative of the myth—from the stones that are cut in order to provide material with which to build the palace. When the king discerns the spring issuing forth, he declares that he can now plant a garden in which he and the world will delight, for the garden will be watered incessantly by the spring that overflows interminably from its source. Precisely in this interminability are the terms of terminability to be sought. Time is linked to the beginning, symbolized by *beit*, the capacity to receive and the potency to overflow, wisdom in its feminine and masculine manifestation, mythopoeically envisioned as garden and spring. The connotation of *shaᶜashuᶜa* relates to this primal dialectic of bestowing and receiving, the division (*maḥloqet*) that stands at the beginning, nay, the division that is the beginning. The way begins with the parting of the way.

In a previous study, I analyzed this pericope in great detail, and it would be impossible to rehearse all the twists and turns that I undertook on that path of listening.[98] I will summarize the points that will be necessary to grasp the issues most pertinent to the present discussion. The embellishment of the rabbinic myth in the bahiric parable, especially the reading of the key verse from Proverbs 8:30, introduces the element of temporality into the consideration of primal *shaʿashuʿa*. When we are to think of God's be/musing himself with Torah, which is the beginning, we are to think of time. A transition is thus noted from the period two thousand years prior to creation to what ensues after creation. The former is alluded to in the part of the verse that speaks of wisdom "being a delight" before God "every day" (*yom yom*), which is interpreted as "everlastingly" (*le-olam*), and the latter in the description of wisdom "playing" in "every time" (*be-khol et*), that is, temporarily, from time to time (*le-ittim*).

Significantly, the transition from *le-olam* ("incessantly") to *le-ittim* ("intermittently") is linked exegetically to "my glory I will hold in for you," *u-tehillati eḥetam lakh* (Isa. 48:9). In the first part of the verse, which is not cited in the bahiric text, God speaks of postponing his wrath for the sake of his name, *le-maʿan shemi aʾarikh appi*. Utilizing the exegetical principle of parallelism, which is operative at the contextual level, we may deduce that the holding in of the glory is an expression of God's compassion, his long-suffering or, to be even more precise, the elongation of his breath. What is held in? The glory, which is identified further as the praise of David, the exaltation of the name. The daughter, who co/habits with both her father and brother, is the praise that is retained, the breath that is held in, yet nothing is lacking—even nothing is no lack for one that lacks nothing but lack—as the spring of blessing erupts perpetually to water the garden.

It is plausible that the parabolic image of a king cutting rocks and carving stones in the effort to build his palace alludes to divine creativity through inscription, since this, too, occurs by removing material or making a space by hollowing out the surface upon which letters are engraved or etched. *Shaʿashuʿa* is a bemusing tied to the act of writing and the object written upon. Especially against this background, the holding in of the glory will become most palpable as the persistence of speech in the silencing of silence, the reverberation of inscription in the erasing of erasure.[99] Moving beyond the positing of two elements that would have to be resolved dialectically, we can imagine a convergence of opposites whereby opposites are identical by reason of being opposites. In the indiscriminate unity of the Godhead, can we picture going-out that is not taking-in, taking-out that is not going-in, inside that is not outside, outside that is not inside, beginning that is not end, end that is not beginning?

Shaʿashuʿa, as we have seen, concomitantly denotes mental activity and sexual desire. One may well translate this term as it is used in *Sefer ha-Bahir* and in later works of kabbalah by the Lacanian expression *jouissance*, that is, the ecstatic state of orgasmic unity wherein the self of consciousness does not relate to the other in its heterogeneity.[100] *Jouissance* is the happiness that does not concern an other, the drive that has no other, the surplus enjoyment that defies signification, what Lacan himself calls "knowledge of the real."[101] No sooner do we inch forward than we are sent back to retrace our steps. What is a drive without an other, a turning-toward without regard for the other? Even in the absence of the self of an other, self-consciousness is predicated on othering the other as the other of self. For Lacan, as I discussed in chapter three, the real is associated with feminine *jouissance*, which, paradoxically, designates both the "substantial hard kernel that precedes and resists symbolization" and the "left-over, which is posited or 'produced' by symbolization itself."[102] Though *jouissance* is the surplus-enjoyment of the feminine, which is nonexistence as such and not some ineffable fullness of being, one is left with the sense that for Lacan, there is no way to get to the impenetrable opacity of the other, the "real" that defies signification or metaphoricization, but through the symbolic structure of the same.[103]

On this account *jouissance* is an expression of the phallic impulse for an other that is identically different in the identity of difference, an other that can be realized only in the fantasy-space of the (homo)erotic imagination of the male seeking himself in the mirror of the other. The primal drive has thus been described aptly as the "self-sufficient closed circuit of the deadly compulsion-to-repeat. The paradox is this: that which cannot ever be memorized, symbolized by way of its inclusion into the narrative frame, is not some fleeting moment of the past, forever lost, but the very insistence of drive as that which *cannot ever be forgotten* in the first place, since it repeats itself incessantly."[104] Žižek astutely draws the implications of this reversal of the imaginary and the real—the other is real only as the metaphorical simulation of reality framed by a fantasy considered to be the fantasy of reality[105]—for the domain of human sexuality: "The whole point of Lacan's insistence on the 'impossibility of sexual relationship' is that this, precisely, is what the 'actual' sexual act is; man's partner is never a woman in the real kernel of her being, but woman qua *a*, reduced to the fantasy-object (let us recall Lacan's definition of the phallic enjoyment as essentially masturbatory)!"[106]

In the incessant compulsion to repeat anew lies the psychical import of the kabbalistic myth of *shaʿashuʿa*, the crisscrossing of time and being, language and eros, in the consciousness that seeks the other as itself and itself as the other.[107] The obsessional drive of the male to reiterate is the beginning that can never be forgotten since it is the locus of memory yet to be remembered. The underpinning of narcissism—the strangeness to difference, to paraphrase Freud[108]—is poetically captured in the mythical image of the uroboros, the serpent biting its tail, consciousness contemplating the self as other in the unconscious prism of the other as self, parting of one in unity of two. The convergence of narcissism, thought, and (auto)eroticism implied in the use of *shaʿashuʿa* in the bahiric text had a profound impact on elaborations of this theme in subsequent kabbalistic treatises.

The symbols of mythic discourse expressing the narcissistic nature of divine eros in kabbalistic works can be translated into philosophical concepts current in the late Middle Ages. We can thus speak of the myth of *shaʿashuʿa* as an articulation of the splintering of the indivisible unity of divine wisdom into the opposite principles of bestowing and receiving, which are valenced respectively as masculine and feminine. More precisely, preserved in the bahiric anthology is a medieval reworking of an archaic mythologoumenon wherein the originary oneness, the one that is even before any thought of God rises to the head, is divided into a unity of three: father, daughter, and son, *alef*, *beit*, and *gimmel*.

This engendering myth, although significantly embellished, persisted as one of the most enduring and influential structures that informed the imagination of later kabbalists.

I will cite here one of countless examples. Ezra of Gerona comments on the rabbinic dictum, "Greater is the one who answers *amen* than the one who makes the blessing,"[109] "for *amen* alludes to wisdom, and thus it says 'I was with him as a confidant' [*amon*] (Prov. 8:30), and *amen* is the integration of the ten emanations [*ḥibbur eser sefirot*] and the unity of everything [*yiḥud ha-kol*]."[110] The intent of this statement is brought into sharper focus by looking at what appears to be a later interpretative gloss on Ezra's text preserved in a manuscript collection of early kabbalistic material. According to this passage, the word *amen* "numerically equals the two names of four letters,"[111] that is *amen* = 91 = *yhwh adonai* = 26 + 54. This is certainly a credible explanation, for Geronese kabbalists, as we may deduce from texts that have been preserved, imaged the unity of ten *sefirot* as the union of the name and its epithet, the masculine and feminine potencies respectively. It seems to me, however, that the intent of Ezra's remark may be cast somewhat differently. The word *amen* denotes the unity of ten *sefirot* circumscribed within the circle that begins and ends with wisdom, the head recalling what will come at the end anticipating what has come at the head. The motif is attested in the following tradition that Jacob ben Sheshet reports in the name of Isaac the Blind:

> Unite [*hitḥabber*] with the supernal faith [*ha-emunah ha-elyonah*] or the supernal wisdom [*ha-ḥokhmah ha-elyonah*], for the name of one is like that of the other, and one is conjoined [*daveq*] to that which comprises all 613 commandments, as they said "Ḥabakuk came and established them on one, as it says, 'the righteous will live in his faith' " (Hab. 2:4).[112] And, in another place, it says, "Wisdom enlivens her masters" (Eccles. 7:12). It follows that faith is wisdom and wisdom is faith, and it is that which envelops the holy One, blessed be he, as it says, "who is mighty like you, O Lord? Your faithfulness surrounds you" (Ps. 89:9), and it says, "in your faithfulness, answer me, in your righteousness" (ibid., 143:1), as if he bound him by an oath. Thus I heard from the mouth of the pious one R. Isaac the son of the great master R. Abraham, may the memory of the righteous be for a blessing, who said it in the name of his father.[113]

If Jacob ben Sheshet is to be trusted, and there seems to be no compelling reason not to do so, the conception of the sefirotic pleroma forming the unbroken circle of wisdom, which is also identified as faith, is a tradition he heard from Isaac the Blind, who received it from his father Abraham ben David of Posquiéres, and he, in turn, from his father. The same idea is affirmed in another statement of Jacob ben Sheshet, but in this case in the name of Ezra: "The saying [*ha-ma'amar*] is Wisdom, which extends from above to below in the edifice, and it was contained in everything [*bi-khelal ha-kol*]."[114] The creative utterance of God is latched to the attribute of wisdom, which comprises all the emanations of the sefirotic edifice. In yet another passage, Jacob ben Sheshet relates the circular portrayal of the *sefirot* to an interpretation of the rabbinic ruling[115] that one must juxtapose the blessing about redemption (*ge'ullah*) with the silent standing prayer (*tefillah*). According to Jacob's explication, the rationale for the liturgical practice is "not because redemption receives from prayer, for prayer is in Ein Sof and redemption is the end of things . . . but rather because their end is fixed in their beginning."[116] Prayer is correlated with the infinite beyond manifestation, which in this context seems to be coextensive with the first manifestation, "the will that is the cause of every thing, hidden and concealed" (*ha-raṣon sibbat kol davar we-hu nistar we-neʿelam*),[117] and redemption with *Shekhinah*, last of the emanations. The aforementioned halakhic decree underscores the mystical ideal of the uroboric unity of the emanations, the beginning fixed in the end and the end in the beginning, according to the oft-cited locution of *Sefer Yeṣirah*.

As it happens, a text written by Ezra's younger colleague Azriel of Gerona confirms this interpretation:

> One may cause the source of blessing to overflow and to draw it down in the measure that is appropriate to it. Thus one should not diminish from its recitation, cut off any of its letters, rush the reading of any of them, or answer *amen* superfluously. . . . Therefore the blessing is called *emunah* in accordance with the one who responds *amen*. . . . The one who answers *amen* is like one who says, "Let God's power be great" (Num. 14:17). Since faith [*emunah*] is from Ein-Sof, he says *amen*, and it is like one who says that in faith the nurse raises the infant steadfastly [*ke-omer ba-emunah ha-omen megaddel ha-umman be-amen*]. . . . The one who answers *amen* faithfully [*ba-emunah*] augments the source of the blessing and this is greater than the one who augments the blessing from the blessing rather than from the source.[118]

In a second passage, Azriel formulates this idea as an interpretation of the aggadic theme that figured prominently in the bahiric pericope discussed above: the delight that God enjoyed with Torah two thousand years prior to the creation of the world. Expressing the matter in a somewhat more technical philosophical manner, Azriel draws out the conceptual correlation between the autogenesis of divine wisdom, portrayed symbolically by the rabbinic notion of the primordial Torah, the eros of *shaʿashuʿa*, and the unfathomable texture of temporality that is beyond the measurable time of physical entities:

> Those days are not the days of humanity [*yemei adam*], for the measure [*middah*] for the days of humanity was not yet made, and those days were from the days whence are the years that cannot be probed, as it is written, "God is greater than we can know; the number of his years cannot be counted" (Job 36:26), and it is written, "Are your days the days of a mortal, are your days the years of a man?" (Job 10:5). Rather, when it arose in thought to bring the will that does not cease into actuality, the Torah was created, which preceded by two thousand years, which are two days. And the Torah came to exist at first and all the paths of the will emanated in it, and it was filled with those days until completion, and its paths were intended to draw forth in truth and candor so that it be perfected in vision [*marʾah*], narration [*sippur*], understanding [*havanah*], knowledge [*yediʿah*], guidance [*hakhanah*], probing [*ḥaqirah*], and proclamation [*amirah*], and this is the delight [*shaʿashuʿa*] as it says, "I delight in your laws" [*be-ḥuqqoteikha eshtaʿasha*] (Ps. 119:16). The one who contemplates

> [*mistakkel*] a matter whence he derives pleasure is referred to as one who is bemused [*mishtaʿasheʿa*] from the expression "he paid no heed" [*lo shaʿah*] (Gen. 4:5), in order to draw forth into it the flux of wisdom [*meshekh ha-ḥokhmah*] without pause from beginning to end.[119]

Spanish kabbalists articulated a philosophical rendering of the older mythic image preserved in *Bahir*—indeed traces of this strategy are already discernible in some of the bahiric fragments that reflect a Provençal redaction—and spoke of the ten *sefirot* as an expression of divine thought, the primordial Torah, the wisdom represented by *yod*, graphically a point, the smallest of all Hebrew letters, but numerically equal to ten and hence the appropriate mathematical cipher to designate the pleroma of divine effluence, the one that is ten in being ten that are one. A striking formulation of this motif is found in *Baddei ha-Aron u-Migdal Ḥananel* of Shem Tov Ibn Gaon, a text that I have mentioned in the preceding chapter:

> This is the principle of the matters said with regard to the twenty-two letters of the Torah, for the number instructs about the form to be remembered, and in this the sage will not err and he will not forget the form of each letter according to its pattern. . . . When the will arose from Ein Sof to create his world and to renew it, the small point was in the *yod* . . . for this is the first letter of the unique name [*shem ha-meyuḥad*] sealed with the primary wisdom. It illustrates in its form two sides corresponding to the two potencies that came to be within it, the first potency, the supernal *Keter*, which is the first of the enumerations, since *Ḥokhmah* emanates from it, and the second, the *yod* itself, which is in its wisdom . . . . Thus it was the head of *alef*, to instruct about the true, perfect unity . . . comprising the forms of all the letters in the mind of every enlightened kabbalist [*be-sekhel kol maskil mequbbal*] upon whom the holy spirit is manifest,[120] the spirit of wisdom by way of the occult truth [*al derekh ha-emet ba-nistar*].[121]

Utilizing the signature expression of Naḥmanides to flag a kabbalistic exposition, *al derekh ha-emet* ("by way of truth"), Shem Tov coins the phrase *al derekh ha-emet ba-nistar* ("by way of the occult truth"), but in his case, the expression denotes the infusion of holy spirit by means of which the enlightened kabbalist gains insight into the nature of the Hebrew letters. All twenty-two letters are comprised in the *yod* that is orthographically set in the head of *alef*, which signifies the "true, perfect unity" (*aḥdut shalem amitti*).[122] Secret gnosis, therefore, is enwrapped, as it were, in knowledge of *yod*, the "inclusion of everything" (*kelal ha-kol*),[123] that is, the totality of the divine pleroma. Elsewhere Shem Tov articulates the matter as a tradition he received with regard to a passage in *Sefer Yeṣirah*[124]: "from *alef* to *yod* are engraved the ten that are known," a reference to the *sefirot*, which correspond to the first ten letters of the alphabet.

Alternatively, *yod*, which orthographically consists of the letter itself and its tip, denotes the first two emanations, *Keter* and *Ḥokhmah*. In the continuation, Shem Tov explains the formation of the rest of *alef*, with the *yod* on top extending through *waw* to *yod* on the bottom.[125] According to the tradition Shem Tov draws upon, the three components of *alef*—*yod-waw-yod*—numerically equal twenty-six, which is the sum of the letters of the Tetragrammaton. The import of the tradition is that the name is hidden within *alef*, the unknowable and ineffable nothing that bears the infinite fullness of divine being.[126] What is crucial for this discussion is that upper and lower *yod* correspond respectively to the upper and lower *Ḥokhmah*, personified as father and daughter, and they are connected by *waw*, which is the son. In the letter *alef* is a semiotic encoding of the older tradition regarding the triune identity of the primal ground, as I discussed at length in my analysis of the myth of the androgyne in *Sefer ha-Bahir*.[127] The totality of the name, encapsulated in the first letter of the alphabet, is expressive of divine wisdom. In the passage where the emergence of *yod* as a separate letter is described, Shem Tov makes the point explicitly: "Since 'their end is in their beginning,' *yod* came forth, for it was is the head of *alef*, and its tail through the overturning [*hippukh*] of its form so that it will be marked and engraved of its own accord, the tenth, the first and last, as it is written, 'wisdoms[128] have built the house' (Prov. 9:1)."[129]

The ontological principle of kabbalistic symbolism par excellence thus relates to the paradox of the one and the many as refracted through the mythic lens of the self-enclosed circle of wisdom, which is identified as faith. This is the intent of Azriel's comments cited above: The one who faithfully answers *amen* augments the source of blessing, the infinite, whence faith issues forth. The unity of *sefirot* is alluded to in the cryptic remark of Azriel, "it is like one who says that in faith the nurse raises the infant steadfastly" (*ke-omer ba-emunah ha-omen megaddel ha-umman be-amen*). I suggest that *omen* denotes the upper wisdom and *umman* the lower wisdom, and *amen* the bond that unifies the two to express the indivisible threefold unity of God.

Another illustration of this orientation is found in the following passage from Todros Abulafia:

> Know that wisdom is at the head and wisdom is at the end [*ḥokhmah ba-ro'sh we-ḥokhmah ba-sof*] as the matter of "I am first and I am last" (Isa. 44:6), and in *Sefer Yeṣirah* they said, "his end is fixed in his beginning."[130] Moreover, for you I will allude to the perfect unity [*yiḥud ha-shalem*] in one small point, the most subtle, the smallest of letters, *yod* that is the name [YHWH], which comprises ten *sefirot belimah*[131] unified and attached to the flame that is bound to the coal[132] . . . and everything is in the power of the inner, pure thought, for all the flames and all the lights are united within it and their being [*qiyyumam*] is in it.[133]

All ten emanations are comprised within the smallest possible point, the letter *yod*, which is divine thought or wisdom. Monosophism is thus an appropriate if somewhat awkward term to demarcate the epistemological basis for the contemplative ideal of mystical union, ascension of human to divine thought, conjunction with wisdom, *yod* extending beyond to the iota crowning its head. But is this monosophism not at the same time monopsychism?[134] If we locate the underlying unity in the self-enclosed circle of divine thought, do we not end with a speculative version of the uroboric myth, thought thinking itself, the mirror mirroring the mirror in the mirrored of the mirror? In emulation of that unity, the kabbalist seeks to be reintegrated within the circle of wisdom to the point that the individual is absorbed in the universal, which, paradoxically, both comprises and is comprised by everything—at the highest point, technically before the emergence of the primary point, *yod*, which is divine wisdom, the *kelal*, the formal principle of inclusion and expansion, becomes the *keli*, the material principle of exclusion and constriction, that is, in language utilized by kabbalists beginning in the sixteenth century, light that encompasses from without (*or maqif*) and light that is encompassed from within (*or penimi*) are no longer distinguishable as autonomous entities.

This is the mystical import of faith, the paradoxical identity of beginning and end, for, in a circle, beginning is end and end beginning, even if, logically speaking, beginning cannot begin nor ending end. Abulafia articulates this view explicitly in his commentary on the rabbinic dictum (which he attributes to R. Ḥisda)[135] regarding one who elongates the response of *amen* to a blessing beyond the specified measure of time: "Know that the word *amen* unites all things from beginning [*ro'sh*] to end [*sof*], and it is from the terminology *emunah omen*, for it unites *emunah* with *amen*. . . . Thus the one who responds *amen* is greater than the one who blesses, for *amen* joins wisdom to wisdom, and hence it says, 'I was with him as a confidant, a source of delight every day' (Prov. 8:30). It follows that *amen* is the unity of everything [*yiḥud ha-kol*]."[136]

The implicit narcissism of the portrayal of God's wisdom is rendered more explicit in the symbolic representations of the Castilian kabbalists responsible for many of the layers that constitute the brocaded weave of the zoharic corpus. The emanation of *sefirot* is described in various passages as proliferation of wisdom; "You made them all through wisdom" (Ps. 104:24) served as a critical prooftext to anchor this idea. The emanative scheme is perceived as the projection of wisdom from concealment to disclosure, a transition that is depicted in mythical and philosophical terms. One of the distinctive contributions of zoharic kabbalists, as I have argued in a previously published study,[137] relates to the imaginary account of the linguistic evolution of God's becoming as a process of spermatogenesis, a mythopoeic analogue to the metaphysical supposition regarding the concept of self-movement on the part of the first and, presumably, unmovable cause,[138] the solipsistic umbilicus of autoaffection interrupted by desire for self-representation. On this account, language in its originary comportment expresses—graphically and phonically—the impulse to overflow, to procreate, the limitless will willfully limited by the unfolding of the other enfolded in the self, an idea greatly expanded and embellished in Lurianic sources.

How do we explain this arousal? We must presume a state of nondifferentiation or equanimity prior to this awakening in which it is not possible to distinguish polarities. Here it is relevant to recall the remark of Simeon Lavi (cited in chapter two) that in the "depths of the Nothing" the masculine force of overflowing and the feminine force of receiving "were in one unity."[139] I have offered what seems to me to be the two approaches to explain the nature of this unity: one that affirms the identity of difference (neither one nor the other is discernible but one and the other are distinguishable) and the other that abrogates difference of identity (neither one nor the other is discernible for the other is completely contained in the one to the point that they are indistinguishable). One way or another, the logic of the symbolism would necessitate that to attain the state of nondifferentiated oneness, it is necessary to go through the polarity that characterizes the emanations that issue forth from the boundless.

The explication of this moment when the limitless is delimited—though not a moment at all, as it is the coming to be of time in the saying-showing of the measure that delimits the limitless in the limitless delimitation, the measure of ten *sefirot* that are infinite, *middatan eser she-ein lahem sof*—can be seen only from the perspective of polarity that is attributed to the One beyond polarity. To express the matter from a different conceptual standpoint, since the infinite is fully present, the only thing from which it can be absent is absence. This, it seems, is the kabbalistic explanation for alterity, which is invariably linked to the emergence and constitution of the feminine (in Lurianic terms, *binyan ha-nuqba*) as a distinct entity, a mythotheosophic reading of the creation narrative in the second chapter of Genesis, as I have previously noted.

Before the beginning—and what makes the beginning possible in the depths of the nondual Nothing—springs forth the phallic impulse to bestow, but in absence of an other, a vessel, to receive the bestowal, this will is hard-pressed to come to fruition. In this sense, paraphrasing the poet William Everson, we can speak of a passion for elseness lurking in the root;[140] otherness must be seen as emerging from the primal need to overflow.[141] *Shaʿashuʿa* is the autoerotic arousal of the male, but this desire is dependent on the construction of a feminine other to receive. In the symbolic language of kabbalists, erotic awakening always begins from the left, an idea linked exegetically in many sources to the verse "his left hand under my head and his right hand embraces me" (Song 2:6). In great measure, the mythopoeic image, as striking and daring as it seems, is an articulation of the philosophical speculation on the emanation of divine wisdom from undifferentiated unity to unified differentiation.

As I explored in length in the previous chapter, the seed of wisdom whence the sefirotic emanations bloom is made up of Hebrew letters, a theosophical principle reflected in the cosmological presumption that all things are made of letters and the more specific anthropological assumption that the fetus of the Jew is constituted by those letters in a special way, a correspondence that is not of the same sort as all other nations, indeed all other created things.[142] Kabbalistic ontology, therefore, presumes that corporeality is constituted most elementally by literality, as we explored in great depth in the previous chapter. Nothing is more fundamentally embodied than the letters of the Hebrew alphabet through which divine, angelic, and all sentient forms are configured, for the letters are the "basic stuff," the flesh of that which is to be accounted real.

The theogonic myth—the eternal becoming-in-time of the temporal being of the eternal—is portrayed as an inscripting of this textual body. At the beginning—before there was a before after which to speak of—is *shaʿashuʿa*, the division within the indivisible, solidifying rupture in the relatedness of God's nothing but everything that appears at-the-moment. Language is disclosed in the opening of that closure—an audible seeing, a visual hearing, phoneme/grapheme, grapheme/phoneme, written as spoken, spoken as written. According to a tradition of Isaac the Blind reported by Jacob ben Sheshet, the intent of the rabbinic locution that God looked at Torah prior to creating the world is that "he saw the essences [*hawwayot*] in himself, for the essences were from Wisdom, and from those essences, which were the essences of Wisdom, he discerned that they would be revealed in the future."[143]

Appropriating and expanding in their cultural key the nexus between eros and noesis, particularly through the influence of the Platonic ideal of intellectual eros,[144] early kabbalists depicted the process of emanation as a progression from the silence of the infinite to the articulation of language in three distinct phases: thought, voice, and speech, which correspond respectively in many passages to the second, sixth, and tenth of the ten gradations of the divine pleroma, *Ḥokhmah, Tif'eret,* and *Malkhut,* also characterized by the symbolic archetypes of father, son, and daughter.[145] The kabbalistic account of the emergence of language—the semiotic configuration of the divine form—is predicated on an erogenic explanation of speech in both written and oral forms, since thought is viewed principally in sexual and indeed phallomorphic terms.[146] God both scripts and declaims the emanations; indeed, as I have already noted, the verbal gesture that engenders the divine body is concurrently spoken and written, written and spoken, two complementary and coterminous events.

Another dimension of the theogonic myth is made explicit in passages that proffer the image of the letters emerging from the womb of *Binah,* the third emanation, whence the lower seven emanations come forth. In terms of historical development, we can mark this spot as the expansion of the archaic triadic structure into the fourfold, the symbol of the mother complementing the father, son, and daughter, a theme that in zoharic literature plays an important role in the imaginary Jewish-Christian polemic, establishing a quaternity in the Godhead according to the Jewish esoteric tradition that is superior to the trinity of the Christian faith. Significantly, the addition of the fourth arises from the demarcation of *Binah* as mother, the womb that receives the seed of *Ḥokhmah,* the composition of which is the Hebrew letters. The pleroma, accordingly, is depicted with the image of four nodules: wisdom (or thought), understanding, voice, and speech, which correspond respectively to *Ḥokhmah* (or *Maḥshavah*), *Binah, Tif'eret,* and *Malkhut.*[147]

On the surface the distinction between *qol* and *dibbur,* voice and speech, is puzzling: Can there be voice without speech? To be sure, the reverse phenomenon is well attested, but what is the logical possibility of unspoken speech? What is a voice without speech but inarticulate, and what is an inarticulate voice, after all is said and done? But that is precisely the point: There can be no voice without speech, just as there can be no male without female. With the articulation of voice, the emanative process reaches its terminus in the engendering of speech. What is from one vantage point graphic inscription is from another oral recitation. Rather than view these as distinct fields of discourse, they must be considered disparate but intersecting vectors of a phenomenal field whose contours are repeatedly changing, evolving, decaying. Indeed, one might say, for the kabbalist language emerges at the intersecting point between oral speech and written text. As Scholem well expressed it: "For the Kabbalists, linguistic mysticism is at the same time a mysticism of writing. Every act of speaking . . . is at once an act of writing and every writing is potential speech."[148] In a second passage, he elaborates:

> For the kabbalist, evidently, language-mysticism is at the same time a mysticism of script and of letters. The relation between script and language is a constitutive prin-

> ciple for the Kabbalah. In the spiritual world, every act of speaking is concurrently an act of writing, and conversely every writing is potential speech, destined to become audible. The speaker engraves, as it were, the three-dimensional space of the word on the plane of the ether. The script, which for the philologist is only a secondary and otherwise rather useless image of real speech, is for the kabbalist the true repository of its secrets.[149]

As is often the case, Scholem's penchant for the dialectical enabled him to embrace what might strike the ear as a contradiction. Affirming both elements of the antinomy, Scholem astutely observed that the kabbalistic understanding of language necessitates the affirmation of the simultaneity of oral and written.[150] The dichotomy of the oral versus writing, which has been used both to legitimate distinct typological approaches and to chart the historical transition from one phase of esoteric cultivation to another, is rendered methodologically problematic, for the complex interplay of these two modalities in kabbalistic theosophy precludes such a polarization, though we can surely find kabbalists speaking (or, as the case may be, writing) of one modality to the exclusion of the other.

In sum, the portrayal of God's creativity is predicated on a mythopoeic conception of language wherein spoken and written are fused together in a prelogical and predialogical moment, if it is at all possible to use the word "moment" to refer to this moment before there is any moment: The written text is spoken even as the spoken word is written. Through the interplay of oral and graphic, word and image converge—image is the word that is the image, and word the image that is the word. Visual imagery, therefore, can be expressed as well in auditory terms and vice versa; as far as I can tell, there is no basis in kabbalistic epistemology to separate the two, even if preference is on occasion given to one over the other.[151]

Poetic Confrontation / Desiring (An)Other

The focus of the contemplative life is the imaginal envisioning of the invisible form, the seeing of the hidden secret revealed in the concealment of its revelation, concealed in the revelation of its concealment. Speech originates from the unspoken, the absence dissembling as present in the presence dissembling as absence. Eros, which kabbalists identify as the phallic potency, overflows, one might say, in the depletion of this dissembling. From this perspective we can, following Blanchot's postmodern retrieval of an archaic insight, speak of mystical consciousness as "thought that thinks more than itself" or desire that "cannot be satisfied and that does not desire union with what it desires" since it "desires what the one who desires has no need of, what is not and what the one who desires has no desire to attain, it being the very desire for what must remain inaccessible and foreign—a desire of the other as other."[152]

Here we hear—or glimpse, as the case may be—a resonance of the Levinasian *l'autre*, the face that can be neither faced for what it is nor effaced for what it is not, an in/essentiality that cannot be met head on but through the veil of the other. Blanchot, at least in this passage, falls short of moving in the direction of Levinas, toward an other for whom I must assume infinite moral responsibility, all things being equal. What is crucial for our discussion is the question of whether there is a way to read kabbalistic symbolism through the prism of desire for the other as other, a desire, perforce, that cannot be fulfilled except as desire deferred, insofar as the other in her or his otherness can never be fully addressed or consumed—the other can never be *my* other and remain other in relation to me. From one perspective it seems the response would be negative, as kabbalists, both theosophic and ecstatic, wrote of and no doubt cultivated meditational practices with the aim of becoming one with the source of all being, reattaching the branches to the root, to use one of various indigenous metaphors employed by the mystical adepts. The logical implication of this trajectory is a metaphysical monism that can be translated psychomythically into the language of narcissism—all that is real is the one that comprises and is comprised by all—the symbolic underpinning of the secret of illicit sexuality, as I suggested in chapter four.

Yet in spite of the well-attested yearning on the part of kabbalists to unite with the divine through contemplative exercises and even the explicit descriptions of the ecstatic experience as cleaving to Ein Sof, the symbolic rendering of divine thought as thought that must be thought as thought that cannot be thought, the unthinkable thought, thought of the unthinkable, yields the paradox of desire attainable only as unattainable and unattainable as attainable.[153] Consider the following account of *devequt* offered by Azriel of Gerona: From the potency of the infinite come forth,

> all the finite existents in the moment that is appropriate for them, and when thought that has a limit clutches the foundation of limit [*yesod ha-gevul*], there is no limit to limit [*ein gevul la-gevul*], for thought is garbed in the light of the spiritual life . . . and it ascends to contemplate [*lehistakkel*] in the inwardness of itself until the negation of its capacity to comprehend it, and its negation is the beginning of the will that comprises all desires.[154]

The "foundation of limit" (*yesod gevul*) is limitless, and hence when one's thought, which is finite, a point that Azriel confirms by appealing to the opinion of the philosophers,[155] is conjoined thereto, it assumes the seemingly paradoxical state of being both limited and unlimited, *ein gevul la-gevul* ("there is no limit to limit"), the very same status that Azriel ascribes to the *sefirot* vis-à-vis Ein Sof, that is, they are *koaḥ bi-gevul mi-beli gevul* ("finite power that is unlimited").[156] Difference of some sort is maintained, as the boundless bounded extends beyond its bounds to the boundless bounded within the boundlessness of the bound. Azriel, as with his older colleague Ezra, does speak of human thought and divine wisdom as being one (*hu we-hi davar eḥad*), though the proof-text to which this idea is linked is important to recall: "Say unto wisdom you are my sister" (Prov. 7:4). The image of "sister" suggests to me the unity of two branches stemming from one root. We can speak of the identity of branch and root precisely because they are different in the manner of siblings who are one in virtue of being separate.

I propose, therefore, that in kabbalistic texts we witness a tension between what Blanchot refers to as metaphysical desire for the other, "desire for that with which one has never been united," on the one hand, and Platonic eros, which is the "nostalgic desire for lost unity, the movement of return toward true Being," on the other.[157] Surely, as I wrote at some length in the previous chapter, medieval kabbalah is indebted to the Neoplatonic principle of return to the source, a return that is framed in decidedly erotological language. The true Being to which one desires to revert is beyond being, *hyperousios*, the surplus that cannot be ontologized. The desire for transcendence, therefore, embraces the eros of the impossible, a desire that must perforce remain unfulfilled if it is to be the desire it seeks to be, the "limit-experience" of "what is outside the whole when the whole excludes every outside; the experience of what is still to be attained when all is attained and of what is still to be known when all is known: the inaccessible, the unknown itself."[158] Blanchot, paradoxically, refers to the "limit-experience" as "the experience of non-experience,"[159] for it is the experience of "thought thinking that which will not let itself be thought; thought thinking more than it is able by an affirmation that affirms more than can be affirmed. This more itself is the experience: affirming only by an excess of affirmation and, in this surplus, affirming without anything being affirmed—finally affirming nothing."[160]

As thought leads not to the unthinkable but to the unthought, so speech leads not to silence but to unsaying, saying nothing, but a *saying* nonetheless, affirmation of negation rather than negation of affirmation, the event of nothing, which is to be distinguished from the nonevent of something, the without-limit in virtue of which every linguistic sign is transposed into a symbol that is the other of itself.[161] Traditional kabbalists (in line with the apophaticism of Neoplatonic speculation) assume there is a reality beyond language, a superessentiality that transcends the finite categories of reason and speech, but this reality is accessible phenomenologically only through language. Silence, therefore, is not to be set in binary opposition to language, but it is rather the margin that demarcates its center. Here it is of relevance to recall a comment of Wittgenstein in the preface to the *Tractatus*:

> The whole sense of the book might be summed up in the following words: what can be said at all can be said clearly, and what we cannot talk about we must pass over in silence. Thus the aim of the book is to draw a limit to thought, or rather—not to thought, but to the expression of thoughts: for in order to be able to draw a limit to thought, we should have to find both sides of the limit thinkable (i.e. we should have to be able to think what cannot be thought). It will therefore only be in language that the limit can be drawn, and what lies on the other side of the limit will simply be nonsense.[162]

Implicit in this remark is the intricate nexus of thought and language, one of the rudiments of the philosophic disposition: What can be thought can be expressed; what cannot be expressed cannot be thought. The *Tractatus*, the reader is told emphatically, deals with the former and not the latter. Yet, as Wittgenstein is quick to point out, to draw the limit (*die Grenze*) of thought or, to be more precise, "expression of thoughts" (*den Ausdruck der Gedanken*), one must know both sides of the thinkable limit, what can and cannot be thought and, by extension, what can and cannot be said. In this context, Wittgenstein labels the unthinkable and unsayable as "nonsense" (*der Unsinn*), a technical term that connotes, strictly speaking, that nothing may be spoken of that which is beyond the limit that may be thought, the unthinkable.

In the concluding remarks of the *Tractatus*, Wittgenstein links the "inexpressible" (*Unaussprechlich*) explicitly with the mystical: "There are, indeed, things that cannot be put into words. They *make themselves manifest.* They are what is mystical [*Dies zeigt sich, es das Mystische*]. . . . What we cannot speak about we must pass over in silence [*Wovon man nicht sprechen kann, darüber muss man schweigen*]."[163] With the mentioning of what cannot be mentioned the reader has come full circle but, having endured the journey, she or he knows that the nonsensical is not unreal; on the contrary, for the one who considers in thought what cannot be thought, the latter is what shows itself, imagined to be real; the nonsense of silence is precisely what accords sense to language, saying nothing that facilitates saying anything.[164]

In another aphorism that appears slightly before the one cited above, Wittgenstein makes the point by linking the inescapable limit of language and confronting the ultimate metaphysical inquiry, the question of being as such, of why there is something rather than nothing: "Not *how* the world is, is the mystical, but *that* it is" (*Nicht wie die Welt ist, ist das Mystische, sondern dass sie ist*).[165] Wittgenstein elaborates the matter in a remark preserved in a different literary context worthy of citation: "Man feels the urge to run up against the limits of language. Think for example of the astonishment that anything at all exists. This astonishment cannot be expressed in the form of a question, and there is no answer whatever. Anything we might say is *a priori* bound to be mere nonsense."[166] In the *Tractatus*, Wittgenstein adds that the mystical consists of feeling the world as a "limited whole" (*begrenztes Ganzes*), a feeling that is linked to the perception of the world from the viewpoint of the eternal (*die Anschauung der Welt* sub specie aeterni). Wittgenstein, doubtless aware of the conceptual link made between "mysticism" and the experience of oneness, accords to the mystical a worldview based on contemplation of the whole, albeit one that is limited.

Needless to say, the universe that emerges from Wittgenstein's *Tractatus* is quite distant from medieval kabbalah. For example, his statement that "God does not reveal himself *in* the world" (*Gott offenbart sich nicht in der Welt*)[167] falls short of grasping the kabbalistic paradox of the veil discussed in the previous chapter: the manner in which the world both is and is not the manifestation of God. His embracing of the mystical, moreover, is tied to his understanding of the role of philosophy "to say nothing except what can be said, i.e. propositions of natural science—i.e. something that has nothing to do with philosophy—and then, whenever someone else wanted to say something metaphysical, to demonstrate to him that he had failed to give a meaning to certain signs in his propositions."[168] The one who receives this response may not be satisfied, but Wittgenstein insists it is the "only strictly correct one." Consequently, Wittgenstein's own propositions "serve as elucidations in the following way: anyone who understands me eventually recognizes them as nonsensical, when he has used them—as steps—to climb up beyond them. (He must, so to speak, throw away the ladder after he has climbed up it)."[169]

Philosophic logic cannot refute skepticism by providing a verbal answer, but it can illustrate that the question itself cannot be verbalized, and when the question cannot be put into words, one should not expect the answer in words.[170] Though Wittgenstein characterized his propositions as a ladder that may be discarded when one has reached the top, having reviewed his thinking in the *Tractatus* and related sources, I think it reasonable to say that, more characteristically, he provides an analytic argument to avoid disentangling the apophatic and kataphatic: Mystical silence is the spoken unspoken determined from the vantage point of the unspoken spoken. As he put it in another work, "Perhaps what is inexpressible (what I find mysterious and am not able to express) is the background against which whatever I could express has its meaning."[171] It is precisely the clarification of this point that justifies the brief excursion into some of the complexities of Wittgenstein's thought. From the ontological standpoint adopted by traditional kabbalists, we can say that the superessential being is conceived only as being-other-than-what-is-conceived—*mah she-ha-maḥshavah einah masseget*, according to the language attributed to Isaac the Blind—but in being so conceived, this being-not, which is to be distinguished from not being, is the object of contemplation.

We remember the account of the *via contemplativa* by Isaac of Acre cited and discussed in chapter three: The name, YHWH, is the ladder to the nameless, a ladder that is not dispensable (as Wittgenstein argued with respect to his own propositions), for the ascent to the nameless on every occasion is through the name. The Tetragrammaton is the model to convey the paradoxical confluence of the hidden and revealed that must always be held together in the middle excluded by the logic of the excluded middle: the prohibition of pronouncing the name as it is written secures the fact that the epithet preserves the ineffability of the name just as the veil conceals the face it reveals by revealing the face it conceals. The main objective of the contemplative path is to be conjoined to Ein Sof, the limitless beyond all representation, but the only way to attain that end is through the agency of the name, which is the ladder that connects the finite to the infinite, the image to the imageless.

In this context, I would like to illustrate the phenomenon from the preamble to the depiction of the seven palaces (*heikhalin*, an Aramaicized form of *heikhalot*) on the side of holiness in the zoharic section on *Pequdei*, the concluding part of Exodus (38:21–40:38), which deals with decrees related to the tabernacle of the pact (*mishkan ha-edut*), the temporary and portable place of divine dwelling that purportedly accompanied the people of Israel in the sojourn in the desert:

> R. Simeon ben Yoḥai said: It has been taught with respect to these palaces that they exist to set the order of the praise [*lesaddera siddura di-shebaḥa*] of the holy One, blessed be he, whether the order that exists through word [*millah*] or the order that exists through intention [*reʿuta*], for there is an order that exists through word and there is an order that exists through intention and the focus of the heart [*reʿuta we-khawwana de-libba*] to know and contemplate [*lemindda u-leʾistakkela*], to contemplate upward until the infinite [*leʾistakkela leʿeila leʿeila ad ein of*]. For there are fixed all the intentions and thoughts, and they do not exist in word at all, but rather just as he is concealed, so all his words are in concealment [*kemah de-ihu satim hakhi kol milloy vi-setimu*].[172]

Attending to the liturgical dimension of the ascent through the palaces, a theme attested in older sources transmitted and studied under the rubric of Heikhalot literature, the author of the zoharic text emphasizes that this dimension is the essential component of the seven holy palaces. For the anonymous Castilian kabbalist, the ascent of prayers has two facets, the liturgical order constituted by the words of traditional prayers, and the second order composed of the inner intention and will that stands behind the words. The text reiterates the contemplative ideal of *maḥshavah ha-deveqah* enunciated by Provençal and Catalonian kabbalists, highlighted by the expression *lemindda u-le'istakkela le'istakkela le'eila le'eila ad ein sof* ("to know and contemplate, to contemplate upward until the infinite"). Particularly important to assessing this zoharic account of the contemplative ascent—the purpose of which is summarized succinctly at the end of the depiction of the first palace, "to unify the one in the other so that all is one in one mystery, to unite above and below as one, so that the holy name is complete"[173]—is the passageway through the seventh palace, which seems, for all intents and purposes, to be identical with *Shekhinah*:

> The seventh palace: This palace is more inward than all the other palaces. This palace is concealed [*setimu*] for there is no icon [*diyoqna*] in it and no body [*gufa*] at all; here is the concealment within the mystery of mysteries [*setimu dego raza de-razin*]. This is the mystery, which is the place to enter, through the supernal channels, the spirit of all spirits, the intention of all intentions, to join everything as one, the spirit of life, to make everything into one arrayment [*tiqquna ḥada*]. This palace is called the holy of holies, the place to receive the supernal soul, and it is called as such to arouse the world-to-come in relation to it. This world [*alma*] is called *olam*, and *olam* means ascent [*seliqa*], for the lower world ascends to the supernal world, and it is hidden within it, and it is concealed there, it is revealed in the concealment [*itgalya bi-setirah*].[174]

There is much that may be retrieved from this passage, but I shall limit my focus to what is most relevant to the themes of this chapter. The seventh palace is the most hidden of all the palaces, a distinction that is framed in terms of the tradition that there was no image in the holy of holies. That there is no image or body connotes in the above passage the secrecy that is associated with the seventh palace, referred to as the "concealment within the mystery of mysteries" (*setimu dego raza de-razin*), that is, the secret entryway through which souls pass in their ascent to the infinite. The ascent of the souls is at the same time an ascent of *Shekhinah*, the inner mystery of the seventh palace. By wordplay the term *olam*, "world," connotes ascent, *seliqa*, which is the Aramaic translation of *aliyyah*, and concealment, *illum*, and both connotations allude to the ascent of *Shekhinah* to *Binah*, the lower to the upper world, wherein she is disclosed in concealment.

The limit-experience knows no limit and thus it escapes the unification that would close the space that differentiates and thereby relates the subject and object of experience. The desire that remains desire is identified more specifically by Blanchot as the interior experience of poetry, which occupies the space,

> not of words but of the relations of words that—always preceding them and nonetheless given by them—is their moving suspension, the appearance of their disap-

pearance; the idea of this space as pure becoming; the idea of image and of shadow, of the double and of an absence "*more real than presence*"; that is, the experience of being that is image before it is object, and the experience of an art that is gripped by the violent difference that is prior to all representation and all knowledge; the idea, finally, of art as revolt—but the most grave revolt, although apparently not real.[175]

Encountering the impossible as immediate, the poet must rely on imagistic thinking that arises from but cannot succumb to mediated categories of human sentience.[176] To trespass the boundaries of speech, the poet has no recourse but to verbal images that are summoned poetically by gazing at the silence that precedes all representation.[177] At the center of the gaze is the blindness that sustains vision—the interminable possibility of seeing the impossible. In this blindness, vision persists not as the "possibility of seeing" but as the "impossibility of not seeing."[178] Poetic language "issues from its own absence, the way the image emerges upon the absence of the thing; a language addressing itself to the shadow of events as well, not to their reality, and this because of the fact that the words which express them are, not signs, but images, images of words, and words where things turn into images."[179]

Much like poets, kabbalists dangle in the confluence of the visual and verbal. Contemplation in the kabbalistic tradition is a poetic envisioning wherein words are seen as images and images are heard as words.[180] In this state, language becomes essential, not in the sense of denoting a reified essence but in terms of becoming an end in itself by no longer designating anything or giving voice to anyone. Blanchot is again particularly useful in expressing kabbalistic poetics in a contemporary idiom:

> The poetic word, then, is no longer opposed only to ordinary language, but also to the language of thought. In poetry we are no longer referred back to the world, neither to the world as shelter nor to the world as goals. In this language the world recedes and goals cease; the world falls silent; beings with their preoccupations, their projects, their activity are no longer ultimately what speaks. Poetry expresses the fact that beings are quiet. . . . The poetic word is no longer someone's word. In it no one speaks, and what speaks is not anyone. It seems rather that the word alone declares itself. Then language takes on all of its importance. It becomes essential. Language speaks as the essential, and that is why the word entrusted to the poet can be called the essential word. This means primarily that words, having the initiative, are not obliged to serve to designate anything or give voice to anyone, but that they have their ends in themselves.[181]

Writing the poem imposes a limit upon what has no limit and thereby allows the unspoken to be heard.[182]

The revolt of the poet against language through language in the attempt to portray what cannot be portrayed can be profitably compared to the desire to envision the invisible and to utter the ineffable on the part of one enlightened in the wisdom of kabbalah. Thus, for example, the matter was articulated at a relatively early stage by Azriel of

Gerona: "From the power of what is hidden [*koaḥ ha-nistar*] there emerges what is heard [*nishma*], and from what is heard what is seen [*nir'eh*]. We have no business with what is hidden,[183] but only with that which is heard."[184] The three levels correspond to different gradations of the divine, the auditory and visual issuing from the concealed. I would venture that the three moments may be correlated along a semiotic grid, the concealed with the unspoken, the heard with the phoneme, and the seen with the grapheme. Beyond what is seen is what is spoken, and beyond what is spoken is what is hidden, but the latter is inaccessible to human cognition except as the trace of what is inaudible and invisible in the gradations associated as the sites of audibility and visibility. In the mythical account of the engendering of the ineffable name is encrypted the esoteric method of transmitting secrets, to speak tacitly, to write invisibly, to cover openly. Beyond the word—inscripted, vocalized, contemplated—there are the letters that carry one into the clamor of silence.

An interesting formulation of the silence beyond language that is nevertheless a language is offered in a commentary on the prayers recently published and attributed to Judah ben Nissim Ibn Malka. According to the schema adopted by this kabbalist, the first of four alphabets is described as "supernal, pure, and holy, the cause of all alphabets, for it is not possible for there to be three sides [*batim*] without four dots. Even though the first point is the cause of the existence of *beit*, it is never to be counted as the first, and concerning this it says in *Sefer Yeṣirah* (1:6) 'before one what do you count?' "[185] To comprehend the point, one must appreciate that the letter *beit* is composed of the same consonants as the word *bayit*; moreover, the plural of the latter is *batim*, which is the term used to denote the three sides that make up the orthography of the letter. To have the three sides connected there must be four points, and hence the first of those points is said to be responsible for the formation of the letter.

That first point, moreover, symbolizes the supernal alphabet, which is described further as the "fount of all springs, which no intellect [*sekhel*] or thought [*maḥshavah*] can comprehend, nor can any eye or idea dominate it, for there is the light of the splendor and hiddenness, for it points to the essence devoid of all combination and mixture."[186] What can one say of an alphabet described as divested of all letter combinations? In the absence of these permutations, there are no words. Thus the first alphabet is one that has no discernible verbal communication. The primordial alphabet instructs us that there is an aspect of language that is not to be judged by the criterion of the scientific mentality in antiquity, the Middle Ages, or the present.

In contemplative envisioning, the kabbalist calls forth speech from silence in a manner that mimics the emanation of the sefirotic gradations from the hidden recesses of the infinite light that is darkness. From this perspective we can speak of the kabbalist poetically giving shape to reality through mystical discourse.[187] In his view, the sacred language of being, Hebrew, the "holy tongue" (*leshon ha-qodesh*) emanates from the "faint silent voice," *qol demamah daqqah* (1 Kings 19:12),[188] a symbolic reference to *Binah*, the locus of divine understanding.[189] Significantly, in one zoharic passage, *qol demamah daqqah* is identified as *tohu*, the primordial chaos, the "place that has no color or image," that which "is not contained in the secret of the image." It follows that when this voice is contemplated (*mistakkelan beih*), "it has no image at all," for "everything has a garment except for this one."[190] Note the conflation of sensory referents: of the "faint silent voice" it is said that it is a place, the empty place, the place of emptiness, *tohu*, the place that has no color or image, no garment, and hence the place that is invisible. There is a natural shift from the acoustic to the ocular, as these are widely considered by kabbalists to be two prisms through which a phenomenon is apprehended. What does one see when one contemplates the *qol demamah daqah*? A vision unseen, dimly clear, a subtle, silent voice, mutely spoken.[191]

In another zoharic passage, the attribution of *qol demamah daqqah* to *Binah* connotes both that the voice is the silence that is not heard on the outside and that the person must be silent when referring to it.[192] But how does the voice not heard on the outside sound, and how is one silent when referring to it? When spoken on the inside, it will be heard as the inaudible voice, "inner vision," in/sight, the image that cannot be seen, the word that cannot be spoken. I am here reminded of a crucial feature in the narrative rescripting of the movement of the living creatures in Ezekiel's chariot vision (Ezek. 1:23–25) in the twelfth of the thirteen *Sabbath Songs of Sacrifice* discovered in the caves of Qumran. The prophetic account inspired a poet-priest of the desert community to envisage the lifting and letting down of the wings on the part of these angelic beings, to attend the corresponding sound they make and the sound of the voice above the firmament;[193] when the cherubim bow before the glory in the "tabernacle of the gods of knowledge" (*mishkan elohei daʿat*),[194] they bless him, but when they rise, the sound of divine stillness, *qol dimmat elohim*, is heard (4Q405, 20 ii-21–22 7–8).[195] From this relatively early Jewish text the discerning ear may gather a first glimpse of an insight that became paramount in medieval kabbalistic tradition: Poetic con/frontation—facing the face that cannot be faced in saying the name that cannot be named—entails both encounter and resistance, embrace and rebuff, approach and withdrawal, revelation and occlusion, communication ensuing from the incommunicable absence, presently absent, in a presence, absently present.

CHAPTER SEVEN

Eunuchs Who Keep Sabbath: Erotic Asceticism / Ascetic Eroticism

What does the man of renunciation do?
He strives for a higher world, he wants to fly further and higher
than all men of affirmation—he throws away much that would encumber his flight,
including not a little that he esteems and likes;
he sacrifices it to his desire for the heights.
This sacrificing, this throwing away, however, is precisely
what alone becomes visible and leads people to call him
the man of renunciation. . . .
But he is quite satisfied with the impression he makes on us:
he wants to conceal from us his desire, his pride,
his intention to soar beyond us.—Yes, he is cleverer
than we thought and so polite to us—this man of affirmation.
For that is what he is, no less than we, even in his renunciation.

—Friedrich Nietzsche, *The Gay Science*

Erotic Asceticism / Ascetic Eroticism

At first glance, it might appear that the title of this chapter brings together two mutually exclusive themes. Asceticism, conventionally understood, implies rigorous discipline of body and mind, the adoption of an austere lifestyle, which can lead to the abrogation of desire, expressed as denial and mortification. Eroticism, by contrast, entails the sense of ecstatic rapture that ensues from inspirited indulgence in bodily matters and the full embrace of the sensual. In the case of both, there is a confluence of life and death, albeit from opposite ends of the spectrum: Asceticism promotes the negation of life in the simulation of death; eroticism, the affirmation of life even to the point of accepting or perhaps even willing death.

When one probes more deeply, however, it becomes apparent that asceticism and eroticism are not necessarily oppositional. Indeed, the ascetic impulse manifest in pious devotion may itself be rooted in erotic desire.[1] Matters pertaining to the sacred can be depicted erotically because there is a presumption regarding the sacred nature of the erotic. It has been commonplace for historians of religion to emphasize, therefore, that the love of God is often expressed in the language of human sexuality.[2] But the issue is not merely one of expression. The texture of intense religious experience, attested in diverse cultural settings, is marked frequently by erotic pathos, the tension between yearning and fulfillment, yearning to fulfill, fulfilling to yearn.[3]

On the face of it, however, the erotic nature of saintly life is to be sharply contrasted with the erotic imagination intent on satiation of physical desire. Traditionally, the pious seeks communion with the plentitude of nonbeing, the ineffable fullness of being, by abnegating the sensual to the point that the latter is a source of shamefulness and degradation. As Bataille put it, "The saint turns from the voluptuary in alarm; she does not know that his unacknowledgeable passions and her own are really one."[4] The simple reading of Bataille's comment implies that even the saint, or perhaps especially the saint, harbors unexpressed passions that are of a sensual nature. Yet upon reflection it becomes apparent that there is a deeper intent, not in contradistinction to the former but distinct from it nonetheless; holy and profane, spiritual devotion and carnal fervor, are not polar opposites but two ways to express the plethora of being, two facets of eros hanging in the balance as indifferently equal, equally indifferent, the road of excess that leads to the palace of wisdom, in Blakean terms.

The "ascetic lust"[5] of the celibate calling can elicit a sexual response no less powerful than that aroused by carnal temptation—renunciation of desire wrought by desire of renunciation, renunciation of renunciation, desire un(filled) to be (un)filled, emptying emptiness, neither empty nor not-empty. For the erotic ascetic, desire not to desire is a potent form of desire, for who, after all, affirms more affirmatively than one who resists affirmation in the affirmation of resistance?[6] In the formulation of Alenka Zupancic, "the thing the ascetic ideal employs in response to displeasure is *jouissance*, (surplus-)enjoyment. . . . Nietzsche repeats this insistently: the ascetic ideal is about excitement—it is, so to speak, a 'passion diet'; it is not about moderation, it counters passions with a surplus of pure passion."[7]

The specifics of ascetic eroticism confirm the "reflective nature" of the phenomenon of desire more generally, which, as Žižek writes, entails that "desire is always also *a desire for desire itself*, a desire to desire or not to desire something."[8] In the polished heart of the ascetic, the two are not separate; desire to desire and desire not to desire are seemingly divergent, but the latter embraces the former and the former the latter in a circular manner not given to a rigidly dichotomous discrimination. Desire not to desire may be compared to the mandate to contemplate the cessation of contemplating; the negation thereof, willy-nilly, is its affirmation, and hence there is no way to attain the goal without revoking its attainment. In the language of an "old poem" transmitted by Takuan Sōhō (1573–1645), the prelate of the Rinzai sect of Zen:

> To think, "I will not think"—
> This, too, is something in one's thoughts.
> Simply do not think
> About not thinking at all.[9]

The application of the logic of paradox to the matter of desire is attested in the words of another anonymous Zen text worthy of citation: "Whether there is no-seeking in seeking or seeking in no-seeking, there is still your seeking. Whether there is no-taking in taking or taking in no-taking, there is still your taking."[10] In the realm of desire, mind is in need of something, even if that something be nothing, desire to have no desire, need to not need; to form the formless, mind must be void of both desire to desire and desire not to desire, indeed, even desire not to desire not to desire.

The homology between eroticism and asceticism is especially prevalent in religious experiences studied and classified under the rubric of mysticism.[11] As many scholars have argued, a central (if not defining) feature of mysticism cultivated within theistic traditions is the experience of communion between the individual soul and personal God. To be sure, the literature studied under the taxon of mysticism exemplifies often enough the extending of the mind beyond the personal God of any particular faith community—in Eckhart's oft-cited formulation, breaking-through (*durchbrechen*) beyond the images of God revealed in Scripture or known through philosophy to the "fathomless ocean of the Godhead" (*in disem gründlosen Mere der Gotheit*) beyond all representation,[12] the nothingness of the "preoriginary origin" (*Ursprunc*) before the emergence of the beginning.[13]

Nevertheless, typically in these traditions, the very mystics who contemplate the ground beyond the theistic image—the image that appears as an idol from the perspective of the ground—have depicted these experiences in the language of love, betrothal, marriage, and sexual consummation.[14] The soul, which is recurrently feminized for both men and women,[15] expresses its desire for the divine, which is personified as the male bridegroom, through amorous images, kissing, caressing, and copulation. It would be misleading, however, to interpret these forms of erotic spirituality in the Freudian sense of libidinal sublimation. Mystics do not fit neatly into the clinical category of the repressed subject. On the contrary, mystics consciously appropriate modes of discourse from the realm of sensual love, as their experience of the sacred is infused with the sexual. It is often the case that eros of mystical experience is dependent on renunciation of carnal eros, but renunciation of carnal eros is predicated on apprehending the mystical nature of eros.[16] In the writings of kabbalists, the convergence of the mystical and erotic renders it necessary to speak of the symbolic transformation of sexual energy in place of the displacement of eros.[17]

Robert C. Zaehner poignantly described the point in his account of the culminating stage of mystical union in which the male mystic is enveloped and penetrated by the spirit of God. Reflecting the androcentric perspective that informs the literary accounts of the predominantly male Christian mystics he studied, Zaehner describes the soul of the mystic in relation to the divine as the bride who passively receives from the masculine potency of God. The soul recognizes its "essential femininity" in relation to God, for in her receptivity she is annihilated, which serves for Zaehner as a paradigm for mystical union in which the autonomy of self is overcome in absorption in the oneness of ultimate reality. Zaehner remarks that in this state the soul of the male mystic is comparable to a "virgin who falls violently in love and desires nothing so much as to be 'ravished,' 'annihilated,' and 'assimilated' into the beloved. There is no point at all in blinking the fact that the raptures of the theistic mystic are closely akin to the transports of sexual union, the soul playing the part of the female and God appearing as the male."[18] Just as the sexual act procures the most intense bodily joy, the ecstasy of mystical union is the most sublime spiritual joy.

Eunuchs for Heaven / Virgins of Christ

The link between asceticism and gender has been well established in scholarly literature. Particularly helpful in charting a theoretical course to discuss the theme in medieval kabbalah are previous treatments of the crisscross of these motifs in the history of Christianity, attested as early as the second century in the link between ascetic behavior and the spectacle of spiritual marriage.[19] Ostensibly, this possibility afforded both women and men the opportunity to overcome not only the limitations of the natural body, imaged in feminine terms, but also the social status determined by gender hierarchy.[20] The empowerment of ascetics could be profitably examined from the broader perspective of the institutionalization of monasticism in the fourth and fifth centuries, which provided the socioeconomic means by which members of Christian communities could negotiate the conflict between otherworldly and worldly sensibilities.[21] There is, however, a critical difference between the experience of men and women. By adopting vows of celibacy in the name of the worship of Christ, women both affirmed and challenged the misogynist debasement of the feminine body and sexuality.[22] It would be helpful to cite the formulation of the clash between androcentric and gynocentric perspectives on the sexuality of ancient Christian ascetic women offered by Virginia Burrus:

> The culturally dominant androcentric construction of virginal sexuality, which crystallizes out of the distinctive needs of the post-Constantinian church, functions to create and defend new communal boundaries and to reassert and strengthen the gender hierarchy; in the process, it rewrites women's bodies with an almost violent disregard for the physical knowledge and experience of women. But at least some ascetic women of antiquity either ignore or resist this interpretation. For them, sexual asceticism represents liberation from precisely such attempts to control women's sexuality, social relationships, and intellectual strivings; and their articulation of their own sexuality remains attentive to the knowledge and experience of their own bodies.[23]

I think it plausible to utilize this theoretical grid to understand the critique of the "ascetic woman" (*ishshah perushah*) in rabbinic literature assigned to the tannaitic period (the closure of which is generally fixed with the completion of some form of the Mishnah, the rabbinic code of custom and law, thought to be redacted and in circulation around 220 C.E.).[24] With regard to ascetic behavior on the part of Jewish men, there is a tension reflected in rabbinic sources, with some dicta expressing ambivalence and others more favorably disposed,[25] but there seems to be no wavering in the critical stance taken vis-à-vis female asceticism. In contrast to early Christianity, where virginity and fasting on the part of women were considered virtuous acts of piety facilitating the angelomorphic transformation of the carnal body and the consequent return to Paradise,[26] rabbinic sages castigated women who embraced a life of renunciation focused primarily on sexuality and eating.

The displeasure on the part of some rabbis is expressed hyperbolically in the ruling that includes ascetic woman in the enumeration of those who bring destruction to the world,[27] an expression meant to convey that female celibacy results in the breakdown of marital life and the bearing of progeny. In a similar vein, we read in another passage of rabbis voicing concern about the abstinent woman whose constant fasting "causes her to lose virginity."[28] Indeed, on account of the reduced intake of food, she is called the "fasting virgin," a term that suggests that the challenge such a woman posed was that she disrupted the societal expectations by abdicating her domestic responsibility.[29] Rabbinic authorities doubtless were aware of the fact that the stereotypical construction of women[30] as sexual objects (expressed most dramatically as the personification of carnal desire in the form of the temptress)[31] and domestic beings (identified principally through the roles of marriage, childbearing, and housekeeping) would be disrupted by the adoption of an ascetic lifestyle on the part of female members of their polity.

In light of this, one must reconsider the argument that the rabbinic utilization of the image of the virgin to describe the ascetic male suggests an "envisioning of female power and autonomy" that challenged the norm. To the best of my knowledge, we do not find anywhere in rabbinic literature an explicit or even an implicit directive that the Jewish male must become female to fulfill God's will. Metaphorical depictions of the rabbis, or even of the Jewish collectivity more generally, as feminine vis-à-vis either God or the Roman imperial power, both engendered as masculine, may surely be considered "symbolic enactments" of femaleness but they do not constitute a genuine change in the construction of Jewish masculinity. I see no justification for the view that in the patriarchal world of talmudic culture the "discourse of self-feminization" should be considered a gesture of "gender bending";[32] it is more reasonable to posit that this form of discourse is a co-opting of feminine images on the part of rabbinic sages that served more to buttress the entrenched androcentrism of the tradition than to challenge it, setting the stage for further subjugation of women.[33]

In the spiritual economy of formative Christianity we find a different symbolic calculus, as the celibate (whether male or female) assumed the status of a martyr, participating through acts of renunciation in the suffering of Jesus and thereby partaking in the penance and purification of humanity. As Foucault observed, underlying the nexus of martyrdom and asceticism is the paradox of the sacrifice of self:

> We have to sacrifice the self in order to discover the truth about ourselves, and we have to discover the truth about ourselves in order to sacrifice ourselves. . . . And we have to understand this sacrifice not only as a radical change in the way of life but as a consequence of a formula like this: you will become the subject of the manifestation of truth when and only when you disappear or you destroy yourself as a real body or as a real existence.[34]

The martyred life of the ascetic evolved into one of the principal forms of *imitatio Christi* that served in turn as the most effective way to attain the angelomorphic state characteristic of the eschaton, the *summum bonum*, communion with God.[35] Given the stereotypical envisioning of docility and submissiveness as female traits, it should come as no surprise that the image of the woman martyr served (even for male celibates) to epitomize the sacrificial victim. Standing before God, both women and men were inclined to depict their ascetic piety in the metaphor of the bride receiving from the bridegroom; in the presence of Christ, men will be as passive and self-effacing as women, reflecting and thereby reifying the stereotypical androcentric portrayal of female behavior as submissive and humble.[36] In this sense, it is legitimate within this cultural matrix to speak of male being female, an ideal that sits alongside the salvific notion of female becoming male.

It would stand to reason, moreover, that the heavenly life, the *vita angelica*, attained by the ascetic regimen would ideally entail erasure of sexual difference, a condition anticipated in the baptismal formula transmitted by Paul,[37] "there is neither male nor female, for you are all one in Christ Jesus" (Gal. 3:28), a theme I have already discussed at some length in chapter two.[38] However, the prevailing gender hierarchy in late antiquity, affirmed by Paul himself and others who followed in his way (1 Cor. 11:2–16, 14:34–36; Rom. 1:26; 1 Tim. 2:8–15),[39] viewed women not only as passive and submissive but as succumbing easily to the sways of the sensual and evocations of the ephemeral. When examined semiotically, renunciation of sexual and other bodily pleasures on the part of early Christian women must be decoded as a mark of the spiritualization, and hence masculinization, of the female.

If this conjecture holds, and I do not see any reason to doubt it, then it would seem implausible to assume that the image of the virgin served as the topos for the feminization of Christian men in their desire to become brides of Christ. In some instances, the "pretence of asceticism" was even displayed by holy women donning the guise of men through change of apparel or other forms of external appearance like cutting the hair.[40] In this effacement, gender difference was overcome, and the angelic status—the true image of God—was attained, the feminine elevated to the masculine, which included women on the social plane becoming overtly like men.[41] As Saint Jerome put the matter in his commentary on *Ephesians*, "when a woman serves birth and children, she is different from a man as the body is from the soul. But if she should wish to serve Christ more than the world, she ceases to be a woman and will be called man."[42]

The gender asymmetry of the ascetic ideal in formative Christianity has been well noted by contemporary scholars. For instance, Alice-Marry M. Talbot put it thus: "What is noteworthy is that the ideal ascetic life, of struggle versus temptation and sin, was always described with male metaphors, a tradition going back at least to John Chrysostom in the fourth century. . . . The ideal for a nun was to rise above her feminine frailty and assume masculine qualities."[43] Reiterating this view, Kim Power writes that the ascetic woman "left the feminine role behind and was engaged in the masculine pursuit of the contemplation of God. Her virginity was not an affirmation of her being as a woman, but an assumption of the nature of the male which is identified with the truly human: rationality, strength and courage, steadfastness and loyalty."[44]

Sexual abstention could be seen as part of the redemptive process by means of which the spiritual order was thought to be restored and the alleged autonomy of the feminine (in the symbolic sense) obliterated. To cast the issue in the language of Simone de Beauvoir, the female body was viewed not only in terms of otherness to man but also in terms of otherness to woman, and hence for a woman to become transcendent (which here denotes identity, personhood, or subjectivity), she had to transcend her own embodiment.[45] Asceticism on the part of women in early Christian communities could be understood, therefore, as a form of veiling the female in an effort to reinforce male hierarchy and the eventual conglomeration of ecclesiastical power; insofar as the female is linked to the veil, we can speak of ascetic self-annihilation as veiling the veil. This veiling is to be taken metaphorically and literally, as there is evidence in the fourth and fifth centuries of virgins putting on the veil as a ritual gesture to enact the consecration.[46] A bold mythic portrayal of this phenomenon, unquestionably fueled by a more overtly negative appraisal of creation, is found in the gnostic figure of Norea, the virgin savior who brings salvation by subverting the power of the male archons, an overturning that comes about by resisting sexual intercourse, which would lead to procreation and further bodily engenderment in the material universe, condemned as the realm of darkness and shadow-images.[47] One can speak of asceticism within this framework as the mechanism by which the demonic feminine, female sensuality, seductive Eve, is transformed into the saintly feminine, male woman, instantiated in and through the symbolic images and poetic tropes of the Virgin Mary and body of the Church.[48]

For Christian male ascetics, by contrast, sexual abstinence was anchored exegetically in the statement attributed to Jesus regarding those who "have made themselves eunuchs for the sake of the kingdom of heaven" (Matt. 19:12).[49] The view that those who dwell in the heavenly realm have overcome sexual desire is reinforced by the response of Jesus to the Sadducees: "When the dead rise, they will neither marry nor be given in marriage; they will be like the angels in heaven" (Mark 12:25). Parallels are found in Matthew 22:30 and Luke 20:34–36. The latter context is especially important, as it is clear that the dictum attributed to Jesus is applied exclusively to men, who shall become like angels in the hereafter: "The sons of this age marry and are given in marriage; but those who are accounted worthy to attain to that age and to the resurrection from the dead neither marry nor are given in marriage, for they cannot die any more, because they are equal to angels and are sons of God, being sons of the resurrection." This exegetical embellishment provided later scriptural interpreters with a model of transfigured masculinity beyond sexual desire but still engendered as masculine.[50]

Heeding the dictum of becoming eunuchs for heaven did not entail, as far as I have been able to research, effeminization but a further empowering of the masculine, which, under the influence of Platonic metaphysics, has been associated from the period of the Church fathers with the incorporeal. The spiritual interpretation of this saying, the "mystical castration" according to the nomenclature of Basil of Ancyra,[51] which prevailed over a literal reading that justified physical self-mutilation, fostered a new ideal of masculinity, the monk or "manly eunuch." To be sure, this model of an ascetic life entailed a rejection of male physiognomy and the conventional masculine social roles implied thereby, an idea captured vividly in the image of the virgin "bride of Christ" applied to monks. To assess whether the figurative understanding of eunuch retains the basic features of the literal meaning, we must probe more deeply into such a claim. Would it not imply that one who takes the vow to abstain unconditionally from sexual intercourse assumes the features associated with the medical condition of castration?[52]

According to some authorities, following an opinion traceable to Aristotle, the ascetic was viewed as an emasculated male, but according to others, echoing a formulation of Galen in *De semine* describing a group of mature animals from whom the testes had been surgically removed, the eunuch, both literal and metaphorical, represents a "third kind" of gender different from male and female[53]—in contemporary scholarly parlance, beyond sexual dimorphism.[54] Notwithstanding this ambiguity, the monastic discipline was depicted as a *vita militaris* that strengthened male virility by fostering the restraint necessary to overcome temptation and the lure of women, to withstand and trample the seductive snare of the serpent. Spiritual castration fostered an alternative model of masculinity marked by the paradox of "manliness in unmanliness."[55]

It is worthwhile recalling that the association of masculinity and monasticism, betraying an encratic milieu, is expressed as "fleeing from femininity"[56] in the Sethian gnostic work *Zostrianos*. I had the occasion to refer briefly to this motif in the second chapter, but it is worthwhile citing here the relevant passage in full:

> Do not baptize yourselves with death
> nor entrust yourselves to those
> who are inferior to you as if to
> those who are better. Flee from the madness
> and the bondage of femaleness,
> and choose for yourselves the salvation
> of maleness. You have
> not come to suffer; rather, you have
> come to escape your bondage.[57]

In another composition, *Allogenes*, also classified as Sethian, Barbelo, the triply powered one,[58] first of the aeons, is depicted in philosophical terms as Intellect, the "eternal light of that knowledge that appeared, the male virginal glory."[59] The second hypostasis of the divine triad, the consort of the Invisible Spirit,[60] is similarly represented as the male virgin. To grasp the import of this expression, it must be recalled that in the mythological architectonic of *Apocryphon of John*, one of the literary sources for the author of *Allogenes* and other Sethian gnostic texts, the supreme divine being,[61] which is characterized in apophatic terms as the "invisible Spirit"[62] or the "invisible, virginal Spirit," is the Monad that is the "pure, immeasurable mind," the "aeon-giving aeon," the "incomprehensible light," the "Father of all," which assumes the likeness of three forms (*morphê*), Father, Mother, and Son.[63]

From the textual evidence I have mentioned (and obviously there is much more that could have been considered), we may deduce that *virginal Spirit* is meant to convey the idea of a male untainted by female otherness, the spirit that is invisible. But how can spirit be virginal or otherwise? One cannot respond if one begins from the premise that the contradiction can and therefore will be resolved; one must approach this by bringing together in mind what must be kept apart, namely, an invisible spirit that is a virgin, a *male virgin*. Given the correlation of spirit and masculinity on the one hand and the correlation of body and femininity on the other, it is reasonable to assume that the male virgin is androgynous, the female being contained in her male progenitor, matter in mind, body in spirit. The implicit logic is drawn explicitly in another Sethian source, *Marsanes*, where the spirit is led by the "third power of the Three-Powered" into the aeon that is Barbelo, the "male virgin." The reader is offered the following explanation of this appellation: "For this reason the / Virgin became male, / because she had been divided from the male."[64] Purity is an ideal attained by means of the noetic transcendence of the (masculine) mind over the pollution of (feminine) matter that issues from carnal desire, an effacing of the feminine other, to return to the time before the division.[65]

With an interesting twist of historical fate, in some gnostic writers the Hellenic outlook meshed with the Hebraic myth preserved in Genesis 2:21–23 depicting the creation of woman (*ishshah*) from man (*ish*). When the ancient Israelite narrative of the female being derived ontically from the male was combined with the philosophical correlation of spirit and masculinity, the consequence is obvious: salvation means to reach the spot or moment—time and place are not distinguishable—before the division of sexes, to restore female materiality to male spirituality. Consider the description of the pneumatics initiated into the mysteries according to the Phrygian system reported by Hippolytus: "And those who come hither ought to cast off their garments, and become all of them bridegrooms, emasculated through the virginal spirit. For this is the virgin who carries in her womb and conceives and brings forth a son, not animal, not corporeal, but blessed forevermore."[66] The mandate for the adept is to become an emasculated bridegroom through the virginal spirit. To be saved, one must emulate the Savior, who was conceived in and born from the womb of a virgin. Virginity, therefore, signifies the pneumatic overcoming of physical appetite, the triumph over femininity, the birth of offspring bypassing the agency of the male or female genitalia.[67]

These examples and others that could have been cited illustrate that spiritual progress was understood as a process of female becoming male, as we find the matter expressed precisely in dicta attributed to Jesus in *Gospel of Thomas* and *Gospel of Egyptians*[68] and implicitly in other works, such as *Second Treatise of the Great Seth*.[69] Ascetic sublimation in early Christian piety did not result in effacing gender difference either sociologically or theologically. On the contrary, destabilization of sociosexual roles of women only reinforced the dominant position of the male in the social and religious order. The androcentric correlation of the psychic/spiritual with masculinity and the somatic/sexual with femininity and the consequent degradation of women prevailed in medieval Christianity, with the occasional exceptions, as important and impressive as they may be, proving rather than refuting the rule.[70]

One thinks, for instance, of the matrilineal literary tradition ostensibly transmitted in medieval lay Christian communities from mother to daughter, emphasizing an alternative model to the scholastic ideal of pedagogy and learning; although literacy of women fostered the production of books written principally in vernacular languages and typically containing more iconographic representations, the link connecting the feminine to the textual artifact is illustrative of the wish to comply in some measure with the dominant logocentrism in both the Greek and Latin traditions, exemplified in the identification of the Word with the carnal body of Jesus, a body that was presumably marked by the circumcised penis, the male member that bears the sign of the covenant with the God of Israel.[71] Even biographical sketches of female saints, when examined in a nonapologetic and nonideological light, indicate the extent to which the denigration of women shaped the binary mentality of Christian communities through the Middle Ages.[72]

I note parenthetically that a similar phenomenon is attested in the mystical ideal promoted in traditional Muslim societies. An interesting formulation of the matter may be gathered from a revealing remark by ʿAṭṭār discussing Rābiʿa of Basra: "When a woman is a man on the path of the Lord Most High, she cannot be called woman."[73] ʿAttār was obviously aware of the potential criticism he was going to face for including Rābiʿa in his list of seventy-five spiritual adepts at a time when Sufism had become, much like contemporary kabbalistic circles, exclusively male. Accordingly, he remarks at the beginning of the section on Rābiʿa, "If anyone asks why her memorial is placed among the ranks of men, we reply that the chief of the prophets—peace and blessing be upon him—declares: *God does not regard your forms*. It is not a matter of form, but of right intention." The sentiment expressed in this *ḥadīth* is surely laudable and does seem on the face of it to problematize any attempt to justify gender inequality by appeal to tradition. It is thus all the more striking that what succeeds the *ḥadīth* is the aforecited comment that a woman on the path to God can no longer be called "woman."

Lest there be any misunderstanding, let me state openly that I am not denying that ʿAṭṭār toiled to accord a more positive value to the feminine, a perspective emphasized by several prominent scholars, beginning with Margaret Smith.[74] This is strengthened by the dictum of ʿAbbāsah Tūsī that he cites in the continuation: "When on the morrow on the plain of resurrection they call out, 'O men,' the first person to step into the ranks of men will be Maryam." The mother of Jesus, who occupies an intriguing place in the imaginary landscape of Muslim poets, philosophers, saints, and mystics, will be first to join the ranks of "men" in the future heralded by the resurrection.[75] And even more strident in support of an egalitarian orientation are the words that follow: "Indeed, when it comes to the truth [*ḥaqīqat*], where this folk is, there is no one—all are unity. In unity, how can your existence or mine remain, much less 'man' or 'woman'?" With respect to the indiscriminate oneness of being, there is no basis to speak of individual, discrete existences, let alone to maintain gender distinctions; "all are unity," all distinctions are abandoned in the consciousness of the oneness of all being.[76]

In light of this conclusion, the underlying bias in the comment "When a woman is a man on the path of the Lord Most High, she cannot be called woman" is all the more striking. It seems that we have a discrepancy here between the metaphysical ideal on the one hand and the sociopolitical reality on the other. In the specific case of Rābiʿa, it will be recalled, her ascetic rejection of marriage, the domestic role to be expected of a faithful Muslim woman, is justified in terms of her having extinguished her self by uniting with the divine, the object of her love and yearning.[77] The overturning of the social mores is implied in ʿAṭṭār's opening depiction of Rābiʿa's veil, as I discussed in chapter five. The very title that Sufi masters attached to Rābiʿa's name—"crown of men," suggesting that she was exalted above male Sufis of previous generations[78]—bespeaks the predominant androcentricism; her exaltation is presented as her being gendered as male. The goal for the Sufi is to become a true "man of God," but manliness (*rajūliyya*) is attained by the ascetic renunciation of carnal desire linked to the vital soul (*nafs*), which is portrayed as feminine, and the consequent strengthening of the intellect, which is masculine.[79] The point is encapsulated in the following saying from the thirteenth century: "Whoever seeks the Lord is a male, whoever seeks the otherworld is a pederast, whoever seeks the world is a female."[80] If walking the path of God required the male adept to eradicate his femininity through ascetic denial of the body, how much more so was it necessary for a woman to efface her womanhood and to become manlike to be on that path. To the best of my knowledge, we cannot find an analogous injunction in Sufi literature for male to become female in order to attain the rank of sainthood.[81]

Expressed in contemporary psychoanalytical terms, which, in my judgment, can be legitimately appropriated in the study of medieval kabbalah, the charge of anachronism being rendered itself anachronistic by the hermeneutic of time reversibility that I laid out at outset of this journey, sexual renunciation on the part of men may be viewed as symbolic castration that maintains control over women even as eros is subjugated to the rule of logos. J. C. Smith and Carla J. Ferstman give a particularly astute account of the matter:

> There are two extreme levels of defense against the seduction, which correspond to the two poles of the phallus within patriphallic psychic reality—logos and penis. At logos, the defense is voluntary castration by the denial of the body leading toward the configuration of religious masochism. By altogether denying the phallus, one can escape the seduction of sacrificing the phallus to the female, thereby allowing the male to simultaneously avoid the *jouissance* of submission while maintaining his control. The religious male would rather castrate himself for the sake of God than for the sake of life, the mother, and the woman. He gives up the erotic but maintains control.[82]

As Smith and Ferstman go on to observe, to the extent that ascetic orientation in religious cultures portrays women primarily as objects of erotic passion, there are grounds to discuss religion in the light of pornography and pornography in the shade of religion:

> Typical pornographic imagery socializes women in terms of a psychic reality that denies them that which men claim as embodiment of the logos. Thus, religion and pornography serve the same basic function: defending men against seduction and the desire to surrender the phallus. . . . Religion and pornography function in a dialectical conjunction at the opposite ends of the phallus—religion at the logos end and pornography at the penis end, and the two are mediated by the Law of the Father.[83]

This text is not affirming—nor is it my personal wish to assert—that religious asceticism and pornographic libertinism are necessarily identical. The point is rather that Smith and Ferstman have accurately perceived that the de-eroticizing tendency of the one and the eroticizing fantasy of the other are dialectically related as two ends of the logocentric spectrum. The ostensible contradictory temperaments of the ascetic and libertine are "part of an integrated patriphallic structure,"[84] that is, both sexual renunciation and pornographic lasciviousness signify the androcentric, if not misogynist, nature of phallic aggression.

Ascetic Sexuality / Sexual Asceticism

The focus of the remainder of this chapter will be the impact of the ascetic ideal of sexual abstinence on the construction of masculinity in kabbalistic symbolism, with a special emphasis on the mystical fraternity surrounding the literary composition in late-thirteenth-century Castile of *Zohar,* which became the dominant social model for traditional kabbalistic circles until the present. Scholars have duly noted the ascetic dimension expressed in the classical rabbinic corpus, ancient throne mysticism, and medieval pietistic treatises of both Iberian and Franco-German extraction as well as in the unique trend of Jewish Sufism that evolved among the descendants of Maimonides in Egypt in the thirteenth and fourteenth centuries.[85] A number of scholars have also commented on the negative (and, at least according to some passages in zoharic literature, demonic) view of the body attested in works of kabbalah (indebted in great measure to the Neoplatonically oriented medieval spirituality) and the consequent necessity for an ascetic life.[86] However, what has been written most extensively on the subject has concentrated on sixteenth-century texts[87] and on the pietistic works composed from the seventeenth to nineteenth centuries based in great measure thereon.[88] Less attention has been paid to the ascetic dimensions of early kabbalah and particularly the zoharic period, let alone to the messianic/eschatological implications of the celibate lifestyle, a theme that I will explore in the next chapter.[89] With respect to the question of gender, other scholars of Jewish mysticism, to the best of my knowledge, have not treated the matter at all.

By contrast, much emphasis has been placed on the sacrality of sexuality in this tradition.[90] Scholem expresses the scholarly consensus with passionate eloquence:

> Chastity is indeed one of the highest moral values of Judaism. But at no time was sexual asceticism accorded the dignity of a religious value, and the mystics make no exception. Too deeply was the first command of the Torah, Be fruitful and multiply, impressed upon their minds. The contrast to other forms of mysticism is striking enough to be worth mentioning: non-Jewish mysticism, which glorified and propagated asceticism, ended sometimes by transplanting eroticism into the relation of man to god. Kabbalism, on the other hand, was tempted to discover the mystery of sex within God himself. For the rest it rejected asceticism and continued to regard marriage not as a concession to the frailty of the flesh but as one of the most sacred mysteries. Every true marriage is a symbolical realization of the union of God and the Shekhinah.[91]

According to the logic of Scholem's argument, the use of erotic imagery to describe the structure of the Godhead is a substitute for the passionate relation of the mystic to

God. It is worth citing his own formulation: "But while in all other instances the Kabbalists refrain from employing sexual imagery in describing the relation between man and God, they show no such hesitation when it comes to describing the relation of God to Himself, in the world of the Sefiroth. . . . In God there is a union of the active and the passive, procreation and conception, from which all mundane life and bliss are derived."[92] The "mystery of sex" for the kabbalist, in Scholem's understanding,[93] is related to the larger claim regarding the symbolic connection that binds human behavior below and what transpires above in the divine realm, a claim that transforms "all human action and expression into a sacral ritual."[94] Intercourse between husband and wife is a mimetic rite that facilitates the conjunction in the Godhead and thereby helps maintain the harmony between restrictive judgment and boundless mercy. From that perspective every sanctioned act of coitus participates in the "sacred marriage," which "is always a ceremony in which redemption is anticipated, in which the exile of the *Shekhinah* is at least momentarily annulled or attenuated."[95] I would challenge the distinction made by Scholem, for the textual evidence overwhelmingly indicates that kabbalists, and particularly as the matter may be adduced from the literary remains of the zoharic and Lurianic circles, endowed ritual with magical efficacy precisely because they cultivated mystical experiences of an intensely erotic nature.[96] The theosophic, ecstatic, and theurgic, I submit, are intertwined branches of one tree.[97]

From other passages in his oeuvre, however, it is clear that Scholem not only recognized that there has been an ascetic dimension in the history of Judaism but was of the opinion that the early kabbalists in twelfth-century Provence emerged from groups of ascetic pietists (referred to variously as *perushim, nezirim, qedoshim*, and *ḥasidism*).[98] Indeed, the contemplative ideal proffered by Isaac the Blind and elaborated by his disciples—a project widely followed in subsequent generations—is predicated on an ascetic renunciation of sensual desire.[99] In this connection, it is important to recall a passage in *Sefer ha-Bahir* that reflects the contemporary ascetic practices of kabbalists in Provence likely responsible for the redaction of the text:

> R. Berachiah sat and expounded, why is it written, "Bring me a heave offering" (Exod. 25:2)? Thus the holy One, blessed be he, said to Israel: I am the heave offering, for you lift me through your prayers. And whom? The one who pledges his heart to be drawn away from this world. Honor him for I rejoice in him, for he knows my name and from him it is appropriate for me to take my lifted offering, as it says, "from every person who pledges his heart you shall accept my heave offering" (ibid.), from the very one that pledges himself, for R. Reḥumai said: It is on account of[100] the righteous and pious in Israel who lift me up over the whole world through their merits.[101]

The biblical injunction to lift up an offering to God is applied specifically to the spiritual elite in Israel, the righteous (*ṣaddiqim*) and pious (*ḥasidim*), who elevate the divine by means of their liturgical utterances.[102] They can accomplish this feat because they possess gnosis of the name, which was considered to be the essence of traditional faith.[103] The description of kabbalists as devout individuals who know the name fits well with other material from twelfth-century Provence and thirteenth-century Catalonia, as I discussed at length in chapter five. Most important for the purposes of the present discussion, masters of esoteric wisdom who can have a theurgical impact upon God are identified as those who pledge their hearts to be removed from mundane matters.

In a second bahiric passage, we read that he who wants to merit Torah, which is true life, "must hate bodily pleasure [*hanaʾat ha-guf*] and receive the yoke of the commandments, and if afflictions come upon him, he should receive them out of love."[104] In an analogous manner, in the commentary on *Sefer Yeṣirah* that records the teachings of Isaac the Blind, the description of the *sefirot* bowing down to God's word is applied to the mystic who contemplates the divine: "The prostration is like he who leaves aside his attributes and he is engaged only with thought, and he is joined to thought, he elevates thought, and he mortifies the body to strengthen his soul."[105] The goal of *Homo religiosus*, according to the kabbalist, is to expand his thought to the point that it will be united to the infinitely extending divine thought. The monopsychic union occurs when one discards the measurable and delimited attributes of God and focuses exclusively on the immeasurable and limitless thought, which is designated "that which thought cannot comprehend." Significantly, the opening of mind, the "expansion of soul to extend in the particulars in the infinite" (*raḥav ha-nefesh lehitpasheṭ bi-feraṭim ba-ein sof*),[106] is linked to the prayer gesture of prostration, since it is predicated on debasing the body, undoubtedly an allusion to the adoption of ascetic practices that weaken the physical and augment the spiritual.[107]

In another context, Isaac reportedly described the initiates as the "enlightened of Israel" (*maskilei yisraʾel*) "who seek God, who call out to him and are answered, who share in the misery of their fellowmen, who supplicate before the face of God on their behalf and mortify themselves, whose prayers are accepted [by God] and through whom many miracles have been performed, both for the benefit of the individual and of the community."[108] Scholem pointed to the historical similarities between the ascetic phenomenon in the Jewish communities of southern France and the monastic tendencies evident in both Catholic clergy and Cathar *perfecti* of the time,[109] but even here he sounded a note of caution, asserting that there are "clear divergences resulting from the different attitudes of Judaism and Christianity toward celibacy."[110]

One cannot disagree with the claim that in the kabbalistic tradition, as in the case of rabbinic Judaism more generally, sexuality is not problematized in the way that it has been in the history of Christianity.[111] The practice of unconditional celibacy was not idealized in Jewish texts in either late antiquity or the Middle Ages, nor was the image of the virgin placed on a spiritual pedestal. Indeed, from the more specific vantage point of the kabbalah articulated especially (but not exclusively) in the zoharic corpus, the Christian ideal of monasticism is demonized, a portrayal familiar from other medieval polemical treatises wherein Christian asceticism is attacked by Jews as an inappropriate form of devotion.[112] The embodiment of impurity, Satan or Samael, is portrayed as the castrated male who is contrasted with the virile, circumcised male Jew.[113] This symbolism underlies the zoharic portrayal (particularly pronounced in the literary strata of *Sifra di-Ṣeniʿuta* and the *Idrot*) of the kings of Edom (Gen. 36:31–39), the archetypal representation of the historical force of Christianity, as emasculated males, a theme that assumed vital importance in the subsequent evolution of kabbalistic symbolism, especially the teachings that disseminated in the name of Luria in the sixteenth century.[114] I cite here one textual illustration from Vital that unfolds faithfully, in my judgment, the intent of the mythologic symbol-complex attested in select zoharic passages:

> They are alluded to in the secret of "The arms of his hands were outstretched" (Gen. 49:24), for this is the secret of the ten drops that were cast from between his nails, as is mentioned in *tiqqun* 69,[115] as is known, for they themselves are the aspects of the kings. The nullification of the kings was on account of the fact that Adam was not yet arrayed as one, male and female. And this is precisely the secret of Joseph's drops of semen that emerged without a female, but rather from the male alone, and they are truly the ten martyrs of the kingdom [*eser harugei melukhah*]. Comprehend the word "kingdom" [*melukhah*], for they are verily the seven kings [*melakhim*] whose vessels and bodies were shattered. And the reason was, similarly, for they were without the arrayment [*tiqqun*] of male and female until Hadar, the eighth king, came, and then they were ameliorated.[116]

Vital develops a sequence of thoughts based on a close reading of the passage in *Tiqqunei Zohar* to which he explicitly refers. In that context, it is affirmed that Joseph sinned with respect to the letter *yod*, the sign of the covenant, that is, the *membrum virile*. More specifically, following an opinion transmitted in the name of R. Isaac in older rabbinic sources,[117] the anonymous fourteenth-century Castilian Jew asserts that the sin ascribed to Joseph consisted of his casting the seminal drop, the *yod*, from between his fingernails, which splintered into ten sparks that were emplaced in the ten rabbinic martyrs of Caesarea who died cruel deaths at the hands of Roman centurions. According to another rabbinic tradition, the ten martyrs (*asarah harugei malkhut*) are depicted as sacrificial substitutes that bear the iniquity of the ten brothers who sold Joseph into slavery.[118] The author of *Tiqqunei Zohar* upholds this connection, but he explains it as a consequence of Joseph's sin of spilling drops of semen in vain.

The conflation of aggadic traditions facilitates linking together Joseph, the martyrs, and the seven Edomite kings, the common denominator being that Joseph and these kings ejaculated semen without a female partner; the martyrs are the result of Joseph's act and thus they are from the same source, the aspect of *malkhut*, the root of the feminine in the uppermost configuration, which is described as a world that is entirely masculine. As I have argued elsewhere,[119] underlying the kabbalistic myth is a psychical inversion typical of an androcentric standpoint: the male desire to ejaculate without a female receptacle is transposed such that the evil is associated more specifically with the woman. That is, the male who ejaculates without a female is transvalued as feminine, and the mercy associated with the seminal overflow is transformed into an act of judgment. In zoharic literature, the primordial kings are portrayed in images that convey emasculation and sterility. The explicit extension of these images to include the impulse to masturbate reflects the peculiar understanding of male sexuality proffered in Lurianic kabbalah.

The point is elucidated in the following passage: "These kings arose in the secret of the female waters for their existence from the beginning was in the secret of ruddiness, for they are the drop of the female. And thus they are called kings [*melakhim*] for they came forth in that *malkhut*, which is the land of Edom, female waters without a masculine."[120] The kings of Edom are engendered as female, for they are a manifestation of judgment, symbolized by the color red. The feminine character is attributed to the Edomite kings, for the first seven of the eight mentioned in Scripture have no female counterparts, and kings without queens are converted symbolically into queens without kings, or, in the language of the aforecited passage, female waters without a masculine. In a state of harmony, the female waters incite the male waters to overflow so that male and female will be united and the latter will be amended by the former.

By contrast, preceding the emanation of the androgynous *sefirot*, the ontic situation is one wherein the female waters have no corresponding male waters, a situation that is depicted by the image of kings who have no queens. Without the feminine receptacle to receive the seminal overflow, the kings cannot actualize their masculinity and thus they are depicted as emasculated beings, kings whose (phallic) weapons are not to be found, which results in the destruction of the (feminine) earth.[121] The death of the kings signifies the purification of judgment to produce *Malkhut*, the aspect of the female that will be balanced by the masculine quality of mercy and will thereby rectify the originary ontic condition of imbalance.

From the perspective of this gender construction, Christianity is correlated with masculine impotence, which is equivalent to the feminine character of judgment. The overcoming of the primordial state of male sterility is related in the zoharic text to Hadar, the last of the Edomite kings delineated in the biblical record, for he is the only one whose wife, Mehetabel, is mentioned. Symbolically, the zoharic authors associate Hadar with the divine attribute that corresponds to the phallus, *Yesod*, which is also called the "fruit of the tree of splendor," *peri eṣ hadar* (Lev. 23:40) and is compared to the date palm (based on Ps. 92:13), which comprises male and female characteristics.[122] The rectification of the celibate condition of the previous seven Edomite kings, who represent the ecclesiastical hierarchy of Roman Catholicism, is connected to the androgynous phallus of God ritually embodied in the circumcised penis of the Jewish male. That heterosexual desire is a component of this rectification is obvious from the fact that the name of Mehetabel is recorded together with Hadar.

Yet, as I argued elsewhere, the theosophical importance of the heterosexual pairing is derived from the fact that the ontological locus of the female is in the male, or, to be even more precise, the ontic source of androgyny and the sexual difference that ensues therefrom is the phallic gradation, represented by Hadar. Erotic yearning on the part of the masculine for the feminine is indicative of the beginning of the redemptive process that overcomes the division of the primal androgyne, but the consummation is marked by restoration of the feminine to the masculine, a restoration that entails the transposition of *Shekhinah* from feminine other to the sign of the covenant inscripted on the corona of the phallus.[123] This matter will be elaborated in the following chapter, but it is necessary to point out at this juncture that corresponding to the crossing of gender identities is a shift in the tenor of the erotic experience from heterosexual to homoerotic, a point to which I will return below.

Repeatedly, as scholars of Jewish mysticism have noted, zoharic authors and other kabbalists emphasize that anthropological completeness is attained in marriage.[124] According to the graphic image found in one passage in *Zohar*, the single male or female is merely "half a body" (*pelag gufa*), a technical term that denotes ontological (and not merely physiological or even psychological) imperfection.[125] Indeed, the distinctive holiness of the Jewish people (based on the biblical mandate in Lev. 19:2) is linked to the sanctity that is attained when husband and wife are joined together in sexual intercourse. Coitus is considered a form of *imitatio dei* insofar as the unity of the divine anthropos is imaged as the coupling of masculine and feminine.[126] Conversely, to refrain from engaging in intercourse is effectively to create a blemish above by interrupting the flow of energy from male to female, which results in the diminution of the phallic potency and the consequent impoverishment of the feminine.[127] Consequently kabbalists, building upon allusions found in some rabbinic dicta, assigned theurgic significance to human sexuality as a means to cause the indwelling of *Shekhinah* or to augment the divine image,[128] understood in the theosophic symbolism as androgynous.[129]

Although the idea that the complete human being comprises male and female is clearly rooted in earlier rabbinic exegesis of the scriptural account of creation, it is possible that the particular form of expression that this idea assumes in medieval kabbalah and especially in *Zohar* serves as a polemic against the Christian affirmation of celibacy as the means to restore humanity to its pristine state. Support for this contention is implied in one context where the ideal of the perfect human is related to the zoharic claim that a priest who is not married cannot enter the Temple to offer sacrifices.[130] *Shekhinah* does not rest on such a person and blessings cannot be transmitted through him since he is blemished. Indeed, he is not even in the category of a human being (*adam*), insofar as the latter comprises both male and female.[131] In passing, I note the convergence of the theurgic-symbolic and erotic-ecstatic elements: the priest cannot draw down blessings that issue from the union of the masculine and feminine aspects of the divine unless he is erotically bound to *Shekhinah*, but only one who is wed can be bound in such a way,[132] for, as it is repeatedly emphasized in the zoharic corpus, *Shekhinah* (or the blessing that emanates therefrom) rests only upon the man who is married.[133] The portrayal of the Jewish priest functions as an antidote to the Catholic priest required to be celibate.

These passages (and many others that could have been cited) unquestionably support the contention of Scholem (and numerous other scholars) that the kabbalistic tradition has unequivocally assigned a positive valence to sexuality as a sacrament that celebrates the union of masculine and feminine energies in the divine, the mythopoeic basis for the kabbalistic interpretation of the religious obligation to procreate. The "body of engenderment," in Mopsik's artful locution, gives linguistic shape to an insight well known to students of Jewish esoteric law: the reproduction of *Homo sapiens* below in the genealogical chain replicates and thereby actualizes the continuous self-becoming of God above, the limitless and hidden one emanating the ten luminous potencies in the form of the imaginal anthropos configured in the quaternity of father, mother, son, and daughter, the ideal human family.[134] Consider, for example, the precise formulation of the theurgical significance of domestic sexuality in the following anonymous text:

> Therefore it says with respect to man "creation" [*beriʿah*] and "planting" [*neṭiʿah*], for man is in this world to bear fruit, and through his good deeds he brings about union [*ziwwug*] above, but when he is not in this world the word "planting" is not appropriate, for above the fruits do not apply since above they do not unite. Thus you must know that when a man does not take a spouse he receives illumination from the backside of the backside, but when they return and offer her to him, he is in the secret of face-to-face.[135]

While in this world, the man must take a wife and cohabit with her to bring about the union above. Sexuality is affirmed as a means by which one unifies the qualities of the divine that result in an efflux of light that sustains the world.

Interestingly, in one zoharic passage, there is a criticism of the rabbinic tradition[136] regarding the voluntary separation of Moses from his wife: "R. Isaac said, Why is the *alef* [in the word] *wa-yiqra* (Lev. 1:1) small? He said to him, Moses existed in perfection but not in everything for he separated from his wife. In the ancient books, they spoke of this as praise, but we learn that the one who ascends above should be bound above and below, and consequently he is perfect."[137] Preserved in this passage, then, is a disputatious stance against the position affirmed elsewhere in zoharic literature regarding the renunciation of conjugal sex on the part of Moses after he had united with *Shekhinah*.[138] According to the aforecited text, this separation is a sign of imperfection, for perfection consists of being bound to the divine presence but still maintaining relations with one's earthly mate. In light of this we can readily understand and accept Scholem's insistence on distinguishing the kabbalistic approach to sexuality and the pietistic ideal proffered by medieval Christian mystics and saints.

From another perspective, however, Scholem's generalization must be qualified. Not only is it the case that there have been Jewish mystics of an ascetic orientation, a point of which Scholem and other scholars are well aware, but the sacralization of human sexuality, which lies at the heart of kabbalistic myth and ritual, is dialectically related to the ascetic impulse.[139] To express the matter in an alternative way, in the kabbalistic tradition, carnal sexuality is celebrated only to the extent that it is transformed by the proper intentionality into a spiritual act. As Jacob ben Sheshet articulates it,

> [Jewish men] must purify themselves when they unite with their wives, for the foetus will be in accord with thought [*ki kefi ha-maḥshavah yihyeh ha-ubbar*], and this is the import of what they said that a man must always sanctify himself at the time of intercourse.[140] . . . The man who is a master of wisdom and who knows how to imagine in his thought what he wants, whether for good or for evil, and he knows how to direct his intention to that form, there is no doubt that he must purify himself at that moment. Concerning this, and things similar to this, Solomon said "the advantage of man to the beast is naught" (Eccles. 3:19).[141]

The purification that ensues from the proper intentionality entails satisfying physical desire after one has annulled physical desire, a detachment attained by burning the craving, even, perhaps especially, the craving to crave no more. The abnegation is alluded to in Jacob ben Sheshet's citation of the verse from Ecclesiastes, "the advantage of man to the beast is naught" (*u-motar ha-adam min ha-behemah ayin*), which, in accord with his reading, signifies that what distinguishes human from animal is *ayin*, the naught that is the fullness of God's infinity, the attribute of *Keter.* The pious man must subdue his physical desire by submitting, commingling, and dissolving his will in the infinite will, which is nothing-that-is-everything-nothing-is, and, in so doing, carnal lust is transformed into the spiritual eros that is characteristic of the subtle essence of the sefirotic gradations.

In the language of one zoharic text:

> Come and see: Concerning the seed of man [*zarʿa de-var nash*], when his desire is aroused vis-à-vis his woman, and his woman is aroused, then the two of them are joined as one, and from them emerges one son comprised of both images [*diyoqnin*] as one, for the holy One, blessed be he, forms him in a form [*ṣiyyura*] that is comprised of both. Thus a man must sanctify himself in that moment [of intercourse] so that the image [*diyoqna*] will be found in the complete form [*ṣiyyura shelim*] as is appropriate.[142]

Minimally, the demand that the Jewish man should sanctify himself when having sex with his wife requires that he not act like an animal and that he should not think of another woman but focus only on his spouse, requirements that were already established in the talmudic code of law;[143] from a mystical standpoint, however, in order to secure that his seed be truthful (*zera emet*), the man must sanctify himself by performing the physical act of intercourse "for the sake of the commandment" (*le-shem miṣwah*) and "direct his heart for the sake of heaven" (*mekhavein libbo le-shem shamayim*), "to build the house and to produce offspring."[144] The model is the rabbinic notion (to be discussed below) that the time for the scholar to engage in the ritual of intercourse (*tashmish de-miṣwah*) is on Sabbath eve,[145] when, according to the medieval kabbalists, the earthly act serves as a theurgic means to activate the *hieros gamos* above, inasmuch as the somatic is aligned with the psychic through the apposite intentionality aimed at the divine will:[146]

> Come and see: When man is sanctified with his wife[147] below in the manner of the fraternity [*ḥavrayya*] who sanctify themselves from Sabbath to Sabbath at the time that the supernal coupling [*ziwwuga ilaʾah*] is enacted, for in that moment the will is found and blessing summoned, then all is conjoined as one, the soul of Sabbath and the body that is summoned on Sabbath. Thus it is written "You shall fear your mother and father" (Lev. 19:3), for they are joined together in one body in the moment that they are sanctified.[148]

The ascetic dimension of the kabbalistic ideal is articulated more fully in one of the most important manuals on sexual etiquette written in the later part of the thirteenth-century, the *Iggeret ha-Qodesh* ("Holy Epistle").[149] It is worthwhile examining some of the key passages from this work, since the attitude expressed therein is rather typical of the position adopted by medieval kabbalists in general and especially the Castilian kabbalists whose views are encoded in zoharic homilies. According to the anonymous author of this text, the ontic condition of humanity prior to the sin in the Garden of Eden was such that Adam and Eve were "engaged with the intelligible matters [*muskkalot*] and all of their intention was for the sake of heaven."[150] The erotic nature of the conjunction of the rational soul and the supernal light is underscored in another passage where it is emphasized that the Hebrew word *yediʿah* can be used to connote both cognition and conjugal intimacy.[151]

In the pristine state of human existence, therefore, the sexual impulse was itself of a spiritual quality, for Adam and Eve were primarily concerned with intelligible realities, which in this context refers to the sefirotic emanations.[152] However, when the aboriginal couple lusted after physical pleasures (*hanaʾot ha-gufaniyyot*) detached from concentration on the spiritual matters, they were lowered to the level of base sexuality, and consequently eros itself became problematized, for the physical was separated from the intelligible. Hence before the sin, Adam and Eve felt no shamefulness with regard to their nakedness (Gen. 2:25); the shamefulness felt after the sin and the need to cover the genitals (ibid., 3:7) result from the fact that sensual desire was severed from its metaphysical basis.[153]

The dichotomization of carnal passion and spiritual eros is reflected, moreover, in the interpretation of the rabbinic tradition that designates Sabbath eve as the proper time for scholars to engage in conjugal sex: the physical act of sex is appropriate for the sages on the eve of Sabbath precisely because it is a time of increased spirituality, the day "that is entirely cessation and repose," the "foundation of the world," which is "in the pattern of the world of souls" (*dugmat olam ha-nefashot*).[154] The offspring produced by the union of husband and wife on that night is endowed with a rational soul that derives ontically from the world of souls, for in the act of coitus the intention of the sage is directed to the divine attribute called the "rational soul."[155] Utilizing language that can be traced to the Catalonian kabbalists, the author of the epistle writes:

> Thus it is known to masters of the tradition [*baʿalei qabbalah*] that the thought of man [*maḥshevet ha-adam*] is from the place of the rational soul [*ha-nefesh ha-sikhlit*] that proceeds from the supernal beings, and there is the potentiality in thought to extend, to ascend, and to reach its place of origin, and then it is conjoined to the supernal secret [*sod ha-elyon*] that emanates from there, and the two become one thing [*naʿasin hi we-hu davar eḥad*], and when thought returns from above to below everything assumes the image of a line.[156]

The operative principle here is the scientific belief of the Middle Ages, based on philosophical works of antiquity, that the mental intention of the parents is one of the key factors that helps determine the nature of the fetus.[157] This is combined with the contemplative ideal of human consciousness ascending to its source in the divine and then descending back to the mundane, causing the overflow of light and blessing. The experience of *devequt* is thus contextualized in the specific context of sexual cohabitation, for the extending line establishes the connection between divine and human and thereby sanctifies the seed-thought of the male in the act of coitus.

So unequivocal is the author of this text in his rejection of carnal sex without this spiritualizing element that in another passage he remarks that if someone marries a woman only on account of her physical beauty, their conjugal union is not for the sake of God; moreover, since his intention during intercourse is focused exclusively on physical pleasure, the child born from their union is considered a "stranger" and "foreigner" in whom God has no portion. The parents cause *Shekhinah* to depart from them as they are rebellious in relation to God.[158] By contrast, the patriarchs are signaled out for their being in constant conjunction with God even when engaged in corporeal matters.[159] Thus Jacob was said to merit the twelve tribes on account of the fact that he was never separated from the supernal light, and they are described as being "in the image of the cosmic order, bearers of the instruments of God, for their thought was not separated from the supernal conjunction even in the moment of union and intercourse."[160]

The kabbalistic ideal articulated by this author can be explained on the basis of the pronounced influence that Platonic dualism of spirit and matter had on the pietists and mystics of Islam, Judaism, and Christianity in medieval society.[161] Even factoring in more recent feminist work that has called attention to a possible divergence of the experience of women and men, the former more affirming of body and sensual images, less encumbered by the philosophical bias, it is still reasonable to say that on the whole the texture of these liturgical faiths, as may be determined by residual cultural formations critically reconstructed (in an apparently open and ongoing manner) by historians of the past, indicates the influence of the Hellenic heritage. In addition to the privileging of the spiritual over the material, Platonic ontology imparted a philosophical account of the correlation of eros and noesis, a correlation that allowed for the expression of the latter in terms of the former, the former, in terms of the latter.[162]

As I will argue below, in zoharic theosophy, a correspondence is established between contemplative ecstasy and seminal emission; indeed, the *semen virile* is understood in scientific terms as the light-seed of the brain—the different elemental forms, water, air, fire, and earth, are all compresent in the seminal drop, which originates as spirit/ether within mind. The reversal of the phallic overflow, from bottom to top, from tail to head, demarcates the ascetic eroticism of the erotic asceticism, a celibate vocation that anticipates the eschatological moment expressed in *Idra Rabba* as the "arousal on the part of the Ancient of Days of the spirit that comes forth from the most hidden brain" (*yitʿar atiq yomin ruḥa de-nafiq mi-moḥa setimaʾah de-khola*).[163] The spirit awakened by *Atiq Yomin*, also called *Arikh Anpin*, is the seventh, which adjoins the other six holy crowns (*kitrin qaddishin*) of *Zeʿeir Anpin* to complete the number of spirits associated with messianic consciousness, derived exegetically from Isaiah 11:2.

I will refrain from engaging in an analysis warranted by this passage and will focus instead on the point most relevant to the present discussion. The semen, which is the life force of the divine emanations, originates in the spirit that emerges from the hidden brain. Against this background, we can understand the practice of withholding the phallic ejaculation and the elevation of the seminal energy flow back to the cavity of the brain cultivated by kabbalists in order to visualize the divine anthropos.

With respect to this issue, there is a striking affinity between theosophic kabbalah and Indian tantric tradition, a theme to which I shall return below.[164] At this juncture, it is worthwhile considering another affinity to the kabbalistic conception of the seminal idea, that is, semen arising in the mind materially as aura, and the Stoic *logos spermatikos*, the generative power of soul, germinating "seeds of virtue" (*semina virtutis*) and "seeds of knowledge" (*semina scientiae*) that are implanted and tended in the garden of mind.[165] From this vantage point, thoughts are, materially, seeds of light. It must also be borne in mind that for the Greek Stoics the generative force applies to the deity and to nature. Indeed, as Maryanne Cline Horowitz has recently articulated the argument, "the offspring are similar to the *logos spermatikos*, or God, and thus the world and human beings in particular are of the nature of God."[166] A contemporary of the zoharic circle, Abraham Abulafia expressed the tacit biological assumption of a contemplative erotics when he wrote:

> It is known that [the word] "desire" [*ha-ta'awah*] is numerically the "essence of light" [*eṣem ha-orah*], the "essence of splendor" [*eṣem ha-zohar*], the "essence of speech" [*eṣem ha-dibbur*].[167] The desire and yearning for something is the cause of the intelligible light [*ma'or ha-sekhel*] coming forth in the intellect [*maskil*], for this is the light that illumines, the light that is the internal light [*ha-or ha-penimi*] that shines from him.[168]

Just as light is the efficient cause of the sense of sight, so it is the impetus that motivates one to fulfill physical craving. Desire, therefore, is intricately bound to light, which is linked to speech and intellect. Hence mental activity assumes a decidedly erotic character, indeed, even more erotic than the carnal, as the intensity of eros is proportionate to the potency of light. When viewed dialectically, however, the intensely erotic representations of the divine, which are characteristic of the theosophic forms of medieval kabbalah, are predicated on the devaluation of the physical body and the senses. Indeed, in kabbalistic theosophy, the symbolic retrieval of the body to characterize incorporeal realities is based on the abnegation of the human body.

The repeated utilization of sexual imagery on the part of kabbalists has nothing to do with celebration of physical pleasure for its own sake. Quite the contrary, the holiness of sexuality is proportionate to the eradication of carnal gratification, as is attested by Vital, who recommends that the man who sets out to study kabbalah "should also sanctify himself in the act of intercourse so that he has no pleasure."[169] Carnal sex is sanctified by the intent that is spiritualized even to the point that one experiences no physical pleasure in arousal or release. The psychological difficulty of attaining this state[170] is underscored in the commentary on Vital's words by the nineteenth-century Hasidic master Zevi Hirsch of Zidachov:

> In truth, not every man can fulfill the sanctity of intercourse [*qedushshat ha-ziwwug*] if he has not studied this wisdom, to know the channels of unity, and to separate his thought from gross matter, and to sanctify himself in his thought through the unifications of his names, blessed be he, in the source of the copulation by sacrificing to the Lord in truth. I heard from my teacher that the essence of sanctification for intercourse is prior to intercourse, to cleave with his thought and to bind himself

> to the Creator, blessed be he and blessed be his name, exalted and elevated, as it is explained in the sacred works, but in the time of intercourse it is not possible not to have pleasure. . . . In accordance with the capacity of a man to distance himself from pleasure, he should certainly do so . . . however, if you have pleasure, you should give thanks to the Creator of the entire world for your portion.[171]

Recognizing the natural tendencies of humankind, Zevi Hirsch softens the harshness of the ascetic ideal endorsed by Vital—not to have any physical pleasure in the act of intercourse—and recommends that one should at least express gratitude to God when one is sexually fulfilled. Even so, we discern in this passage that the ascetic orientation persisted, for the most laudable station on the pietistic path is to distance oneself entirely from sensual pleasure, which is depicted as an act of mortification (*mesirat ha-nefesh*) for God, language that draws on the nexus between martyrdom and eroticism, another well-attested theme in various forms of medieval Jewish mystical pietism.[172] The kabbalist experiences God in erotic terms, but such an experience is dependent on the subjugation of physical eros: the spiritualization of the erotic leads to the eroticization of the spiritual.[173]

The erotic characterization of the noetic thus serves seemingly antithetical goals: the mental concentration required of the man in the act of coitus transforms the generative force of physical desire into the creative energy of contemplation, but the latter is experienced in a distinctively sensual manner.[174] The erotic nature of mystical ecstasy is based on an ascetic denial of the body that facilitated the spiritual marriage of the kabbalist and the divine. In that sense, it is appropriate to posit an ideal of celibacy developed by the zoharic circle, albeit one that is far more limited than Christian monasticism. Indeed, for these kabbalists, and for hosts of others through the centuries influenced by their imaginary construction of gender and sexual identity, the very process of becoming male was predicated to some degree on the ascetic transformation of eros and the upward channeling of the phallic energy from the genitals to the mind.

Symbolic Castration, Phallic Empowerment, Mystical Enlightenment

The key passage in *Zohar* wherein the ascetic ideal is expressed is an extraordinarily bold reading of the verses "For thus said the Lord: As far as the eunuchs who keep my Sabbaths, who have chosen what I desire and they hold fast to my covenant, I will give them, in my house and within my walls, a monument and a name better than sons and daughters, I will give them an everlasting name that shall not perish" (Isa. 56:4–5):

> Who are the eunuchs? These are the comrades engaged in Torah. They castrate themselves the six days of the week and study Torah, and on the night of Sabbath they prepare themselves for intercourse, for they know the supernal secret concerning the time when the Matrona unites with the King. The comrades who know this secret direct their hearts to the Faith of their Master and they are blessed with the fruit of their loins on that night. . . . They are truly called eunuchs because they

> wait for the Sabbath, to discover the desire of their Master, as it is written, "who have chosen what I desire." What is [the meaning of] "what I desire"? It is intercourse with the Matrona. "And they hold fast to my covenant," it is all one. "My covenant," without qualification. Praiseworthy is the portion of the one who is sanctified in this holiness and who knows this mystery.[175]

The scriptural reference to eunuchs who keep the Sabbath is applied allegorically to members of the kabbalistic fraternity. In the course of the six weekdays, the kabbalists abstain from sexual intercourse, but on the eve of Sabbath they engage in marital sex because they know the secret of the holy union of the feminine and masculine aspects of God that is consummated precisely at that time.[176] The zoharic passage is based on the rabbinic recommendation (mentioned above) that Torah scholars ideally should fulfill their conjugal obligations on Friday evening.[177] Going beyond the talmudic injunction, however, the kabbalistic idea is linked to the assumption that the abstinence of those occupied in the study of Torah reflects the ontological condition of the divine potencies. During the days of the week *Shekhinah* is entrapped in the demonic shells (symbolic of exile), and she is thus compared to a gate that is closed so that the unholy male will not be afforded the opportunity to have intercourse with the holy female. By contrast, on Sabbath *Shekhinah* is liberated and the gate is opened to allow the holy male to have intercourse with the holy female (symbolic of redemption).[178]

On Friday evening, therefore, it is the task of the comrades to direct their intention to *Shekhinah*, referred to by the technical term "Faith of the Master," when they are having intercourse with their wives, for by so doing they will draw down the blessing of the divine in their procreative act and thereby merit having righteous children.[179] The intention of the kabbalist in the act of coitus facilitates the union above between the King and Matrona, a theurgic deed referred to in the scriptural expression, "they hold fast to my covenant," that is, by means of his sexual activity the kabbalist fortifies the phallic aspect of God.[180]

Kabbalists are called eunuchs, therefore, for their sexual abstinence during the week is a metaphorical castration. On this account there is basic agreement in the figurative connotation of "eunuch" in the Christian and kabbalistic traditions. There is, however, an obvious difference in that kabbalists are encouraged to engage in carnal sex albeit at the time that the spiritual force is heightened in the world—the eve of Sabbath. The zoharic imagery underscores a deep ambivalence about celibacy as a religious ideal for the mystical elite and about the marital obligation to procreate.[181] A careful examination of the relevant passages has led me to the conclusion that the ascetic dimension is not pitted against the erotic; on the contrary, asceticism and eroticism in zoharic literature (and other kabbalistic sources) are dialectically interrelated: the impulse to chastity is itself a sexual impulse.[182] The symbolic castration of the kabbalist does not imply sexual impotence, which would be equivalent to effeminization,[183] but the transformation of the phallic energy from carnal intercourse with one's earthly wife to spiritual intercourse with *Shekhinah*. The imaginal contemplation of the divine ensues from the erotic attachment of the mystic to God.[184] The price of mystical enlightenment is symbolic castration.[185]

The erotic and ultimately phallic nature of the image of the eunuch can be gathered only from a careful scrutiny of the passages that describe in more detail the activities of the comrades in the weekdays, when others are engaged in marital intercourse. According to *Zohar,* the propitious time for the conjugal act is midnight,[186] which is the hour when God is said to visit the souls of the righteous in the Garden of Eden in order to take delight in them.[187] In almost every instance, the delight that is attributed to God is related to the study of Torah on part of the kabbalists.[188] Hence at the very moment that most Jewish males engage in marital sex, the mystical elite renounce physical sexuality in favor of a spiritualized relationship with God that is consummated through midrashic activity of an intensely erotic nature. One passage in particular underscores the nexus of different motifs:

> The sexual intercourse of [the Jewish] male is restricted to designated times so that he may direct his will to be conjoined to the holy One, blessed be he. Thus they have taught: At midnight the holy One, blessed be he, enters the Garden of Eden to take delight with the righteous, and the Community of Israel praises the holy One, blessed be he, and this is the acceptable time to be conjoined to them. The comrades who are engaged in [study of] Torah join the Community of Israel in praising the holy King as they are occupied with the Torah. For the rest of the [Jewish] males this is the acceptable time to be sanctified in the sanctity of the holy One, blessed be he, and to direct their intention to be conjoined to him. With respect to the comrades who are engaged in [study of] Torah, the time for their sexual intercourse is the time that another intercourse takes place, and this is on the eve of Sabbath.[189]

The mystics rise at midnight to study Torah at precisely the time that other Jewish males should ideally engage in sexual intercourse. The hermeneutical activity of the kabbalist is viewed as distinct from yet isomorphic to the conjugal sex of the layman; just as the latter is conjoined to God through the proper intention in sexual intercourse, so the former attains the state of conjunction by means of textual exegesis. The phenomenological structure of the two experiences is identical; by uniting with the female (in the case of the ordinary male, his wife, and in the case of the mystic, *Shekhinah*) the male gains access to the masculine potency of the divine. Thus in another passage the zoharic author states that at midnight the scholars "rise to study Torah, to be united to *Shekhinah* in order to praise the holy King."[190] The act of self-castration suggested by the use of the metaphor of the eunuch in no way implies emasculation of the male mystic. On the contrary, according to the members of the zoharic fraternity, the kabbalist who abstains from carnal sex is united with the feminine *Shekhinah.* The masculine virility of the kabbalist is left intact, indeed augmented, albeit translated from the physical to the spiritual. The renunciation of sexual power results in the empowerment of the mystic.[191] As the author of the following zoharic passage puts the matter:

> With respect to the sages who separate from their wives all the days of the week in order to be involved in [the study of] Torah, the supernal union [*ziwwuga ila'ah*] is

conjoined to them and it is not separated from them so that male and female will be found. When the Sabbath arrives, the sages must bring joy to their homes[192] on account of the glory of the supernal union, and they must direct their hearts to the will of their master.[193]

The zoharic perspective was well understood by the sixteenth-century kabbalist Elijah de Vidas, who thus commented: "The time of the intercourse of the rest of the people during the week, which is at midnight, is the time that the scholar is sanctified through intercourse with the Community of Israel, to rise to study Torah. Thus he is sanctified through the holy, spiritual intercourse [*ziwwug ruḥani we-qadosh*], just as the rest of the people are sanctified through the physical intercourse [*ziwwug gashmi*]."[194] One can speak of the kabbalist's spiritual marriage to *Shekhinah*, a matrimonial bond predicated on the separation from one's physical wife.[195] To be sure, only the kabbalist who is married can attain a state of conjunction with *Shekhinah*, but to achieve that experience it is necessary to abstain from conjugal intercourse.[196] A number of scholars have noted, the model of the abstinent mystic was Moses, who, according to older rabbinic sources, separated from his wife after having received the Torah.[197] As I noted above in passing, the aggadic tradition is the basis for the zoharic idea that the union of Moses and *Shekhinah* is consequent upon his adopting a life of celibacy.[198] The primary means by which the kabbalist emulates Moses and is united with *Shekhinah* is study of Torah, a spiritually erotic experience that presupposes the negation of physical eros.

The image of the eunuch by which the kabbalist is portrayed is paradoxically transformed into a symbol of masculine fecundity. Indeed, for the Castilian kabbalists who participated in the zoharic circle, becoming male in the full sense was predicated on the ascetic sublimation of the erotic. As I have already indicated, the form that this forbearance took may be referred to as the upward displacement of the phallic energy from the genitals to the brain. Contemplative study of Torah, which for the zoharic authors involved visually meditating on the shape of God embodied in the script of Torah, is predicated on the correlation of the psychomental and erogenic.[199]

To a degree this correspondence is derived from the zoharic understanding of the divine anatomy, which naturally reflects the conception of the human anatomy prevalent in the time of the composition of this literature. Of particular relevance is the entity that is named by the zoharic authorship *boṣina de-qardinuta* (the "hardened spark"), which is the aspect of the divine that gives shape to the luminous forms of being, a process that is depicted metaphorically as the act of writing or engraving. In several studies, I have argued that this spark functions like an upper phallus in the mind of God.[200] Moreover, the zoharic authors depict the very seed whence the sefirotic emanations come to be as made up of the letters of the Hebrew alphabet. The linguistic evolution of God's becoming, therefore, is a process of spermatogenesis.[201]

It goes without saying that the authors of *Zohar* understood the operation of the human mind in terms that correspond to the divine mind. Thus the hermeneutical activity of the kabbalist, which is linked to the phallic imagination, is comparable in structure and function to the creative effort of God. The prooftext that serves in zoharic literature to anchor both divine illumination and mystical enlightenment is Daniel 12:3: "And the enlightened will shine like the splendor of the sky."[202] The radiant ecstasy that arises from textual engagement involves the erotic union of kabbalist and *Shekhinah*, an experience that takes the place of conjugal sex with one's earthly wife.[203] From that vantage point, eroticism and asceticism can be seen in dialectical, not oppositional, relationship. Becoming male for the mystical elite entails metaphorical self-castration. The true male is he who willfully adopts the posture of the eunuch, for only the castrated mystic can accomplish the ultimate act of masculine virility, the telos of the (homo)erotic impulse, by becoming one with the divine feminine. The most potent form of erotic discharge is through retention of the seminal fluid from the genitals and its restoration to the aura of the brain.

Contemplative Envisioning / Raising Foot to Head

With respect to the interdependence of asceticism and eroticism, there is an interesting parallelism between *Zohar* and Tantrism, although there is no explicit instruction in the former (or in kabbalistic literature in general) to immobilize the emission of semen in the act of coitus as part of a spiritual exercise of mental concentration, as we find in the latter.[204] Nevertheless, the proscribed behavior of the kabbalist in refraining from sexual intercourse at the precise moment that he contemplates the divine in his imagination suggests that in zoharic kabbalah there is a comparable phenomenon to the tantric practice in *hatha yoga* of awakening and driving the *kuṇḍalinī* (the feminine vital energy in the form of a coiled snake at the base of the spine) by drawing up the semen (*biṇḍu*) from the genitals through the spinal cord to the spiritual center of the brain, the "mind of enlightenment" (*bodhicitta*), the source in the crown *cakra* whence the seminal fluid originated and proceeded in its downward flow through the subtle body to the sexual organ.[205]

That is, only after having mastered physical eros can the kabbalist creatively interpret Scripture and contemplate the symbolically anthropomorphic image of the divine form. Exposition of esoteric doctrines, both in oral and written discourse, is itself a reified type of sexual copulation in the mind.[206] The splendor of mystical insight is the light-seed in the head that corresponds to the *semen virile* of the genitals, an idea that is buttressed by the widespread assumption in medieval society, traceable to medical treatises from antiquity, that the seminal fluid originates in the brain, the anatomical conception that served as the model to depict the emanation of the *sefirot*.[207] The aim of the kabbalist, therefore, is not only to cause the seminal energy to flow from the brain to the phallus, whence it overflows to the feminine receptacle wherein the holy union is realized. The moment of mystical assimilation into the Godhead is attained by a reverse flow of semen from the phallus back to its source in the brain. What sets the upward trajectory into motion is the withholding of the ejaculation of seed on the part of the kabbalist. The ultimate theurgic role of the kabbalists who rise to study at midnight is to draw down the influx of divine energy from the upper recesses of the Godhead upon the masculine attribute of *Tif'eret* and from there to the feminine *Malkhut*.[208] I would argue, nonetheless, that the downward motion of the seminal light in the embodied mindfulness of the divine anthropos is occasioned by the upward motion of the *semen virile* in the mindful embodiment of the kabbalist.

From yet another perspective there is a striking similarity between the kabbalistic orientation and tantric "*yoga* of drawing up the drop."[209] It has been argued that the conjunction of masculine and feminine is fundamentally different in the two traditions: the kabbalist affirms carnal sex as a means to foster procreation below and to mimic the mystical coupling of the male *Tif'eret* and female *Shekhinah* above; by contrast, the yogin seeks to overcome gender polarity by reintegrating the feminine power of *sakti* and the masculine power of *siva* in the uppermost *cakra* (center) of the subtle body called *sahasrāra* (lotus of a thousand petals) or *brahmarandhra* (located on the crown of the skull) so that the primary state of nonduality is attained in the reconfiguration of the androgyne.[210] In this state, masculine and feminine are logically distinguishable without signifying duality or division; in the oneness of the Absolute the polarity of gender is transcended but not negated. Although it is certainly true, as I have previously noted, that in the theosophic kabbalah great emphasis is placed on the sacrality of heterosexual union, a close reading of the sources indicates that the spiritual ideal for the kabbalist likewise entails the overcoming of the duality of gender, which is achieved by reintegrating the feminine in the masculine.[211]

Ontological fission within the Godhead, reflected in the historical condition of Israel's exile, results in the bifurcation of the male androgyne into the masculine and feminine hypostases, which in turn yields the desire of the masculine to overcome duality and separation, a desire that is manifest in images of heterosexual fantasy. The lust of the male for the female is interpreted in *Zohar* (and related kabbalistic literature) as the attempt of the male to restore the part of himself that has been severed.[212] In the state of redemption, the otherness of the feminine is transcended and the primordial male androgyne is reconfigured. In the overcoming of duality, however, gender is not abolished in the face of a neutered unity. On the contrary, the union of the sexes results in the feminine being transformed into an aspect of the masculine. More specifically, kabbalists embrace the idea that the male and female are united through the phallus: the organ itself corresponds to the male and the corona to the female.

With respect to this structure, we again find an interesting phenomenological parallel to the symbol of the androgynous *linga* in tantric doctrine. Consider, for example, the following description of the unity achieved through the union of the sexes according to the method of *kulayāga*:

> Since the stem of the median channel is also visualized as inseparably linked to the sex organs—as it indeed is in the esoteric experience—there results a symbolic identification of the male and female united through the phallus with the sexually polarized triangular lotuses strung on and united through the median channel. It is no doubt here, in the reciprocal "sexualization" of the median channel and the "spiritualization" of the coital exchange, that the mythical identity of the *axis mundi* with the *linga* has its true rationale.[213]

Bracketing the obvious differences between Tantrism and zoharic kabbalah, the conceptual similarities are indeed conspicuous: the union of the sexes in both traditions results in the integration of the feminine in the phallus. According to my interpretation of the zoharic texts, the phallicization of the feminine implies that heterosexual eros (desire for the other as self) gives way to homoeroticism (love of self as other). In the symbolic worldview of the circle of kabbalists responsible for the production of *Zohar* in its diverse literary segments, the same-sex union is possible to the degree that physical sexuality has been abandoned for the sake of spiritualized erotics. To put the matter somewhat differently: homoeroticism is the carnality of celibate renunciation. A prolepsis of the eschatological transmutation of erotic energy from the bisexual to the monosexual is found in the fraternity of mystics whose Torah study takes the place of sexual mating with their female partners.[214]

Homoeroticism / Carnality of Celibate Renunciation

What are the implications of this dynamic for the question of the masculine identity of the medieval kabbalist? In previous scholarly discussions on the nature of eros in *Zohar*, attention has been paid almost exclusively to the heterosexual nature of the relationship of the male mystic either to the feminine *Shekhinah* or to his wife, who stands symbolically for the former. The erotic bonding of kabbalist and the divine and/or human feminine, however, must be seen as only the first stage in an integrative process that culminates in a restitution of the feminine to the phallus. To rectify a misunderstanding of my work promulgated by a number of colleagues,[215] let me emphasize that I do not deny the obvious fact that eros in the theosophic symbolism of *Zohar* entails the heterosexual yearning of male for female. The task before the scholar, however, is to evaluate how gender types are constructed in the particular cultural context of medieval kabbalists. The mystery of faith, as the zoharic authors remind the reader time and again, consists of the unification of male and female. But what is the nature of masculinity and femininity in light of the kabbalistic understanding of coitus? As I have already noted, the goal of sexual intercourse is to restore the feminine to the masculine. The most startling image used to convey this restoration is the symbol of the penal corona, which is identified with the feminine.

To highlight the hermeneutical value of this approach, let me review a topic that a number of scholars have previously analyzed: According to the view affirmed in a number of zoharic passages, the righteous man stands between two females, his earthly wife and *Shekhinah*.[216] In that respect, the mystic emulates the pattern of the divine gradations, for the masculine *Tif'eret* is situated between *Binah* and *Malkhut*, the upper and lower *Shekhinah*. But just as *Tif'eret* is between two females, so the lower *Shekhinah* occupies a position between two righteous males, *Yesod* and the mystic sage.[217] The primary function of the righteous man below is to stimulate *Shekhinah* so that she arouses the desire of the masculine above. From this vantage point, the eroticism is to be viewed in purely heterosexual terms. However, this arousal is also expressed in the homoerotically charged image of the righteous below causing the divine phallus to become erect. Two zoharic passages are particularly noteworthy:

> Come and see the secret of the matter: When the righteous man is in the world, *Shekhinah* does not depart from him, and her desire is for him. Consequently, the desire of love for her from above is like the desire of a male for a female when he is jealous of her.[218]

> Rachel gave birth to two righteous men, and this was appropriate for *Shemiṭṭah*[219] always sits between two righteous men, as it is written, "The righteous men shall inherit the land" (Ps. 37:29), the righteous above and the righteous below. From the righteous above the supernal waters flow and from the righteous below the feminine emits fluid in relation to the masculine in complete desire.[220]

The critical point here, which has been ignored by scholars, is the shifting gender valences implied by this chain of desire: the erotic conjunction of the mystic with *Shekhinah* transforms the latter from passive female to active male and the former from active male to passive female. To arouse the supernal male, the female must assume a role that is characteristically masculine; what facilitates this role is the insemination of the female by the male mystic. In the language of one zoharic passage, a homiletical reflection on "And your people, all of them righteous, shall possess the land for all time" (Isa. 60:21): "There is none to possess that land except for the one that is called righteous, for the Matrona is conjoined to him in order to be sweetened, and the righteous man verily possesses the Matrona."[221] The esoteric meaning of the prophetic claim that the righteous shall inherit the land is that only the righteous male can be mystically conjoined to *Shekhinah*. The effect that this conjunction has on *Shekhinah* is (in the technical zoharic terminology)[222] that it sweetens her, that is, the union with the righteous male ameliorates feminine judgment by masculine mercy. The ultimate goal of the mystic's interpretative efforts is the union of the masculine and feminine aspects of the divine, but this union results in the restoration of the latter to the former.

The mystery of the gender transformation is related in another zoharic passage on the verse, "Isaac then brought her into the tent of his mother Sarah, and he took Rebekah as his wife" (Gen. 24:67):

> The secret of the matter: The supernal mother [*Binah*] is found with the male [*Tif'eret*] only when the home [*Malkhut*] is in order, and the male and female are united. Then the supernal mother showers blessings upon them. In a similar way, the lower mother [*Malkhut*] is found with the male only when the home is in order, and the male comes to the female and they are joined as one. Then the lower mother showers blessings upon them. Thus the male in his home is crowned by two females in the manner of the world above.[223]

The complexity of gender symbolism reflected in the above citation (as well as numerous other passages) renders it far too simplistic to say that the dominant orientation in the zoharic composition is that the mystic is masculine in relation to the feminine *Shekhinah*.[224] The erotic union of the male mystic and the feminine *Shekhinah* results in the mutual transformation of the two: the masculine below is feminized, and the feminine above is masculinized. In the language of *Zohar*, the man is crowned by two females, one above and one below; the upper feminine assumes a masculine role and showers blessings upon him, whereas the lower feminine receives sustenance from him.

A fascinating account of this gender transformation is found in the extended passage in *Zohar* that proffers a simple meditational technique for one "who desires to know the wisdom of the holy unity" (*ma'n de-va'ei lemindda ḥokhmata di-yeḥuda qaddisha*).[225] The zoharic author recommends that one should contemplate the flame that rises from the coal or gaze upon a candle that is burning. It is the second image that engages the imagination of the author, but the importance of the first image, which can be traced to *Sefer Yeṣirah*, is that it underscores the point that a flame rises only when it is united with gross matter. In accord with the standard medieval hierarchy, the flame is the spiritual element that is sustained by the material. It is also evident that this can be transmuted into gender terms: the flame is the masculine, and the coal is the feminine. Even if this correlation is not stated explicitly, it is consistent with the symbolism attested in many other zoharic passages and within the larger intellectual world of the late Middle Ages.

But the example of the candle offers a somewhat more complex symbolism. There are three flames: "concealed flame," "white flame," and "blue-black flame." This particular text is an example of a ubiquitous phenomenon in zoharic literature of referring to the sefirotic potencies in terms derived from sense experience. Hence this passage implicitly alludes to the unification of the *sefirot*, the "wisdom of the holy unity." Most of the discussion concerns the white and blue-black flames; the concealed flame refers to one of the higher *sefirot*, most likely *Binah*. The radiant white flame rises above in a direct line, and the blue-black flame serves as the throne of glory for the white flame. The white flame is thus described as resting upon the blue-black flame and uniting with it so that everything is one.

The symbolic intent of this imagery is given in the zoharic text itself through the voice of Simeon ben Yoḥai: the blue-black flame is the final *he* of the Tetragrammaton, that is, the feminine *Shekhinah*, which is united with the white flame or the *yod-he-waw* of the name, that is, the masculine *Tif'eret*. The unification of the two flames, therefore, represents the perfection of the name, the expansion of the threefold into a quaternity.[226] But the blue-black flame is the final *he* of the Tetragrammaton only when the righteous men of the community of Israel are conjoined to *Shekhinah* from below so that she is united with the masculine potency from above. When Israel is not conjoined to *Shekhinah*, she is in the form of *dalet*, which clearly symbolizes her state of impoverishment or weakness (related to the word *dal*).

Significantly, the verse that the zoharic author quotes to make this point is "If there be a damsel that is a virgin," *ki yihyeh na'arah betulah* (Deut. 22:23). According to the masoretic orthography, the word *na'arah* ("damsel")is written *na'ar*, that is, without the final *he*. In response to the query why this is so, the zoharic author writes: "Because she is not united with the masculine, and wherever male and female do not exist, the *he* does not exist. It departs from there and she is left *dalet*. When she is united with the radiant white flame, she is called *he*, for then everything is united as one." When *Shekhinah* is united with Israel from below, she is united with the male above, and this unification transforms her semiotic status from *dalet* to *he*. Underlying this linguistic symbolism is an ontological presumption: *Shekhinah* is transformed from the impoverished feminine (the virgin written as *naʿar*) to the enriched feminine, the virgin that has united with and transformed into the male (symbolically represented as *naʿarah*).

The esoteric exegesis proffered here overtly contradicts the literal sense of Scripture. The damsel, *naʿarah*, is not only not a virgin but the female who has been metamorphosed into a male as a result of sexual intercourse. Concomitantly, the body politic of Israel is transformed from masculine to feminine as the righteous males are assimilated into *Shekhinah* in the image of the material wax that feeds the flame. The term *naʿarah*, therefore, symbolically denotes both Israel below (feminized male) and *Shekhinah* above (masculinized female).

In line with this gender metamorphosis, we should expect a shift from the heterosexual to the homoerotic. As I have already indicated, the position articulated in zoharic homilies is that the mystic becomes fully male when he abstains from heterosexual intercourse, an abstinence that facilitates the reintegration of the feminine into the masculine. The masculinization of the feminine effects a change in the texture of the erotic experience: heterosexual desire is fulfilled in the homoerotic bonding of the mystic to the male body of God,[227] which is constituted by the members of the kabbalistic fraternity. One passage in particular is noteworthy, for there is an explicit link between the ascetic denial of the world and cleaving to the phallic gradation of the divine:

> "[The Lord spoke to Moses, saying: Tell the Israelite people] to bring me gifts" (Exod. 25:1–2). Here is the unity in one containment, above and below. It does not say, "bring gifts," but "bring me gifts," above and below in one containment without any separation. "From every man whose heart so moves him you shall accept gifts for me" (ibid., 2). This verse should have said "every man whose heart so moves him." What is the meaning of "from every man" [*meʾet kol ish*]? This is a secret here for those masters of judgment. Praiseworthy are the righteous who know how to set the will of their hearts towards the holy, supernal king. All of the will of their hearts is not toward this world and its vacuous desire. Rather, they know and they try to set their intentions to cleave above in order to draw down the will of their master towards them from above to below. From what place do they draw the will of their master towards them? They take it from the one holy and supernal place whence emerge all the holy intentions. And who is it? "Every man" [*kol ish*], this is the righteous one who is called "all" [*kol*], as it is written, "the advantage of the land is in the all [*ba-kol*] (Eccles. 5:8). "Truly by all [*kol*] your precepts I walk straight" (Ps. 11:128). And [the word] "man" [*ish*], as it is written, "the righteous man" [*ish ṣaddiq*] (Gen. 6:9). This is the righteous one [*ṣaddiq*], master of the house, whose intention is constantly toward his woman as a husband loves his wife constantly. "Whose heart so moves him," he loves her, and "his heart" is his woman, "So moves him," to cleave to it.[228]

The mystical interpretation of the command to bring a gift offering to God yields the following esoteric knowledge to the kabbalists designated "masters of judgment."[229] The righteous men turn their attention from the vain cravings of the physical world and direct the intention of their hearts to the supernal king. More specifically, the object of their intent is the phallic potency of God, the source of all intention, which is designated by the terms "all" (*kol*), "man" (*ish*), and "righteous" (*ṣaddiq*). The cleaving of male kabbalists to the phallus surely suggests a homoerotic underpinning to the ascetic renunciation, the very means that facilitates the union above between the male and female potencies of the Godhead.

The homoerotic nature of the ascetic lifestyle is conveyed most vividly in zoharic homilies by means of the mythical image (to which I referred above) of God taking delight in the souls of the righteous in the Garden of Eden at midnight. One may presume that the souls referred to in these contexts are those of the departed who dwell in the Garden of Eden. Yet from a number of these passages it may be concluded that the reference is also to the righteous souls of the living who rise at midnight to study Torah. Let us consider as representative the following text:

> R. Isaac said: It is written, "A river issues from Eden to water the garden" (Gen. 2:10). This is the pillar upon which the world stands, and it waters the garden and the garden is irrigated by it. By means of it she produces fruits and all the fruits disseminate in the world, and they are the pillar of the world, the pillar of Torah. Who are they? The souls of the righteous for they are the fruit of the actions of the holy One, blessed be he. Thus every night the souls of the righteous ascend and at midnight the holy One, blessed be he, comes to the Garden of Eden to take delight in them. In which ones? R. Yose said: In all of them, those whose dwelling is in that world and those who reside in their dwelling in this world. At midnight the holy One, blessed be he, takes delight in all of them.[230]

The homoerotic implication of this passage cannot be ignored: God delights in the souls of the righteous, which include both the dead who have a permanent residence in the Garden of Eden and the living who are visiting there temporarily. In the first instance, it would appear that the word *ishtaᶜsha* (or, in the infinitive, *leᶜishtaᶜsheᶜa*) signifies a form of delight related to the exercise of the mind, which would be appropriate in light of the fact that the righteous souls are involved in the study of Torah when God comes to visit them. Hence the image of God's taking delight with the righteous is certainly meant to convey the idea of intellectual joy. On the other hand, the erotic connotation of this term is also quite evident.[231] Indeed, the two significations are not ultimately separable, given the homology of the noetic and erotic to which I have already referred.

There is another important dimension to this relationship that is made clear in the continuation of the aforecited passage:

> When the souls of the righteous depart from this world and ascend above, they are all garbed in the supernal light, in the glorious image, and the holy One, blessed be he, delights in them and desires them, for they are the fruit of his actions. Thus they are called "Israel," for they have holy souls, and they are the sons of the holy One, blessed be he, as it is said, "You are sons of the Lord your God" (Deut. 14:1), sons in truth, the fruit of his actions.[232]

The righteous souls in whom God delights are the fruits of his own labor and indeed his own sons who are in his image. Taking delight in the righteous mystics who study Torah is tantamount to God taking delight in himself. The erotic bond between God and the righteous, therefore, should not be construed as incestuous but, rather, as narcissistic: God's love of the righteous is an expression of self-love.[233] God delights in his own image reflected in the faces of the mystics even as the mystics delight in their own image reflected in the face of God. From this perspective, moreover, it can be said that the homoeroticism is an aspect of divine autoeroticism.[234]

One might argue that even if I am correct in asserting that from the human perspective heterosexual eros is fulfilled in the homoerotic union of the male mystic and God, surely from the divine perspective homoeroticism serves only as a catalyst to bring about the heterosexual union of the male and female attributes within the sefirotic pleroma. Thus according to one zoharic passage, when God enters the Garden of Eden to take delight in the righteous, *Shekhinah* brings forth words of innovative Torah study that were stored away, and God is said to contemplate these words in joy. As a result of this contemplation, God is crowned with the supernal crowns and is united with *Shekhinah*.[235] In this case, it would seem, the homoerotic relation of God and the righteous facilitates the heterosexual mating of God and *Shekhinah*. Upon closer examination, however, it becomes apparent that the feminine *Shekhinah* is made up essentially of the members of the kabbalistic fraternity and she is thus constructed as masculine. This is the esoteric significance of the repeated claim that God's heterosexual relationship to *Shekhinah* is actualized through his homoerotic bonding with kabbalists. For example, according to the conclusion of an intricate zoharic discourse on the verse, "How good and how pleasant it is that brothers dwell together" (Ps. 133:1), the word *gam* in the expression *gam yaḥad* ("together") signifies the inclusion of *Shekhinah* with the mystical brothers in whom God takes joy, for their words of study are pleasing to him.[236]

The degree to which *Shekhinah* is composed ontically of the male mystics is underscored in a second passage that is an exegetical reflection on the verse, "O my dove, in the cranny of the rocks, hidden by the cliff, let me see your face, let me hear your voice; for your voice is sweet and your face is comely" (Song 2:14): *Shekhinah* (referred to by the technical name "Community of Israel" and symbolized by the scriptural image of the "dove") is described as being constantly with the scholars who have no rest in the world (hence they are "in the cranny of the rocks") and who are "modest" and "pious" (signified by the expression "hidden by the cliff"). God desires *Shekhinah* on account of the sages who have adopted an ascetic lifestyle (implied by the designations "modest" [*ṣenuʿin*] and the "pious who fear the holy One, blessed be he" [*ḥasidin daḥalei qudsha verikh hu*]), a yearning that is linked to the words, "let me see your face, let me hear your voice." The voice of the feminine *Shekhinah* turns out to be the voice of the male mystics engaged in nocturnal study of Torah.

That the face of *Shekhinah* likewise is related to the male mystics[237] is implied in the continuation of the passage: "It has been taught: The images of those engaged in [the study of] Torah at night are engraved above before the holy One, blessed be he, and the holy One, blessed be he, takes delight in them all day and he gazes upon them. That voice [of Torah] rises and breaks through all the heavens until it ascends before the holy One, blessed be he."[238] The voice and face of *Shekhinah* that God desires to encounter refer respectively to the voices and iconic representations of kabbalists involved in exegesis of Torah according to the theosophic secrets. That the homosocial bonding of the male deity and the male community of kabbalists, which constitutes the textual body of the feminine, is the ultimate goal of the midnight study is stated explicitly in the following passage:

> R. Simeon began [to expound the verse] and said, "He gives food to those who fear him; he is ever mindful of his covenant" (Ps. 111:5). "He gives food to those who fear him," this refers to the righteous, those who fear the holy One, blessed be he, for whoever fears him is designated as one of the men of the king's house, and concerning him it is written, "Praiseworthy is one man who fears the Lord" (ibid., 112:1). What is [the meaning of] "he gives food to those who fear him?" It is as it is written, "She rises while it is still night, and supplies food for her household" (Prov. 31:15). From here we learn that every man who studies Torah at night, and who rises at midnight when the Community of Israel is aroused to prepare the house for the King, such a person participates with her, and he is named as one from the house of the King, and all day they bestow upon him from the provisions of the house, as it is written, "and supplies food for her household, the allotted portion for her maids." What is "her household?" All those who participate with her at night are called "her household," members of her household. Therefore "he gives food to those who fear him." What is [the meaning of] "food?" Verily food that she receives from a supernal remote place, as it is written, "from afar she brings her bread" (ibid., 14). And who merits this food? The end of the verse offers proof as it is written, "he is ever mindful of his covenant," the one who contemplates[239] the Torah, to participate with her in the night. Moreover, [the verse indicates that] the holy One, blessed be he, has a supernal righteous man [*ṣaddiq ḥad ila'ah*], and he participates with him, and both of them bestow upon the Community of Israel, as it is written, "the righteous shall possess the land for all time" (Isa. 60:21).[240]

The fraternity of male mystics who rise at midnight to engage in the nocturnal study of Torah join together with the feminine presence, the Community of Israel. The kabbalists are referred to as the household of *Shekhinah*, for they assist her in preparing the house for the King, which is a euphemistic way of speaking about the intercourse of the masculine and feminine potencies of the Godhead, that is, preparing the house means preparing the female receptacle to receive the seminal discharge, the breath/light-seed of the divine potency. On account of this union kabbalists acquire the divine overflow, which is designated symbolically as the food (*ṭeref*) that *Shekhinah* obtains from a higher source in the sefirotic pleroma. The symbolic connotation of food is underscored by the exegetical aside that the term *ṭeref* is to be taken in its precise sense, *mammash*, which is one of the technical ways the zoharic authors express the idea that the literal is symbolical in its literalness and the symbolic is literal in its symbolism.[241]

The ontological assimilation of male mystics into the feminine presence results in their being accorded the status of God's covenant, of which he is ever mindful. Additionally, the attribution of the title "covenant" to kabbalists signifies that their behavior below parallels the action of the *ṣaddiq* above, which corresponds to *Yesod,* the ninth gradation or the phallic potency, which is also called "covenant" on account of the rite of circumcision. The contemplative study of Torah affords the opportunity for the male kabbalists to be conjoined to the feminine presence, which receives the influx from *Yesod.* The double intercourse—from the *ṣaddiq* below and the *ṣaddiq* above—is the underlying meaning of the verse that speaks of the righteous in the plural (*ṣaddiqim*) inheriting the land, which is the *Shekhinah. Prima facie,* it would seem that this passage unequivocally affirms the appropriateness of heterosexual language to depict both the relationship between the mystic and the divine and the relationship between the different aspects of the divine. Upon closer reflection, however, one may conclude that insofar as the earthly righteous constitute the household of the King, which is the body of the feminine presence, the union of the King and his house can be seen ultimately as providing the context whereby the masculine aspect of God is united with the group of male kabbalists.

Heterosexual language is used, therefore, to describe the homoerotic relationship between God and kabbalist, but this is to be expected, since—given the gender stereotypes that prevailed in medieval society at large and were affirmed by the rabbinic elite as well—the weaker party will be valorized as female.[242] By this same logic, it is possible for God's erotic union with the righteous male to be portrayed by quintessentially heterosexual images such as that of the king and the queen. Indeed, we find a remarkable articulation of this phenomenon in a passage from Gikatilla, which occurs in the context of his delineating the different phases of divine disclosure in the world in terms of the Tetragrammaton and the various cognomens.[243] When God appears before the nations of the world, he does so "in the image of a king who stands before his ministers and all his servants, garbed in the attire of royalty or the attire of warfare." Gikatilla concludes, therefore, that God in his essence is not seen by the worldly nations, for he is concealed in the garb of the cognomens when he is revealed to them. By contrast, when God stands before the Jewish people, "he stands with them like a king with the members of his household and he removes something of his clothing as is the way of the king to remove some of his clothing when he stands with the members of his household." Gikatilla links this phase to the verse, "Three times a year—on the feast of unleavened bread, on the feast of weeks, and on the feast of booths—all your males shall appear before the Lord your God in the place that he will choose" (Deut. 16:16), and to the talmudic principle underlying the ruling that one who is blind in one eye is exempt from the commandment to be seen in the Temple during the three festivals, "just as one comes to see so one comes to be seen."[244]

The biblical commandment and the rabbinic dictum as understood by Gikatilla involve the obligation to see God, a seeing that is connected more specifically to the disclosure of God in his true essence, the Tetragrammaton. The disclosure is a form of divestiture, a removal of the garments that are the cognomens that conceal the essential name. But even when God appears before Israel there must be a measure of concealment, since there are some who are not worthy to apprehend the truth of the Tetragrammaton.

Only when God is alone with the righteous (*ṣaddiqim*) and pious (*ḥasidim*) of Israel, the mystical elite, is the disclosure complete. Here it is worth citing Gikatilla's language verbatim:

> When God, blessed be he, unites with the righteous and pious, the patriarchs of the world and the mighty ones, he removes from himself all cognomens and the Tetragrammaton alone is exalted.[245] Thus the Tetragrammaton alone stands with Israel like a king who has removed all his garments and unites with his wife. This is the secret, "Turn back, O rebellious children, for I have united with you" (Jer. 3:22), and it says, "I will espouse you forever" (Hosea 2:21). "I will espouse you"—like a king who removes his garments and unites with his wife, so too the Tetragrammaton removes all cognomens and garments, and unites with Israel, with their pious [*ḥasidim*], ascetics [*perushim*], and the pure ones [*ṭehorim*]. This is the secret, "I had taken off my robe, was I to don it again?" (Song 5:3).[246]

The unique relation that God has to the spiritual elite of Israel is depicted metaphorically as the erotic relationship of the king and queen.[247] Gikatilla articulates in a lucid manner an orientation found in *Zohar* as well: the homoerotic bond between God and mystic is expressed in heterosexual images.[248] From the fact that the homoerotic is embedded in heterosexual images—another illustration of this dynamic is the relationship of master to disciple, for the former is portrayed as the phallic potency disseminating the seminal teaching to the latter, who assumes the role of the feminine vessel receiving the light-seed[249]—we may deduce that relationships depicted heterosexually can be understood homoerotically.

The overtly feminine characterizations of the divine in kabbalistic texts do not in and of themselves instruct us about a positive valence imputed to the female gender by medieval mystics. It is more tenable, as I have argued, that the feminine images must be seen as part of an androcentric, indeed, phallocentric perspective whereby the female is conceived ontically (and this is a biological as well as a metaphysical assumption) as part of the masculine. The attitude toward gender had a profound impact on the nature of the mystic's experience with God. The preponderance of heterosexual imagery in the tradition and the positive affirmation of carnal sexuality as a means for procreation cannot be denied.

On the other hand, being male for kabbalists meant restricting conjugal intercourse to the eve of Sabbath and adopting an ascetic lifestyle during the week. Ironically enough, self-inflicted castration augmented rather than weakened the kabbalist's masculine virility, for the vow of abstinence facilitates participation in a nocturnal ritual of Torah study that leads to mystical communion with *Shekhinah* and an erotic relationship with her masculine consort, the holy One. Celibacy of this circumscribed nature has provided members of kabbalistic fraternities an opportunity to transpose the heterosexual into the homoerotic. However, by expressing the homoerotic in heterosexual terms, the medieval kabbalist was able to appropriate standard Jewish sexual norms even as he radically transfigured them. This transfiguration has afforded kabbalists the opportunity to anticipate the overcoming of gender dimorphism characteristic of the eschaton, an overcoming by coming-over, to be explored in the next chapter.

CHAPTER EIGHT

Coming-to-Head, Returning-to-Womb: (E)Soteric Gnosis and Overcoming Gender Dimorphism

Renunciation—is a piercing Virtue—
The letting go
A Presence—for an Expectation—
Not now—
The putting out of Eyes—
Just Sunrise—
Lest Day—
Day's Great Progenitor—
Outvie
Renunciation—is the Choosing
Against itself—
Itself to justify
Unto itself—
When larger function—
Make that appear—
Smaller—that Covered Vision—Here—

—Emily Dickinson

There is a variety of literary settings in which the ideal of spiritual eroticism cultivated in the mystical piety of various traditions has found expression, but one medium that has been especially significant in the history of Judaism and Christianity is the commentarial tradition on the Song of Songs, the biblical book that most overtly employs tropes of sensual love and carnal sexuality.[1] As Bernard McGinn astutely articulated the matter, "Among the many intimate bonds between Jewish and Christian mystical traditions none is more important than the fact that both found in the Song of Songs the mystical text par excellence. For Jews and Christians, the Song was not some excuse for the surreptitious use of forbidden themes, but was the authorized model that guided their personal appropriation of the divine-human encounter."[2]

From the formative period when rabbinic Judaism and Christianity evolved as distinct faith communities, the Song presented a unique hermeneutical problem: How does one interpret the exclusively sensual language of a book canonized as part of sacred Scripture? From the standpoint of the leitmotif of this book, the Song embodied for medieval kabbalists, and in a unique way for the members of the fraternity responsible for the production of the zoharic anthology, the convergence of language, eros, and being that has informed their mystical-esoteric orientation.[3]

Eroticization of Allegory in Rabbinic and Christian Interpretation

Early rabbinic interpreters, as with their Christian counterparts, adopted exegetical strategies to deal with the problem of how to infuse a work that on the surface is not about God, Israel, or the covenantal bond between them with sacred meaning. One strategy formulated in the rabbinic academies was the allegorical approach: to interpret the erotic imagery of the earthly lover and beloved as a reference to the relationship between God and Israel.[4] This is the approach that is most frequently mentioned in conjunction with the rabbis, but it must be noted that the exegetical comments on the Song scattered in literature of both the tannaitic and amoraic periods indicates that the rabbinic reading was not uniform or monolithic. On the contrary, even the key metaphor adopted by the rabbis splintered into smaller symbolic applications that do not add up to one coherent picture, although each is predicated on locating the liturgical utterance of the poem at a particular moment in Israel's sacred history.[5] The correlation of the Song and historical events, beginning with creation and ending with messianic redemption, is implicit in some of the rabbinic comments but fully developed in the Aramaic Targum.[6]

The prevailing approach to the Song attested in patristic documents involved a figurative understanding of the explicit eroticism, but here it is necessary to differentiate the allegorical and tropological approaches: the dialogue refers either to the relationship of the soul and God or that of the Church and Jesus.[7] The theological interpretations proffered by rabbis and Church fathers shared a common agenda, as both provided a cultic-liturgical framework for the Song, which may have been a retrieval of its original Canaanite background.[8] Notwithstanding the parallel intent, an important distinction must be made. The allegorical interpretation adopted by the rabbis did not entail, as in the case of the Church fathers (typified, for example, by Origen), in an evidently Platonic-Philonic manner, a negation of the carnality linked to the literal sense of the biblical text,[9] nor the presumed correspondence between the spiritual realm and the inner sense, so that one can, indeed must, proceed from visible to invisible. As has been recently argued, a "controlling hermeneutic" in the patristic reading of the Song was the doctrine of Incarnation, the "meeting of the divine and human in Christ," for the biblical text provided "a series of icons/similes which actually have a surreal—that is defined as the juxtaposition of natural and supernatural—quality."[10] The Song's erotic imagery is interpreted as a figurative depiction of the soul's ascetic yearning to unite with Christ, a spiritual union that is made possible by the epiphany of the Word in the person of Jesus; the soteriological message of the Song, therefore, is that the transubstantiation of the human into the divine is made possible by the mystery of the divine becoming human.

In spite of the Christological avowal of bodily images in the Song, the task of the reader is to surpass the literalness of carnal love and affirm the spiritual love expressed in the mystical union that binds the soul and Logos or the Church and Christ.[11] Even if one were to agree with Patricia Cox Miller that according to Origen, the allegorical reading intensifies the erotic nature of the text,[12] the eroticism is subsumed under the body of the text rather than the text of the body, which is to say that this approach diminishes the concrete sensuality implied by the contextual meaning.[13] The overtly sexual eroticism of the Song thus provided an argument for Origen (and those who followed him) for the allegorical interpretation of Scripture as a whole and not just in this one case. In some of the later patristic writers, for example, Jerome and Ambrose of the fourth century, the hermeneutical posture is employed to advocate on behalf of ascetic renunciation.[14]

For rabbinic exegetes, by contrast, the internal meaning of the Song is not predicated on undermining the external form of the scriptural metaphor. On the contrary, the allegoresis intended by the midrashic reading is an intensification of the literal carnality and the consequent application of erotic imagery to the divine.[15] Elsewhere I have suggested that a number of aphoristic comments scattered throughout talmudic and midrashic literature, including the critical exegetical remark that every Solomon mentioned in the Song is holy, for the name refers to God, the "one to whom peace belongs" (*li-mi she-ha-shalom shelo*),[16] indicate that the allegorical interpretation of the Song for some rabbis seems to have been predicated on a theosophical conception that attributed gender and sexual images to God.[17] The esoteric tradition I presumed to have uncovered was apparently independent of the *Shiʿur Qomah* speculation, which has also been linked by a number of scholars to the Song (especially the detailed description of the lover in the fifth chapter).[18] If my suggestion proves to be correct, then the midrashic reading reflected in a few isolated passages anticipates the kabbalistic orientation that developed more fully and systematically at a later point in Jewish history.[19]

Even if one were not prepared to accept my hypothesis regarding the theosophic implications of the interpretation of the Song implied in select rabbinic authorities, there is another feature of their allegorical perspective that had an influential role in the subsequent evolution of medieval kabbalah. The allegorical reading of the Song, which is attributed to Aqiva and several other rabbinic figures, is predicated on the assumption that the Song is equivalent to the Torah in its entirety. This, it seems, is the underlying meaning of the oft-cited remark attributed to Aqiva that all of Scripture is holy, but the Song is the holy of holies.[20] That is, just as the sanctity of the holy of holies outweighs the sanctity of all other holy places, so too the Song is the most sacred book of holy writ, for it encapsulates the holiness of the entire canon. The Song is the inner sanctum wherein lay the measure of holiness that marks the parameters of sacred space in the textual topography.

The erotic drama of the Song, therefore, reveals something fundamental about the mystery of revelation. The point is poignantly made in another comment attributed to Aqiva in the midrashic anthology *Shir ha-Shirim Zuṭa*, which is linked exegetically to the opening verse, "The Song of Songs by Solomon" (Song 1:1): "This is to teach you that all the wisdom of Solomon was equal to the Torah. R. Aqiva said: Had the Torah not been given, the Song of Songs would have been sufficient to guide the world."[21] The notion that the Song is commensurate with the entire Torah was no doubt presumed as well by the rabbis who located the utterance of the Song at Sinai.[22] Recitation of the poem, which expresses figuratively the love between God and Israel, occurred precisely when the divine glory was manifest in the giving of Torah to his people. To locate the narration of the Song at the Sinaitic epiphany underscores the fact that the moment that Torah was revealed to Israel is itself erotically charged. This can be explained in terms of the prevalent depiction of the theophany at Sinai in matrimonial language,[23] but it also embraces the more esoteric claim that the very notion of Torah as revealed word entails the structure of the parable, which is predicated on the paradox of metaphorical representation that is basic to the dynamic of eros, with its disclosure of truth through the appearance of image.

The equation of Torah and the Song opens a path that uncovers the ground of rabbinic poetics: Just as in the particular case of the Song the contextual meaning is figurative, so the hermeneutical pattern of Scripture in general is related to the poetic structure of metaphor, the *mashal* in Hebrew, which presumes an interplay of inner and outer signification, the duplicity of meaning, the secret hidden beneath the veil. In the midrashic anthology *Shir ha-Shirim Rabbah*, the nature of the Song is elucidated by a discussion of the parables (*meshalim*) that Solomon composed in order to clarify the meaning of Scripture,[24] an activity that is epitomized in the statement, "Until Solomon arose there was no similitude" (*dugma*).[25] Hence, interpreting the description of Solomon in Ecclesiastes 12:9 as one who "weighed, pondered, and composed many parables" (*izzen we-ḥiqqer tiqqen meshalim harbeh*), the anonymous midrashist remarks, "He made handles for the Torah." The parables composed by Solomon are depicted idiomatically as handles (*oznayim*), for just as one can carry a basket more effectively if it has a handle, so the parables make the meaning of Torah comprehensible to one who possesses a discerning ear (*ozen*).

The Song itself is the *dugma* of the *dugma*, that is, the paradigm of paradigms, the metaphorical figuration that likens dissimilar things through the prism of symbolic imagination. Alternatively expressed, the Song is the poem par excellence, for the contextual sense (*peshaṭ*) overlaps with the figurative (*mashal*). The convergence of *peshaṭ* and *mashal* is indicative of the larger hermeneutical claim regarding the poetic nature of Torah,[26] which in turn expresses and is expressed by the erotic desire that resonates in the language of the Song. The implication of the symbolic reading of the Song proffered by rabbinic interpreters is well captured in Rosenzweig's recognition of the essentially metaphorical nature of eros and the concurrent affirmation of the essentially erotic nature of metaphor. In his words, "love is not 'but a metaphor;' it is metaphor in its entirety and its essence; it is only apparently transitory: in truth, it is eternal. The appearance is as essential as the truth here, for love could not be eternal as love if it did not appear to be transitory. But in the mirror of appearance, truth is directly mirrored."[27]

Contemplative Eros: Scriptural Exegesis and Christian Monasticism

Not only is it the case that Jews and Christians through the centuries have shared an abiding exegetical interest in the Song, but precisely this venue served as one of the most important ways in which the polemic between the two faiths was expressed. Inasmuch as clerical authorities and lay practitioners in both faith communities doggedly maintained the covenantal privilege of being the special recipient of divine love, it was only natural that commentaries and sermons on the Song would serve as a prism to refract theological controversies and debates.[28] As one might expect, however, the polemical element was apt to enhance the intrigue of the other and thereby increase the possibility of mutual influence.[29] It is thus appropriate for me to include this brief section on the contemplative explanation of the erotic images of the Song reflected in medieval monastic culture, for, as I will argue below, these texts or, better, the ideas they purport serve as the theological other to interpretations of the Song enunciated by medieval Jewish philosophers and kabbalists.

The interpretation of the Song in the Christian Middle Ages on the part of male readers basically continued the two exegetical lines established by the Church fathers (subsequently I shall address the difference in orientation between men and women readers): The narrative dialogue between bride and bridegroom was applied allegorically to the soul and Jesus or tropologically to the Church and God.[30] In either case, but especially the former, a decidedly mystical understanding of the erotic language of the Song evolved. The vicissitudes of eros characteristic of the Song—periodic presence and absence of the beloved, yearning of lover incessantly hounded by eventual separation, burning desire to consummate love tempered by the advice not to arouse it before its time—were treated as a perfectly apt way to describe the soul's contemplative life and its quest for union with the divine.[31]

Particularly important was the image of the kiss, suggested by the opening verse "Let him kiss me with the kisses of his mouth" (Song 1:2). The importance of this motif in the history of Christian mysticism, related specifically to the exegesis of the Song, is well summarized by Nicholas Perella:

> The language of the Song of Songs is indeed daring, and if it is asked how far the Church fathers and medieval mystics could go in adopting it in their symbolism of the conjugal relationship between the soul and God, the answer must be that they could go even beyond the amatory expressions of the Song, for we should note that almost invariably what begins as an exegetical treatment becomes a description of experiential knowledge or affective mysticism in which the Song serves as a stepping-stone and point of reference. . . . At the very beginning of the Song of Songs, the mystics and theologians found they had to contend with the bride's bold request for kisses. . . . Even so, the mystics, unlike ordinary lovers, tend to make of the kiss not merely a preliminary of the love relationship, but love's very terminus.[32]

The implications of this interpretative strategy for the gender valence of the mystical experience should be obvious: the biblical text becomes a mirror reflecting the erotic relationship of male writers, in most cases celibate monks, to the male aspect of the divine. To be sure, in relation to the Logos, the soul assumes the rank of the feminine, but male exegetes nonetheless relate to the male Jesus through interpreting the erotic language of the Song.[33] The heterosexual imagery of the scriptural narrative, therefore, is hermeneutically transposed into a male homoeroticism.[34] A particularly striking illustration of the point is found in the case of Bernard of Clairvaux (1090–1153) who thus addressed his fellow monks in the opening sermon on the nature of the Song:

> Only the touch of the Spirit can inspire a song like this, and only personal experience can unfold its meaning. Let those who are versed in the mystery revel in it; let all others burn with desire rather to attain to this experience than merely to learn about it. . . . It is preeminently a marriage song telling of chaste souls in loving embrace of their wills in sweet concord, of the mutual exchange of the heart's affections.[35]

Similarly, in the third sermon, prior to explicating the verse of the Song according to the rendering of the Vulgate text, *Osculetur me osculo oris sui*, "Let him kiss me with the kiss of his mouth," Bernard commented:

> Today the text we are to study is the book of our own experience. You must therefore turn your attention inwards. . . . I am attempting to discover if any of you has been privileged to say from his heart: "Let him kiss me with the kiss of his mouth." Those to whom it is given to utter these words sincerely are comparatively few, but any one who has received this mystical kiss from the mouth of Christ at least once, seeks again that intimate experience, and eagerly looks for its frequent renewal.[36]

Reflecting on this passage, Grace Jantzen noted a shift in Bernard's language to an emphasis on experience as the distinguishing mark of the mystical. But, as she also points out, the experience here, which is linked especially to the kiss, is mediated through the text of Scripture.[37] To be sure, Bernard himself informs us that the "experience of the kiss tells more than any words,"[38] and in a second passage he reminds the reader that even if one were granted the experience of the Word, one could not describe it, as it is beyond description.[39] The ineffability of the unitive experience notwithstanding, the primary way to attain it is through the text of Scripture, the Word incarnate: "The man who thirsts for God eagerly studies and meditates on the inspired word, knowing that there he is certain to find the one for whom he thirsts. Let the garden, then, represent the plain, unadorned, historical sense of Scripture, the storeroom its moral sense, and the bedroom the mystery of divine contemplation."[40]

For Bernard, the task is to transform the erotic imagery of the Song into mental images that serve as the catalyst that fosters the experience of union on the part of the soul of the male reader with the masculine Logos.[41] In a passage from the second sermon on the Song, Bernard passionately writes: "If it really be true, as you prophets have said, that God has determined to show mercy, to reveal himself in a more favorable light, let him establish a covenant of peace, an everlasting covenant with me by the kiss of his mouth. If he will not revoke his given word, let him empty himself, let him humble himself, let him bend to me and kiss me with the kiss of his mouth."[42]

Reading the verse from the Song provides the hermeneutical framework within which an experiential reliving of that which is encoded in the text can recur. Hence to meditate on the verse "Let him kiss me with the kiss of his mouth" is to activate the text in a such a way that contemplation of the revealed word facilitates the mystical union of the reader with God experienced in the erotic intimacy of the kiss, or, to be more precise, the kiss of the mouth, which Bernard contrasts in one sermon with the kiss of the feet and the kiss of the hand, respectively signifying forgiveness that is consequent to contrition felt in response to recognition of one's transgressions and the marking of repentance occasioned and sustained by the flow of undeserved grace.

Once the soul has attained the preliminary stages on the path—conversion and penance—it is ready for the "mystical kiss" that issues from the mouth of Christ.[43] Being kissed by the mouth of Christ symbolically depicts receiving the "living, active word . . . an unreserved infusion of joys, a revealing of mysteries, a marvelous and indistinguishable mingling of the divine light with the enlightened mind, which, joined in truth to God, is one spirit with him."[44] To attain this state, the soul must no longer be burdened with sin or be subject to carnal passions.[45] Bernard, following a long-standing tradition going back to Origen, asserts that ascetic renunciation is the prerequisite for study of the Song, which for him is the means to bring about the experience of contemplative union: "Before the flesh has been tamed and the spirit set free by zeal for truth, before the world's glamour and entanglements have been firmly repudiated, it is a rash enterprise on any man's part to presume to study spiritual doctrines."[46] Bernard constantly emphasizes the vision of God as an integral component of the union, but it is clear that this seeing is akin to the *visio intellectualis* of Augustine, a mental vision that transcends both the senses and imagination. To have this vision one must adhere to God, but only one who has mastered the passions is capable of this perfection: "That is the prerogative reserved to that supreme and infinite Spirit, who alone . . . communicates himself directly to the mind, he makes himself known directly; a pure spirit himself, he is received by us in proportion to our rectitude."[47]

The love that the soul has for the divine is a "holy love, the impulse of an upright spirit rather than of carnal desire."[48] In the seventy-first sermon, Bernard describes the matter of spiritual union in the following way: just as the Son dwells in the Father and the Father in the Son, the soul and God are conjoined reciprocally in mutual cohabitation: "Who is there who cleaves perfectly to God, unless he who, dwelling in God, is loved by God, and reciprocating that love, draws God into himself. Therefore, when God and man cleave wholly to each other—it is when they are incorporated into each other by mutual love that they cleave wholly to each other—I would say beyond all doubt that God is in man and man in God."[49] In the eighty-third sermon, love is described in terms of the way up and the way down—the task is to restore love to its origin so that it overflows with new vigor upon the soul and upon the world. Of all affections of the soul, love is the one in and through which there may be parity between God and human, for in loving, God wants to be loved, just as the human who loves wants to be loved. The gifting of love is in the loving itself.[50] The union symbolized by the kiss is thus "holy and chaste," the spiritual marriage that "joins two beings, not in one flesh, but in one spirit, making them no longer two but one."[51]

The ultimate yearning on the part of the soul is to be kissed by the kiss of the mouth of Jesus. Indeed, on occasion the kiss itself is identified as Jesus, as we find in the conclusion of the second sermon: "Moreover, this kiss is no other than the Mediator between God and man, himself a man, Christ Jesus,[52] who with the Father and Holy Spirit lives and reigns as God for ever and ever."[53] According to this line of interpretation, the rhetorical opening of the Song relays the soul's quest to unite directly with Christ. Bernard, however, is not always consistent on this matter, as may be gathered from a passage in the eighth sermon:

> Hence the bride is satisfied to receive the kiss of the Bridegroom, though she be not kissed with his mouth. For her it is no mean or contemptible thing to be kissed by the kiss, because it is nothing less than the gift of the Holy Spirit. If, as is properly understood, the Father is he who kisses, the Son he who is kissed, then it cannot be wrong to see in the kiss the Holy Spirit, for he is the imperturbable peace of the Father and the Son, their unshakable bond, their undivided love, their indivisible unity.[54]

The ostensible conflict between the two explanations may be resolved by bearing in mind that the kiss signifies, in Bernard's own words, the "mystery of the incarnate Word."[55] Hence the second sermon, which deals extensively with the different meanings of the kiss, begins with the heading *De Incarnatione Christi per patriarchas et prophetas nuntiata, et ardentissime ab eis exspectata* ("Regarding the incarnation of Christ announced by the patriarchs and prophets, and most ardently awaited by them"). In the continuation of the sermon, Bernard refers explicitly to the symbolic intent of the kiss, a point that by his own admission demands the full attention of the reader: "The mouth that kisses signifies the Word who assumes human nature; the nature assumed receives the kiss; the kiss, however, that takes its being both from the giver and the receiver, is a person that is formed by both, none other than 'the one mediator between God and mankind, himself a man, Christ Jesus.'"[56] The mouth, then, is identified as the Word that assumes human nature, and the kiss, the union of the Word and flesh. To receive the kiss would denote human participation in the mystery, wording the flesh in place of fleshing the word, so to speak. The possibility of the soul receiving the kiss of God's mouth is dependent on the humbling of self, which parallels the emptying of the divine, a central tenet of the theological enigma of incarnation based on the language of Philippians 2:3–8.[57] In sermon fifteen, the act of Jesus emptying himself is linked to "Your name is poured out like oil" (Song 1:2):

> And what wonder if the name of the Bridegroom is poured out, since he himself is poured out? For he emptied himself to assume the condition of a slave. Did he not even say, "I am poured out like water"?[58] The fullness of divine life was poured out and lived on earth in bodily form that all of us who live in this body doomed to death may receive from that fullness, and being filled with its life-giving odor say "Your name is poured out like oil." Such is what is meant by the outpouring of the name, such its manner, such its extent.[59]

The incarnation is thus expressed as the pouring of the oil that is the name of Christ—a formulation that embodies the kenotic paradox, the fullness emptying itself and remaining full. From the perspective of the pietistic ideal reflective of the mythopoeic image, this may be expressed as the emptiness filling itself by remaining empty—the suffering and humiliation that mark the path of one who bears the cross. Interestingly, in sermon fifty-six, commenting on the verse "There he stands behind our wall, gazing through the window, peering through the lattice" (Song 2:9), Bernard refers to the self-deprecation on the part of Jesus as the "experience" that the Bridegroom undergoes, which corresponds to the experience of the Bride suffering the vicissitudes of corporeal existence:

> He drew near the wall, therefore, when he joined himself to our flesh. Our flesh is the wall, and the Bridegroom's approach is the incarnation of the Word. The windows and lattices through which he is said to gaze can be understood, I think, as the bodily senses and human feelings by which he began to experience all our human needs. . . . On being made man, therefore, he has used our bodily feelings and senses as openings or windows, so that he would know by experience the miseries of men and might become merciful.[60]

We may conclude, therefore, that behind the metaphor of the kiss is the mystery of incarnation, the divine assuming human form, which is depicted as Jesus emptying himself by donning the garb of the corporeal world. From the anthropological viewpoint, union with Christ in spiritual marriage is linked to the ascetic denial of carnality, a mimetic participation in the incarnational kenosis. As Jantzen points out, for Bernard, the "vocabulary of passionate spirituality" was a "substitute for actual bodily love."[61] It is not unreasonable to extend the scope of this remark to other medieval male Christian commentators on the Song. The ancient Israelite understanding of monotheism as monogamy (reaffirmed in both rabbinic and patristic theology) gives way in the monastic culture of medieval Christianity (based in part on passages in the New Testament) to the encratic idea that the exclusive love of God demands the repudiation of physical sexuality. But the matter is more complex for Bernard. In his opinion, as I have already emphasized, the bodily images applied to Christ in the Song should be interpreted as a reference to the incarnation, to the saving activities of Jesus when he is in the flesh, activities that are essential to the economy of salvation. In this regard, there is a major difference between Origen and Bernard: anthropomorphic language about God is literally and not only metaphorically true.[62] Even though the love of Jesus is not sensual but always a matter of the spirit, the engendering mystery of Christianity is that God takes on a body.

While it is true that the sweetness of spirit can be experienced only by one not laden by the weight of sensual passions and the pursuit of fleshly pleasure, one must nonetheless emulate Jesus by loving Jesus with the senses, for this will help one overcome the lure of carnal temptation: "Do not let the glory of the world or the pleasure of the flesh lead you astray; the wisdom of Christ should become sweeter to you than these. . . . Your affection for your Lord Jesus should be both tender and intimate, to oppose the sweet enticements of sensual life. Sweetness conquers sweetness as one nail drives out another."[63] This, according to Bernard, is the import of the injunction to love God with all one's heart (Deut. 6:5): "For there is no love of Christ at all without the Holy Spirit, even if this love is in the flesh, and without its fullness. The measure of such love is this: its sweetness seizes the whole heart, and draws it completely from the love of all flesh and every sensual pleasure."[64] The love of the body of Christ helps the soul raise physical eros into the spiritual realm.[65]

Assuredly, there is no celebration of the physical here, and no sense that by engaging in carnal sex one spiritually unites with God. On the contrary, unless one breaks one's body through ascetic discipline, one will not be able to see the radiance of Christ splintered in the body of Scripture. Of all biblical books, the Song epitomizes the mystery of the Word made flesh, which is described as well in the metaphor of the bread that is broken. Thus Bernard advises the reader in the first of his sermons: "Be ready then to feed on bread rather than milk. Solomon has bread to give that is splendid and delicious, the bread of that book called the Song of Songs. Let us bring it forth then if you please, and break it. . . . But who is going to divide this loaf? The Master of the house is present, it is the Lord you must see in the breaking of the bread."[66]

To grasp this admonition, we must take note of the fact that Bernard has blended together two distinct themes from New Testament. The first, which is derived from the Gospel of John, involves the exegetical application of an older Jewish homiletical theme, the symbolic identification of manna, the bread from heaven, as wisdom or Torah.[67] For John, the bread from heaven or the bread of life, which is wisdom/Torah, is identified with the Word incarnate in Jesus.[68] Bernard combines this Johannine image with the section of Luke where the breaking of bread on the part of Jesus leads to the opening of the eyes of the disciples so that they would recognize him (24:30–31). Breaking the bread is to be taken as a ritual sign of the incarnation, the sacrament of the Eucharist. In Bernard's reading, influenced by an older tradition, the spiritual meaning of the Johannine doctrine of word-made-flesh is that God suffers by assuming corporeal form in the textual body of Scripture, a point epitomized in the Song, the "book of experience" (*libro experientiae*); the Song, we are to imagine, is the one part metonymically representative of the body of Scripture as a whole, a conception that resonates with the trajectory of rabbinic interpretation of the Song being parallel to or encompassing all of Torah, the revealed word, as noted above.

The one who wants to experience the mystery of incarnation, to see Jesus in the breaking of the "bread of the book called the Song of Songs," is exhorted to "feed on bread rather than milk," that is, to give up or curb the fleshly appetite in exchange for the "bread," identified as the book of the Song. This book must be broken; in response to the query, who shall break the bread, comes the response, "The Master of the house is present, it is the Lord you must see in the breaking of the bread." This would seem to imply that the symbolic meaning of the bread-breaking justifies viewing Jesus as agent of the breaking. In breaking the bread, interpreting the text, one emulates the Word broken doing the breaking. How so? By renouncing the milk in exchange for the bread.

Renunciation of carnality is an emulation of incarnation. Humility is presented as an especially good agency by means of which the soul participates in the mystery of incarnation: just as Jesus emptied himself by assuming incarnate form, so one becomes divine by emptying oneself.[69] This, for Bernard, is the mystical intent of the Song, which can be known only by one who has had communion with Christ. Of all the erotic images employed in the Song, none is more pertinent than the kiss of the mouth, for the reciprocity of this gesture symbolizes the debasement of the elevated Christ in the human body that makes possible the elevation of the human body in the glorified spirit of Christ.

The position articulated by Jantzen is affirmed as well by Amy Hollywood in the context of expressing a general methodological claim pertaining to the reciprocity between exegesis and revelatory experience, which she relates more specifically to interpreting the erotic imagery of the Song. In Hollywood's opinion, meditation on devotional images and biblical texts provides the phenomenological foundation for medieval Christian visionary and unitive experience:

> The use and subversion of biblical images to describe and evoke the experience of God's presence and union with God must be understood in this context, for through meditation on such biblical images, and in particular the erotic language of desire in the Song of Songs, such experiences are brought about in the mystic. . . . The bridal language of the Song of Songs . . . is not a later addition, a vain attempt through the application of biblical images to convey the ineffable experience of God's presence and union, but rather is intrinsic to that experience in its very ineffability.[70]

The particular example of the Song is illustrative of a larger hermeneutical point pertaining to the study of mysticism. The older tendency to distinguish sharply between text and experience should be modified in light of the epistemological assumption that mystical experiences—whether visionary or unitive in nature—are occasioned by meditational study of images, often recorded in devotional texts.[71] If we assume (following those who posit a contextualist perspective with respect to human knowledge)[72] that all experience is mediated through language, then it makes little sense to speak of access to unmediated experience. Moreover, in mystical accounts that take shape within the matrix of scriptural religious cultures, one of the most important ways that the visionary and unitive experiences are mediated is through study of the canonical texts. The experiences themselves may transcend the limits of language, but it is only through language that those limits are surpassed.

The apophatic tendency to submerge all forms of sentient imaging in the formlessness of pure consciousness cannot be completely severed from the kataphatic insistence on the possibility of being in the presence of the divine.[73] To quote Hollywood again, "The turn to apophasis, then, is not a denial of the validity of the visionary imagination, but rather an attempt to transcend its limitations."[74] The language of the Song provided imagery that was perfectly apt to convey the mystical dialectic of apophasis and kataphasis, unsaying and saying, the paradox of uttering a statement of ineffability.[75] The mutual yearning of beloved and lover, the desire to consummate the union that is present through its absence, provided a narrative framework within which to experience the concealing that ensues from the light that is unveiled.

In an extensive study on medieval exegesis of the Song, Denys Turner commented on the ostensibly puzzling fact that men who were committed to a life of sexual abstinence expressed their spiritual aspirations in the amatory imagery of this biblical book. Turner insightfully argues that it was precisely the renunciation of carnal sexuality that allowed the monks to exploit the eroticism of the Song. The true image of union between Christ and the soul or union between Christ and the Church, two ways of instantiating the mystery of spiritual marriage, is linked to the denial of carnality.[76] We shall see to what extent this formulation applies to the kabbalistic attitude regarding asceticism, sexuality, and the worship of God.

Before turning to the medieval Jewish material, it is necessary to address briefly the question of female readers of the Song in the history of Christianity. Jantzen has convincingly argued that there is a basic difference between male and female mystics with respect to the erotic nature of the experience of union, which relates more generally to their respective positions regarding the body.[77] For men, carnal sexuality at best served as an allegorical depiction of the spiritual union, which entails the ascetic abnegation of the flesh. For women, by contrast, sexual tropes are far more explicit and less intellectualized or spiritualized. The mind/body dichotomy, which is correlated with the male/female gender binary, is not as sharp or rigid in the case of women mystics.[78]

Nevertheless, as Jantzen herself duly notes, even in the case of women mystics, such as Hildegard of Bingen, the precondition for the spiritual union of the female and Jesus, interpreted through the erotic lens of the Song, was ascetic renunciation. To be the bride of Christ, the earthly woman had to be a virgin like Mary.[79] The emphasis on virginity on the part of women reflects to some degree the internalization of the dominant misogynist orientation, which can be traced back to the Platonic devaluation of the body and of sexuality, linked to the passive female, as opposed to reason, associated with the active male.[80] The monastic culture of medieval Christianity is marked by a patent asymmetry: chastity for a man meant divesting himself of an effeminate weakness, whereas for a woman it meant denying her female nature in a more radical and fundamental way.

However, asceticism on the part of Christian women in medieval times should not be reduced entirely to an internalized misogyny; on the contrary, as Caroline Walker Bynum has shown, the matter is far more complex, insofar as women's radical asceticism was a rejection not only of the physical world but also of the Church.[81] Moreover, Bynum has suggested that the androcentric notion of the female as flesh was inverted by some women to an argument that the feminine is the most perfect symbol for humanity and hence the way to imitate Christ is through physicality.[82] It is nonetheless valid, as Bynum herself readily acknowledges, to assume that the self-perception of medieval women was at least in part informed by the dualistic conception of men with a misogynist tendency. The ideal of the holy virgin reflects one of the ways in which the female could symbolically become male such that the natural and cultural hierarchy of gender roles would be reversed. The acceptance on the part of women mystics of the cultural association of women with eroticism led to the spiritualization and ultimate subversion of this stereotype.[83]

It is reasonable to conclude, therefore, that despite the different orientations of men and women to the body and sexuality, with respect to the spiritual union occasioned by the erotic images of the Song, there is no appreciable difference. Certainly in the case of the Jewish approach to the Song in the Middle Ages, the matter is even more monolithic in nature, since there is no credible way to retrieve the voices of women and thus the historical analysis is limited to an androcentric perspective on the issues of gender and sexuality as they emerge from the biblical text.[84]

Allegorization of the Erotic in Medieval Jewish Exegesis

Medieval rabbinic exegesis of the Song of Songs exemplified an array of possible readings.[85] In the first instance, the midrashic approach to the Song with a tendency toward historical allegory was preserved and expanded, particularly in the Ashkenazi tradition exemplified by Solomon ben Isaac.[86] The reading of the Song in this light has to be seen against the background of the tendency of Jewish exegetes in the Middle Ages, building on earlier rabbinic dicta but also inspired by contemporary polemical attacks, to portray the relationship between God and Israel "as a most intimate mutual dependence approximating to a mystic union."[87] Recently it has been pointed out that the allegorical approach of rabbinic interpreters embellished with an intensified apocalyptic messianism is attested in two tenth-century commentators, Salmon ben Jeroḥam and Japeth ben Eli, members of the Karaite sectarian group known as *avelei ṣiyyon*, the "Mourners for Zion," a term derived from Isaiah 61:3.[88] In spite of borrowing the central exegetical tenet of the rabbis to read the literal sense of the Song as metaphorical, these authors were able to use the biblical text as the platform to proffer the Karaitic understanding of Jewish history, which involved a fundamental polemic against rabbanite authority. The polemical stance is most conspicuous in the messianic posture adopted by the sectarians, a posture supported by their interpretation of this biblical book, demonstrated most poignantly in the derivation of the name *shoshanim* from Song 2:1–2 to designate their prophetic calling.[89]

In addition to the allegorical-apocalyptic approach, philosophical and mystical interpretations of the Song emerged in the Jewish Middle Ages. In spite of the substantial differences between the philosophical and kabbalistic perspectives on many doctrinal issues, with respect to the spiritualized understanding of the erotic images of the Song there is an important affinity between philosopher and kabbalist.[90] Indeed, the mystical conception of the union of the soul and God expressed in kabbalistic works of thirteenth-century Spain and Italy—and on this point I see no difference between the authors of *Zohar* and the disciples of Abulafia—is indebted to the philosophical interpretation of the Song as an allegorical depiction of the relationship of the soul to God, generally personified as the Active Intellect, and engendered respectively as feminine and masculine.[91]

By contrast, as noted in the previous chapter, Scholem has argued that the Spanish kabbalah in its early period is to be distinguished from other forms of mysticism, especially that of Christianity, by the fact that man's relation to God is not portrayed in erotic images. In support of his claim, Scholem asserts that the interpretation of the Song as an allegorical depiction of the soul's yearning for union with the divine is lacking in kabbalistic sources until the sixteenth century.[92] Idel has argued that Scholem's view is valid with respect to theosophic kabbalah, but not in the case of ecstatic kabbalah.[93] As I argue below, even in thirteenth-century theosophic kabbalah one can find evidence for the allegorical interpretation of the Song as an erotic dialogue between the soul and God.

Brief allusions to the philosophical stance are already found in Baḥya Ibn Paquda's classical work of Jewish pietism, *Ḥovot ha-Levavot*, which is clearly modeled on a Sufi paradigm. In particular, Baḥya cites from the Song in support of the notion that the pietistic ideal entails the all-consuming love of God, which is realized only in a state of contemplative isolation (*hitbodedut*).[94] Interestingly enough, in the introduction to his commentary on the Song, Abraham Ibn Ezra specifically rejects the philosophers (*anshei meḥqar*) who interpret the biblical narrative as a reference to the union of the supernal, masculine soul and the female body as antithetical to the allegorical approach adopted by the rabbis.[95] I note parenthetically that Ibn Ezra's remark is rendered problematic by the fact that in his own poetry as well as in his *Iggeret Ḥay ben Meqiṣ*, an adaptation of Avicenna's *Ḥayy ibn Yaqzān*,[96] he does adopt an allegorical interpretation of verses from the Song in a philosophical vein, a posture that is consonant with his approach to other parts of Scripture.[97] Indeed, as has been argued, the third interpretation of the Song proffered by Ibn Ezra, the midrashic, is in some places a theological allegory that reflects the Neoplatonic worldview.[98] In any event, the comment of Ibn Ezra, regardless of its sincerity, is clear evidence that by the twelfth century an allegorical explanation of the Song of a philosophical nature took its place alongside the allegorical interpretations of the rabbis. Thus we find, for example, that in *Torat ha-Nefesh*, falsely attributed to Baḥya, the soul is identified explicitly as the female voice of the Song, Shulamit, on account of her peaceful return from the world to her ontological source in the divine. The erotic content of the Song, therefore, relates to the desire and love of the rational soul for the Creator.[99]

The philosophical approach is attested as well in the works of Maimonides. In the *Mishneh Torah*, Maimonides explicitly states that the entire Song of Songs is a parable (*mashal*) for the all-consuming love of the soul for God.[100] Along similar lines, in the context of explicating the ideal of the intellectual worship of God toward the denouement of the *Guide of the Perplexed*, Maimonides cites the verse "I was asleep, but my heart was wakeful" (Song 5:2) to provide scriptural support for the idea that those of a prophetic nature experience the union of the rational soul and the divine,[101] an exegesis that is repeated by Abraham Maimonides in his treatise on Jewish Sufism, the *Highways to Perfection*.[102] In the continuation of the aforementioned passage from the *Guide*, Maimonides interprets the kiss mentioned in Song 1:2 as a reference to the comprehension that arises as a result of the passionate love (*ʿishq*) for God,[103] which is followed by the experience of ecstatic death (related to the rabbinic trope of the death of the righteous by a kiss),[104] which is in fact deliverance from physical mortality and the limitations of the body.[105] Maimonides, therefore, appropriates the erotic symbolism to depict the contemplative ideal of union, the intellectual love, which is also identified as true worship and the highest level of prophecy, a state of mindfulness that is consequent to quelling carnal desire originating in the imagination.[106]

The philosophical reading is given its fullest expression in the commentaries on the Song composed in the thirteenth century by Joseph Ibn Aqnin and Moses Ibn Tibbon.[107] Ibn Aqnin proposed three approaches to the book: *peshaṭ, derash*, and *sod*, which correspond respectively to the philological, homiletical, and philosophical. The three hermeneutical approaches are also related to the three human faculties: the natural, animalistic, and rational. The last approach, which is presented as the truly esoteric or internal meaning of the text, assumes that the erotic dialogue between bride and bridegroom relates to the desire of the human soul to become one with the Active Intellect.[108] The attainment of this state is clearly facilitated by the liberation of the intellect from the subjugation of physical pleasures.[109] Nevertheless, erotic imagery is the most appropriate way to characterize the longing of the soul for union with the Active Intellect, even if there is no precise parallel between the contemplative and carnal forms of eros. To cite one example, in his interpretation of the kiss mentioned in Song 1:2, Ibn Aqnin writes: "Its explanation according to my approach is that the rational [soul] compares the dissemination of the lights of the [Active] Intellect upon her to the kisses of the mouth . . . and this is intellectual pleasure."[110]

In spite of some minor differences in interpreting certain images and phrases in the Song, Moses Ibn Tibbon adopts the same hermeneutical approach as that of Ibn Aqnin; that is, he similarly affirms that the ultimate meaning of the Song is related to the "belief in the conjunction of the soul of man, that is, the rational [soul], with the Separate Intellect, for through this faith is the survival of the soul of man after death possible."[111] Solomon composed the Song to "strengthen belief in conjunction of the human soul with the Separate Intellect [*devequt nefesh ha-adam im ha-sekhel ha-nifrad*] and the immortality of the soul, which is the 'abundant good hidden away for those who fear you, for those who take refuge in you' (Ps. 31:20)."[112] Commenting on the image of the kiss in Song 1:2, Ibn Tibbon writes: " 'Let him kiss me' alludes to the fact that conjunction of the soul of man and the Separate Intellect is possible. . . . The conjunction of man with the Separate Intellect involves the intellect alone, for when he comprehends it, it is conjoined to him. The reality of the forms is in the intellect alone, for they are not matter so that the one is conjoined to the other, body to body."[113] Ibn Tibbon accepts the standard medieval notion (with roots in antiquity) that the weaker party of any pair is depicted as feminine, and the stronger, as masculine. Thus, as is to be expected in this cultural context, matter is configured as female, and form, male; the soul, female, and the intellect, male; the intellect of man, female, and the Separate Intellect, male.[114] In a state of potentiality, the soul is characterized as female, but when it is actualized it is male.[115]

In a manner similar to the exegetical strategy prevalent in Christian authors, a resemblance explicable on the basis of the shared indebtedness to Aristotelian and Neoplatonic sources, the sensual images of the biblical text were applied figuratively by these Jewish exegetes to the contemplative desire of the human intellect for union with God (or the Active Intellect).[116] The philosophical orientation took root in the cultural climate of the golden age of Hispanic Jewry, reflecting the particular impact of Graeco-Arabic philosophy. To appreciate the unique contribution of the Sephardic thinkers in formulating a philosophical-mystical interpretation of the Song, however, it is necessary to bear in mind that the new secular poetry composed by the Hispano-Jewish poets undoubtedly revived the erotic element in the literal reading of this biblical book. On the other hand, the attempt to combine Arabic love poetry and the rabbinic liturgical use of the Song also lead to the allegorization of the love poems.[117] More important, the same poets who utilized the erotic symbolism of the Song in their secular love poetry also applied a philosophical allegory to it, understanding the overtly erotic imagery as a figurative depiction of the rational soul's longing for union with God. The application of images culled from the Song to refer to the relationship between God and the soul shifted the focus from national eschatology to personal salvation.[118]

Ecstatic and Theosophic Elements in Kabbalistic Allegoresis

In the history of scholarship on medieval kabbalah, it is generally assumed that the individualizing interpretation[119] of the Song as an imaginative representation of the love of soul for matters spiritual, which was cultivated by a rabbinic elite given to a kind of philosophical mysticism,[120] had its greatest impact on the prophetic kabbalah developed by Abraham Abulafia.[121] In a measure this is true, insofar as Abulafia's mystical teaching is a unique blend of Maimonidean philosophy and ancient Jewish esotericism (principally mediated through the writings of the German Pietists).[122] Following Maimonides, Abulafia affirms the love of God as the apex of intellectual worship, portraying the passionate relationship between mystic and God as well in the erotic images of the Song, especially the symbol of the kiss. Abulafia relates the bride and bridegroom to the rational soul and the Active Intellect respectively, the erotic union of the two constituting the mystical significance of prophecy.[123] Abulafia even goes so far as to interpret the midrashic understanding of the Song in these terms; that is, on an exoteric level the Song is a parable about the community of Israel and God, but esoterically it alludes to the relationship of the rational soul and the Active Intellect.

The influence of the philosophical approach to the Song is evident in a passage in the work composed in the later part of the thirteenth century by Abulafia's disciple, Joseph Gikatilla, *Ginnat Egoz*, which is a synthesis of Maimonidean thought and various forms of linguistic and numerical mysticism.[124] In line with the philosophical interpretation, Gikatilla describes the experience of prophecy as the separation of the rational soul from the body and its consequent conjunction with the intelligible world (*olam ha-sekhel*), identified further as the angelic beings that are incorporeal light. Gikatilla relates these immaterial and translucent forms to the waters mentioned by Aqiva in his warning to those who entered Pardes (according to the version of the legend in the Babylonian Talmud, Ḥagigah 14b) not to say "water, water" when they come upon the pure marble stones. "These are the waters," writes Gikatilla, "that are entirely the inner, intelligible, spiritual, subtle light. . . . Concerning these waters it says, 'Abundant waters cannot quench love' (Song 8:7). Love is not a corporeal matter that the waters could quench, but rather the waters are intelligible waters and the love is intelligible love."[125] *Ahavah sikhlit*, a love that comes by way of intellect, commands the intense passion of the soul for the object of its longing. The Song expresses poetically the fervor of mind in its desire to be conjoined to the intelligible world of incorporeal light.

It would be wrong, however, to limit the impact of the philosophical interpretation exclusively to the trend of kabbalah cultivated by Abulafia and his followers. Indeed, there is ample evidence that other kabbalists in the formative period acknowledged the individualizing orientation with respect to the Song.[126] I do not wish to argue with the standard and certainly valid point of view that many kabbalists (early on and through the generations) have theosophically applied the erotic imagery of the Song to the masculine and feminine potencies of the divine.[127] As Joseph of Hamadan expressed the matter, "By way of the true kabbalah, every bridegroom and bride mentioned in the Song of Songs and every love is between the king, Lord of hosts, and the bride, Community of Israel, perfect in all perfection and comprised of every beauty, and this is the secret of the cherubim, which are male and female."[128] It is nevertheless the case that kabbalists who accepted the theosophic interpretation of the Song have also affirmed a more personalistic and mystical stance. By way of illustration let me cite the following remark from the earliest kabbalistic commentary on the Song by Ezra ben Solomon of Gerona:

> "Oh, give me of the kisses of his mouth" (Song 1:2): These are the words of the glory, which desires and yearns to ascend, to be conjoined and to be illuminated in the supernal light that has no image and is elevated in consciousness of thought [*maḥshevet ha-raʿayon*], and thus it speaks in the third person. The kiss is a symbol for the joy of the conjunction of the soul [*taʿanug devequt ha-neshamah*] in the source of life and for the abundance of the holy spirit [*tosefet ruaḥ ha-qodesh*]. Thus it says, "of the kisses of his mouth," for each and every cause receives the emanation [*hamshakhah*] and the increase from the light of the source [*tosefet min ha-or ha-maqor*] and this resplendent splendor. When he speaks with the glory, which is the gate to the entities, he speaks in the third person.[129]

The verse from the Song can be read in two ways, referring either to the intradivine relationship between the feminine and masculine glories or to the ecstatic encounter of the soul and the glory.[130] According to the first reading, the kiss signifies the aspiration of the lower, feminine glory (*Shekhinah*) to ascend and to be united with the upper, masculine glory (*Tifʾeret*).[131] By contrast, according to the second reading, the kiss is symbolic of the delight that the soul experiences when it is conjoined to the divine glory, referred to as the "gateway to the words" (*shaʿar la-devarim*), that is, the opening to the emanations.[132] In this case, then, the soul of the male mystic assumes the persona of the feminine lover, and the divine glory, that of the male beloved.

With respect to the second interpretation of the kiss, there is affinity between the kabbalistic and philosophic approaches. Ezra himself was keenly aware of this kinship; in the first of three introductions to his commentary, Ezra chooses the example of the kiss to illustrate that in the Song the literal meaning is figurative:

> Thus I will call your attention to one verse of the verses of this book, "Oh, give me of the kisses [of his mouth]" (Song 1:2), the kiss is figurative [*mashal*] for the conjunction of the soul [*devequt ha-neshamah*] as will be explained, and it says, "his mouth," and it has no relevance here, but since the conjunction of the soul was compared to the kiss of the mouth, it was necessary to say "his mouth" to tie the

> figurative expression to it, as one of the sages of the generation has already written in his book.[133]

The comments by Ezra confirm that at a relatively early literary stage, the feminization of the male mystic in relation to the masculine God is found in the symbolism of theosophic kabbalah and is not associated exclusively with ecstatic kabbalah.[134] Consistent with other mystical traditions, theosophic and ecstatic kabbalists portrayed the soul of the mystic as feminine in relation to the male deity. In particular, I would note that with respect to this reversal of gender roles, there is a striking phenomenological similarity between medieval kabbalah and Christian scholastic mysticism, for the latter, as I have already remarked, is based in great measure on the appropriation of the erotic imagery of the Song to depict the soul's relationship to Christ: the male mystic assumes the voice of the female beloved, and Jesus, that of the male lover. According to the mystical exegesis of the Song in both traditions, the overtly heterosexual language of the biblical narrative is transmuted into a spiritualized homoeroticism.[135] Moreover, as I suggested at length in the previous chapter, the homoerotic bond of the male kabbalist and the divine presence is predicated ideally on the ascetic abrogation of carnal desire. In the course of this chapter, it shall become clear that the erotic asceticism is most fully realized (at least as the matter is articulated in zoharic literature, which had a profound impact on subsequent kabbalists) in the eschaton.

In the final analysis, the theosophic and ecstatic readings offered by Ezra cannot be separated, because the realm of divine potencies provides the ontological structure that occasions the mystical experience of union, an experience poetically rendered by the image of the kiss.[136] The kiss of *Shekhinah* symbolizes the conjunction of the soul in the source of life and the consequent overflow of the holy spirit.[137] The point is underscored in another kabbalistic commentary on the Song composed by Isaac Ibn Sahula at a somewhat later date in thirteenth-century Castile. Ibn Sahula is explicitly critical of Ibn Aqnin's philosophical interpretation of the Song as a dialogue between the rational soul and the Active Intellect. However, in spite of Ibn Sahula's criticism, he was greatly influenced by Ibn Aqnin and indeed incorporated his allegorical interpretation as the "revealed way" (*derekh ha-nigleh*) in his own commentary, which stands in contrast to the "hidden way" (*derekh nistar*).[138] More important, the esoteric interpretation presented by Ibn Sahula is not merely theosophical in nature. His kabbalistic viewpoint entails a mystical-ecstatic dimension, which shares much in common with the philosophical outlook, especially as it relates to the conjunction of the soul and God. Consider, for example, Ibn Sahula's explanation of the title, *shir ha-shirim* ("song of songs"):

> By means of the pleasantness of the song in the mouth and through the instrument the soul is aroused, and the holy spirit is illuminated in her, and she comprehends the supernal concepts in a manner that was not the case previously. . . . All of this is to arouse the soul to its gradation, to reach its characteristic. The holy spirit, then, is aroused, and it shines and yearns for her in desire, affection, and great love. Consequently, she comprehends the extra gradation, the power and the strength. . . .

When one begins the song the supernal beings augment the spirit to know, to understand, and to comprehend that which heaven and earth did not comprehend. They augment the power through that song. Fortunate is the one who is worthy to know that very song.[139]

From my perspective, what is essential about this passage is the fact that Ibn Sahula, who is critical of Ibn Aqnin's philosophical allegory, explains the mystical mechanics of the song that underlie the book as a whole in terms of a process that is very close in spirit (if not terminology) to the philosophic idea of conjunction. Indeed, in the continuation of the passage, Ibn Sahula explicitly states that the soul of the one who hears the song is "escorted and conjoined to that which is above."[140] The theosophic interpretation, which is quantitatively more prevalent, cannot be understood properly without taking into account the mystical dimension.

The intersection of the two hermeneutical tracks is most evident in Ibn Sahula's treatment of the image of the kiss related in Song 1:2. In a manner similar to Ezra, Ibn Sahula presents two explanations, which I have dubbed theosophic and ecstatic. The symbolic meaning of the kiss is the "emanation of the spirit from its source," but this can be applied to *Shekhinah* in relation to the potencies above her or to the soul in relation to *Shekhinah*. The Song begins with the verse, "Oh, give me of the kisses of his mouth" (*yishshaqeni mi-neshiqot pihu*) "in order to arouse man so that he yearns for this supernal gradation . . . to provide him with the support to assist him in being conjoined to him in the manner of lovers who out of the abundance of their affection are conjoined to one another."[141]

Evidence for the persistence of the theosophic and ecstatic understanding of the poetic language of the Song among Spanish kabbalists of the late-thirteenth and early-fourteenth centuries is found in the brief composition *Ma'amar al Penimiyyut ha-Torah* (*Treatise on the Inwardness of Torah*), which has been (in my view, correctly) attributed to Gikatilla:[142] "Even though the Song of Songs is build on the foundation of the supernal chariot and on the roots of the emanation and the knots of the gradations, and the secret of two lovers as they are known to the masters of kabbalah, they also allude to the way of sensible and intelligible desire."[143] It seems that preserved here is an allusion to three ways of interpreting the Song: the theosophic, which entails decoding the biblical book as a dialogue between the "two lovers" known to the masters of kabbalah, that is, *Tif'eret* and *Malkhut*; the allegorical, which interprets the narrative as an expression of intelligible desire; and the literal, which presumes the book is an account of the sensible desire between man and woman.

Love Is as Strong as Death: Erotic Be/Longing

The same claim can be made with respect to the interpretation of the Song found in many passage in the corpus of *Zohar*. The theosophic reading of the Song as a symbolic narrative about the relationship of the male and female potencies of the divine—the interpretation most often noted by scholars[144]—is combined with the ecstatic rendering of the Song as a dialogue between the human soul (personified as female) and the divine (imaged as male).[145] Thus, following the earlier examples of Ezra and Ibn Sahula, the zoharic authorship provides two concurrent explanations for Song 1:2.[146] According to one line of interpretation, the one who utters the verse, "Oh, give me of the kisses of his mouth," is *Shekhinah*, designated by the technical expression "Community of Israel" (*kenesset yisra'el*), and the one addressed is *Tif'eret*. In that case, the kiss denotes the conjunction of *Shekhinah*, imaged as the feminine beloved, with *Tif'eret*, the masculine lover.[147]

According to another interpretation, the one uttering the verse is the human soul (or, in terms specific to the historical context of the formative period in the crystallization of zoharic literature, the soul of the male Jew) who addresses *Shekhinah*. In even more specific terms, the kiss signifies the union of the lower spirit of the *ṣaddiq*, the righteous Jewish man, and the upper spirit of the divine, *itdabquta de-ruḥa be-ruḥa*,[148] a union that is also represented by the kiss of death. In a manner consonant with Maimonides, the author of the zoharic passage assumes that the kiss of death signifies the passionate union of the soul and God, which is in fact true life, salvation from the death of body.[149] From this vantage point we must consider the confluence of eros and thanatos that marks the erotic asceticism embraced by kabbalists behind the composition of zoharic literature in their yearning to be conjoined to the divine.

The point is captured succinctly in Joseph of Hamadan's interpretation of "for love is as strong as death" (Song 8:6): "That is to say, from the abundance of passion and love that there is between us and our father in heaven, we await the day of death, the time when *Shekhinah* will be seen face-to-face."[150] The vision of God's presence is presented as the culmination of desire realized with the death of the body, what is called in Sufism "death before dying" based on the prophetic tradition "Die before you die!"[151] Building on the older rabbinic theme linking death and the vision of the divine presence, a vision rendered possible only with the demise of the corporeal, Joseph of Hamadan, as other kabbalists of his time, locates the vision at the moment of death. The ascetic lifestyle prepares one in the expectation of the day of death, a dying-of-body that is true life, uniting with God like the coal bound to the flame.[152]

With the concluding image, which is derived from a description of the ten *sefirot* in the first part of *Sefer Yeṣirah*, Joseph of Hamadan wishes to demarcate the critical spot where the erotic and ascetic crisscross. In the binding of flame to coal, there can be no experiential way to separate one from the other. In the mind, one can differentiate flame and coal, but not tactically. What is even more pressing to our immediate concern is to consider more carefully the erotic undertone of the death imagery utilized by Joseph of Hamadan to depict the soul's conjunction with God: just as the coal endures as that which is utterly devoured by the flame, so the soul that cleaves to God endures in God by being consumed by God; to endure in this union, one must be consumed, but to be consumed, one must endure—the paradoxical challenge of erotic be/longing, to persist in passing, to pass in persisting.[153] The point may be discerned better if one considers the image of the flame bound to the coal in light of the scriptural mystery of the burning bush that was not consumed, *ha-seneh boʿer ba-esh we-ha-seneh einennu ukkal* (Exod. 3:2), the phenomenal event that marked the inaugural vision of Moses, his call to prophecy. The bush burns continually but is not consumed; just so, the eternality of the soul is attained in its being annihilated in the flame.[154] The mystical reading of the Song conveys this hope for the death of eros experienced through the eros of death and the consequent crowning vision of the glory.

The two interpretations in *Zohar* cannot be isolated, for it is precisely the ecstatic union of the male mystic and *Shekhinah* that promotes the unification of the latter and her masculine partner in the divine realm. Indeed, basic to the zoharic symbology is the view that the erotic impulse of the divine feminine to cohabit with the masculine is triggered by the arousal from below, which is brought about by the communion of the group of enlightened (*maskilim*) with the divine feminine.[155] The principle is stated in one passage that explicates the conjunction of David to the three patriarchs who constitute the divine chariot: "The desire of the female towards the male occurs only when a spirit enters into her and casts fluid corresponding to the supernal, masculine waters. Analogously, the Community of Israel is not aroused in relation to the holy One, blessed be he, except by means of the spirit of the righteous who enter into her."[156]

The emphasis on the erotic arousal in the divine realm stemming from the female in relation to the male is the kabbalistic reworking of the idea expressed in rabbinic literature (based on Hippocrates and Galen) to the effect that if the woman produces the orgiastic fluid first, she gives birth to a male, an idea that is linked exegetically to the verse "When a woman brings forth seed and bears a male" (Lev. 12:2).[157] From the vantage point of the arousal of the left side, the feminine potency occupies a privileged position. But even with respect to this issue, if one reads kabbalistic texts carefully, the androcentric bias in the construction of the feminine, which is linked with the left, associated with judgment, darkness, and impurity, becomes clear enough. Let us consider the articulation of this matter in the anonymous sixteenth-century composition *Galya Raza*, a representation that is by no means idiosyncratic. Significantly, the theme of erotic arousal from the left is framed exegetically in terms of a verse from the Song:

> Know that with respect to all things that need existence, felicity, and blessing, the arousal must come from the side of the feminine, which is the left side, as it is written, "Awake, O north wind, come O south wind, blow upon my garden, that its perfume may spread' (Song 4:16). Therefore it is written "When a woman brings forth seed and bears a male" (Lev. 12:2). Moreover, the Torah begins with the letter *beit*, which is the feminine, and the reason is that the light was hidden in the darkness, and before the world was created the darkness ruled, as it is written, "the earth was unformed and void, and darkness was on the surface of the deep" (Gen. 1:2). The spirit of all aspects of impurity, whether amongst spiritual or physical beings, comes from the side of darkness, and from the side of the light that was hidden in the darkness all aspects of purity and holiness emerge.[158]

The theosophic insight expressed in this text is based on the obvious empirical observation that the female is the one who bears progeny in the world, an anatomical fact encoded orthographically in *beit*, the first letter of Torah, which signifies the feminine potency, left side, aspect of impurity, that hovered above the primordial waters and reigned prior to the creation of the world. The negative implications of the correlation of *beit* and the feminine are underscored in a passage cited in the name of *Sefer ha-Qanah*[159] toward the beginning of the text:

> Moses our master, peace be upon him, asked of Metatron, "Why didn't the holy One, blessed be he, begin the Torah with the letter *alef*?" He answered him, "It was not appropriate for the lower world, which is the world of death, to be created by means of the letter *alef*, for it is from the supernal world, the world of life and masculinity, but rather by means of *beit*, which is from the world of the feminine, for the *beit* denotes the woman." From the point of the *alef* below there emerge the twenty-two letters of *Ze'eir Anpin*, and from them the world below was created. The arousal must start from the side of the feminine and a sign for this matter is "When a woman brings forth seed and bears a male" (Lev. 12:2), *zakhar* is numerically equal to *berakhah*.[160]

Reproduction ensues only on the basis of the arousal of the feminine, and from that perspective priority can be assigned the feminine, even though ontologically the masculine is prior, just as the primordial darkness preceded the light, but the latter is the true reality. The feminine is associated with the world of death, whereas the masculine is the world of life; the positive value of the woman is judged strictly from the perspective of her capacity to give birth to a male, a point underscored by the numerical equivalence of *zakhar* and *berakhah* (both equal 227), that is, blessing is linked to masculinity. The interpretation of the metaphor of the kiss in the Song is a specific exegetical application of the larger ontological principle widely embraced by kabbalists through the generations.[161] However, as I have suggested in the previous chapter, the erotic encounter with *Shekhinah* on the part of the righteous inverts the gender attribution, for the male kabbalist is feminized, and the female glory, masculinized.[162] I shall return to the reversal of gender prompted by the erotic dynamic of the mystical experience of communion (*devequt*).

The theosophic reading, which is obviously central to the understanding of the Song in *Zohar*,[163] cannot be separated from the psychological-ecstatic interpretation, nor can it be severed from the historical-allegorical sense, which in fact would have been understood by medieval kabbalists as *peshaṭ*, the contextual sense, of the Song.[164] The socioeconomic and political condition of Israel in this world reflects the ontological state of the divine above. The erotic yearning of the Song aptly depicts the exile, which in its deepest symbolic sense alludes to the separation of masculine and feminine aspects of the divine, the unification of which characterizes redemption. To cite but one of countless texts that illustrate the point:

> "The Lord spoke to Moses, saying: [Speak to the Israelite people thus:] When a woman brings forth seed and bears a male [she shall be unclean seven days]" (Lev. 12:1–2). R. Eleazar began to expound: "Upon my couch at night [I sought the one I love—I sought, but found him not]" (Song 3:1). "Upon my couch" [*al mishkavi*],

but it should have said "in my couch" [*be-mishkavi*]. What is [the meaning of] *al mishkavi*? The Community of Israel uttered this before the holy One, blessed be he, and she requested of him regarding the exile, for she dwelt with her children amidst the other nations, and she lay in the dust. Because she was dwelling in another impure land, she said "concerning my couch" [*al mishkavi*], I am asking for I am dwelling in exile. Therefore "I sought the one," so that he might take me out from it. "I sought, but found him not," for it is not his way to cohabit with me except in his palace. "I called, but he did not answer" (Song 5:6), for I am dwelling amidst the other nations, and his children alone hear his voice, as it is written, "Has any people heard the voice of God [speaking out of the fire, as you have, and survived?]" (Deut. 4:33). R. Isaac said: "Upon my couch at night." The Community of Israel said "concerning my couch" I pleaded with him so that he will cohabit with me, to take joy in me, and to bless me with a complete joyfulness. For we have learned that when the King is united with the Community of Israel several righteous inherit the portion of their holy inheritance, and several blessings are found in the world.[165]

The erotic desire spoken by the female persona in the Song is applied by the zoharic authorship to the divine feminine, *Shekhinah*, which is identified further as the Community of Israel, the symbolic collective constituted paradigmatically by the fraternity of male mystics.[166] *Shekhinah* utters words of longing before the masculine potency, for in the state of exile she is separated from him. The *hieros gamos* occurs within the spatial confines of the holy of holies, the innermost sanctum of the Temple, but since in the time of exile the latter is not standing, there is no space wherein the union can be fully realized. Hence the feminine expresses her yearning to cohabit with the masculine, to inhabit the same space, nay to be the *secret* space wherein the phallic foundation is laid. Ever mindful of the standard medieval Christian triumphalist claim regarding God's rejection of Israel, the zoharic author is quick to point out that even though *Shekhinah* is in a lowly state, which reflects the depraved condition of Israel in exile, the Jews are still the only ones among the nations who can truly hear the word of God. The calling out on the part of Israel in an effort to respond to heeding the divine voice is correlated with the erotic longing expressed by *Shekhinah* in relation to *Tif'eret*. Symbolically, the eroticism of the Song—marked by the movement betwixt the pull of attraction and push of deferment—must be interpreted in light of this theosophic dynamic.

According to other passages in *Zohar*, the utterance of the Song celebrates not only the desire of female for male, which is appropriate to the transition from exile to redemption, but the moment of consummation wherein the fragmentary state of being is overcome and a sense of ontic integration is realized. The matter is expressed as follows in one context: "In that moment, when everything was removed from the world, and the wife remained face-to-face with her husband, the Song of Songs was revealed."[167] Building upon the midrashic tradition that located the recitation of the Song by Solomon on the day of the dedication of the Jerusalem Temple,[168] the zoharic author interprets that historical moment in theosophic terms as a reference to the positioning of the masculine king in the feminine palace, the *hieros gamos* of enthronement, which is depicted by other symbols, for example, illumination of the moon by light of the sun.[169] Thus in one passage the author of a zoharic homily distinguishes the efficacy of the songs uttered respectively by Moses, David, and Solomon: the song of Moses ascended to the heights but it did not descend, for the ultimate purpose of his song was to offer praise to the supernal King so that miracles would be performed to save Israel; the song of David was an attempt to adorn the Matrona and her maiden; the song of Solomon was aimed at bringing the Matrona under the bridal canopy to unite with her masculine consort. Whereas Moses united with *Shekhinah* below to consummate the union in the terrestrial realm, Solomon at first facilitated union above between the bride and bridegroom in the canopy, and only then did he invite them to the Temple built below.[170]

Elevation of Shekhinah / Gender Transposition of Daughter to Mother

The recitation of the Song signifies the moment of erotic coupling that occurs in both realms of being, but it is particularly the effect that this unification has on *Shekhinah* that most engaged the imagination of the kabbalists behind the composition of the zoharic texts. The mystical significance of the Song relates principally to the ontological transformation of *Shekhinah*, which is portrayed in a number of different figurative tropes. For example, in one zoharic passage, the purification (*berur*) of the "lower point," *Shekhinah*, from all the other hymns that are gathered within the celestial palace that is called Zevul is depicted in terms of the image of the female being prepared for her union with the male, a process that is also related exegetically to the account of the building of the Temple from stones cut from the quarry. The cutting of the stone, therefore, alludes symbolically to the mystery of the severance of the primordial androgyne so that the female other could be constructed through which the male could procreate and thereby extend his masculine lineage through time, chain of engenderment, bearer of covenantal seal:

> And when it is purified from everything, it ascends above in the secret of the song, and it is called the "Song of Songs," and it rises above all those praises, and it is purified from them all. It is written, "When the House was built only the finished stone [cut at the quarry was used, so that no hammer or ax or any iron tool was heard in the House while it was being built]" (1 Kings 6:7). "When the House was built," when male and female were joined as one, then [we can speak of the] "finished stone" [*even shelemah*], for it was perfected [*ishtalimat*] as was necessary. It was not perfected until it was "cut at the quarry," for the holy One, blessed be he, severed her, adorned her, decorated her, and brought her to Adam, and thus she was constructed and she was perfected from everything.[171]

The ontological elevation of the status of *Shekhinah* related to the Song is expressed in slightly different terms in another passage: "When Solomon built the Temple and the lower world was perfected in the manner of the upper world, all of Israel were righteous, and they ascended in several supernal gradations, and then the throne of glory ascended in joy with several joys and several ascensions."[172] Utterance of the Song at the time of the building of the Temple is associated with the ascent of the throne, one of the standard symbols employed by kabbalists to describe the positioning of *Shekhinah* in the pleroma of divine gradations. To be more precise, the mounting of *Shekhinah* in the form of the ascending throne signifies the transformation of gender that is consequent to her reunion with the masculine potency.[173] In one passage, the motif of the dedication of the Temple is marked by the elevation of the wisdom of Solomon, which similarly signifies the *hieros gamos* of the King and Matrona. The consequence of the union is the illumination of the face of Matrona and the augmentation of her gradation:

> Come and see: Joy has not been found before the holy One, blessed be he, like on the day that Solomon was elevated to wisdom and he uttered the Song of Songs. As a result, the face of the Matrona shone, and the King came to dwell with her in his habitation, as it is written, "Solomon's wisdom was greater" (1 Kings 5:10). What [is the meaning of] "was greater?" The beauty of the Matrona arose and was augmented in her gradations over all the other gradations on account of the fact that the King placed his habitation within her.[174]

In another passage, the alteration in the ontological status of *Shekhinah* is represented as the transmogrification of *yod* into *he*, the opening of the female space to receive the male, as a result of which the female herself overflows and thereby sustains beings beneath her:

> Initially, she was only a single dark point, for she had no other place, and it was concealed within her. Now that she has ascended and she is conjoined to her husband, he says to her, "Go out" (Song 1:8), "Enlarge the site of your tent" (Isa. 54:2), extend yourself, and, consequently, you shall "graze your kids" (Song 1:8), you will be capable of gathering the pleasures and delights. For when she was a single point and she ascended above, the supernal King descends to her in order to enter into her. He strikes that very point, and it spreads forth to all sides, and that point becomes a letter *he*, and she is perfected from all sides to gather the pleasures and delights. . . . It is written, "In her palaces, *Elohim* is known as a refuge" (Ps. 48:4), for the great King comes to her, and he pulls her above to enter into her, and he strikes that point. When he strikes that point, it spreads forth and opens up to all sides, and it becomes a letter *he*, the opening to the palaces on every side, through which the great King can enter.[175]

The esoteric meaning of the Song alludes to the gender transformation of *Shekhinah* that is consequent to the union of female and male. In the process of her elevation and augmentation, *Shekhinah* assumes the demiurgical characteristics of the upper female, *Binah*.[176] This is the implication of the semiotic metamorphosis of *Shekhinah* from the diminished *yod* to the enlarged *he*, for *Binah*, too, is symbolized by the letter *he*—a homology is thus envisioned between the second and fourth letters of the Tetragrammaton: "There are two *he'in*, one above and one below, one is the world of the masculine and the other the lower world, which is the world of the feminine."[177] The extension of the point that was hidden signifies the transmutation of *Shekhinah* from a passive receptacle to an active force that overflows. In overflowing to the terrestrial world of differentiation (*alma di-peruda*), *Shekhinah* mirrors the activity of *Binah* in the supernal world of unity (*alma de-yiḥuda*).

The eschatological valence of the Song celebrates the restitution of *Shekhinah* to *Binah*, the reunion of mother and daughter through the ascent of the latter to the former.[178] This appears to be the symbolic import of the following statement, which attributes the utterance of the Song to Elijah,[179] an attribution that undoubtedly carries an implicit messianic insinuation:

> When [*Shekhinah*] ascends, it ascends from gradation to gradation, and from crown to crown, until everything is united above. And this is the secret of the "Song of Songs of Solomon." The Song of Songs was decreed by the mouth of Elijah by means of the supernal authority. The "Song of Songs," the praise of praises to the King to whom peace belongs, for this is the place that desires joy, for no anger or judgment is there. The world-to-come is entirely joyous, and it gladdens everyone, and thus it dispenses joy and happiness to all the gradations. Just as the joy must be aroused from this world above, so the happiness and joy must be aroused from the world of the moon in relation to the supernal world. Consequently, the worlds exist in one pattern, and the arousal ascends only from below to above.[180]

According to this passage, the Song is directed to *Binah*, the "supernal world" or the "world-to-come," which is also identified as Solomon (*shelomo*), based on the rabbinic interpretation of the name as a reference to God who is the one to whom peace belongs (*li-mi she-ha-shalom shelo*).[181] The rabbinic remark can be interpreted in this way theosophically, for *Binah* is the king whose creative potency reaches fruition, attains climax, in the phallic gradation of *Yesod*, designated as *shalom* ("peace" or "wholeness"),[182] and then overflows to *Shekhinah*, irrigating the garden, as it were. The "king" in this context does not refer, as one might expect, to the sixth emanation or the masculine potency of *Tif'eret*, the divine son who emerges from the union of *Ḥokhmah* and *Binah*, the father and mother. On the contrary, the "king" is *Binah*, who is called by this name on account of her demiurgical role in birthing the lower seven *sefirot*.[183] The shift in symbolism underscores the fact that the theurgical purpose of the Song is to arouse the joy of *Shekhinah*, the "world of the moon," in relation to *Binah*, the "upper world," so that the two worlds may be aligned in one pattern.[184]

Gikatilla expresses the eschatological import of the ontological alignment of the upper and lower female in a poignant way:

> Contemplate how the two occurrences of the letter *he* in the name [*YHWH*] correspond to one another, and the keys of the name are placed in their hands—the one above and the other below. . . . From here you can understand the mystery of *Shekhinah* in the unity of the two occurrences of the letter *he*, and the two of them are one intention, the one draws from the other, and everything is one unity in God, blessed be he. The one who knows how to intend these two occurrences of

> the letter *he* in the name must intend in the moment of unification [*sheʿat ha-yiḥud*] that the secret of the perfect unity is in the two of them. Concerning the two of them, it says, "The Lord will be one and his name will be one" (Zech. 14:9), to set one corresponding to the other, and to unify the *sefirot* one with the other.[185]

According to the symbology adopted by Gikatilla, which resonates with what is expressed in a large section of the zoharic literature, this alignment should be interpreted in gender terms as the transformation of the lower feminine into the upper, which is depicted in the overtly masculine image of the king to whom the (phallic) peace belongs. The masculinization of *Shekhinah*, occasioned by her unification with *Tif'eret*, reaches its fullest expression when *Shekhinah* unites with and is integrated in *Binah*, the ontological condition associated with the eschaton. The messianic significance of the Song lies precisely in the gender transposition of *Shekhinah* occasioned by her restitution to *Binah*.

In another passage, the image of the kiss at the beginning of the Song is interpreted as a reference to the union of *Binah* and *Malkhut*, the lower light igniting the upper.[186] The application of the ostensibly heterosexual setting of the metaphor of the kiss to the intimate relationship between these two attributes is rendered meaningful if one bears in mind the transformation of gender to which I have alluded. *Binah* assumes the persona of Solomon in relation to *Shekhinah*, who is the Shulamite woman; the desire of the latter to receive the kiss of the former denotes the longing on the part of the lower world to be united with the upper, a union that portends one of the clear signs of redemption.

In this respect, the zoharic authorship continued the older midrashic tradition that assigned messianic significance to the Song. Refracted through the kabbalistic prism, however, the messianism is linked primarily to the ontological elevation of *Shekhinah* to *Binah*. It is from this eschatological perspective, moreover, that we can understand the zoharic utilization of the view attributed to Aqiva (discussed above) to the effect that the Song is the holy of holies in relation to the rest of Scripture, as well as the implicit claim (also discussed above) that the Song is equivalent to all of Torah:[187]

> This Song is the song that contains all of the Torah, the song in relation to which the upper and lower beings are aroused, the song that is in the pattern of the world above, which is the supernal Sabbath, the song on account of which the supernal, holy name is crowned. Therefore it is the holy of holies. Why? Because all of its words are in love and in the joy of everything.[188]

The eros of the Song conveys not only the heterosexual bonding of the King and the Matrona, but also the restoration of the holy pair to the womb whence they emerged.[189] The consummation of desire, the first phase in the messianic drama, involves the union of the lower world of the feminine (*Shekhinah*) and the upper world of the masculine (*Binah*), the eschatological re/turn of the daughter to the mother, the overcoming of phallic *jouissance* in the reparation of the phallic womb.[190] When *Shekhinah* is conjoined to *Binah*, the process is semantically marked by the completion of the name YHWH Elohim.[191] Here the historical allegorization itself reaches fullest articulation, inasmuch as the Song is read as a figurative depiction of the drama in the divine realm that corresponds to events in time, culminating with the coming of Messiah. The symbolic approach articulated by the zoharic authorship does not preclude or supplant the historical allegory of the earlier rabbinic-targumic tradition; on the contrary, the former enhances and deepens the latter.[192] Thus in one passage we read:

> On the day [of the dedication of the Jerusalem Temple] the Song was revealed and *Shekhinah* descended upon earth. . . . On that day verily this Song was revealed, and by means of the holy spirit Solomon uttered the hymn of the Song, which is the principle of all the Torah, the principle of the entire account of creation, the principle of the mystery of the patriarchs, the principle of the exile of Egypt. . . . the principle of the coronation of the supernal, holy name in love and in joy, the principle of the expulsions of Israel amongst the nations and their redemption, the principle of the resurrection of the dead until that day that is the "Sabbath unto the Lord" (Lev. 25:4).[193]

The Song encompasses every aspect of the *Heilsgeschichte* of the Jews, including the messianic redemption, resurrection of the dead, and the eschatological world-to-come, which is described as the Lord's Sabbath. The ultimate rectification involves the unification of all things in the world-to-come, the attribute of *Binah*, which is the "supernal Sabbath" that transcends the division of Sabbath into night and day, alluding symbolically to the binary of female and male.[194] "Sabbath unto the Lord" signifies the transcending of gender dimorphism in the restitution of all polarity in the world of the masculine, the day that is entirely Sabbath.

The apocalyptic reading of the Song as the depiction of the ontological restoration of *Shekhinah* to *Binah*, the lower female to the upper female, is expressed somewhat differently in another context: the Song begins in the third person, "Oh, give me of the kisses of his mouth," for the initiation of love entails the arousal of kisses in the one who is not seen, the concealed of the concealed (*setima de-khol setimin*), who is conjoined to the gradation that corresponds to Jacob, the sun (*Tif'eret*), which illumines the moon (*Shekhinah*) with the supernal lights that shine from the place of the hidden wine, the attribute of *Binah*, or the world-to-come.[195] According to this passage, the Song is a poetic encoding of the efflux of light from the first of the luminous emanations to the last, from the "concealed of the concealed" overflowing to *Shekhinah*, the moon, by way of *Binah* through *Tif'eret*, the sun. In this context, the process is interpreted from above to below, rather than the reverse. The common denominator nonetheless is the view that the Song in its innermost structure reflects the unification of the divine emanations, and particularly the union of the upper and lower female attributes.

This thought is articulated in a somewhat different way in another zoharic passage wherein the content of the Song is related to the "supernal chariot," which is constituted by the four names, Adonai, Ṣeva'ot, YHWH, and Ehyeh. The divine names correspond respectively to four kinds of splendor, an allusion to the four sefirotic emanations in ascending order, *Shekhinah, Yesod, Tif'eret*, and *Binah*. The "mystery of the four inscribed names of the four splendors" entails, according to the zoharic text, that "each splendor is contained in the other, and the desire of the one is to enter the other, so that one may be contained in the other. These four splendors are specified in their names as they are known."[196]

The nature of the Song, which conveys the erotic pattern of the poetic word in general, is related to the desire of each splendor, to which corresponds a particular name of God, to be contained in the other. The eros for the other is here related to the impetus for unity in the divine realm, a unity that underlies the mystical import of the Song. The symbolic reading of the poem, therefore, imparts information about the "mysteries of the wisdom of the supernal, inscribed name," which is the Tetragrammaton.[197] Indeed, the Song itself is the very name that, given the identification of Torah as the name, is an alternative way of expressing the equivalency of the Song and Torah.[198] From this perspective, it is appropriate to speak of the Song as the "extreme point of zoharic intuition," for this part of Scripture is the holy of holies that is poetically envisioned as the "absolute interiority" of the divine edifice of Torah.[199] Alternatively expressed, it is possible to view *Zohar* as an extended and multivalent commentary on the erotic mysticism celebrated in the Song.[200]

The intrinsic connection between the Song, the four-letter name, and the erotic nature of the kiss as the union of the four spirits, which translates symbolically to the elevation of *Shekhinah* to *Binah*, is made explicit in the following interpretation of the opening verse of the Song, "Oh, give me of the kisses of his mouth" (Song 1:2):

> What did King Solomon perceive such that he placed words of love between the supernal world and the lower world, and at the beginning of the poem of love he placed between them [the words] "Oh, give me of the kisses [of his mouth]"? Rather, it has been established and it is the case that there is no love, conjunction of spirit with spirit [*devequt de-ruḥa be-ruḥa*], except through the kiss, and the kiss is through the mouth, the wellspring of spirit and its overflow. When the one kisses the other, these spirits are conjoined to these spirits, and they are one, and consequently there is one love. In the book of the ancient Rav Hamnuna Sava, it is said concerning this verse, the kiss of love divides into four spirits, and the four spirits are joined as one, and they are within the mystery of faith [*raza di-meheimanuta*], and they arise in the four letters, and these are the letters upon which depend the letters of the holy name, and the supernal and lower beings depend on them, and the praise of the Song of Songs depends on them. And what are they? [The four letters of the word] *ahavah*, and they are the supernal chariot, and they are the union, conjunction, and perfection of everything. These letters are four spirits, and these are the spirits of love and joy of all the parts of the body that has no sadness at all. Four spirits are in the kiss, each one is contained in the other. When the one spirit is contained in the other and the other is contained in it, the two spirits become one, and consequently the four [spirits] are joined perfectly in one conjunction.[201]

The essence of the Song is thus related to the desire of the four spirits to be united in the one bond of love, which is related to the four letters of the word *ahavah*, which in turn are correlated with the four letters of the most sacred name, YHWH, the name that signifies what cannot be signified, the garment of Torah unveiled in its mystical core to the one properly attired. The four spirits relate to the four divine attributes, alternatively referred to as the four splendors, but also to the fourfold that is born from the union of the spirit/breath of the male and the spirit/breath of the female. Each gender contains the other in itself, the principle that is basic to the kabbalistic notion of androgyny.[202] The conjunction of male and female yields the intertwining, cohabiting, of male in female and female in male. Mathematically framed, the twofold that is one becomes four.

In another context, the matter is expressed in similar but somewhat different terms, related exegetically to the four spirits (*ruhoṭ*) that shall alight upon the shoot to grow out of the stump of Jesse (Isa. 11:2) and to the breath (*ruaḥ*) of prophecy that comes forth from the four winds (Ezek. 37:9):

> The kiss of love is only through the mouth, the spirit is joined to the spirit, and each of them is comprised of two spirits, its spirit and the spirit of its counterpart. Thus the two are in four spirits, and all the more so the male and female in conjunction of four spirits together. The son that comes out from them, this is the breath that comes forth from the four winds, as it says, "Come, O breath, from the four winds" (Ezek. 37:9), this is the perfect spirit.[203]

The eros of the kiss is thus associated with the emanative process by means of which the androgynous being emerges from the union of the spirits of the mouth, male and female. This being is the perfect spirit, the son that contains the daughter as his sister, or as the breath of prophecy, the inarticulate masculine voice articulated through the articulation of feminine speech.[204]

Corresponding to the upper union of the breaths is the lower union of the genitals, but even with respect to this lower union, the depiction embraces the symbolism of language to express the texture of the erotic experience. The point is accentuated in the description of the second splendor, Ṣevaʾot, or the "living splendor" (*zohar ḥai*), the phallic gradation of *Yesod*. "His desire is to praise constantly the first splendor, which is called song [*shir*], and thus they are contained as one in a single bond without separation, with a complete desire. As a result, the all [*kola*] is called Song of Songs [*shir ha-shirim*]."[205] The plural of the expression *shir ha-shirim* ("song of the songs") alludes to the mystery of the sacred copulation between the first and second splendors, *Shekhinah* and *Yesod*. This union, a transformation that is encoded in the linguistic transition from the singular *shir* to the plural *shir ha-shirim*, transforms the former.[206] The theosophic interpretation of the title of the scriptural book indicates that the mystical constitution of the Song is related to the holy union of male and female. The final attainment of that union, however, is realized only in the restoration of the various splendors to the fourth splendor, the "hidden splendor that is not visible at all" except by means of "contemplation of the heart" (*sukhlatenu de-libba*), "for the heart knows and contemplates it even though it is not seen at all."[207]

The Song of Songs is thus contrasted with the song of Moses uttered at the splitting of the Reed Sea, for the latter is the "song of the feminine" (*Shekhinah*) whereas the former is the "song that ascends to the world of the masculine" (*Binah*).[208] The Song is identified with the apocalyptic moment wherein the feminine potency ascends to the world of the masculine and is thereby transformed. The inspiration for the Song, the augmentation of the wisdom of Solomon, derives from the gesticulation by which the "lower world ascends to the supernal world and is hidden within it, and it is concealed in it, revealed in secrecy [*itggalya vi-settirah*]."[209] The secret of the Song is captured in the richly paradoxical phrase *itggalya vi-settirah*, an appreciation of which requires one to take note of the fuller context of the passage wherein it occurs. When the world of the feminine, the seventh of the seven palaces of holiness, is elevated and incorporated into the world of the masculine, the "world that is exposed" in the "world that is concealed," what is revealed is revealed in secrecy, not as binary opposites but as the unification of opposites held together by their difference.

Spiritual Eroticism, Ascetic Renunciation, and the Eschatological Re/Turn

The legacy of the Hispano-Jewish philosophical orientation on the kabbalistic understanding of the Song was quite profound. The negative attitude toward bodily pleasure fostered an allegorical interpretation that replaced the literal eroticism of the text by a spiritualized eroticism related to the contemplative ideal of conjunction. Going beyond philosophers and poets, however, kabbalists intensified the nexus of asceticism and eroticism. As I argued at length in the previous chapter, the sacralization of human sexuality attested in kabbalistic lore cannot be understood in isolation from the ascetic impulse. On the contrary, as kabbalists have emphasized repeatedly, carnal sexuality is celebrated only to the extent it is transformed spiritually by proper intentionality.

To be sure, as Scholem noted, kabbalah is to be contrasted with non-Jewish mysticism, and in particular the spiritual ideal of Christianity, on the grounds that kabbalists resisted a monastic ideal of absolute abstinence. Marriage is viewed within the kabbalistic tradition not as a concession to the weakness of the flesh but as a symbolical realization of the union of the masculine and feminine potencies of the divine. Scholem thus distinguished the ascetic dimension of Christian mysticism, which led to the transplanting of eroticism into the relation of man to God, and the affirmation of human sexuality on the part of kabbalists, which was viewed as one of the central means to discover the mystery of sex within the divine.[210]

While I would not disagree with the claim that Jewish and Christian approaches to asceticism must be kept distinct in light of the respective values placed on human sexuality and the engenderment of the divine image, my own research has led me to the conclusion that the medieval kabbalistic tradition does share something closer to the Christian demeanor related to the problematization of the corporeal body and its gender correlation with the feminine. In particular, the symbolic reading of the Song, which is expressive of both theosophic and ecstatic elements, underscores the extent to which kabbalists sought to augment and in some measure displace carnal sexuality with spiritual eroticism.[211] Functioning within the confines of normative halakhah, kabbalists could not affirm celibacy as an absolute ideal, but they nevertheless boldly posited an austere lifestyle for themselves wherein the intensity of their contemplative regimen was linked to an erotic passion that demanded in turn abrogation of physical desire.

The ascetic renunciation of carnal sexuality for the sake of spiritual eros anticipates the condition of the eschaton, which must be a retrieval of the primordial beginning. If we can believe that an actual circle of mystics in Castile lay behind the narrative tales recorded in the zoharic texts, a belief that I think is entirely justified on scholarly grounds, then it is possible to refer to an eschatological community of ascetic mystics who believed they were already living at the end of days.[212] This pattern was repeated in each community of kabbalists who relived the zoharic myth and envisioned themselves to be a textual embodiment of the fraternity of Simeon ben Yoḥai.

The nexus between asceticism and redemption, I submit, is one of the central tenets of zoharic spirituality, if I may be allowed such an inadequate formulation. The redemptive character of the ascetic dimension is especially highlighted by the symbolic association of *Binah*, the world-to-come, and Yom Kippur, the Day of Atonement in which five primary physical pleasures are prohibited (eating, drinking, bathing, sexual intercourse, and wearing leather). The theosophic symbolism intensifies the rabbinic depiction of the world-to-come as a state beyond sensual joy, an idea doubtless with older roots in a priestly related pietism cultivated in what is known in Jewish historiography as the late Second Temple period.[213]

According to one zoharic text, on Yom Kippur the people of Israel "all exist in the soul more than the body, for on that day there is affliction of the soul [*innuya de-nafsha*] and not of the body, as it says, 'you shall deny your souls' (Lev. 16:31) and 'every soul that is not afflicted' (ibid., 23:26)."[214] The hyperliteral reading underscores in the first instance that abstention from physical pleasure is an affliction of the soul and not merely of the body. It insinuates, moreover, that ascetic denial is endowed with transformative power, for it is on account of denying the somatic body its pleasures that the people of Israel are ensouled in a different body of a higher ontic status, a more subtle and refined embodiment. The psychic metamorphosis is portrayed as a restoration of the Jew to the gradation of the divine to which the day of atonement symbolically corresponds, an idea expressed by the zoharic author in the description of this day as "taking all the souls . . . that are in his power."[215] As it happens, according to this passage, Yom Kippur stands symbolically for *Shekhinah*, and not the more typical sefirotic referent *Binah*, for on this day the moon receives light from the ten *sefirot* in the form of a hundred lights (since each of the ten comprises ten, the sum of the ten equals one hundred).

The implication of this passage, then, is that on Yom Kippur Jewish souls are absorbed into *Shekhinah*, the pneumatic integration facilitated by ascetic renunciation. The distinctive quality of this day rendered theosophically is the union of *Binah* and *Malkhut*, the upper and lower feminine configurations of the divine. According to another homily, the point is derived exegetically from the biblical locution *yom ha-kippurim* (Lev. 23:27); the plural form is used instead of the singular (*yom ha-kippur*) to impart that this day is marked by the bonding of mother and daughter. It is precisely on account of this dynamic in the imaginal realm of the sefirotic emanations that intercourse is forbidden on the Day of Atonement, that is, since *Malkhut* is illumined from *Binah*, the house of the mother, rather than *Ḥokhmah*, the house of the father, it is inappropriate, indeed prohibited, for husband and wife—in truth, brother and sister—to cohabit. The coupling of brother and sister, king and queen, is possible only when *Malkhut* receives from *Ḥokhmah* and is thereby rendered "holy" (*qodesh*).[216]

One can detect here the trace of the archaic mythologoumenon concerning the bestowal of the daughter by the father to the son, a bestowal that facilitates the union of wisdom that constitutes the fullness of the divine realm. I have discussed the psychosexual implication of the theosophic myth and the secret of illicit sexual relations (*sod arayot*) in chapter four. What is crucial to emphasize in this context is that union of mother and daughter renders sexual intercourse forbidden, whereas union of father and daughter renders it permissible. The return to the womb carries with it the overcoming of heterosexual eros.

A particularly important passage, which addresses the eschatological significance of the ascetic quality of the Day of Atonement,[217] is found in one of the later strata of zoharic literature:

> Therefore on Yom Kippur . . . sexual intercourse is forbidden. There the sign of the covenant, which is the *yod*, is the crown on the Torah scroll [*taga al sefer torah*] . . . as it has been established, "In the world-to-come there is no eating, drinking, or sexual intercourse. Rather the righteous sit with their crowns upon their heads."[218] Since there is no intercourse [*shimmush*] in this world with the crown [*taga*], the masters of the Mishnah established,[219] "the one who makes use of the crown perishes" [*kol ha-mishttammesh be-taga ḥalaf*].[220]

In this context, sexual abstinence required on Yom Kippur is linked explicitly with the feminine assuming the posture of the crown. As I have analyzed in a number of studies, the image of the crown atop the head of the righteous signifies repeatedly in kabbalistic sources, with little variance in time or place, the gender transformation of the feminine, the restoration of the female to the male whence she was taken. For the immediate purpose, it is sufficient to note two passages written by the same hand that penned the afore-cited text. In the introduction to *Tiqqunei Zohar*, it is stated that when *Shekhinah* "takes from *Keter*, she is called the 'crown of splendor' [*aṭeret tif'eret*], the crown on the head of every righteous man, the crown of the Torah scroll, and concerning her it has been said 'whoever makes use of the crown perishes.'"[221]

A similar description of *Shekhinah* occurs in a second passage from this work, but in that context the pressing concern involves the imaginal representation of *Shekhinah* as the *yod* on top and bottom of *alef* when it is decomposed into *yod* on top, *waw* in the middle, and *yod* on the bottom. Rendered symbolically, *Malkhut* stretches from the upper to the lower point of emanation, a theme that is portrayed as well in the two images applied to *Shekhinah*, the earth that is the footstool (Isa. 66:1) and the discarded foundation stone (Ps. 118:22) that rises to be a crown on the head of the three patriarchs.[222] Additionally, the theme is related exegetically to the words "from the first the last will be told," *maggid me-re'shit aḥarit* (Isa. 46:10), that is, the end is known from the beginning.[223] Just as in the beginning the feminine was in the position of the crown on the head of the male, an ontic state that is cast in the image of the corona of the phallus—even though there is no phallus in this configuration, since at the top of the chain is the thought-beyond-thought that may be represented only in the figure of the head—so in the end the seemingly autonomous feminine will be restored to the male androgyne.

Kabbalistic literature widely attests that masters of the Jewish esoteric tradition have believed the eschaton would be marked by the overcoming of gender dimorphism in the repairing of the male androgyne, the restitution of the feminine to the masculine.[224] For my immediate purpose what is important to note is that in the aforecited zoharic passage, the eschatological image of the righteous sitting with crowns on their heads is a symbolic depiction of their celibacy. The elevation of *Shekhinah*, which is designated as the sign of the covenant, the phallic marking of the *yod*, to the position of the crown on the scroll of Torah or on the head of the righteous indicates the reintegration of the feminine as an aspect of the masculine. Significantly, according to another passage in *Tiqqunei Zohar*, the images of the "locked garden" (*gan naʿul*) and "sealed spring" (*maʿayan ḥatum*) from Song 4:12 are applied to the "lower *Shekhinah*," for she is " 'the virgin that no man had known' (Gen. 24:16), and she is the wisdom of Solomon concerning whom it is said 'Solomon's wisdom was greater' (1 Kings 5:10), she was filled with the irrigation of each and every *sefirah* by means of that channel, which is the *waw*, until she reaches that supernal fount, which is the supernal *yod*, 'the wisdom of all the Kedemites' (ibid.), and at that moment she becomes a crown [*taga*] on the head of the letter *waw*."[225] *Shekhinah*, "the virgin that no man had known" (*betulah we-ish lo yedaʿah*), receives the overflow of the *sefirot* via the channel of *Yesod*, and consequently ascends to the supernal wellspring of *Ḥokhmah*, where she assumes the posture of the crown on the head of the phallus, the *yod* atop the *waw*. In the social plane, the kabbalist mimics the indigenous virginal state of *Shekhinah* and her subsequent gender metamorphosis by abstaining from physical sex and engaging in contemplative envisioning of the sefirotic emanations in explicitly erotic terms. Even when the man enlightened in the ways of kabbalah engages in domestic intercourse, it is necessary for him to avoid all thoughts of sensual pleasure, focusing instead on cleaving to the divine through the medium of his wife and thereby drawing down the flow of energy from on high.[226]

The state of conjunction is imaged as a myth of reciprocal coronation: *Shekhinah* is crowned by the kabbalists as the former assumes the posture of crown on the head of the latter. This motif is linked exegetically by kabbalists, including members of the zoharic circle, to the verse "O maidens of Zion, go forth and gaze upon King Solomon wearing the crown that his mother gave him on his wedding day, on his day of bliss" (Song 3:11). The interpretation of this passage, attested in several zoharic pericopae, underscores the convergence of theosophic and ecstatic elements, for the coronation of Solomon by his mother on the day of his wedding is applied simultaneously to an event within the Godhead and to the experience of the mystic vis-à-vis the divine presence.[227] Most important, that experience involves the assimilation of the male mystic into the feminine presence that has been transposed into the corona of the phallus.

The overtly heterosexual images, therefore, must be decoded as a veiled allusion to the homoerotic bond between the male mystic and the reconstituted male androgyne in the divine realm, a consequence of the phallo-narcissistic vision that has informed kabbalistic ontology apparently from its inception. Insofar as the homoeroticism is ideationally predicated on abrogation of carnal sexuality, it seems reasonable to distinguish the homosocial texture of mystical experience from homosexuality.[228] Indeed, the kabbalist bound to God presumably experiences the life of the world-to-come, which is a plane of being beyond the gender bifurcation that erotic yearning presupposes for its fulfillment. Alternatively expressed, the Song celebrates the great Sabbath, the "Sabbath of Sabbaths" (*shabbat shabbaton*), one of the biblical designations of Yom Kippur (Lev. 16:31), in which the division of Sabbath into night and day is overcome. The great Sabbath, the world-to-come, is the day that is entirely Sabbath, a day that is not measured by the alternating nocturnal and diurnal rhythms.[229]

The reading of the Song proffered in zoharic literature is expressive of the eschatological vision wherein the end is marked by the restitution of the holy pair to the womb of the divine mother, *Binah*, the place of return, *teshuvah*, the world of the masculine, the world that is coming, Yom Kippur, the Day of Atonement, the day of a/mends, that is, the day on which there is the mending of what has been torn.[230] The re/pairing achieved in the eschaton is portrayed as well as the symbolic import of forgiveness—the giving before that ensues from the womb of all-that-is-to-come. By thinking philosophically about forgiveness and atonement, one can grasp the mythic import of Yom Kippur as the time of return to the womb, the mending of the sore by a reversal of eros, the wheel of be/coming revolving from *nega* to *oneg*, in the language of *Sefer Yeṣirah*, from pain to pleasure.

In some measure, the eschatological reparation unfolds each Sabbath. Thus, according to one relevant passage, the letters of the word *shabbat* (*shin beit taw*) are interpreted as a reference to the ascent of *Shekhinah* to *Binah*, for the letters *beit* and *taw* spell the word *bat*, "daughter," which symbolizes *Shekhinah*, and the letter *shin* alludes to the three patriarchs or the fourth, fifth, and sixth emanations, *Ḥesed*, *Gevurah*, and *Raḥamim*. When the *bat* rises as a crown on the head of the *shin*, the chariot is completed by the unity of the four, and they in turn ascend to be united in the world-to-come, which is the "great Sabbath" (*shabbat ha-gadol*).[231] This is precisely the theosophic dynamic that the zoharic authorship assigns to the Song. Hence in one passage the four words of the first verse of the Song, *shir ha-shirim asher li-shelomo*, are related to the "perfect, holy chariot," which consists of the three patriarchs and David, that is, the central three *sefirot* of *Ḥesed, Gevurah*, and *Raḥamim*, conjoined with *Shekhinah*.[232] Contained in the first verse, therefore, is the mystery of the entire Song, which relates to the elevation of *Shekhinah* to form, together with the patriarchs, the holy chariot for King Solomon, that is, *Binah*, the king to whom peace belongs. The symbolic import of the Song is thus identical to the mystical meaning attributed to Sabbath.

The liturgical rhythm of Sabbath moves from the sacrality of sexual union, which is necessary to overcome the state of exile, to the ascetic denial of sexual gratification, which is characteristic of the eschaton. This transition is reflected in the intradivine dynamic. The eve of Sabbath is the time of the *hieros gamos* and hence the focus is on the heterosexual coupling of the king and queen, *Zeʿeir Anpin* and *Nuqba*, also symbolized as brother and sister. On the day of Sabbath, by contrast, the principal union is between *Arikh Anpin* and *Zeʿeir Anpin*, which translates mythopoeically into the homoerotic pairing of father and son. The reign of *Arikh Anpin*, the realm of complete mercy, over *Zeʿeir Anpin*, a mixture of mercy and judgment, signifies the messianic state, which is proleptically anticipated in the present historical epoch. Thus, for example, in one zoharic passage[233] the second of the three festive meals of faith (*seʿudatei di-meheimanuta*) on Sabbath is the banquet of *Atiqa Qaddisha*, for at that time this attribute is revealed "and all the worlds are joyous." In the same passage the time of the afternoon service on Sabbath is described as a "propitious moment" (*et raṣon*) when the "will of wills is found and *Atiqa Qaddisha* reveals his will, and all judgments are subdued and desire and elation are found in everything." The zoharic perspective is well captured by Isaac Luria in his hymn for the third meal of Sabbath: "Thus I will summon / the ancient of days / to his forehead until / they are interchangeable" (*we-ha azmin / atiq yomin / lemiṣḥeh ad / yehon ḥolfin*).[234] According to another zoharic passage, the mystical significance of repentance is explicated in terms of the restoration of the lower emanations to *Binah*, the divine mother who is called *teshuvah*, which activates the uppermost attribute of the divine, *Atiqa Qaddisha*, to illumine *Zeʿeir Anpin*:

> It has been taught that when all actions below are proper and the mother [*Binah*] is joyous, *Atiqa Qaddisha* is revealed and the light is restored to *Zeʿeir Anpin*, and everything is joyous, everything is perfect, everything is blessed, mercy is summoned, and all the worlds are joyous, as it is written, "He will return and he will love us, he will suppress our iniquities" (Micah 7:19). What is "He will return?" *Atiqa Qaddisha* will return to be revealed in *Zeʿeir*. He will return to be revealed for at first he was hidden, and everything is called repentance [*teshuvah*].[235]

The disclosure of *Atiqa Qaddisha* from its state of concealment is cast as the theosophic meaning assigned to the act of repentance.[236] The relationship between *Atiqa Qaddisha* and *Zeʿeir Anpin*, which is the leitmotif of the third meal on Sabbath, figures prominently in the *Idrot* sections of zoharic literature, expressed especially in the image of the illumination of the forehead or face of one upon the other.[237] The homoerotic bond in the Godhead betokens a state of compassion, the propitious moment when the mercy of the supernal male configuration overflows to the lower male configuration and thence to the world at large. Significantly, the homoeroticism achieves its climax in the highest manifestation of the divine, the "primordial nothingness" (*ayin qadmaʾah*), the "supernal will," the "will of wills," the "concealed of the concealed," that "knows and does not know" the infinite (*ein sof*) within which there "are no desires, no lights, and no sparks."[238] We can speak of this will as the will that eternally empties itself of will in its extending beyond itself infinitely. The ascetic posture below on the part of the kabbalist, the kenotic impulse to empty oneself of impulse, is an emulation of the divine volition, to be immersed in that which has no limit by divesting oneself of all that is limited.

The soteriological import of the homoerotic conjunction of *Arikh Anpin* and *Zeʿeir Anpin*, the upper and lower masculine configurations (*parṣufim*) of the Godhead, is drawn explicitly in the following explanation offered by Ḥayyim Vital of the talmudic legend of the four rabbis who entered Pardes, which he connects to the primordial sin of Adam in the Garden of Eden:

> "It has been taught by the rabbis: Four entered Pardes, and they are Ben Azzai, Ben Zoma, Elisha Aḥer, and R. Aqiva."[239] As a consequence of primal Adam having transgressed in this grave transgression, the fruits of which we are still eating in this world, it will not be rectified until the coming of Messiah. These four sages were distinguished in wisdom and piety, as is known, and they contemplated through the holy spirit and the account of the chariot, and it arose in their minds to rectify this blemish brought about by the transgression of primal Adam or at least to rectify the parts of the roots of their souls affixed in primal Adam. The blemish caused by the transgression of Adam was that he enlarged the crown [*keter*] of *Zeʿeir Anpin* before the suitable time, prior to the entry of the facets of consciousness [*moḥin*] of *Abba*, and as a consequence the mind [*daʿat*] of *Zeʿeir Anpin* fell down from the side of *Imma* to between the shoulders in the upper third of *Tifʾeret*. . . . It follows that it was impossible to rectify this blemish and to elevate the mind above to its place until they drew forth the facets of consciousness of *Abba* into *Zeʿeir Anpin*, and then the *Keter* within him will be rectified, and the mind can ascend to its place. Hence, it was necessary for them to draw forth the four aspects of consciousness of *Abba*, which are *Ḥokhmah, Binah*, and the two crowns of *Daʿat*, aspects of mercy [*ḥasadim*] and aspects of severity [*gevurot*], everything together. However, it arose in the mind of these four sages that between the four of them together they would rectify this blemish, and each one would rectify and draw forth one facet of consciousness from the four since there was not enough power in them so that each one would draw forth all four facets, but they erred in this matter, for it was necessary that all four facets be perfected by one of them alone. . . . Thus, even with respect to R. Aqiva who entered in peace and who did not sin at all, the ministering angels desired to push him away. *Prima facie*, the matter is strange, but even though through him only one facet of consciousness was drawn forth, by means of his rectification all four facets of consciousness were, willy-nilly, drawn forth, as will be explained. In any event, he alone was worthy to rectify all of them and to draw them forth to *Zeʿeir Anpin*, and thus they desired to push him away, and God, may he be blessed, saved him by saying that all four facets of consciousness were drawn forth on account of him, as will be explained, even though he only rectified one facet alone.[240]

Vital explains the rudimentary transgression of humanity in theosophic terms that have a decidedly sexual nuance: Adam's sin consisted of his expanding the crown of *Zeʿeir Anpin* prior to the entry thereto of the four facets of consciousness of *Abba*, which correspond to *Ḥokhmah, Binah, Ḥesed* and *Gevurah*, the latter two being the dual manifestation of *Daʿat*. As a consequence of this premature elongation of the crown, the mind (*daʿat*) of *Zeʿeir Anpin* fell down from the side of *Imma* to between the shoulders in the upper third of *Tifʾeret*, and hence it could not occupy its proper position in the head. Accordingly, the rectification (*tiqqun*), which entails elevating the mind of *Zeʿeir Anpin* above the shoulders, cannot take place until the four facets of consciousness of *Abba* are drawn down and inserted into *Zeʿeir Anpin*.

It lies beyond the immediate concern of this discussion to elaborate on the symbolic intricacies of this passage. Suffice it here to say that sin and its rectification are understood in terms of a homoerotic dynamic between *Abba* and *Zeʿeir Anpin*, configurations of the divine that personify the father and son respectively. A prolepsis of this pairing occurs every Sabbath afternoon when *Arikh Anpin* begins to illumine *Zeʿeir Anpin*, a process that reaches its climax at the time of the third meal before the closing of Sabbath, and unmitigated mercy disseminates in the world. Needless to say, I am aware that the description of the originary offense does not directly involve the configuration of *Arikh Anpin* but rather *Abba*. The justification for interpreting Vital's account in the way that I have proposed, however, lies in the fact that the Lurianic doctrine transmitted and expounded by him (as well as by other disciples) presumes that the *moḥin* are ontically sustained by the light that *Abba* receives from *Arikh Anpin*. Significantly, the final augmentation is not represented as the embrace of male and female but as the elevation of the mind of the son to the consciousness of the father.

The phallomorphic texture of the *tiqqun* is underscored in Vital's exegesis of the fate ascribed to Aqiva in the rabbinic narrative: "This is the secret of R. Aqiva who entered in peace [*nikhnas be-shalom*], that is, he brought down the *Yesod* of *Abba*, which is called 'peace' [*shalom*], together with the crown of mercy [*iṭara de-ḥesed*] that is in it, and afterward he raised the lower *Yesod* of *Imma*, which is called 'peace' [*shalom*], and elevated it above."[241] Utilizing the phallic connotation of the term "peace" (*shalom*) which can be traced back to classical rabbinic sources,[242] Vital interprets the talmudic locution applied to Aqiva as an encoded symbolic reference to the double gesture of the messianic rectification: he entered and exited Pardes by means of the phallic potency, or, to be more precise, his entry consisted of lowering the upper phallus, *yesod de-abba*, literally, "foundation of the father," and the exit consisted of elevating the lower phallus, *yesod de-imma* "foundation of the mother," the womb,[243] which is the locus of knowledge, *daʿat*, in the divine anatomy. "*Yesod* is always in the aspect of knowledge, for we have found that *yesod de-imma* is the knowledge of *Zeʿeir Anpin*."[244] The genital repairing of male and female is a necessary precondition for *tiqqun*, but the final rectification is attained when *yesod de-imma* is uplifted to be rejoined with *yesod de-abba* and thereby restored as the phallic gradation whence the mind of God is conceived.[245] When the esoteric nature of this matter is properly apprehended, the implicit homoerotic underpinnings of the heteroerotic symbolism come to light.

The homoerotic nature of the messianic unification is expressed as well in terms of the nexus between the great Sabbath, the world-to-come, and Yom Kippur, a chain of symbolic images that indicates that the eschatological vision is predicated on ascetic renunciation, a ritual feature of the holiest day of the Jewish calendar. In the rhythm of each Sabbath, night is the time for sexual union of man and his wife, since this is the time of the *hieros gamos* above between the holy King and the Matrona,[246] but in the progression of the day, the sanctity of physical copulation gives way to the abnegation of sexuality, a state of purity that anticipates the holiness of the world-to-come, which is Yom Kippur.[247] The zoharic symbolism is expressed succinctly by Gikatilla:

> From the Sabbath a man can enter into the life of the world-to-come, which is the secret of the jubilee . . . and the world-to-come is called the great Sabbath. . . . Open your eyes and see how you must observe the Sabbath, if you desire to merit life, redemption, and to enter into the life of the world-to-come. . . . When you comprehend this matter, then [you may understand] "If you call the Sabbath delight"—this is our Sabbath, "The Lord's holy day is honored" (Isa. 58:13)—this is the supernal Sabbath, which is called the jubilee. Therefore the rabbis, blessed be their memory explained,[248] "The Lord's holy day is honored"—this is Yom Kippur.[249]

The reading of the Song that emerges from the different literary settings of *Zohar* suggests that the thirteenth-century kabbalists responsible for this work imagined that the celebrated love poem is an allusion to the very same transition from the currently acceptable observance of Sabbath, which features prominently engaging in carnal intercourse in an effort to facilitate the sacred union above, to the eschatological Sabbath, which involves a state of holiness that is predicated on the abolition of physical desire. The zoharic interpretation of the Song, therefore, embraces an erotic mysticism that affirms the ideal of ascetic eschatology, an ideal that is proleptically realized by kabbalists in their pietistic fraternities principally through communal study of the secrets of Torah. No scriptural text afforded kabbalists a better opportunity to express the homoerotic asceticism of their mystical piety than the Song, the book that is the holy of holies, the speculum through which the invisible glory is seen and the ineffable name spoken.

Epilogue

R. Pinḥeas said:
"On the eve of Sabbath Israel stood at Mount Sinai,
men and women were arranged separately."
The holy One, blessed be he, said to Moses:
"Go and inquire of the daughters of Israel whether they
want to receive the Torah, for the way of men is to follow the opinion of women,
as it says, 'Thus it has been spoken to the house of Jacob' (Exod. 19:3),
this refers to women, 'and declare unto the sons of Israel' (ibid.), this refers to men."
They answered unanimously, "All that the Lord will speak we will fulfill" (ibid., 8),
and it says, "Singers and dancers alike will say, All my roots are in you" (Ps. 87:7).

—*Pirqei Rabbi Eliʿezer*, chap. 41

The sway of thought, like the trajectory of time at once circular and linear, seems always to lead one back to where one has not been, retracing steps yet to be imprinted. In this book, I have once again labored long in the orchard of kabbalistic texts to articulate philosophically the poetic imagination and hermeneutic orientation of the medieval Jewish esoteric lore. In great measure, my effort herein, reflective of my scholarly project since I began graduate school in 1980, has been impelled by a keen sense that kabbalah—not to speak of the spiritual comportment of Judaism more generally—is in need of mending that cannot be attained by way of apologetic thinking or obfuscation shaped by winds of political correctness. As the seventeenth-century Polish kabbalist, Naftali Bachrach, put it, "There is no repair [*tiqqun*] except in a place where there was fracture [*qilqul*] previously."[1] Repair, if it is to be more than the proverbial bandage on a broken limb, comes not through forgetfulness, lest it issue forth from remembering the root that must remain oblivious to memory and, in that sense, rootless. I have sought to remember in this way, to take hold of the root and thereby uproot, to re/collect something of what has been disseminated. Admittedly, the focus is on one tradition, with an occasional venturing into other traditions for comparative purposes, but this study, as all my work, is informed by the sincere belief that delving deeply into the ground of one tradition opens paths to explore others.

In spite of the noteworthy expansion of the boundaries of the mythopoeic imagination on the part of kabbalists, attested in the explicit characterizations of the divine as male and female, there is no textual or conceptual basis to argue that they were able to overcome the androcentric bias of medieval rabbinic culture according to which man, and not woman, was upheld as the more perfect ideal of human existence, both somatically and psychically.[2] In light of this understanding, one would be hard pressed to identify *Shekhinah*, configured as the great goddess mother, as the locus of the erotic. On the contrary, as I have argued repeatedly, the phallus is the focal point of the erotic for the kabbalists, that is, when examined beneath the lens of critical theory, the texture of eros at play in traditional kabbalah has to be seen from the perspective of the sexual desires and anxieties of a man shaped by a very limited sociocultural but at the same time broad philosophical perspective, one literate with the basic texts of the medieval rabbinic elite. The imaging of the feminine has to be seen as part of the male erotic fantasy to attain psychosomatic wholeness, to enter the other so that the other is restored to one's self. In a typically androcentric orientation, the feminine is demarcated in the erotic drama of redemption as the dwelling place of the phallic potency.

As it happens, the redemptive task understood by kabbalists is captured succinctly in the idiom of *Gospel of Thomas*: to "make the female male."[3] Traditional kabbalists read the account of God having created Adam male (*zakhar*) and female (*neqevah*) in the first chapter in Genesis in light of the second account, wherein the derivative ontic status of woman (*ishshah*) from man (*ish*) is made explicit, the woman having been constructed from the body of man. Accordingly, the protohuman *adam*, derived from the word *adammah* ("earth"), is conceived imaginally as a male androgyne, the single gender that contains its other as part of itself, a typical patriarchal construction. For kabbalists, therefore, we can speak properly of an Edenic state of the androgynous prelapsarian man, a condition to be retrieved at the end of time. In the *conjunctio oppositorum*, two sexes are unified and woman is restored to man, the ideal unification that tolerates no difference, redemption understood as assimilation of the other to the same.[4] In this condition, eschatological repair is complete—in the absence of an other, there is no pair to re/pair, identity of difference is no longer different from nor identical to difference of identity, identically different, differently identical.

Based on this principle, which is substantiated by a plethora of sources that I have studied carefully and critically in the course of more than two decades, it should become apparent to the nonpartisan reader that the positive attributes associated with *Shekhinah* entail her masculinization, the transformation of judgment into mercy, a transposition depicted in a number of symbolic figures, to wit, the midpoint of the circle, the sign of the covenant inscribed on the circumcised phallus, the footstool of the throne rising to be the crown on the head of the king. Representations of the feminine, and especially in erotic images crafted by a phallocentric imagination, bespeak the sexual dimorphism characteristic of a state of exile wherein the unity of the male androgyne has been severed, and as a consequence the male seeks his other, to restore the part of his self that has been taken and rendered independent. Redemption entails the overcoming of this dimorphic condition, the reconstitution of the androgynous male, the unseeing of *Shekhinah* in the guise of an autonomous feminine imaginary, the speculum that is the other, an eschatological vision of the occluded, seeing of nothing-to-be-seen, the covenant of peace, the prismatic bow enveloped in the cloud, unveiling of the veil in veiling the unveiled.

The intricate imaging of *Shekhinah* on the part of male kabbalists signifies the mental state of one hovering midway betwixt ecstasy and collapse, fragmentation and restoration, oblivion and remembrance—if I no longer remember forgetfulness, I cannot forget remembrance, and consequently, there would be no need or even possibility for making symbols other than as tokens of memory to remember what to forget so as not to forget what to remember. When the imaginal configuration ascribes autonomy to the female, forgetting that her memorialization—her capacity to be re/membered, that is, to be incorporated into the covenant—is dependent on her image being affixed as a seal upon the body of the male,[5] she assumes a demonic character that dons multiple masks, two of the most emblematic being the rageful warrior wielding a sword of vengeance and the alluring Gentile female sexually baiting the male member of the covenantal community.[6] Therein lies the psychological root of idolatry, for to worship the feminine in isolation from the masculine, to focus the heart's intention on adoration of the goddess separate from the god, to conceive of the female as anything but the space that contains the male so that she may be contained by the male, is the quintessential act of heresy, variously referred to as cutting the shoots, plucking the fruit, building a tower to heaven, crafting the golden calf.[7]

As scholars have long noted, depictions of *Shekhinah* as daughter who has fallen into captivity or as mother weeping over her children are figurative tropes employed by kabbalists to express the rabbinic teaching that *Shekhinah* accompanies the Jewish people in exile. These mythopoeic images convey the broken, fragmented nature of the divine, the displacement of *Shekhinah*, cast down from the realm of light into the world of shadow, the gnoseological symbol of the pearl sunk to the bottom of the sea, which is linked exegetically by kabbalists to the scriptural topos of the forbidden woman whose "feet go down to death" (Prov. 5:5), *Shekhinah* in the bereaved state of tottering about in the world, typified historically by the banishment of Jews from the land of Israel but meant to convey something more basic about the existential plight of the human condition. The walking of the mystical fellows in the zoharic homilies, as Cordovero's *Sefer Gerushin* well attests, captures poetically the gesture of redemptive reading, to traverse the hermeneutical path, to accompany *Shekhinah* in her exilic meanderings, to lift her from dust and restore the crown to its glory.[8]

In my own thinking, I have raised the issue of gender that belies the imaginal construct, interpreting the exile of *Shekhinah* as a symbolic rendering of the suffering of eros as the indifferent identity (one-that-is-all) becoming identical difference (all-that-is-one), a process that is collectively conceived by kabbalists as amelioration of feminine judgment, her restoration to and elevation through the morphological prism of the divine, culminating in the reconstitution of the male androgyne in *Keter*, the place that is no-place (*atar law atar*), unity of what cannot be counted before the one, neither one nor many, a world that is all right, the left contained in the right, reparation of Adam by restoring the female to the male, the tip of the *yod*, sign of the covenant, corona of the phallus, in its upper position situated in the single eye set in the forehead of *Arikh Anpin* that has no companion, the open eye that is never shut, like the eye of a fish, the fount of light whence springs forth in/sight.[9]

Even the image of the bedecked bride waiting for her groom in the nuptial chamber is a symbol of liminality delimiting the initial phase of redemption, the transition from separation to unification, which is consummated when the feminine is reintegrated into the masculine and the visionary gaze is no longer focused on *Shekhinah* as an autonomous female persona but as the diadem that encircles the head of the male. The encircling is also portrayed as the ascent of *Malkhut* to *Keter*, the last to the first emanation, the reconfiguration of the constellation of divine potencies in the imaginal symbol *keter malkhut*, crown of kingship. The eschatological intent of the symbol is captured poignantly by Luzzatto, a kabbalist to whom I have referred intermittently in the course of this book. Commenting on the verse "For they will bestow on you length of days, years of life and well-being" (Prov. 3:2), Luzzatto writes: "For surely all throughout the time of exile the great rectifications [*tiqqunim gedolim*] go forth and are summoned for the time of the redemption, which is accomplished through the power of *Arikh Anpin*—the supernal mystery, and then all the feminine forces [*nuqvin*], which are exclusively in the aspect of *Malkhut*, will be in the aspect of *keter malkhut*."[10] In a passage from another treatise, Luzzatto articulates the eschatological transformation of *Shekhinah* in the scriptural image of *aṭeret baʿlah* ("a crown for her husband"), which underscores the gender hierarchy that has prevailed in traditional kabbalistic symbolism even as it provides the terms that notionally lead to its subversion:

> The matter of "a woman of valor is a crown for her husband" (Prov. 12:4), for the feminine [*nuqba*] is a single point alone [*nequddah aḥat levad*] and the nine *sefirot* come to her by the secret of the supplement [*be-sod tosefet*], that is, *Malkhut*, which is verily the root of the lower beings [*shoresh ha-taḥtonim mammash*], is the one that alone gives a place to darkness in the providential act [*be-hanhagah*], and verily to evil, for deficiency [*ha-ḥissaron*] is not due to the force that overflows to the world [*ha-mashpiʿa le-olam*], but due to what receives [*ha-meqabbel*]. Indeed, from one perspective this is surely her lowliness, but from another perspective this is praise and elevation, for this is not done except to reveal the supernal unity [*legallot yiḥud ha-elyon*] . . . and the praise of Lord, blessed be he, is not disclosed except through her.[11]

Scholars of kabbalah have correctly focused on the female imaging of *Shekhinah* as one of the distinctive and most influential facets of this lore, and in particular the images of bride, princess, and Matrona have most captivated their imagination. In the course of this study, I have tried to contextualize these symbolic representations by examining the theme of language, eros, and being in kabbalistic literature from a philosophical standpoint. When the hermeneutical foundations of the gender construction are properly attended to, it becomes clear that the female personifications of *Shekhinah* are liminal images, marking the space between dark and light, separation and union, difference and identity. Consider, for example, the following comment of Ezra of Gerona on the verse, "Your cheeks are comely with plaited wreaths" (Song 1:10): "The figurative language refers to *Shekhinah* coming out from exile and she is like a bride that enters the nuptial chamber."[12] The depiction of *Shekhinah* as bride is appropriate to the moment she comes forth from exile, a moment overflowing with desire. The texture of the erotic at this juncture is fantasized by the male in heterosexual terms, the king longing for the queen, the bridegroom lusting for the bride, a desire dependent on the construction of woman as an autonomous entity from the body of man. As the cosmological narrative of the creation of man and woman is recounted in the following zoharic passage:

> When Adam rose up, his female was fixed in his side, and the holy soul that was in him expanded to this side and to that side, and it was sufficient for the one and the other. Since she was thus contained, the holy One, blessed be he, later severed Adam and arrayed [*taqqin*] the female, as it is written, "The Lord God constructed the side etc." (Gen. 2:22). It has been established *et ha-ṣela*, "the side," as it says, *u-le-ṣela ha-mishkan*, "the side of the Tabernacle" (Exod. 26:20). "And he brought her to Adam" (Gen. 2:22), in her arrayment [*be-tiqqunaha] as a bride to the nuptial chamber.*[13]

In the originary state, the female was contained in the male; when the primordial androgyne is severed, the female is brought to the male, adorned like a bride entering the nuptial chamber. Once the male androgyne is split into the gender binary of male and female, the heteroerotic division of sexual labor ensues—the desire of man to cohabit with woman so that the original unity of Adam will be reinstated. The essence of the arrayment of the feminine, *tiqqun ha-nuqba*, consists of the construction of the woman as the other who stands face-to-face with man,[14] the female vessel that receives the seminal flow from the male channel so the female will be returned to the male and the re/pair will be complete,[15] the "one flesh," *basar eḥad* (Gen. 2:24), reconstituted.

One of the most dramatic applications of the mythical symbol is the ritual of *tiqqun haṣot*, the "midnight reparation," a vigil characterized by forms of prayer and study by means of which kabbalists participate in mourning and lamenting the suffering of *Shekhinah* in exile, portrayed imagistically in the matriarchal figure of Rachel weeping over her children.[16] In this theurgical rite great emphasis is placed on conjugal union, since the task at hand is to repair the separation of feminine and masculine in the divine, the casting of earth (*Shekhinah*) from heaven (*Tif'eret*), which is paralleled in the mundane sphere by the desolation of the land of Israel and the scattering of the Jewish people among the nations of the world.[17] The initial phase of redemption entails envisioning *Shekhinah* as the female other desirous of and desired by her male consort, *Tif'eret*, but the final goal is the integration of female into male, symbolized most poignantly by the image of the ascent of *Malkhut* to the rank of *aṭeret ba'lah*, positioned as a crown on the head of *Keter*, the "female surrounding the male," *neqevah tesovev gever* (Jer. 31:21), an othering of the other that yields the unity of the same and thereby renders indifference indifferent to all but perhaps its own indifference.

In these concluding remarks I will limit myself to the eschatological portrayal of this drama in the zoharic interpretation of the sign of the covenant established between God and Noah.[18] A key passage occurs in a homily that purports to be delivered by an anonymous and unassuming Jewish merchant who is traveling about with two sacks of clothes. (We later learn that he is engaged in business to support two sons who study in a rabbinic academy.) One midnight, in a hotel in Mehaseyah, the merchant happens upon R. Judah when he rises to study Torah. Prior to the section that I will cite, R. Judah had begun to expound the verse "And this stone, which I have set up as a pillar, shall be God's abode" (Gen. 28:22). After an exchange between R. Judah and the merchant, including exegetical queries that the former could not answer, the latter is encouraged to expound the verse. The initial homily is built on the connection between the aforecited verse and the words ascribed to David, "Justifiably, I will behold your face; awake, I am filled with your image" (Ps. 17:15). The kabbalistic reading turns the adverbial expression *be-ṣedeq* ("justifiably") into a nominal "through righteousness." To grasp the import of the grammatical misreading, one must bear in mind that *ṣedeq* typically symbolizes *Shekhinah*. The psalmist is reporting, therefore, that he beheld God's face by way of *Shekhinah*, which is also identified as the stone lifted by Jacob (Gen. 28:22) and the foundation stone rejected by the fathers (Ps. 118:22). David's love and longing for conjunction (*ḥavivuta u-devequta*) were directed toward that stone, and thus "when he desired to contemplate the vision of the glory of his master [*le'isttakkela ve-ḥizu yeqara de-mareih*], initially he took hold of that stone in his hand, and afterward he entered."[19]

Both verses inform us about the mystery of worship, thus formulated by the zoharic authorship: "whoever desires to be seen before his master should not enter except by means of this stone, as it is written, 'through this [*be-zo't*] Aaron entered the shrine' (Lev. 16:3)."[20] The purpose of prayer is cast primarily in visionary terms—to be seen before the master—but this can come about only through the agency of *Shekhinah*, symbolized by the physical stone (*even*), the attribute of righteousness (*ṣedeq*), and the pronoun "this" in the feminine form (*zo't*). *Shekhinah* is the gateway through which the worshipper must enter to reach the holy One—a basic tenet of the mystical understanding of ritual promulgated by kabbalists, already expressed in the recommendation in *Sefer ha-Bahir* that before one inquires about the king, one should ask about his dwelling,[21] with the entry thereto portrayed in explicitly erotic terms.[22] Mystical communion (*devequt*) cannot be severed from visualization (*histakkelut*), nor is it profitable to align them in a linear or causal sequence.[23] When the mechanics of contemplative prayer are viewed within a theistic framework, as must be the case in kabbalistic tradition, then communion can ensue only from envisioning, and envisioning, only from communion.

The exegetical excursus on prayer and envisioning *Shekhinah* sets the stage for the divulgence of the messianic secret of the rainbow:[24]

> He began to expound, "Solomon sat upon the throne of his father David, and his rule was firmly established" (1 Kings 2:12). What praise is this? Rather he laid the

foundation stone and he placed over it the holy of holies, and then "his rule was firmly established." And it is written, "[When the bow is in the clouds] I will see it and remember the everlasting covenant" (Gen. 9:16), for the desire of the holy One, blessed be he, is towards it[25] constantly and the one who is not worthy through it cannot enter before the master. Thus it is written, "I will see it and remember the everlasting covenant." "I will see it," what [is the meaning of] "I will see it"? This is a secret, as it is said, "Put a mark on the foreheads etc." (Ezek. 9:4), to be manifest on them. Others say that this is the inscription of the holy sign on the flesh. R. Judah said: Certainly everything is this way, but the rainbow that is seen in the world exists in a supernal mystery. When Israel will go out from the exile, this rainbow will be adorned in the colors of the bride who is adorned for her husband. That Jew said to him: Thus my father said to me when he departed from this world: Do not expect the feet of Messiah until that rainbow is seen in the world, adorned in bright colors, and illuminating the world. Then you can expect the Messiah. From where do you know? As it is written, "I will see it and remember the everlasting covenant." Now it is seen in darkened colors to be a reminder that a flood will not come. However, in that time, it will be seen in bright colors and it will be adorned in the ornamentation of a bride who is adorned for her husband. Then [is it appropriate to say] "and remember the everlasting covenant" [*lizkor berit olam*]. The holy One, blessed be he, remembers that covenant that is in exile and he lifts her up from the dust, as it is written, "they will seek the Lord their God and David their king" (Hosea 3:5), and it is written, "they shall serve the Lord their God and David, the king whom I will raise up for them" (Jer. 30:9). "I will raise up" from the dust, as it says, "I will raise up again the fallen booth of David" (Amos 9:11). Thus "I will see it and remember the everlasting covenant," to raise her up from the dust.[26]

The homily begins with a theosophic interpretation of Solomon's being seated on the throne of David: Enthronement is one of the symbolic portrayals of the union of masculine and feminine potencies in the divine, the potency to bestow abundantly and the capacity to receive restrictively. The matter is also conveyed in the biblical locution of Solomon establishing his rule, *malkhuto*, that is, *Shekhinah* assumes the name *malkhut* when the king is enthroned, when male is conjoined to female, the potency to bestow with the capacity to receive, the river and the ocean. This is the symbolic intent of God's gazing at the rainbow to remember the sign of the covenant.[27] We are justified in translating the medieval kabbalistic symbolism into the idiom of contemporary feminist theory and in speaking of the phallomorphic gaze. The glance of the male vis-à-vis the female is to be evaluated repeatedly from the standpoint of phallic desire to project into space, to be enframed by the other.

As we have seen, the phallomorphism goes a step further, as the gaze transforms the feminine to the point that she is reincorporated into the phallus in the form of the corona. The adornment of the rainbow as bride, which heralds the coming of messianic redemption, denotes the initial gesture that will culminate in the uplifting of *Shekhinah*, which signifies her gender transposition. In accord with the widely attested correlation of gender and moral disposition, male corresponding to mercy and female to judgment, we might expect that the transformation implied in the embellishment of the bride in the garb of the rainbow would symbolically convey as well a transvaluation of values. The motif is transmitted in another zoharic homily in the guise of a parable:

> R. Jose said: The rainbow came to protect the world. [This may be compared] to a king who, in all times that his son sins against him, comes to beat him, but the Matrona is revealed to him in glorious garments of royalty [*levushei yeqar de-malkhu*], and the king looks at her, and the anger towards his son dissipates as he is gladdened by her, as it is written, "I will see her and remember the everlasting covenant" (Gen. 9:16). Thus the rainbow is not seen in the world except in glorious garments of royalty. When there is a righteous man [*ṣaddiq*] in the world, he is a covenant to uphold the covenant [*berit lemeiqam berit*] and to protect the world. When there is no righteous man, the rainbow is revealed, for the world is set to be destroyed if not for this rainbow. R. Eleazar said: This rainbow is never attired except in the garment of the patriarchs: green, red, and white. . . . It takes hold of the colors to be crowned by means of them atop the patriarchs. In these garments, the rainbow is attired when she appears before the king. Come and see: The secret of the holy covenant is the letter *yod*, which is crowned in the supernal marking, and this is perpetually inscribed on the covenant. Because Phineḥas was zealous with respect to this covenant, this letter was inscripted in his name, Phineḥas, a diminished *yod*, which is verily the *yod* of the covenant that emerges from the supernal, holy *yod*. And thus he stood perfectly before the holy king and he was not obliterated from the world. [28]

Ideally, peace reigns when the lower covenant, the righteous man below, fortifies the upper covenant, the corresponding attribute above,[29] but in the absence of the former, the rainbow serves as the protective sign. Following the language of the opening parable, the appearance of the rainbow functions as the means to appease God's wrath just as the king's anger toward a rebellious son is quelled when he gazes on the queen adorned in her royal garments. The statement that the "rainbow is not seen in the world except in glorious garments of royalty" signifies the investiture of *Shekhinah* in the attribute of *malkhut*.

The full intent of that image is exposed in the ensuing discussion set into play by the remark attributed to R. Eleazar: the rainbow, which is *Shekhinah*, is adorned in the colors of the three patriarchs, green, red, and white. Two interpretations to explain the relationship between the colors and the patriarchs are offered in a portion of the zoharic text that I did not translate. In my judgment, this is a later accretion to the text. Be that as it may, what is essential is that the patriarchs correspond to the central three *sefirot*, the attributes of mercy, judgment, and compassion. The radiance of the rainbow is the physical expression of *Shekhinah* reflecting the light of the upper emanations. This process is described as well in the image of *Shekhinah* crowning the patriarchs, an image we have encountered previously, especially with respect to the inner theosophic meaning of Sabbath. The elevation of the rainbow to the position of crown on the head of the patriarchs may also be decoded as an allusion to the gender transformation of *Shekhinah*. This facet of the phenomenon is made explicit in the concluding part of the homily, where the rainbow is related to the "secret of the holy covenant" (*raza di-verit qaddisha*), which is the letter *yod* that is "crowned in the supernal marking" (*de-mitʿaṭṭera vi-reshimu illaʾah*), that is, the mark of circumcision. Thus we may conclude that the theosophic import of remembering the covenant, occasioned by seeing the rainbow, is the manifestation of *Shekhinah* in the form of the letter *yod*, the letter/sign of circumcision inscripted on the flesh.

A similar usage of the word *qeshet* is attested in other zoharic passages, of which I will here mention two more examples most pertinent to the discussion underway:

> It is written, "Like the appearance of the bow [*ke-marʾeh ha-qeshet*] that shines in the clouds on a day of rain, such was the appearance of the surrounding radiance. That was the appearance of the semblance of the glory of the Lord" (Ezek. 1:28), the appearance of all the colors, and thus [it is written] "I have set my bow [*qashtti*] in the clouds" (Gen. 9:13). What is "my bow"? As it is said with respect to Joseph, "Yet his bow [*qashtto*] stayed taut" (ibid., 49:24), for Joseph is called righteous [*ṣaddiq*]. Therefore "his bow" is the covenant of the bow [*berit de-qeshet*] that is contained in the righteous, for in the covenant the one is united with the other. Since Noah was righteous, his covenant was a bow.[30]

In the second relevant passage, it is asserted that peering at the rainbow is prohibited because it is akin to looking at *Shekhinah*, the same rationale that is used to explain the rabbinic prohibition of looking at the fingers of the priests during the priestly blessing.[31] Explaining this dictum, the zoharic kabbalist posits a bow above and a corresponding bow below. With respect to the former, it is forbidden to look at its colors because "he who looks at its colors it is as if he looked at the place above and it is forbidden to look at it so as not to cause shame to *Shekhinah*." On the other hand, the bow below refers to "that sign of the covenant inscribed on a person, for he who looks at it causes shame above."[32] The parallelism between lower bow and upper bow instructs about the nature of the latter: just as the *qeshet* below is the sign of the covenant inscribed on the phallus, so the *qeshet* above refers to the phallic potency of God.[33] When God beholds the sign inscribed on the place that must be hidden, he remembers the everlasting covenant.

The gender transposition implied by remembering the covenant informs one about the ultimate goal of messianic redemption. From the claim that the rainbow will be "adorned in the ornamentation of a bride," it would appear that this symbol corresponds to the feminine *Shekhinah* and not to the masculine *Yesod*.[34] This is a reasonable deduction, but before one jumps to conclusions regarding the imaginary constructions of the female aspect of God, it is necessary to situate this passage in the larger framework of assumptions regarding gender that one finds in *Zohar* and related theosophic literature. The rainbow is a liminal symbol, for it demarcates the transition from exile to redemption. The exilic state is characterized by separation of male and female, and hence the rainbow appears in darkened colors; the redemptive state, by contrast, is marked by reunion of male and female, and hence the rainbow at first shines in bright colors like a bride adorned before the bridegroom.

The adorning of the rainbow as a bride indicates the imaginal representation of *Shekhinah* as the feminine other of masculine desire.[35] The heterosexual union cannot be effected in the absence of reciprocal yearning on the part of male and female, but from the psychosexual perspective adopted by kabbalists, eros is linked essentially to man's desire to be contained by the woman. In a typically androcentric maneuver, the author of the following zoharic exegesis of Song 7:11 expresses this desire through the voice of the feminine, "'I am my beloved's' is first and afterwards 'his desire is for me.' 'I am my beloved's,' to establish a place for him initially and afterwards 'his desire is for me.'"[36] In the gender symbolism promulgated by kabbalists, the purported female need to contain the male results in her becoming part of what is contained. Alternatively expressed, the female who provides the space to enclose the male becomes thereby the encircling part of the male.[37] The mutual desire can be seen, therefore, as the initial stage of redemption whereby the severance of male and female is mended; once the union is effected, the reintegration of the female into the male is accomplished. In the state of exile, the rainbow is depicted as the forsaken covenant buried in the dust, whereas in the time of redemption the covenant is uplifted and restored to the phallus. The gender transposition implied by the uplifting of the covenant is the theosophic intent assigned to the biblical idiom of God's remembering the covenant by beholding the rainbow. The point is clarified in another zoharic passage:

> Then the rainbow will be seen in the cloud in bright colors like a wife that is adorned for her husband, as it is written, "I will see it and remember the everlasting covenant." . . . "I will see it," in the bright colors, as is appropriate, and then [I will] "remember the everlasting covenant." What is the everlasting covenant [*berit olam*]? This is the Community of Israel, and *waw* will be united with *he*, and she will be lifted from the dust, as it says, "and God remembered His covenant" (Exod. 2:24), this is the Community of Israel, for she is the covenant, as it says, "and it shall serve as a sign of the covenant" (Gen. 9:13). When *waw* is aroused in relation to *he*, then supernal miracles will be aroused in the world . . . and he will lift the Community of Israel from the dust, and the holy One, blessed be he, will remember her.[38]

At the beginning of the redemption, it is appropriate for the rainbow to appear in the form of the bride (or wife) so that the erotic yearning of the male will be aroused and the union of the two consummated. The conjugal mating of male and female, represented respectively by the letters *waw* and *he* of the Tetragrammaton, rectifies the ontological separation of exile.[39] But the reunion of male and female is a process of reintegration of the latter in the former, an othering of the psychic projection of the feminine as other.[40] The phallocentric morphology is expressed in the image of God's remembering the covenant, which must be construed as an act of re/membering, that is, of ontically restoring the female to the *membrum virile*.[41] From a passage in one of Moses de León's Hebrew writings the intent of the zoharic text becomes clearer: the memory engendered by God's looking upon the rainbow signifies the gender transformation of *Shekhinah*, which is expressed as well as the amelioration of judgment by mercy:

> When the rainbow is seen, then the sign of the covenant [*ot berit*] is within and judgment vanishes from the world. . . . Whenever the rainbow is seen in the cloud, then the sign of the covenant is within her. And the secret is "I will remember My covenant etc." (Gen. 9:15), for there is no memory [*zekhirah*] without the sign of the covenant. Therefore they established its blessing,[42] "Blessed be the one who remembers the covenant" [*zokher ha-berit*],[43] for then she comprises the colors that are seen within her from the All [*ha-kol*]. Thus God, blessed be he, has mercy over the creatures and over the earth. Know that the secret of the matter of the rainbow and the covenant are joined together. Therefore they established that it is forbidden for a person to look at the rainbow so that he will not shame the *Shekhinah* and not peer within her. Thus the prophet said "Like the appearance of the bow that shines in the clouds on a day of rain, such was the appearance of the surrounding radiance. That was the appearance of the semblance of the glory of the Lord" (Ezek. 1:28).[44]

The theophany of Ezekiel culminates in the vision of the anthropomorphic glory encompassed by the radiance that shines like the rainbow in the cloud. In the passages from both *Zohar* and de León, the use of this image in the chariot-vision is to call to mind the sign of the covenant seen by Noah after the flood. But when does *Shekhinah* appear in the guise of the rainbow? When she reflects the light from *Yesod*, the gradation referred to as "All" (*ha-kol*) since it contains within itself all of the upper potencies. When *Shekhinah* receives the overflow from *Yesod*, judgments are removed from her. The aura of the bow enveloping the glory signifies the restoration of the female to the male in the form of the corona of the phallus. Accordingly, the pietistic directive derived from the theosophic tenet is that one is prohibited from looking at the male organ, which is connected to the rabbinic injunction not to fix one's gaze on Noah's rainbow.

One of the more interesting implications of the texts that I have cited and analyzed, and a plethora of others that could have been added, is the tension between seeing and unseeing that characterizes messianic enlightenment, that is, the manifestation of the rainbow as a sign of redemption, on the one hand, and the prohibition of looking at it, on the other. With all the emphasis placed on the visual—and as I have maintained in my work, the kabbalistic orientation is decidedly ocularcentric—there is ambivalence with respect to the visionary. To see is the goal, but the goal is not to see. Indeed, in a number of critical passages in the zoharic corpus, vision is indicative of exile, a fissure within the divine edifice that facilitates the seeing of that which should be concealed. We have previously encountered the paradox—visualizing the hidden in hiding the visual—especially as it pertains to the kabbalistic understanding of circumcision.[45] In phenomenological terms, we can speak of circumcision and redemption mirroring one another in an inverse image: circumcision, mystically understood, induces seeing the unseen, redemption, unseeing the seen. In the redemptive state, the feminine is sheltered securely within her boundaries like the point enclosed in the center of a circle, and the glory that was exposed is modestly occluded.[46] The securing of the feminine as the nucleus in the infinite circle is a reinstatement of the condition of the feminine before the emanation of the divine potencies as male and female.

The status of the feminine before the beginning, signified by the letter *beit*, is captured in brilliant brevity at the start of the nineteenth of the seventy homilies on the first word of Torah, *bere'shit*, that make up the work known as *Tiqqunei Zohar*: "*Bere'shit*—[contained] there are [the letters of the word] *bat* [daughter]. This *bat* is the point hidden in the ether [*nequddah setima ba-awwira*], concerning which it says 'Guard me like the apple of your eye [*shomreni ke-ishon bat ayin*] (Ps. 17:8). She was certainly hidden in the light [*genizah be-or*] and through her the ether [*awwir*] was made."[47] The feminine potency is concealed in the beginning, in *bere'shit*, as the *bat*, that is, the letters of the word *bat*—*beit* and *taw*—are the first and last letters of *bere'shit* ("in the beginning") a point confirmed by the scriptural idiom *bat ayin*, literally, "the daughter of the eye," but here read metaphorically as that which is most hidden in the eye. Before the emanation of *beit*, the second *sefirah* or *Ḥokhmah*, the *bat* was a "point hidden in the ether," the *yod* in the word *awwir*. When the *yod* is removed from *awwir*, one is left with *alef*, *waw*, and *reish*, which spells *or*, the light that emerged from the ether. What is most significant for our purposes is the depiction of the feminine at the beginning as the point occluded within the ether, one of the technical names of *Keter*; it is precisely this status that the feminine is to attain at the end.

The matter is brought into sharp focus by comparing two passages from Joseph of Hamadan. In the first, the view we have chronicled from other kabbalistic compositions is reiterated:

> The covenant [*berit*] that is seen in the cloud on a rainy day signifies the colors of the attribute of the *Ṣaddiq*. . . . Ezekiel the prophet, may peace be upon him, alluded to this when he said "Like the appearance of the bow which shines in the clouds on a day of rain, such was the appearance of the surrounding radiance. This was the appearance of the semblance of the Presence of the Lord. When I beheld it, I flung myself down on my face" (Ezek. 1:28). From here it is forbidden to look at the phallus [*berit*] and the one who sees the phallus should fall on his face.[48]

The nexus between prophetic envisioning and exile is further elucidated in a second passage, but, in that context, Joseph of Hamadan emphasizes the necessity for the rainbow to be concealed. By heeding this text we will be able to take hold of the paradox that characterizes redemption: the glory is rendered most conspicuous in the occlusion of its sign. The rainbow, we are told, can serve as testimony that the world will not be destroyed again by floodwaters because the deluge arose from the "attribute of the phallus [*middat berit*] of the supernal pure and holy form," that is, in consonance with the principle of measure for measure, "they sinned against the phallus and therefore they were punished by the phallus." And thus it says, "I will remember my covenant," *we-zakharti et beriti* (Gen. 9:15), "for verily it is the masculine [*zakhar*], the golden bowl [*gullat zahav*] that overflows to *Shekhinah*."[49] In the continuation of the passage, Joseph of Hamadan asserts that this attribute is called both "rainbow" (*qeshet*) and "covenant" (*berit*) because it respectfully exemplifies judgment (*din*) and mercy (*raḥamim*).

The messianic dimension is introduced as an exposition of the aggadic statement that in the days of R. Joshua ben Levi the rainbow was not seen.[50] According to Joseph of Hamadan, this alludes to the "secret of the mysteries of our Torah." When the pious and righteous are in the world, unifying the bridegroom and bride, then the covenant [*ha-berit*] is not seen with the eye of the intellect [*ein ha-sekhel*] from *Shekhinah*, for the attributes coalesce and the rainbow is not seen alone, for it is comprised in the rest of the attributes and they become one thing, blessed be he, and it is swallowed up and comprised in *Shekhinah* like a flame in the coal, blessed be he, and the rainbow is not seen as an attribute unto itself since it is comprised in the rest of the attributes."[51] In the continuation, we read that the "pure, holy, supernal phallus [*ha-gid ha-elyon ha-qadosh we-ha-ṭahor*] is called 'covenant' [*berit*] when it is manifest as the attribute of mercy and 'rainbow' [*qeshet*] when it is manifest as the attribute of judgment." From this we may deduce that when the rainbow, the female aspect of the phallus, is seen independently, it is a time of judgment, but in a time of mercy, the rainbow is not visible since it is contained in the phallic covenant that is hidden.[52] Seeing the sign secreted signifies the moment of salvation wherein the female is restored to the male and the androgynous phallus is reconstituted.

The dialectic of which I spoke is predicated on the confluence of concealment and disclosure, a convergence that characterizes kabbalistic ontology and epistemology—both the nature of being and the way it is known display the paradoxical leveling of opposites. From this perspective a positive role must be accorded the feminine as the garment that reveals the light it conceals, the ring that envelops the glory it exposes, the mirror that veils the unveiling of the veil, the imagination that endows the formless with form.[53] A passage from *Tiqqunei Zohar* poetically relates the philosophical tenet through the prism of Simeon ben Yoḥai's homiletical reflection (a prism within a prism, as it were, since the historical veracity of the rabbinic master is refracted through the lens of kabbalistic symbolism) on the verse "This is the book of the account of human beings," *zeh sefer toledot adam* (Gen. 5:1).

> He began to expound and said, *zeh sefer toledot adam*, verily *zeh*, comprising the twelve signs of the supernal Adam concerning which it is said "the tribes of Yah, a testimony to Israel" (Ps. 122:4). Verily *zeh*, this refers to the four lion-faces, four ox-faces, and four eagle-faces, through which human countenances [*parṣufin di-venei nasha*] are known, and all of these faces are inscribed with four letters, which are YHWH. What is *adam*? *Yod he waw he*, and concerning him it is said, "as the splendor of Adam, to dwell in the house" [*ke-tif'eret adam lashevet bayit*] (Isa. 44:13). To what does his "house" refer? *Shekhinah* who is called "image of Adam" [*demut adam*], for all the images and countenances of human beings [*dimyonin u-parṣufin di-venei nasha*], and all the forms of the upper and lower beings, are known through her. In relation to her, it is said, "and imaged through the prophets" [*u-ve-yad ha-nevi'im adammeh*] (Hosea 12:11).[54]
>
> All the marks, forms, and actions were seen through the lower *Shekhinah*, which is the image of Adam [*demut adam*], concerning whom it is said, "and imaged through

the prophets" [*u-ve-yad ha-nevi'im adammeh*], all were seen through her below. There is no one who could know and envision[55] the marks, forms, and actions above except through her. In relation to her, it is said, "You will see my back" (Exod. 33:23), but above me "you shall not see my face" (ibid.), for no created being can envision there on account of the power of the radiances and the light of the facets. Concerning them it says, "no man shall see me and live" (ibid., 20). If they could not gaze upon the face of Moses, how much more so the central pillar, which comprises all marks, forms, and facets, and in it everything shines, and it comprises all of them.[56]

It lies beyond the mandate of this epilogue to explore all the important themes in this homily. What is most significant for our purposes is the fact that the feminine is linked epistemically to the image, that is, *Shekhinah* is portrayed as the imaginal representation through which the invisible God is visually apprehended. The hidden dimension—the veiled face—is engendered as masculine, and the revealed dimension—the exposed back—as feminine; the former is identified near the conclusion of the passage as the "central pillar" of the sefirotic edifice. This central pillar comprises all forms, but the latter are seen only through *Shekhinah*, the "image of man" (*demut adam*), which consists of the four-letter name YHWH. The image is also depicted as the "house" where the splendor of the anthropos (*tif'eret adam*) dwells, that is, the feminine is the shelter that reveals the masculine potency concealed therein. The anonymous author of this passage—and the number of parallels that I could have cited is copious—imparts that the kabbalistic practice of contemplatively visualizing God conceives the female primarily as the vessel that delimits the limitlessly overflowing potency of the male, the fringe, we might say, that allows us to apprehend dimly the indeterminate reality of YHWH. We are thus justified in concluding that the role assigned the feminine in the imaginal envisioning of the divine enhances rather than diminishes the androcentric nature of kabbalistic symbolism, falling far short of what we would consider a genuine celebration of the female.[57]

Practitioners of the tradition deem any act or thought that separates male from female as transgressive, but the reification of the female as autonomous is judged to be idolatrous in a manner that is not so with regard to the reification of the male. The demonization of the female is expressed as well in terms of the male becoming female. Indeed, as I discussed above in chapter seven, one of the more influential symbols to depict evil in kabbalistic sources is the impotent or celibate male, mythically portrayed in *Zohar* and other kabbalistic works from late-thirteenth-century Castile as the Edomite kings manifest on the historical plane in the guise of Christianity, which upheld ascetic renunciation as the pietistic ideal.[58] The impotent male has the same ontic status as the female unbalanced by the male, for in that condition the male does not have a ground in which to lay his weapon.[59] Implicit here is a psychosexual explanation of the nature of these kings, which accounts for the dying. That is, these kings are swayed by the temptation to ejaculate with no female mate to receive their seminal discharge.

The act of spilling seed in vain, therefore, is viewed as the primordial transgression, the sin whose rectification summons forth the chain of being. The point is expressed in striking terms at the very beginning of *Sifra di-Ṣeniʿuta*: "Before there was a balance[60] they did not look face-to-face, and the primordial kings died, their weapons were not found and the land was destroyed."[61] The decoding of this text seems not too formidable a task: The image of the "weapons" functions as a metaphor for the *membrum virile*, and that of the "land," for the feminine potency. Before there was balance in the Godhead, there was no union of male and female—signified by the face-to-face glance—and consequently the primordial kings died and the earth was destroyed. The first seven of the eight Edomite kings are mentioned in Scripture without any female counterparts, which signifies symbolically that they were emasculated and thus have the symbolic stature of females, that is, untempered forces of judgment. When the mythical image is applied historically, it is evident that Edom symbolizes Roman Christianity, and the kings without weapons refer to celibate priests. Unqualified celibacy as a religious ideal precludes the possibility of procreation, and hence it is a kind of emasculation, which is linked to the demonic "other side."[62]

The sixteenth-century kabbalistic master Isaac Luria, who taught that the ultimate rectification of the break in the Godhead is attained when there is a reconstitution of the female as male, brings the full implication of the zoharic myth to light. Purification of the demonic, depicted most dramatically by the image of uplifting the sparks entrapped in the shells, involves a restoration of judgmental forces into mercy, for the initial catharsis involved the removal of the impure feminine from the economy of the masculine Godhead. As Luria's disciple, Ḥayyim Vital, astutely observed: "Thus you will understand why the aspect of the feminine is always judgments [*dinin*], for her root is in the aspect of the kings who died, and consequently they are called kings [*melakhim*] from the word *malkhut*."[63]

Underlying the zoharic myth of the Edomite kings, symbolic of the forces of impurity within the Godhead, is the ontological problem of the feminine. The death of the kings represents the purification of the feminine quality of judgment, the attribute of restriction necessary to balance the masculine beneficence, the vessel that contains and thereby circumscribes the phallic issue. Again to quote Vital: "'These are the kings who ruled in the land of Edom' (Gen. 36: 31), for when they emerged the aspect of these kings immediately began to be purified to produce the aspect of the feminine for him."[64] The ontological condition of these primordial kings was such that there was no balance between male and female, no correlation between the impulse to bestow and the desire to receive. Although the emasculated kings, who are, according to the narrative, kings without queens, are portrayed ontically as feminine, the psychological disposition that corresponds to this primordial situation, as I have already noted, is the urge of the man to ejaculate without any ground wherein the seminal fluid may be contained. From that vantage point the primal transgression is masturbation. The link between this act and the Edomite kings is drawn explicitly in the following Lurianic text:

> "The arms of his hands were spread out" (Gen. 49:24), this refers to the secret of ten drops that were cast out from between the nails,[65] as is mentioned in *tiqqun* 69,[66]

as is known . . . for they are themselves the aspect of the kings, or the nullification of the kings [*biṭṭul ha-melakhim*] was on account of the fact that Adam was not yet arrayed as one, male and female. This is the secret of the seminal drops of Joseph that were discharged without a female, but from the male alone. And these are the ten martyrs of royalty [*asarah harugei melukhah*]. Contemplate the word *melukhah*, for they were verily the seven kings [*melakhim*] whose vessels and bodies were broken. The reason was also because they were without the arrayment [*tiqqun*] of male and female, until Hadar, the eighth king, came, and then they were arrayed.[67]

The death of the Edomite kings is mythicized as the sin of spilling seed in vain, for they were males without female partners to receive the seminal discharge. By a psychical inversion typical of an androcentric standpoint, the male desire to ejaculate without a female receptacle is transposed such that the evil is associated more specifically with the woman. That is, the male who ejaculates without a female is transvalued as feminine. Thus these primordial kings are portrayed in zoharic literature in images that convey emasculation and sterility.

The hermeneutical extension of these images to include the masturbatory impulse reflects the peculiar understanding of male sexuality proffered in Lurianic kabbalah. The extent of the misogyny is brought into sharp relief insofar as the man's casting semen without a woman is understood as a transgressive act that symbolically feminizes the male. To be sure, the ultimate purpose of the divine catharsis is to purify the feminine aspect of the divine, but the purification is attained only when the feminine is restored to the male, when the other is obliterated in the identity of sameness. The messianic era is described as the final obliteration of the evil force (related exegetically to Isa. 25:8) that entails a restitution of the world to a primeval state of chaos. In that stage, the feminine is completely integrated in the masculine, a point represented symbolically by the overcoming of the divine name that numerically equals fifty-two (the force of the feminine operating independently of the male) by the names that equal sixty-three and seventy-two, which correspond respectively to the feminine and masculine.[68]

The reconstitution of the female as male is represented as well by the image of the wife being the crown of her husband[69] or the eschatological teaching of the rabbis that in the future the righteous sit with their crowns on their heads.[70] The eschaton signifies the reintegration of the feminine as part of the masculine, an ontic unity that was rendered asunder in the beginning of creation. The deeply mythical element of kabbalistic cosmogony (reflected as well in the eschatology) is such that fission of the Godhead is a cathartic process by means of which the (feminine) "other" is discarded so that it may be purified and ultimately restored to its ontological source in the male androgyne. Both the image of the wife being the crown of her husband and that of the righteous sitting with their crowns on their heads signify the ultimate unification which involves the recontextualization of the feminine as part of the phallus, a mystery related by Vital to the eighth of the Edomite kings who survived, Hadar, who corresponds to "*Yesod* that comprises male and female, which is the crown that is in him."

As I argued at length in the third chapter of this book, the engendering myth of theosophic kabbalah hinges on positing an androgynous phallus. There is thus a perfect symmetry between the beginning and end, the cosmogonic and eschatological poles of the temporal process. Just as the beginning is marked by the containment of the female in the male, symbolized by the phallus that comprises both genders, so in the end the female is restored to the male and the androgynous phallus is reconstituted. Hence, in the imagination of the kabbalists, the male organ is concomitantly the locus of sexual duality and the unity that overcomes that duality.

In an oft-cited remark in *Major Trends in Jewish Mysticism* to which I referred in chapter two, Scholem noted the dubious distinction of Judaism in the history of religions regarding the lack of women mystics. Scholem explained the "exclusive masculinity" in the history of kabbalah in terms of "an inherent tendency to lay stress on the demonic nature of woman and the feminine element of the cosmos."[71] I would express matters in a slightly different way, but there is little question that the male domination of kabbalists is due to the ontologically subservient role attributed to women. There is an essential homology between the structure of the myth of divine unity predicated on the transcendence of sexual opposites, on the one hand, and the hierarchical constitution of social relationships, on the other. That is, just as in the former case the female is subordinated to the male, so too in the latter. To be sure, male kabbalists have recognized that the woman plays an important role as the vehicle that facilitates procreation, and thus there is always a need for the feminine. Moreover, we can even say that theurgic efficacy is accorded the Jewish woman in the act of domestic intercourse, a role that is predicated on the symbolic correlation of the female below and the divine feminine. Notwithstanding the legitimacy of this claim, the role assigned to the woman is reflective of an androcentric bias, her worth determined exclusively from the vantage point of the man. In the final analysis, the female was considered part of the male, a reversal of what empirical evidence would suggest.

The perfection or wholeness depicted in heterosexual terms as the union of male and female, the mystery of the androgyne, is realized in the mystical bonding of the male fraternity, the circle of mystics that assemble around the figurehead of the *ṣaddiq*, the righteous soul who corresponds to the divine phallus.[72] The symbolic structure of this homoerotic fraternity is dramatically portrayed in the imaginary fellowship of Simeon ben Yoḥai and his colleagues according to zoharic literature. This mythic portrayal in turn served as the basis for the social fabric of subsequent groups of kabbalists who were active in history, including the circles of Isaac Luria in sixteenth-century Safed, Moses Ḥayyim Luzzatto in seventeenth-century Italy, and Israel ben Eliezer, the Baʿal Shem Tov, in eighteenth-century Ukraine.

The homoerotic element of mystical ecstasy—the "joy of the fraternity" (*ḥedwah de-ḥavruta*) according to the locution of one zoharic passage[73]—underlies the relationship of the individual male mystic to the feminine aspect of the divine, which is ontologically restored as part of the phallus. As I have argued at length elsewhere, the peak mystical experience of coronation is to be understood in symbolic terms as cleaving to the corona of the male organ.[74] There is no question that a central element of the lived experience of the kabbalist is the special relationship that he has with *Shekhinah*. In a telling phrase,

Ezra of Gerona refers to the kabbalists generically as "the group who receive the presence" (*kat meqabbelei ha-shekhinah*),[75] an allusion to the standard rabbinic idiom, "to receive the face of the presence" (*lehaqbil penei ha-shekhinah*).[76] In a second passage, Ezra designates the mystic who experiences communion with the Presence (*devequt ba-shekhinah*) as rising to the supernal level and being counted among the *meqabbelei penei ha-shekhinah*.[77]

Receiving the presence truly marks the *Weltanschauung* of the kabbalist, the world perspective that informs his cognition and valuation of reality. From that perspective it is correct, as scholars have long noted, that the kabbalist must imagine himself to be wedded to *Shekhinah*, the prototype of that experience being Moses.[78] The complex transvaluation, however, calls for a more nuanced understanding of the status of the feminine in a heterosexual union. For the kabbalist, the female is masculinized in the moment of sexual union. It is this transvaluation that underlies the symbolic depiction of coitus by the image of the crown: the male is crowned by the female, for the female is the crown of the male, that is, the female is assimilated into the corona of the phallus (*aṭeret berit*). Phenomenologically, the erotic fantasy revolves about the envisioning of God not as an autonomous female but rather as incorporated into the male. Thus Ezra comments on the description of King Solomon "wearing the crown that his mother gave him on his wedding day, on his day of bliss" (Song 3:11):

> For the entire [sefirotic] edifice will be conjoined to, unified with, and ascend to Ein Sof . . . and the diadem [*aṭarah*] is the emanation of the blessing and the surplus from the spirit of the living God. . . . Therefore blessing, holiness, and unity, which emanate from the Nothingness of Thought [*afisat ha-maḥshavah*], are called diadem [*aṭarah*] and crown [*keter*], as the rabbis, blessed be their memory, said in *Midrash Tehillim*,[79] "the angel who is appointed over prayer waits until the last congregation of Jews prays and he makes from [their prayers] a diadem for the head of the holy One, blessed be he, as it says, 'blessings for the head of the righteous' (Prov. 10:6)," the eternally living one.[80]

The ontic restoration of all divine grades, which is most fully realized in the eschaton, is portrayed in terms of the image of the ascending crown,[81] a central motif that recurs throughout the history of kabbalistic speculation. The male mystic is effeminized, and the feminine aspect of the divine, masculinized, the classical psychological complex of the homoerotic dynamic. The eroticism appropriate to the time of redemption—the time, that is, when time itself is redeemed in time—not only precludes the necessity of the female as part of the experience for the male but also excludes the female as such, that is, the female without being transmuted into a male, from having the experience of communion with the divine.[82]

In the symbolic view of medieval kabbalah, as in a variety of ancient gnostic sources, especially of Valentinian provenance, the cultic retrieval of sexual unity is in fact a "reconstituted masculinity"; that is, the union of the sexes results in making the female male.[83] The yearning to transcend otherness and separation (signs of exile and death) manifests itself in the initial stage in the heterosexual desire of female for male and male for female, which leads to the ultimate phase of redemption, the restitution of the female to the male whence she was severed. Reunification culminates in the abolition of the polarity of male and female, the overcoming of gender dimorphism. We may conclude, therefore, that the myth of the divine androgyne in kabbalistic sources, as in Gnostic compositions of late antiquity, is yet another expression of a socially dominant androcentrism. Salvation comes about through the containment of the feminine in the masculine, the neutralization of female power. Suffering the suffering of this axiom is a first step on the path to redeeming an ancient wisdom, tiredly waiting to be liberated from the confinement of its own textual embodiment.

Notes

Preface

1. Scholem, *On the Possibility of Jewish Mysticism*, p. 48. I was reminded of this passage through its citation in Wasserstrom, *Religion after Religion*, pp. 108–109. A more detailed account of the poetic dimension of Scholem's literary imagination is now offered by Wasserstrom in the introduction and notes to Scholem, *Fullness of Time*, pp. 25–26, 35, 39–40. Regarding Scholem's understanding of the relationship between mystical experience attested in works of kabbalah and poetic sensibility, see further, chap. 1, n. 245.

2. On the etymological connection between thinking and thanking, see Heidegger, *What Is Called Thinking?*, pp. 138–147.

3. See, in particular, the comment of Muḥyīddīn Ibn ʿArabī on the imagination's capacity for embodiment (*tajassud*) cited in Chittick, *Sufi Path of Knowledge*, p. 116: "The Prophet said, 'I saw my Lord in the form of a youth.' This is like the meanings that a sleeper sees in his dreams within sensory forms. The reason for this is that the reality of imagination is to embody that which is not properly a body [*jasad*]; it does this because its presence [*ḥaḍra*] gives this to it." Ibn ʿArabī conveys the capacity of the imagination to image the imageless also in terms of its ability to bring together opposites (*al-jamʿ bayn al-aḍḍād*); see citation in Chittick, *Sufi Path of Knowledge*, p. 115; and brief remarks in Sviri, *Taste of Hidden Things*, p. 56. Needless to say, the research of Chittick continues the pioneering work of Corbin on the role of the spiritual imagination in giving form to the formless through the theophanic envisioning or visionary knowledge (*la connaissance visionnaire*) of the imaginal world, *mundus imaginalis*, *ʿālam al-mithāl*, the world that is intermediate between the corporeal and spiritual. See, for instance, Corbin, *Creative Imagination*, pp. 190–195; idem, *Face de Dieu*, pp. 7–40; idem, *L'Iran et la Philosophie*, pp. 127–145. On the role of poetic imagination in medieval Islamic thought, with special reference to Avicenna, see Kemal, *The Poetics of Alfarabi and Avicenna*, pp. 89–103, 141–200; and idem, *The Philosophical Poetics*, pp. 82–127.

4. Hobbes, *Leviathan*, I:2, p. 11; on the inherent lack of veridicality associated with imagination, a theme well attested in medieval scholasticism, see IV:45, pp. 424–425. On the role of poetic imagination in medieval Islamic thought, with special reference to Avicenna, see Kemal, *The Poetics of Alfarabi and Avicenna*, pp. 89–103, 141–200; and idem, *The Philosophical Poetics*, pp. 82–127.

5. Corbin, *Creative Imagination*, p. 249. Corbin links this encounter specifically to prayer, a claim that may be compared profitably to the contemplative visualization of medieval kabbalists, more or less, contemporary with Ibn ʿArabī. See E. Wolfson, *Through a Speculum*, pp. 198–203, 290–293. On the virtual identification of prayer and imagination, see Corbin, *Creative Imagination*, p. 214: "For one and the same agent underlies the secret of Prayer and the secret of the Imagination." Following the lead of Corbin, I have studied the rabbinic conception of prayer from the vantage point of the theophanic imagination. See E. Wolfson, "Iconic Visualization," and (this time adding Torah study) idem, "Judaism and Incarnation: The Imaginal Body of God." For a similar approach, see Ehrlich, "Place of the *Shekhina*"; idem, *Non-Verbal Language*. On the centrality of the image of enthronement and worship in ancient Israelite mythology and its impact on later Jewish and Christian liturgical practices, see Bauckham, "Throne of God," pp. 43–69.

6. See the survey offered by Philip S. Alexander in the introduction to his translation of *3 Enoch* in Charlesworth, *Old Testament Pseudepigrapha*, vol. 1, pp. 225–229.

7. Ibid., p. 228.

8. Ibid., p. 256.

9. E. Wolfson, "Yeridah la-Merkavah," pp. 13–44.

10. For a rich discussion based on this hypothesis, see Kutsko, *Between Heaven and Earth*. Seemingly unbeknownst to the author, his analysis of Ezekiel fits in perfectly well with the thesis of my *Speculum* regarding the merging of ostensibly conflicting cultural tendencies in the history of Jewish mysticism, the need to configure God's form in the imagination, and the aniconic rejection of its physical representation.

11. Here I am influenced by the comments by Corbin, *History of Islamic Philosophy*, p. 307. Suhrawardī, *Book of Radiance*, sec. 90, p. 82, describes the faculty of imagination being "imprinted" from the forms that inhere in the *sensus communis* "as between two facing mirrors." On the relation of the *sensus communis*, the faculty (traceable to Aristotle's κοινὸν αἰσθητήριον) that integrates all sense data, and the retentive imagination, see op. cit., sec. 35, pp. 30–32, and the learned philological discussion in H. Wolfson, *Studies in the History of Philosophy and Religion*, vol. 1, pp. 250–314, esp. pp. 278–294.

12. It goes without saying that the expression "traditional kabbalah" is a verbal redundancy, but one that is necessary given the multiple interpretations and applications of the term in contemporary times. Those who wish to be genuine interlocutors need to bear this is mind: in the mode of classical philology, I seek in my work to render poetically the teachings promulgated by kabbalists primarily from the thirteenth to the seventeenth centuries, though on occasion I may cite or refer to a kabbalist from before or after the aforementioned time line.

13. Heidegger, *Elucidations of Hölderin's Poetry*, p. 176.

Prologue: Timeswerve/Hermeneutic Reversibility

1. On the affinities between Böhme and Jewish esotericism, see Schulze, "Jacob Boehme und die Kabbala," pp. 12–29; Benz, *Mystical Sources*, pp. 47–58; Schulitz, *Jakob Böhme und die Kabbalah*; and O'Regan, *Gnostic Apocalypse*, pp. 193–209. See also Wilhelm Schmidt-Biggemann, "Jakob Böhme und die Kabbala," in *Christliche Kabbala*, pp. 157–181.

2. On the influence of kabbalistic sources on Schelling, see Scholem, *Major Trends in Jewish Mysticism*, pp. 409 n. 19 and 412 n. 77; idem, *Kabbalah*, pp. 134 and 200; Schulze, "Schelling und die Kabbala," pp. 65–99, 143–170, 210–232; Idel, *Kabbalah: New Perspectives*, p. 264; A. Olson, *Hegel and the Spirit*, pp. 42–44; Schulte, "Zimzum in the Works of Schelling," pp. 21–40; E. Beach, *Potencies of God(s)*, pp. 1–2, 6–13, 25–45, 226–230; Drob, *Kabbalistic Metaphors*, pp. 83–85; Gibbons, *Spirituality and the Occult*, pp. 12–13; Kosolowski, *Philosophien der Offenbarung*, pp. 565–771. On the presumed affinity between Schelling and Luria, see the important comment in the "Urzelle" to *The Star of Redemption* in Franz Rosenzweig, *Philosophical and Theological Writings*, pp. 56–57 (see reference to Haberman cited p. 57 n. 23). In describing the "God that is before all relation, whether to the world or to Himself," the "seed-point of the actuality of God," Rosenzweig mentions Schelling's "dark ground," "an interiorization of God, which *precedes* not merely His self-externalization, but rather even His self," an idea that he further associates with what "Lurianic kabbalah teaches." For analysis of the text, see Idel, "Franz Rosenzweig and the Kabbalah," pp. 166–167. Regarding the influence of Lurianic kabbalah through the channel of Schelling in Rosenzweig's discussion in the first part of *The Star* of the self-negation of the divine Naught that yields the positive Aught of creation, see E. Wolfson, "Facing the Effaced," pp. 75–76. See also the brief comment in idem, "Divine Suffering and the Hermeneutics of Reading," p. 151 n. 87. For the influence of kabbalah on German thought, see Gardt, *Sprachreflexion in Barock*, pp. 108–128. The impact of kabbalah on romantic figures, especially connected to theories of language, is also discussed in Kilcher, *Sprachtheorie der Kabbala*, pp. 239–327, and idem, "Die Kabbala als Trope," pp. 135–166. See also Kremer, "Kabbalistische Signaturen," pp. 197–221; Schulte, "Kabbala in der deutschen Romantik," pp. 1–19; Cahnman, "Friedrich Wilhelm Schelling and the New Thinking," pp. 167–205. Also relevant is the monograph by Magee, *Hegel and the Hermetic Tradition*. The author duly notes the influence of kabbalah on nineteenth-century German philosophical thought, largely transmitted through intermediary channels. See also O'Regan, "Hegel and Anti-Judaism," pp. 141–182, esp. pp. 156–172, 178–

182. In this connection, it is of interest to note as well the passing remark by Derrida, *Dissemination*, p. 344, that the doctrine of *ṣimṣum*—the contraction into a point in the original ether—is "linked to the mythology of 'Louria,' but it can also arise by way of 'Hegel,' 'Boehme,' etc." And consider the passing parenthetical comment in Stuckrad, "Relative, Contigent, Determined," p. 906: "Schelling is an example of the deep impregnation of philosophy with religious ideas, for he described universal history in cabbalistic terms and spoke of *zimzum* and restoration." The thesis that Schelling's thought is a form of theosophic Gnosticism was put forth by Jaspers, *Schelling*, and see, more recently, Kosolowski, *Philosophie der Offenbarung*. The particular impact of Böhme has been discussed in R. Brown, *Later Philosophy of Schelling*. A still-interesting and informative discussion of the mystical elements in Schelling can be found in Tillich, *Mysticism and Guilt-Consciousness*. On the question of Schelling's general mystical leanings and their impact on Heidegger, see Hedley, "Schelling and Heidegger," pp. 141–155. On the relation of Heidegger and Gnosticism, see chap. 3, n. 6, and for Scholem's engagement with and reaction to Heidegger, see Magid, "Gershom Scholem's Ambivalence," pp. 245–269; and Wasserstrom, *Religion after Religion*, pp. 136 and 310 nn. 60–61.

3. Lusthaus, *Buddhist Phenomenology*, p. ix (emphasis in original). See also Huntington, *Emptiness of Emptiness*, pp. 5–15, esp. pp. 12–13. An analogous approach is adopted by Arkoun, *Unthought in Contemporary Islamic Thought*. As the author states explicitly in the methodological introduction, his book proposes a "way of thinking, rather than essays in traditional scholarship based on primary sources." To be sure, Arkoun does not ignore original texts; his aim, however, is to provide a "systematic deconstruction" of them rather than a "descriptive, narrative presentation." The term he assigns to his methodology is "historical epistemology" (pp. 9–10).

4. On time and interpretative activity, see S. Rosenthal, *Time, Continuity, and Indeterminacy*, pp. 119–131. For an analysis of the hermeneutical enterprise and the primary attention directed toward the temporal structure of objects of interpretation, see also Wood, *Deconstruction of Time*, pp. 319–334. The structural dynamic of time inherent in human logic, inspired especially by the Platonic tradition as explicated by Hegel, is explored by Kojève, *Le concept, le temps et le discours*, pp. 173–300.

5. The description of *chronos* as the "space of time" is derived from Cicero, *De Natura Deorum*, II, xxv.

6. My reflection was inspired by Dastur, *Telling Time*, pp. 12–13.

7. Park, *Image of Eternity*, p. 82.

8. Christensen, *Space-Like Time*, pp. 242–289, esp. pp. 274–279. For a learned discussion of the metaphysical presuppositions underlying Einstein's theory, see Craig, *Time and the Metaphysics of Relativity*. P. Davies, *About Time*, pp. 204–207, 219–232, offers a readable account of the sundry implications of the theorized imaging of time running backwards. A careful discussion of the historian's task and the tacit assumption regarding an absolute time of a linear character, a supposition that accords with Newtonian physics but is at odds with quantum theory, is offered by Wilcox, *Measures of Times Past*, pp. 1–15. I thank Charlotte E. Fonrobert for kindly drawing my attention to this study. Wilcox raises many pertinent issues but he does not deal explicitly with the phenomenon of reversibility, which is the thrust of my analysis. For an alternative approach that defends Newton's conception of absolute metaphysical time set over and against relative physical time, see Craig, "Relativity and the 'Elimination' of Absolute Time," pp. 91–127.

9. P. Davies, *About Time*, p. 236.

10. Weyl, *Continuum*, p. 49.

11. Weyl, *Continuum*, p. 104; J. Bell, "Hermann Weyl on Intuition and the Continuum," pp. 1–13, esp. pp. 6–8.

12. Weyl, *Continuum*, p. 102 (emphasis in original).

13. Ibid., p. 104.

14. Ibid., pp. 101 and 103. See Weyl, *Space—Time—Matter*, p. 246: "But the light-waves emitted by an atom will have, of course, the same frequency, measured in *cosmic* time, at all points in space" (emphasis in original).

15. P. Davies, *About Time*, pp. 241–243. The theoretical possibilities emerging from general relative theory render plausible the closing of the time line both in terms of time loops and space loops. The latter would be associated more precisely with the imaginary wormhole, the term coined by John Wheeler to designate

the alternative route connecting two points in space. The wormhole, in other words, is the bridge or tunnel that provides a supplementary way to link two points spatially. My summary is indebted to P. Davies, *About Time*, pp. 245–246. See also Yourgrau, *Disappearance of Time*, pp. 42–56; Faye, "When Time Gets Off Track," pp. 1–17, and Arntzenius and Maudlin, "Time Travel and Modern Physics," pp. 169–200.

16. Malin, *Nature Loves to Hide*, p. 23. For discussion of simultaneity in Einstein's theory of special relativity and curved spacetime, see Sklar, *Space, Time, and Spacetime*, pp. 244–296. See as well Healey, "Can Physics Coherently Deny," pp. 293–316.

17. Plato, *Statesman* 270a; Brumbaugh, *Unreality and Time*, pp. 36–37.

18. Whitehead, *Process and Reality*, p. 237.

19. Ibid., p. 211.

20. Whitehead, *Adventures of Ideas*, p. 191. For discussions of Whitehead's notion of time and process philosophy, see I. Leclerc, *Whitehead's Metaphysics*, pp. 161–162; and Neville, *Eternity and Time*, pp. 39–43.

21. I have borrowed the expression "temporal atomicity" from Jones, *Intensity*, p. 91.

22. Christian, *Interpretation of Whitehead's Metaphysics*, pp. 60–72, 123–128; Emmet, *Whitehead's Philosophy of Organism*, pp. 175–183; Neville, *Eternity and Time*, pp. 56–59.

23. Corbin, *Avicenna and the Visionary Recital*, p. 17. On the nexus between time as a curve and the symbolic imagination, see idem, *Creative Imagination*, pp. 38–77, esp. p. 53: "These privileged theophanic moments cut across the continuity of profane, quantified and irreversible time, but their *tempus discretum* (the time of angelology) does not enter into that continuity." The formulation "hierophanic time" is, as Corbin notes, derived from Eliade, whose understanding of the sacred as the overcoming of time was embraced by Corbin. See Dudley, *Religion on Trial*, pp. 65–72; Wasserstrom, *Religion after Religion*, pp. 161–163. On the ahistorical bias of postmodern hermeneutics and problematizing the return to history, see Hutcheon, *Poetics of Postmodernism*, pp. 87–101.

24. Corbin, *Creative Imagination*, p. 35. On the discontinuous nature of sacred history as opposed to the continuous nature of the time of secular history, see idem, *Temple and Contemplation*, p. 286: "The only history we are concerned with here—sacred history or hierohistory or hierology—does not come to pass in the continuous time of chronological causality which is the time of secular history. Each manifestation of the *Imago* constitutes a unity in itself. . . . It is itself its own time. . . . These unities of discontinuous time are the times of the *Imago Templi*; they irrupt into our own time and confer the dimension of eternity upon the scissions they produce. It is through this rupturing of time that the truth of all history can finally shine forth; for through it history is liberated and transmuted into parable."

25. Corbin, *Creative Imagination*, pp. 35–36. The theme is repeated in many of Corbin's writings. For instance, see idem, *Voyage and the Messenger*, pp. 54–55. For discussion of the abolition of time in the respective phenomenologies of Eliade and Corbin, see Wasserstrom, *Religion after Religion*, pp. 161–163, and on Corbin's indebtedness to Eliade, ibid., pp. 176–177. The reversibility of time as a *regressus ad uterum*, especially in Yogic and Buddhist thought, is a hallmark of Eliade's hermeneutics of religious experience. See Eliade, *Myths, Dreams, and Mysteries*, pp. 47–56; idem, *Myth and Reality*, pp. 75–91; and idem, *Images and Symbols*, pp. 57–91, esp. pp. 79–82.

26. I have drawn on the account of this matter found in Dainton, *Time and Space*, pp. 53–55. See also P. Davies, *About Time*, pp. 220–221, 228–229; and L. Krauss, *Quintessence*, pp. 244–245.

27. Dainton, *Time and Space*, p. 54.

28. For extensive discussion on the "asymmetries of time," see Dainton, *Time and Space*, pp. 44–62, and see the brief summation on p. 364; Sklar, *Space, Time, and Spacetime*, pp. 351–358, 398–411; Mansfield, "Time in Madhyamika Buddhism," pp. 10–27; idem, "Time and Impermanence," pp. 305–321. On the indeterminacy of time in quantum physics, see also Spisani, *Significato e Struttura del Tempo*, pp. 12–15, 20–23, 24–27. For discussion of the respective concepts of reversible and irreversible time in thermodynamics, see Park, *Image of Eternity*, pp. 45–58; Cramer, "Plane of the Present," pp. 177–189; and Sandbothe, *Temporalization of Time*, pp. 7–62.

29. On the reversal of the sequence of causal events, see discussion in Plotnitsky, *Knowable and the Unknowable*, pp. 182 and 283 n. 83.

30. What I have argued here can be favorably compared with the attempt to relate Blake's wish to combine opposites to the mathematical recipe of chaos theory proposed by Steenburg, "Chaos at the Marriage of Heaven and Hell," pp. 447–466.

31. To be sure, scientific knowledge encompasses two inseparable components, the empirical and rational, or in Kantian terms, intuition and judgment, and hence one must avoid positivism and rationalism as appropriate methodological perspectives. My point is, rather, that forms of understanding are mental constructs—shaped as much by imagination as by reason—that are not derivable from empirical phenomena. This seems to have been Einstein's philosophical approach. See Beller, "Kant's Impact on Einstein's Thought," pp. 83–106, esp. pp. 86–89.

32. Lloyd, "Principle that the Cause Is Greater," pp. 146–151.

33. Dainton, *Time and Space*, pp. 77–78.

34. Interestingly, precisely this view has been attributed to Eriugena, the Carolingian Neoplatonist whose thought bears striking similarities to the theosophic metaphysics articulated by Provençal and Catalan kabbalists. See Otten, "Dialectic of the Return," pp. 399–421. For the possible influence of Eriugena on the formation of Jewish mysticism in the twelfth and thirteenth centuries, see sources cited in E. Wolfson, *Through a Speculum*, pp. 204 n. 57, and 293–294 n. 88.

35. The reader will undoubtedly be familiar with a similar enunciation of time's reversibility in T. S. Eliot's "Four Quartets" and perhaps also with the ecstatic character of temporality described on numerous occasions and in a myriad of thought-images in the writings of Martin Heidegger. For a representative sampling of scholarly discussions of Heidegger's notion of ecstatic temporality, see Dastur, *Heidegger and the Question of Time*, pp. 17–51; Blattner, *Heidegger's Temporal Idealism*, pp. 89–126; Boer, *Thinking in the Light of Time*, pp. 79–113. For the discernment of a similar structure in later Hasidic sources, based, however, on earlier kabbalistic texts, see E. Wolfson, "Cut That Binds," pp. 103–154, esp. pp. 106–112, 119–120, 123–124.

36. The catalyst for writing this section was a conversation I had with Charlotte E. Fonrobert in July 2002, for which I am most grateful.

37. I have obviously chosen to portray the matter figuratively in terms of three kinds of lines. The issue could have been depicted in other geometric images as well—for instance, the circle—but I do not think that this change in detail would affect the overall argument, as, in four-dimensional space, two shapes relate to one another in one of three ways, skewed, intersecting, or parallel.

38. McCall, "Time Flow," pp. 143–151.

39. On the epistemological symmetry of the macrolevel and microlevel, see Papa-Grimaldi, *Time and Reality*, pp. 135–140.

40. See Mazis, "Merleau-Ponty and the 'Backward Flow,'" pp. 53–68; Gallagher, "Disrupting Seriality," pp. 97–119, esp. pp. 100–108.

41. See D. Davis, "Reversible Subjectivity," pp. 31–45; Hass, "Sense and Alterity," pp. 91–105; G. Johnson, "Introduction: Alterity as a Reversibility," pp. xvii–xxxiv.

42. Lefort, "Flesh and Otherness," pp. 3–13.

43. Merleau-Ponty, *Signs*, p. 86. I have also consulted the original version of the essay in idem, *Signes*, pp. 105–122.

44. Merleau-Ponty, *Signs*, p. 87. For more detailed analysis of this theme, see Low, *Merleau-Ponty's Last Vision*, pp. 86–90.

45. The locution is borrowed from Waelhens, *Philosophie de l'ambiguïté*. See also Cueille, "Profondeur du négatif," pp. 301–335, esp. pp. 307–312.

46. Merleau-Ponty, *Phenomenology of Perception*, p. 169. I have consulted as well the original *Phénoménologie de la perception*. All parenthetical references to the French version are taken from this edition.

47. Merleau-Ponty, *Visible and the Invisible*, p. 182. I have consulted as well the original *Le visible et l'invisible*. All parenthetical references to the French version are taken from this edition.

48. Ibid., p. 96.

49. For a sustained study on the affinity between chiasm and speech, see Herkert, *Das Chiasma*.

50. Merleau-Ponty, *Visible and Invisible*, p. 192.
51. Ibid., p. 217.
52. Ibid., p. 260 (French ed., pp. 313–314).
53. Ibid., p. 273.
54. Ibid., p. 182.
55. Ibid., p. 170.
56. Ibid., p. 203 (French ed., p. 257).
57. Ibid., pp. 270–271.
58. Ibid., p. 178 (French ed., p. 232).
59. Ibid., p. 181 (French ed., pp. 234–235).
60. Ibid.
61. Ibid., p. 178.
62. Ibid., p. 183 (French ed., p. 237). See Weihe, "Merleau-Ponty's Doubt," pp. 99–107; Wurzer, ". . . wild being/*écart*/capital," pp. 234–244.
63. Merleau-Ponty, *Visible and Invisible*, p. 203.
64. Ibid., p. 195.
65. This topic has been discussed from multiple interpretative perspectives. For a representative list arranged chronologically, see J. Klein, "Phenomenological Concept of 'Horizon,'" pp. 143–163; Natanson, *Literature, Philosophy and the Social Sciences*, pp. 172–194; F. Kaufmann, "Phenomenological Approach to History," pp. 159–172; Boehm, "La phénoménologie de l'histoire," pp. 55–73; Nota, *Phenomenology and History*; Ricoeur, *Husserl*, pp. 143–174; Kersten, "Phenomenology, History and Myth," pp. 234–269; Funke, "Phenomenology and History," vol. 2, pp. 3–101; D. Lowe, "Intentionality and the Method of History," vol. 2, pp. 103–130; Natanson, *Edmund Husserl*, pp. 50–54, 70–72; David Carr, *Phenomenology and the Problem of History*; idem, *Interpreting Husserl*, pp. 97–114, 249–266; idem, "Phenomenology and Philosophy of History," pp. 103–112; Landgrebe, "Phenomenology as Transcendental Theory," pp. 101–113; Krombach, "Husserl and the Phenomenology of History," pp. 89–112; Nuki, "Temporality and Historicity," pp. 149–165. See also the perceptive remarks of Ricoeur in "History of Religions," pp. 13–30; and for the analysis of the relation between historicity, the assumption regarding the radically temporal dimension of human existence, and historicism, the relativistic presumption that what is true is true only from the context of a particular point in time, see McPartland, *Lonergan and the Philosophy of Historical Existence*, pp. 76–107. The author, in my view, is correct to point out that it is possible to have an operative notion of historicity without historicism. On this score, albeit from a slightly different perspective, see the discussion of the philosophical task and historicity in Ricoeur, *History and Truth*, pp. 63–77. I present a fuller discussion of the interface of time and hermeneutics in E. Wolfson, *Alef, Mem, Tau*, based on the Taubman Lectures in Jewish Studies delivered at the University of California, Berkeley, February–March 2001.
66. Merleau-Ponty, *Signs*, p. 87.
67. Tréguier, *Corps selon la chair*, pp. 183–190. For a detailed philosophical analysis of the thematic nexus between desire and temporality, see Grimaldi, *Désir et le temps*.
68. See Gallagher, *Inordinance of Time*, pp. 90–91.
69. On the convergence of the three temporal modalities in the present, see Priest, *Merleau-Ponty*, p. 412. For alternative explanations, see Madison, *Phenomenology of Merleau-Ponty*, pp. 180–181; G. Johnson, "Generosity and Forgetting," pp. 196–212; idem, "Desire and Invisibility," pp. 85–96; Fóti, *Vision's Invisibles*, pp. 69–80. It strikes me that the thinking of Merleau-Ponty resonates with Jean-Luc Marion's insights regarding the necessity of the invisible or unseen (*l'invu*)—the "visible in excess"—in the phenomenological constitution of the visible; alternatively expressed, visibility "conceals and reveals an invisibility"; see Marion, *In Excess*, pp. 104–113; idem, *Crossing of the Invisible*, pp. 1–45. Finally, I note in passing that the philosophic-poetic meditations of Merleau-Ponty bear interesting similarities to ancient Buddhist reflections on the nature of time, being, and consciousness; see C. Olson, "Human Body as a Boundary Symbol," pp. 107–120, esp. pp. 112–114 where the specific issue of time and body in the two is discussed; Lusthaus, *Buddhist Phenomenology*, pp. 11–39. On the comparison of Merleau-Ponty and Eastern philosophical thought, see further references in chap. 1, n. 229, and chap. 5, n. 9.

70. Merleau-Ponty, *Visible and Invisible*, p. 184.

71. Ibid., p. 184 (French ed., p. 238)

72. Ibid., p. 191.

73. The importance of this taxon in reading Merleau-Ponty is explored by Richir, "Merleau-Ponty and the Question of Phenomenological Architectonics," pp. 37–50.

74. Mallin, *Merleau-Ponty's Philosophy*, pp. 91–107.

75. Gadamer, *Truth and Method*, pp. 108–109, correctly observed that the notion of the fullness of time, a suprahistorical or sacred time, is a conception of timelessness that arises dialectically out of the idea of historical time. In Gadamer's opinion, one cannot move beyond a dialectical tension of the two. The notion of the transcendence of the moment that I have proffered, based on a close reading of Merleau-Ponty, does, I think, present one with a way to move beyond the dialectic.

76. Dillon, "Preface: Merleau-Ponty and Postmodernity," pp. xviii–xix.

77. Merleau-Ponty, *Phenomenology of Perception*, p. 411.

78. Ibid., p. 412.

79. Ibid., pp. 414–415 (French ed., p. 474)

80. Ibid., p. 411 (French ed., p. 470).

81. The original French, *Les événements découpés*, intones a somewhat different resonance from the English rendering, "shapes cut out."

82. Merleau-Ponty, *Phenomenology of Perception*, p. 411.

83. Merleau-Ponty, *Visible and Invisible*, p. 158.

84. Ibid., p. 173 (French ed., p. 227). On Merleau-Ponty's critique of Husserl, see Steinbock, "Merleau-Ponty, Husserl, and Saturated Intentionality," pp. 53–74; Barbaras, *Tournant de l'expérience*, pp. 63–79. For an interesting account of Merleau-Ponty's "bricolage" approach to Husserl and the impact of this method on his own philosophical reflections, see Rajan, *Deconstruction and the Remainders*, pp. 18–19.

85. Priest, *Merleau-Ponty*, pp. 123–131. The idea articulated by Merleau-Ponty resonates with the following account in Rospatt, *Buddhist Doctrine of Momentariness*, p. 39: "Thus, the Sarvāstivādins do not contend that all conditioned entities only *exist* for a moment, but merely that they are only *present* for a moment, namely when they are causally efficient. Before this moment they exist in the future and thereafter in the past so that they are not momentary in the sense that they only exist for a moment" (emphasis in original). If I have understood Merleau-Ponty correctly, he would embrace the idea that the criterion for differentiating the three temporal modes is casual efficiency, but in truth, the time that is most real is the present that encompasses past and future respectively as potential cause and effect.

86. See Olkowski, "Merleau-Ponty and Bergson," pp. 27–36.

87. See Gallagher, "On the Pre-Noetic Reality of Time," pp. 134–148.

88. Merleau-Ponty, *Phenomenology of Perception*, p. 415.

89. Schnell, "Das Problem der Zeit bei Husserl," pp. 89–122.

90. Merleau-Ponty, *Visible and Invisible*, p. 160.

91. Mallin, *Merleau-Ponty's Philosophy*, p. 91.

92. Merleau-Ponty, *Phenomenology of Perception*, p. 411.

93. Ibid., p. 415.

94. See *Visible and Invisible*, p. 179, where Merleau-Ponty refers to his "indirect method," which departs from the presumption that we can establish a "direct ontology," as "negative philosophy" or "negative theology." On this dimension of Merleau-Ponty's philosophy, see Madison, *Phenomenology of Merleau-Ponty*, p. 196; O'Connor, "Reconstructive Time," pp. 149–166, esp. pp. 154–155.

95. Merleau-Ponty, *Visible and Invisible*, p. 173. From this vantage point it is instructive to compare and contrast Merleau-Ponty's notion of time as indeterminate, especially in his later writings—though by his own understanding of time, one must be on guard against privileging a hermeneutic rigidly based on a linear, chronological temporality—and similar theories in quantum physics. See Mazis, "Chaos Theory," pp. 219–241; Bernet, "Le sujet dans la nature," pp. 57–77; Cassou-Noguès, "Merleau-Ponty et les sciences de la nature," pp. 119–141. For a nuanced discussion of the evolution in Merleau-Ponty's thought from "phe-

nomenological positivism" to "negative ontology," see Madison, *Phenomenology of Merleau-Ponty*, pp. 166–203.

96. Merleau-Ponty, *Phenomenology of Perception*, p. 412.

97. One is reminded of Rosenzweig's insight regarding the breakthrough of revelation, which is always of the moment, the eternal coming-to-be of that-which-has-already-not-been.

98. Merleau-Ponty, *Visible and Invisible*, pp. 40–41. I have also consulted the original version, *Le visible et l'invisible.*

99. See B Flynn, "Merleau-Ponty et la position philosophique du scepticisme," pp. 147–161.

100. Merleau-Ponty, *Visible and Invisible*, pp. 181–182 (emphasis in original).

101. Ibid., pp. 177–178. On circularity and being-in-the-world in Merleau-Ponty's thought, see Madison, *Phenomenology of Merleau-Ponty*, pp. 21–45.

102. I discuss this Derridean theme in chap. 2.

103. On the image of the field of being, see Madison, *Phenomenology of Merleau-Ponty*, pp. 204–265.

104. Merleau-Ponty, *Phenomenology of Perception*, p. 416.

105. Bruzina, "Aporia of Time-Analysis," pp. 105–132, esp. pp. 107–115.

106. Merleau-Ponty, *Phenomenology of Perception*, p. 412.

107. Ibid., p. 414.

108. Ibid., p. 419.

109. Ibid., pp. 419–420.

110. Ibid., p. 424.

111. Ibid., p. 426.

112. Ibid., p. 420.

113. Ibid., p. 421.

114. Ibid., p. 422.

115. Ibid., p. 423.

116. See, for example, *Visible and Invisible*, pp. 148–149; Natanson, *Edmund Husserl*, pp. 37, 82, 137; Nagataki, "Husserl and Merleau-Ponty," pp. 29–45, esp. pp. 32–34. With regard to the notion of "horizon," there are also interesting affinities between Merleau-Ponty and William James that demand elaboration. For a preliminary study, see Kazashi, "On the 'Horizon,'" pp. 49–64.

117. The French is a bit more ambiguous: *il se prémédite au-devant de lui* (p. 471).

118. Merleau-Ponty, *Phenomenology of Perception*, p. 411.

119. Ibid., p. 68.

120. Ibid., p. 69.

121. Merleau-Ponty, *Visible and Invisible*, p. 185.

122. Merleau-Ponty, *Phenomenology of Perception*, p. 412.

123. Ibid.

124. Ibid., p. 414.

125. Ibid., p. 415.

126. Merleau-Ponty, *Visible and Invisible*, pp. 111, 117.

Chapter One
Showing the Saying: Laying Interpretative Ground

1. Idel, *Kabbalah: New Perspectives*, pp. 263–264; idem, "Introduction to the Bison Book Edition," pp. xv–xvi, xviii–xix. The impact of Christian kabbalah as an inspirational factor shaping Scholem's understanding of kabbalah is also addressed by Wasserstrom, *Religion after Religion*, pp. 39–41.

2. On the theurgical dimensions of Reuchlin's kabbalah, see Celenza, "Search for Ancient Wisdom," pp. 115–133, esp. pp. 129–131. I have explored the matter in "Language, Secrecy, and the Mysteries of Law."

3. The following account of gnosis in the Sethian text *Trimorphic protennoia* given by G. Robinson,

"The Trimorphic Protennoia and the Prologue," p. 40, provides a remarkably suitable description of medieval kabbalah: "Knowing about the secrets effects salvation. But this knowledge is attained in concrete practice. Secret teaching and secret practice in any case belong together and correspond to each other."

4. In this I follow the deeply entrenched German philosophic tradition wherein hermeneutics and phenomenology are inextricably interwoven—the task of the one, as the other, is to uncover meaning. Husserl's *epoché* epitomizes the point, as the question of the factuality (*Tatlichkeit*) of the phenomenon is put into brackets so that what matters is the pursuit of the meaning of the phenomenon enframed within those brackets. The point is well understood by Merleau-Ponty, *Visible and Invisible*, p. 172: "Every negation of the world, *but also* every neutrality with regard to the existence of the world, has as its immediate consequence that one misses the transcendental. The *epoché* has the right to be a neutralization only with regard to the world as effective in itself, to the pure exteriority: it must leave extant the phenomenon of this effective in itself, of this exteriority." For a more recent formulation, see Byers, *Intentionality and Transcendence*, p. 82: "The fundamental principle of phenomenology is expressed in the method of phenomenological reduction: it is experience that must be allowed to determine the meaning and status of what is; conversely, no predetermination of the meaning of what is can be allowed to determine the meaning of experience, nor the meaning of what is given experientially."

5. Scholem, "Zehn unhistorische Sätze über Kabbala," in *Judaica 3*, p. 264. See Dan, "Beyond the Kabbalistic Symbol," pp. 363–385; D. Biale, "Gershom Scholem's Ten Unhistorical Aphorisms," pp. 102–104; Schäfer, "'Die Philologie der Kabbala,'" pp. 19–21; E. Wolfson, *Abraham Abulafia*, pp. 26–30; Bouretz, "Gershom Scholem und das Schreiben," pp. 124–125; Habermas, *Liberating Power of Symbols*, p. 58. On the aura of secrecy and the role of the symbolic for Scholem, see Wasserstrom, *Religion after Religion*, pp. 34–35.

6. I have explored the phenomenon of esotericism in much of my work, highlighting especially the nexus between the secret and erotic imagery; see E. Wolfson, *Through a Speculum*; idem, "Occultation of the Feminine," pp. 113–154; idem, *Abraham Abulafia*, pp. 3–29. On the nexus of hermeneutics and esotericism, see also idem, "Beyond the Spoken Word," pp. 166–224, esp. pp. 168–170. For discussion of this theme in a different cultural context but one that parallels my own account in a number of striking ways, see Corbin, *En Islam Iranien*, pp. 186–218.

7. Foucault, *Language, Counter-Memory, Practice*, p. 139.

8. For a sustained analysis of Foucault's genealogical approach and Heidegger's critique of the ontotheological, see Spanos, *Heidegger and Criticism*, pp. 132–180, esp. pp. 151–152. See also Hoff, *Spiritualität und Sprachverlust*, pp. 64–82.

9. My discussion has been enhanced by Chartier, "Chimera of the Origin," pp. 167–186, esp. pp. 170–171. For alternative discussions of the notion of genealogy and the archaeological in Foucault, see Racevskis, *Michel Foucault and the Subversion of Intellect*, pp. 67–89; G. Shapiro, "Translating, Repeating, Naming," pp. 39–55; Mahon, *Foucault's Nietzschean Genealogy*, pp. 81–155; Visker, *Michel Foucault*, pp. 30–73; Hough, *Nietzsche's Noontide Friend*, pp. 48–50; Shumway, "Genealogies of Knowledge," pp. 82–98; Strozier, *Foucault, Subjectivity, and Identity*, pp. 21–49. Jantzen, *Power, Gender and Christian Mysticism*, pp. 12–18, adopts the model of Foucault to develop a genealogy of mysticism that rests on the theoretical presumption that mysticism is a social construct reflecting varying historical contingencies retrievable hermeneutically from the study of texts and artifacts. My own approach accords with this interpretative strategy.

10. Foucault, *Language, Counter-Memory, Practice*, pp. 145–146.

11. In my work, I have challenged the rigid typological distinction between theosophic and ecstatic kabbalah on grounds that the former is predicated on an experience of communion that properly speaking may be called ecstatic and that the latter entails a theosophic conception whereby gnosis of the divine name is thought to impart one with wisdom about God. Notwithstanding this challenge, I accept the heuristic value of isolating a current of Jewish esotericism focused on contemplative envisioning of the sefirotic emanations. However, as will be shown intermittently in the course of this book, the typological distinction collapses under the weight of its own textual specificity. For other independent critiques of the reigning typological distinction between theosophic and ecstatic kabbalah, see S. Brody, "Human Hands Dwell in Heavenly Heights," pp. 249–250, 396, 682–683; Pedaya, "'Possessed by Speech,'" pp. 565–636, and idem,

Vision and Speech, pp. 91–207. Mention should also be made of the use of the word "theurgy" to describe the kabbalah of Abraham Abulafia in Beitchman, *Alchemy of the Word*, pp. 72, 81. For Beitchman, however, this term connotes meditational practices leading to personal transformation rather than the idea of having an impact on the nature of the divine, and thus his view is not in conflict with the perspective advanced by Scholem and Idel.

12. To be more precise, *Sefer Yeṣirah* is a composite work made up of independent textual strands that were woven together at some point in the redactional process. The notion of thirty-two paths of wisdom, which appears in the opening paragraph of all known versions of the text, is an attempt on the part of the redactor to combine two separate units, one that deals with ten *sefirot* and the other with the twenty-two letters. See Gruenwald, "Preliminary Critical Edition," pp. 132–177 (all references to *Sefer Yeṣirah* in this book are based on this edition and thus if the reader discovers a discrepancy between the paragraph number that I use and the standard text, which follows the layout of the *editio princeps*, Mantua 1562, it is to be explained by the fact that I follow the division utilized in Gruenwald's edition); idem, "Some Critical Notes on the First Part of *Sefer Yeẓira*," p. 479. Scholem, "Name of God," pp. 72–73, noted that in *Sefer Yeṣirah* no attempt is made to determine the precise relationship between *sefirot*, which he interpreted as "numbers," and letters. The enigma to which Scholem pointed is easily resolved if one lets go of the presumption that *Sefer Yeṣirah* is one integral text. It is obvious, as Gruenwald correctly noted, that we have two discrete sections that were combined in the process of redaction for reasons that remain unclear. For a recent attempt to articulate the shared numerical emphasis in the description of *sefirot* and letters, see Liebes, *Ars Poetica in Sefer Yetsira*, pp. 16–22. Liebes does discuss the contradictions and inconsistencies in the respective treatments of *sefirot* and letters (pp. 23–30), but his analysis, in my opinion, is flawed methodologically, for he assumes textual unity and compositional integrity, an orientation that seems highly questionable if not indefensible. For a more detailed discussion of this matter, see Hayman, "Original Text," pp. 434–449. For a more nuanced approach to the redactional history of the text, see Wasserstrom, "*Sefer Yeṣira* and Early Islam," pp. 1–30; and idem, "Further Thoughts on the Origins of *Sefer Yeṣirah*," pp. 201–221.

13. See Idel, "*Sefirot* above the *Sefirot*," pp. 239–280; and idem, *Kabbalah: New Perspectives*, pp. 119–120.

14. Scholem, *Major Trends in Jewish Mysticism*, p. 403 n. 75, characterized the work of S. Rubin, *Heidenthum und Kabbala*, as a "well documented but very superficial treatise." Interestingly, in *On the Kabbalah and Its Symbolism*, p. 94, Scholem refers to the "promising title" of Rubin's composition, which he then proceeds to characterize as demonstrating "an abundance of source material but little insight." I cannot ascertain confidently why Scholem thought the title promising, but his aside is certainly suggestive. There is no room to quarrel with the observation that Rubin's rationalist temperament led him to seek the roots of kabbalah outside Judaism, albeit in antiquity, and led him to sundry negative assessments about the esoteric tradition. Nevertheless, Scholem too hastily dismissed Rubin's work, which, in my judgment, is replete with valuable insights, some of which have been substantiated in more current research.

15. S. Rubin, *Heidenthum und Kabbala*, pp. 36–80.

16. Scholem, "Name of God," p. 165. See idem, *On the Kabbalah and Its Symbolism*, pp. 35–36; idem, *Origins of the Kabbalah*, p. 449.

17. The philosophical point I am making applies equally to the two major approaches to the question of the nature of the first emanation and the infinite. Whether one were to assume that the first emanation is ontically distinct from Ein Sof or one were to assume that they were coeval, we still have to entertain an image of the boundless assuming boundary. This paradox seems to be shared universally by kabbalists who embrace the theosophic system.

18. Scholem, "Name of God," p. 71, notes that the "mystique of language," the presumption that the "creative force" is to be sought in words and names, entails that "for the mystic, the image of sound and the written image coincide reciprocally." On the convergence of speech and writing, the verbal and visual, see Scholem, "Name of God," pp. 167–168, and discussion below, chap. 6. In light of the synesthesia attested in kabbalistic literature, I would take issue with the phenomenological typology developed by Pedaya, *Vision and Speech*, based on a distinction between hearing, which is correlated with holiness, and seeing, which is linked to the glory (see pp. 238–241). It is certainly true that some kabbalists distinguish the two modalities

and thus speak of the priority of vision over hearing, or vice versa, but even for kabbalists who speak this way there is an overall acceptance of the convergence of the two—the object of mystical experience is at the same time seen and heard, I would say, seen as heard and heard as seen. No traditional kabbalist, to the best of my knowledge, would reject this claim. Finally, it is of interest to consider the Sufi dictum cited by Corbin, *Creative Imagination*, p. 251: "When He shows Himself to me, my whole being is vision; when He speaks to me in secret, my whole being is hearing." Compare the remark of Suhrawardī cited in chap. 5, n. 136.

19. The comment of Jakobson on the poetic function of language is cited and briefly analyzed in Kristeva, *Language*, p. 288. For a more elaborate discussion of this subject, see Bradford, *Roman Jakobson*, pp. 9–73. See also Waugh, "Poetic Function," pp. 57–82, repr. in Jakobson, *Verbal Art*, pp. 143–168.

20. Jakobson, *Verbal Art*, p. 39. On the relationship between poetic and ordinary modes of discourse, see Ormsby, *Poetry as Isotope*, pp. 20–21: "Poetry is but a heightened, an isotopic, instance of a miracle which occurs every time we engage in speech. . . . The very fact that our words do correspond to recognizable realities in daily converse also corresponds to what happens in poetry. The difference is, that in poetry the words do not merely point to the reality, they seek to recreate, to replicate, to incorporate and inhabit, the very reality to which they point. Poetry is speech reified, speech made as real, as concrete, as dense with implication, as things are themselves while at the same time remaining crystalline in transparency. . . . If poetry is but an 'isotope' of human language, language itself is the ultimate mystery."

21. Jakobson, *Language in Literature*, p. 374.

22. Dilthey, *Poetry and Experience*, pp. 44–46.

23. Ibid., p. 129. On the relation of lived experience to poetry in the particular case of Goethe, see ibid., pp. 278–283.

24. Ibid., p. 56.

25. Ibid., p. 164 (emphasis in original).

26. Ibid., p. 223.

27. Ibid., p. 226 (emphasis in original).

28. Ibid., pp. 225, 227. For an amplification of this theme, see analysis of Dilthey, Husserl, and Heidegger in Bowie, *From Romanticism to Critical Theory*, pp. 138–163.

29. For a richly nuanced discussion of the ineffability of music, with particular focus on the inherently temporal nature of the musical score, see Jankélévitch, *Music and the Ineffable*.

30. Several recent studies that explore the intricate relationship of philosophical thinking and poetry include Wood, *Philosophers' Poets*; Eldridge, *Beyond Representation*; Colilli, *Idea of a Living Spirit*; Lacoue-Labarthe, *Poetry as Experience*; K. Hart, "Experience of Poetry."

31. The expression is utilized by Johnstone, *Rationalized Epistemology*, p. 175.

32. Jameson, *Prison-House of Language*, pp. 30–31; Holdcroft, *Saussure*, pp. 52–56, 61–68, 93–95, 112–115, 158–159.

33. Corrington, *Ecstatic Naturalism*, pp. 67–115.

34. Cassirer, *Essay on Man*, p. 25. The identification of symbol-making as the unique trait of human consciousness is further developed by S. Langer, *Mind*, pp. 265–355.

35. Cassirer, *Language and Myth*, p. 7.

36. Heidegger, *Being and Time*, p. 30; German edition: *Sein und Zeit*, p. 34. See also the passage from Heidegger's *Nachlaß*, "Über das Prinzip 'Zu den Sachen selbst,' " pp. 5–8, and the analysis by Sallis, "Identities of the Things Themselves," pp. 113–126.

37. Ihde, *Sense and Significance*, pp. 119–120 (emphasis in original).

38. Walton, "World-experience," pp. 1–20, esp. pp. 12–14.

39. Sallis, "Image and Phenomenon," pp. 61–75.

40. Some of the affinities and disparities between Cassirer and Schelling were noted by Heidegger, "Das mythische Denken von Cassirer," pp. 1000–1012; English version in *Piety of Thinking*, pp. 32–45. For discussion of Cassirer's view and Heidegger's critique, see Doherty, *Sein, Mensch und Symbol*, pp. 15–59; Krois, "Cassirer's Unpublished Critique," pp. 147–159.

41. Cassirer, *Philosophy of Symbolic Forms*, vol. 1, p. 178; vol. 2, pp. 20, 23, 99. On Cassirer's approach to

myth as symbolic form, see Baeten, *Magic Mirror,* pp. 41–93; Lofts, *Cassirer,* pp. 35–59; Bayer, *Cassirer's Metaphysics,* pp. 56–68, 85–86.

42. For an attempt to distinguish myth and symbol in kabbalistic literature, see Liebes, "Myth vs. Symbol," pp. 212–242. The author's distinction is anticipated in some of his earlier studies. For example, consider the contrast between "symbolic level" and "total identity" in Liebes, *Studies in the Zohar,* pp. 19 and 179 n. 116 (see below, n. 340). My own thinking is indebted to Paul Ricoeur, for whom myth and symbol are not easily distinguishable, surely inseparable. See Ricoeur, *Symbolism of Evil,* p. 18; idem, *Conflict of Interpretations,* pp. 28, 293; Kearney, "Paul Ricoeur and the Hermeneutic Imagination," pp. 1–31; Champagne, *Structuralists on Myth,* pp. 13, 46–47, 75; E. Deutsch, "Truth and Mythology," pp. 46–47.

43. Cassirer, *Philosophy of Symbolic Forms,* vol. 4, pp. 78–79.

44. Sallis, *Delimitations,* p. 66.

45. See Burckhardt, *Alchemy,* pp. 196–197; Coudert, *Alchemy,* pp. 27–28; G. Roberts, *Mirror of Alchemy,* pp. 68–70.

46. Read, *Prelude to Chemistry,* p. 54.

47. Quispel, "Gnosis and Alchemy," pp. 304–333.

48. *De Somniis* I, 187–188, in *Philo,* vol. 5, pp. 395–397.

49. Böhme, *Signature of All Things,* p. 12. See Stoudt, *Jacob Boehme,* p. 141; Weeks, *Boehme,* pp. 4, 34, 76, 119, 188–190; Bianchi, "Visible and the Invisible," p. 28 and other references cited on pp. 46–47 n. 70.

50. D. Biale, "Gershom Scholem's Ten Unhistorical Aphorisms," p. 113. Also relevant are the passages explicating the immanence of Ein Sof in Abraham Herrera, *Tiqqunei Zohar,* and Moses Cordovero that are cited and analyzed by Scholem, *On the Mystical Shape,* pp. 40–42. Although kabbalists attempt to preserve the ontological difference of the infinite by maintaining its transcendence, the fact is that once the immanence is affirmed, the ontic independence of the cosmos is seriously challenged, and one is led invariably into a pantheistic or panentheistic posture.

51. Scholem, *Origins,* p. 448.

52. *Zohar* 3:120a.

53. *Zohar* 3:291b (*Idra Zuṭa*). For an alternative translation and explication of this passage, see Tishby, *Wisdom of the Zohar,* p. 246.

54. Tishby, *Wisdom of the Zohar,* pp. 295–298.

55. *Zohar* 3:139b (*Idra Rabba*).

56. An expression used by Nietzsche in *Birth of Tragedy,* sec. 4, to characterize a dream and a work of art. See Nietzsche, *Basic Writings of Nietzsche,* p. 45.

57. Scholem, *On the Possibility of Jewish Mysticism,* p. 140. For further references in Scholem's *oeuvre* in which he characterizes the symbol as the communication of the incommunicable, see below, n. 88. Idel, *Absorbing Perfections,* pp. 274–275, is critical of the "pansymbolic school that Scholem established" based on an "overemphasis on the radical transcendence of the referent to which the symbols point." For a variant formulation of this critique, see Idel, "Hieroglyphs, Keys, Enigmas," pp. 232–233. Idel's sweeping claim that this perspective is "hardly sustained even by the Kabbalistic texts alone" (*Absorbing Perfections,* p. 275) is not supported by any documentation, and even if it were, I do not think it is a fair presentation of Scholem's view; on the contrary, the symbol, by Scholem's account, always points to what cannot be declaimed and therefore must be polychromatic. Finally, and perhaps most important, I see no evidence from either Idel's work or from my independent study of kabbalistic texts that undermines the philosophical claim regarding the inherently symbolic nature of language as the expression of the inexpressible. The Tetragrammaton, according to the theosophic, ecstatic, and magical streams of kabbalah, according to Idel's own taxonomy, conveys this point. The term "noetic insufficiency," which Idel dubs a "Neokantian approach," presumably based on Kant's insistence that we can know only phenomena, the appearances of things, and not noumena, the things in themselves, is not entirely accurate as it fails to capture the paradoxical nature of the mystical claim regarding language leading through itself to its own surpassing, a theme I explore in chapter 6. Idel presents his critique in other terms as well, for example, the distinction between "negativity" and "plentitude" (see *Absorbing Perfections,* pp. 423–427). This binary, however, is problematic inasmuch as kabbalists

conceive of ultimate truth as the *coincidentia oppositorum*, and consequently negativity and plentitude, absence and presence, are not separable. For discussion of the paradoxical identification of the vacuum and plenum, absolute emptiness and absolute fullness, in mystical experience, see Stace, *Mysticism and Philosophy*, pp. 161–178.

58. Scholem, *Origins*, p. 408.

59. For fuller discussion of this motif, see E. Wolfson, "Mirror of Nature," pp. 305–331, esp. pp. 306–316.

60. See, for instance, the categorical assertion of Ajzenstat, *Driven Back to the Text*, p. 140, that many (!) kabbalists "take up what Levinas calls the skeptical attitude towards ontology." An inquiry into the relationship of Levinas to kabbalistic esotericism remains a scholarly desideratum, and it is my hope to return to this challenge at a later date. For another account of the thought of Levinas and Jewish mysticism, including kabbalistic and Hasidic sources, related to the themes of the trace, divine absence, temporality, eschatology, and righteousness, see Chalier, *Trace de l'infini*, pp. 77–106, 156–158, 189–201, 208–231.

61. The apophatic depiction is articulated in the anonymous commentary on the *sefirot* that has been falsely attributed to a number of kabbalists; see Scholem, "Traditions of R. Jacob," pp. 174–175. The long recension was published in *Liqquṭei Shikheḥah u-Fe'ah*, 21a–22a, and then again in the short and long recensions by Scholem, "Traditions of R. Jacob," pp. 227–230. The expanded version has been recently reprinted in *Sha'ar ha-Qabbalah we-Sidrah*. I here translate the text extant in MS London, British Museum 1087, published in Scholem, "Traditions of R. Jacob," p. 227: "The beginning of every matter, which is first and prior to everything, is hidden from all, and it is called the 'cause of causes' [*illat ha-illot*], and concerning it one does not say either something [*yesh*] or nothing [*ayin*], for it is concealed." To predicate neither something nor nothing is to occupy a middle ground between polar opposites in a manner that is reminiscent of the middle way (Mādhyamika) philosophy cultivated by Nāgārjuna, the third-century Indian Brahmin who became a Buddhist monk, the door of nonduality through which one attains (the) nothing there is to attain, neither something nor nothing, the form that exists, does not exist, and does not not exist. Needless to say, many studies have been written on this figure and the main tenets and repercussions of his thought. See, e.g., Kalupahana, *Nāgārjuna*. On the question of the appropriateness of speaking about a "Buddhist ontology," see Nagao, *Mādhyamika and Yogācāra*, pp. 155–187. The conclusion reached by Nagao may be applied profitably to the question of kabbalah and ontology: "It would seem, therefore, that if an ontology of a Buddhist kind is to be considered seriously, then it would have to be based, not on an ontology of 'being'—that is, not in an ontic sense, but on transcending both existence and non-existence—that is, in the movement toward sūnyatā" (p. 187). *Sūnyatā*, which is to be translated as "emptiness," is the technical term not for the absence of being, but for the discernment that neither being nor nonbeing is real, that is, the middle ground that transcends both existence and nonexistence. While I have clearly incorporated the logic of Mādhyamika to elucidate kabbalistic texts, I am not prepared to understand Ein Sof as a cognate to *sūnyatā*, for, in my understanding, the former term functions in kabbalistic literature as a marker for the ultimate ground of being, albeit a ground that is innately inaccessible to human comprehension, whereas the latter term is precisely a rejection of such a metaphysical construct. On this score, see the comment of Lusthaus, *Buddhist Phenomenology*, p. 375 n. 16: "*Sūnyatā* is not a *via negativa* for revealing or uncovering the 'True Ground of Being' or any other such fantasy; nor is *sūnyatā* itself that ground. The term signifies the activity of 'emptying out' such notions, not merely as concepts, but in terms of the festering inner compulsions which lead one to posit such things in the first place. Emptiness is not an ontological ground, but a methodological tool to be discarded, i.e., 'emptied,' when its task is completed." The kabbalistic notion is closer in spirit to the apophatic logic displayed by Dionysius the Areopagite. See, for instance, *Divine Names*, chap. 1, 588B, in *Divine Names and Mystical Theology*, pp. 108–109: "The indefiniteness beyond being lies beyond beings [ὑπέρκειται τῶν οὐσιῶν ἡ ὑπερούσιος ἀπειρία] . . . be-ing according to no being [κατὰ μηδὲν τῶν ὄντων οὖσα], cause of *being* to all; but itself: non-be-ing, as it is beyond every being [αὐτὸ δὲ μὴ ὂν ὡς πάσης οὐσίς ἐπέκεινα]." And in *Divine Names*, chap. 5, 817D, p. 165: "God neither was, nor will be, nor has come to be, nor is come to be, nor will come to be, nor, indeed, is not." See the concluding litany of negative attributions of the "cause of all things" in *Mystical Theology*, chap. 5, 1048A, p. 222: "not something among

what is not [οὐδέ τι τῶν οὐκ ὄντων], not something among what is [οὐδέ τι τῶν ὄντων ἐστίν]. . . . There is neither logos, name, or knowledge of it. It is not dark nor light, not error, and not truth. There is universally neither position [θέσεις] nor denial [ἀφαιρέσεις] of it." The Greek is supplied on the basis of the critical texts published in the *Corpus Dionysiacum I*, p. 109, and *Corpus Dionysiacum II*, p. 150.

62. Marion, "In the Name," pp. 20–53, and a slightly revised version in idem, *In Excess*, pp. 128–162. See also idem, "Saturated Phenomenon," pp. 176–216; and idem, "Introduction," pp. 1–7. A constructive theological application of this phenomenological orientation is found in Marion, *God without Being*. A discussion of Dionysius along these lines is also found in idem, *The Idol and Distance*, pp. 139–195. For a suggestive discussion of the kataphatic and apophatic elements in the writings of Dionysius in terms of a convergence between "Hebrew and Greek allegory," see D. Turner, *Darkness of God*, pp. 19–49; and Golitzin, "Suddenly Christ," pp. 8–37. Although the middle ground staked by Dionysius resonates with the logic of Mādhyamika expounded by Nāgārjuna, there are also subtle and important differences; see note 61.

63. The *Gospel of Truth* provides an extraordinary lens by which to refocus our thinking about later kabbalistic wisdom. I explore this in more detail in chap. 5.

64. Tishby, *Wisdom of the Zohar*, p. 274, notes that the two most common images in *Zohar* used to depict the emanation were the shining of light and flowing of water. To do justice to the kabbalistic sources it is necessary to include the third prism as well, the vocalization of the ineffable name.

65. I have borrowed these formulations from the analysis of Husserl's idea of prototemporalization in Bruzina, "Aporia of Time-Analysis," p. 106. The author's immediate concern was clarification of Husserl's internal-time consciousness. I have applied the terms, and what they imply, to account for the nature of the excess-of-being that is the prototemporal, protospatial source of all beings.

66. See Froment-Meurice, *That Is To Say*.

67. For a discussion of language in the new thinking of Rosenzweig with particular sensitivity to the poetic, see Galli, *Franz Rosenzweig and Jehuda Halevi*, pp. 360–398.

68. For discussions of the place of poetry in Gadamer's philosophical hermeneutics, see Misgeld, "Poetry, Dialogue, and Negotiation." pp. 161–181 (the convergence of Gadamer's insight with regard to the survival of hope through confronting the hopeless with the radical thought of Heidegger and Benjamin is noted on p. 180 n. 42); Schmidt, "Poetry and the Political," pp. 209–228; Bruns, "The Remembrance of Language," pp. 1–51; Risser, *Hermeneutics and the Voice of the Other*, pp. 185–208.

69. E. Wolfson, "Occultation of the Feminine." One might protest that kabbalists do affirm the independent existence of Ein Sof, which would be appropriately delineated as the being divested of all garments. Such a characterization, based on Hebraic sources, is found, for instance, in Reuchlin, *On the Art of the Kabbalah*, pp. 248, where Ein Sof is described as *deitas ipsa sine indumento*, the "deity without vestment." Reuchlin has correctly understood the tradition, but even in this case it could be argued that there is no "naked truth" to behold, for the Ein Sof, divested of all garments, cannot be seen in any form or image and cannot be spoken of in any manner. Properly speaking, or perhaps I should say "unspeaking," with regard to Ein Sof—the one beyond affirmation and denial—there can only be "negation of imagery," which would have to include even "negative images," for the latter, though they be negative, are no less imagistic than the affirmative images they negate. On this important philosophical insight into apophatic discourse, see Turner, *Darkness of God*, p. 35.

70. See E. Wolfson, *Through a Speculum*, p. 62, and references to philosophic sources given in n. 45. On the confluence of speech and perception, language and experience, in human consciousness, see Ihde, *Sense and Significance*, pp. 155–161. On the essentially linguistic nature of imagination, related especially to the function of constructing metaphors, see Madison, *Hermeneutics of Postmodernity*, pp. 183–191. For an analysis of the rhetoric of the image, see Barthes, *Image—Music—Text*, pp. 32–51. The notion of myth as a semiological system is also emphasized in the thought of Barthes. See Baeten, *Magic Mirror*, pp. 95–117. On the semiotic understanding of myth as the symbolic displacement and reanimation of cultural values of signification, see Liszka, *Semiotic Myth*. I am aware of the fact that in contemporary linguistics a more expansive and comprehensive use of "language" is employed to include animal communication; indeed, the "birth" of language is traced by some to the stage of the evolutionary process wherein the need for the preservation of the species

necessitated forms of communication to facilitate procreation. For a lucid account of this hypothesis, see Fischer, *History of Language,* pp. 11–34. Nevertheless, I am using "language" in the more restricted sense to encompass the linguistic abilities, verbal and graphic, distinctive to *Homo sapiens*, though these may be traced to the earliest stage of hominid language development marked by the appearance of *Homo erectus* in the chain of evolution. See Fischer, *History of Language,* pp. 35–59, and especially his comment on p. 56: "There was never an *Ursprache*, a 'primeval language.' Still, a capacity for language of some kind was present among the earliest hominids. Humans evolved from creatures without language and for this reason brain areas with other functions, such as gesturing, were called upon for the new task of speech. . . . Language was superimposed and elaborated on top of these more primitive cerebral systems and, in addition, appears to be parasitic to them." From this vantage point it seems even scientifically plausible to distinguish qualitatively nonhuman and human forms of communication, and perhaps the word "language" should be applied only to the latter.

71. Cited in Dastur, *Telling Time*, p. 96 n. 3.

72. Husserl, *Logical Investigations* vol. 1, p. 250 (emphasis in the original).

73. Agamben, *Potentialities*, pp. 39–47, esp. p. 45: "Thus we finally find ourselves alone with our words; for the first time we are truly alone with language, abandoned without any final foundation. This is the Copernican revolution that the thought of our time inherits from nihilism: we are the first human beings who have become completely conscious of language." See ibid., p. 68: "The pure existence . . . that constitutes the sole object of philosophy is something to which philosophy has no access other than through reflection on the *factum loquendi* and the construction of an experience in which this *factum* is thematically at issue. Only the *experience of the pure experience of language allows thought to consider the pure existence of the world*" (emphasis in original). A similar hypothesis is presented within an entirely different theoretical framework by Grace, *Linguistic Construction of Reality.* See also Hottois, *L'Inflation du langage*; and the comment by Murti, *Studies in Indian Thought,* p. 358: "What is amply borne upon us by linguistic philosophers and others is that the philosophy of language is not one aspect or branch of philosophy, but is all philosophy. . . . Philosophy may be re-defined as Critique of Language. . . . Language is not an accidental, dispensable garb which could be put on and put off. It grows with thought, or rather thought grows with it. In the ultimate analysis they may be identical." The presentation of the contemporary philosophic predicament accords well with the semiotic orientation in kabbalistic ontology.

74. The essay arose as a response of Benjamin to a letter from Scholem in which the latter raised some philosophical questions regarding the nature of language. See Benjamin, *Correspondence*, no. 46, p. 81. On Scholem's enthusiastic reaction to Benjamin's letter, see the comment from his diary cited in Scholem, *Gershom Scholem*, p. 19, and also Scholem's letter from 3 August 1917 to Werner Kraft, p. 51, in which he acknowledges that his own reflections on the philosophy of language "went in the very same direction as Benjamin's" and that he translated large sections of the latter's essay into Hebrew in order to discern better its "immanent relation to Judaism." See also Scholem, *Walter Benjamin: The Story of a Friendship*, p. 38, where Scholem acknowledges that he attempted to translate into Hebrew portions of Benjamin's study on language, which was "very close" to his heart. Scholem's plan was to offer the translation to Walter and Dora as a wedding gift (the date of their ceremony was 16 April 1917). Benjamin insisted that Scholem read the first pages of the translation "so that he might hear how his sentences sounded in the Ursprache, as he put it half-jokingly." For recent discussion of the impact of Benjamin's essay on Scholem, see E. Jacobson, *Metaphysics of the Profane*, pp. 123–153. On pp. 124–125 Jacobson reproduces pages from the Jewish National and University Library, Jerusalem, in Scholem's own hand of the two attempted translations of Benjamin.

75. Benjamin, *Reflections*, p. 316. The essay is reprinted in Benjamin, *Selected Writings, Volume 1*, pp. 62–74.

76. Benjamin, *Reflections*, p. 316 (emphasis in original).

77. Ibid.

78. Ibid., p. 324. It would seem that this remark indicates unequivocally that Benjamin would have rejected the identification of ontology and language that has informed the kabbalistic worldview (I note parenthetically that with regard to this matter there is no substantial difference between the so-called theosophic and ecstatic kabbalists). In spite of this unequivocal remark, Wolin, *Walter Benjamin,* pp. 39–41, has

raised the possibility that Benjamin's philosophy of language from the early period was indebted to the kabbalistic conception of language as the "divine substance of reality." In particular, Wolin focuses on the influence of Abulafia's conception of language, correctly reminding the reader (p. 281 n. 26) that Scholem, *Walter Benjamin: Die Geshichte einer Freundschaft*, pp. 118–119, reports "having discussed Abulafia's philosophy of language with Benjamin in connection with the linguistico-philosophical interests of his planned *Habilitationsschrift* on *Trauerspiel.*" For the English version, see Scholem, *Walter Benjamin: The Story of a Friendship*, p. 92. See also Handelman, *Fragments of Redemption*, pp. 17–18; Alter, *Necessary Angels*, pp. 45–46, 63; Mosès, *Der Engel der Geschichte*, pp. 87–111, 215–234; Idel, "A. Abulafia, G. Scholem, and W. Benjamin on Language," pp. 130–138. On the suspected impact of kabbalistic linguistic theory on Benjamin's notion of the original, pure language, see also Steiner, *After Babel*, pp. 66–67; Eco, *Experiences in Translation*, p. 10. On the more specific surmise that Benjamin was influenced by Christian kabbalah as transmitted by Franz Joseph Molitor, see E. Jacobson, *Metaphysics of the Profane*, pp. 114–122. For a different approach, see Gasché, "Saturnine Vision," p. 87, and the more recent discussion in Agamben, *Potentialities*, pp. 57–58. According to Agamben, the supremacy accorded the orthographic form in the kabbalistic conception of language is at odds with Benjamin's notion of a universal language based on pure speech, the definitive utterance of the divine name, and the cancellation of any written representation. Agamben's view can be challenged, however, on the basis that in *Ursprung des deutschen Trauerspiels*, Benjamin, following in the footsteps of Johann Wilhelm Ritter, considered the written word to be the universal intelligible image that requires no translation. Moreover, in that context music is upheld as the source whence word and script emerge. See Benjamin, *Origin of German Tragic Drama*, p. 214. For another critique of viewing Benjamin's theory of language in mystical or kabbalistic terms related primarily to the notion of language as the potential for communicability, which establishes a sense of difference or otherness, see Gasché, *Of Minimal Things*, pp. 61–82.

79. Benjamin, *Reflections*, p. 323. See idem, *Origin of German Tragic Drama*, p. 214, where Benjamin cites the following words of Ritter: "In reality the whole of creation is language, and so is literally created by the word, the created and creating word itself."

80. Benjamin, *Reflections*, p. 321: "The incomparable feature of human language is that its magical community with things is immaterial and purely mental, and the symbol of this is sound. The Bible expresses this symbolic fact when it says that God breathes his breath into man: this is at once life and mind and language."

81. Ibid., pp. 325–326.

82. Benjamin, *Origin of German Tragic Drama*, p. 32.

83. Ibid., p. 36.

84. Ibid., p. 37. On the subordination of philosophy to poetry, and the romantic sacralization of the latter, in the poetological thinking of Novalis and Schlegel, see Schaeffer, *Art of the Modern Age*, pp. 72–90, 94–95, 104–106.

85. Benjamin, *Reflections*, pp. 318–319. It strikes me that there are interesting parallels between Benjamin and Wittgenstein's notion of the language game according to which the power of language resides not in its descriptive modality but in its constitutive role in determining the ways human beings respond in the world. See Wittgenstein, *Tractatus Logico-Philosophicus*, p. 21, secs. 4.021–4.023, p. 47, secs. 5.471–5.4711 (for the original I consulted idem, *Tractatus Logico-Philosophicus*, German text; all German references to the *Tractatus* are from this volume); idem, *Philosophical Investigations*, vol. I, p. 9, sec. 19, p. 11, sec. 23, p. 88, sec. 241, p. 146, sec. 546, p. 167, sec. 654; idem, *Philosophical Grammar*, p. 42. On the competing interpretations of the relationship between life-forms and language games, particularly in Wittgenstein's later philosophy, see Gier, *Wittgenstein and Phenomenology*, pp. 17–32. An in-depth examination of Wittgenstein's elucidation of language as the projection of reality is offered by Hunnings, *World and Language*. For a richly nuanced discussion of language and ontology in Wittgenstein, see Stokhof, *World and Life as One*, pp. 104–185; Wabel, "Die Hineinnahme der Sprachgrenzen," pp. 85–106. Also worthy of consideration are the monographs by Staten, *Wittgenstein and Derrida*, and Garver and Lee, *Derrida and Wittgenstein*. The authors explore the common elements in Wittgenstein and Derrida, emphasizing in particular that both men affirm language as the key to understanding philosophy and the quest to understand the nature of being, without, however, reverting to a totalizing ontology or metaphysic. For an implicit critique of the Derridean notion of the play of signification

based on Wittgenstein's conception of the grammatical form of language, see Guetti, *Wittgenstein and the Grammar of Literary Experience*. On the comparison between Wittgenstein and Heidegger, see below, nn. 127–129.

86. On the notion of "pure language" and the task of translation, see the essay "The Task of the Translator," in Benjamin, *Illuminations*, pp. 69–82, esp. pp. 74–75; and see Fynsk, *Language and Relation*, pp. 177–210; Jacobs, *In the Language of Walter Benjamin*, pp. 75–90. The disentanglement of the idea of a natural language, that is, the notion of primordial language to which all other languages may be traced but that is not identifiable with any specific language, including Hebrew, from a theological basis was already entertained by Leibniz, in part in dialogue with older esoteric themes. See Rutherford, "Philosophy and Language in Leibniz," pp. 224–269, esp. pp. 240–248.

87. Benjamin, *Reflections*, p. 331. See Cacciari, "Problem of Representation," pp. 155–165; E. Jacobson, *Metaphysics of the Profane*, pp. 85–106.

88. See Scholem, *Major Trends*, p. 27; idem, "Name of God," pp. 61–65; idem, *On the Kabbalah and Its Symbolism*, pp. 8–11, 22–23, 35–36. Scholem's understanding of the symbolic valence of language has been well discussed in scholarly literature, and here I offer a modest sampling of the relevant studies: D. Biale, *Scholem*, pp. 89–92; Schweid, *Judaism and Mysticism*, pp. 43–44, 126–127; Idel, *Kabbalah: New Perspectives*, pp. 231–232; Handelman, *Fragments of Redemption*, pp. 104–109. See also reference to Idel above, n. 57. On the centrality of naming in Scholem's conception of language, see Derrida, *Acts of Religion*, p. 197, based on Scholem's own remarks in a letter to Rosenzweig dated December 26, 1926, cited on p. 227: "Language is Name [*Sprache ist Namen*]. In the names, the power of language is enclosed; in them, its abyss is sealed." For a comparison of the respective theories of language in Scholem and Benjamin, see D. Biale, *Scholem*, pp. 80–81, 103–108; Kilcher, *Sprachtheorie der Kabbala*, p. 46 n. 59; Weigel, "Scholems Gedichte," pp. 24–28; Bouretz, "Gershom Scholem und das Schreiben," pp. 108–115, esp. p. 109 n. 34.

89. On the proximity of Heidegger and Benjamin with regard to the question of truth and the inner form revealed in the act of creation, particularly the poem, see Bowie, *From Romanticism to Critical Theory*, pp. 194–195. See also Adorno's comment in a letter of 17 April 1963 to Scholem in Scholem, *Gershom Scholem*, p. 392, on the "astounding, mostly linguistic, similarities between Benjamin and Heidegger" with respect to the matter of poetics. For a nuanced analysis of the thinking of Benjamin and Heidegger centered around the linguisticality of experience, see Ziarek, *Historicity of Experience*, pp. 42–71, and see below, n. 189.

90. Gadamer, "Text and Interpretation," p. 28. See idem, *Truth and Method*, pp. 397–447, where Gadamer analyzed in detail the linguistic nature of human experience of the world under the rubric of "language as horizon of a hermeneutic ontology." See, in particular, p. 432: "Being that can be understood is language. The hermeneutical phenomenon here draws into its own universality the nature of what is understood, by determining it in a universal sense as language, and its own relation to beings, as interpretation." Gadamer comments on this passage in "Text and Interpretation," p. 25. The resemblance of Gadamer's notion of the inseparability of being and language to the view expressed by Schelling, which in turn may have affinity with the attitude of kabbalists, has been noted by Bowie, *Schelling and Modern European Philosophy*, p. 117.

91. Gadamer, *Truth and Method*, p. 423. In that context, Gadamer acknowledges that the hermeneutical dialectic, which is conceived from the "centre of language," and the metaphysical dialectic of Plato and Hegel, which privileges the form of the philosophical proposition based on the attribution of a predicate to a subject, both share in the "speculative element." This element relates more specifically to the presumption that meaning is linked to the image reflected through language like a visual image in a mirror. On the one hand, mirroring, it would seem, is dependent on the substitution of one thing for another, for the mirror image is merely the appearance and not the thing itself. On the other hand, precisely this appearance makes possible the proper vision of the thing in relation to an observer. Gadamer thus speaks of the "actual mystery" of reflection, which entails the "intangibility of the picture, the unreal quality of sheer reproduction." See Wachterhauser, "Gadamer's Realism," pp. 148–171. In this matter, Gadamer follows the lead of Heidegger, *Being and Time*, pp. 29–30: "But everything depends on staying clear of any concept of truth construed in the sense of 'correspondence' or 'accordance' [*Übereinstimmung*]. This idea is by no means the primary one

in the concept of *alētheia*. The 'being true' of *logos* as *aletheuein* means: to take beings that are being talked *about* in *legein* as *apophainesthai* out of their concealment; to let them be seen as something unconcealed (*alethes*); to *discover* them. . . . What no longer takes the form of a pure letting be seen, but rather in its indicating always has recourse to something else and so always lets something be seen *as* something, acquires with this structure of synthesis the possibility of covering up" (emphasis in original). For a brief but insightful discussion of the difference between *alētheia* and the correspondence theory of truth, see Levin, *Opening of Vision*, pp. 419–424.

92. For an analysis of Heidegger and Gadamer, see Riedel, *Hören auf die Sprache*, pp. 96–130; Bernasconi, *Heidegger in Question*, pp. 170–189; Coltman, *Language of Hermeneutics*; Lafont, *Linguistic Turn in Hermeneutic Philosophy*, pp. 55–116.

93. Heidegger, *Early Greek Thinking*, p. 37.

94. Heidegger, *Basic Writings*, p. 193. See also idem, *On the Way to Language*, p. 63. Heidegger's words resonate with the following remark of the fourteenth-century Persian poet Ḥāfiẓ from *The Gift*, p. 281: "What /We speak /Becomes the house we live in."

95. Heidegger, *Introduction to Metaphysics*, p. 15; German edition: *Einführung in die Metaphysik*, p. 11. Heidegger's thought, as several scholars have noted (see below, n. 182), resonates with several streams of Chinese philosophy. Particularly relevant to Heidegger's notion of language as the matrix within which things come into being is the statement of the *Zhuangzi*, cited in the introduction of Ames and Hall, *Focusing the Familiar*, p. 31: "The way is forged in the walking; things and events become so in the saying." See Tzu, *Complete Works of Chuang Tzu*, p. 40: "A road is made by people walking on it; things are so because they are called so. What makes them so? Making them so makes them so. What makes them not so? Making them not so makes them not so." The thought is captured succinctly in the dictum, technically known as *jakugo*, translated in Hori, *Zen Sand*, p. 125: "To think of it—is it."

96. Heidegger, *Contributions to Philosophy*, p. 350 (emphasis in the original). The theme is repeated in many of Heidegger's later writings; see, e.g., *Poetry, Language, Thought*, p. 73: "language alone brings what is, as something that is, into the Open for the first time. Where there is no language . . . there is also no openness of what is, and consequently no openness either of that which is not and of the empty. Language, by naming beings for the first time, first brings beings to word and appearance." See Heidegger, *Poetry, Language, Thought*, pp. 189–210.

97. Heidegger, *Contributions*, p. 324; German edition: *Beiträge zur Philosophie*, p. 460. On "enthinking" being and language, see Heidegger, *Contributions*, p. 54.

98. Heidegger, *Beiträge*, p. 497.

99. Heidegger, *Introduction to Metaphysics*, p. 7; *Einführung in die Metaphysik*, p. 5.

100. Heidegger, *Contributions*, p. 39; *Beiträge*, p. 56. For discussion of the theme of "inceptual thinking," see Vallega, "'Beyng-Historical Thinking,'" pp. 48–65, esp. pp. 54–59.

101. Heidegger, *Contributions*, p. 39; *Beiträge*, p. 56.

102. Heidegger, *Contributions*, p. 119.

103. For clarification of these critical terms in Heidegger's thinking, see Zarader, *Heidegger et les paroles de l'origine*, pp. 17–30; Schürmann, *Heidegger On Being and Acting*, pp. 120–151. The underlying political implications of the Heideggerian distinction are drawn clearly by Janicaud, *Shadow of That Thought*, pp. 57–58.

104. Heidegger and Fink, *Heraclitus Seminar*, p. 17: "Philosophy can only speak and say, but it cannot paint pictures. . . . There is an old Chinese proverb that runs, 'Once pointed out is better than a hundred times said.' To the contrary, philosophy is obligated to point out precisely through the saying."

105. Heidegger, *Contributions*, p. 40; *Beiträge*, p. 57.

106. Heidegger, *Contributions*, p. 41; *Beiträge*, p. 58.

107. Heidegger, *Contributions*, p. 39.

108. Heidegger, *Contributions*, p. 45; *Beiträge*, p. 64.

109. Heidegger, *Contributions*, p. 216.

110. On the distinction between speaking and saying, see D. A. White, *Heidegger and the Language of Poetry*, pp. 35–52.

111. Roth, *Poetics of Resistance*, pp. 57–124. The influence of Heidegger is discernible in the comments by Ricoeur, *Conflict of Interpretations*, p. 91: "It would appear then that the sign is not only that which is lacking to things, it is not simply absent from things and other than them; it is what wishes to be applied, in order to express, grasp, apprehend, and finally to show, to manifest. That is why a philosophy of language need not be limited to the conditions of possibility of a semiology: to account for the absence of the sign from things, the *reduction* of relations of nature and their mutation into signifying relations suffices. It is necessary in addition to satisfy conditions of possibility of discourse insofar as it is an endeavor, renewed ceaselessly, to express integrally the thinkable and the sayable in our experience. Reduction—or any act comparable to it by reason of its negativity—no longer suffices, Reduction is only the inverse, the negative side, of a wanting-to-say which aspires to become a wanting-to-show" (emphasis in original).

112. Heidegger, *On the Way to Language*, p. 123. Reference to the original German is taken from *Unterwegs zur Sprache*, p. 254.

113. Heidegger, *On the Way to Language*, p. 76; *Unterwegs*, p. 181.

114. Heidegger, *On the Way to Language*, p. 96.

115. Heidegger, *On the Way to Language*, p. 94; *Unterwegs*, p. 200.

116. Heidegger, *Zollikon Seminars*, p. 185.

117. *Birth of Tragedy*, in Nietzsche, *Basic Writings*, sec. 4, p. 45.

118. See *Birth of Tragedy*, in Nietzsche, *Basic Writings*, sec. 1, p. 34: "The beautiful semblance [I have modified Kaufmann's translation of *Schein* as 'illusion'] of the dream worlds, in the creation of which every man is truly an artist, is the prerequisite of all plastic art, and, as we shall see, of an important part of poetry also. In our dreams we delight in the immediate understanding of figures; all forms speak to us; there is nothing unimportant or superfluous. But even when this dream reality is most intense, we still have, glimmering through it, the sensation that it is mere appearance: at least this is my experience, and for its frequency—indeed, normality—I could adduce many proofs, including the sayings of the poets." Compare the brief but brimming fragment of Benjamin entitled "On Semblance" in which he explicates Nietzsche's definition of *Schein*, translated in Benjamin, *Selected Writings*, vol. 1, pp. 223–225. And consider the measured statement of Buchler, *Nature and Judgment*, p. 127: "Philosophically, the intrinsic, fixed distinction between appearance and reality or shadow and substance is inexcusable, reflecting an indulgent bias for one form of reality as against every other form. If, as has sometimes been suggested, this bias is the symptom of one kind of valuational preference in opposition to another, there is still no reason for conceptually ordering the cosmos in accordance with such a preference." Also relevant is Lacoste, "Work and Complement of Appearing," pp. 68–93.

119. Nietzsche, *Will to Power*, p. 433, sec. 817. See below, n. 379.

120. Heidegger, *Nietzsche, Volume I*, pp. 118–119; *Nietzsche, Erster Band*, pp. 118–119.

121. Ibid., p. 119.

122. Ibid., p. 215.

123. See Proimos, "Martin Heidegger on *Mimesis*," pp. 153–163. Also relevant is the discussion on the phenomenon of the simulacrum and Heidegger's refutation of the metaphysical conception of appearance in Perniola, *Ritual Thinking*, pp. 175–193. On the "deep structure of the controversy" between "mimesis and meaning," see Menke-Eggers, *Sovereignty of Art*, pp. 87–105. While the blurring of the line separating imagined and real is not without epistemological and ontological consequences, it seems to me far more sophisticated than the continued analytic struggle to differentiate the imaginary and real, fictional and nonfictional narratives. For a recent example of this kind of study, see Sutrop, "Imagination and the Act of Fiction-Making," pp. 332–344.

124. The passage of Nietzsche is cited by Heidegger from the *Grossoktavausgabe*, XIII, 50. Nietzsche articulates the obliteration of the opposition between appearance and reality in the aphorism "How the 'Real World' at last Became a Myth" in *Twilight of the Idols*, pp. 40–41: "The 'real world'—an idea no longer of any use, not even a duty any longer—an idea grown useless, superfluous, *consequently* a refuted idea: let us abolish it! . . . We have abolished the real world: what world is left? the apparent world perhaps? . . . But no! *with the real world we have also abolished the apparent world*!" (emphasis in the original). On Heidegger's reading

of this passage and the implied "inversion" (*Umdrehung*) of the hierarchy of Platonic metaphysics, see Derrida, *Spurs*, pp. 80–81. For a discussion of different interpretations of Nietzsche's comment, see M. Clark, *Nietzsche on Truth and Philosophy*, pp. 95–125. On the relationship of art and truth in Schopenhauer and Nietzsche, see Taminiaux, *Poetics, Speculation, and Judgment*, pp. 111–126.

125. Heidegger, *Nietzsche, Volume I*, p. 215. For discussion and critique of Heidegger's interpretation of Nietzsche's perspectivism, see Hough, *Nietzsche's Noontide Friend*, pp. 32–34.

126. Nietzsche, *Gay Science*, p. 70, sec. 58.

127. Johnstone, *Rationalized Epistemology*, pp. 99–104. *Inter alia*, the author notes the "remarkable" similarity of Heidegger to Wittgenstein on this issue.

128. Wittgenstein, *Philosophical Remarks*, p. 51. For discussion of the phenomenological dimensions of Wittgenstein's thought in conversation with Heidegger, see Guest, "Phénoménologie de Wittgenstein," pp. 53–74. See the analysis of Wittgenstein's "phenomenological reduction" in Ihde, *Sense and Significance*, pp. 142–154, esp. p. 149: "The 'reductions' employed by Wittgenstein *invert* the emphasis of Husserlian phenomenology. Where Husserl reduced things to transcendental experience, Wittgenstein reduces things to linguistic usages—*the meaning is the use*. What must be seen here is that this 'reduction' is one which wants to get back to the structures of language" (emphasis in original). See also Bermes, "Wittgensteins Phänomenologie," pp. 5–21 and other references cited on pp. 12–13 n. 21. On the question of truth and language games in Wittgenstein, see Martin, *From Nietzsche to Wittgenstein*, pp. 257–289.

129. Still useful is the observation of Ihde, *Sense and Significance*, p. 155, that the "methodological bases of phenomenology and linguistic analysis begin with inverse weightings of an essentially paired phenomenon, *language-experience*. The methodological drift of phenomenology is to begin with experience and attempt to deal with language from a description of experience in its movement toward expression. The methodological drift of linguistic analysis is, to begin with, a description of language and its structure from which experience is to be understood" (emphasis in the original). Mandel, "Heidegger and Wittgenstein," pp. 259–270. For a sampling of studies exploring the thought of Heidegger and Wittgenstein, in addition to the study by Guest cited in n. 128, see Rentsch, *Heidegger und Wittgenstein*; Fay, "Ontological Difference," pp. 319–328; Standish, *Beyond the Self*; Rorty, "Wittgenstein, Heidegger, and the Reification of Language," pp. 337–357; Apel, "Wittgenstein and Heidegger," pp. 241–274; Furuta, *Wittgenstein und Heidegger*; D. G. Stern, "Heidegger and Wittgenstein," pp. 245–259. A more recent analysis of Heidegger's thought from the perspective of analytic philosophy is found in Lafont, *Heidegger, Language, and World-Disclosure*. The hypothesis that the limit of language and logic is a shared feature in the ostensibly disparate philosophical approaches of Heidegger and analytic thought is argued as well by Witherspoon, "Logic and the Inexpressible," pp. 89–113. See below, n. 206. On the genealogical analysis of language and reality in Nietzsche's own thought, framed within the larger question of the epistemology of nihilism, see Strong, *Friedrich Nietzsche*, pp. 55–78; a comparative analysis of Nietzsche and Wittgenstein is offered, op. cit., pp. 78–86.

130. Paraphrasing the remark of Heraclitus, "Nature loves to hide," in Kahn, *Art and Thought of Heraclitus*, p. 33.

131. On the nexus of suspicion, deception, and concealment as the basis for philosophical esotericism, see S. Rosen, *Metaphysics in Ordinary Language*, pp. 1–14.

132. Derrida, *Margins of Philosophy*, p. 132, notes that Heidegger's privileging the "phenomenological metaphor" of *Lichtung* and the consequent emphasis on presence as self-presence are in consonance with the priority accorded to speech over writing. There is surely validity to this claim, as Heidegger's writings are saturated with phonocentric claims such as we find, for instance, in *On the Way to Language*, p. 120: "The point is to approach more closely language's own peculiar character. Here, too, language shows itself first as our way of speaking." In spite of the evidence that supports Derrida's critique, a case may be made for an alternative reading of Heidegger that would problematize the label of phonocentrism. The essential feature of language is in the saying in virtue of which beings show themselves. This saying, however, is not necessarily limited to verbal speech, as writing itself is a form of showing. On the nonphonic dimension of saying, see the remark of Heidegger cited above at n. 116. One must bear in mind, moreover, that for Heidegger the priority accorded saying is challenged by positing silence as the source of language, and hence the meta-

physical is undermined not by affirming the graphic over the phonic but by subverting all forms of language in the unspoken. A defense of Heidegger along these lines is offered by Bernasconi, "Transformation of Language," pp. 1–23. On the theme of presence in Heidegger, see also Schuback, "Perplexité de la presence," pp. 257–279.

133. Heidegger, *Hölderin's Hymn "The Ister,"* p. 21; see p. 26: "naming first elevates and poetizes what is named into its essence."

134. I borrow this expression from W. Wimsatt, *Verbal Icon*. On the conflation of the verbal and visual, see also the description of poetry in Jung, *Spirit in Man*, pp. 75–76, as "a language pregnant with meanings, and images that are true symbols because they are the best possible expressions for something unknown—bridges thrown out towards an unseen shore."

135. In several of his writings, Heidegger employs the locution of poetic dwelling based on Hölderin's image "poetically man dwells." For instance, see Heidegger, *Poetry, Language, Thought*, pp. 213–229; idem, *Elucidations*, pp. 172, 187; Pierson, "Sur l'habitation poétique," pp. 107–113; Coltman, *Language of Hermeneutics*, pp. 88–94.

136. Heidegger specifies the meaning of this term in *On the Way to Language*, p. 92: "The country offers ways only because it is country. It gives way, moves us. We hear the words 'give way' in this sense: to be the original giver and founder of ways." The poetic motion of the original German is virtually impossible to capture adequately in translation: *Die Gegend ergibt als Gegend erst Wege. Sie be-wegt. Wir hören das Wort Bewegung im Sinne von: Wege allererst ergeben und stiften* (*Unterwegs*, pp. 197–198).

137. Heidegger, *On the Way to Language*, p. 77; *Unterwegs*, p. 181. On the belonging-together of poetizing and thinking, see idem, *Hölderin's Hymn "The Ister,"* pp. 111–115. Various scholars have discussed this dimension of Heidegger's thought. For instance, see Biemel, "Poetry and Language in Heidegger," pp. 65–105, esp. pp. 82–93; D. A. White, *Heidegger and the Language of Poetry*, pp. 143–167; Bernasconi, *Question of Language*, pp. 49–64; Bruns, *Heidegger's Estrangements*, pp. 99–122; Ziarek, *Inflected Language*, pp. 21–42; Botet, *Langue, langage, et stratégies linguistiques*, pp. 71–80; Fynsk, *Language and Relation*, pp. 39–85. In some measure, Heidegger's poetizing of thought brings him close to the romantic ideal of the poet-thinker (*dichtender Denker*), embodied for him by Hölderin. See Schaeffer, *Art of the Modern Age*, pp. 237–238, 259–265.

138. Heidegger, *On the Way to Language*, p. 86; *Unterwegs*, p. 191.

139. Heidegger, *On the Way to Language*, p. 82; *Unterwegs*, p. 187. MacLeish, *Poetry and Experience*, p. 9, commenting on the words of the Chinese poet Lu Chi (d. 303), "We poets struggle with Non-Being to force it to yield to Being /We knock upon silence for an answering music," writes: "The poet's labor is to struggle with the meaninglessness and silence of the world until he can force it to mean: until he can make the silence answer and the non-Being *be*." It is worthwhile noting as well the comment of Sri Aurobindo recorded in Gokak, *Integral View of Poetry*, p. 1, that poetry is the "mantra of the Real—a rhythmic revelation of Reality in language." Or, again, in something of a poetic flourish, the author writes: "Poetry is mantra. It is incarnation. In it is revealed the closest possible union of music and meaning, of thought and image, of sense and suggestion, of imagination and intuition . . . poetry is a mantra of the Real, an interpretative incarnation of some aspect of Reality." Lest one attribute naïve essentialism to this author based on the remarks concerning reality, consider the following comment: "There are as many interpretations and representations of Reality as there are poets. The poet ascends into the world of pure vision on the wings of an attitude or attitudes" (p. 2). This comment attests unequivocally that the presupposed notion of the real is a multifaceted and ever-changing phantasmagoria of images, not a monolithic and reified constellation of fixed forms.

140. Heidegger, *On the Way to Language*, p. 155; *Unterwegs*, p. 237 (I have modified the translation slightly in accord with the original).

141. Heidegger, *On the Way to Language*, p. 90.

142. Ricoeur, *Conflict of Interpretations*, p. 266. On the circularity of interpretation, see chap. 3, n. 6.

143. Heidegger, *On the Way to Language*, p. 107.

144. See my preliminary remarks in E. Wolfson, *Abraham Abulafia*, pp. 28–29. On revealing and concealing in Heidegger's thought, see Vail, *Heidegger and Ontological Difference*, pp. 25–46. The mystical implications of Heidegger's treatment of this theme are noted by K. Hart, *Trespass of the Sign*, pp. 237–252.

145. Heidegger, *Zollikon Seminars*, p. 171.

146. Heidegger, *Early Greek Thinking*, p. 77.

147. Ibid., p. 60.

148. See the citations from Heidegger, *Hölderin's Hymn "The Ister"* below at nn. 164–165. On the shift from proposition to saying in Heidegger's thinking about language, see the nuanced discussion in Vallega-Neu, "Poietic Saying," pp. 66–80.

149. Heidegger, *What Is Called Thinking?* pp. 198–199.

150. Ibid., pp. 206–207.

151. Heidegger, *Early Greek Thinking*, p. 37 (emphasis in original). Original German in *Holzwege*, p. 350.

152. Heidegger, *Early Greek Thinking*, pp. 41–42; *Holzwege*, pp. 354–355. On the paradox of belonging and withdrawal, see Taminiaux, *The Thracian Maid and the Professional Thinker*, pp. 122–139.

153. Heidegger, *Early Greek Thinking*, p. 43; *Holzwege*, p. 356.

154. Heidegger, *Early Greek Thinking*, p. 77.

155. On this critical Heideggerian term, see Amoroso, *Lichtung*. Magee, *Hegel and the Hermetic Tradition*, p. 229 n. 12, remarks that there are "striking analogies between Luria's *tsimtsum*, the 'clearing' in which beings come to be, and Heidegger's notion of the *Lichtung*, the clearing in which Being itself comes to presence." In my own thinking, I have considered this resemblance as well, which is enhanced by the recognition that in both Lurianic kabbalah and Heideggerian thought the clearing manifests by concealing, that is, what comes to presence does so in virtue of being absent. For a detailed exploration of this theme, see E. Wolfson, "Divine Suffering," pp. 107–117, and the comparison of Lurianic kabbalah and Heidegger offered on p. 154 n. 112.

156. Heidegger, *Poetry, Language, Thought*, p. 53 (emphasis in the original). Reference to the German taken from *Holzwege*, p. 40.

157. Heidegger, *Poetry, Language, Thought*, p. 178: "Thinging, the thing stays the united four, earth and sky, divinities and mortals, in the simple onefold of their self-unified fourfold." On the fourfold, see below, n. 188.

158. Ibid., p. 179.

159. On the thematic link between saying and showing in Heidegger's thought, see Kockelmans, "Language, Meaning, and Ek-sistence," pp. 3–32, esp. pp. 24–28. On the understanding of speaking as a kind of seeing in the phenomenological philosophy of Merleau-Ponty, see Dufrenne, *In the Presence of the Sensuous*, p. 70.

160. Heidegger, *Piety of Thinking*, p. 132.

161. Sugarman, *Rancor against Time*, pp. 120–128; Roth, *Poetics of Resistance*, pp. 87–108. It stands to reason that the dialectic of absence and presence in Heidegger's notion of *Lichtung* and the (un)concealedness of truth reflects, in part, the phenomenology of Husserl. For an application of this dimension of Husserlian phenomenology that is particularly relevant to the theme of this chapter, see Sokolowski, *Presence and Absence*.

162. Heidegger, *Early Greek Thinking*, p. 34.

163. Ibid., pp. 35–36.

164. Heidegger, *Hölderin's Hymn "The Ister,"* pp. 119–120.

165. Ibid., p. 19.

166. Heidegger, *On the Way to Language*, p. 160. For the fuller context of the Heideggerian notion of the "single poetic statement," see chap. 3, n. 97.

167. Heidegger, *Hölderin's Hymn "The Ister,"* p. 165. Heidegger's view is captured succinctly and incisively by Levinas, *Collected Philosophical Papers*, p. 83: "And in Heidegger being is revealed out of the hiddenness and mystery of the unsaid which the poets and philosophers bring to speech, without ever saying everything." On the interface of the verbal and ocular, see Stankiewicz, "Poetics and Verbal Art," pp. 54–76.

168. Heidegger, *Pathways*, pp. 136–154. See idem, *What Is Called Thinking?* p. 153: "But language is not a tool. Language is not this and that, is not also something else besides itself. Language is language." On the trace of mimesis in Heidegger's notion of truth as opening, see Sallis, *Echoes*, p. 174: "I shall propose a certain reinscription of mimesis, a reinscription that will follow the lines of a trace of mimesis discernible in those

turns in Heidegger's text. Mimesis, thus reinscribed, will serve to name the connection where Heidegger thinks, perhaps most rigorously, the necessity of the doubling return from the truth of Being back to beings." See Sallis, *Echoes*, pp. 173, 178, 185.

169. Consider Heidegger's remark that "Language is the clearing-concealing advent of Being itself," cited in Sallis, *Echoes*, p. 195. See also Heidegger, *Identity and Difference*, p. 65: "The difference of Being and beings, as the differentiation of overwhelming and arrival, is the perdurance of the two in *unconcealing keeping in concealment [entbergend-bergender Austrag]*. Within this perdurance there prevails a clearing of what veils and closes itself off—and this its prevalence bestows the being apart, and the being toward each other, of overwhelming and arrival" (emphasis in original).

170. Heidegger, *Early Greek Thinking*, p. 39.

171. Heidegger, *Poetry, Language, Thought*, p. 54; original German, *Holzwege*, p. 41.

172. Ibid. On the exposure of the double concealment, see Protevi, "Stilling of the Aufhebung," pp. 67–83, esp. pp. 79–80.

173. Heidegger, *Contributions to Philosophy*, pp. 245, 249. Heidegger returns to the nexus between untruth, the concealedness of beings as a whole, and the disclosure or letting-be of beings, in his essay "On the Essence of Truth"; see Heidegger, *Pathways*, pp. 147–150. The seed of the convergence of truth and untruth in Heidegger's later thought is already planted in *Being and Time*, pp. 204–205: "Truth (discoveredness) must always first be wrested from beings. Beings are torn from concealment. . . . Is it a matter of chance that the Greeks express themselves about the essence of truth with a *privative* expression [*a-letheia*]? Does not a primordial understanding of its own being make itself known in such an expression—the understanding . . . that being-in-untruth constitutes an essential determination of being-in-the-world? The fact that the goddess of truth who leads Parmenides places him before two paths, that of discovering and that of concealment, signifies nothing other than the fact that Da-sein is always already both in the truth and the untruth." For an extended discussion of Heidegger's statement that "the essence of truth is un-truth," see Sallis, "Interrupting Truth," pp. 19–30, and the analysis in Biemel, "Marginal Notes on Sallis's Peculiar Interpretation," pp. 221–239. See also Derrida, "Silkworm of One's Own," p. 39. On double concealment, the concealment of concealing, implied in Heidegger's notion of truth as *aletheia*, see Bernasconi, *Question of Language*, pp. 15–27; Tugendhat, "Heidegger's Idea of Truth," pp. 83–97. For discussion of the epistemological aspects of Heidegger's notion of truth, see J. Anderson, "Truth, Process, and Creature," pp. 28–61. Let me say briefly that understanding the belonging-together of truth and untruth in Heidegger's thought is the apt response to the thesis of Edwards, *Authority of Language*, which rests on the presumed contrast between the "linguistic fascism" of Heidegger that "elevates the *Logos* to the status of a god" and the "decentralized account of linguistic authority" offered by Wittgenstein in his depiction of the "scene for our language-game" (p. 3), the necessary and sufficient conditions that make intersubjective communication possible. Edwards fails to take into consideration that Heidegger identifies infinite transcendence with finitude and temporality, that is, the power of the infinite transcendence bestows upon human finitude its temporal comportment, rendering possible openness to the ecstatic horizon of temporality. My formulation here is indebted to the analysis of Horosz, *Search without Idols*, pp. 308–309. On the openness to being and the temporal comportment of Dasein in Heidegger, see also Rapaport, "Time's Cinders," pp. 218–233; and G. Rose, *Mourning Becomes the Law*, p. 55. Insofar as Heidegger located the work of infinite transcendence in the domain of finitude, he is not subject to the critique of totalitarian logocentrism offered by Edwards. See the discussion on totalizing thinking and totalitarianism in Boeder, *Seditions*, pp. 241–254. The view that Heidegger could not escape the ontotheological assumptions he sought to expose was also expressed by Derrida, *Margins of Philosophy*, pp. 130–131. On the "scandalous" implications of Heidegger's essentialism and the "mythologic of being," see Caputo, *Demythologizing Heidegger*, pp. 118–147. For a more nuanced discussion of the relationship between thinking and the foundation in Heidegger's later thought, with some emphasis paid to the relationship between Heidegger and Wittgenstein, see Vattimo, *Adventure of Difference*, pp. 110–136. A provocative account of the Heideggerian notion of the abyss as the ground of thought is offered by Cristin, *Heidegger and Leibniz*. See also McCumber, "Essence and Subversion," pp. 13–29; and the discussion of Heidegger's critique of metaphysical presence in Chanter, *Time, Death, and the Feminine*, pp. 123–139.

174. Heidegger, *Poetry, Language, Thought*, p. 54 (emphasis in original); *Holzwege*, p. 41.

175. Heidegger, *Poetry, Language, Thought*, p. 60. The conflation of truth and untruth on the part of Heidegger, which signifies the necessary concealment of all that is revealed, is to be distinguished from the confounding of truth and lies, connected especially to the promotion of political ideology on the part of the German fascists, discussed by Adorno, *Minima Moralia*, pp. 108–109. See also the interpretation of the ancient philosophical maxim *veritas patefacit se ipsam et falsum* in Agamben, *Coming Community*, p. 13: "Truth cannot be shown except by showing the false, which is not, however, cut off and cast aside somewhere else. On the contrary, according to the etymology of the verb *patefacere*, which means 'to open' and is linked to *spatium*, truth is revealed only by giving space or giving place to non-truth—that is, as a taking-place of the false, as an exposure of its own innermost impropriety."

176. Heidegger, *Poetry, Language, Thought*, p. 218.

177. Heidegger, *Early Greek Thinking*, p. 107.

178. Heidegger, *On the Way to Language*, p. 122: "To say and to speak are not identical. A man may speak, speak endlessly, and all the time say nothing. Another man may remain silent, not speak at all and yet, without speaking, say a great deal. . . . What is unspoken is not merely something that lacks voice, it is what remains unsaid, what is not yet shown, what has not yet reached its appearance." In *Heraclitus Seminar*, p. 52, Heidegger comments: "But how about thinking and saying? We will also have to say for Heraclitus that there is a saying to which the unsaid belongs, but not the unsayable. The unsaid, however, is no lack and no barrier for saying."

179. Heidegger, *On the Way to Language*, p. 59.

180. Ibid., p. 81.

181. Similarly, Gadamer, *Truth and Method*, p. 416, writes: "Thus every word, in its momentariness, carries with it the unsaid, to which it is related by responding and indicating. . . . All human speaking is finite in such a way that there is within it an infinity of meaning to be elaborated and interpreted. That is why the hermeneutical phenomenon also can be illuminated only in the light of this fundamental finitude of being, which is wholly linguistic in character." Gadamer, "Text and Interpretation," p. 24, acknowledges his indebtedness to Heidegger: "Thus, I tried to hold fast to the inexhaustibility of the experience of meaning by developing the implications for hermeneutics of the Heideggerian insight into the central significance of finitude." A trace of Heidegger can also be discerned in the account of the unique quality of philosophical discourse, with special emphasis placed on the mode of interrogation, in Merleau-Ponty, *Visible and the Invisible*, p. 102: "if philosophy can speak, it is because language is not only the depository of fixed and acquired significations, because its cumulative power itself results from a power of anticipation or of prepossession, because one speaks not only of what one knows, so as to set out a display of it—but also of what one does not know, in order to know it—and because language in forming itself expresses, at least laterally, an ontogenesis of which it is a part. But from this it follows that the words most charged with philosophy are not necessarily those that contain what they say, but rather those that most energetically open upon Being, because they more closely convey the life of the whole and make our habitual evidences vibrate until they disjoin." Merleau-Ponty's claim regarding philosophical speech as speaking that which one does not know is related to his idea of the dialectic of the negative and positive, the invisible and visible: in the openness of being, what is rendered visible remains for the most part hidden, and thus just as we speak of invisibility as the depth of the visible, so silence is the fount of speech. See Merleau-Ponty, *Prose of the World*, p. 37: "Things perceived would not be evident for us and present in flesh and blood if they were not inexhaustible, never entirely given. . . . In the same way, expression is never absolutely expression, what is expressed is never completely expressed." See also pp. 45–46: "Speech does choose only one sign for one already defined signification. . . . And if we want to grasp speech in its most authentic operation . . . we must evoke all those words that could have come in its place that have been omitted. . . . In brief, we should consider speech before it has been pronounced, against the ground of the silence which precedes it, which never ceases to accompany it, and without which it would say nothing. Moreover, we should be sensitive to the thread of silence from which the tissue of speech is woven." Just as the body is the vehicle by which we apprehend the beings in the world that transcend the body, so speech is the vehicle by which we move toward the truth

that surpasses speech (p. 129). For fuller discussion of indirect language and voices of silence, see idem, *Signs*, pp. 39–83. Significantly, Merleau-Ponty compares the writer and the painter in his effort to explain the interplay between speech and silence. The point is epitomized in the statement, "In short, language speaks, and the voices of painting are the voices of silence" (*Signs*, p. 81). On the invisible and the logos, see Low, *Merleau-Ponty's Last Vision*, pp. 71–112. For an intentional analysis of silence based in great measure on Merleau-Ponty and Heidegger, see Dauenhauer, *Silence*.

182. Heidegger, *On the Way to Language*, p. 120. For analysis of this Heideggerian motif, see W. Richardson, *Heidegger through Phenomenology*, pp. 21–22, 221–223, 609–610, 638; D. A. White, *Heidegger and the Language of Poetry*, pp. 43–49, 70–71. See also the study of Bernasconi cited above, n. 137. It is plausible that the "unspoken" in Heidegger's thinking reflects the influence of Taoist philosophy. See R. May, *Heidegger's Hidden Sources*, pp. 21–34. See also Pöggeler, "West-East Dialogue," pp. 48–50, 59, 61–62; Stambaugh, "Heidegger, Taoism, and the Question of Metaphysics," pp. 79–91; Parkes, "Thoughts on the Way," pp. 120–124, 131; Nishitani, "Reflections on Two Addresses," pp. 145–153; Zhang, "Heidegger and Taoism," pp. 307–320; and consider the repeated references to Heidegger offered by Chung-yuan, *Tao*. For a comparison of Heidegger to other elements of Chinese thought, see, for instance, Cheng, "Confucius, Heidegger, and the Philosophy of the I-Ching," pp. 51–70. Heidegger has also been placed in dialogue with Zen Buddhism (especially the thirteenth-century figure Dōgen) by a number of scholars. See Steffney, "Transmetaphysical Thinking in Heidegger and Zen Buddhism," pp. 323–336; idem, "Man and Being in Heidegger and Zen Buddhism," pp. 46–54; C. Olson, "Leap of Thinking," pp. 55–62; Heine, *Existential and Ontological Dimensions*; Abe, *Zen and Western Thought*, pp. 47, 67, 119, 134; idem, *A Study of Dōgen*, pp. 55–57, 74–76, 107–144; Kotoh, "Language and Silence," pp. 201–211; Carter, "Zen and Ontotheology via Heidegger," pp. 167–182; Stambaugh, *Impermanence Is Buddha-Nature*; Dallmayr, *The Other Heidegger*, pp. 200–226; Maraldo, "Rethinking God," pp. 31–49. Murti, *Studies in Indian Thought*, p. 360, remarks that Heidegger's characterization of language as the house of being "comes very close to the Indian conception of language." On the latter, see Aklujkar, "The Word *Is* the World," pp. 452–473. The analogies between Heidegger and ancient Indian and Asian thought, on the one hand, and the resemblance of the latter to the Jewish esoteric gnosis, on the other, may prove to be another important avenue to pursue in the attempt to explain the methodological rationale for using Heidegger as an interpretative lens to illumine the paths of kabbalah. On Taoism and kabbalah, see discussion in chap. 2, nn. 416–419.

183. See Heidegger, *On the Way to Language*, p. 93: "Neighborhood means: dwelling in nearness. Poetry and thinking are modes of saying. The nearness that brings poetry and thinking together into neighborhood we call Saying." See also pp. 103–104.

184. Surely my characterization of Heidegger demands explanation, but to pursue this matter responsibly would take me too far afield. As a preliminary observation, however, I note that Heidegger's thought after the self-proclaimed turn demands a new method for staying on the path, a method that strikes me as congruent in some respects with the midrashic mentality, a playfulness of language that rests on the assumption that heeding the word gives one access to being. (Needless to say, I am well aware that I am relating to only one of the connotations of the term "midrashic.") See, e.g., Heidegger's formulation in *What Is Called Thinking?* p. 119: "Is it playing with words when we attempt to give heed to this game of language and to hear what language really says when it speaks? If we succeed in hearing that, then it may happen—provided we proceed carefully—that we get more truly to the matter that is expressed in any telling and asking." In this context, it is of interest to recall the denunciation of Heidegger as a "German talmudist" offered by Erich Jaensch, a professor at Marburg, in a letter to Ernst Krieck. It is, wrote Jaensch, "typical that the Avocassiero-talmudic thought of the Jews is felt to be so close to Heidegger's philosophy. In fact he owes his fame to Jewish propaganda. . . . It is a scandal that Jewish doctors themselves bastardize medicine by using Heidegger's terminology. But in fact the language is in total harmony with the rabbinic way of thinking, which would want to make natural science a kind of Talmudic exegesis." The passage is cited in Farías, *Heidegger and Nazism*, p. 167; and see discussion in Lyotard, *Heidegger and "the jews,"* pp. 59–60. The comments of Jaensch were obviously written in a spirit of condemnation in a climate where exaggeration and anti-Semitism were far from exceptional and hence they must be taken with the proverbial grain of salt. See, e.g., the distorted

characterization of Einstein's theory of relativity as a "Jewish physics" promoted by Bruno Thüring and Hans Alfred Grunsky, discussed by Jammer, *Einstein and Religion,* pp. 59–61. Nevertheless, I would contend that the comments of Jaensch betray insight into the tenor and texture of Heidegger's philosophical thought and willy-nilly point to the uncanny resemblance between it and rabbinic modes of midrashic interpretation. The matter is explored in detail by Zarader, *La dette impensée.*

185. Heidegger, *On the Way to Language,* p. 108; *Unterwegs,* p. 216.

186. Ibid.

187. Heidegger, *Poetry, Language, Thought,* p. 173.

188. Ibid., p. 178. Original German in Heidegger, *Vorträge und Aufsätze, II,* p. 50. On the notion of the fourfold, see Kockelmans, *On the Truth of Being,* pp. 94–121; Bruns, *Heidegger's Estrangements,* pp. 77–85; Roth, *Poetics of Resistance,* pp. 113–122; and especially the richly nuanced analysis in Levin, *The Philosopher's Gaze,* pp. 116–169. In particular, Levin discusses *Gestalt, Gestell,* and *Geviert,* the three words in Heidegger's poetic thinking that elucidate the way of the lighting. At one point, he offers the following account of the three terms, which is well worth citing in full: "If *Gestalt* refers to a gathering for a while of the lighting, of the visible and the invisible, into a practical structure, *Gestell* names a gathering of the lighting, of the visible and the invisible, into the nihilism of a phantasmagoric reification, and *Geviert* attempts to think the historically new possibility of a gathering of the lighting into a configuration of the most dynamic openness. *Geviert* would thus be the name of a certain dream, the vision of another beginning, a time coming after the overcoming of the *Gestell,* when perception, assuming a radically different *Gestalt* configuration, would take place as a hermeneutical λέγειν, a gathering of earth and sky, mortals and gods, a gathering outside our present order of time and history, a gathering in which, because of our response-ability, our *Wahr-nehmung,* our care for the hermeneutics of truth as beings gifted with sight, it might somehow become possible for each of the four to become a realm of inconceivable disclosure, opening beyond the reach of representation into the depths of the invisible" (pp. 159–160).

189. Heidegger, *Elucidations,* p. 109. The notion of origin, for Heidegger, does not connote the temporal beginning of something but its essence, which is not, however, a reified nature but the taking-hold of thinking, the appropriation, the enowning (*Ereignis*) through which something becomes the being that it is, always in the form of what is to come as what has been. See Heidegger, *Poetry, Language, and Thought,* p. 17, and detailed discussion of the terms *Ursprung, Anfang,* and *Beginn* in Schürmann, *Heidegger on Being and Acting,* pp. 120–151. The point is made succinctly by Marx, *Reason and World,* p. 80: "For Heidegger the traditional concept of essence is one of those determinations which must be overcome because they derive from metaphysics. Accordingly, he is convinced that 'thinking' is also something which, unlike a *ti* or *quid,* cannot be defined in its 'what' by determining its essence (*Wesensbestimmung*)." On the paradox of origin in Heidegger's thinking, see Marrati-Guénoun, *La genèse et la trace,* pp. 126–132. It is of interest to compare Heidegger's notion of *Ursprung* with the comments by Benjamin in the *Origin of German Tragic Drama,* pp. 45–46 regarding the "dialectic which is inherent in origin": "Origin [*Ursprung*], although an entirely historical category, has, nevertheless, nothing to with genesis [*Entstehung*]. The term origin is not intended to describe the process by which the existent came into being, but rather to describe that which emerges from the process of becoming and disappearance. . . . That which is original is never revealed in the named and manifest existence of the factual; its rhythm is apparent only to a dual insight. On the one hand it needs to be recognized as a process of restoration and reestablishment, but, on the other hand, and precisely because of this, as something imperfect and incomplete. There takes place in every original phenomenon a determination of the form in which an idea will constantly confront the historical world, until it is revealed fulfilled, in the totality of its history. Origin is not, therefore, discovered by the examination of actual findings, but it is related to their history and their subsequent development." For an illuminating discussion of the affinities between Benjamin and Heidegger, in spite of Benjamin's sense of irreconcilable differences separating the two, see Levin, *Philosopher's Gaze,* pp. 343–374, esp. pp. 356–357, where the author discusses the topic of origin in conjunction with the aforecited passage from the *Trauerspiel.* See above, n. 78. On Benjamin's concerns for origin and his suspicion of claims to novelty, see Frisby, "Walter Benjamin's Prehistory of Modernity," pp. 15–32.

190. Heidegger, *Hölderin's Hymn "The Ister,"* p. 151.

191. Ibid., pp. 28–30.

192. Heidegger, *Concept of Time*, p. 13; see p. 15: "Running ahead seizes the past as the authentic possibility of every moment of insight, as what is now certain. Being futural, as a possibility of Dasein as specific, gives time, because it is time itself"; and pp. 19–20: "The past remains closed off from any present so long as such a present, Dasein, is not itself historical. Dasein, however, is in itself historical insofar as it is its possibility. In being futural Dasein is its past. . . . The past—experienced as authentic historicity—is anything but what is past. It is something to which I can return again and again. . . . *The possibility of history is grounded in the possibility according to which any specific present understands how to be futural. This is the first principle of all hermeneutics.* It says something about the being of Dasein, which is historicity itself" (emphasis in original). For a comprehensive analysis of the role of historical thinking in Heidegger's intellectual biography, see Barash, *Martin Heidegger and the Problem of Historical Meaning*,. On the intricate relationship between phenomenology and history, see studies cited in the Prologue, n. 65.

193. Heidegger, *Hölderin's Hymn "The Ister,"* p. 29.

194. Heidegger, *Poetry, Language, Thought*, pp. 173–174.

195. Particularly relevant is Heidegger's preface to the lecture "Hölderlin's Earth and Heaven," delivered in Stuttgart on 14 July 1959, included in Heidegger, *Elucidations*, p. 176: "Our reflection is concerned solely with Hölderin's poem. It is an attempt to transform our accustomed way of representing things into an unaccustomed, because simple, thinking experience. (The transformation into the thinking experience of the center of the infinite relation—out of the collected framework [*Ge-stell*] as the self-dissimulating event [*Ereignis*] of the fourfold.)"

196. Heidegger, *Poetry, Language, Thought*, p. 179.

197. Ibid. See the brief but incisive comments on this Heideggerian motif in Abe, *Study of Dōgen*, pp. 109–110.

198. Heidegger, *Early Greek Thinking*, p. 43.

199. Kudszus, *Poetic Process*, p. 33, ends the chapter on Heidegger's poetics with the observation that "pain marks the joys of lightness with the cleavage of language torn apart and cast into silence." Dilthey, p. 227, depicts the lived experience of the poet in terms of the "great capacity for suffering. He becomes engrossed in this suffering and fashions it into a lasting mood. Precisely because of this he is able to liberate others by allowing suffering to be resolved in tranquility." For a sustained analysis of the economy of pain and suffering in Heidegger's notion of poetizing (*Dichten*), albeit with a decidedly different valence from my own, see Caputo, *Demythologizing Heidegger*, pp. 148–168.

200. Heidegger, *On the Way to Language*, p. 82. I note that on this point Heidegger was not always consistent. In some passages, he seems to emphasize the identity of poetizing (*Dichten*) and thinking (*Denken*), whereas in other passages he insists that their very proximity implies difference. See idem, *What Is Called Thinking?* p. 134: "The essential closeness of poesy and thinking is so far from excluding their difference that, on the contrary, it establishes that difference in an abysmal manner. . . . But precisely because thinking does not make poetry, but is a primal telling and speaking of language, it must stay close to poesy." See also idem, *Principle of Reason*, p. 35. Commenting on the remark by Angelus Silesius in *The Cherubic Wanderer* that the "rose is without why," which ostensibly conflicts with the Leibnizian principle of reason, *Nihil sine ratione*, "Nothing is without reason," Heidegger wrote: "But one might immediately point out that this source is indeed mystical and poetic. The one as well as the other belong equally little in thinking. Certainly not *in* thinking, but perhaps *before* thinking." On the essential link between philosophical reflection and poetry, consider the remark by Wittgenstein, *Culture and Value*, p. 24: "I think I summed up my attitude to philosophy when I said: philosophy ought really to be written only as a poetic composition."

201. Heidegger, *On the Way to Language*, p. 84.

202. Heidegger, *Poetry, Language, Thought*, p. 218; original in *Vorträge und Aufsätze*, p. 187.

203. Heidegger, *On the Way to Language*, p. 85.

204. Heidegger, *Poetry, Language, Thought*, p. 74.

205. Heidegger, *On the Way to Language*, p. 59.

206. See Heidegger, *Elucidations*, p. 186: "Art, as the pointing that allows the appearance of what is invisible, is the highest kind of showing. The ground and the summit of such showing again unfold themselves in saying as poetic song." The demarcation of the task of the poet and the thinker "to make sense of the enigmatic, unfathomable face of life" is made by Dilthey, *Poetry and Experience*, p. 222. On the depiction of poetry as the disclosure of what must be concealed, see N. Brown, *Apocalypse and/or Metamorphosis*, pp. 3–4. The paradox of disclosure as concealment is also characteristic of the poetic sensibility of Edmond Jabès. See Derrida, *Writing and Difference*, pp. 67–69. On visible representation of the invisible in the writings of Jabès, see Hawkins, *Reluctant Theologians*, pp. 220–224. On the characterization of the abyss—the music box—whence the song of poetry emerges as concomitantly invisible and inaudible, consider the poem "In den Geräuschen," in Celan, *Fathomsuns and Benighted*, p. 63: "In the sounds, as our beginning / in the abyss, / where you feel to me, / I wind it up again, the/ music box—you / know: the invisible, / the / inaudible."

207. The matter can be expressed in terms of the radical empiricism of William James: language can be considered the "house" of pure experience insofar as language makes pure experience available—in the evolutionary scheme, human consciousness as it is cannot be disentangled from language, and in that respect we cannot get out from under Kant's emphasis on the constructed nature of the phenomenal realm—what we experience as world—but language cannot describe the pure experience adequately, as the purity of that experience does not lend itself to discursive or analytic classification. See Stevens, *James and Husserl*, pp. 33–34, 136; and, more recently, Gavin, *William James and the Reinstatement of the Vague*, pp. 78–95. Gavin distinguishes two positions regarding language in James: a negative one (in line with Romanticism) that emphasizes the insufficiency of language to depict the concreteness and immediacy of life experience (pp. 47–50) and a more positive one based on the intentional and contextual aspects of language as the mode by which reality is constructed in individual consciousness (pp. 69–76). Language is not an objective copy of reality but a way of molding the world. The positive view of language is central to the pragmatism of James, even though in the end he would maintain that human consciousness experiences more than the mind could conceptualize or describe linguistically (pp. 95, 170–172). For an elaboration of this point, see Kress, "Contesting Metaphors," pp. 263–283, esp. pp. 264–266. On the insufficiency of language to capture the concrete texture of "pure experience" or the "thickness of reality" in the philosophy of James, see also Taylor, *William James on Consciousness*, pp. 82–96; Lamberth, *William James and the Metaphysics of Experience*, pp. 213–214. On the aversion of idealism to language and the affirmation of logic independent of grammar, see the insightful comments of Rosenzweig, *Star of Redemption*, pp. 140–141.

208. Heidegger, *Identity and Difference*, p. 142; Stambaugh renders the German on p. 73, *sagenden Nichtsagen*, as "a telling silence." I have followed the translation offered by Bernasconi, *Question of Language*, p. 77. Heidegger's view of the poetic is captured in the Zen teaching cited in Hori, *Zen Sand*, p. 440: "On the road, if you meet an expert in the Way,/ Do not greet him with either words or silence." What lies between words and silence but the "saying not-saying," the unspoken that is spoken in speaking the unspoken? This seems to be the message implied in another adage in Hori, *Zen Sand*, p. 126: "Speech silenced." The simple reading would be that one's speaking is followed by silence, but a deeper understanding would cut through the duality such that speaking itself conveys silence. See also p. 187: "Close your mouth and say one word."

209. Heidegger, *Poetry, Language, Thought*, p. 11.

210. Raschke, *Fire and Roses*, pp. 4–5; Muldoon, "Silence Revisited," pp. 275–298, esp. pp. 289–292. For an interesting comparative discussion of the deconstructive tendency of language to transcend itself in its enunciation, see Loy, "Language against Its Own Mystifications," pp. 245–260. For discussion of the "poetics of the possible" in Heidegger's thought in relation to Kant's analysis of imagination, time, and the transcendental horizon of experience, see Kearney, *Poetics of Modernity*, pp. 14–17, 35–49.

211. See Heidegger, *History of the Concept of Time*, p. 267: "Just as hearing is constituitive of discourse, so also is silence. Only an entity whose being is defined by the ability to discourse can also be silent." For an instructive treatment of the role of silence in human discourse as the horizon of sound, which is influenced by Heidegger, see Ihde, *Sense and Significance*, pp. 61–68, 75–76; and Fiumara, *Other Side of Language*. In some measure, Heidegger's notion of silence as the condition for authentic language bespeaks the influence of the apophatic tradition in medieval Christian mysticism and especially the thought of Meister Eckhart. See, for

instance, Eckhart, *Sermons and Treatises*, vol. I, pp. 20–21: "Accordingly a master says: 'To achieve an interior act, a man must collect all his powers as if into a corner of his soul where, hiding away from all images and forms, he can get to work.' Here, he must come to a forgetting and an unknowing. There must be a stillness and a silence for this Word to make itself heard. We cannot serve this Word better than in stillness and in silence: *there* we can hear it, and there too we will understand it aright—in the unknowing. To him who knows nothing it appears and reveals itself" (emphasis in original). The influence is noted but qualified by Caputo, *Mystical Element*, pp. 224–225. According to Caputo, Heidegger pursued the renewal of language, the bringing of language into language, rather than the discovery of the primal word that is spoken eternally in its absolute silence which characterizes the mystical yearning of Eckhart. With respect to this matter, as Caputo also notes (p. 216), Eckhart is closer to the spirit of enlightenment in Zen Buddhism. For comparative analysis of Eckhart and Zen Buddhism, see Suzuki, *Mysticism*, pp. 3–35; and the remarks by Schürmann, "Trois penseurs du délaissement," pp. 56–60, English version in *Wandering Joy*, pp. 217–222. On the influence of Eckhart on Heidegger, see Helting, *Heidegger und Meister Eckehart;* and further references cited in chap. 3, n. 6. The primary emphasis placed on language as the house of being situates Heidegger's thinking in close proximity to the kabbalistic presumption regarding the effability of the ineffable and the linguistic articulation of mystical silence, saying the unsayable. Finally, it is worthwhile considering the Heideggerian perspective in conjunction with the statements of Wittgenstein cited and briefly discussed in chap. 6, nn. 162, 163, 165, 166, 168, 169, 171.

212. Heidegger, *Contributions*, p. 26.

213. Ibid., pp. 54–55.

214. Heidegger, *Parmenides*, p. 12.

215. Heidegger, *Identity and Difference*, p. 57.

216. Heidegger, *Being and Time*, p. 142.

217. Heidegger, *Poetry, Language, Thought*, p. 92.

218. Heidegger, *Contributions*, pp. 214, 228–229, 314–320.

219. Sallis, *Echoes*, pp. 98–100.

220. Heidegger, *On Time and Being*, pp. 4–5: "Time—a matter, presumably *the* matter of thinking, if indeed something like time speaks in Being as presence. Being *and* time, time *and* Being, name the relation of both issues, the matter at stake which holds both issues toward each other and endures their relation. To reflect upon this situation is the task of thinking, assuming that thinking remains intent on persisting in its matter. . . . Being, by which all beings as such are marked, means presencing. Thought with regard to what presences, presencing shows itself as letting-presence. . . . Letting shows its character in bringing into unconcealment. To let presence means: to unconceal, to bring to openness. In unconcealing prevails a giving, the giving that gives presencing, that is, Being, in letting-presence." See also pp. 12–14: "Presence means: the constant abiding that approaches man, reaches him, is extended to him. . . . With this presencing, there opens up what we call time-space. But with the word 'time' we no longer mean the succession of a sequence of nows. Accordingly, time-space no longer means merely the distance between two now-points of calculated time . . . . Time-space now is the name for the openness which opens up in the mutual self-extending of futural approach, past and present. This openness exclusively and primarily provides the space in which space as we usually know it can unfold."

221. Heidegger, *Contributions*, pp. 230–231, 259–271.

222. Sallis, *Echoes*, p. 172.

223. Merleau-Ponty, *Prose of the World*, pp. 5–6. I have also utilized the French edition *Prose du monde*. For a succinct but nuanced discussion of Merleau-Ponty's theory of language, see Ihde, *Sense and Significance*, pp. 162–178, and the more detailed analysis in Bucher, *Zwischen Phänomenologie und Sprachwissenschaft*.

224. Merleau-Ponty, *Prose of the World*, p. 14 (French ed., p. 22).

225. Merleau-Ponty, *Signs*, pp. 88–89.

226. Merleau-Ponty, *Visible and Invisible*, p. 52.

227. Ibid., p. 178 (French ed., p. 232). For a comparative study on the relationship of embodiment, language, and prelinguistic meaning in the writings of Merleau-Ponty and Wittgenstein, see Poppe, "*Monde vécu* and *Lebensform*."

228. Merleau-Ponty, *Visible and Invisible*, p. 35.

229. Ibid., p. 52 (French ed., p. 78). I have modified the translation "capacity for receiving the plentitude etc." by striking the word "receiving." It is worthwhile comparing Merleau-Ponty's notion of a prereflective consciousness that is "without inhabitant," the "nothing" or the "void," with eastern meditation techniques aimed at overcoming the dualism of subject and object by divesting the mind of all forms including the form of emptiness. For an interesting study along these lines, see Morley, "Inspiration and Expiration," pp. 73–82. Also worthy of consideration is Nagatomo, *Attunement through the Body*, index, s.v. Merleau-Ponty, and reference to study of Olson cited in Prologue, n. 69. It is of interest to note in this connection the observation of Kojima, *Monad and Thou*, pp. 141–143, that Merleau-Ponty's view of body has close affinity to his own conception of the somatic ego that inhabits the lifeworld, a perspective shaped in part by the legacy of Japanese philosophy. See also Guenther, *Teachings of Padmasambhava*, p. 166 n. 100.

230. Merleau-Ponty, *Visible and Invisible*, p. 185. It would be of interest to compare Merleau-Ponty's view to the depiction of epistemological phenomenalism given by Weyl, *Open World*, pp. 26–27: "The beginning of all philosophical thought is the realization that the perceptual world is but an image, a vision, a phenomenon of our consciousness; our consciousness does not directly grasp a transcendental real world as it appears. . . . The postulation of the real ego, of the thou and of the world, is a metaphysical matter, not judgment, but an act of acknowledgment and belief. But this belief after all is the soul of all knowledge. It was an error of idealism to assume that the phenomena of consciousness guarantee the reality of the ego in an essentially different and somehow more certain manner than the reality of the external world; in the transition from consciousness to reality the ego, the thou and the world rise into existence indissolubly connected and, as it were, at one stroke."

231. Merleau-Ponty, *Visible and Invisible*, p. 174.

232. For discussion of this critical term, see Kwant, *From Phenomenology to Metaphysics*, pp. 63–70.

233. On language as gesture, see Gill, *Merleau-Ponty and Metaphor*, pp. 82–104.

234. Merleau-Ponty, *Visible and Invisible*, pp. 130–155; on the distinction between "speech" and "language," see p. 175. On Merleau-Ponty's notion of intertwining whereby every object becomes a mirror for all other objects, see Levin, *Opening of Vision*, pp. 163.

235. Dastur, "World, Flesh, Vision," pp. 23–49; idem, *Chair et langage*, pp. 69–107.

236. Merleau-Ponty, *Visible and Invisible*, p. 235.

237. Many have written about the interface of body and language in Merleau-Ponty's writings. I offer a modest sampling of what is available: Kwant, *Phenomenological Philosophy of Merleau-Ponty*, pp. 46–62; idem, *From Phenomenology to Metaphysics*, pp. 54–63; Edie, *Merleau-Ponty's Philosophy of Language*; Dillon, *Merleau-Ponty's Ontology*, pp. 178–223; idem, "The Unconscious," pp. 67–83; Sato, "Incarnation of Consciousness," pp. 3–15; Maldiney, "Flesh and Verb," pp. 51–76. For a detailed study of the chiasm and speech, see Herkert, *Das Chiasma*.

238. Merleau-Ponty, *Visible and Invisible*, p. 171.

239. Ibid., p. 176 (French ed., p. 230). On the play of language and silence in Merleau-Ponty, see Kwant, *From Phenomenology to Metaphysics*, pp. 184–190.

240. Merleau-Ponty, *Visible and Invisible*, p. 179. See Waldenfels, "Paradox of Expression," pp. 89–102. With respect to the issue of the inherent ineffability of language, which is correlated with the invisibility at the heart of all that is visible, Merleau-Ponty anticipates a central concern of Derrida's deconstruction. See Margolis, "Philosophical Extravagance," pp. 112–132, esp. pp. 125–127.

241. I am not unaware of the many complicated issues raised by a scholar of Jewish mysticism utilizing a Heideggerian poetics to illumine the kabbalistic tradition, which, for the most part, crystallized in the Middle Ages. To do justice to these issues, however, would require a separate study. Perhaps one day my path shall lead me there, but suffice it here to say that I do not naïvely assume that Heidegger's thought can be entirely divorced from its historical context nor do I condone him for his moral failings. At the same time, I would not subscribe to the view that his thought can be reduced simply to his political engagement with Nazism. Here the turn of my thinking accords with the words uttered by Cornelius Castoriadis, a distinguished

French philosopher, political activist, and psychoanalyst, in *Critical Sense*, p. 8: "I don't think you can draw directly from philosophy, as such, political conclusions." This is not to deny the intricate links between the two but only to avoid setting up a simplistic causal relationship. See also the sage comments of Barash, *Heidegger and the Problem of Historical Meaning*, p. 225: "As reprehensible as Heidegger's political attitude and activity in 1933–34 might be, it in no way justifies explaining away the significance of his thought. Indeed, the attitude that would dismiss Heidegger's thought at a distance through labels such as the 'irrationalism of the times' and a 'destruction of reason' (Lukács) is vulnerable to the very accusations it makes—not only because Heidegger clearly came to appreciate the bankruptcy of Nazism, but, more fundamentally, because of the unwillingness of such an attitude to comprehend the seriousness of Heidegger's questioning of Western rationality and of Western intellectual traditions in general." From my perspective what is striking is that, repeatedly, Heidegger's thinking has provided useful language for philosophical discourse about kabbalistic esotericism. It is plausible that he was indeed influenced by this stream of thought, probably through an intermediary channel such as Böhme or Schelling (see Prologue, n. 2), but even that is not the central point as far as I am concerned. For representative studies that deal with the question of Heidegger's involvement with National Socialism, see Farías, *Heidegger and Nazism*; Bourdieu, *Political Ontology of Martin Heidegger*; Rockmore, *On Heidegger's Nazism and Philosophy*; Rockmore and Margolis, *Heidegger Case*; Löwith, *Martin Heidegger and European Nihilism*; Lang, *Heidegger's Silence*; Beistegui, *Heidegger and the Political*; Rickey, *Revolutionary Saints*. Also pertinent is the essay by Gibbs, "Reading Heidegger," pp. 157–172. For what appears to me to be a balanced approach that neither ignores the historical context of Heidegger's thought nor adopts a reductionist posture that subsumes the entirety of the philosophical project under the guise of the ideological, see Kovacs, "Being Truth, and the Political," pp. 31–48. The question of Heidegger's anti-Semitism has to be engaged in a broader conversation about attitudes toward Jews and Judaism expressed in German philosophy in the eighteenth and nineteenth centuries. For an illuminating study, see Mack, *German Idealism and the Jew*. See also Brumlik, *Deutscher Geist und Judenhaß*.

242. See Ouaknin, *Mysteries of the Kabbalah*, pp. 97–98: "For the kabbalah, the essence of the world is poetic. When speaking of the Kabbalah, one needs to find a language that offers an opening onto infinity. The great texts of the Kabbalah, especially the texts of the literature of the Palaces and later the Zohar, used poetic language. . . . Language and our understanding of the world begin in this preliminary region in which a set of complex correspondences echo each other and succeed in enabling us to experience the most infinite subtleties of our presence in the world. . . . Of course, the Kabbalah cannot be reduced merely to a piece of poetry, but its first language is that of poetry."

243. Interestingly, in his brief but incisive account of the "kabbalistic drift" of language, largely based on Scholem, Eco, *Semiotics and the Philosophy of Language*, p. 154, writes: "Language can be the place where things come authentically to begin: in Heidegger's hermeneutics the word is not 'sign' (*Zeichen*) but 'to show' (*Zeigen*), and what is shown is the true voice of Being." For this reference I am indebted to Idel, "Reification of Language in Jewish Mysticism," p. 50, who cites the comment of Eco in support of his presentation of the prominence of the visual dimension of letters as the image of God in theosophic kabbalah.

244. Thus, for instance, Knysh, *Islamic Mysticism*, pp. 150–151, discusses affinities between poetic expression and mystical experience as an introduction to an analysis of Sufi poetry. *Inter alia*, Knysh notes that poetry is often deemed the preferred vehicle to express mystical experience inasmuch as the "open-endedness" and "elasticity" of poetic language can suitably communicate the ineffable. For discussion of revelation and poetry, see Chittick, *Imaginal Worlds*, pp. 67–82. Scholem's distinguishing kabbalists on this score does not appear to me to be materially justifiable. Consider as well the intricate analysis of the shared "linguistic skepticism" of philosopher, mystic, and poet, which fosters an assault on language through language, in Zhang, *Tao and the Logos*, pp. 37–70.

245. Scholem, "Name of God," p. 194. For discussion of this passage, see Weigel, "Scholems Gedichte," pp. 21–23. See also the discussion of poiesis or *ars poetica* in Liebes, "Zohar and Eros," pp. 78–79. Other scholars who have focused on the poetical dimensions of kabbalah include Meged, "Kabbalah as Poetry," pp. 558–564; Grözinger, "Tradition and Innovation," pp. 347–355; Lévy-Valensi, *Poétique du Zohar*; Anidjar, *"Our Place in al-Andalus,"* pp. 166–245. See reference to Ouaknin above, n. 242. Also relevant here is the

argument proffered by Yates, *Occult Philosophy in the Elizabethan Age*, to the effect that English poetry was influenced by kabbalistic thought mediated through Renaissance Hermeticism and, in particular, the intriguing suggestion that the belief in the coincidence of darkness and light in the Godhead may lay behind the theme of the conjunction of Jerusalem and Albion. Beyond the significance of this conjecture for the diachronic charting of the history of ideas, the linkage of the poetic sensibility to the paradoxical identification of opposites provides a critical element in discerning the poiesis of kabbalah. On this score, it is worthwhile mentioning the view affirmed by Isaac ben Ḥayyim ha-Kohen of Sativa, *Eṣ Ḥayyim*, pp. 14–17, that music, which is identified in this treatise with poetry, has the ability to arouse in its listeners opposite emotional and psychological responses, to wit, joy and trepidation, strength and weakness. To the extent that this is case, one can speak of music as a coincidence of opposites. Consider also the following comment by Karel Sabina, "true poetry—the more original and alive its world, the more contradictory the contrasts in which the secret kinship occurs," cited in Jakobson, *Language in Literature*, p. 368.

246. Such an argument is advanced by Liebes, "Zohar and Eros," pp. 71–72.

247. Buber, *Ecstatic Confessions*, p. 10, noted that poet and mystic share the "impossible task" of "saying the unsayable." For an attempt to construct a theory of comparative mystical experience centered around this theme, which is presented as a way to explain the historical manifestation of mysticism amongst Muslims, Jews, and Christians in Spain from the twelfth to the sixteenth centuries, see McGaha, "Naming the Nameless," pp. 37–52. The effort of McGaha to highlight the possibility of a greater influence of Sufism on Spanish kabbalists, who in turn influenced Christian mystics, many of whom descended from Jewish converts, is laudable but, in my opinion, flawed, which is not to deny the importance of examining in more detail the influence and affinity between Islamic and Jewish esotericism in the Middle Ages (see my own discussion on the image of the veil below in chap. 5). This is a matter that lies beyond the scope of this study, and hence I shall refrain from commenting at length. Another attempt, also problematic in my judgment, to consider the two traditions is presented by Mir, "Kabbalah and Sufism," pp. 165–179. What is of interest to the discussion here is the fact that in McGaha's working taxonomy of mysticism he focused on the paradoxical naming of the nameless and numbering the infinite, traits (especially the former) that Scholem incorrectly marked as distinctive to kabbalists. For a comparative analysis of the use of silence in poetic and mystical discourse, see Longxi, *Tao and Logos*, pp. 73–129. Also consider the discussion of language, ontology, the doctrine of emptiness, ineffability, and silence in Cabezón, *Buddhism and Language*, pp. 153–187. For an incisive analysis of the import of words in medieval Buddhist thought, see Mookerjee, *Buddhist Philosophy of Universal Flux*, pp. 107–139. Though the author focuses on one school, he contends that the theory of *Apoha* he expounds, which denies that words possess a factual meaning either subjectively or objectively, applies universally to all Buddhist thinkers (pp. 112–113, 134). Language is a "convenient instrument for communication of concepts, which however are fictitious representatives of reality" (p. 139).

248. The orientation I am ascribing to medieval kabbalists bears a notable affinity to the following attempt of Dionysius the Areopagite to explain the Christological doctrine of incarnation in Neoplatonic emanationist terms, in the third letter addressed to Gaius, included in *Divine Names*, p. 226, 1069B: "I believe the theology has declared this in reference to the love of man in Christ: the beyond being [ὑπερούσιον] had proceeded from hiddenness into a manifest taking on of being in a human way. It is hidden after the manifestation; or, to speak more divinely, it is hidden in the manifestation. For this remains hidden about Jesus: the mystery in him is not brought forward by any logos or intellect, rather it remains ineffable in being spoken, and unknown in being thought [ἀλλὰ καὶ λεγόμενον ἄῤῥητον μένει καὶ νοούμενον ἄγνωστον]." A similar paradox related to the Incarnation is affirmed by Maximus the Confessor; see Balthasar, *Cosmic Liturgy*, pp. 96–97.

249. The postmodern logic, as it is formulated in the body of this chapter, resonates with the Mādhyamika philosophy cultivated by Nāgārjuna (see above, n. 61) whereby one discerns that identity and nonidentity are equally empty of meaningful significance, let alone ontic status.

250. For a fuller exposition of these themes, see E. Wolfson, "Divine Suffering."

251. For discussion of this principle of kabbalistic ontology and hermeneutics, see Scholem, *On the Kabbalah and Its Symbolism*, pp. 37–44; idem, "Name of God," pp. 78–80, 178–180, 193–194; Idel, "Concept of Torah," pp. 23–84, esp. pp. 49–58; Tishby, *Wisdom of the Zohar*, pp. 1079–1082.

252. Particularly pertinent is the brilliant analysis in Sandywell, *Reflexivity and the Crisis of Western Reason.*

253. The expression, which is perfectly appropriate to describe the medieval kabbalistic conception of Ein Sof, is derived from the explication of the apophatic theology of Dionysius the Areopagite offered by Nicholas of Cusa, *De Venatione Sapientiae,* 30, in *Complete Philosophical and Theological Treatises,* p. 1334.

254. Consider the remark of Plotinus, *Enneads* VI.1.9: "And some are what they are called by the same form, but others by opposed forms: for the double comes to one thing and the half to another simultaneously, and largeness comes to one thing at the same time as smallness to the other. Or both are in each thing, both likeness and unlikeness and, in a general sense, sameness and otherness."

255. An interesting example of this principle is offered by the Zen master Keizan (1268–1325), *Transmission of Light,* p. 81: "So you do not stay in the realm of nondiscrimination, you are not confined to the sphere of inconceivability. It is not permanent, not impermanent; it is not that the original mind has ignorance, nor is it that it is pure. When you arrive at the realm of pure clear complete illumination . . . everything conditioned and unconditioned is all ended and is like a dream, an illusion. Though you try to grasp, your hand is empty; though you try to see, nothing catches the eye."

256. Tishby, *Wisdom of the Zohar,* p. 275.

257. Abraham Abulafia, *Sitrei Torah,* MS Paris, Bibliothèque Nationale 774, fol. 149a (printed ed., p. 118). For further discussion of Abulafia's paradoxical approach to the problem of eternity versus creation, see chap. 2, n. 288. On the esoteric method of the concurrent concealment and disclosure of the secret in Abulafia, see E. Wolfson, *Abraham Abulafia,* pp. 81–88.

258. Sack, *Kabbalah of Rabbi Moshe Cordovero,* p. 57 n. 2. At the final stages of preparing this monograph, I received a copy of Fine, *Physician of the Soul.* Fine eloquently notes that the "vitality of Lurianic mysticism," at the level of "mythic imagination and ritual performance," is grounded in the dialectical tension between the messianic urge to disclose the secrets of Torah as a source of "life-giving nourishment" in the process of *tiqqun* (rectification), on one hand, and the recognition of the implicit lethal danger of revealing the esoteric meaning to the unworthy, on the other (p. 356). This is surely an important anthropological element that should be considered in addition to the mythopoeic hermeneutic that I have espoused; I see the approaches as complimentary and not contradictory.

259. For citation and discussion of some relevant sources, see E. Wolfson, "Divine Suffering," pp. 110–115. Scholem, *Messianic Idea in Judaism,* p. 293, duly noted, "those secret signatures (*rishumim*) that God had placed upon things are as much concealments of His revelation as revelation of His concealment." On the possible source for Scholem's term *rishumim* in Böhme's conception of *signatura rerum,* see Idel, "Hieroglyphs," p. 231.

260. For a richly nuanced study of this theme, see Chittick, "Paradox of the Veil in Sufism," pp. 59–85. See also idem, *Sufi Path of Knowledge,* pp. 230–231; idem, *Self-Disclosure of God,* pp. 104–108, 120–163; and the discussion in chap. 5 in the section entitled "Unveiling the Veil/Veiling the Unveiled."

261. Ibn Rushd, *Averroes' Tahafut al-Tahafut,* vol. 1, p. 281.

262. Wensinck, *Pensée de Ghazali,* p. 9, cited in Fakhry, *History of Islamic Philosophy,* p. 251.

263. Corbin, *Paradoxe du monothéisme,* pp. 7–18. It is relevant here to recall the comments of Mopsik, "Body of Engenderment," pp. 50–51: "There has been too marked a tendency to make a radical distinction between monotheism and polytheism, whether archaic or still practiced today. . . . At least where Judaism in concerned, we are able, thanks to the so-called esoteric literature it has produced, to undertake a radical critique of the so-called monotheistic split, a critique that serves the interests of religious reasoning through the theological power of the deepest aspirations of homo religiosus, perhaps the highest form of homo sapiens." See p. 60, where Mopsik refers explicitly to the expression "metaphysical idol of orthodox monotheism" used by Corbin in *Paradoxe du monothéisme.*

264. Corbin, *History of Islamic Philosophy,* p. 295.

265. For an extensive discussion of this concept, especially as it evolved in Iranian philosophy, see Izutsu, *Concept and Reality of Existence,* pp. 35–55. See also Chittick, *Imaginal Worlds,* pp. 15–29; idem, "Rūmī and *waḥdat al-wujūd,*" pp. 70–111.

266. Ibn al ʿArabi, *Meccan Revelations,* p. 182.

267. Ibid., p. 183. On the expression "He/not He" (*huwa lā huwa*), see Chittick, *Self-Disclosure*, pp. xxvi–xxvii, 29, 58.

268. Corbin, *History of Islamic Philosophy*, p. 307.

269. Scholem, *Origins*, p. 438 n. 170.

270. Chittick, *Sufi Path of Knowledge*, p. 364. For a more detailed discussion of this theme, see the elaborate treatment by Meier, "Problem of Nature," pp. 149–203.

271. Nasafī, "Kashf ul-ḥaqāʿiq," cited by Meier, "Problem of Nature," p. 176.

272. Nasafī, "Tanzīl ul-arwāḥ," cited by Meier, "Problem of Nature," p. 175. See the articulation of this point by Suhrawardī, *Book of Radiance*, pp. 41–42: "And, since the Necessary Being is unique, It has no equal or opposite. The multitude mean by 'opposite' that which is either contrary to something or equal to it in terms of power. Since all things are caused by the Necessary of Being, nothing is Its opposite."

273. Corbin, *Creative Imagination*, p. 215.

274. Ibid.

275. A number of writers have pointed to the central role of paradox in mystical expression, but a particularly relevant discussion is found in Stace, *Mysticism and Philosophy*, pp. 161–178. Stace's comment that this paradox is not found in Islamic mysticism (p. 177) cannot be upheld as even the brief discussion of the matter in this chapter proves beyond any shadow of doubt.

276. Izutsu, *Concept and Reality*, p. 17.

277. Ibid., p. 14.

278. Cupitt, *Mysticism after Modernity*, p. 58.

279. Jasper Hopkins, *On Learned Ignorance*, III:1–2, pp. 125–130; McGinn, "*Maximum Contractum et Absolutum*," pp. 151–175; idem, "*Unitrinum Seu Triunum*," pp. 90–117, esp. pp. 96–98. Needless to say, for Cusanus, a committed Christian, Jesus as the *Verbum incarnatum*, both divine and human, is the embodiment of the *coincidentia oppositorum* of the "absolute maximum" and the "contracted maximum," the "contracted maximum individual." See *On Learned Ignorance*, III:4, pp. 133–135.

280. *De Visione Dei*, in Jasper Hopkins, *Nicholas of Cusa's Dialectical Mysticism*, chap. 3, p. 123. See also Nicholas of Cusa, *On Learned Ignorance*, II:3, pp. 93–96; *De Quaerendo Deum* I:31, in Jasper Hopkins, *A Miscellany on Nicholas of Cusa*, p. 147: "the Beginning from which things flow forth, the Middle in which we are moved, and the End unto which things flow back."

281. *De Venatione Sapientae* 29, in Nicholas of Cusa, *Complete Philosophical and Theological Treatises*, p. 1332.

282. *De Visione Dei*, in Jasper Hopkins, *Nicholas of Cusa's Dialectical Mysticism*, chap. 5, p. 133 and chap. 12, p. 175. On the gaze of Jesus in which "human vision," a vision limited by a bodily organ, and the "absolute and infinite" vision are combined, see ibid., chap. 22, pp. 237–247; and the analysis by Bond, "'Icon' and the 'Iconic Text,'" pp. 177–197.

283. Jasper Hopkins, *Nicholas of Cusa's Dialectical Mysticism*, chap. 2, p. 121.

284. *De Dato Patris Luminum*, 4, translated in Jasper Hopkins, *Nicholas of Cusa's Metaphysic of Contraction*, p. 126.

285. Harries, *Infinity and Perspective*, pp. 260–261.

286. See, for instance, *De Deo Abscondito*, 9, in Jasper Hopkins, *Miscellany*, p. 134.

287. Nicholas of Cusa, *On Learned Ignorance*, I:16, p. 68.

288. Ibid., II:2, pp. 92–93.

289. Stace, *Mysticism and Philosophy*, p. 212, refers to the "proposition that the world is both identical with, and different from, God" as the "pantheistic paradox." I do not see any substantial difference between this view and the one I have articulated, but for semantic reasons I have preferred "panenhenic" to "pantheistic." See below, n. 325.

290. Babylonian Talmud, Pesaḥim 50a. The influence of this dictum is evident in *Zohar* 3:143a (*Idra Rabba*), as noted in Scholem, *Gershom Scholem's Annotated Zohar*, vol. 3, p. 1475.

291. *Zohar* 2:100b.

292. To offer another formulation, in some of the manuscript versions of *Shaʿarei Ṣedeq*, a treatise composed in the latter part of the thirteenth or early part of fourteenth century by a disciple of Abraham Abulafia

(Idel, *Le Porte della Giustizia,* pp. 47–51, identifies the author as Natan ben Saʿadyah Harʾar), we find the following comment on the letters *alef, mem, shin,* the three "mothers" according to the threefold division of the twenty-two Hebrew letters in the second part of *Sefer Yeṣirah,* three mothers (*immot*), seven doubles (*kefulot*), and twelve singles (*peshuṭot*): "*Alef, mem, shin,* for the supernal fire [*ha-esh ha-elyon*] acts upon the lower [*ha-poʿel ba-taḥton*], and his will is above and below, for when the two are conjoined [*be-hidabbequt*] the supernal rests on the lower," translated from *Shaʿarei Ṣedeq: Beʾur Sefer Yeṣirah,* p. 40.

293. On the image of mirroring as a creative redoubling and reflecting in the artistic process of imitation, see Burwick, "Reflections in the Mirror," pp. 122–140. Burwick's thesis is a response to M. Abrams, *Mirror and the Lamp.*

294. My formulation is indebted to the insightful comments by M. Roberts, *Poetry and the Cult of the Martyrs,* p. 194 n. 11, which are based in turn on the definition of metaphor offered by Eco, *Semiotics and the Philosophy of Language,* pp. 87–129, esp. pp. 104–106. An interesting exception is found in Azriel of Gerona's exegetical gloss on the warning in *Sefer Yeṣirah* to impede the heart from contemplating the *sefirot* (1:5), "not to compare the hidden to the revealed" (*she-lo ledammot ha-nistar la-gilluy*), in *Kitvei Ramban,* 2:458. It is fair to say that no kabbalist, including Azriel, heeded this warning faithfully, for if that were the case, there would be no depiction of the concealed reality, and, consequently, there would be no written or verbal account of the divine realm, whether allusive or discursive. Indeed, in several passages in the very same treatise, Azriel recommends that one must contemplate the concealed from the revealed. See citation in chap. 5, n. 58.

295. Based on the suggestive language used to describe the journey of Moses in Qurʾān 18: 60. For a rich analysis of this motif, see Sviri, *Taste of Hidden Things,* pp. 77–101.

296. Baḥya ben Asher, *Rabbenu Baḥya,* 3:472 (ad Lev. 12:2).

297. See, for instance, Maimonides, *Mishneh Torah,* Yesodei ha-Torah 1:10, 4:8–9. For discussion of the legacy of Platonic logocentrism in Jewish philosophical speculation, see Jospe, "Superiority of Oral over Written Communication," pp. 127–156.

298. E. Wolfson, "Ontology, Alterity, and Ethics," pp. 129–155. See chap. 5, n. 127.

299. This is not to deny the anthropocentric tendency of kabbalistic symbolism, which accords a special status to the human being (understood as referring ideally to the Jewish male) in the sublunar world. See, for instance, Moses de León, *Sefer ha-Mishkal,* p. 39. Nevertheless, the same kabbalists affirm a more monistic or panentheistic approach, viewing all beings as an expression of the one divine substance. In the mystical expression of Islam, one finds a similar identification of God, human, and world. See Fakhry, *History of Islamic Philosophy,* p. 249.

300. A typical account is offered by Azriel of Gerona, *Commentary on Talmudic Aggadoth,* pp. 32–33: "Each and every person has a root (*shoresh*) in the divine, and in accord with the level of his attributes he is rooted in him, and he is conjoined to his holiness, for the soul (*neshamah*) emanates from the holy spirit, and it is the form of the body, bestowing upon it the power to carry out its deeds, and if it were not so, man would not have the power to do good or evil or to fulfill his desire."

301. Jacob ben Sheshet, *Sefer Meshiv Devarim Nekhoḥim,* p. 74.

302. See Scholem, *Major Trends,* pp. 216–217 (in that context, Scholem advances the interesting argument that the identification of the development of "God's personality" with human experience prevented kabbalists from focusing on divine immanence and depersonalizing God, which he considers "one of the main pitfalls of pantheism"); idem, *On the Kabbalah and Its Symbolism,* pp. 127–128; and the wide-ranging essay by Altmann, *Studies in Religious Philosophy,* pp. 1–40, esp. pp. 14–28. I detect the influence of Altmann's approach in the comments by Daniel Matt in the introduction to his edition of David ben Yehudah he-Ḥasid, *Book of Mirrors,* pp. 21–22, a revised version of the doctorate written under Altmann's supervision: "In tracing the reality of each *sefirah,* the mystic uncovers layers of being within himself and throughout the cosmos." See also the evocative but underdeveloped insight of Tishby, *Wisdom of the Zohar,* p. 271, that the *sefirot* "are seen as spiritual forces, as attributes of the soul, or as means of activity within the Godhead, that is to say, as revelations of the hidden God, both to Himself and to that which is other than He. The fundamental element in this revelation is His emergence from the depths of limitless infinity."

303. The term is borrowed from Panikkar, *Cosmotheandric Experience.*

304. *Kitvei Ramban*, 2:395.

305. On the use of the word *dugma* to denote the sefirotic "archetype," see the passage from Menaḥem Recanati cited by Scholem, *On the Kabbalah and Its Symbolism*, p. 124. In zoharic texts and in the Hebrew writings of Moses de León, *dugma* denotes the mundane instantiation of the sefirotic archetype. See, e.g., *Zohar* 1:59b; Moses de León, *Shushan Edut*, pp. 350 and 363; idem, *Book of the Pomegranate*, pp. 161, 206, 243, 316; idem, *R. Moses de Leon's Sefer Sheqel ha-Qodesh*, p. 51; idem, *She'elot u-Teshuvot le-R. Moshe di li'on be-Inyyenei Qabbalah*, pp. 40 and 44; idem, *Sefer ha-Mishkal*, pp. 42, 45. The use of the word *dugma* in kabbalistic literature reflects the long and varied history of the term in the lexicon of Jewish textual interpretation from late antiquity through the Middle Ages. See Kamin, *Jews and Christians*, pp. 13–30. Kamin focuses on *dugma* in Rashi's commentary on the Song, but her insights are helpful for understanding something of the exegetical legacy inherited by kabbalists. See reference cited in chap. 8, n. 25.

306. For discussion of this motif, see my study on the interpretative evolution of the mythopoeic theme of the image of Jacob engraved on the throne in *Along the Path*, pp. 1–62, esp. pp. 4–9.

307. Kirk and Raven, *Presocratic Philosophers*, p. 344; Empedocles, *Extant Fragments*, pp. 44, 72–73, 76, 233–235.

308. *Zohar* 1:137b; cf. Hebrew parallel in Moses de León, *Book of the Pomegranate*, p. 144. Similar formulations appear in other zoharic passages; see *Zohar* 1:20b, 126b, 167b; 2:111a, 141a; 3:169a, 234b (*Ra'aya Meheimna*), 263b (*Piqqudin*); *Zohar Ḥadash*, 18b.

309. Moses de León, *Book of the Pomegranate*, p. 244; see idem, *Sefer ha-Mishkal*, p. 46.

310. The idea I am attributing to kabbalists is made on numerous occasions by Meister Eckhart; see, e.g., *Sermons and Treatises*, 1:163: "Our masters say union presupposes likeness. Union cannot be without likeness." Insofar as there can be no real resemblance between God and all other beings in the ontological chain, the likeness to God is achieved through the soul withdrawing from all images, a kenotic act that transforms the soul into the virgin ground wherein the Son is eternally born. See pp. 4–5: "And you must know too that inwardly the soul is free and void of all means and all images—which is *why* God can freely unite with her without form or likeness. . . . But God needs *no* image and has no image: without any means, likeness or image God operates in the soul—right in the ground where no image ever got in, but only He Himself with His own being. . . . See, it is like this and in no other way that God the Father gives birth to the Son in the ground and essence of the soul, and thus unites with her. For if any image were present there would be no real union, and in that real union lies the soul's whole beatitude" (emphasis in original). See chap. 5, n. 162. Compare as well the formulation of this idea in the fifteenth century by Nicholas of Cusa, *De Dato Patris Luminum*, in Jasper Hopkins, *Nicholas of Cusa's Metaphysic of Contraction*, pp. 118–120: "The Giver of forms does not give something other than Himself; rather, His gift is best and is His own maximal goodness, which is absolute and in every respect maximum. But it cannot be received as it is given, because the receiving of the gift occurs in a descending manner. . . . For [one thing] cannot be received in another thing except in a manner other than [it is in itself]. For example, your face, in the course of multiplying from itself a close resemblance [*aequalitas*] of the facial features, is received in a mirror otherwise [than your face is in itself]—according as the mirror (i.e., [according as] the receiving) varies. In the one [mirror the face is received] more clearly, for the mirror-reception is clearer; in another, [it is received] more dimly; but in no [mirror] is it ever [received] as it is. For it will have to be received in something other [than itself] in a manner other [than it is in itself]. There is only one Mirror without flaw, viz., God Himself, in whom [what is received] is received as it is. For it is not the case that this Mirror is *other* than any existing thing; rather, in every existing thing, it is that which is, for it is the Universal Form of being. . . . By means of such a likeness [we see that] as the form of light is related to the form of colors, so God (who is Infinite Light) is related as the Universal Form of being to the forms of created things." The depiction of God as the "Form of forms" or as the "Absolute form," the "maximum actual being," is repeated on several occasions in the writings of Cusanus. See Jasper Hopkins, *On Learned Ignorance*, I:70, p. 78; idem, *Nicholas of Cusa's Dialectical Mysticism*, p. 123. Insofar as God is the Universal Form of being, the forms of all beings are enfolded within him in the manner that the form of all colors is contained in the form of light. Accordingly, the mind of God may be characterized metaphorically as the mirror in which everything is reflected. The forms, moreover, are mani-

fest in nature, and hence the latter can be viewed as well as the mirror through which the image of God as the one that is "all in all" is seen. For discussion of the "world as theophany" in Nicholas of Cusa, see Hopkins, *Nicholas of Cusa's Metaphysic of Contraction*, pp. 33–57. For a different perspective on the question of omnipresence and divine immanence, see the comparative analysis of Brient, "Meister Eckhart and Nicholas of Cusa," pp. 127–150.

311. *Kitvei Ramban*, 2: 511.

312. For discussion of creation and emanation in medieval kabbalah, see Hayoun, *Zohar aux origins*, pp. 219–259.

313. The terminology *sheteim esreh zero*ʿ*ot olam* is derived from *Sefer Yeṣirah* 5:1, where it is used to describe the twelve diagonals, *gevulei ukhlusin*, the spatial boundaries of the world, which are related, in turn, to the twelve simples, one of the three divisions of the twenty-two letters, the other two being the three mothers and seven doubles.

314. Ezra does not elaborate on the meaning of *zayin*, but Vajda, *Commentaire*, p. 122, translates it as "sept continents."

315. *Zohar* 1:129a. See 145b: "R. Jose said, Certainly, all that the holy One, blessed be he, made in the earth was through the mystery of wisdom, and it was entirely to illustrate the supernal wisdom to humankind."

316. *Zohar* 1:38a. See as well *Zohar* 1:158b, 240b; 2:20a (*Midrash ha-Ne*ʿ*elam*).

317. *Zohar* 2:15b.

318. Coulter, *Literary Microcosm*, pp. 32–72.

319. *Zohar* 1:70b.

320. Moses de León is explicating the expression *eser sefirot belimah* in the first part of *Sefer Yeṣirah*, rendering the last word as *beli mah*, "without being," and, apparently, applying it to the infinite source whence the *sefirot* emanate, the faceless light illumined by the luminous faces of the *sefirot*. The apophatic interpretation of the expression *sefirot belimah* is found as well in de León's *Book of the Pomegranate*, p. 376. In an earlier treatise, de León offered a diametrically opposite explanation for the expression *belimah*. See Moses de León, "Moses de León's *Sefer Or Zaru*ʿ*a*," p. 254: "And here you can understand the secret of the matter of the ten *sefirot belimah*, without his being [*beli mahuto*], blessed be he." For a slightly different explanation, see p. 266. The gloss *beli mahuto* is meant to challenge those who would claim that the *sefirot* are of the same substance as God, a position that de León himself affirmed in his later theosophic compositions. As Altmann observed, "*Sefer Or Zaru*ʿ*a*," p. 254 n. 81, a similar exegesis of *belimah* is found in Gikatilla, *Ginnat Egoz*.

321. Moses de León, *Shushan Edut*, p. 333.

322. The imaging of weighing on the holy scale alludes here to the process of symbolization by means of which two disparate things are rendered equal without compromising their difference just as two entities are balanced on a scale. See chap. 5, n. 219.

323. Moses de León, *Shushan Edut*, pp. 354–355; see parallel in idem, *Book of the Pomegranate*, p. 243.

324. Scholem, *Major Trends*, p. 223; see idem, *Kabbalah*, pp. 147–152. Scholem's position is reaffirmed by Tishby, *Wisdom of the Zohar*, p. 549: "Kabbalistic cosmogony, therefore, is really a framework for theogonic processes, that is, for stages in the revelation and embodiment of divine forces in the world of emanation." See ibid., p. 272. In spite of recognizing the convergence of the cosmogonic and theogonic, Tishby, p. 549, maintained that kabbalists distinguished the "divine cosmos in the system of the *sefirot*" and the "nondivine cosmos, that is, a system of worlds and of spiritual and corporeal entities outside the realm of the Godhead." Tishby's approach has been reiterated recently by Oron, "Three Commentaries to the Story of Genesis," pp. 183–184. While I would not deny that kabbalists struggled with this question and that they did develop a terminology that lends itself to such a distinction, I would nonetheless contend that in the final analysis there cannot be a being, let alone a universe of beings, that is nondivine. I am well aware of the fact that the genre of commentaries on *ma*ʿ*aseh bere*ʾ*shit* suggests different approaches, some kabbalists emphasizing a continuous emanation and others distinguishing emanation from volitional creation. See Gottlieb, *Studies in the Kabbala Literature*, pp. 18–28, 59–87. Many of the relevant texts are conveniently described and partially

transcribed in Asher ben David, *R. Asher ben David: His Complete Works*, pp. 301–353. See also S. Brody, "Human Hands Dwell in Heavenly Heights," p. 126: "On an ontological level, the divine and phenomenal realms constitute a single interlinked continuum."

325. Scholem, *Major Trends*, pp. 221–224, used the term "pantheism" when discussing passages from zoharic and related kabbalistic literature that affirm the unbroken chain of being. In the main, I am in agreement with Scholem's analysis, but I have used the word "panenhenism" instead of "pantheism" to avoid the theological quagmire traditionally associated with the latter term. I readily admit, however, that "panenhenism" may not fare any better. On this term, see above, n. 289.

326. Moses de León, *She'elot u-Teshuvot*, pp. 40 and 44.

327. Moses de León, *Book of the Pomegranate*, pp. 102–103.

328. Moses de León, *Sefer ha-Mishkal*, pp. 42 and 45.

329. Scholem, *On the Kabbalah and Its Symbolism*, pp. 122–123.

330. Liebes, *Studies in the Zohar*, p. 38. Consider also Tishby's depiction of the "model" (*dugma*) or "image" (*demut*) as "static," in *Wisdom of the Zohar*, p. 1159. The context in which this occurs is his discussion of the relationship between the commandments and *sefirot*. While I surely have no qualms with the notion of a "dynamic conception" of this relationship (see brief discussion in E. Wolfson, "Mystical Rationalization," p. 225), I do not think it necessary to set this in contrast to the symbolic, here demarcated philologically in the terms *dugmah* and *demut*. In this matter, I concur with Liebes as well as with Idel, *Kabbalah: New Perspectives*, pp. 222–234, who has emphasized the dynamism of kabbalistic symbolism, epitomized in the remark that for the kabbalist a symbol invites "one to act rather than to think" (p. 223). I do not think, however, that the dynamism can be affirmed only at the expense of rejecting Scholem's insight that the symbol in kabbalistic tradition is related to the expression of an inexpressible reality. Indeed, I would argue that the dynamism stems precisely from the paradox of naming the nameless, ascribing form to the formless.

331. Eco, *Search for the Perfect Language*, p. 25.

332. *Zohar* 2:190b.

333. *Book Bahir*, sec. 92, p. 177. All references in this book to the *Bahir* are taken from this edition; translations are my own.

334. I am not generally in the habit of using such militaristic language when describing a phenomenon hermeneutically, but I have here followed the path laid out by Liebes, *Ars Poetica*, pp. 9–30, where the matter of interpretation is described as destruction (*harisah*) of the other's point of view. This is not the place to unpack this rather alarming metaphorical way of depicting the hermeneutical task, but let me surmise that, in part, Liebes is influenced by an account of interpretation as waging battle found on occasion in zoharic texts, especially the beginning of *Idra Rabba*, 3:127b, based on earlier rabbinic descriptions of the *beit midrash*, the rabbinic study-house, as Liebes himself notes, *Studies in the Zohar*, pp. 21–22. In a preliminary way, I have dealt with the substance of the claim in E. Wolfson, "Text, Context, and Pretext." On this score, compare Heidegger, *Kant and the Problem of Metaphysics*, p. 138: "every interpretation must necessarily use violence. Such violence, however, cannot be roving arbitrariness. The power of an idea which shines forth must drive and guide the laying-out [*Auslegung*]. Only in the power of this idea can an interpretation risk what is always audacious, namely, entrusting itself to the concealed inner passion of a work in order to be able, through this, to place itself within the unsaid and force it into speech." For discussion of Heidegger's notion of strife (*Streit*) related especially to the poet's violence, understood as the task to wrest phenomena out of the reification of everyday experience and to return them to the "interplay of concealment and unconcealment," the "ekstatic intertwining of the visible and the invisible," see Levin, *Philosopher's Gaze*, pp. 129–132.

335. For scholarly discussions of the geometric aspect of the kabbalistic symbolism, see Pachter, "Circles and Straightness," pp. 59–90; Elior, "Metaphorical Relation," pp. 54–55.

336. I have utilized the expression "linear circularity" to characterize time in a number of previous studies, but the fullest exposition thereof is to be found in the second chapter of the forthcoming volume, *Alef, Mem, Tau*. See E. Wolfson, "Assaulting the Border," p. 502; idem, "Before Alef / Where Beginnings End," p. 147. In "Cut That Binds," p. 104, I offer a brief account of recollection as that which "transcends the linearity of time by gathering together past, present, and future in the circular resumption of what has never

been." Since penning those words, I have found support for my conception in the writings of Nicholas of Cusa, who similarly envisioned the compresence of circularity and linearity, or in the precise language that he utilizes, "in a circle oneness and infinity coincide—a oneness of essence and an infinity of angles. . . . Thus, the circle is both one and infinite; and it is the actuality of all the angles that are formable from a line"; *De Theologicis Complementis* 9, in *Complete Philosophical and Theological Treatises*, p. 761. See the extended discussion of the infinity of man and the infinity of God in Harries, *Infinity and Perspective*, pp. 160–183, with particular sensitivity to the emphasis placed "on the human power of self-transcendence that links Petrarch to a mystic like Meister Eckhart (1260–ca. 1328), and links both to St. Augustine" (p. 160).

337. *Zohar* 3:187a (for reference to Liebes, see below, n. 340).

338. In the Mantua edition of *Zohar* and all subsequent printings based thereon, the *yanuqa* discourses are placed in the section on *Balaq*, 3:186a–192a, whereas in the Cremona edition they appear in the section on *Devarim*, 485–496. The discrepancy is reflective of two distinct manuscript traditions, as noted by Scholem, *Major Trends*, p. 161; Tishby, *Wisdom of the Zohar*, p. 3.

339. An enigmatic figure mentioned sporadically in zoharic literature; see *Zohar* 1:6a, 7a, 8a; 2:124a; 3:145b (*Idra Rabba*); *Zohar Ḥadash* 97b–c (*Tiqqunim*).

340. Liebes, *Studies in the Zohar*, p. 179 n. 116.

341. In my judgment, this statement is equally true for the so-called theosophic and ecstatic kabbalists, though, of course, the way the nature of the *sefirot* is explained by devotees of each respective group may differ. For a different approach, see Idel, *Kabbalah: New Perspectives*, pp. 200–210.

342. Moses de León, *She'elot u-Teshuvot*, p. 40.

343. *Zohar* 1:22a. The relevant sources were cited and explained in the doctoral dissertation by Yehuda Liebes published as *Sections of the Zohar Lexicon*, p. 182 n. 45.

344. Dillon, "Aletheia, Poiesis, and Eros," p. 17, defines poiesis as the "generation of a narrative that, once espoused by a community, becomes a social form." This seems to me an appropriate use of the term when applied to the kabbalistic material.

345. It is possible to view the convergence of the theomorphic and anthropomorphic as emerging exegetically from Hebrew scripture, and, in particular, from the Priestly account of man having been created in God's image (Gen. 1:26–27) and Ezekiel's depiction of the enthroned glory "in the image of the appearance of a man" (Ezek. 1:26). For an insightful comparison of the two accounts, see Kutsko, *Between Heaven and Earth*, pp. 59–70.

346. Chittick, *Imaginal Worlds*, p. 89, uses the expression "imaginal embodiment," a term that obviously resonates with Corbin, who has influenced my own conception of "imaginal body." Additionally, the view I am expressing parallels the comments of Waghorne, "Body for God," pp. 20–47. See also Rudhart, "Coherence and Incoherence," pp. 14–42, esp. pp. 38–39. By accepting this understanding of the symbol as the means by which one envisions the invisible, I do not mean to suggest that this constitutes in and of itself the essence of the religious phenomenon. To explain the dynamic of religion as a cultural phenomenon, one must take into account social factors that would explain the specific needs to which this envisioning might respond. Here one would do well to consider the remarks of Gauchet, *Disenchantment of the World*, p. 102: "In order for religion to exist, it was necessary for individuals' spontaneous psychological and intellectual functioning to adapt itself specifically to its investment in the invisible. And the otherworldly perspective, and the confrontation with otherness, most certainly constitute a major organizing factor of the human imagination. Similarly, the encounter with the undifferentiated, unrepresentable infinite presents an ineradicable horizon for structuring thought, just as the double-edged and contradictory experience of self-abrogation and inextinguishable self-presence echoes, at the deepest level, the problematic tension determines being-a-subject. But that tension does not make this substratum a creative principle. It does not tell us what religions' essential function was, and consequently tells us nothing about their internal logic and the possible ramifications of successive changes to their content."

347. The eloquently simple phrase "real but not actual" is utilized by Wieseltier, *Kaddish*, p. 122, to describe the existence of "immaterial" and "intelligible" objects or propositions that constitute the "realm of reason," which, in his opinion, "leads directly to the realm of religion, in the sense that religion, too,

traffics in real but not actual entities." Wieseltier contends, moreover, that this notion of reason poses a challenge to the materialist conception of mind and hence it is "not the enemy of mysticism" (p. 123). Wieseltier alludes to the same idea when he remarks in another passage, "Rationalists are more like mystics than like materialists" (p. 359). In the session dedicated to Wieseltier's *Kaddish* at the 34th Annual Association for Jewish Studies Conference, held in Los Angeles, December 2002, I explored in some detail the embryonic understanding of mysticism implicit in these remarks, but suffice it here to say that what interested me most is the understanding that the mystical is not synonymous with the irrational or even the suprarational; it is, rather, congruent with the rational inasmuch as it presupposes an idealized realm of "real" but not "actual" objects that are subject to critical scrutiny even if belief ultimately cannot be reduced to a matter of demonstrative reason.

348. For some relatively recent discussions of the phenomenon, see Finney, *Invisible God*; Kessler, *Spiritual Seeing*; Besançon, *Forbidden Image*.

349. Corbin, *Paradoxe du monothéisme*, pp. 9–10; idem, *History of Islamic Philosophy*, p. 161.

350. The view I have espoused accords with the notion of "metaphorical thinking in mysticism" promoted by Izutsu, *Creation and the Timeless Order of Things*, pp. 39–42.

351. Jacob ben Sheshet, *Sefer Meshiv Devarim Nekhoḥim*, p. 75.

352. Ibid., p. 76.

353. On this score it is of interest to note that the fourteenth-century apostate Abner of Burgos signaled out the doctrine of incarnation as the "root of faith of the kabbalah" (*la rayz de la fe de la cabala*). See Scholem, "The Beginnings of Christian Kabbalah," p. 27.

354. See above, n. 251. This is not to rule out the possibility that the scriptural roots of the Christological doctrine of incarnation in the prologue to the Gospel of John may preserve an ancient Jewish esoteric motif centered on the embodiment of wisdom/Torah in human form. The identification of the latter with Jesus may represent the specific Christian application of the Logos theology of Judaic gnosis. For two recent philologically competent and theoretically sophisticated studies advocating this approach, see Eskola, *Messiah and the Throne*; and Endo, *Creation and Christology*. See also Schimanowski, *Die himmlische Liturgie*. The thesis that the prologue of the fourth evangelist should be studied as an exegesis of the first chapter of Genesis was explored by Borgen, *Philo, John and Paul*, pp. 75–101. On the possible connection between the Logos Christology in the Gospel of John and the Jewish Christian conception of the hypostasized name expressed, for instance, in the *Gospel of Truth* and *Gospel of Philip*, see Longenecker, *Christology of Early Jewish Christianity*, pp. 41–46; Fossum, *Name of God and the Angel of the Lord*, pp. 106–112, 125–127; Quispel, "Qumran, John and Jewish Christianity," pp. 137–155, esp. pp. 149–154. For other representative studies that emphasize the Jewish milieu of the fourth gospel, see Schoneveld, "Torah in the Flesh," pp. 77–94; B. Mack, "The Christ and Jewish Wisdom," pp. 192–221; Boyarin, "The Gospel of the *Memra*," pp. 243–284. The Jewish milieu of the fourth gospel, including the suggestion that Hebrew-Aramaic idioms are detectable beneath the surface of the Greek, was a prime focus of the work of Dodd, *Interpretation of the Fourth Gospel*, and especially pertinent is his discussion of the doctrine of the Logos in the prologue (pp. 263–285). On the possible background of the fourth gospel in the synagogue rite of the Palestinian triennial cycle, see Guilding, *The Fourth Gospel and Jewish Worship*. Also relevant to this discussion is the presentation of Jesus as an angelic form implied in some passages in the fourth gospel (see comments of Augustine, *De Trinitate* 2.5.23), an idea that may be rooted in the soil of Jewish apocalyptic, wherein the righteous soul is depicted as one who is angelically transformed. For references, see chap. 5, n. 134. Hurtado, *One God, One Lord*, argues for a Jewish matrix to explain the binitarian pattern of devotion in early Christian piety, linked, as it was, with the representation of God through the garb of angelic mediation. See idem, "Binitarian Shape of Early Christian Worship," pp. 187–213; and the later assessment in idem, *Lord Jesus Christ*, pp. 32–53; on the depiction of Jesus as the glory of God and as the divine name, see pp. 374–389. O'Neill, *Who Did Jesus Think He Was?* pp. 94–114, suggests that the trinity and incarnation were "Jewish doctrines." On the Jewish milieu of the incarnational doctrine of early Christianity, see also Dearman, "Theophany, Anthropomorphism, and the *Imago Dei*," pp. 31–46; and A. Segal, "The Incarnation," pp. 116–139. Also pertinent here is the study by Jonge, "Monotheism and Christology," pp. 225–237. On the divine status accorded the glorious angel in the history of Judaism and its

impact on Christianity, see Barker, *Great Angel*; idem, "High Priest and the Worship of Jesus," pp. 93–111; idem, *Great High Priest*, pp. 103–145; Gieschen, *Angelomorphic Christology*. In *Through a Speculum*, pp. 255–263, I discussed the impact of this archaic exegetical tradition on the depiction of the glorious angel and angelic glory in various streams of medieval Jewish esotericism. See chap. 5, n. 134. In emphasizing the Jewish background to the Johannine Christology, one should not neglect to take into account the preponderant negative stance toward Jews and Judaism sponsored by the author of this gospel. See the proceedings of an international conference dedicated to this theme published in Bieringer, et al., *Against Judaism and the Fourth Gospel*. In fact, one might even argue that it is precisely the Jewish background and foreground of the fourth evangelist that accounts for such strident opposition to "the Jews." On the Jewish background of John, see W. Davies, *Christian Engagements*, pp. 188–209. I have explored incarnational elements in classical rabbinic texts, related specifically to prayer; for references, see Preface, n. 5.

355. *Zohar* 1:134b.

356. Meir Ibn Gabbai, *Avodat ha-Qodesh*, pt. 2, chap. 20, p. 129.

357. Scholem, *On the Kabbalah and Its Symbolism*, p. 65. See *Zohar* 1:21b–22a, where the 600,000 male Israelites over the age of twenty are correlated with aspects of the supernal Jubilee, *Binah*. We are also told in this passage that after the death of his body, Moses ascended by means of the holy spirit to *Binah* to join these 600,000 aspects that belong to him. It is likely that these aspects correspond to the lower six *sefirot* centered in *Tif'eret*, which corresponds symbolically to Moses. The kabbalistic association of Moses and the 600,000 Israelites is based on the earlier aggadic motif that the clan of Moses equaled the number of Israelites. For references, see Ginzberg, *Legends of the Jews*, vol. 6, p. 97 n. 540. An interesting variation on the kabbalistic interpretation of the aggadic theme is found in Bachrach, *Emeq ha-Melekh*, chap. 16, p. 843: "The totality of souls is 600,000, and the Torah is the root of the souls of Israel, and thus there are 600,000 explanations, and from each and every one of the 600,000 a root of one soul in Israel comes to be."

358. *Zohar* 1:2b; 2:126b; 3:145a (*Piqqudin*); Moses de León, *Book of the Pomegranate*, pp. 6, 137, 354; E. Wolfson, "Mystical Rationalization," p. 242.

359. Lefebvre, *Introduction to Modernity*, pp. 174–175. On the link of the poet and incarnation in Baudelaire's aesthetic, see Starobinski, *Largesse*, pp. 127–129.

360. For an interesting application of the kabbalistic orientation in modern Jewish art, see Wechsler, "Eli Lissitzky's 'Interchange Stations,'" pp. 187–200. I am grateful to the author for drawing my attention to her study.

361. I am using the term "abyss" as synonymous with Ein Sof, the limitless that determines the limit of what cannot be delimited. On the identification of abyss and the infinite, see Reuchlin, *On the Art of the Kabbalah*, p. 285.

362. This description of the poem is indebted to the view of Paul Celan, which in turn has affinity with the thought of Heidegger. See Lacoue-Labarthe, *Poetry as Experience*, p. 67: "In other words, poetry's questioning is meta-physical questioning itself, in the sense that it is the repetition of the meta-physical as Heidegger understands it. It questions in the direction of being as 'transcendence as such.' Just such a 'transcendent' is sought in the singular thing or being it is incumbent upon poetry—the poem—to perceive (think): it is the 'wholly other' . . . . In this sense, the poetic act is ecstatic. The exorbitant is the pure transcendence of being. It follows that the poem, as a questioning, is turned toward the open, offered up to it. And the open is itself open, after a fashion, to u-topia, to the place without place of the advent. To put it in other terms, the poetic act is catastrophic: an upsetting relation to what is an upset, in the direction of no-thingness (the abyss)." For a different perspective on the relationship between Heidegger and Celan with respect to the proximity of poetry and thought, see Joris, "Celan/Heidegger," pp. 155–166. See also Hatley, "Grund and Abgrund," pp. 176–195. On the task of hermeneutics to heed the unsaid in what is spoken, to mark the inscription of otherness, see Ziarek, *Inflected Language*, pp. 133–160. See also Wolosky, "Mystical Language and Mystical Silence," pp. 364–375; and the fuller analysis in idem, *Language Mysticism*, pp. 197–263; Mosès, "Patterns of Negativity in Paul Celan's 'The Trumpet Place,'" pp. 209–224; Fioretos, "Nothing," pp. 295–341; Olschner, "Poetic Mutations of Silence," pp. 369–385; Gadamer, "Meaning and Concealment of Meaning," pp. 167–178; and Broda, "Traduit du silence," pp. 139–143. With respect to the silence of the poetic

word, there is also an important affinity between Celan and Jabès. See Shillony, "Métaphores de la négation," pp. 23–30; Gardaz, "Rhétorique et figures du silence," pp. 31–43; Walter, "La spiritualité du silence," pp. 71–88; Folin, "La figure du silence," pp. 147–156; Stamelman, "Le dialogue de l'absence," pp. 201–217; Mole, *Lévinas, Blanchot, Jabès* pp. 112–113; Hawkins, "Perpetuating the Death of God," pp. 289–372, esp. pp. 371–372, and in greater detail in idem, *Reluctant Theologians*, pp. 155–241 For a different approach to Celan that minimizes the ontological partiality of Heidegger and the consequent idealization of poetry as the saying that entrusts beings with being, see Levinas, *Proper Names*, pp. 40–46, and the further elaboration of the Levinasian perspective in Fóti, *Heidegger and the Poets*, pp. 114–124. On the other hand, it must be noted that Levinas himself accords special status to poetry as the form of language that best expresses the ontological state of "existing without existence," the "anonymity of existence," events of being that turn the unnameable verb "to be" into substantives. See Chanter, "Reading Hegel as a Mediating Master," pp. 1–21, esp. pp. 6–10. In the poetic musings of Celan, silence, or the breakdown of language, is integral to the task of witnessing the suffering of the other. The poetic gesture springs from the desire to address the other, but the other being addressed cannot be addressed and remain other. The other, therefore, is continually on the way to becoming the other the other must always (not) be. See Hatley, *Suffering Witness*, pp. 137–165.

363. Schmidt, "Black Milk and Blue," p. 110.

364. Certeau, *Heterologies*, p. 81. On the role of absence, difference, and mystical patterns of speech in Certeau's thought, see Ahearne, *Michel de Certeau*, pp. 95–128. On yielding as a key component in Heidegger's appropriation of *Gelassenheit* as a hermeneutical gesture, see T. Davis, "*Deinon* of Yielding," pp. 161–174.

365. In this matter, too, my thinking has been informed by Heideggerian poetics. On "imagining invisibles" as a topos to converse about "Heidegger's meditation," see Fóti, *Vision's Invisibles*, pp. 81–98.

366. Lacoue-Labarthe, *Poetry as Experience*, p. 68. It is of interest to consider the following remark of Kerouac, *Poems All Sizes*, p. 68: "The monument in the park / For the institute of the blind / Because it is not seen / Is truly a great monument / Would to God that I could make one / So artistically fabulous / As that with my hands." The poet expresses the desire to create in his poetic utterance something akin to the invisible monument to the blind. Consider as well the observation of Kierkegaard, *Concluding Unscientific Postscript*, pp. 409–409: "Poesy is the illusion which precedes the understanding; religiosity, the illusion which comes after the understanding. Between poesy and religiosity, worldly wisdom presents its vaudeville performance. Every individual who does not live either poetically or religiously is stupid." Implicit in Kierkegaard's remark is his belief that the faculty of reason cannot grasp truth; the distinction between poetry and religion is simply that the former is the "illusion" that precedes understanding while the latter is the "illusion" that succeeds understanding; to live without one or the other is to be completely unenlightened or "stupid" in the author's own language.

367. E. Wolfson, "Sacred Space and Mental Iconography," pp. 605–606 n. 36. On the attainment of a "pure and all-consuming" vision that results in the absorption of the self in God, predicated on an ascetic praxis, the "polishing of a dirty mirror," in the *Ḥayy Ibn Yaqzān*, the visionary cycle in the version of Abū Bakr Ibn Ṭufayl (c. 1116–1185), see Hughes, *Texture of The Divine*, p. 101. The kabbalistic notion has a striking analogue in the mystical pietism of Rūmī. See, for instance, Rūmī, *Mystical Poems of Rumi*, p. 37: "The soul, like a mirror, has received your image in its heart; the heart has sunk like a comb into the tip of your tress"; idem, *Rumi Collection*, p. 83: "Someone with a clear and empty heart / mirrors images of the Invisible. / He becomes intuitive and certain / of our innermost thought, / because 'the faithful are a mirror for the faithful' "; idem, *Selected Poems From the Dīvāni Shamsi Tabrīz*, p. 53: "Dismiss cares and be utterly clear of heart, / Like the face of a mirror without image and picture. / When it becomes clear of images, all images are contained in it; / No man's face is ashamed of that clear-faced one." On the image in Rūmī's poems of the human being—with special emphasis on Adam, the perfect man—as a mirror that reflects the divine attributes, see Chittick, *Sufi Path of Love*, pp. 62–65, 139–143. Significantly, Rūmī maintains that the image of the beloved conjured in the imagination facilitates union with the beloved beyond the image. See sources translated and analyzed by Chittick, *Sufi Path of Love*, pp. 259–267. With regard to the relationship between imaginal representation and unitive experience, I again note a conspicuous similarity to kabbalistic

sources. On the polishing of the heart and the ascetic path in Rūmī, see Renard, *All the King's Falcons*, pp. 37–38. Interestingly, according to Rūmī, the prophets of ancient Israel—Abraham, Joseph, and Moses—serve as models of perfection for initiates inasmuch as they possessed a polished mirror in which the imageless God could behold his image. See Renard, *All the King's Falcons,* p. 54, 64, 70. The image of the heart as a polished mirror wherein the divine glory is revealed has been repeated by other Sufi masters through the ages. For some examples, see Sviri, *Taste of Hidden Things*, pp. 5, 14, 19–20, 125, 170–171.

368. Hale, "Taste and See, For God Is Sweet," pp. 7–8.

369. Bloom, *Kabbalah and Criticism*, p. 51.

370. This expression is used to depict Nietzsche's asceticism in Lingis, *Deathbound Subjectivity*, pp. 59–70.

371. See *On the Genealogy of Morals*, bk. 3, secs. 5–8, in Nietzsche, *Basic Writings*, pp. 538–548. On Nietzsche's approach to asceticism, in addition to the work of Lingis cited in note 370, see Hulin, "Nietzsche and the Suffering of the Indian Ascetic," pp. 64–75; C. Scott, "Mask of Nietzsche's Self-Overcoming," pp. 217–229; J. Richardson, *Nietzsche's System*, pp. 174–179, 275–278; Ansell-Pearson, *Viroid Life*, pp. 37–39; T. Roberts, *Contesting Spirit,* pp. 77–102; Murray, *Nietzsche's Affirmative Morality,* pp. 72–73, 184, 187–188, 212–213, 243; D. B. Allison, *Reading the New Nietzsche,* pp. 141–142, 240–247; Zupancic, *Shortest Shadow*, pp. 47–61. The influence of Nietzsche is discernible in Foucault's remarks concerning self-overcoming through ascetic pleasures. See McWhorter, *Bodies and Pleasures,* pp. 176–192; A. Davidson, "Ethics as Ascetics," pp. 63–80.

372. Nietzsche, *Gay Science*, pp. 50–51, sec. 27. For a recent study that emphasizes Nietzsche's conception of tragic joy as an overcoming of nihilism by embracing suffering and loss, see McIntyre, *Sovereignty of Joy*; the author's thesis is summarized in the following statement: "As a political vision that celebrates a tragic conception of joy, Nietzsche's poetry of the future overcomes modernity not by withdrawing from it, but by accentuating and intensifying its nihilism. . . . This constitutes the atopia of grand politics: the poet of the future stands outside of the existing culture through the critique of morality and the politics of subjective freedom: hence, the ease with which it is read as an apology for tyranny or as a new form of utopianism" (p. 155).

373. Schelling, *Ages of the World*, p. 14.

374. Ibid., p. 107.

375. My language is derived from Keller, *Hammer and the Flute*, who utilizes the images of the "hammer" and the "flute" to convey the paradoxical situation of the possessed woman as one who becomes powerful because she has become the instrument of an overpowering force. In my judgment, this paradox of "instrumental agency" applies as well to kabbalists in their imaginal visualization of what has no image.

376. Deleuze, *Nietzsche and Philosophy*, p. 145.

377. Nietzsche, *Will to Power*, p. 377, sec. 708.

378. The matter is expressed in slightly different terms by Ansell-Pearson, *Viroid Life*, p. 54: "Overcoming one's own time in oneself involves overcoming one's prior aversion to it, one's suffering from it, the kind of suffering that gave birth to romanticism. Again, the eternal return speaks not to the liberation from this time but only of its enigma." On self-creation, self-overcoming, and the task of the poet in Nietzsche to articulate the "voiceless voice," see also Rorty, *Contingency, Irony, and Solidarity*, pp. 27–28; Hough, *Nietzsche's Noontide Friend*, pp. 111–112; Muneto, "Eloquent Silence of Zarathustra," pp. 226–243.

379. Nietzsche, *Will to Power*, p. 306, sec. 567. See n. 124.

380. Nietzsche, *Thus Spoke Zarathustra*, p. 111.

381. Rilke, *Sonnets to Orpheus,* II, 3, pp. 74–75. On the temporal dimension of the poetic in Rilke, see Jacobs, *Telling Time*, pp. 188–205.

382. Nietzsche, *Philosophy and Truth*, p. 39, sec. 110.

383. Ibid., p. 39, sec.107. Cf. ibid. p. 37, sec. 99, where Nietzsche depicted knowing as a "process of measuring according to a criterion." In other writings, Nietzsche signals out reason as the measure by means of which reality is created. See, for instance, *Will to Power*, p. 279, sec. 516, where Nietzsche raised the question whether axioms of logic were "adequate to reality" or a "means and measure for us to *create* reality" (emphasis in original).

384. Joós, *Poetic Truth and Transvaluation*, pp. 71–81.

385. For extensive discussion of the motif of being and time in Nietzsche's studies on ancient rhythm and meter (1870–1872), see Porter, *Nietzsche and the Philology of the Future*, pp. 127–166. On the centrality to music in the shaping of Nietzsche's thought, especially in the aforementioned period, see Liébert, *Nietzsche and Music*, pp. 71–93.

386. Cited in Porter, *Nietzsche and the Philology of the Future*, p. 143 (emphasis in original). In *Philosophy in the Tragic Age of the Greeks*, p. 50, Nietzsche referred to the notion of becoming in the thought of Heraclitus as the "everlasting wavebeat and rhythm of things." From the continuation of Nietzsche's account of Heraclitus, it is evident that he perceived in this Presocratic thinker the views that he would later proffer as his own, viz., the rejection of a duality between the physical and metaphysical worlds and the consequent denial of a realm of being over and against becoming. Reality consists solely of a perpetual flowing in which "every moment . . . exists only insofar as it has just consumed the preceding one, its father, and is then immediately consumed likewise" (pp. 52–53). Even closer to Nietzsche's own aesthetic is his comment that playfulness in Heraclitus "exhibits coming-to-be and passing away, structuring and destroying, without any moral additive, in forever equal innocence" (p. 62). For an alternative account of the thought of Heraclitus, see Nietzsche, *Pre-Platonic Philosophers*, pp. 53–74, esp. pp. 62–63.

387. Nietzsche, *Will to Power*, p. 380, sec. 715.

388. Nietzsche, *Gay Science*, p. 176, sec. 311, and p. 181, sec. 325.

389. My analysis has benefited from C. Scott, "Mask of Nietzsche's Self-Overcoming," pp. 217–218. See also Deleuze, *Pure Immanence*, p. 59: "With Nietzsche, everything is mask. His health was a first mask for his genius; his suffering, a second mask, both for his genius and for his health. Nietzsche didn't believe in the unity of a self and didn't experience it. Subtle relations of power and of evaluation between different 'selves' that conceal but also express other kinds of forces—forces of life, forces of thought—such is Nietzsche's conception, his way of living."

390. The expression *voilante dissimulation* is used to describe Nietzsche's view by Derrida in *Spurs*, p. 57.

391. Nietzsche, *Beyond Good and Evil*, Preface, p. 2 and pp. 163–164, sec. 232; idem, *Gay Science*, Preface, p. 8, and p. 72, sec. 64. On the link between truth and woman in Nietzsche, a figurative representation that underscores the polysemous and dissimulating nature of truth as a veil hiding another veil, see Derrida, *Spurs*, pp. 47–67, 101–109; Doane, "Veiling over Desire," pp. 119–126; Joós, *Poetic Truth* , pp. 169–180; Ansell-Pearson, "Who is the Übermensch?" pp. 23–45, esp. pp. 40–43; Burgard, "Introduction: Figures of Excess," pp. 1–32, esp. pp. 11–12. On the artistic propensity of woman, associated with "inner longing for a role and mask, for an appearance (*Schein*)," attributed as well to the Jews, the "people possessing the art of adaptability par excellence," see Nietzsche, *Gay Science*, pp. 225–226, sec. 361. In discussing this passage, Derrida, *Spurs*, p. 69, suggests: "parallel roles might in fact be related to the motif of castration and simulacrum for which circumcision is the mark, indeed the name of the mark." For further discussion of these motifs, see chap. 3, nn. 143 and 173. On the inseparability of truth and falsity in Nietzsche's philosophy, see J. Richardson, *Nietzsche's System*, p. 278.

392. Derrida, *Spurs*, p. 51.

393. Nietzsche, *Gay Science*, p. 8. In this connection, it is of interest to recall Nietzsche's description in *Thus Spoke Zarathustra*, p. 109, of "wild wisdom" as a "lioness" that "became pregnant upon lonely mountains."

394. Nietzsche, *Gay Science*, p. 144, sec. 222. Compare p. 70, sec. 59, where artists are described as the ones "who conceal naturalness." On the poet's exerting attraction through imperfection, see p. 79, sec. 79.

395. Nietzsche, *Will to Power*, p. 330, sec. 616.

396. Harr, *Nietzsche and Metaphysics*, pp. 69–81, esp. pp. 70–73.

397. Nietzsche, *Will to Power*, p. 35, sec. 55.

398. Ibid., p. 273, sec. 499 (emphasis in original).

399. Ibid., p. 293 n. 18, sec. 544.

400. For discussion of the aphorism *Wie man wird, was man ist*, which is the subtitle of *Ecce Homo*, see Nehamas, "How One Becomes What One Is," pp. 255–280.

401. I have borrowed this expression from Ansell-Pearson, *Viroid Life*, to characterize Nietzsche's celebrated image of the *Übermensch*.

402. In *Will to Power*, p. 277, sec. 513, Nietzsche wrote of the "greatest artists in abstraction who created the categories." The taxonomic enterprise by which names of things are placed into law is viewed, therefore, as an illustration of artistic power.

403. Ibid., p. 330, sec. 617.

404. Nietzsche, *Thus Spoke Zarathustra*, p. 216. See Leiter, "Paradox of Fatalism," pp. 217–255. See also the comparative discussion of Spinoza's *amor dei* and Nietzsche's *amor fati* in Stambaugh, *Other Nietzsche*, pp. 75–93.

405. Bloom, *Kabbalah and Criticism*, p. 52. See idem, *Poetry and Repression*, p. 140; idem, "Lying against Time," pp. 57–72, esp. pp. 60, 68, 70–72.

Chapter Two
Differentiating (In) Difference: Heresy, Gender, and Kabbalah Study

1. Lawrence Kushner utilizes this formulation in his praise for Matt, *Essential Kabbalah*. Kushner's comments, together with the remarks of other scholars and rabbis, are included on the first page of the book. The pervasiveness of this misconception may be gauged from the cavalier comment of Julia Kristeva to Catherine Clément (Clément and Kristeva, *Feminine and the Sacred*,, p. 98), concerning the "female deity" or "Hebrew goddess" of Jewish mysticism.

2. A number of religious thinkers and charismatic leaders (from a variety of different segments of the Jewish population) have emphasized the feminization of the divine in kabbalistic theosophy, which supposedly stands in marked contrast to the male-centered theology of legalistic rabbinism. For discussion of Scholem's dichotomous perspective, see Idel, "Rabbinism Versus Kabbalism," pp. 281–296. For a somewhat different view, see the brief discussion in E. Wolfson, *Abraham Abulafia*, pp. 34–35. Finally, it is of interest to consider the account given by Eliade, *Journal II*, pp. 266–267 (entry of 30 June 1965): "[I]n the Kabbala we have to do with a new, real creation of the Judaic religious genius, due to the need to recover a part of the cosmic religiosity smothered and persecuted as much by the prophets as by the later Talmudic rigorists. What is significant is that the Kabbala redevelops very ancient, cosmic symbols and images (the Tree, the Sun, Fertility, etc.) alongside gnostic, almost 'heretical,' ideas. Even better: introduced into the idea of God are feminine elements (*Shekhinah*) and dramatic ones (God's withdrawal, His exile, etc.). It would be interesting to compare cosmic Christianity, that is, the beliefs of the rural populations of southeast Europe and of the Mediterranean, with these medieval and postmedieval Judaic religious creations. Surprising parallelisms: devotion to the Virgin Mary and the importance of the *Shekhinah*, the Christological drama and Yahweh's exile, paradigm of Israel's exile, etc." I will resist the temptation to engage Eliade's overall assessment of Judaism as a religious culture, for my main point is to draw attention to the potential distortion that has and can continue to emerge from Scholem's portrayal of kabbalah. For more recent attempts of Schäfer and Green to consider the symbolic portrayal of *Shekhinah* on the part of kabbalists in light of imaginative representations of Mary, see below, n. 224. Neither scholar mentions Eliade's brief but suggestive comment. The matter deserves to be analyzed independently.

3. Schwarz, *Kabbalah and Alchemy*, p. 8. The author follows the interpretation of gender symbolism and tropes of sexuality offered by scholars of kabbalah and especially Idel, who contributed the foreword (entitled "The Sexualizing Vector in Jewish Mysticism") to the volume and also allowed his study "The Origin of Alchemy according to Zosimos and a Hebrew Parallel" to be reprinted therein.

4. Perhaps the most telling rite that is indicative of the phallomorphic nature of rabbinic androcentricism is the covenant of circumcision, which from its priestly articulation in the biblical canon forged an opposition and a discrepancy in the social status between Israelite men and women, not to mention the polarity established between Israelite and non-Israelite men, who are classified as the alien other. See Eilberg-Schwartz, *Savage in Judaism*, pp. 167–176; idem, *God's Phallus*, pp. 141–142, 207; L. Hoffman, *Covenant of Blood*, pp. 22–23; Olyan, *Rites and Rank*, pp. 64–68. For an alternative and less androcentric reading of the

rite of circumcision in rabbinic sources, see Boyarin, *Radical Jew*, pp. 126–130, 225–226. Eilberg-Schwartz, *God's Phallus*, pp. 157, 170–174, also affirmed the link between circumcision and feminization of the male body. Baskin, *Midrashic Women*, marshals many texts in support of her claim regarding the androcentric construction of women as ancillary beings in the aggadic ruminations of the rabbis. For an attempt to minimize rabbinic androcentrism, see also Boyarin, *Carnal Israel*; idem, "Women's Bodies," pp. 88–100 (in this study, Boyarin shifts his thinking somewhat and is careful to note that the abolishment of a misogynist ritual sanctioned by Scripture and hence the improvement of the social status of women occur at precisely the same moment and within the same space as rabbinic authority begins to be anchored on the study of Torah, the "epistemic regime" [p. 97], from which women are basically excluded); and the works of Tal Ilan cited below, n. 207. On the complex portrayal of gender construction in the economy of the early rabbinic period, see as well Satlow, "Texts of Terror," pp. 273–297, Peskowitz, *Spinning Fantasies*; Fonrobert, *Menstrual Purity*; idem, "Beginnings of Rabbinic Textuality," pp. 49–68; Stein, "Maidservant," pp. 375–397. For a sympathetic reconstruction of the rabbinic attitude toward women, see also Valler, *Women and Womanhood*; Hauptman, *Rereading the Rabbis*; Novak, *Covenantal Rights*, pp. 133–142. On the ambivalent attitude toward Jewish women reflected in rabbinic halakhah, see R. Biale, *Women and Jewish Law*; and Wegner, *Chattel or Person?* For a critical review of the scholarly project to interpret rabbinic culture through a feminist lens, see E. Alexander, "Impact of Feminism," pp. 101–118.

5. On the history of the composition, redaction, and literary structure of zoharic literature, see Scholem, *Major Trends*, pp. 156–204; Tishby, *Wisdom of the Zohar*, pp. 1–12; Liebes, *Studies in the Zohar*, pp. 85–138; Huss, "*Sefer ha-Zohar* as a Canonical, Sacred and Holy Text," pp. 257–307; idem, "Appearance of *Sefer ha-Zohar*," pp. 507–542; Mopsik, "Corpus Zoharique ses titres et ses amplifications," pp. 75–105; idem, "Moïse de León, le Sheqel ha-Qodesh et la rédaction du Zohar," pp. 117–218; D. Abrams, "Critical and Post-Critical Textual Scholarship," pp. 17–71, esp. pp. 61–64; Meroz, "Zoharic Narratives," pp. 3–63; Giller, *Reading the Zohar.*

6. This material is derived from a more extended discussion in the introduction to a forthcoming collection of my essays, *Luminal Darkness*.

7. Kumin, *Logic of Incest*, p. 278.

8. *Zohar* 1:228b. The connection between an earthly woman and *Shekhinah* is implied in the narrative describing R. Joseph; whenever he heard the footsteps of his mother, he would say "Let me rise before the *Shekhinah* who has arrived" (Babylonian Talmud, Qiddushin 31b).

9. Lamentably, scholarly discussions of ethics and kabbalah have been virtually blind and deaf to the issue of gender and the construction of a cultural axiology. Here, too, I have stood alone in an effort to investigate kabbalistic symbolism from this perspective. I have explored the relation of ethics and mysticism in my monograph *Venturing Beyond*, based on the Shoshana Shier Lectures in Jewish Studies delivered at the University of Toronto, February–March 1998. I am currently in the last stages of preparing the manuscript for publication. For an illuminating study of postmodern gender theory and the ethics of difference, see S. Parsons, *Ethics of Gender.*

10. A careful reading discloses that the three models discussed by Idel, "Female Beauty," pp. 317–334, are all predicated on an instrumentalist representation of the feminine.

11. I borrow this expression from Lee, "Problems of Religious Pluralism," pp. 453–477.

12. This line of reasoning is adopted, for instance, by Barlas, *"Believing Women" in Islam*, pp. 101–103. As part of the effort to demonstrate the hypothesis that the "teachings of the Qur'an (see, for example, 40:40) are radically egalitarian and even antipatriarchal" (p. 93), Barlas argues that the Islamic idea of unity (*tawḥīd*) runs contrary to a binary construction of reality that is linked to patriarchy. Sufism is presented as an extreme expression of the monistic truth implied in the monotheism of Islam. From a gender perspective, according to this reading, the monotheistic orientation logically entails a principle of ontological sameness applied to men and women, and hence "man" is to be taken as a paradigm for women and men, and women are viewed as the other of the true self instantiated in men. In short, for Barlas, the scriptural roots of Islam affirm sexual difference without sexual inequality. Apposite here is the suggestion of Hassan, "Islamic Perspective," p. 346, that in the Qur'ān the original human creation was that of an "undifferentiated humanity," neither male nor female. For a positive valorization of the feminine in Islam against the background of the avowed

"male supremacy," see Bouhdiba, *Sexuality in Islam*, pp. 19–29. On the depiction of Sufism as the discernment of the ultimate truth that transcends confessional differences, see Goldziher, *Introduction to Islamic Theology and Law*, pp. 150–152. See also Nicholson, *Mystics of Islam*, pp. 86–88. For a more attenuated attempt to present Sufism as empowering women spiritually without denying the dominance of male agency in Islam, see Butorovic, "Between the Tariqa and the Shari'a," pp. 135–150. See chap. 7, n. 76. A philosophically rich analysis of the symbolic constructions of masculinity and femininity is presented in Murata, *Tao of Islam*. For a good survey of the social, political, and cultural standing of women in Islamic countries during the Middle Ages, see Hambly, "Becoming Visible," pp. 3–27. On the negative assessment of the feminine as the source of sexual temptation in Islamic literature, see Calderini, "Women, 'Sin,' and 'Lust,'" pp. 49–63.

13. A similar argument has been made by Schott, *Cognition and Eros*, pp. 60–61, with respect to the medieval worship of Mary. According to Schott, there is no correspondence between Mary figuring prominently in religious beliefs and practices and the social status of Christian women. On the contrary, Marian cults intensified misogynist tendencies, inasmuch as Mary was elevated as a semi-divine object of veneration precisely on account of her giving birth as a virgin and herself having been born of immaculate conception, the notion of virginity being rooted in a denigration of femininity, which was associated with the senses and the physical world as opposed to masculinity, the site of reason and rationality. The need on the part of Christian men, predominantly monks and clerics, to sever the textual and visual representations of Mary, on the one hand, and the existential condition of women in social context, on the other, is emphasized by Gold, *Lady and the Virgin*, pp. 43–75.

14. I have examined this phenomenon in great detail in the concluding essay in *Circle in the Square*, pp. 79–121.

15. See Meeks, "Image of the Androgyne," pp. 166, 180–185; idem, *First Urban Christians*, pp. 87–89; Luedemann, *Paul, Apostle to the Gentiles*, pp. 66–67; A. Segal, *Paul the Convert*, pp. 137, 146, 181–182; Boyarin, *Radical Jew*, pp. 180–200. See, by contrast, MacDonald, *There Is No Male and Female*; idem, "Corinthian Veils and Gnostic Androgynes," pp. 283–285. According to MacDonald, Galatians 3:28 proves only that the overcoming of sexual differentiation results in the constitution of one male person, an interpretation that resonates with my own perspective on the paradigm of sexual sameness implicit in kabbalistic symbolism. For a different approach, see W. Walker, "Corinthians 11:2–16 and Paul's Views regarding Women," pp. 94–110. See also Mortley, *Womanhood*, pp. 50–54, and the judicious weighing of contradictory evidence in Doran, *Birth of a Worldview*, pp. 145–156. Meeks, "Images of the Androgyne," pp. 189–197, discusses other rituals in gnostic sources—including, most importantly, the mystery of the bridal chamber—intended to renew or restore the androgynous image. I am not aware of any rituals of this sort initiated by early kabbalists as a means of uniting masculine and feminine, although the traditional customs of rabbinic halakhah were transformed symbolically into mystical rites. For examples of the phenomenon of bisexualism in the history of shamanism, see Eliade, *Two and the One*, pp. 116–117. A similar explanation is offered for the gender transformation of the female into male in Mahāyāna Buddhism by Ueki, *Gender Equality in Buddhism*, pp. 87–105. Ueki's thesis that statements affirming the need for the female body to be transformed into a male so that women can attain enlightenment actually affirm the equality of the sexes seems to me forced and apologetic. See the more critical and, in my judgment, historically accurate view of Gross cited below at n. 68, and the negative portrayals of women catalogued by Kloppenborg, "Female Stereotypes in Early Buddhism," pp. 151–169. For a more egalitarian approach to this material, see Murcott, *First Buddhist Women*.

16. Needless to say, many scholars have weighed in on the issue of the authenticity of the Pauline authorship of Colossians. Cannon, *Use of Traditional Materials*, pp. 1–9, presents a useful and judicious account of the evidence and refers the reader to the relevant discussions in the accompanying notes.

17. A measured judgment is offered by Barth and Blanke, *Colossians*, p. 71: "Whether Colossians was written by Paul himself or by one of his disciples, its intention includes a confirmation and reinforcement of the apostle's authority, not a correction of his teachings."

18. On the spiritual transformation from the "old human" to the "new human," see also Ephesians 4:22–24. In Romans 8:15, the matter is expressed in terms of the transition from the "spirit of slavery" to the "spirit of sonship." For a comprehensive philological analysis of the relevant nomenclature, see Jewett, *Paul's Anthropological Terms*.

19. Even if one were to accept the prevailing opinion amongst New Testament scholars that the epistle to the Colossians is not an authentic Pauline document, it is safe to conclude that with regard to the passage I have cited, there is an exact parallel to Galatians 3:28. Inasmuch as the latter likely reflects the older baptismal formula, the same may be said with respect to the former. See discussion in Barth and Blanke, pp. 415–417.

20. Meeks, *First Urban Christians*, pp. 89–90.

21. For a discussion of Paul's notion of the "new creation" against the backdrop of the sexual mores of his time and place, see P. Brown, *Body and Society*, pp. 44–57.

22. J. Z. Smith, *Imagining Religion*, pp. 11–12. Needless to say, Paul himself is not always consistent regarding the erasure of gender difference and on occasion affirms the conventional view of his time that ascribed a subordinate and submissive role to the woman (1 Cor. 11:2–16, 14:34–36; Rom. 1:26). See discussion below, chap. 7. Consider also the observation of Gaston, *Paul and the Torah*, pp. 33–34, that the statement that there is neither Greek nor Jew in Christ actually implies that there are both Greek and Jew, which is to say, Paul's remark affirms the legitimacy of both groups as autonomous units rather than signifying the erasure of their difference. Despite the avowed moral urgency on the author's part to encourage Christians in the post-Holocaust era to allow Israel to remain Israel and still be genuine faith partners, I am not certain of his ecumenical interpretation. For a review of Gaston's position, see Gager, *Reinventing Paul*, pp. 52–53, 56–57.

23. The rabbinic response (discernible from a textual viewpoint at a somewhat later date) is to insist, as do the Pharisees in *Acts*, on Torah as being the only way to break down difference. The outsider must come inside, and he does so by circumcision and submission to the ways of Torah. The overcoming of difference is related more specifically to the phenomenon of conversion, which is accorded eschatological significance, a point linked exegetically to the tracing of the lineage of the Davidic messiah to Ruth the Moabite. Inasmuch as this seed comes forth as a consequence of the trespassing of the boundary separating Moabite and Israelite, the messianic figure embodies the mystery of conversion, the "othering of the other," as I refer to it in the third chapter of *Venturing Beyond*. For a succinct account of this aspect of rabbinic eschatology, see Jacob Neusner's assessment of *Ruth Rabba*, the midrashic compilation organized about the book of Ruth, in Neusner, *Midrash Compilations*, pp. 148–149.

24. *Coptic Gnostic Library*, vol. 2, pp. 63. For an alternative rendering, see *Gospel of Thomas: Hidden Sayings*, p. 35, and parallel sources from early Christian documents cited and analyzed on pp. 79–80. On the disruption of the androcentric positioning of women in the household and a challenge to patriarchal norms in the early stages of the Jesus movement, see Schottroff, "Itinerant Prophetesses," pp. 347–360.

25. *Apostolic Fathers* vol. 1, p. 147.

26. Hennecke, *New Testament Apocrypha*, vol. 2, pp. 319–320.

27. P. Brown, *Body and Society*, pp. 49–50; S. Davis, "'Pauline' Defense," pp. 453–459. Also relevant to the question of the status of women in Christian origins is the cultivation of female disciples on the part of Jesus. See Munro, "Women Disciples," pp. 47–64.

28. Gibson, "Could Christ Have Been Born a Woman?" pp. 65–82. Needless to say, the metaphorical representation of Jesus in female imagery has its literary roots in much older sources, including Christologies indebted to Jewish wisdom speculation. See, for instance, Guillemin, "Jesus/Holy Mother Wisdom," pp. 244–267.

29. Bynum, *Jesus as Mother*; idem, *Holy Feast and Holy Fast*, pp. 260–269.

30. Stendahl, *Bible and the Role of Women*; Fiorenza, *In Memory of Her*; Scroggs, "Paul and the Eschatological Woman," pp. 283–303; and the reaction by Pagels, "Paul and Women," pp. 538–549.

31. Schottroff, *Lydia's Impatient Sisters*, pp. 41, 124–128.

32. D'Angelo, "Veils, Virgins, and the Tongues of Men and Angels," pp. 389–419, esp. pp. 390–399.

33. Clement of Alexandria, *Stromateis*, 3.92.2, p. 314. Regarding the text from the *Gospel of the Egyptians*, see the comments by Jung, *Mysterium Coniunctionis*, pp. 373–374. For citation of the relevant passages from this apocryphal gospel and discussion about its literary-historical provenance, see *New Testament Apocrypha*, vol. 1, pp. 166–178.

34. Fletcher-Louis, "Worship of Divine Humanity," pp. 112–128, esp. pp. 120–125.

35. See Fatum, "Image of God and Glory of Man," pp. 50–133. See also the studies by MacDonald and Mortley cited above, n. 15. For a different interpretation emphasizing that Paul's "spiritual body" is a restoration of the androgynous image of primal Adam, see A. Segal, "Paul's '*Soma Pneumatikon*,'" pp. 265–266. At the final stages of revising this chapter, Hindy Najman kindly drew my attention to D'Angelo, "Gender Refusers in the Early Christian Mission," pp. 149–173. In this study, D'Angelo weighs the evidence carefully and concludes that the baptismal formula, even when interpreted as a basis for sexual asceticism, did not necessarily translate into a rejection of patriarchal marriage and the establishment of community based on egalitarianism. However, she does refer to the proclamation of inclusion in Christ as a "knock-down argument" (pp. 164–166) inasmuch as it leaves open the possibility for future generations to affirm an overcoming of gender difference, which entails not subsuming the female into perfect manhood but recognizing the autonomy and equality of the two genders in the image of God. For an interesting case example of gender differentiation presumed to profess equality of gender in the face of recognizing essential differences between women and men, see Wallace, "Priesthood and Motherhood," pp. 117–140.

36. Clement of Alexandria, *Stromateis* 3.45.3, p. 284. See parallel in Clement, *Excerpta ex Theodoto* 67, cited in *New Testament Apocrypha*, p. 169.

37. Clement of Alexandria, 3.63.2, p. 295.

38. Ibid., 3.64.1, p. 296.

39. Genesis 2:6; and see 2 Corinthians 11:3. By contrast, in Roman 5:12–14, Paul ascribed responsibility for the primal sin to Adam and not only to his female helpmate. For detailed philological exegesis of the passage in 1 Timothy cast in a comparative perspective with contemporary historical documents, see Quinn and Walker, *First and Second Letters to Timothy*, pp. 226–230.

40. Clement of Alexandria , 3.12.89–90, p. 312. To be precise, in this passage, Clement exegetically links 1 Timothy 2:15 with 5:14–15.

41. By "Pauline" I do not mean to suggest that one accept the traditional attribution of the epistle to Paul. The connotation of this term conveys rather the assumption that the document was composed and redacted by individuals who thought of themselves as promoting the traditions and expounding the teachings of the apostle. See discussion on assessing the authorship of the pastoral epistles in L. Johnson, *First and Second Letters to Timothy*, pp. 55–90.

42. Consider the detailed analysis of multiple readings of 1 Timothy 2:15 offered by Köstenberger, *Studies on John and Gender*, pp. 283–322.

43. See Quinn and Walker, *First and Second Letters to Timothy*, pp. 230–243.

44. As we find, for instance, in the following comment of Quinn and Walker, *First and Second Letters to Timothy*, p. 225: "The equality of male and female before God and in Christ does not contradict a further ordering within the marriage relationship, also created by God. The equality of the sexes belongs to nature; the subordination of one to the other comes by the choice of the marriage relationship."

45. J. Cooper, "Gendered Sexuality," p. 91 n. 30.

46. *Coptic Gnostic Library*, vol. 2, p. 93. Valantasis, *Gospel of Thomas*, pp. 194–195, remarks that sayings 22 and 114 must be seen in the broader context of gender transformations attested in Hermetic literature that involved the male becoming female as well as the female becoming male, the ultimate goal being "supervening the masculine and feminine genders altogether." For the view that the two sayings refer to different stages in the redemptive process, see Buckley, "Interpretation of Logion 114," pp. 245–272, esp. pp. 253–254. For further discussion of these texts, see Eliade, *Two and the One*, pp. 105–107; Klijn, "Single One," pp. 271–278; Meyer, "Making Mary Male," pp. 554–570; idem, "*Gospel of Thomas* Logion 114," pp. 101–111; both of Meyer's studies are reprinted in Meyer, *Secret Gospels*, pp. 76–106; P. Brown, *Body and Society*, pp. 103–121. A more critical feminist approach, in line with my own reading, is attested in a number of studies, including Vogt, "Becoming Male," pp. 172–187; Børresen, "God's Image, Man's Image?" pp. 188–207; McGuire, "Women, Gender, and Gnosis," pp. 277–282, esp. pp. 277–282; Meltzer, "Re-embodying," pp. 274–277; Nash, "Language of Mother Work," pp. 174–195, esp. the précis of the author's contention on p. 175: "I argue that, in the *Gospel of Thomas*, the act of gaining the Kingdom, being saved, is a harsh and violent

process for women, amounting to psychic rape, a lobotomy of the female self." K. King, *Gospel of Mary*, p. 147, suggests that logion 114, the final saying in *Gospel of Thomas*, was "probably tacked onto the end of the work by a later scribe." It seems to me, however, that the conceptual thread that links sayings 22 and 114 weakens the plausibility of this suggestion.

47. K. King, *Gospel of Mary*, pp. 147–148.

48. Koester, "Gnostic Writings as Witnesses," pp. 238–261; idem, *Ancient Christian Gospels*, pp. 181–186; Koester and Pagels, "Report on the Dialogue of the Savior," pp. 66–74; idem, "Introduction," vol. 3, pp. 1–17.

49. *Nag Hammadi Codex III*, 5, 3:79.

50. Ibid., 3:81.

51. K. King, "Why All the Controversy?" pp. 53–74; idem, *Gospel of Mary*, pp. 3–7, 32–34, 67, 83–90, 141–154, 170–187.

52. *Nag Hammadi Codex III*, 5, 3:83.

53. Ibid., 3:87.

54. Ibid., 3:91; K. King, *Gospel of Mary*, pp. 146–147.

55. Koester, *Ancient Christian Gospels*, p. 186, already suggested that the question of the "works of womanhood" in the *Dialogue of the Savior* is a "topic that belongs to the overarching concern of wearing a body," that is, the "continuation of existence in the body through child-bearing," and is thus "possibly a commentary on the final saying of the *Gospel of Thomas* (114) about Mary, the woman who is not worthy of the kingdom unless she is made male." Koester's remark that "rejection of the works of womanhood does not imply a degradation of women as such" is not acceptable. He correctly notes the contrast between the mandate in the *Gospel of Thomas* for the female to become male by ceasing from bearing children and the assertion in 1 Timothy 2:13–15 that women will be saved by bearing children. It does not seem to me, however, that one can persuasively argue that the directive for the female to become a male is not degrading to women; at most one can say that this transformation eradicates a negative stereotype of femininity.

56. For further discussion of this motif, see Pagels, "Exegesis of Genesis 1," pp. 477–496; and idem, *Beyond Belief*, pp. 40–41, 55–58, 66–69.

57. Meeks, "Image of the Androgyne," pp. 194–195, and reaffirmed more recently by DeConick, *Seek to See Him*, pp. 17–20. See also E. Castelli, "I Will Make Mary Male," pp. 29–49, esp. p. 33: "The female can and should strive to become male—to overcome gender distinction, since the male embodies the generic 'human' and therefore the potential for human existence to transcend differences and return to the same. . . . 'Becoming male' marks for these thinkers the transcendence of differences, but it does so only by reinscribing the traditional gender hierarchies of male over female, masculine over feminine; the possibility that women can 'become male,' paradoxically however, also reveals the tenuousness and malleability of the naturalized categories of male and female. . . . I would argue that these discourses do not simply rearticulate the hegemonic gendered order, nor do they simply deconstruct it; rather, they stretch its boundaries and, if only for a moment, call it into question—even if, ultimately, things return to 'normal.'" See, by contrast, Meyer, *Secret Gospels*, pp. 91–92 and 103–104. Without denying the patriarchal dominance in late antiquity and the devaluing of femaleness based on the theory of a single sex, Meyer nevertheless insists that the injunction for the female to become male is to be interpreted symbolically; the message of liberation, therefore, is not limited to a biological woman, but extends to the transformation of what is earthly and corporeal (female) into what is heavenly and spiritual (male). An egalitarian reading of logion 114 is also proffered by Marjanen, "Women Disciples in the *Gospel of Thomas*," pp. 89–106. See as well *Gospel of Thomas: Annotated and Explained*, translated by Stevan Davies, p. 138. According to Davies, the final saying "was added to the text of Thomas at some later date. . . . In any event, saying 114 is contradicted by saying 22, which requires the union of the sexes rather than preference for one over the other." For a similar orientation regarding the masculinization of the feminine as a sign of perfection in Philo, see Philo, *Supplement I*, II.49, p. 131; *Supplement II*, I.8, pp. 15–16. It must be noted that, according to Philo, the ideal anthropos created in the image of God is an incorporeal and incorruptible "object of thought" that is "neither male nor female" in contrast to the corporeal and corruptible man that is an "object of sense perception . . . consisting of body and soul, man or woman" (*On the Creation* 134 in *Philo*, vol. 1, p. 107). However, given the fact that the incorporeal

mind is gendered as masculine in Philo as opposed to the corporeal senses, which are feminine, it follows that the ideal anthropos depicted in the first chapter of Genesis is a male beyond gender bifurcation, an idea that corresponds, in my opinion, to the male androgyne that has informed the thinking of kabbalists. See Jervell, *Imago Dei*, pp. 161–163; R. Baer, *Philo's Use of the Categories*, pp. 45–49, 69–71; Aspegren, *Male Woman*, pp. 79–98. For a different approach, see Boyarin, *Carnal Israel*, pp. 37–42, 78–80. On the myth of the androgyne in ancient Graeco-Roman literature, see also Delcourt, *Hermaphrodite*, pp. 27–61; and D'Angelo, "Transcribing Sexual Politics," pp. 115–146 (I thank the author for providing me with a copy of her essay). Consider the statement transmitted in the name of Jesus in the *Second Treatise of the Great Seth*, a Christian Gnostic revelation dialogue, cited in chap. 7, n. 69.

58. On the eschatological renunciation of the female body and the transvestite motif of becoming male, see also T. Shaw, *Burden of the Flesh*, pp. 235–252. On the encratic background of the motif of the female becoming male, see Aspegren, *Male Woman*, pp. 115–143.

59. For discussion of the encratic elements in the *Gospel of Thomas*, see Uro, "Is *Thomas* an Encratite Gospel?" pp. 140–162.

60. Patterson, *Gospel of Thomas and Jesus*, pp. 153–155.

61. For a relatively recent review of this question, see Marjanen, "Is *Thomas* a Gnostic Gospel?" pp. 107–139.

62. *Zostrianos* 131, 5–6, text and translation in *Coptic Gnostic Library*, 4: 222–223. See Wisse, "Flee Femininity," pp. 297–307. For the depiction of asceticism as an escape from the femaleness of somatic desire, see also M. Williams, *Immovable Race*, pp. 99–102.

63. *Zostrianos* 1, 11–13, in *Coptic Gnostic Library*, 4: 31.

64. *Zostrianos* 7, 5–6, in *Coptic Gnostic Library*, 4: 43.

65. See chap. 7, n. 40.

66. D. Paul, *Women in Buddhism*, p. 236. A version of the narrative appears in *Lotus Sutra*, pp. 187–188. Needless to say, the ideal of a gender-neutral enlightenment is affirmed in other parts of this text. See, for instance, the comment attributed to Buddha, "the great sage, the World-honored One," *Lotus Sutra*, p. 103: "I look upon all things / as being universally equal, / I have no mind to favor this or that, / to love or hate another. / I am without greed or attachment / and without limitation or hindrance. / At all times, for all things / I preach the Law equally; / as I would for a single person, / that same way I do for numerous persons." The pietistic application of the ideal is laid out in the chapter of the sutra that deals with "peaceful practices" of the bodhisattva: "Again one should not make distinctions / by saying, 'This is a man,' 'This is a woman.' / Do not try to apprehend phenomena, / to understand or to see them" (p. 200). For another articulation of this Mahāyāna teaching, see Shāntideva, *Way of the Bodhisattva*, p. 149: "All form, therefore, is like a dream, / And who will be attached to it, who thus investigates? / The body, in this way, has no existence; / What is male, therefore, and what is female?" See also L. Wilson, "Buddhist Views on Gender and Desire," pp. 151–158.

67. For a representative listing of studies that treat the Mahāyāna concept of emptiness from various theoretical perspectives and historical instantiations, see Nāgārjuna, *Twelve Gate Treatise*, pp. 4–26; Jeffrey Hopkins, *Meditation on Emptiness*; idem, *Emptiness in the Mind-Only School*; Lopez, *Heart Sutra Explained*, pp. 57–93; Fenner, *Ontology of the Middle Way*, pp. 35–44; Swanson, "Spirituality of Emptiness," pp. 373–396; A. Klein, *Path to the Middle*, pp. 43–89; Huntington and Wangchen, *Emptiness of Emptiness*, pp. 40–59; Varela, "Pour une phénoménologie," pp. 121–148; Ganeri, *Philosophy in Classical India*, pp. 42–70; Garfield and Priest, "Nāgārjuna and the Limits of Thought," pp. 1–21, esp. pp. 7–10. On the attempt to use the concept of zero, thought to be derived from the Sanskrit *sūnya*, to articulate the notion of the "unsexed" that precedes the division into gender binaries, see Weston, *Gender in Real Time*, pp. 32–41.

68. R. Gross, *Buddhism after Patriarchy*, p. 73. See idem, "Some Buddhist Perspectives on the Goddess," pp. 406–425.

69. *Buddhism after Patriarchy*, pp. 67–73.

70. Ibid., p. 117.

71. R. Gross, *Feminism and Religion*, p. 138. Consider also the observations by Campbell, *Traveller in Space*, pp. 147–148: "As I have shown, in the Vajrayana Buddhist scriptures, 'otherness' is commonly repre-

sented as either demon or woman, or both. In the spiritual realm, the Tibetan Buddhist's ultimate goal is to realise all phenomena (both external experience and the mind itself) as emptiness. . . . However, as I will show, the promise on a non-dual philosophy, applicable to men and women, is not fulfilled, for in the allocation of symbolic femaleness to the concepts of both 'otherness' and 'emptiness,' the application of the philosophy is rendered problematic for women. . . . The monastic tradition emphasised the polluting aspect of women, and encouraged celibacy and physical distance from women. On the other hand, women were viewed as essential components to advanced Tantric practice, which addressed the understanding of man's being through his sexuality. In both respects, however, woman is 'other,' either through her negative potential or through her female being and sexuality with which man had to associate in order to reach his full potential (Buddhahood)." See also L. Wilson, *Charming Cadavers*; and the discussion of the "hermeneutics of desire" in Faure, *Red Thread*, pp. 15–63, esp. pp. 29–34, 55–58. See also Sponberg, "Atttitudes toward Women," pp. 3–36. For a more positive account of women and the feminine imaginary, see M. Shaw, *Passionate Enlightenment*; Cleary and Aziz, *Twilight Goddess*; Simmer-Brown, *Dakini's Warm Breath*. For discussion of the Tibetan ideal of enlightenment and the feminist project of undoing dualisms, see A. Klein, *Meeting the Great Bliss Queen*, pp. 149–169. An intermediate position, which acknowledges negative stereotypes of the feminine but nonetheless discerns an ideal of spiritual enlightenment whereby gender differences are overcome, is taken in the survey offered by N. Barnes, "Women and Buddhism in India," pp. 38–69; and in the careful study by Peach, "Social Responsibility," pp. 50–74. I am not in a position to judge between these approaches, but what is important to me is that Campbell's assessment presents a perfectly apt description of the symbolic representation of the female and the status of women in traditional kabbalah. See above, n. 15 and below, n. 231.

72. D. Paul, *Women in Buddhism*, pp. 175–176. Consider the exchange between Shariputra and the goddess in the Mahāyāna text, Vimalakīrti, *Vimalakirti Sutra*, pp. 90–92. After the goddess instructs Shariputra in the ways of the Dharma, he inquires of her, "Why don't you change out of this female body?" assuming that "enlightenment can be obtained only by men and that women must first reincarnate in male form to reach the highest goal" (Vimalakīrti, *Holy Teaching of Vimalakīrti*, p. 128 n. 24.) The goddess responds by eliciting from Shariputra the insight that the form of a phantom (indeed, the form of all things) has no permanence, and hence it is meaningless to ask why she has not given up her female form to become male. To deepen the insight, the goddess employs the supernatural power of magic, clothing Shariputra in her female body while she takes on his male form. The goddess, then, turns the table on Shariputra and asks him what he had initially asked her, to which he responded "I don't know why I have suddenly changed and taken on a female body!" (The Tibetan version, presumed by some scholars to be closer to the original Sanskrit, is more loquacious. See *Holy Teaching of Vimalakīrti*, p. 62: "I no longer appear in the form of a male! My body has changed into the body of a woman! I do not know what to transform!") At this juncture the goddess discloses her intent and reveals the moral: "Shariputra, who is not a woman, appears in a woman's body, and the same is true of all women—though they appear in women's bodies, they are not women. Therefore the Buddha teaches that all phenomena are neither male nor female." (According to *Holy Teaching of Vimalakīrti*, p. 62: "All women appear in the form of women in just the same way as the elder appears in the form of a woman. While they are not women in reality, they appear in the form of women. With this in mind, the Buddha said, 'In all things, there is neither male nor female.' ") The denigrated state of women is also attested in the comment in *Lotus Sutra* included in a litany of exhortations for one who aspires to be enlightened as a bodhisattva: "Never go alone into an enclosed place / to preach the Law to a woman" (p. 199). On similar expressions of the spiritual ideal in Islamic mysticism, see chap. 7, n. 81.

73. D. Paul, *Women in Buddhism*, p. 308.

74. Peach, "Social Responsibility," p. 57.

75. Note the observation of Jantzen, *Power, Gender and Christian Mysticism*, p. 28, that the "identification of the fertile earth with the female body did not mean that Hesiod thought well of actual women." Quite the contrary, Hesiod characterized the earth as the womb whence all life springs forth and at the same time used overtly misogynist language to depict women. This insight ought to give pause to the desire on the part of some contemporary feminists to utilize the kabbalistic symbol of *Shekhinah* to develop an ecologically sound theology of nature as the mother goddess. Analogously, Warner, *Alone of All Her Sex*, p. 191, has

argued that under the influence of the Franciscans the adoration of the Virgin's femininity was transformed into a social code of behavior that kept women relegated to the domestic domain. For different perspectives on the gender dynamic, see Wefelmeyer, "Raphael's *Sistine Madonna*," pp. 105–118, esp. pp. 107–108; and Palumbo, "Gender Difference."

76. A similar argument with regard to the disjuncture between feminine images applied to the divine and the social value accorded women is made by Mortley, *Womanhood*, pp. 24–25, 40–43.

77. Peach, "Social Responsibility," p. 69.

78. Babylonian Talmud, Shabbat 145b–146a; Yevamot 103b; Avodah Zarah 22b.

79. *Zohar* 1:126b. The ontic connection between the woman's soul, the serpent, and the force of evil on the north side, is made explicitly in *Book Bahir*, sec. 140, p. 223. On the serpentine nature of women in the medieval context, see Chandès, *Le serpent, la femme et l'épée*, and Gregg, *Devils, Women, and Jews*, pp. 86–87, 90–93, 99–101, 119–121. A fascinating study combining linguistics and anthropology, on the nexus of woman, womb, and worm, focusing particularly on mythological depictions of the Great Mother as a serpent, is offered by Thōng, *Golden Serpent*. As a total surprise I received a copy of the work directly from the author, and to the best my knowledge I do not think the work was ever published for public consumption. The dual role of the serpent in symbolizing male and female demonic potencies is consistent with the twofold character of this symbol in a host of varied societies. For a useful review, see Mundkur, *Cult of the Serpent*, pp. 172–208. On the nexus between serpent, women, and fecundity in erotic and initiatory symbolism, see D. Allen, *Structure and Creativity in Religion*, pp. 150–153.

80. The severe nature of the view proffered in this zoharic passage can be appreciated if we bear in mind that Jewish women in medieval European communities did have a more active role in traditional ritual life, both communal and private. On this point, see Grossman, *Pious and Rebellious*, pp. 304–345.

81. In traditional zoharic commentaries, one can discern an attempt to interpret the statement in *Zohar* in light of the more standard rabbinic taxonomy. See, for instance, the commentarial gloss on the zoharic formulation "women are exempt from the commands of Torah" by Moses Cordovero in Abraham Azulai, *Or ha-Ḥamnah*, 1:106d: "from the positive commandments dependent on time."

82. For an elaboration of this fundamental tenet of kabbalistic anthropology, unfortunately neglected by many scholars, see E. Wolfson, "Ontology, Alterity, and Ethics."

83. Exod. 22:17; 2 Kings 9:22; Ezek. 13:17–23; Mishnah, Avot 2:7; Palestinian Talmud, Ḥagigah 2:2, 77d, Sanhedrin 14:19, 25d; Babylonian Talmud, Shabbat 66b, Pesaḥim 111a, Sanhedrin 67a; Eruvin 64b; *Massekhet Soferim*, 15:7, p. 282; Maimonides, *Guide of the Perplexed*, III.37, pp. 541–542. On the association of women and magic in Jewish tradition, see Blau, *Das Altjüdische Zauberwesen*, pp. 18–19, 23–26; Trachtenberg, *Jewish Magic and Superstition*, pp. 16, 50–51, 115–116; S. Fishbane, "Most Woman Engage in Sorcery," pp. 27–42; Lesses, "Exe(o)rcising Power," pp. 343–375; Baskin, *Midrashic Women*, pp. 10–11, 33–34, 141–143, 160, 162. For references to this motif in other cultural contexts, see J. Ward, "Women, Witchcraft and Social Patterning," pp. 99–118; Kieckhefer, *Magic in the Middle Ages*, pp. 31–33, 39, 187; Abusch, "Demonic Image of the Witch," pp. 27–58; Scarborough, "Pharmacology of Sacred Plants," pp. 140, 144–145, 161–162; Breyfogle, "Magic, Women, and Heresy," pp. 435–454; Graf, *Magic in the Ancient World*, pp. 185–186; Cryer, "Magic in Ancient Syria-Palestine," pp. 134–137, 140–141; Janowitz, *Magic in the Roman World*, pp. 86–96; Stephens, *Demon Lovers*, pp. 32–57. Closely connected to the misogynist stereotype of the female magician is the persistent belief that has been felicitously referred to as the "witch fantasy in men's imagination." See Winkler, "Constraints of Eros," p. 228; see also Kieckhefer, *Magic in the Middle Ages*, p. 198; and Hanegraaff, "From the Devil's Gateway," pp. 213–242.

84. On the identification of creation of woman and the ontic arousal of the evil inclination, see *Zohar* 1:49a. For discussion of the theme of magic and the left side of feminine judgment, see E. Wolfson, "Left Contained in the Right," pp. 33–37. For a more comprehensive discussion of the phenomenon of magic in zoharic literature, see Cohen-Alloro, "Magic and Sorcery in the Zohar." On pp. 63–64 and 68–69, the author discusses the correlation of women and magic in zoharic texts (including the passage that I have cited in the body of this chapter). The symbolic valence accorded Egypt as the locus of the demonic power of magic is discussed by Cohen-Alloro, pp. 93–94. For a varied approach to models of magical activity in zoharic literature, see Garb, "Power and Kavvanah in Kabbalah," pp. 154–171.

85. *Zohar* 1:126a. On the link between women and sorcery, see also the passage from *Midrash ha-Ne'elam* on Ruth in *Zohar Ḥadash*, 81b–c.

86. Babylonian Talmud, Shabbat 145b–146a; Yevamot 103b; Avodah Zarah 22b; *Pirqei Rabbi Eli'ezer*, chap. 21, 48a. On the related tradition that Cain was the progeny of Samael and Eve, see Targum Pseudo-Jonathan to Genesis 4:3; Bowker, *Targums and Rabbinic Literature*, pp. 132 and 136 n. 1. For discussion of the aggadic motif of the insemination of Eve by the serpent and its resonance with gnostic texts, see Stroumsa, *Another Seed*, pp. 45–52. G. Anderson, *Genesis of Perfection*, pp. 89–90, raises the possibility that the aggadic motif of Cain being born from the serpent's deflowering of Eve came into Jewish materials from a Christian source wherein it served as the antitype to Mary's virginal conception of Jesus, as we find, for example, in the *Protevangelium of James* 13:1.

87. Such an argument has been made about the treatment of women's ritual obligations in *Sefer ha-Qanah*, an anonymous kabbalistic work composed in all likelihood in late-fourteenth- or early-fifteenth-century Byzantine; see Fishman, "Kabbalistic Perspective," pp. 199–245. For an elaborate treatment of this work, see Kushnir-Oron, "*Sefer ha-Peli'ah* and the *Sefer ha-Kanah*."

88. Scholem, *Major Trends*, pp. 37–38. It should be noted that the exclusion of women was not unique to kabbalah. It seems that medieval Jewry, dominated as it was by rabbinic hegemony, had the distinctive quality of being more exclusive of women than the neighboring cultures. On this point, see the observation regarding the virtual lack of medieval Jewish women writers in comparison to Christian and Muslim women made by T. Rosen, *Unveiling Eve*, pp. 2–3.

89. See Rapoport-Albert, "On Women in Hasidism," p. 523 n. 80; Polen, "Miriam's Dance," pp. 17–18 n. 26; Idel, "Beloved and the Concubine," pp. 141–143. See below, n. 115.

90. Grossman, *Pious and Rebellious*, pp. 344–345, 505, similarly links Scholem's remark about the exclusion of Jewish women from mystical fraternities based on the presumed demonic nature of the feminine to an intensified concern with laws of menstrual purity.

91. See Humbert, "La femme étrangère du livre des Proverbes," pp. 40–64; Archer, "Evil Women," pp. 239–246; Skehan, *Wisdom of Ben Sira*, pp. 78, 90–92, 139, 171, 263–265; Newsom, "Woman and the Discourse of Patriarchal Wisdom," pp. 142–160; Blenkinsopp, "Social Context of the 'Outsider Woman,'" pp. 457–473; Horst, "Images of Women in Ancient Judaism," pp. 43–60; Camp, "Woman Wisdom and the Strange Woman," pp. 85–112; idem, "The Strange Woman of Proverbs," pp. 310–329; Crawford, "Lady Wisdom and Dame Folly," pp. 355–366. On the negative stereotype of the imprudent woman, see Yee, "I Have Perfumed My Bed with Myrrh," pp. 110–126, and Washington, "The Strange Woman," pp. 157–185. On the use of the image of the evil woman as a symbol for the heretical other, see Aubin, "She is the Beginning of All the Ways," pp. 1–23. On the duplicitous nature of the scriptural representation of the feminine, see also Toorn, "Torn between Vice and Virtue," pp. 1–13. The Janus quality of the female in Proverbs is reflected in the contrast in the book of Revelation between Babylon, mother of all harlots (17:4–6), and New Jerusalem, bride of the Lamb (21:1–2). For a psychoanalytic and literary study on the twofold nature of the feminine in Jewish folklore, see Abarbanell, *Eve and Lilith*. Against this background, it is of interest to consider the following characterization of Sarai in *Genesis Apocryphon*, "Indeed, her beauty surpasses that of all women; her beauty is high above all of them. Yet with all this beauty there is much wisdom in her; and whatever she has is lovely" (20 6–8). I have utilized the text and translation prepared by Fitzmyer, *Genesis Apocryphon*, pp. 62–63. The ancient author seems almost surprised that Sarai exemplified both wisdom and physical beauty.

92. Moi, *Sexual/Textual Politics*, p. 167.

93. Loraux, *Mothers in Mourning*, p. 77.

94. Koren, "Woman from Whom God Wanders," pp. 150–208; idem, "Mystical Rationales for the Laws of *Niddah*," pp. 101–121. See also E. Wolfson, "Face of Jacob in the Moon," pp. 267–268 n. 59.

95. As noted by Koren, "Woman from Whom God Wanders," pp. 178–181, 192–194. On the dual nature of *Shekhinah* and her interchangeability with Lilith, see Scholem, *On the Kabbalah and Its Symbolism*, p. 105; idem, *On the Mystical Shape*, pp. 190–192; Tishby, *Wisdom of the Zohar*, pp. 376–379.

96. Regarding the complex compositional and redactional status of the introduction to the printed editions of *Zohar*, see D. Abrams, "When Was the Introduction to the *Zohar* Written?" pp. 211–226.

97. *Zohar* 1:1a; on the image of the red rose as a symbol for the demonic potency, see *Zohar* 1:148a (*Sitrei Torah*). See also *Zohar* 3:107a; *Tiqqunei Zohar*, sec. 19, 39b. On the implicit sexual intent of the symbol of the rose in zoharic literature, see Scholem, *On the Mystical Shape*, pp. 184–185. For a general account of the evocative image from the Song, see McGrady, "More on the Image of the 'Rose among Thorns,'" pp. 33–37. See also Anidjar, *"Our Place in Al-Andalus,"* pp. 196–213.

98. This is the formulation of Asher ben David in *Sefer ha-Yiḥud*. See *R. Asher ben David: His Complete Works*, p. 52; see p. 61: *kol aḥat mehen kelulah be-ḥevratah*, and p. 63 for further discussion on the unification of mercy and judgment in the execution of the divine will, and p. 77, where Asher observes with respect to the three central *sefirot*, the "patriarchs" (*avot*), referred to as the "interior attributes" (*middot ha-penimiyyot*), *kol aḥat mehem poʿelet sheloshtan ke-aḥat . . . we-kollelet bo et kulan*. See Idel, *Kabbalah: New Perspectives*, p. 331. Drob, *Kabbalistic Metaphors*, pp. 131–132, suggests that this kabbalistic principle should be viewed in light of the Neoplatonic idea of "all contained in all." The formulation of Asher ben David (combined with a passage from *Zohar* 2:26b–27a; see chap. 4, n. 195) is discernible in *Book of the Pomegranate*, p. 101; the containment of judgment and mercy in each attribute is affirmed on p. 146. See additional references cited by Idel, "Kabbalistic Material," p. 182 n. 65. See also the text of Gikatilla cited below at n. 122. Finally, it is worth mentioning the observation of Moses Cordovero, *Sefer Yeṣirah im Perush Or Yaqar*, p. 104, that just as in the case of the *sefirot* each one is comprised of all the others, so, too, in the case of the letters.

99. *Kitvei Ramban*, 2:359. See the text attributed to the Rabad cited in chap. 4, n. 185.

100. It is possible that the kabbalistic notion influenced Jung, who articulated a similar hybridity or, in a locution closer to the tenor of his thought, a synchronicity of gender, with masculine traits in the female, feminine traits in the male. For an elaborate discussion of this dimension of Jungian psychology, see Singer, *Androgyny*.

101. Scholem, *On the Kabbalah and Its Symbolism*, p. 107.

102. Babylonian Talmud Berakhot 58a; *Zohar* 3:176b.

103. Babylonian Talmud, Ḥullin 60b; Shavuʿot 9a.

104. Based on the rabbinic idea (attributed to Simeon ben Yoḥai) that all of days of the week exist in pairs with the exception of Sabbath, whose mate is the community of Israel (*kenesset yisraʾel*). Cf. *Genesis Rabbah* 11:8, pp. 95–96. When refracted through the prism of medieval kabbalistic symbolism, the midrashic tradition is interpreted as an allusion to the sacred union of masculine and feminine potencies of the divine, the former signified by the Sabbath and the latter by the Community of Israel. See Ginsburg, *Sabbath in Classical Kabbalah*, pp. 102–103, 109, 110, 111, 167 n. 179, 190.

105. The printed text reads "his desire," but this is clearly a scribal error, as the content demands that the reference is to the desire of woman for man on the basis of Genesis 3:16.

106. Isaac ben Samuel of Acre, *Sefer Meʾirat Einayion*, p. 8.

107. On the "economics of marriage" that evolved in rabbinic literature, see Satlow, *Jewish Marriage*, pp. 199–224.

108. Babylonian Talmud, Berakhot 24a; Yevamot 62a; Sanhedrin 76b, Bekhorot 38b.

109. Babylonian Talmud, Yevamot 62a; see also Sanhedrin 76b transmitted with an alternative introductory formula, reflecting a different redactional stratum.

110. There is, of course, the larger hermeneutical question of whether underlying the halakhic discourse is an ontological premise regarding what the rabbinic elite considered to be the "nature" of woman and man. I fear this is a matter upon which the philosophically oriented and the historically inclined may never agree, but perhaps the field can continue to evolve to the point that genuine dialogue is possible. On the increasing tendency in prerabbinic and rabbinic sources to see contemporary marriage patterned on the biblical primal marriage, see Satlow, *Jewish Marriage*, pp. 60–66.

111. See *Zohar* 1:49b, "Come and see: What is the import of what is written here 'Then the man said, This one at last etc.' (Gen. 2:23)? . . . 'Bone of my bones, and flesh of my flesh,' in order to show her that they are one and there is no separation at all between them."

112. A similar ontological rationale for marriage and the love of women is found in Sufi texts, which begin from the same exegetical standpoint. See Murata, "Mysteries of Marriage," pp. 347–348.

113. Scholem, *Sabbatai Ṣevi*, pp. 403–405. Scholem refers to Sabbatai Ṣevi's efforts on behalf of women's reform as a "striking and very revealing sign of the messianic transformation of the old order, and of the substitution of a messianic Judaism for the traditional and imperfect one." His choice of words discloses much about his own hermeneutical bias. For a recent and expansive treatment of the topic, see Rapoport-Albert, "On the Role of Women in Sabbatianism." My statement regarding the lack of change in the status of women in the ideology of the Sabbatian movement does not apply to the Frankist resurgence of Sabbatianism, which would require an independent analysis.

114. On this point, I find myself in basic disagreement with the claim of Idel, "Eros in der Kabbala," p. 59 (my gratitude to Daniel Abrams for bringing this study to my attention), who speaks of the difficulty of discussing the theme of eros in kabbalistic literature given the diversity of opinions in the "conglomerate of different schools and tendencies." While I certainly concur that kabbalah (as any literary-cultural phenomenon) is marked by multivocality, I maintain that with respect to critical structures of thought, including the complex nexus of eros, gender, and sexuality, the uniformity of approach is more telling than diversity. Moreover, as I argue later on in this chapter, it is precisely the repetition of structure that accounts for the innovation and proliferation of viewpoints. In many of his writings, Idel has repeated his "models" for the study of Jewish mysticism that are presented as ostensibly more pluralistic and multivalent than the so-called Scholemian school. For instance, see Idel, "Kabbalah-Research," pp. 15–46; idem, *Messianic Mystics*, p. 33, where Idel proposes his "theory of models" based on "different paradigms of Kabbalistic messianism" as an alternative to the "essentialistic view" and "monolithic phenomenology" of Scholem's approach. In my judgment, polymorphism and monochromatism as methodological paradigms should not be set in opposition, as the seeing of multiple forms is possible only against the background of remembering what has already been visually apprehended, a point well attested in phenomenological studies of human perception, memory, and imagination.

115. See Vital, *Sefer ha-Ḥezyonot*, pp. 6–7, 10, and text by Abraham Galante cited by Fine, *Physician of the Soul*, p. 67; Faierstein, "*Maggidim*, Spirits, and Women," pp. 186–196; Chajes, *Between Worlds*, pp. 97–118. There is also evidence that in the Sabbatian movement both men and women had prophetic visions. See Scholem, *Sabbatai Ṣevi*, pp. 254, 418–423. Rapoport-Albert, "On Women in Hasidism," p. 496, points out, however, that these women were not central to the phenomenon of mass prophecy and they certainly were not mystical leaders of the messianic movement. For a more detailed discussion, see idem, "On the Role of Women in Sabbatianism." In the case of the Frankist heresy, a significant role is accorded to the feminine aspect of God and there is also evidence of female participants in visionary experiences (see Weinryb, *Jews of Poland*, pp. 236–261), but here too we are dealing with isolated incidents and would therefore be ill advised to draw any general conclusion about the role of women's participation in the history of Jewish mysticism. On the attribution of prophecy and other supernatural powers such as clairvoyance to Jewish women, see also Ben-Naeh, "Tried and Tested Spell," pp. 99–100.

116. Following the conjecture by S. A. Horodecky, several scholars have maintained that in Hasidism women were accorded a more positive and equal social role due to the popularization of esotericism and the overcoming of rabbinic intellectualism by pietistic emotionalism. For a critique of this romantic portrait of Hasidism and the assertion that the social position of women was actually weakened, see J. Katz, *Tradition and Crisis*, p. 212; Rapoport-Albert, "On Women in Hasidism," pp. 495–525. For a more positive depiction of women in Hasidic spirituality and a partial rejoinder to Rapoport-Albert, see Polen, "Miriam's Dance," pp. 1–21. A more balanced and methodologically sophisticated account is offered by N. Deutsch, *Maiden of Ludmir*, pp. 124–143. An astonishingly—and, in my judgment, exaggerated—affirmative role is accorded women in the history of twentieth-century Ḥabad by Lowenthal, "Daughter/Wife of Hasid," pp. 21–28; and see idem, "Women and the Dialectic of Spirituality," pp. 7–65. Wiskind-Elper, *Tradition and Fantasy*, pp. 103–114, attributes a feminist sensibility to Naḥman's teachings based on depictions of *Shekhinah* in his parabolic stories. For a criticism of this tendentious portrayal of Naḥman, see E. Wolfson, "Cut That Binds," pp. 134–135 n. 26.

117. An interesting illustration of the point may be deduced from the study by Weissler, *Voices of the Matriarchs*. Weissler examines Yiddish supplications, *tkhines*, composed by women in an effort to reconstruct

something of women's religious experiences in the Ashkenazi orbit of the late seventeenth to the early nineteenth centuries. Beyond the issue of women's religious devotion and the construction of gender in modern Ashkenazic culture, Weissler's research attempts to redress the imbalance in Judaic scholarship by including a genre of literature that was not written and studied exclusively by male elites of the rabbinic establishment. In one passage, Weissler optimistically states her conclusion: "Ashkenazic Judaism as reflected in Yiddish devotional literature is less rigid in its gender categories than the halakhah and tends to involve them in more playful and symbolic ways" (p. 65). This optimism is tempered, however, by the sober realization that many of the more daring motifs found in these texts, such as the depiction of righteous women in paradise studying Torah (pp. 76–85) or the transformation of the woman who lights the Sabbath candles into a high priest (pp. 89–103), indicate that the androcentric inclination of traditional rabbinic culture is reinforced. Weissler herself admits that the *tkhines* at best present a "complicated web of resistance and accommodation, valorization and abnegation" that makes it impossible to distinguish sharply between women's popular culture and men's elitist culture (p. 175). In the final analysis, the "religious world" that can be inferred from the *tkhine* literature "is, essentially, a set of female variants of male Jewish culture. It does not comprise a Judaism that takes women as the starting point" (pp. 185–186).

118. Consider the formulation of this motif in the sixteenth-century kabbalist, Joseph Ibn Ṣayyaḥ, *Even ha-Shoham*, fol. 4a: "Each of the attributes from the ten *sefirot* is comprised of judgment and mercy except for the supernal *Keter*, which is complete mercy, and it mediates all of them to act with judgment or mercy." For detailed studies of this kabbalist, see Garb, "Kabbalah of Rabbi Joseph Ibn Ṣayyaḥ," pp. 255–313; idem, "Trance Techniques in the Kabbalistic Tradition," pp. 47–67. For some kabbalists even *Keter* must display the androgynous character of bestowing and constricting, a logical consequence of the view that the first of the emanations embodies the coincidence of opposites. An interesting example of this tendency is found in the writings of Moses Cordovero: see *Pardes Rimmonim*, 15:5, 77b–c, 23:11, 24a; *Elimah Rabbati*, 20b–c; Ben-Shlomo, *Mystical Theology of Moses Cordovero*, pp. 271, 277–280. See chap. 4, n. 243. It must be noted, however, that in other passages in his compositions Cordovero emphasizes (following earlier sources, principally the Idrot strata of zoharic literature) that *Keter* is entirely right without any opposing left. See, for instance, *Elimah Rabbati*, 67b–c. The two approaches are not necessarily contradictory, as it is plausible to maintain that within *Keter* the feminine left is so completely integrated in the masculine right that we can speak of this attribute as having only one side. Cordovero adopts this approach in *Shiʿur Qomah*, 9a.

119. Liebes, *Studies in the Zohar*, pp. 99–105, and references to other scholars cited on pp. 203 nn. 77–79 and 204 n. 87.

120. This is one of the technical terms Gikatilla uses to designate the sefirotic emanations. See Gikatilla, *Shaʿarei Orah*, 1:65; Scholem, *On the Mystical Shape*, p. 177; Gikatilla, *Secret du Mariage*, p. 16. It is clear from this particular context that the term *maʿalot* more broadly connotes all levels of being, including the sefirotic gradations.

121. That is, the *sefirah* of *Keter*, which is hidden so that it can be demarcated only by the scribal jot on top of *yod*, the first letter of YHWH, the name that comprises the sefirotic emanations.

122. Gikatilla, *Shaʿarei Orah*, 1: 238. Compare idem, *Secret du Mariage*, pp. 42–43 (the English rendering of the Hebrew text is my own): "Know that the one who knows the secret of the supernal grades [*maʿalot*] and the emanation of the *sefirot* in the secret of that which overflows [*mashpiʿa*] and that which receives [*meqabbel*], in the secret of earth and heaven and heaven and earth, knows the secret of the bond of all the *sefirot*, and the secret of all created beings in the world, how they receive from one another." See analysis by Mopsik in Gikatilla, *Secret du Mariage*, pp. 16–33. Similar language is found in Gikatilla, *Shaʿarei Ṣedeq*, 25a. On the secret of androgyny applied to the human soul, see idem, *R. Joseph Gikatilla's Commentary*, p. 53. The "secret of the androgyne" and the dual capacity of each of the *sefirot* to bestow and to receive are also affirmed by Joseph of Hamadan, *Fragment d'un commentaire sur la Genèse*, p. 5 (Hebrew section). In the French section, pp. 52–53 n. 32, Mopsik asserts that the view of Joseph of Hamadan stands in opposition to my thesis regarding the male androgyne since androgyny is clearly linked to both male and female. The argument is repeated in Mopsik, *Le sexe des âmes*, p. 60. In my opinion, just the opposite is the case, for the nature of the androgyny

formulated here is decidedly androcentric insofar as the feminine receives and the masculine bestows. Moreover, the overflow of the male is inscribed in the female like the flame in the coal. The notion of the male androgyne that I have suggested applies to the kabbalistic sources does not negate the view that each *sefirah* comprehends mercy and judgment, bestowing and receiving. The issue, rather, is the ontically derivative status of the feminine vis-à-vis the masculine and the inflexible linkage of bestowal and the male, on one hand, and reception and the female, on the other. The most recent skewed characterization of my thesis is presented by Schäfer, *Mirror of His Beauty*, p. 285 n. 37. In chapter 4, I shall deal with Schäfer's specific challenge to my interpretation of the relevant bahiric passages, but here I wish only to draw the reader's attention to the author's comment that he sees no basis for my "repeated claim that God's allegedly primordial androgyny is only superficial, that in reality the feminine emanates from and depends on the masculine." To claim, as I do, that medieval kabbalah is suffused in an ontology that recognizes only one gender that comprises two sexes, what I call the male androgyne (for this I am indebted to Wendy Doniger O'Flaherty's study of the androgyne motif in Hindu mythology, as I acknowledged explicitly in "Woman—The Feminine as Other," p. 192 n. 4) is not to say that I have ever suggested that the myth of the primordial androgyne is "only superficial." Perhaps Schäfer imparts a meaning to this term of which I am unaware, but in the dozens of studies that I have written that deal with the topic of gender and kabbalistic symbolism, I have never once referred to the myth of androgyny as "superficial." Regrettably, what is superficial is Schäfer's rendering of my portrayal of the androcentric construction of androgyny on the part of traditional kabbalists and his lack of engagement with feminist studies that have shown the androcentric underpinnings of the image of the androgyne as a privileging of male subjectivity. For representative studies, see O'Flaherty, *Women, Androgynes, and Other Mythical Beasts*; Warren, "Is Androgyny the Answer to Sexual Stereotyping?" pp. 170–196; Weil, *Androgyny and the Denial of Difference*; E. Goldberg, *Lord Who Is Half Woman*, pp. 113–132. I gladly situate my work within this vector of contemporary scholarship.

123. See Farber-Ginat, "Shell Precedes the Fruit," pp. 121–124.

124. See the introduction by Ben-Shlomo in his edition of Gikatilla, *Shaʿarei Orah*, 1:30–31; and the discussion of this philosophical issue in Tishby, *Wisdom of the Zohar*, pp. 242–246.

125. I have qualified this claim with the word "ostensibly" since there are passages in Gikatilla's writings that suggest that *Keter* is portrayed in decisively masculine or, to be more precise, phallic terms, for example, the white head or the beard of thirteen curls, images that bear a resemblance to the imagery found in the Idrot sections of zoharic literature. See Gikatilla, *Shaʿarei Orah*, 1:31–33, and E. Wolfson, "Beyond Good and Evil," pp. 118–122. A revised version of this study will appear in my forthcoming *Venturing Beyond*. On the purely masculine nature of *Keter*, see also the passage from Joseph of Hamadan cited in chap. 4, n. 230.

126. Babylonian Talmud, Yoma 54a. See Idel, *Kabbalah: New Perspectives*, pp. 130–134; idem, "Sexual Metaphors and Praxis," pp. 202–204. In light of the esoteric interpretation of the cherubim that may be elicited from Jewish sources in late antiquity, it is of interest to consider the comment in Hebrews 9:5 that it is not appropriate to speak in detail about the "cherubim of glory." On the divine attributes in rabbinic and kabbalistic sources, see also Liebes, *Studies in Jewish Myth*, pp. 27–42.

127. See text of Joseph ben Shalom Ashkenazi cited in chap. 4, n. 233.

128. *Sefer Yeṣirah* 23a (pseudo-RaBaD commentary).

129. For discussion of this matter, see E. Wolfson, *Through a Speculum*, pp. 70–73.

130. *Sefer Yeṣirah*, 24b.

131. Proclus, *Proclus' Commentary on Plato's Parmenides*, I, 668, pp. 53–54.

132. For discussion of the different facets of the concept of activity in the thought of Proclus, see Gersh, ΚΙΝΗΣΙΣ ΑΚΙΝΗΤΟΣ, pp. 81–102. On the theme of participation in Platonic thought, see Brisson, *Même et l'Autre*, pp. 116–125.

133. Proclus, *Proclus' Commentary on Plato's Parmenides*, II, 740, p. 114. For an informative discussion on the notion of contrariety in Greek philosophic thought, which undoubtedly influenced Neoplatonic thinkers, see Anton, *Aristotle's Theory of Contrariety*, pp. 1–67.

134. Proclus, *Procli Diadochi In Platonis Timaeum Commentaria*, 17A, p. 18. All renderings of this text are

my own, though I have consulted the following translations: Proclus, *Commentaire sur le Timée*, vol. 1, p. 45; idem, *Commentaries of Proclus on the Timaeus of Plato*, vol. 1, p. 14.

135. An illustration of the point is found in Proclus, *On the Existence of Evils*, 13.13–17, p. 67: "For the good is measure and light, whereas evil is darkness and absence of measure; the former is the cause of all foundation and all power, the latter is without foundation and weak; the former is that which sustains everything, the latter that which corrupts each thing in which it is present, each according to its own rank; for, as we have explained, not everything has the same mode of corruption."

136. Cornford, *Plato's Cosmology*, p. 10.

137. In the final stages of preparation of this chapter, Mopsik's *Le sexe des âmes* came across my desk. On pp. 76–75, Mopsik cites a portion of the same passage from Proclus as textual support for his contention that gender is located not in the body but in the soul, and hence it is possible to conceive of heterosexual and homosexual yearning as legitimate or "natural" possibilities in the economy of desire embraced by kabbalists. I concur with this claim, but I would contend that the shift from body to soul as the site for *différence sexuelle* does not alter the androcentric bias of the gender construction, which in fact calls into question whether it is credible to speak of a genuine sense of sexual difference rather than a one-sex theory, with the feminine derived ontically from the masculine, a point that Mopsik assiduously ignores as he repeatedly emphasizes the unity of the primal androgyne as masculine and feminine interpreted as autonomous powers (ibid., p. 77). It is also curious that Mopsik is completely silent with respect to the misogynist characterizations of the feminine offered by Proclus; it is reasonable to expect a scholar writing on the issue of masculinity and femininity to heed the specific depictions of male and female before rushing to promote a doctrine of androgyny that challenges the engendering structure of the primal male androgyne. It is lamentable that Mopsik did not realize that his claim for shifting the locus of gender identity is consonant with my own view. I believe a more sympathetic reading from him would have gone a great distance in advancing the field, but sadly, with his untimely passing, this is not to be, and even colleagues who embrace my work more generously are left with the impression that Mopsik's discussion of homosexuality is a radical departure.

138. Proclus, *In Platonis Timaeum Commentaria*, 18c, p. 46; idem, *Commentaire sur le Timée*, vol. 1, pp. 77–78; idem, *Commentaries of Proclus on the Timaeus*, vol. 1, pp. 38–39.

139. Proclus, *Proclus' Commentary on Plato's Parmenides*, II, 740, p. 114.

140. Proclus, *Elements of Theology*, prop. 123, p. 109.

141. Ibid., prop. 129, p. 115. On the motif of participation, see De Ruk, "Causation and Participation in Proclus," pp. 1–34; Meijer, "Participation in Henads and Monads," pp. 65–87; Siorvanes, *Proclus*, pp. 71–86.

142. Neumann, *Origins*, p. 75; for more detailed discussion of the maternal uroboros, see pp. 13–18.

143. Neumann, *Great Mother*, p. 7.

144. Neumann, *Origins*, p. 371.

145. Neumann, *Great Mother*, p. 6.

146. Ibid.

147. Neumann, *Origins*, pp. 5–6, 367–369.

148. Ibid., p. 276.

149. Ibid., pp. 276–277.

150. Neumann's position is captured succinctly in the remark of Jacobi, *Complex/ Archetype/ Symbol*, p. 146, that in the Great Mother "the male principle is not yet operative . . . the opposites, male and female, are not yet separate." The engendering mythos of traditional kabbalistic symbolism, according to my understanding, is predicated on the notion of the male androgyne in which the female principle is "not yet operative" as a distinct and actualized potency.

151. Neumann, *Origins*, pp. 322–323.

152. Neumann, *Origins*, p. 331, notes, "In the patriarchal development of the Judaeo-Christian west, with its masculine, monotheistic trend toward abstraction, the goddess, as a feminine figure of wisdom, was disenthroned and repressed. She survived only secretly, for the most part on heretical and revolutionary bypaths." It is likely that in the case of Judaism, Neumann has in mind the kabbalistic symbol of *Shekhinah*.

153. Although Neumann consistently speaks of the Great Mother in a manner that justifies the locution

"female androgyne," which is to say, the male is contained in the female, it behooves me to note that Neumann's depiction of the archetypal feminine as a vessel and the association of the latter with the body and the material world (Neumann, *Great Mother,* pp. 39–47, 95–96, 120–146, 162–164, 171–172, 282–287, 325–329; idem, *Origins,* pp. 13–14) bespeak a typical androcentric depiction of the female as a container or orifice the value of which is determined by what is received from the male. Finally, it is incumbent on me to underscore that for Neumann the archetype of the Great Mother is a psychological and not a sociological structure; thus it lives in man as well as woman, individually or collectively, and hence the archetype can take form in a patriarchal society just as the archetype of the Father God can take form in a matriarchal society (Neumann, *Great Mother,* pp. 91, 94–95).

154. Neumann, *Fear of the Feminine,* pp. 102–103.

155. Scholem, *On the Mystical Shape,* pp. 185–186.

156. In the zoharic context, *Shekhinah* is identified both as the "redeeming angel," *ha-mal'akh ha-go'el* (based on Gen. 48:16) and as the angel who bore the name of God in his entrails (*ki shemi be-qirbo,* "for my name is in him," words attributed to the divine voice) as he accompanied the Israelites in the desert (Exod. 23:20–23). On the identification of *Shekhinah* (designated Matronita) and the angel of God (*mal'akh ha-elohim*), see *Zohar* 2:51a.

157. *Zohar* 1:232a. In the continuation of the text, the dual nature of *Shekhinah* is related to the belief that angels appear in this world as both male and female, an idea linked exegetically to the biblical image of the "fiery ever-turning sword," *lahaṭ ha-ḥerev ha-mithapekhet* (Gen. 3:24). Regarding the zoharic passage, see Tishby, *Wisdom of the Zohar,* p. 372; E. Wolfson, "Woman—The Feminine as Other," p. 188. The extent to which the contemporary need to find a voice for the feminine in traditional kabbalistic symbolism blinds the scholar is exemplified in the comment by Daniel C. Matt in the introduction to his critical edition of David ben Yehudah he-Ḥasid, *Book of Mirrors,* p. 28. After citing a portion of the zoharic text wherein *Shekhinah* is described as assuming a male character when she bestows blessings on the world, Matt writes, "From the perspective of the lower worlds, She is a powerful governess; from a higher perspective, She is simply transmitting divine blessing or chastisement." How is it that the contemporary interpreter employs the word "governess" to depict the status of *Shekhinah* that the zoharic text itself portrays as masculine? The one example is, sadly, illustrative of a much larger tendentious reading of the medieval kabbalistic sources predicated on attenuating or obscuring their androcentric orientation in the name of political correctness.

158. In the course of teaching kabbalistic religious philosophy over the last two decades, I have found that audiences are always struck by the symbolic correlation of masculinity/mercy and femininity/judgment, expecting the reverse. This was indeed the more typical association in the medieval Christian ideal of the two faces of divine justice—the punitive dimension linked to the father and the merciful to the mother. See Semple, "Male Psyche," p. 186.

159. It is possible, although the matter is not stated explicitly in the zoharic homily, that there is allusion here to the two stages of pregnancy and giving birth. With regard to the former, the female is engendered as feminine, the vessel that holds in, and with regard to the latter, the female is masculinized, the opening of the womb to discharge. On the use of the image of a pregnant woman to describe *Shekhinah* when she is filled with the souls of the righteous, see *Zohar* 2213b, 259a.

160. The pronoun is in the third person singular masculine, *ihu,* but I have accepted the practice of translators, scholarly and traditional (for instance, Tishby, *Wisdom of Zohar,* p. 202), in rendering it in the feminine, which is demanded by the language of the rest of the passage.

161. *Zohar* 3:187a.

162. *Zohar* 1:60a–b.

163. *Zohar* 1:33b–34a. See *Zohar* 2:235b, where the "mystery of Adonai," the ark of the covenant, *Shekhinah,* is linked to the "mystery of the tabernacle." In that context, the epithet Adonai is said to be in the "likeness of the mystery of the supernal holy name, YHWH." Although the symbolic associations are somewhat different, the main point is the same.

164. Moses de León, *Book of the Pomegranate,* pp. 203–204.

165. Tishby, *Wisdom of Zohar,* pp. 379–381.

166. Moses de León, *Sheqel ha-Qodesh*, p. 26.

167. Ibid., p. 72.

168. Pattai, *Hebrew Goddess*, pp. 186–206.

169. See Liebes, *Studies in the Zohar*, pp. 103–126.

170. In chapter 5, I discuss the import of the book's title for understanding the author's worldview.

171. Joseph of Hamadan, *Sefer Tashak*, p. 436.

172. Ibid., pp. 97, 356; see p. 70, where *Ḥokhmah* is similarly described as "occasionally overflowing and occasionally receiving."

173. *Genesis Rabbah* 1:3, pp. 21–22; Babylonian Talmud, Ḥagigah 12a.

174. Babylonian Talmud, Megillah 15b; Sanhedrin 111b.

175. Joseph of Hamadan, *Sefer Tashak*, p. 355.

176. Ibid., pp. 69, 73, 103–104, and see discussion in E. Wolfson, *Circle in the Square*, pp. 211–212 n. 85, 224–225 n. 152. On the identification of the encircling spirit as the wellspring and source of all things created, the "pattern in the pure and holy chain," which I assume should be decoded as a reference to the phallic potency, see Joseph of Hamadan, *Sefer Tashak*, p. 64. Consider also the passage from Joseph of Hamadan cited in E. Wolfson, *Through a Speculum*, p. 340 and discussion in n. 48 *ad locum*. An alternative explanation of the eschatological symbol of the crown perched on the head of the righteous is offered by Jacob ben Sheshet, *Sefer Meshiv Devarim Nekhoḥim*, pp. 71–72. If I understand this text properly, then a distinction is drawn between the status of the righteous in this world and in the world-to-come: in the former state, they are crowned by *Shekhinah* (linked exegetically to Ps. 8:6) whereas, in the latter, they are crowned by *Tif'eret*, which ascends to *Keter* (linked to Ps. 103:4). In support of the depiction of the conjunction of the righteous and *Shekhinah*, Jacob ben Sheshet mentions a tradition concerning the drawing forth of the *dalet* in the word *eḥad* of the *Shema*, which he ascribes to Isaac the Blind. The author adds "as I have written his language in the second chapter with respect to the verse 'Hear O Israel' (Deut. 6:4)." Vajda, op. cit., p. 72 n. 44, remarks that he did not find this reference in the manuscript he utilized. The reference seems to be the third (and not second) chapter of *Sefer ha-Emunah we-ha-Biṭṭaḥon*, where Jacob ben Sheshet does explicate the liturgical practice connected to the word *eḥad*, including a tradition he heard in the name of Isaac the Blind. See *Kitvei Ramban*, 2:362.

177. Joseph of Hamadan, *Sefer Tashak*, pp. 166–168.

178. E. Wolfson, *Through a Speculum*, pp. 357–368.

179. For discussion of this motif elicited from a text of Cordovero, see E. Wolfson, "Coronation of the Sabbath Bride," pp. 336–338, and references to zoharic sources cited on p. 337 n. 97.

180. This is not to deny that Scholem was well aware of the centrality of phallic imagery in kabbalistic tradition connected especially to the ninth emanation, *Yesod*, to which in fact he dedicated a separate treatment; see Scholem, *On the Mystical Shape*, pp. 88–139. See also idem, *Origins*, pp. 152–158; idem, *On the Kabbalah and Its Symbolism*, pp. 104–105.

181. Scholem, *On the Mystical Shape*, p. 188. For a less nuanced presentation of the feminine character of *Shekhinah*, see idem, *Major Trends*, p. 230.

182. Scholem, *Mystical Shape*, p. 174. Interestingly, in *On the Kabbalah and Its Symbolism*, p. 105, Scholem notes that the third *sefirah* is the "upper mother or upper *Shekhinah*, but also, strange to say, the demiurgic potency." Though Scholem does not elaborate, I would surmise that what struck him as "strange" was the amalgamation of demiurgical and maternal characteristics in the same potency, the former typically associated with the paternal; see p. 107, where Scholem contrasts the demiurgical qualities of *Binah* and *Malkhut* on the grounds that the former are purely positive, whereas the latter are combined with pejorative, even demonic, aspects.

183. MS Munich 47, fol. 338b. For discussion of this text, see Scholem, "Eine unbekannte mystische Schrift des Mose de Leon," pp. 109–123. The verse is interpreted in an analogous manner in *Zohar* 3:39b, 46b.

184. In Moses de León's writings, *Tif'eret* is identified as the living creature whose name is "Israel," a

tradition preserved in the Heikhalot corpus; see E. Wolfson, *Along the Path*, p. 7 and references cited p. 118 n. 48. See *Shushan Edut*, p. 336.

185. E. Wolfson, *Through a Speculum*, pp. 339–345; idem, *Circle in the Square*, pp. 116–119; idem, "*Tiqqun ha-Shekhinah*," pp. 313–329; idem, "The Engenderment of Messianic Politics," pp. 203–258, esp. pp. 230–247.

186. Babylonian Talmud, Sanhedrin 22b.

187. Luzzatto, *Adir ba-Marom*, p. 134. For a slightly different translation and brief analysis of this passage, see E. Wolfson, "*Tiqqun ha-Shekhinah*," p. 325.

188. Needless to say, Luzzatto explicates this theme in many of his writings. Particularly helpful is the discussion in *Pitḥei Ḥokhmah wa-Daʿat*, secs. 92–94, pp. 226–229.

189. See E. Wolfson, *Circle in the Square*, pp. 110–112, and references to primary and secondary sources given, pp. 227 nn. 158–160 and 228 n. 168.

190. See E. Wolfson, *Circle in the Square*, pp. 213–214 n. 96. The androcentric, if not misogynist, tendency reflected in this talmudic dictum was influential in shaping attitudes toward women in medieval rabbinic texts and beyond. See, for instance, Abraham Ibn Ezra's comment on the prohibition of a woman wearing a "man's apparel" (Deut. 22:5), "for the woman is not created except to establish progeny, and if she were to go out to war with men she would be led in the way to harlotry." Text cited from Ibn Ezra, *Perushei ha-Torah*, 3:287.

191. For translation and analysis of a representative list of sources, see E. Wolfson, *Circle in the Square*, pp. 85–89, and idem, "Divine Suffering," pp. 126–128 (some of these passages are repeated in chap. 4 of this monograph). In Luzzatto's kabbalah, closely following his Lurianic sources, there is a perfect symmetry between creation and redemption: just as in the originary state, the female is contained in the male in the image of the corona of the phallus, so the end is characterized by the restoration of the feminine to the masculine. See E. Wolfson, "*Tiqqun ha-Shekhinah*," pp. 322–332.

192. Here it is incumbent on me to correct the view of Tishby, *Wisdom of the Zohar*, p. 372, that *Shekhinah* is called *aṭarah* because "all the worlds are crowned by it." For a different explanation, see Liebes, *Studies in Jewish Myth*, p. 47. According to Liebes, citing the work of Asi Farber-Ginat and Moshe Idel (references on p. 264 n. 108), the symbol of the diadem (*aṭarah*) in early kabbalah "derived from mythical ideas . . . such as wreathing the divine crown from the prayers offered by His people and the phylacteries laid by God." This seems to be the understanding embraced as well by A. Green, *Keter*, pp. 141–144. The precise intent of the term *aṭarah* and the masculine transvaluation of the feminine implied thereby, which has been a cornerstone of my own interpretation of the kabbalistic symbol, is stated explicitly in an anonymous commentary on the *sefirot* published by Scholem, "Traditions of R. Jacob and R. Isaac," p. 230: "The tenth *sefirah, Shekhinah*, is the diadem [*aṭeret*], and she is alluded to in the feminine language, and it is this world, for this world is guided by her through the efflux that she receives from the masculine, which is the sixth attribute . . . and it is called the angel of God [*mal'akh elohim*], and Rabbi Moses explained that it is apposite rather than in the construct state, and the meaning is the angel that is called *elohim*, the angel that is called YHWH, 'The angel that is the Lord appeared to him' (Exod. 3:2). The Rabbi said, 'Therefore she is called *aṭeret*, for the providence of the world [*hanhagat ha-olam*] is by means of her,' as we have explained." The author of this text alludes to two passages in the commentary on the Torah by Naḥmanides, references that are lacking in the short recension. The first is to Exod. 14:19 (Moses ben Naḥman, *Perushei ha-Torah*, 1:351) and the second to Exod. 23:20 (vol. 1, p. 442). For my purposes, the latter is crucial. The exact language of Naḥmanides is: "By way of truth, the angel about whom promises are made here is the redeeming angel [*mal'akh ha-go'el*] in whose midst is the great name . . . and the verse refers to it as an angel since the entire providence of the world is dependent on this attribute." Significantly, Naḥmanides himself does not utilize the word *aṭeret* (the version printed in *Liqquṭei Shikhehah u-Fe'ah* is more faithful to the language of Naḥmanides). It is nevertheless accurate on the part of the latter kabbalist to interpret Naḥmanides in this fashion, for the designation *aṭarah* indeed relates to the providential role assumed by *Shekhinah*, which is also the esoteric sense of the title *mal'akh* applied to her. Both "diadem" and "angel" denote the masculine transposition of the feminine presence vis-à-vis the cosmos. Finally, I note the attention drawn to the symbol of *aṭarah*, especially in the anonymous *Maʿarekhet*

ha-Elohut, in Neumark, *History of Jewish Philosophy*, vol. 1, pp. 191, 196–199. Neumark clearly understood that the significance of this symbol was connected to the mystery of androgyny in the divine. Thus he observed that *Malkhut* "is called *aṭarah* because it is the last of the *sefirot* and it serves as the final channel for all of the influx that comes from above. But, in truth, the power of *aṭarah* is in the middle bar that mediates between all the *sefirot* and unites them as one. The activity of *aṭarah*, which is the overflow of the potencies from the androgynous source, from within the inner unity of the elements of masculinity and femininity, is an activity shared by all the *sefirot*, and therefore *aṭarah* is the motif shared by every movement in the world of emanation" (pp. 196–197).

193. E. Wolfson, "Engenderment of Messianic Politics," pp. 223–224.

194. Tishby, *Wisdom of the Zohar*, pp. 245–246.

195. *Zohar* 3:128b.

196. Luzzatto, *Adir ba-Marom*, pp. 133–134.

197. It seems that an allusion to this doctrine is found in *Zohar* 2:177a (*Sifra di-Ṣeniʿuta*): "The supernal *yod*, which is crowned in the crown of *Atiqa*, is the supernal membrane that is pure and sealed." The image of the *yod* in the brain to symbolize the attribute of wisdom set in the middle and encompassing everything is found in the commentary to *Sefer Yeṣirah* that preserves the teachings of Isaac the Blind. See Isaac the Blind, *Perush Sefer Yeṣirah*, p. 2. The conventional wisdom of experts in the field is that the aforementioned commentary is properly attributable to Isaac, though Scholem did surmise on the basis of a reference in one passage to "our teacher says" (ibid., p. 12) that the text was a transcription on the part of a disciple of Isaac's teaching (presumably from a text) or written from the master's dictation. See Scholem, *Origins*, pp. 257–258. For further weighing of the evidence, see Sendor, "Emergence of Provençal Kabbalah," vol. 1, pp. 45–50. I concur with Sendor's conclusion, "whether the writer was R. Isaac himself or a student copyist, the text can be considered an accurate record of R. Isaac's thought" (p. 50), and thus I refer to the commentary as "preserving the teachings of Isaac the Blind."

198. In distinguishing "phallus" (the cultural mark of signification) from "penis" (the physical organ), I am following the suggestion of Lacan; see chap. 3, n. 119.

199. The text of Luzzatto illustrates a larger point that is true of kabbalistic symbolism more generally and particularly pronounced in the intricacies of Lurianic theosophy. Somatic images such as *aṭeret berit*, the corona of the phallus, or, alternatively, *aṭeret yesod*, do not denote only the lower gradations of the divine anthropos. On the contrary, they are semiotic markers of aspects of the highest realm of the divine, even applicable to Ein Sof, according to some texts. In kabbalistic lore, hardly altered by time or place, the myth of the ascent of *aṭarah*, which draws upon much older material describing the coronation of God by the prayers of Israel, denotes the elevation of the lowest gradation to the highest, which signifies the reconstitution of the broken circle of divine unity. Moreover, in the relevant sources, this process denotes as well the gender transformation of the feminine by her restoration to the masculine in the form of the corona or crown. A. Green, *Keter*, pp. 151–153, presents the former meaning, but he has not appreciated the gender implications of the mythical image, a point that has been central to my own reflections. See below, n. 256.

200. E. Wolfson, "Divine Suffering," p. 156 n. 128.

201. I am in agreement with the formulation of Eilberg-Schwartz, *Savage in Judaism*, p. 27: "Since the historical anthropologist cannot question natives about the meaning of practices, she or he is in the position of doing cultural archaeology, a mode of interpretation that involves imagining what practices meant from incomplete and partial remains. These unstated meanings can often be detected from symbolic artifacts such as metaphors, which point to larger complexes of unarticulated meaning." See also pp. 143–144: "Symbolic exegesis is the attempt to tease out implicit meanings that are embedded in the practice in question. . . . Since the historical anthropologist cannot question natives about the meaning of practices, she or he is in the position of doing cultural archaeology, a mode of interpretation which involves imagining what practices meant from incomplete cultural remains. Unstated meanings can often be detected from symbolic artifacts such as metaphors which point to larger complexes of meaning that never found explicit articulation."

202. The philosophical point is well stated by Salvaggio, *Enlightened Absence*, p. x: "Yet while my primary concern is with representations of woman, implicit in my argument is the belief that configuration and reality

are always infused in each other—making it impossible to talk about the plight of women without also understanding the ways in which they and their gender have been represented, and just as it is impossible to talk about schemes of representation without constantly keeping in mind the effects of these configurations in the real world."

203. Grossman's *Pious and Rebellious* is a comprehensive attempt to reconstruct the lives of women in medieval Europe (in both the Ashkenazic and Sephardic cultural milieu) based exclusively on documents written by men of the rabbinic elite. See also Baskin, "Jewish Women in the Middle Ages," pp. 94–114. On the use of Geniza sources, see Goitein, "Sexual Mores of the Common People," pp. 43–61; idem, *Mediterranean Society*; Kraemer, "Women's Letters from the Cairo Geniza," pp. 161–182. For additional studies that treat in some measure the sexual lives and domestic rights of women in the Jewish middle ages, see Z. Falk, *Jewish Matrimonial Law*; Assis, "Sexual Behaviour," pp. 25–59; M. Friedman, "Ethics of Medieval Jewish Marriage," pp. 83–101; idem, "Halacha as Evidence for the Study of Sexual Mores," pp. 143–160; Barkaï, *Les infortunes de Dinah*; Westreich, *Transitions in the Legal Status of the Wife*, pp. 62–198.

204. For an elaborate discussion of this subject, see Spiro, *Gender Ideology*.

205. See N. Miller, "Text's Heroine," pp. 112–120.

206. Gold, *Lady and the Virgin*, pp. 73–74. See also Ellington, *From Sacred Body*, pp. 47–76, esp. pp. 69–70.

207. An excellent illustration of this methodological strategy is found in the trilogy produced by Ilan, *Jewish Women in Greco-Roman Palestine*; *Mine Are Yours Are Hers*; and *Integrating Women into Second Temple History*. Consider also the review of scholarly literature offered by S. Heschel, "Genre et historiographie juive," pp. 157–180, and the monograph by Grossman, *Pious and Rebellious*. Grossman offers a balanced account of historical changes that affected Jewish women in medieval Europe, noting both improvement and decline. There is an enormous amount that one can learn from this work, but it is still marred theoretically by privileging a materialist historicism that fails to take into account the difference between sexual and gender identification. Many of the changes he notes should be examined in terms of the former and not the latter, which, in my view, would not alter substantially the construction of gender that informed rabbinic culture in medieval societies. An exception to this prevalent tendency in Jewish studies is found in Fonrobert, *Menstrual Purity*. In this work, Fonrobert offers the reader a sophisticated gender analysis that attempts to locate a "counterdiscourse" that "disturbs the talmudic metaphoric imagination of the women's body even within talmudic literature" (p. 67), that is, the portrayal of woman's body as a subject rather than an object determined functionally in relation to man, an "alternative constellation" that may lie on the "margins of the androcentric universe" of the rabbis but that nevertheless presents a "corrosion of the 'center' of androcentrism" (p. 101). Following the feminist theorists Cixous and Irigaray, Fonrobert attempts to "move beyond the strategy of critique to a constructivist mode" (p. 66) based on discerning a rupture within the fold of rabbinic literature itself. Although I am sympathetic to this approach, I am not convinced of the argument on textual grounds nor am I hopeful that ruptures of this sort are enveloping of the feminine. Surely this is not evident in kabbalistic texts. Notwithstanding my reservation, I would not consider a continual effort to discern cracks in the edifice futile. In my judgment, a sophisticated approach to this question is displayed in Exum, *Fragmented Women*. The interpretative strategy of recovering the voice of the feminine adopted by Exum is predicated on exhuming the subversion of negative portrayals of women preserved in the scripture of ancient Israel.

208. T. Rosen, *Unveiling Eve*, p. 3.

209. Ibid., p. 5.

210. For a more detailed analysis of this theme and a critique of the oral/written binary that has dominated the field, see E. Wolfson, "Beyond the Spoken Word."

211. E. Wolfson, *Circle in the Square*, pp. 49–78. On the images of writing (*kitāba*) or the book (*kitāb*) as metaphorical tropes for sexual union in the thought of Ibn ʿArabī, see Chittick, *Self-Disclosure*, p. 5.

212. Isaac Luria, *Perush Sifra di-Ṣeniʿuta*, in Vital, *Shaʿar Maʾamerei Rashbi*, 27c; printed anew in Vital, *Sefer ha-Derushim*, p. 257. See also *Shaʿar Maʾamerei Rashbi*, 28a; *Sefer ha-Derushim*, p. 259.

213. Moi, *Sexual/Textual Politics*, p. 44.

214. Bourdieu, *Masculine Domination*, pp. 41–42.

215. Ibid., p. 11.

216. Orr, *Donors, Devotees, and Daughters of God*, p. 179.

217. Feminist Jewish theologians such as Judith Plaskow, Lynn Gottlieb, and Marcia Falk have expressed this hesitancy. See the concise but insightful discussion in Oppenheim, *Speaking/Writing of God*, pp. 77–78. Scholars of kabbalah would benefit from the discussion on the compatibility of feminism and women's mystical writings in Mazzoni, *Saint Hysteria*, pp. 156–196. Kabbalistic literature from the Middle Ages (and, for the most part, continuing in the modern period even to the present) leaves one with an even more difficult task as we do not have literary compositions or any historical documentation written or even inspired by Jewish women's mystical experiences.

218. See the preliminary remarks of Tirosh-Rothschild, "Continuity and Revision," pp. 182 and 186. Far more perceptive was the observation of Neumann, *Great Mother*, p. 50, regarding the "patriarchal world of India, as of the cabala and Christianity." The problematic nature of the mistaken perceptions on the part of leading scholars in the field is most acutely felt in the influence they have had on other fields. A noteworthy example of this phenomenon is the comparison of the Mesopotamian goddess Ishtar, gnostic Sophia, and kabbalistic *Shekhinah* in Parpola, *Assyrian Prophecies*, pp. xxxv–xxxvi, lxxxix n. 98. Particularly troublesome is Parpola's uncritical acceptance of the feminine characterization of *Shekhinah*, which he then compares to what he considers to be similar depictions of Ishtar. In my judgment, this approach is methodologically flawed on several fronts, but this is not the place to elaborate. See idem, "The Assyrian Tree of Life," pp. 161–208. In spite of my critique of Parpola's attempts to use later Jewish esotericism to explain the contours of biblical monotheism, I would not deny the fact that the range of the mythical imagination and actual ritual practices based thereon in ancient Israel were far greater than what has been preserved in the literary confines of Scripture. The relationship of this older material to kabbalah, however, is another matter. For a thorough and careful analysis of the polytheism of the ancient Near East and the emerging monotheism of biblical Israel, with special focus on the ways in which gender assumptions about the divine are mirrored in the social roles assigned to men and women of a particular cult, see Henshaw, *Female and Male*. See also references in chap. 4, nn. 3 and 4.

219. Vital, *Sefer ha-Gilgulim*, chap. 19, 21a.

220. I have benefited from the discussion of Foucault in Braidotti, "Body-Images," pp. 17–19. See also McLaren, *Feminism, Foucault, and Embodied Subjectivity*, pp. 81–116.

221. Fausto-Sterling, *Sexing the Body*, pp. 3–4, 20.

222. Ibid., p. 21 (emphasis in original). For a recent attempt to essentialize gender difference in neurobiological terms, see Baron-Cohen, *Truth about the Male and Female Brain*.

223. Grosz, *Volatile Bodies*, pp. 138–159.

224. For instance, Tishby, *Wisdom of the Zohar*, pp. 379–381, discerns that maternal images applied to *Shekhinah* signify her mercy in relation to Israel in particular and to the lower worlds in general, but he is oblivious to the fact that this implies masculinization of the feminine. Liebes, "Zohar and Eros," p. 105 n. 250, refers to the attribution of the idiom "world of masculinity" to *Binah*, which is personified as the mother (he relates specifically to the image of the mother lending her clothes to the daughter in *Zohar* 1:2a; see below at n. 252), in zoharic literature, as a paradox. I do not think this is paradoxical at all, since "motherhood" is engendered precisely and consistently as masculine in kabbalistic symbolism. Schäfer, "Daughter, Sister, Bride, and Mother," pp. 221–242, similarly displays no engagement with critical or theoretical accounts of the imaginary construction of gender. The essay has been published in revised form, but with little substantive change, in Schäfer, *Mirror of His Beauty*, pp. 118–134. I commend Schäfer for raising the important issue of the possible influence of the veneration of Mary in Christian piety on the formation of the symbol of *Shekhinah* in European centers of kabbalah in the late Middle Ages, but he has not evaluated the phenomenon utilizing contemporary gender theory. A. Green, "*Shekhinah*, the Virgin Mary, and the Song of Songs," pp. 1–52, has independently explored the conjecture regarding the impact of Marian imagery on the kabbalistic symbolization of *Shekhinah*. Both Schäfer and Green neglect to mention previous scholars who have made this connection, for instance, Pattai, *Hebrew Goddess*, pp. 191–192, 202–203; Pope, *Song of Songs*, pp. 168–

171. See also the remark of Eliade cited above, n. 2, and my comments in chap. 5, n. 454. For a thorough analysis of the divinization of Mary in textual and iconic sources, at roughly the time when kabbalistic symbolism began to crystallize, see Newman, *God and the Goddesses*, pp. 245–290.

225. A stereotypical example of this approach is found in the moral admonition offered by A. Harvey, *Return of the Mother*, pp. 17–18: "The tragic imbalance of the masculine has brought humankind to the point of disaster, and unless we recover the feminine powers of the psyche, the powers of intuition, patience, reverence for nature, and knowledge of the holy unity of things, and marry in our depths these powers with the masculine energies of rule, reason, passion for order and control, life on the planet will end. This sacred marriage of the masculine with the feminine has to take place in all our hearts and minds, whether we are male or female." His study of the image of the mother in various traditions, to wit, Christianity, Sufism, Taoism, and Buddhism, represents an effort to correct this disparity. I am sympathetic to the ethical dimension of the scholarly enterprise, responding to the demands of the moment in particular cultural settings, but I cannot justify philological inexactitude on this basis.

226. As a matter of fact, there are kabbalistic texts, including passages in the zoharic corpus, wherein *Binah*, the third gradation in the divine pleroma, is identified as the ontic source whence the demonic potencies emerge. For a sampling of relevant references, see E. Wolfson, "Left Contained in the Right," p. 29 n. 10.

227. Idel, "Beloved and the Concubine," p. 144. Grossman, *Pious and Rebellious*, pp. 499–500, lists as the last of the ten enhancements of the status of Jewish women in the European Middle Ages the "important place of women in the teachings of kabbalists, in the life of the family and in the future paradise." The author compares the change in the position of Jewish women in the twelfth century to the general atmosphere of Christian Europe. In support of his claim regarding kabbalists, Grossman relies exclusively on texts cited and analyzed by Idel.

228. Scholem, *On the Mystical Shape*, pp. 174–176, and see brief discussion in E. Wolfson, *Circle in the Square*, p. 99. See also Scholem, *Major Trends*, p. 219; idem, *On the Kabbalah and Its Symbolism*, p. 105.

229. For select references, see above, n. 224.

230. Bynum, *Jesus as Mother*, pp. 143–144. The "rift between symbolic exaltation and pragmatic subjection" of women in the writings of Hildegard of Bingen is also noted by Newman, *Sister of Wisdom*, p. 197; see also pp. 214–215.

231. On the "uroboric coincidence of opposites" attributed to the androgynous mother, who comprises the feminine aspect of containing (womb-vessel) and the masculine aspect of bestowing (breast-phallus), see Neumann, *Great Mother*, pp. 45–49, 64–83; idem, *Origins*, pp. 43–44, 54–58, 73–75, 94–98, 322–323. For in-depth studies of the phallic portrayal of the mother, see Gallop, *Daughter's Seduction*, pp. 113–131; Ian, *Remembering the Phallic Mother*. On the phallus of the mother and the narcissistic-incestuous complex, see Kristeva, *Desire in Language*, pp. 191–200, 206, 238, 242–243; idem, *Tales of Love*, pp. 41–45. Another facet of this complex issue is the extent to which images of motherhood reflect the institution of patriarchy in a given sociocultural framework. The naïve assumption on the part of some scholars of kabbalah that the symbol of mother necessarily points to the adulation of the feminine reflects a complete ignorance of contemporary feminist theorizing of motherhood. For a useful discussion of this theme, see Nnaemeka, "Introduction," pp. 1–25, esp. pp. 4–6. See also the description of Buddha as mother in a biographical text translated by Gombrich, "Feminine Elements in Sinhalese Buddhism," cited and analyzed in L. Wilson, *Charming Cadavers*, pp. 30–31. As Wilson makes clear, particularly from a passage in *Gotamī Apadāna* in which the spiritual nurturing of Buddha in teaching the Dharma, on the one hand, and the physical nourishment provided by his foster mother, Gotamī Mahāpajāpatī, on the other, are contrasted, the ascription of the role of mother to Buddha is actually a devaluation of worldly motherhood, which is associated with the female body. Hence there is no basis to conclude that the appropriation of the maternal symbol is meant as an affirmation of the feminine. On this score, I would also add that maternal representations of Jesus in the late Middle Ages are not necessarily indicative of the positive valorization of the feminine, or of what Bynum, *Jesus as Mother*, p. 129, called a reflection of "affective spirituality," but rather they may provide another indication of even women succumbing to the androcentric strategy of ascribing the role of nurturing to the

male figure of Christ. See Bynum's own warning quoted above and cited at n. 230. This, at least as it seems to me, is the import of the ascription of the symbol of mother to Jesus, identified as well with wisdom, in the revelatory accounts of Julian of Norwich. See especially the following passage from the fifty-seventh chapter of the long text in *Julian of Norwich's Showings*, p. 292: "So our Lady is our mother, in whom we are all enclosed and born of her in Christ, for she who is mother of our saviour is mother of all who are saved in our saviour; and our saviour is our true Mother, in whom we are endlessly born and out of whom we shall never come." For the original text, see Julian of Norwich, *Book of Showings* p. 580. Julian acknowledges that Mary must be considered the mother of all Christians from the (presumed) biological fact that she gave birth (without phallic insemination), but Jesus is the "true Mother," that is, the being in and through whom Christians are reborn and consequently eternally saved. In simple terms, Mary is the physical mother and Jesus the spiritual, the womb of wisdom, even though I would accept the point raised by a number of scholars that Julian's emphasis on the maternal character of Jesus provides an androgynous model of personhood reflective of the *imago dei* and thus problematizes the standard binary opposition of sexual difference, the male correlated with reason, which is the divine aspect of the soul, and the female with the body, pleasure, or the senses. I would also agree that the marginal societal status of Julian as a woman lends credibility to her claim of being the vessel or medium to transmit the message of Jesus, though I do not concur with the view that this marginality is mapped onto the bodily humanity of Christ. See further references in n. 232. On Hildegard of Bingen's application of imagery connected to the motherhood of God to the male clergy, see Newman, *Sister of Wisdom*, pp. 188–195, 228–238. Finally, let me adduce the following passage from the section on the "mystery of reincarnation and impregnation" (*sod ha-gilgul we-ha-ibbur*) in Abraham Azulai, *Ḥesed le-Avraham*, 5:20, 55c, as a textual example that illustrates the need to maintain the difference between the semiotic/gender and anatomic/sexual conceptions of motherhood operative in kabbalistic sources: "Know that when the male reincarnates in a female, he cannot give birth unless the soul of a female impregnates in him, and for this reason it is also impossible that the male reincarnated in a female can give birth to males, for the man and woman are males, but it is written 'When a woman brings forth seed' (Lev. 12:2)." For parallel discussion, see Vital, *Shaʿar ha-Gilgulim*, sec. 9, 10b. Azulai's comment indicates that from a biological standpoint it is the woman who gives birth, and thus when the soul of a male reincarnates as a female (the author previously made the point that only male souls suffer the cycle of reincarnation), that being must receive an additional female soul by way of impregnation. From a gendered perspective, the soul in the body of the woman is male even after it receives the female soul.

232. Julian of Norwich, *Julian of Norwich's Showings*, pp. 293–299, 300–305, 340; Bynum, *Jesus as Mother*, pp. 129–135, 140–141, 148 n. 130, 151, 159 n. 160, 168, 195; McNamer, "Exploratory Image," pp. 21–28; D. Baker, *Julian of Norwich's Showings*, pp. 108, 112–113,118–120, 124, 128–134, 166; Bauerschmidt, *Julian of Norwich*, pp. 59, 76, 89–95, 110–111, 155–156, 160; Jantzen, *Julian of Norwich*, pp. 104, 111, 115–124, 143, 158; Newman, *God and the Goddesses*, pp. 222–234. On the application of feminine images to Jesus, see also Leclercq, *Women and St Bernard of Clairvaux*, pp. 109–114. Finally, mention should be made here of the application of "a motherly name" (*ein müeterlich Name*) to the Father on the part of Meister Eckhart to designate the pure potentiality of the divine to conceive the Son, the Nothingness of the "natural power" (*nâtiurlîchen Kraft*) for generation, as opposed to "fatherhood" (*Vaterlicheit*), which is the primordial fullness of the "personal power" (*persônlichen Kraft*), the active source of bearing. See McGinn, *Mystical Thought of Meister Eckhart*, pp. 84–86; see also pp. 139–140.

233. Scholem, *On the Kabbalah and Its Symbolism*, p. 107.

234. E. Wolfson, *Circle in the Square*, pp. 89, 99, 103, and references given on p. 205 n. 47.

235. In the original Aramaic, *de-salqa*; the author of the zoharic text is playing on the word *olah*, "burnt offering," which is from a root that means to ascend.

236. The zoharic interpretation of *tamim* as a reference to circumcision, particularly associated with Abraham on the basis of Genesis 17:1, is based on older sources. See *Genesis Rabbah* 46:4–5, pp. 461–463; Babylonian Talmud, Makkot 24a; Nedarim 32a. For an elaboration of this exegetical motif, see *Zohar* 1:161a; 3:165b–166a; Moses de León, *Book of the Pomegranate*, pp. 375–376, 380–381.

237. Cf. *Zohar* 2:137a.

238. *Zohar* 1:246a–b.

239. The principle is stated in *Zohar* 2:224a: "Moses and Bezalel are one, Moses above and Bezalel below, the terminus of the body is as the body" (*siyyuma de-gufa ke-gufa*). Decoded symbolically, Moses corresponds to *Tif'eret*, the torso of the body, and Bezalel to *Yesod*, the terminus of the body; see *Zohar* 2:214b, 225a. The zoharic idea is based on the expression *guf u-verit ḥad hu*, "the body and the phallus are one," in *Book Bahir*, sec. 114, p. 199. The bahiric locution is evident in the interpretation of the scriptural phrase *ish tam* in *Zohar* 3:223b (*Ra'aya Meheimna*): *guf u-verit ḥashvinan ḥad*, "the body and phallus are considered as one." For further discussion of the phallocentric implications of this motif, see E. Wolfson, "Cut That Binds," pp. 132–133 n. 25.

240. Utilizing this approach, we can explain why the term "mother" is on occasion applied in early kabbalistic sources to *Ḥokhmah*, the second emanation, which is more often depicted as the father of the divine pantheon. See, for instance, Azriel of Gerona, *Commentary on the Talmudic Aggadoth*, p. 82 n. 7; Bos and Pellow, "*Ma'amar Rabbi Barzillai*," p. 371 and references cited in n. 15 *ad locum*. Concerning this somewhat enigmatic thirteenth-century kabbalist, apparently from Gerona, see Scholem, *Origins*, pp. 392–393; Jacob ben Sheshet, *Sefer Meshiv Devarim Nekhoḥim*, p. 14. On the scriptural roots for the masculine transvaluation of the anatomical process of conception and birth, see Levine, "'Seed' versus 'Womb,'" pp. 337–343.

241. E. Wolfson, *Circle in the Square*, pp. 98–106. I note that the locution "phallic womb" well captures the idiom used by disciples of Isaac Luria and many subsequent kabbalists, *yesod de-nuqba*, literally, "foundation of the female," but metaphorically the phallic potency of the female, or the part of the woman's anatomy that corresponds functionally to the male organ, viz., the womb. The utilization of the word "phallic" to depict the womb does not make sense biologically; the meaningfulness rests, rather, in the realm of gender construction. In this regard, there is continuity with the psychoanalytic category of the penis of the mother, which is a form of representation in the psychic landscape of desire and not a claim about nature. See the brief but illuminating discussion in Leclaire, *Psychoanalyzing*, pp. 42–43.

242. In line with an archaic metaphorical expression, the zoharic authors employ the image of being in one's house as a figurative trope for sexual cohabitation. See C. Baker, *Rebuilding the House of Israel*, pp. 34–76. The metaphorical depiction of the feminine in spatial metaphors, and especially interior spaces, is not unique to Jewish sources but is, rather, fairly well attested in texts from diverse cultural and literary contexts. For recent discussion of the symbolic nexus of femininity and spatiality in zoharic literature, see the work of my student, Greenstein, "Aimless Pilgrimage," pp. 262–273.

243. The expression *iqqar ha-bayit* is applied to Rachel based on the description of her as "infertile," *aqarah* (Gen. 29:31) in Moses de León, *She'elot u-Teshuvot*, p. 44. The wordplay may have been suggested by the exegesis of "The Lord supports all those who have fallen" (Ps. 145:14) in *Genesis Rabbah* 71:2, p. 821, "These are the barren women [*aqarot*] who fall within their houses [*bateihem*]." Clearly, the term "house" in this context refers metaphorically to the womb.

244. *Genesis Rabbah* 60:16, p. 656.

245. *Zohar* 1:50a.

246. *Zohar* 1:153b; Moses de León, *Book of the Pomegranate*, pp. 138 and 142; Tishby, *Wisdom of the Zohar*, pp. 1357–58; Liebes, *Studies in the Zohar*, pp. 15, 72–73; idem, "Zohar and Eros," pp. 101–103; Idel, "Sexual Metaphors," p. 206. None of the scholars mentioned in this note has been attentive to the gender dynamics implicit in this motif.

247. E. Wolfson, *Circle in the Square*, p. 217 n. 118; and discussion of this motif below, chap. 7. The absurdity of the androcentric orientation is attested in striking terms in the following remark in Vital, *Liqquṭei Torah Nevi'im Ketuvim*, p. 291 (ad 1 Sam. 1:6): "Know that whoever comes from the side of the female has no life." Under the weight of the kabbalistic symbolism, the very source of life in the natural world becomes its opposite.

248. Moses de León, *Shushan Edut*, p. 331.

249. For a similar masculine appropriation of the symbol of motherhood to express the male fantasy of reproduction and the creation of a homoerotic world in Tibetan Buddhism, see Campbell, *Traveller in Space*, pp. 76–77, 148, 185.

250. For example, *Zohar* 1:178b, and analysis in Hellner-Eshed, "Language of Mystical Experience," p. 73. The symbolic correlation of David and *Shekhinah* is expressed in other images; for example, *Shekhinah* is

portrayed as the jewel clasped by David, the foundation stone rejected by the fathers (Ps. 118:22), by means of which he entered before the Lord (*Zohar* 1:7a). In this instance, the biblical king serves as a model to instruct the pious that *Shekhinah*, the attribute of righteousness, is the portal through which one enters to behold God. See also *Zohar* 1:72a–b, discussed in the Epilogue of this monograph. To be sure, on occasion the link between the feminine and David is emphasized, for example, *Zohar* 2:103b: "When King David arrived, he remained in the lower tree of the feminine and he had to receive the lifeforce from another." For parallel language, see *Zohar* 1:168a, and extended discussion in Vital, *Shaʿar ha-Gilgulim*, sec. 7, 10b–11a. The ontic linkage of David to the "lower tree of the feminine" does not contradict the claim that *Shekhinah* is symbolically represented by the figure of David on account of his royal pedigree, which is gendered as masculine. The failure to comprehend the gender valence underlying the association of the figure of David and *Shekhinah* is conspicuous in the remark by A. Green in his introduction to *The Zohar: Pritzker Edition*, p. lii: "The biblical personage associated with *Malkhut* is David (somewhat surprisingly, given its usual femininity), the symbol of kingship." There is nothing surprising here if one apprehends that the term *malkhut* denotes providence, and this attribute is applied to *Shekhinah* in her role as the womb that overflows, a role that is predicated on her assuming the masculine trait of bestowing. It thus makes perfectly good sense that David, who emblematizes kingship, would be associated with *Shekhinah* in her providential posture. See E. Wolfson, *Circle in the Square*, pp. 103 and 221 n. 133. Also pertinent to this discussion is the association of Ephraim and the feminine in *Zohar* 2:246b: "Since Joseph is the mark of the masculine [*reshimu di-dekhura*] he is called 'Joseph the righteous' [*yosef ha-ṣaddiq*], for he is surely the righteous one . . . and since all the arrayments of *Shekhinah* [*tiqqunei shekhinta*] are females [*nuqvan*], Joseph departed from there, and Ephraim was appointed in his place, and he is the female of her arrayments [*nuqva le-tiqqunaha*]." Finally, let me note one more example from Vital, *Sefer ha-Gilgulim*, chap. 19, 21a, which sheds much light on the methodological issue at hand. Vital reports that he heard from his teacher that the five aspects of soul—*yeḥidah, ḥayyah, neshamah, nefesh*, and *ruaḥ*—correspond respectively to Enoch, Adam, Eve, Abel, and Cain. Why, then, does Cain emerge before Abel? "Since Adam sinned and the shells [*qelippot*] that come forth from the powers of judgment [*gevurot*] were augmented, the attribute of the feminine [*beḥinat ha-nuqba*], which is Cain, is revealed first, in the secret of 'a women of valor is a crown for her husband' (Prov. 12:4)." Obviously, the ascription of the attribute of the feminine to Cain cannot be understood in a biological manner; the mark of femininity, which is the aspect of judgment, is culturally determined, and since Cain embodies that quality, he is referred to as the "attribute of the feminine," which emerges prior to Abel on account of Adam's transgression and the consequent augmentation of judgment in the world. Cain is thus linked exegetically to the symbol of the "woman of valor" (*eshet ḥayyil*) who is a "crown for her husband" (*aṭeret baʿlah*).

251. In opposition to the explicit words of the zoharic authors and other kabbalists who followed their path, Tishby, *Wisdom of the Zohar*, p. 372, writes "*Malkhut*'s activity as ruler of the world . . . presents us with a completely new view of its status. . . . In relation to the upper world it is the last link in the chain of emanation, acting as a receptacle for the supernal flow of influence, and representing the extreme limit of the divine being. In relation to the lower world, however, it is the very beginning and highest point, assuming the role of mother and ruler of the world. . . . The parallel with *Binah* is mainly one of femininity and motherhood: the upper mother and the lower mother." See ibid., p. 550. In the imagination of kabbalists, motherhood is valenced as a masculine activity.

252. *Zohar* 1:2a. For translation and analysis of this text as well as its ramifications in Lurianic kabbalah, see E. Wolfson, *Circle in the Square*, pp. 104–106. See also Moses de León, *Sefer Sheqel ha-Qodesh*, p. 26; Luzzatto, *Adir ba-Marom*, pp. 16–17.

253. *Zohar* 1:156a.

254. *Zohar* 1:156a–b.

255. Tishby, *Wisdom of the Zohar*, pp. 288, 588–589.

256. E. Wolfson, "Coronation of the Sabbath Bride," pp. 301–343. The matter is discussed in greater detail in the concluding chapter of this monograph.

257. See the review of this problem in the introduction of Epstein and Straub, *Body Guards*, pp. 1–28. A poststructuralist feminist perspective that attempts to get beyond the essentialist/contextualist opposition is

offered by Fuss, *Essentially Speaking*. Summarizing her thesis, Fuss remarks, "This book will make the claim that there is no essence to essentialism, that (historically, philosophically, and politically) we can only speak of *essentialisms*. Correlatively, it will also make the claim that constructionism (the position that differences are constructed, not innate) really operates as a more sophisticated form of essentialism. The bar between essentialism and constructionism is by no means as solid and unassailable as advocates of both sides assume it to be" (p. xii; emphasis in the original). See also the astute observation by Moi, *What Is a Woman?* p. 167: "In their style and mode of writing, postmodern theories tend to be as generalizing and universalizing as the Enlightenment theory they oppose (as if there were such a thing as *one* monolithic Enlightenment theory, any more than there is *one* postmodern theory)" (emphasis in original).

258. For a critique of the sex/gender distinction, see Gatens, *Imaginary Bodies*, pp. 3–20. The author is correct to argue that the assumption underlying many theorists of the sex/gender distinction that body and psyche are neutral, passive entities is untenable. See also Nadeau, *S/He Brain*. For opposition to positing biology and social conditioning as distinct ways to explain feminine identity, see Irigaray, *Democracy Begins between Two*, pp. 30–39. According to Irigaray, the identity of a woman should be determined by recognition of her "belonging to a different sex or gender that makes up half of the human species" (p. 34). That is, as Irigaray has argued in numerous publications, we must accept "sexual difference" as a given in the very nature of human embodiment, a sex that is not essentially one but two, for only by discerning the essential otherness of the opposing gender can there be unity and relationship. A succinct account of her orientation is found in Irigaray, *Sexes and Genealogies*, pp. 169–170: "Gender as index and mark of the *subjectivity* and the ethical responsibility of the speaker. In fact gender is not just a question of biology and physiology, a matter of private life, of animal habits or vegetal fertility. It constitutes the irreducible differentiation that occurs *on the inside of 'the human race.'* Gender stands for the unsubstitutable position of the *I* and the *you* [*le tu*] and of their modes of expression. Once the difference between I and you is gone, then asking, thanking, appealing, questioning . . . also disappear" (emphasis in the original). Needless to say, this notion of dual subjectivity is repeated in many of Irigaray's writings. To name a few of the relevant titles: *Speculum of the Other Woman*; *This Sex Which Is Not One*; *An Ethics of Sexual Difference*; *To Be Two*; *Why Different?* For a critique of treating nature and nurture as dichotomous, see Tuana, "Re-Fusing Nature/Nurture," pp. 70–89; see also Elam, *Feminism and Deconstruction*, pp. 42–58; Felski, *Doing Time*, pp. 116–136. Notwithstanding the important corrective of the feminist theory of difference, it still seems valid to distinguish biological sex and the sociocultural specification of gender as an epistemic category. On the complex interplay of biological constitution and sociocultural organization, see Jaggar, "Human Biology in Feminist Theory," pp. 78–89. For a review of the criticism of the essentializing tendency implicit in Irigaray's notion of a distinct feminine subjectivity, see Fuss, "Essentially Speaking," pp. 94–112.

259. J. Scott, *Gender and the Politics of History*, p. 2. See idem, "Deconstructing Equality," pp. 134–148. A similar position is offered by Butler, *Gender Trouble*, p. 7: "Gender ought not to be conceived merely as the cultural inscription of meaning upon a pregiven sex (a juridical conception); gender must also designate the very apparatus of production whereby the sexes themselves are established. As a result, gender is not to culture as sex is to nature; gender is also the discursive/cultural means by which 'sexed nature' or 'a natural sex' is produced and established as 'prediscursive,' prior to culture, a politically neutral surface *on which* culture acts" (emphasis in the original). See also Jaggar, "Sexual Difference and Sexual Equality," pp. 18–28.

260. Here is not the place to enter into a lengthy discussion, but it seems to me that the contemporary feminist demand to balance the theological language of traditional Judaism, particularly evident in the realm of prayer, should be viewed in the larger context of the phenomenology of religious experience in a theistic framework, that is, the task remains envisioning what cannot be envisioned in imaginal forms that appropriately reflect the moral and sociopolitical needs of the contemporary cultural moment. The change in imaginal representation demands a corresponding change in modes of theological discourse. This has been the working assumption of a number of feminist thinkers who have sought to traverse beyond the masculinized God of patriarchal philosophy and religion. For instance, Daly, *Beyond God the Father*, p. 8: "To exist humanly is to name the self, the world, and God. The 'method' of the evolving spiritual consciousness of women is nothing less than this beginning to speak humanly—a reclaiming of the right to name. The liberation of

language is rooted in the liberation of ourselves." For specific application of this approach to contemporary Judaism, see Plaskow, "Language, God, and Liturgy," pp. 3–14.

261. An eloquent expression of this theme is found in Scholem, "Revelation and Tradition as Religious Categories in Judaism," in *Messianic Idea*, pp. 282–303. My emphasis on the constitution of tradition in Judaism should not be construed as if I were saying that the process is unique to this religious culture. On the contrary, I assume a similar process is at work in other cultural settings, though in each it will bear an inimitable quality reflective of its own irreducible particularity. For a thoughtful account of the use of the midrashic method to construct a feminist revision, see Myers, "Midrashic Enterprise," pp. 119–141.

262. This does not mean that I think it advisable to isolate the moral fabric of a tradition and its attitude toward gender in the sociopolitical arena, as we find, for instance, in the following comment of Frymer-Kensky, *Reading the Women of the Bible*, p. xiv: "Readers can accept the Bible's moral structure without conforming to the patriarchal social structure within it." Frymer-Kensky is honest enough to stress that the Bible did not eliminate or question patriarchy, even if it did not create it. The author is also to be given credit for stressing that slavery and poverty were not eradicated from ancient Israel in spite of the biblical concerns with these matters. Nonetheless, it seems to me, her comment regarding accepting a moral structure without conforming to the patriarchal structure within it is problematic and perhaps even apologetic. The hermeneutical basis for her statement is the view that "the idea of social revolution is integral to biblical thought" (p. xv). Without denying that Scripture is a product of a patriarchal society, Frymer-Kensky uses the narratives about women to suggest that ancient Israelite religion includes within its parameters a challenge to the status quo. I can accept this argument but I think it is precarious to offer the reader the possibility of separating "moral stature" and the "patriarchal social structure." An attempt to reconstruct the subjectivity of the feminine from scriptural texts on the basis of an essentialist feminism is found in Sawyer, *God, Gender and the Bible*. For an engaging discussion of the manner in which a feminist agenda can be appropriated as consistent with the hermeneutical presuppositions of rabbinic tradition, see Ross, "Modern Orthodoxy," pp. 3–38.

263. See M. Falk, "Notes on Composing New Blessings," p. 129, cited by Oppenheim, *Speaking/Writing of God*, p. 67.

264. The complexity of the task, which requires the creation of a new feminist symbolic reflected in both modes of discourse and patterns of behavior, is set out lucidly by Jantzen, *Becoming Divine*. See also the discussion of the possibility of a "feminist linguistics" in Nye, *Philosophy and Feminism at the Border*, pp. 47–81; and idem, "Voice of the Serpent," pp. 323–338. The philosophical challenge of getting beyond anthropomorphic representationalism—viewed as a form of narcissism—by substituting a matriarchal for a patriarchal imaginary, is set out by Kristeva, "Women's Time," pp. 13–35.

265. Plaskow, *Standing Again at Sinai*, pp. 139–140.

266. Raphael, "Goddess Religion," pp. 198 and 211 n. 3.

267. Ibid., p. 213 n. 21.

268. Irigaray, *This Sex Which Is Not One*, p. 164. The approach is exemplified in the collection of essays edited by Haddad and Esposito, *Daughters of Abraham*.

269. For an elaboration of this point, see Adler, *Engendering Judaism*.

270. I am indebted to Heidegger, who articulated the nexus between phenomenology and philology by arguing that Western philosophical concepts must be understood in light of the Greek language out of which they arose. This is certainly the case if one is to hear the thought unthought in archaic forms of poetic utterance. Since these thoughts were transmitted largely through the medium of translation into Latin, the originary experience underlying the concepts has been concealed, a condition that Heidegger refers to as the "rootlessness of Western thought." See *Poetry, Language, Thought*, p. 23. It is the task of the thinker to recover that experience through a translation that opens the space in which the matter first came to show itself, and in this respect translation belongs essentially to language. See Sallis, *Echoes*, pp. 195–199. For a succinct account of this dimension of Heideggerian thought, see Erickson, *Language and Being*, pp. 7–8.

271. The use of philology, in my judgment, ought to be seen as a way of openly concealing philosophical views of a decidedly phenomenological pattern. For a similar argument with respect to the philological schol-

arship of Gershom Scholem on the history of Jewish mysticism, see D. Kaufmann, "Imageless Refuge for All Images," pp. 147–158, esp. pp. 147–148.

272. The element of traditional kabbalah that has most escaped the attention of contemporary, popular presentations of this lore is the ascetic rejection of the sensual world. This particular example fits in with the more general this-worldly orientation of modern New Age spirituality. See Hanegraaff, *New Age Religion and Western Culture*, pp. 113–119, 515–516. On the intimate relationship between mysticism and asceticism, see the cogent and still relevant remarks of Hügel, *Mystical Element of Religion*, pt. 3, pp. 341–351.

273. My articulation is indebted to Feder and Zakin, "Flirting with the Truth," p. 25. Their remarks concerning Derrida's attempt to deconstruct the gender categories of traditional masculine philosophy apply perfectly to my own project. For a nuanced analysis of Derrida's critique of phallocentrism, see Spivak, "Displacement and the Discourse of Woman," pp. 43–71. For different perspectives on this question, see Marrati, "Le rêve et le danger," pp. 194–211; Deutscher, *Yielding Gender*, pp. 34–58; Armour, "Crossing the Boundaries," pp. 193–214; and the study by Elam, *Feminism and Deconstruction*. Consider Derrida's own words cited below in n. 275.

274. The point is articulated clearly by Jantzen, *Becoming Divine*, pp. 25–26: "From a feminist perspective, it is self-evident that a critique of Anglo-American philosophy of religion is long overdue. Yet in my opinion such a critique can be counter-productive unless it derives from a creative alternative. This is because a consequence of remaining at the level of critique means that effectively we stay at the same old level as those whom we critique: we do not change the ground. But if we do not change the ground, then in fact, though we may not intend it, we are reinforcing it. . . . This is not to say that we should always wait to develop a critique until we see what the future possibilities are: sometimes it is necessary to do the former task before the latter becomes clear. Nevertheless, the move to develop creative alternatives is both to claim the right to develop our own identities rather than have them imposed on us, and to change the ground of debate so that it may become more liberative."

275. My own scholarly enterprise is mirrored in the following comment of Derrida, *Acts of Literature*, p. 58: "Following this logic, if we come back to the question of what is called 'feminist' literature or criticism, we risk finding the same paradoxes: sometimes the texts which are most phallocentric or phallogocentric in their themes (in a certain way no text completely escapes this rubric) can also be, in some cases, the most deconstructive. And their authors can be, in statutory terms, men or women. . . . Because of the literary dimension, what 'phallogocentric' texts display is immediately suspended. When someone stages a hyperbolically phallocentric discourse or mode of behavior, s/he does not subscribe to it by signing the work, s/he describes it as such, s/he exposes it, displays it. Whatever the assumed attitude of the author on the matter, the *effect* can be paradoxical and sometimes 'deconstructive.'"

276. Beal, "Opening," pp. 1–12.

277. The role of appropriation in the hermeneutics of deconstruction, usually associated with Derrida, is traceable to Heidegger. See Glendinning, *On Being with Others*, p. 77, and further discussion below. My use of "appropriation" also bears the influence of Ricoeur, *Hermeneutics and the Human Sciences*, pp. 182–193. On the event of appropriation in philosophical hermeneutics, see Wallulis, *Hermeneutics of Life History*, pp. 15–30. For utilization of this technical term to depict the nature of reading in zoharic texts, see E. Wolfson, "Beautiful Maiden without Eyes," p. 172.

278. Critchey, *Ethics of Deconstruction*, pp. 20–21.

279. Ibid., p. 89.

280. A typical expression of this sentiment is offered by Peskowitz, *Spinning Fantasies*, p. 9, who thus explains her use of the expression "gendered knowledges" in reference to Roman antiquity: "I use 'knowledges' as an explicitly plural form precisely because different knowledges about gender and sexuality circulated simultaneously. . . . I use the plural 'knowledges' to resist suggesting that there was one singular hegemonic gender culture in 'the Roman world,' or (moving toward the specific focus of this book) 'the world of early rabbinic Judaism and Roman Palestine.' Especially when I turn to study the texts of rabbis and other Jews from Roman Palestine, I read these texts from an ethos that recognizes multiple notions of gender, and looks for both their texture and contexts." I, too, embrace an ethos that recognizes multiple notions of

gender; however, the hegemonic character of traditional kabbalistic symbolism lamentably does not allow for the desired diversity. It should be noted, finally, that some feminist theorists have expressed concern over the postmodern emphasis on plurality of perspective and diversity of voice. A consequence of the logic of the postmodernist hermeneutic is that the very categories of gender analysis can be dislodged as a primary tool of cultural explication inasmuch as no single metatheory can claim the status of unequivocal referentiality. See Hare-Mustin and Mareck, "Beyond Difference," pp. 196–197.

281. Irigaray, *This Sex Which Is Not One*, p. 68.

282. Ibid., pp. 74–75.

283. Moi, *Sexual/Textual Politics*, p. 108.

284. On the question of essentialism and constructivism in feminist theory, see Lazreg, "Women's Experience," pp. 45–62, and Fricker, "Knowledge as Construct," pp. 95–109. On the charge of essentialism leveled at Irigaray, see reference to the study of Fuss cited above, n. 257.

285. Grosz, *Space, Time, and Perversion*, p. 16.

286. My formulation here draws on the distinction between "women's texts," "feminine texts," and "feminist texts" offered by Grosz, *Space, Time, and Perversion*, p. 11. The claim I have made for the texture of medieval kabbalism stands in contrast to the history of mysticism in both medieval Christianity and Islam, where we find that visionary experiences of women apparently had the effect of challenging more conventional patriarchal norms and their misogynist tendencies.

287. See the preliminary and somewhat primitive attempt on my part to articulate this matter in E. Wolfson, *Abraham Abulafia*, pp. 4–5.

288. Abulafia, *Sitrei Torah*, fol. 149b (printed ed., p. 119).

289. Rosenzweig, *Briefe*, p. 263 (emphasis in original). An English translation is found in idem, *Philosophical and Theological Writings*, pp. 51–52 n. 11: "[S]ystem is *not architecture*, where the stones assemble the structure and are there for the sake of the structure (and otherwise for no reason); rather, system means that every individual has the drive and will to *relation* to all other individuals; the 'whole' lies beyond its conscious field of vision, it sees only the chaos of individuals into which it stretches out its feelers." The innovation of Rosenzweig's approach to system, still understood as the impulse for wholeness but without subsuming particulars to an ontological unity of being, can be appreciated especially in light of Schelling's later philosophy. Concerning the latter, see Vater, "Schelling's Neoplatonic System-Notion," pp. 275–299.

290. Jakobson, *Verbal Art*, p. 12.

291. Chevalier, *Scorpions and the Anatomy of Time*, p. 4 (emphasis in original).

292. Derrida, "Living On: Border Lines," p. 84. For a valuable discussion of the pertinent hermeneutical issues, see M. Taylor, "Introduction: System . . . ," pp. 373–404.

293. Derrida, *Dissemination*, pp. 316–317.

294. Derrida, *Acts of Literature*, pp. 44–45. On the issue of play and the indeterminacy of meaning in Derridean thought, see C. Johnson, *System and Writing*, pp. 109–141; Amdor, "Interpretive Unicity," pp. 48–62.

295. Derrida, *Acts of Literature*, p. 47.

296. Ibid., p. 50.

297. Lisse, "Donner à lire," pp. 133–151. For a critique of Derrida's notion of trace and the act of "transcendental writing," see Pavel, *Spell of Language*, pp. 38–73.

298. Derrida and Ferraris, *Taste for the Secret*, p. 30. For a somewhat different perspective on the characterization of his work as unreadable, see Derrida's comments in an interview included in Wood and Bernasconi, *Derrida and Différance*, pp. 71–72. On the presentation of hermeneutics and writing as getting lost in a labyrinth, see Krajewski, *Traveling with Hermes*, pp. 96–114. For a sharp critique of the ambiguity of language in Derrida's thinking, see McCarthy, *Ideals and Illusions*, pp. 97–119.

299. Derrida and Ferraris, *Taste for the Secret*, p. 47. With regard to the convergence of endurance and change, it is instructive to compare Derrida's notion of iteration to Nietzsche's doctrine of the eternal recurrence of the same. See Pfeffer, *Nietzsche: Disciple of Dionysus*, p. 137; Deleuze, *Pure Immanence*, p. 87.

300. Howells, *Derrida: Deconstruction*, p. 3.

301. Derrida, *Acts of Literature*, p. 54. As Wyschogrod, "Texts in Transit," p. 47, has duly noted, for Derrida the process of reading "does not provide a warrant for indiscriminate interpretation, but rather presupposes passing through the discipline of historical analysis." I would simply add that this "passing through" is not accomplished once and for all; on the contrary, each event of reading implicates one in the transgressive moment of bypassing the historical. Alternatively expressed, philology is the way beyond the philological, a way that must be traversed constantly if one is to be centered in the margins of the text.

302. Derrida and Ferraris, *Taste for the Secret*, p. 47.

303. Wood and Bernasconi, *Derrida and Différance*, p. 73. In the continuation of this comment, Derrida mentions the fact that the oldest synagogue in Prague is called "Old-New."

304. Derrida and Ferraris, *Taste for the Secret*, p. 31. On the inability to re/present the present, see Derrida, *Dissemination*, pp. 302–303.

305. Derrida and Ferraris, *Taste for the Secret*, pp. 56–57.

306. Derrida, ". . . and Pomegranates," p. 326.

307. Derrida and Ferraris, *Taste for the Secret*, p. 68. On the Derridean notion of iterability, see T. May, *Reconsidering Difference*, pp. 96–99; Hobson, *Jacques Derrida: Opening Lines*, pp. 97–106. The interplay between repetition and difference in Derrida's wrestling with traditions is aptly noted by T. Wright, "Midrash and Intertexuality," pp. 113–115.

308. This locution is derived from Felstiner, *Paul Celan*, p. 204. For an extended discussion of the motif of translation in Derrida's work, see Dünkelsbühler, *Reframing the Frame of Reason*.

309. Derrida, "Living On: Border Lines," p. 81. On the interplay of "repetitions and differenciations," see C. Scott, *Time of Memory*, pp. 185–204.

310. Derrida and Ferraris, *Taste for the Secret*, p. 4.

311. Ibid. On the paradoxical quality of the institution of philosophy, "whose space has to be administrated without a symmetrical contract—an institution in which thought on the subject of the institutionality of the institution has to remain open and have a future," see ibid., p. 50. Derrida further characterizes the "double bind" of philosophy as a "way of being home with itself [*chez elle*] that consists in not being at home with itself" in ibid., p. 55. The quality of the *unheimlich*, the belonging of unbelonging, is connected as well to the secret; indeed, in one place, Derrida even refers to this as his taste for secrecy; see ibid., p. 59.

312. See, for example, the account of various renderings of Plato's use of *pharmakon* in Derrida, *Dissemination*, pp. 71–72, and the analysis of B. Johnson, "Taking Fidelity Philosophically," pp. 145–146. On the question of context, text, and authorial intent, see also S. Wheeler, *Deconstruction as Analytic Philosophy*, pp. 79–84.

313. Derrida, "Sending: On Representation," p. 108. Compare Derrida's enunciation in Derrida et al., *Life. After. Theory*, p. 13: "Even when we want to *break* with the discourse, or logic, or grammar—that is, to reach a point of a-grammaticality—we have to *follow* the grammar. That is what I try to do when I read a text. Even when, as I said at the beginning, I try to locate an interruption, a break, an inconsistency, or some inarticulation, I have, in order to locate this, to think of this, I have to respect the grammar. I have to know the language. I cannot deconstruct Heidegger if I don't read Heidegger, if I don't read German, if I don't respect the grammaticality of the discourse" (emphasis in original).

314. Derrida and Ferraris, *Taste for the Secret*, p. 43.

315. See Derrida, "Devant la loi," pp. 128–149, and idem, "Sending: On Representation," pp. 135–137.

316. Derrida and Ferraris, *Taste for the Secret*, p. 43.

317. Ibid., p. 55.

318. By assuming "structures," I do not suppose that there is a logical consistency or an attempt to resolve contradictory views. My sentiment about the logic of kabbalistic symbolism accords with the following observation of Rospatt, *Buddhist Doctrine of Momentariness*, p. 115: "Canonical Buddhism is not a systematic philosophy aiming at maximum coherency. Therefore, it is not self-evident that two disconnected teachings are seen in the context of each other and that the bearing they may have upon each other is worked out."

319. For discussion of this issue in Derrida's writings, see C. Johnson, *System and Writing*, pp. 142–187.

320. Idel, "Kabbalah-Research," pp. 27–32, offers a sharp contrast between what he calls the monochro-

matic nature of Scholem's approach and the supposedly variegated approach of the new perspectives, which refers mostly to his own work. See above, n. 114. In *Messianic Mystics*, p. 17, Idel characterizes his approach as "synchronic polychromatism," a typology that takes into account a diversity of models, to wit, theosophical-theurgical, ecstatic, and magical.

321. Simeon Lavi, *Ketem Paz*, vol. 1, p. 27c. The passage is mentioned by Idel, *Kabbalah: New Perspectives*, p. 136. For further discussion of the orientation of this kabbalist, see chap. 4.

322. My language is a paraphrase of Yiṣḥaq Isaac Ḥaver, *Pitḥei Sheʿarim*, pt. 1, *Seder ha-parṣufim*, sec. 11, 84a. Careful analysis of this text suggests that even in this setting, where the eschaton is blatantly described as an equalizing of gender difference, the account is still phallomorphic. Hence the overcoming of difference is predicated on elevating the feminine as a crown to be restored to the head of the male, the mystery of *keter malkhut*, "crown of royalty."

323. E. Wolfson, *Through a Speculum*, p. 275 n. 14.

324. Scholem, *On the Mystical Shape*, p. 176. Interestingly, Scholem felt the need here to emphasize that the symmetry between creation and redemption arises from indigenous Jewish sources and hence need not be traced to Christian influence. This is a matter that requires an analysis beyond the parameters of this study.

325. Vital, *Liqquṭei Torah*, p. 21 (ad Gen. 3:1).

326. As one finds, for example, in Coulmas, "Principles masculin et feminin," pp. 41–70, esp. p. 52. An exemplary textual illustration of the distinction I make between gender ambivalence and the dynamic of intermingling or crossing gender boundaries is found in the following passage from an exposition of the symbolic significance of erotic foreplay as it pertains to the divine configurations of *Abba* ("Father") and *Imma* ("Mother") in Lurianic kabbalah, preserved in MS Oxford, Bodleian Library 1791 (Opp. 467), fols. 11a–b: "Know that when *Abba* and *Imma* wish to be conjoined [*lehizddawweq*], there are kisses [*neshiqot*] from one to the other, 'and from my flesh I would behold God' (Job 19:26), for it is the way of man to return initially to his loss [*ki darko shel ish laḥazor teḥillah al avedato*]. Therefore, *Abba* first kisses *Imma*, and afterward *Imma* kisses *Abba* in response. Know that when *Abba* kisses *Imma*, he receives the breath [*hevel*] from her, for she sits without any motion [*yoshevet beli shum tenuʿah*]. Similarly, when *Imma* kisses *Abba*, she verily receives the breath from him, for *Abba* sits without any movement [*yoshev beli shum tenuʿah*]. It follows from this that *Abba* has a kiss and breath that he receives from *Imma*, and *Imma* has a kiss and breath that she receives from *Abba*. . . . there are two kisses and two breaths in relation to what is given and to what is received, for each of them gives a kiss and receives a kiss, gives breath and receives breath. With respect to the kisses and breaths, they are equal. Yet, there is one thing found in *Abba* and not in *Imma*, and it is speech [*ha-dibbur*], for the rule [*din*] is thus that he must appease her [with words], but silence is appropriate for women." The author of this text clearly acknowledges a crossing of gender boundaries as both male and female impart and receive, but he nevertheless maintains a supremacy for the male by affirming that speech (*dibbur*) is assigned only to the man, and he thereby stops short of affirming a leveling of gender difference to the point of positing the ontic position of indifference.

327. Armstrong, "Womanly Men and Manly Women," pp. 107–115. I am equally unconvinced of Mopsik's *la femme masculine*, a locution he employs in *Le sexes des âmes*, pp. 19–105, to name the construction of masculine and feminine in kabbalistic symbolism with special emphasis on Ḥayyim Vital. Mopsik follows the standard viewpoint, making a case once again for an affirmation of genuine sexual difference on the part of traditional (male) kabbalists. I detect in *la femme masculine* an implicit response to my analytic category *male androgyne*, which does not, as Mopsik and others have claimed, deny that gender dimorphism is a central component of the kabbalistic perspective; my claim, rather, has always been that since the feminine is ontically derived from the masculine, in the unified ground of being there can be no real difference to speak of but the difference of indifference, wherein same and other are no longer distinguishable as contrary.

328. *Zohar* 2:176b.

329. *Perush Sifra di-Ṣeniʾuta*, in Vital, *Sefer ha-Derushim*, pp. 237–238; *Shaʿar Maʾamerei Rashbi*, 22a. The degree to which a feminist predisposition can lead a scholar to offer an entirely erroneous view can be gauged from the following account of *Shekhinah* in kabbalistic lore offered by Beitchman, *Alchemy of the Word*, p. 38: "The purpose of this feminine divine avatar or emanation is to attenuate the severity, cruelty, and violence

of the jealous, possessive, military, and aggressive Old Testament Jehovah. It is certainly through the *Shekhinah*, or the feminine, that the cabalist is in relation with the male Godhead." While it is true that the feminine *Shekhinah* is the medium through which the male kabbalist is conjoined to the masculine gradations of the divine (see discussion in chap. 7), it is manifestly incorrect to say that the role of *Shekhinah* is to attenuate the severity of the judgmental male deity. Apart from the questionable use of this somewhat biased language to characterize traditional kabbalah, the symbolism of the latter associates judgment and severity precisely with the feminine, and mercy and compassion with the masculine. Another illustration of this erroneous approach is found in Shoham, *Bridge to Nothingness*, p. 190: "When projected onto transcendence, there is the Kabalist *Malkhut-Schechina* hovering ethereally around the coagulating and hence profane self. She is the graceful and pure early oral mother, as structured in the cosmogonic myths of Lurianic Kabala." To the degree that the sources themselves depict *Malkhut* as graceful, it is the masculine aspect of this emanation that warrants such a description, and not the feminine component of divinity.

330. Luzzatto, *Pitḥei Ḥokhmah wa-Da'at*, sec. 92, p. 226.

331. Consider, for example, the words of Luzzatto in a letter to his teacher, Isaiah Bassan, composed in Padua on the 22nd of the month of Elul 1729, *Iggerot Ramḥal u-Venei Doro*, p. 15: "The withdrawal [*ṣimṣum*] is the first limit placed on the actions, and it is not privation [*he'eder*] but existence [*meṣi'ut*], for the shimmering [*hitnoṣeṣut*] is the source of judgment that is revealed and that imparts boundary on the action to guide it, and the rest of the gradations similarly descend one from the other in the progression of potencies." Luzzatto incisively notes that the primal act of withdrawal, denoted by the technical term *ṣimṣum*, which semiotically marks the paradoxical delimitation of the limitless, is an expression of divine judgment, but the constriction itself is a form of illumination, a shimmering, a bursting-forth, *hitnoṣeṣut*, being and not the privation thereof.

332. Ezra ben Solomon of Gerona, *Perush Shir ha-Shirim*, in *Kitvei Ramban*, 2:521.

333. Text of Ezra published in Azriel of Gerona, "New Fragments" p. 222.

334. Azriel of Gerona, "New Fragments," p. 215. For an alternative and somewhat less precise rendering, see Scholem, *Origins*, p. 416.

335. Azriel of Gerona, "New Fragments," p. 208.

336. *Sefer Yeṣirah* 2:5.

337. Azriel of Gerona, "R. Azriel of Gerona—*Perush ha-Tefillah*," p. 21; Sed-Rajna, *Commentaire*, p. 67.

338. Jasper Hopkins, *Concise Introduction*, p. 31.

339. *Trialogus de possest*, 16, translated in Jasper Hopkins, *Concise Introduction*, p. 81.

340. Nicholas of Cusa, *On Learned Ignorance*, I.21, p. 76.

341. My summary is indebted to Bond, "Changing Face of Posse," pp. 35–46.

342. Azriel of Gerona, "New Fragments," p. 215.

343. On the use of the term *efes* in Azriel's writings to designate either Ein Sof or *Keter*, see Azriel of Gerona, *Commentary on the Talmudic Aggadoth*, p. 103, and further references cited in n. 4 *ad locum*; Idel, *Kabbalah: New Perspectives*, pp. 220–221.

344. Azriel of Gerona, "New Fragments," p. 215.

345. Scholem, *Origins*, pp. 422–425, 438 n. 170, where the analogy to Eriugena's *praeter eum nihil est*, is duly noted.

346. Dionysius the Areopagite, *Divine Names*, chap. 5, 825A, p. 171. Compare the depiction of the "cause of all things" in idem, *Mystical Theology*, chap. 5, 1048A, p. 222, cited in chap. 1, n. 61.

347. Palestinian Talmud, Berakhot 2:4, 5a; Mishnah, Oqṣim, 3:12; *Siphre ad Numeros*, sec. 42, p. 46; *Numbers Rabbah* 21:1.

348. Azriel of Gerona, *Perush ha-Tefillah*, fol. 232a; "R. Azriel of Gerona—*Perush ha-Tefillah*," p. 46; Sed-Rajna, *Commentaire*, p. 123.

349. Heidegger, *Poetry, Language, Thought*, p. 218; idem, *Vorträge und Aufsätze*, p. 187.

350. Consider the following account of the Chinese understanding of calligraphy and poetry in Jullien, *Propensity of Things*, p. 127: "just as the guiding principle of calligraphy is to create a combined relation of attraction and repulsion between the two complementary elements of a single ideogram . . . similarly the art of the poet is to introduce a relation of both affinity and contrast between two succeeding lines."

351. Azriel of Gerona, *Perush Eser Sefirot,* 2a. Scholem, *Origins,* p. 440, utilizes the expression "indifferent *'en-sof'* " to characterize the viewpoint of Azriel of Gerona, which Reuchlin compares in *De Arte Cabalistica* to Nicholas of Cusa's *coincidentia oppositorum.* See, for example, Nicholas of Cusa, *On Learned Ignorance,* II:1, p. 89: "pure oppositeness of the opposites . . . agree precisely and equally." The technical term "indifferent," however, must be distinguished from coincidence; that is, as I argue below, indifference means precisely that the opposites do not coincide but remain distinct. Scholem, *Origins,* p. 312, remarks that the Iyyun term *aḥdut ha-shaweh* (see below, n. 355) "refers to that unity in which all oppositions become 'equal,' that is, identical." See also Sed-Rajna, *Commentaire,* pp. 160–161.

352. This is a very large topic that demands a separate monograph, if not several. For a good introduction to the taxonomic issue, see Hayman, "Monotheism," pp. 1–15. See further references cited in chap. 1, n. 263.

353. Azriel of Gerona, *Perush Sefer Yeṣirah,* in *Kitvei Ramban,* 2:254. *Kitvei Ramban,* 2:454. For a more recent discussion of this aspect of Azriel's thinking, see J. Goldberg, "Mystical Union," pp. 516–522.

354. Azriel of Gerona, *Perush Sefer Yeṣirah,* in *Kitvei Ramban,* 2:455. See idem, *Perush ha-Tefillah,* fol. 200b (Sed-Rajna, *Commentaire,* p. 26; for a slightly different version, see "R. Azriel of Gerona—*Perush ha-Tefillah,*" p. 1). Commenting on the second-person masculine singular pronoun *atah,* which is part of the standard liturgical formula, Azriel observes that all the letters of the Hebrew alphabet are comprised within this word, a claim substantiated by the fact that two of the three consonants that make up this word are *alef* and *tau,* the first and last letters. The additional letter is *he*; although not stated explicitly, I suggest that Azriel interpreted this letter as a metonymic reference to the name YHWH, a stock scribal circumlocution for the Tetragrammaton. In Azriel's own words: "All the letters of the name are comprised in *atah,* and when we make a blessing we do not intend to bless the separate letters [*otiyyot ha-nifradot*] even though they are from him, but rather the distinctive and unifying letters [*ha-otiyyot ha-meyuḥadot ha-mit'aḥdot*], for all are blessed from them, and this is what they said in *Midrash Tehillim* [16:8, p. 122] 'The one who prays must say "you" [*atah*] on account of 'I have placed YHWH' [Ps. 16:8], and the meaning of 'I have placed' [*shiwwiti*] is [the aspect of] indifference [*hashwa'ah*], for this word [*atah*] is equal to every name and every praise, and it alludes to all of reality."

355. Scholem, *Origins,* pp. 312, 439 n. 174; Verman, *Books of Contemplation,* pp. 39 n. 10 and 195.

356. Azriel of Gerona, *Commentary on the Talmudic Aggadoth,* p. 116.

357. Azriel of Gerona, "New Fragments," p. 208.

358. An interpretation of Micah 2:13 based on *Book Bahir,* sec. 48, p. 145.

359. Based on the description of Jericho in Joshua 6:1.

360. Compare Jacob ben Sheshet, *Sefer ha-Emunah we-ha-Biṭṭaḥon, Kitvei Ramban,* 2:361: "The *alef* alludes to that which thought cannot comprehend" (*le-mah she-ein ha-maḥshavah masseget*); p. 364: "The pious one [*he-ḥasid*], R. Isaac ben Abraham, may the memory of the righteous and holy one be for a blessing, explained that the beginning of the essences [*hawwayot*] is *alef*"; and pp. 385–386: "And *alef* alludes to the infinite will [*remez le-raṣon ad ein sof*] from which is the potency of arousal [*koaḥ ha-mit'orer*]." See Jacob ben Sheshet, *Sefer Meshiv Devarim Nekhoḥim,* p. 153: "*Ḥokhmah* exists from *Ayin,* that is, the one subtle essence that thought cannot comprehend [*hawwayah aḥat daqqah she-ein ha-maḥshavah yekholah lehasiggah*] . . . and the *alef* alludes to the subtle essence from which is the existence of *Ḥokhmah* . . . and it is the beginning of all essences."

361. Jacob ben Sheshet, *Sha'ar ha-Shamayim,* p. 155; "Sefer Sha'ar ha-Shamayim (The Book Gate of Heaven)," p. 104.

362. Plotinus, *Enneads* III.7.6.

363. Nicholas of Cusa, *Of Learned Ignorance,* I.19, p. 73.

364. Ibid., I.21, p. 75.

365. *De Visione Dei,* in Jasper Hopkins, *Nicholas of Cusa's Dialectical Mysticism,* chap. 3, p. 123.

366. Jasper Hopkins, *Nicholas of Cusa on God as Not-Other,* p. 69; *De Venatione Sapientiae,* 14, in Nicholas of Cusa, *Complete Philosophical and Theological Treatises,* p. 1303.

367. See Prologue, n. 2.

368. Schelling, *Philosophical Investigations,* p. 276 (emphasis in original).

369. Ibid., p. 277.

370. Hegel, *Phenomenology of Spirit*, p. 99.

371. Ibid., pp. 99–100.

372. Hegel, *Hegel's Logic*, p. 168 (emphasis in original). There were three editions of the *Encyclopaedia* in Hegel's life: 1816, 1827, and 1830. For discussion of the literary evolution of the text, see Wallace's bibliographical notice, op. cit., pp. xxxi–xliii.

373. Ibid., p. 169.

374. Ibid., p. 170.

375. Ibid., p. 171.

376. Ibid., pp. 171–172 (emphasis in original).

377. Ibid., p. 173.

378. Ibid., p. 175.

379. See Rang, *Identität und Indifferenz*.

380. There is a critical shift in the connotation of the term "indifference" in the various stages of Schelling's thought. In the early phase of the Identity Philosophy, "indifference" names the absolute identity of freedom and necessity in the first principle or "ground" (*Grund*), the "source" (*Quelle*) and "root" (*Wurzel*) of all beings. In the latter phase of the post–Identity Philosophy, "indifference" denotes the nonground in which all oppositions shatter not through the identity of difference but through the difference of identity. See Marx, *Philosophy of F. W. J. Schelling*, pp. 10, 67, 84. On the "indifference of *différance*," see the rich analysis of Spanos, *Heidegger and Criticism*, pp. 81–131.

381. Schelling, *Ages of the World*, p. 6.

382. Ibid., p. 12.

383. Ibid., p. 6.

384. Ibid., p. 9 (emphasis in original).

385. Ibid., p. 6.

386. Ibid., p. 10.

387. Heidegger, *Schelling's Treatise*, p. 51. For further discussion of the theme of the ontotheological and the thought of Schelling, see Courtine, *Extase de la raison*, pp. 263–311.

388. Schelling, *Ages of the World*, p. 85.

389. Ibid., p. 87.

390. In my judgment, the logic articulated by Schelling to account for the Godhead, A + B, can be viewed as a source for the dialogical philosophy that runs its course from Hermann Cohen through Martin Buber and Franz Rosenzweig to Emmanuel Levinas and beyond. From another standpoint, the Schellingian logic anticipates the move of Irigaray to speak of the sex that is not one, that is, the affirmation of a binary of difference that cannot be transcended in the identity of the same.

391. Schelling, *Ages of the World*, p. 42.

392. Berdyaev, "Unground and Freedom," pp. v–xxxvii, esp. pp. xxvii–xxviii; D. Walsh, *Mysticism of Innerworldly Fulfillment*, pp. 68–70; Magee, *Hegel and the Hermetic Tradition*, pp. 38–42. Böhme himself may have been influenced by Christian kabbalah; see Weeks, *German Mysticism*, p. 171, and the detailed analysis in Schulitz, *Jakob Böhme und die Kabbalah*, and Schmidt-Biggerman, "Jakob Böhme und die Kabbala," pp. 157–181. The resemblance of Azriel of Gerona's characterizations of the infinite nought and Böhme's *Ungrund* is noted by Scholem, *Origins*, p. 436; see pp. 442–443, where Ein Sof is depicted as the "abyss and *Ungrund* hidden in the absolute nothingness of which we have only a vague intimation."

393. See the brief comments on this work by Scholem, *Kabbalah*, pp. 200, 416–419, and the more detailed treatment in Coudert, *Impact of the Kabbalah*, pp. 100–136, esp. pp. 118–119. For a similar argument regarding this anthology serving as the source for Hegel's knowledge of kabbalah, see Magee, *Hegel and the Hermetic Tradition*, p. 167.

394. Schulze, "Friedrich Christoph Oetinger," pp. 268–274; Weeks, *German Mysticism*, pp. 196–198; Kilcher, *Sprachtheorie der Kabbala*, pp. 199–201; Magee, *Hegel and the Hermetic Tradition*, pp. 65–67, 167, 173.

395. For an elaborate explication of the problem of the identity of the Absolute in Schelling's philosophy and its repercussions, see Bowie, *Schelling and Modern European Philosophy*, pp. 55–90.

396. Scholem, *Origins*, p. 439. Apparently reflecting the influence of Schelling, Scholem uses the expressions "indifferent with regard to the opposites" and "indifference of unity" to render the notion of *hashwa'ah* as applied to Ein Sof. As Scholem emphasizes, the notion of God's indistinctness implies equalization or coincidence, and not merely a conjoining, of opposites (he refers the reader to Judah Halevi's *Kuzari* 4:25 as an illustration of the alternative). I would argue that Scholem has incorrectly equated the "indifference" of Schelling and "coincidence" of Cusanus, for the former connotes the indeterminate that contains all determination in the preservation of opposites, whereas the latter signifies the rendering of all determination indeterminate in the collapse of opposites.

397. Schelling, *Ages of the World*, p. 7.

398. Ibid., p. 8.

399. Ibid., p. 7.

400. Ibid., p. 9.

401. Ibid., p. 10.

402. *Zohar* 2:239a.

403. For citation of some of the relevant sources, see E. Wolfson, "Beyond Good and Evil," pp. 112–122; idem, "Gender and Heresy," pp. 234–235 n. 17, 244–259; idem, "Divine Suffering," pp. 123–128.

404. Neumann, *Origins*, p. 18.

405. See, for example, Waite, *Holy Kabbalah*, pp. 377–405; Scholem, *Major Trends*, pp. 225–235; Tishby, *Wisdom of the Zohar*, pp. 298–302, 957–959, 1355–1379; Liebes, *Studies in the Zohar*, pp. 67–71; Mopsik, *Lettre sur la sainteté*, pp. 41–163; idem, *Grands textes de la Cabale*, s.v. *hiérogamie*.

406. For further discussion of the theurgical significance accorded to each gender in the play of carnal sexuality, see below, chap. 7.

407. Schelling articulates this position in *Ages of the World*, p. 89: "Sweetness is inverted into bitterness, gentleness into ire, and love into hate, because a root of bitterness lies even in sweetness and a root of hatred lies in love and, although concealed, it is necessary for its support."

408. E. Wolfson, *Circle in the Square*, pp. 92–98.

409. Naḥman of Bratslav, *Liqquṭei MoHaRaN*, II, 23.

410. Literally, "black bile" (*marah sheḥorah*), which I have rendered in accordance with its intended connotation.

411. Nathan of Nemirov, *Liqquṭei Halakhot*, Even ha-Ezer: Peri'ah u-Reviyyah, 3, 8c–9b.

412. *Sefer ha-Peli'ah*, pt. 1, 28b.

413. One would do well here to recall the description of the myth of divine androgyny offered by Eliade, *Patterns in Comparative Religion*, pp. 420–421: "Divine androgyny is simply a primitive formula for the divine bi-unity; mythological and religious thought, before expressing this concept of divine two-in-oneness in metaphysical terms (*esse* and *non esse*), or theological terms (the revealed and the unrevealed), expressed it first in the biological terms of bisexuality." Bracketing the question of the validity of Eliade's belief that his comment applies to the history of religions in general, it seems to me his insight regarding the expression of an ontological principle in biological terms is appropriate to kabbalistic symbolism in particular. For a recent analysis of the uses of androgyny in the history of religions, see Wasserstrom, *Religion after Religion*, pp. 204–214.

414. For an interesting attempt to locate the origins of medieval Jewish esotericism in ancient Greece, see Barry, *Greek Qabalah*. Although the title of this work is anachronistic and potentially misleading, as the author himself acknowledges (p. xiii), the hypothesis that medieval kabbalah is a Jewish manifestation of gnosis that is traceable to ancient Greek speculation on alphabetic numerals, which in turn is based on the adoption of Phoenician letters written in cuneiform script, is argued in a convincing and historically plausible manner. On the affinity between Pythagoras and kabbalah, see also the somewhat speculative account offered by Ouaknin, *Mysteries of the Kabbalah*, pp. 355–360.

415. Kirk and Raven, *Presocratic Philosophers*, p. 285.

416. Laozi, *Tao Te Ching*, sec. 28, p. 41. See the comments of Roberts, in Laozi, *Dao de Jing*, pp. 88–89: "This stanza is about controlling the excess of a positive quality (the proud male stance) by preserving the

opposite (meek female reserve). By holding to the 'female' or submissive course while aware of the opposite 'male' or dominant course, one can approach the unity underlying the differences and thus balance the dialectic." Consider the commentary on this passage by the third-century scholar Wang Bi cited in Laozi, *The Classic of the Way and Virtue*, p. 103: "The male belongs to that category of being that is in front; the female belongs to that category of being that is in the rear." This schematization has an analogue in kabbalistic symbolism, based on earlier midrashic precedent, whereby the front is correlated with the male and the rear with the female, a theme linked exegetically to Psalms 139:5. On the balance of opposites in ancient Chinese thought, see the remarks by Jung in the introduction to *Secret of the Golden Flower*, p. 85.

417. Laozi, *Tao Te Ching*, sec. 42, p. 55.

418. Grigg, *Tao of Zen*, p. 4. See also the comment by Roberts in Laozi, *Dao de Jing*, p. 117: "For Laozi *yin* and *yang* seem to be equal and, like heaven and earth, subordinate functions of Dao. *Yin* and *yang* became dominant concepts in the philosophical schools of the eastern Qi kingdom when the understanding of them as natural, equal forces interacting in a balanced manner was revised and they were each assigned to sets of social factors. . . . In this way *yang* became associated with dominance and dynamism, *yin* with submissiveness and quietism." See also Yao, "Harmony of Yin and Yang," pp. 67–99. For the view that the theory concerning the interaction of two opposing principles, *yin* and *yang*, is due to the influence of a metaphysical dualism that is not Taoist in origin, see Waley, *Way and Its Power*, pp. 51, 110–112.

419. Robinet, *Taoist Meditation*, pp. 83–85. Another similarity between Taoist doctrine and the kabbalistic understanding of gender polarity consists of the fact that even though both systems of thought understand reality as the endless play of female and male as interactive forces, light takes precedence over darkness. As Robinet expressed it in her *Taoism: Growth of a Religion*, p. 10, when viewed horizontally, *yin* and *yang* are complementary poles, but if aligned vertically, the latter is superior to the former. Given the gender valence of each pole, it is fair to say that the masculine dominates the feminine. Surely, the same can be said about the orientation of traditional kabbalah. Consider, however, the formulation in the Huanglao Taoist text, "The Canon" (*Jing*), in *Five Lost Classics*, p. 125: "Punishment is dark and virtue bright; / punishment is Yin and virtue is Yang; / punishment is obscure and virtue conspicuous. / It is the bright that is taken as a model, / but it is the obscure Dao that is to be carried out. / The brightest clarity becomes obscure, / the seasons revolve and act as the key." See also the passage from another text, "Designations" (*Cheng*), p. 161: "The Dao of Heaven and Earth has left and right, has female and male." According to this text, the feminine is aligned on the right and the masculine on the left; see p. 274 n. 465. On the hierarchical classification of *yin-yang*, see pp. 167–169.

420. Idel, "Beloved and the Concubine," p. 144.

421. Coudert, *Alchemy*, pp. 179–180.

422. The imagery is derived from a parable in *Book Bahir*, sec. 36, pp. 137–139, and see analysis in chap. 4.

423. Babylonian Talmud, Bava Meṣiʿa 59a.

424. Mishnah, Yoma 2:4; Tamid 5:2.

425. Babylonian Talmud, Yevamot 63b.

426. *Sefer ha-Peliʾah*, pt. 2, 7a-b.

427. This is precisely the argument put forth by Idel, "Beloved and the Concubine," pp. 146–148.

428. On the discrepancy between the intentions assigned respectively to man and woman in the act of intercourse, see discussion in chap. 7. With regard to this matter, kabbalists continue and expand the androcentrism of the rabbinic portrayal of the subservient role of women in marriage. See Satlow, *Jewish Marriage in Antiquity*, pp. 248–249.

429. My formulation here is indebted to the thesis propounded by Deutscher, *Yielding Gender*. The author readily acknowledges the internal instability of gender and more specifically the meanings of "female" and "woman," but she also insists that this instability has been constitutive of phallocentricism in the history of Western philosophy. In my judgment, this is an important corrective to those who use the ambiguity of gender to stabilize instability.

430. I have borrowed this expression from R. Smith, *Derrida and Autobiography*, p. 91.

431. Neumann, *Great Mother*, p. 50, refers to the scriptural account of Eve emerging from Adam as an

"unnatural" symbol rooted in a "patriarchal spirit" that expresses "hostility to the nature symbol." On this "patriarchal revaluation," see op. cit., p. 58.

432. Stordalen, *Echoes of Eden*, p. 199, points out that in the second chapter of Genesis the parallel wordplays *ish/ishshah* and *adam/adamah* indicate that just as "man" (*adam*), is created from "earth" (*adamah*), so "female" (*ishshah*), is constructed from "male" (*ish*). Stordalen contends that the "narrative subtly lets humankind encounter its essence when returning to humus, and men find their origin when abandoning their parents for their wives." Androcentrically construed, the coupling of man and woman is portrayed as a domestication of man's narcissistic impulse to be conjoined with woman in order to restore the unity of his being. See Bal, "Sexuality, Sin, and Sorrow," pp. 149–173.

433. See E. Wolfson, "*Tiqqun ha-Shekhinah,*" pp. 313–329; idem, "Coronation of the Sabbath Bride"; and the final chapter of this book.

434. McGuire, "Women, Gender, and Gnosis," p. 262.

435. My interpretation of the kabbalistic conception of the image of God as it is configured in the beginning and in the end is comparable to the following account of the anthropological notion according to Pauline eschatology offered by Meeks, "Images of the Androgyne," p. 185: "Where the image of God is restored, there, it seems, man is no longer divided—not even by the most fundamental division of all, male and female. The baptismal reunification formula thus belongs to the familiar *Urzeit-Endzeit* pattern, and it presupposes an interpretation of the creation story in which the divine image after which Adam was modeled was masculofeminine." I would simply add that the "masculofeminine" model corresponds to my own locution, "male androgyne," an ideal that presumes the incorporation of the feminine in the masculine. See also the account of the myth of the androgyne in Eliade, *Two and the One*, pp. 103–108. Finally, it is of interest to consider the kabbalistic symbol in conjunction with the following comment by Böhme, *Mysterium Magnum*, 18.2, vol. 1, p. 121: "Adam was a man and also a woman, and yet none of them [distinct], but a virgin [*eine Jungfrau*], full of chastity, modesty and purity, viz. the image of God. He had both the tinctures of the fire and the light in him; in the conjunction of which the own love, viz. the virginal centre [*Jungfrauliche Centrum*], stood, viz. the fair Paradisical rose-garden of delight, wherein he loved himself. As we also, in the resurrection of the dead, shall be such; as Christ telleth us, that *we shall neither marry, nor be given in marriage, but be like the angels of God*" (emphasis in original). I have also consulted the original German in Böhme, *Sämtliche Schriften*. For Böhme, the original Adamic figure was both androgynous and genderless, a pristine virgin, chaste, modest, and pure, created in the image of God, the "tinctures of fire and light." In the paradisaical state, Adam stood alone in the "virginal centre," that is, "the rose-garden of delight, wherein he loved himself"—self-delight, but no desire for the other, as there is no other to desire. That center, the rose-garden, is doubtless an allusion to the feminine capacity incorporated within the primal Adam, the Divine Virgin, not yet a separate entity to be desired; in time, according to Böhme's understanding, Satan tempts Adam to the point that he lusts for the Virgin, an act that brings about the departure of the Virgin from Adam and her replacement by the figure of Eve, the earthly woman with whom he will cohabit physically. In the future resurrection, the primal state will be restored and gender dimorphism overcome; hence the admonition of Jesus to shun marriage, the angelic status of the resurrected body linked to the celibate conquest of desire for the other (Mark 12:25; Matt. 22:30; Luke 20:34–36), as the angel is "neither flesh nor bones, but is constituted or composed by the divine power in the shape, *form* and manner of a man, and hath all members like man, except the members of generation, and the fundament or *going out of the draff*, neither hath an angel need of them" (Böhme, *Aurora*, 6.23, p. 124). For discussion of the motif of the androgynous Adam in Böhme, see Weeks, *Boehme*, pp. 114–121.

436. See chap. 4. My assumption regarding the monolithic character of the symbol of the androgyne in kabbalistic doctrine stands in sharp contrast to those who would argue that androgyny is a semiotic marker of gender ambiguity. See, for instance, Levinson, "Cultural Androgyny," pp. 119–140. It is beyond the scope of this note to assess Levinson's claim critically, but let me say that the position I have attributed to kabbalists is not unique. See studies mentioned at the end of n. 122 above. See also the brief but incisive comments on the rabbinic fear of the hermaphrodite or androgyne—making a man into a woman capable of becoming a wife—in Satlow, "They Abused Him Like a Woman," pp. 17–18.

Chapter Three
Phallomorphic Exposure: Concealing Soteric Esotericism

1. Heidegger, *Being and Time*, p. 141. The hermeneutical discussion in this section is a reworking of my earlier analysis in "Lying on the Path."

2. Heidegger, *Being and Time*, p. 141. See Gadamer, *Truth and Method* p. 236: "The point of Heidegger's hermeneutical thinking is not so much to prove that there is a circle as to show that this circle possesses an ontologically positive significance. . . . All correct interpretation must be on guard against arbitrary fancies and the limitations imposed by imperceptible habits of thought and direct its gaze 'on the things themselves' (which, in the case of the literary critic, are meaningful texts, which themselves are again concerned with objects). It is clear that to let the object take over in this way is not a matter for the interpreter of a single decision, but is 'the first, last and constant task.' . . . A person who is trying to understand a text is always performing an act of projecting. He projects before himself a meaning for the text as a whole as soon as some initial meaning emerges in the text. Again, the latter emerges only because he is reading the text with particular expectations in regard to a certain meaning. The working out of this fore-project, which is constantly revised in terms of what emerges as he penetrates into the meaning, is understanding what is there."

3. Gadamer, *Truth and Method*, p. 274. It is of interest to note that Ricoeur, *Time and Narrative*, vol. 3, p. 158, drew the analogy between his notion of appropriation and Gadamer's problem of application.

4. Gadamer, *Truth and Method*, pp. 273–274.

5. Ricoeur, *Time and Narrative*, pp. 178–179.

6. Here my thinking betrays the influence of Heidegger's analysis of the temporal character of human comportment in the world. On temporality and thinking in Heidegger's thought, see Dastur, *Heidegger and the Question of Time*, pp. 17–51; Blattner, *Heidegger's Temporal Idealism*, pp. 89–126, esp. p. 124; Boer, *Thinking in the Light of Time*, pp. 79–113. Sikka, *Forms of Transcendence*, pp. 177–180, raised the possibility that Heidegger's notion of temporality as the event of appropriation of being wherein the three dimensions of time are unified in the future as "anticipatory resoluteness" (*vorlaufende Entschlossenheit*) that "makes present in the process of having been" (*Being and Time*, pp. 299–300) may parallel Eckhart's conception of eternity as the fullness of the now (*nunc, nū*) in which all modes of time are comprehended. For a different view, see Caputo, *Mystical Element*, pp. 216–217, 225–226. A mystical understanding of Heidegger's thought is explored from another perspective in idem, *Heidegger and Aquinas*, pp. 246–287. A comparative analysis of Heidegger and Eckhart with particular focus on the notion of *Gelassenheit* (releasement) as the way to let beings be is offered by Schürmann in *Wandering Joy*, pp. 188–209. See also Helting, *Heidegger und Meister Eckehart;* and the brief but insightful comments regarding the circular logic of identity in Heidegger and the mystics offered by Taubes, "Gnostic Foundations," pp. 165–166 (my thanks to Charlotte E. Fonrobert for drawing my attention to this study); and the remarks by Albert, *Mystik und Philosophie*, pp. 193–202. For a more detailed analysis of the affinities between Heidegger and ancient Gnosticism, see Jonas, *Gnostic Religion*, pp. 64–65, 333–337; Baum, *Gnostische Elemente*. Also relevant is the more imaginative work by Avens, *New Gnosis*; and the study of the impact of Heidegger and Bultmann, and in particular the notion of *Entweltlichung* (acosmism), on the early conception of gnosticism proffered by Hans Jonas in Waldstein, "Hans Jonas' Construct 'Gnosticism'," pp. 341–372, esp. pp. 343–345.

7. Heidegger, *What Is Called Thinking?*, pp. 174, 180–181; idem, *On the Way to Language*, p. 129; idem, *Parmenides*, pp. 12–13. Regarding the significance of translation in Heidegger's philosophy as the means by which one thinks the unthought in the history of ontology, see Emad, "Thinking More Deeply," pp. 341–347. See also Gondek, "Das Übersetzen denken," pp. 37–55. Heidegger's view on translation as interpretation shares much in common with Franz Rosenzweig. Regarding the latter, see Galli, *Franz Rosenzweig and Jehuda Halevi*, pp. 322–359; idem, "Introduction," pp. 3–57; Batnitzky, *Idolatry and Representation*, pp. 105–141. Galli, "Introduction," pp. 12–54, discusses the respective views of Benjamin and Rosenzweig on translation against their cultural background with special emphasis on the thought of Kafka. For discussion of the views of Benjamin and Rosenzweig on translation, see E. Wolfson, "Lying on the Path," pp. 19–23; Jacobs, *Telling Time*, pp. 128–141; P. E. Gordon, *Rosenzweig and Heidegger*, pp. 248–274, esp. pp. 267–272, where the author notes the proximity of Rosenzweig and Heidegger on the hermeneutical nature of speech as

translation. See also Barnstone, *Poetics of Translation*, pp. 20–24, 261–262. On the relationship of Heidegger and Rosenzweig, see E. Wolfson, "Facing the Effaced," pp. 41–42, and references to other scholars cited on p. 41 n. 10. See also the brief but poignant remarks on this relationship in Gadamer, *On Education, Poetry, and History*, pp. 161–163. A sustained comparison of the two thinkers is also found in Düttmann, *Gift of Language*, pp. 5–34. Curiously, in the author's chapter on translation, Benjamin's views are discussed in conjunction with Heidegger but no mention is made of Rosenzweig. On translation as a mode of interpretation, see Iser, *Range of Interpretation*, pp. 5–12, 19; and Eco, *Experiences in Translation*, pp. 13–14, 67–132.

8. Gadamer, *Truth and Method*, p. 349. See idem, "Text and Interpretation," p. 32: "every translation, even the so-called literal reproduction, is a sort of interpretation."

9. Gadamer, "Text and Interpretation," p. 34.

10. These taxonomies are, as thinking in general, politically driven. It would be naïve to think of thinking without political context, as even this formulation occurs within a specific political context.

11. Wood, *Deconstruction of Time*, pp. 319–334; Bennington, *Interrupting Derrida*, pp. 137–140.

12. Mosès, "Rosenzweig et Lévinas," pp. 137–155. For other references to the impact of Rosenzweig on Levinas, see E. Wolfson, "Facing the Effaced," p. 43 n. 17, to which many more studies could be added.

13. Barthes, *Pleasure of the Text*, p. 64 (emphasis in original).

14. Blanchot, *Space of Literature*, pp. 22–23. A similar view is espoused by Derrida, *Demeure*, pp. 28–29: "There is no essence or substance of literature: literature is not. It does not exist. . . . The contradiction is its very existence, its ecstatic process. Before coming to writing, literature depends on reading and the right conferred on it by an experience of reading." It is important to note that Derrida's work is published together with Blanchot's *Instant of My Death*, to which it is a response. The title of the original French work is *Demeure: Maurice Blanchot* (Paris: Editions Galilée, 1998).

15. Borges, *Seven Nights*, p. 76.

16. On the nexus of time, eros, and hermeneutics, see the preliminary remarks in E. Wolfson, "From Sealed Book to Open Text," pp. 145–178. I have explored the matter in more depth in *Alef, Mem, Tau*. See also E. Wolfson, "Cut That Binds," pp. 112–122.

17. A presentation of hermeneutics from this vantage point is found in Vattimo, *Beyond Interpretation*.

18. Nietzsche, *Will to Power*, p. 291, sec. 540. See Granier, "Perspectivism and Interpretation," pp. 190–200; Bergoffen, "Nietzsche's Madman," pp. 57–71. For a more recent analysis, see Hales and Welshon, *Nietzsche's Perspectivism*; and Poellner, "Perspectival Truth," pp. 85–117.

19. For a striking polarization of cultural construction and the epistemological belief in truth, see Veyne, *Did the Greeks Believe In Their Myths?*, pp. 117–129.

20. Gadamer, *Truth and Method*, p. 238. On the role of openness and questioning in Gadamer's hermeneutical orientation, see Coltman, *Language of Hermeneutics*, pp. 52–57, 109–110; S.-J. Hoffmann, "Gadamer's Philosophical Hermeneutics," pp. 88–90; and Freudenberger, "Hermeneutic Conversation," pp. 262–264.

21. Betti, "Hermeneutics as the General Methodology," p. 173.

22. Harpham, *Ascetic Imperative*, p. xvi.

23. Rogers, *Interpreting Interpretation*, p. 135.

24. Regosin, *Montaigne's Unruly Brood*, p. 85.

25. An appreciation and judicious characterization of my work can be found in S. Shapiro, "Toward a Postmodern Judaism," p. 89 n. 7. Two recent sensitive interpretations for which I am grateful may be found in Bruckstein, *Die Maske des Moses*, pp. 115–135, esp. pp. 120–124; and Kripal, *Roads of Excess*, pp. 258–298.

26. On the relationship between philology and philosophical speculation in Nietzsche, which may be applied more broadly, see Porter, *Nietzsche and the Philology of the Future*. See also Blondel, *Nietzsche, the Body and Culture*, pp. 88–200.

27. My formulation is indebted to Caputo, *Radical Hermeneutics*; idem, "Radical Hermeneutics and Religious Truth," pp. 146–172. See also R. Martinez, *Very Idea of Radical Hermeneutics*; Caputo, *More Radical Hermeneutics*; Safranski, *Martin Heidegger*, p. 155. The only other scholar of whom I am aware who has employed this term in the study of kabbalah is Idel, "Radical Hermeneutics," pp. 165–210. Idel, however,

uses the term in a manner that is different from my own. For Idel, the expression "radical hermeneutics" connotes an aggressive form of reading that may even lead to the destruction of the semantic form of the canonical text. My use of the term, which is in conformity with the way the expression is used by philosophers in the hermeneutical tradition, connotes a manner of reading that seeks to establish the ground by breaking through the foundation. The positing of a "foundation" should not be construed as embracing a foundationalist hermeneutic, that is, I am not suggesting that there is a reified essence that constitutes the immutable origin of meaning and truth, the fixed point of departure. On the contrary, the act of establishing the ground by breaking the foundation is meant to convey the sense of disruption at the beginning, a splintering of the rock into manifold sparks, to utilize the well-known image from ancient rabbinic lore. I would thus distinguish between "origin" and beginning," the latter term denoting the doubling, the retrieval of what has always not been, that lies at the inception. For an account of this distinction applied specifically to *Sefer ha-Bahir*, presumed by Scholem to be the "first" text of medieval kabbalah, see E. Wolfson, "Before Alef." A revised and expanded version of this essay appears as the third chapter of *Alef, Mem, Tau*.

28. Frey, "Hölderlin's Marginalization of Language," p. 356. For an illuminating study of the cultural significance of the margin from a different conceptual standpoint, see Camille, *Image on the Edge*.

29. Derrida, *Archeology of the Frivolous*, p. 71 (emphasis in original).

30. Cacciari, *Icone della legge*, p. 143, cited in Colilli, *Idea of a Living Spirit*, p. 15 (emphasis in original).

31. Steiner, *Real Presences*, p. 40.

32. For an introductory treatment of the hermeneutical methodology implied by the felicitous expression "textual reasoning," see Ochs, "Introduction to Postcritical Scriptural Interpretation," pp. 3–51; and the more technical account in idem, *Peirce, Pragmatism and the Logic of Scripture*, pp. 246–325. See also Meskin, "Textual Reasoning," pp. 475–490; and the relevant discussion on Scripture and philosophical analysis in Novak, *Election of Israel*, pp. 108–115.

33. Schimmel, *As through a Veil*, p. 34. See idem, "Eros—Heavenly and Not So Heavenly," pp. 119–141. The intricate connection of the sacral and sexual has been emphasized by a number of other scholars, of whom I will here mention only a representative sampling: Sutter, *Mystik und Erotik*; B. Goldberg, *Sacred Fire*; Bleeker, *Rainbow*, pp. 208–224; Evola, *Eros and the Mysteries of Love*; Bouhdiba, *Sexuality in Islam*, pp. 88–100. On the more specific nexus between eroticism and esotericism in language that is compatible with my own thinking, see Kripal, *Kali's Child*; and idem, *Roads of Excess*, pp. ix–xv, 15–23, passim; Freimark, *Okkultismus und Sexualität*.

34. On the distinction between eros and the libidinal drive, see the useful discussion in Irwin, *Eros toward the World*, pp. 6–8. A key question, which lies beyond the scope of this book, concerns the precise moral value of the erotic, a determination that depends in great measure on the epistemic and ontic presuppositions of the unitive experience. Briefly put, is the union attained on the basis of accepting the other in the otherness of the other's being or on the basis of effacement of the other in the nondifferentiated sameness of the one? See discussion in chap. 4.

35. See Milka Rubin, "Language of Creation," pp. 306–333. The author deftly examines the nexus between claims to cultural and ethnic superiority and primacy accorded to a particular language as the language of creation in Judaism, Christianity, and Islam respectively. Regarding the latter, see also Ess, "Verbal Inspiration?" pp. 177–194. On the possibility of a semiotic interpretation of the world without falling into the ethnocentric hole of medieval kabbalah, see the discussion of Renaissance thinkers in Steiner, *After Babel*, pp. 64–65, and Hallyn, *Poetic Structure of the World*, pp. 163–182. I note in passing that one of the interesting features of Christian kabbalah and its aftermath as an intellectual force in Western thought, from Romantic to postmodern hermeneutics, is the attempt to universalize the ontologizing understanding of Hebrew as the mother tongue, the source of all language, by identifying it with the Logos, the name of the invisible Father incarnate in the glorious Son. See Schmidt-Biggemann, "Christian Kabbala," pp. 81–121; and Kuntz, "Original Language as a Paradigm," pp. 123–149.

36. For a richly nuanced discussion of this aspect of the Jewish esoteric tradition, see Scholem, "Name of God."

37. Steiner, *After Babel*, pp. 39–40.

38. Ibid., pp. 61–64.

39. The symbolic nature of the erotic provides a specific example of the larger epistemological claim that corporeal metaphors lie at the origin of human language. See M. Johnson, *Body in the Mind*; Bouvet, "Metaphors of the Body," pp. 27–39.

40. One would do well to compare the nexus between sexuality and speech, which is an integral aspect of the kabbalistic tradition (in both the theosophic and the ecstatic streams), to a similar tendency in the esoteric current of Indian religion that served as the basis for Tantric practices. See Dange, *Sexual Symbolism*, pp. xiii–xiv, 99–115; D. G. White, "Tantric Sects and Tantric Sex," pp. 249–270.

41. Woods, *Articulate Flesh*, p. 1.

42. See the relevant remarks of Ouaknin, *Burnt Book*, p. 198.

43. See E. Wolfson, "Anthropomorphic Imagery," pp. 147–181; and further discussion in chap. 5.

44. On this score, see the illuminating discussion of Eckhart in D. Turner, *Darkness of God*, pp. 168–185. For an attempt to consider the apophatic/kataphatic distinction from the perspective of the aniconic/iconic polarity, see Gerhart, "Word Image Opposition," pp. 63–79.

45. Freud, *Moses and Monotheism*, p. 144. See Eilberg-Schwartz, *God's Phallus*, pp. 32–33. For discussion of the larger German-Jewish cultural context to explain the aniconism adopted by Freud, see Bland, "Antisemitism and Aniconism," pp. 41–66; idem, *Artless Jew*, pp. 24–26; and the applicable remarks of Mendelsohn, "People of the Image," pp. 305–312, esp. pp. 307–308. For a different approach to Freud, see Boyarin, "Imaginary and Desirable Converse," pp. 184–204.

46. For a brief discussion of the matter, see E. Wolfson, "Sacred Space," pp. 599–600 n. 15 and 605–606 n. 36. I have explored the theme in greater detail in "Imaging the Imageless." The kabbalistic perspective can be profitably compared to the view of Suhrawardī, *Shape of Light*, p. 35: "With these spiritual efforts, man can be elevated to the level of annihilation, leaving the material tastes of the world, the flesh, and worldly knowledge, cutting all relationship with the exterior. That is when the soul becomes a mirror upon which Allah's light reflects, and the soul sees the images of Light." For a similar account affirming the nexus between abrogation of the material body and the visionary conjuration of corporeal images, compare the explanation of a vision by the anonymous author of *Sefer ha-Qanah* offered by Eliezer ben Abraham ha-Levi, *Iggeret Sod ha-Geʾullah*, in *Shalosh Maʿamerei Geʾullah*, p.45: "We should not push away the words of the *Qanah* concerning what he said about the act he executed and the visions he saw upon the sea . . . his words were like metaphor and simile [*mashal we-ḥiddah*], for he conjoined his soul to the supernal beings, and he entered to navigate the sea of wisdom [*yam ha-ḥokhmah*], and he performed a deed by the agency of a name so that he would see with his eyes, hear with his ears, and understand with his heart that the deed of the Lord is wondrous, and he would not be injured or damaged. All of this was only because he removed the garment of matter [*kettonet ha-ḥomer*] that was on him and he remained an actualized intellect [*sekhel be-foʿal*], as this is known to those who traverse the ways of contemplation [*hitbodedut*] and disembodiment [*hafshaṭah*] to bind their souls to the supernal light. The great light that comes to his eyes is a figurative representation [*mashal*] of the light of the efflux [*or ha-shefa*] that overflows upon him from God, and the splendor [*ziw*] that emanates upon him is from the place to which his mind is conjoined [*she-hidbiq bo maḥshavto*]."

47. For a psychoanalytic study of the image of the mirror as mediating symbol, see Legendre, *Dieu au miroir*, and the relevant material extracted from this work in idem, *Law and the Unconscious*, pp. 211–254.

48. Scholem's assessment, in *On the Possibility of Jewish Mysticism*, p. 143, that the kabbalists' use of anthropomorphic symbols bespeaks their role as "theoretical defenders of the concept of God by the simple and naïve pious Jew" against the claims of the philosophical elite is problematic. Closer to the mark is the characterization he offers in *On the Mystical Shape*, p. 39.

49. On occasion Scholem explicitly mentioned the affinity between Schelling's thought and a kabbalistic idea. For references, see Prologue, n. 2. As Kilcher, *Sprachtheorie der Kabbala*, pp. 45–46, points out, in *Major Trends*, p. 27, Scholem cites from Friedrich Creuzer's *Symbolik und Mythologie der alten Völker*, a work bearing the influence of Schelling, in an effort to articulate the transformative power of the symbol to unify the life of God and creation. For the influence of Schelling's narrative philosophy on Scholem, see also Wasserstrom, *Religion after Religion*, pp. 100–101. On the role of imagination in Schelling's privileging of the mythopoeic over the philosophical, see the recent analysis of Llewelyn, *HypoCritical Imagination*, pp. 50–68.

50. See Weigel, *Body- and Image-Space*, pp. ix–xvii, 8–11, 21–22, 49–60, 80–83. The influence of both Schelling and Benjamin on Scholem has been noted by Kilcher, *Sprachtheorie der Kabbala*, pp. 45–46. Here it is also important to recall Scholem's reference to Schelling in his depiction of Benjamin's autobiographical *A Berlin Childhood around 1900* in a lecture delivered at the Leo Baeck Institute, New York, October 1964, printed in English translation in Scholem, *On Jews and Judaism in Crisis*, p. 176: "It has often been asserted that Schelling, the philosopher, at the height of his creative powers wrote *Nachtwachen* (*Night Vigils*) . . . under the pseudonym of 'Bonaventura.' It is not certain whether this is correct. If it were, it would be the most exact parallel to Benjamin's book . . . a prose that could only have been conceived in the mind of a philosopher turned storyteller. 'Narrative philosophy' was Schelling's ideal. In this book by Benjamin it has been achieved in an undreamt-of manner." It is significant that in the same context Scholem notes that in Benjamin's work "poetry and reality have become one."

51. Scholem, *On the Kabbalah and Its Symbolism*, p. 96.

52. Scholem, *Kabbalah*, pp. 87–88; see p. 117, where Scholem concludes that the philosophers did not deal at all with the divine emanations, although kabbalists were influenced by philosophical cosmology when discussing the world below the last of the *sefirot*. This statement must be qualified, however, in light of the fact that some of the early kabbalists identified either the *sefirot* collectively with the separate intellects or one of the *sefirot* (usually the second or the tenth) with the Active Intellect.

53. The question of the relationship between philosophy and kabbalah or Jewish mysticism more generally in Scholem's *oeuvre* is a complex matter, the clarification of which lies beyond the scope of this study. For brief analysis and citation of some other relevant scholarly discussions, see E. Wolfson, "Hebraic and Hellenic Conceptions," pp. 151–156. This subject has to be seen against a broader polarization of mysticism and philosophy, the former associated with the irrational or nonrational intuition and the latter with rational argumentation, a somewhat antiquated dichotomy that has its roots in post-Kantian Western thought. See R. King, *Orientalism and Religion*, pp. 26–34.

54. See, for instance, Scholem, *Kabbalah*, p. 370, and discussion in E. Wolfson, *Through a Speculum*, pp. 278–279.

55. Scholem, *Kabbalah in Provence*, Appendix, p. 4. Particularly relevant is a passage wherein Benjamin describes the imagination in terms of a Hasidic saying that everything in the world-to-come is arranged in the pattern of this world. "Everything will be the same as here—only a little bit different. Thus it is with the imagination. It merely draws a veil over the distance. Everything remains just as it is, but the veil flutters and everything changes imperceptibly beneath it." See Benjamin, *Selected Writings, Volume 2*, p. 664. For a different account of the imagination, which emphasizes the role of de-formation or dissolution of forms, see Benjamin, *Selected Writings, Volume 1*, pp. 280–282. In that context as well, however, Benjamin argues that "pure imagination" is not an "inventive power" because it does not create a new nature. A similar approach is taken by Bachelard, *Air and Dreams*, p. 72: "We always think of the imagination as the faculty that *forms* images. On the contrary, it *deforms* what we perceive; it is, above all, the faculty that frees us from immediate images and *changes* them. If there is no change, or unexpected fusion of images, there is no imagination; there is no *imaginative act*" (emphasis in original).

56. For a description of this part of *Sha'arei Qedushah*, including a list of the major sources utilized by Vital, see Fine, "Recitation of Mishnah," pp. 188–189. The mystical techniques recommended by Vital to attain a contemplative state of communion, consisting mainly of unifications (*yiḥudim*), conjurations (*hashba'ot*), and adjurations by divine or angelic names (*hazkarot ha-shemot*), are discussed in Werblowsky, *Joseph Karo*, pp. 71–83. See also Pachter, "Concept of Devekut," pp. 225–229; Fine, "Maggidic Revelation," pp. 141–157; idem, "Contemplative Practice of Yihudim," pp. 64–98; idem, *Physician of the Soul*, pp. 259–299.

57. *Sha'arei Qedushah*, 4:2, in Vital, *Ketavim Ḥadashim*, p. 10.

58. Ibid., p. 9.

59. See, for instance, Vital, *Sha'ar ha-Gilgulim*, sec. 38, 52a. In that passage, Vital reports that Luria instructed him to fast three days before Pentecost, a theme linked exegetically to the scriptural admonition to the male Israelites to prepare themselves three days prior to the theophany at Sinai by separating from

their wives (Exod. 19:15), for just as the pollution of the serpent was removed from the Israelites at that time, so the "filth of matter" (*zuhamat ha-ḥomer*) would be eradicated from Vital and he would consequently be empowered in "knowledge of the secrets of Torah" (*yediʿat sodot ha-torah*) on the night of the festival. On the role of asceticism in kabbalistic pietism, especially expressed in sixteenth-century texts, see Werblowsky, *Joseph Karo*, pp. 38–83, 113–118, 149–152, 161–165; Pachter, "Concept of Devekut," pp. 200–210; Fine, "Purifying the Body," pp. 117–142.

60. The point is stated explicitly in another passage in *Shaʿarei Qedushah*, 4:2, p. 5: "The person must meditate in his thought (*yitboded be-maḥshavto*) until the utmost limit, and he should separate his body from his soul as if he does not feel that he is he garbed in matter at all, but he is entirely a soul. To the degree that he separates from matter his comprehension is augmented . . . if any corporeal thought comes to him, the thought of his soul ceases to be conjoined to the supernal entities and he does not comprehend anything, for the supernal holiness does not dwell on a person when he is attached to matter even [in the measure of] a hairsbreadth." For an alternative translation, see Fine, "Recitation of Mishnah," pp. 189–190.

61. *Maʿarekhet ha-Elohut*, chap. 10, 142b–144b; for discussion of this passage, see E. Wolfson, *Through a Speculum*, p. 325.

62. Consider the following passage in the anonymous kabbalistic treatise, *Sullam ha-Aliyyah*, p. 73: "All this is in order to separate the soul and to purify it from all the physical forms and entities. . . . And when it is in this condition, he will prepare his true thought to form in his heart and in his intellect as if he were sitting above in the heaven of heavens before the holy One, blessed be he, and in the midst of the splendor, the effulgence, and the majesty of his *Shekhinah*, and it is as if he were to see the holy One, blessed be he, sitting like a high and exalted king."

63. *Shaʿarei Qedushah*, 4:2, p. 12.

64. *Maʿarekhet ha-Elohut*, 143a.

65. *Shaʿarei Qedushah*, 3:5, p. 89.

66. Ibid., 3:8, p. 101. For discussion of this passage, see M. Fishbane, *Kiss of God*, pp. 44–45.

67. *Shaʿarei Qedushah*, 3:5, pp. 89–90; and see analysis of this passage in E. Wolfson, *Through a Speculum*, pp. 320–323. See also Werblowsky, *Joseph Karo*, pp. 65–71; E. Wolfson, "Weeping, Death, and Spiritual Ascent," pp. 209–247. On the description of *devequt* as an ecstatic separation of the soul from the body and its consequent restoration to the divine, cf. *Shaʿarei Qedushah*, 3:2, pp. 80 and 84.

68. See, by contrast, the characterization of *kawwanah* in sixteenth-century Lurianic material given by Scholem, *Major Trends*, pp. 276–278. Scholem emphasizes that for the Lurianic kabbalists, *kawwanah*, which involves concentrating on the mystical meaning associated with each word, is the way that leads to *devequt*, the kabbalistic equivalent of *unio mystica*. True to fashion, however, he does not mention the visionary quality of the experience.

69. *Olat Tamid*, 46a–b. This passage appears in some editions of *Shaʿar Ruaḥ ha-Qodesh*, for example, the version of this text published in *Kitvei Rabbenu ha-Ari*, 11:39. For discussion of this text, see E. Wolfson, *Through a Speculum*, pp. 323–324, and Fine, "Purifying the Body," pp. 131–132. Cf. *Shaʿarei Qedushah*, 4:2, p. 15.

70. *Shaʿarei Qedushah*, 3:4, pp. 87–88.

71. This aspect of *devequt* in the writings of Jewish mystics was duly noted by Werblowsky, *Joseph Karo*, pp. 58–59. Interestingly, Werblowsky suggests that the idea expressed by kabbalists that the mystic's heart is the true dwelling of God may betray the influence of Sufism. For more recent studies that reconsider this possibility, see Fenton, "La 'Hitbodedut' chez les premiers Qabbalists," pp. 133–157, and idem, "Influences of Sufism," pp. 170–179.

72. My orientation to the history of Jewish mysticism, which has served as the theoretical underpinning of much of my work, including *Through a Speculum*, bears a close resemblance to Bernard McGinn's approach to the history of Western Christian mysticism, which he has aptly called *The Presence of God*. Contrary to the widely held view, McGinn argues that "union with God" is not the most central category for understanding mysticism. The mystical element in Christianity relates to the "belief and practices that concerns the preparation for, the consciousness of, and the reaction to what can be described as the immediate or direct presence

of God." See McGinn, *Foundations of Mysticism*, p. xvii; see p. xix: "When I speak of mysticism as involving an immediate consciousness of the presence of God I am trying to highlight a central claim that appears in almost all mystical texts." See also idem, *Growth of Mysticism*, pp. x–xi: "It also seems necessary to insist that the mystical element of the Christian religion be seen primarily as a *process* or way of life rather than being defined solely in terms of some experience of union with God. . . . Though this encounter is often expressed in terms of some form of union with God, I have argued that a more flexible understanding of this goal in terms of the consciousness of the immediate or direct presence of God—a presence that paradoxically is often expressed through such thoroughgoing negation of all created forms of being and awareness that it appears as absence—is a better way of looking at the entire story of the Christian mystical tradition" (emphasis in original). On the dialectical relation of absence and presence, see idem, *Foundations of Mysticism*, pp. xviii–xix.

73. See the reference to Corbin's notion of "metaphysical idolatry" in chap. 1, n. 349.

74. This is a summary account of my thesis presented in *Through a Speculum*. For a more recent discussion of this theme, see E. Wolfson, "Iconicity of the Text." The matter is discussed from a different vantage point by Adams, "Idolatry and the Invisibility of God," pp. 39–52. For a richly nuanced and sophisticated discussion of idolatry and aniconism in the biblical literary context, which is cast in terms of the larger question concerning literal versus metaphorical explanations of language, see Aaron, *Biblical Ambiguities*, pp. 125–192. Kochan, *Beyond the Graven Image*, presents the more conventional and hackneyed approach to the topic.

75. This is the depiction of Jesus in Colossians 1:15. On Christ's image as the icon of God, see Raw, *Trinity and Incarnation*, pp. 120–142; and the studies cited in chap. 1, n. 348. For an illuminating theological discussion of the idol, icon, and visibility of the invisible, see Marion, *God without Being*, pp. 7–24; idem, *Idol and Distance*, pp. 1–9; idem, "Event, the Phenomenon, and the Revealed," pp. 87–105. A challenge to the possibility of a "pure" experience, the epistemological condition necessary for the appearance of the Other, the giving/showing of the non-phenomenalizable, is presented by Zarader, "Phenomenality and Transcendence," pp. 106–119. For an alternative approach to the nexus of the image and idol in the theistic religious imagination, see Mommaers, *Riddle of Christian Mystical Experience*, pp. 5–41.

76. Benz, "Color in Christian Visionary Experience," pp. 95–101; Heiler, "Contemplation in Christian Mysticism," pp. 195–196.

77. For an interesting study that illumines the same tension in a different cultural context, see Stewart, "Imageless Prayer," pp. 173–204. I am indebted to Stewart for the expression "imageless prayer."

78. On the relationship of the kataphatic and apophatic in kabbalistic symbolism, see E. Wolfson, "Negative Theology," pp. v–xxii.

79. Scholem, *On the Mystical Shape*, pp. 41–42. German expressions are derived from Scholem, *Von der mystischen Gestalt*, p. 34.

80. For discussion of this dimension of Scholem's theory of mystical experience and citation of some of the relevant sources, see E. Wolfson, *Through a Speculum*, pp. 55–57.

81. The English translation is a fairly precise rendering of the original German in *Von der mystischen Gestalt*, p. 47: "*mit der sie in ihrer Gleichsetzung der Emanationstheorie mit der mystischen Sprachtheorie im Namen Gottes zugleich auch das Bildlose ergriffen.*" See, however, the Hebrew version in Scholem, *Pirqei Yesod be-Havanat*, p. 186: "*she-mitokh hashwwa'atam we-zihuyam et torat ha-aṣilut le-torat ha-lashon ha-mistit hissigu be-shem hwy"h gam et neʿedar ha-demut.*" Ben-Shlomo added the phrase *hissigu be-shem hwy"h*, which should rendered as "they contemplated the name YHWH." It is significant that there is nothing in the original to which the gloss corresponds, but it nevertheless reflects a proper understanding of the kabbalistic tradition described by Scholem, for there is an intricate link between contemplation of the ineffable name and envisioning the imageless form.

82. Scholem, *On the Mystical Shape*, p. 55.

83. Benjamin, *Selected Writings, Volume 2*, p. 269.

84. For an illuminating study of this theme in Taoism and Zen Buddhism, see Izutsu, "Between Image and No-Image," pp. 427–461, reprinted in idem, *On Images*, pp. 3–37.

85. For a description of this literary stratum of zoharic literature, see Scholem, *Major Trends*, p. 161; Tishby, *Wisdom of Zohar*, pp. 2–3.

86. *Zohar* 1:147b (*Sitrei Torah*).

87. Dionysius the Areopagite, *Divine Names*, 1, 596A, p. 114.

88. E. Gottlieb, *Studies in the Kabbala Literature*, p. 236, identifies this as R. David Kohen.

89. In my judgment, this verse was already utilized exegetically by rabbis of the talmudic period as a scriptural prooftext to anchor the meditation practice of envisioning the divine in prayer. See E. Wolfson, "Iconic Visualization," pp. 141–142.

90. The passage is cited in E. Gottlieb, *Studies in the Kabbala Literature*, p. 236. On the Abulafian background for this image, see Idel, *Mystical Experience in Abraham Abulafia*, p. 116. For recent discussion of visualization techniques and contemplation of the divine name in Isaac of Acre, see E. Fishbane, "Contemplative Practice," pp. 271–299.

91. I have appropriated the term *autrement qu'être*, utilized by Levinas in his rejection of the ontological understanding of self as an entity or event that manifests itself in being; the self, such that it is, is shaped by the movement of alterity, which is otherwise than being, a key notion that Levinas returns to repeatedly in his writings, for instance, *Otherwise Than Being*. The defense of its suitability in characterizing the metaphysical position of medieval kabbalists is not an easy matter and would require an independent treatment that would have to delve more deeply into the "kenosis of discourse" in thinkers like Heidegger, Levinas, and Derrida, and its relationship to the Neoplatonic apophatic tradition. For references to scholars who have tackled this issue, see E. Wolfson, "Assaulting the Border," p. 476 n. 1; and in particular Vries, *Philosophy and the Turn to Religion*, pp. 305–358, whence I derived the redolent locution "kenosis of discourse." See also the thoughtful discussion of the "anarchy of transcendence" in Peperzak, *Beyond*, pp. 72–120; and the pertinent analysis in Crignon, "Figuration," pp. 100–125.

92. Isaac ben Samuel of Acre, *Sefer Me'irat Einayim*, p. 91.

93. E. Wolfson, *Through a Speculum*, pp. 291–293.

94. See, for instance, Verman, "Kabbalah Refracted," pp. 123–130; and Elior, "Jewish Studies in Israel," pp. 1–11.

95. Horkheimer, *Studien über Autorität*, p. 13, cited in Rudolph, *Historical Fundamentals*, p. 31. On the relationship between psychology and religious experience, see Goodenough, *Psychology of Religious Experiences*; Taves, *Fits, Trances, and Visions*, pp. 261–307; and Vaidyanathan and Kripal, *Vishnu on Freud's Desk*, esp. pt. 5, "Psychoanalytic Approaches to Hindu Mysticism, Myth and Ritual," pp. 233–398, and the afterword by Kripal, "Psychoanalysis and Hinduism: Thinking through Each Other," pp. 438–452. Another side of the argument consists of a more nuanced understanding of the religious underpinnings (and especially in the area of mysticism) of modern psychoanalysis. For an early attempt to articulate this complex relationship, see Dunlap, *Mysticism, Freudianism, and Scientific Psychology*; and the more recent discussion in W. Parsons, *Enigma of the Oceanic Feeling*. Freud's complex relationship to religion has been discussed by a number of scholars. See, for instance, Gay, *Godless Jew*; Kristeva, *In the Beginning Was Love*; Scharfenberg, *Sigmund Freud*; and Vitz, *Sigmund Freud's Christian Unconscious*. For a review essay of these studies, see Jonte-Pace, "Quest for the Religious Freud," pp. 493–505. For more recent discussions on religion and psychoanalytic theory, see Kirschner, *Religious and Romantic Origins*; and DiCenso, *Other Freud*.

96. Hillman, "On Paranoia," p. 307. Interestingly enough, Hillman further noted that the interpenetrating of psychology and theology was the "Eranos tradition since its inception with C. G. Jung and Rudolf Otto, continued by Gershom Scholem, Henry Corbin and Ernst Benz, and now by Ulrich Mann, David L. Miller and Wolfgang Giegerich." His insight regarding Scholem is particularly illuminating, and it stands as a corrective to the overly simplistic claims of Joseph Dan that Scholem the historian distanced himself entirely from psychological paradigms, especially Jungian archetypes. For discussion and citation of some relevant passages, see E. Wolfson, *Through a Speculum*, pp. 56–57 n. 21; and more recently the analysis of Scholem's relationship to depth psychology in Wasserstrom, *Religion after Religion*, pp. 187–190. On this score, it is important to recall that Altmann, "God and Self in Jewish Mysticism," p. 143, remarked that the world of *sefirot* as depicted in zoharic literature "must be understood as a projection into the outer realm of the unconscious archetype of Self." Altmann goes on to say that kabbalists—he mentioned the mystics of Gerona in particular—did not realize the character of the *sefirot* as a projection of self, but it is nevertheless feasible for

scholars to speak of the matter in these terms. It should be evident that his remarks embrace the technical terminology of Jungian psychology. Several scholars with varying degrees of success have also advanced the comparison of Freudian psychoanalysis and kabbalistic symbolism. See Bakan, *Sigmund Freud*; Bloom, *Kabbalah and Criticism*, pp. 43–44, 83–84. For a recent attempt to apply the Jungian notion of individuation to kabbalistic symbolism, see Shokek, *Kabbalah and the Art of Being*, pp. 62–76. A different attempt to analyze kabbalistic symbolism in a psychological light can be found in Shoham, *Bridge to Nothingness*. See also Drob, *Symbols of the Kabbalah*; and idem, *Kabbalistic Metaphors*.

97. The repeated emphasis of a certain theme in a thinker's writings is not necessarily indicative of a reductionist posture. On the contrary, such repetition may underscore the very opposite tendency of intellectual expansiveness. Here it would be worthwhile to recall Heidegger's remark that every essential thinker thinks one essential thought. Every thought, therefore, is a station on the pathway of thinking that facilitates the return to the single thought that informs that thinker's worldview in its entirety. Each step on the journey is an act of recollection, a gathering-in, that leads to a homecoming of that which is repeatedly new. See Heidegger, *Nietzsche, Volume 3*, pp. 4–5. Consider also idem, *Contributions to Philosophy*, pp. 15–16: "All essential thinking requires that its thoughts and sentences be mined, like ore, every time anew out of the grounding-attunement. If the grounding-attunement stays away, then everything is a forced rattling of concepts and empty words." A comparable view is attributed to Bergson in Kolakowski, *Husserl and the Search for Certitude*, p. 4: "Bergson was probably right in saying that every philosopher in his life says only one thing, one leading idea or intention that endows all his works with meaning." For a similar description of poetry, see Heidegger, *On the Way to Language*, p. 160: "Every great poet creates his poetry out of one single poetic statement only. The measure of his greatness is the extent to which he becomes so committed to that singleness that he is able to keep his poetic Saying wholly within it. The poet's statement remains unspoken. None of his individual poems, nor their totality, says it all. Nonetheless, every poem speaks from the whole of one single statement, and in each instance says that statement." The Heideggerian notion of the essential thought provides a model of an intellectual single-mindedness that is expansive rather than reductive in nature. On the question of reductionism and the study of religion, see R. Segal, "In Defense of Reductionism," pp. 97–124; Idinopulos and Yonan, *Religion and Reductionism*; Flood, *Beyond Phenomenology*, pp. 65–90.

98. Freud, *Group Psychology*, p. 30.

99. For a still useful discussion of the transformation of sexuality into eros in Freudian psychoanalysis, see Marcuse, *Eros and Civilization*, pp. 197–221.

100. On this matter there is again much affinity between my own thinking and the remarks by Kripal, *Roads of Excess*, pp. 21–23.

101. I referred to Neumann's text in my response, printed as a "Letter to the Editor," *Shofar* 14 (1996): 155, to Verman's review of *Through a Speculum*.

102. Neumann, *Origins*, p. 19. Jung makes a similar claim with regard to the multivalence of the Hindu symbol of the lingam. See Jung, *Symbolic Life*, pp. 249–250. See chap. 2, n. 231. See also Eliade, *Patterns in Comparative Religion*, p. 421: "We have already noted on more than one occasion how archaic ontology was expressed in biological terms. But we must not make the mistake of taking the terminology superficially in the concrete, profane ('modern') sense of the words." For a more recent study of ancient Egyptian cosmology and images of reproductive sexuality, see Troy, "Engendering Creation in Ancient Egypt," pp. 238–268.

103. Neumann is here drawing on the terminology in several passages in Hebrew scripture where *qedesha* (from the root *qdsh*) denotes the cultic prostitute (Gen. 38:21–22; Deut. 23:18; Hosea 4:14).

104. Neumann, *Origins*, p. 53; see p. 53 n. 53, where the author, in an attempt to avoid potential misunderstanding, makes a clear distinction between "symbolic castration" and "personalistic castration," which is acquired in childhood and has a concrete reference to male genitalia.

105. It is of interest to note that D. Biale, *Gershom Scholem*, p. 146, cites Neumann in an effort to draw an analogy between Scholem's reevaluation of myth in Judaism through the prism of kabbalistic symbolism and the Jungian attack on a repressive psychoanalytic reductionism regarding the ultimate religious meaning of mythical symbols. Bracketing for a moment the validity of this comparison, I would say that Neumann's own understanding is helpful in articulating kabbalists' deployment of erotic symbols to convey the divine

reality. For a recent attempt to interpret kabbalistic symbolism through a psychological prism, with particular emphasis on interpreting the creation myth as the paradigm for an ethical praxis, see Shokek, *Kabbalah and the Art of Being*.

106. A similar point was made already by Underhill, *Mysticism*, p. 80: "All kinds of symbolic language come naturally to the articulate mystic, who is often a literary artist as well: so naturally, that he sometimes forgets to explain that his utterance is but symbolic—a desperate attempt to translate the truth of that world into the beauty of this. . . . Symbol—the clothing which the spiritual borrows from the material plane—is a form of artistic expression. That is not say, it is not literal but suggestive. . . . Hence the persons who imagine that the 'Spiritual Marriage' of St. Catherine or St. Teresa veils a perverted sexuality, that the vision of the Sacred Heart involved an incredible anatomical experience, or that the divine inebriation of the Sufis is the apotheosis of drunkenness, do but advertise their ignorance of the mechanism of the arts." While I would explain the recourse to symbolic language on the part of mystics in different terms, I agree with Underhill's assessment that the use of embodied symbols to depict mystical experience is comparable to a similar process in artistic creativity.

107. G. Scott, *Phallic Worship*, p. xviii.

108. The expression is derived from Whitman's "Song of Myself," p. 26: "Out of the dimness opposite equals advance, always substance and increase, always sex, / Always a knit of identity, always distinction, always a breed of life."

109. See E. Wolfson, *Through a Speculum*, pp. 61–67. A view quite similar to my own has been expressed by Trías, "Thinking Religion," p. 103: "The symbol is thus a (*sym-ballic*) unity that presupposes a break. There is in principle a disjunction between the symbolizing form as a manifest and manifestative aspect of the symbol (given to vision, to perception or hearing) and the symbolized form in the symbol, which constitutes the horizons of meaning." For an analogous account of the symbolic imagination, see the remark by Allen Tate cited by Donoghue, *Adam's Curse*, pp. 69–70.

110. On the dialectic of concealment and disclosure in the kabbalistic approach to the symbol, see E. Wolfson, "Occultation of the Feminine," pp. 113–121; idem, *Abraham Abulafia*, pp. 9–38.

111. See Inge, *Mysticism in Religion*, p. 72.

112. Esmail, *Poetics of Religious Experience*, pp. 23–24.

113. See chap. 1, n. 251.

114. On the characterization of poetry as the experience of the letter in the death of language, see Agamben, *End of the Poem*, pp. 62–75.

115. Many have written on circumcision, but especially important for our discussion of kabbalistic androcentrism are the remarks in Sacha Stern, *Jewish Identity*, p. 239, and the extensive analysis in L. Hoffman, *Covenant of Blood*. For other references, see chap. 2, n. 4.

116. It is worth recalling that in the satire of Juvenal (verses 102–104) there is mention of the secret book that Moses transmits only to the circumcised, which I assume discounts Jewish women along with Gentiles. See Collins, *Between Athens and Jerusalem*, p. 213.

117. I have argued this thesis with much textual support in *Through a Speculum*. By locating the object of contemplative envisioning in the phallic potency, I do not deny that other attributes of the divine pleroma served as objects of meditational intention (*kawwanah*) in kabbalistic practice. Needless to say, the overarching goal of the meditation was to envision the unified body of the divine anthropos lest one be guilty of creating division in the Godhead, a transgression troped by the traditional idiom "cutting the shoots." I would still maintain, however, that the central focal point of contemplative visualization is the phallic potency, *Yesod*, which is called *kol*, "all," inasmuch as it was thought to have comprised all the potencies within itself. There is also ample evidence that in kabbalistic texts the body is metonymically understood as the phallus, an insight supported philologically by the fact that the word *guf*, usually translated as "body," was applied more specifically to the phallus. For example, consider the passage from *Sefer ha-Bahir* translated and analyzed in E. Wolfson, *Along the Path*, pp. 87–88. See also examples of this usage from zoharic literature cited by Liebes, *Sections of the Zohar Lexicon*, pp. 170 n. 2, 178 n. 32, and 182 n. 45.

118. E. Wolfson, "Circumcision and the Divine Name," pp. 77–112.

119. See Lacan, *Écrits*, pp. 281–291. Lest my utilization of Lacanian ideas to elucidate medieval kabbalah be labeled anachronistic, it is significant to recall the following comment in idem, *Seminar of Jacques Lacan, Book XI*, p. 5: "This remark is not without relevance to my subject—the fundamentals of psycho-analysis—for *fundamentum* has more than one meaning, and I do not need to remind you that in the Kabbala it designates one of the modes of divine manifestation, which, in this register, is strictly identified with the *pudendum*. All the same, it would be extraordinary if, in an analytic discourse, we were to stop at the *pudendum*. In this context, no doubt, the fundamentals would take the form of the bottom parts, were it not that those parts were already to some extent exposed." It should also be recalled that Lacan was indebted to Christian mystics and to philosophers who influenced the mystical tradition in the West. Consider, for example, the citation from *The Cherubinic Wanderer* by Angelus Silesius at the end of the lecture "The Symbolic Order" in Lacan, *Seminar of Jacques Lacan, Book I*, pp. 232–233; the reference to Cornelius Agrippa in *Book XI*, p. 88; and especially the interpretation of mystical experience in light of the *jouissance* of the woman that is beyond the phallus in *Seminar of Jacques Lacan, Book XX*, pp. 76–77. See Webb and Sells, "Lacan and Bion," pp. 195–215; W. Parsons, *Enigma of the Oceanic Feeling*, pp. 132, 134; and the elaborate discussion in Hollywood, *Sensible Ecstasy*, pp. 64–66, 146–170. On the convergence between mysticism and psychoanalysis, with specific reference to Lacan, see Certeau, *Heterologies*, pp. 36–37. Kakar, *Analyst and the Mystic*, p. 5, characterizes Lacan as an "ironic mystic." An explanation of this depiction may be elicited from the author's discussion of Lacan's notions of the real, the imaginary, and the symbolic order of language to articulate the mystic's quest to get beyond the rupture of this world (p. 27).

120. Irigaray, *This Sex Which Is Not One*, pp. 60–61.

121. D. Brody, "Levinas and Lacan," pp. 56–78, esp. pp. 56–57; Bergoffen, "Queering the Phallus," pp. 273–291, esp. pp. 281–286.

122. Lacan, *Écrits*, pp. 285–287.

123. Lacan, "Les formations de l'inconscient," cited in Lacan, *Language of the Self*, p. 187.

124. Lemaire, *Jacques Lacan*, p. 86. See also Frosh, *Sexual Difference*, pp. 65–88; Smith and Ferstman, *Castration of Oedipus*, pp. 154–158; H. Lang, *Language and the Unconscious*, pp. 118–121. On the suppression of the spatially located body implied in Lacan's insistence on the distinction between the symbolic phallus and bodily penis, see Lefebvre, *Production of Space*, pp. 36 and 185 n. 19, and, in more detail, Blum and Nast, "Jacques Lacan's Two-Dimensional Subjectivity," pp. 184, 196–200.

125. Ragland-Sullivan, *Jacques Lacan*, p. 55. On the inscription of the Other through the letter of the phallic signifier, which reduces the feminine to a projection of the masculine insofar as the other is demarcated as lack or absence, the space wherein the phallus thrusts its presence, see Butler, *Gender Trouble*, p. 44; Julien, *Jacques Lacan's Return to Freud*, p. 124. A critique of Lacan's "heterosexist structuralism" is given by Butler, *Gender Trouble*, pp. 43–57; and idem, *Bodies That Matter*, pp. 57–91. The debate amongst feminist theorists regarding Lacan's phallocentricism and the related question of separating the phallus and penis is discussed by Fuss, *Essentially Speaking*, p. 65. For a more recent assessment, see Luepnitz, "Beyond the Phallus," pp. 221–237.

126. It is of interest to consider here the following remark of Derrida, ". . . and pomegranates," p. 327: "This double value—is it not, for example, that signified by a phallus in its differentiality, or rather by the phallic, the effect of the phallus, which is not necessarily the property of man? Is it not the phenomenon, the *phainesthai*, the day of the phallus?—but also, by virtue of the law of iterability or of duplication that can detach it from its pure and proper presence, is it not also its *phantasma*, in Greek, its ghost, its specter, its double or its fetish? . . . The phallic—is it not also, as distinct from the penis and once detached from the body, the marionette that is erected, exhibited, fetishized, and paraded in processions?"

127. See Boothby, *Death and Desire*, pp. 188–191.

128. On the double meaning of *aufheben* as to annul and to preserve, see esp. Hegel, *Hegel's Logic*, p. 142. Derrida, *Taste for the Secret*, p. 55, refers to *Aufhebung* as a "poetic signature" that means at the same time to preserve and to destroy.

129. Lacan, *Écrits*, p. 288.

130. Blum and Nast, "Jacque Lacan's Two-Dimensional Subjectivity," p. 184.

131. Jacqueline Rose, "Introduction—II," in Lacan, *Feminine Sexuality,* p. 40.

132. Ibid., p. 42: "Sexual difference is then assigned according to whether individual subjects do or do not possess the phallus, which means not that anatomical difference *is* sexual difference (the one as strictly deducible from the other), but that anatomical difference comes to *figure* sexual difference, that is, it becomes the sole representative of what that difference is allowed to be" (emphasis in original).

133. Lacan, *Écrits,* p. 288; see p. 285, where Lacan addresses the Freudian notion of the "splitting" (*Spaltung*) by which the phallus (as signifier) is constituted. See Lacan, *Seminar of Jacques Lacan, Book VII,* pp. 102 and 209. Freud addressed this phenomenon in the unfinished fragment dated January 2, 1938, and published posthumously in 1940 as "Die Ichspaltung im Abwehrvorgang." An English translation is included in Freud, *Collected Papers,* vol. 5, pp. 372–375.

134. Lacan, *Écrits,* p. 290.

135. In an alternative translation of this piece, included in Lacan, *Seminar of Jacques Lacan, Book XX,* p. 73, the French is rendered more felicitously as "not-whole."

136. *Feminine Sexuality,* p. 144.

137. Ibid., p. 147.

138. Žižek, *Tarrying with the Negative,* pp. 57–58.

139. I have appropriated this locution from Kristeva, *Sense and Non-Sense of Revolt,* pp. 65–90, esp. pp. 72–76.

140. On the charge of phallocentrism in Lacan's thought, see Gallop, *Daughter's Seduction,* pp. 15–32; idem, *Reading Lacan,* pp. 133–156. See also Cixous, "Castration or Decapitation?" pp. 41–55, esp. pp. 45–46, and the brief but insightful discussion in Roudinesco, *Jacques Lacan,* pp. 369–370. Consider as well the comment by Žižek, *Tarrying with the Negative,* p. 43: "The whole point of Lacan's insistence on the 'impossibility of sexual relationship' is that this, precisely, is what the 'actual' sexual act is; man's partner is never a woman in the real kernel of her being, but woman qua *a*, reduced to the fantasy-object (let us recall Lacan's definition of the phallic enjoyment as essentially masturbatory)!"

141. Jacqueline Rose, "Introduction—II," in Lacan, *Feminine Sexuality,* p. 49: "For Lacan, men and women are only ever in language. . . . All speaking beings must line themselves up on one side or the other of this division, but anyone can cross over and inscribe themselves on the opposite side from that to which they are anatomically destined." In fairness to the author, it must be noted that she emphasizes the subservient nature accorded women in Lacan's phallic definition of sexual identity.

142. Žižek, *For They Know Not What They Do,* pp. 25–26.

143. Jacqueline Rose, "Introduction—II," in Lacan, *Feminine Sexuality,* p. 38; Boothby, "Lacanian Castration," pp. 215–234; Žižek, *Tarrying with the Negative,* p. 60; Barzilai, *Lacan and the Matter of Origins,* p. 201.

144. Consider Lacan's depiction of the word made from the symbolic object in *Écrits,* p. 65: "Through the word—already a presence made of absence—absence itself gives itself a name in that moment of origin whose perpetual recreation Freud's genius detected in the play of the child. And from this pair of sounds modulated on presence and absence . . . there is born the world of meaning of a particular language in which the world of things will come to be arranged." This is exactly the function of the phallus as the signifier without a signified.

145. Lacan, *Seminar of Jacques Lacan, Book XX,* p. 35.

146. Lacan, *Feminine Sexuality,* p. 143.

147. Ibid.

148. Brivic, *Veil of Signs,* pp. 97–98.

149. Nancy and Lacoue-Labarthe, *Title of the Letter,* pp. 45–46.

150. Lacan, *Seminar of Jacques Lacan. Book XI,* p. 89; and see Hassoun, *Cruelty of Depression,* pp. 49–50.

151. H. Lang, *Language and the Unconscious,* p. 121.

152. Žižek, *Puppet and the Dwarf,* p. 61.

153. Vital, *Eṣ Ḥayyim,* 46:3, 103b. See discussion and citation of relevant texts in E. Wolfson, *Through a Speculum,* pp. 336–345. On the dialectic of concealment and disclosure as it pertains to the divine phallus, see also Liebes, *Studies in the Zohar,* pp. 26–30. Countless other sources could have been cited to support my

depiction of the phallic gradation as being paradoxically the concealed disclosure of the disclosed concealment. An extraordinary application of this older symbolism is found in the Yemenite kabbalist Azariah Ḥai Amrani, *Shemen ha-Sullam,* pt. 2, p. 83: "The righteous man is considered to be an angel in relation to the people below even though he still holds on to the supernal secret, and he is cloaked and clad in a garment and hidden, but he is a king here. Even the *alef* is a mystery [*pele*], for then he is an angel in truth, and according to his way he will be blessed and they will reveal to him secrets, for he does not fear and he believes." The righteous man is recipient of secrets that he reveals, but precisely for this reason he must be concealed in the manner of angels in relation to human beings. Interestingly, the book contains pictures of the author in which his face is veiled (see pt. 2, pp. 5 and 96), a rather uncommon practice amongst Jews, including kabbalists, to the best of my knowledge, although the custom of men wearing veils, which can be traced to the Berbers, is well attested among Arabs. See Meier, *Essays on Islamic Piety and Mysticism,* pp. 400–420, and esp. pp. 408–409, where the veil is treated as a symbol of the mystery of sanctity or even as a sign of incarnation (I am grateful to Steven Wasserstrom for this reference). On the symbol of the veil in Sufism, see discussion in chap. 1 and relevant studies cited in n. 260, and discussion in chap. 5. On the veiling of men in Arab culture, see also El Guindi, *Veil,* pp. 117–128. I assume that for Amrani, the veil is a concretization of the notion that the righteous man corresponds symbolically to the attribute of God that must be hidden, even though or especially on account of the fact that it is the ontic locus of mystery; indeed, the veil is the vehicle of disclosure.

154. *Zohar* 3:187b.

155. *Zohar* 1:64b; an exact parallel appears in *Zohar* 2:227b.

156. Tishby, *Wisdom of the Zohar,* p. 1364.

157. *Tiqqunei Zohar,* sec. 19, 38a.

158. Babylonian Talmud, Ḥagigah 15a.

159. See chap. 2, n. 189.

160. The exegetical reference is to "And they saw the God of Israel and under his feet there was the likeness of a pavement of sapphire, like the very sky for purity" (Exod. 24:10). Needless to say, the symbolic interpretation is found in earlier kabbalistic sources. For instance, see the commentary by Judah Ḥayyat, *Minḥat Yehudah,* in *Maʿarekhet ha-Elohut,* 179a.

161. Vital, *Shaʿar ha-Kawwanot,* 18d, previously translated in E. Wolfson, *Circle in the Square,* p. 117.

162. Isaac ben Samuel of Acre, *Sefer Meʾirat Einayim,* p. 44.

163. See E. Wolfson, "Woman—The Feminine as Other," pp. 185–188; idem, *Through a Speculum,* pp. 274–275 n. 14, 315–317, 339, 341–344, 357–360, 363–364, 369–370, 396–397; idem, *Circle in the Square,* pp. 20, 81, 88–89, 108–110, 117–121, 198–199 n. 11, 202–203 n. 33, 205 n. 42, 224–226 n. 152, 231–232 n. 198.

164. On the dual nature of *Shekhinah* as revealed and hidden, connected to the name Esther, see Joseph of Hamadan, *Sefer Tashak,* p. 45. Particularly interesting is the following text of Cordovero, which contrasts the visibility of the male and the invisibility of the female. The passage, which has been published in Sack, *Kabbalah of Rabbi Moshe Cordovero,* p. 334, is a commentary on the description of the letter *gimmel* in *Zohar Ḥadash,* 122a, as "revealed in day and hidden in night": "This is verily the emanation of *Yesod,* for he emanates and is revealed from the side of *Tifʾeret,* for he is the male, the limb through which is disclosed the mercy that is within the mercy. However, the night is *Malkhut,* which is hidden, for it is the feminine, surely the hidden limb, submerged and invisible. Therefore, *Malkhut* is not comprised within *Yesod,* and this is the secret of the concealed light." The concluding remark that the feminine *Malkhut* is not contained within the phallic *Yesod* is especially noteworthy as it goes against the grain of the tradition that Cordovero himself affirms on many occasions regarding the ultimate containment of *Malkhut* in *Yesod* in the form of the corona. The matter requires further reflection.

165. I have dealt preliminarily with the theme of manifestation and concealment of *Shekhinah* in "Occultation of the Feminine," but more work needs to be done in unpacking the symbolic intricacies of this motif.

166. See chap. 2, n. 242. Mention should be made of the symbolic application of the image of the sealed garden in Song 4:12 to Mary in the Christian tradition, which draws on a similar cluster of motifs

applied to the feminine. See Stokstad, "Garden as Art," pp. 179–180; and Daley, "Closed Garden," pp. 255–278.

167. *Zohar* 1:50a, 122a.

168. *Zohar* 1:245a.

169. See Loraux, *Tragic Ways of Killing a Woman*, pp. ix, 2–3, 21–22; Wogan-Browne, "Chaste Bodies," pp. 24–42; Mews, "Virginity, Theology, and Pedagogy," pp. 23–24.

170. M. Green, "From 'Diseases of Women,'" pp. 5–39.

171. Ibid., p. 12.

172. E. Wolfson, *Circle in the Square*, pp. 42–47; idem, *Through a Speculum*, pp. 359–360; and esp. idem, "Occultation of the Feminine," pp. 120–121.

173. In this matter, Irigaray is responding to the connection between circumcision and castration in Freud, which is a specific example of the psychoanalytical approach to ritual initiation as an expression of the Oedipal complex. According to Freud's thinking, circumcision is a symbolic substitute for castration, which relates to neurotic repression of the child's masturbatory activity. See Freud, *Complete Introductory Lectures*, pp. 165, 550–551; idem, *Moses and Monotheism*, p. 156; idem, *Totem and Taboo*, p. 189 n. 61. See Ozturk, "Ritual Circumcision," pp. 49–60; Kern, "Prehistory of Freud's Theory," pp. 309–314; Gilman, *Freud, Race, and Gender*, pp. 70–92; Bull, "Re-Interpretation of a Male Initiation Ritual," pp. 83–104. On the depiction of circumcision as a symbolic castration, which is related to inscription in language, see Derrida, *Glas*, pp. 41–46. On the depiction of circumcision as the name of the mark of the simulacrum, which is linked to castration, see Derrida, *Spurs*, p. 69 (for the fuller literary context of this remark, see chap. 1, n. 391). By contrast, see idem, *Archive Fever*, p. 42, where Derrida emphasizes the irreducibility of circumcision to castration in opposition to the Freudian view that circumcision is a symbolic substitute of the castration of the son by the primitive father. The change in Derrida's writing with regard to the relationship between circumcision and castration has been duly noted by Caputo, *Prayers and Tears of Jacques Derrida*, pp. 234, 240, 259, 262, 306–307. On the treatment of castration, which is linked to the phallus as opposed to the penis, as a metaphor or simulacrum for emasculation of *logos* in Kantian thought, see Derrida, "Of an Apocalyptic Tone," pp. 42–43. For discussion of Derrida's view, see also M. Taylor, *Tears*, pp. 164–165; Ofrat, *Jewish Derrida*, pp. 44–50 (where the influence of Lacan's phallocentrism on Derrida is duly noted); Cixous, *Portrait of Jacques Derrida*, pp. 67–87. On castration as resistance to writing, see Cixous, *Readings*, pp. 10–11. An anthropological explanation of circumcision as ritualized castration is offered by Paige and Paige, *Politics of Reproductive Ritual*, pp. 147–157. A summary of their view and what seems to me to be a justified hesitation regarding its applicability to the priestly rite of circumcision in ancient Israel is found in L. Hoffman, *Covenant of Blood*, pp. 39–40.

174. Irigaray, *Marine Lover of Friedrich Nietzsche*, p. 82.

175. *Tanḥuma, Lekh Lekha* 19.

176. Sacha Stern, *Jewish Identity*, pp. 229–231.

177. Restriction of the secret to the humble is implied in the statements in Babylonian Talmud, Qiddushin 71a, regarding either the transmission of the twelve-letter name of God to the modest priests or the transmission of the forty-two-letter name to the modest and humble middle-aged man. On the use of the term *ṣeniʿu* to designate the hidden and incomprehensible nature of Ein Sof, see *Zohar* 3:26b.

178. Irigaray, *Marine Lover*, pp. 81–82.

179. For fuller discussion of this motif, see E. Wolfson, "Circumcision, Vision of God," pp. 189–215; idem, *Through a Speculum*, pp. 104, 249 n. 251, 330, 342 n. 52, 357, 397.

180. Consider the midrashic passages from *Genesis Rabbah* and *Numbers Rabbah* translated and analyzed in E. Wolfson, "Circumcision, Vision of God," pp. 192–198. It is of interest to consider the interpretation of the theophany in Genesis 18 offered by Jacob Böhme, *Mysterium Magnum*, p. 449. According to Böhme, reflecting a much older exegetical tradition attested by Christian homilists, the appearance of the three men is rendered in Trinitarian terms. Significantly, and what appears to me somewhat exceptional, according to Böhme, Abraham merited seeing the incarnation of the Trinity on account of the covenant of circumcision. In this matter the German mystic and theosophist follows the kabbalistic path in emphasizing the nexus

between circumcision of the flesh and revelatory experience of divine embodiment. It should be further noted, however, that for Böhme, the spiritual intent of circumcision is to cast aside man's base bestiality, epitomized in the sexual urge expressed through the penis, which parallels the death of Jesus, the ultimate sacrifice that overcomes the bestial will and desire. Circumcision, in a word, is a sign that to receive Christ one must cut off the natural urge to procreate (see *Mysterium Magnum*, pp. 432–433).

181. Marks, "On Prophetic Stammering," pp. 60–80, esp. pp. 63, 71–73.

182. See E. Wolfson, *Through a Speculum*, pp. 339–345.

183. I refer here to a process that elsewhere I have called "erasing of the erasure." See E. Wolfson, *Circle in the Square*, pp. 49–78.

184. The link between circumcision and sexual renunciation is based on an ancient belief widely repeated in medieval Jewish literature that removal of the foreskin diminishes the sexual drive. See Judah Halevi, *Sefer ha-Kuzari*, I:115; Abraham Ibn Ezra, *Yesod Mora*, chap. 7, 29a; Maimonides, *Guide*, III:49; A. Gross, "Reasons for the Commandment of Circumcision," pp. 25–46, esp. pp. 25–34; D. Biale, *Eros and the Jews*, pp. 91–92; J. Diamond, *Maimonides and the Hermeneutics of Concealment*, p. 35. For an allegorical interpretation of circumcision along these lines in early Christian sources, see E. Clark, *Reading Renunciation*, pp. 225–230. See also the suggestive remark by Scetis, *Abba Isaiah of Scetis Ascetic Discourses*, p. 163: "Abraham was the first to be circumcised. This signified that the left was no longer alive in him."

185. My remarks here are indebted to the discussion in Hassoun, *Cruelty of Depression*, p. 50.

186. On asceticism as a means to intensify rather than weaken the phallic potency, see the following description of the man who embraces Tao in Laozi, *Tao Te Ching*, no. 55, p. 68: "He is oblivious to the union of male and female / yet his vitality is full / his inner spirit is complete." The life force of man's virility is not in the least diminished by the renunciation of physical sex.

187. Lacan, *The Seminar of Jacques Lacan. Book XI*, pp. 234–235 (emphasis in original).

188. I have here borrowed a distinction made by Nasio, *Five Lessons*, p. 38. On circumcision, the symbolic correlate to castration, as a sign of phallic empowerment, see the analysis of the "circumcision of Moses" (Exod. 4:24–26) in Pierre Gordon, *Sex and Religion*, pp. 69–71.

189. Daly, *Pure Lust*, p. 72.

190. Miles, "Textual Harassment," p. 50.

191. Verman, "Kabbalah Refracted," p. 129. A. Green, "Kabbalistic Re-Vision," p. 272 n. 16, also resorts to a pornographic reference when describing my work. This is a regrettable association that does justice neither to my scholarship nor to future discourse on matters of body and sexuality as they apply to the symbolic world of kabbalah. Alas, the latest name to be added to the list of scholars of Jewish mysticism who feel the need to use pornographic imagery to attack my work on gender comes from the pen of Peter Schäfer. For discussion, see chap. 4, n. 111. I would like to note, however, that a plausible argument can be made that erotic representations in pornography have something in common with sexual symbolism pervasive in religious texts and rituals. Consider, for example, the observation of Michelson, *Speaking the Unspeakable*, pp. 95–96: "There is a verbal strategy common to both religious and pornographic literature, what Eric Auerbach in *Mimesis* has defined as the figural interpretation of reality. . . . The important point here is that the figural method is a way of articulating an abstract reality (God, for example) by means of imagistic reference to an experiential reality (God as father, shepherd, or lover). . . . But, unlike figurative language, it is not simply a rhetorical way of speaking; it is a means of getting at reality. . . . My thesis here is that pornographic imagery is best understood in terms of its figural structure, that it has that structure in common with religious literature, and that both use it as a device of moral statement." In the continuation of his analysis (pp. 96–99), Michelson discusses in particular the use of sexual figures in mystical literature, his primary examples being derived from the writings of John of the Cross. While acknowledging the critical difference between "naturalistic figuration of sex" in pornography and the "figural use of sex" to depict spiritual love in mysticism, the author nonetheless concludes that there is a similarity with regard to the privileged place accorded sexual images in the figural representation of reality. In my judgment, this is a useful insight that can be profitably applied to the erotic imagery in kabbalistic texts, but this is a far cry from the crude understanding attested in the aforementioned comments of Green and Verman.

192. Verman's response in "Kabbalah Refracted," p. 167, to my rejoinder, which is printed in *Shofar* 14 (1996): 167.

193. See E. Wolfson, *Circle in the Square*, pp. 196–197 n. 6, and my discussion in *Shofar* 14 (1996): 158–160.

194. Let me take this opportunity to correct another misunderstanding of my interpretation of *aṭarah* as the corona of the phallus. Both Verman and Green, to mention two of the more obvious examples, have assumed that I have said that this symbolic interpretation has to be applied in every occurrence of this term in kabbalistic texts. I have nowhere in my scholarly writings suggested that this is the case. On the contrary, my symbolic decoding is always relative to a particular textual context. The absurdity of assuming that I have made general claims for this symbol is epitomized in a remark by A. Green, *Keter*, p. 143 n. 30. In the context of discussing a passage from *Sefer ha-Bahir* wherein the image of *aṭarah* is used, Green notes that he is aware of my "phallic reading of *aṭarah* references in the Kabbalistic corpus," and he has tried to imagine such a reading in the bahiric text that he has cited. Alas, he concludes, such a reading would make no sense in this context. Bracketing the accuracy of Green's claim with respect to the bahiric passage that he mentions, I would like to point out that he incorrectly presumes that my decoding of *aṭarah* as phallic crown is meant to be applied universally and indiscriminately. This runs counter to my methodology, which allows for generalization only on the basis of retracing specific textual markings.

195. Ṣemaḥ, *Ṣemaḥ Ṣaddiq*, 37b.

196. On the identification of the *yod* of the covenant and the corona (*aṭarah*), see ibid., 37c, and on the analogy between the exposure of the corona and the disclosure of the rainbow, see ibid., 38b.

197. E. Wolfson, *Through a Speculum*, pp. 336–345, 357–377, 384–392; idem, *Circle in the Square*, pp. 29–48.

198. E. Wolfson, "Woman—The Feminine as Other," pp. 179–180; idem, *Through a Speculum*, pp. 382 n. 204, 388–390. See also Liebes, "Zohar and Eros," p. 80.

199. E. Wolfson, "Circumcision and the Divine Name," pp. 103–106.

200. The original Hebrew in this context is not entirely clear, but I have rendered the verse in accordance with the meaning implied by Gikatilla's interpretation.

201. Gikatilla, *Shaʿarei Orah*, 1:103.

202. See chap. 1, n. 251.

203. See texts cited and analyzed by E. Gottlieb, *Studies in the Kabbala Literature*, p. 130; and Idel, "Infinities of Torah in Kabbalah," pp. 141–157, esp. pp. 148–151.

204. For citation of some of the relevant sources, see E. Wolfson, "Circumcision and the Divine Name," p. 104 nn. 84–85.

205. Gikatilla, *Shaʿarei Orah*, 1:114–115.

206. See discussion of this redactional matter in E. Wolfson, *Circle in the Square*, pp. 12–14.

207. Gikatilla, *Shaʿarei Orah*, 1:115.

208. Abulafia, *Oṣar Eden Ganuz*, fol. 129b (printed ed., p. 285).

209. Underlying the identification of *ha-shem* and *mosheh* is the assumption that Moses is the personification of the Active Intellect, a point that is underscored further by decoding the letters of *mosheh* as *meṭaṭron sar ha-panim*, "Metatron the angel of the presence." On this identification, see, for instance, Abulafia, *Imrei Shefer*, fol. 241a (printed ed., p. 81). For the identification of *mosheh* and *ha-shem*, see, for instance, Abulafia, *Sitrei Torah*, fol. 171a (printed ed., p. 186). Both elucidations of the name *mosheh* are found in Abulafia, *Sheva Netivot ha-Torah*, p. 18. See Idel, "Writings of Abraham Abulafia," p. 93 and references to primary sources given on p. 115 nn. 60–62. For a later attestation of these identifications, see Sabba, *Ṣeror ha-Mor*, 2:456 (ad Deut. 34:6). The possible influence of Abulafia in this matter has been noted by A. Gross, *Iberian Jewry*, p. 146 nn. 69 and 71. On the identification of Moses and Metatron, see E. Wolfson, "Metatron and Shiʿur Qomah," p. 91 and references to other studies cited in n. 151. On the desire of Moses to behold Metatron, the angel of the presence, *sar ha-panim*, which is linked exegetically to the request to see the face of God's glory (Exod. 33:18–23), see the passage from *Midrash ha-Neʿelam* in *Zohar Ḥadash*, 9d–10a.

210. See, however, Abulafia, *Oṣar Eden Ganuz*, fol. 129a (printed ed., p. 284), where Abulafia writes that the new covenant (*berit ḥadashah*) given to Abraham and his descendants comprised the covenant of circumcision (*berit milah*) and the covenant of the tongue (*berit lashon*). For a slightly different formulation of the two covenants, see Abulafia, *Ḥayyei ha-Olam ha-Ba*, fols. 28b–29b (printed ed., pp. 107–109): "The blood attests that the foundation of man is the blood, and this is the blood of circumcision, as they speak of the blood of the paschal sacrifice [*dam pesaḥ*] and the blood of circumcision [*dam milah*]. . . . The blood of the male is superior in the secret of the mouth that speaks [*peh saḥ*] and the blood of the female is in the image of the blood of circumcision."

211. See Abulafia, *Imrei Shefer*, fol. 231b (printed ed., p. 48): "Abraham our patriarch, the beginning for every master of the covenant [*ha-hatḥalah le-khol baʿal berit*], was circumcised through the commandment of God, and since in the secret of circumcision [*be-sod berit milah*] there is the first principle regarding knowledge of the explicit name, the verse said 'The secret of the Lord is with those who fear him, to them he makes his covenant known' (Ps. 55:14), and this secret will be revealed from the words *eser sefirot belimah*." On the nexus between circumcision and the contemplative ideal of intellectual conjunction, which is expressed mystically as cleaving to the name, see additional Abulafian sources cited and analyzed in E. Wolfson, *Abraham Abulafia*, pp. 87–90, 194–195, 216–220.

212. Abulafia, *Oṣar Eden Ganuz*, fol. 130a (printed ed., p. 286).

213. Gikatilla, *Shaʿarei Orah*, 1:116.

214. Ibid., p. 117.

215. Neumann, *Great Mother*, p. 3.

216. See the concise summary in Madison, *Hermeneutics of Postmodernity*, pp. 178–179.

217. See Iser, "Representation," pp. 217–232.

Chapter Four
Male Androgyne: Engendering E/masculation

1. Pattai, *Hebrew Goddess*, p. 18.

2. Eilberg-Schwartz, *God's Phallus*.

3. Pattai, *Hebrew Goddess*, pp. 29–100; Frymer-Kensky, *In the Wake of the Goddesses*; Gruber, *Motherhood of God*, pp. 3–107; Brenner, "Hebrew God," pp. 56–71; Ackerman, "Queen Mother and the Cult in Ancient Israel," pp. 385–401; idem, "Queen Mother and the Cult in the Ancient Near East," pp. 179–209; E. F. Beach, "Transforming Goddess Iconography," pp. 239–263. For review of the evidence regarding Asherah as a goddess of ancient Israel, see M. S. Smith, *Origins of Biblical Monotheism*, pp. 72–74. For a useful discussion of the role of feminist theory and the discipline of archaeology, related especially to the goddess motif, see Conkey and Tringham, "Archaeology and the Goddess," pp. 199–247.

4. Hadley, "From Goddess to Literary Construct," pp. 360–399, and Bernhard Lang, "Lady Wisdom," pp. 400–423; idem, *Hebrew God*, pp. 25–28. See further references, chap. 2, n. 91. Also relevant is the study on the "divine lady" by Bleeker, *Sacred Bridge*, pp. 83–111.

5. In spite of the many challenges and modifications to Scholem's account of Heikhalot mysticism, on this point his insights have stood the test of time. See Scholem, *Major Trends*, pp. 54–56.

6. For discussion of the feminization of the throne, see E. Wolfson, *Through a Speculum*, pp. 100–101 and other references to scholarly literature cited on p. 100 n. 120. For a psychoanalytic confirmation of this symbolism, see Neumann, *Origins*, pp. 98–100. Scholem's remark in *Origins*, p. 162, that one would look in vain in the "literature of the Merkabah gnosis" for feminine images of the Godhead cannot be upheld in light of the textual evidence that the throne itself is treated hypostatically and assumes a quasi-divine status in contradistinction to the masculine glory. On the possible roots for the *hieros gamos* in ancient Israel, see Weinfeld, "Feminine Elements," pp. 348–358.

7. On the female imaging of Torah, see E. Wolfson, *Circle in the Square*, pp. 1–28, and references to other scholars cited on pp. 123–124 n. 1. The identification of Torah as the preexistent sapiential order of being, so vital in the mythopoeic imagination retrievable from latter rabbinic texts, is found already in some

Second Temple literary sources, as has been argued persuasively by Lange, "Wisdom and Predestination," pp. 342–343; and in fuller detail in idem, *Weisheit und Prädestination.*

8. M. Cohen, *Shi'ur Qomah*, pp. 210–211 n. 47 and p. 217 n. 6.

9. Here I am following the argument of several scholars reviewed and expanded by Wasserstrom, "*Sefer Yeṣira* and Early Islam," pp. 1–30. The dating of the intensive period of redaction of this text to between the eighth and ninth centuries in an Islamic/Arabic environment makes perfectly good sense.

10. Gruenwald, "Preliminary Critical Edition," p. 141. The reading of *Sefer Yeṣirah* that I have proposed is a departure from most scholarly interpretations, which do not interpret the doctrine of *sefirot* in *Sefer Yeṣirah* theosophically. On this question, the common view is still the one expressed by Scholem, *Origins*, pp. 81, 139. For a more elaborate presentation of this interpretation, see E. Wolfson, *Through a Speculum*, pp. 70–72. A theosophic explication of the *sefirot* in *Sefer Yeṣirah* is supported by Pines, "Points of Similarity," pp. 63–142.

11. E. Wolfson, "Circumcision and the Divine Name."

12. See chap. 3, nn. 210–211.

13. Several scholars, in varying degrees and for ulterior motives, have noted the gender/sexual implications of the gnosis of the secret of the nut and the implicit correlation of eroticism and esotericism. For two of the more recent studies, see Farber, "Concept of the Merkabah"; D. Abrams, *Sexual Symbolism.*

14. E. Wolfson, "Image of Jacob."

15. Ibid., p. 4.

16. For a more detailed account of this process, see E. Wolfson, "Face of Jacob in the Moon," pp. 240–245; idem, "Sacred Space," pp. 593–634.

17. I am here responding to a critique of my position offered by D. Abrams, *Sexual Symbolism*, pp. 55–56. The gist of the criticism is that I supposedly build my argument from passages in Eleazar's work wherein the four beasts of the chariot are seen as a single beast, which is the form that sits on the throne. According to Abrams, in the Pietistic writings there is no connection between the image of Jacob, the motif of the beast named "Israel," and the enthroned figure. Again, in apparent contradiction to my position, Abrams suggests that the image of Jacob is part of the throne and not an entity or form that sits upon it. Regrettably, I must say that this criticism fails to grasp not only the text of my argument but also the texture of my approach to the study of gender symbolism in esoteric literature. Without entering into a lengthy rejoinder, let me state briefly that I did not build my argument on the basis of the idea that the four beasts who bear the throne are identical with the one beast that sits upon the throne nor did I conflate the views of Eleazar with those expressed in the material that derives from the group of Pietists known as the circle of the Special Cherub (*ḥug keruv ha-meyuḥad*). With respect to the latter, I simply conjecture that it is plausible that the various pietistic groups were working on similar traditions and hence the ideational chasm separating them is not as wide as some previous scholars (principally Joseph Dan) have maintained. With respect to the former, I propose through a very complex textual reconstruction that there are earlier sources utilized by Eleazar wherein the image of Jacob is linked either to the human form of the glory enthroned on the chariot or to the human form of the celestial beast that comprises the four faces of the beasts who bear the throne. Naturally, I recognize that these are distinct traditions that were fused together in the minds of the Pietists, but in either case there is the blurring of difference between throne and glory, which is precisely the point of the motif of the glory erotically interacting with the icon of Jacob engraved on the throne—the iconic form functions both as mirror reflecting image and image reflected in mirror. I still harbor the opinion that this is a foundational myth of ancient Jewish esotericism that evolved exegetically in the religious imagination of the Rhineland Pietists in the late Middle Ages.

18. My conclusions regarding this rabbinic motif have been corroborated by the independent study by S. Friedman, "Graven Images," pp. 233–238. As Friedman remarks, p. 237, he became aware of my study (written in 1989 but not published until 1994) after he had completed his own. I am grateful to Friedman for referring to my study as "outstanding" but I must take issue with his presentation of my thesis. In an apparent attempt to demarcate his own work from mine, he has misrepresented my view by downplaying the extent to which I myself considered the motif of Jacob's image engraved on the throne an attestation in rabbinic

literature of the idea that God has an incarnate and iconic form. The point is already evident in the original Hebrew version of my study seen by Friedman but it is even more conspicuous in the English translation, prepared in 1992 but not published until 1995.

19. *Genesis Rabbah* 8:1, pp. 54–56; *Leviticus Rabbah*, 14:1, pp. 295–299; Babylonian Talmud, Berakhot 61b; Eruvin 18a. For discussion of the motif of the creation of Adam as an androgyne in some of the relevant rabbinic sources, see Aaron, "Imagery of the Divine and the Human," pp. 1–62, esp. pp. 22–33. See also Boyarin, *Carnal Israel*, pp. 42–46; Teugels, "Creation of the Human," pp. 107–127. On the utilization of this motif in kabbalistic sources, see Mopsik, "Recherches autour de la *Lettre sur la sainteté*," pp. 29–73; idem, "Genèse 1:26–27," pp. 341–361; Idel, *Kabbalah: New Perspectives*, pp. 128–136. The kabbalistic symbol of the androgyne may also reflect the impact of the myth of Aristophanes articulated by Plato in the *Symposium*. For an illuminating study of this source in medieval Arabic literature, see Gutas, "Plato's *Symposion*," pp. 36–60.

20. Todros ben Joseph Abulafia, *Oṣar ha-Kavod ha-Shalem*, 9b.

21. Concerning the use of the word "mishnah" in zoharic texts to refer to alleged older sources, see Matt, "Matnita Dilan," pp. 123–145. On p. 139, Matt correctly notes that the reference to the Mishnah in this case is an attempt to present a kabbalistic motif, derived from either a prior literary source or the imagination, as a statement of the rabbis. It may be the case, as Matt also notes, that the zoharic authorship is expanding the statement attributed to Rav in Babylonian Talmud, Baba Batra 74b.

22. See Babylonian Talmud, Yevamot 62a; *Zohar* 3:5a.

23. *Zohar* 1:55b.

24. For references, see chap. 2, n. 192.

25. Grosz, "Histories of the Present and Future," p. 22 (emphasis in original).

26. For representative studies on the *Bahir*, see Scholem, *Origins*, pp. 49–198; Lehmann, "Theology of the Mystical Book Bahir," pp. 477–483; Weinstock, *Studies in Jewish Philosophy*, pp. 15–50; Idel, "Problem of the Sources of the *Bahir*," pp. 55–72; idem, *Kabbalah: New Perspectives*, pp. 122–128; Pedaya, "Provençal Stratum," pp. 139–164; E. Wolfson, *Along the Path*, pp. 63–88. See also the survey of scholarship on the *Bahir* presented by D. Abrams in *Book Bahir*, pp. 1–54, and the comprehensive bibliography on pp. 293–336. For a challenge to the conventional scholarly view regarding twelfth-century Provence as the likely setting for the redaction of the *Bahir*, see Verman, *Books of Contemplation*, pp. 166–169; idem, "Evolution of the Circle," pp. 168–169. For a Spanish as opposed to a Provençal setting, see also McGaha, "*Sefer ha-Bahir* and Andalusian Sufism," pp. 20–57. McGaha argues that the *Bahir* was written in the thirteenth century by an Andalusian who fled to Northern Spain to escape Almohad persecution. On the possible "oriental" provenance, see Ariel, "Eastern Dawn of Wisdom," pp. 149–167, esp. pp. 160–165; and more recently Meroz, "Bright Light in the East," pp. 137–180.

27. Many of the passages cited below have been noted and discussed by Scholem, *Origins*, pp. 139–142; and see idem, *On the Mystical Shape*, pp. 44–45.

28. The interpretation of the biblical notion of the divine image with which Adam was created as a reference to the body, implying thereby that God has a somatic human shape, is one of the distinctive doctrines promulgated by medieval kabbalists, even though there were some kabbalists who recoiled from this idea and tried to explain it in a nonliteral way. I note in passing that the somatic interpretation of the divine image is attested in older gnostic sources that became a major bone of contention for Church authorities by the fourth century. See Gould, "Image of God," pp. 549–557; E. Clark, *Origenist Controversy*, pp. 43–84. A similar idea is attributed by Epiphanius to the Audians, a possible Jewish-Christian group that articulated views of an esoteric nature. See Stroumsa, "Jewish and Gnostic Traditions," pp. 97–108, esp. p. 101. Finally, I note that the somatic interpretation of the divine image as the literal meaning of Scripture figured in medieval Muslim polemical attacks on Jews. See, for instance, Pulcini, *Exegesis as Polemical Discourse*, p. 84.

29. In my opinion, the seven limbs should be interpreted as an autonomous theosophic tradition based on a conception of the divine represented by seven potencies. There is no need to assume, as Scholem does, that the limbs of the Primordial Anthropos are the lower seven of ten *sefirot*. Although Scholem does emphasize that the seven potencies are treated as a "separate whole," he nevertheless maintains that these seven are part of the decade, with the upper three potencies corresponding to intellectual powers or spiritual forces and the lower seven to the anatomical limbs. See Scholem, *Origins*, pp. 138–139, and *On the Mystical Shape*,

p. 45. (In *Origins*, p. 140, however, Scholem acknowledges the wavering of numerical symbolism related to different theosophies in the *Bahir*, and in *On the Mystical Shape*, p. 162, he correctly observes that "we cannot expect systematic uniformity among all of the highly disparate fragments scattered throughout the book." On the presumption of different and at times even contradictory traditions preserved in the bahiric text, see also *Origins*, pp. 56–57 and 147; *On the Mystical Shape*, p. 93.) Such an interpretation presupposes a doctrine of ten *sefirot* in sections of the book where it is not stated explicitly or even implicitly. It is more plausible to assume, as I have argued, that the bahiric text preserves different theosophic structures, and one of those involves imaging the divine in terms of seven potencies that are described in different symbolic ways, to wit, seven limbs, seven days of creation, seven voices of revelation, seven holy forms, and seven gardens. See E. Wolfson, *Along the Path*, pp. 69–70.

30. *Book Bahir*, sec. 55, p. 151.

31. Ibid., sec. 114, p. 199. Cf. secs. 64–65, pp. 157–159, where a group of eight powers, added to the sixty-four forms in order to equal the sum of the seventy-two names of God, are said to comprise the seven days of the week (on the hypostatic nature of the days of creation, see secs. 39, p. 139; 55, p. 151; 74, p. 163; and 105, p. 189) with the eighth called (on the basis of Eccles. 5:8) *yitron*, the place whence the earth is hewn and from which the inhabitants of the world receive the splendor. In sec. 65, p. 159, this "earth" is identified further as the throne of God, the precious jewel, and the sea of wisdom that corresponds to the blue thread of the fringe garment. All of these symbols are obvious references to the feminine potency. On the structure of seven forms or potencies plus the eighth, which is the ruler, see the comments by Idel, *Kabbalah: New Perspectives*, pp. 125–126.

32. For the impact of this bahiric expression on later kabbalistic sources, especially the zoharic corpus, see Liebes, *Sections of the Zohar Lexicon*, p. 185 n. 52.

33. Regarding the expression "holy forms" (*ṣurot qedoshot*) in the *Bahir* and some interesting parallels in gnostic literature as well as several medieval Jewish sources, see Idel, *Kabbalah: New Perspectives*, pp. 122–128. Idel discusses the particular bahiric text that deals with the seven holy forms, identified further as the seven sons, on pp. 126–127.

34. In accordance with the reading of MS Munich, Bayerische Staatsbibliothek 209, fol. 33a, *guf bi-verito*. The reading in MS Vatican-Barberini Or. 110, cited in *Book Bahir*, p. 201, is *guf u-verit milah* ("the body and the phallus"). The reading preserved in the Margaliot edition, sec. 172, is *guf berit*. In the *editio princeps* of the *Bahir* (Amsterdam, 1651), 10b, reproduced in *Book Bahir*, p. 281, the reading is: *ha-guf u-verit* ("the body and the phallus"). According to that text, the "head" is not delineated as a separate item, and hence the six limbs, which correspond to the six forms, consist of the right and left thighs, the right and left hands, the body and the phallus. This reading also appears in the passage of the *Bahir* copied in the Cremona edition of the *Zohar* (1559–1560), 32a, reproduced in *Book Bahir*, p. 246.

35. *Book Bahir*, sec. 116, p. 201.

36. It is of interest to note the depiction of the androgynous Christ in the fragment from *Interrogationes maiores Mariae* preserved by Epiphanius, *Panarium*, 26:8. The relevant passage is discussed by Jung, *Aion*, pp. 202–206. As Jung correctly notes (p. 204), the production of the woman from the side of Christ, with whom he engages in sexual intercourse, suggests that Christ is here identified typologically with Adam. The androgyny of Jesus reflects the standpoint of the creation account in the second chapter of Genesis insofar as the male regains the original wholeness by cohabiting with his feminine counterpart after she is separated from him. On the depiction of the birth of Jesus from the virgin Mary in terms of Adam's creation from the virgin earth and Eve's creation from the virgin Adam, see Newman, *Sister of Wisdom*, p. 171. On the androgynous Christ, see as well Jung, *Mysterium Coniunctionis*, pp. 184–185 (the mystical androgyny of Christ is depicted in the image of the "man encompassed by the woman," which is reminiscent of the language used by kabbalists derived from Jeremiah 31:21 to characterize the union of male and female in the Godhead), 208–217, 373–374, 393, 404–405 (in this context, Jung compares the unity of the dual nature of Christ as male and female to the Tantric iconography that depicts Shiva and Shakti in permanent cohabitation; see also p. 185 n. 384), 421–434. It is instructive to consider as well Jung's use of the dictum from the *Hermetis Trismegisti Tractatus vere Aureus de Lapide philosophici secreto* of Dominicus Gnosius that every man "carries Eve, his wife, hidden in his body" as a reference to the *anima* or the feminine element in every man. See Jung, *Symbolic*

Life, p. 189. The psychoanalytic appropriation of the dictum in some measure preserves the androcentric dimension of the original, albeit in a manner sufficiently transformed by the new context. See, however, Jung, *Symbols of Transformation*, p. 221: "Not only the gods, but the goddesses, too, are libido-symbols, when regarded from the point of view of their dynamism. The libido expresses itself in images of sun, light, fire, sex, fertility, and growth. In this way, the goddesses . . . come to possess phallic symbols, even though the latter are essentially masculine. One of the main reasons for this is that, just as the female lies hidden in the male, so the male lies hidden in the female." For a constructive application of the symbol of the androgyne in Jungian analysis, see the work of Singer cited in chap. 2, n. 100. Finally, it should be noted that in the fifth of the "Seven Sermons on the Dead," which were composed in 1916, Jung associated spirituality with the feminine, *mater coelestis* (the celestial mother), and sexuality with the masculine, *phallos* (earthly father). This obviously represents a reversal of the standard gender stereotypes that have been influential in Western thought in general and in gnostic symbolism in particular. In the same context, however, Jung contrasts the earthly sexuality of man and the spiritual sexuality of woman, while he also affirms that the spirituality of man is heavenly and the spirituality of woman is earthly. See Jung, *Memories, Dreams, Reflections*, pp. 386–387, and analysis in *Gnostic Jung*, p. 42.

37. *Book Bahir*, sec. 116, p. 201.

38. See E. Wolfson, *Circle in the Square*, pp. 92–98. An interesting and somewhat atypical remark that underscores the tenuous nature of heterosexual union is found in *Sefer ha-Yiḥud*, in *R. Asher ben David: His Complete Works*, p. 62, where the author contrasts the unity of the three central *sefirot*, *Ḥesed*, *Din*, and *Raḥamim*, linked exegetically to the three names of God mentioned in Deuteronomy 6:4, and the unity of the *sefirot* in *Shekhinah*, related to the unity of the Tabernacle (*mishkan*) mentioned in Exodus 26:6, as well as the unity of husband and wife in one flesh according to Genesis 2:24: " 'And couple the cloths to one another with the clasps, so that the tabernacle will be one' (Exod. 26:6), this union is not like that union, for the union of the Tabernacle was from discrete things, and when they are joined one to the other, it is as if it were one, but it is not so, for this union can break apart and it will be as it was at first, and there will be a multiplicity of things, and thus 'and they will be one flesh' (Gen. 2:24). But the 'one' of the verse 'Hear, O, Israel' (Deut. 6:4) is one from every perspective and in all of his attributes without any division and without any composition [*be-lo shum perud uve-lo shum ḥibbur*] even though it appears as if they are distinct attributes [*middot nifradot*], for this one activates loving-kindness [*ḥesed*], this one judgment [*din*], and this one compassion [*raḥamim*], but it is not so for he is one in every aspect and in each and every attribute, he is mercy, he is judgment, and he is compassion." For the zoharic parallel, see chap. 5, n. 452. It is of interest to note that in another passage from *Sefer ha-Yiḥud*, p. 106, Asher ben David affirms a threefold unity in the first of the *sefirot*, which he links to the description of the first *sefirah* in *Sefer Yeṣirah* (1:10) as the "spirit of the living God" (*ruaḥ elohim ḥayyim*), which is further identified as the "holy spirit" (*ruaḥ ha-qodesh*) divided into three components, voice (*qol*), spirit (*ruaḥ*), and speech (*dibbur*). It appears that this is a formulation of the idea expressed by other kabbalists (for instance, by the anonymous author of the epistle erroneously attributed to Hai Gaon on the three hidden lights above the *sefirot*; see Scholem, *Origins*, pp. 347–354) concerning three attributes comprised in the first of the *sefirot*, an idea that may have arisen out of the attempt to harmonize the rabbinic doctrine of God's thirteen attributes of mercy (*yod-gimmel middot raḥamim*)—derived exegetically from Exodus 34:6–7—and the esoteric notion of the ten *sefirot*, which were also identified as divine attributes (*middot*). See Matt, "Introduction," in David ben Yehudah he-Ḥasid, *Book of Mirrors*, pp. 23–24.

39. The Hebrew word that I have rendered as phallus is *gewiyyah*, which can refer to the body in general or to the male organ in particular. This signification of the term is reflected, for instance, in the expression *ro'sh ha-gewiyyah*, the "head of the body," in Babylonian Talmud, Nedarim 32b, as noted by Liebes, *Sections of the Zohar Lexicon*, p. 258 n. 382. A similar semantic usage is associated with the word *guf* in kabbalistic literature and is perhaps already implicit in rabbinic literature. See Liebes, pp. 170 n. 2, 178 n. 32, 273 n. 442; Eilberg-Schwartz, *God's Phallus*, p. 182 (the author refers explicitly to Palestinian Talmud, Berakhot 1:3, 3:3, and *Leviticus Rabbah* 25:6, to support his contention).

40. MS New York, Jewish Theological Seminary of America Mic. 2324, fol. 172b. Abrams, in *Book Bahir*, p. 42, cites this text, as well as three parallel versions. Independently, in *Circle in the Square*, pp. 97–98,

I translated and analyzed an almost identical text preserved in MSS Vatican, Biblioteca Apostolica ebr. 236, fols. 76a–b and Parma, Biblioteca Palatina 2704 (De Rossi 68), fol. 87a, as a kabbalistic commentary on levirate marriage, *sod ha-yibbum*. It is worth noting the affinity of the kabbalistic perspective and the following depiction of the Sufi view in Murata, "Witnessing the Rose," pp. 353–354: "Love with its two sides—loverness and belovedness—is an attribute of the Real at root, and it has permeated the existent entities in keeping with permeation by existence. . . . The fountainhead of love between a couple is that the woman is derived from the man and the relationship of wholeness and partness and the intimacy of rootness and branchness are established between them. . . . Especially since the woman was derived from the left side of the man—which is the place of the heart—the heart inclines helplessly toward her." For a similar mystical interpretation in Ibn ʿArabī's reading of the scriptural account of the woman's creation from man and man's desire to unite with the woman as an analogue to the soul's yearning to become one with God, see Nettler, *Sufi Metaphysics*, pp. 181–192.

41. Lacan, "Positions of the Unconscious," p. 276.

42. See chap. 2, n. 408.

43. The preference on the part of medieval kabbalists for monogamy, which is a cultural innovation of the Ashkenazic rabbinate, is to be explained by the theosophic meaning they assigned to sexual relations between husband and wife. See Y. Baer, *History of the Jews in Christian Spain*, vol. 1, p. 437 n. 19.

44. See, for instance, the dictum of R. Jeremiah ben Eleazar preserved in Babylonian Talmud, Berakhot 61a (parallel to Eruvin 18a) concerning the androgynous nature of Adam: "The first Adam had two faces [*diyo parṣuf panim hayah lo le-adam ha-riʾshon*] as it says, 'You formed me in front and from behind' (Ps. 139:5), and it is written 'The Lord God fashioned the side that he had taken from the man into a woman' (Gen. 2:22)." The account of the female being constructed from the male in Genesis 2:22 is read as an exegetical gloss on Psalms 139:5, which is equivalent to the account of the bisexual nature of Adam in Genesis 1:27. See also Ketuvot 8a, where the following exegetical tradition is reported in the name of R. Judah (in Eruvin 18a, the exegesis is attributed to R. Abbahu): "It is written 'And God created Adam in his image' (Gen. 1:27) and it is written 'male and female he created them' (ibid., 5:2). How is this possible? Initially, it arose in thought to create two but in the end one was created." The context wherein this teaching is transmitted is a halakhic discussion concerning the intent of the first two of the seven nuptial blessings.

45. For a different interpretation, see the studies by Mopsik cited above, n. 19. It is of interest to consider the following remark by Eliade, *History of Religious Ideas*, vol. 1, p. 165: "The creation of woman from a rib taken from Adam can be interpreted as indicating the androgyny of the primordial man. . . . The myth of the androgyne illustrates a comparatively widespread belief: human perfection, identified in the mythical ancestor, comprises a unity that is at the same time a *totality*. We shall gauge the importance of androgyny when we come to discuss certain gnostic and hermetic speculations. We should note that human androgyny has as its model divine bisexuality, a conception shared by a number of cultures" (emphasis in original). Eliade's depiction of the biblical text accords with the exegetical strategy adopted by most kabbalists. On the use of the symbol of the androgyne in the work of Eliade, see Altizer, *Mircea Eliade and the Dialectic of the Sacred*, pp. 99–104; Wasserstrom, *Religion after Religion*, pp. 204–214. Also pertinent is the comment of Lacan, "Positions of the Unconscious," p, 276: "It is not true that God made them male and female, even if the couple Adam and Eve said so; such a notion is also explicitly contradicted by the highly condensed myth found in the same text on the creation of Adam's companion."

46. Gikatilla, *Sefer ha-Niqqud*, p. 21.

47. *Book Bahir*, sec. 116, p. 201. See Scholem, *On the Mystical Shape*, p. 169. I take this opportunity to respond to the criticism of my interpretation offered by Schäfer, *Mirror of His Beauty*, p. 285 n. 37, based on an earlier version of this material in my "Hebraic and Hellenic Conceptions of Wisdom." Schäfer begins his note by saying that he sees no basis for "E. Wolfson's repeated claim that God's allegedly primordial androgyny is only superficial." I have already responded to this skewed characterization of my work in chap. 2, n. 122. Schäfer further proclaims that I have "strangely" read "a lot of phallic symbolism into the bahiric sources" and that the "proofs" (placed in quotes to indicate to the reader that he does not consider them proofs at all) I have adduced "are all weak or forced interpretations." Schäfer's principle line of attack is to

say that the bahiric parables I have interpreted are not "concerned with the ontic status of the *Shekhinah*, but simply [include] her among the king's sons." In my judgment, not only does this comment not make sense, it illustrates a fundamental lack of understanding, as the parabolic form is precisely the way in which the bahiric authors engage in discourse about the nature of ontology. The parable is the key that transforms language into a mimetic discourse that allows one access to the imaginal realm of divine being. Along similar lines, Schäfer rejects my surmise that the parable concerning the change in status of the last emanation, the *etrog*, from male to female, alludes to the containment of the female in the male, on the grounds that "the plain meaning of the text suggests that God simply changed his mind; he originally planned 'his garden' to be completely male, but realized that an all-male garden (i.e., an all-male God) would not be able to survive." Schäfer's comments serve only to buttress the androcentrism that I have uncovered in the bahiric imagery—the female, by his own account, is viewed solely from the procreative perspective. Surely, no one would argue with the claim that there can be no generation if there were only one sex, but dual sex does not necessarily mean two genders that are legitimately autonomous.

48. Regarding this symbolic image for the divine pleroma, see *Book Bahir*, sec. 4, pp. 119–121, sec. 15, pp. 125–127, sec. 62, p. 155, and sec. 90, pp. 175–177. The feminine character of the garden, an archaic trope attested in a variety of cultural contexts, is especially linked to a plethora of erotic images on occasion stemming from fertility rites enacted in sites of vegetation. On the garden as a setting for eroticism, see the evidence adduced by Stordalen, *Echoes of Eden*, pp. 107–111, 128–130.

49. On the bisexual nature of the symbol of the tree, see Jung, *Symbols of Transformation*, p. 221.

50. See Scholem, *Origins*, pp. 171–173, and discussion below in chap. 8.

51. *Book Bahir*, sec. 117, p. 203. See Scholem, *Origins*, p. 142.

52. See Targum Onkelos and Targum Pseudo-Jonathan *ad locum*; *Sifra*, Emor, 16:4; *Leviticus Rabba* 30:8; Palestinian Talmud, Sukkah 3:7; Babylonian Talmud, Sukkah 35a.

53. Scholem, *Das Buch Bahir*, p. 126, sec. 117 n. 3, suggests that the expression *hadar ha-kol* may be an ellipsis of *hadar kol ha-illanot*, the "splendor of all the trees," and thus has the signification of *hadar al ha-kol*, the "most splendid of all." On p. 127 n. 1, Scholem suggests that the word *kol* in the expression *hadar ha-kol* may be a technical name for the last *sefirah*, the *Shekhinah*. In support of this he refers to the reader to sec. 52 (p. 149 in the Abrams edition). In my opinion, however, the term *kol* in that context denotes the phallus, and hence I have rendered the expression *hadar ha-kol* as the "splendor of the All." Similarly, in sec. 52, the daughter given to Abraham is called *ba-kol* (based on the rabbinic reading of Genesis 24:1 in Babylonian Talmud, Baba Batra 16b) and not simply *kol*. That is, the feminine is in the masculine, literally, "in the All," *ba-kol*, a state that is retrieved or reenacted by the reverse, viz., by the male entering into the female, the container becoming that which is contained. The point was well understood by subsequent interpreters of the bahiric text. See, e.g., commentary of Naḥmanides to Genesis 24:1 and Numbers 15:31 and discussion in E. Wolfson, "By Way of Truth," pp. 134 n. 90, 144 n. 116, and 166–167. On the demiurgic and phallic connotation of the term *kol* in the *Bahir*, see my study, "Tree That Is All" in *Along the Path*, pp. 63–88.

54. The bahiric exegesis is elaborated in *Zohar* 3:24a.

55. My formulation reflects the widely affirmed distinction between nature and culture, gendered respectively as female and male. See Ortner, "Is Female to Male as Nature is to Culture?" pp. 67–87.

56. Babylonian Talmud, Pesaḥim 56a. The characterization of the palm tree as androgynous should be viewed as one aspect of a broader anthropomorphic perspective that may be elicited from rabbinic literature. For instance, see Visotzky, "The Conversation of Palm Trees," pp. 205–214.

57. *Book Bahir*, secs. 139–140, p. 223.

58. Needless to say, the symbolic correlation of the moon and the feminine, particularly the archetype of the mother, is known from a variety of religious societies. See Harley, *Moon Lore*, pp. 53–68; Eliade, *Patterns in Comparative Religion*, pp. 163–169; Neumann, "Moon and Matriarchal Consciousness," pp. 64–118. Particularly important for the history of Western culture is the influence of the kabbalistic symbol of the moon on alchemy. See Jung, *Alchemical Studies*, pp. 79 n. 64, 161; idem, *Psychology and Alchemy*, pp. 383 and 404; idem, *Archetypes and the Collective Unconscious*, p. 81; idem, *Mysterium Coniunctionis*, pp. 24–29.

59. It is of interest to note the following comment by Abraham Abulafia, *Imrei Shefer*, fol. 238a (printed

ed., p. 70): "The testicles are two spheres filled with semen and the two of them are male and female and the semen is the matter whence the particular body is generated."

60. *Book Bahir*, sec. 42, p. 141. For a more extended discussion of this passage, see E. Wolfson, *Along the Path*, p. 84.

61. *Book Bahir*, sec. 67, p. 159.

62. Consider the following description of the tenth *sefirah* in an anonymous kabbalistic text extant in MS Moscow, Günzberg 407, fol. 64b: "[It is called] heart [*lev*], for she is the completion of everything, and this is the *beit* from [the word] *bere'shit* (Gen. 1:1) and the *lamed* from [the word] *yisra'el* (Deut. 33:12). Therefore the tenth *sefirah* is called *lev* because she is the bride comprised of everything" (*kallah ha-kelulah min ha-kol*). Cf. ibid., fol. 66a. The heart is associated with the feminine potency, which is constituted by what she receives from the masculine. The heart, moreover, comprises the whole of Torah, which is represented by the letters that make up the word *lev*, the *lamed* and *beit*, respectively the last and first letters of the Torah. For an analogous approach in the esoteric theosophy of the Rhineland Jewish Pietists, see E. Wolfson, *Through a Speculum*, pp. 253–254.

63. That is, that which dwells. A similar play on the word *hadar* is found already in classical rabbinic sources. See *Leviticus Rabbah* 30:8; Babylonian Talmud, Sukkah 31b and 35a. See also commentary of Rashi to Lev. 23:40, s.v., *hadar*.

64. *Book Bahir* sec. 118, p. 203.

65. Ibid., secs. 87–88, p. 173.

66. Ibid., sec. 88, pp. 173–175. On the proposed gnostic origin and the fragmentary condition of this passage, see Scholem, *Origins*, pp. 119–120.

67. *Book Bahir*, sec. 89, p. 175.

68. Scholem, *Das Buch Bahir*, sec. 89, p. 96, renders *daveq u-meyuḥad* as *verbunden und geeint ist*. For a similar rendering, see Gottfarstein, *Bahir*, sec. 128, p. 97: *"qui se trouve attaché et uni avec tous."* Schäfer, "Daughter, Sister, Bride, and Mother" pp. 227–228, duly notes the "twofold function" of the last *sefirah* implied by the expression *daveq u-meyuḥad*. The point is repeated in idem, *Mirror of His Beauty*, pp. 127–128. See, however, pp. 120–121, where Schäfer asserts that the third *qadosh*, which is described as "united and special in (= separate from) all of them," refers to *Binah*, the third of the ten emanations. His justification for applying this description to both *Binah* and *Shekhinah* seems to rest on the assumption that in bahiric symbolism a "perfect harmony seems to exist between the third Sefirah (*binah*), as the lowest of the three upper Sefirot, and the tenth Sefirah (*Shekhinah*), as the lowest of the seven lower Sefirot" (p. 126). It is certainly the case that, according to one passage in the *Bahir*, *Shekhinah* is treated as twofold, below and above, the "light that emanated from the first light" (*Book Bahir*, sec. 116, p. 201; Schäfer's account is basically a paraphrase of Scholem's discussion of the double *Shekhinah*; see *Origins*, pp. 178–180; *On the Mystical Shape*, pp. 173–175; see below, n. 88). I would argue, however, that it is not relevant or appropriate to introduce this motif in interpreting the depiction of the third *qadosh*, for discernible here is an attempt to combine an older mythic teaching that presumed the pleroma consisted of three potencies.

69. *Mishta'asha'in bah*. On the sexual connotation of this and related words, see E. Wolfson, *Circle in the Square*, pp. 70–71, and further references to both primary and secondary sources given on pp. 190–192 nn. 175–180. On the symbolic intent of *sha'ashu'a* in the bahiric text, see E. Wolfson, "Before Alef," pp. 142–150, and discussion below, chap. 6.

70. Babylonian Talmud, Ḥagigah 13b.

71. In subsequent kabbalistic literature, the expression *eshet ḥayyil* (Prov. 31:10) became a standard symbol for *Malkhut*.

72. On the feminine aspect of the field, with a decidedly sexual component connected to the motif of walking, cf. *Book Bahir*, sec. 43, p. 141; Scholem, *On the Mystical Shape*, p. 162. The image of the field as a metaphor for the feminine is not uncommon in classical texts. See DuBois, *Sowing the Body*, pp. 39–64; O'Flaherty, *Women, Androgynes, and Other Mythical Beasts*, pp. 29–30.

73. *Book Bahir*, sec. 90, p. 175.

74. On this point, there are striking analogies between the bahiric symbolism and ancient Zoroastrian-

ism, but I cannot elaborate on these matters here. For discussion of some of the relevant themes in Persian literature, see Corbin, *Spiritual Body and Celestial Earth*, pp. 36–50. Also relevant to this motif is the study by P. Berger, *Goddess Obscured*, pp. 5–47; and Newman, *God and the Goddesses*, pp. 190–244.

75. Scholem, *Origins*, pp. 94–96; idem, *On the Mystical Shape*, pp. 166–167.

76. Jacob ben Sheshet, *Shaʿar ha-Shamayim*, p. 156; "Sefer Shaʿar ha-Shamayim," p. 105 and see discussion, pp. 70–71. As Gabay properly notes, the three-letter name, YHW, is referred to as the "great name" (*shem ha-gadol*) in *Sefer Yeṣirah* 1:13. See also the formulation in Asher ben David, *Sefer ha-Yiḥud*, in *R. Asher ben David: His Complete Works*, pp. 112–113: "Moreover, this name is called the explicit name [*shem ha-meforash*] for it elucidates everything [*mefaresh ha-kol*], and within it is written his great name [*shemo ha-gadol*], which is *yod he waw*, and the second *he* that is in it alludes to God's glory [*le-khivodo shel maqom*], the *Shekhinah*, which is the tenth *sefirah*. The *yod*, as we said, refers to *Ḥokhmah* together with the efflux that flows to it from the *alef* [i.e., *Keter*]; they are two even though they appear as one. The *he* [i.e., *Binah*] is one, and hence there are here three. The *waw* refers to six *sefirot* corresponding to six extremities [i.e., from *Ḥesed* to *Yesod*], and thus there are nine, and the second *he*, which corresponds to the place [*ha-maqom*], and there are ten. She completes the matter of the one [*inyan ha-eḥad*], for the matter of the one is not concluded except in the tenth, no less and no more. Therefore, the author of *Sefer Yeṣirah* [1:4] said 'Ten and not nine, ten and not eleven.' The illustration [*mashal*] of this is that there is no point [*nequddah*] in the world that does not have nine [aspects], and they are length, width, and depth, and each of these has a beginning, end, and middle. Thus there are three times three so that there are nine. And every point needs a place [*maqom*], and this is called in the language of the tradition [*be-lashon ha-qabbalah*] the topos of place [*geder ha-maqom*], and together with it they are ten, and through it the enumeration of the one [*minyan ha-eḥad*] is terminated, for it is not terminated with less than ten. Therefore the great name begins with *yod*, for the *yod* completes the enumeration of the one, as I have explained, not by less nor more, to allude to the fact that everything derives from the *alef*, which is transmitted with respect to the unity [*ha-mesurah al ha-aḥdut*]." See citation below at n. 205.

77. Jung, *Psychology and Alchemy*, pp. 26–27; see pp. 205 (where reference is made by Jung to the "masculine trinity" and the "feminine quaternity"), 229–230. On the symbol of the quaternity, see idem, *Aion*, pp. 222–265, esp. pp. 251–252, where the author discusses the duplex nature of one of the factors of the quaternity, that is the doubling of an original member of a trinity to transpose the threefold into a fourfold, a move that invariably leads to the theme of marriage between brother and sister that emulates the conjunction of father and mother. See idem, *Mysterium Coniunctionis*, pp. 6–17, 47–48, 101–103, and esp. pp. 185–188. On the tendency in Indian symbolism to perceive things through the lens of four axes structured about a central point of origin, see Bucknell and Stuart-Fox, *Twilight Language*, p. 139.

78. Knorr von Rosenroth, *Kabbala Denudata*, I, pt. 3, chap. 8, sec. 3, p. 116.

79. Pattai, *Jewish Alchemists*, pp. 60–80, esp. pp. 69–74.

80. Jung, *Mysterium Coniunctionis*, pp. 429–430.

81. See *Book Bahir*, secs. 3, p. 119, 36, pp. 137–139, 43–44, pp. 141–143, 51, pp. 147–149. Some of the relevant texts are discussed by Scholem, *On the Mystical Shape*, pp. 163–164. The structure revolving about the father, son, and daughter that I have discerned in *Bahir* may be seen as a theosophic mythologization of the book of Proverbs itself wherein the feminine wisdom (*ḥokhmah*) mediates between God and Israel, imaged respectively as father and son. Eilberg-Schwartz, *God's Phallus*, pp. 130–132, remarks that one of the functions of the female image of wisdom in this text is to restore the heterosexual imagery and thereby keep the homoerotic associations of God's love for Israel and Israel's love for God at bay. In the case of the *Bahir*, and subsequent kabbalistic sources informed by the mythical structure attested in this text, it is the heterosexual relationship of son and daughter that militates against the incestuous relationship of father and daughter. The homoerotic relationship of father and son, as well as that of mother and daughter, are developed independently of the wisdom motif.

82. See *Book Bahir*, secs. 3, p. 119, 37, p. 139, 43–44, pp. 141–143, 51–52, pp. 147–149, 74, p. 163; Scholem, *Origins*, pp. 70, 92; David Stern, *Parables in Midrash*, p. 221; E. Wolfson, *Circle n the Square*, pp. 11–12. In *Book Bahir*, sec. 96, p. 181, which is part of the section in which the ten divine sayings are delineated, wisdom is identified as the second of these hypostases.

83. The relationship of father and daughter, upper and lower wisdom, is a theme repeated often in later kabbalistic literature and is especially prominent in the zoharic corpus. See, for instance, Isaac ha-Kohen, *Maʾamar al ha-Aṣilut ha-Semoʾlit*, in Scholem, "Traditions of R. Jacob," pp. 246–247: "They placed the throne . . . in the bosom of the primordial wisdom, and he received her in the language 'Come O bride,' and he delighted [*mishtaʿasheʿa*] in her like a father delighting with his only daughter amongst his sons." Of the many relevant passages in zoharic literature that could be cited, I mention one from *Zohar* 1:156b (*Sitrei Torah*) for it clearly draws on the language of the *Bahir*: "The desire of the father is constantly towards his daughter, for the daughter, his beloved, is always near him since she is the only daughter amongst the six sons." Apparently, this passage underlies the comment in Moses de León's *Sheʾelot u-Teshuvot*, p. 43: "They said there is no love greater than that of a father for the daughter, for she is the only daughter amongst six brothers." The likely connection between this passage and the aforecited zoharic text was already noted by Tishby, *Wisdom of the Zohar*, p. 43 n. 46. An even more striking repetition of the structure underlying the bahiric myth is found in *Tiqqunei Zohar*, sec. 64, 95b: "When [Solomon] ascended in his kingship, it said concerning him, 'Solomon's wisdom was greater [than the wisdom of all the Kedemites and than all the wisdom of the Egyptians]' (1 Kings 5:10). It increased until it reached that place whence it was taken, the place of the supernal wisdom, for he is the wisdom in the beginning and she is the wisdom in the end"; cf. sec. 21, 44b, where the elevation of *Shekhinah* to the supernal *yod* or *ḥokhmah*, which is designated as the father, is related exegetically to the verse, "The Lord founded the earth by wisdom" (Prov. 3:19). And see sec. 21, 61b: "When Israel contemplate wisdom [*maskilim be-ḥokhmah*], which is the *yod*, supernal thought [*maḥshavah ilaʾah*], they know how to cast [*lezarqa*] that stone, which is an only daughter, to the place whence she was taken, for the daughter is made in the father [*di-beratta be-abba itʿavidat*], as it is written, 'The Lord in wisdom established the earth,' [*yhwh be-ḥokhmah yasad areṣ*] (Prov. 3:19), in wisdom, which is the father, he established the daughter, which the earth, his footstool [based on Isa. 66:1]. Her thread is the *waw*, for the stone is a crown, the diadem on his head, the crown of the Torah scroll, and concerning it was said 'the one who makes use of the crown perishes' [Mishnah Avot 1:13], this is verily the crown of Torah, for there are three crowns [Mishnah Avot 4:13], the crown of Torah, the crown of priesthood, and the crown of kingship, and the crown of Torah is over the others." I note parenthetically that in the original dictum the crown of a good name is said to rise above the other three crowns.

84. The relationship of the father and daughter is also expressed in the theosophic reworking of the aggadic motif (Babylonian Talmud, Baba Batra 16b) regarding the daughter given to Abraham in *Book Bahir*, sec. 52, p. 149. See Scholem, *Origins*, pp. 87–88; idem, *On the Mystical Shape*, p. 168. Consider also the parabolic reference to the signs (*simanim*) of the king and of his daughter in *Book Bahir* sec. 62, p. 155, and the parable in sec. 104, pp. 187–189, about the prince who hides the riches of his father's house in the inner chamber where his bride is hidden. In that context, the phallic potency is identified with the east, which stores its semen in the feminine west. On the occultation of the feminine in order to protect her from Satan, cf. the parable of the king and his daughter in sec. 109, pp. 193–195. The restoration of the original unity of the feminine in the masculine is also implied in the symbol of the crown ascending to the head in sec. 61, pp. 153–155. (Cf. also the depiction of the precious pearl that served as a crown in sec. 49, p. 145.) The use of this image to depict the masculine transformation of the feminine became a standard motif in subsequent kabbalistic literature. See E. Wolfson, *Through a Speculum*, pp. 275 n. 14, 362 n. 123, 363; idem, *Circle in the Square*, pp. 116–120, 231–232 n. 198. I have also explored this symbolism in the writings of Ḥasidei Ashkenaz in "Sacred Space," pp. 624–634. Finally, let me note that my analysis of the father-daughter relationship depicted in bahiric parables confirms the insight of Zeitlin, *Playing the Other* p. 113, that "the father-daughter relationship is the purest form of female dependence."

85. As various commentators have pointed out, what immediately follows is not a direct citation of a biblical verse. See Scholem, *Das Buch Bahir*, p. 6, sec. 3 n. 2; and the Margaliot edition of *Sefer ha-Bahir*, sec. 3 n. 6.

86. Here I follow the reading in MS Munich, Bayerische Staatsbibliothek 209, fol. 2b, reproduced in *Book Bahir*, p. 118, *be-matanah*, "as a gift," rather than the reading in other versions, including the edition of Margaliot, *be-ḥatunah*, "in the wedding."

87. *Book Bahir,* sec. 3, p. 119.

88. See Scholem, *Origins*, pp. 91–94. A particularly interesting mythologoumenon is preserved in the *Gospel of Philip* 60:10–12, in Layton, *Gnostic Scriptures*, p. 336: "Ekhamoth is one thing; and ekh-moth another. Ekhamoth refers to wisdom proper; But ekh-moth, to the wisdom of death—that is, the wisdom who is acquainted with death, and who is called the little wisdom." The proximity of this mythical teaching to the symbology of the *Bahir* and subsequent kabbalistic authors is obvious and does not require elaboration. The relationship of this ancient text and medieval kabbalah has been noted by several scholars. See Scholem, *On the Mystical Shape*, p. 300 n. 99; Liebes, "Messiah of the Zohar," pp. 230–232; Idel, "Sexual Metaphors," pp. 203–204; idem, "Jerusalem in Thirteenth-Century Jewish Thought," pp. 266–267. See below, n. 170.

89. See the introduction by William C. Robinson, Jr., to his translation and edition of the *Expository Treatise on the Soul*, in *Coptic Gnostic Library*, vol. 2, pp. 138–139. On the utilization of Hebrew Scripture in this composition, see R. Wilson, "Old Testament Exegesis," pp. 217–224. I added discussion of this text at the final stage of preparation of this monograph based on a comment of Hindy Najman. The conversation had nothing to do with my own work, but it did inspire me to review this gnostic treatise and in the process I discovered what I consider to be a remarkable affinity to the theologoumenon I have reconstructed from the *Bahir.* I am grateful to Professor Najman for goading me, albeit unwittingly, to this key source.

90. Ibid., p. 145.

91. Ibid., pp. 147, 153.

92. Ibid., p. 151. The specific formulation that is interpreted symbolically is "the sons of Egypt, men of great flesh" (Ezek. 16:26).

93. Ibid., p. 145.

94. The experience of the soul in the corporeal realm is portrayed in the image of the desolate widow. See ibid., pp. 147, 157.

95. Ibid., p. 155.

96. Ibid., pp. 155, 159, 161, 163.

97. This is not to say that in the synoptic gospels the depiction of Jesus as the son of God implies, as it does in the fourth gospel and other documents reflecting the thought of the early Church, divine status. See Friedrich, *Theological Dictionary*, vol. 8, pp. 367–368, 374–376; Charlesworth, *Jesus within Judaism*, pp. 148–153; E. Sanders, *Historical Figure of Jesus*, pp. 161–162; Flusser, *Jesus*, pp. 113–123. For a different perspective with respect to the Gospel of Mark, see Jonge, *Christology in Context*, pp. 56–63, 86–87.

98. The image of redemption through the bridal chamber calls to mind several other gnostic texts: *Gospel of Philip, Dialogue of the Savior,* the apocryphal *Acts of Thomas*, as well as accounts of the Valentinians offered in Irenaeus, Clement of Alexandria, and Heracleon. See Marcovich, *Studies in Graeco-Roman Religions*, pp. 163–167. Of special interest is the *Gospel of Philip*, 70:18–24, in *Nag Hammadi Codex II, 2–7*, vol. 1, p. 183, where it is emphasized that the husband and wife united in the bridal chamber cannot be separated. On the motif of the bridal chamber, see also LaFargue, *Language and Gnosis*, pp. 107–108 n. 60. For reference to other scholarly treatments, see below n. 173. See, in particular, *Gospel of Philip* 71:5–10, in *Nag Hammadi Codex II, 2–7*, vol. 1, p. 183. According to that passage, the mystery consists of the "father of everything" uniting with the "virgin who came down" in the bridal chamber. From the context, however, it appears that the male form uniting with the virgin is in fact Jesus, for it is the task of the anointed one to come "to repair the separation which was from the beginning and again unite the two, and to give life to those who died as a result of the separation and unite them" (70:14–16, vol. 1, p. 183).

99. *Nag Hammadi Codex II, 2–7*, vol. 2, p. 157.

100. For a sustained analysis of the apophatic dimensions of this treatise, expressed in both philosophical and mythological modes of discourse, see Trakatellis, *Transcendent God of Eugnostos.*

101. The Coptic is a borrowing from Greek, *archè*, which can be rendered either as "beginning" or "principle." Both meanings are attested in *Eugnostos the Blessed*; see Trakatellis, *Transcendent God*, pp. 81–82.

102. *Nag Hammadi Codices III, 3–4 and V, 1*, pp. 80–86. Also worthy of consideration is the speculation of the sect known as the Peratae described by Hippolytus, *Refutation*, 5.12: the three principles of being are the father, son, and matter. The son, identified as the word, is compared to a serpent that is always in motion,

snaking its way to the father or to matter. The serpentine son turns to the father to receive the powers, or the "paternal marks," and he then turns toward matter to discharge these powers, as matter is said to be "devoid of attribute, and being unfashioned, moulds (into itself) forms from the son which the son moulded from the father." The gender character of the third principle is not made explicit, but given the overwhelming cultural assumption of late-antique thinkers, it stands to reason that matter is feminine is nature. Even if we assume the correctness of this surmise, the triad as a whole is gendered as male. Consider the description offered by Hippolytus, *Refutation*, 5:7, of the "first segment" in the thought of the Peratae as the "triad" that is called a "perfect good" and "paternal magnitude." Böhlig, "Triade und Trinität," pp. 617–634, presents a wide-ranging analysis of the centrality of the tripartite structure as a non-Christian gnostic theologoumenon. See also Pétrement, *Separate God*, pp. 75–77. According to Pétrement, two stages in the evolution of the gnostic trinity can be distinguished; the former stage, which involved the triad of father, mother, and son, is in all probability pre-Christian in origin, deriving from Jewish wisdom speculation, and hence the mother is holy spirit (*ruaḥ ha-qodesh*), and the second stage, properly gnostic, involves the doubling of the mother, extending the triad to a quaternity, the lower mother corresponding to Sophia, the demiurgical potency responsible for the creation of the inferior material world. For other references to the trinitarian aspects of gnostic myth, see chap. 7, n. 63. In the wedding hymn of the apocryphal *Acts of Thomas*, one can discern a similar threefold structure of father, son, and daughter. See LaFargue, *Language and Gnosis*, pp. 91–112. The author utilizes Jewish esoteric literature, including *Sefer Yeṣirah* and *Sefer ha-Bahir*, in an effort to reconstruct the intellectual milieu of the wedding hymn; see pp. 110–111, 122–128.

103. *Nag Hammadi Codices III, 3–4 and V, 1*, pp. 110–124. Idel, *Kabbalah: New Perspectives*, pp. 123–127, discusses the affinity of the image of the seventy-two powers in the text of *Eugnostos* as well as the image of the seventy-two names in the *Origin of the World* and passages in *Sefer ha-Bahir*. The mythologic structure of the triad that I have adduced provides another striking resemblance between the gnostic and bahiric sources.

104. *Nag Hammadi Codex II, 2–7*, vol. 2, p. 161 (citing John 6:44 as exegetical prooftext). On receiving the name as a gift through baptism, see *Gospel of Philip* 64:25–30, in *Nag Hammadi Codex II, 2–7*, vol. 1, p. 169.

105. E. Wolfson, *Along the Path*, pp. 84–86.

106. Ibid., pp. 73–75 (note that I am modifying my remark on p. 74 that the second potency of the triad, symbolized by the letter *beit*, represents either the mother or daughter); E. Wolfson, "Before Alef."

107. It is on account of this feature of generosity—giving without any thought of return—that Cixous associates the realm of the gift with the feminine in contrast to the masculine, which is linked with the realm of the proper. See Moi, *Sexual/Textual Politics*, pp. 110–113.

108. Derrida, *Gift of Death*, p. 7. See Derrida's comment in his discussion with Jean-Luc Marion on the nature of the gift in Kearney, *God, the Gift, and Postmodernism*, p. 59: "As soon as a gift—not a *Gegebenheit*, but a gift—as soon as a gift is identified as a gift, with the meaning of a gift, then it is cancelled as a gift. It is reintroduced into the circle of an exchange and destroyed as a gift." On the analysis of gift-giving in terms of sacred objects that are not exchangeable, see Godelier, *Enigma of the Gift*.

109. Derrida, *Given Time*, pp. 79–81 (emphasis in original).

110. The nexus of the image of the gift and the androcentric theme of treating the woman as a vessel to receive the male seed is illustrated in the following passage in *Ha-Ketavim ha-Ivriyyim shel Ba'al Tiqqunei Zohar we-Ru'aya Meheimna*, p. 1: "The kabbalah is the *Shekhinah* . . . when she is given into the hands of Moses she is called *qabbalah*, and this is the import of 'Moses received [*qibbel*] the Torah from Sinai' [Mishnah, Avot 1:1], and when he turned her into something that could receive [*hiqbil otah*], she is called 'gift' [*matanah*], as it says [in the Sabbath liturgy] 'Moses took joy in his allocated portion' [*be-matnat ḥelqo*]."

111. See David Stern, *Parables in Midrash*, p. 222. Schäfer, *Mirror of His Beauty*, p. 285 n. 47, offers the following pronouncement regarding my Derridean analysis of the gift (based on the earlier version of this material in my study "Hebraic and Hellenic Conception"): "The incestuous relationship, on which Wolfson feasts, is the 'logical' conclusion of the daring imagery, but not its essence." A firm grasp of the function of parable as it pertains to the hermeneutics of secrecy expressed in medieval kabbalah, exemplified in a striking manner by the bahiric example wherein incestuous relationships—particularly the relationship of father and

daughter, which is supplanted by the relationship of daughter and son, sister and brother—does not allow for the distinction made by Schäfer. The logic of the parables in the *Bahir* conveys the meaning of the essence of the parables, as the parabolic formulation provides the way to approach the metaphysical truth of the divine reality and the ontological problem of alterity, the possibility of affirming the difference of identity from within the identity of difference.

112. Derrida, *Gift of Death*, p. 9.

113. Ibid., pp. 29–30. In *Spurs*, p. 121, Derrida draws a connection between the feminine and the gift on the basis that both defy essentializing and therefore they cannot be thought from the perspective of Being.

114. Derrida, *Given Time*, p. 147 (emphasis in original). For a rehashing of the argument, see idem, *Taste for the Secret*, p. 34.

115. Derrida, *On the Name*, p. 25.

116. Derrida, *On the Name*, p. 26. See idem, *Glas*, pp. 49–50. In that context, Derrida engages Hegel's depiction of the Jewish aversion to iconic representation. He remarks that the characteristic feature of the inner sanctum in the tabernacle and temple was that at the center was nothing, an empty space devoid of all content. The nothingness that lies at the sacred center, the hearth, which is the mystery (*Geheimnis*), arises from the attempt to provide a dwelling for that which cannot be contained, to delimit the limitless, to assign a figure to the infinite. "One undoes the bands, displaces the tissues, pulls off the veils, parts [*écarte*] the curtains: nothing but a black hole or a deep regard, without color, form, and life. . . . The Jewish *Geheimnis*, the hearth in which one looks for the center under a sensible cover [*enveloppe*]—the tent of the tabernacle, the stone of the temple, a robe that clothes the text of the covenant—is finally discovered as an empty room, is not uncovered, never ends being uncovered, as it has nothing to show." The Jewish notion of the inner sanctum alludes to the hermeneutical dynamic of secrecy: That which is covered can never cease being uncovered since nothing is there to be recovered. Significantly, Derrida applies this notion of mystery to the text of the covenant veiled behind the curtain.

117. Derrida, *On the Name*, p. 59.

118. Ibid., pp. 26–27. On the impossibility of testifying to a secret, see Derrida, *Demeure*, pp. 30–31.

119. Derrida, *Taste for the Secret*, pp. 57–58.

120. Derrida, *Gift of Death*, p. 59.

121. See E. Wolfson, "Occultation of the Feminine," pp. 118–119; idem, *Abraham Abulafia*, pp. 21–33.

122. Derrida, "Of an Apocalyptic Tone," p. 26 (emphasis in original).

123. For discussion of this Derridean notion, see Foshay, "Introduction," pp. 1–24. On the relationship of Derrida, mysticism, and the apophatic orientation of traditional negative theology, see K. Hart, *Trespass of the Sign*, pp. 183–194.

124. Derrida, "How To Avoid Speaking: Denials," p. 25. On the "negativity of the secret" and the "secret of denegation," see ibid., p. 18.

125. See Caputo, *Prayers and Tears*, p. 33.

126. In "Of an Apocalyptic Tone," p. 26, Derrida relates this process to the act of translation, rendering one language in terms of another: "translation-proof, grace would perhaps come when the writing of the other absolves you, from time to time, from the infinite *double bind* and first of all, such is a gift's condition, absolves itself, unbinds itself from the double bind, unburdens or clears itself, it, the language [*langue*] of writing, this given trace that always comes from the other, even if it is no one."

127. The point is made explicitly in the exegetical homilies on Leviticus 18:9 in *Zohar* 3:77a–b. For partial translation and analysis, see Tishby, *Wisdom of the Zohar*, p. 1368. My formulation of the insight regarding the symbolic meaning of incest is indebted to Neumann, *Origins*, pp. 16–17. See also Layard, "Incest Taboo," pp. 254–307; Héritier, "Symbolics of Incest," pp. 152–179. Jung, *Practice of Psychotherapy*, pp. 228–230. As Jung correctly notes, the mystical reading of the Song in Christian exegesis, according to which the love narrative is transposed into a dialogue between Christ and the Church, *sponsus* and *sponsa* (see below, chap. 8), is a good example of the use of an incestuous relation, deplorable in the social sphere, to express the supreme spiritual ideal. An analogous situation is found in kabbalistic sources with respect to the secret of illicit sexual relations, *sod arayot*. For an elaborate discussion of this topic, see Idel, "Kabbalistic Interpretation," pp. 89–199. On the evolution of incest symbolism, understood as the regressive urge to get back to

childhood, see Jung, *Symbols of Transformation*, pp. 158–159, 204–205, 213, 235 n. 42. A different approach, albeit one that exemplifies considerable theoretical sophistication and that may prove advantageous in considering incestuous motifs in rabbinic and kabbalistic literature, is offered by Kumin, *Logic of Incest*. On the primitive ritual of incest and its sociological consequences, see Pierre Gordon, *Sex and Religion*, pp. 137–157, and for other anthropological examples of ritual incest, especially involving the figure of the king, see Girard, *Violence and the Sacred*, pp. 104–107, 114–116. Finally, it is worth recalling that in the delineation of incestuous relationships in Lev. 6–18 the one prohibition that is not explicitly mentioned is sex between father and daughter. See Berquist, *Controlling Corporeality*, pp. 87–88. Worthy of consideration here as well is the discrepancy in medieval ecclesiastic penitential literature noted by Gregg, *Devils, Women, and Jews*, p. 134: mother-son incest required specific penances, while father-daughter sexual relations did not.

128. Girard, *Violence and the Sacred*, p. 74.

129. Based on the statement in Babylonian Talmud, Ḥagigah 15a.

130. That is, the numerical value of the consonants of the word *lev* equals thirty-two, *lamed* (30) and *beit* (2).

131. *Sefer Yeṣirah* 1:1.

132. *Book Bahir*, sec. 43, p. 141. See Scholem, *Origins*, pp. 168–169; idem, *On the Mystical Shape*, 162–163.

133. *Book Bahir*, secs. 67, p. 159 (in that context, the heart of the tree is identified as the citron, for it comprises the thirty-two paths of mysterious wisdom), 75. p. 163, 91, p. 177 (in that context, the heart is identified as the glory, based on the numerical equivalence of *lev* and *kavod*). See Scholem, *Origins*, p. 92; idem, *On the Mystical Shape*, p. 162.

134. The image of the daughter is used in other parabolic contexts in the *Bahir*. See secs. 3, p. 119, 36, pp. 137–139, 44, pp. 141–142, 52, p. 149. In light of this obvious sexual innuendo, I cannot agree with Scholem, *On the Mystical Shape*, p. 163, that in the *Bahir* the "explicitly sexual sphere of female symbolism is here quite clearly and visibly rejected." Scholem notes one exception, a passage that refers to the feminine as the matrona of the king (sec. 90, p. 175), but he neglects to note the sexual aspects of other feminine images, including most significantly the relationship of father and daughter. Incest is also implied in the parable in sec. 124, p. 207, which explains the sexual praxis related to the Sabbath: The king invites his sons to join him in rejoicing with his bride on the day of his joy.

135. Compare the parable of the king's garden with thirty-two paths in sec. 62, p. 155. The phallic connotation of the paths is suggested by the statement that the king utters to the guard appointed over the paths: "Guard them and traverse them each day, and at any time that you tread through them peace will be upon you." I assume that the word "peace" (*shalom*) also has a phallic connotation in this context as it does elsewhere in the *Bahir* and other kabbalistic writings. For the possibility regarding the archaic use of this usage, see E. Wolfson, *Along the Path*, p. 205 n. 71. On the notion of the thirty-two paths and the forms that guard them, see also *Book Bahir*, sec. 67, p. 159.

136. Cf. the interpretation of "the land is full of His glory" (Isa. 6:3) in *Book Bahir*, sec. 90, p. 175: "That land that was created on the first day, which is above corresponding to the land of Israel, is filled from the glory of the name." It seems to me that the "glory of the name" (*kevod ha-shem*) should here be interpreted phallically, and hence the point of the passage is that the feminine potency, symbolized as the land, is filled with the overflow of the divine phallus. The phallic signification of the word *kavod* obviously has far-reaching implications for Jewish religious thought.

137. See *Pesiqta de-Rav Kahana*, 1:3, 7; *Shir ha-Shirim Rabbah* 3:21; *Exodus Rabbah* 52:5; *Numbers Rabbah* 12:8; *Midrash Tanḥuma*, Pequde, sec. 8, p. 133.

138. Elsewhere in the *Bahir* (sec. 74, p. 163) the mother (given the name *Binah* on the basis of Prov. 2:3) is depicted as the source of the seven hypostases, which are rendered symbolically as the seven sons or the seven days of Tabernacles. In the parable employed in sec. 51, p. 147, the mother acts as the mediating force between the king and his sons who have disobeyed his will. The mother implores the father to have mercy for his wayward children. See also the parabolic use of the symbol of mother to characterize the divine glory in sec. 90, p. 175. It is not uncommon in the mythic imagination for the mother and daughter to be identified as one persona. See discussion of the identification of Demeter and Kore in the Eleusian mysteries in Neumann, *Great Mother*, pp. 142, 197, 305–309, 332, and Kerényi, *Eleusis*, pp. 32–33, 130.

139. The five names are *neshamah, ruaḥ, ḥayyah, yeḥidah*, and *nefesh*. Cf. *Genesis Rabbah* 14:9, p. 132.

140. *Book Bahir*, sec. 36, p. 137. See Scholem, *On the Mystical Shape*, pp. 165–166.

141. *Book Bahir*, sec. 36, pp. 137–139. The bahiric passage is based on a midrashic parable in *Exodus Rabbah* 33:1. See Scholem, *Das Buch Bahir*, p. 40, sec. 36 n. 2; idem, *Origins*, p. 170; Margaliot's note in his edition of *Sefer ha-Bahir*, sec. 54 n. 3; E. Wolfson, *Circle in the Square*, pp. 11–12. For a different interpretation of this parable, see Scholem, *On the Mystical Shape*, p. 164.

142. See Liebes, *Sections of the Zohar Lexicon*, p. 358 n. 13. The implicit intent of the bahiric passage is made explicit in *Zohar* 1:56a, wherein the "secret of the covenant" (*raza di-verit*), the phallic potency, is identified as the letter *beit*, which completes the name "Seth" (*shin-taw*) to form the word "Sabbath" (*shin-beit-taw*).

143. Support for this interpretation may be elicited from a number of kabbalistic sources. See, for example, Ibn Gaon, *Sefer Baddei ha-Aron u-Migdal Ḥananel*, p. 55. In his explication of *ṭeit*, the ninth letter that corresponds to the ninth gradation, Shem Tov writes: "In the secret of *Yesod*, in the form of a throne to show there is a throne to the throne. And see that the emanation that it had from the east returned to the west, and the opening that it had from the west returned from the east. And I have seen that it is in the form of an open window to receive light from the east." See also the Lurianic text *Shaʿar ha-Kelalim*, chap. 1, printed in Vital, *Eṣ Ḥayyim*, 8a: "When the light of Ein Sof enters into *Keter*, it does not have the capacity to bear it except by means of spatial distance. Yet, from *Keter* to *Ḥokhmah* there is no distance at all, but rather it comes by way of a window, that is, from *Yesod* of *Arikh Anpin*, which is called 'window' [*ḥalon*], for the light is diminished from what it was. From *Ḥokhmah* to *Binah* it comes as well by way of a window, that is, from *Yesod* of *Abba*, which is another small window. However, in the six extremities [*Ḥesed* to *Yesod*] themselves their windows are identical to one another for they are all one aspect. Subsequently, from *Yesod* to *Malkhut*, the light comes from a small and very narrow window in the pattern of a small perforation."

144. Babylonian Talmud, Shavuʿot 35b. According to some versions of the bahiric text, e.g., MS Munich, Bayerische Staatsbibliothek 209, fol. 8a (reproduced in *Book Bahir*, p. 140), the rabbinic comment is transmitted in the name of R. Yoḥanan. Concerning this talmudic text and the possibility that it preserves an older theosophic tradition, see E. Wolfson, *Along the Path*, p. 205 n. 71.

145. MS Munich, Bayerische Staatsbibliothek 209, fol. 8b (reproduced in *Book Bahir*, p. 142) reads: "the very wisdom that was given to God." Scholem, *Origins*, p. 92, prefers this reading and suggests that it was changed in later manuscripts because of the bold theological implication regarding God's union with the feminine *ḥokhmah*. I am not convinced, however, that this alternative reading actually makes better sense in context, and hence I have followed the version, *ottah ḥokhmah she-natan lo elohim*, "the very wisdom that God had given to him," which is preserved in the *editio princeps* of the *Bahir* (Amsterdam, 1651), 4c, reproduced in *Book Bahir*, p. 270. See the reading in MS Vatican-Barberini Or. 110, cited in *Book Bahir*, p. 143, as well as Margaliot's edition of *Sefer ha-Bahir*, sec. 65.

146. *Book Bahir*, sec. 44, pp. 141–143.

147. Scholem, *Origins*, p. 92. Scholem's interpretation is accepted by David Stern, *Parables in Midrash*, p. 222.

148. Babylonian Talmud, Shabbat 10b, Sanhedrin 55b.

149. Babylonian Talmud, Shavuʿot 35b.

150. *Book Bahir*, secs. 9, p. 123, 40, p. 141, 50, p. 147, and 62, p. 155. See E. Wolfson, *Along the Path*, pp. 204–205 n. 71.

151. Cf. the use of the term *kavod* in *Book Bahir*, sec. 33, p. 137, analyzed in E. Wolfson, *Along the Path*, p. 209 n. 85.

152. I thus take issue with Scholem's remark that the Solomon to whom Sophia is given as a gift is "the Solomon of history and not a symbolic Solomon" (*Origins*, p. 92). In fact, the bahiric parable (in both secs. 3 and 44) makes little sense if one does not appreciate the symbolic character of Solomon.

153. *Book Bahir*, sec. 19, pp. 127–129.

154. See, for instance, *Zohar* 2:218b; 3:223a.

155. It appears that *dalet* symbolizes the feminine in other sections of the *Bahir*; see secs. 20, p. 129, and 25, p. 131.

156. Scholem, *On the Mystical Shape*, p. 165, already suggested that the twofold description of the one king who is wealthy but poor signifies the active and passive elements in the *Shekhinah*. Although my locution differs from that of Scholem there is a common element to the two approaches.

157. Based on a passage in *Seder Rabbah di-Vere'shit*; see Schäfer, *Synopse zur Hekhalot-Literatur*, sec. 440 (cf. sec. 745): "Just as his *Shekhinah* is above so it is below." See Scholem, *Origins*, pp. 178–179; idem, *On the Mystical Shape*, pp. 173 and 296 n. 59. On the distinction between the lower and upper *Shekhinah*, see also the magical text, *Sidrei de-Shimmusha Rabba we-Sidrei Heikhalot*, in Jellinek, *Beit Midrash*, 6:110, previously cited by Scholem, *Das Buch Bahir*, p. 124, sec. 116 n. 2. Scholem's statement that according to the predominant theosophic symbolism, the double *Shekhinah* refers respectively to the third and tenth of the *sefirot*, is valid for latter kabbalistic texts but it does not reflect the approach of the bahiric passage. As I have argued, in the context of the *Bahir* itself, the upper *Shekhinah* is wisdom or the first light, and the lower *Shekhinah* is the light that emanated from that light, the divine glory that is immanent in the world and the aspect of wisdom that is imaged as feminine. The assumption here is that the divine comprises eight powers consisting of seven sons and one king.

158. It is noteworthy that the expression "encompassing everything" (*sovevet ha-kol*) is used to describe the attribute of divine wisdom in some of the Provençal kabbalists, e.g., Isaac the Blind and Asher ben David. See Isaac the Blind, *Perush Sefer Yeṣirah*, p. 2; Asher ben David, *Sefer ha-Yiḥud*, in *R. Asher ben David: His Complete Works*, p. 113. For discussion of this expression, see Scholem, *Kabbalah in Provence*, p. 177. The relationship between *Sefer ha-Bahir* and strands of theosophic kabbalah that crystallized in Provence is a complex issue that has been addressed by various scholars. See Scholem, *Reshit ha-Qabbalah*, pp. 64–65; idem, *Origins*, pp. 209–211; Idel, "*Sefirot* above the *Sefirot*," p. 239; and Pedaya, "Provençal Stratum."

159. *Book Bahir*, sec. 116, p. 201. See Scholem, *On the Mystical Shape*, p. 173.

160. *Book Bahir*, sec. 116, p. 201. See E. Wolfson, "Woman—The Feminine as Other," p. 171.

161. Babylonian Talmud, Sanhedrin 98b.

162. *Book Bahir*, sec. 58, p. 153.

163. Scholem, *Origins*, p. 142.

164. *Gospel of Thomas*, 114, in *Nag Hammadi Codex II, 2–7*, p. 93. See chap. 2, n. 46 and chap. 7, nn. 68–69.

165. Scholem, *Origins*, p. 142. Scholem's approach is reiterated by Idel, "Sexual Metaphor," p. 211: "The return to the primal androgyne state of humans, which was commonly described by Gnostics, or the endeavor to transcend the feminine plight by mystic transformations of the female into a 'male,' recurring in ancient Christian thought and Gnosticism, is alien to talmudic and theosophical kabbalistic weltanschauung." Idel repeats his opinion regarding the androgyne in the symbolism of theosophic kabbalah in "Eros in der Kabbala," pp. 68–85. See also Mopsik, *Lettre sur la sainteté*, pp. 324–325 n. 218. Schwarz, *Kabbalah and Alchemy*, pp. 35–43, uncritically follows the view espoused by Idel and Mopsik that androgyny does not mean eradication or neutralization of either gender.

166. See chap. 2, n. 15.

167. As described by Ginsburg, *Sabbath in Classical Kabbalah*, p. 107.

168. I borrow this locution from Mircea Eliade, who employs it, for instance, in *Quest*, p. 134: "On the religious level, the solution of the sexual antagonism does not always imply a ritual enactment of the *hieros gamos*; in many cases, the antagonism is transcended by a ritual androgynization."

169. See Mopsik, *Lettre sur la sainteté*, pp. 214–215.

170. See above, n. 88. In addition to the references listed there, see also DeConick, "True Mysteries," pp. 225–261, esp. pp. 253–256; and idem, "Great Mystery of Marriage," pp. 307–342, esp. pp. 339–340.

171. *Nag Hammadi Codex II, 2–7*, vol. 1, p. 179.

172. Ibid., vol. 1, p. 183. A slightly different explanation is offered in *Gospel of Philip*, 71:18–20, *Nag Hammadi Codex II, 2–7*, vol. 1, p. 185: "Adam came into being from two virgins, from the spirit and from the virgin earth. Christ, therefore, was born from a virgin to rectify the fall which occurred in the beginning." Consider as well the contrast between Adam and Jesus in Constas, *Proclus of Constantinople*, p. 169: "That one had a woman as his accomplice, but this one had a virgin as his bridal chamber." In the case of

Adam, the female is taken out from the male, and the two become one flesh through intercourse, whereas in the case of Jesus, the male is taken from the female, and union is achieved by the passion, the means by which the corporeal Jesus is transfigured into the spiritual Christ. Significantly, the virginal womb of Mary is referred to as the "bridal chamber."

173. Pagels, "Mystery of Marriage," pp. 107–116, esp. pp. 108–110. For other scholarly discussions, see Grant, "Mystery of Marriage," pp. 129–140, esp. pp. 134–138; Meeks, "Image of the Androgyne," pp. 189, 195–196; Sevrin, "Noces spiritueles," pp. 143–193; M. Williams, "Uses of Gender Imagery," pp. 205–211; and references to studies of DeConick cited above, n. 170. See Rudolph, *Gnosis*, p. 80: "For the Gnostics bisexuality is an expression of perfection; it is only the earthly creation which leads to a separation of the original divine unity, which holds for the whole pleroma." The choice of the term "bisexuality" is somewhat misleading, but the basic point is well taken, that is, in the perfect state, there is no union between male and female. What Rudolph does not sufficiently note is that the primordial androgyne, which symbolizes perfection, is gendered as the male that contains within himself the female. In this regard, it is of interest to consider the bearded, androgynous figure of the Goddess in Assyrian texts and iconography, which symbolizes purity and perfection. See Parpola, *Assyrian Prophecies*, pp. xxix and lxxxix n. 97.

174. *Nag Hammadi Codex II, 2–7*, vol. 1, p. 179.

175. Ibid., vol. 1, p. 195.

176. It would appear from *Book Bahir*, sec. 42, p. 141, that the bent *nun* represents the female, the *neqevah*. Compare Baḥya ben Asher, *Rabbenu Baḥya*, 2:123 (ad Exod. 14:31): "You already know that the word *amen* is an acronym for *el melekh ne'eman* ["God the trustworthy king;" see Babylonian Talmud, Sanhedrin 111a]. You must consider that in the word *ne'eman* there is a bent *nun* and a straight *nun* . . . the straight *nun* in the word *amen* comprises male and female since the bent *nun* is female and the straight *nun* male, and inasmuch as the bent *nun* is contained in the straight it comprises male and female."

177. *Book Bahir*, sec. 57, p. 151.

178. On the symbol of the open *mem*, see also *Book Bahir*, sec. 25, p. 131. In that context, the open *mem* is associated with an aspect of the head upon which is placed the crown, which also functions parabolically as the throne upon which the king sits and the phylacteries that he places upon his arm. While the language of this text is truly enigmatic, in general it seems to be depicting the *hieros gamos* in the divine world through various images, including that of coronation: the crown is the feminine potency and the head, or more specifically the open *mem* of the head, is the masculine. Scholem, *Origins*, p. 60, interprets the open *mem* as a symbol of the feminine. See also David Stern, *Parables in Midrash*, p. 221. For discussion of this bahiric parable and the other passages that utilize these images, see E. Wolfson, "Images of God's Feet," p. 161.

179. See E. Wolfson, *Circle in the Square*, pp. 98–106.

180. For discussion of the two Creation narratives from the vantage point of human sexuality and gender, see Bird, "Images of Women," pp. 71–74; idem, "Sexual Differentiation," pp. 11–34. For a convenient review of various feminist readings of the creation of the female in the biblical narrative, see Pardes, *Countertraditions in the Bible*, pp. 13–38.

181. On the chain of tradition, see Scholem, *Origins*, p. 37; Twersky, *Rabad of Posquières*, pp. 286–287; E. Wolfson, "Beyond the Spoken Word," pp. 190–192.

182. Babylonian Talmud, Berakhot 61a, Eruvin 18a. The text attributed to Rabad is translated and discussed in Scholem, *Origins*, pp. 216–218. See also Idel, *Kabbalah: New Perspectives*, pp. 128–134; idem, "Eros in der Kabbala," pp. 70–74.

183. That is, the sun and moon, which here stand symbolically for the male and female aspects of God. See Scholem, *Origins*, p. 217 n. 30; Idel, *Kabbalah: New Perspectives*, p. 338 n. 151.

184. A similar exegetical point is made by Abraham Abulafia, *Imrei Shefer*, fol. 235b (printed ed., p. 62).

185. I have translated the text from the version published in Scholem, *Reshit ha-Qabbalah*, p. 79, n. 1, from MSS London, British Museum 768, fol. 14a and Oxford, Bodleian Library 1956, fol. 7a.

186. See the text of Jacob ben Sheshet cited in chap. 2, n. 99.

187. See chap. 2, n. 103.

188. The text is cited in Pedaya, *Name and Sanctuary*, p. 103.

189. *Genesis Rabbah* 13:3, p 113; 15:1, p. 135.

190. Ezra ben Solomon of Gerona, *Perush Shir ha-Shirim*, in *Kitvei Ramban*, 2:510. Cf. the language of Asher ben David in his commentary on the account of creation, *Perush Maʿaseh Bereʾshit*, transcribed in *R. Asher ben David: His Complete Works*, p. 327: "On the sixth day the edifice was completed in a perfect form, as it says, 'in our image and in our likeness' (Gen. 1:26), the completion of the edifice to produce offspring. This is [the meaning of] what is said, '[God ceased from all the work of creation] that He had done' (Gen. 2:3). Up to this point [Scripture] did not mention the Tetragrammaton in all of the six days of creation, for the ten *sefirot* are contained in it . . . and how could the name be mentioned until the edifice was completed?"

191. Ezra ben Solomon of Gerona, *Perush Shir ha-Shirim*, in *Kitvei Ramban*, 2:513.

192. See above, n. 56.

193. See M. Cohen, *Shiʿur Qomah*, pp. 77–78.

194. Based on earlier rabbinic sources, for example, Mishnah, Berakhot 9:5.

195. *Zohar* 2:26b–27a. For analysis of this passage, see E. Wolfson, "Light through Darkness," pp. 89–91. A parallel is found in Moses de León, *Book of the Pomegranate*, p. 101; see chap. 2, n. 98. Of the many texts influenced by the zoharic approach, consider Vital, *Sefer ha-Derushim*, p. 204: "Know that in the heart there are two cavities, right and left, and they allude to two hearts, the evil inclination and the good inclination, which correspond to the two houses of Israel, the lower *Shekhinah* and the upper *Shekhinah*, and these are the two [occurrences of] *he* [in YHWH], and this is *zakhor*, 'remember' (Exod. 20:8) and *shamor*, 'observe' (Deut. 5:12), for the first *he* terminates with the masculine and this is YHWH, and the second is *shamor* and it is Adonai and it is also Elohim, and this is YHWH Elohim, and they are the Tree of Life and the Tree of Knowledge. . . . Thus you have the secret of Abel and Cain, the one is the Tree of Life [on the right] and the other the Tree [of Knowledge] on the left in one root. This is [the import of] 'when YHWH Elohim are unified,' and this is the mystery of faith [*raza di-meheimanuta*], and there is a root that unifies acts of mercy and strength, and it is the mystery of Jacob, which is the secret of *waw* that stands between the two [occurrences of] *he*, and thus he is called the 'elect of the patriarchs.' "

196. Abraham Abulafia, *Imrei Shefer*, fol. 236a (printed ed., p. 62), relates the rabbinic idea of *du-parṣufim* to the binary of matter and form, which respectively represent female and male. The association of masculinity with form and femininity with matter is a commonplace in medieval philosophical literature. See chap. 6, n. 29.

197. See the formulations of Asher ben David and Moses de León mentioned in chap. 2, n. 98. In this connection, it is of interest to recall the remark of Ibn ʿArabi, *Divine Governance of the Human Kingdom*, p. 9: "Thus the whole of creation in all its perfection is manifested in humankind. We are placed, in the connecting stage of our corporeal existence, between the divine attributes of Might and Grace. We are granted generosity, which we may dispense freely, and power to rule over all and everything." In a manner consonant with kabbalistic symbolism, the Spanish Sufi relates the ethical task to the two corresponding divine attributes, the execution of power related to might and the exercise of generosity issuing from grace.

198. Abraham ben David, *Baʿalei ha-Nefesh*, pp. 13–15. The passage is paraphrased and cited in Jacob ben Asher, *Arbaʿah Ṭurim*, Even ha-Ezer, Introduction, 1b. The text from *Baʿalei ha-Nefesh* is partially cited and discussed by Idel, "Eros in der Kabbala," pp. 75–77.

199. *Zohar* 2:200a.

200. See E. Wolfson, "Iconicity of the Text." Perhaps the most striking illustration of the connection between exclusive worship of the feminine and idolatry is the widespread linkage in kabbalistic literature of the golden calf and *Shekhinah*. See, for instance, Isaac of Acre, *Sefer Meʾirat Einayim*, p. 185: "The intent of the act of the generation of the desert in making the calf was directed to *Aṭarah* because the essence of her reception is from the side of the calf and the ox." According to this explanation, the sin of idol worship is not venerating a false god but rather the female aspect of the divine, which is sustained by the attribute of judgment, in separation from the male aspect, which is the attribute of mercy. See Isaac of Acre, *Sefer Meʾirat Einayim*, pp. 38–39.

201. The linkage of heresy and the female attested in traditional kabbalistic lore is based in part on a topos

for engendering sectarian heresy as the unchaste female, the "estranged woman" (*ishshah zarah*) in the book of Proverbs, attested in classical rabbinic sources. See Boyarin, *Dying For God*, pp. 67–68. The engendering of the heretic as the wayward woman is known from religious symbolism cultivated in other patriarchal societies. One thinks, for instance, of the role accorded Sophia in the core mythologoumenon of Valentinian Gnosticism as well as the ambivalent attitude toward Mary in the history of Christianity. See Burrus, "Heretical Woman as Symbol," pp. 229–248; idem, *Making of a Heretic*; Trevett, "Spiritual Authority and the 'Heretical' Woman," pp. 45–62. For discussion of this theme in Christian mysticism at roughly the same time and place as the formative period of medieval kabbalah, see McNamara, "Rhetoric of Orthodoxy," pp. 9–27. Also pertinent is the discussion of the strategy of embodying heresy as a female figure, often linked more specifically to sexuality, in Lipton, "Tanquam effeminatum," pp. 107–129. For a more comprehensive study of this theme in a later historical period, see McSheffrey, *Gender and Heresy.*

202. Liebes, "How the Zohar Was Written," p. 4 n. 12, argues that this passage was not composed by the "main author" of the zoharic text. Interestingly, this observation was not included in the English translation of Liebes's study, *Studies in the Zohar*, p. 195 n. 12. For my purposes, the question of authorship is not relevant.

203. For discussion of the kabbalistic interpretation of this biblical idiom, deduced from another zoharic passage, see E. Wolfson, "Left Contained in the Right," p. 40.

204. *Zohar* 2:38b. The dictum is repeated on 39b and applied exegetically to other verses.

205. *Sefer ha-Yiḥud*, in *R. Asher ben David: His Complete Works*, p. 103. See above, n. 76.

206. The kabbalistic perspective preserves and extends the androcentric posture expressed in rabbinic texts, exemplified in the following statement in Babylonian Talmud, Yevamot 63a: "R. Eleazar said: Every man who has no wife is not a man [*adam*], as it says, 'Male and female He created them . . . and he called their name Adam' (Gen. 5:2)."

207. This passage is based on the maxim, *teḥillat ha-maḥshavah hu sof ha-maʿaseh* ("the beginning of thought is the end of action"), which was influential in medieval philosophical texts. The saying is cited in the name of the rabbis in another section of *Maʿarekhet ha-Elohut*, chap. 3, 36a; cf. chap. 4, 50a, and chap. 8, 86b. Idel, *Kabbalah: New Perspectives*, p. 197, refers to an anonymous kabbalist of the fourteenth century who employs the same dictum to underscore the reversibility of the *sefirot* predicated on the fact that there can be no beginning or end with respect to that which is divine. A version of this saying, *sof maʿaseh be-maḥshavah teḥillah* ("the end of action is in thought first"), was popularized in the liturgical hymn for Sabbath, *Lekhah Dodi*, written by the sixteenth-century mystic, Solomon Alkabets. See Kimelman, *Mystical Meaning of Lekhah Dodi*, pp. 47–48. The evolution of this maxim from Greek to Arabic and Hebrew sources has been traced by Samuel Stern, "First in Thought is the Last in Action," pp. 234–252; the relevant passages from *Maʿarekhet ha-Elohut* are cited on p. 251 n. 1.

208. The image of man ruling his house as symbolic of the masculine dominance over women is based on an archaic locution attested in classical rabbinic literature. See C. Baker, *Rebuilding the House*, pp. 56–59.

209. *Maʿarekhet ha-Elohut*, chap. 8, 88b.

210. *Zohar* 1:48b.

211. This reflects the heretical claim attributed to Elisha ben Abuyah (Aḥer) in Babylonian Talmud, Ḥagigah 15a. See A. Segal, *Two Powers in Heaven*, pp. 60–67.

212. MS Cambridge Dd. 10. 11, fols. 27a-b. Cf. Baḥya ben Asher, *Beʾur al ha-Torah*, 1:47 (ad Gen. 1:27).

213. Implicit here is a central idea embraced by kabbalists concerning the unity of the first and tenth emanations, *Keter* and *Malkhut*, a unity that underscores the ultimate oneness of the multiplicity of potencies.

214. On the symbolic portrayal of woman as a house in classical rabbinic sources, which informed medieval kabbalists, see C. Baker, *Rebuilding the House*, pp. 34–76.

215. *Zohar* 3:18b–19a. For an extended discussion of the motif of the containment of the female in the male in zoharic literature, see my study referred to above, n. 38.

216. *Zohar* 1:31a.

217. The zoharic expression reflects a technical Spanish idiom, *endulzar*, as noted by Scholem, *Major Trends*, p. 388 n. 44.

218. *Zohar* 3:142b–143a (*Idra Rabba*); cf. Liebes, "Messiah of the Zohar," p. 191.

219. The text here is elliptical, for it should read that the female alone is all-judgmental just as the male separated from the female is all-merciful.

220. *Zohar* 3:296a (*Idra Zuṭa*).

221. Interestingly, a similar critique has been made with respect to the conception of the alterity of the feminine in Levinas. See Irigaray, "Questions to Emmanuel Levinas," pp. 109–118, and the more recent analysis in idem, "What Other Are We Talking About?" pp. 67–81. For a more conciliatory, although decidedly nonapologetic, approach to the issue of "sexual difference" and the status of women in the ethical philosophy of Levinas, see C. Katz, *Levinas, Judaism, and the Feminine*, pp. 35–77.

222. *Zohar* 3:56a.

223. My citation of this passage is indebted to Elqayam, "On the 'Knowledge of Messiah'," p. 665. Referring to this passage, Elqayam remarks that Lavi "abrogates the distinction between male and female in the depths of nothingness." I agree with this claim, but as I will argue below, even this abrogation does not do away with the androcentric privileging of the masculine in this state of transcendence.

224. On the use of the aggadic motif of the hidden light in Lavi's writings, see Huss, "*Genizat Ha-Or*," pp. 341–362; idem, *Sockets of Fine Gold*, pp. 108–146.

225. Based on the interpretation of Genesis 1:2 in *Zohar* 1:24b. An alternative interpretation appears in 1:31a.

226. *Genesis Rabbah* 2:2, p. 15.

227. Lavi, *Ketem Paz*, vol. 1, p. 27c–d.

228. This is the gist of the criticism leveled against me by Elqayam, "On the 'Knowledge of Messiah,'" p. 665 n. 107. A similar critique has been offered more recently by Gamlieli, "Stages of 'Becoming' in the Creation," pp. 316–320. Gamlieli's attempt to challenge my interpretation of the androcentric nature of gender construction in traditional kabbalah with her own egalitarian approach on the basis that I follow a "biological" model in contrast to her "philosophical" understanding of form and matter is misguided on two counts; first, because I have cast the issue of masculinity and femininity in these very philosophical terms, and second, because medieval philosophical hylomorphism, which is the foundation for the kabbalistic symbolism, is not gender-neutral.

229. MS Munich 47, fols. 340a–b.

230. *Toledot Adam*, printed in *Sefer ha-Malkhut*, pp. 95d–96a.

231. See chap. 2, n. 354.

232. On the use of this phrase in thirteenth-century kabbalah, derived from the medieval Hebrew philosophical lexicon of Judah Ibn Tibbon, see David ben Yehudah he-Ḥasid, *Book of Mirrors*, p. 21 n. 151 (Introduction).

233. *Sefer Yeṣirah*, 28b.

234. For references, see David ben Yehudah he-Ḥasid, *Book of Mirrors*, p. 22 n. 163 (Introduction). It should be pointed out, however, that in some contexts, this kabbalist insists on not reversing the linear relation that pertains between cause and effect. For instance, in *Book of Mirrors*, p. 98, David ben Yehudah he-Ḥasid notes that the import of the biblical details about kindling lights to burn from evening to morning on the lampstand in the tabernacle, the tent of meeting (Exod. 27:20–21; see also Lev. 24:2–4), as well as the daily burning of the incense on the altar (Exod. 25:6, 30:1–10, 31:8, 11, 37:29; Lev. 2:16, 4:7, 16:12; Num. 4:16), challenges the one who would argue that the "supernal event arouses the event below" (*she-ha-maʿaseh ha-elyon meʿorer maʿaseh ha-taḥton*). The truth is the reverse: "The kindling of the lamps and the aromatic incense [*hatlaqat ha-nerot u-qeṭoret ha-besamim*] above, bound as one, as is appropriate, and the action below arouses the action above." A similar, if not identical, exegesis of Exodus 27:20–21 is found in *Zohar* 3:104b–105a. In the final analysis, for David ben Yehudah he-Ḥasid, the circular nature of truth renders this hierarchical alignment insufficient. Consider his comment, *Book of Mirrors*, p. 279: "The blessings descend from the supernal source [*ha-maqor ha-elyon*], as it is known, which is the Supernal Crown [*keter elyon*], which discharges blessings to all of the worlds, as it is written, 'the river goes forth from Eden to irrigate the garden' (Gen. 2:10), and *Shekhinah* dwells in the world. When does *Shekhinah* dwell below? When Israel constructs

the Tabernacle [*mishkan*], and they made it in accord with the supernal pattern [*al derekh dugma elyonah*], as it is written, 'as it has been shown you on the mountain' (Exod. 25:30), for Moses contemplated and comprehended [*mistakkel u-massig*] in the world of *Malkhut*, and the Tabernacle below was made in the pattern of the Tabernacle above, and this is sufficient for the one who understands."

235. Adamson, "Aristotelianism and the Soul," p. 217.

236. *Sefer Yeṣirah*, 23b.

237. Ibid., 2c.

238. Compare David ben Yehudah he-Ḥasid, *Book of Mirrors*, p. 98 (Hebrew section): "We bind together the top of the palm branch [Mishnah, Sukkah 3:1] to allude to the fact that the Supernal Crown is bound and tied to the knot of the Cause of Causes [*be-qesher illat ha-illot*], for there is no separation [*perud*] or division [*qiṣṣuṣ*] there, but rather all is whole in the limit of wholeness [*ha-kol shalem be-takhlit ha-sheleimut*] so that all will be like the supernal paradigm [*dugma elyonah*]."

239. *Sefer Yeṣirah*, 2c.

240. *Zohar* 3:129a.

241. Vital, *Eṣ Ḥayyim*, 13:13, 68c.

242. *Zohar* 3:129b–130a, 137b, 293b. A similar characterization of *Keter* is found in David ben Yehudah he-Ḥasid, *Book of Mirrors*, pp. 212, 259–260, 271–272 (Hebrew section). For a later Hasidic application of the zoharic image of the single eye to denote the world of pure mercy in which the left is contained in the right, see Qalonymous Qalman ha-Levi Epstein, *Ma'or wa-Shemesh*, p. 48. A comparative analysis of the kabbalistic idea and the symbol of the "third eye" in Tantric Buddhist sources would prove instructive, but it clearly lies beyond the scope of this note. See, however, D. G. White, *Kiss of the Yoginī*, p. 101, who expresses the opinion that "the third eye is itself an emblem of the female vulva on the forehead of the male Siva," and see references to other scholars cited on p. 300 n. 33. See also the representation of Siddhaloka as a crescent moon in the forehead of Jain Loka Purusa, the "Universal Man," reproduced in D. G. White, *Kiss of the Yoginī*, p. 176. While it is possible that the eye can function as a symbol for female genitalia in Jewish esotericism (see discussion in E. Wolfson, *Through a Speculum*, pp. 103–104, including the suggestion by David Halperin to this effect), it seems to me beyond question that in the relevant kabbalistic texts the third eye, which is correlated with *Keter*, is masculine in nature, corresponding to the upper phallus.

243. Cordovero, *Elimah Rabbati*, 66b–c.

244. It should be noted that in other passages Cordovero affirms that *Keter* is androgynous, exemplifying both qualities of overflowing (in relation to the emanations below it) and receiving (in relation to the infinite above it). See chap. 2, n. 118, where some of the relevant sources are mentioned. It is of interest to consider in this context the tradition of Israel Sarug reported by Abraham Cohen de Herrera, *Gate of Heaven*, 8:4, p. 326, to the effect that *Adam Qadmon*, the first emanation from Ein Sof, is called *adam* because the three letters of that word, *alef, dalet, mem*, can be transposed into *alef, mem, dalet*, which is vocalized as *em dalet*, literally "mother of the four," that is, according to this tradition, the name of the first emanation signifies that it is the matrix of the four worlds in the ontological chain of being, emanation (*aṣilut*), creation (*beri'ah*), formation (*yeṣirah*), and doing (*asiyyah*). Commenting on the attribution of the maternal symbol to *Adam Qadmon*, Herrera writes, "I believe he is called mother and not father of the worlds so that no one should think that he is the First Cause but rather its female, instrument, vessel, and receptacle which, like a life that came out of Adam the first man and with his efficacy, was mother of all living human beings. The first and most perfect effect of the uncaused Causal Agent of everything, as if pregnant with its power and efficacy, therefore gave birth to all of the worlds, receiving them from it as if from the male in a very superior and hidden way and later producing or giving birth to them in a more coarse and diverse composite out of the male's uniform diminutive seed." For the corresponding Hebrew text, see Herrera, *House of Divinity (Casa de la Divinidad). Gate of Heaven (Puerta del Cielo)*, p. 510. I acknowledge that, in a manner that diverges from my explanatory model, Herrera links pregnancy and motherhood to the female, but the real agency of creation nonetheless resides in the male seed. Hence *Adam Qadmon* is depicted as the female receptacle vis-à-vis the masculine Ein-Sof, the First Cause and ultimate source of all being. The explanation of the word *adam* as *em dalet*, "mother of four," is reiterated by Herrera in *Beit Elohim*, 5:12; see *House of Divinity*, p. 168. I note, however,

that in *Gate of Heaven*, 8:14, pp. 370–372 (Hebrew edition by Yosha, pp. 539–541), Herrera offers an extensive depiction of the chain of being from the First Cause to the material world of *asiyah* in the image of an anthropos that is masculine in gender. Thus the First Cause is described as the "mind" (*haskkel*) or "thought" (*maḥshavah*) "of all the worlds, what the Platonic philosophers call the mental world, Son of God, and first mind, and Zoroaster calls fatherly and deep, in which they locate the causative representational unities and ideas to which the supreme unity and unmoving mind correspond in man." From the First Cause there emanates the "perfect effect," the "great Universal man" (*ha-adam ha-gadol we-ha-kolel*), in Lurianic terminology, *Adam Qadmon*, the "first mind" (*haskkel ha-ri'shon*). The five configurations of the world of emanation (*parṣufei aṣilut*) are identified as "five ranks of spirit" of the "macrocosmic man" that "give being, life, and perfection to all the worlds." *Atiqa Qaddisha* (or *Arikh Anpin*) corresponds to *yeḥidah*; *Abba* to *ḥayyah* or the *neshamah* of *neshamah*; *Imma* to *neshamah*; *Ze'eir Anpin* to *ruaḥ*; and *Nuqba* to *nefesh*. The world of emanation (*aṣilut*) thus constitutes the psychic component of the "singular universal man" (*adam ha-yaḥid we-ha-kolel*), whereas the remaining three worlds constitute his body: the world of creation (*beri'ah*) corresponds to the head, the world of formation (*yeṣirah*) to the chest, stomach, arms and hands, and the world of making (*asiyyah*) to the penis, called the "procreative member" (*eiver ha-holadah*), and the legs. Significantly, there is no mention of a female counterpart to the male persona nor is there even a reference to the feminine part incorporated in the anthropomorphic structure that metaphorically represents the chain of being; on the contrary, *Shekhinah* is described as the image of the mouth of *Adam Qadmon* (*Gate of Heaven*, 8:14, p. 373). When Herrera does relate to the feminine representation of *Shekhinah*, he does so in the context of articulating the ideal of elevating all the potencies back to their source in Ein Sof, "attaining the final end for which everything was produced, which is the communication and revelation of the First Cause in and to its effects, which is achieved by this union alone" (ibid., p. 372). The positive agency accorded the feminine relates, therefore, to the symbol of the *mayyin nuqbin*, the female waters that stimulate the arousal from below. The phallocentric nature of this configuration is abundantly clear from Herrera's own language: "And that mankind corresponds to the procreative member is proved by the fact that man is the most perfect of the lower ones, like the member in comparison to the legs, and he is the cause (just as the member contains the whole human being by virtue of its procreative power) of a complete perfect man through whom alone the Deity communicates to the human race. . . . Like the tongue and the heart, the latter of which is located between the arms and the former in the center of the body, it is located between the legs and along the axis of man's body, and according to what one reads in the *Book of Yeṣirah* attributed to our Father Abraham, it is the point of the scale, balance, or mediator" (ibid., pp. 372–373). Finally, let me note that in the concluding part of this chapter Herrera, paraphrasing a passage from Sarug's version of Lurianic kabbalah anthologized as *Seder Aṣilut* or *Kanfei Yonah* (for bibliographic detail, see Hebrew edition by Yosha, p. 532 n. 55), characterizes the projection of *Malkhut* from the world of emanation into the three lower worlds of creation, formation, and making in terms of the letter *he* broken orthographically into *dalet* and *waw*, which respectively represent the feminine and masculine, the "mystery of the cherubim." The three worlds are contained in the cherubim in the following manner: the world of creation corresponds to their heads; the world of formation to the six extremities (two arms, two legs, torso, and the phallus); and the world of making to the corona of the phallus, *aṭeret berit*, which is identified further as *Malkhut*. Recapping the discussion, Herrera writes, "In summary, by making *Malkhut* the spirit of the three worlds, the mental, rational, and material, as she really is, he establishes *beri'ah* the seat of glory as the head of this great body; *yeṣirah* the angelical world as the body with its six extremities, top and bottom, right and left, front and back; and *asiyyah* the material world as the extreme, end-point, and subject of all, like the tip of the member, appropriating their unions or copulation as if taking over those that consist of male and female, giver and receiver, all of which is largely symbolic of what we have said" (*Gate of Heaven*, 8:14, p. 376).

245. See above, n. 84.

246. That is, the combination of YHWH and Elohim, which correspond respectively to the masculine and feminine.

247. I have followed here the reading preserved in the Mantua edition of *Zohar*, which is also found in parentheses in the Cremona edition, 21a. The main reading in the Cremona edition is *ba-imma be-fumeih de-*

imma, that is, "in the mother in the mouth of the mother," an apparently corrupt version. In the *Zohar* prepared by Margaliot, the two readings are conflated, *ke-imma de-fumeih de-amah*, which should be rendered "like the mother in the mouth of the penis." The conflated reading is also found in other editions such as *Sefer ha-Zohar im Perush ha-Sullam*. In my study "Gender and Heresy," p. 239 n. 42, I was misled by following this flawed version. Giller, *Reading the Zohar*, p. 134, rendered the zoharic idiom "like a mother in the mouth of a maidservant." In addition to being misled (as I was) by the mistaken reading of *imma* in place of *amah*, Giller incorrectly translated *amah* as "maidservant," a translation that obscures the intent of the passage. The expression *pumeih de-amah*, "mouth of the penis," appears in several zoharic contexts as a designation of the phallic corona. See *Zohar* 2:60b; 3:38a, 142a.

248. *Zohar* 2:178a.

249. Support for this interpretation is found in the explication of this passage in Elijah ben Solomon, *Commentary of the Gaon Rabbi Elijah of Vilna*, p. 96: "'In the measure of the mouth of the penis' [*be-amah be-fumeih de-amah*], and thus the essence of the rectifications [*tiqqunin*] is to ameliorate the feminine in the masculine for this is the rectification in the world of chaos in which there was no balance [*matqela*], and the balance is in *Yesod* . . . for the balance consists of a side of merit and a side of guilt, the masculine and feminine, the masculine is the side of merit and the feminine the side of guilt, *Ḥesed* and *Gevurah*, and the tongue that is the law mediating in between, and this is *Yesod*, which is called 'tongue' [*lashon*] . . . in the secret of the covenant of the tongue and the covenant of the foreskin. The mediator needs to comprise both male and female and this is the penis and the mouth of the penis, which is *Yesod* and *Malkhut*, as is known." For further elaboration of these themes in the Vilna Gaon's kabbalistic thought, see E. Wolfson, "From Sealed Book," pp. 148–150.

250. For references to this motif, see chap. 7, n. 114.

251. *Zohar* 3:142a.

252. *Genesis Rabbah* 14:9, pp. 132–133.

253. Vital, *Liqquṭim Ḥadashim*, p. 63.

254. Vital, *Eṣ Ḥayyim*, 6:5, 28a. Cf. Vital, *Shaʿar ha-Gilgulim*, sec. 19, 10b–11a.

255. Vital, *Liqquṭim Ḥadashim*, p. 22.

256. The word I have translated as "genitals" is *yesod*, literally, "foundation." The choice of this term should be obvious: The genitalia engender offspring since it is through them that procreation and begetting are effected. They are thus both appropriately referred to as *yesod*.

257. Vital, *Eṣ Ḥayyim*, 39:2, 67d.

258. For discussion of this motif and citation of representative texts, see E. Wolfson, *Circle in the Square*, pp. 69–72.

259. Based on Job 19:26.

260. Vital, *Sefer ha-Derushim*, p. 263.

261. Meroz, "Early Lurianic Compositions," p. 315, raises the possibility that the attribution of *shaʿashuʿa* to Ein Sof may suggest an androgynous nature. My own interpretation concurs with this suggestion, although I have utilized the expression "male androgyne" to capture the autoerotic quality of the sexual act that accounts for the division of the indivisible one into male and female. See E. Wolfson, *Circle in the Square*, pp. 69–70. Y. Jacobson, "Aspect of the Feminine," p. 242, concludes that we can say that Ein Sof is neither male nor female or that it comprises both male and female.

262. Neumann, *Origins*, pp. 31, 207–208, 301–302.

263. The severity of spilling semen in vain is attested in a rabbinic dictum that compares this transgression to the shedding of blood (Babylonian Talmud, Niddah 13a; consider also the ruling preserved in Tosefta, Berakhot 2:12, where men who have had a seminal emission, in contrast to gonorrheics, menstruants, and parturients, are prohibited from reading Torah and studying Mishnah, midrash, halakhah, or aggadah) and another where the punishment for having an erotic fantasy (*hirhur*) that leads to an act of lewdness with the hand, i.e., masturbation, is being denied entry (presumably after death) into the antechamber of God (Babylonian Talmud, Niddah 13b, and the commentary of Rashi, *ad locum*, s.v. *be-yad*). See D. Biale, *Eros and the Jews*, pp. 55–57, 252 n. 148; Satlow, "'Wasted Seed,'" pp. 137–175; Laqueur, *Solitary Sex*, pp. 111–122. The

focus, indeed obsession, with this act as the severest of sins—according to some, the original transgression of Adam (in an earlier aggadic tradition, Adam begot demons and evil spirits through the semen he emitted accidentally, and not volitionally, in the course of the 130 years when he was separated from Eve; see Babylonian Talmud, Eruvin 18b, and other sources mentioned by Ginzberg, *Legends*, vol. 5, p. 148 n. 47)—is a distinctive feature of kabbalah, inspired principally by passages in zoharic literature, which have had a lasting impact on the formation of Jewish piety. For select references, see following note.

264. *Zohar* 1:57a, 62a, 69a, 188a, 219b; 3:90a; *Shushan Edut*, p. 353; *Book of the Pomegranate*, pp. 230–231, 242; Scholem, *On the Kabbalah and Its Symbolism*, pp. 154–156; Tishby, *Wisdom of the Zohar*, pp. 1365–1366, 1377 n. 119; D. Biale, *Eros and the Jews*, pp. 107, 110; Fine, *Physician of the Soul*, pp. 177–179; Laqueur, *Solitary Sex*, pp. 122–124. Especially significant in this regard are the compositions dedicated exclusively to *tiqqun ha-berit*, the rectification of sexual sins of which voluntary masturbation and involuntary nocturnal emissions are treated as the most severe. Such works, which began to appear in the seventeenth century in the wake of the influence of kabbalah, especially due to the legendary status of Isaac Luria, in wider circles of rabbinic leadership, were an important part of the spiritual and ideational climate of Sabbatianism and Hasidism. See D. Biale, *Eros and the Jews*, pp. 116–117 and treatises delineated on p. 269 n. 74, to which many more sources could have been added. See now Hundert, *Jews in Poland-Lithuania*, pp. 131–137.

265. Moses de León, *She'elot u-Teshuvot*, p. 40.

266. See discussion of this motif in chap. 7.

267. Consider the following comment in the compilation of Nathan of Gaza, *Liqquṭei Raza de-Malka Qaddisha*, fol. 1b: "Furthermore, we must ask, it is known to us that no configuration [*parṣuf*] comes to be except from male and female, so how can it be said that *Atiqa Qaddisha* has no female and that Ein Sof also has no female? We must respond that in truth there is no female there in actuality, but there is a female in potentiality . . . and with respect to Ein Sof as well there is no [female] in actuality but the aspect of the female is connected there to the point that we do not mention her for everything is one." What Nathan expresses is the philosophical insight that even autoeroticism entails the construction of the other in the imagination. On this point, see Marion, *Le phénomène érotique*, p. 194, and further discussion in chap. 6. See Nathan of Gaza, *Sefer ha-Beri'ah*, fols. 1b–2a: "In the time of the contraction (*ṣimṣum*), several roots for the beings that are differentiated in the worlds were produced, and one instance of them is the root of the right and left. Why is one place called 'right' and one place called 'left'? Know that when there was the contraction (*ṣimṣum*) in the will of Ein Sof, in that very void (*ḥalal*) there remained a trace (*reshimu*), as is known. In the elevation of the light above, that trace did not remain as it was initially, that is, in its first place, for the movement of the elevation of the light above it was removed from its place. The depth of Ein Sof was great and wondrous to transfer the trace from its place to another place, that is, the trace that stands there today was not there from the beginning when Ein Sof filled the entire world, but rather it went to another place. Thus from one side it stood as it was, and that side is called 'right,' and comprised within it stood Ein Sof, for every left that is contained there in the right produces motion for the trace that remains from the great light, and with respect to this it is left. When the light of the straight line (*or qaw ha-yosher*) comes to the primordial space (*ṭehiru*), in every light that stands in its place are constructed the mercies (*ha-ḥasadim*) on the right side, and when motion from its place is produced the powers (*ha-gevurot*) on the left side are constructed."

268. *Zohar* 3:129a; and see Vital, *Eṣ Ḥayyim* 13:13, 68c.

269. That is, the numerical value of the letters of the Tetragrammaton, when it is spelled as *ywd he waw he*, is forty-five (10+6+4+5+1+6+1+6+5+1), which signifies the masculine aspect of mercy.

270. That is, the numerical value of the letters of the Tetragrammaton, when it is spelled as *ywd hh ww hh*, is fifty-two (10+6+4+5+5+6+6+5+5). This signifies the feminine aspect of judgment.

271. Vital, *Sha'ar ha-Haqdamot*, 29c.

272. It behooves me to note that in the continuation of the passage in *Sha'ar ha-Haqdamot*, 29c–d, it does appear that Vital makes a distinction between the status of duality in *Atiq Yomin* and *Arikh Anpin*: "This was the intention of what was said in the *Idra*, 'accordingly, there is no right or left at all in *Atiqa*.' That is, the [permutation of] forty-five and the [permutation of] fifty-two that are in him are joined together in his right

side and in his left side. Thus there is no left or right there, as is found in *Arikh*, for his right side is masculine and his left side is feminine."

273. The philosophical issue here is reminiscent of descriptions in Gnostic (especially Valentinian) and Neoplatonic sources of the First Principle as the solitary and alone Father. See Pépin, "Theories of Procession," pp. 297–335, esp. pp. 301–307.

274. Vital, *Eṣ Ḥayyim*, 17:3, 85a.

275. For translation and discussion of some of the relevant texts, see E. Wolfson, *Circle in the Square*, pp. 85–92; idem, "Gender and Heresy," pp. 255–259.

276. Vital, *Shaʿar ha-Haqdamot*, 20c. Compare Vital, Eṣ Ḥayyim, 28:2, 18c (parallel in *Sefer ha-Derushim*, p. 234): "In *Arikh Anpin* there are only nine *sefirot*, and the aspect of *Malkhut* is not mentioned there. However, *Yesod* that is within him is comprised of male and female, in the image of the date-palm that encompasses male and female, in the secret of 'the righteous shall bloom like a date-palm' (Ps. 92:13)."

277. I have not found this exact formulation in the *Zohar*. The closest passage to this citation is the reworking of the aggadic motif that when it arose in God's will to create the world, he took counsel with the Torah. See *Zohar* 3:61b.

278. "Commentary on *Idra Rabba*," p. 142.

279. To be more precise, the rabbinic expression is "thus it arose in thought" (*kakh alah ba-maḥshavah*). See Babylonian Talmud, Menaḥot 29b; Ketuvot 8a.

280. See, for instance, the following passage in Luria's commentary on *Sifra di-Ṣeniʿuta* in *Sefer ha-Derushim*, p. 261 (*Shaʿar Maʾamerei Rashbi*, 28c): "*Yesod* is male and it is not from the side of *Binah* for she is female. . . . Nevertheless, the supernal point of Zion that is in *Binah* is in him even though it is not discernible. Accordingly, within him the potency of femininity is hidden and the potency of masculinity revealed . . . and these two aspects are Joseph and Benjamin, the one is the female waters . . . and the other the male waters in the secret of Joseph the righteous, he is above and he is below, he enters and exits, he enters to bestow the male waters and he exits to take out the female waters corresponding to the male waters, and this is so every time there is copulation." The translation and interpretation of this passage are slightly different from what I presented in *Circle of the Square*, p. 106.

281. Vital, *Eṣ Ḥayyim*, 35:1, 50c–d.

282. *Shaʿar ha-Pesuqim*, 5a–b.

283. Vital, *Liqquṭim Ḥadashim*, p. 47.

284. I have not located a precise parallel to the exegesis of Isaiah 44:6 in *Tiqqunei Zohar*, but something quite close appears in sec. 70, 120a.

285. Fano, *Maʾamerei ha-*RAMA, vol. 1, pp. 30–31.

286. See, for example, Vital, *Mavo Sheʿarim*, 28a; idem, *Eṣ Ḥayyim*, 6:5, 28a, 39:2, 67d; idem, *Liqquṭim Ḥadashim*, pp. 22–23, 63. I have translated and analyzed these texts in "Beyond Good and Evil," pp. 116–117. For a revised and expanded version, see the third chapter of *Venturing Beyond*.

287. *Yonat Elem*, chap. 29, in Fano, *Maʾamerei ha-RaMa*, vol. 2, p. 37. I had the occasion to cite this passage in *Circle in the Square*, pp. 119–120.

288. Brenner, *Intercourse of Knowledge*, p. 12. The persistence of this ancient bias is discernible in the more modern correlation of the masculine with culture, on the one hand, and the feminine and nature, on the other.

289. E. Wolfson, "Re/membering."

290. *Book Bahir*, sec. 83, p. 169. The expression is derived from Babylonian Talmud, Eruvin 76b.

291. *Zohar* 2:180a. To be more precise, in that context, the *yod*, which signifies the second emanation or *Ḥokhmah*, is said to be supported by the nine pillars, which are also identified as nine points arranged in the shape of the final *mem* or a square with three points on each of the four sides. The image of the point supported by these pillars, which are also depicted as the chariot, conveys the motif of the male resting upon the female. It is of interest to consider the following comment by Derrida, *Dissemination*, p. 353: "here, the *squaring of the circle* is the uniting of the masculine sex and the feminine sex into a whole, just as it is possible to unite into a single figure the framed circle or the circle square" (emphasis in original). In the continuation of the passage, the "squaring of the circle" is identified as the "philosopher's stone," the object of the alchemical quest. Concerning this image, see also Jung, *Psychology and Alchemy*, p. 169; idem, *Aion*, pp. 224–225.

292. On the gender implications of the symbol of the point related specifically to the masculine transformation of the feminine, see E. Wolfson, "Coronation of the Sabbath Bride," pp. 315–324.

293. Literally, "whenever the male and female come as one."

294. *Zohar* 2:147b. See as well *Zohar* 1:49a, previously cited in E. Wolfson, *Circle in the Square*, p. 210 n. 76: "when a woman is joined to her husband she is called by the name of her husband."

295. On the phenomenon of gender metamorphosis in Jewish mysticism, see E. Wolfson, *Circle in the Square*, pp. 79–121 and notes on pp. 195–232.

Chapter Five
Flesh Become Word: Textual Embodiment and Poetic Incarnation

1. Wiethaus, "Introduction," p. 1; Hale, "'Taste and See,'" pp. 3–14. The polarizing of the carnal and spiritual had grave implications for the implementation of ecclesiastical discipline in the High Middle Ages. For discussion of this theme, see Peters, "Destruction of the Flesh," pp. 131–148.

2. Jaouën and Semple, "Editors' Preface," pp. 1–4. On the Eucharist, the glorified flesh of Christ, and the indwelling of the divine presence in the saintly body, see Lubac, *Corpus mysticum*; Kantorowicz, *King's Two Bodies*, pp. 193–272; R. Williams, "Troubled Breasts," pp. 63–78, esp. pp. 67–72. D. Power, *Eucharistic Mystery*, pp. 184–240, discusses Eucharistic devotion and representation of Christ's passion contemporary with the time and place of the early kabbalist fraternities in Europe. On the "swell of eucharistic devotion" in the later twelfth and thirteenth centuries, see Bynum, *Jesus as Mother*, pp. 192–193, 256–257, and Miri Rubin, *Corpus Christi*.

3. Jager, *Book of the Heart*. For an illuminating study on the corporealization and fetishization of the book in a fourteenth-century Christian milieu, see Camille, "Book as Flesh," pp. 34–77.

4. I have discussed this notion in chaps. 1 and 2.

5. This account is a philosophic synopsis of my exegetical presentation of the imaginal body of God in "Judaism and Incarnation." For a similar account in a different cultural context, see Lagerwey, "Écriture et corps divin," pp. 383–398. It is of interest to note that the author begins his essay with an epigram from Jeremiah 7:23–24.

6. Barbaras, *Tournant de l'expérience*, pp. 95–136.

7. On poetry as the embodiment of the mystery of incarnation, see R. Schwartz, "From Ritual to Poetry," pp. 138–160.

8. Merleau-Ponty, *Visible and Invisible*, p. 193.

9. Ibid., p. 28. Sarukkai, "Inside/Outside," pp. 459–478, thematizes the overcoming of the internal-external binary in Merleau-Ponty's thought in conversation with the yogic practice of attaining the inner body that does not yield to or foster transcendent/immanent duality. The comparative analysis of Merleau-Ponty and Asian religions has been a fruitful area of scholarly inquiry; see references cited in Prologue, n. 69.

10. On the nexus between perceptual faith and the invisible, see Dastur, *Chair et langage*, pp. 111–126; see also G. Johnson, "Desire and Invisibility."

11. Merleau-Ponty, *Visible and Invisible*, p. 28.

12. Ibid., pp. 226–227 (French ed., p. 280).

13. Ibid., pp. 252–253.

14. Ibid., p. 167.

15. Ibid., p. 37.

16. Levin, *Opening of Vision*, p. 331.

17. Merleau-Ponty, *Visible and Invisible*, pp. 127–128.

18. Lingis, "Intentionality and Corporeity," pp. 75–90, esp. pp. 83–87; Ihde, *Sense and Significance*, pp. 124–127.

19. Merleau-Ponty, *Visible and Invisible*, pp. 147–148.

20. Ibid., p. 142.

21. Ibid., p. 148.

22. Ibid., pp. 248–249.

23. Ibid., p. 118.

24. Ibid.

25. Ibid., p. 119. On the entwining of the visible and invisible, see Levin, *Opening of Vision*, pp. 175, 211–323.

26. Merleau-Ponty, *Visible and Invisible*, p. 107 (emphasis in original). Various scholars have written about the nexus of body and language in Merleau-Ponty's thought. For a representative list, see Kwant, *Phenomenological Philosophy*, pp. 46–62; Barral, *Body in Interpersonal Relations*, pp. 171–212; Dillon, *Merleau-Ponty's Ontology*, pp. 130–150; Priest, *Merleau-Ponty*, pp. 73–74, 166–178. On the isomorphic relation between language and world, see Kwant, *From Phenomenology to Metaphysics*, pp. 54–61; Dillon, *Merleau-Ponty's Ontology*, pp. 178–223, esp. pp. 209–219; and idem, "Unconscious," pp. 67–83. On the inextricable link between language and silence, see Kwant, *From Phenomenology to Metaphysics*, pp. 184–190. On language as gesture, see also discussion in Gill, *Merleau-Ponty and Metaphor*, pp. 82–104.

27. Merleau-Ponty, *Visible and Invisible*, pp. 216–217.

28. Ibid., p. 139 (emphasis in original).

29. Ibid., p. 138.

30. Ibid., p. 249.

31. Ibid., p. 140 (emphasis in original).

32. Ibid., p. 147.

33. Ibid., p. 146.

34. Cantillon, "Corpus Pascalis," pp. 44–45.

35. Merleau-Ponty, *Visible and Invisible*, p. 271. See Lingis, "Sensitive Flesh," pp. 225–240.

36. For discussion of the fuller context and implications of this theme in Merleau-Ponty's hermeneutical phenomenology, see Barbaras, "Dédoublement de l'originaire," pp. 289–303; and idem, *Tournant de l'expérience*, 81–94.

37. My English renderings of *Urpräsentiert* and *Nichturpräsentierbar* are indebted to the suggestions made by Charlotte E. Fonrobert.

38. Merleau-Ponty, *Visible and Invisible*, p. 228. See P. Burke, "Flesh as *Urpräsentierbarkeit* in the Interrogative," pp. 60–70.

39. Merleau-Ponty, *Visible and Invisible*, p. 251 (emphasis in original).

40. Ibid., p. 228 (emphasis in original).

41. It is important to recall here Merleau-Ponty's exploration of the metaphysical implications of human sexuality and the play of eroticism in the fifth chapter of *Phénoménologie de la perception*: "The importance we attach to the body and the contradictions of love are . . . related to a more general drama which arises from the metaphysical structure of my body, which is both an object for others and a subject for myself. The intensity of sexual pleasure would not be sufficient to explain the place occupied by sexuality in human life or, for example, the phenomenon of eroticism, if sexual experience were not, as it were, an opportunity, vouchsafed to all and always available, of acquainting oneself with the human lot in its most general aspects of autonomy and dependence. . . . Metaphysics—the coming to light of something beyond nature—is not localized at the level of knowledge: it begins with the opening out upon 'another,' and is to be found everywhere, and already, in the specific development of sexuality" (pp. 167–168). For a constructive, feminist reading of Merleau-Ponty's notion of lived bodies and the phenomenon of the flesh, see Grosz, *Volatile Bodies*, pp. 86–111; and the nuanced analysis of Heinämaa, *Toward a Phenomenology of Sexual Difference*, pp. 21–79. By contrast, a feminist critique of Merleau-Ponty's thinking about sexual difference is offered by Chanter, "Wild Meaning," pp. 219–236.

42. Merleau-Ponty, *Visible and Invisible*, p. 132. See Tréguier, *Corps selon la chair*, pp. 135–148.

43. Merleau-Ponty, *Visible and Invisible*, p. 263.

44. For an elaboration, see E. Wolfson, "Before Alef."

45. Böhme, *Aurora*, 8.123–126, p. 173. For other pertinent references, see chap. 1, n. 49.

46. E. Wolfson, "Anthropomorphic Imagery," pp. 147–181; idem, "Letter Symbolism," pp. 195–236. The reader interested in gathering more information about the molecular biological image of the genome would do well to consult the wide-ranging study by Verma, *Genome*.

47. *Book Bahir*, sec. 53, p. 149. Scholem, "Name of God," duly noted that kabbalists draw no distinction between a thing and its proper name (p. 77) and that the most proper of all names is YHWH, the "essential name" that is the "original source of all language" (p. 194). It is of interest to note here that the number twenty-two was used to signify perfection in Christian devotional texts. This numerical symbolism was based both on the letters of the Hebrew alphabet and the Platonic tradition that twenty-two terms compose the double interval series related to the formation of the soul and the principle of order in the cosmos. See Frost, *Holy Delight*, pp. 109–110.

48. The point was well understood by Shem Tov Ibn Shem Tov, *Sefer ha-Emunot*, 19b, who cites and briefly explicates the bahiric text.

49. Lipiner, *Metaphysics of the Hebrew Alphabet*, pp. 124–140, presents a thorough summary of the linguistic theory in the second part of *Sefer Yeṣirah*. See also Idel, "Reification of Language," pp. 45–49; idem, *Absorbing Perfections*, pp. 34–37.

50. Scholem, "Name of God," pp. 65–66. The ancient Israelite tradition about the power of the name crossed over into syncretistic Hellenistic magic. See Gager, *Moses in Greco-Roman Paganism*, pp. 142–146. Another facet of the correlation of letters and limbs that I will not discuss in this chapter is the richly evocative traditions about the golem that have been cultivated and transmitted through the centuries. For analysis of this motif, see Scholem, *On the Kabbalah and Its Symbolism*, pp. 158–204; Idel, *Golem*; Liebes, "*Golem* in Numerology is *Ḥokhmah*," pp. 1305–1322; idem, *Ars Poetica*, pp. 63–71.

51. Jacob ben Sheshet, *Sefer Meshiv Devarim Nekhoḥim*, p. 154; see idem, *Sefer ha-Emunah we-ha-Biṭṭaḥon*, in *Kitvei Ramban*, 2:392–393: "There is no letter in the *alef-beit* that does not allude to the holy One, blessed be he."

52. Technically, the word "enstatic" is from the Greek *en-stasis*, "standing within," the etymological opposite of "ecstatic" from *ek-stasis*, "standing without." For a brief account of these terms, see Griffiths, *On Being Mindless*, p. 149 n. 27.

53. Merleau-Ponty, *Signs*, p. 89.

54. My language respectfully modifies the saying discussed by Perrett, "Is Whatever Exists Knowable and Nameable?" pp. 401–414, being influenced in particular by Blanchot's notion of the limit-experience to be discussed in more detail in the next chapter.

55. Shem Tov Ibn Gaon, *Sefer Baddei ha-Aron*, p. 14.

56. For a thorough treatment of this matter, and citation of other relevant scholarly analyses, see Idel, "Maimonides and Kabbalah," pp. 31–81. And see now E. Wolfson, "Beneath the Wings," pp. 209–237, esp. pp. 212–221. Scholars of medieval kabbalah and Jewish philosophy would benefit from the nuanced and sophisticated discussion on the interplay of the mystical and philosophical enunciated in the essay by F. Rosenthal, "Ibn ʿArabī between 'Philosophy' and 'Mysticism,'" pp. 1–35.

57. *Lirmoz* literally means to hint, to allude, to represent symbolically. I have rendered it "to imagine," out of the conviction that in kabbalistic sources there is no disjuncture between the verbal and visual.

58. *Kitvei Ramban*, 2:454.

59. Scholem, *Origins*, p. 452; J. Goldberg, "Mystical Union," pp. 518 n. 104 and 520 n. 109.

60. *Kitvei Ramban*, 2:453 (commentary on *Sefer Yeṣirah* 1:1).

61. *Kitvei Ramban*, 2:454; see also p. 455, where Azriel frames the ontological chain in terms of visionary ascent (in his commentary on *Sefer Yeṣirah* 1:6), that is, the natural (*muṭba*) ascends in order to contemplate the sensible (*murgash*), and the sensible ascends to contemplate the intelligible (*muskkal*), and the intelligible ascends to contemplate the hidden (*neʿelam*). According to Azriel, the word *ṣefiyyah* ("vision") denotes the effluence of the "potency that extends from above to below."

62. Scholem, *Origins*, p. 265, refers to Azriel's composition as a "Neoplatonic catechism."

63. See E. Wolfson, "Negative Theology," p. xi.

64. *Perush Eser Sefirot*, in Ibn Gabbai, *Derekh Emunah*, 3a.

65. *Devarim*; this is one of the technical terms in the lexicon of Isaac the Blind and his disciples to refer to the *sefirot*. See Scholem, "Name of God," pp. 166–167; idem, *Origins*, pp. 265, 277–278.

66. *Sefer Yeṣirah* 1:6.

67. Scholem, "New Document," p. 143.

68. Ibid., p. 146; see also Scholem, *Origins*, pp. 394–395.

69. Gersh, *Middle Platonism and Neoplatonism*, vol. 1, pp. 170–174.

70. Vanderkam, *Book of Jubilees*, p. 73.

71. Many competent scholars have turned their attention to the evolution of the sapiential tradition in ancient Israelite religion and Second-Temple Judaism. For a useful survey and relevant bibliography, see Collins, *Jewish Wisdom*.

72. It should come as no surprise that this matter has been the focus of many important studies. Here I mention but one study, S. Sanders, "Writing, Ritual, and Apocalypse." I am indebted to the author, who graciously sent me a copy of his informative and impressive work. Needless to say, one will find in Sanders a judicious engagement with other relevant scholarly accounts.

73. For discussion of the depiction of wisdom as the image of fullness, see Liesen, *Full of Praise*, pp. 145–187.

74. Skehan, *Wisdom of Ben Sira*, p. 138. On the myth of the descent of the personified wisdom, see Argall, *1 Enoch and Sirach*, pp. 53–98.

75. P. Davies, *About Time*, p. 248.

76. I offer this remark as a rhetorical prod to stimulate thinking about kabbalah in a somewhat broader conceptual framework and not as a commitment to the belief that medieval kabbalists anticipated current developments in quantum physics, as is sometimes suggested by the overly zealous preachers of the gospel of New Age Jewish spirituality. For a helpful and measured account of the philosophical issues that emerge from the depictions of space and time in string theory, see Dainton, *Time and Space*, pp. 320–334.

77. Scholem, *Explications and Implications*, p. 38. For other passages in Scholem's oeuvre that express this idea, see chap. 1, nn. 50–51.

78. Kabbalistic lore preserves and intensifies the nexus between the chosenness of the Jewish people and the privileging of Hebrew as the ontological language. For a comprehensive and nuanced study of the development of this "metasemantic" notion of *leshon ha-qodesh*, see Aaron, "Judaism's Holy Language," pp. 49–107, and esp. pp. 96–105, where the author discusses the mythological conception of Hebrew as a cosmogonic force in *Genesis Rabbah* and select mystical and magical texts. On the related but conceptually distinct topic of the holiness of the divine word, see Harrington, *Holiness: Rabbinic Judaism*, pp. 130–160.

79. *Genesis Rabbah*, 18:4, p. 164. For other sources, see Ginzberg, *Legends*, vol. 5, pp. 205–206 n. 91.

80. On the theme of the heavenly tablets, see S. Paul, "Heavenly Tablets," pp. 345–353; and other references cited in E. Wolfson, *Circle in the Square*, p. 161 n. 31. I note here two worthwhile discussions of this imaginal symbol in more recent studies: F. Martinez, "Heavenly Tablets," pp. 243–260; Najman, "Interpretation as Primordial Writing," pp. 379–410.

81. For a still-useful review of the image of the world as a book, see Josipovici, *World and Book*, pp. 25–51. The augmented use of the metaphor of the book of nature has been traced to the renaissance of twelfth-century humanism; see Curtius, *European Literature*, pp. 302–347; Pai, "Varying Degrees of Light," pp. 3–19. On the later reverberation of this motif as a key to understanding the respective convergence and divergence of science and theology, two fundamental fountainheads of knowledge, see Howell, *God's Two Books*.

82. On the textualization of God in kabbalistic symbolism, see E. Wolfson, *Circle in the Square*, pp. 49–78; idem, "From Sealed Book to Open Text"; and the recent remarks in Idel, *Absorbing Perfections*, pp. 44, 116–124, 483–487. On the link between representation of nature as a text or book in medieval Christian sources, a belief that rests on the assumption that things in nature and words in Scripture are to be interpreted as metaphorical signs denoting God's existence, and on the doctrine of incarnation, see Gellrich, *Idea of the Book*, pp. 29–50; Melchior-Bonnet, *Mirror*, pp. 108–118; Newman, *God and Goddesses*, pp. 51–137. On the impact of this motif in occult philosophies that crystallized in the Renaissance and early modern periods, in part under the influence of kabbalah, see Bono, *Word of God and the Languages of Man*, pp. 72–84, 123–166; Harkness, *John Dee's Conversations with Angels*, pp. 64–97, 157–194.

83. Rosenzweig, *Star of Redemption*, p. 409.

84. For a comprehensive study of this influence, see Lobel, *Between Mysticism and Philosophy.* The author provides a brief review of previous scholars who have discussed the influence of Islamic mysticism on Halevi (pp. 6–9). The theme of the sacrality of Arabic, the language of God's revelation transmitted to Muḥammad and preserved in the Qur'ān, in Sufism and its proximity to Halevi's view, not to mention Jewish mystical texts, is not discussed by Lobel. In spite of the justified emphasis placed on the auditory-verbal dimension of language attested to in the central role accorded recitation of the Qur'ān in Muslim ritual, one should not ignore the importance of the graphic-visual dimension; indeed, there is a subtle and dialectical relationship between the recited *qur'ān* and the written *kitāb*. See Graham, *Beyond the Written Word*, pp. 81–115; Madigan, *Qur'ān's Self-Image*. Furthermore, Muslim belief in the Qur'ān as the primal text, the heavenly "guarded tablet," *al-lawḥ al-maḥfūẓ* (Q 85:21–22), an archaic mythical notion (see above, n. 80), surely complicates the relation between the written and oral aspects of scriptural language even at the revelatory stage. It has even been suggested that the notion of the uncreated Qur'ān as the embodied word of God amounts to a doctrine of "illibration" that corresponds to the Christian concept of incarnation; see H. Wolfson, *Philosophy of the Kalam*, pp. 235–263; Wild, "We Have Sent Down," pp. 137–153. See the incisive and rich analysis of logocentrism and the construction of religious truth in Islam offered by Arkoun, *Unthought in Contemporary Islamic Thought*, pp. 170–203, esp. the discussion on writing, text, and reading, pp. 171–178. The sacred nature of the written script is also attested in the central place accorded calligraphy in Islamic culture as well as in the sustained impact of magical talismans, which feature the sundry names of God written in Arabic. See Schimmel, *Deciphering the Signs of God*, pp. 150–158; idem, *Mystical Dimensions of Islam*, pp. 411–425. For a somewhat different perspective on the efficacy assigned to the isolated letters of the Qur'ān, see Massignon, *Passion of al-Hallāj*, vol. 3, p. 98.

85. Halevi, *Sefer ha-Kuzari*, 4:25.

86. The influence of Halevi is conspicuous in *Zohar* 2:129b, where the "holy language" of the Jews is contrasted with the "foreign language" of the "other nations," i.e., the language of the other side, identified in the continuation of the passage as the "language of the Targum," i.e., Aramaic. The fact that most of *Zohar* was composed in the language attributed to the demonic potency is a matter that demands analysis. For a related motif, attested in earlier sources, that may have influenced the formation of the zoharic topos, see below, n. 88. In *Zohar* 3:204a, the supremacy of the Jews vis-à-vis the idolatrous nations is emphasized by the claim that only the former possess the written and oral form of the language whence one can know the truth of reality. Part of the text is cited below, at n. 100.

87. Halevi, *Sefer ha-Kuzari*, 2:68. The resemblance, indeed underlying unity, of the three languages, Hebrew, Aramaic, and Arabic, is also noted in the writings of Halevi's contemporary, Abraham Ibn Ezra, but he is of the opinion that Aramaic is the "primordial language." See discussion in Idel, "Infant Experiment," pp. 59–61. On the contrast between the views of Halevi and Ibn Ezra on the nature of language, see Simon, *Four Approaches*, pp. 267–268 n. 53. See below, n. 102.

88. Halevi follows a line of thinking in rabbinic literature according to which the language of the angels is Hebrew and not Aramaic. See Babylonian Talmud, Shabbat 12b, Soṭah 33a; *Avot de-Rabbi Natan*, version A, chap. 37, 55a; Yahalom, "Angels Do Not Understand Aramaic," pp. 33–44. The motif is repeated on a number of occasions in zoharic literature. See, for example, *Zohar* 1:9b, 74b, 88b, 89a.

89. Halevi, *Sefer ha-Kuzari*, 1:53–56; Silman, *Philosopher and Prophet*, pp. 90 n. 29 and 292 n. 7; Jospe, "Superiority of Oral," pp. 127–129. Another twelfth-century author who demonstrates affinity with the mystical tradition on this account is the Yemenite Nathanel Ibn al-Fayyūmī. In his *Bustan al-ʿuqul* (Ibn al-Fayyūmī, *Bustan Al-Ukul*, pp. 3–4, English section; p. 2, Judeo-Arabic section), al-Fayyūmī relates the view in the name of "some of the learned" that the "characters of the alphabet [*ḥuruf al-otiyyot*] . . . were originated before the world of changeable things, inasmuch as every rational being needs them in discourse and in uttering the praise of God." In the continuation of this passage, al-Fayyūmī links this thought exegetically to the first verse in Genesis, "In the beginning God created the heavens and the earth" (*bere'shit bara elohim et ha-shamayim we-et ha-areṣ*). It is possible that the exegetical point is related to the particle *et*, which consists of *alef* and *tau*, the first and last letters of the Hebrew alphabet. The technical term used by al-Fayyūmī reflects the Shiʿite notion of the "science of letters" (*ʿilm al-ḥuruf*), that is, the "magical and divinatory application of

the numerical value of the alphabet" (Moezzi, *Divine Guide*, p. 95). A possible source for al-Fayyūmī may have been Saadiah Gaon's commentary on *Sefer Yeṣirah*, especially the eighth of the nine positions he delineates in the introduction to this work, a position that he identifies as compatible with the one expressed in *Sefer Yeṣirah*, viz., that the first of all things created were the numbers and letters. For some representative studies of al-Fayyūmī, see Pines, "Nathanael ben al-Fayyūmī et la théologie ismaëlienne," pp. 5–22; Kiener, "Jewish Ismaʿilism," pp. 249–266; and the comments by Idel, *Kabbalah: New Perspectives*, pp. 121 and 334 nn. 76–77.

90. In light of this long-standing belief attested in works of Jewish esotericism, it is of interest to consider the remark of Dastur, *Telling Time*, p. 99 n. 14, that the "inflection" of Semitic languages "concerns a root which—contrary to the Indo-European radical which is merely a product of analysis and becomes apparent only through etymological research—is part of the living linguistic consciousness of the speaker without, however, being embodied otherwise than in consonantal script."

91. Some relevant passages from Gikatilla on this point are cited by Idel, "Abulafia's Secrets," pp. 298–299.

92. Halevi's influence is detectable in Joseph ben Shalom Ashkenazi, *Kabbalistic Commentary*, p. 44: "On account of our sins we are mixed together with the nations and we have seen that their letters are only signs [*simanim*]. . . . The people of our nation made a great error and thought erroneously about God, his Torah, and the letters of Torah by saying they are only signs. God forbid that our holy Torah, that is, its letters, are signs fabricated in the hearts of men. How could the letters engraved by the finger of God be fabricated letters?"; compare p. 146. The former passage is cited by Lipiner, *Metaphysics of Hebrew*, pp. 48–49. See also the commentary to *Sefer Yeṣirah* by the same kabbalist erroneously attributed to Abraham ben David in *Sefer Yeṣirah*, 31a: "Thus it should be clear to you that there are letters of spirit [*otiyyot shel ruaḥ*], and they are the letters of the Holy Spirit [*otiyyot shel ruaḥ ha-qodesh*]. Therefore [Hebrew] is called the holy language [*leshon ha-qodesh*], which is not the case with any other language of the seventy languages, because it comes forth and emanates from the source of holiness."

93. Scholem, "Name of God," pp. 134–135; Idel, *Language, Torah, and Hermeneutics*, pp. 12–14, 16–27; idem, "Abulafia's Secrets," pp. 300–304; E. Wolfson, *Abraham Abulafia*, pp. 58–65. On the possible impact the Maimonidean conception of language had in eliciting a response on the part of kabbalists, see Idel, *Absorbing Perfections*, p. 106.

94. For instance, consider Abulafia's depiction of prophecy in *Sitrei Torah*, fol. 155a (printed ed., p. 138): "The beginning of the truth of prophecy is the inner speech [*dibbur penimi*] created in the soul in the seventy languages by means of the twenty-two holy letters, and all of them are combined in the heart through the permutation of letters." On the relation of the seventy languages to Hebrew in Abulafia's writings, see E. Wolfson, *Abraham Abulafia*, pp. 62–64 and reference to studies of Scholem and Idel cited p. 62 n. 178.

95. Abulafia, *Imrei Shefer*, fol. 238a (printed ed., pp. 69–70; I have translated from the manuscript version). Compare Abulafia's comment in *Oṣar Eden Ganuz*, fol. 25a (printed edition, p. 51) on the statement in *Sefer Yeṣirah* that God created the soul of all that exists by means of the twenty-two Hebrew letters: "This is a great secret that God revealed to his prophets, and his prophets revealed it to his people Israel, and it is not known by any nation except this one." In the continuation of the passage, Abulafia refers to this "wondrous secret" as the "stake upon which everything is hung."

96. Idel, "Infant Experiment," p. 70.

97. Ibid., p. 71.

98. I am not engaging the third model, which Idel identifies as magic, since in my opinion the tripartite typological structure is a variation of the earlier twofold structure, that is, the magical is operative in either the theosophic or prophetic framework and one therefore does not gain much by according it an independent taxonomic status.

99. On occasion Abulafia limited somewhat the claim about the "natural" state of Hebrew by ascribing this quality only to the verbal dimension of the letters, as opposed to the written forms, which are considered to be conventional. The distinction is made, for instance, in Abulafia, *Oṣar Eden Ganuz*, fol. 62a (printed ed., p. 124): "I will speak now initially about the matter of the letters. That which is written in books are merely

signs and that which is mentioned by mouth are also signs, but the difference between them is that the written letter *alef* is a conventional sign [*simman muskkam*], and even if it is prophetic [*nevu'i*] it is conventional, However, the *alef* that is mentioned through pronunciation that comes forth from the throat is natural [*muṭba*] and not conventional."

100. *Zohar* 3:204a.

101. On the identification of word and will, see Halevi, *Sefer ha-Kuzari*, 2:6.

102. Halevi, *Sefer ha-Kuzari*, 1:101; 4:25. The insistence that the exclusive language of prophecy is Hebrew (see also 5:20) is a corollary of the claims that it is limited to the Jewish people and that it must occur within the boundaries of the land of Israel. See Silman, *Philosopher and Prophet*, pp. 178–179. The distinctiveness of Halevi's approach and its similarity to Jewish mysticism are underscored when he is compared to other thinkers of his time. For a comparison of Halevi and Abraham Ibn Ezra, see the reference in n. 87 above to Simon, *Four Approaches*. In contrast to Halevi's classification of Hebrew as the divine language, Ibn Ezra views it as the "first language," created by Adam, though he maintains the unique sanctity of Hebrew as the "holy tongue" exemplified by the divine name. See Idel, "A la recherché de la langue originelle," pp. 416–420. An even sharper contrast to Halevi is Maimonides, who incontrovertibly affirms that language is a matter of convention; no special status is accorded Hebrew. See Jospe, "Superiority of Oral," p. 128 n. 2; Silman, *Philosopher and Prophet*, pp. 90–91 n. 29. For another example of a philosopher affirming the conventionalist view, see Dotan, "Saadia Gaon on the Origins of Language," pp. 237–249. The similarity of Halevi's identification of Hebrew as the divine language and the linguistic theory formulated by kabbalists, especially Isaac the Blind, is noted by Sendor, "Emergence," vol. 1, pp. 244–246.

103. Manetti, *Theories of the Sign*, pp. 166–167.

104. See chap. 1, n. 331.

105. R. Corrington, *Ecstatic Naturalism*, p. 67.

106. Schimmel, *Deciphering the Signs*, pp. xii–xiii. On the nexus of body and writing in Islamic sources, see also Chebel, *Corps en Islam*, pp. 175–190.

107. Schimmel, *Mystical Dimensions*, p. 411. For the introduction of gender and specifically the feminine character to depict the nature of the sign and the spirit, see Sells, *Approaching the Qur'ān*, pp. 201–204.

108. It is of interest to consider the following prophetic tradition on the special status accorded the Qur'ān in Merlin Swartz, *Medieval Critique of Anthropomorphism*, sec. 170, p. 239: "In a tradition reported by ʿUthmān, the Prophet said: 'The superiority of the Quran to other forms of speech is comparable to God's superiority over His creatures, for the Quran proceeded from Him (*minhu kharaja*) and will return to Him.' The point of the saying is that the Quran has come (*waṣala*) to us from Him (*min ʿindahu*) and will return to Him again; moreover, [the saying] is to be taken as resting on the authority of the Prophet." The qualitative difference between God and the Qur'ān must be upheld, even though the latter is to be accorded a special status since it proceeded from and will return to God and thus it stands apart from the world of created things. The issue of the divinization of the qur'ānic text and the implied corporeality of God is underscored in sec. 237, p. 276: "As for the prophetic tradition: 'God's servants do not approach Him with anything like what proceeds from Him,' the expression 'what proceeds from Him' (*mā kharaja minhu*) should be construed to mean what becomes manifest through Him (*ẓahara ʿanhu*). We are not to suppose that the expression implies one body coming out of another, for God is not a body (*jism*) and His word (*kalām*) is not a body (*jism*)." On the charge of heresy on the part of Muslims who refused to acknowledge the created nature of the Qur'ān, thereby affirming a view akin to the Christian depiction of Jesus as the uncreated Word of God, see the evidence adduced by Hawting, *Ideal of Idolatry*, p.80.

109. My analysis is indebted to the discussion of Augustine's semiology in Manetti, *Theories of the Sign*, where the author asserts that Augustine's semiology shows "a striking anticipation of some of the most recent semantic research tendencies (instructional model) in the contemporary world" (p. 168).

110. Cited in Chittick, *Self-Disclosure*, p. 5.

111. Cited in Nicholson, *Studies in Islamic Mysticism*, p. 140 n. 1.

112. Scholem, *Major Trends*, pp. 152–153. In that context, Scholem is describing the prophetic kabbalah of Abraham Abulafia, but his words could easily be applied to the theosophic kabbalah propounded, for

instance, by Moses de León, Moses of Burgos, or Joseph Gikatilla, to mention just a few of the prominent figures active in the latter part of the thirteenth century. For an attempt to distinguish different views of language in theosophic and prophetic kabbalah while affirming the shared assumption regarding the ontologized or reified nature of language and the assumption that the Hebrew letters are the constitutive elements of creation, see Idel, "Reification of Language."

113. Babylonian Talmud, Menaḥot 29b. Regarding this text and other cognate rabbinic dicta, see E. Wolfson, *Circle in the Square*, pp. 159–160 n. 23.

114. Gikatilla, *Sefer ha-Niqqud*, p. 4.

115. See references cited in chap. 1, n. 251.

116. Gruenwald, "Preliminary Critical Edition," sec. 19, p. 148. Scholem, "Name of God," p. 75, suggests three possible interpretations of this passage: the name refers to the Tetragrammaton; the reference is to the alphabet itself, which constitutes a mystical name; or the term *shem* does not denote a name in a precise sense but a method of the formation of words. I do not think the first two possibilities need be treated as distinct. That is, the mystical name can refer simultaneously to the divine name and to the letters of the Hebrew alphabet, for the latter are comprised within the former. Kaplan, *Sefer Yetzirah*, p. 125, advances the interpretation of the "one name" as a reference to the Tetragrammaton. Although Kaplan is often anachronistic in his approach, it seems to me that in this particular instance he is not far off the mark. However, I do not agree with his assessment that this passage alludes to the process of combining the twenty-two letters with the letters of the Tetragrammaton, a technique we find in medieval prescriptions for creating the golem. This possibility is suggested as well by Idel, *Golem*, p. 11. In my estimation, the intent of the text in *Sefer Yeṣirah* is that the twenty-two letters themselves constitute the one divine name, which is the source of all that exists.

117. I am in agreement with Pedaya, "'Flaw' and 'Correction,'" p. 160 n. 17, that the "one name" here refers to the Tetragrammaton, the root word of the metaphysical language, Hebrew, the divine source whence all being comes to be. See Pedaya, *Name and Sanctuary*, p. 75. See also S. Brody, "Human Hands Dwell in Heavenly Heights," Ph.D. dissertation, pp. 431–432. In my judgment, this is the original meaning of the expression in *Sefer Yeṣirah*. For a different approach, see Scholem, "Name of God," p. 75; and Idel, *Golem*, p. 13.

118. Scholem, *Kabbalah in Provence*, Appendix, p. 10.

119. See above, n. 65.

120. Azriel of Gerona. *Commentary on Talmudic Aggadoth*, p. 99.

121. See chap. 2, n. 197.

122. Scholem, *Kabbalah in Provence*, Appendix, p. 13; Mopsik, *Grands textes de la Cabale*, pp. 74–75. For analysis of the emanationist doctrine articulated in this passage, see Sendor, "Emergence," vol. 1, pp. 120–121.

123. Lipiner, *Metaphysics of Hebrew*, pp. 100–103; E. Wolfson, "Anthropomorphic Imagery." In *Oṣar Eden Ganuz*, fol. 46a (printed edition, p. 94), Abulafia asserts that it is known to the "enlightened ones of our faith who receive from the truths" (*maskilei dateinu ha-mequbbalim min ha-amitiyyot*) that the "compositions of the body" (*harkavot ha-golem*) are identical to the "compositions of the letters" (*harkavot ha-otiyyot*).

124. *Kitvei Ramban*, 2:454. The linguistic conception of the human body is a principle affirmed by so-called theosophic and ecstatic kabbalists (see below, n. 338), and hence it may be considered an axiom of the esoteric tradition that cuts across the typological lines that have dominated contemporary scholarship.

125. See chap. 1, n. 345.

126. Some kabbalists have affirmed the view that the soul, and not the body, is the image of God, an approach well attested in philosophically inspired exegesis traceable as far back as Philo. See Tishby, *Wisdom of the Zohar*, pp. 679–682.

127. E. Wolfson, "Ontology." It is regrettable that other scholars who have written on this subject have neglected to mention this critical point, thereby leaving the impression that the kabbalists have advocated a humanistic anthropology more equitable towards Jewish women and non-Jews. While this apologetic orientation is understandable and perhaps even desirable in certain homiletical circumstances, I find it to be a

moral failing when scholars tender such a gross and blatant misrepresentation of kabbalistic tradition. An exception is the essay by Ḥallamish, "Relation to the Nations," pp. 289–311. Working independently, we have reached similar conclusions, albeit expressed differently.

128. On the taxonomic centrality of knowledge of the name to understanding the phenomenological contours of kabbalah, see Idel, "Defining Kabbalah," pp. 97–122.

129. Scholem, "Concept of Kavvanah," pp. 165–180; idem, *Origins*, pp. 299–309, 414–430; Idel, *Kabbalah: New Perspectives*, pp. 42–49, 51–55; Pedaya, *Name and Sanctuary*, pp. 73–102; idem, *Vision and Speech*, pp. 137–207; S. Brody, "Human Hands," Ph.D. dissertation, pp. 123–158; Mopsik, *Grands textes*, pp. 88–95.

130. Idel, *Kabbalah: New Perspectives*, pp. 41–42. See also the detailed study by J. Goldberg, "Mystical Union." A similar argument with regard to Sufism in relation to Arab-Islamic philosophy is made by Ernst, "Mystical Language," pp. 192–194.

131. With respect to this dimension of the lived religious experience, Provençal and Spanish kabbalists were indebted to the ideal of contemplative worship cultivated by thinkers of a philosophical bent. A particularly interesting use of the account of intention in Maimonides is cited and explicated in a mystical vein in Asher ben David's *Sefer ha-Yiḥud*. See *R. Asher ben David: His Complete Works*, p. 80; and analysis in E. Wolfson, "Beneath the Wings," pp. 222–223.

132. See below, n. 385.

133. Years ago I began to utilize the term "morphology" as a theoretical alternative to the typological approach championed by Scholem and Idel. For an elaboration of this terminological shift, see J. Goldberg, "Mystical Union," pp. 32–54.

134. Charlesworth, "Portrayal of the Righteous," pp. 135–151; Smelik, "On Mystical Transformation," pp. 122–144; Dimant, "Men as Angels," pp. 93–103; Fletcher-Louis, "4Q374: A Discourse," pp. 236–252; idem, *Luke-Acts*, pp. 185–198; idem, "Some Reflections on Angelomorphic Humanity," pp. 292–312; idem, *All the Glory of Adam*. On angelomorphic Christology, see Barker, *Great Angel*; Longenecker, *Christology of Early Jewish Christianity*, pp. 26–32; Fletcher-Louis, *Luke-Acts*; Bock, *Blasphemy and Exaltation*, pp. 113–183; Gieschen, *Angelomorphic Christology*; Hannah, *Michael and Christ*; Constas, *Proclus of Constantinople*, pp. 300–307. For other pertinent references, see chap. 1, n. 354. On angelification as an ideal of mystical piety, see Morray-Jones, "Transformational Mysticism," pp. 1–31; and E. Wolfson, "*Yeridah la-Merkavah*," pp. 23–26. As one might expect, in later rabbinic texts the angelic status is absorbed into their pietistic conception. Hence the one garbed in a fringed garment for the sake of prayer, study, or other ritual behavior is said to resemble the ministering angels of God. See *Pesiqta Rabbati* 14, 61b–63a; Babylonian Talmud, Shabbat 25b; Nedarim 20b; Qiddushin 72b; Rubin and Kosman, "Clothing of the Primordial Adam," pp. 155–174, esp. pp. 166–168.

135. In some rabbinic texts, inferential knowledge—"understanding one thing from another"—is accorded a privileged place in the epistemological hierarchy. See, for instance, Babylonian Talmud, Shabbat 31a: According to the dictum attributed to Rava, the last of five queries that every Jewish male will be asked at the moment of judgment is *hevanta davar mi-tokh davar* ("have you understood one thing from another?"). And compare Ḥagigah 14a, where the word *nevon* in Isaiah 3:3 is interpreted as *ha-mevin davar mi-tokh davar* ("the one who understands one thing from another"), which is superceded only by "words of Torah that are transmitted silently" (*divrei torah she-nittenah be-laḥash*), a mode of learning encoded in the word *laḥash* from the aforementioned verse, which literally connotes enchanting. In his talmudic commentary, Solomon ben Isaac (Rashi) explains this as a reference to *sitrei torah*, the "mysteries of Torah," communicated clandestinely. According to the teaching attributed to R. Ami in Ḥagigah 13a, the expression *nevon laḥash* is listed as the last of five things (all derived from the same verse in Isaiah) that one must possess before one receives secrets of Torah. In the immediate context, no attempt is made to explain the idiom. On the use of *leḥishah* as a *terminus technicus* in the rabbinic lexicon to demarcate communication of esoteric lore "in a whisper," see Scholem, *Jewish Gnosticism*, p. 58 (consider especially the comment of Hai Gaon cited in n. 10 *ad locum*); Altmann, *Studies in Religious Philosophy*, pp. 129–130; E. Wolfson, "Beyond the Spoken Word," pp. 173–174.

136. Scholem, "Name of God," pp. 71, 167–168. Sendor, "Emergence," vol. 2, p. 57 n. 163, remarks that *ṣefiyyah* for Isaac the Blind "refers to the contemplation or inference of one thing from another, in this

case, an object of inner hearing grasped through an object of inner sight." Basing himself on an explicit remark of Abulafia, Idel, "Reification of Language," pp. 52–53, distinguishes the presumed two types of kabbalah, theosophic and ecstatic, on the grounds that the visual aspect of language is paramount for the former and the vocal aspect for the latter. Assuredly, there is cogency to this typological distinction, but the matter is more complex, inasmuch as both theosophic and ecstatic kabbalists (to use the nomenclature for the sake of the argument) affirm the phenomenon of synesthesia, which is predicated on the mélange of the visual and auditory fields, ontically and experientially. See E. Wolfson, *Through a Speculum*, pp. 287–288. While it is true that some kabbalists emphasize the visual and others the auditory, or it may even be the case that the same kabbalist will at one point stress the former and at another point the latter, the texture of the experience should thwart any proposed dichotomization of the two epistemic modes along presumed typological lines. Even more vexing is the recent formulation in Idel, *Absorbing Perfections*, p. 76. Challenging my thesis regarding the centrality of the iconic dimension of Jewish mysticism, related specifically to contemplation of Torah as a technique for seeing God (some of my work is mentioned on p. 510 n. 158 together with one of Idel's own studies), Idel writes that the visual "should be understood as a less influential tradition in the general economy of Jewish mystical literatures . . . than the recurrent resort to the recitation of the Torah as another technique to induce a mystical experience." Apart from the dubious scholarly practice of making a general pronouncement with no textual backing, this claim rests on the false separation of the visual and auditory; I contend that in the mystical experience, seeing is hearing, and hearing, seeing. Another attempt, learned though it may be, based on an equally faulty dichotomy is found in Pedaya, *Vision and Speech*. The remark of Suhrawardī, cited in Schimmel, *Deciphering the Signs*, p. 156, encapsulates the collapse of the dichotomy precisely: "To listen to the Koran means to listen to God; hearing becomes seeing, seeing becomes hearing, knowing turns into action, action turns into knowing—that is the 'fine hearing.'" Though the conclusion of this statement would seem to privilege hearing, which indeed reflects the central role accorded the oral recitation of the Qur'ān in Muslim prayer ritual (see above, n. 84), the mystical wisdom imparted by Suhrawardī is that listening to the recital of the inscripted word of God is like listening to God, and in listening to God, hearing is seeing and seeing is hearing, just as knowing becomes acting and acting becomes knowing. This succinct formulation well captures what I have tried to articulate with respect to the phenomenology of vision and imagination in kabbalistic sources. See also Graham, "Das Schriftprinzip," pp. 209–226, esp. pp. 220–221. For a well-informed discussion of a similar phenomenon in early Christianity, see Chidester, *Word and Light*. The tendency of kabbalists not to distinguish absolutely between writing and speech was duly noted by Scholem, "Name of God," pp. 71, 167–168; idem, *Origins*, p. 277; D. Biale, *Gershom Scholem*, pp. 99–100. Scholem's view is repeated by Bloom, *Kabbalah and Criticism*, p. 52. The ritual basis for the mystical wisdom can be sought in the fact that the word for Scripture, *miqra*, literally means "what is recited." Hence just as in the case of the Qur'ān in Islam, so Torah in Judaism embodies the oral and written in an inseparable confluence.

137. These words are repeated verbatim in Ezra's commentary to Song 6:3, *Kitvei Ramban* 2:504.

138. That is, the composite and individual entities in the world of differentiation (*olam ha-perud*) which is beneath the world of unity (*olam ha-yiḥud*), the realm of *sefirot*, which are not ontically distinct from the infinite divine being. As Scholem observed ("Concept of Kavvanah," pp. 35, 62–65), the expression *nifradim* to designate differentiated beings reflects an interesting misuse of a technical medieval philosophical Hebraism, *nifrad*, which denotes the incorporeal being; for instance, the nomenclature *sekhalim nifradim* refers to the immaterial intellects attached to each of the spheres. See also extended discussion in Sendor, "Emergence," vol. 1, pp. 130–136.

139. Scholem, *Kabbalah in Provence*, Appendix, pp. 5–6. For analysis of this passage, see Scholem, "Concept of Kavvanah," pp. 165–166; idem, *Origins*, pp. 300–301; S. Brody, "Human Hands," Ph.D. dissertation, pp. 429–430.

140. We can distinguish between writing and speaking, the former associated with a higher emanation than the latter and which thus can be thought of as preceding it. However, just as the emanative scheme can be imagined in a linear way, it also can be imagined cyclically, and when viewed through that prism, there is no lower or higher, before or after. To apply this to the particular example of language, every spoken utter-

ance is an inscripted word and every inscripted word, a spoken utterance, a critical dimension of the kabbalistic worldview duly noted by Scholem. See above, n. 136.

141. Scholem, *Origins*, pp. 264–265.

142. E. Wolfson, *Through a Speculum*, p. 285 n. 54.

143. Scholem, *Kabbalah in Provence*, Appendix, p. 1.

144. Scholem, *Kabbalah in Provence*, Appendix, p. 1; idem, *Origins*, p. 275. Elsewhere in the *Sefer Yeṣirah* commentary, the term *yeniqah* is used to depict the manner by which the lower entities draw the efflux from the sefirotic potencies. See Scholem, *Kabbalah in Provence*, Appendix, p. 9; Sendor, "Emergence," vol. 1, pp. 122–123.

145. The distinction between *yediʿah* and *yeniqah* is not meant to convey anti-intellectualism, a mystical sensibility that is pitted against a speculative or philosophic orientation. On the contrary, the contrast between discursive and intuitive forms of apprehension is an integral part of the Platonic tradition, especially significant in Neoplatonism. See Rappe, *Reading Neoplatonism*, pp. 25–66. Consider also the pertinent discussion on the divergence of discursive philosophy (*al-baḥth*, literally, "investigation") and "divine philosophy" (*taʾalluh*, literally, "becoming God") in Walbridge, *Leaven of the Ancients*, p. 176. The intuitive philosopher attains a higher state than the discursive philosopher, but supreme perfection belongs to one who has mastered both. One can apply a similar model to the speculative kabbalah traced to Isaac the Blind.

146. To be more precise, for the most part Plotinus describes the One in apophatic terms as the "what" that is beyond being, thought, and language, but there are places where he describes the One in kataphatic terms (reminiscent of Aristotle's account of the first principle) as intelligible and as capable of thought. The inconsistency in Plotinus yielded two different approaches in Neoplatonic thought as it evolved in Islamic and then latter Jewish and Christian philosophy, one emphasizing the transcendence of the One (as in the Plotinian *Theology of Aristotle*) and the other identifying the One with the intellect and the ground of being (as in the Proclan *Liber de causis*). See Peterson, "Ḥamīd al-Dīn al-Kirmānī on Creation," pp. 555–567, esp. pp. 560–561. An extensive discussion of the One in Plotinian thought is provided by Bussanich, "Plotinus's Metaphysics of the One," pp. 38–65.

147. Plato, *Republic* 509b 9–10. See also the characterization of the One as above being and description in Plato, *Parmenides* 142a 3.

148. For reference, see chap. 1, n. 307.

149. Aristotle, *De anima* 429a, 13–17. On the appropriation of the Aristotelian epistemology by Plotinus, see Inge, *Philosophy of Plotinus*, vol. 1, pp. 137–138; H. Blumenthal, "Plotinus' Adaptation of Aristotle's Psychology," pp. 41–58.

150. Plotinus, *Enneads* I.6.8. The passage may be viewed as an interpretation of Plato's *Symposium*, 218e–219a. In the context of discussing the distinction between the "semblance of beauty" and the "thing itself," Plato remarks that the "mind's eye begins to see clearly when the outer eyes grow dim."

151. For a detailed study of this theme in late antiquity, see Culianu, *Psychanodia*.

152. Blake, *Complete Poetry and Prose*, p. 225.

153. Plotinus, *Enneads* I.6.9. A similar sentiment is expressed in *Gospel of Philip* 61:21–25, in *Nag Hammadi Codex II, 2–7*, vol. 1, p. 163: In the pleroma, in contrast to this world, when one sees something, one becomes that which one sees even to the point of becoming the Father.

154. Plotinus, *Enneads* I.6.6.

155. For discussion of divine simplicity in Plotinus, see Kenney, *Mystical Monotheism*, pp. 93–111.

156. Plotinus, *Enneads* V.5.6; see also V.3.14, V.4.1–2, VI.7.38.

157. Plotinus, *Enneads* V.5.6.

158. Schroeder, "Vigil of the One," pp. 61–74.

159. E. Wolfson, *Through a Speculum*, pp. 270–272.

160. Wallis, "ΝΟΥΣ as Experience," pp. 121–153.

161. See Miles, *Plotinus on Body and Beauty*.

162. Kingsley, *In the Dark Places*, p. 6. For parallel formulations of the mandate to experience death before one dies in Jewish and Islamic traditions, see chap. 8, n. 151. The theme is expressed as well in Meister

Eckhart, *Sermons and Treatises*, vol. 1, p. 140: "Our Lord ascended into heaven, beyond all light, beyond all understanding and all human ken. . . . Therefore a man must be slain and wholly dead, devoid of self and wholly without likeness, like to none, and then he is really God-like. For it is God's character, His nature, to be peerless and like no man." The theme is rendered in a poem either composed by Eckhart or by one of his disciples, cited p. xxxi: "My soul within / come out, God in! / Sink all my aught / in God's own naught, / sink down in bottomless abyss. / Should I flee thee, / thou wilt come to me; / when self is done, / then Thou art won, / thou transcendental highest bliss!"

163. Hadot, *Plotinus*, p. 32. The passage upon which Hadot bases his comments is *Enneads* IV.4.2: "when one contemplates, especially when the contemplation is clear, one does not turn to oneself in the act of intelligence, but one possesses oneself; one's activity, however, is directed towards the object of contemplation, and one becomes this, offering himself to it as a kind of matter, being formed according to what one sees, and being oneself then only potentially." In *Enneads* VI.8.13, Plotinus expresses the same paradox in volitional terms. The desire of each being is to participate in the Good, but this must be both a freely willed act and reflective of a merging or synchronicity of wills that effaces the ontic independence of the individual will vis-à-vis the will of the Good whence all things emerge and to which they return: "Observe this also: every being in its desire for the Good wants to be that Good rather than what it is, and thinks that it is in the highest degree when it participates in the Good, and in such a state each being will choose for itself to be in so far as it has being from the Good; so the nature of the Good is obviously far more worthy of choice for himself, if it is true that whatever share of the Good there may be in something else is most worthy of choice, and is its freely willed substance which comes to it in accordance with its will and is one and the same thing as its will and is established in existence through its will."

164. Dionysius the Areopagite, *Divine Names*, chap. 5, 825B, p. 171.

165. Ibid., chap. 7, 872A, p. 179. A similar negative dialectic is affirmed in John Scotus Eriugena, the ninth-century Neoplatonic thinker whose Latin translation of the *Corpus Dionysianum* had a decisive influence on medieval philosophy and theology. Eriugena's own *Periphyseon*, which betrays the Dionysian teaching, is presumed to have had a major impact on thinkers in the twelfth and thirteenth centuries, including kabbalists. See Moran, *Philosophy of John Scotus Eriugena*, pp. 186–187, 208. On Eriugena's influence on kabbalists in the thirteenth century, see Prologue, n. 34.

166. From another perspective, contemplation on the part of the human mind can be seen as the mirror opposite of contemplation on the part of the One, that is, the former has the goal of purging the mind of multiplicity and restoring it to unity, whereas the latter is the process by which the unity becomes a multiplicity. See Plotinus, *Enneads* VI.2.6, where contemplation on the part of the One is described as being "the cause of its appearing many, that it may think: for if it appears as one, it did not think, but is that One." To be other than one, the other must not be part of the one, but if there is an other that is not part of the one, the one cannot be one. In the effort to explain the one and the many, one is forced logically to posit two aspects of the one, or two ones, as it were, if one adopts an emanationist scheme, such that the one both is and is not, it is one but it is not many, and yet the many could not be unless it were the one it cannot be. In great measure, the speculative trajectory of these matters springs from Plato's dialectical hypotheses about unity in his dialogue on Parmenides. For relevant texts and detailed analyses, see Plato, *Plato's Parmenides*, pp. 207–339. See also Plato, *Plato and Parmenides: Parmenides' Way of Truth*, pp. 109–115; Tarrant, *Thrasyllan Platonism*, pp. 150–161.

167. The influence of the Plotinian account was quite pronounced in Christian mysticism and occult philosophy. For instance, consider the depiction of the soul's immediate vision of God occasioned by the mental ascent that is consequent to leaving aside cultivation of the body in Ficino, *Platonic Theology*, p. 185: "Having returned thither, it sees God through what is now the very light of God like someone who uses the sun's ray to look at the sun itself and no longer at the colors of bodies."

168. Plotinus, *Enneads* V.8.11.

169. It lies beyond the scope of this chapter to engage the critical question of whether the mystical vision propounded by Plotinus should be viewed as "monistic" or "theistic." For representative studies, see Mamo, "Is Plotinian Mysticism Monistic?" pp. 199–215; Rist, "Back to the Mysticism of Plotinus," pp. 183–197.

See also Oosthout, *Modes of Knowledge*, pp. 75–164, and the discussion in Kristeva, *Tales of Love*, pp. 119–121, on Plotinian ecstasy and the loss of self.

170. Plotinus, *Enneads* V.8.12; on intellect as an image of the first principle, see also V. 4. 2.

171. On the One as everything and nothing, see Bussanich, "Plotinus's Metaphysics," pp. 57–61.

172. Plotinus, *Enneads* V.2.1.

173. Ibid., V.3.13.

174. Ibid., V.8.6; see Schroeder, "Plotinus and Language," pp. 336–355, esp. pp. 350–351.

175. Plotinus, *Enneads* V.8.21.

176. Ibid., V.5.7. For a later influence of these Neoplatonic themes in the *Golshan-e Rāz* of the fourteenth-century Persian poet Mahmūd Shabestarī, explicated in the commentary of Shamsoddin Lāhījī, see Corbin, *Man of Light*, pp. 110–120, esp. p. 116: "The black light . . . is that which cannot itself be seen, because it is the cause of seeing; it cannot be object, since it is absolute Subject. It dazzles, as the light of *superconsciousness* dazzles. . . . Only a knowledge which is a theophanic experience can be knowledge of the divine Being. But in relation to the divine Ipseity, black light, excludes this correlation" (emphasis in original).

177. A learned treatment of the Western apophatic orientation is presented by Carabine, *Unknown God*.

178. Plotinus, *Enneads* V.5.6; see VI.9.5.

179. Ibid., V.3.17. For discussion of the development of this theme, see Brenk, "Darkly beyond the Glass," pp. 39–60.

180. Hancock, "Negative Theology in Gnosticism and Neoplatonism," p. 180. Hancock's study is important for it provides a model to problematize the schematic polarization of the "two philosophical Hellenistic schools" (p. 167), Neoplatonism and Gnosticism, by demonstrating the affinity of the two with regard to the inability to converse or to speculate about the highest God. Hancock suggests, moreover, that respect for the "transcendent goal of moral life" entailed by the negative theology in both schools helps explain the influence of these two trends on medieval Christian apophasis. This approach could prove helpful in understanding the complex interweave of different threads that make up the intellectual cloth of medieval kabbalah in such a manner that one would avoid the radical split between Neoplatonic and Gnostic influences such as we occasionally find in Scholem, for instance in *Origins*, p. 264. Also apposite is the opinion of Jonas, *Gnostic Religion*, pp. 91–92, that gnostic imagery has to be contextualized in the history of allegory in Greek philosophy, an exegetical strategy that facilitated the appropriation of concrete tales and figures of mythical lore as a symbolic mode to express abstract ideas. Jonas goes on to distinguish "gnostic allegory" from the more conventional type inasmuch as the former is often of a subversive nature and hence does not uphold the primary aim of integration and synthesis. I am not certain of the necessity to contrast subversive and conventional uses of allegory, but what is important for my purposes is the recognition on the part of Jonas that an intrinsic component of the gnostic imagination is the rendering of philosophical ideas in concrete mythic symbols. In this regard, there is once again a striking correspondence between late-antique Gnosticism and medieval kabbalah. For a fuller discussion of Gnosticism and the "classical mind," see Jonas, pp. 239–289.

181. McGinn, *Foundations of Mysticism*, pp. 118, 141.

182. Compare Gregory of Nyssa, *Commentary on the Song of Songs*, I.331, p. 206: "through baptism the bride has once and for all removed her sandals." On Gregory's interpretation of the blatantly erotic images of the Song as instruments by which carnal desire can be domesticated into the spiritual love of Christ, symbolized by the male lover, culminating in the discarding of images altogether as one enters the "apophatic space" of the Holy of Holies, which is identified as the Song, to encounter God in the luminal darkness of unknowing, see G. Ward, "Allegoria," pp. 286–287; R. Norris, "Soul Takes Flight," p. 526; Laird, "Under Solomon's Tutelage," pp. 81–88.

183. Gregory of Nyssa, *Life of Moses*, 2.19, p. 59. I have availed myself of the Greek text printed together with the French translation in idem, *La vie de Moïse*. All references to Greek marked parenthetically are taken from and refer to the pagination of this edition. For a nuanced gender analysis of Gregory's account of the vision of Moses at the "virginal" thorny bush and his subsequent entry into the cloud of thick darkness, see Burrus, *"Begotten, Not Made,"* pp. 125–129.

184. Gregory of Nyssa, *Life of Moses*, 2.24, p. 60 (Gk text, p. 120).
185. Ibid., 2.25, p. 60 (Gk text, p. 120).
186. Ibid., 2.26, p. 60.
187. Ibid., 2.27, p. 61 (Gk text, p. 122).
188. Gregory of Nyssa, *Contra eunomium libri*, I:11, 416A; and see discussion on the theme of the transposition of the image in Balthasar, *Presence and Thought*, 163–169. See also Pottier, *Dieu et le Christ*, pp. 233–243.
189. Gregory of Nyssa, *Life of Moses*, 2.162, pp. 94–95.
190. Ibid., 2.162, p. 95 (Gk text, p. 210).
191. Ibid., 2.163, p. 95 (Gk text, p. 210). Gregory's exegesis of the entry of Moses into a cloud of darkness as symbolic of the soul's contemplation of the unseen and unattainable realm, the mystery in which God dwells, is repeated in his *Commentary on the Song of Songs*, J.181, p. 130, and J.322–323, p. 202. See also Gregory's explication of the sixth beatitude, "Blessed are the pure in heart, for they shall see God" (Matt. 5:6), printed in Gregory of Nyssa, *Lord's Prayer*, pp. 143–153.
192. *De mutatione nominum* 7–8; *De posteritate Caini* 14; *De gigantibus* 54; *De vita Mosis* I, 158; H. Wolfson, *Philo*, vol. 2, p. 155; Gregory of Nyssa, *Life of Moses*, p. 177 n. 192.
193. D. Hart, "Mirror of the infinite," pp. 111–131.
194. McGinn, *Foundations of Mysticism*, pp. 157–182. For other references, see chap. 1, n. 61.
195. Dionysius the Areopagite, *Pseudo-Dionysius*, pp. 49–50.
196. Ibid., p. 53.
197. Ibid., pp. 108–109. The Dionysian perspective is elaborated in less technical terms in the fourteenth-century anonymous English treatise *The Cloud of Unknowing*; see Walsh, *Cloud of Unknowing*, chap. 70, p. 256.
198. Dionysius the Areopagite, *Pseudo-Dionysius*, p. 54.
199. Ibid., p. 109.
200. Ibid., p. 137.
201. Ibid., p. 109.
202. Ibid., p. 263.
203. For a detailed study of this kabbalistic doctrine, see Idel, "*Sefirot* above the *Sefirot*."
204. Scholem, *Kabbalah in Provence*, Appendix, p. 3.
205. I borrow this richly ambiguous locution from Sells, *Mystical Languages*.
206. On this important philosophical point, see D. Turner, *Darkness of God*, p. 35. See also S. Katz, "Mystical Speech and Mystical Meaning," pp. 3–41; idem, "Utterance and Ineffability," pp. 279–298; E. Wolfson, "Negative Theology and Positive Assertion," pp. v–xxii.
207. The meaning of the expression *remez ha-maḥshavah* is clarified by its use in the commentary on the *sefirot* by Azriel of Gerona, cited above at n. 64.
208. *Kitvei Ramban*, 2:409. For further explication of this passage, see Idel, "*Sefirot* above the *Sefirot*," pp. 265–267; idem, *Absorbing Perfections*, pp. 119–120; E. Wolfson, "Beyond the Spoken Word," p. 199.
209. Maimonides, *Mishneh Torah*, Yesodei ha-Torah 2:10.
210. Maimonides, *Guide* II:6, pp. 262–263.
211. Consider Scholem's sketch, *Origins*, p. 377: "With Jacob ben Shesheth, the kabbalists appear on the battlefield for the first time, undisguised. The enemy is unmistakable: the radical philosophic enlightenment of the adherents of Maimonides." In support of his characterization, Scholem cites one of Jacob's works, *Meshiv Devarim Nekhoḥim*, which is an explicit rebuttal of Samuel Ibn Tibbon's *Ma'amar Yeqqawu ha-Mayim*, a cosmology (*ma'aseh bere'shit*) based on Maimonidean thought. Scholem himself nuances his argument when he notes that the polemical thrust is directed more at Ibn Tibbon than Maimonides. The heretical views were introduced into the "system" of Maimonides, which in itself was "in Jacob's opinion very close to the true theology and therefore to the Kabbalah, as he frequently and triumphantly notes whenever he believes that he can demonstrate that his adversary misunderstood the views of Maimonides" (p. 378); see p. 381, where Scholem notes that Jacob ben Sheshet sides with Maimonides with respect to the right of each interpreter to devise his own reasons for the commandments.
212. Scholem, *Kabbalah in Provence*, Appendix, p. 5.

213. My reflections here were inspired by the observations of W. Lowe, *Theology and Difference*, pp. 79–80. A similar affirmation of ostensible clashing views is found in the Sufi antinomy of *tanzīh* and *tashbīḥ*, the former declaring the incomparability of the one true entity (*wujūd*), the essence whose existence is necessary, vis-à-vis all other things, which are considered contingent, and the latter declaring the similarity between God and all things. See below, n. 280.

214. See chap. 1, n. 263.

215. *Zohar* 3:152a.

216. Liebes, *Studies in the Zohar*, pp. 45–46. This is one of several attempts in zoharic literature to delineate four levels of meaning in Scripture. Whatever the historical or textual origins of this seminal idea, from the relevant kabbalistic sources it is evident that it was formulated as an elaboration of the principle of dual meaning, the internal and external, esoteric and exoteric. See Bacher, "L'exegese biblique," pp. 33–46, esp. pp. 37–40; idem, "Das Merkwort PRDS," pp. 294–305; Scholem, *On the Kabbalah and Its Symbolism*, pp. 50–65; Tishby, *Wisdom of the Zohar*, pp. 1077–1089; Heide, "Pardes," pp. 147–159; Idel, "Pardes: Some Reflections," pp. 249–268; idem, "Zohar as Exegesis," pp. 89–91; idem, *Absorbing Perfections*, pp. 429–437; Huss, "NiSAN," pp. 155–181; S. Katz, "Mysticism and the Interpretation of Sacred Scripture," pp. 21–32. Some scholars, including Bacher and Scholem, suggested the kabbalists derived the four levels of meaning from parallel Christian modes of interpretation. Regarding the fourfold sense of Scripture in Christian mysticism, see the lucid and relatively recent account in Cousins, "Fourfold Sense of Scripture," pp. 118–137.

217. *Zohar* 1:20b; 2:75b–76a; *Sefer ha-Mishkal*, pp. 44, 159.

218. For an insightful exposition of kabbalistic hermeneutics against a broader framework of religious culture in the Middle Ages, see Talmage, "Apples of Gold," pp. 313–355.

219. See the language employed by de León in the passage from *Shushan Edut* cited in chap. 1, n. 323. Another relevant passage appears in *Zohar* 2:61b, where the following response is given to the hypothetical question of whether it is really the case that the members of the mystical fraternity engaged in Torah study are sustained by the spiritual food that angels eat, the "bread of the mighty," *leḥem abirim* (Ps. 78:25), the overflow of divine wisdom: "No, it is like that very food, for two are balanced on one" (*de-shaqil al ḥad terein*). The concluding phrase conveys the image of the scale upon which two independent things are weighed together and brought into balance. The food consumed by kabbalists is not exactly what is eaten by angels, but it is plausible to say that the former is in the likeness of the latter. For extended discussion of the motif of eating in zoharic kabbalah, see Hecker, "Each Man Ate An Angel's Meal"; idem, "Eating Gestures," pp. 125–152. The word *shaqil* in the sense of comparing one thing to another is used in other passages in zoharic literature. See *Zohar* 1:153b, where the word is employed in the context of discussing the parallelism between the mundane and divine spheres, and especially *Zohar* 3:64a, where the three books traditionally ascribed to Solomon—Song of Songs, Ecclesiastes, and Proverbs—are correlated respectively with Wisdom (*ḥokhmah*), Understanding (*tevunah*), and Knowledge (*daʿat*). The description of the latter sheds light on the zoharic approach to parables: "Proverbs corresponds to Knowledge. How is this manifest? All of the verses have two aspects [*terei gawwenei*], the beginning and end, two aspects that are disclosed [*itḥazyyan*]. When one contemplates the verses, the [beginning] is contained in the [end], and the [end] is contained in the [beginning]. Thus it corresponds to Knowledge [*shaqil laqableih de-daʿat*]." Interestingly, the author of this passage follows the standard view regarding the twofold structure of the parable, as one finds, for instance, in the introduction to the *Guide of the Perplexed* by Maimonides, but there is a shift from the inner/outer orientation to the beginning/end distinction. The nature of parabolic truth illumines one in the wisdom that the one is contained in the other. Finally, it is worth mentioning the title of a treatise composed by Moses de León in 1290, *Sefer ha-Mishqal*, literally the "Book of Balance." The author gave the work another name, *Sefer Nefesh ha-Ḥokhmah*, which was used in the edition of the work published in Basel 1608. The latter title signals the main purpose of the book, which is to elucidate the kabbalistic mysteries pertaining to the nature of the Jewish soul. The former title, I surmise, relates to the enterprise of speaking about the divine emanations, which by necessity requires the symbolic correlation of disparate realities, the figural representation of the incorporeal God in anthropomorphic terms, an envisioning that makes possible the more specific discourse about the soul and its resemblance to the divine. It is possible that de León has this poetic process in

mind when he uses the expression *mishqal ha-ḥokhmah*, the "balance of wisdom." See Moses de León, *Sefer ha-Mishkal*, pp. 34–35. It is of interest to recall as well that Moses de León begins *Sheqel ha-Qodesh*, pp. 1–3, with a philosophical discussion (in the vein of Maimonides) on the incorporeality of God and the meaning of biblical anthropomorphism. Perhaps the meaning of the title is not "sacred coin" but "holy weight," the imaginal envisioning of God based on the inherently analogical nature of language. For a somewhat different explanation of the titles of Moses de León's works, see E. Wolfson, *Circle in the Square*, p. 182 n. 128. In that context, I suggested that the words *mishqal* and *sheqel* denote the phallic potency, which is compared to the "tongue" that balances two sides of the scale.

220. *Zohar* 2:98b. For fuller discussion of this passage, see E. Wolfson, "Beautiful Maiden," pp. 169–172. The more typical approach on the part of scholars has been to dichotomize the exoteric and esoteric layers of meaning. See, for instance, the discussion of *sod* as "coded meaning" in Rojtman, *Black Fire on White Fire*, pp. 68–98.

221. See chap. 1, n. 260.

222. My analysis finds support in Marion's discussion of the paradox of the face, *In Excess*, pp. 113–119, esp. pp. 115–116.

223. Perhaps implicit in the symbol of the tongue when associated with *Shekhinah* is the kabbalistic understanding of Oral Torah. For an explicit correlation along these lines, see Joseph of Hamadan, *Sefer Tashak*, p. 318.

224. My explication is supported by *Zohar* 1:228a: "The holy spirit is called *zo't*, which is the mystery of the covenant [*raza di-verit*], the holy inscription [*reshima qaddisha*] that is found constantly with the person." The exact formulation recurs in *Zohar* 2:236b. The gender transposition of *Shekhinah* is thus related to the fact that the word *zo't*, the feminine demonstrative pronoun, is identified as the covenantal sign affixed to the male organ. It is in this capacity that *Shekhinah* assumes the character of the holy spirit. Needless to say, the symbolism is older than the period of the zoharic fraternity. See, for instance, Azriel of Gerona, *Commentary on Talmudic Aggadoth*, p. 49.

225. *Zohar* 3:60b–61a.

226. A number of scholars have analyzed this section of zoharic literature. See Oron, "Place Me as a Seal upon Your Heart," pp. 1–24; Giller, *Reading the Zohar*, pp. 35–68; D. Abrams, "Knowing the Maiden," pp. lix–lxxxiii; and further references in following note.

227. Scholem, *On the Kabbalah and Its Symbolism*, pp. 55–56; Talmage, "Apples of Gold," pp. 316–318; Idel, *Kabbalah: New Perspectives*, pp. 227–229; Tishby, *Wisdom of the Zohar*, pp. 1084–1085; David Stern, *Parables in Midrash*, pp. 230–231; Liebes, "Zohar and Eros," pp. 87–98; E. Wolfson, *Through a Speculum*, pp. 384–387. On the representation of the female body as text, see Scholes, *Semiotics and Interpretation*, 127–141; and Benstock, *Textualizing the Feminine*.

228. For instance, see the commentary on "And Adam knew his wife Eve" (Gen. 4:1) in *Zohar Ḥadash*, 63c: "'And Adam'—this is the hidden, primordial Adam, engraved in the supernal, subtle engravings. 'Knew'—what he did not comprehended of it before. He knew how to be face-to-face. When they gazed face-to-face for the sake of intercourse, it is written 'knew,' for he knew how to irrigate her, to inseminate her with seed, to produce offspring."

229. E. Wolfson, "Beautiful Maiden," pp. 169–170, 185–187. On the twofold task of the mask to veil and to reveal, see the study "Die Maske: Verhüllung oder Offenbarung?" in Bleeker, *Sacred Bridge*, pp. 236–249.

230. The point is captured in the Arabic *taʿbīr* ("interpretation") from *ʿubūr* ("crossing over"). For the enlightened mystics, the "Folk of Allah," as opposed to the rationalist philosophers and theologians, the crossing over from exoteric to esoteric is not predicated on discarding the former. See Chittick, *Sufi Path of Knowledge*, p. 245; see also Corbin, *Creative Imagination*, pp. 28–29.

231. My analysis of the zoharic passage accords with the insights of Izutsu, *Creation and the Timeless Order*, pp. 40–41, regarding the metaphorical understanding of the Sufi use of the word *nūr* ("light"). Izutsu begins the argument by following an Aristotelian interpretation of metaphor as a word with a "double role," "pointing at the same time to two different meanings [A and B], the first being its literal or conventional meaning and the second its non-conventional or figurative meaning" (p. 40). Having established that, he

proposes *nūr* in the Sufi context as an example of metaphor, inasmuch as the term refers concurrently to physical and spiritual light. Izutsu proceeds to show how the Sufi hermeneutic reverses the relationship between literal and metaphorical—the real, the supreme metaphysical reality, is the light seen with the "eye of spiritual vision" (*ʿayn al-basīrah*), whereas physical light is merely a figure of speech. It follows that the term *nūr* "functions as an *immediate sign* for the spiritual light and as a *mediate sign* for the physical" (p. 41; emphasis in original). Finally, it would be instructive to explore in more detail the connotation of the term *remiza* in the zoharic context and the use of *ramz* in Islamic esotericism to denote "symbolic speech," that is, speaking through parable or allusion. For discussion of this technical terminology, see Bürgel, "Symbols and Hints," pp. 114–132, esp. pp. 117–122; Gutas, *Avicenna and the Aristotelian Tradition*, pp. 299–307; Heath, *Allegory and Philosophy in Avicenna*, pp. 151–155.

232. Consider the comment of Neumann, *Origins*, p. 53: "The 'bridal veil' must be understood in this sense, as the symbol of *kedesha*, the harlot. She is 'unknown,' i.e., anonymous. To be 'unveiled' means to be naked, but this is only another form of anonymity. Always the goddess, the transpersonal, is the real and operative factor." Neumann insightfully grasps that the unveiling of the harlot is not a form of exposure but another masquerade, not a disclosure of her name but an ascription of anonymity. But why is this so? How can we conceive of unveiling as masking? That which is real—whose face we seek to expose and whose name we seek to disclose—is the goddess, the transpersonal that is forever beyond the confines of any particular manifestation. To translate Neumann's language into a kabbalistic idiom, every gradation is a mask by which that which has no face appears, the transpersonal, Ein Sof, that which is beyond any and all representation and hence may be considered the catalyst for the multifaceted imaginary representations, the drawing of verbal icons—visual signs—in the poetic imagination of the contemplative kabbalist.

233. The paradox is captured in the Zen maxim, "Face to face a thousand miles away" (Hori, *Zen Sand*, p. 143), read in correlation with a second dictum, "When you're face to face, it's hard to hide" (p. 147).

234. On the nexus of woman, text, veil, poetry, and the elusive nature of (un)truth, see T. Rosen, *Unveiling Eve*, pp. 64–82.

235. See Mernissi, *Beyond the Veil*; idem, *Veil and the Male Elite*, pp. 85–101; A.-E. Berger, "Newly Veiled Woman," pp. 93–119; Hoodfar, "Veil in Their Minds," pp. 420–446; Minces, *La femme voilée*; Hekmat, *Women and the Koran*, pp. 181–213. For a similar phenomenon in the case of Jewish women, see Stillman, "Cover Her Face," pp. 13–31. On the connection of the veil and scopic desire in contemporary texts, see Hitchcock, "Eye and the Other," pp. 69–81.

236. Knysh, *Islamic Mysticism*, pp. 311–314.

237. It is worth noting in this context the use of the image of garbing on the part of kabbalists to denote the emanative process, a theme they connect with the midrashic dictum in *Genesis Rabbah* 3:4 (linked exegetically to Ps. 104:2) that God created the primordial light by donning a garment and shining forth the brilliance of his splendor. See, for instance, the remark of Ezra of Gerona in *Perush Shir ha-Shirim, Kitvei Ramban*, 2:493, that the word *salmah* ("cloak") denotes "the summoning of the emanation of wisdom that encompasses everything" (*hazmanat hamshakhat ha-ḥokhmah ha-sovevet et ha-kol*). The rabbinic image of God wrapping himself with the garment signifies that "he received the splendor from this effluence and the light verily sparkled." In his letter to Abraham ben Isaac, the cantor of Gerona, published by Scholem, "New Document," pp. 157–158, Ezra employs very similar language to depict the emanative process, the "splendor of wisdom, which is his garment" (*zohar ha-ḥokhmah she-hu levusho*). The same interpretation is attributed to Isaac the Blind, referred to by the honorific title "our master, the pious one" (*rabbenu he-ḥasid*) by Azriel of Gerona, *Commentary on Talmudic Aggadoth*, pp. 110–111. For analysis of this theme and its exegetical trajectory, see Altmann, *Studies*, pp. 128–139.

238. In light of the qur'ānic emphasis on the removal of the veil on the day of reckoning, it is of interest to consider the remark in Merlin Swartz, *Medieval Critique of Anthropomorphism*, p. 277: "I heard the following tradition [from ʿAbd al-Wahhāb b. al-Mubārak] in which Sahl b. Saʿd reports that the Prophet said: '[On the day of judgment] God will be concealed by seventy thousand veils of light and darkness. No one will hear even the slightest sound from [behind?] those veils else he would perish.'"

239. Ziai, *Knowledge and Illumination*, pp. 155–166; idem, "Ḥāfeẓ, Lisān al-Ghayb," p. 463. On the Sufi

notion of the time-atom severed from past and future, see Massignon, "Time in Islamic Thought," pp. 108–114, esp. pp. 110–111; Böwering, "Ideas of Time in Persian Sufism," pp. 223–225. I have discussed the matter elsewhere (chap. 2 of *Alef, Mem, Tau*) and thus will not repeat all of the intricate details related to this rudimentary Sufi notion. Let me simply state that the atomistic conception of time is the temporal correlate to the ontological paradox of *fanā'* and *baqā'* the identity of perishing and abiding. To grasp the mystical ideal of passing away and enduring in the oneness of what is, one must take hold of the mystery of time disclosed in the moment that endures in its elapsing. Consider Ibn ʿArabī's explication of the qur'ānic verse "Everything will perish except his own face" (28:88) in his *Futūḥāt al-makkiyya*, cited in Chittick, *Self-Disclosure*, p. 156: "The pronoun that modifies 'face' goes back to 'thing' and it also goes back to the Real. You accord with that in which you stand, for you are the companion of a [present] moment [*waqt*]." See F. Rosenthal, "Ibn ʿArabī between 'Philosophy' and 'Mysticism,'" p. 29.

240. Sells, *Early Islamic Mysticism*, p. 284.

241. Izutsu, *Creation and the Timeless Order*, pp. 11–13, 76–77; Sells, *Early Islamic Mysticism*, pp. 43–45; Abrahamov, *Divine Love in Islamic Mysticism*, pp. 27 and 61–66.

242. Margaret Smith, *Rābiʿa the Mystic*, p. 121; Abrahamov, *Divine Love*, p. 27.

243. Sells, *Early Islamic Mysticism*, p. 155.

244. For discussion of the different facets of Rābiʿa's asceticism, see Margaret Smith, *Rābiʿa*, pp. 40–52, and her account of the celibate lifestyle of other women saints in Islam, pp. 195–205.

245. On depictions of Mary in the Qur'ān and subsequent Islamic tradition, see Robson, "Stories of Jesus and Mary," pp. 236–243; Smith and Haddad, "Virgin Mary in Islamic Tradition," pp. 161–187; N. Robinson, "Jesus and Mary in the Qur'ān," pp. 161–175; idem, *Christ in Islam and Christianity*, pp. 4–7, 45; Hagemann and Pulsfort, *Maria, die Mutter Jesu*; Ayoub, *Qur'an and Its Interpreters*, vol. 2, pp. 93–107, 122–135; Schimmel, *Mystical Dimensions*, p. 429; idem, "Jesus and Mary as Poetical Images," pp. 143–157; Schleifer, *Mary the Blessed Virgin*;; Leirvik, *Images of Jesus Christ*, pp. 23–27; Austin, "Sophianic Feminine," pp. 243–244; Marshall, "Christianity in the Qur'ān," pp. 4–7, 11–18; Hammad, *Mary, the Chosen Woman*. It is worth mentioning in this connection that the affirmation of the Virgin Birth in Islamic tradition was utilized by medieval Christian polemicists, for example, Peter the Venerable, to bolster the claim that Jews are worse than Muslims. On this point, see A. Abulafia, "Intellectual and Spiritual Quest," p. 63. On the reverence for Mary in contemporary Sufi teaching, see, for instance, al-Jerrahi, *Blessed Virgin Mary*.

246. Margaret Smith, *Rābiʿa*, p. 21.

247. In Q 3:35–36, Maryam is identified as the daughter of ʿImrān and in 19:28 she is referred to as the "sister of Aaron," indicating that there was a conflation of Miriam of the Old Testament, the daughter of Amran and sister of Moses and Aaron (Num. 26:59), and Mary of the New Testament, the wife of Joseph and mother of Jesus. The confusion was noted from a relatively early period by Christians as a polemical strategy to underscore misrepresentations of the New Testament in the Qur'ān, although it is possible that the conflation in its inception was not a distortion but reflects a typological interpretation, perhaps traceable to some branch of Syrian Christianity, that linked Miriam and Mary. See N. Robinson, *Christ in Islam*, pp. 9, 18–19, and Ayoub, *Qur'an and Its Interpreters*, vol. 2, pp. 88–92; Bauschke, *Jesus im Koran*, pp. 13–33.

248. In Q 4:156, the people of the book (*ahl al-kitāb*), which in this context refers exclusively to the Jews and not to Jews and Christians (for a thorough discussion of this appellation, see Busse, *Islam, Judaism, and Christianity*, pp. 29–62, and see below, n. 275), are said to be punished for various reasons, including "their disbelief and their imputing to Mary a great falsehood." The nature of the falsehood is not specified, but it is likely that there is an allusion here to one of the disparaging ways that Jews cast Mary in order to discredit the Christian narrative, for example, dismissing the belief in the virginal conception by identifying the father of Jesus as a Roman soldier, implying thereby that Mary was guilty of adultery, or depicting Jesus as *ben niddah*, literally "son of a menstruant," a title that not only challenges the alleged virginity of Mary but also suggests that Jesus was conceived while she was menstruating, an accusation that implies her failure to observe traditional Jewish purity laws. For select references to these themes, see E. Wolfson, "Re/membering the Covenant," pp. 234 n. 23 and 236–237 n. 39. Along with the sources mentioned there, see as well Y. Deut-

sch, "New Evidence," pp. 177–197, esp. p. 182. Deutsch raises the possibility that the designation *ben niddah* is a later interpolation dating from the fifteenth century, with the earlier texts emphasizing that Jesus was the offspring of an adulterous act. The insinuation of sexual immorality on the part of Mary is also implied in Q 19:28. It is of interest to consider in this connection the exegesis of Q 19:16–17 that links the retreat of Mary behind the curtain to her purifying herself from menstrual impurity. See Kisāʾi, *Tales of the Prophets*, p. 328; B. Wheeler, *Moses in the Quran*, pp. 77–79, 120. Finally, it is worth recalling the comment in Q 33:53 about the proper etiquette of requesting something from a woman who is situated "before a screen."

249. Jesus, or as he is referred to in the Qurʾān, ʿĪsā ibn Maryam or simply ibn Maryam, is identified as a prophet (*nabī*), servant (*ʿabd*), messenger (*rasūl*), word (*kalima*), spirit (*rūḥ*), and the anointed one (*al-masīḥ*), but there is a categorical rejection of identifying him as the son of God or as a member of the Trinity. See Q 9:30, where Jews and Christians are both condemned for identifying a human figure as the son of God, for the former, ʿUzair (that is, Ezra), and for the latter, Jesus. For a representative list of studies dedicated to the portrayals of Jesus in Islam, see Parrinder, *Jesus in the Qurʾan*; Wismer, *Islamic Jesus*; Räisänen, "Portrait of Jesus," pp. 122–133; Nurbakhsh, *Jesus in the Eyes of the Sufis*; Busse, *Islam, Judaism, and Christianity*, pp. 113–137; ur-Raḥim, *Jesus: Prophet of Islam*; N. Robinson, *Christ in Islam*; Leuze, *Christentum und Islam*, pp. 56–71; Cragg, *Jesus and the Muslim*; Zebiri, "Contemporary Muslim Understanding," pp. 71–90; Leirvik, *Images of Jesus Christ*; Bauschke, *Jesus im Koran*. On the question of the divinity of Christ from the Muslim perspective, see also Ljamai, *Ibn Hazm et la polémique*, pp. 103–109.

250. See as well Q 5:116–117, where worship of Jesus or Mary is steadfastly rejected. On the possibility that the presentation of Christian faith in the relevant qurʾānic verses reflects some heterodox interpretation, for example, identifying the Trinity as God, Jesus, and Mary (who is sometimes referred to as "Theotokos," the God-bearer), see Goddard, *Muslim Perceptions of Christianity*, pp. 14–15. Needless to say, the question of the representations of Jesus and Mary in Islamic scripture, tradition, and commentaries is a vast and complex subject that has been discussed by several notable scholars. The view I have expressed is based solely on qurʾānic verses and hence does not deal adequately with the phenomenon of Islamic Christology. In addition to the relevant scholarly discussions mentioned in nn. 245 and 249, see Mahmud Mustafa Ayoub, "Jesus the Son of God," pp. 65–81.

251. Cragg, *Jesus and the Muslim*, p. 32.

252. Leirvik, *Images of Jesus Christ*, p. 96. Schimmel, "Jesus and Mary," pp. 143–145, emphasizes the importance of the portrayal of Jesus as the ideal ascetic in Sufi sources.

253. On the impact of the figure of Virgin Mary on the formation of the narrative accounts of Rābiʿa, see Baldick, "Legend of Rābiʿa of Basra," pp. 233–247. Relevant to this orientation is Rūmī's comparison of the body to Mary and the spirit to Jesus, as noted by Ridgeon, *Crescents on the Cross*, pp. 38–39.

254. Qushayrī, *Principles of Sufism*, p. 143.

255. Schimmel, *Mystical Dimensions*, pp. 167–178.

256. Schimmel, *Mystical Dimensions*, p. 112; Knysh, *Islamic Mysticism*, pp. 71–72.

257. The paradox is poetically captured by al-Junayd, as cited in Sells, *Early Islamic Mysticism*, pp. 254–255: "My annihilation is my abiding. From the reality of my annihilation, he annihilated me from both my abiding and my annihilation. I was, upon the reality of annihilation, without being or annihilation, through my abiding and annihilation, for the existence (*wujūd*) of annihilation in abiding, for the existence of my other is my annihilation. . . . He abides in your abiding, that is, the unity of the affirmer of unity abides through the abiding of the one who is one, even as the affirmer of unity passes away. Then you are you. You lacked yourself, and then you came to abide insofar as you passed away." See also p. 260: "He annihilated my construction just as he constructed me originally in the condition of my annihilation."

258. Ibid., p. 255. Compare the formulation of al-Qushayrī translated by Sells, *Early Islamic Mysticism*, p. 120: "Whoever is seized by the sovereign power of reality, to the point that he no longer witnesses any vision, vestige, trace, or ruin of the others, is said to have passed away from creatures and to endure through the real."

259. Ibid., p. 223.

260. Ibid., p. 121. On the Sufi ideal of extinction in and unity with God, see Ritter, *Ocean of the Soul*, pp. 593–614.

261. Böwering, "Ideas of Time," pp. 223–225.

262. Nicholson, *Kashf al-Maḥjūb*, p. 250. On the distinction between the "veil of covering" (*ḥijāb-i raynī*), which can never be removed, and the "veil of clouding" (*ḥijāb-i ghaynī*), which is removable, see Nicholson, *Kashf al-Maḥjūb*, pp. 4–5, 391; Chittick, "Paradox of the Veil," pp. 65–67.

263. Nicholson, *Kashf al-Maḥjūb*, p. 274.

264. Ibid., p. 22.

265. Ibid., p. 149; see also p. 325. On the use of the image of being hidden behind the veil to denote ignorance, see Moezzi, *Divine Guide*, pp. 166–167 n. 197.

266. Nicholson, *Kashf al-Maḥjūb*, p. 374. The Sufi terms *qabḍ* and *basṭ* are reminiscent of two pairs of terms in Lurianic kabbalah, *hitpashṭut* and *histalqut* (expansion and withdrawal), and *gadlut* and *qaṭnut* (augmentation and diminution). Both pairs denote states of the theogonic myth, but they also apply psychologically to the consciousness of individuals. Although the later is more commonly associated with the metamorphosis of Lurianic theosophy in Hasidism, a careful reading of the sixteenth- and seventeenth-century kabbalistic sources yields no sound reason to separate the ontological and psychological. As I discussed in chapter 1, kabbalists affirm a consubstantiality of divine and human, and hence to contemplate the one is to contemplate the other, an idea that I developed on the basis of the essay by my teacher, Alexander Altmann (see chap. 1, n. 302). If that insight is properly heeded, there is no conceptual basis for the distinction between the theosophical and psychological when one considers the phenomenological orientation of medieval kabbalists.

267. Nicholson, *Kashf al-Maḥjūb*, p. 414.

268. Chittick, *Self-Disclosure*, pp. 106–108. One of the most elaborate accounts of the revelatory experience of unveiling (*kashf*) is found in *Ḥikmat al-ishrāq*, the "Wisdom of Illumination," by the twelfth-century Persian mystic, Suhrawardī. I cannot possibly do justice to Suhrawardī's complex blending of eastern spirituality and Neoplatonic philosophy in this note. Let me simply remark that, in accord with the latter, he affirms the possibility of the soul separating from the body and ascending mentally to the higher realm, where it contemplates by way of "unveiling and intuition" the intelligible lights without veils linked to the hindrance of corporeality, culminating in a pure vision of the Light of Lights, the formless and imageless source of all being, the "true King" who "possesses the essence of everything but whose essence is possessed by none." See Suhrawardī, *Philosophy of Illumination*, p. 96; Razavi, *Suhrawardi and the School of Illumination*, pp. 87–92.

269. I note, parenthetically, as Meier has pointed out in *Essays on Islamic Piety and Mysticism*, pp. 400–420, esp. pp. 408–409, as early as the ninth century the practice of veiling the face could also symbolize the mystery of sanctity, that is, he who veiled his face was thought to be the incarnation of the hidden and impenetrable light of the divine. Like Moses, according to Hebrew scriptures (Exod. 34:33–35), the holy man in Islam had to veil his face so that the radiance of his countenance would not harm others. See chap. 3, n. 153. On the use of this theme in later Islamic exegesis, see B. Wheeler, *Moses in the Quran*, p. 32.

270. On the creed that God spoke directly to Moses in Muslim faith, see Merlin Swartz, *Medieval Critique of Anthropomorphism*, p. 276 n. 480.

271. Nicholson, *Mathnawī*, 5:233–234.

272. Babylonian Talmud, Yevamot 49b.

273. Sells, *Early Islamic Mysticism*, p. 80.

274. al-Kalābādhī, *Doctrine of the Ṣūfīs*, p. 117.

275. See above, n. 248.

276. For other accounts of the sin of the golden calf, see Q 7:138–140, 148–153, 20:83–98; U. Rubin, *Between Bible and Qur'ān*, pp. 100–113; idem, "Traditions in Transformation," pp. 196–214, esp. pp. 201–209. The depiction of Jews as idolaters and promoters of anthropomorphic-corporealist views of God, in part supported by the scriptural narrative regarding the golden calf, continued to be a major ploy in the medieval Islamic polemic against Judaism. See Hawting, *Idea of Idolatry*, pp. 75–85. For an attenuated reading of the golden calf episode that challenges a rigid distinction between idolatry and true worship, see the analysis of Ibn ʿArabī's exegesis in Nettler, *Sufi Metaphysics*, pp. 64–66.

277. See chap. 3, n. 89.

278. Nicholson, *Mathnawī*, 1:1435–1436. I note the similarity of the imagery used by Rūmī and the language of Joseph Gikatilla; for reference, see chap. 7, n. 246.

279. Ibid., 1:3146. On the polished mirror as a symbol of the "purified heart of the lover" that facilitates the "mysterious union" of the lover and beloved in Sufism, see Schimmel, "Mawlānā Rūm ī," p. 17. On the emptying of all images from the heart and Rumi's poetics of silence, see Keshavarz, *Reading Mystical Lyric*, pp. 49–71.

280. Chittick, *Self-Disclosure*, pp. xxi–xxii; idem, *Sufi Path of Knowledge*, pp. 68–76; idem, *Imaginal Worlds*, pp. 23–29. See also Nicholson, *Studies in Islamic Mysticism*, p. 140; Nettler, *Sufī Metaphysics*, pp. 7–11, 18–22, 80–88, 116–122.

281. Ibn ʿArabī, *Bezels of Wisdom*, pp. 74–75.

282. Schimmel, *Mystical Dimensions*, p. 268. On the narrowing of the ontic gap between God, world, and soul in Sufi mysticism, see the wealth of material translated and analyzed by Ritter, *Ocean of the Soul*, pp. 615–636.

283. See chap. 1, n. 270. It is of interest to recall the conjecture by Nasr, *Sufi Essays*, pp. 159–163, that the derivation of the "unicity of nature" from the "unity of the Divine principle" affirmed by masters of Islamic gnosis, the presumption that unity *(al-tawḥīd)* "pervades all things and all forms of knowledge," is indebted to a basic axiom of Eastern science expressed in Chinese and Japanese traditions in terms of the unity of the ten thousand things in the one substance of the whole. Nasr suggests, moreover, that just as Islam geographically "covers the middle belt of the world, intellectually and spiritually it occupies a position half way between the mental climate of the Occident and the intellectual climate of the Indian and Far Eastern worlds" (p. 160).

284. Several interesting traditions concerning the veil are cited in the section on the symbols of the throne and footstool in Heinen, *Islamic Cosmology*, pp. 133–134.

285. Ghazālī, *Niche of Lights*, p. 44.

286. Ibid., p. 51. The boldness of al-Ghazālī's text is attested by the fact that some considered it a heretical affirmation of multiplicity within the divine. See Colville, *Two Andalusian Philosophers*, pp. 9 and 69–70 n. 17.

287. Ghazālī, *Niche of Lights*, p. 52. See Fakhry, *History of Islamic Philosophy*, pp. 248–249. A similar depiction is given by Ibn Ṭufayl in his account of the third and final type of mimesis that ends in a vision of the One wherein the self as an autonomous being vanishes; see Hughes, *Texture of the Divine*, p. 101.

288. Heinen, *Islamic Cosmology*, p. 133.

289. Sells, *Early Islamic Mysticism*, p. 291.

290. Chittick, "Paradox of the Veil," p. 83.

291. Chittick, *Self-Disclosure*, p. 110; idem, "Paradox of the Veil," p. 74.

292. Chittick, *Self-Disclosure*, p. 129; idem, "Paradox of the Veil," pp. 81–82.

293. Chittick, *Self-Disclosure*, p. 156; idem, "Paradox of the Veil," pp. 74–75.

294. Chittick, *Self-Disclosure*, pp. 105, 107–108, 113, 115, 156.

295. Ibn ʿArabī, *Divine Governance of the Human Kingdom*, p. 239. For a detailed rationalist interpretation of Q 28:88, see Abrahamov, *Anthropomorphism*, pp. 98–109.

296. Ibn ʿArabī, *Divine Governance*, p. 239.

297. Chittick, *Sufi Path of Knowledge*, p. 230. The Sufi wisdom brings to mind the poem of enlightenment composed by the Zen master Tōzan Ryōkai after having caught a glimpse of his reflection in the water, cited in Jōkin, Keizan, and Kennett, *Denkōroku*, p. 209: "Truly I should not seek for the TRUTH from others / For then it will be far from me; / Now I am going alone, / Everywhere I am able to meet HIM. / HE is ME now, / I am not HIM; / When we understand this, / We are instantaneously with the TRUTH."

298. On the identity of veil and face, see the relevant texts cited and analyzed in Chittick, *Self-Disclosure*, pp. 128–135.

299. A similar claim is made for Buddhist phenomenology by Laycock, *Mind as Mirror*, pp. 49–50. This comparison is worthy of further reflection, but this is not the appropriate context; perhaps one day I shall return to it.

300. Cited in Ziai, "Ḥāfeẓ, Lisān al-Ghayb," p. 466: "There is no veil blinding the lover's vision of the beloved, / Thou art thyself the veil Ḥāfeẓ! Remove thyself from the midst." Maria Subtelny graciously provided me with an alternative rendering of this passage, which has helped me refine my exposition: "Between [*miyān*] the lover and the beloved there is no barrier [*ḥāyil*] / You yourself are the veil [*ḥijāb*] of selfhood, Ḥāfeẓ, remove yourself from this midst [*miyān*]."

301. Shayegan, "The Visionary Typography of Ḥáfiẓ," p. 17. See also Glünz, "Poet's Heart," pp. 53–68; my thanks to Maria Subtelny for drawing my attention to this study.

302. The medium for visualization is most often designated as the veil, mirror, or heart of the visionary, but in the Persian tradition, it is also associated with the world-revealing cup of Jamshīd. See, for instance, Suhrawardī, *Philosophical Allegories*, p. 81; Ḥāfiẓ, *Fifty Poems*, no. 11 p. 94, no. 15 p. 97; Glünz, "Poet's Heart," pp. 54 and 62. In the poetry of Ḥāfiẓ, the cup of the mythical king seems often conflated with the cup of wine whence the visionary enjoys the ecstasy of intoxication. See, for instance, Ḥāfiẓ, *Fifty Poems*, no. 16 p. 100, no. 46 p. 129. In mystical and philosophical works, moreover, the cup is applied allegorically to the Active Intellect, identified as well as the Holy Spirit and the archangel Gabriel. See Ziai, "Ḥāfeẓ, Lisān al-Ghayb," pp. 454 n. 16 and 465; Ritter, *Ocean of the Soul*, pp. 602–603.

303. Ziai, "Ḥāfeẓ, Lisān al-Ghayb," pp. 467–469.

304. Ḥāfiẓ, *The Gift*, p. 148.

305. This is reminiscent of the wisdom of the "gateless gate" (*wu-wen kuan*)—the title of a work by the Chinese master Wu-men Hui-hai (1183–1269)—articulated in the Zen Buddhist tradition: only after having passed through the gate does one know that there is no gate through which to pass.

306. *Zohar* 1:161b. The language of annihilation, *avaddon*, is derived from Job 28:22, where the word personifies a force of destruction, and hence it is paired with *mawet*, the personification of death. In scriptural context, these forces say of the wisdom hidden from all living beings (Job 28:20–21) that they have heard about it (*be-ozneinu shamaʿnu shimʿah*), evidently an inferior form of discernment. God alone comprehends its way and knows its place and thus employs it as the means of creation, a measuring by the way of wisdom, culminating in the instruction to man that wisdom is the fear of the Lord and understanding the shunning of evil (Job 28:23–28). The zoharic author obviously interprets *avaddon* in his own kabbalistic way, using the term to demarcate the mystical passing away into the attribute of the divine that is no/thing that is everything, the emptiness that is full, the fullness that is empty. I have thus taken the liberty to compare this to the Sufi *fanāʾ al-fanāʾ*, the passing of passing. I should note, in passing, that in the continuation of the zoharic text (3:161b–162a), *avaddon* and *mawet* are applied respectively to the male and female powers of the demonic, Samael and his female cohort, the "primordial snake" (*naḥash qadmaʾah*), the "woman of harlotry" (*eshet zenunim*), whose "feet descend down to death" (Prov. 5:5). In the fifth chapter of *Alef, Mem, Tau*, I exegete this turn on the path, which leads the mystic hermeneut, the *maskil*, in emulation of Jacob, "to draw near truth, the signet of the holy king," *leʾitqarva ba-emet ḥotama de-malka qaddisha* (*Zohar* 1:162a).

307. The identification of the heart and throne is a crucial dimension of Sufi piety and is well attested in medieval Jewish philosophic, poetic, and mystical works. See E. Wolfson, *Through a Speculum*, pp. 178–180, in addition to which many more examples could be adduced as illustration of the motif.

308. My translation is based on the Hebrew text published in Idel, *Le Porte della Giustizia*, p. 482; Italian translation by Maurizio Mottolese appears on p. 424. See also *Shaʿarei Ṣedeq*, ed. Parush, p. 27. For alternative English renderings, see Scholem, *Major Trends*, p. 155; Idel, *Mystical Experience*, p. 108.

309. The breakdown of the inside-outside polarity is also expressed by Abulafia and the author of *Shaʿarei Ṣedeq* (traceable to earlier figures, for example, Abraham Ibn Ezra) with respect to the source of prophetic speech: the divine word is conceived of as originating in the human heart, but the human heart does naught but reflect back the luster and timbre of the divine word. See Scholem, *Major Trends*, pp. 141–142; idem, "Eine kabbalistische Erklärung," pp. 285–290. Some of the pertinent sources are cited and analyzed by Idel, *Mystical Experience*, pp. 84–85, 89–91. It is relevant here to recall as well the discussion of *ek-stasis* in Buber, *Ecstatic Confessions*, pp. 2–3, 7, 8. Buber insightfully articulated the view that ecstasy is the turning inward that entails projection outward, indeed, because it is an experience (*Erlebnis*) of the "most inward" it is placed the "furthest outward," an experience of I cast as an experience of God. See Mendes-Flohr, *From Mysticism to Dialogue*, pp. 62–66; E. Wolfson, "Problem of Unity," pp. 423–444, esp. pp. 424–428.

310. Zimmer, "On the Significance," p. 13. The affinity between Yoga and Abulafian kabbalah, indeed the bold claim that prophetic kabbalah is, in truth, a "Judaized version" of Indian yogic practice, was proffered by Scholem, *Major Trends*, pp. 139 and 144. Idel, *Mystical Experience*, pp. 14, 24, notes other interesting similarities between the meditational practice of Abulafia and Yoga techniques of breathing. See, however, Idel's more cautionary attitude, pp. 39–40.

311. My formulation is indebted to Aquila, "Self as Matter and Form," pp. 31–54, esp. p. 44.

312. I translate from the text transcribed by Scholem, "Eine kabbalistische Erklärung," p. 287: "The enlightened sage [*he-ḥakham ha-maskil*], his honor, R. Nathan, blessed be his memory, said: Know that the perfection of the secret of prophecy for the prophet is when suddenly he sees the image of himself standing before him, and he forgets himself and it disappears from him, and he sees his image before him speaking to him and informing him of future events. Concerning this secret the sages, blessed be their memory said [*Genesis Rabbah* 27:1, pp. 255–256] 'Great is the power of the prophets for they compare the form to its creator.'" For an alternative English translation, see idem, *Major Trends*, p. 142. A version of the text was published in *Shoshan Sodot*, 69b, noted and cited by Idel, *Mystical Experience*, pp. 91–92. According to the interpretation of the aggadic dictum transmitted in the name of R. Nathan, disciple of Abulafia and teacher of Isaac of Acre (see Idel, *Mystical Experience*, pp. 91–92; idem, *Studies in Ecstatic Kabbalah*, pp. 73–89, 98 n. 18, 149 n. 42, 151 nn. 61–62), the peak of prophecy consists of the spontaneous dissolution of the distinction between inside and outside: the form that the prophet sees communicating information about the future of his own image. It is worth comparing this feature of prophetic kabbalah to the description of the final stage of the mystical ideal set forth by Ibn Sīnā cited by Ibn Ṭufayl, *Story of Ḥayy ibn Yaqzān*, in Colville, *Two Andalusian Philosophers*, pp. 4–5: "his deepest being becomes like a flawless mirror facing the truth. . . . At this level, he sees the truth and he sees his own soul—as it is seeing—and looks from one to the other. He then loses all consciousness of himself, seeing only paradise, and there achieves union."

313. Idel, *Le Porte della Giustizia*, pp. 245–250.

314. It is likely that implied here is the identification of Torah and the Active Intellect, a central idea in Abulafian kabbalah. If this surmise is correct, then the symbol of *malbush* applies as well to the Active Intellect. A similar notion is expressed by Ibn Latif, *Shaʿar ha-Shamayim*, fol. 28a, in his description of the Active Intellect, based in part on the depiction of Maimonides, *Mishneh Torah*, Yesodei ha-Torah 2:7: "Perhaps this tenth intellect is called '[the man] clothed in linen' [*levush ha-baddim*] (Dan. 12:6) on account of the fact that it clothes [*malbush*] form in matter and matter in form."

315. Abulafia, *Oṣar Eden Ganuz*, fol. 66b (printed ed., p. 132).

316. On the tension between the apophatic and kataphatic in Abulafia's treatises, see E. Wolfson, *Abraham Abulafia*, pp. 152–177.

317. Maimonides, *Guide* I:26, p. 56.

318. Abulafia, *Or ha-Sekhel*, fol. 71b (printed ed., p. 70).

319. Abulafia, *Or ha-Sekhel*, fol. 72b (printed ed., p. 69).

320. Idel, *Language, Torah, Hermeneutics*, pp. 34–38, 79, 163 n. 33.

321. Here I take issue with Scholem's assessment in *Major Trends*, p. 139, of Abulafia's use of the "theory of prophecy" derived from medieval philosophical sources. For an elaboration of the difference in approach between Scholem and myself with regard to the relationship between philosophy and kabbalah, see E. Wolfson, "Conceptions of Wisdom," pp. 151–156. For further references, see above, n. 56.

322. Scholem, *Major Trends*, p. 141. The staying power of this conception is reflected in a comment of the sixteenth-century homilist in Padua, Menaḥem ben Moses Rabba, *Beit Moʿed*, 155a, interpreting the aggadic tradition attributed to R. Simai (Babylonian Talmud, Shabbat 88a) that when Israel responded to Moses "all that the Lord shall speak we shall do and we shall listen" (Exod. 24:7) "600,000 ministering angels affixed on each and every Israelite two crowns, one for 'we shall do' and one for 'we shall listen'": "This teaches us that Torah brings forth the potentiality of man to complete actuality until he is like an angel of the Lord, which is the Active Intellect [*sekhel ha-poʿel*]. And the proof that Israel acquired perfection [*sheleimut*] by means of Torah is that they became the Active Intellect to the point that even their matter was transformed into the intellectual [*maskil*], as if the two parts were one alone. . . . Thus they put 'we shall do' first, which

is comparable to matter, to 'we shall listen,' which is comparable to intellect, and as a consequence they were like the angels in complete actuality."

323. Abulafia, *Or ha-Sekhel*, fol. 75a (printed ed., p. 72).

324. Here I have followed the reading preserved in the manuscript; the printed version reads *ṣiyyurit gashmit*, which should be translated as "corporeal image" (see next note for references).

325. Abulafia, *Ḥayyei ha-Olam ha-Ba*, fols. 4a–b (printed ed., pp. 48–49).

326. E. Wolfson, *Through a Speculum*, pp. 160–181, esp. pp. 166–167.

327. Abulafia, *Ḥayyei ha-Olam ha-Ba*, fols. 4b–5a (printed ed., p. 49).

328. Abulafia, *Sitrei Torah*, fol. 135b (printed ed., p. 73).

329. On the name YHWA, see E. Wolfson, *Through a Speculum*, p. 252 n. 264.

330. Corbin, *Creative Imagination*, pp. 22, 33, passim; see p. 27, where Corbin remarks that the "dominant" aspect of Shiʿite thought is "the idea of the Theophany in Human form, the divine anthropomorphosis which fills the gulf left open by abstract monotheism . . . the manifestation of the unknowable God in the angelic form of the celestial anthropos." This axiom of Islamic esotericism resonates with the figure of *Christos Angelos* in the angelomorphic Christology that has been traced to Jewish Christians in the formative period known in scholarly parlance as Christian origins. See Corbin, *Paradoxe du monothéisme*, pp. 83–96. For other references to angelic Christology, see chap. 1, n. 354.

331. Corbin, *Creative Imagination*, p. 63. On the holy spirit and the anthropomorphic manifestation of the angel, see idem, *Paradoxe du monothéisme*, pp. 50–63, 143–150. On Ibn Sīnā's *al-ḥikma al-mashriqīya*, see Gutas, *Avicenna and the Aristotelian Tradition*, pp. 115–130; idem, "Ibn Ṭufayl on Ibn Sīnā's Eastern Philosophy," pp. 222–241.

332. Corbin, *Creative Imagination*, p. 35, cites the exegesis of Jacob's contest with the angel (Gen. 32:25–29) by the "Jewish mystic Joseph ben Judah," i.e., Joseph ben Judah Ibn Aqnin, as an example of the soul's quest for union with the Active Intellect, personified as the angel in the form of an anthropos. Corbin then makes the following remark: "A whole series of Jewish speculative mystics found the same symbolism in the *Song of Songs*, where the Beloved plays the role of the active Intelligence, while the heroine is the thinking human soul." In a manner far more astute than many scholars of medieval Jewish mysticism, Corbin insightfully discerned that the philosophical interpretation of the Song as a figurative account of the conjunction of the human and Active Intellect may be demarcated as a form of speculative mysticism. See my discussion below, chap. 8.

333. Corbin, *Avicenna*, p. 8; for more extensive discussion of the process of individuation and angelic epiphany, see pp. 77–93.

334. Ibid., pp. 19–20.

335. Abulafia, *Ḥayyei ha-Olam ha-Ba*, fol. 3b (printed ed., p. 47).

336. Scholem, *Major Trends*, p. 140; Idel, *Mystical Experience*, pp. 116–119.

337. Abulafia, *Ḥayyei ha-Olam ha-Ba*, fol. 12a (printed ed., p. 63).

338. Abulafia, *Sitrei Torah*, fol. 155b (printed ed., pp. 139–140).

339. *Sefer Yeṣirah* 2:2. For further references to this motif in Abulafia's writings, see E. Wolfson, *Abraham Abulafia*, pp. 141–142 n. 127.

340. E. Wolfson, "Anthropomorphic Imagery," pp. 155–158.

341. See E. Wolfson, *Through a Speculum*, p. 245 n. 235.

342. A scriptural locution that appears in 1 Sam. 24:6, 10, 26:9, 11,16, 23; 2 Sam. 1:14, 16, 19:22; Lam. 4:20.

343. Gen. 21:17, 31:11; Exod. 14:19; Judg. 13:6, 9; 1 Sam. 29:9; 2 Sam. 14:17, 20, 19:28.

344. I propose that, for Abulafia, the title *sar ha-panim* signifies that Metatron is the angel within whom opposites cohere, a coherence—note that I speak of "coherence," not "coincidence" or "confluence"—that marks the unity of the divine vis-à-vis the world, the mystery of providence (*hanhagah*), which is related soterically to the mystical name of seventy-two letters, identified as the "thick cloud" (*av anan*) within and through which the divine was revealed to the Israelites at Sinai according to Exodus 19:9—the consonants of the word *av* have the numerical value of seventy-two. This is one of the principle secrets disclosed in Abulafia, *Ḥayyei Olam ha-Ba*, fols. 3b–4a (printed ed., p. 47). The secret is implied in the grammatical oddity

that the plural form *panim* ("faces") is the word for the singular "face." The two-faced nature of Metatron is expressed through various images scattered about in Abulafia's voluminous corpus: he is the secret of the Tree of Knowledge that comprises good and evil (Abulafia, *Oṣar Eden Ganuz*, fol. 64b; printed ed., p. 128); he bears the attributes of mercy and judgment; he is the balance that mediates between the side of merit, *kaf zekhut*, and the side of debt, *kaf ḥovah* (Abulafia, *Or ha-Sekhel*, fol. 185b; printed ed., p. 82); he appears as *naʿar* and *zaqen*, youth and elder—a symbolic configuration adduced exegetically from the verse "I was young and now I am old" (*naʿar hayyiti gam zaqanti*; Ps. 37:25) and instantiated in the image of the "spiritual mentor" who is visualized either as a young or as an old man (Scholem, *Major Trends*, pp. 139–140; Idel, *Mystical Experience*, pp. 117–118; it is worthwhile to underscore the comparative gesture on Scholem's part in his identifying the path laid out by Abulafia to be "a Judaized version of that ancient spiritual technique which has found its classical expression in the practices of the Indian mystics who follow the system known as *Yoga*," an insight embellished by Idel, *Mystical Experience*, pp. 25–26. It behooves me to note that Idel's criticism of Scholem's referring to Abulafia's path as "magic" rather than "technique," op. cit., p. 41, obviously needs to be modified in light of the aforecited comment. Beyond the ostensibly pedantic scholarly quibble over terminology, it is conceptually erroneous and misleading to present Scholem's discussion of Abulafia as if he did not appreciate the fact that the primary intent of the meditational path was internal transformation rather than external alteration); he is the first and last of the ten separate intellects or, alternatively expressed, the head and tail of the sefirotic edifice, *Keter* and *Malkhut*, the front and back (*panim we-aḥor*), the warp and woof (*sheti wa-erev*), also related respectively to the two names Israel and Jacob, *yisraʾel* decoded as *leroʾshi* ("to my head") and *yaʿaqov* as *aqevi* ("my heel") (Abulafia, *Or ha-Sekhel*, fol. 97b; printed ed., p. 94); a conception doubtlessly suggested to Abulafia by the depiction of the *sefirot* in *Sefer Yeṣirah*, "the end is fixed in their beginning and their beginning in their end" (E. Wolfson, *Abraham Abulafia*, pp. 83–85 n. 264).

345. Babylonian Talmud, Sanhedrin 38b.

346. There is still much to be elicited from Hugo Odeberg's exhaustive philological and textual presentation of conceptions of Metatron in various genre of exoteric and esoteric Jewish texts in Odeberg, *Enoch*, pp. 79–146.

347. On the interposition of speech in between imagination and intellect, see Abulafia, *Ḥayyei ha-Nefesh*, fol. 91a–b (printed ed., p. 158), and discussion in Idel, "Abulafia's Secrets," pp. 304–306.

348. Abulafia utilizes a common saying in medieval Hebrew texts, *ke-shemo ken hu*, that is, the name of a thing instructs one about the nature of the thing that is so named, which is based on a larger assumption regarding the homology of language and being.

349. On the nexus between imagination (*dimyon*), *daemon*, *mediyun* (medium) and the political (*medini*), see Idel, *Language, Torah, Hermeneutics*, pp. 56–67. Idel cites the same passage from *Oṣar Eden Ganuz* (see below, n. 351), but offers a slightly different interpretation than my own.

350. See above, n. 116.

351. Abulafia, *Oṣar Eden Ganuz*, fols. 60a–b (printed ed., pp. 120–121; discrepancies between my rendering and the published text can be accounted for by the fact that I translated from the manuscript).

352. I have found an interesting conceptual analogy in an account of the visionary meditation according to the Nyingmapa school of Tibetan Buddhism in the teachings of Dzogchen expounded by Garab Dorje. The relevant text occurs in the commentary to the third statement of "The Last Testament of Garab Dorje," in Dorje, *Golden Letters*, p. 164, but before I cite this passage, it would be helpful to the reader to summarize briefly the "secret of self-liberation" laid out in the first statement. The state of "immediate intrinsic Awareness" (*Rigpa*), the "Primordial Base or Dharmakaya" (p. 130), is attained as a result of the Son (*bu*), symbolic of "knowledge or cognition (*ye-shes*) of the vision or phenomena directly," searching for and encountering the Mother (*ma*), "its source or origin." The Son's visionary encounter with the Mother, which is described both as the "immediate pure presence" (p. 130) and as "emptiness" (p. 132), occasions the process of self-liberation, that is, "the vision is self liberated by means of the vision, like melted butter dissolving into butter. . . . The Awareness itself is self-liberated by means of Awareness; just like water dissolving into water. When searching for the unique state (of Rigpa), one encounters only one's own unique state. That is to say, one's own nature (Rigpa) simply encounters itself. . . . If that is the case, then when one recognizes one's essence,

everything is brought together in a single moment within which a cognition is present that does not go beyond the knowledge of that singular unique essence (which is Rigpa). This is like a man and woman who are in love and who meet together secretly in solitude in order to make love" (pp. 131–132). For discussion of this theme, see Rossi, *Philosophical View*, pp. 61–64, and references to other scholarly treatments on pp. 61–62 n. 184. The shift from the image of mother and son to man and woman is instructive and shares a basic similarity with the symbolic presentation of different phases of the unitive experience in kabbalistic tradition, but this is not the place to enter into detail on this matter (for a brief discussion of some of the relevant issues, see the section entitled "Spiritual Eroticism, Ascetic Renunciation, and the Eschatological Re/turn" below in chap. 8 as well as my studies cited in chap. 8, n. 224.) What is significant to emphasize is the self-liberation of the Son through the visualization process that results in the overcoming of ontic difference, a return to the emptiness of the Mother, portrayed as butter dissolving into butter or water into water. Now we can appreciate the comment on the description of the "realization of the Body of Light" (*'od lus*) in the third statement: "And having such a concrete experience with respect to the state of liberation, one's confidence becomes like the experience of space dissolving into space. . . . In this unique state of immediate Awareness, everything is liberated into this single understanding of the state of immediate intrinsic Awareness. This is like taking fire from fire, or like transferring water into water, or like adding melted butter to butter. Thus the Mother (the Primordial State) and her Son (knowledge) become united. Because one's own Mother, as the origin or source, is just itself (and nothing else, existing in its own state of existence, and this brings emptiness), one can say that emptiness itself is liberated by means of emptiness. Thus, one individual's presence of Awareness dissolves (at the time of the realization of the Body of Light) and becomes integrated into the vision itself" (pp. 134–135). Commenting on this statement, especially the opening part, and applying it to anyone seeking enlightenment, Reynolds writes, "When a Siddha, like the master Garab Dorje, attains the Body of Light, it appears as if the material body dissolves into the vast space of the sky, or else dissolves into pure radiant energy, the lights of the rainbow. Matter is transformed into energy, and this radiant energy remains the vehicle of awareness. . . . The Siddha, however, does not really ascend in a physical sense to some extraterrestrial heaven world—but simply returns to the center of his or her being, the Primordial State. The Siddha lives in the condition of the mirror, rather than in the reflections, the world illusion" (p. 164). For an in-depth philosophical analysis, see Guenther, *Matrix of Mystery*; idem, *From Reductionism to Creativity*. I do not think it frivolous to compare the account in the prophetic kabbalah to this description: the visualization that is bestowed on one who attains the unitive experience with the divine intellect as a consequence of following the path of meditation entails seeing an external image of that reality as a projection of the internal; the mind, therefore, may be likened to a mirror empty of all form so that which is formless may assume form in the form that has been rendered formless by donning the luminous, angelic body.

353. See Corbin's depiction of the imaginal world, *ʿālam al-mithāl*, in *Paradoxe du monothéisme*, p. 120: "le monde où se spiritualisent les corps et où se corporalisent les Espirits."

354. For a more literal understanding of "unveiling" in kabbalistic hermeneutics, see Rojtman, *Black Fire on White Fire*, pp. 84–85. Rojtman cites a passage from Gikatilla that ostensibly presents a different model from zoharic literature, which affirms the act of disrobing or unveiling and the consequent seeing of the naked body or exposed face. However, see my comments on Gikatilla's text in "Occultation," p. 116 n. 8, and in chap. 7, nn. 246–247. Compare the images used by Rūmī in the passage cited in chap. 1, n. 367.

355. *Zohar Ḥadash*, 73b; Liebes, *Sections of the Zohar Lexicon*, p. 230.

356. Mishnah, Ḥagigah 1:8; Tosefta, Shabbat 2:10; Babylonian Talmud, Berakhot 63a, Shabbat 32a, Ḥagigah 11b; Ḥullin 60b, Keritut 5a; *Sifra de-vei Rav*, Qedoshim 1:1, 86a; *Leviticus Rabbah* 24:5, p. 557; *Numbers Rabbah* 13:15; *Avot de-Rabbi Natan*, version A, chap. 27, p. 84. On occasion we find in rabbinic literature the expression *gufei halakhot*, literally "bodies of the laws," which is more or less synonymous with *gufei torah*. See Mishnah, Avot 3:18; Tosefta, Eruvin 11:24, Ḥagigah 1:9; *Avot de-Rabbi Natan*, version A, chap. 27, p. 84.

357. The zoharic formulation is also based on metaphorical depictions of letters as the body and vowels as the soul that are widespread in medieval Hebrew texts. See Liebes, *Sections of the Zohar Lexicon*, pp. 174–176.

358. E. Wolfson, "Occultation," pp. 124–135.

359. J. Katz, *Exclusiveness and Tolerance*, pp. 22–23.

360. Liebes, *Sections of the Zohar Lexicon*, pp. 173–174, already suggested that the use of the term *gufa* ("body") to refer to Torah in some zoharic texts might reflect the influence of the Christian idea of *corpus mysticum*. On the phenomenological use of the term "docetic" to demarcate the image of the body that is real, an interpretative stance that is commensurate with my own, see Depraz, "Phénoménologie et docétisme," pp. 87–105.

361. Liebes, *Studies in the Zohar*, pp. 103–110.

362. The reference is to the commentary by Naḥmanides on Deut. 27:26. See Moses ben Naḥman, *Perushei ha-Torah*, 2:472. The earlier rabbinic source cited by Naḥmanides as a basis for the custom to lift the Torah scroll is *Massekhet Soferim*, 14:8, pp. 261–262.

363. Joseph of Hamadan, "Critical Edition of the *Sefer Ṭaʿamey ha-Miẓwoth*," p. 58.

364. Idel, "Torah," pp. 197–236; idem, *Absorbing Perfections*, pp. 69–74, 76.

365. Joseph of Hamadan, *Sefer Tashak*, p. xx.

366. Ibid., p. 13.

367. Ibid., p. 72.

368. E. Wolfson, "Ontology," pp. 138–140.

369. *Zohar* 3:73a.

370. Liebes, Sections of the *Zohar Lexicon*, pp. 400–401; Tishby, *Wisdom of the Zohar*, p. 1086; idem, *Studies in Kabbalah*, pp. 941–960; Sack, *Kabbalah of Rabbi Moshe Cordovero*, pp. 103–109; Idel, "Two Remarks," pp. 213–214; idem, *Absorbing Perfections*, pp. 20, 99–101, 118–119, 349, 497 n. 49.

371. A similar esoteric explanation for the obligation incumbent upon every male Jew to write a Torah scroll, which represents the "shape" of God, is offered by the anonymous author of *Sefer ha-Yiḥud*, a kabbalistic treatise, more or less, from the period of the *Zohar*. For citation of the relevant passage, see Idel, "Concept of Torah," pp. 62–64; idem, "Infinities," p. 145; idem, *Absorbing Perfections*, p. 70.

372. Joseph of Hamadan, "Critical Edition of the *Sefer Ṭaʿamey ha-Miẓwoth*," pp. 78–80.

373. See, for example, *Zohar* 3:170a; Tishby, *Wisdom of the Zohar*, pp. 764–765.

374. Safran, "Rabbi Azriel and Naḥmanides," pp. 75–106; see below, chap. 7.

375. Idel, *Kabbalah: New Perspectives*, pp. 184–185; E. Wolfson, "Mystical Rationalization," pp. 231–235.

376. The kabbalistic representation of Torah as body is supported by the idea that the 248 positive commandments correspond to the 248 limbs, and the 365 negative commandments, to the 365 sinews. This formulation is a modification of the tradition attributed to R. Simlai (Babylonian Talmud, Makkot 23b), according to which the 248 positive commandments correspond to the limbs and the 365 negative commandments to the days of the year. See Scholem, *On the Kabbalah and Its Symbolism*, p. 128. It is worth noting, however, that the 248 limbs and 365 sinews are mentioned in Targum Pseudo-Jonathan to Genesis 1:27 as an explication of the "divine image" with which Adam was created. See E. Wolfson, "Mystical Rationalization," p. 231 n. 78. Concerning Simlai's dictum and particularly its impact on select medieval Jewish philosophers, see Hyman, "Rabbi Simlai's Saying," pp. 49–62.

377. Benin, *Footprints of God*, pp. 147–162.

378. It is also possible to explain this matter in terms of the distinction between spiritual and corporeal substance, a Neoplatonic motif that was known by kabbalists in Provence and Northern Spain. If we adopt this hermeneutical framework, we could say that for kabbalists the mystery of incarnation entails the transformation of the former into the latter, a transformation facilitated by the mystical conversion of the latter into the former. See discussion of a similar theme in Ismaʿili Neoplatonism in Alibhai, "Transformation of Spiritual Substance," pp. 167–177.

379. On the use of poetry as a literary model to articulate an incarnational language from within a Christological framework, see Norris, "Word Made Flesh," pp. 303–312.

380. The point was well grasped in the lecture "The Kabbalah," by Borges, *Seven Nights*, pp. 95–98: "The diverse, and occasionally contradictory, teachings grouped under the name of the Kabbalah derive from a concept alien to the Western mind, that of the sacred book. . . . The idea is this: the Pentateuch, the Torah,

is a sacred book. An infinite intelligence has condescended to the human task of producing a book. The Holy Spirit has condescended to literature which is as incredible as imagining that God condescended to become a man." For extended discussion of the kabbalistic influence on Borges, see Sosnowski, *Borges y la Cabala.*

381. Focusing primarily on passages in the *oeuvre* of Ezra of Gerona, Idel, "Some Remarks on Ritual," pp. 111–130, has argued that we need to consider the kabbalistic approach to ritual without being burdened by a negative assessment of rabbinic halakhah as demythologized legalism, on one hand, and by an overemphasis on a symbolic narrative of a gnostic nature, on the other. I am in general agreement with this contention, but I would argue that in the final analysis, the spiritualized understanding of ritual cannot be separated from the theosophic orientation and its implicit theurgy. Using anthropological terminology that Idel himself summons, one could counter that the sensory and ideological poles of ritual should be examined in a manner that avoids polarization, that is, the efficacy of the performance of a commandment cannot be entertained without assuming an underlying symbolic-mythic complex that explains the dynamics of the world order. For Ezra to claim that one is immersed in the divine light as a consequence of fulfilling the ritual is dependent on a certain presupposition regarding the mechanics of being, which is connected in turn to a particular theosophy and its accompanying symbolism. To be sure, Idel himself ("Some Remarks," pp. 120–121) asserts that the somatic experience of being enveloped by the light of the commandments is related to Ezra's theosophic conception of the divine attributes "arranged in an anthropomorphic order." Nevertheless, he concludes, Ezra "attempted to convey his understanding of the effect of the commandments in terms that are not symbolic but strive to point to the efficacy of the ritual in terms understandable to his contemporaries." Even if the matter of intentionality (*kawwanah*) is not stated explicitly, it is valid to assume that Ezra would have presumed that the experience of conjunction is not possible if one is not cognizant of the technicalities of the theosophic drama. Indeed, his imparting the wisdom of kabbalah is intended to provide the informational data necessary for one to cultivate the proper intention.

382. *Kitvei Ramban*, 2:497. Some of the passages from Ezra have been cited previously by Matt, "Mystic and the *Mizwot*," p. 378, but in this study all translations are my own. For a more recent discussion of the role of ritual practice in Ezra's kabbalah, including a critical edition and translation of the section of his *Perush Shir ha-Shirim* that deals extensively with the commandments, see Travis, "Kabbalistic Foundations of Jewish Spiritual Practice." I thank the author for providing me with a copy of his work. The passage I cite occurs on p. 4 of the Hebrew section and the author's independent translation on p. 175 of the English section.

383. For explication of this theme, see Idel, "In the Light of Life," pp. 192–198; idem, "Some Remarks," pp. 118–119.

384. *Kitvei Ramban*, 2:528–529. Ezra alludes in this passage to the aggadic tradition transmitted in the name of R. Sheila that two ministering angels (*mal'akhei ha-sharet*) accompany a person (Babylonian Talmud, Ta'anit 11a). The full intent of the kabbalistic embellishment of the rabbinic teaching is made clear in Azriel of Gerona's explication of R. Sheila's dictum in his *Commentary on Talmudic Aggadoth*, pp. 32–33.

385. Mopsik, *Grands textes*, pp. 116–119. According to Mopsik's interpretation of the text of Ezra, the "theosophic signification" is secondary to the primary emphasis on the "identity between the concrete rite and the divine reality" (p. 117). Pedaya, *Vision and Speech*, p. 150 n. 27, similarly argues that mystical conjunction and theurgy should not be seen in a causal manner but rather as two aspects of the one prophetic experience of ecstasy. Though my work is not cited by her in this context, I too have emphasized the need to view the theurgical and mystical as two facets of a phenomenon that I have designated as ecstatic. See E. Wolfson, "Forms of Visionary Ascent," pp. 209–235, esp. pp. 219–221, and idem, *Through a Speculum*, p. 374, "It is necessary to reintegrate the theurgical and mystical elements of the religious experience of the kabbalist, for it makes no sense to speak of effecting the nature of God if one is not experiencing God in some immediate and direct sense." The point was made forcefully in the dissertation by S. Brody, "Human Hands," pp. 249–250: "the theurgic efficacy of a ritual act is profoundly intertwined with the Kabbalist's attainment of mystical adhesion, howsoever that might be conceived"; and the summary account on p. 396: "Careful analysis of many of our sources has consequently indicated that the transformative and theurgic sides of Kabbalistic experience and practice are all but inseparably interlinked. Contemporary scholarly literature has been far

too facile in its differentiation between the 'mystical' and the 'theurgic' aspects of spiritual praxis, as if they represented two distinct foci of Kabbalistic interest and endeavor. On the contrary, they represent the two sides of a unified spiritual enterprise." On the interface of theurgic activity and mystical union as two stages of unification, see also J. Goldberg, "Mystical Union," pp. 7–12, 83 n. 31.

386. From here until the end of this sentence is lacking in the printed text; my translation is based on MS Oxford, Bodleian 1947, fol. 26b.

387. That is, "righteousness" is a technical term for *Malkhut* or *Shekhinah*, and hence the force of Ezra's exegesis of the verse "his righteousness lasts forever" (Ps. 112:9) is that the last of the emanations acts as a magnet to draw the disembodied soul back into the divine realm.

388. Mishnah, Avot 5:2; *Avot de-Rabbi Natan*, version A, chap. 25, p. 81.

389. The kabbalists utilize the rabbinic distinction between the "speculum that shines" and the "speculum that does not shine" (Babylonian Talmud, Yevamot 49b) to characterize respectively the sixth and tenth emanations, the masculine *Tif'eret* and the feminine *Malkhut.*

390. Mishnah, Avot 1:3.

391. *Liqquṭei Shikheḥah u-Fe'ah*, 17b–18a. The concluding phrase "it is not so" is a translation of the version in MS Oxford, Bodleian 1947, fol. 27a, *eino khen.* The printed text here reads *setumim*, which means "closed," an obvious corruption.

392. *Kitvei Ramban*, 2:538.

393. See above, n. 376.

394. Note the variant reading in MS Vatican 211, fol. 24b, *yihyeh ha-guf we-ha-neshamah shawin* ("the body and soul will be equal")

395. This is the reading in the printed text by Chavel as well as the *editio princeps* (Altona 1764, 16a), but note the variant *binyan elohi* in MS Leiden, Warner 32, fol. 23a, cited and discussed by Scholem, *On the Kabbalah and Its Symbolism*, pp. 44–45. In the German version of this essay included in Scholem, *Zur Kabbalah*, p. 65, the reading is *binyan elohi*, as we find in the English translation. However, in the Hebrew edition, Scholem, *Pirqei Yesod*, p. 47, the expression is transcribed as *binyan eloha*. Idel, "Concept of Torah," pp. 49–50 n. 81, follows this emendation. The reading *binyan elohi* is confirmed in the manuscript version of Ezra's commentary transcribed in Tishby, *Mishnat ha-Zohar*, vol. 2, p. 366; for English translation, see idem, *Wisdom of the Zohar*, p. 1080.

396. On the identification of Torah as the name of God, see the statement from Ezra's *Perush ha-Aggadot* in *Liqquṭei Shikheḥah u-Fe'ah*, 19b, cited in Tishby, *Wisdom of the Zohar*, p. 1080.

397. *Kitvei Ramban*, 2:548.

398. See, for instance, Scholem, "Name of God," p. 165; and idem, *On the Kabbalah and Its Symbolism*, pp. 35–36.

399. The original text is transcribed in Scholem, *Pirqei Yesod*, p. 196. For an alternative translation and analysis, see Scholem, *On the Mystical Shape*, pp. 68–71.

400. It is of interest to compare the kabbalistic *guf ruḥani* to the depiction of the spirit (*al-rūḥ*) as a "subtle body" (*jismī laṭīf*) in Nicholson, *Kashf al-Maḥjūb*, p. 262. See also the account of al-Ghazālī's view regarding resurrection of the body in Ibn Rushd, *Averroës' Tahafut al-Tahafut*, p. 362: "it must be assumed that what arises from the dead is simulacra of these earthly bodies, not these bodies themselves, for that which has perished does not return individually and a thing can only return as an image of that which has perished, not as a being identical with what has perished." On the pneumatic or astral body, composed of air or fire, see Plotinus, *Enneads* III.5.6. On the daemonic body composed of fire, see Iamblichus, *De mysteriis*, vol. 12, pp. 246–247. The language in the *Tahafut al-Tahafut* by Averroës bears an evocative similarity to terminology employed by thirteenth-century kabbalists, attested especially in the zoharic compilation. See Scholem, *On the Mystical Shape*, pp. 260–272. For a detailed analysis of al-Ghazālī's mystical eschatology, see Gianotti, *Al-Ghazālī's Unspeakable Doctrine of the Soul.*

401. This is based on a rabbinic exegesis of Genesis 3:21; see *Genesis Rabbah* 20:12, pp. 196–197; G. Anderson, "Garments of Skin," pp. 101–143; idem, *Genesis of Perfection*, pp. 117–134. See also Lambden, "From Fig Leaves to Fingernails," pp. 74–90; Ricks, "Garment of Adam," pp. 203–225.

402. For this useful terminology I am indebted to Elqayam, "Between Referentialism and Performativism," pp. 5–40.

403. To understand the wordplay in Azriel's comment, one must bear in mind that the custom among pious Jews is to refer to God as *ha-shem*, which literally means "the name," an honorific title that alludes to the Tetragrammaton, the most sacred divine name. As Tishby remarks in Azriel of Gerona, *Commentary on Talmudic Aggadoth*, p. 37 n. 9 (in the name of Scholem), the source for this formulation is the older Heikhalot literature. See also Scholem, *On the Kabbalah and Its Symbolism*, p. 44.

404. Azriel is here interpreting a rabbinic passage that deals with the placing of dust on a Torah scroll (Babylonian Talmud, Taᶜanit 16a).

405. Based on Ps. 19:8.

406. Azriel of Gerona, *Commentary on Talmudic Aggadoth*, p. 37. On the equation of Torah and the name, compare Azriel, *Perush ha-Tefillah*, fol. 206a: "'The Torah of the Lord is his delight' (Ps. 1:2), for this is the knowledge of his name [*yediᶜat shemo*]." See Sed-Rajna, *Commentaire*, p. 46; Azriel of Gerona, *"Perush ha-Tefillah,"* p. 11.

407. This usage is attested in *Zohar* 3:152a, where, in the schematization of four levels of meaning, the commandments are referred to as "bodies of Torah" beneath the garments, which are the scriptural narratives. Liebes, *Studies in Zohar*, p. 181 n. 133, concludes that in this zoharic passage those involved with practical commandments are accorded a lower status than those engaged in kabbalah. While there is surely a hierarchical delineation of the four levels at work here, I would be loath to express matters in the way suggested by Liebes. Just as garment, body, soul, and soul of souls coalesce to form an organic unity in which no layer is dispensable, so the stories, laws, mystical secrets, and messianic mysteries cohere together in one textual organism. See also Liebes, *Sections of the Zohar Lexicon*, p. 173.

408. Here it seems that Azriel is using the expression *gufei torah* both in the traditional sense to denote the fundamentals of Torah and in the kabbalistic sense as the corporeal form of Torah, which is the incarnation of God or the embodiment of the name.

409. Azriel of Gerona, *Commentary on Talmudic Aggadoth*, pp. 37–39. In his *Perush ha-Tefillah*, fol. 206a, Azriel writes that one must be engaged in observing the commandments "to extend his imaginings and all his thoughts in the reasons for the law [*ṭeᶜamei torah*] for there is an abundance of holiness [*tosefet qiddush*] in them" (Sed-Rajna, *Commentaire*, p. 45).

410. *Kitvei Ramban*, 1:203.

411. *Sefer Yeṣirah*, 6:4. The slight variations probably do not reflect an alternative text in the possession of Naḥmanides but rather the fact that he was recalling the passage from memory, as was the custom of Jewish learning in the Middle Ages.

412. Moses ben Naḥman, *Perushei ha-Torah*, 1:494 (ad Exod. 30:19).

413. *Kitvei Ramban*, 2:513, slightly emended according to MS Vatican 211, fol. 26a.

414. Moses ben Naḥman, *Perushei ha-Torah*, 2:115–116 (ad Lev. 19:2); Safran, "Rabbi Azriel and Naḥmanides," pp. 82–106; Henoch, *Ramban*, pp. 98–100; and the detailed analysis of asceticism and the transformation of the body in Feldman, "Power of the Soul." On the modified asceticism of Naḥmanides, which includes codifying sexual restraint as part of the command to be holy, see Feldman's discussion, pp. 106–122.

415. Moses ben Naḥman, *Perushei ha-Torah*, 2:395 (ad Deut. 11:22); see the pertinent comments of Scholem, *Messianic Idea*, pp. 204–205.

416. Moses ben Naḥman, *Perushei ha-Torah*, 2:100 (ad Lev. 18:4).

417. Naḥmanides distinguishes between the righteous (*ṣaddiq*) and the pious (*ḥasid*): the former cleaves to *shem ha-meyuḥad*, the Tetragrammaton, presumably a reference to *Tifᵓeret*, the sixth emanation, and the latter to *shem ha-nikhbad*, the epithet Adonai, which is linked symbolically to *Shekhinah*. See Safran, "Rabbi Azriel and Naḥmanides," pp. 83–85, 102–103 n. 101; Idel, *Kabbalah: New Perspectives*, p. 46; E. Wolfson, "By Way of Truth," pp. 151–153 and sources cited on p. 152 n. 141.

418. Moses ben Naḥman, *Perushei ha-Torah*, 1:275–276 (ad Gen. 49:33).

419. See E. Wolfson, "Secret of the Garment," p. xl. For extended discussion of the eschatological motif

of the "rabbinic garment," see Scholem, "Paradise Garb of Souls," pp. 290–306; and idem, *On the Mystical Shape*, pp. 264–265.

420. Moses ben Naḥman, *Perushei ha-Torah*, 1:6–7. For parallel, albeit in a considerably different terminological register, see the sermon of Naḥmanides, *Torat ha-Shem Teminah*, in *Kitvei Ramban*, 1:167–168. The view I have expressed here is a modification of my remarks concerning the relationship of the exoteric and esoteric understanding of the text as hermeneutically elaborated by Naḥmanides in E. Wolfson, "By Way of Truth," p. 117 n. 44. For a different understanding of the two readings proffered by Naḥmanides, see Scholem, *On the Kabbalah and Its Symbolism*, pp. 38–39; idem, "Name of God," pp. 77–79; Idel, "Concept of Torah," pp. 52–55; idem, *Absorbing Perfections*, p. 322. On the aggadic image of the primordial Torah being inscripted as black fire upon white fire in Jewish mystical hermeneutics, see Scholem, *On the Kabbalah and Its Symbolism*, pp. 48–49; Idel, "Concept of Torah," pp. 43–45; idem, *Absorbing Perfections*, pp. 45–69.

421. E. Wolfson, "Secret of the Garment," pp. xli–xlii; idem, *Through a Speculum*, pp. 63–64. On the glorious angel in Naḥmanidean kabbalah, see the text translated by Scholem, *On the Mystical Shape*, p. 171. For discussion of this motif in thirteenth-century kabbalistic literature, see Scholem, *Origins*, pp. 184–187, 214–216; idem, *On the Mystical Shape*, pp. 186–187. On the centrality of this theme as an ancient trope of Jewish esotericism, see E. Wolfson, *Through a Speculum*, pp. 184 n. 247, 216, 224–228, 255–263, 310 n. 147, 312–313, and the summary account offered by Idel, *Messianic Mystics*, p. 85.

422. Moses ben Naḥman, *Perushei ha-Torah*, 2:395 (ad Deut. 11:22).

423. *Kitvei Ramban*, 2:303.

424. Ibid., 2:304–305.

425. Babylonian Talmud, Yoma 75b.

426. Moses ben Naḥman, *Perushei ha-Torah*, 1:365 (ad Exod. 16:6). For a parallel explanation in *Shaʿar ha-Gemul*, see *Kitvei Ramban*, 2:305.

427. Babylonian Talmud, Berakhot 17a.

428. Moses ben Naḥman, *Perushei ha-Torah*, 1:365 (ad Exod. 16:6). For discussion of the manna and bodily transformation in Naḥmanides, see Feldman, "Power of the Soul," pp. 195–210.

429. E. Wolfson, *Through a Speculum*, pp. 361–363 (the passage from Naḥmanides is cited on p. 361 n. 122); idem, "Coronation," pp. 335–342.

430. *Kitvei Ramban*, 1:304.

431. Chernus, *Mysticism in Rabbinic Judaism*, pp. 83–86; E. Wolfson, *Through a Speculum*, pp. 42–43.

432. S. Krauss, *Jewish-Christian Controversy*, pp. 70, 229, 238.

433. Feldman, "Power of the Soul," p. 197 n. 2, raises the issue of a contemporary Christian influence on Naḥmanides. In his opinion, however, this possibility should not be overemphasized, given the earlier rabbinic sources whence Naḥmanides derived his ideas. I would be less hesitant to stress the Christological affinities, as the likelihood of older sources influencing Naḥmanides does not preempt or preclude contemporary analogues. On the appropriation of the Christian symbol of the consecrated Host in a Jewish context, inspired in part by kabbalistic imagery, see the illuminating study by Batterman, "Bread of Affliction," pp. 53–89. For representative discussions of the variegated symbolism pertaining to the mystery of the Eucharist, see Camporesi, "Consecrated Host," pp. 221–237; D. Power, *Eucharistic Mystery*; Bynum, *Resurrection of the Body*, pp. 156–199.

434. For a representative study of this theme in Islamic thought, with special emphasis on Ismaʿili Neoplatonism, see Alibhai, "Transformation of Spiritual Substance," pp. 167–177.

435. Camille, "Image and the Self," pp. 62–99, esp. pp. 74–77; see also Otten, "Parallelism of Nature and Scripture," pp. 81–102.

436. Idel, "Some Remarks," pp. 120–121, compares Ezra's description of the one who fulfills the commandments being encompassed by light and donning the pure and holy body to the Christian notion of the aura that encircles the body of Christ, known as the *mandorla*. In my opinion, this is a very evocative suggestion that is corroborated by the independent approach I have taken. Mention here should also be made of Sendor's observation, "Emergence," vol. 1, pp. 154–164, that the discussion of the unity of the divine in early Provençal kabbalists such as Isaac the Blind and his nephew Asher ben David should be seen as respond-

ing to the apparent polytheism implied by the Neoplatonist doctrine of the primordial causes of John Scotus Eriugena. On the charge of the doctrinal similarity of kabbalah and Christianity leveled at kabbalists by opponents in the thirteenth century and the possible impact this may have had on Isaac, see Sendor, "Emergence," vol. 1, pp. 164–167.

437. *Zohar* 2:60b, 87a, 90b, 3:13b, 19a, 21a, 35b–36a, 73a, 89b, 98b, 159a, 265b, 298b; Scholem, *On the Kabbalah and Its Symbolism*, p. 44; Idel, "Concept of Torah," pp. 58–73; Tishby, *Wisdom of the Zohar*, pp. 284, 293–294, 1086; Mopsik, *Grands textes*, pp. 278–280; E. Wolfson, "Mystical Significance," pp. 59–60.

438. *Zohar* 2:60b.

439. For discussion of these associations and citation of some relevant sources, see E. Wolfson, "Mystical Rationalization," pp. 224–225 and the accompanying notes.

440. *Zohar* 2:90b.

441. *Zohar* 3:89b. In my judgment, the full force of the claim made in numerous zoharic passages and corroborated from the words of other kabbalists from this period is that the incarnation of the divine in the Torah scroll is to be understood ontologically. Consider, by way of contrast, the assessment in Rorem, *Biblical and Liturgical Symbols*, p. 66: "For Dionysius, the divine procession 'down' to the scriptures and the liturgy is not an ontological bestowal of being, as in some Neoplatonists, but more a matter of revelation and manifestation. In itself, the divine is absolutely transcendent and unknowable." In the kabbalistic sources with which I am engaged, I see no justification in distinguishing between the *substantial presence* of God in the letters of the text and his disclosure.

442. Regarding this theme, see E. Wolfson, "Mystical Significance," pp. 69–72; idem, "Gender and Heresy," pp. 252–253 n. 107; idem, "Before Alef," pp. 146–150.

443. See E. Wolfson, *Along the Path*, p. 242 n. 114.

444. On the symbolic background for this symbolism, see E. Wolfson, "Images of God's Feet," pp. 143–181.

445. For references, see E. Wolfson, *Abraham Abulafia*, p. 154 n. 28.

446. The orthography of the letter was also the subject of midrashic interpretation. For a sampling of sources, see E. Wolfson, "Before Alef," p. 154 n. 33.

447. *Gagin*, literally, "roofs," but one of the connotations of this term attested already in rabbinic literature is the orthographic line that is part of the letter (see, for example, Babylonian Talmud, Shabbat 104b).

448. *Zohar* 3:36a.

449. Liebes, *Sections of the Zohar Lexicon*, p. 401, suggests that heaven, earth, and the divine mediating between them, symbolized by the three lines of the *beit*, may correspond to *Binah* and *Malkhut* with *Tif'eret* in the middle, an interpretation found in the traditional commentary on *Zohar* by Buzaglo, *Miqdash Melekh*, p. 60. Implied in this approach is the belief that the opinion attributed to R. Eleazar reiterates and supports the view of R. Judah. I am doubtful of this suggestion, as it seems that zoharic hermeneutics is predicated on positing an exoteric interpretation followed by an esoteric, though I am not alleging that these two levels are in any absolute sense independent from one another.

450. The mystery of the threefold unity is linked to the orthography of *alef* in *Zohar* 3:193b: "The image [*diyoqna*] of *alef* consists of three sides, the beginning of the supernal mystery of primordial Adam, for the image of *alef* is composed of two arms, one from here and the other from here, and the body in the middle, and all is one mystery, it is the mystery of unity, and therefore *alef* has the numerical value of one." A similar decoding of the shape of *alef* appears in *Sha'rei Ṣedeq*, pp. 18–19; Idel, *Le Porte della Giustizia*, pp. 473–474.

451. I have argued that an older mythopoeic complex extractable from the bahiric text posits a primal triad depicted imaginally as father, son, and daughter. The father regains the unity with the daughter through the agency of the son, that is, the daughter is given in matrimony to the son, brother weds sister. In some passages, the son represents the male potency, the phallic channel that connects father and daughter. See E. Wolfson, *Along the Path*, pp. 63–88; idem, "Before Alef"; and discussion in previous chapter of this monograph.

452. Liebes, *Sections of the Zohar Lexicon*, p. 400. Curiously, when Liebes mentions the part of the zoharic passage that I have investigated, referring to the three lines that make up the letter *beit*, the beginning of

Torah and the totality of the name, he makes no mention of the Christological element. On the threefold unity in the "mystery of the voice" (*raza de-qol*), i.e., *Tif'eret*, which comprises water, fire, and air (the central *sefirot* of *Ḥesed, Din*, and *Raḥamim*), discerned through the "vision of the holy spirit" (*ḥezyona de-ruaḥ qudsha*) linked exegetically to the three names of God mentioned in the *Shema* (Deut. 6:4), see *Zohar* 2:43b, and parallel in Moses de León, *Sheqel ha-Qodesh*, pp. 103–106; Liebes, *Studies in Zohar*, pp. 140–145; E. Wolfson, *Through a Speculum*, pp. 380–383. Compare passage from Asher ben David's *Sefer ha-Yiḥud* cited in chap. 4, n. 38.

453. Liebes, *Studies in Zohar*, pp. 66–67; E. Wolfson, "Re/membering the Covenant." For a relatively early attempt at a critical assessment of the affinities between kabbalah and Christianity, especially esoteric strands of the latter, see Franck, *Die Kabbala*, pp. 249–260.

454. Liebes, *Studies in Zohar*, pp. 139–161. Recently, Schäfer and Green have independently adopted a similar strategy to explain the kabbalistic fascination with the feminine image of *Shekhinah* in light of the augmented Marian imagery in Christian piety during the twelfth and thirteenth centuries; see references in chap. 2, n. 224. On my own conjecture that a critical passage in *Sefer ha-Bahir* should be decoded as a polemic against the Christian myth of the virgin birth of the Messiah, deplorably ignored by both Schäfer and Green, see E. Wolfson, *Along the Path*, pp. 83–86. If my surmise is correct, it would support the orientation of Schäfer and Green, who have both looked to Christian portrayals of Mary in order to explain one possible and too often neglected channel of influence on the early kabbalists.

455. Liebes, *Studies in Zohar*, pp. 41–43, 79, 171 n. 65, 174 n. 90, 180 n. 126, 191 n. 209.

456. *Zohar* 2:162b.

457. Babylonian Talmud, Berakhot 55a, and see Scholem, *On the Kabbalah and Its Symbolism*, pp. 166–167; E. Wolfson, *Along the Path*, p. 159 n. 23.

458. For an exemplary study of this theme, see Jeffrey, *People of the Book*. On the attempt to forge a nexus between interpretation and incarnation, see Bozarth-Campbell, *The Word's Body*. See also discussion of the metaphorical conjunction between *corpus* and *verba* in Augustine by Gellrich, *Idea of the Book*, pp. 116–122. According to this insightful analysis, Augustine draws a parallel between his own writing and the incarnational Word that became flesh so that saving words could be spoken and written. In short, Augustine's *verba* become the *corpus* to explain God's *Verbum*. For further elucidation of these points, see Troup, *Temporality, Eternity, and Wisdom*, pp. 82–116.

459. A. Abulafia, "Jewish Carnality," pp. 59–75.

Chapter Six
Envisioning Eros: Poiesis and Heeding Silence

1. This dimension of medieval kabbalah has been well documented in scholarly literature. For a limited list of representative studies, see Waite, *Holy Kabbalah*, pp. 377–405; G. Langer, *Die Erotik der Kabbala*; Scholem, *Major Trends*, pp. 225–229; Tishby, *Wisdom of the Zohar*, pp. 1355–1379; Mopsik, *Lettre sur la sainteté*; Idel, "Sexual Metaphors and Praxis," pp. 197–224; Liebes, "Zohar and Eros"; Rotenberg, *The Yetzer*. For a brief discussion of the erotic symbolism of language, see G. Langer, *Liebesmystik der Kabbala*, pp. 84–95.

2. The paradoxical nature of the ecstatic experience as a standing-out that is concurrently a turning-in was duly noted by Buber, *Ecstatic Confessions*, p. 2: "This most inward of all experiences is what the Greeks call *ek-stasis*, a stepping out."

3. I am in full agreement with the assessment on this topic offered by Kripal, *Kali's Child*, p. 23. Kripal reflects on the use of the erotic to characterize the "dimension of human experience that is simultaneously related both to the physical and emotional experience of sexuality and to the deepest ontological levels of religious experience." On the convergence of eros and religious ecstasy, see other references cited in chap. 3, n. 33. For a nuanced analysis of sacred eroticism with a primary focus on Renaissance devotional literature, see Rambuss, *Closet Devotions*.

4. G. Scott, *Phallic Worship*, p. xxi.

5. On the centrality of *coincidentia oppositorum* in Eliade's philosophy of religion as the phenomenologi-

cal modality that reveals the highest attainment of *Homo religiosus*, the experience of the totality that transcends the limits of conditional being, see Altizer, *Mircea Eliade and the Dialectic of the Sacred*, pp. 17–20, 81–104; D. Allen, *Structure and Creativity in Religion*, pp. 121, 165–166, 184–185, 221–222; Rennie, *Reconstructing Eliade*, pp. 33–40; and Wasserstrom, *Religion after Religion*, pp. 67–82.

6. Eliade, *Journal III*, p. 148, entry dated 27 February 1974 (emphasis in original).

7. See further Eliade, *Yoga*, p. 134, and consider the insightful remark on Eliade's attraction to Tantra in Wasserstrom, *Religion after Religion*, p. 292 n. 54.

8. It must be said, however, that more recent scholarship on tantrism has confirmed Eliade's perception regarding the intricate nexus of the sexual and spiritual. Consider, for example, Brooks, *Secret of the Three Cities*, p. 70: "However, intoxicating substances, sensuality, and even ritual sex, do more than force the Tantric to break down the distinctions between the ultimate reality of Brahman and the mundane physical and material world. These distinctive Kaula tradition elements intend to propel the adept to the realization of Brahman's blissful nature (*ananda*) in both physical and spiritual realms." See also David G. White's hyperbolic remark regarding the "erotico-mystical tantric operations" in *Alchemical Body*, p. 6: "In the end, all is a continuity of sexual fluids." The erotic practices of tantric alchemy are rooted in a cosmology affirming the sexual nature of reality. See ibid., pp. 54, 172–173, 191–202, 207–211; and the discussion on vital and sexual fluids as well as other sexual transactions connected especially to the mouth in idem, *Kiss of the Yoginī*, pp. 67–122. On the homology between transformation of the subtle body, orgasm in sexual intercourse, and mystical enlightenment, see Kvaerne, "On the Concept of Sahaja," pp. 88–135. On the use of sexuality as spiritual technique in the Hindu and Buddhist tantric traditions, see also Samuel, "Body in Buddhist and Hindu Tantra," pp. 197–210, esp. pp. 205–207.

9. For example, the introduction to M. Taylor, *Critical Terms*, pp. 1–19. See also Arnal, "Definition," pp. 21–34, and the relevant bibliography cited at the conclusion of his essay, especially the study by Asad, "Construction of Religion," pp. 27–54. See also Joy, "Beyond Essence and Intuition," pp. 69–86.

10. The idiom is taken from Smart, *Dimensions of the Sacred*.

11. See, for instance, Proudfoot, *Religious Experience*; Sharf, "Buddhist Modernism," pp. 228–283; and esp. Flood, *Beyond Phenomenology*, who develops a "critique of phenomenology and the ghost of essentialism in religious studies" on the basis of a "dialogical tradition in relation to narrativism," arguing therefore for the "demise of the ahistorical, philosophy of consciousness within the academic study of religions in favour of a historically contingent philosophy of the sign" (p. 11). See also R. King, *Orientalism and Religion*, pp. 35–61. While the critique of an ahistorical, phenomenological essentialism in the study of religion is in order, it must be pointed out that the issue of history or historical consciousness and Husserlian phenomenology is more complex than the presentation by Flood would allot. On this question, see, for instance, Funke, "Phenomenology and History," pp. 3–101; Lyotard, *Phenomenology*, pp. 111–132. For an approach to Husserl's transcendental reduction, which emphasizes the universal and timeless character of apodictic judgments regarding the world of phenomenality, see Sokolowski, "Truth within Phenomenological Speech," pp. 188–217; idem, *Husserlian Meditations*, pp. 233–270.

12. *Kitvei Ramban*, 2:522, corrected in part in accordance with MS Vatican 211, fol. 18a. See E. Wolfson, *Through a Speculum*, pp. 290–291. I have modified my translation here, which has altered my interpretation as well. For a verbatim parallel, see Azriel of Gerona, *Commentary on Talmudic Aggadoth*, p. 16. Scholem, *Origins*, p. 302 n. 204, tentatively suggested that the "cardinal principle" transmitted by Ezra in the name of Isaac the Blind signified that "in the meditation on the name of God the mystic brings the ten sefiroth—from the first to the last—into harmony."

13. See *Book Bahir*, sec. 61, pp. 153–155.

14. Ezra ben Solomon of Gerona, *Perush Shir ha-Shirim*, *Kitvei Ramban*, 2:477–478.

15. Maimonides, *Guide*, III.51, pp. 627–628; M. Fishbane, *Kiss of God*, pp. 24–26; and further references in chap. 7, n. 151.

16. Ezra ben Solomon of Gerona, *Perush Shir ha-Shirim*, *Kitvei Ramban*, 2:485.

17. Ibid., pp. 510–511.

18. Jacob ben Sheshet, *Sefer ha-Emunah we-ha-Biṭṭaḥon*, *Kitvei Ramban*, 2:387. In that passage, Jacob ben

Sheshet relates the notion of spiritual pleasure to the midrashic idea of "actual eating" (*akhilah wada'it*), which is linked exegetically to Exodus 24:11. See E. Wolfson, *Through a Speculum*, p. 294 and references given there, n. 89.

19. The roots for this way of thinking are found in *Sefer ha-Bahir.* See E. Wolfson, "Hebraic and Hellenic Conceptions," pp. 168–172.

20. The elitist nature of the medieval kabbalists has been long recognized in scholarly literature. For an attempt to discuss this phenomenon in a different way with particular focus on the period when works of kabbalah and references to kabbalists began to proliferate, see Idel, "Kabbalah and Elites," pp. 5–19.

21. Satlow, "Try To Be A Man," pp. 19–40. On the nexus between masculinity and self-control in Roman sources contemporary with the formative period of rabbinic literature, see C. Williams, *Roman Homosexuality*, pp. 138–142. Also pertinent to an assessment of the rabbinic construction of maleness is the analysis in D'Angelo, "Knowing How to Preside," pp. 265–295, esp. pp. 276–278, 290–293.

22. Mishnah, Avot 4:1.

23. For fuller discussion, see chap. 7.

24. A sustained argument to this effect, more nuanced than my brief summary, is mounted by Boyarin, *Unheroic Conduct*, pp. 81–185.

25. *Genesis Rabbah*, 65:20–21, pp. 733–740.

26. See Rist, *Eros and Psyche*; Nussbaum, *Love's Knowledge*, pp. 106–124; C. Osborne, *Eros Unveiled*; Finkelberg, "Plato's Language of Love and the Female," pp. 231–261; Calame, *Poetics of Eros*, pp. 177–191. For the development of this philosophical ideal in medieval Western Christianity, see Scaglione, *Nature and Love*.

27. G. Lloyd, *Man of Reason*, pp. 18–28; Thornton, *Eros*, pp. 127–138, 210–212. On the Graeco-Roman conception of the excessive emotionality of women, illustrated by the particular case of anger, see W. Harris, *Restraining Rage*, pp. 264–282. For an interesting attempt to overcome the traditional binary of mind/reason as masculine and the body/imagination as feminine, see Labouvie-Vief, *Psyche and Eros*. Finally, it must be mentioned that there is evidence from classical Greek literature suggesting that women were involved in philosophical pursuits. The misogynist tendencies of Plato and Aristotle, therefore, were not necessarily the norm. See Pomeroy, *Women in Hellenistic Egypt*, pp. 61–71; R. Hawley, "Problem of Women Philosophers," pp. 70–87; Snyder, *Woman and the Lyre*, pp. 99–121, cited by Richlin, "Foucault's *History of Sexuality*," p. 157 n. 37.

28. The matter is explored in detail in Schott, *Cognition and Eros*. See also Songe-Møller, *Philosophy without Women*, pp. 21–48, 89–112. On the role of philosophical asceticism in the shaping of the Christian monastic ideal, see Lohse, *Askese und Mönchtum*, pp. 41–78. For a nuanced discussion of the Greek philosophical ideal of the subordination of women and the domination of men in Christian sources, indebted in part to the influence of Hellenistic Judaism, see Jantzen, *Power, Gender and Christian Mysticism*, pp. 30–58. A different approach to sexual conduct is discernible in Stoic philosophy, in which the act is deemed virtuous or malevolent in accord with the nature of the agent rather than the action. See Nussbaum, "Eros and the Wise," pp. 290–291. An interesting exception to the general pattern in medieval literature is the allegorical personification of Reason as a female in the *Roman de la Rose*, although a debate regarding the precise identity of Reason (whether divine wisdom or human intellect) persists in modern scholarship; see Gunn, *Mirror of Love*, pp. 145–150, 179–180; Huot, *Romance of the Rose*, pp. 12–13, 97–98, 172–173. (The personification of Reason as female may reflect the allegorical depiction of Philosophy as a female in the *Philosophiae consolationis* of Boethius.) On the personification of nature as feminine, see Gunn, *Mirror of Love*, pp. 155–156; Huot, *Romance of the Rose*, pp. 223–224. But see Gunn, pp. 225–226, where he notes the use of phallic symbols (especially the images of the hammer, anvil, and pen) to represent nature's creative activity and power in *De planctu naturae* by Alain de Lille.

29. One of the most important channels for explaining the transmission of the ancient engendering of form as masculine and matter as feminine to the medieval kabbalists was Maimonides. See *Guide*, I:Introduction, pp. 13–14; I:6, p. 31; I:17, p. 43; II:30, pp. 355–356; III:8, p. 431. See Abulafia, *Ḥayyei ha-Olam ha-Ba*, fol. 6a (printed ed., pp. 51–52): "From the secret of Adam and Eve, for they are in every person in the image of matter and form, for they are the principle and beginning of the entire account of creation. Thus primal

Adam is in the image of form and Eve, his wife who was created from his side, in the image of matter." For extended discussion of the Maimonidean perspective, see Gikatilla, *Be'urim le-Sefer Moreh Nevukhim la-Rambam*, 22b–c. The standard medieval philosophical conception is expressed succinctly in the allegorical interpretation (*al derekh ha-sekhel*) given by Baḥya ben Asher to the narrative about Adam, Eve, and the serpent in the Garden of Eden. See *Rabbenu Baḥya: Be'ur al ha-Torah*, 1:83 (ad Gen. 3:21): "The man alludes to the intellect, and it is not good for the intellect to be alone [based on Gen. 2:18], for it needs an instrument through which its actions would be visible and that would be an aid to it in the fulfillment of Torah and the commandments. This instrument is matter. Just as man who is created in body and soul has a need for an aid in the establishment of the species, so the body is an aid to the intellect in intellectual matters, and this aid is the woman, and in her there is an allusion to the body. Thus Solomon compared matter to a woman . . . for the woman receives the action in a manner similar to the matter that receives the forms and bears the images. The serpent alludes to the evil inclination." For discussion of the correlation of masculinity/intellect and femininity/body in medieval Jewish philosophy, especially in the thought of Maimonides, see S. P. Allen, "Plato, Aristotle and the Concept of Woman," pp. 89–111; Klein-Braslavy, *Maimonides' Interpretation of the Adam Stories*, pp. 193–208; Dobbs-Weinstein, "Matter as Creature," pp. 217–235; Shapiro, "Matter of Discipline," pp. 158–173. For a different approach to the status of the woman in Maimonidean thought, see Melamed, "Maimonides on Women," pp. 99–134; Rudavsky, "To Know What Is," pp. 192–200. See also Kellner, "Philosophical Misogyny," pp. 113–128. Although Maimonides unquestionably appropriates the hierarchical distinction between reason and matter along gender lines, the hierarchy is mitigated to a degree insofar as both intellect and body are presented in the thought of Maimonides as attributes of God, a viewpoint that was articulated in a distinctive way at a later point by Spinoza. See Goodman, "Matter and Form as Attributes of God," pp. 86–97. For a more positive role assigned to the feminine as the embodiment of wisdom in later Jewish philosophy, see Melamed, "Women as Philosophers," pp. 113–130.

30. Bachofen, *Das Mutterrecht*, vol. 1, p. 412, cited by Neumann, *Great Mother*, p. 57.

31. See D. Biale, *Eros and the Jews*, pp. 33–59; Boyarin, *Carnal Israel*, pp. 53–57, 71–75, 142; Satlow, *Jewish Marriage*, pp. 12–21. Needless to say, the evaluation of human sexuality exclusively from the perspective of fertility is part of the scriptural legacy. See Berquist, *Controlling Corporeality*, pp. 51–79.

32. *Zohar* 2:108b, 112a. On the depiction of Satan as the emasculated male, see the discussion in chap. 7.

33. Scholem, *On the Mystical Shape*, p. 209; Tishby, *Wisdom of the Zohar*, p. 1362; Liebes, *Studies in the Zohar*, p. 71; E. Wolfson, *Circle in the Square*, p. 93.

34. *Leviticus Rabbah* 20:9, pp. 463–464. In this midrashic source, the views that the sons of Aaron had no children and that they were not married are offered as distinct explanations to explain their death; in the zoharic context, the two are blended together.

35. *Zohar* 1:55b, 165b.

36. *Zohar* 3:57a. See ibid., 3:5b, 6b. Mention should be made of the fact that preserved in zoharic literature as well (3:56b) is a positive portrayal of Nadab and Abihu as righteous men whose death atones for the sins of Jews through the ages.

37. Matt, "Matnita Dilan," pp. 130–144, considers this rhetorical trope as one of the veiled allusions in zoharic literature to the homiletical technique of innovation.

38. *Zohar* 3:57b. The reincarnation of Nadab and Abihu in Phineḥas is alluded to in 3:61b; for an alternative decoding of the name Phineḥas as *penei ḥas*, the countenances of mercy, see 3:237b (*Ra'aya Meheimna*). Vital, *Sha'ar ha-Gilgulim*, sec. 36, 42a, reports another tradition in the name of his teacher according to which Shimshon the Nazirite was the reincarnation of Nadab. Mention should also be made of Vital's assertion, sec. 27, 28a, that when Nadab and Abihu entered the world, there was the "beginning and inception of the rectification of the root of Cain, the second aspect of the root of the first Adam, which is the most supreme." These matters are too complex to engage here, and perhaps time and inclination will admit me to return to them someday.

39. *Zohar* 3:57b.

40. *Zohar* 3:7b, 109b (*Ra'aya Meheimna*), 264b, 296a; Tishby, *Wisdom of the Zohar*, p. 1355; Liebes, *Sections of the Zohar Lexicon*, pp. 277–278 n. 459; E. Wolfson, *Circle in the Square*, pp. 94–95.

41. The *yod* in Phineḥas is associated in *Zohar* 3:213b, 220a with the fervor he exhibited with respect to the sign of the holy covenant.

42. Babylonian Talmud, Shevuᶜot 18b.

43. *Zohar Ḥadash*, 11a (*Midrash ha-Neᶜelam*); *Zohar* 1:90b, 112a (*Midrash ha-Neᶜelam*), 3:56a. In some passages, based on a discussion in Babylonian Talmud, Nedarim 20b, the wrong intent during intercourse is related more specifically to thinking about another woman while making love to one's wife. See *Zohar* 1:155a (*Sitrei Torah*), *Zohar Ḥadash*, 11a (*Midrash ha-Neᶜelam*).

44. See E. Wolfson, *Circle in the Square*, pp. 92–98.

45. See chap. 8.

46. See D. Schwartz, "Avicenna and Maimonides," pp. 185–197.

47. Desmond, *Being and the Between*, p. 7.

48. Ibid., p. 31.

49. See chap. 3, n. 53.

50. Aristotle, *Metaphysics* 1072b, 20–23.

51. For elaboration of this Platonic theme in German Idealism, see Velkley, "Realizing Nature in the Self," pp. 151–152.

52. Lacan, *Reading Seminar XI*, pp. 234–235; and see Braunstein, "Desire and Jouissance," pp. 102–115.

53. *Zohar* 3:288b.

54. The point is elaborated in Butler, *Subjects of Desire*.

55. See Brenner, *Intercourse of Knowledge*, pp. 23, 29. The author duly notes the discrepancy between male and female; men are the "*knowing* subjects of the supreme act of knowledge," whereas women are "more passive, less knowing and less discerning in their 'love,' from love for children to sexual desire" (emphasis in original).

56. Barr, *Garden of Eden*, pp. 57–73; Veenker, "Forbidden Fruit," pp. 57–73, esp. pp. 69–73. See as well the discussion of "carnal knowledge" in Malul, *Knowledge, Control and Sex*, pp. 233–252.

57. *Book Bahir*, sec. 13, p. 125, sec. 56, p. 151, sec. 104, p. 187; E. Wolfson, *Along the Path*, pp. 73 and 209 n. 85.

58. Vital, *Shaᶜar ha-Kawwanot*, 79b. Compare Vital, *Shaᶜar ha-Pesuqim*, 3a: "Know that all the souls come forth from the supernal copulation [*ziwwug elyon*] from the drop of the five mercies and five strengths that are in the mind [*daᶜat*], as is known from the verse 'And Adam knew his wife Eve' (Gen. 4:1), for copulation is referred to as knowledge [*yediᶜah*] since the drop of the copulation [*tippat ha-ziwwug*] is drawn forth from the brain of the mind [*moaḥ ha-daᶜat*]." Needless to say, the erotic understanding of *daᶜat* is attested in older kabbalistic sources that influenced the Lurianic kabbalists. For instance, see *Tiqqunei Zohar* sec. 69, 99a: "*Bereʾshit*, *beit* is two, *Ḥokhmah* and *Tevunah*, and the third is 'the fear of the Lord is the beginning of knowledge' (Prov. 1:7). Concerning this knowledge it is said 'And Adam knew Eve his wife' (Gen. 4:1), for there is no copulation [*ziwwug*] except through knowledge [*daᶜat*], which is the central pillar, the unity of *Abba* and *Imma*. Thus it is below, *Ṣaddiq* is the unity of the central pillar and *Shekhinah* below. With respect to the body and the phallus [*guf u-verit*] it is said 'the Lord is a God of knowledge' [*el deᶜot*] (1 Sam. 2:3), and both of them constitute testimony [*edut*] for there is no testimony with less than two."

59. *Shaᶜar ha-Pesuqim*, 6c.

60. *Perush Sifra di-Ṣeniʿuta*, in Vital, *Shaᶜar Maʾamerei Rashbi*, 28b; *Sefer ha-Derushim*, p. 260.

61. *Shaᶜar ha-Pesuqim*, 38a.

62. Vital, *Eṣ Ḥayyim*, 39:2, 67d; for fuller citation and analysis of this passage, see E. Wolfson, "Divine Suffering," p. 124.

63. It is useful to compare the nexus of eros and language in kabbalistic lore to a similar labyrinth of themes in Benjamin, as discussed by Weigel, *Entstellte Ähnlichkeit*, pp. 147–179.

64. Aristotle's depiction of the divine mind relates to a larger presumption regarding the circular nature of human thought. An informed discussion on this matter may be found in Bontekoe, *Dimensions of the Hermeneutic Circle*. The author states the operative hermeneutical principle at the outset of his inquiry: "All human understanding, by virtue of its occurring in time, is hermeneutically circular" (p. 2). The example I

have provided is one specific application of this sentiment. For discussion of the origin of the idea regarding the inescapable circularity of human consciousness in nineteenth-century German thought, see Breazeale, "Circles and Grounds," pp. 43–70; Perrinjaquet, "Some Remarks," pp. 71–95; and Rockmore, "Antifoundationalism, Circularity, and the Spirit of Fichte," pp. 96–112.

65. Further textual support for this claim may be elicited from the fact that the motif of the uroboros is attested in zoharic literature. See *Zohar* 2:176b, 179b; 3:205b; Scholem, *Sabbatai Ṣevi*, p. 236.

66. Gruenwald, "Critical Notes," p. 492, suggested a possible link between the description of *sefirot* in *Sefer Yeṣirah* and the image of the serpent eating its own tail in the Ophite sect, but he casts doubt on the idea that that the author of the passage incorporated into *Sefer Yeṣirah* was promoting a gnostic worldview. Gruenwald thus suggests a second interpretation (there is a third as well, but I will not be concerned with it here): the image of the end fixed in the beginning and the beginning in the end calls to mind the form of a circle. In my judgment, there is no theoretical justification or need to distinguish these as distinct explanations. The symbol of the uroboros conveys the circular morphology; indeed, many scholars have noted that the primary significance of this image is to express the unbroken unity of nondifferentiated being.

67. Dionysius the Areopagite, *Divine Names*, chap. 4, 709C–D, p. 144; on eros as a unifying and binding power, see p. 147.

68. Ibid., 712C–D, p. 146.

69. Ibid., 712D–713A, pp. 146–147.

70. Neumann, *Origins*, p. 50.

71. *Nag Hammadi Codex I* in *The Coptic Gnostic* Library, vol. 1, p. 89.

72. Here it is worthwhile recalling Freud's account of mystical experience in terms of the primary narcissism that the child feels vis-à-vis the mother. See Kripal, *Roads of Excess*, pp. 88–89. It is also of interest to compare the kabbalistic ideal as I have presented it with the contemplative ideal of *jouissance* described by P. Rose, *Bodin and the Great God of Nature*, pp. 104–106. Finally, it is noteworthy to recall the locution "narcissistic autoeroticism," which Kristeva, *Tales of Love*, p. 109, uses to describe Plotinus, although she argues that the speculative element in the Plotinian plan transforms the narcissistic process into an internal state of "autoerotic reflection." Kristeva's analysis of Plotinus seems to me to be an entirely appropriate way to depict the contemplative state proferred by medieval male kabbalists.

73. Also noteworthy is the use of *shiʿasha* (Isa. 11:8) in the sense of "infant."

74. Babylonian Talmud, Shabbat 89a.

75. E. Wolfson, *Circle in the Square*, p. 2.

76. The point is implicit as well in the tradition preserved in *Avot de-Rabbi Natan*, version A, chap. 31, p. 91: "R. Eliezer the son of R. Yose the Galilean said: 974 generations prior to the world's having been created the Torah was written and it rested in the bosom of the holy One, blessed be he, and it uttered song together with the ministering angels, as it says, 'I was with him as a confidant, and I was delighted every day, rejoicing before him' (Prov. 8:30), and it says, 'Rejoicing in his inhabited world, finding delight with human beings' (Prov. 8:31)." In this text, the comparison of the Torah to the angels underscores the hypostatic nature underlying the feminine personification. See also *Midrash Tehillim*, 90:12, p. 391. The Torah, which is one of seven things that preceded the world, is described as being written as "black fire upon white fire and resting on the knee of the holy One, blessed be he."

77. *Genesis Rabbah*, 1:1, p. 2. It is worth noting a parallel in the Islamic tradition, based in part on Jewish teachings reflected in several qurʾānic verses, regarding the throne of God (*al-ʿarsh*), the pen (*al-qalam*), and the guarded tablet (*al-lawḥ al-mahfūẓ*). See Kisāʾi, *Tales of the Prophets*, p. 5; Nicholson, *Studies in Islamic Mysticism*, pp. 106, 111–112 n. 3, 116; Schimmel, *Mystical Dimensions*, pp. 413–416. Consider the formulation of this older motif cited in a fifteenth-century Arabic cosmological text: "The first thing God Most High created was the throne, consisting of light. Then came the footstool; then the guarded tablet from a white pearl, with its two sides being made of a ruby. Its stylus is light, and its writing is light. Every day God looks at it 360 times; and with every look He creates"; Heinen, *Islamic Cosmology*, p. 137. See chap. 5, n. 84.

78. Yosse ben Yosse, *Poems*, p. 178. This source and the ones cited in the following two notes are already noted in E. Wolfson, *Circle in the Square*, pp. 124–125 n. 6.

79. Yosse ben Yosse, *Poems*, p. 189.

80. Ibid., p. 128.

81. D. Castelli, *Il Commento di Sabbatai Donnolo*, p. 32. For analysis of this passage, see E. Wolfson, "Theosophy of Shabbetai Donnolo," pp. 296–297.

82. Bernstein, *New Poems and Poets*, p. 20.

83. Babylonian Talmud, Menaḥot 29b; Ketuvot 8a.

84. One may hear here a resonance of Tantra. For a fuller, albeit still preliminary, examination comparing the kabbalistic and tantric symbolism, see the section "Ascetic Sexuality/Sexual Asceticism" in chap. 7.

85. Shelomo ha-Bavli, *Poems*, p. 292.

86. The matter seems to have been given an eschatological significance in *eikhah tif'arti*, a lamentation for the destruction of the Temple attributed to Eleazar Kallir: *niḥumav meherah yesha'she'uni*, "let his consolations swiftly comfort me." For a contemporary edition, see *Seder Qinnot ha-Meforash le-Tish'ah ba-Av*, p. 130.

87. Shelomo ha-Bavli, *Poems*, p. 336. In this connection it is of interest to consider the language of the liturgical poem *ashrei ha-am*, which is part of the *Sidrei Avodah*, the genre related to the description of the priest's service on the Day of Atonement. In this poem, we read *hagar avnet / ka-ezor la-matnayim / lehadbiq beit esh / le-esh okhlah esh* ("he girded a sash [Exod. 29:9] / like a loincloth on the loins [Jer. 13:11] / to cleave the house of fire [Obad. 1:18] / to the fire consuming fire [Deut. 4:24]." The imagery of girding is thus applied to the cleaving of Israel to God, the house of fire to the fire consuming fire.

88. The same triad is used in Deuteronomy 26:19 to depict Israel's special status vis-à-vis the nations; see also Jeremiah 33:9.

89. Yannai, *Liturgical Poems*, p. 316.

90. For the philological background pertaining to this term, see E. Wolfson, "Circumcision and the Divine Name," pp. 82–83 and accompanying notes.

91. See *Mekhilta de-Rabbi Ishmael*, p. 14, and references to a plethora of other rabbinic sources offered in n. 10 *ad locum*; and see discussion in L. Hoffman, *Covenant of Blood*, pp. 92–93, 99–101.

92. Yannai, *Liturgical Poems*, p. 316 n. 12.

93. Consider, by contrast, the formulation in the poem by Kallir that begins *we-atah amarta heiṭev*, in *Seder Qinnot ha-Meforash*, p. 198: *attah giddalta we-romamta banim lehaneq / ka'asher yissa ha-omen et ha-yoneq*. Here the language is closer to Numbers 12:11.

94. The language of Yannai, as noted by Rabinovitz (see n. 92), is based on Isaiah 66:1.

95. Liss, *El'azar Ben Yehuda von Worms*, sec. 50, p. 46.

96. *Genesis Rabbah*, 1:1, pp. 1–2, 8:2, p. 57; *Exodus Rabbah*, 30:9; *Leviticus Rabbah*, 19:1, pp. 412–413; *Shir ha-Shirim Rabbah*, 5:7, p. 131.

97. *Book Bahir*, sec. 4, pp. 119–121.

98. E. Wolfson, "Before Alef."

99. Here one would do well to consider the following observation of Schelling, *Ages of the World*, p. 17: "But the divine nature does not allow that it is just an eternal No and an eternal denial of itself. It is an equally valid part of its nature that it is a being of all beings, the infinitely self-granting and self-communicating being. In that it therefore conceals its being, there thereby appears, by force of the eternal necessity of its nature, the eternal affirmation of its being as it opposes the negation (which is not sublimated but abiding, albeit now receding into the negative). In contrast, the negating force represses itself and precisely thereby intensified itself into an independent being." In the divine, opposites coalesce and thus there is no basis to distinguish negation and affirmation. However, it is possible to speak of affirmation arising as negation of negation, and consequently, the disclosure of God may be portrayed as concealment of concealment or, in the langage I have employed to account for the kabbalistic doctrine, writing of the name ensues from erasure of erasure. On the coincidence of opposites, see Schelling, *Ages of the World*, p. 74: "But precisely because the Godhead is whole and undivided, the eternal Yes and the eternal No, the Godhead is again neither one nor the other, but the unity of both. This is not an actual trinity of separately located principles, but here the Godhead *is* as the One, and precisely because it is the One, it is both the No and the Yes and the unity of both" (emphasis in original).

100. See Julien, *Jacques Lacan's Return to Freud*, pp. 174–175; Ragland-Sullivan, *Jacques Lacan and the Philosophy of Psychoanalysis*, pp. 75–76. There are obvious structural similarities between the mythic teachings of

medieval kabbalah and older gnostic sources on the issue of the autoeroticism of the primal aspect of the divine, framed, moreover, in terms of the combination of thought and desire, a similarity that may be explained by the influence of Neoplatonism on both. See, for example, the depiction of the One in the *Apocryphon of John*, in *Coptic Gnostic Library*, vol. 2, p. 26: "He desires (αἰτεῖν) himself alone in the perfection of the light. He will contemplate (νοεῖν) the pure (ἀκέραιον) light, the immeasurable majesty."

101. Salecl, *(Per)versions of Love and Hate*, pp. 59–78, esp. pp. 63–64 (emphasis in original).

102. Žižek, *Tarrying*, p. 36.

103. Ibid., p. 69.

104. Salecl, *(Per)versions of Love and Hate*, p. 63.

105. Žižek, *Tarrying*, pp. 43–44: "This reversal relies on a kind of realization of the metaphor: what at first appears as a mere metaphorical simulation, a pale imitation, of the true reality . . . becomes the original paradigm imitated by blood-and-flesh reality. . . . What we experience as 'reality' is constituted by such a reversal: as Lacan puts it, 'reality' is always framed by a fantasy, i.e., for something real to be experienced as part of 'reality,' it must fit the preordained coordinates of our fantasy-space. . . . This way, we can propose a second definition of the Real: a surplus, a hard kernel, which resists any process of modeling, simulation, or metaphoricization."

106. Ibid., p. 43.

107. This characterization of union would raise questions regarding the ultimate moral valence of the experience of erotic contemplation. In the intersubjective sphere, erotic union can have an ethical dimension if it is attained on the basis of the acceptance of the other in the otherness of the other's being. See, in particular, Farley, *Eros for the Other.*.

108. Bass, *Difference and Disavowal*, p. 53.

109. Babylonian Talmud, Berakhot 53b.

110. Ezra's text as cited in Azriel of Gerona, *Commentary on Talmudic Aggadoth*, p. 20.

111. Ibid., p. 20 n. 22. The text to which Tishby refers is found in MS, Oxford-Bodleian 1947, fol. 18a.

112. Babylonian Talmud, Makkot 24a.

113. Jacob ben Sheshet, *Sefer ha-Emunah we-ha-Biṭṭaḥon*, *Kitvei Ramban*, 2:357.

114. Ibid., 2:411.

115. Babylonian Talmud, Berakhot 9b.

116. Jacob ben Sheshet, *Sefer ha-Emunah we-ha-Biṭṭaḥon*, *Kitvei Ramban*, 2:368.

117. Ibid. On the notion of the will in Jacob ben Sheshet, see Scholem, *Origins*, pp. 381–382. For discussion of the status of the primordial will and the infinite in early kabbalah more generally, see Scholem, "Traces of Gabirol," pp. 160–178, esp. pp. 165–170, reprinted with updated bibliography in idem, *Studies in Kabbalah*, pp. 39–66, esp. pp. 46–53; idem, *Origins*, pp. 341–343, 430–439; Wijnhoven, "Mysticism of Solomon Ibn Gabirol," pp. 137–152, esp. pp. 146–149; Wilensky, "Isaac Ibn Laṭif," pp. 185–223, esp. pp. 202–205, 212–215; Tishby, *Wisdom of Zohar*, p. 270.

118. Azriel of Gerona, *Commentary on Talmudic Aggadoth*, pp. 23–25.

119. Ibid., p. 101. Commenting in his *Perush ha-Tefillah*, fol. 201b (Sed-Rajna, *Commentaire*, p. 30; "*Perush ha-Tefillah*," p. 3), on the depiction of God as the one "who has formed" (*asher yaṣar*), Azriel writes, "and he formed his creation in wisdom, the hidden potential for beings is called 'wisdom' [*ḥokhmah*] as the philosophers [*ḥakhmei meḥqar*] say matter [*shoresh*] and form [*ṣurah*] were seals [*ḥotamot*] concealed in thought [*maḥshavah*] prior to their being. They were concealed like a scribe who forms on the outside forms that were within." In *Commentary on Talmudic Aggadoth*, p. 82, this formulation is attributed to Plato; for references, see Sed-Rajna, *Commentaire*, p. 30 n. 5. On the ascription of the image of a scribe to divine thought, see *Commentary on Talmudic Aggadoth*, p. 116 and the references to Solomon Ibn Gabirol and Jacob ben Sheshet cited in n. 10 *ad locum*, and E. Wolfson, *Circle in the Square*, pp. 58 and 172–173 n. 73.

120. Similar language is found in Ezra's commentary to Song 4:12, *Kitvei Ramban*, 2:498: "Thus it is appropriate to the sages like them, for all their words are spoken in the holy spirit through allusion to arouse the hearts of the enlightened kabbalists [*ha-maskilim ha-mequbbalim*]." Compare the commentary on Song 7:2, ibid., p. 513: "Thus I received its explanation from the mouth of an enlightened kabbalist [*maskil mequbbal*]."

121. *Baddei ha-Aron*, pp. 42–43.

122. See ibid., pp. 50–51.

123. Ibid., p. 82.

124. The expression *qibbalti be-ma᾽amar sefer yeṣirah* ("I received with respect to a passage in the *Book of Creation*") succinctly captures the interface of oral and written that is implied in the technical term *qabbalah*. See E. Wolfson, "Beyond the Spoken Word"; on p. 200 I mention Shem Tov explicitly. Further confirmation of this understanding can be elicited from Shem Tov's comment in *Baddei ha-Aron*, p. 32: "if a man receives from a well-known kabbalist [*im qibbel ish mi-pi mequbbal mefursam*] *Sefer Yeṣirah, Sefer ha-Bahir*, and *Pereq Shiᶜur Qomah*." We see again that oral tradition consists of exposition of a written text. On this score, consider as well the comment of Shem Tov, p. 35, "I did not receive *Sefer Yeṣirah* from the mouth of my teachers until after many days when I was in the middle of my days."

125. *Baddei ha-Aron*, p. 44.

126. See ibid., pp. 199–201. The inclusion of all the *sefirot* orthographically in the letter *alef* is affirmed by the author of *Shaᶜarei Ṣedeq*; see Idel, *Le Porte della Giustizia*, p. 474.

127. An allusion to this tradition is discernible in *Zohar* 1:21a. The decoding of *alef* as encompassing the totality of the sefirotic pleroma, the *waw* connecting the upper *yod* and the lower *yod*, wisdom at the beginning (*ḥokhmah ba-ro᾽sh*) and wisdom at the end (*ḥokhmah ba-sof*) is found in *Tiqqunei Zohar*, sec. 40, 80b.

128. The author or a scribe mistakenly added the word *nashim* ("women") here. While it is possible that this insertion was an intentional gloss on the word *ḥokhmot* ("wisdoms"), on balance I think it was due to an error and hence I have decided to delete it.

129. *Baddei ha-Aron*, p. 58.

130. Gruenwald, "Preliminary Critical Edition," sec. 6, p. 142. Abulafia was most likely citing the text from memory, since his rendering does not correspond precisely to the received text, "their end is fixed in their beginning and their beginning in their end." See Gruenwald, "Some Critical Notes," p. 492.

131. This is the technical way the *sefirot* are designated in the first part of *Sefer Yeṣirah*. For what still seems to be a reasonable explanation to account for this somewhat enigmatic expression, see Gruenwald, "Some Critical Notes," p. 485.

132. This, too, is derived from the *Sefer Yeṣirah* passage cited in n. 130.

133. Todros ben Joseph Abulafia, *Oṣar ha-Kavod*, 4a. Gikatilla, *Shaᶜarei Orah*, 2:87, elaborates on the kabbalistic dictum *ḥokhmah ba-ro᾽sh ḥokhmah ba-sof*. On the motif of the double wisdom, see Scholem, *Origins*, pp. 92–93, 178–180; and further references in E. Wolfson, "Coronation," p. 317 n. 55.

134. Here I am deliberately playing with the terminology of Merlan, *Monopsychism*.

135. The variant recorded by Abulafia is attested as well in Tosafot, Soṭah 39b, s.v. *ad she-yikhleh amen mipi ha-ṣibbur*.

136. Todros ben Joseph Abulafia, *Oṣar ha-Kavod*, 7d.

137. See E. Wolfson, *Circle in the Square*, pp. 62–74. Even in kabbalistic sources where this term (or any of its cognates) is applied to conditions that cannot be interpreted in terms of adult sexuality, for instance the babe sucking from his mother's breast, the implication is erotic in nature. See, for example, Galante, *Qol Bokhim*, 94b: "This is the secret of 'A babe [*shiᶜashaᶜ*] shall play [*yoneq*] over a viper's hole, and an infant pass his hand over an adder's den' (Isa. 11:8). You already know that the secret of union and copulation [*sod ha-yiḥud we-ha-ziwwug*] is called *shaᶜashuᶜa*." In the continuation, Galante appropriates a zoharic motif and explains that *shaᶜashuᶜa* applies to Metatron, the babe who sucks from the breasts of his mother, *Shekhinah*, and through whom unity in the six weekdays is accomplished.

138. Regarding this principle, see Choufrine, "On Eriguena's Appropriation," pp. 19–58.

139. See chap. 2, n. 321.

140. Everson, seemingly operating out of an independent symbolic matrix, has articulated the understanding of male desire that resonates with the engendering theosophic myth in kabbalistic thinking through the generations. Consider the depiction of the river as the primordial impulse of masculine eros in Everson, *River-Root*, p. 14: "For the River is male. / He is raking down ridges . . . / And bringing down to bring on has but one resolve: to deliver. / It is this that makes up his elemental need, / Constitutes his primal ground,

the under-aching sex of the River. / For deep in his groin he carries the fore-thrusting phallos of his might / That sucks up a continent, pouring it into the sea. / A passion for elseness lurks in his root. As the father in child-getting / . . .—so does the river-phallos draw on the land." From the continuation of the poem, it becomes clear that Everson sees in the image of the river a symbol for the divine potency that vibrates through nature: "The male god draws, serpentine giant, phallic thrust and vengeance, / The sex-enduring, life-bestowing, father of waters: the River" (p. 15). In a manner analogous to kabbalistic symbolism, Everson articulated a poetic vision predicated on an intimate nexus between the erotic and mystical, the basic impulse of being troped in intensely sensual terms. See, for example, Everson, *Excesses of God*, pp. 148–149, and especially the passage in idem, *Prodigious Thrust*, p. 83, reprinted in idem, *Dark God of Eros*, p. 192: "And the whole of the universe had but one proclivity: to be consumed—formed and destroyed, formed and destroyed, endlessly. Thus sex: the divine power exploding out of the tissue of being, the male-flesh, seeking the counter-thrusting ground, driven like a shaft into the vascular orifice, their orgasm the uncontainable volcanic force breaking its own way out; birth an inscrutability, a smudge of the blind power clotted like a chance infection in the entrails of the female and sucked up into creaturehood. So too with the creative psychic act, a glint struck off the dynamic core, fragment of the divine preponderance burning like a jewel in the plasm of the brain; man's whole meaning, brain and plexus, twin polarities, radiating each its own pulsation of the uncheckable energy, two gouts of the supreme majestic force, locked together in a terrible oscillation, flashing back and forth between them the fitful signals of their hunger, an oscillation forever unresolvable, an oscillation which in the end would devour him, and cast him down, and the husk of his flesh be sloughed back to earth." See also idem, *Veritable Years*, p. 215: "All the daughters of Eve / Stamped and twisted, / Swinging the orgiastic strut, / Inducing the final insuperable subjugation: / The phallos of God." For discussion of the contours of the poet's erotic mysticism, see Gelpi's introduction to *Dark God of Eros*, pp. xv–xxxvii.

141. This is a summary account of a longer argument, supported by citation and analysis of primary texts, in the section "Suffering and the *jouissance* of becoming-other," in E. Wolfson, "Divine Suffering," pp. 117–135.

142. This principle is expressed as well by Abulafia, *Oṣar Eden Ganuz*, fol. 74a (printed ed., p. 146): "The seed is the matter that exists from the existence of the Active Intellect, which is the overflow that the intellect receives, and it is in the image of the seed that is born from man and woman."

143. Jacob ben Sheshet, *Sefer ha-Emunah we-ha-Biṭṭaḥon*, *Kitvei Ramban*, 2:409.

144. Equally important and influential on medieval intellectuals was the Aristotelian idea that the ultimate efficient cause in the universe is the desire for the intellect, which finally accounts for the circular motion of heaven and earth. See Russell, *History of Heaven*, pp. 125–140.

145. See Mopsik, "Pensée, voix et parole," pp. 385–414. The kabbalists' emphasis on the progression from thought to speech bears resemblance to depictions of Jesus as the uttered word that expresses the thought of the Father in some Christian theologians. See K. Burke, *Rhetoric of Religion*, p. 13.

146. With respect to the erogenic nature of thought, there is a striking similarity between the kabbalistic symbolism and the approach that informed Tantric traditions and practices in Eastern religions. A number of scholars have touched upon this intriguing parallelism. See chap. 7, n. 204. See also the study of Dange, *Sexual Symbolism*.

147. *Zohar* 1:246b.

148. See Scholem, "Name of God," p. 167. See chap. 1, n. 18. The point is made as well by Bloom, *Kabbalah and Criticism*, p. 52: "Kabbalah is a theory of *writing*, but this is a theory that denies the absolute distinction between writing and inspired speech, even as it denies human distinctions between presence and absence. Kabbalah speaks of a writing before writing . . . but also of a speech before speech, a Primal Introduction preceding all traces of speech." In the continuation of that analysis, Bloom contrasts Derrida's privileging of writing over speech, as a corrective to Occidental logocentrism, and the linguistic orientation of the kabbalah according to which writing and speech cannot be separated.

149. Scholem, *Origins*, p. 277.

150. See D. Biale, *Gershom Scholem*, pp. 99–100.

151. E. Wolfson, *Through a Speculum*, pp. 287–288. Idel, *Messianic Mystics*, p. 355 n. 72, cites the emphasis on the auditory in the ecstatic kabbalah of Abraham Abulafia and Beshtian Hasidism as counterevidence to my claim regarding the dominant impact of the visual in the history of Jewish mysticism. Idel fails to take into account that I stated explicitly that the auditory and visual cannot really be separated. I would apply this synesthesia of vision and hearing to the different currents of Jewish mysticism, including ecstatic kabbalah and Beshtian Hasidism. In my judgment, the confluence of the two epistemic modes stems from the fact that the ultimate datum of mystical experience is the Tetragrammaton, which can be heard as a vocalized name or seen as an envisioned form. In this regard, it is of interest to consider the following remark in *Zohar Ḥadash*, 120b: "'The Lord appeared to him' (Gen. 18:1): Come and see: There is prophecy from seeing, prophecy from scent, prophecy from hearing, and prophecy from speech, and these are the four chariots of the name YHWH." In this taxonomy of prophecy, there is a convergence of the visual, auditory, olfactory, and verbal, the four main prisms through which the divine may be envisioned, prisms correlated with and functioning therefore as chariots in relation to the four letters of the name. In spite of references to the other senses in kabbalistic texts (especially hearing) and my own acknowledgment of the phenomenon of synesthesia, the visual is accorded primacy. The ocularcentrism attested in kabbalistic sources is on a par with a tendency in Western thought that has been studied by a number of scholars from a variety of methodological perspectives. For representative studies, see Jay, *Downcast Eyes*; Brennan and Jay, *Vision in Context*; Levin, *Modernity and the Hegemony of Vision*; idem, *Sites of Vision*; idem, *Philosopher's Gaze*. The philosophical insight is corroborated by the neuroanatomical thesis proffered by J. Turner, *On the Origins of Human Emotions*, pp. 22–23: "Often visual and tactile body language is considered a supplement to verbal and auditory forms of communication, but I believe the reverse to be the case: visual body language is the more primal and basic aspect of face-to-face interaction. Auditory cues simply fine-tune the motional overtones communicated through the visual sense modality; our brains are wired to see and to subordinate the auditory to the visual. . . . Moreover, because we expose our full bodies to visual inspection and because our facial movements are generated by striated muscles rapidly activated by the emotion centers in the brain . . . interpersonal attunement is achieved primarily via the visual senses, with other senses—touch, hearing, and olfaction—being secondary." On the joining of the visual and auditory in Christian visionary sources, see Benz, "Color in Christian Visionary Experience," p. 83.

152. Blanchot, *infinite Conversation*, p. 53.

153. Perhaps this is what Scholem had in mind when he noted (based on a passage in Azriel) that the kabbalistic ideal of conjunction (*devequt*) "does not . . . erase the boundaries between Creator and creature but preserves them in this particular form of communion" (*Origins*, p. 416). I concur with Idel, *Kabbalah: New Perspectives*, pp. 42–49, that the unitive dimension of *devequt* in kabbalistic literature was improperly downplayed by Scholem, but I do see some merit to the latter's caution. The insistence on rendering *devequt* as "communion" in contradistinction to "union" is an attempt to preserve the tension of absolving and preserving a sense of individuated difference.

154. Azriel of Gerona, *Commentary on Talmudic Aggadoth*, p, 116.

155. See passage of Azriel of Gerona cited in chap. 5, at n. 64.

156. See chap. 5, n. 63.

157. Blanchot, *infinite Conversation*, p. 53.

158. Ibid., p. 205.

159. Ibid., p. 210. For discussion of this motif, see K. Hart, "Experience of Nonexperience," pp. 188–206.

160. Blanchot, *infinite Conversation*, p. 209. See also the analysis of the utility of language and the place of silence in P. Russell, "Ephraem the Syrian," pp. 21–37.

161. My formulation is indebted to the language of Carlo Sini cited and analyzed in Carrera, "Consequences of Unlimited Semiosis," pp. 48–62, esp. pp. 54–58.

162. Wittgenstein, *Tractatus*, p. 3.

163. Wittgenstein, *Tractatus*, ed. Pears and McGuinness, secs. 6.522–6.53, pp. 73–74; Wittgenstein, *Tractatus*, ed. Ogden, pp. 186 and 188. On the mystical dimension of Wittgenstein's thought and the limits of

language, see Bouveresse, *Wittgenstein*, pp. 21–72; Nieli, *Wittgenstein*; Martin, *From Nietzsche to Wittgenstein*, pp. 173–219; Weeks, *German Mysticism*, pp. 233–237; Sontag, *Wittgenstein and the Mystical*; and Popov, "Wittgenstein's Analytic." For further exploration of the inexpressible and the limits of reason according to Wittgenstein, see Bouveresse, *Dire et ne rien dire*. On the possibility that Wittgenstein studied kabbalistic lore mediated through the channel of Christian Knorr von Rosenroth's *Cabbala denudata*, see Benz, *Mystical Sources*, p. 48.

164. On the characterization of art in similar terms, see Wittgenstein, *Culture and Value*, p. 23: "In art it is hard to say anything as good as: saying nothing." For an extended discussion of art and the unsayable, see Hagberg, *Art as Language*, pp. 8–30.

165. Wittgenstein, *Tractatus*, ed. Ogden, sec. 6.44, pp. 186–187. In this case, I have preferred Ogden's more literal translation to the rendering in Wittgenstein, *Tractatus*, ed. Pears and McGuinness, p. 73.

166. McGuinness, *Wittgenstein and the Vienna Circle*, p. 68.

167. Wittgenstein, *Tractatus*, ed. Pears and McGuinness, sec. 6.432, p. 73; Wittgenstein, *Tractatus*, ed. Ogden, p. 186.

168. Wittgenstein, *Tractatus*, ed. Pears and McGuinness, sec. 6.53, p. 74.

169. Wittgenstein, *Tractatus*, ed. Pears and McGuinness, sec. 6.54, p. 74.

170. Wittgenstein, *Tractatus*, ed. Pears and McGuinness, sec. 6.5–51, p. 73.

171. Wittgenstein, *Culture and Value*, p. 16.

172. *Zohar* 2:244b.

173. Ibid., 2:246b.

174. Ibid., 2:258b.

175. Blanchot, *infinite Conversation*, pp. 295–296 (emphasis in original).

176. See Bruns, *Maurice Blanchot*, pp. 46–55, 128–129.

177. On the identification of poetic language as the heterovalent surplus of semiotic meaning vis-à-vis the monovalent symbolic discourse dominated by patriarchal images, see Kristeva, *Revolution in Poetic Language*, pp. 64–65, 80–85; Leland, "Lacanian Psychoanalysis," pp. 125–128.

178. Blanchot, *Space of Literature*, p. 32.

179. Ibid., p. 34 n. 3. On blindness as the vision of the invisible, the seeing of the icon as the kenosis of the image, see the elaborate discussion in Marion, *Crossing of the Visible*, pp. 46–65.

180. On the confluence of the auditory and ocular, see the discussion of verbal imagery in Mitchell, *Iconology*, pp. 19–31. See also Gerhart, "Word Image Opposition," pp. 72–77; Bryson, "Semiology and Visual Interpretation," pp. 61–73.

181. Blanchot, *Space of Literature*, p. 41.

182. Ibid., pp. 33, 37. On the centrality of the theme of inexpressibility and poetic utterance, see Wolosky, *Language Mysticism*.

183. Based on the rabbinic dictum in Babylonian Talmud, Ḥagigah 13a.

184. Azriel of Gerona, *Iggeret le-Burgos*, p. 233.

185. Ibn Malka, *Perush ha-Tefillot*, p. 246.

186. Ibid., pp. 246–247.

187. Liebes, "Zohar and Eros," has stressed the creative nature of exegesis in zoharic literature. See also M. Fishbane, *Exegetical Imagination*, pp. 105–122.

188. The description of Elijah's epiphany was on occasion applied in midrashic and kabbalistic exegesis to the Sinaitic theophany, in some cases based on the presumed connection between the "mighty voice," *qol gadol* (Deut. 5:19) of God at Sinai and the "faint silent voice," *qol demamah daqqah* (1 Kings 19:12) of God on Mount Horeb. See *Siphre ad Numeros*, sec. 58, p. 56; *Zohar* 2:81b. An interesting use of the language of Elijah's epiphany with special reference to the *qol demamah daqqah* is found in the narrative about R. Sheshet the Blind and the heretic (*min*) in Babylonian Talmud, Berakhot 58a. The story centers on the rabbi and the heretic going out with others to greet the monarch. As the story unfolds, it becomes clear that the one of true insight is the blind rabbi who, on the basis of interpreting 1 Kings 19:11–13, informs the heretic that one knows the arrival of the royal authority not through a great tumult but by means of the silent sound that

is the appropriate token of respect. That silence is the apt response to God's epiphany is an oft-repeated theme in biblical and postbiblical sources. See Isa. 41:1, Hab. 2:20, Zech. 2:17; Rev. 8:1; Babylonian Talmud, Ḥagigah 13b; *Exodus Rabbah* 29:9 (related specifically to the Sinaitic theophany). For a different approach to the idiom *qol demamah daqqah,* see B. Levine, "Silence, Sound, and the Phenomenology of Mourning," pp. 101–102. See also Sommer, "Revelation at Sinai," pp. 422–451; on pp. 441–444, Sommer discusses the expression *qol demamah daqqah,* which he translates as the "thin utter silence." I concur with the drift of Sommer's thinking and accept that the expression *qol demamah daqqah* alludes to the "sound of silence," the voice of God that is inaudible. Sommer surmises, moreover, that this is a modification of the earlier Israelite portrayal of the Sinaitic theophany wherein God is manifest in loud noises (pp. 442–443).

189. In an ostensibly different symbolic framework, Eleazar of Worms remarks that the unusual locution *qol demamah* denotes that "the custom [*minhag*] of the supernal ones is that when they advise the glory, first there is silence and afterwards the voice of the announcer [*qol ha-karuz*] goes forth to the external ones." We can thus speak of the voice being heard through silence. There is no conflict between Elijah's *qol demamah* and Eliphaz the Temanite's *demamah wa-qol eshma,* "I heard silence and a voice" (Job 4:16), for both relate to the voice without that gives expression to the silence within. See Eleazar ben Judah, *Perush ha-Merkavah,* fol. 40b. Eleazar's view shares much affinity with kabbalistic texts wherein *qol demamah daqqah* denotes the inner voice of silence that is heard outside.

190. *Zohar* 1:16a. Compare *Tiqqunei Zohar,* sec. 30, 74b: *Binah,* the "supernal mother," is depicted as the "concealed vision that has no image," in contrast to *Shekhinah,* the "lower mother," which is the "revealed vision that has an image."

191. For a similar conflation of the visual and auditory, see passage from *Shushan Edut* cited in chap. 2, n. 248.

192. *Zohar* 2:81b. See also *Zohar* 3:30a. In part, the zoharic interpretation may reflect the targumic rendering of *qol demamah daqqah* as *qal di-meshabbeḥin ba-ḥashsha'i,* the "voice that they praise in silence." From the context it is evident that this voice must be understood hypostatically as the manifestation of the divine presence. See also Moses de León, *Sheqel ha-Qodesh,* pp. 6–7: "the inner subtle voice [*qol ha-daq ha-penimi*] is not heard at all on the outside." A nuanced account of the elevation of speech to silence linked to the tenor of esotericism is offered in the following explanation of the dictum transmitted in the name of Aqiva, "Silence is a fence for wisdom" (Mishnah, Avot 3:13) in Elijah de Vidas, *Re'shit Ḥokhmah,* Sha'ar ha-Qedushah, chap. 11, 169a: "For by means of his being silent he is elevated above the actions of the six extremities, which are the voice [*qol*] and speech [*dibbur*], and he ascends to the place of silence [*meqom ha-shetiqah*], which is thought [*maḥshavah*], the secret of wisdom [*sod ha-ḥokhmah*], and as they said [Babylonian Talmud, Menaḥot 29b], 'Be silent for thus it arose in thought'. . . . Another explanation of this matter is that when a man is silent he makes himself a chariot for the place of wisdom, and he will merit that the secrets of Torah will overflow upon him, for they are in silence as they are not allowed to be revealed."

193. It is possible that the exegetical revision was also inspired by the second account of the chariot vision in Ezek. 10:15–17; especially significant is the fact that in that context the four-faced living creature (*ḥayyah*) is identified as the cherub (*keruv*). The interpretative elaboration of the scriptural text attested in the Qumran text can be profitably compared to the targumic rendering of the prophet's account, as has been noted by Newsom, *Songs of the Sabbath Sacrifice,* p. 314. See *Targum of Ezekiel,* p. 22: "And I heard the sound of their wings, like the sound of many waters, like a sound from *before Shaddai*; as they went, *the sound of their words were as though they were thanking and blessing their Master, the everliving King of the worlds*; like the sound of the hosts *of the angels on high*; when they stood still, their wings became silent *before the Dibbur. And at such time when it was His will to make the Dibbur audible to His servants the prophets of Israel,* there was a voice which was heard from the above the firmament which was above their heads. When they stood still, their wings became silent *before the Dibbur*" (emphasis in the original to mark the targumic additions to the scriptural text).

194. This is one of several designations used by the priestly members of the *yaḥad* ("the community") established in Qumran to refer to the heavenly temple. A central part of the attempt of these priests to construct a priestly regimen after having rejected the main institution of priestly power and authority was focused on poetic composition and liturgical worship directed to the celestial throne-chariot. The fact that this

occurred in a time when the Jerusalem temple stood and sacrifices were still being offered complicates the view expressed by Levey in his introduction to *Targum of Ezekiel*, p. 3, that "Merkabah Mysticism becomes the instrumentality for the preservation of the ego-structure of the Jewish people in the face of the critical threats to its survival." Leaving aside the whole genre of apocalyptic visions, Levey's portrayal is complicated by the evidence that has emerged from the caves at Qumran. It is also not clear if the priestly scribes at Qumran did not interpret the vision of the restored temple in Ezek. 40–48 exclusively in terms of the heavenly temple. See E. Wolfson, "Seven Mysteries of Knowledge," pp. 177–213, and reference to other scholars cited pp. 191 n. 32 and 212–213 n. 111.

195. For transcription, translation, and commentary, see Newsom, *Songs of the Sabbath Sacrifice*, pp. 303–307, 312–314. I have accepted Newsom's reconstruction, *qol dimmat elohim*, and her translation based on the reasonable supposition that the locution is based on *qol demamah daqqah*, the "subtle still voice," the depiction of the presence of God in 1 Kings 19:12. See also Allison, "Silence of Angels," pp. 189–197.

Chapter Seven
Eunuchs Who Keep Sabbath: Erotic Asceticism / Ascetic Eroticism

1. See O'Flaherty, *Asceticism and Eroticism*; Masson, "Sex and Yoga," pp. 307–320. The paradoxical role of desire in asceticism is noted by Harpham, *Ascetic Imperative*, p. 45. On the homology between transformation of the subtle body through sexual intercourse and the attainment of enlightenment, see Kvaerne, "On the Concept of Sahaja," pp. 88–135. On the use of physical sexuality as a spiritual technique, see also Samuel, "Body in Buddhist and Hindu Tantra," pp. 197–210, esp. pp. 205–207. Rotenberg, *Yetzer*, pp. 53–78, offers a psychological discussion of the relationship of asceticism and eroticism in the kabbalistic tradition.

2. A typical expression of this approach is found in the essays collected in Gupta, *Sexual Archetypes*; see also Pierre Gordon, *Sex and Religion*, and the more recent collections of essays in Hayes, Porter, and Tombs, *Religion and Sexuality*; and Machacek and Wilcox, *Sexuality and the World's Religions*.

3. The point is conveyed superbly by Bürgel, "Love, Lust, and Longing," pp. 81–117; see also Cameron, "Sacred and Profane Love," pp. 1–23.

4. Bataille, *Death and Sensuality*, p. 7. See LaFountain, "Bataille's Eroticism," pp. 26–41.

5. The expression is borrowed from Faure, *Red Thread*, p. 29.

6. Here it is useful to recall the observation of Jung, *Symbols of Transformation*, p. 229: "The fact that primitive Christianity resolutely turned away from nature and the instincts in general, and through its asceticism, from sex in particular, clearly indicates the source from which its motive forces came. So it is not surprising that this transformation has left noticeable traces in Christian symbolism. Had it not done so, Christianity would never have been able to transform libido. It succeeded in this largely because its archetypal analogies were for the most part in tune with the instinctual forces it wanted to transform." The nexus between the erotic and the ascetic in the history of Christianity is a specific example of Jung's thesis regarding the symbol's power of attraction being the "equivalent quantum of the libido." See Jung, *On the Nature of the Psyche*, p. 24.

7. Zupancic, *Shortest Shadow*, p. 48.

8. Žižek, *For They Know Not What They Do*, p. 144.

9. Sōhō, *Unfettered Mind*, p. 34.

10. Broughton, *Bodhidharma Anthology*, p. 16. For another formulation of the paradox, see the Mahāyāna text Kambala, *Garland of Light*, p. 25: "Being thus convinced that the two of them, i.e., passion as well as dispassion, are false, [a yogin] neither desires or detests anything, because [both of them] are [empty like] an opened fist. One who is dispassioned will no doubt also become passionate again. Therefore, in order to get rid of passions, one should not even come in contact with dispassion." The paradox of desiring not to desire in Buddhist teachings has been the focal point of several studies. See Visvader, "Use of Paradox," pp. 455–467; Herman, "Solution to the Paradox," pp. 91–94; Alt, "There Is No Paradox," pp. 521–530, and the responses by Herman and Visvader in Alt, "There Is No Paradox," pp. 529–534.

11. For select references, see chap. 3, n. 33. See also the poignant remarks regarding this matter in Scholem, *Major Trends*, pp. 225–226. On the relationship of mystical experience and the language of passion in

medieval Christendom, see de Rougemont, *Love in the Western World*, pp. 141–170. On the interplay of the carnal and spiritual in the Sufi ideal of mystical love, see Bouhdiba, *Sexuality in Islam*, pp. 122–125.

12. The distinction is already anticipated in Dionysius the Areopagite, *Divine Names*, chap. 2, 641A, p. 120, where reference is made to the "divinity beyond God," that is, the "ground beyond being," the undifferentiated unity of the Godhead.

13. Schürmann, *Wandering Joy*, pp. 108–118; Forman, *Meister Eckhart*, pp. 170–172, 177–182; McGinn, *Mystical Thought*, pp. 142–146. See also the perceptive assessment given by Walshe in the "Introduction" to his translation of Eckhart, *Sermons and Treatises*, vol. 1, p. xxxvii. Walshe's comment occurs in the context of his effort to criticize scholars who pushed the comparison of Eckhart and Zen Buddhism: "If mysticism in the traditional Western sense implies communion with God, then there is a real sense in which Eckhart may be said to go beyond this, for according to him the soul has to proceed beyond 'God' to the nameless Oneness of the 'Godhead.' Nevertheless, the theistic 'sub-structure' remains an essential part of Eckhart's thought, and this, in Zen as in other schools of Buddhism, is wholly lacking."

14. See Underhill, *Mysticism*, pp. 425–426; and the study by Schimmel, "Eros."

15. In terms of the spirit/flesh or mind/body dichotomy typical in the Middle Ages, the spiritual or rational is symbolically associated with the male, and the material or emotional, with the female. For references, see chap. 2, n. 57. See also Bynum, *Holy Feast*, pp. 216–217, 262. On the other hand, in relationship to the divine, the soul itself is feminized, an experience that was shared by men and women. Although it was not uncommon for women in medieval Christian society to assume a symbolic maleness in order to advance spiritually, it is also the case, as Bynum has argued, that basic images of women's religious experience were feminine in nature, or at the very least androgynous. For medieval women ascetics, the body has a positive function and hence does not necessarily reflect a Platonic dualism. See Bynum, *Holy Feast*, pp. 28, 291, 294–296; see as well Culianu, "Corpus for the Body," pp. 61–80, esp. pp. 64–65.

16. The view I have articulated accords with the "Blakean" perspective on the "mystico-erotic" proposed by Kripal, *Roads of Excess*, pp. 21–22. See also the nuanced analysis of the psychoanalytic approach to eros in Kalsched, "Limits of Desire," pp. 66–93.

17. The nexus between eroticism and asceticism is an integral aspect of Tantrism, which bears interesting comparisons to kabbalistic spirituality, as I argue in more detail in the continuation of this chapter. For example, see the account of *kamakaladhyana*, "meditation on the aspect of desire," in the eighteenth-century Vedic brahman, Bhaskararaya, in Brooks, *Secret of the Three Cities*, p. 82: "Underlying this practice is the notion that the Tantric, by meditating on the erotic feminine form, partakes of the bliss (*ānanda*) of the divine and transforms sensual, worldly experience into a vehicle of liberation. In what may seem an ironic twist to the uninitiated, Bhaskararaya grounds the practice in a rigorously ascetical ritual interpretation. . . . Nevertheless, it is this dual relationship between the erotic and the ascetic that characterizes Tantric discipline, much as it does the mythology of Siva in nonesoteric traditions." See above, n. 1, and below, n. 205.

18. Zaehner, *Mysticism Sacred and Profane*, p. 151. Negative images of the feminine are occasionally found as well in the writings of female visionaries. See J. Miller, "Eroticized Violence," pp. 25–49; Salih, "When Is a Bosom Not a Bosom?,'" pp. 14–32.

19. This locution is indebted to the analogy drawn between late-antique theatre and spiritual marriage in Leyerle, *Theatrical Shows*, pp. 75–99.

20. See P. Brown, *Body and Society*, p. 61; Salisbury, *Church Fathers*, pp. 60–125; G. Corrington, "Defense of the Body," pp. 65–74; Burrus, "Word and Flesh," pp. 27–51; Elm, *"Virgins of God"*; Schulenburg, *Forgetful of Their Sex*, pp. 59–125; and further references below, n. 26.

21. For a Weberian analysis of the triumph of asceticism judged from this perspective, see Friedrich-Silber, *Virtuosity, Charisma, and Social Order.* The link between ascetic renunciation and social disengagement (primarily on the part of men) in Buddhism is explored by L. Wilson, *Charming Cadavers*, pp. 15–39.

22. To appreciate the novel element introduced by the possibility of a celibate lifestyle that challenged the stereotypical domestic role assigned to women, consider the reflection of Loraux, *Tragic Ways*, p. 23, regarding the suicide of women in ancient Greece: "They are free enough to kill themselves, but they are not free enough to escape the space to which they belong, and the remote sanctum where they meet their death is equally the symbol of their life—a life that finds its meaning outside the self and is fulfilled only in

the institutions of marriage and maternity, which tie women to the world and lives of men. It is by men that women meet their death, and it is for men, usually, that they kill themselves."

23. Burrus, "Word and Flesh," p. 51.

24. Mishnah, Soṭah 3:4; Babylonian Talmud, Soṭah 22a. See also the censure of the "fasting virgin" in Palestinian Talmud, Soṭah 3:4, 9a. Weinstein, *Piety and Fanaticism*, p. 113, suggests that the term "fasting" may be a euphemism for sexual abstinence, just as its opposite, "eating," is employed by the rabbis as a euphemism for sexual relations. On fasting in early Christian asceticism as an aid to reduce the sexual drive and thereby facilitate a life of abstinence, see P. Brown, *Body and Society*, pp. 78. 224–225, 236, 419. It may be useful to compare the difficulties faced by women ascetics within rabbinic culture and the complex social dimensions of women becoming official members of the monastic institutions in Hindu society, as studied in detail by Sinclair-Brull, *Female Ascetics*.

25. See Urbach, "Askesis and Suffering," pp. 48–68; idem, *Sages*, pp. 251, 444–448, 478; Halivni, "On the Supposed Anti-Asceticism," pp. 243–252; Fraade, "Ascetical Aspects," pp. 253–288; McArthur, "Celibacy in Judaism," pp. 163–181; D. Biale, *Eros and the Jews*, pp. 34–36; Satlow, "Shame and Sex," pp. 535–543; idem, *Tasting the Dish*, pp. 243–246; Weinstein, *Piety and Fanaticism*, pp. 65–105; Naeh, "Freedom and Celibacy," pp. 73–89; Horst, *Japheth in the Tents of Shem*, pp. 191–201; E. Diamond, *Holy Men and Hunger Artists*. See also Soloveitchik, "Halakhic Approach to Suffering," pp. 3–24. In line with Maimonides, Soloveitchik offers a Platonic interpretation of the rabbinic distinction between this world and the world-to-come; the loftier telos of commitment to ritual is escape from the physical realm of sensual desire.

26. P. Brown, *Body and Society*, pp. 223–224, 269; T. Shaw, *Burden of the Flesh*, pp. 161–253. On women ascetics and fasting, see also Bynum, *Holy Feast*, pp. 78–93.

27. Mishnah, Soṭah 3:4.

28. Palestinian Talmud, Soṭah 3:4, 19a.

29. See Weinstein, *Piety and Fanaticism*, pp. 107–144. On the subsidiary role of women as silent partners delegated the exclusive task of bearing children according to the rabbinic construction, see Baskin, *Midrashic Women*, pp. 88–118. P. Brown, *Body and Society*, pp. 62–63, perceptively noted that the rabbinic acceptance of marriage as the means to insure survival of the community was in part a reaction to expressions of radical asceticism. The attack on women ascetics in rabbinic literature stands in sharp contrast to the portrayal of women by the rabbis as lacking the ability to control their impulses as well as the more negative depiction of women as temptresses and seductresses. See Satlow, *Tasting the Dish*, pp. 155–159; idem, "Try to Be a Man," pp. 35–36.

30. Salisbury, *Church Fathers*, pp. 11–38; H. Bloch, "Medieval Misogyny," pp. 87–117. For a later example of this bias, see the description of the "feminine secrets" in the discourse of La Vieille in *Roman de la Rose* as summarized by Huot, *Romance of the Rose*, pp. 92–93.

31. This image of the feminine, which has had an enduring influence on generations of Jewish male exegetes, has its roots in Scripture. See Bach, *Women, Seduction, and Betrayal*.

32. Boyarin, *Dying for God*, pp. 67–92, esp. pp. 74–78. For an independent discussion of the process of feminization of Jacob vis-à-vis Edom in rabbinic thought, see E. Wolfson, "Face of Jacob," pp. 237–238.

33. My formulation is indebted to M. Green, "From 'Diseases of Women,'" p. 7, who makes a similar argument with regard to the genre of *secrets of women* in late medieval gynecological literature. As Green notes, the adoption of this title by men "did not enshroud women's bodies with a protective barrier to the male gaze; rather, it rendered women's bodies open for intellectual scrutiny in ways that, quite understandably, may have left certain observers with concern that medical discourse had more power to harm women than to help them." In my estimation, this assessment can be applied to rabbinic and kabbalistic accounts of the female body.

34. Foucault, *Religion and Culture*, p. 179. On the nexus between martyrdom and asceticism in early Christian sources, see Viller, "Martyre et perfection," pp. 3–25; idem, "Martyre et l'ascèse," pp. 105–142; Ladner, *Idea of Reform*, pp. 319–373. These sources are cited in Friedrich-Silber, *Virtuosity, Charisma, and Social Order*, p. 120 n. 4. See also Binns, *Ascetics and Ambassadors of Christ*, pp. 140, 230–231. For an exploration of a similar confluence of themes, see E. Wolfson, "Martyrdom, Eroticism, and Asceticism," pp. 171–220.

35. See Luke 20:34–40, and discussion in Fletcher-Louis, *Luke-Acts*, pp. 78–86; on angelomorphic celi-

bacy in Qumran, that is, the nexus between the angelic status of the ideal human nature and sectarian asceticism, see pp. 193–195; idem, *All the Glory of Adam*, pp. 131–134. On the ascetic tendencies in Qumran sectarianism and the desire to overcome sexual pollution, which fostered the anointing of males into angelic perfection and the pledging of select female virgins in a ceremony of immaculate conception, see Sheres and Blau, *Truth about the Virgin*. On the question of celibacy, marriage, and the place of women in the community reflected in the fragments retrieved from the caves at Qumran, see also Daniel, "Esséniens et Eunuques," pp. 353–390; Baumgarten, "On the Testimony of Women," pp. 125–136; idem, "4Q502," pp. 125–136; idem, "Qumran-Essene Restraints on Marriage," p. 13; idem, "Cave 4 Versions," pp. 268–276; idem, "Celibacy," pp. 122–125; Qimron, "Celibacy in the Dead Sea Scrolls," pp. 287–294; Elder, "Woman Question," pp. 220–234; Talmon, "Community of the Renewed Covenant," pp. 9–10; Schuller, "Evidence for Women," pp. 252–265; Stegemann, *Library of Qumran*, pp. 193–198; Thiede, *Dead Sea Scrolls*, pp. 28–33; Harrington, "Holiness and Law," pp. 124–135, esp. pp. 126 and 131; and the material evidence adduced to support the view that the sectarian community was predominantly made up of male celibates in Zias, "Cemeteries of Qumran," pp. 220–253; Magness, *Archaeology of Qumran*, pp. 38, 163–187. The link between celibacy and the original angelic state of humankind seems to be implied in the tradition attributed to R. Meir that after the sin in the Garden of Eden, Adam adopted the life of a pious soul (*ḥasid*), which included refraining from sexual relations with his wife. Ascetic renunciation, with a special focus on sexual denial, is thus presented as atonement for transgression. For citation and analysis of relevant sources, see Ginzberg, *Legends*, vol. 5, pp. 115 n. 106, 148 n. 46.

36. Aspegren, *Male Woman*, pp. 132–133.

37. See references cited in chap. 2, n. 15; Scroggs, "Paul and the Eschatological Woman," pp. 283–303; idem, "Paul and the Eschatological Woman Revisited," pp. 532–537. The position implied in some of Paul's comments was affirmed more explicitly in the application of the expression *demuta de-mala'ke* ("likeness of angels") to celibate priests in the Syrian Christian tradition. Inasmuch as angels were thought to be nongendered beings, the monastic life afforded men and women the opportunity to become angelic and thereby transcend gender dimorphism. See P. Brown, *Authority and the Sacred*, p. 78; idem, "Arbiters of Ambiguity," pp. 123–142, esp. pp. 140–142; idem, "Rise and Function," pp. 353–376, esp. pp. 371–372; Barstad, "Body, Soul, and Image," pp. 262–266. Exhortations to virginity through the Middle Ages continued to focus on the nexus between chastity and purity of the angelic life. See Mews, "Virginity, Theology, and Pedagogy," pp. 21–22, and the passages from *Speculum Virginum* in the Appendix, pp. 275, 283, and 290.

38. See Ruether, "Misogynism and Virginal Feminism," pp. 150–183; idem, "Mothers of the Church," pp. 71–98; idem, *Women and Redemption*, pp. 13–43; E. Clark, *Ascetic Piety and Women's Faith*, pp. 175–208; idem, *Reading Renunciation*, pp. 95, 127, 345–347; Elm, *"Virgins of God,"* pp. 47–51, 106–136; G. Clark, "Women and Asceticism," pp. 33–48; Boyarin, *Radical Jew*, pp. 180–200; C. Cooper, *Virgin and the Bride*, pp. 45–67; Streete, "Women as Sources of Redemption," pp. 347–350; Clack, "Virgins and Vessels," pp. 193–202. On women ascetics and mystical piety in the Christian Middle Ages, see Bynum, *Holy Feast and Holy Fast*, pp. 82–87, 103–104; idem, *Fragmentation and Redemption*, pp. 53–78, 131–134; Petroff, *Body and Soul*, pp. 205–206.

39. MacDonald, *There Is No Male and Female*, pp. 72–91; Wire, *Corinthian Women Prophets*, pp. 116–180; Gritz, *Paul, Women Teachers, and the Mother Goddess*, pp. 79–93; L. Johnson, *First and Second Letters*, pp. 198–211; and Köstenberger, *Studies on John and Gender*. See also Eph. 5:22–24, and the analysis by Dawes, *Body in Question*. See also Økland, "Man Is the Measure of all Things," pp. 59–82; Peerbolte, "Man, Woman, and the Angels," pp. 76–92. On the continued impact of Paul's negative assessment of women on the shaping of medieval clerical misogyny, see Gregg, *Devils, Women, and Jews*, pp. 89–91.

40. E. Clark, *Jerome, Chrysostom, and Friends*, pp. 15, 19, 55–56; idem, *Ascetic Piety*, pp. 180 and 199 n. 38; Cloke, *Female Man of God*; Brooten, "Paul's Views on the Nature of Women," pp. 61–87; idem, *Love between Women*, pp. 215–266; Elm, *"Virgins of God,"* pp. 108–111; E. Castelli, "Paul on Women and Gender," pp. 221–235; Aspegren, *Male Woman*; D Leclerc, *Singleness of Heart*, pp. 25–59; S. Davis, "Crossed Texts, Crossed Sex," pp. 1–36; Schulenburg, *Forgetful of Their Sex*, pp. 155–166. For a useful review of the attitude toward women promoted by the Church in late-antique Graeco-Roman culture, see K. Power, *Veiled Desire*, pp. 23–68.

41. The connection between martyrdom, asceticism, and the ideal of becoming male is discussed at length by Miles, *Carnal Knowing*, pp. 53–77. On Augustine's steadfast denial that women bear the image of God, see Power, *Veiled Desire*, pp. 131–1168. On the anthropological question as to whether women were considered to have been created in God's image, like men, or at best, in the likeness of the image, which is restricted to men, a view linked exegetically to a reading of Gen. 1:26 in light of 1 Cor. 11:7, see Børresen, "God's Image, Man's Image?" pp. 192–194; Hunter, "Paradise of Patriarchy," pp. 447–469; N. Harrison, "Women, Human Identity, and the Image of God," pp. 205–249. See also the analysis of the patristic topos "she will be called man" in Jantzen, *Power, Gender and Christian Mysticism*, pp. 43–58.

42. *Patrilogiae Latina*, edited by Jean-Paul Migne, 26:533, cited in Rapp, "Woman Speaks," p. 4; see also E. Clark, *Reading Renunciation*, pp. 167, 335, 360.

43. Talbot, "Comparison of the Monastic Experience," p. 9; and compare the discussion of "frightful women" in Leyerle, *Theatrical Shows*, pp. 143–182.

44. Power, *Veiled Desire*, p. 166. On the persistence of the virginal strategies adopted by women saints within medieval Christian societies, see the learned and balanced discussion in Schulenburg, *Forgetful of Their Sex*, pp. 127–175.

45. Beauvoir, *Second Sex*, pp. 675–678; and see Gatens, *Feminism and Philosophy*, p. 55.

46. See Hunter, "Clerical Celibacy," pp. 139–152.

47. McGuire, "Virginity and Subversion," pp. 241–258. On the possible evolution and transformation of this mythical discourse in a later Jewish magical document, see Leicht, "Gnostic Myth in Jewish Garb," pp. 133–140. In this text, the gnostic virgin savior becomes the evil witch who, by rendering men impotent, brings sin and corruption rather than redemption and liberation. On the transformations of the gnostic figure of Norea, itself rooted in the ancient Near Eastern *Lichtjungfrau*, "maiden of light," in medieval Islamic and Jewish esoteric sources, see the evidence adduced by Wasserstrom, "Jewish Pseudepigrapha in Muslim Literature," pp. 97–99 (my gratitude to the author for calling my attention to his work).

48. On the roots of the dual portrayal of woman as sacred and demonic, see chap. 2, n. 91. For a provocative example in the history of European Christianity of the blurring of gender identity in the visual and verbal representations of a figure who is both masculine and feminine, including the striking image of a bearded woman, see Friesen, *Female Crucifix*. Friesen is of the opinion that the depictions and veneration of St. Wilgefortis are illustrative of the Pauline new order based on transcending gender polarity (pp. 19–33). It is not clear to me that becoming Christlike actually entailed (in historical perspective) the total and unqualified abolishment of gender difference. It seems to me equally plausible theoretically and perhaps far more accurate historically to view the transvestite saint as an illustration of the androcentric bias (promoted as well by the patriarchal ecclesiastic authorities) according to which femininity is itself expressive of the masculine rather than interpreting it as an indication of gender ambiguity.

49. Ranke-Heinemann, *Eunuchs for the Kingdom of Heaven*, pp. 9–152. Regarding the theme of the "male virgin" and citation of some of the relevant sources, see Ford, *Revelation*, pp. 242–244. I am reluctant to accept Ford's argument that "virgin" in this context has nothing to do with being unmarried but is a symbol used to express fidelity to God. The ascetic reading in which the metaphoric and literal meanings would converge seems to be more plausible, and on the face of it the virginal beings are exclusively male. This is not to deny the effort of subsequent exegetes to extend the description in Rev. 14:3–5 so that the "men" denoted women as well. Consider the example of Cyprian discussed by E. Clark, *Reading Renunciation*, p. 139.

50. Compare the description in Rev. 14:1–5 of 144,000 men standing together with the Lamb on Mount Zion. These men, who had the names of the Lamb and the Father inscribed on their foreheads (14:1), are described as having been "redeemed from the earth" since they were virgins who had not defiled themselves with women (14:3–4). Despite the fact that entry into this heavenly realm is offered only to those who are redeemed from the bondage of the material world by adopting a celibate lifestyle, the gender identity remains critical, as it is clear that the virgins (*parthenoi*) referred to are only male since the demonstrative pronoun *outoi*, "these," is masculine. The angelification of these male virgins is underscored in the description of the new song they utter before the throne, the living creatures, and the elders (14:3).

51. Elm, *"Virgins of God,"* p. 123.

52. Horstmanshoff, "Who Is the True Eunuch?" pp. 101–118. For a different approach, see Stevenson, "Rise of Eunuchs," pp. 495–511. For the phenomenon of castration as a gesture of "cutting off desire at the root" in the Buddhist cultural settings of China and Japan, see Faure, *Red Thread*, pp. 34–37.

53. Ringrose, "Living in the Shadows," pp. 85–109, esp. pp. 87–88; idem, *Perfect Servant*; Horstmanshoff, "Who Is the True Eunuch?," p. 108.

54. See Herdt, "Introduction," pp. 21–81.

55. Kuefler, *Manly Eunuch*, pp. 245–282. Also relevant here is the discussion in Foucault, *History of Sexuality*, vol. 3, p. 121, of authors in late antiquity who viewed abstention, and particularly the retention of semen, as a means of augmenting male potency.

56. Wisse, "Flee Femininity."

57. *Coptic Gnostic Library*, vol. 4, p. 223.

58. On the "Triple Powered One," see John Turner, *Sethian Gnosticism*, pp. 512–531.

59. K. King, *Revelation of the Unknowable God*, pp. 78–81. For an alternative rendering of this text, see *Coptic Gnostic Library*, vol. 5, p. 193.

60. See K. King, *Revelation of the Unknowable God*, p. 29 and sources cited in n. 120.

61. It behooves me to note that in several passages there is an explicit refusal to refer to the invisible, ineffable, unfathomable, and immeasurable monad as "god" or "divine" being. See *Coptic Gnostic Library*, vol. 2, pp. 20, 24–25.

62. Ibid., p. 21.

63. Ibid., pp. 16–19. See Waldstein, "Primal Triad," pp. 154–187. Also relevant for an appreciation of the trinitarian speculation attested in Gnostic sources is the study by Manchester, "Noetic Triad," pp. 207–222.

64. *Coptic Gnostic Library*, vol. 5, p. 275.

65. As noted by K. King, *Revelation of the Unknowable God*, p. 80, note to 45.17b–22a. See also John Turner, "Time and History in Sethian Gnosticism," pp. 209–211.

66. Hippolytus, *Refutation of All Heresies*, V.3, p. 56.

67. T. Shaw, *Burden of the Flesh*, pp. 247–252, suggests that the transvestite motif of becoming male is to be qualified by the fact that female virgins were valorized as brides of Christ. Shaw acknowledges that this metaphor was applied to the souls of men or to the Church, but she contends that in fourth-century ascetic writings it became increasingly the demarcation of female virginity, that is, in virtue of choosing a life of chastity, the virgin becomes the spouse of Christ. I am not persuaded by Shaw's argument that the attribution of the title "bride of Christ" to women ascetics conveys a positive valorization of the female that balances the eschatological transvestitism implied by the demand that the female become male. On the contrary, virginity itself is a cultural rejection of femaleness, as a number of scholars have argued.

68. See chap. 2, n. 24, and chap. 4, n. 164.

69. J. M. Robinson, *Nag Hammadi Library*, p. 369: "And do not become female, lest you give birth to evil and (its) brothers: jealousy and division, anger and wrath, fear and a divided heart, and empty, nonexistent desire."

70. LeGoff, *Medieval Imagination*, p. 83.

71. S. Bell, "Medieval Women Book Owners," pp. 742–768, esp. pp. 762–763.

72. For instance, see Semple, "Male Psyche and Female Sacred Body."

73. Sells, *Early Islamic Mysticism*, p. 155.

74. Margaret Smith, *Rābiʿa*, 19–21; Schimmel, *Mystical Dimensions*, pp. 426–435; idem, *My Soul Is a Woman*, pp. 34–37; Chittick, *Self-Disclosure*, pp. 374–376.

75. On the images of Mary in Islamic tradition, see chap. 5, n. 245.

76. Schimmel, *My Soul Is a Woman*, pp. 77–80. See chap. 2, n. 12. Consider the response of Abida Parvin to the query concerning women having a part in singing Sufi poetry, cited in Abbas, *Female Voice in Sufi Ritual*, p. 22: "Male and female does not even come to it—what you call Allah is one—God is the *mehver* [center] of everything—you make a roundabout and whatever way it goes . . . it will go to it—it really does not matter whether it is male or female—in fact we can really say that in the Sufi's terminology—if someone is not a male—he is called a female."

77. Sells, *Early Islamic Mysticism*, pp. 161–162.

78. Butorovic, "Between the Tariqa and the Shari'a," p. 144.

79. Schimmel, *My Soul Is a Woman*, pp. 69–88.

80. Cited in Schimmel, *My Soul Is a Woman*, p. 76. For a decidedly negative assessment of the status of women in Islam, with special reference to issues pertaining to sexuality, see Warraq, *Why I Am Not a Muslim*, pp. 290–327.

81. This is not to ignore the fact that there are Sufi sayings that emphasize that in matters pertaining to the worship of God there should be no distinction between male and female and hence no privilege given to one over the other. See, for instance, the comment in Nasafī, *Persian Metaphysics and Mysticism*, p. 48, wherein one who belongs to the "people of reality" (*ahl-i-ḥaqīqa*), also identified as the "people of unity" (*ahl-i-waḥdat*), is described as disregarding the ethnic divisions that separate one group from others and thus such a person considers no one an enemy. In light of the ultimate unity in which all differentiation is overcome, all peoples must be deemed the same. For the overcoming of doctrinal differences that leads to a "mystical ideal of tolerance" in Ibn ʿArabī, see Schimmel, *Mystical Dimensions*, pp. 271–272. Needless to say, the dicta proclaiming gender equality must be scrutinized carefully, but the point I would emphasize here is that there is no account of the transformation of male into female as a sign of spiritual perfection in the manner we find with respect to female becoming male. On the positive symbolic role accorded the feminine in Islamic mystical symbolism, and especially in the works of Ibn ʿArabī and Rūmī, see Austin, "Sophianic Feminine."

82. Smith and Ferstman, *Castration of Oedipus*, p. 160.

83. Ibid., pp. 160–161; on the authors' notion of the "Law of the Father," which is depicted as the misogynist foundation of male authority, see pp. 195, 211.

84. Ibid., p. 161.

85. On asceticism in rabbinic sources, see references above, n. 25. The ascetic dimensions of ancient throne mysticism have been noted by Scholem, *On the Possibility*, pp. 128–129; Idel, *Kabbalah: New Perspectives*, pp. 87–88; Michael Swartz, *Scholastic Magic*, pp. 153–172; Lesses, *Ritual Practices to Gain Power*, pp. 117–160. On the ascetic dimension of the medieval philosophical tradition, see Vajda, *Théologie ascétique*; Lazeroff, "Baḥya's Asceticism," pp. 11–38; Schweid, *Judaism and Mysticism*, pp. 102–116; Kreisel, "Asceticism in the Thought of Baḥya and Maimonides," pp. 5–22; Silman, *Philosopher and Prophet*, pp. 97–98, 233. On asceticism and medieval Ashkenazi pietism, see Scholem, *Major Trends*, pp. 92–97; Ben-Arzi, "Asceticism in Sefer Ḥasidim," pp. 39–45; and the comprehensive analysis in Kanarfogel, *Peering through the Lattices*, pp. 33–92. On the Sufi-like pietism cultivated by the descendants of Maimonides, see Rosenblatt, *High Ways to Perfection*, pp. 48–53, 66, 82–85; Fenton, *Treatise of the Pool*, pp. 1–24. On Halevi's negative attitude toward asceticism, in part expressed by appropriating Sufi terminology, see Fenton, *Treatise of the Pool*, p. 54 n. 3; Lobel, *Between Mysticism and Philosophy*, pp. 17, 45–48, 51–53, 67, 78–80, 158, 168. A useful discussion of the various shades of asceticism in the rabbinic traditions of the classical and medieval periods is found in Sokol, "Attitudes toward Pleasure," pp. 293–314.

86. Safran, "Rabbi Azriel and Naḥmanides," pp. 75–106; Tishby, *Wisdom of the Zohar*, pp. 764–765; D. Biale, *Eros and the Jews*, pp. 99–113. Note the perceptive remark of A. Heschel, *Earth Is the Lord's*, p. 103 concerning the "ascetic obstinacy of the Kabbalists."

87. See Scholem, *Major Trends*, p. 286; idem, *On the Kabbalah and Its Symbolism*, p. 146; idem, *Kabbalah*, p. 245; and references to Werblowsky, Pachter, and Fine cited in chap. 3, n. 56.

88. See Piekarz, *Beginning of Hasidism*, pp. 37–39, 48–49, 62–63, 74, 78, 113, 153, 157, 168, 230–231, 262, 339–340; A. Green, *Tormented Master*, pp. 27–28, 35–40; D. Biale, *Eros and the Jews*, pp. 121–148; Rosman, *Founder of Ḥasidism*, pp. 30, 33–35, 37–38, 115; Faierstein, "Personal Redemption in Hasidism," pp. 216–217; Nadler, *Faith of the Mithnagdim*, pp. 80–87; Krassen, *Uniter of Heaven and Earth*, pp. 55, 108–121. On the rejection of extreme asceticism in early Hasidism, which is traced back to the views expressed by Isaiah ben Abraham Horowitz, author of the highly influential kabbalistic-moralistic compendium *Shenei Luḥot ha-Berit*, see Piekarz, "Hasidism as a Socio-Religious Movement," pp. 236–237.

89. Scholem, *On the Kabbalah and Its Symbolism*, p. 153, briefly notes (in the context of discussing the seventeenth-century compendium of kabbalistic piety, *Ḥemdat Yamim*) the link between asceticism and mes-

sianism. On asceticism and Sabbatian eschatology, see Scholem, *Kabbalah*, pp. 251 and 261; E. Wolfson, "Engenderment," pp. 255–258.

90. See Solomon Rubin, *Heidenthum und Kabbala*; G. Langer, *Die Erotik der Kabbala*; Waite, *Holy Kabbalah*, pp. 377–405; Scholem, *Major Trends*, pp. 225–229; idem, *On the Kabbalah and Its Symbolism*, pp. 138–146; idem, *On the Mystical Shape*, pp. 183–196; Tishby, *Wisdom of the Zohar*, pp. 300–302, 992–993, 1355–1379; Mopsik, *Lettre sur la sainteté*, pp. 45–219; idem, "Union and Unity in the Kabbala," pp. 223–242; Idel, "Sexual Metaphors," pp. 197–224; Liebes, *Studies in the Zohar*, pp. 67–71; idem, "Zohar and Eros," pp. 99–103.

91. Scholem, *Major Trends*, p. 235.

92. Ibid., p. 227.

93. See Scholem, *On the Kabbalah and Its Symbolism*, p. 155: "To the Kabbalists, the union between man and woman, within its holy limits, was a venerable mystery, as one may judge from the fact that the most classical and widely circulated Kabbalistic definition of mystical meditation is to be found in a treatise about the meaning of sexual union in marriage." The treatise to which Scholem refers is the anonymous *Iggeret ha-Qodesh*, which he attributes to Joseph Gikatilla.

94. Scholem, *On the Kabbalah and Its Symbolism*, p. 131.

95. Ibid., p. 153.

96. For a critique of Scholem, see Tishby, *Wisdom of the Zohar*, pp. 991–993. On the correlation of mystical union (*devequt*) and the theurgical task of rectifying the divine (*tiqqun*), see Liebes, *Studies in the Zohar*, pp. 52–55. On the erotic ecstasy of the zoharic circle, see idem, "Zohar and Eros," pp. 70–80, 87–98, 104–112. Consider also the insightful, if laconic, remark by Bloom, *Kabbalah and Criticism*, p. 32: "The Kabbalist encounters the *Sefirot* only through *Malkhut*, which makes of Kabbalism necessarily a sexual mysticism or erotic theosophy."

97. See chap. 5, n. 381. The confluence of the theosophic and ecstatic in the kabbalistic utilization of sexual imagery was well understood by Jung, *Mysterium Coniunctionis*, p. 23: "The Cabala develops an elaborate hieros gamos fantasy which expatiates on the union of the soul with the Sefiroth of the worlds of light and darkness. . . . Conversely, the Shekhinah is present in the sexual act."

98. See Scholem, *Origins*, pp. 229–233; idem, *Kabbalah*, p. 44. On pietistic and ascetic tendencies in the Provençal rabbinic academies, see also Twersky, *Rabad of Posquières*, pp. 25–29; and Pedaya, *Name and Sanctuary*, pp. 26–34. See, in particular, the depiction of the "pious sage," *he-ḥakham he-ḥasid*, by Abraham bar Ḥiyya, *Hegyon ha-Nephesch ha-Atzuvah*, p. 49: "They said with respect to the one who is a sage [*ḥakham*] and a saint [*ḥasid*] that when he departs from this world his soul from the aspect of his wisdom [*ḥokhmato*] separates from the creation and exists in its form as it was before and from the aspect of its saintliness [*ḥasadah*] in its abhorring the ways of this world, will ascend from the lower world to the supernal world and it will be saved from all the created entities below, and it reaches the supernal, pure, and primordial form, and it enters within it and is never separated from it. This is the level of the saintly sage [*he-ḥakham he-ḥasid*]." At a later point in this treatise (p. 54), bar Ḥiyya raises the question regarding who among human beings is worthy of attaining the world-to-come. From his response (pp. 55–57) it is unambiguously clear that the Jewish people are distinguished from all other human beings in virtue of being called by the divine name, whence ensues their obligation to unify the divine, and of having received the Torah. Yet he also asserts emphatically that he does not believe the superior level of spiritual attainment is categorically denied the other nations; on the contrary, the gates of repentance (*shaʿarei teshuvah*) are always open, and hence non-Jews can achieve the supreme state of perfection associated with the people of Israel. See Efros, *Studies in Medieval Jewish Philosophy*, p. 197. Notwithstanding this critical difference, the ascetically oriented ideal articulated by bar Ḥiyya, with roots in Stoic and Neoplatonic philosophy (see Efros, p. 174), is phenomenologically on a par with the contemplative ideal alluded to in the bahiric text and developed at greater length by Provençal and Catalonian kabbalists.

99. Scholem, *Origins*, p. 307. Consider also *Major Trends*, p. 328, where Scholem describes kabbalists in eighteenth-century Poland "who entirely renounced the more popular aspects of Lurianism and tried to lead Kabbalah back from the market place to the solitude of the mystic's semi-monastic cell."

100. The Hebrew text here literally should be translated as "If not for" (*ilmale*), but this reading would not make sense since the clause is not completed. I have translated the word in accord with what I take to be the meaning of the passage. Regarding the lacuna in this text, see Scholem, *Das Buch Bahir*, sec. 66, p. 70 n. 3.

101. *Book Bahir,* sec. 66, p. 159.

102. Scholem, *Origins,* p. 178, suggests that *terumah* here denotes more specifically the *Shekhinah,* who "through asceticism and detachment from the world, must be 'elevated' in prayer. Divine things are indicated by the process of setting aside the offering, that is, the detachment of the mystic from the world in order to seek God, as well as by the offering itself, the symbol of that which is to be elevated, that is, the Glory of God that is lifted up." The theurgical explanation of the heave offering as the elevation of *Shekhinah* is made explicitly in sec. 72, pp. 161–162 (and not sec. 71 as Scholem suggests). It is probable that this is indeed the intent of sec. 66.

103. See *Book Bahir,* sec. 95, p. 181: "When the enlightened ones [*maskilim*] in Israel who know the secret of the honorable name [*sod ha-shem ha-nikhbad*] lift up their palms, they are immediately answered."

104. *Book Bahir,* sec. 100, p. 185.

105. Scholem, *Kabbalah in Provence,* p. 6, Appendix.

106. Ibid., p. 5. To be precise, these words are used to describe the presumed expansion of thought (*harḥavat ha-maḥshavah*) on the part of prophets. I am justified in applying these words to the contemplative exercise more generally, insofar as the content of the experience of enlightenment and prophecy is one and the same, as I have emphasized in many studies on the poetic visualization fostered by kabbalists.

107. Consider the fifth of ten conditions, delineated by Ibn Gaon, *Baddei ha-Aron,* p. 16, required for one who wishes to gain esoteric wisdom: "he should despise all the lusts of this world and its desires." By fulfilling these ten conditions, one is rendered worthy to be conjoined to the enlightened master (*lehidabbeq le-maskil*) so that the teachings one is to receive from him can be inscribed on the "tablet of his heart," an idiom derived from Prov. 7:3 (p. 32).

108. Translated in Scholem, *Origins,* pp. 256–257.

109. In part, the intensified cultivation of ascetic pietism by the few who belonged to the rabbinic elite in medieval Europe can be explained as a psychological response to the monastic ideal of Christianity. Support for this may be gathered from the fact that in contemporary rabbinic texts, such as *Malmad ha-Talmidim* of Jacob Anatoli, excessive ascetic practices adopted by Jews are criticized in language that is comparable to the polemic against extreme forms of Christian asceticism. See Saperstein, *"Your Voice Like a Ram's Horn,"* pp. 67–70. On the attack against the monastic ideal in Jewish polemics, see also D. Berger, *Jewish-Christian Debate,* p. 27; and other sources cited in Kimḥi, *Book of the Covenant,* p. 35 n. 21.

110. Scholem, *Origins,*, p. 230. For an imbalanced, exaggerated account of the alleged difference between Jewish (with particular emphasis on kabbalah in the late Middle Ages) and Christian mysticism along lines similar to those pursued by Scholem, see Mendel, *Vision and Violence,* pp. 70–78.

111. Matt. 19:3–12; 1 Cor. 7:1–9, 25–38. See Rousselle, *Porneia,* pp. 129–193; Pagels, *Adam, Eve, and the Serpent,* pp. 78–97; Boyarin, *Radical Jew,* pp. 158–179; Payer, *Bridling of Desire,* pp. 42–60, 132–178.

112. S. Krauss, *Jewish-Christian Controversy,* pp. 102–103, 156.

113. *Zohar* 2:103a, 108b–109a.

114. *Zohar* 1:108b, 177a–b; 2:108b, 111a; 3:128a, 135a, 142a, 292a; Tishby, *Wisdom of the Zohar,* pp. 276–277, 289–290; Liebes, *Studies in the Zohar,* pp. 65–68, 149, 190 n. 201; E. Wolfson, "Woman—The Feminine as Other," pp. 168–169, 189–190; idem, "Divine Suffering," pp. 129–133. I have expanded on the role of gender in the zoharic polemic against Christianity in "Re/membering the Covenant."

115. *Tiqqunei Zohar,* sec. 69, 110a.

116. Vital, *Eṣ Ḥayyim,* 8:3, 37b; see also 31:2, 33b–c; Vital, *Liqquṭei Torah,* pp. 116–117 (ad Gen. 49:24). In *Shaʿar ha-Gilgulim,* sec. 39, 67b, Vital elaborates on the emission of semen in vain in the sefirotic realm that parallels the act below at the hands of Joseph, the symbolic correlate (*dugma*) to the phallic potency of *Yesod.* In light of this passage, which follows closely older kabbalistic teaching, including that which is reiterated on numerous occasions in *Sefer ha-Zohar,* I take issue with the comment on a zoharic homily dealing with Joseph and Potiphar's wife (given the name Zuleikha) offered by Goldman, *Wiles of Women,* p. 138: "In the Zohar's reading we are no longer in the domain of personal passion and court intrigue. Zuleikha is here demonized, and the seduction attempt symbolizes and foreshadows a cosmic drama, one in which Satan threatens to gain dominion over mankind." A proper understanding of the kabbalistic approach to human behavior and the cosmic drama precludes dichotomizing the historical and symbolic. For a detailed account

of the pernicious effect of the Jewish man's spilling seed in vain, see *Sha'ar ha-Kawwanot*, 56b–c. According to that passage, casting semen without a (female) vessel to contain it is described as both tarnishing divine thought (a notion that flows naturally out of the widespread presumption that semen originates in the brain) and bringing about the creation of demonic spirits.

117. *Genesis Rabbah* 87:7, pp. 1072–1073; Palestinian Talmud, Horayot 2:5, 46d; Babylonian Talmud, Soṭah 36b. The author of *Tiqqunei Zohar* conflates the opinion ascribed to R. Isaac that Joseph emitted the semen on the ground rather than engage in sexual intercourse with the wife of Potiphar and a second opinion in *Genesis Rabbah* 87:7, p. 1073, transmitted by R. Huna in the name of R. Mattena, that reinforces the scriptural portrayal of Joseph's steadfast capacity to withstand the sexual advances of Potiphar's wife (Gen. 39:7–12) by emphasizing that at the moment of seduction Joseph "saw the icon of his father and his blood was cooled." For discussion of the biblical narrative and its interpretative embellishment in rabbinic and targumic legend, see Kugel, *In Potiphar's House*, pp. 106–112; Niehoff, *Figure of Joseph*, pp. 131–134, 149–151; Goldman, *Wiles of Women*, pp. 84–86. In the Lurianic sources (delineated at the beginning of the previous note), the rabbinic gloss that Joseph was saved by seeing the image of Jacob is utilized to differentiate his spilling semen in vain and his engaging in intercourse with the Gentile woman, the locus of demonic power. Spilling semen in vain, usually viewed by kabbalists as a horrific transgression, becomes the lesser of two evils and hence, in this context, marks Joseph's righteousness. The righteousness notwithstanding, there is a price to be exacted, as is attested by the link made between the seminal drop that came from Joseph and the ten rabbinic martyrs, who are said to be from the same ontic root as the Edomite kings.

118. *Midrash Mishle*, chap. 1, p. 18, and see other references cited in the note to lines 172–174.

119. E. Wolfson. "Divine Suffering," pp. 131–133. Some of the material there is repeated verbatim in this context.

120. MS London, British Museum 10627, fol. 64b.

121. Y. Jacobson, "Aspect of the Feminine," pp. 250–255, suggests that the reason no wife is mentioned in the case of the first seven kings is "not because they were male, but because their fertile femininity was actualized only after their revival and reconstruction." In fact, the Edomite kings are emasculated males and thus they are symbolically equivalent to females without male partners. The underlying issue in this myth is not feminine fertility but rather masculine virility.

122. *Zohar* 3:292a; cf. 1:223b. According to a passage in the *Idra Rabba* (3:142a), Hadar is identified as the attribute of *Ḥesed*, but in that context the rectification of the Edomite kings is depicted as the sweetening of feminine judgment by forces of mercy revealed in the "mouth of the penis" (*puma de-amah*). For an elaboration of the zoharic symbolism in sixteenth-century Lurianic kabbalah, see E. Wolfson, *Circle in the Square*, pp. 116–119.

123. I have discussed the symbol of the androgynous phallus in a number of studies. See *Through a Speculum*, pp. 274–275 n. 14, 315–317, 342, 344, 357–359, 371 n. 155; "Woman—The Feminine as Other," p. 187; *Circle in the Square*, pp. 85–92; *Along the Path*, pp. 84–88, 175 n. 329, 186 n. 376, 222 n. 172; "Re/membering the Covenant," pp. 226–231; and discussion above, chaps. 3–4.

124. Scholem, *Major Trends*, pp. 225–235; Tishby, *Wisdom of the Zohar*, pp. 298–302, 1355–1379; Liebes, *Studies in the Zohar*, pp. 67–71.

125. See chap. 5, n. 220.

126. *Zohar* 3:37b, 81a–b.

127. A particularly lucid formulation of this motif is found in Chani, *Me'ah She'arim* p. 48a, translated and analyzed by Mopsik, *Grands textes*, pp. 358–359.

128. Mopsik, "Body of Engenderment," pp. 56–57; Idel, "Sexual Metaphors," pp. 202–203; Liebes, *Studies in the Zohar*, pp. 71 and 190 n. 199.

129. Tishby, *Wisdom of the Zohar*, pp. 298–300.

130. Cf. *Zohar* 1:239b; 3:90b, 145b.

131. *Zohar* 3:5b; cf. 1:55b; 2:55a; 3:7a.

132. *Zohar* 3:37b.

133. *Zohar* 1:49a–50a, 55b, 122a, 165a, 182a, 228b, 233a–b; 3:5b, 109b (*Ra'aya Meheimna*), 145b, 148a, 296a; *Zohar Ḥadash*, 50c, 65b. For an earlier rabbinic precedent, cf. Babylonian Talmud, Soṭah 17a.

134. Mopsik, "Body of Engenderment," pp. 58–59.

135. MS Oxford-Bodleian 1784, fol. 37a.

136. Babylonian Talmud, Shabbat 87a; Yevamot 42a.

137. *Zohar* 1:234b.

138. *Zohar* 1:21b, 22a, 236b, 239a; 2:5b, 245a; 3:4b, 148a, 180a. See below, n. 198.

139. The dialectic of which I speak in kabbalistic literature is related to the medieval scholastic notion of the intellectual love of God, expressed, for instance, in the writings of Maimonides (see below, n. 151). For discussion of this phenomenon in medieval Christian sources, see Leclercq, *Love of Learning*, pp. 212–217. The importance of this dialectic for understanding the erotic characterization of cleaving to God in thirteenth-century kabbalistic sources has been noted by Shokek, *Jewish Ethics*, pp. 219–224.

140. The closest formulation to this dictum, which is cited by other kabbalists in the thirteenth and fourteenth centuries, for example, the anonymous author of a passage in the *Midrash ha-Ne'elam* stratum of zoharic literature (see below, n. 144), Baḥya ben Asher, and Menaḥem Recanaṭi (see below, n. 152), is found in Babylonian Talmud, Shevu'ot 18b: "He who sanctifies himself in time of intercourse will have male children."

141. Jacob ben Sheshet, *Sefer ha-Emunah we-ha-Biṭṭahon, Kitvei Ramban* 2:395.

142. *Zohar* 1:90b; see 1:155a (*Sitrei Torah*); 3:43a, 104a–b.

143. Babylonian Talmud, Nedarim 20b; Niddah 70b–71a.

144. *Zohar Ḥadash*, 11a–b (*Midrash ha-Neʿelam*). In Zohar 3:19a, the task of directing the intention of the heart to the holiness of God in the moment of sexual intercourse is preserved as part of an incantational remedy (*asuwata*) to protect the couple from the malevolence of Lilith. See Scholem, *On the Kabbalah and Its Symbolism*, p. 157; Tishby, *Wisdom of the Zohar*, p. 1364.

145. Palestinian Talmud, Ketuvot 5:8, 30b; Babylonian Talmud, Ketuvot 62b; Bava Qama, 82a; Maimonides, *Mishneh Torah*, Deʿot 5:4; Shabbat 30:14; Ishut 14:1; Jacob ben Asher, *Arbaʿah Ṭurim*, Oraḥ Ḥayyim, 240; Even ha-Ezer, 25, 76; Joseph Karo, *Shulḥan Arukh*, Oraḥ Ḥayyim, 240:1; Even ha-Ezer, 76:2. The recommendation that a Jewish man in general fulfill his conjugal obligation on Friday evening is intimated in several other talmudic sources. See Palestinian Talmud, Ketuvot 5:13, 30b; Megillah 4:1, 75a; Babylonian Talmud, Ketuvot 65b; Satlow, *Tasting the Dish*, pp. 278–280. Goitein, *Mediterranean Society*, vol. 5, pp. 312–313, notes that from the Genizah material one can conclude that the talmudic recommendation that scholars engage in their conjugal obligations on Friday night was extended to the Jewish population more generally. Additionally, Goitein notes the conflict between this Rabbanite view and that of the Karaites, who regarded sexual intercourse as a desecration of the holiness of the Sabbath. The approach of the Karaites resonates with a pietistic orientation expressed at a much earlier point in history. According to Qimron, "Halacha of Damascus Covenant," pp. 9–15, the prohibition of sexual relations on Sabbath is implied by the injunction *al yitʿarev ish mi-reṣono be-shabbat* (CD 11:4–5). On the controversy over sexual relations on Sabbath, see also Broshi, "Anti-Qumranic Polemics," pp. 596–597. For discussion of celibacy at Qumran, see above, n. 35. On the connection between observance of the Sabbath and the ascetic renunciation of the physical world, which leads to a vision of God, see Valantasis, *Gospel of Thomas*, pp. 100–101.

146. *Zohar* 1:112a (*Midrash ha-Neʿelam*); *Zohar* 3:56a.

147. The expression "with his wife" (*be-ittetteih*) is added on the basis of the citation of this zoharic text in Recanati, *Be'ur al ha-Torah*, 63c (ad Lev. 19:2).

148. *Zohar* 3:82a.

149. D. Biale, *Eros and the Jews*, pp. 105–113; Sokol, "Attitudes toward Pleasure," pp. 305–306. Regarding this text, see also M. Harris, "Marriage as Metaphysics," pp. 197–226; Guberman, "Language of Love," pp. 53–95; Idel, "Sexual Metaphors," pp. 205–206. A similar tension between the use of erotic language and the ideal of sexual abstention in Christian mysticism has been noted by McGinn, "Language of Love," p. 209.

150. *Kitvei Ramban*, 2:323.

151. *Kitvei Ramban*, 2:334. It is likely that the erotic characterization of the intellectual conjunction of the soul and the divine intelligibles reflects Maimonides' notion of *ʿishq*, the intellectual love of God, which is identified as the contemplative ideal of prayer, the true worship of the heart. See Maimonides, *Guide*, III:51; *Mishneh Torah*, Teshuvah 10:6. For recent discussions of this aspect of the contemplative pietism advocated

by Maimonides, see M. Fishbane, *Kiss of God*, pp. 24–30; Benor, *Worship of the Heart*, pp. 52–53; Peter Gordon, "Erotics of Negative Theology," pp. 1–38.

152. According to the author of *Iggeret ha-Qodesh*, the ideal Adam was not a disembodied spirituality but a spiritualized body. Regarding these two anthropological approaches in thirteenth-century kabbalah, see Safran, "Rabbi Azriel and Naḥmanides." See also Pines, "Naḥmanides on Adam," pp. 159–164. On the presumption regarding sexual desire in the Garden of Eden, see Baḥya ben Asher, *Rabbenu Baḥya: Be'ur al ha-Torah*, 1:84 (ad Gen. 3:21); on the need for man to purify his thoughts in the act of coitus, see 1:266 (ad Gen. 30:38); 2:521 (ad Lev. 19:2); Recanati, *Be'ur al ha-Torah*, 30b (ad Gen. 30:37).

153. *Kitvei Ramban*, 2:323–324.

154. *Kitvei Ramban*, 2:327. Isaac ben Samuel of Acre, a contemporary of the author of *Iggeret ha-Qodesh*, put the matter as follows in *Sefer Me'irat Einayim*, p. 20: on Friday evening the enlightened mystics can "sense" through their "intellectual eyes" the "augmentation of the joy of the heart and the power of reproduction."

155. The utilization of the philosophical locution "rational soul" (*nefesh ha-sikhlit*) to denote the divine emanation is attested in Catalonian kabbalistic texts. For instance, see Jacob ben Sheshet, *Sefer ha-Emunah we-ha-Biṭṭahon, Kitvei Ramban*, 2:386: "This emanation [*hitpashṭut*] corresponds to what is called in the language of the philosophers the 'rational soul' [*ha-nefesh ha-sikhlit*]."

156. *Kitvei Ramban*, 2:333. The language of this text is based on a passage in Azriel of Gerona, *Commentary on Talmudic Aggadoth*, p. 20.

157. *Kitvei Ramban*, 2:331. For discussion of this philosophical view, see the evidence adduced by Mopsik, *Lettre sur la sainteté*, pp. 300–302 n. 133; D. Biale, *Eros and the Jews*, p. 106.

158. *Kitvei Ramban*, 2:332.

159. This, too, seems to reflect the influence of Maimonides' characterization of the patriarchs in *Guide* III:51 as being in constant intellectual conjunction with God. The ideal set forth by the author of *Iggeret ha-Qodesh* also bears a similarity to the characterization of *devequt* in the commentary of Naḥmanides to Deut. 11:22. The resemblance between Maimonides and Naḥmanides was noted by Scholem, *Messianic Idea*, pp. 204–205.

160. *Kitvei Ramban*, 2:333–334; cf. pp. 336–337. The kabbalistic perspective elaborates an earlier rabbinic ideal epitomized in the remark in *Tanḥuma*, Naso, 7: "When a woman is united with her husband in holiness, the holy One, blessed be he, causes her to bring forth righteous children."

161. In some zoharic passages, the association of the body and the demonic force necessitates the ascetic life. See *Zohar* 1:180b; Tishby, *Wisdom of the Zohar*, pp. 764–765.

162. On the Platonic tradition of eros and its impact on the Christian idea of love, see the still useful discussion by Nygren, *Agape and Eros*.

163. *Zohar* 3:130b.

164. Eliade, *Yoga*, pp. 200–273; idem, *Occultism, Witchcraft, and Cultural Fashions*, pp. 93–119.

165. For a wide-ranging study of this imagery, see Horowitz, *Seeds of Virtue*. It is also important to recall that attested in the long recension of the *Theology of Aristotle* is the idea that God sows or seeds things in their entirety in the intellect. See P. Walker, *Wellsprings of Wisdom*, pp. 80 and 167.

166. Horowitz, *Seeds of Virtue*, p. 28.

167. That is, each of these expressions equals 417.

168. Abulafia, *Oṣar Eden Ganuz*, fol. 127b (printed ed., p. 280).

169. Vital, *Eṣ Ḥayyim*, 5c.

170. For discussion of rabbinic texts where a similar dilemma is raised, see Urbach, *The Sages*, pp. 478–479.

171. Zevi Hirsch of Zidachov, *Ṣur me-Ra we-Aseh Ṭov*, p. 47.

172. See above, n. 34.

173. On a similar use of erotic imagery in Christian mysticism, see McGinn, "Language of Love." On the fusion of asceticism and eroticism in medieval women mystics depicted as the bride or lover united with the humanity of Christ through the ecstatic ingestion of the Eucharist, see Bynum, *Fragmentation and Redemption*, pp. 133–134, 184–186.

174. An excellent example of this phenomenon can be found in the passage from Moses Cordovero cited in Mopsik, "Union and Unity," pp. 234–236. It must be pointed out, however, that Cordovero's elaborate description of the meditational practice linked to conjugal sex is limited to the intercourse of scholars on the eve of Sabbath and does not apply to the general practice of most people, an impression that one gets from reading Mopsik's analysis of the text.

175. *Zohar* 2:89a; cf. 2:204b–205a; 3:82a. See Waite, *Holy Kabbalah*, p. 382; Tishby, *Wisdom of the Zohar*, pp. 1232–1233, 1357; Liebes, *Studies in the Zohar*, p. 15.

176. A similar interpretation of Isaiah 56:4 is found in Moses de León, *Sefer ha-Mishkal*, p. 142; Joseph Gikatilla, *Shaʿarei Oraḥ*, 1:107; idem, *Sod ha-Shabbat*, 40a; Baḥya ben Asher, *Rabbenu Baḥya: Beʾur al ha-Torah*, 2:521–522. It is of interest to recall in this connection the description in *Zohar Ḥadash*, 8d (*Midrash ha-Neʿelam*), of a group of ascetics (*perishei alma*) who supposedly hid during the week in caves and returned on Sabbath eve to their homes. See Tishby, *Wisdom of the Zohar*, p. 1331. One may infer that with respect to the issue of sexual practice, what is attributed to these ascetics matches the lifestyle of the mystical fraternity described in other parts of the *Zohar*. Regarding those who abstain from wine, cf. *Zohar Ḥadash*, 22c (*Midrash ha-Neʿelam*). In *Zohar* 2:187a there is a reference to a band of ascetics (*perushim*) who meet Simeon ben Yoḥai.

177. For talmudic references, see above, n. 145. The rabbinic passage figures prominently in the zoharic anthology. Cf. *Zohar* 1:14a–b, 50a, 112a (*Midrash ha-Neʿelam*); 2:63b, 89a, 136a, 204b–205a; 3:49b, 78a, 81a, 82a, 143a; *Tiqqunei Zohar*, sec. 16, 38b; sec. 21, 57a, 61a; sec. 36, 78a; sec. 56, 90a.

178. *Zohar* 1:75a–b; *Tiqqunei Zohar*, sec. 18, 34a; sec. 19, 38a; sec. 21, 61a; sec. 30, 73a–b; sec. 36, 78a; Tishby, *Wisdom of the Zohar*, pp. 438–439, 1226–1227; Ginsburg, *Sabbath*, pp. 115–116, 292–293; Kimelman, *Mystical Meaning*, pp. 66–67, 142–145. The *Zohar* is not totally consistent on this point because it does describe a form of union between the masculine and feminine potencies of the divine even during the week, albeit in a less complete manner than the union on the eve of Sabbath, which is the most appropriate time for the *hieros gamos*. Moreover, the recommended time for conjugal relations is based on the assumption that at midnight God visits the Garden of Eden, which must be understood as a symbolic depiction of the erotic union of the male and female. Cf. *Zohar* 3:81a; Tishby, *Wisdom of the Zohar*, p. 1357.

179. Tishby, *Wisdom of the Zohar*, p. 1391 n. 101.

180. The arousal of the divine phallus by means of the sexual activity of the kabbalist in relation to his earthly wife and to *Shekhinah* is a recurrent theme in *Zohar* and related theosophic literature. See Tishby, *Wisdom of the Zohar*, p. 301; Liebes, *Sections of the Zohar Lexicon*, pp. 378–379 n. 92; idem, "Tsaddiq Yesod Olam," p. 107 n. 171; E. Wolfson, *Through a Speculum*, pp. 371–372 n. 155. In another kabbalistic text that transmits material from the zoharic period, *Shoshan Sodot*, 79a, the author states that the righteous person engages in conjugal sex on Friday evening not for the sake of his own pleasure but to assist in the conjunction of the supernal righteous one, the phallic *Yesod*, and the feminine persona of the divine, the attribute of *Malkhut*.

181. David Biale, *Eros and the Jews*, p. 111. An interesting application of the kabbalistic ideal of sexual renunciation is found in the teaching of Naḥman of Bratslav expressed in *Liqquṭei Eṣot*, sec. 8. There are two kinds of guarding of the phallic covenant: the lower unity, which refers to refraining from sexual transgression, and in particular spilling seed in vain, for one who engages in sex during the week, and the upper unity, which refers to those who engage in sex only on Sabbath.

182. My formulation is indebted to O'Flaherty's description of a Tantric Sahajiya sect of Bengal in O'Flaherty, *Asceticism and Eroticism*, p. 261.

183. As has been argued, for instance, with respect to the ideal man in Buddhist societies who acts in this world after having achieved detachment from the world. See Keyes, "Ambiguous Gender," pp. 66–96.

184. On the erotic nature of the contemplative state described in zoharic literature, related especially to exegetical activity, see E. Wolfson, *Circle in the Square*, pp. 16–19; idem, *Through a Speculum*, pp. 326–392; and see the reference to studies of Liebes at the end of n. 90 above.

185. On the nexus between enlightenment and castration, see Smith and Ferstman, *Castration of Oedipus*, p. 205. Also worthy of consideration is the explanation of Neumann, *Origins*, p. 53, regarding why priests of the Mother Goddess had to be eunuchs: "They have sacrificed the thing that is for her the most important—

the phallus. . . . For her, loving, dying, and being emasculated are the same thing. Only the priests, at least in later times, escape being put to death because, by castrating themselves, they have voluntarily submitted to a symbolical death for her sake"; see pp. 59–61. In zoharic literature, the conjunction of kabbalist and *Shekhinah* is depicted as a simulated death, a motif obviously based on a presumed relation of eros and thanatos, and in some passages, the death experience is linked to the supplication prayer (*taḥanun*) traditionally uttered on Monday and Thursday; the customary gesture of falling on one's face (*nefilat appayim*) is a way of expressing the death that ensues from union with *Shekhinah*. See Liebes, *Studies in Zoharic Literature*, pp. 52–53, 63–65, 184 n. 154; M. Fishbane, *Kiss of God*, pp. 38–39, 104–120; E. Wolfson, *Through a Speculum*, pp. 335–336. Given the fact that the kabbalist is considered a eunuch, it is plausible to apply Neumann's explanation to the Jewish esoteric symbolism.

186. That midnight is the appropriate time for sexual intercourse is implied in a statement attributed to the wife of R. Eliezer in the Babylonian Talmud, Nedarim 20b. This practice is codified in the standard codes of Jewish law. Cf. *Mishneh Torah*, Issurei Bi'ah 21:10; *Arbaʿah Ṭurim*, Oraḥ Ḥayyim, 240; Even ha-Ezer, 25, 76; *Shulḥan Arukh*, Oraḥ Ḥayyim, 240:7; Even ha-Ezer, 25:3. On the basis of the zoharic passages (see n. 187) it became a standard theme in kabbalistic literature. On the prohibition of engaging in intercourse during the day, see *Zohar* 1:49b.

187. *Zohar* 1:72a, 82b, 92a, 136b, 231b, 243a; 2:46a, 130b, 136a, 195b; 3:13a, 67b–68a, 193a–b, 260a; *Zohar Ḥadash* 13b, 18a, 47d. See E. Wolfson, "Forms of Visionary Ascent," pp. 227–228; idem, *Through a Speculum*, p. 371 n. 154; idem, *Circle in the Square*, pp. 190 n. 175 and 228 n. 167.

188. On the ritual of midnight Torah study, see Scholem, *On the Kabbalah and Its Symbolism*, pp. 147–148; E. Wolfson, "Forms of Visionary Ascent." For the later development of the zoharic tradition in the sixteenth-century Lurianic kabbalah, see Magid, "Conjugal Union," pp. xvi–xlv.

189. *Zohar* 3:49b.

190. Ibid., 3:81a. My translation follows the version of this passage in Recanati, *Beʾur al ha-Torah*, 11d and 90b.

191. For recent discussion of this theme, see Valantasis, "Constructions of Power," pp. 775–821. The kabbalistic sources illustrate the "concomitancy of male asceticism and misogyny" noted by Gregg, *Devils, Women, and Jews*, p. 89, with respect to male clerics in medieval Christian societies.

192. A euphemism for engaging in conjugal intercourse.

193. *Zohar* 1:50a.

194. Vidas, *Reʾshit Ḥokhmah*, Shaʿar ha-Qedushah, chap. 7, 149b.

195. This is implied as well in the zoharic description of the union of *Shekhinah* and the righteous man who goes on a journey and separates from his earthly wife. See *Zohar* 1:49b–50a; Tishby, *Wisdom of the Zohar*, p. 1357.

196. Idel, "Sexual Metaphors," p. 206, provides an interesting example of this phenomenon from Isaac of Acre. In my opinion, however, there is no need to explain Isaac's view—that spiritual union with God is achieved only after physical union with one's wife is severed—as a synthesis of the positive valorization of marriage in theosophic kabbalah and the emphasis on the spiritual nature of man's relationship to God in ecstatic kabbalah. One can find the same dialectical overcoming of carnal sex through ascetic attachment to the divine in the theosophic material. An interesting example of this phenomenon in Christian mysticism is Margery Kempe, who could not be a bride of Christ while she was still a bride of her earthly husband. Jesus was not only a substitute husband, but he subverted the social function of husbandry. See Beckwith, *Christ's Body*, pp. 84–86.

197. See above, n. 136.

198. Waite, *Holy Kabbalah*, pp. 355–356; Scholem, *Major Trends*, pp. 226–227; Tishby, *Wisdom of the Zohar*, p. 1333; Idel, "Sexual Metaphors," p. 206; Liebes, *Studies in the Zohar*, p. 15; idem, "Zohar and Eros," p. 102. For references to the relevant zoharic passages, see above, n. 138.

199. For fuller discussion of this motif, see E. Wolfson, *Through a Speculum*, pp. 383–392.

200. E. Wolfson, "Woman—The Feminine as Other," pp. 179–182; *Circle in the Square*, pp. 60–69; Liebes, "Zohar and Eros," p. 80. See the comment of Neumann, *Origins*, p. 158: "But the masculinity and ego of the hero are no longer identified with the phallus and sexuality. On this level, another part of the

body erects itself symbolically as the 'higher phallus' or the 'higher masculinity': the head, symbol of consciousness, with the eye for its ruling organ—and with this the ego now identifies itself." Bracketing the psychoanalytic dimension of Neumann's observations, it is of interest to note that his insight confirms my interpretation of the head and eye as symbolic circumlocutions of the upper phallic potency.

201. See E. Wolfson, *Circle in the Square*, pp. 68–69.

202. E. Wolfson, *Through a Speculum*, pp. 356–357, 389–391; Liebes, "Zohar and Eros," pp. 73–80.

203. On the erotic nature of Torah study, see Idel, *Kabbalah: New Perspectives*, pp. 227–229; E. Wolfson, *Circle in the Square*, pp. 16–19; idem, "Beautiful Maiden," pp. 169–170, 185–187; Liebes, "Zohar and Eros," pp. 97–98.

204. The kabbalistic and tantric approaches to human sexuality are compared and contrasted in Patai, *Jewish Mind*, pp. 134–151; Mopsik, *Lettre sur la sainteté*, pp. 159–160; idem, *Grands textes*, p. 323 n. 60; idem, "Union and Unity," pp. 238–240; Idel, "Sexual Metaphors," pp. 205–206; Beitchman, *Alchemy of the Word*, p. 71; McGinn, "Language of Love," p. 221. McGinn perceptively noted that the kabbalistic affirmation of human sexuality as an *imitatio dei* bears a resemblance to the Latin Hermetic text, *Asclepius* 21, where the conjunction of male and female is portrayed as a means of imitating the fecundity of the divine androgyne.

205. Regarding this tantric practice, see Eliade, *Yoga*, pp. 134–135, 245–249; O'Flaherty, *Asceticism and Eroticism*, pp. 261–277; Chalier-Visusalingam, "Union and Unity in Hindu Tantrism," pp. 195–222; McEvilley, "The Spinal Serpent," pp. 93–113; Brooks, *Secret of the Three Cities*, pp. 83–129; idem, *Auspicious Wisdom*, pp. 147–188; David G. White, *Alchemical Body*; idem, "Tantric Sects and Tantric Sex," pp. 249–270; idem, *Kiss of the Yoginī*; Feurstein, *Tantra*, pp. 120–183; Goudriaan, "Stages of Awakening," pp. 139–173; R. Davidson, *Indian Esoteric Buddhism*, pp. 131–153, 194–206, 224–292, 327–330. See further references cited in n. 1 above. From the perspective of gender, there is an interesting ambivalence in the tantric philosophy. On the one hand, *kuṇḍalinī*, which must be drawn up through the different *cakras* from the base of the spinal column to the top of the head, is identified with *sakti*, the feminine aspect of the creative force. On the other hand, the most critical part of the yogic meditational practice is drawing up the semen, which leads to enstasis and the reintegration of feminine and masculine. See Srinivasan, "Polar Principles," pp. 106–115, esp. pp. 108–111. Similarly, in *Zohar*, the vital energy is depicted as a coiled snake that is feminine in nature yet incarnate in the male's semen. On the active nature of the female pole of the ultimate reality in tantric Hinduism as opposed to the passive nature of the male, see Jacobsen, "Female Pole of the Godhead," pp. 56–81. See also Lidke, "Union of Fire and Water," pp. 117–123.

206. See E. Wolfson, "From Sealed Book to Open Text," pp. 149–150; and the text of Cordovero analyzed by Mopsik, "Union and Unity," pp. 240–241.

207. See, for instance, Ezra's *Persuh Shir ha-Shirim*, *Kitvei Ramban*, 2:492. According to the formulation of a passage in *Raʿaya Meheimna*, a later stratum of zoharic literature, the casting of breadcrumbs in vain is interpreted as referring to either "drops of semen," which are "crumbs of the brain" that are spilled in vain or placed in an undeserving vessel (a woman in her menstrual period, a prostitute, or a Gentile), or the "crumbs of the bread of Torah," which are the "the strokes and crownlets of the letters," transmitted to one unworthy of receiving them (*Zohar* 3:244a).

208. *Zohar* 1:92a; 3:13a.

209. Siklós, *Vajrabhairava Tantras*, p. 58.

210. See reference to the studies of Mopsik given in n. 204.

211. See E. Wolfson, "Woman—The Feminine as Other," pp. 185–191; idem, *Circle in the Square*, pp. 92–98.

212. See E. Wolfson, *Circle in the Square*, pp. 80, 195–196 n. 3.

213. Chalier-Visusalingam, "Union and Unity in Hindu Tantrism," p. 207. On the androgynous linga of the Hindu tradition, see O'Flaherty, *Women, Androgynes, and Other Mythical Beasts*, pp. 317–318.

214. I have discussed the homoerotic nature of the mystical fraternity in *Through a Speculum*, pp. 357–377; and *Circle in the Square*, pp. 107–110. The phenomenon has been discussed independently by Liebes, "Zohar and Eros," pp. 104–112, although he still privileges the heterosexual as the most perfect expression of the erotic orientation. The homoerotic tendencies in zoharic literature should be examined in a larger cultural appreciation of sexual mores in the time and place when this corpus began to take shape. See, for instance, González-Casanovas, "Male Bonding as Cultural Construction," pp. 157–192.

215. For references, see chap. 2, n. 122.

216. See references in chap. 2, n. 246.

217. *Zohar* 1:153b; see parallel in Moses de León, *Book of the Pomegranate*, pp. 138 and 142.

218. *Zohar* 1:66b.

219. Literally, the "sabbatical year," which is one of the names of *Shekhinah* in kabbalistic symbolism.

220. *Zohar* 1:153b.

221. *Zohar* 1:216a. Cf. Gikatilla, *Sha'arei Orah*, 1:98–99.

222. See Scholem, *Major Trends*, pp. 165 and 388 n. 44.

223. *Zohar* 1:50a. Cf. Moses de León, *Book of the Pomegranate*, p. 223.

224. See Idel, "Sexual Metaphors," p. 206; idem, *Kabbalah: New Perspectives*, pp. 209–210. The experience of the mystics being female in relation to God, who is male, which Idel associates with ecstatic kabbalah, can be found as well in the theosophic kabbalah. Consistent with other mystical traditions, both theosophic and ecstatic kabbalists portrayed the soul of the mystic as feminine in relation to the male deity. The reversal of gender roles is particularly significant in the Christian mystical tradition, based in great measure on the appropriation of Song of Songs to depict the soul's relationship to Christ: the male mystic assumes the voice of the female beloved, and Jesus, that of the male lover. See McGinn, "Language of Love," pp. 202–203, 207, 211–212.

225. *Zohar* 1:50b–51b.

226. See chap. 4, nn. 76 and 205.

227. On the zoharic locution of being conjoined to the "body of the king," see Liebes, *Sections of the Zohar Lexicon*, p. 227 n. 250. In some of the relevant passages (1:219a; 3:294b), the primary concern is the return of the soul to the divine after the death of the body, but in other contexts (1:216a; 223b, 2:86a) the issue is clearly the conjunction of the righteous to the divine, especially the phallic aspect of God.

228. *Zohar* 2:134b.

229. The expression "masters of judgment" is used to refer to the kabbalists in *Zohar* 2:34a. In that context, the specific gnosis that the masters of judgment possess is the secret wisdom of the demonic power personified as the great sea monster (based on Ezek. 29:3). Given the judgmental character of the demonic force, it makes sense to refer to the kabbalists in this passage as "masters of judgment." For the background of this zoharic text, see Liebes, *Studies in the Zohar*, pp. 15–16.

230. *Zohar* 1:82b.

231. On the dual signification of this term, see E. Wolfson, *Circle in the Square*, pp. 69–70, 124–125 n. 6, 189–190 n. 174, 190–192, nn. 175–180. See also Liebes, "Zohar and Eros," p. 81; Magid, "Conjugal Union," pp. xxix–xxxi.

232. *Zohar* 1:82b.

233. A similar argument has been made by Segal, *Poimandres as Myth*, pp. 33–34, with respect to a passage in *Poimandres* regarding God's love of his son's beauty.

234. In E. Wolfson, *Circle in the Square*, pp. 49–78, I explore the motif of divine autoeroticism in the kabbalistic tradition, principally in zoharic and Lurianic sources, as it pertains to the emanative process by means of which the infinite comes to be in the differentiated world of the *sefirot*. The autoeroticism of which I here speak occurs on a lower ontic level, but it clearly reflects what takes place in the initial phase of divine creativity.

235. *Zohar* 1:243a. God's erotic relationship to the words of innovative Torah study is also described in *Zohar* 1:4b.

236. *Zohar* 3:59b; and see extended analysis in E. Wolfson, *Through a Speculum*, pp. 370–372.

237. On the members of the fraternity constituting the face of *Shekhinah*, cf. the zoharic sources cited and analyzed in E. Wolfson, *Through a Speculum*, pp. 368–369.

238. *Zohar* 3:61a.

239. My translation renders the Aramaic *de-istakkel*; an alternative reading is *de-ishtaddel*, which should be translated as "one who is engaged in." Both readings are found in the first two printed editions of *Zohar* (Mantua and Cremona).

240. *Zohar* 3:90a. This passage is cited in the name of a "midrash" in Isaac of Acre, *Sefer Me'irat Einayim*, p. 6.

241. On this exegetical device, see E. Wolfson, "Beautiful Maiden," pp. 175–178.

242. Needless to say, the correlation of masculinity with penetration and the consequent effeminization of the male who receives is attested in much older sexual ideologies based on an oppositional symbolic. See C. Williams, *Roman Homosexuality*, pp. 125–159. The homoerotic images in kabbalistic symbolism are also indebted to the bipolar approach implied in biblical and rabbinic sources. See Satlow, " 'They Abused Him Like a Woman,' " 1–25; Olyan, "And with a Male," pp. 179–206.

243. Gikatilla, *Sha'arei Orah*, 1:205–206.

244. Babylonian Talmud, Ḥagigah 2a.

245. Based on Ps. 148:13.

246. Gikatilla, *Sha'arei Orah*, 1:206.

247. See, however, *Sha'arei Orah*, 1:196, where Gikatilla employs the image of the king and queen to characterize the erotic relationship of the masculine and feminine aspects of the divine.

248. A comparable tendency is prominent in the Christian mystical tradition wherein the relationship of Jesus and the soul of the male mystic, frequently a celibate monk or priest, is portrayed as the erotic union of the bridegroom and bride as described in the Song. See above, n. 224.

249. See E. Wolfson, *Through a Speculum*, pp. 368–377. For a similar phenomenon in Islamic mystical piety, see Malamud, "Gender and Spiritual Self-Fashioning," pp. 89–117.

Chapter Eight
Coming-to-Head, Returning-to-Womb: (E)soteric Gnosis and Overcoming Gender Dimorphism

1. For two recent sensitive treatments of the interplay of the sensual and spiritual in the imagery of the Song, see Walsh, *Exquisite Desire*; David M. Carr, *Erotic Word*, pp. 109–151.

2. McGinn, "Language of Love," p. 217. See also the comments of Scholem, *On the Mystical Shape*, p. 31, regarding the restriction of the public study of the Song due to the potential usurpation by the servant, the Church, in place of the mistress, the Synagogue. See the interesting if somewhat overstated contrast between Islam on the one hand and Judaism and Christianity on the other made by E. Bloch, *Principle of Hope*, p. 1135: "Indeed even real mysticism was never repelled by such so-called crudely sensual depictions of the other world. . . . Because almost more than the Mohammedan, the Christian and Jewish love of God incorporated voluptuous images, without wishful maidens but with Allah himself."

3. In this context, it is of interest to note the characterization of the Song as the "paradigm of cultural change" in Shmueli, *Seven Jewish Cultures*, p. 65: "Commentaries on the Song of Songs furnish a most revealing illustration for the comparative approach to the study of Jewish cultures and their divergent conceptions of God, man, and the world. No other Biblical book so patently exemplifies each culture's unique interpretation of the spiritual and vital forces which fashioned the nation's character." These words are certainly applicable to the variety of interpretations of this biblical book in Jewish mystical sources across the generations.

4. See Buzy, "L'allegorie matrimoniale," pp. 77–90; Vajda, *L'amour de Dieu*, pp. 44–47; Urbach, "Homiletical Interpretations," pp. 247–275; Pope, *Song of Songs*, pp. 89–132; Kimelman, "Rabbi Yoḥanan and Origen," pp. 567–595; E. Clark, *Ascetic Piety*, pp. 386–427; Hirshman, *Rivalry of Genius*, pp. 83–94. See also the reference to Cohen cited below, n. 15.

5. See I. Gottlieb, "Jewish Allegory of Love," pp. 1–18.

6. See Loewe, "Apologetic Motifs," pp. 159–196; Alonso-Fontela, "El Targum al Cantar," pp. 2–24; P. Alexander, "Tradition and Originality," pp. 318–339, esp. pp. 336–338.

7. The allegorical reading of the Song as a reference to Christ and the Church was doubtless inspired by Eph. 5:21–33. Especially relevant is the use of the term "mystery" in verse 32 to refer to the relationship between husband and wife, which symbolically alludes to Christ and the church. The mystery (in the full sacramental sense of the word) of the Song was read in an analogous fashion. For the possibility that the word

"mystery" here denotes primarily an exegetical secret that is related more specifically to the Christological interpretation of Gen. 2:24, see Bockmuehl, *Revelation and Mystery,* pp. 204–205.

8. For a review of the relevant scholarly literature, see Pope, *Song of Songs,* pp. 145–153.

9. See Boyarin, "Two Introductions to the Midrash," pp. 479–500, esp. pp. 480–491; idem, *Intertextuality,* pp. 108–110. For a somewhat different perspective regarding the rabbinic and patristic allegorical approaches to the Song, see D. Biale, *Eros and the Jews.* p. 59. Biale recognizes the obvious fact that Christian thinkers took a much more radical stance vis-à-vis human sexuality than did the rabbis, and he also notes that the midrashic reading of the Song "did not efface the eroticism of the text," although he insists that it did not fully embrace eroticism on the human plane. My own sense is that the erotic nature of allegory affirmed in the rabbinic texts is predicated on a full embrace of human sexuality, albeit one that is infused with semiological significance. The real issue at stake is not eros, but the construction of body.

10. Elliott, *Song of Songs,* p. 12.

11. See Matter, *Voice of My Beloved,* pp. 20–48; Astell, *Song of Songs,* pp. 2–5, 18–19.

12. P. Miller, "'Pleasure of the Text," pp. 241–253. See also Cameron, "Sacred and Profane Love," pp. 10–12; V. Harrison, "Allegory and Eroticism," pp. 113–130, esp. pp. 123–124.

13. My remarks reflect the critique of Miller in Matter, *Voice of My Beloved,* p. 33. Compare Dawson, "Allegorical Reading," pp. 26–43. See also Asiedu, "Song of Songs," pp. 299–317.

14. E. Clark, *Ascetic Piety,* pp. 401–405.

15. See G. Cohen, *Studies in the Varieties of Rabbinic Cultures,* pp. 3–17, esp. p. 13. Cohen distinguishes two kinds of allegorical reading of the Song of Songs in the classical rabbinic period: the public exposition of the book, which emphasized the different stages of Jewish history and the contacts between the collectivity of Israel and the divine, and the innermost allegory, which involved the erotic relationship of the individual and God, an interpretation limited to the select few who entered the chambers of mystical knowledge in solitude. For an elaboration of the two allegorical readings, see M. Fishbane, "Song of Songs and Ancient Jewish Religiosity," pp. 69–81.

16. Babylonian Talmud, Shevu'ot 35b. In that context (see n. 17), I cited Babylonia Talmud, Shabbat 152a, as a rabbinic source that attests to the use of the term *shalom* as a euphemism for the penis. See also *Leviticus Rabbah,* 18:1, p. 396, where the idiom of placing peace in the house is interpreted as sexual desire of a man to cohabit with a woman.

17. See E. Wolfson, *Along the Path,* pp. 204–205 n. 71. On the possibility of a hypostatic theosophy underlying the rabbinic reading of the Song, related especially to the symbol of *kenesset yisra'el* ("community of Israel") see the preliminary remarks by Idel, "Rabbinism versus Kabbalism," pp. 286–288. Regarding the use of the symbol *kenesset yisra'el* in rabbinic and kabbalistic sources, see also Liebes, *Studies in Jewish Myth,* pp. 42–54.

18. The linkage between the overtly anthropomorphic theosophic speculation of the *Shi'ur Qomah* texts and the mystical reading of the Song has been affirmed by a number of scholars, including, most prominently, Adolf Jellinek, Gershom Scholem, and Saul Lieberman. For a critical review of the relevant literature, see M. Cohen, *Shi'ur Qomah,* pp. 19–31, 111–112. Lieberman's view regarding a mystical midrash on the Song, which is related to the *Shi'ur Qomah* tradition, is also criticized by Boyarin, "Two Introductions," pp. 492–500.

19. It is of interest to note the following remark made by Vulliaud, *Cantique des Cantiques,* p. 116, in the context of comparing the treatment of the Song in *Zohar* and in *Shir ha-Shirim Rabbah*: "Encore une fois, comparant Midrasch et Kabbale, je ne constate dans la Kabbale qu'une systématisation et une plus complète exposition des enseignements du Midrasch. Mêmes théories, mêmes symboles, mêmes regrets et mêmes aspirations, la force de l'exaltation mystique est toutefois plus vivement entretenue et surexcitée par l'école kabbalistique, tandis qu'elle rattache ses doctrines au système qui lui est particulier et qui forme la théosophie séphirothique." Although Vulliaud does not focus on the specific traditions that figure prominently in my own analysis, I share his assumption regarding the relationship of the theosophic kabbalah and earlier midrashic theology.

20. Mishnah, Yadayim 3:5. Here it is worth noting the Islamic tradition, "The entire Koran is a symbolic,

allusive [*ramz*] story, between the Lover and the Beloved, and no one except the two of them understands the truth or reality of its intention," and the interpretation offered by Corbin, *Creative Imagination*, p. 251: "Clearly the entire 'science of the heart' and all the creativity of the heart are needed to set in motion the *ta'wīl*, the mystic interpretation which makes it possible to read and to practice the Koran as though it were a variant of the Song of Songs."

21. *Agadath Shir Hashirim*, p. 5. The original Hebrew of this passage is somewhat enigmatic: *illu lo nitnah ba-torah shir ha-shirim keda'y hayyetah linhog et ha-olam*. My rendering presumes that the word *ba-torah* is a corruption of *ha-torah*, a reading that is confirmed by the passage cited by the thirteenth-century kabbalist, Isaac Ibn Sahula, in his commentary on the Song, which is mentioned by Schechter in *Agadath Shir Hashirim*, p. 49. See also Lieberman, *Midreshei Teiman*, p. 14 n. 1. Lieberman suggests that the correct reading is *illu lo nitnah ba-torah ela shir ha-shirim*, which should be translated as "Had nothing been given in the Torah except for the Song of Songs."

22. See Lieberman, "Mishnath Shir ha-Shirim," pp. 118–121. The influence of this rabbinic tradition is reflected, for instance, in a liturgical poem for Pentecost composed by Eleazar bi-R. Qillir that is organized around verses from the Song. See Elizur, "On the Role of the *Yoẓer*," pp. 351–394.

23. See E. Wolfson, *Circle in the Square*, pp. 4–7.

24. See David Stern, *Parables in Midrash*, pp. 63–67.

25. *Shir ha-Shirim Rabbah*, 1:8, p. 5. Many of the pericopae included in this anthology are predicated on the implicit identification of the Song and the Torah. Only such an assumption can account for the specific application of verses from the Song to the Torah. An early articulation of the essential parabolic nature of Torah linked to Solomon's literary productions, and especially the Song of Songs, is found in Abulafia, *Oṣar Eden Ganuz*, fols. 59b–60a (printed ed., p. 120): "Thus Solomon [proceeded] from parable to parable, and from word to word, until he understood the words of Torah. Hence, they acknowledged that Proverbs was first, and then the words of Ecclesiastes, and subsequent to the two of them the parables [that illumine] the clarity of Torah, which is the Song of Songs." Abulafia goes on to say that this is the order of study that must be followed by one seeking perfection: initially one must attain moral excellence (Proverbs), and then one must master matters pertaining to nature (Ecclesiastes), and finally one attains metaphysical felicity in the "secret of the poem," *be-sod ha-shir* (Song).

26. This idea, which occupied a central role in rabbinic readings of the Song, is expressed in a particularly poignant way in David ben Ḥayyim, *Shirah le-Dawid*, 1d: "King Solomon cherished the holy Torah even though he was a great wise man, as it says, 'He was the wisest of all men, he composed three thousand proverbs, and his songs numbered one thousand and five' (1 Kings 5:11–12). Notwithstanding all of this, the holy Torah, which was given from heaven, is better, for the Torah is also referred to as 'song,' as it says, 'Therefore, write down this song' (Deut. 31:19). This is the 'Song of Songs' [*shir ha-shirim*], the five books of Torah, 'by Solomon' [*asher li-shelomo*], for by means of the holy Torah one can acquire perfection [*sheleimut*], by means of Torah and the commandments one can be conjoined to the holy One, blessed be he. This is the import of what is said, 'Oh, let him kiss me with the kisses of his mouth,' for by means of Torah one is conjoined to the holy One, blessed be he, in one moment."

27. Rosenzweig, *Star of Redemption*, p. 201. For discussion of this passage, see E. Wolfson, "Facing the Effaced," pp. 77–78.

28. Many examples could be cited to prove the point that Jewish interpreters through the ages have been keenly aware of the struggle between Church and Synagogue over the Song. Here I will mention briefly one example. In the introduction to his commentary on the Song, *Sefer Sar Shalom*, 3b–4a, Samuel Aripul affirms the standard allegorical reading of the scroll as a dialogue between God and the community of Israel, but he also emphasizes that the true meaning of this text can be ascertained only by Israel, whereas the other books traditionally ascribed to Solomon can be understood by other nations. I assume that the metaphorical comparison of the Song to the pure flour of which only Israel can partake is a veiled allusion to the fact that Christians cannot penetrate the inner depths of this poem. See ibid., 16a, where Aripul reiterates the point that the hidden secrets of the Song, which are connected to the amorous imagery, can be known only by Israel.

29. An interesting case study along these lines is found in Saltman, "Jewish Exegetical Material," pp. 421–452.

30. Leclercq, *Love of Learning*, p. 84, thus distinguishes between the medieval Christian scholastic approach and the monastic approach to the Song: the former was basically collective in nature, emphasizing God's relations to the entire Church, whereas the latter was individualistic in orientation, focusing primarily on God's relations with each soul. I am deliberately ignoring the Marian interpretation of the female persona of the Song, which is also attested in the history of Christian exegesis and liturgy, beginning with Origen and Gregory of Nyssa in the East and Ambrose in the West, eventually becoming a formal part of the commentary genre, especially in the twelfth and thirteenth centuries. In particular, the biblical text was used to extol the virtue of Mary's virginity as the Mother-Bride (an important verse in this regard was Song 4:12). See Beumer, "Die marianische Deutung," pp. 411–439; Ohly, *Hohelied-Studien*, pp. 124–134; Perella, *Kiss Sacred and Profane*, pp. 70–73; Wechsler, "Change in the Iconography," pp. 73–93; E. Clark, *Ascetic Piety*, pp. 405–407; Pope, *Song of Songs*, pp. 188–192; Matter, *Voice of My Beloved*, pp. 151–177; Astell, *Song of Songs*, pp. 15–16, 42–50, 60–72, 138–143, 168–176; Hamburger, *Rothschild Canticles*, pp. 71, 88–104; Fulton, "Virgin Mary and Song of Songs"; idem, *From Judgment to Passion*; Ebertshäuser, Haag, Kirchberger, and Sölle, *Mary*, pp. 175–176. For a later reflex of this exegetical tradition, see Engammare, *Qu'il me baise*, pp. 260–266; and for an interesting devotional application of the symbol, see Winston-Allen, *Stories of the Rose*, pp. 88–92, 145–146.

31. On the description of the Song as a "contemplative text" (*theoricus sermo*), expressive of the eschatological desire in medieval monastic culture, see Leclercq, *Love of Learning*, pp. 85–86.

32. Perella, *Kiss Sacred and Profane*, p. 40. The importance of the kiss in the history of Christian spirituality should not be limited to exegetical support for the mystical imagination. On the contrary, there is evidence that the kiss as union with Christ was part of the communion ritual. See Taft, "Byzantine Communion Rites," pp. 307–345, esp. pp. 337–342.

33. See McGinn, "Language of Love," pp. 202–203, 207, 211–212. See also Moore, "Song of Songs in the History of Sexuality," pp. 328–349. The gender reversal implied by the portrayal of the soul as feminine vis-à-vis the divine or the earthly incarnation of God depicted as male is also found in Islamic esotericism. As a representative study of this phenomenon, see Asani, "Bridal Symbolism," pp. 389–404, esp. pp. 398–399. See also Schimmel, *Mystical Dimensions*, pp. 152–155, who notes that the use of feminine images to depict the soul of men in their yearning for the deity imaged as masculine in some Islamic mystical sources reflects the influence of Hinduism, in contrast to other Sufi authors for whom the soul is masculinized and God, the object of yearning, is feminine.

34. For discussion of the process of homosocial bonding with God through exegesis of biblical texts in a fourteenth-century literary setting, see Keiser, *Courtly Desire*, pp. 165–200. Keiser's insight that the celebration of the homosocial bonding between God and men rests upon an unequivocal rejection of homosexual deviance corresponds to my view that the homoerotic relationship of the male kabbalist with the masculine God is predicated on an abnegation of carnal sexuality. See E. Wolfson, *Circle in the Square*, pp. 107–110, 223–224 n. 145.

35. Bernard of Clairvaux, *On the Song of Songs I*, 1:11, pp. 6–7.

36. Ibid., 3:1, p. 16. The emphasis placed on experience is repeated on many occasions in Bernard's sermons; for example, see 6:9, p. 37, where Bernard refers to experience as a "teacher." See idem, *On the Song of Songs II*, 22:2, p. 15: "In matters of this kind, understanding can follow only where experience leads, and I shall be the last to intrude rashly where the bride alone may enter"; idem, *On the Song of Songs II*, 39:3, p. 193: "I have no doubt that some of you understand what I am saying from your own experience, which enables you even to anticipate my words"; idem, *On the Song of Songs II*, 41:3, p. 206: "The things we speak of are divine, totally unknown except to those who have experienced them." See also idem, *On the Song of Songs III*, 51:3, p. 42: "I am telling you of what comes within my own experience"; idem, *On the Song of Songs IV*, 68:1, p. 17: "Hear now what I held over from yesterday; hear of the joy which I have experienced. . . . I experienced this joy in just one word of the Bride. . . . The Bride has spoken, and has said that the Bridegroom inclines himself to her; who then is the Bride, and who is the Bridegroom? The Bridegroom is

our God, and we, I say in all humility, are the Bride—we, and the whole multitude of captives whom he acknowledges"; idem, *On the Song of Songs IV*, 74:5, pp. 89–90: "I want to tell you of my own experience. . . . I admit that the Word has also come to me . . . and has come many times. But although he has come to me, I have never been conscious of the moment of his coming."

37. Jantzen, *Power, Gender and Christian Mysticism*, p. 126. See idem, "Mysticism and Experience," pp. 295–315. On the theme of mystical union in the writings of Bernard, see Gilson, *Mystical Theology*, pp. 101–118. The manner in which the circular process of writing and reading construct the monastic site according to Bernard is explored by Pranger, *Bernard of Clairvaux*, pp. 47–84. On the role of experience and the spiritual senses in Bernard's mystical orientation, see McGinn, *Growth of Mysticism*, pp. 185–190. On the kiss as a symbol for the union between the soul and the divine in Bernard's reading of the Song, see Perella, *Kiss Sacred and Profane*, pp. 52–57; Astell, *Song of Songs*, pp. 17–20.

38. Bernard of Clairvaux, *On the Song of Songs I*, 9:3, p. 55.

39. Bernard of Clairvaux, *On the Song of Songs IV*, 85:14, p. 210. For discussion of the various nuances of mystical union in Bernard's religious philosophy, see Tamburello, *Union with Christ*, pp. 64–83.

40. Bernard of Clairvaux, *On the Song of Songs II*, 23:3, p. 28.

41. On the meditational practice of Bernard as it relates especially to his sermons on the Song of Songs, see Carruthers, *Craft of Thought*, pp. 84–87.

42. Bernard of Clairvaux, *On the Song of Songs I*, 2:6, p. 12.

43. Ibid., 3:2–5, pp. 16–20. See McGinn, *Growth of Mysticism*, p. 166.

44. Bernard of Clairvaux, *On the Song of Songs I*, 2:2, p. 9; see 3:5, p. 20: "and he who is joined to him in a holy kiss becomes through his good pleasure, one spirit with him." Bernard's words are based in part on 1 Cor. 16:17.

45. On the role of asceticism in the Cistercian spirituality appropriated by Bernard, see Gilson, *Mystical Theology*, pp. 68–69.

46. Bernard of Clairvaux, *On the Song of Songs I*, 1:3, p. 2.

47. Ibid., 5:8, p. 30.

48. Ibid., 7:3, p. 39.

49. Bernard of Clairvaux, *On the Song of Songs IV*, 71:10, pp. 56–57.

50. Ibid., 83:4, p. 184. The emphasis on mystical union in Bernard's sermons is not to foster unmitigated withdrawal from the world. On the contrary, the monastic ideal of the Cistercian and Franciscan orders was socially oriented. The spiritual program of Bernard in particular was to restore God's love to its origin so that it might overflow again with a revitalized strength. The effect of union with God is augmentation of charity in the world. The contemplative ideal is seen as part of the process by means of which divine love is disseminated. See Bernard of Clairvaux, *On the Song of Songs II*, 23:2, p. 26; commenting on the verse "The king has brought me into his chambers" (Song 1:3), Bernard remarked, "Even though I alone seem to have been introduced, it is not for my sole advantage. Every preferment I enjoy is a joy for you all; the progress that I make is for you, and with you I shall divide all that I shall merit above your measure"; idem, *On the Song of Songs III*, 57:9, p. 103: "It is characteristic of true and pure contemplation that when the mind is ardently aglow with God's love, it is sometimes so filled with zeal and the desire to gather to God those who will love him with equal abandon that it gladly foregoes contemplative leisure for the endeavor of preaching"; idem, *On the Song of Songs IV*, 68:1, p. 17: "Hear now what I held over from yesterday; hear of the joy which I have experienced. Yet it is your joy also." See J. Wimsatt, "St. Bernard, the Canticle of Canticles, and Mystical Poetry," pp. 77–95; McGinn, *Growth of Mysticism*, pp. 207–215.

51. Bernard of Clairvaux, *On the Song of Songs IV*, 83:6, p. 186. The utilization of the kiss as symbolic of spiritual fellowship is attested in the ritual kiss of peace affirmed by Dionysius the Areopagite in his *The Ecclesiastical Hierarchy* in conjunction with mystery of *synaxis* or communion; see *Pseudo-Dionysius*, pp. 211 and 218.

52. Based on 1 Tim. 2:5.

53. Bernard of Clairvaux, *On the Song of Songs I*, 2:9, p. 15.

54. Ibid., 8:2, p. 46.

55. Ibid., 2:7, p. 12.

56. Ibid., 2:3, p. 10.

57. The matter is expanded in ibid., 11:7, pp. 74–75. See also Bernard of Clairvaux, *On the Song of Songs IV*, 69:6, pp. 32–33.

58. Ps. 22:15.

59. Bernard of Clairvaux, *On the Song of Songs I*, 15:4, pp. 108–109.

60. Bernard of Clairvaux, *On the Song of Songs III*, 56:1, pp. 87–88.

61. Jantzen, *Power, Gender and Christian Mysticism*, p. 129.

62. This is not to say that Bernard does not at times adopt the more conventional view that would deny the literal ascription of anthropomorphic images to God. For instance, see the apophatic orientation affirmed by Bernard, *On the Song of Songs I*, 4:4, pp. 23–24.

63. Ibid., 20:4, pp. 149–150.

64. Ibid., 20:7, p. 153.

65. A particularly important application of this is Bernard's explanation of the iconic image one must have in prayer of God as human; see ibid., 20:6, p. 152: "The soul at prayer should have before it a sacred image of the God-man, in his birth or infancy or as he was teaching, or dying, or rising, or ascending. Whatever form it takes this image must bind the soul with love of virtue and expel carnal vices, eliminate temptations and quiet desires. I think this is the principle reason why the invisible God willed to be seen in the flesh and to converse with men as a man. He wanted to recapture the affections of carnal men who were unable to love in any other way, by first drawing them to salutary love of his own humanity, and then gradually to raise them to a spiritual love. . . . So it was only by his physical presence that their hearts were detached from carnal love."

66. Ibid., 1:1, 4, pp. 1–3.

67. See Borgen, *Bread from Heaven*.

68. John 6:25–59, esp. 33: "For the bread of God is he who comes down from heaven and gives life to the world." And ibid., 51: "I am the living bread that came down from heaven. If anyone eats of this bread, he will live forever. This bread is my flesh, which I will give for the life of the world." On the hidden manna, see Rev. 2:17.

69. Bernard of Clairvaux, *On the Song of Songs II*, 34:1–4, pp. 160–164, 45:3–4, pp. 234–235. The emphasis on humility can be traced back to the exhortation attributed to Jesus, "He who is greatest among you shall be your servant; whoever exalts himself will be humbled, and whoever humbles himself will be exalted" (Matt. 23:11–12). In the reworking of the statement attributed to Jesus in James 4:4–10, an explicit connection is established between humility and denial of worldly pleasures. See also *Ecclesiastical Hierarchy*, 3.12, in Dionysius the Areopagite, *Pseudo-Dionysius*, p. 222.

70. Hollywood, *Soul as Virgin Wife*, p. 21. See also Hamburger, *Rothschild Canticles*, pp. 1–7, 23–26, 71–72, 105–117.

71. See E. Wolfson, *Through a Speculum*, pp. 119–124, 326–332.

72. Although a number of scholars in this century have adopted the contextualist approach in one form or another, the most outspoken and oft-cited champion of this position has been Steven Katz; see the two collection of essays edited by him: *Mysticism and Philosophical Analysis*, and *Mysticism and Religious Traditions*. For a response to the contextualist argument, see the essays in Forman, *Problem of Pure Consciousness*; see also Forgie, "Hyper-Kantianism," pp. 205–218; and Evans, "Can Philosophers Limit," pp. 53–60. For a modified contextualism, see my own discussion in *Through a Speculum*, pp. 52–73; see also the studies by Sells and Kripal in the following note.

73. On the phenomenon of apophatic imagery, which embodies the dialectic of revelation and concealment, see Hamburger, *Rothschild Canticles*, pp. 133–142. This dialectic is at the foundation of the richly nuanced analysis in Sells, *Mystical Languages of Unsaying*. See also the pertinent remarks of Kripal, *Kali's Child*, pp. 17–21.

74. Hollywood, *Soul as Virgin Wife*, p. 22.

75. The point is made quite profoundly in a passage from the *Midrash ha-Ne'elam*, a relatively early stra-

tum of zoharic literature, in *Zohar* 1:98b. According to the narrative setting of that passage, on a particular Friday when the health of Eliezer ben Hyrcanus was failing, several sages of the generation came to pay him a visit. Amongst those sages was Aqiva, who requested Eliezer to teach some Torah. The master began to expound the account of the chariot, as a result of which a fire surrounded those who were gathered about his bed. After the others departed from the room, Eliezer continued to instruct Aqiva in nine hundred legal decisions (*halakhot pesuqot*) and 216 explanations (*teʿamim*) for the verses of the Song. However, when Eliezer reached the verse, "Sustain me with raisin cakes, refresh me with apples, for I am faint with love" (Song 2:5), Aqiva could no longer endure the experience. He wept and he cried out, and no more was said "out of respect for the *Shekhinah* who was there." Eliezer's exposition of the mysteries embedded in the Song led to Aqiva's ecstatic experience, depicted primarily by his weeping in the face of the fiery presence of the divine. See the interesting use of this zoharic passage in the comments by David ben Samuel Halevi, *Ṭurei Zahav*, on the marginal gloss of Moses Isserles to Joseph Karo, *Shulḥan Arukh*, Oraḥ Ḥayyim, 288:2. According to Isserles, if one derives pleasure from weeping, then it is permissible to weep on Sabbath. Commenting on this, David ben Samuel Halevi writes, "As it says in the *Aggadah*, the disciples of Aqiva found him weeping on Sabbath, and he said, 'I have pleasure in this.' It appears that out of the abundance of his cleaving to the holy One, blessed be he, his eyes shed tears. Thus we find in *Zohar Ḥadash* that Aqiva would weep intensely when he uttered the Song of Songs, for he knew where these matters reached." On the nexus of weeping and ecstasy, see Idel, *Kabbalah: New Perspectives*, pp. 75–88; and E. Wolfson, "Weeping, Death, and Spiritual Ascent," pp. 209–247. For a nuanced analysis of the motif of weeping in zoharic literature, see also E. Fishbane, "Tears of Disclosure," pp. 25–47.

76. D. Turner, *Eros and Allegory*, pp. 19–21.

77. On the use of erotic images and the centrality of the body in the case of Christian women mystics in the later Middle Ages, see Bynum, *Holy Feast*, pp. 26, 246–276. The more positive role accorded the body and sexuality in theological discourse is echoed in contemporary feminist theory. See Sands, "Uses of the Thea(o)logian," pp. 7–33; Gudorf, *Body, Sex, and Pleasure*; Cooey, *Religious Imagination and the Body*.

78. Jantzen, *Power, Gender and Christian Mysticism*, pp. 90–92, 126, 133–146. Weber, *Teresa of Avila*, pp. 114–122, suggests that the language of erotic spirituality in Teresa's *Las Moradas des castillo interior* was enhanced in great measure by a reading of the Song distinctive to women exegetes. For the suggestion that the nuptial mysticism of Teresa and John of the Cross betrays the influence of kabbalists' utilization of erotic images of the Song, see Swietlicki, *Spanish Christian Cabala*, pp. 169–171.

79. Jantzen, *Power, Gender and Christian Mysticism*, pp. 236–238. For a later development of this motif, see St. J. Flynn, "Saint of the Womanly Body," pp. 91–109.

80. See Thornton, *Eros*, pp. 128–134. For a presumed challenge in the twelfth and thirteenth centuries to the equations between femininity and carnality, on the one hand, and masculinity and the spiritual, on the other, see Kay, "Women's Body of Knowledge."

81. Bynum, *Holy Feast*, pp. 217–218. See also the balanced account in P. Johnson, *Equal in Monastic Profession*.

82. Bynum, *Holy Feast*, pp. 262–269, 290–294.

83. See Hollywood, *Soul as Virgin Wife*, p. 7. For discussion of the adoption of the ascetic ideal on the part of early Christian women and the subversion of the social order of the Roman Empire based on marriage as the proper role assigned to women, see E. Clark, *Ascetic Piety*, pp. 175–208; G. Clark, "Women and Asceticism in Late Antiquity," pp. 33–48; C. Cooper, *Virgin and the Bride*.

84. To avoid potential misunderstanding, let me make clear that I am not saying that Jewish women in the Middle Ages were not capable of interpreting the Song in erotic terms that may have occasioned mystical experiences of an ecstatic nature. The difficulty lies in finding the sources for the historian to construct a methodologically sound argument.

85. The range of exegetical strategies in reading the Song can easily be gauged from even a cursory glance at Walfish, "Annotated Bibliography," pp. 518–571.

86. See Kamin, *Jews and Christians*, pp. 13–61. The rendering of Rashi's historico-allegorical approach to the Song as the literal sense (*exposito hystorica*) in the thirteenth-century Latin commentary on the Song is

described in Smalley, *Study of the Bible*, pp. 352–355; see also Signer, "Thirteenth Century Christian Hebraism," pp. 89–100; Kamin and Saltman, *Secundum Salomonem*. On the historical approach to the allegorical reading of the Song, referred to as the concealed meaning (*nistar*), in contrast to the literal or revealed sense (*nigleh*), see Tamakh, *R. Abraham b. Isaac ha-Levi Tamakh*, pp. 39–42. In this chapter I am deliberately ignoring the utilization of verses from the Song in the formulation of the mystical theosophy articulated by the Jewish Pietists of the Rhineland in the twelfth and thirteenth centuries, as we find, for instance, in their articulation of chariot speculation in terms of the image of the secret of the nut (*sod ha-egoz*), which is derived from Song 6:11. See references above, chap. 4, n. 13. In my various attempts at decoding the Pietistic esotericism, which involved the attribution of an erotic drama to the divine realm, I have noted the central role played by key passages from the Song. See, in particular, the comments in E. Wolfson, *Along the Path*, pp. 185–186 n. 364. See also Marcus, "Song of Songs," pp. 181–189.

87. J. Katz, *Exclusiveness and Tolerance*, p. 21.

88. Frank, "'Voice of the Turtledove." My brief summary is indebted to the author's skilled textual analysis. See idem, "Karaite Commentaries," pp. 51–69.

89. Frank, "*Shoshanim*," pp. 199–245, esp. pp. 200–201.

90. See, by contrast, A. Green, "Song of Songs," p. 49: "With the contraction of midrashic thinking in the Middle Ages and its displacement by philosophical theology as the dominant Jewish way of speaking about God, the traditions of sacred eros, scandalous to the philosophers, became virtually the unique legacy of the mystics." I see little evidence to support the surmise concerning a "contraction of midrashic thinking" in medieval Jewish academies nor do I think it valid to speak of "philosophical theology" as a dominant mode of discourse about God, but what I find most objectionable in Green's statement is the notion that the philosophers would have been scandalized by the "sacred eros" articulated in kabbalistic literature. On the contrary, the sacred eroticism so pronounced in works of kabbalah is related to and in a measure derived from the idea of an intellectual eros that informed the medieval philosophical conception of conjunction (*devequt*). The contrast between the approach of Maimonides to the image of the kiss in the Song as a metaphor for the union between the rational soul and the Active Intellect and the erotic spirituality of kabbalistic symbolism (especially as it may be excavated from the various strata of *Zohar*) is also drawn too sharply by Perella, *Kiss Sacred and Profane*, pp. 75–83. By contrast, Rosenberg, "Philosophical Hermeneutics," pp. 133–151, proposes a typological distinction between the philosophical exegesis of the Song as a figurative dialogue between the individual soul and the divine, on the one hand, and the kabbalistic exegesis that reads the Song as a description of the relationship of the male and the female attributes of the divine, on the other, but he readily acknowledges that the philosophical interpretation appears in works that would be classified as kabbalistic (p. 134).

91. See Vajda, *L'amour de Dieu*, pp. 142, 144–145, 168–169, 179–180, 242–247, 254–255; Corbin, *Creative Imagination*, p.35. An interesting departure from the norm is found in a passage in some versions of *Shaʿarei Ṣedeq*, for example, MS Leiden 24.3, Cod. Or. 4762 Warner. A translation of the passage into Italian appears in Idel, *Le Porte della Giustizia*, p. 449, but the original text is not provided. I translate from the Hebrew version edited by Parush, *Shaʿarei Ṣedeq*, p. 38, adding parenthetical remarks to explicate the text: "Your name will be called Israel [*yisraʾel* = 541] in accord with my name, which numerically is the Active Intellect [*sekhel ha-poʿel* = 541], for I and you are one thing [*ani we-atah davar eḥad*]. Moreover, he joins the name of twenty-six [i.e., YHWH] with Rebekah and the name of twenty-six with Jacob, and when he joins the four of them they equal *yisraʾel* [the sum of *rivqah* is 307 and *yaʿaqov* 182, to which one adds 52, that is, 2 x YHWH, and the sum of all four is 541, the numerical value of *yisraʾel*]. The secret is 'Rebekah loves Jacob' (Gen. 25:28), the matter is the conjunction [*ḥibbur*] of the soul [*nefesh*], which is the mother, with her true son, whose intellect, by means of the names, is together with the Active Intellect, and they are one thing, for 'Jacob the son of Rebekah' [*yaʿaqov ben rivqah* = 541] is 'Israel' [*yisraʾel* = 541]." According to this text, the intellectual conjunction of the human soul and the Active Intellect is cast in the mold of the relationship of Rebekah and Jacob, the mother associated with the Active Intellect and the son with the human soul.

92. Scholem, *Major Trends*, p. 226.

93. Idel, *Kabbalah: New Perspectives*, p. 206.

94. Ibn Paquda, *Sefer Torat Ḥovot ha-Levavot*, 10.1, p. 412.

95. See Vajda, *L'amour de Dieu*, p. 115 n. 6.

96. The relevant passages are cited by Rosenberg, "Philosophical Hermeneutics," pp. 136–137. See also Hughes, *Texture of the Divine*, pp. 38, 61, 121–122.

97. See Scheindlin, *Gazelle*, pp. 49, 128–129; and the poem by Judah Halevi translated and analyzed in T. Rosen, *Unveiling Eve*, p. 89, and the comments of the author, p. 221 n. 20.

98. Reif, "Abraham ibn Ezra on Canticles," p. 247.

99. Pseudo-Baḥya, *Réflexions sur l'âme*, pp. 38 and 40; see also p. 35; Rosenberg, "Philosophical Hermeneutics," p. 137.

100. *Mishneh Torah*, Hilkhot Teshuvah 10.3.

101. Maimonides, *Guide*, III:51. On the reappropriation of the language of eros in the thought of Maimonides (and other philosophical thinkers influenced by him) as the most compelling metaphorical expression to depict the intellectual conjunction of the soul and the divine, see M. Fishbane, *Kiss of God*, pp. 24–30; and the philological-historical analysis by S. Harvey, "Meaning of Terms Designating Love," pp. 175–196. See also the study of Gordon cited in chap. 7, n. 151.

102. Rosenblatt, *Highways to Perfection*, p. 395.

103. Saadya Gaon, *Kitāb al-Amānāt wa'l-I'tiqādāt*, 10:4, pp. 300–303, discusses individuals who are dedicated to passionate love (*'ishq*), which serves as the model for their relationship to God. For the social and intellectual background of Saadya's use of this term, including the possibility that it is borrowed from Islamic mysticism, see Goitein, *Mediterranean Society*, vol. 5, pp. 317–320. On the use of *'ishq* in Sufism to connote the passionate love of the soul for God, see Schimmel, *Mystical Dimensions*, p. 137; Massignon, *Passion of al-Hallāj*, vol. 1, pp. 340–343, 523 n. 64; vol. 2, pp. 412; vol. 3, pp. 102–104; Wafer, "Vision and Passion," pp. 111, 122, 128 n. 4; Abrahamov, *Divine Love in Islamic Mysticism*, pp. 18–23, 32. On the discrediting of *'ishq* on the part of Islamic philosophers, see Giffen, *Theory of Profane Love*, pp. 64–65.

104. Babylonian Talmud, Baba Batra 17a; *Shir ha-Shirim Rabbah*, 1:16, p. 16. On the description of the kiss of death as the "union of the soul in the root," see *Zohar* 1:168a.

105. See Rawidowicz, *Studies in Jewish Thought*, pp. 291–298; and other references cited in chap. 7, n. 151. The influence of Maimonides is clearly discernible in Baḥya ben Asher's description in *Kad ha-Qemaḥ* of *ḥesheq*, intense desire, which he contrasts with *ahavah*, love. See Baḥya ben Asher, *Kitvei Rabbenu Baḥya*, pp. 34–35: "The intense desire [*ḥesheq*] is the conjunction of thought [*devequt ha-maḥshavah*] to the great and powerful love, for the thought of the one who desires is not at all separated from that which is desired. . . . The book of the Song of Songs is based on this level of intense desire, as it begins 'Oh, give me of the kisses of his mouth' (Song 1:2), and the rabbis, blessed be their memory, explained that all of Scripture is holy, but the Song of Songs is the holy of the holies, for the desired goal of human beings is to conjoin the thought to the holy of holies. The word 'kiss' [*neshiqah*] has the meaning of conjunction [*devequt*]. . . . Concerning the one whose death is by the kiss of *Shekhinah*, his body is pure and his soul is pure."

106. Maimonides, *Guide*, I:5; III:51. On the origin of the expression "intellectual love" in Plotinus, see Ivry, "Neoplatonic Currents in Maimonides' Thought," p. 125.

107. In the introduction to his commentary to the Song, Moses Ibn Tibbon states that his explanations will be based on the teachings of Maimonides related to select verses from the book and on the more extensive explication of his father, Samuel; see Ibn Tibbon, *Perush al Shir ha-Shirim*, 3b (Fraisse, "Hohelied-Kommentar," pp. 103–104). The reference to what his father said concerning the literary production of Solomon in *Perush al Shir ha-Shirim*, 5a (Fraisse, "Hohelied-Kommentar," pp. 127–130) corresponds to a comment in Samuel's commentary on Ecclesiastes, as noted by Fraisse, p. 128 n. 80. For a more comprehensive delineation of the parallels between the commentary on Ecclesiastes by Samuel and the commentary on the Song by Moses, see James T. Robinson, "Samuel Ibn Tibbon's *Commentary*," pp. 482–488. In his comments on Song 8:10, *Perush al Shir ha-Shirim*, 23a, Ibn Tibbon refers to what "my master, my uncle, the sage wrote in the commentary" (*we-adoni dodi he-ḥakham katav be-feirush*). But see the variant reading from MSS Vatican ebr. 549, fol. 30b, and Oxford heb f. 109, fol. 39a, recorded by Fraisse, "Hohelied-Kommentar," p.

332, *we-katav adoni avi* ("my master, my father, wrote"). The question of Samuel Ibn Tibbon's approach to the Song is complicated by a comment he makes in his *Perush Qohelet*, MS Parma 272, fol. 20b, cited by Fraisse, "Hohelied-Kommentar," p. 12 n. 27: "the words [of Solomon] in [the Song of Songs] were not by way of wisdom [*derekh ha-ḥokhmah*] but by way of the words of two lovers, one to the other [*derekh divrei shenei ḥoshqim zeh la-zeh*]."

108. Ibn Aqnin, *Divulgatio Mysteriorum*, pp. 18–19. See Halkin, "Ibn Aknin's Commentary," pp. 389–420; Vajda, *L'amour de Dieu*, pp. 144–145.

109. Ibn Aqnin, *Divulgatio Mysteriorum*, pp. 14–15.

110. Ibid., pp. 24–25.

111. Ibn Tibbon, *Perush al Shir ha-Shirim*, 4b (Fraisse, "Hohelied-Kommentar," pp. 125–126); see also 6a, 6b (Fraisse, "Hohelied-Kommentar," pp. 129–131).

112. Ibn Tibbon, *Perush al Shir ha-Shirim*, 5a (Fraisse, "Hohelied-Kommentar," pp. 127–128).

113. Ibn Tibbon, *Perush al Shir ha-Shirim*, 7b–8a (Fraisse, "Hohelied-Kommentar," pp. 169–170); see Vajda, *L'amour de Dieu*, pp. 179–180.

114. Ibn Tibbon, *Perush al Shir ha-Shirim*, 5a (Fraisse, "Hohelied-Kommentar," pp. 129–132).

115. Ibn Tibbon, *Perush al Shir ha-Shirim*, 6a (Fraisse, "Hohelied-Kommentar," pp. 137–140).

116. Subsequent philosophical and mystical authors continued this allegorical approach. See, for instance, Ravitsky, "Immanuel of Rome"; Narboni, *Epistle on the Possibility of Conjunction*, p. 96, English section, pp. 128–129, Hebrew section; Kellner, "Gersonides' Commentary," pp. 81–107; idem, "Gersonides on the Song," pp. 1–22.

117. For a similar process in Christian authors, see C. S. Wright, "Influence of the Exegetical Tradition"; Brückmann and Couchman, "Du 'Cantique des cantiques,'" pp. 35–50.

118. My brief analysis of the use of the Song in medieval Hebrew poetry is indebted to Scheindlin, *Gazelle*, pp. 20–21, 37–41, 48–49. See also Vajda, *L'amour de Dieu*, pp. 86, 91, 99, 115.

119. I have borrowed this term from McGinn, "Language of Love," p. 217, who bases his own remarks on the formulation of Idel, "Sexual Metaphors," pp. 199–200.

120. See Ḥoter ben Shelomo, *Philosophic Questions*, pp. 72–73. In his introduction, Blumenthal cites several examples from the so-called "eastern school of Maimonidean interpretation" (see p. ix), represented by Zekharya ha-Rofe and Saʿid Ibn Daʾud, who interpreted the Song as affirmation of the ideal of conjunction typical for medieval philosophical mysticism.

121. Idel, "Sexual Metaphors," pp. 200–201; idem, *Kabbalah: New Perspectives*, p. 206.

122. See Scholem, *Major Trends*, pp. 126, 138–139, 144, 383 n. 76; idem, *Kabbalah of Sefer ha-Temunah*, pp. 87–90, 107, 127–128, 151–152, 161, 164; idem, *Kabbalah*, p. 54; Idel, *Mystical Experience*, pp. 16–17, 22–24; idem, *Kabbalah: New Perspectives*, pp. 98–101; idem, "Contribution of Abraham Abulafia's Kabbalah," pp. 124–125.

123. See, for instance, Abraham Abulafia, *Oṣar Eden Ganuz*, fol. 130b (printed ed., p. 288). In addition to the studies of Idel cited above, n. 122, see Idel, *Mystical Experience*, pp. 180–187, 203–205; idem, *Kabbalah: New Perspectives*, p. 151. See also M. Fishbane, *Kiss of God*, pp. 39–43.

124. A thorough account of Gikatilla's religious philosophy still remains a desideratum. In the meantime, one may consult E. Gottlieb, *Studies in the Kabbala Literature*, pp. 263–279; Weiler, "Studies in the Kabbalistic Terminology," pp. 13–44; idem, "Kabbalistic Doctrine," pp. 157–186; Blickstein, "Between Philosophy and Mysticism," for the specific assessment of the influence of Maimonides, see pp. 48–49. See also Farber, "On the Sources," pp. 67–96; and idem, "Traces of the *Zohar*," pp. 70–83.

125. Gikatilla, *Ginnat Egoz*, pp. 280–281. It is of interest to note that in his later work on the symbolism of the *sefirot*, Gikatilla reaffirms the contemplative ideal of *devequt* that is consequent to the passionate love of God, but in that context it is related to knowledge of the names, which is interpreted in a theosophic way as a reference to the divine attributes. See Gikatilla, *Shaʿarei Orah*, 1:47: "When one contemplates these names one will find that all of the Torah and the commandments are dependent on them, and when one knows the intention of each and every one of these names, one will discern and know the greatness of the One who spoke and the world came into being, and one will have fear and awe before him, and one will desire, yearn, and long to cleave to him through knowledge of his names, blessed be he"; see p. 83.

126. This has been duly recognized by McGinn, "Language of Love," pp. 217–218. McGinn, following Idel, contrasts the mystical orientation to the Song in the two branches of kabbalah, the ecstatic and theosophic, on the grounds that in the former the mystic, like the Christian saint, is conceived of as female in relation to the masculine divine lover, whereas in the latter the mystic is male in relation to the female aspect of the Godhead. I take issue with this depiction insofar as there is sufficient proof that in theosophic kabbalah there is a gender metamorphosis whereby the male mystic is feminized in relation to the divine. See below (especially n. 134), and the discussion in the previous chapter.

127. See Vulliaud, *Cantique des Cantiques*, pp. 118–133, 183–185, 191–204, 219–225; Pope, *Song of Songs*, 153–179; A. Green, "Song of Songs," pp. 48–63; *Le Zohar: Cantique des cantiques*, pp. 18, 20–21. It should be noted that the theosophic interpretation of the male and female personae of the Song as referring respectively to the masculine and feminine potencies of the Godhead is already implied in several sections of the *Bahir.* See reference in chap. 4, n. 50.

128. Joseph of Hamadan, *Sefer Tashak*, p. 33. See ibid., pp. 7–8, 27, 50–51, 60–61, 103. In the formulation of Shem Tov Ibn Shem Tov, *Sefer ha-Emunot*, 28b, "We have learnt that the book of Song of Songs in its rhetoric and figurative speech is a symbol [*mashal*] for the hidden and revealed glory [*ha-kavod ha-neʿelam we-ha-nigleh*], and in it is the secret of existent beings, and it is the secret of *shiʿur qomah.*" The hidden and revealed glory refer respectively to *Tifʾeret* and *Malkhut*, and hence the Song is essentially a symbolic depiction of the dialogue between the masculine and feminine personifications of the divine, which are referred to by the technical idiom that denotes the measure of the bodily stature of God, *shiʿur qomah.*

129. *Kitvei Ramban*, 2:485, corrected in part by MS Vatican ebr. 211, fol. 13a.

130. To a degree this is implicit in A. Green's comment on this passage in "Song of Songs," p. 57: "The 'Glory' here is the devoted bride whose longings for union with her spouse also represent the longing of the worshipper's soul for reunion with God." Green does not, however, pay attention to the gender reversal implied in the application of the verse to the soul in relation to the divine potency. The merging of the symbolic and ecstatic ways of reading the Song in Ezra's commentary is also noted by Pedaya, "'Possessed by Speech,'" pp. 594–595.

131. The theme is reiterated in Ezra's commentary on the verse "He brought me into the banquet room" (Song 2:4), in *Kitvei Ramban*, 2:489: "This alludes figuratively to the elevation of the glory [*mashal le-hitʿallut ha-kavod*], and the abundance of joy and pleasure in the supernal light." On the elevation of the glory, see also Ezra's commentary on "where do you rest them at noon" (Song 1:7), in *Kitvei Ramban*, 2:486: "This alludes figuratively to the disappearance of the glory and its elevation to the supernal heights" (*ha-mashal al silluq ha-kavod we-hitʿalluto le-marom meromim*).

132. Cf. Ezra's comment on "Your ointments yield a sweet fragrance" (Song 1:3), in *Kitvei Ramban*, 2:485: "[Scripture] calls the influx that overflows to the glory, which is the gateway to the words, 'fragrance,' and from [the glory] it increases and descends upon the seventy branches that surround the median line, and together with it they are seventy-one." From this text it is clear that *kavod* is *Shekhinah*, which is also portrayed as the median line, an expression that is more often associated in kabbalistic literature with the masculine gradation of *Tifʾeret.*

133. *Kitvei Ramban*, 2:480. Scholem, *Origins*, pp. 377–378, surmised that Ezra is referring to a commentary on the Song reportedly penned by Samuel Ibn Tibbon. For a recent discussion of the historical background, intellectual profile, and literary achievements of this figure, see James T. Robinson, "Samuel Ibn Tibbon's *Commentary*," pp. 2–54.

134. The contrast between theosophic and ecstatic trends of kabbalah along these lines is the position adopted by Idel, "Sexual Metaphors," p. 206; idem, *Kabbalah: New Perspectives*, pp. 209–210.

135. A. Green, *Keter*, pp. 161–162 n. 35, argues that the hypostatization of *Shekhinah* as the Community of Israel as an entity distinct from the earthly community of Jews is a "key part of the Kabbalistic promulgation of a feminine divinity who is both the spouse of the male deity and the object of the Kabbalists' own devotions." Green suggests, moreover, that there is a relationship between this theosophical development and changes in the interpretation of the Song in the twelfth century in both Jewish and Christian circles. Green contends that in the case of Jewish readers, the "interposition of a new feminine divine self" was

occasioned by the "erotic (and potentially homoerotic) pressures" brought about by reading the Song as referring to the "individual soul's love of God rather than that of the historical community." Although this is not the place to enter into a lengthy critique of Green's remarks, let me note two flaws in the argument. Firstly, there is no reason to dichotomize the individualistic and communal application of the symbol of the community of Israel employed in the Song. That is, for kabbalists, the Song is read simultaneously on both planes. Secondly, the so-called "feminine divine self" to which Green refers is an overly simplistic interpretation of the engendered symbol of *Shekhinah* in medieval kabbalistic sources. *Shekhinah* is indeed portrayed in feminine terms, but she can be transvalued as masculine in relation to the soul of the male mystic who becomes female in relation to her. I do not, of course, deny the obvious fact that the relationship of the male kabbalist to *Shekhinah* is portrayed in standard heterosexual terms. The essential point, however, ignored by Green, is that this relationship results in the transformation of *Shekhinah*, a transformation that entails, as I have argued, the ontic restoration of the feminine to the masculine (particularly as the corona of the phallus). As a consequence of the destabilization of gender boundaries, the heterosexual terminology must be transmuted into homoerotic discourse. See E. Wolfson, *Through a Speculum*, pp. 357–368; idem, *Circle in the Square*, pp. 80–110. The wishful attempt to avoid homoeroticism by reifying the feminine quality of the divine will not work, for in the contemplative visualization *Shekhinah* is masculinized, and kabbalist, feminized.

136. See Vajda, *Commentaire d'Ezra*, pp. 141–144.

137. The reading proffered by Ezra, which is reiterated by any number of other kabbalists, has a striking resonance with the philosophical mysticism, particularly as it has been expressed in Sufi-influenced authors. As a way of illustration, see Fenton, "Daniel Ibn al-Māshiṭa's 'Taqwīm al-Adyān,'" p. 79.

138. See Vajda, *L'amour de Dieu*, pp. 233–235; Ibn Sahula, "Rabbi Isaac Sahula's Commentary," pp. 396–397; A. Green, "Song of Songs," p. 57.

139. Ibn Sahula, "Rabbi Isaac Sahula's Commentary," pp. 408–409. For more on the background of this passage, see Idel, *Mystical Experience*, pp. 59–60.

140. Ibn Sahula, "Rabbi Isaac Sahula's Commentary," p. 409.

141. Ibid., p. 410. See A. Green, "Song of Songs," pp. 57–58.

142. E. Gottlieb, *Studies*, pp. 128–131.

143. *Kitvei Ramban*, 2:469. For a different interpretation of this passage from the one I proffered, see E. Gottlieb, *Studies*, p. 131.

144. See above, n. 128. The centrality of the Song in shaping the theosophic worldview of the zoharic anthology was also duly noted by S. Katz, "'Conservative' Character," pp. 9–10. As one might expect, Katz focuses on how the religious imagination of the zoharic kabbalist "was saturated with this structural architectonic and the sexual-anthropomorphic imagery that was interwoven with it." The "secret doctrine" that "lay at the heart of Zoharic Kabbalah" involves the portrayal of the drama of divine unity in the explicitly erotic terms of separation, yearning, and copulation.

145. Vajda, *L'amour de Dieu*, p. 210. Schimmel, *As through a Veil*, pp. 152–155, noted the depiction of the souls of men as feminine in their yearning for the male God in the Indo-Muslim tradition. In her opinion, this reflects the influence of Hinduism in contrast to other forms of mystical expression within Islam (for example, Ibn al-ʿArabī), wherein the soul is depicted as male and the divine as feminine.

146. *Zohar* 2:124b.

147. On the use of the kiss to symbolize the union of *Tifʾeret* and *Malkhut*, male and female spirits, in the divine realm, see *Zohar* 1:44b, 70a; 2:124b, 146a–b, 253b–254a, 256b; 3:287a; *Zohar Ḥadash*, 51c, 63c–64a.

148. *Zohar Ḥadash*, 63a.

149. See Maimonides, *Guide*, III.51, p. 628. In *Zohar* 1:137a (*Midrash ha-Neʿelam*) the desire for the kiss expressed in Song 1:2 is interpreted as the yearning of the soul to derive sustenance and pleasure from the splendor of the *Shekhinah*. See, by contrast, M. Fishbane, *Kiss of God*, pp. 38–39. Although Fishbane readily acknowledges that in *Zohar*, as in the case of Ibn Sahula, there are two explanations for the kiss, ecstatic and hypostatic, he concludes that the "zoharic tradition of ecstatic death by divine kiss is not affected by philosophical notions or vocabulary, which distinguishes it from the Maimonidean reworking of the talmudic

tradition, as well as from the mystical adaptation of Maimonides by Abraham Abulafia . . . and his disciples." I do not concur with this observation and contend that the Maimonidean influence is detectable in the relevant zoharic passages as well. On the application of the motif of "death by a kiss" in the sixteenth-century circle of Luria, see Fine, *Physician of the Soul*, pp. 350–353.

150. Joseph of Hamadan, *Sefer Tashak*, p. 34. The characterization of death as the occasion for the soul to behold *Shekhinah* is a theme repeated often in kabbalistic literature, based on earlier midrashic sources. For instance, see *Zohar* 1:98a, 126b; 3:53a, 88a.

151. On this *ḥadīth* and its impact on Sufi piety, see Schimmel, *Mystical Dimensions*, pp. 70 and 135; Sviri, *Taste of Hidden Things*, pp. 210 and 230 n. 94 (en passant, the author makes an interesting and important claim that the tradition attributed to Muḥammad "can be traced back to even older Jewish sources," but she offers no textual support; see, however, the passage from the rabbinic tractate *Derekh Ereṣ* cited by Jonah Gerondi, *Shaʿarei Teshuvah* 2:17, *mut ad shelo tamut* ("die before you die"), as noted by M. Fishbane, *Kiss of Death*, p. 22); Elias, *Death before Dying*, p. 3; Ritter, *Ocean of the Soul*, p. 601.

152. Joseph of Hamadan, *Sefer Tashak*, p. 37. The same imagery is used to describe the relationship between male and female potencies within the divine. See ibid., pp. 51, 55, 66.

153. One is reminded here of the technical Sufi terms *fanāʾ* and *baqāʾ*, annihilation and perdurance; according to the formulation of many masters, the two states are related cyclically, coexisting in their confluence, diverging in their convergence, converging in their divergence. See brief discussion in chap. 5.

154. The reading of Joseph of Hamadan that I have presented—and a plethora of collateral examples from the oeuvre of this kabbalist and others could have been supplied—challenges the claim of S. Katz, "'Conservative' Character," pp. 13–14, that the "pre-conditions" and "pre-conditioning" of Jewish experience precludes the possibility of a Jewish mystical reading of the Song that would proffer union with God in an intimate and absorptive manner known, for example, from Christian mysticism. The nexus of love and death, inspired scripturally, points to the very possibility of a unitive experience on the part of kabbalists vis-à-vis God that Katz emphatically and categorically denies.

155. In a number of studies, Yehuda Liebes has explored the nature of eros in the kabbalah in general and in the zoharic literature in particular. See, for example, "Zohar and Eros."

156. *Zohar* 1:60b. The zoharic attitude is well captured in the brief remark of Gikatilla, *Shaʿarei Orah*, 2:51: "This is the secret of the conjunction of the tenth emanation in the ninth without any doubt, for he who causes the Community of Israel to be united with the emanation of *Yesod* is himself conjoined to her, and she is conjoined to *Yesod*, and the two of them as one are conjoined to YHWH."

157. E. Wolfson, *Circle in the Square*, p. 97 and references given on p. 213 n. 91.

158. *Galya Raza*, p. 20.

159. On the author's use of *Sefer ha-Qanah*, see the comments of Elior in the introduction to her edition of *Galya Raza*, p. 14. I have not been able to locate the citation in the printed versions of *Sefer ha-Qanah*, although *Sefer ha-Peliʾah* begins with Moses asking questions of Metatron related to the creation narrative in the context of his ascent to receive the Torah. The passage cited by the author of *Galya Raza* would seem to fit into this section, but I have not found an exact parallel. On the textual complications of the beginning of this text, see Oron, "Introduction of *Sefer ha-Peliʾah*," pp. 273–295.

160. *Galya Raza*, p. 1.

161. The point is well expressed in the interpretation of Song 1:2 found in Ibn Gabbai, *Tolaʿat Yaʿaqov*, p. 91. For translation and analysis of this passage, see Ginsburg, *Sabbath*, pp. 293–294.

162. An interesting example of the reversal of gender is found in a passage in *Zohar* 2:97a (in what follows I base my analysis and partial translation on the version of the passage preserved in *Zohar* [Cremona, 1558–1559], 173–174). In that context, the soul of the righteous male that departs from this world is connected exegetically with the daughter sold into slavery by her father (Exod. 21:7–11). The relationship between the divine and the soul is described in the following way: "When the King enters that palace, of which it is written, 'And Jacob kissed Rachel' (Gen. 29:11), he finds that soul, embraces it, elevates it, and takes delight with it. This is [the import of] 'he shall deal with her as is the practice of free maidens' (Exod. 21:9), in the manner that the father acts in relationship to his daughter, for she is beloved to him. He kisses her, embraces

her, and bestows gifts upon her." The male soul is thus treated as feminine when it erotically embraces the male aspect of the godhead after the death of the body. See Scholem, *Major Trends*, p. 226. Reflecting on this text, Scholem notes the difference between the union of the soul and the divine, on the one hand, and the bridal symbolism of contemporary Christian mysticism, on the other. I cannot agree with the basic premise of Scholem's argument: in zoharic kabbalah, descriptions of love of God for the soul take the form of love of the father for the child rather than that of the lover for his beloved. The text I cited above is sufficient to perceive the shortcomings of this line of argument: The father-child imagery itself may be connected to more overtly erotic terminology between the lover and the beloved. Moreover, the zoharic authorship does seem to maintain, contrary to Scholem's assessment (*Major Trends*, p. 403 n. 71), that mystical union between God and the soul is attainable.

163. Vajda, *L'amour de Dieu*, pp. 217–221, 223–228. The theosophic reading is the mythical basis for the ritual instituted by Safedian kabbalists in the sixteenth century to chant the Song every Friday evening, the time of the *hieros gamos* in the divine realm, which is facilitated by the sexual intercourse below between a man and his wife. This custom assumed an especially important place in Hasidic ritual. For sources, see Benayahu, *Toledoth ha-Ari*, p. 350 n. 3; Ḥallamish, "Place of Kabbalah in Ritual," p. 209 n. 170.

164. For example, in *Sefer Tashak*, p. 43, Joseph of Hamadan labels the allegorical reading of the Song as the love between God and Israel the "contextual sense" (*derekh ha-peshaṭ*). It is also of interest to note the following remark of Abraham Azulai, *Ḥesed le-Avraham*, 4:48, 44d: "Know that the book of the Song of Songs speaks about the matter of the bridegroom and bride, the bridegroom alluding to *Shekhinah* and the bride to Israel."

165. *Zohar* 3:42a–b.

166. See E. Wolfson, *Through a Speculum*, pp. 368–377.

167. *Zohar Ḥadash*, 62c; see 63d, 72b.

168. See Lieberman, "Mishnath Shir ha-Shirim," p. 119.

169. *Zohar* 2:143a.

170. *Zohar* 2:144b–145a.

171. *Zohar Ḥadash*, 62b.

172. Ibid., 62d.

173. I have discussed this motif in more detail in E. Wolfson, *Circle in the Square*, pp. 92–98.

174. *Zohar* 3:74b.

175. *Zohar Ḥadash*, 71b.

176. For a more elaborate discussion of this gender transposition, see E. Wolfson, *Circle in the Square*, pp. 103–106.

177. *Zohar Ḥadash*, 72b.

178. Elsewhere the zoharic text expresses the idea that the Song relates concomitantly to *Binah* and *Shekhinah*. See especially *Zohar* 1:240b: "In the Song of Songs, Solomon mentioned the two arrayments of the feminine [*tiqqunei de-nuqvei*], one for the beloved above, the jubilee, and one for the bride, the Sabbatical year, an arrayment above and an arrayment below. The account of creation similarly is in these two places, an account above and an account below. Thus the Torah begins with a *beit*, the account below in the pattern of that which is above, the one produced the supernal world and the other the lower world. In this manner, Solomon mentioned the two arrayments of the feminine, one above and one below, the one above in the supernal arrayment of the holy name, and the one below in the lower arrayment in the likeness of that which is above." See also *Zohar* 3:290b.

179. On the significance of Elijah in the zoharic commentary on the Song, see *Le Zohar: Cantique des cantiques*, pp. 8–10. According to a passage in *Zohar Ḥadash*, 59c, Elijah clandestinely came to instruct Simeon ben Yoḥai and his son Eleazar (presumably concerning esoteric matters) twice a day during the time they were hidden in a cave, a rabbinic legend appropriated by zoharic kabbalists. For a convenient list of references, see *Tiqqunei Zohar*, Introduction, 1a, n. 1.On the importance of the revelation of Elijah (*gilluy eliyahu*) to early kabbalists, see Scholem, *Origins*, pp. 39–44, 49–53; A. Heschel, *Prophetic Inspiration*, pp. 33–35. See also Hames, "Elijah and a Shepherd," pp. 93–102. On the importance of the revelation of Elijah in classical

rabbinical literature, see Cohn, "Mystic Experience and Elijah-Revelation," pp. 34–44. On the appearance of Elijah and dream inquiries in other medieval Jewish sources, see A. Heschel, *Prophetic Inspiration*, pp. 48–67.

180. *Zohar Ḥadash*, 62b. For a slightly different symbolic interpretation of the theosophic import of the Song, consider the comment in 60c–d: "The *shin* is the mystery of the supernal chariot, and thus it has three sides, for the patriarchs were the chariot. All the Song of Songs is the mystery of the supernal chariot, and thus it begins with a *shin*." In this case, the Song seems to be linked to the three central emanations, depicted as the three patriarchs who are the supernal chariot.

181. See above, n. 16.

182. See *Zohar* 1:29a; 2:5a, 100b, 127b. In *Zohar Ḥadash*, 63a, the word *shalom* is interpreted as a reference either to *Tif'eret*, the sixth emanation, for it establishes harmony between left and right, or to *Yesod*, the ninth emanation, which is responsible for the "peace of the house," a euphemistic depiction of union with the feminine; see ibid., 64b.

183. The identification of *Binah* as king is attested in Moses de León's Hebrew writings. See, for example, Moses de León, *Shushan Edut*, p. 331. It is of interest to consider the following observation in a kabbalistic commentary on the Song, *Zimrat Yah*, fol. 1a, attributed to Jacob Shalish. In the context of offering various symbolic interpretations of the Song, the author remarks, "In the *Zohar*, it seems that Song of Songs relates to *Binah*, which is the king [*melekh*], for *Tif'eret* is called peace [*shalom*] as is known."

184. See E. Wolfson, "*Tiqqun ha-Shekhinah*," pp. 313–322; idem, "Fore/giveness On the Way," pp. 153–169.

185. Gikatilla, *Sha'arei Orah*, 2:76.

186. *Zohar* 1:70a–b. A similar interpretation is proffered in *Zohar Ḥadash*, 64b, but in that context the emphasis is on the desire of the lower world, *Shekhinah*, to join the upper world, *Binah*.

187. It is also possible to interpret this older rabbinic idea in a theosophic way as a reference to the union of the Oral Torah and the Written Torah, which correspond respectively to the *Shekhinah* and *Tif'eret*. That is, the Song is equivalent to the Torah in its entirety because the Song is about the relationship between male and female, which relate to the dual Torah. See *Zohar Ḥadash*, 63d–64a; Gikatilla, *Sha'arei Orah*, 1:86.

188. *Zohar* 2:143b. For analysis of this passage, see *Le Zohar: Cantique des Cantiques*, pp. 13–14. A parallel expression of this motif appears in *Zohar* 2:18b: "Song of Songs [*shir ha-shirim*], that is, the song of the archons [*sarim*] above, the song that comprises all the matters of Torah, wisdom, power, and strength, concerning what was and what will be." Liebes, *Ars Poetica*, p. 124, suggests this zoharic passage may be connected to the stratum of *Midrash ha-Ne'elam*, a suggestion that seems reasonable to me.

189. See *Le Zohar: Cantique des Cantiques*, pp. 22–23.

190. This idea is on occasion related exegetically by the zoharic authorship to the expression *mi zo't* ("who is this one"), which is found three times in The Song (3:6, 6:6, and 8:5). See *Zohar* 1:10a; 2:126b.

191. *Zohar Ḥadash*, 67a; and see parallel discussion in Gikatilla, *Sha'arei Orah*, 2:51–56.

192. Hence one finds strewn throughout the zoharic corpus exegetical applications of specific verses in the Song to moments in Israel's sacred history. For instance, see *Zohar* 1:170a, 176b.

193. *Zohar* 2:143b–144a.

194. E. Wolfson, "Coronation."

195. *Zohar* 2:146b–147a.

196. *Zohar Ḥadash*, 61d.

197. On the identification of the Song and the four letters of the name, see Joseph of Hamadan, *Sefer Tashak*, pp. 7–8. To be more specific, in that context the matter is expressed in terms of the correspondence of the first four words, *shir ha-shirim asher li-shlomo*, and the four letters of the name.

198. See chap. 1, n. 251.

199. Lévy-Valensi, *La poétique du Zohar*, p. 94.

200. Vulliaud, *Cantique des Cantiques*, 183; *Le Zohar: Cantique des Cantiques*, p. 13.

201. *Zohar* 2:146a–b. The passage is interpreted as well by Liebes, "Zohar and Eros," p. 79.

202. See discussion in chap. 2.

203. *Zohar Ḥadash*, 60d.

204. E. Wolfson, *Circle in the Square*, pp. 73–74.

205. *Zohar Ḥadash*, 61d.

206. Consider the formulation of Joseph of Hamadan, *Sefer Tashak*, pp. 5–6: "All the songs [*shirim*] were uttered from the attribute of *Malkhut*, but the song of songs [*shir ha-shirim*] was from the attribute of *Ṣaddiq*. Therefore, the rabbis, blessed be their memory, said the Song of Songs renders hands impure, for it is the supernal phallus [*ha-berit ha-elyon*], and it was not given to men to make use of the pure and holy supernal phallus [*we-hu lo natan lehishtammesh li-venei adam bi-verit ha-elyon ha-qadosh we-ha-ṭahor*]. . . . Moreover, this alludes to the matter of unity [*inyan ha-yiḥud*]."

207. *Zohar Ḥadash*, 62a.

208. Ibid., 63a.

209. *Zohar* 2:258b. According to this passage, the mystical conception of worldhood (*olam*) is connected to the elevation (the Hebrew *oleh*) of the lower world to the upper world, which entails a concealment (*illum*) of what is disclosed in the disclosure of what is concealed.

210. Scholem, *Major Trends*, p. 235.

211. D. Biale, *Eros and the Jews*, pp. 101–120.

212. This is essentially the claim of Liebes, *Studies in the Zohar*, pp. 1–84, although he does not emphasize the ascetic dimension in the manner that I have in my own reflections.

213. See the brief but informative discussion of this matter in Ginzberg, *Legends*, vol. 5, pp. 43–44 n. 127.

214. *Zohar* 2:185b. I have rendered the biblical verses in a hyperliteral way in order to capture the nuance of the zoharic exegesis. On the nexus between *Binah*, Yom Kippur, and ascetic renunciation, see *Zohar Ḥadash* 93c.

215. *Zohar* 2:185b.

216. *Zohar* 3:100b.

217. The connection between Yom Kippur and sexual purity is underscored in the custom attributed to Luria to say the verse "The light is sown for the righteous" (Ps. 97:11) prior to the *Kol Nidrei* service on the evening of the fast, for this prayer was believed to have special efficacy in effecting rectification of the phallus (*tiqqun ha-yesod*). To be even more precise, the purpose of *Kol Nidrei* is to rectify the covenant of the tongue (*berit ha-lashon*), but this covenant cannot be rectified until the covenant of the foreskin (*berit ha-maʿor*), upon which it is dependent, is rectified properly. See Menaḥem Mendel, *Aṭeret Shalom*, 76a.

218. Babylonian Talmud, Berakhot 17a.

219. Mishnah, Avot 1:13.

220. *Zohar* 2:116a (*Raʿaya Meheimna*).

221. *Tiqqunei Zohar*, 11b.

222. See below, n. 233.

223. *Tiqqunei Zohar*, sec. 21, 61b.

224. See E. Wolfson, "*Tiqqun ha-Shekhinah*;" idem, "Coronation." See also idem, "The Engenderment of Messianic Politics," pp. 203–258.

225. *Tiqqunei Zohar*, sec. 16, 39a. On the elevation of *Shekhinah* by means of *Tif'eret* to *Keter*, where she receives the status of being the crown, represented orthographically as the decomposition of *zayin* into *yod* on the head of *waw*, see *Zohar* 3:257a (*Raʿaya Meheimna*). In that context, the transposition of *Shekhinah* is related to the rite of circumcision. On the depiction of *Shekhinah* as the "virgin of Israel" (*betulat yisra'el*), an expression derived from Amos 5:2, see *Zohar* 3:6a, 257a–b (*Raʿaya Meheimna*); *Ha-Ketavim ha-Ivriyyim shel Baʿal Tiqqunei Zohar we-Raʿaya Meheimna*, p. 24. On the description of the angels who escort *Shekhinah* to join her consort as "virgins" (*betulot*) based on Ps. 45:15, see *Zohar* 2:197b; see also *Zohar* 2:112b, 238a; *Zohar Ḥadash*, 67b; *Ha-Ketavim ha-Ivriyyim*, p. 46.

226. The matter is expressed succinctly by Menaḥem Mendel of Shklov in his commentary on *Berit Menuḥah* called *Derekh ha-Qodesh*, p. 9: "The essence of everything is the secret of the feminine and the Oral Torah . . . and she is revealed in the guarding of the sign of the glorious crown of the phallus [*nitgalah bi-*

shemirat ot aṭeret tif'eret ha-berit], and this is the second river called Gihon, but one should not elaborate and the enlightened one will understand."

227. E. Wolfson, *Through a Speculum*, pp. 363–364.

228. See above, n. 34.

229. Babylonian Talmud, Sanhedrin 97a.

230. See E. Wolfson, *Circle in the Square*, pp. 102–103.

231. *Zohar* 2:204a. For fuller discussion of this motif, see E. Wolfson, "Coronation," pp. 314–316.

232. *Zohar* 2:144a.

233. *Zohar* 2:88b. A parallel passage is found in *Zohar* 3:288b (*Idra Zuṭa*).

234. Liebes, "Poems for Meals," pp. 554–555.

235. *Zohar* 3:16a.

236. See Tishby, *Wisdom of the Zohar*, p. 1502.

237. *Zohar* 3:129a, 136b, 288b, 293a.

238. *Zohar* 3:26b.

239. Babylonian Talmud, Ḥagigah 14b.

240. Vital, *Sha'ar Ma'amerei Razal*, p. 3b. See parallel with slight variations in Vital, *Liqquṭei Torah*, pp. 17–18 (ad Gen. 3:1); and idem, *Sefer ha-Derushim*, p. 147.

241. Vital, *Sha'ar Ma'amerei Razal*, p. 3d; idem, *Liqquṭei Torah*, p. 19; idem, *Sefer ha-Derushim*, p. 148.

242. See above, n. 16.

243. See, for instance, Vital, *Eṣ Ḥayyim*, 22:2, 104b–c: "In the secret of the womb of the woman, which is the place of her foundation [*yesod*], there are three aspects, one, the skin, two, the flesh, and, three, that which is more inward in the inwardness of the womb."

244. Vital, *Eṣ Ḥayyim*, 8:3, 37d. See ibid., 29:8, 24d: "*Yesod de-imma* is garbed in the knowledge [*da'at*] of *Ze'eir Anpin*, and the corona [*aṭarah*] is in *Tif'eret* only until the chest." Ibid., 32:2, 36a: "These two staffs were given to the hand of Moses, and they are also called by his name 'the staff of Moses' [*maṭṭeh mosheh*], and this is on account of the reason mentioned above, for both of them emerge from *yesod de-abba*, which is the locus of the aspect of Moses, peace be upon him, when he is concealed in *Ze'eir Anpin*, as is known, for the knowledge of *Ze'eir Anpin* is given to him from the side of *Abba*." On the technical connotation of the term *yesod*, see chap. 4, n. 256.

245. Vital, *Eṣ Ḥayyim*, 29:8, 25b; 39:10, 74c–d.

246. On the linkage of Sabbath evening and carnal intercourse in rabbinic and kabbalistic sources, see discussion in previous chapter.

247. See E. Wolfson, "Coronation," pp. 325–332.

248. *Leviticus Rabbah*, 34:16, p. 815; Babylonian Talmud, Shabbat 119a.

249. Gikatilla, *Sha'arei Orah*, 1:111–112.

Epilogue

1. Bachrach, *Emeq ha-Melekh*, 7:1, p. 331.

2. Consider, as one of numerous illustrations, the following remark in a Lurianic commentary on the zoharic section *Sabba de-Mishpaṭim*, in *Zohar ha-Raqi'a*, 78b: "Eli was the reincarnation of the wife of Heber the Kenite . . . her name was Yael, that is, she rose [*ta'alah*] to the gradation of a man [*madregat ish*], and in this she was more blessed than the women of the world who did not merit this, and thus Yael served in the tent of Shiloh in the place of Eli the priest." The statement is based on the tradition of Luria transmitted by Vital, *Sha'ar ha-Gilgulim*, sec. 36, 43a: The biblical account of Yael's murdering Sisera, the army commander of Jabin, the king of Canaan (Judg. 4:17–21), is explained by the fact that she was the wife of Heber the Kenite, who was from the root of Cain situated in the shell of Sisera. Moreover, according to the Lurianic teaching, Yael was reincarnated in the person of Eli, the high priest in Shiloh (1 Sam. 1:3). What is significant for the purposes of my analysis is the use made of this tradition by the author of the aforecited passage: Yael attains a level of distinction by reaching the graduation of, that is, being transformed into, a man.

3. See chap. 4, n. 164.

4. Pagels, "Exegesis of Genesis 1," pp. 477–496, esp. p. 480.

5. *Zohar* 2:114a. In that passage, the theme of the reintegration of the feminine into the masculine is expressed as an interpretation of the verse "Place me as a seal upon your heart, like the seal upon our hand" (Song 8:6). It is presumed by the author of this text, in accord with the exegetical view adopted by a number of kabbalists in the thirteenth century, as was discussed in the previous chapter, that the dialogue between the female beloved and male lover is to be read symbolically as a conversation between *Shekhinah* and *Tif'eret*. Hence the aforecited verse is explicated as the plea of *Shekhinah*, referred to by the technical term *kenesset yisra'el*, at the moment that she cleaves to her consort, *Tif'eret*. Significantly, the metaphor used to depict the conjunction (*devequt*) of male and female is seal (*ḥotam*), for "the way of a seal is that when it is conjoined to the place to which it is conjoined [*de-itddevaq be-hahu atar de-itddevaq*], it leaves all of its image [*diyoqneih*] within it even though the seal goes hither and thither, and does not subsist there as it is removed from there, it leaves all of its image there, and there it persists. So, too, here the Community of Israel says 'Since I have been conjoined to you, all of my image [*diyoqni*] is engraved therein, for even though I go hither and thither, my image is found engraved in you and you will remember me." In my judgment, this is an alternative way of expressing the motif of the female being restored to the male as a consequence of coital union, though I readily admit that in this passage the conjunction is not complete, a point underscored by the topos of the seal itself, that is, through the impression of the seal the female is restored to the male, but she also is separate from the very male to and in which her image is affixed. Finally, it is worth wondering if the term *ḥotam* is meant to conjure the image of circumcision, as this term is used in conjunction with the rite in earlier rabbinic literature and in liturgical compositions based thereon. For more extensive discussion of the phallomorphic nature of the restoration of female to male, see E. Wolfson, "Re/membering the Covenant."

6. *Zohar* 1:35b, 52a–b, 53a–b, 75a–b, 83a, 221a–b, 262a; 2:191a, 237a; 3:42a.

7. Altmann, *Studies in Religious Philosophy*, p. 193 n. 60.

8. The motif of walking and the related image of the path have been central to my thinking, a point demonstrated in my publications and teaching. Though I have come to this motif on many occasions, to date I have dedicated only one study exclusively to this theme. See E. Wolfson, "Walking as a Sacred Duty," pp. 180–207, reprinted in idem, *Along the Path*, pp. 89–109 and accompanying notes on pp. 223–245. The matter has been more recently explored in imaginative ways by Greenstein, "Aimless Pilgrimage," pp. 101–198.

9. E. Wolfson, "Divine Suffering."

10. Luzzatto, *Oṣerot Ramḥal*, p. 180.

11. Luzzatto, *Sefer ha-Kelalim*, sec. 26, p. 275. Luzzatto returns to the eschatological transformation of gender in many of his compositions, often linked exegetically to the image of *eshet ḥayyil aṭeret ba'lah* (Prov. 12:4). See, in particular, the lengthy passage from *Adir ba-Marom* translated in E. Wolfson, "Constructions of the *Shekhinah*," pp. 71–72 n. 180. The text in its original Hebrew is transcribed in idem, "Gender and Heresy," pp. 261–262. For fuller discussion and reference to other sources, see idem, "*Tiqqun ha-Shekhinah*," pp. 322–332.

12. *Perush Shir ha-Shirim*, in *Kitvei Ramban*, 2:487.

13. *Zohar* 3:19a; see *Zohar* 1:28a.

14. *Zohar* 1:35a–b: "What is [the import of] 'and he closed up the flesh at that spot' (Gen. 2:21)? [She was] in his side, and the one was in the side of the other. Surely, the holy One, blessed be he, uprooted them and planted them in another place, and they turned face-to-face for the sake of existence."

15. See *Zohar* 1:50a, where the unification of the female and male is expressed in terms of the former's house being established (*ittaqqenat beita*) to receive the latter.

16. Scholem, *On the Kabbalah and Its Symbolism*, pp. 146–150; Magid, "Conjugal Union"; Idel, *Messianic Mystics*, pp. 308–320. Idel's remark that my view of kabbalah as "phallocentric lore" cannot be corroborated from the ritual of the midnight reparation (p. 320) rests on an erroneous presentation of my thinking. I have never denied that in the state of exile the primary emphasis, reflected both in the symbolic language and the theurgic forms of action, is on reuniting male and female. *Tiqqun haṣot* is appropriate to the first phase of

redemption, which involves the heterosexual pairing. The goal of the union, however, is the amelioration of judgment by mercy and the consequent restoration of the female to the male, which marks the second phase of redemption. Both phases are phallocentric, but this becomes more explicit in characterizations of the latter. The same response can be offered to the remark in Idel, "Zohar as Exegesis," p. 100 n. 26. After summarizing my view as "a tendency to obliterate the difference between male and female divine powers, as part of the absorption of the female within the male," Idel concludes: "This thesis, which may sometimes be helpful in understanding some few texts of Zoharic Kabbalah, does not hold, however, for many other Zoharic treatments of sexual polarity." The demeaning assessment that my thesis at best "may sometimes be helpful in understanding some few texts" whereas "many other" passages in zoharic literature provide counterevidence does not provide any verification and, as such, has limited value for the reader. It is not sufficient to issue such pronouncements without offering textual corroboration; this mode of argumentation amounts to an appeal to multivocality from behind a screen of hegemonic authority, that is, assuming the role of the one who will undermine the views of others by a plea for hermeneutic diversity. Beyond the question of scholarly propriety, I must say, lamentably, that Idel's feigned criticism of my position again demonstrates a fundamental lack of understanding. When I speak of the containment of female in male, this reflects the idealized gender construction assumed by kabbalists to be operative at the beginning and at the end. Of course, there will be many passages that speak of male and female as separate entities that need to be paired together to effect the unity of the divine, to re/pair what has been severed. The issue is in evaluating the nature of that separateness over and against the understanding of gender identity. I have shown in a host of studies—always making my case from close reading of specific texts—that the engendering myth adopted by traditional kabbalists without noticeable exception is that of a single gender that comprises the polarity within itself in the vein of the identity of difference, the "androgynous male" or the "androgynous phallus."

17. *Zohar* 1:219a.

18. The discussion on the messianic implications of the symbol of the rainbow is a (re)vision of my analysis in E. Wolfson, "Re/membering," pp. 228–231.

19. *Zohar* 1:72a.

20. Ibid.

21. *Book Bahir*, sec. 3, p. 119. For translation and analysis, see E. Wolfson, "Before Alef," pp. 138–140.

22. This theme is attested in numerous sources. For discussion of some key zoharic texts, see Tishby, *Wisdom of the Zohar*, pp. 957–958, 991–993.

23. The nexus between communion and contemplation is duly noted by Tishby, *Wisdom of the Zohar*, p. 996, but I take issue with his characterization of the latter as "an act of will usually leading to concentration . . . and the ascent of the soul." Tishby cannot determine if the act of will "means a volitional impulse or an emotional desire." What he does not consider is that contemplation involves envisioning the imaginal form. Trying to understand the willfulness related to contemplation as either volitional impulse or emotional desire misses the point; the will spoken of here is concurrently a will to create, to envision, and to give form.

24. Against this background, it is of interest consider the following passage from the *Tiqqunim* in *Zohar Ḥadash*, 97a: "When prayer is a propitious time [*et raṣon*] before the Lord, the rainbow is seen in luminous colors in the cloud. Concerning that time [it is said] 'I will see it and remember the everlasting covenant' (Gen. 9:16), for it is known that in these luminous colors *Shekhinah* ascends before the Lord through the benevolent acts of Israel. But if the rainbow is not seen in luminous colors, it is said 'You have covered yourself with a cloud so that no prayer may pass through' (Lam. 3:44)."

25. The word that I have translated as "it" is *bah*, which is in the feminine form. I have not rendered the word as "her" because this would give the impression that the point of the passage is that the desire of God is perpetually for *Shekhinah* in its feminine configuration. The referent here, however, is the masculine aspect of *Shekhinah* related to the phallic covenant. The feminine grammatical form is used because it relates to the word *qeshet*, the visible sign of the covenant, but in terms of theosophic symbolism, *qeshet* corresponds to the female aspect of God localized in the phallus, the sign of the covenant (*ot berit*).

26. *Zohar* 1:72b. cf. ibid., 2:11a; *Tiqqunei Zohar*, sec. 18, 36b.

27. *Zohar* 1:65b, 93b; 2:57b, 66b, 87b, 180b, 195a; Moses de León, *Shushan Edut*, pp. 363–364; idem,

Sefer ha-Mishkal, p. 132. In some passages, the "sign of the covenant" refers symbolically to *Yesod* rather than *Shekhinah*. Cf. *Zohar* 1:47b, 94a, 114b, 153b, 222b, 236b, 246a, 247b; 2:23a, 200a, 225a; 3:84a.

28. *Zohar* 3:215a.

29. This fortification is expressed on occasion in homoerotic terms as the phallic bond between the righteous man below and the corresponding potency above. See E. Wolfson, *Through a Speculum*, pp. 371–372 n. 155.

30. *Zohar* 1:71b. The view expressed by Tishby, *Wisdom of the Zohar*, p. 617 n. 215, that in this passage the bow refers symbolically to *Malkhut* can be accepted only if it is understood that it is the aspect of *Malkhut* comprised within *Yesod*, which is precisely the point of the comment that the "covenant of the bow" is "contained in the righteous." By contrast, compare the interpretation of Gen. 49:24 in *Zohar* 1:247a, where *qeshet* is said to refer to the female spouse of Joseph, presumably a reference to the feminine personification of *Shekhinah*. On the phallic connotation of *qeshet*, cf. *Zohar* 1:18a, 72b; 3:84a; and see E. Wolfson, *Through a Speculum*, pp. 286, 334 n. 30, 337–338 n. 40, 340–341, 368–369 n. 149, 386–387.

31. Babylonian Talmud, Ḥagigah 16a.

32. *Zohar* 2:66b. I discussed this passage in E. Wolfson, *Through a Speculum*, p. 334, but I did not go far enough in my understanding of the phallic nature of the rainbow.

33. Cf. *Zohar* 1:71b: "Permission is not given to gaze with the eye upon the rainbow when it appears in the world so that no shame will appear before the *Shekhinah*." For a Hebrew parallel to this passage, cf. Moses de León, *Shushan Edut*, p. 364. The zoharic analogue was noted by Scholem in his edition of *Shushan Edut*, p. 364 n. 266.

34. Liebes, *Studies in the Zohar*, p. 15, asserts that in *Zohar* the rainbow generally alludes to *Yesod*, but he acknowledges that in this context (the reference to *Zohar* 1:62b should be corrected to 72b; in the original Hebrew version the reference is correct) the rainbow appears to represent *Malkhut*, or the feminine *Shekhinah*. I have adopted a similar approach, but I have provided the ontological structure that resolves the tension between these two interpretations. That is, the rainbow, like the phallus, is an androgynous symbol and thus it can represent both male and female. Indeed, in my opinion, the latter is ontically part of the former.

35. Cf. *Tiqqunei Zohar*, sec. 12, 27a: "The lilies refer to the children of Israel who shall be in exile amongst the mixed multitude who are the thorns. This is the secret of 'I will make an end [*khalah*] of all the nations among which I have banished you, but I will not make an end of you' (Jer. 46:28). He showed him the reward of the general assembly of study [*agra de-khallah*], and it is the 'blazing fire' (Exod. 3:2) amongst the thorns, which are the sinners when they oppress *Shekhinah* and Israel. Their reward is the bride [*kallah*], for the *Shekhinah* goes from them as a bride and the groom comes on account of her. This is the meaning of 'the profit of the public lectures is the pushing' [*agra de-khallah duḥaqa*], that is, he will bring them out of exile on account of her." For a different use of the talmudic dictum *agra de-khallah duḥaqa* (Babylonian Talmud, Berakhot 6b), cf. *Zohar* 3:239a (*Raʿaya Meheimna*). In that context, the dictum is interpreted as support for the idea that those engaged in study of Torah suffer on behalf of *Shekhinah* in exile.

36. *Zohar* 1:88b.

37. E. Wolfson, *Circle in the Square*, pp. 92–98. See also my remarks in *Through a Speculum*, pp. 274–275 n. 14. On the role of the female to contain the male, cf. the interpretation of the expression *aron ha-berit* in *Zohar* 2:214b, as a reference to *Shekhinah*, which contains the holy body of the divine anthropos, also depicted as the secret of the Torah. In that context, moreover, the symbolic nexus is applied to the custom of placing the corpse of the righteous man in a coffin, for he alone is worthy of such an honor since he was careful with respect to the "sign of the holy covenant." The biblical paradigm is Joseph, of whom it says that "he was embalmed and placed in a coffin in Egypt" (Gen. 50:26). Commenting on the double *yod* in the word *wayyisem*, the author of the zoharic passage writes that the "covenant was joined to the covenant, the secret below in the secret above, and he entered the coffin." The funerary rite is thus portrayed as the occasion for the homoerotic bonding of the righteous man below and the phallic gradation above, a conjunction of secret to secret. On secrecy and the phallus, see chap. 3, n. 153.

38. *Zohar* 1:117a.

39. *Zohar* 1:119a, 145b–146a. In the latter context, it is stated explicitly that rectification for the sin of

the primordial serpent is through union of male and female. On the use of this zoharic text by the Frankists, see Scholem, *Messianic Idea*, p. 139.

40. Consider the account of the creation of Eve out of Adam given in *Zohar* 3:83b: "The holy One, blessed be he, took her from his side, shaped her, and brought her before him. Then Adam had sexual intercourse with his wife and she was a support to him." According to this passage, there is a transition from the original androgynous state (Gen. 1:26–28), in which the female was contained in the male, to a separation of the female from the male (Gen. 2:18–24). What is significant about the kabbalistic reading is that even in the second account of the creation of woman from the body of man, the female gender is described strictly from the point of view of heterosexual desire, presumably driven by the procreative mandate of the male. The zoharic author thus understands the biblical locution of God making a "fitting helper" for Adam in terms of separating female from male so that the latter can have sexual relations with the former. Cf. *Zohar* 3:296a (*Idra Zuṭa*), translated and discussed in E. Wolfson, "Woman—The Feminine as Other," pp. 175–176. Given the repeated emphasis in *Zohar* on coitus as the masculinization of the female (see chap. 2, n. 408), there is no textual justification to interpret the second account of creation as more egalitarian than the first. The consistent androcentric reading proffered by kabbalists is brought into sharp relief when compared and contrasted with the interpretation of the creation of Adam and Eve presented by Heinrich Cornelius Agrippa von Nettesheim, *De nobilitate*, pp. 53–54, translated and analyzed in Newman, *From Virile Woman*, pp. 230–231. According to Agrippa's reading of the second chapter of Genesis, the fact that the woman is created from man and is thus the last of all created things is an indication of her superior status. "As the final work of God, woman was brought into this world by God, led as its queen led to the palace already prepared for her, embellished and perfected with every gift. Rightly, therefore, every creature loves, venerates and serves her, and all creation is rightly subject and obeys her, the queen and end of all creatures, their perfection and consummate glory in all respects." The superiority of Eve to Adam is also indicated by the etymology of their respective names; the former signifies "life," whereas the latter is related to the "earth." The point is enhanced by Agrippa's observation that "according to the mystical symbols of the kabbalists, the woman's name has a greater affinity than the man's with the ineffable name of the divine omnipotence, the Tetragrammaton, for the man's name does not accord with the divine name in characters, in figure or in number" (*De nobilitate*, p. 52, cited in Newman, *From Virile Woman*, p. 230). I am unaware of any statement in a traditional Jewish kabbalistic text that accords such unequivocal supremacy to the female over the male, identifying the woman, as opposed to the man, as the locus of the divine potency represented by the Tetragrammaton.

41. See E. Wolfson, *Circle in the Square*, pp. 116–121. In part, the kabbalistic understanding of remembering reflects one of the uses of the root *pqd* in talmudic parlance, for example, in the dictum (attributed to Joshua ben Levi) in Babylonian Talmud, Yevamot 62b, "every man is obligated to have conjugal relations with [literally, to remember] his wife [*lifqod et ishto*] when he goes on a journey." Cf. *Shulḥan Arukh*, Oraḥ Ḥayyim 240; Yoreh Deʿah 184; Even ha-Ezer 76. This euphemistic usage is biblical in origin; cf. Judg. 15:1. One must also bear in mind those biblical passages where the root *pqd* is used in conjunction with God visiting the barren woman, an act that results in the opening of the womb. Cf. Gen. 21:1; 2 Sam. 2:21.

42. That is, the blessing to be cited when one sees a rainbow. See following note for textual references.

43. Tosefta, Berakhot 6:5; Palestinian Talmud, Berakhot 9:3; Babylonian Talmud, Berakhot 59a. Cf. Moses de León, *Book of the Pomegranate*, p. 161.

44. Moses de León, *Shushan Edut*, pp. 363–364.

45. See chap. 3.

46. *Zohar* 1:84b, 115b–116a; 2:170b–171a; 3:74b, 125b; and discussion in E. Wolfson, "Occultation of the Feminine," pp. 135–148.

47. *Tiqqunei Zohar*, sec. 19, 38a.

48. Joseph of Hamadan, *Sefer Tashak*, pp. 52–53.

49. Ibid., p. 67.

50. *Genesis Rabbah* 35:2, pp. 328–329.

51. Joseph of Hamadan, *Sefer Tashak*, p. 68.

52. Against this background, it is of interest to consider ibid., p. 113, where, according to Joseph of

Hamadan's interpretation, the aggadic tradition that in the eschatological future the righteous will have wings (Babylonian Talmud, Sanhedrin 92b) signifies that they will be concealed in the "holy body" and "in the bosom of holy king." The emphasis on concealment is not part of the original tradition. The intent of this remark can be understood only if we bear in mind that for this kabbalist the "holy body" designates the phallic potency. For example, see Joseph of Hamadan, *Sefer Tashak*, p. 118.

53. The point has been recently made by Hellner-Eshed, "Language of Mystical Experience," p. 57 n. 24. Curiously, the author presents this view as an alternative to my own. While I acknowledge that my emphasis on the containment of the feminine in the masculine presents a starker portrait than the one that emerges from the more positive role accorded the feminine in the imaginal garbing of the divine, the latter has been affirmed by me as well as part of my understanding of the coincidence of concealment and disclosure in kabbalistic representations of truth. On the feminine as the locus of imaginal representation, see E. Wolfson, *Through a Speculum*, pp. 306–317. Concerning the role of the feminine in the dialectic of re/covering the uncovered, see idem, "Occultation." Hellner-Eshed mentions the latter work in her note but she does not consider it as affirmation of the point she makes as an alleged challenge to me. Compare, by contrast, the way she refers to this essay on p. 132 n. 47. I note, finally, that the kabbalistic association of the feminine with the imagination and the depiction of the latter in the image of the speculum relates to the widely attested linkage of the female, the mirror, and sensual lust or temptation. Regarding these themes, see Melchior-Bonnet, *Mirror*, pp. 200–221. The association of the mirror and the feminine can also have a positive connotation, as we see, for instance, in the description of the Virgin Mary in the liturgical hymn "O virga ac diadema," in Hildegard of Bingen, *Symphonia*, pp. 130–131: "O quam magnum est / in viribus suis latus virir, / de quo Deus formam mulieris produxit, / quam fecit speculum / omnis ornamenti sui / et amplexionem / omnis creature sue" (O how great / in its strength is the side of man, / from which God produced the form of woman. / He made her the mirror / of all his beauty / and the embrace / of his whole creation). The point of the hymn is that Mary rectifies the transgression of Eve and thereby restores woman to her original glory as the mirror in which the beauty of God and his creation can be seen. In this sense, the Virgin is portrayed as *salvatrix*, the "feminine savior." The point is made explicitly in another antiphon included in Hildegard's liturgical song cycle, "Qui ergo femina," op. cit., pp. 116–117. On the identification of Mary and Eve, see also "O quam magnum miraculum," op. cit., pp. 120–121. On Hildegard's identification with Mary as the female savior, realized in her poetic composition of the new songs of the Psalter, see Newman, "Poet," pp. 176–177.

54. *Tiqqunei Zohar*, sec. 70, 121a. For parallel texts in this stratum of zoharic literature, see E. Wolfson, *Through a Speculum*, pp. 312–316.

55. According to the original, *leminda u-le'istakkala*. Rendering the latter term as "envision" reflects my understanding of contemplation (*histakkelut*) in kabbalistic sources as a kind of visionary gnosis or illuminative exegesis. Hence one of the technical self-referential designations of the kabbalists is *maskilim*, the enlightened ones or, to render the idiom more precisely, those who visually contemplate what cannot be envisioned. See E. Wolfson, *Through a Speculum*, pp. 276–277, 285–287, 356–357, 367, 379–380, 383–384, 389–390; and chap. 6, n. 120.

56. *Tiqqunei Zohar*, sec. 70, 133b.

57. For point of contrast, it is helpful to consider what seems to me to be an authentic celebration of the feminine in the poetry of Walt Whitman, a bard who had mystical leanings. For instance, see Whitman's assertion in "Song of Myself," in *Leaves of Grass*, p. 40: "I am the poet of the woman the same as the man, / And I say it is as great to be a woman as to be a man, / And I say there is nothing greater than the mother of men." See also the account of the "female form" in "Sing the Body Electric," op. cit., p. 80: "Be not ashamed women, your privilege encloses the rest, and is the exit of the rest, / You are the gates of the body, and you are the gates of the soul. / The female contains all qualities and tempers them, / She is in her place and moves with perfect balance, / She is all things duly veil'd, she is both passive and active, / She is to conceive daughters as well as sons, and sons as well as daughters." And in "Unfolded out of the Folds," op. cit., p. 307: "Unfolded only out of the inimitable poems of woman can come the poems of man, (only thence have my poems come;) / . . . A man is a great thing upon the earth and through eternity, but every

jot of the greatness of man is unfolded out of woman; / First the man is shaped in the woman, he can then be shaped in himself." See also the description of the "Mother of All" or the "Maternal" in "Return of the Heroes," op. cit., p. 287. In my estimation, these pronouncements, in contrast to the statements in kabbalistic literature, reflect a genuine adoration of the feminine and a reversal of the androcentrism that has informed Western consciousness.

58. See *Zohar* 3:128a, 135a, 142a, 292a; Liebes, *Studies in the Zohar*, pp. 66–67.

59. The symbolic significance of the zoharic myth is elaborated in Lurianic texts wherein the primordial Edomite kings are identified as "points" (*nequddim*) that are female in nature and collectively constitute the "world of chaos" (*olam ha-tohu*), i.e., destructive and negative judgment. See Y. Jacobson, "Aspect of the Feminine," pp. 250–255. I must, however, respectfully disagree with Jacobson's observation that the reason no wife is mentioned in the case of the first seven kings is "not because they were male, but because their fertile femininity was actualized only after their revival and reconstruction." On the contrary, I would contend that the Edomite kings are emasculated males, symbolically equivalent to females without male partners. The underlying issue in this myth is not feminine fertility but masculine virility.

60. The word I have rendered as balance is *matqela*, which means weight (in Hebrew, *mishqal*), from the root *teqal* ("to weigh"). See *Zohar* 2:255a. Regarding this term in its zoharic context and a possible precedent in the writings of Isaac the Blind, see Liebes, *Sections of the Zohar Lexicon*, pp. 329–330; idem, *Studies in the Zohar*, p. 68.

61. *Zohar* 2:176b.

62. See Tishby, *Wisdom of the Zohar*, p. 1362.

63. Vital, *Eṣ Ḥayyim*, 10:3, 49a. See as well idem, *Mavo Sheʿarim*, 2:3:2, 12c, cited by Y. Jacobson, "Aspect of the Feminine," p. 251.

64. Vital, *Eṣ Ḥayyim*, 10:3, 48d.

65. According to the interpretation of "The arms of his hands were spread out" (Gen. 49:24) attributed to R. Isaac in *Genesis Rabbah* 87:7, p. 1072: "his seed was dispersed and it went out by way of his nails." From the exegetical context, it would appear that the nails refers to the fingers. For a later discussion regarding whether this refers to the hands or to the feet, see Vital, *Eṣ Ḥayyim*, 15:2, 33b–c.

66. *Tiqqunei Zohar*, sec. 69, 110a. In that context, a link is established between the ten seminal drops discharged by Joseph through his nails and the ten martyrs, the *asarah harugei malkhut*. For the development of this motif in Lurianic sources, see Meroz, "Redemption in the Lurianic Teaching," pp. 257–261.

67. Vital, *Eṣ Ḥayyim* 8:3, 37b.

68. Ibid., 10:3, 49a–b.

69. Vital, *Shaʿar ha-Haqdamot*, 28c.

70. Vital, *Mavo Sheʿarim*, 2:3:2, 12a. See Meroz, "Redemption," pp. 244–245.

71. Scholem, *Major Trends*, p. 37.

72. The homoerotic aspect is not unique to kabbalistic fraternities; on the contrary, it is a phenomenon well attested in other religious societies. For an illuminating discussion of the homoerotic texture of mystical experience in different cultural settings, see Kripal, *Roads of Excess*.

73. *Zohar* 3:162a.

74. See E. Wolfson, *Through a Speculum*, pp. 357–377; idem, *Circle in the Square*, pp. 107–110.

75. *Kitvei Ramban*, 2:480.

76. See, in particular, Babylonian Talmud, Sukkah 45b, where the righteous are referred to as "those who receive the face of the presence" (*meqabbelei appei shekhinah*). This source was already noted by Chavel in his annotations to Ezra's text; see *Kitvei Ramban*, 2:480 n. 57.

77. *Kitvei Ramban*, 2:514.

78. See Tishby, *Wisdom of the Zohar*, p. 374; Liebes, *Studies in the Zohar*, pp. 67–74; Idel, *Studies in Ecstatic Kabbalah*, pp. 19 and 152–153 n. 66.

79. *Midrash Tehillim*, 19:7, 84a.

80. *Kitvei Ramban*, 2:494.

81. See Vajda, *L'amour de Dieu*, pp. 213–214 n. 5.

82. I am thus in basic agreement with the observation of Tirosh-Rothschild, "Continuity and Revision," p. 182: "I suspect that Kabbalah exacerbated the marginalization of women in traditional Jewish society precisely because it expressed (or satisfied) the sexual and erotic needs of Jewish men." Although these remarks are cast within a framework of heterosexuality, I think the author correctly understood that the exclusion of women from the history of kabbalah is related to male sexual fantasies that I consider to be profoundly homoerotic.

83. See chap. 2, n. 46. It behooves me to note a passage from a section in *Zohar* 3:161b–168a in which the mysteries of the righteous souls in the celestial paradise are revealed. At a critical point in the narrative account, Simeon ben Yoḥai poses the question to the master of the heavenly academy regarding the status of women in this realm (167a), and after a digression it is revealed to him that there is a distinct area exclusively for women. The area is divided into four palaces, associated respectively with Bitya, the daughter of Pharoah, Serach bat Asher, the granddaughter of Jacob, Yocheved, the mother of Moses, and Deborah. Within these four palaces are the "four hidden palaces of the holy matriarchs that have not been allowed to be revealed and that have not been seen by anyone" (167b). A full analysis of this text will have to await a separate study; suffice it here to remark that this passage does offer a genuine portrait of women predicated on some form of autonomy, a point underscored by the fact that they are accorded eight palaces to which men can have no access. Yet the activities assigned to the righteous women in these palaces are the ones typically associated with men, fulfillment of ritual obligations and study of Torah, especially the reasons for the commandments, a topic that medieval kabbalists considered part of the esoteric lore. Moreover, in the first of the palaces, the women are described as being "engaged with the commandments of Torah, all of them in those images [*diyoqnin*] as they were in this world, in the garment of light, as the garment of males [*bi-levusha di-nehora ki-levusha di-dekhurin*] (167b). Although this comment is associated only with the first palace, I do not think it would be incorrect to assume that the gender transformation indicated by this description would apply to the souls of the righteous women in all of the palaces. The women are not reduced to men, but their eschatological status is delimited nonetheless in the language of transposition, the donning of garments of light, which are garments of the males. To inhabit the space apart from men, therefore, female souls had to be garbed as masculine. It seems to me, therefore, that what is conveyed in this zoharic passage is the kabbalistic equivalent of the gnostic motif of the female becoming male.

Bibliography

Primary Sources

Abraham ben David. *Baʿalei ha-Nefesh.* Edited by Yosef Kafiḥ. Jerusalem: Mosad ha-Rav Kook, 1982.

Abulafia, Abraham. *Ḥayyei ha-Nefesh.* MS Munich, Bayerische Staatsbibliothek 408. Printed ed., Jerusalem, 2001.

———. *Ḥayyei ha-Olam ha-Ba.* MS Oxford, Bodleian Library 1582. Printed ed., Jerusalem, 1999.

———. *Imrei Shefer.* MS Munich, Bayerische Staatsbibliothek 40. Printed ed., Jerusalem, 1999.

———. *Or ha-Sekhel.* MS Vatican, Biblioteca Apostolica 233. Printed ed., Jerusalem, 2001.

———. *Oṣar Eden Ganuz.* MS Oxford, Bodleian Library 1580. Printed ed., Jerusalem, 2000.

———. *Sheva Netivot ha-Torah.* In Adolph Jellinek, *Philosophie und Kabbala,* 1:1–25. Leipzig, Heinrich Hunger, 1854.

———. *Sitrei Torah.* MS Paris, Bibliothèque Nationale 774. Printed ed., Jerusalem, 2001.

Abulafia, Todros ben Joseph. *Oṣar ha-Kavod ha-Shalem.* Warsaw, 1879.

Agadath Shir Hashirim. Edited by Solomon Schechter. Cambridge: Deighton Bell, 1896.

Amrani, Azariah Ḥai. *Shemen ha-Sullam.* Jerusalem, 1999.

Aripul, Samuel. *Sefer Sar Shalom.* Safed, 1579.

Asher ben David. *R. Asher ben David: His Complete Works and Studies in His Kabbalistic Thought.* Edited by Daniel Abrams. Los Angeles: Cherub Press, 1996 (Hebrew).

Avot de-Rabbi Natan. Edited by Solomon Schechter. Vienna: Ch. D. Lippe, 1887.

Azriel of Gerona. *Commentary on Talmudic Aggadoth.* Edited by Isaiah Tishby. Jerusalem: Mekize Nirdamim, 1945 (Hebrew).

———. *Iggeret le-Burgos.* In *Maddaʿei Yahadut* 2 (1927): 233–240.

———. "New Fragments in the Writings of R. Azriel of Gerona." In *Sefer Zikkaron le-Asher Gulak we-li Shemuʾel Klein,* edited by Gershom Scholem, 201–222. Jerusalem: Hebrew University, 1942 (Hebrew).

———. *Perush Eser Sefirot.* In Meir Ibn Gabbai, *Derekh Emunah.* Berlin, 1850.

———. *Perush ha-Tefillah.* MS Oxford-Bodleian 1938.

———. *Perush Sefer Yeṣirah.* In *Kitvei Ramban,* 2 vols., edited by Ḥayyim D. Chavel, 2:453–461. Jerusalem: Mosad ha-Rav Kook, 1964.

———. "R. Azriel of Gerona—*Perush ha-Tefillah*: A Critical Edition of MS Ferrera 1." Edited by Martel Gavarin. MA thesis, Hebrew University, 1984.

Azulai, Abraham. *Ḥesed le-Avraham*. Amsterdam, 1685.
———. *Or ha-Ḥammah*. 3 vols. Jerusalem, 1973.
Bachrach, Naftali. *Emeq ha-Melekh*. Jerusalem, Yerid ha-Sefarim, 2003.
Baḥya ben Asher. *Kitvei Rabbenu Baḥya*. Edited by Ḥayyim D. Chavel. Jerusalem: Mosad ha-Rav Kook, 1970.
———. *Rabbenu Baḥya: Be'ur al ha-Torah*. 3 vols. Edited by Ḥayyim D. Chavel. Jerusalem: Mosad ha-Rav Kook, 1981.
Bar Ḥiyya, Abraham. *Hegyon ha-Nephesch ha-Atzuvah*. Edited with introduction and notes by Geoffrey Wigoder. Jerusalem: Bialik Insitute, 1971.
The Book Bahir: An Edition Based on the Earliest Manuscripts. Edited by Daniel Abrams with an introduction by Moshe Idel. Los Angeles: Cherub Press, 1994 (Hebrew).
Buzaglo, Shalom. *Miqdash Melekh ha-Shalem*. 5 vols. Jerusalem: Makhon Benei Yissaschar, 1995–2000.
Chani, Isaac. *Me'ah She'arim*. Lublin, 1924.
Cordovero, Moses. *Elimah Rabbati*. Brody, 1881.
———. *Pardes Rimmonim*. Jerusalem, 1962.
———. *Sefer Yeṣirah im Perush Or Yaqar*. Jerusalem, Mif'al Or Yaqar, 1989.
———. *Shi'ur Qomah*. Warsaw, 1883.
David ben Ḥayyim. *Shirah le-Dawid*. Grodno, 1797.
David ben Yehudah he-Ḥasid. *The Book of Mirrors: Sefer Mar'ot ha-Ẓove'ot*. Edited by Daniel Chanan Matt. Chico: Scholar's Press, 1982.
Eleazar ben Judah of Worms. *Perush ha-Merkavah*. MS Bar-Ilan 1037.
Eliezer ben Abraham ha-Levi. *Shalosh Ma'amerei Ge'ullah*. Jerusalem, 2000.
Elijah ben Solomon. *The Commentary of the Gaon Rabbi Elijah of Vilna to Sifra di-Ẓeni'uta*. Edited by Bezalel Naor. Jerusalem, 1997 (Hebrew).
Ezra ben Solomon of Gerona. *Perush ha-Aggadot*. MS Oxford, Bodleian 1947. Partially printed in *Liqquṭei Shikheḥah u-Fe'ah*. Ferrara, 1556.
———. *Perush Shir ha-Shirim*. In *Kitvei Ramban*, 2 vols., edited by Ḥayyim D. Chavel, 2:476–548. Jerusalem: Mosad ha-Rav Kook, 1964.
Fano, Menahem Azariah. *Ma'amerei ha-RAMA*. 2 vols. Jerusalem: Yismaḥ Lev—Torat Moshe, 1997.
Galante, Abraham. *Qol Bokhim*. Venice, 1589.
Galya Raza. Edited by Rachel Elior. Jerusalem: Hebrew University, 1981.
Genesis Rabbah. Edited by Julius Theodor and Chanoch Albeck. Jerusalem: Wahrmann Books, 1965.
Gikatilla, Joseph. *Be'urim le-Sefer Moreh Nevukhim la-Rambam*. In Isaac Abarbanel, *Ketavim al Maḥshevet Yisra'el*, vol. 3, Jerusalem: Sifriyyah le-Maḥshevet Yisra'el, 1967.
———. *Ginnat Egoz*. Jerusalem: Yeshivat ha-Ḥayyim we-ha-Shalom, 1989.
———. *R. Joseph Gikatilla's Commentary to Ezekiel's Chariot*. Critically edited and introduced by Asi Farber-Ginat, edited by Daniel Abrams. Los Angeles: Cherub Press, 1998 (Hebrew).
———. *Le Secret du Mariage de David et Bethsabée*. Hebrew text edited and translated by Charles Mopsik. Paris: Éditions de l'Éclat, 1994.
———. *Sefer ha-Niqqud*. Jerusalem: Yerid ha-Sefarim, 1994.
———. *Sha'arei Orah*. 2 vols. Edited by Joseph Ben-Shlomo. Jerusalem: Bialik Institute, 1981.
———. *Sha'arei Ṣedeq*. Cracow, 1881.
———. *Sod ha-Shabbat*. In *Heikhal ha-Shem*. Venice: Daniel Zaniti, 1601.

Gruenwald, Ithamar. "A Preliminary Critical Edition of *Sefer Yeẓira*." *Israel Oriental Studies* 1 (1971): 132–177 (Hebrew).

Ha-Ketavim ha-Ivriyyim shel Baʿal Tiqqunei Zohar we-Raʿaya Meheimna. Edited and annotated by Efraim Gottlieb, introduction by Moshe Idel, prepared for press by Shmuel Reem, indexes prepared by Michal Oron. Jerusalem: Israel Academy of Sciences and Humanities, 2003.

Halevi, Judah. *Sefer ha-Kuzari*. Translated by Yehudah Even Shmuel. Tel-Aviv: Dvir, 1972.

Ḥaver, Yiṣḥaq Isaac. *Pitḥei Sheʿarim*. Tel-Aviv, 1964.

Herrera, Abraham Cohen de. *Gate of Heaven*. Translated from the Spanish with introduction and notes by Kenneth Krabbenhoft. Leiden: Brill, 2002.

———. *House of Divinity (Casa de la Divinidad). Gate of Heaven (Puerta del Cielo)*. Annotated translation from Spanish into Hebrew with introduction by Nissim Yosha. Jerusalem: Ben-Zvi Institute, 2002.

Hippolytus. *Refutation of All Heresies*. Translated by J. H. Macmahon. In *The Ante-Nicene Fathers*, edited by Alexander Roberts and James Donaldson. Grand Rapids: William B. Eerdmans, 1981.

Ḥoter ben Shelomo. *The Philosophic Questions and Answers of Ḥoter ben Shelomo*. Edited, translated, and annotated by David R. Blumenthal. Leiden: E. J. Brill, 1981.

Ibn al-Fayyūmī, Nathanael. *The Bustan Al-Ukul by Nathanael Ibn Al-Fayyūmī*. Edited and translated by David Levine. New York: Columbia University Press, 1908.

Ibn Aqnin, Joseph ben Judah ben Jacob. *Divulgatio mysteriorum luminumque apparentia: Commentarius in Canticum Canticorum*. Edited and translated by Abraham S. Halkin. Jerusalem: Mekize Nirdamim, 1964.

Ibn Ezra, Abraham. *Perushei ha-Torah le-Rabbenu Avraham Ibn Ezra*. 3 vols. Edited by Asher Weiser. Jerusalem: Mosad ha-Rav Kook, 1977.

———. *Yesod Mora*. Prague, 1833.

Ibn Gabbai, Meir. *Avodat ha-Qodesh*. Jerusalem: Shevilei Orḥot ha-Ḥayyim, 1992.

———. *Derekh Emunah*. Berlin, 1850.

———. *Tolaʿat Yaʿaqov*. Jerusalem: Shevilei Orḥot ha-Ḥayyim, 1996.

Ibn Gaon, Shem Tov ben Abraham. *Sefer Baddei Aron u-Migdal Ḥananel*. A limited facsimile edition of Codex Paris Bibliothèque nationale no. 40. Edited by D. S. Löwinger. Jerusalem: Makor, 1977.

Ibn Latif, Isaac. *Shaʿar ha-Shamayim*, MS Vatican ebr. 335.

Ibn Malka, Judah ben Nissim. *Perush ha-Tefillot*. Edited with an introduction by Saverio Campanini. In Giulio Busi, *Catalogue of the Kabbalistic Manuscripts in the Library of the Jewish Community of Mantua*, 243–371. Firenze: Edizioni Cadmo, 2001.

Ibn Paquda, Baḥya. *Sefer Torat Ḥovot ha-Levavot*. Translated by Joseph Kafiḥ. Jerusalem, 1973.

Ibn Sahula, Isaac. "Rabbi Isaac Sahula's Commentary on the Song of Songs." Edited by Arthur Green. *Jerusalem Studies in Jewish Thought* 6:3–4 (1987): 393–491 (Hebrew).

Ibn Ṣayyaḥ, Joseph. *Even ha-Shoham*, MS Ramat Gan, Bar-Ilan University 598.

Ibn Shem Tov, Shem Tov. *Sefer ha-Emunot*. Ferrara, 1556.

Ibn Tabul, Joseph. "Commentary on *Idra Raba*." In *Temirin: Texts and Studies in Kabbala and Hasidism*, edited by Israel Weinstock, 2:123–167. Jerusalem: Mosad ha-Rav Kook, 1981 (Hebrew).

Ibn Tibbon, Moses. "Moses Ibn Tibbons Hohelied-Kommentar (Edition, Übersetzung und Analyse): Ein Beitrag zur philosophische orientierten Schriftauslegung im Südfrankreich des 13. Jahrhunderts." Submitted by Otfried Fraisse. Ph.D. dissertation, Freie Universität, 2002.

———. *Perush al Shir ha-Shirim*. Lyck: Mekize Nirdamim, 1874.

Isaac ben Ḥayyim ha-Kohen of Sativa. *Eṣ Ḥayyim*. Edited by Raphael Cohen. Jerusalem, 2001.
Isaac ben Samuel of Acre. *Sefer Me'irat Einayim by R. Isaac of Acre: A Critical Edition*. Edited by Amos Goldreich. Jerusalem: Akkadamon, 1981 (Hebrew).
Isaac the Blind. *Perush Sefer Yeṣirah*. "Appendix" in Gershom Scholem, *The Kabbalah in Provence*. Edited by Rivka Schatz. Jerusalem: Akkadamon, 1970 (Hebrew).
Jacob ben Asher. *Arbaʿah Ṭurim*. New York: M. P. Press, 1975.
Jacob ben Sheshet. *Sefer ha-Emunah we-ha-Biṭṭaḥon*. In *Kitvei Ramban*. 2 vols. Edited by Ḥayyim D. Chavel, vol. 2, 353–448. Jerusalem: Mosad ha-Rav Kook, 1964.
———. *Sefer Meshiv Devarim Nekhoḥim*. Edited by Georges Vajda, introduction by Georges Vajda and Efraim Gottlieb. Jerusalem: Israel Academy of Sciences and Humanities, 1968.
———. "Sefer Shaʿar ha-Shamayim (The Book Gate of Heaven) by Rabbi Yacov Ben Sheshet Girondi: Scientific Edition including Foreword and Annotations." Edited by Nahora Gabay. MA thesis, Tel-Aviv University, 1993 (Hebrew).
———. *Shaʿar ha-Shamayim*. In *Oṣar Neḥmad* 3 (1860): 153–165.
Jellinek, Adolf. *Beit Midrash*. 3rd ed., 2 vols. Jerusalem: Wahrmann Books, 1967.
Joseph ben Shalom Ashkenazi. *Commentary on Sefer Yeṣirah* (attributed to Abraham ben David). In *Sefer Yeṣirah*. Jerusalem, 1962 (Hebrew).
———. *A Kabbalistic Commentary of Rabbi Yoseph Ben Shalom Ashkenazi on Genesis Rabbah*. Edited by Moshe Ḥallamish. Jerusalem: Magnes Press, 1984 (Hebrew).
Joseph of Hamadan. "A Critical Edition of the *Sefer Ṭaʿamey ha-Miẓwoth* (Book of Reasons of the Commandments) Attributed to Isaac Ibn Farḥi. Section I—Positive Commandments with Introduction and Notes." Menachem Meier, Ph.D. dissertation, Brandeis University, 1974.
———. *Fragment d'un commentaire sur la Genèse*. Edited and translated by Charles Mopsik. Paris: Éditions Verdier, 1998.
———. "Joseph of Hamadan's *Sefer Tashak*: Critical Text Edition with Introduction." Edited by Jeremy Zwelling. Ph.D. dissertation, Brandeis University, 1975.
Kimḥi, Joseph. *The Book of the Covenant of Joseph Kimḥi*. Translated by Frank Talmage. Toronto: Pontifical Institute of Mediaeval Studies, 1972.
Lavi, Simeon. *Ketem Paz*. 2 vols. Jerusalem, 1981.
Leviticus Rabbah. Edited by Mordecai Margulies. New York and Jerusalem: Jewish Theological Seminary of America, 1993.
Liqquṭei Shikheḥah u-Fe'ah. Ferrara, 1556.
Luzzatto, Moses Ḥayyim. *Adir ba-Marom*. Jerusalem, 1990.
———. *Iggerot Ramḥal u-Venei Doro*. Edited by Mordecai Chirqi. Jerusalem: Makhon Ramḥal, 2001.
———. *Oṣerot Ramḥal*. Edited by Ḥayyim Friedlander. Benei Beraq, 1986.
———. *Pitḥei Ḥokhmah wa-Daʿat*. In *Shaʿarei Ramḥal*. Edited by Ḥayyim Friedlander. Benei Beraq, 1986.
———. *Sefer ha-Kelalim*. Edited by Ḥayyim Friedlander. Benei Beraq, 1989.
Maʿarekhet ha-Elohut. Jerusalem, 1963.
Massekhet Soferim. Edited by Michael Higger. New York: Debe Rabbanan, 1937.
Mekhilta de-Rabbi Ishmael. Edited by H. S. Horovitz and I. A. Rabin. Jerusalem: Wahrmann Books, 1970.
Menaḥem Mendel, *Aṭeret Shalom*. Lemberg, 1893.
Midrash Mishle: A Critical Edition based on Vatican Ebr. 44, with Variant Readings from All Known Manuscripts and Early Editions, and with an Introduction, References and a Short Commentary. Edited by Burton Visotzky. New York: Jewish Theological Seminary of America, 1990.

Midrash Tanḥuma. Edited by Solomon Buber. New York: Sefer, 1946.
Midrash Tehillim. Edited by Solomon Buber. Vilna: Rom, 1891.
Midreshei Teiman. Edited by Saul Lieberman. Jerusalem: Wahrmann Books, 1970.
Moses ben Maimon (Maimonides). *The Guide of the Perplexed*. Translated with an introduction and notes by Shlomo Pines, with an introductory essay by Leo Strauss. Chicago and London: University of Chicago Press, 1963.
———. *Mishneh Torah*. New York: Schlusinger, 1947.
Moses ben Naḥman (Naḥmanides). *Kitvei Ramban*. 2 vols. Edited by Ḥayyim D. Chavel. Jerusalem: Mosad ha-Rav Kook, 1964.
———. *Perushei ha-Torah le-R. Mosheh ben Naḥman*. 2 vols. Edited by Ḥayyim D. Chavel. Jerusalem: Mosad ha-Rav Kook, 1959–1960.
Moses ben Shem Ṭov de León. *The Book of the Pomegranate: Moses de León's Sefer ha-Rimmon*. Edited by Elliot R. Wolfson. Brown Judaic Studies, no. 144. Atlanta: Scholars Press, 1988.
———. Fragment of an Untitled Work. MS Munich 47.
———. "Moses de León's *Sefer Or Zaruʿa*: Introduction, Critical Text, and Notes." Edited by Alexander Altmann. *Qoveṣ al Yad* 9 (1980): 219–293 (Hebrew).
———. *R. Moses de Leon's Sefer Sheqel ha-Qodesh*. Critically edited and introduced by Charles Mopsik, with an introduction by Moshe Idel. Los Angeles: Cherub Press, 1996 (Hebrew).
———. "*Sefer ha-Mishkal*: Text and Study." Edited by Jochanan H. A. Wijnhoven. Ph.D. dissertation, Brandeis University, 1964.
———. *Sheʾelot u-Teshuvot le-R. Moshe di liʾon be-Inyyenei Qabbalah*. Edited by Isaiah Tishby. *Studies in Kabbalah and Its Branches: Researches and Sources*, vol. 1, 36–75. Jerusalem: Magnes Press, 1982 (Hebrew).
———. *Shushan Edut*. Edited by Gershom Scholem. "Two Treatises of R. Moses de León." *Qoveṣ al Yad* n.s. 8 (1976): 325–370 (Hebrew).
Naḥman of Bratslav. *Liqquṭei Eṣot*. Jerusalem, 1976.
———. *Liqquṭei MoHaRaN*. Benei Beraq, 1972.
Narboni, Moses. *The Epistle on the Possibility of Conjunction with the Active Intellect by Ibn Rushd with the Commentary of Moses Narboni*. Edited and translated by Kalman P. Bland. New York: Jewish Theological Seminary of America, 1982.
Nathan of Gaza. *Liqquṭei Raza de-Malka Qaddisha*. MS New York, Jewish Theological Seminary of America Mic. 1549.
———. *Sefer ha-Beriʾah*. MS New York, Jewish Theological Seminary of America 1581.
Nathan of Nemirov. *Liqquṭei Halakhot*. Jerusalem, 1974.
Olat Tamid. Jerusalem, 1907.
Pesiqta de-Rav Kahana. Edited by Bernard Mandelbaum. 2 vols. New York: Jewish Theological Seminary of America, 1962.
Pesiqta Rabbati. Edited by Meir Friedmann. Vienna: Josef Kaiser, 1880.
Pirqei Rabbi Eliʿezer. Warsaw, 1852.
Pseudo-Baḥya. *Les Réflexions sur l'âme par Bahya ben Joseph Ibn Pakouda*. Translated by I. Broydé. Paris, 1896.
Qalonymos Qalman ha-Levi Epstein. *Maʾor wa-Shemesh*. New York, 1985.
Rabba, Menaḥem ben Moses. *Beit Moʿed*. Venice, 1605.
Recanati, Menaḥem. *Beʾur al ha-Torah*. Jerusalem, 1961.
Saadya ben Joseph Gaon. *Kitāb al-Amānāt wal-iʿtiqādāt*. Edited by Joseph Kafiḥ. Jerusalem: Sura Institute for Research and Publication, 1970.

Sabba, Abraham. *Ṣeror ha-Mor.* 2 vols. Benei Beraq: Heikkal ha-Sefer, 1990.
Seder Qinnot ha-Meforash le-Tishʿah ba-Av. Edited by Jacob Weingarten. Jerusalem: Gefen, 1988.
Sefer ha-Bahir. Edited by Reuven Margaliot. Jerusalem: Mosad ha-Rav Kook, 1978.
Sefer ha-Malkhut. Casablanca, 1930.
Sefer ha-Peliʾah. Przemysl, 1884.
Sefer Yeṣirah. Jerusalem, 1962.
Sefer ha-Zohar. Edited by Reuven Margaliot. 6th ed., 3 vols. Jerusalem: Mosad ha-Rav Kook, 1984.
Ṣemaḥ, Jacob. *Ṣemaḥ Ṣaddiq.* Korets, 1785.
Shaʿarei Ṣedeq: Beʾur Sefer Yeṣirah. Edited by Yosef E. Parush. Jerusalem: Sha'ar ha-Shamayim, 1989.
Shaʿar ha-Pesuqim. Jerusalem, 1868.
Shaʿar ha-Qabbalah we-Sidrah. Edited and annotated by Joseph Parush. Jerusalem, 2002.
Shelomo ha-Bavli. *The Poems of Shelomo Ha-Bavli: Critical Edition with Introduction and Commentary.* Edited by Fleischer, Ezra. Jerusalem: Israel Academy of Sciences and Humanities, 1973 (Hebrew).
Shir ha-Shirim Rabbah. Edited by Shimshon Dunasky. Jerusalem and Tel-Aviv: Dvir, 1980.
Shklov, Menaḥem Mendel of. *Derekh ha-Qodesh.* Jerusalem, 1999.
Shoshan Sodot. Korets, 1784.
Sifra de-vei Rav—Torat Kohanim. Jerusalem: Sifra Publications, 1959.
Siphre ad Numeros. Edited by Ḥayyim S. Horovitz. Jerusalem: Wahrmann Books, 1966.
Sullam ha-Aliyyah. Edited by Joseph E. Parush. Jerusalem, 1989.
Tamakh, Abraham ben. Isaac ha-Levi. *R. Abraham b. Isaac ha-Levi Tamakh: Commentary on the Song of Songs.* Edited by Leon A. Feldman. Assen: Van Gorcum, 1970.
The Targum of Ezekiel. Translated, with a critical introduction, apparatus, and notes by Samson H. Levey. Collegeville: Liturgical Press, 1987.
Tiqqunei Zohar. Edited by Reuven Margaliot. Jerusalem: Mosad ha-Rav Kook, 1978.
Vidas, Elijah de. *Reʾshit Ḥokhmah.* New York, 1965.
Vital, Ḥayyim. *Eṣ Ḥayyim.* Jerusalem, 1910.
———. *Ketavim Ḥadashim le-Rabbenu Ḥayyim Viṭal.* Jerusalem, 1988.
———. *Liqquṭei Torah Neviʾim Ketuvim.* Jerusalem, 1995.
———. *Liqquṭim Ḥadashim.* Edited by Daniel Touitou. Jerusalem, 1985.
———. *Mavo Sheʿarim.* Jerusalem, 1904.
———. *Sefer ha-Derushim.* Jerusalem: Ahavat Shalom, 1996.
———. *Sefer ha-Gilgulim.* Jerusalem, 1903.
———. *Sefer ha-Ḥezyonot.* Edited by A. Aescoli. Jerusalem: Mosad ha-Rav Kook, 1954.
———. *Shaʿar Maʾamerei Razal.* Jerusalem, 1898.
———. *Shaʿar ha-Gilgulim.* Jerusalem, 1903.
———. *Shaʿar ha-Haqdamot.* Jerusalem, 1901.
———. *Shaʿar ha-Kawwanot.* Jerusalem, 1963.
———. *Shaʿar Maʾamerei Rashbi.* Jerusalem, 1898.
———. *Shaʿar ha-Pesuqim.* Jerusalem, 1912.
———. *Shaʿar Ruaḥ ha-Qodesh.* In *Kitvei Rabbenu ha-Ari,* vol. 11. Jerusalem: Yeshivat Kol Yehuda, 1963.
Yannai. *The Liturgical Poems of Rabbi Yannai according to the Triennial Cycle of the Pentateuch and the Holidays.* Critical edition with introduction and commentary by Zvi Meir Rabinovitz. Jerusalem: Bialik Institute, 1985 (Hebrew).

Yosse ben Yosse. *Yosse ben Yosse: Poems*. Edited with an introduction, commentary, and notes by Aharon Mirsky. 2nd ed. Jerusalem: Bialik Institute, 1991 (Hebrew).
Zevi Hirsch of Zidachov. *Ṣur me-Ra we-Aseh Ṭov*. With notes by Zevi Elimelekh Shapira of Dinuv. Tel-Aviv, 1969.
Zimrat Yah. MS New York, Columbia University X893 M6856.
Le Zohar: Cantique des cantiques. Translation from Aramaic and Hebrew, annotation and introduction by Charles Mopsik. Paris: Verdier, 1999.
Zohar Ḥadash. Edited by Reuven Margaliot. Jerusalem: Mosad ha-Rav Kook, 1978.
Zohar ha-Raqiʿa. Korets, 1785.

Secondary Sources

Aaron, David H. *Biblical Ambiguities: Metaphor, Semantics, and Divine Imagery*. Leiden: E. J. Brill, 2001.
———. "Imagery of the Divine and the Human: On the Mythology of Genesis Rabba 8 § 1." *Journal of Jewish Thought and Philosophy* 5 (1995): 1–62.
———. "Judaism's Holy Language." In *Approaches to Ancient Judaism*, edited by Jacob Neusner, new series, 16, 49–107. Atlanta: Scholars Press, 1999.
Abarbanell, Nitza. *Eve and Lilith*. Ramat Gan: Bar-Ilan University Press, 1994 (Hebrew).
Abbas, Shemeem Burney. *The Female Voice in Sufi Ritual: Devotional Practices of Pakistan and India*. Austin: University of Texas Press, 2002.
Abe, Masao. *A Study of Dōgen: His Philosophy and Religion*. Edited by Steven Heine. Albany: State University of New York Press, 1992.
———. *Zen and Western Thought*. Edited by William R. LaFleur. Foreword by John Hick. Honolulu: University of Hawaii Press, 1985.
Abrahamov, Binyamin, ed. *Anthropomorpism and Interpretation of the Qurʾān in the Theology of Al-Qāsim Ibn Ibrāhīm: Kitāb al-Mustarshid*. With translation, introduction, and notes by Binyamin Abrahamov. Leiden: E. J. Brill, 1996.
———. *Divine Love in Islamic Mysticism: The Teachings of Al-Ghazāli and Al-Dabbāgh*. New York: RoutledgeCurzon, 2002.
Abrams, Daniel. "Critical and Post-Critical Textual Scholarship of Jewish Mystical Literature: Notes on the History and Development of Modern Editing Techniques." *Kabbalah: Journal for the Study of Jewish Mystical Texts* 1 (1996): 17–71.
———. "Knowing the Maiden without Eyes: Reading the Sexual Reconstruction of the Jewish Mystic in a Zoharic Parable." *Daʿat* 50–52 (2003): lix–lxxxiii.
———. *Sexual Symbolism and Merkavah Speculation in Medieval Germany: A Study of the Sod Ha-Egoz Texts*. Tübingen: Mohr Siebeck, 1997.
———. "When Was the Introduction to the *Zohar* Written? With Variants in the Different Versions of the Introduction in the Mantua Print." *Asufot* 8 (1994): 211–226 (Hebrew).
Abrams, Meyer H. *The Mirror and the Lamp: Romantic Theory and the Cultural Tradition*. New York: Oxford University Press, 1953.
Abulafia, Anna Sapir. "The Intellectual and Spiritual Quest for Christ and Central Medieval Persecution of Jews." In *Religious Violence between Christians and Jews: Medieval Roots, Modern Perspectives*, edited by Anna Sapir Abulafia, 61–85. Hampshire: Palgrave, 2002.
———. "Jewish Carnality in Twelfth-Century Renaissance Thought." In *Christianity and Judaism: Papers Read at the 1991 Summer Meeting and the 1992 Winter Meeting of the Ecclesiastical History Society*, edited by Diana Wood, 59–75. Oxford: Blackwell, 1992.

Abusch, Tzvi. "The Demonic Image of the Witch in Standard Babylonian Literature: The Reworking of Popular Conceptions by Learned Exorcists." In *Religion, Science, and Magic: In Concert and In Conflict*, edited by Jacob Neusner, Ernest S. Frerichs, and Paul Virgil McCracken Flesher, 27–58. New York and Oxford: Oxford University Press, 1989.

Ackerman, Susan. "The Queen Mother and the Cult in Ancient Israel." *Journal of Biblical Literature* 112 (1993): 385–401.

———. "The Queen Mother and the Cult in the Ancient Near East." In *Women and Goddess Traditions in Antiquity and Today*, edited by Karen L. King, 179–209. Minneapolis: Fortress Press, 1997.

Adams, Robert M. "Idolatry and the Invisibility of God." In *Interpretation in Religion*, edited by Shlomo Biderman and Ben-Ami Scharfstein, 39–52. Leiden: E. J. Brill, 1993.

Adamson, Peter. "Aristotelianism and the Soul in the Arabic Plotinus." *Journal of the History of Ideas* 62 (2001): 212–232.

Adler, Rachel. *Engendering Judaism: An Inclusive Theology and Ethics*. Philadelphia and Jerusalem: Jewish Publication Society of America, 1998.

Adorno, Theodor. *Minima Moralia: Reflections from Damaged Life*. Translated by E. F. N. Jephcott. London: Verso, 1974.

Agamben, Giorgio. *The Coming Community*. Translated by Michael Hardt. Minneapolis and London: University of Minnesota Press, 1993.

———. *The End of the Poem: Studies in Poetics*. Translated by Daniel Heller-Roazen. Stanford: Stanford University Press, 1999.

———. *Potentialities: Collected Essays in Philosophy*. Edited and translated with an introduction by Daniel Heller-Roazen. Stanford: Stanford University Press, 1999.

Agrippa von Nettesheim, Heinrich Cornelius. *De nobilitate et praecellentia foeminei sexus*. Edited by Charles Béné. Geneva: Droz, 1990.

Ahearne, Jeremy. *Michel de Certeau: Interpretation and Its Other*. Stanford: Stanford University Press, 1995.

Ailes, Marianne J. "The Medieval Male Couple and the Language of Homosociality." In *Masculinity in Medieval Europe*, edited by Dawn M. Hadley, 214–237. London and New York: Longman, 1999.

Ajzenstat, Oona. *Driven Back to the Text: The Premodern Sources of Levinas's Postmodernism*. Pittsburgh: Duquesne University Press, 2001.

Aklujkar, Ashok. "The Word *Is* the World: Nondualism in Indian Philosophy of Language." *Philosophy East and West* 51 (2001): 452–473.

Albert, Karl. *Mystik und Philosophie*. Sankt Augustin: Verlag Hans Richarz, 1986.

Alexander, Elizabeth Shanks. "The Impact of Feminism on Rabbinic Studies: The Impossible Paradox of Reading Women into Rabbinic Literature." *Studies in Contemporary Jewry: An Annual* 16 (2000): 101–118.

Alexander, Phillip S. "Tradition and Originality in the Targum of the Song of Songs." In *The Aramaic Bible: Targums in their Historical Context*, edited by Derek R. G. Beattie and Martin J. McNamara, 318–339. Sheffield: Sheffield Academic Press, 1994.

Alibhai, Mohamed A. "The Transformation of Spiritual Substance into Bodily Substance in Isma'ili Neoplatonism." In *Neoplatonism and Islamic Thought*, edited by Parviz Morewedge, 167–177. Albany: State University of New York Press, 1992.

al-Jerrahi, Sheikh Muzaffer Ozak. *Blessed Virgin Mary*. Translated by Muhtar Holland, foreword, introduction, and afterword by Nur al-Jerrahi. Westport: Pir, 1991.

al-Kalābādhī, Abū Bakr. *The Doctrine of the Ṣūfīs (Kitāb al-Taʿarruf li-madhhab ahl al-taṣawwuf).* Translated by Arthur J. Arberry. Cambridge: Cambridge University Press, 1935.

Allen, Douglas. *Structure and Creativity in Religion: Hermeneutics in Mircea Eliade's Phenomenology and New Directions.* Foreword by Mircea Eliade. The Hague: Mouton, 1978.

Allen, S. P. "Plato, Aristotle and the Concept of Woman in Early Jewish Philosophy." *Florilegium* 9 (1987): 89–111.

Allison, Dale C., Jr. "The Silence of Angels: Reflections on the Songs of the Sabbath Sacrifice." *Revue de Qumran* 13 (1988): 189–197.

Allison, David B. *Reading the New Nietzsche: The Birth of Tragedy, The Gay Science, Thus Spoke Zarathustra, and On the Genealogy of Morals.* Lanham: Rowman & Littlefield, 2001.

Alonso-Fontela, C. "El Targum al Cantar de los Cantares (Edicion Critica)." Ph.D. dissertation, Universidad Complutense de Madrid, 1987.

Alt, Wayne. "There Is No Paradox of Desire in Buddhism." *Philosophy East and West* 30 (1980): 521–530.

Alter, Robert. *Necessary Angels: Tradition and Modernity in Kafka, Benjamin, and Scholem.* Cambridge, Mass.: Harvard University Press, 1991.

Altizer, Thomas J. *Mircea Eliade and the Dialectic of the Sacred.* Westport: Greenwood Press, 1975.

Altmann, Alexander. "God and Self in Jewish Mysticism." *Judaism* 3 (1954): 1–5.

———. *Studies in Religious Philosophy and Mysticism.* Ithaca: Cornell University Press, 1969.

Amado Lévy-Valensi, Eliane. *La Poétique du Zohar.* Preface by Charles Mopsik. Paris: Éditions de l'Éclat, 1996.

Amdor, J. D. H. "Interpretive Unicity: The Drive toward Monological (Monotheistic) Rhetoric." In *The Rhetorical Interpretation of Scripture: Essays from the 1996 Malibu Conference*, edited by Stanley E. Porter and Dennis L. Stamps, 48–62. Sheffield: Sheffield Academic Press, 1999.

Ames Roger T., and David L. Hall. *Focusing the Familiar: A Translation and Philosophical Interpretation of the Zhongyong.* Honolulu: University of Hawaii Press, 2001.

Amoroso, Leonardo. *Lichtung: Leggere Heidegger.* Torino: Rosenberg & Sellier, 1993.

Anderson, Gary A. "The Garments of Skin in Apocryphal Narrative and Biblical Commentary." In *Studies in Ancient Midrash*, edited by James L. Kugel, 101–143. Cambridge, Mass.: Harvard University Press, 2001.

———. *The Genesis of Perfection: Adam and Eve in Jewish and Christian Imagination.* Louisville: Westminster John Knox Press, 2001.

Anderson, John M. "Truth, Process, and Creature in Heidegger's Thought." In *Heidegger and the Quest for Truth*, edited with an introduction by Manfred S. Frings, 28–61. Chicago: Quadrangle Books, 1968.

Anidjar, Gil. *"Our Place in Al-Andalus": Kabbalah, Philosophy, Literature in Arab Jewish Letters.* Stanford: Stanford University Press, 2002.

Ansell-Pearson, Keith. *Viroid Life: Perspectives on Nietzsche and the Transhuman Condition.* London and New York: Routledge, 1997.

———. "Who Is the Übermensch? Time, Truth and Woman in Nietzsche." In *Figures on the Horizon*, edited by Jerrold Seigel, 23–45. Rochester: University of Rochester Press, 1993.

Anton, John P. *Aristotle's Theory of Contrariety.* London: Routledge and Kegan Paul, 1957.

Apel, Karl-Otto. "Wittgenstein and Heidegger: Language Games and Life Forms." In *Critical Heidegger*, edited by Christopher Macann, 241–274. London and New York: Routledge, 1996.

The Apostolic Fathers. Translated by Kirsopp Lake. 2 vols. Cambridge, Mass.: Harvard University Press, 1985.

Aquila, Richard E. "Self as Matter and Form: Some Reflections on Kant's View of the Soul." In *Figuring the Self: Subject, Absolute, and Others in Classical German Philosophy*, edited by David E. Klemm and Günter Zöller, 31–54. Albany: State University of New York Press, 1997.

Archer, Léoni. "The 'Evil Women' in Apocryphal and Pseudepigraphical Writings." In *Proceedings of the Ninth World Congress of Jewish Studies, August 4–12, 1985. Division A: The Period of the Bible*, 239–246. Jerusalem: World Union of Jewish Studies, 1986.

Argall, Randal A. *1 Enoch and Sirach: A Comparative Literary and Conceptual Analysis of the Themes of Revelation, Creation, and Judgment*. Atlanta: Scholars Press, 1995.

Ariel, David S. "'The Eastern Dawn of Wisdom': The Problem of the Relation between Islamic and Jewish Mysticism." In *Approaches to Judaism in Medieval Times*, vol. 2, edited by David R. Blumenthal, 149–167. Chico: Scholars Press, 1985.

Aristotle. *De anima*. Edited with introduction and commentary by David Ross. Oxford: Oxford University Press, 1961.

Aristotle. *Metaphysics*. Translated by Richard Hope, with an analytic index of technical terms. Ann Arbor: University of Michigan Press, 1978.

Arkoun, Mohammed. *The Unthought in Contemporary Islamic Thought*. London: Saqi Books, 2002.

Armour, Ellen T. "Crossing the Boundaries between Deconstruction, Feminism, and Religion." In *Feminist Interpretations of Jacques Derrida*, edited by Nancy J. Holland, 193–214. University Park: Pennsylvania State University Press, 1997.

Armstrong, Elizabeth Psakis. "Womanly Men and Manly Women in Thomas à Kempis and St. Teresa." In *Vox Mystica: Essays on Medieval Mysticism in Honor of Professor Valerie M. Lagorio*, edited by Anne Clark Bartlett, with Thomas H. Bestul, Janet Goebel, and William F. Pollard, 107–115. Cambridge: D. S. Brewer, 1995.

Arnal, William E. "Definition." In *Guide to the Study of Religion*, edited by Willi Braun and Russell T. McCutcheon, 21–34. London and New York: Cassell, 2000.

Arntzenius, Frank, and Tim Maudlin, "Time Travel and Modern Physics." In *Time, Reality & Experience*, edited by Craig Callender, 169–200. Cambridge: Cambridge University Press, 2002.

Asad, Talal. *Genealogies of Religion: Discipline and Reasons of Power in Christianity and Islam*. Baltimore: Johns Hopkins University Press, 1993.

Asani, Ali S. "Bridal Symbolism in Ismaʿili Mystical Literature of Indo-Pakistan." In *Mystics of the Book: Themes, Topics, and Typologies*, edited with an Introduction by Robert A. Herrera, 389–404. New York: Peter Lang, 1993.

Asiedu, F. B. A. "The Song of Songs and the Ascent of the Soul: Ambrose, Augustine, and the Language of Mysticism." *Vigiliae Christianae* 55 (2001): 299–317.

Aspegren, Kerstin. *The Male Woman: A Feminine Ideal in the Early Church*. Edited by René Kieffer. Uppsala: Acta Universitatis Upsaliensis, 1990.

Assis, Yom Tov. "Sexual Behaviour in Medieval Hispano-Jewish Society." In *Jewish History: Essays in Honour of Chimen Abramsky*, edited by Ada Rapoport-Albert and Steven J. Zipperstein, 25–59. London: P. Halban, 1988.

Astell, Ann W. *The Song of Songs in the Middle Ages*. Ithaca: Cornell University Press, 1990.

Aubin, Melissa "'She Is the Beginning of All the Ways of Perversity': Femininity and Metaphor in 4Q184." *Women in Judaism: A Multidisciplinary Journal* 2 (2001): 1–23.

Austin, Ralph W. J. "The Sophianic Feminine in the Work of Ibn ʿArabī and Rumi." In *The Heritage of Sufism: Volume II, The Legacy of Medieval Persian Sufism (1150–1500)*, edited by Leonard Lewisohn, 233–245. Oxford: Oneworld Publication, 1999.

Avens, Robert. *The New Gnosis: Heidegger, Hillman, and Angels*. Dallas: Spring, 1984.

Ayoub, Mahmoud. *The Qur'an and Its Interpreters*. 2 vols. Albany: State University of New York Press, 1984.
Ayoub, Mahmud Mustafa. "Jesus the Son of God: A Study of the Terms *Ibn* and *Walad* in the Qur'an and *Tafsīr* Tradition." In *Christian-Muslim Encounters*, edited by Yvonne Y. Haddad and Wadi Z. Haddad, 65–81. Gainesville: University of Florida Press, 1995.
Bach, Alice. *Women, Seduction, and Betrayal in Biblical Narrative*. Cambridge: Cambridge University Press, 1997.
Bachelard, Gaston. *Air and Dreams: An Essay on the Imagination of Movement*. Translated by E. R. Farrell and C. F. Farrell. Dallas: Dallas Institute of Humanities and Culture, 1988.
Bacher, Wilhelm. "L'exegese biblique dans le Zohar." *Revue des études juives* 22 (1891): 33–46.
———. "Das Merkwort PRDS in der Jüdischen Bibelexegese." *Zeitschrift für die alttestamentliche Wissenschaft* 13 (1893): 294–305.
Bachofen, Johann Jakob. *Das Mutterrecht*. 2 vols. Basel: B. Schwabe, 1948.
Baer, Richard A., Jr. *Philo's Use of the Categories Male and Female*. Leiden: E. J. Brill, 1970.
Baer, Yitzhak. *A History of the Jews in Christian Spain*. Translated by Louis Schoffman. 2 vols. Philadelphia: Jewish Publication Society of America, 1961.
Baeten, Elizabeth M. *The Magic Mirror: Myth's Abiding Power*. Albany: State University of New York Press, 1996.
Bakan, David. *Sigmund Freud and the Jewish Mystical Tradition*. Boston: Beacon Press, 1958.
Baker, Cynthia M. *Rebuilding the House of Israel: Architectures of Gender in Jewish Antiquity*. Stanford: Stanford University Press, 2002.
Baker, Denise Nowakowski. *Julian of Norwich's Showings: From Vision to Book*. Princeton: Princeton University Press, 1994.
Bal, Mieke. "Sexuality, Sin, and Sorrow: The Emergence of the Female Character." In *Women, Gender, Religion: A Reader*, edited by Elizabeth A. Castelli with the assistance of Rosamond C. Rodman, 149–173. New York: Palgrave, 2001.
Baldick, Julian. "The Legend of Rābiʿa of Basra: Christian Antecedents, Muslim Counterparts." *Religion* 20 (1990): 233–247.
Balthasar, Hans Urs von. *Cosmic Liturgy: The Universe according to Maximus the Confessor*. Translated by Brian E. Daley. San Francisco: Ignatius Press, 2003.
———. *Presence and Thought: An Essay on the Religious Philosophy of Gregory of Nyssa*. San Francisco: Ignatius Press, 1995.
Barash, Jeffrey Andrew. *Martin Heidegger and the Problem of Historical Meaning*. Rev. and expanded ed. New York: Fordham University Press, 2003.
Barbaras, Renaud. "Le dédoublement de l'originaire." In *Notes de cours sur* L'origine de la géométrie *de Husserl suivi de recherches sur la phénoménologie de Merleau-Ponty*, edited by Renaud Barbaras, 289–303. Paris: Presses Universitaires de France, 1998.
———. *Le tournant de l'expérience: Recherches sur la philosophie de Merleau-Ponty*. Paris: Librairie Philosophique J. Vrin, 1998.
Barkaï, Ron. *Les infortunes de Dinah: Le livre de la génération: La gynécology juive au moyen âge*. Paris: Les Éditions du Cerf, 1991.
Barker, Margaret. *The Great Angel: A Study of Israel's Second God*. London: SPCK, 1992.
———. *The Great High Priest: The Temple Roots of Christian Liturgy*. London and New York: T & T Clark, 2003.
———. "The High Priest and the Worship of Jesus." In *The Jewish Roots of Christological Monotheism: Papers from the St. Andrews Conference on the Historical Origins of the Worship of Jesus*, edited by Carey C. Newman, James R. Davila, and Gladys S. Lewis, 93–111. Leiden: E. J. Brill, 1999.

Barlas, Asma. *"Believing Women" in Islam: Unreading Patriarchal Interpretations of the Qur'an*. Austin: University of Texas, 2002.

Barnes, Jonathan. *The Presocratic Philosophers*. 2 vols. London and Boston: Routledge and Paul, 1979.

Barnes, Nancy J. "Women and Buddhism in India." In *Women in Indian Religions*, edited by Arvind Sharma, 38–69. Oxford and New York: Oxford University Press, 2002.

Barnstone, Willis. *The Poetics of Translation: History, Theory, Practice*. New Haven and London: Yale University Press, 1993.

Baron-Cohen, Simon. *The Truth about the Male and Female Brain: The Essential Difference*. New York: Basic Books, 2003.

Barr, James. *The Garden of Eden and the Hope of Immortality*. Minneapolis: Fortress Press, 1993.

Barral, Mary Rose. *The Body in Interpersonal Relations: Merleau-Ponty*. Lanham: University Press of America, 1984.

Barry, Kiren. *The Greek Qabalah: Alphabetic Mysticism and Numerology in the Ancient World*. York Beach: Samuel Weiser, 1999.

Barstad, Joel Irving. "Body, Soul, and Image: Gregory of Nyssa's Influence on Eriugena." Ph.D. dissertation, University of Notre Dame, 1997.

Barth, Markus, and Helmut Blanke, *Colossians: A New Translation with Introduction and Commentary*. Translated by Astrid B. Beck. New York: Doubleday, 1994.

Barthes, Roland. *Image—Music—Text*. Selected and translated by Stephen Heath. New York: Hill and Wang, 1999.

———. *The Pleasure of the Text*. Translated by Richard Miller. New York: Hill and Wang, 1975.

Barzilai, Shuli. *Lacan and the Matter of Origins*. Stanford: Stanford University Press, 1999.

Baskin, Judith R. "Jewish Women in the Middle Ages." In *Jewish Women in Historical Perspective*, edited by Judith R. Baskin, 94–114. Detroit: Wayne State University Press, 1991.

———. *Midrashic Women: Formations of the Feminine in Rabbinic Literature*. Hanover and London: University Press of New England, 2002.

Bass, Alan. *Difference and Disavowal: The Trauma of Eros*. Stanford: Stanford University Press, 2000.

Bataille, Georges. *Death and Sensuality: A Study of Eroticism and the Taboo*. New York: Walker, 1962.

Batnitzky, Leora. *Idolatry and Representation: The Philosophy of Franz Rosenzweig Reconsidered*. Princeton: Princeton University Press, 2000.

Batterman, Michael. "Bread of Affliction, Emblem of Power: The Passover Matzah in Haggadah Manuscripts from Christian Spain." In *Imagining the Self, Imagining the Other: Visual Representation and Jewish-Christian Dynamics in the Middle Ages and Early Modern Period*, edited by Eva Frojmovic, 53–89. Leiden: Brill, 2002.

Bauckham, Richard. "The Throne of God and the Worship of Jesus." In *The Jewish Roots of Christological Monotheism: Papers from the St. Andrews Conference on the Historical Origins of the Worship of Jesus*, edited by Carey C. Newman, James R. Davila, and Gladys S. Lewis, 43–69. Leiden: E. J. Brill, 1999.

Bauerschmidt, Frederick Christian. *Julian of Norwich and the Mystical Body Politic of Christ*. Notre Dame and London: University of Notre Dame Press, 1999.

Baum, Wolfgang. *Gnostische Elemente im Denken Martin Heideggers? Eine Studie auf der Grundlage der Religionsphilosophie von Hans Jonas*. Neuried: Ars Una, 1997.

Baumgarten, Joseph. "4Q502, Marriage or Golden Age Ritual?" *Journal of Jewish Studies* 43 (1983): 125–136.

———. "The Cave 4 Versions of the Qumran Penal Code." *Journal of Jewish Studies* 53 (1993): 268–276.
———. "Celibacy." In *Encyclopedia of Dead Sea Scrolls*, vol. 1, edited Lawrence H. Schiffman and James C. Vanderkam, 122–125. Oxford: Oxford University Press, 2000.
———. "On the Testimony of Women in 1Qsa." *Journal of Biblical Literature* 43 (1983): 125–136.
———. "The Qumran-Essene Restraints on Marriage." In *Archaeology and History in the Dead Sea Scrolls: The New York University Conference in Memory of Yigael Yadin*, edited by Lawrence H. Schiffman, 13–24. Sheffield: JSOT Press, 1990.
Bauschke, Martin. *Jesus im Koran*. Cologne: Böhlau, 2001.
Bayer, Thora Ilin. *Cassirer's Metaphysics of Symbolic Forms: A Philosophical Commentary*. Introductory essay by Donald Phillip Verene. New Haven and London: Yale University Press, 2001.
Beach, Edward A. *The Potencies of God(s): Schelling's Philosophy of Mythology*. Albany: State University of New York Press, 1994.
Beach, Eleanor Ferris. "Transforming Goddess Iconography in Hebrew Narrative." In *Women and Goddess Traditions in Antiquity and Today*, edited by Karen L. King, 239–263. Minneapolis: Fortress Press, 1997.
Beal, Timothy K. "Opening: Cracking the Binding." In *Reading Bibles, Writing Bodies: Identity and the Book*, edited by Timothy K. Beal and David M. Gunn, 1–12. London and New York: Routledge, 1997.
Beattie, Derek R. G., and Martin J. McNamara, eds. *The Aramaic Bible: Targums in Their Historical Context*. Sheffield: Sheffield Academic Press, 1994.
Beauvoir, Simone de. *The Second Sex*. Translated by Howard M. Parshley. New York: Vintage Books, 1989.
Beckwith, Sarah. *Christ's Body: Identity, Culture, and Society in Late Medieval Writings*. London and New York: Routledge, 1993.
Beistegui, Miguel de. *Heidegger and the Political: Dystopias, Thinking the Political*. London and New York: Routledge, 1998.
Beitchman, Philip. *Alchemy of the Word: Cabala of the Renaissance*. Albany: State University of New York Press, 1998.
Bell, John L. "Hermann Weyl on Intuition and the Continuum." *Philosophia Mathematica* 3 (2000): 1–13.
Bell, Susan G. "Medieval Women Book Owners: Arbiters of Lay Piety and Ambassadors of Culture." *Signs: Journal of Women in Culture and Society* 7 (1982): 742–768.
Beller, Mara. "Kant's Impact on Einstein's Thought." In *Einstein: The Formative Years, 1879–1909*, edited by Don Howard and John Stachel, 83–106. Boston: Birkhäuser, 2000.
Ben-Arzi, Hagi. "Asceticism in Sefer Ḥasidim." *Daʿat* 11 (1983): 39–45 (Hebrew).
Benayahu, Meir. *The Toledoth ha-Ari and Luria's "Manner of Life" (Hanhagoth)*. Jerusalem: Ben Zvi Institute, 1967 (Hebrew).
Benin, Stephen D. *The Footprints of God: Divine Accommodation in Jewish and Christian Thought*. Albany: State University of New York Press, 1993.
Benjamin, Walter. *The Correspondence of Walter Benjamin 1910–1940*. Edited and annotated by Gershom Scholem and Theodor W. Adorno, translated by Manfred R. Jacobson and Evelyn M. Jacobson. Chicago and London: University of Chicago Press, 1994.
———. *Illuminations*. Edited and with an introduction by Hannah Arendt, translated by Harry Zohn. New York: Schocken Books, 1969.
———. *The Origin of German Tragic Drama*. Translated by John Osborne, with an introduction by George Steiner. London and New York: Verso, 1998.

———. *Reflections: Essays, Aphorisms, Autobiographical Writings*. Edited and with an introduction by Peter Demetz, translated by Edmund Jephcott. New York: Schocken Books, 1986.

———. *Selected Writings, Volume 1: 1913–1926*. Edited by Marcus Bullock and Michael W. Jennings. Cambridge, Mass., and London: Harvard University Press, 1996.

———. *Selected Writings, Volume 2: 1927–1934*. Edited by Michael W. Jennings, Howard Eiland, and Gary Smith. Cambridge, Mass., and London: Harvard University Press, 1999.

Ben-Naeh, Yaron. "'A Tried and Tested Spell': Magic Beliefs and Acts among Ottoman Jews." *Peʿamim* 85 (2000): 89–111 (Hebrew).

Bennington, Geoffrey. *Interrupting Derrida*. London and New York: Routledge, 2000.

Benor, Ehud. *Worship of the Heart: A Study of Maimonides' Philosophy of Religion*. Albany: State University of New York Press, 1995.

Ben-Shlomo, Joseph. *The Mystical Theology of Moses Cordovero*. Jerusalem: Bialik Institute, 1965 (Hebrew).

Benstock, Shari. *Textualizing the Feminine: On the Limits of Genre*. Norman and London: University of Oklahoma Press, 1991.

Benz, Ernst. "Color in Christian Visionary Experience." In *Color Symbolism: Six Excerpts from the Eranos Yearbook 1972*, 95–101. Dallas: Spring, 1977.

———. *The Mystical Sources of German Romantic Philosophy*. Translated by Balir R. Reynolds and Eunice M. Paul. Allison Park: Pickwick Publications, 1983.

Berdyaev, Nicolas. "Unground and Freedom." In Jacob Böhme, *Six Theosophic Points and Other Writings*, v–xxxvii. Ann Arbor: University of Michigan Press, 1958.

Berger, Anne-Emmanuelle. "The Newly Veiled Woman: Irigaray, Specularity, and the Islamic Veil." *Diacritics* 28 (1993): 93–119.

Berger, David. *The Jewish-Christian Debate in the High Middle Ages: A Critical Edition of the Nizzaḥon Vetus*. Philadelphia: Jewish Publication Society of America, 1979.

Berger, Pamela C. *The Goddess Obscured: Transformation of the Grain Protectress from Goddess to Saint*. Boston: Beacon Press, 1985.

Bergoffen, Debra B. "Nietzsche's Madman: Perspectivism without Nihilism." In *Nietzsche as Postmodernist: Essays Pro and Contra*, edited and with an introduction by Clayton Koelb, 57–71. Albany: State University of New York, 1990.

———. "Queering the Phallus." In *Disseminating Lacan*, edited by David Pettigrew and François Raffoul, 273–291. Albany: State University of New York Press, 1996.

Bermes, Christian. "Wittgensteins Phänomenologie. Phänomenologie als Motiv und Motivation Wittgensteinscher Philosophie." *Phänomenologische Forschungen*, new series 1 (1996): 5–21.

Bernard of Clairvaux. *On the Song of Songs I*. Translated by Kilian Walsh, introduction by M. Corneille Halflants. Kalamazoo: Cistercian, 1977.

———. *On the Song of Songs II*. Translated by Kilian Walsh, introduction by Jean Leclercq. Kalamazoo: Cistercian, 1983.

———. *On the Song of Songs III*. Translated by Kilian Walsh and Irene M. Edmonds, introduction by Emero Stiegman. Kalamazoo: Cistercian, 1979.

———. *On the Song of Songs IV*. Translated by Irene Edmonds, introduction by Jean Leclercq. Kalamazoo: Cistercian, 1980.

Bernasconi, Robert. *Heidegger in Question: The Art of Existing*. Atlantic Highlands: Humanities Press, 1993.

———. *The Question of Language in Heidegger's History of Being*. Atlantic Highlands: Humanities Press, 1985.

———. "The Transformation of Language at Another Beginning." *Research in Phenomenology* 13 (1983): 1–23.

Bernet, Rudolf. "Le sujet dans la nature: Réflexions sur la phénoménologie de la perception chez Merleau-Ponty." In *Merleau-Ponty: Phénoménologie et expériences*, edited by Marc Richir and Etienne Tassin, 57–77. Grenoble: Éditions Jérôme Millon, 1992.

Bernstein, Simon. *New Poems and Poets from the Byzantine Period*. Jerusalem: Darom, 1941 (Hebrew).

Berquist, Jon L. *Controlling Corporeality: The Body and the Household in Ancient Israel*. New Brunswick: Rutgers University Press, 2002.

Besançon, Alain. *The Forbidden Image: An Intellectual History of Iconoclasm*. Translated by Jane Marie Todd. Chicago and London: University of Chicago Press, 2000.

Betti, Emilio. "Hermeneutics as the General Methodology of the *Geisteswissenschaften*." In *The Hermeneutic Tradition: From Ast to Ricoeur*, edited by Gayle L. Ormiston and Alan D. Schrift, 159–197. Albany: State University of New York Press, 1990.

Beumer, Johannes. "Die marianische Deutung des Hohen Liedes in der Frühscholastik." *Zeitschrift für katholische Theologie* 76 (1954): 411–439.

Biale, David. *Eros and the Jews: From Biblical Israel to Contemporary America*. New York: Basic Books, 1992.

———. *Gershom Scholem: Kabbalah and Counter-History*. Cambridge, Mass., and London: Harvard University Press, 1979.

———. "Gershom Scholem's Ten Unhistorical Aphorisms on Kabbalah." In *Gershom Scholem*, edited and with an introduction by Harold Bloom, 99–123. New York: Chelsea, 1987.

Biale, Rachel. *Women and Jewish Law: An Exploration of Women's Issues in Halakhic Sources*. New York: Schocken Books, 1984.

Bianchi, Massimo L. "The Visible and the Invisible: From Alchemy to Paracelsus." In *Alchemy and Chemistry in the 16th and 17th Centuries*, edited by Piyo Rattansi and Antonio Clericuzio. Dordrecht: Kluwer Academic, 1994.

Biemel, Walter. "Marginal Notes on Sallis's Peculiar Interpretation of Heidegger's 'Vom Wesen der Wahrheit.'" In *The Path of Archaic Thinking: Unfolding the Work of John Sallis*, edited by Kenneth Maly, 221–239. Albany: State University of New York Press, 1995.

———. "Poetry and Language in Heidegger." In *On Heidegger and Language*, edited by Joseph J. Kockelmans, 65–105. Evanston: Northwestern University Press, 1972.

Bieringer, Reimund, Didier Pollefeyt, and Frederique Vandecasteele-Vanneuville, eds. *Against Judaism and the Fourth Gospel*. Louisville: Westminster John Knox Press, 2001.

Bingen, Hildegard of. *Symphonia: A Critical Edition of the Symphonia Armonie Celestium Revelationum [Symphony of the Harmony of Celestial Revelations]*. Translated by Barbara Newman. 2nd ed. Ithaca and London: Cornell University Press, 1998.

Binns, John. *Ascetics and Ambassadors of Christ: The Monasteries of Palestine, 314–631*. Oxford: Oxford University Press, 1994.

Bird, Phyllis. "Images of Women in the Old Testament." In *Religion and Sexism: Images of Woman in the Jewish and Christian Traditions*. Edited by Rosemary R. Ruether. New York: Simon and Schuster, 1974.

———. "Sexual Differentiation and Divine Image in the Genesis Creation Texts." In *Image of God and Gender Models in Judaeo-Christian Tradition*, edited by Kari Elisabeth Børresen, 11–34. Oslo: Solum Forlag, 1991.

Blake, William. *The Complete Poetry and Prose of William Blake*. Edited by David V. Erdman, commentary by Harold Bloom. Rev. ed. Berkeley: University of California Press, 1982.

Blanchot, Maurice. *The infinite Conversation*. Translated by Susan Hanson. Minneapolis: University of Minnesota Press, 1993.

———. *The Space of Literature*. Translated with an introduction by Ann Smock. Lincoln and London: University of Nebraska Press, 1982.

Bland, Kalman P. "Antisemitism and Aniconism: The Germanophone Requiem for Jewish Visual Art." In *Jewish Identity and Modern Art History*, edited by Catherine M. Soussloff, 41–66. Berkeley: University of California Press, 1999.

———. *The Artless Jew: Medieval and Modern Affirmations and Denials of the Visual*. Princeton: Princeton University Press, 2000.

Blattner, William D. *Heidegger's Temporal Idealism*. Cambridge: Cambridge University Press, 1999.

Blau, Ludwig. *Das altjüdische Zauberwesen*. Strassburg: Karl J. Trübner, 1898.

Bleeker, Class J. *The Rainbow: A Collection of Studies in the Science of Religion*. Leiden: E. J. Brill, 1975.

———. *The Sacred Bridge: Researches into the Nature and Structure of Religion*. Leiden: E. J. Brill, 1963.

Blenkinsopp, Joseph. "The Social Context of the 'Outsider Woman' in Proverbs 1–9." *Biblica* 72 (1991): 457–473.

Blickstein, Shlomo. "Between Philosophy and Mysticism: A Study of the Philosophical-Qabbalistic Writings of Joseph Giqatila (1248–c. 1322)." Ph.D. dissertation, Jewish Theological Seminary of America, 1983.

Bloch, Ernst. *The Principle of Hope*. Translated by Neville Plaice, Stephen Plaice, and Paul Knight. 3 vols. Cambridge, Mass.: MIT Press, 1986.

Bloch, Howard. "Medieval Misogyny." In *Continuity and Change: Political Institutions and Literary Movements in the Middle Ages: A Symposium*, edited by Elizabeth Vestergaard, 87–117. Odense: Odense University Press, 1986.

Bloechl, Jeffrey. *Religious Experience and the End of Metaphysics*. Bloomington: Indiana University Press, 2003.

Bloom, Harold. *Kabbalah and Criticism*. New York: Seabury Press, 1975.

———. "Lying against Time: Gnosis, Poetry, Criticism." In *The School of Valentinus*, edited by Bentley Layton, 57–72. Vol. 1 of *The Rediscovery of Gnosticism: Proceedings of the International Conference on Gnosticism at Yale, New Haven, Connecticut, March 28–31, 1978*. Leiden: E. J. Brill, 1980.

———. *Poetry and Repression: Revisionism from Blake to Stevens*. New Haven and London: Yale University Press, 1976.

Blondel, Eric. *Nietzsche, the Body and Culture: Philosophy as a Philological Genealogy*. Translated by Seán Hand. Stanford: Stanford University Press, 1991.

Blum, Virginia, and Heidi Nast. "Jacques Lacan's Two-Dimensional Subjectivity." In *Thinking Space*, edited by Mike Crang and Nigel Thrift, 183–204. London and New York: Routledge, 2000.

Blumenthal, David R., ed. *The Philosophic Questions and Answers of Ḥoter Ben Shelomo*. Leiden: E. J. Brill, 1981.

Blumenthal, Henry J. "Plotinus' Adaptation of Aristotle's Psychology." In *The Significance of Neoplatonism*, edited by R. Baine Harris, 41–58. Norfolk: Old Dominion University, 1976.

Bock, Darrell L. *Blasphemy and Exaltation in Judaism and the Final Examination of Jesus*. Tübingen: Mohr Siebeck, 1998.

Bockmuehl, Markus N. A. *Revelation and Mystery in Ancient Judaism and Pauline Christianity*. Tübingen: J. C. B. Mohr, 1990.

Boeder, Heribert. *Seditions: Heidegger and the Limit of Modernity.* Translated, edited, and with an introduction by Marcus Brainard. Albany: State University of New York Press, 1997.

Boehm, Rudolf. "La phénoménologie de l'histoire." *Revue internationale de philosophie* 71–72 (1965): 55–73.

Boer, Karin de. *Thinking in the Light of Time: Heidegger's Encounter with Hegel.* Albany: State University of New York Press, 2000.

Böhlig, Alexander. "Triade und Trinität in den Schriften von Nag Hammadi." In *The Rediscovery of Gnosticism: Proceedings of the International Conference on Gnosticism at Yale, New Haven, Connecticut, March 28–31, 1978*, vol. 2, edited by Bentley Layton, 617–634. Leiden: E. J. Brill, 1981.

Böhme, Jacob. *The Aurora.* Translated by John Sparrow. London: John M. Watkins, 1960.

———. *Mysterium Magnum, or An Exposition of the First Book of Moses called Genesis.* Translated by John Sparrow. 2 vols. London: John M. Watkins, 1924.

———. *Sämtliche Schriften.* Vol. 7. Edited by Will-Erich Peuckert. Stuttgart: Friedrich Frommann, 1958.

———. *The Signature of All Things and Other Writings.* Cambridge and London: James Clarke, 1969.

———. *Six Theosophic Points and Other Writings.* Ann Arbor: University of Michigan Press, 1958.

Bond, Hugh L. "The Changing Face of Posse: Another Look at Nicholas Cusanus' *De apice theoriae* (1464)." In *Nicholas of Cusa: A Medieval Thinker for the Modern Age*, edited by Kazuhiko Yamaki, 35–46. Richmond: Curzon Press, 2002.

———. "The 'Icon' and the 'Iconic Text' in Nicholas of Cusa's *De visione Dei* I–XVII." In *Nicholas of Cusa and His Age: Intellect and Spirituality: Essays Dedicated to the Memory of F. Edward Cranz, Thomas P. McTighe and Charles Trinkaus*, edited by Thomas M. Izbicki and Christopher M. Bellitto, 177–197. Leiden: Brill, 2002.

Bono, James J. *Ficino to Descartes.* Vol. 1 of *The Word of God and the Languages of Man: Interpreting Nature in Early Modern Science and Medicine.* Madison: University of Wisconsin Press, 1995.

Bontekoe, Ronald. *Dimensions of the Hermeneutic Circle.* Atlantic Highlands: Humanities Press International, 1996.

Boothby, Richard. *Death and Desire: Psychoanalytic Theory in Lacan's Return to Freud.* New York and London: Routledge, 1991.

———. "Lacanian Castration: Body-Image and Signification in Psychoanalysis." In *Crises in Continental Philosophy*, edited by Arleen B. Dallery and Charles E. Scott, 215–234. Albany: State University of New York Press, 1990.

Borgen, Peder. *Bread from Heaven: An Exegetical Study of the Concept of Manna in the Gospel of John and the Writings of Philo.* Leiden: E. J. Brill, 1981.

———. *Philo, John and Paul: New Perspectives on Judaism and Early Christianity.* Atlanta: Scholars Press, 1987.

Borges, Jorge Luis. *Seven Nights.* Translated by Eliot Weinberger, introduction by Alastair Reid. New York: New Directions, 1984.

Borradori, Giovanna. *Recoding Metaphysics: The New Italian Philosophy.* Evanston: Northwestern University Press, 1988.

Børresen, Kari Elisabeth. "God's Image, Man's Image? Patristic Interpretation of Gen. 1:27 and I Cor. 11:7." In *Image of God and Gender Models in Judaeo-Christian Tradition*, edited by Kari Elisabeth Børresen, 188–207. Oslo: Solum Forlag, 1991.

Bos, Gerrit, and Eric Pellow, "*Maʾamar Rabbi Barzillai*: A Commentary on the Ten *Sefirot* by Rabbi Barzillai of Gerona." *Sefunot* 22 (1999): 367–377 (Hebrew).

Botet, Serge. *Langue, langage, et stratégies linguistiques chez Heidegger.* Bern: Peter Lang, 1997.

Bouhdiba, Abdelwahab. *Sexuality in Islam.* Translated by Alan Sheridan. London: Saqi Books, 1998.

Bourdieu, Pierre. *Masculine Domination.* Translated by Richard Nice. Stanford: Stanford University Press, 2001.

———. *The Political Ontology of Martin Heidegger.* Translated by Peter Collier. Stanford: Stanford University Press, 1991.

Bouretz, Pierre. "Gershom Scholem und das Schreiben der Geschichte." In *Gershom Scholem: Literatur und Rhetorik*, edited by Stéphane Mosès and Sigrid Weigel, 93–129. Cologne: Böhlau, 2000.

Bouveresse, Jacques. *Dire et ne rien dire: L'illogisme, l'impossibilité et le non-sens.* Nîmes: Éditions Jacqueline Chambon, 1997.

———. *Wittgenstein: La rime et la raison. Science, éthique et esthétique.* Paris: Éditions de Minuit, 1973.

Bouvet, Danielle. "Metaphors of the Body in Gestural Languages." *Diogenes* 175 (1996): 27–39.

Böwering, Gerhard. "Ideas of Time in Persian Sufism." In *Classical Persian Sufism from its Origins to Rumi (700–1300)*, edited by Leonard Lewisohn, 199–233. Vol. 1 of *The Heritage of Sufism.* Oxford: One World, 1999.

Bowie, Andrew. *From Romanticism to Critical Theory: The Philosophy of German Literary Theory.* London and New York: Routledge, 1997.

———. *Schelling and Modern European Philosophy: An Introduction.* London and New York: Routledge, 1993.

Bowker, John. *The Targums and Rabbinic Literature: An Introduction to Jewish Interpretations of Scripture.* Cambridge: Cambridge University Press, 1969.

Boyarin, Daniel. *Carnal Israel: Reading Sex in Talmudic Culture.* Berkeley: University of California Press, 1993.

———. *Dying for God: Martyrdom and the Making of Christianity and Judaism.* Stanford: Stanford University Press, 1999.

———. "The Gospel of the *Memra*: Jewish Binitarianism and the Prologue to John." *Harvard Theological Review* 94 (2001): 243–284.

———. "'An Imaginary and Desirable Converse': Moses and Monotheism as Family Romance." In *Reading Bibles, Writing Bodies: Identity and the Book*, edited by Timothy K. Beal and David M. Gunn, 184–204. London and New York: Routledge, 1997.

———. *Intertextuality and the Reading of Midrash.* Indiana Studies in Biblical Literature. Bloomington: Indiana University Press, 1990.

———. *A Radical Jew: Paul and the Politics of Identity.* Berkeley: University of California Press, 1994.

———. "Two Introductions to the Midrash on the *Song of Songs.*" *Tarbiz* 56 (1987): 479–500 (Hebrew).

———. *Unheroic Conduct: The Rise of Heterosexuality and the Invention of the Jewish Man.* Berkeley: University of California Press, 1997.

———. "Women's Bodies and the Rise of the Rabbis: The Case of Sotah." *Studies in Contemporary Jewry: An Annual* 16 (2000): 88–100.

Bozarth-Campbell, Alla. *The Word's Body: An Incarnational Aesthetic of Interpretation.* Tuscaloosa: University of Alabama Press, 1979.

Bradford, Richard. *Roman Jakobson: Life, Language, Art.* London and New York: Routledge, 1994.

Braidotti, Rosi. "Body-Images and the Pornography of Representation." In *Knowing the Difference: Feminist Perspectives in Epistemology,* edited by Kathleen Lennon and Margaret Whitford, 17–30. London and New York: Routledge, 1994.

Braunstein, Néstor. "Desire and Jouissance in the Teachings of Lacan." In *The Cambridge Companion to Lacan,* edited by Jean-Michel Rabaté, 102–115. Cambridge: Cambridge University Press, 2003.

Breazeale, Daniel. "Circles and Grounds in the Jena Wissenschaftslehre." In *Fichte: Historical Contexts/Contemporary Controversies,* edited by Daniel Breazeale and Tom Rockmore, 43–70. Atlantic Highlands: Humanities Press, 1994.

Brenk, Frederick E. "Darkly beyond the Glass: Middle Platonism and the Vision of the Soul." In *Platonism in Late Antiquity,* edited by Stephen Gersh and Charles Kannengiesser, 39–60. Notre Dame: University of Notre Dame Press, 1992.

Brennan, Teresa, and Martin Jay, eds. *Vision in Context: Historical and Contemporary Perspectives on Sight.* New York and London: Routledge, 1996.

Brenner, Athalya. "The Hebrew God and His Female Complements." In *Reading Bibles, Writing Bodies: Identity and the Book, Biblical Limits,* edited by Timothy K. Beal and D. M. Gunn, 56–71. London and New York: Routledge, 1997.

———. *The Intercourse of Knowledge: On Gendering Desire and "Sexuality" in the Hebrew Bible.* Leiden: E. J. Brill, 1997.

Breyfogle, Todd. "Magic, Women, and Heresy in the Late Empire: The Case of the Priscillianists." In *Ancient Magic and Ritual Power,* edited by Marvin Meyer and Paul Mirecki, 435–454. Leiden: E. J. Brill, 1995.

Brient, Elizabeth. "Meister Eckhart and Nicholas of Cusa on the 'Where' of God." In *Nicholas of Cusa and His Age: Intellect and Spirituality: Essays Dedicated to the Memory of F. Edward Cranz, Thomas P. McTighe and Charles Trinkaus,* edited by Thomas M. Izbicki and Christopher M. Bellitto, 127–150. Leiden: Brill, 2002.

Brisson, Luc. *Le même et l'autre dans la structure ontologique du Timée de Platon: Un commentaire systématique du Timée de Platon.* Sankt Augustin: Academia, 1994.

———. "Neutrum utrumque: La bisexualité dans l'antiquité gréco-romaine." In *L'androgyne,* 27–61. Paris: Éditions Albin Michel, 1986.

Brivic, Sheldon. *The Veil of Signs: Joyce, Lacan, and Perception.* Urbana and Chicago: University of Illinois Press, 1991.

Broda, Martine. "Traduit du silence: Les langues de Paul Celan." *Poetik der Transformation: Paul Celan—Übersetzer und übersetzt,* edited by Alfred Bodenheimer and Shimon Sandbank, 139–143. Tübingen: Max Niemeyer, 1999.

Brody, Donna. "Levinas and Lacan: Facing the Real." In *Levinas and Lacan: The Missed Encounter,* edited by Sarah Harasym, 56–78. Albany: State University of New York Press, 1998.

Brody, Seth L. "Human Hands Dwell in Heavenly Heights: Contemplative Ascent and Theurgic Power in Thirteenth Century Kabbalah." In *Mystics of the Book: Themes, Topics and Typologies,* edited by Robert A. Herrera, 123–158. New York: Peter Lang, 1993.

———. "Human Hands Dwell in Heavenly Heights: Worship and Mystical Experience in Thirteenth-Century Kabbalah." Ph.D. dissertation, University of Pennsylvania, 1991.

Brooks, Douglas R. *Auspicious Wisdom: The Texts and Traditions of Śrīvidyā Śākta Tantrism in South India.* Albany: State University of New York Press, 1992.

———. *The Secret of the Three Cities: An Introduction to Hindu Śākta Tantrism.* Chicago: University of Chicago Press, 1990.

Brooten, Bernadette J. *Love between Women: Early Christian Responses to Female Homoeroticism*. Chicago: University of Chicago Press, 1996.

———. "Paul's Views on the Nature of Women and Female Homoeroticism." In *Immaculate and Powerful: The Female in Sacred Image and Social Reality*, edited by Clarissa W. Atkinson, Constance H. Buchanan, and Margaret R. Miles, 61–87. Boston: Beacon Press, 1985.

Broshi, Magen. "Anti-Qumranic Polemics in the Talmud." In *The Madrid Qumran Congress: Proceedings of the International Congress on the Dead Sea Scrolls, Madrid, 18–21 March, 1991*, edited by Julio Trebolle Barrera and Luis Vegas Montaner, 589–600. Leiden: E. J. Brill, 1992.

Broughton, Jeffrey L. *The Bodhidharma Anthology: The Earliest Records of Zen*. Berkeley: University of California Press, 1999.

Brown, Norman O. *Apocalypse and/or Metamorphosis*. Berkeley: University of California Press, 1991.

Brown, Peter Robert Lamont. "Arbiters of Ambiguity: A Role of the Late Antique Holy Man." *Cassiodorus: Rivista di studi sulla tarda antichità* 2 (1996): 123–142.

———. *Authority and the Sacred: Aspects of the Christianisation of the Roman World*. Cambridge: Cambridge University Press, 1995.

———. *The Body and Society: Men, Women, and Sexual Renunciation in Early Christianity*. New York: Columbia University Press, 1988.

———. "The Rise and Function of the Holy Man in Late Antiquity, 1971–1997." *Journal of Early Christian Studies* 6 (1998): 353–376.

Brown, Robert F. *The Later Philosophy of Schelling: The Influence of Böhme on the Works of 1809–15*. Lewisburg: University of Pennsylvania Press, 1990.

Brückmann, J., and J. Couchman. "Du 'Cantique des Cantiques' aux 'Carmina Burana': Amour sacré et amour érotique." In *L'érotisme au Moyen Âge: Études présentées au troisième colloque de l'Institut d'Études Médiévales*, edited by Bruno Roy, 35–50. Montreal: Aurore, 1977.

Bruckstein, Almut Sh. *Die Maske des Moses: Studien zur jüdischen Hermeneutik*. Berlin: Philo, 2001.

Brumbaugh, Robert S. *Unreality and Time*. Albany: State University of New York Press, 1984.

Brumlik, Micha. *Deutscher Geist und Judenhaß: Das Verhältnis des philosophischen Idealismus zum Judentum*. Munich: Luchterhand, 2000.

Bruns, Gerald L. *Heidegger's Estrangements: Language, Truth, and Poetry in the Later Writings*. New Haven and London: Yale University Press, 1989.

———. *Maurice Blanchot: The Refusal of Philosophy*. Baltimore and London: Johns Hopkins University Press, 1997.

———. "The Remembrance of Language: An Introduction to Gadamer's Poetics." In *Gadamer on Celan: "Who Am I and Who Are You? and Other Essays*, Hans-Georg Gadamer, 1–51. Translated and edited by Richard Heinemann and Bruce Krajewski. Albany: State University of New York Press, 1997.

Bruzina, Ronald. "The Aporia of Time-Analysis—Reflection across the Transcendental Divide." In *Phenomenology: Japanese and American Perspectives*, 105–132. Edited by Burt C. Hopkins. Dordrecht: Kluwer Academic, 1999.

Bryson, Norman. "Semiology and Visual Interpretation." In *Visual Theory: Painting and Interpretation*, edited by Norman Bryson, Michael Ann Holly, and Keith Moxey, 61–73. New York: HarperCollins Publishers, 1991.

Buber, Martin. *Ecstatic Confessions*. Edited by Paul Mendes-Flohr, translated by Esther Cameron. San Francisco: Harper & Row, 1985.

Bucher, Stefan. *Zwischen Phänomenologie und Sprachwissenschaft: Zu Merleau-Pontys Theorie der Sprache*. Münster: Nodus, 1991.

Buchler, Justus. *Nature and Judgment*. New York and London: Columbia University Press, 1955.

Buckley, Jorunn J. "An Interpretation of Logion 114 in *The Gospel of Thomas*." *Novum Testamentum* 27 (1985): 245–272.

Bucknell, Roderick S. and Martin Stuart-Fox, *The Twilight Language: Explorations in Buddhist Meditation and Symbolism*. Surrey: Curzon Press, 1993.

Bull, Graham E. "A Re-Interpretation of a Male Initiation Ritual: Back to Freud via Lacan." *Journal of European Psychoanalysis* 3–4 (1996–1997): 83–104.

Burckhardt, Titus. *Alchemy: Science of the Cosmos, Science of the Soul*. Translated by William Stoddart. London: Stuart & Watkins, 1967.

Burgard, Peter J. "Introduction: Figures of Excess." In *Nietzsche and the Feminine*, edited by Peter J. Burgard, 1–32. Charlottesville and London: University Press of Virginia, 1994.

Bürgel, Johann Christoph. "Love, Lust, and Longing: Eroticism in Early Islam as Reflected in Literary Sources." In *Society and the Sexes in Medieval Islam*, edited by Afaf Al-Sayyid-Marsot, 81–117. Malibu: Undena Publications, 1979.

———. "'Symbols and Hints:' Some Considerations Concerning the Meaning of Ibn Ṭufayl's *Ḥayy ibn Yaqẓān*." In *The World of Ibn Ṭufayl: Interdisciplinary Perspectives on Ḥayy ibn Yaqẓān*, edited by Lawrence I. Conrad, 114–132. Leiden: E. J. Brill, 1996.

Burke, Kenneth. *The Rhetoric of Religion: Studies in Logology*. Berkeley: University of California Press, 1970.

Burke, Patrick. "The Flesh as *Urpräsentierbarkeit* in the Interrogative: The Absence of a Question in Derrida." In *Écart & Différance: Merleau-Ponty and Derrida on Seeing and Writing*, edited by Martin C. Dillon, 60–70. Atlantic Highlands: Humanities Press, 1997.

Burrus, Virginia. *"Begotten, Not Made": Conceiving Manhood in Late Antiquity*. Stanford: Stanford University Press, 2000.

———. "The Heretical Woman as Symbol in Alexander, Athanasius, Epiphanius, and Jerome." *Harvard Theological Review* 84 (1991): 229–248.

———. *The Making of a Heretic: Gender, Authority, and the Priscillianist Controversy*. Berkeley: University of California Press, 1995.

———. *The Sex Lives of Saints: An Erotics of Ancient Hagiography*. Philadephia: University of Pennsylvania Press, 2004.

———. "Word and Flesh: The Bodies and Sexuality of Ascetic Women in Christian Antiquity." *Journal of Feminist Studies in Religion* 10 (1994): 27–51.

Burwick, Frederick. "Reflections in the Mirror: Wordsworth." In *Reflecting Senses: Perception and Appearance in Literature, Culture, and the Arts*, edited by Walter Page and Frederick Burwick, 122–140. Berlin and New York: Walter de Gruyter, 1995.

Bussanich, John. "Plotinus's Metaphysics of the One." In *The Cambridge Companion to Plotinus*, edited by Lloyd P. Gerson, 38–65. Cambridge: Cambridge University Press, 1996.

Busse, Heribert. *Islam, Judaism and Christianity: The Theological and Historical Affilliations*. Princeton: Markus Wiener, 1998.

Butler, Judith. *Bodies That Matter: On the Discursive Limits of "Sex."* New York: Routledge, 1993.

———. *Gender Trouble: Feminism and the Subversion of Identity*. New York: Routledge, 1990.

———. *Subjects of Desire: Hegelian Reflections in Twentieth-Century France*. New York: Columbia University Press, 1987.

Butorovic, Amila. "Between the Tariqa and the Shari'a." In *Feminist Poetics of the Sacred: Creative Suspicions*, edited by Frances Devlin-Glass and Lyn McCredden, 135–150. Oxford: Oxford University Press, 2001.

Buzy, T. R. Denis. "L'allegorie matrimoniale de Jahve d'Israel et la Cantique des Cantiques." *Revue biblique* 52 (1944): 77–90.

Byers, Damian. *Intentionality and Transcendence: Closure and Openness in Husserl's Phenomenology.* Madison: University of Wisconsin Press, 2002.

Bynum, Caroline Walker. *Fragmentation and Redemption: Essays on Gender and the Human Body in Medieval Religion.* New York: Zone Books, 1991.

———. *Holy Feast and Holy Fast: The Religious Significance of Food to Medieval Women.* Berkeley: University of California Press, 1987.

———. *Jesus as Mother: Studies in the Spirituality of the High Middle Ages.* Berkeley: University of California Press, 1982.

———. *The Resurrection of the Body in Western Christianity, 200–1336.* New York: Columbia University Press, 1995.

Cabezón, José Ignacio. *Buddhism and Language: A Study of Indo-Tibetan Scholasticism.* Albany: State University of New York Press, 1994.

Cacciari, Massimo. *Icone della legge.* Milan: Adelphi, 1985.

———. "The Problem of Representation." In *Recoding Metaphysics: The New Italian Philosophy,* edited by Giovanna Borradori, 155–165. Evanston: Northwestern University Press, 1988.

Cahnman, Werner J. "Friedrich Wilhelm Schelling and the New Thinking of Judaism." In *Kabbala und Romantik,* edited by Eveline Goodman-Thau, Gert Mattenklott, and Christoph Schulte, 167–205. Tübingen: Max Niemeyer, 1994.

Calame, Claude. *The Poetics of Eros in Ancient Greece.* Princeton: Princeton University Press, 1999.

Calderini, Simonetta. "Women, 'Sin,' and 'Lust': The Fall of Adam and Eve According to Classical and Medieval Islamic Exegesis," 49–63. In *Religion and Sexuality,* edited by Michael A. Hayes, Wendy Porter, and David Tombs. Sheffield: Sheffield Academic Press, 1998.

Cameron, Averil. "Sacred and Profane Love: Thoughts on Byzantine Gender." In *Women, Men and Eunuchs: Gender in Byzantium,* edited by Liz James, 1–23. London and New York: Routledge, 1997.

Camille, Michael. "The Book as Flesh and Fetish in Richard de Bury's *Philobiblon.*" In *The Book and the Body,* edited by Dolores Warwick Frese and Katherine O'Brien O'Keeffe, 34–77. Notre Dame and London: University of Notre Dame Press, 1997.

———. "The Image and the Self: Unwriting Late Medieval Bodies." In *Framing Medieval Bodies,* edited by Sarah Kay and Miri Rubin, 62–99. Manchester and New York: Manchester University Press 1994.

———. *Image on the Edge: The Margins of Medieval Art.* Cambridge, Mass.: Harvard University Press, 1992.

Camp, Claudia V. "The Strange Woman of Proverbs: A Study in the Feminization and Divinization of Evil in Biblical Thought." In *Women and Goddess Traditions in Antiquity and Today,* edited by Karen L. King, 310–329. Minneapolis: Fortress Press, 1997.

———. "Woman Wisdom and the Strange Woman: Where Is Power to Be Found?" In *Reading Bibles, Writing Bodies: Identity and the Book,* edited by Timothy K. Beal and David M. Gunn, 85–112. London and New York: Routledge, 1997.

Campbell, June. *Traveller in Space: In Search of Female Identity in Tibetan Buddhism.* New York: George Braziller, 1996.

Camporesi, Piero. "The Consecrated Host: A Wondrous Excess." In *Fragments for a History of the Human Body, Part One,* edited by Michel Feher with Ramona Naddaff and Nadia Tazi, 221–237. New York: Zone, 1989.

Cannon, George E. *The Use of Traditional Materials in Colossians*. Macon: Mercer University Press, 1983.
Cantillon, Alain. "Corpus Pascalis." *Yale French Studies* 86 (1994): 39–55.
Caputo, John D. *Demythologizing Heidegger*. Bloomington and Indianapolis: Indiana University Press, 1993.
———. *Heidegger and Aquinas: An Essay on Overcoming Metaphysics*. New York: Fordham University Press, 1982.
———. *More Radical Hermeneutics: On Not Knowing Who We Are*. Bloomington and Indianapolis: Indiana University Press, 2000.
———. *The Mystical Element in Heidegger's Thought*. Athens: Ohio University Press, 1978.
———. *The Prayers and Tears of Jacques Derrida: Religion without Religion*. Bloomington and Indianapolis: Indiana University Press, 1997.
———. "Radical Hermeneutics and Religious Truth: The Case of Sheehan and Schillebeeckx." In *Phenomenology of the Truth Proper to Religion*, edited by Daniel Guerrière, 146–172. Albany: State University of New York Press, 1990.
———. *Radical Hermeneutics: Repetition, Deconstruction, and the Hermeneutic Project*. Bloomington and Indianapolis: Indiana University Press, 1987.
Carabine, Deirdre. *The Unknown God, Negative Theology in the Platonic Tradition: Plato to Eriugena*. Louvain: Peeters Press, 1995.
Carr, David. *Interpreting Husserl: Critical and Comparative Studies*. Dordrecht: Martinus Nijhoff, 1987.
———. "Phenomenology and Philosophy of History." In *Phenomenology and Indian Philosophy*, edited by Debi Prasad Chattopadhyaya, Lester Embree, and Jitendranath Mohanty, 103–112. Albany: State University of New York Press, 1992.
———. *Phenomenology and the Problem of History: A Study of Husserl's Transcendental Philosophy*. Evanston: Northwestern University Press, 1974.
Carr, David M. *The Erotic Word: Sexuality, Spirituality, and the Bible*. Oxford and New York: Oxford University Press, 2003.
Carrera, Alessandro. "Consequences of Unlimited Semiosis: Carlo Sini's Metaphysics of the Sign and Semiotical Hermeneutics." In *Cultural Semiosis: Tracing the Signifier*, edited with an Introduction by Hugh J. Silverman, 48–62. New York and London: Routledge, 1998.
Carruthers, Mary. *The Craft of Thought: Meditation, Rhetoric, and the Making of Images, 400–1200*. Cambridge: Cambridge University Press, 1998.
Carter, Robert E. "Zen and Ontotheology via Heidegger." In *Religion, Ontotheology, and Deconstruction*, edited by Henry Ruf, 167–182. New York: Paragon House, 1989.
Castelli, David. *Il Commento di Sabbatai Donnolo sul Libro della creazione*. Firenze: 1880.
Castelli, Elizabeth A. "'I Will Make Mary Male': Pieties of the Body and Gender Transformation of Christian Women in Late Antiquity." In *Body Guards: The Cultural Politics of Gender Ambiguity*, edited by Julia Epstein and Kristina Straub, 29–49. New York and London: Routledge, 1991.
———. "Paul on Women and Gender." In *Women & Christian Origins*, edited by Ross Shepard Kraemer and Mary Rose D'Angelo, 221–235. New York and Oxford: Oxford University Press, 1999.
Cassirer, Ernst. *An Essay on Man: An Introduction to the Philosophy of Culture*. New Haven and London: Yale University Press, 1944.
———. *Language and Myth*. Translated by Susanne K. Langer. New York: Dover Publications, 1946.

———. *The Philosophy of Symbolic Forms.* Translated by Ralph Manheim, preface and introduction by Charles W. Hendel. 3 vols. New Haven: Yale University Press, 1955.

———. *The Philosophy of Symbolic Forms.* Vol. 4. Edited by John M. Krois and Donald P. Verene, translated by John M. Krois. New Haven and London: Yale University Press, 1996.

Cassou-Noguès, Pierre. "Merleau-Ponty et les sciences de la nature: Lecture de la physique moderne; confrontation à Bergson et à Whitehead." In *Merleau-Ponty: De la nature à l'ontologie,* 119–141. Paris: Philosophique J. Vrin, 2000.

Celan, Paul. *Fathomsuns and Benighted.* Translated by Ian Fairley. Riverdale-on-Hudson: Sheep Meadow Press, 2001.

Celenza, Christopher S. "The Search for Ancient Wisdom in Early Modern Europe: Reuchlin and the Late Ancient Esoteric Paradigm." *Journal of Religious History* 25 (2001): 115–133.

Certeau, Michel de. *Heterologies: Discourse on the Other.* Translated by Brian Massumi, foreword by Wlad Godzich. Minneapolis and London: University of Minnesota Press, 1986.

Chajes, Jeffrey H. *Between Worlds: Dybbuks, Exorcists, and Early Modern Judaism.* Philadelphia: University of Pennsylvania Press, 2003.

Chalier, Catherine. *La trace de l'infini: Emmanuel Levinas et la source hébraïque.* Paris: Éditions du Cerf, 2002.

Chalier-Visusalingam, Elisabeth. "Union and Unity in Hindu Tantrism." In *Between Jerusalem and Benares: Comparative Studies in Judaism and Hinduism,* edited by Hananya Goodman, 195–222. Albany: State University of New York Press, 1994.

Champagne, Roland A. *The Structuralists on Myth: An Introduction.* New York: Garland, 1992.

Chandès, Gerard. *Le serpent, la femme et l'épée: recherches sur l'imagination symbolique d'un romancier medieval, Chrétien de Troyes.* Amsterdam: Rodopi, 1986.

Chanter, Tina. "Reading Hegel as a Mediating Master: Lacan and Levinas." In *Levinas and Lacan: The Missed Encounter,* edited by Sarah Harasym, 1–21. Albany: State University of New York Press, 1998.

———. *Time, Death, and the Feminine: Levinas with Heidegger.* Stanford: Stanford University Press, 2001.

———. "Wild Meaning: Luce Irigaray's Reading of Merleau-Ponty." In *Chiasms: Merleau-Ponty's Notion of Flesh,* edited by Fred Evans and Leonard Lawlor, 219–236. Albany: State University of New York Press, 2000.

Charlesworth, James H. *Jesus within Judaism: New Light from Exciting Archaeological Discoveries.* New York: Doubleday, 1988.

———. *The Messiah: Developments in Earliest Judaism and Christianity.* Minneapolis: Fortress Press, 1992.

———, ed. *The Old Testament Pseudepigrapha.* 2 vols. New York: Doubleday, 1983.

———. "The Portrayal of the Righteous as an Angel." In *Ideal Figures in Ancient Judaism,* edited by John J. Collins and George W. E. Nickelsburg, 135–151. Chico: Scholars Press, 1980.

Chartier, Roger. "The Chimera of the Origin: Archaeology, Cultural History, and the French Revolution." In *Foucault and the Writing of History,* edited by Jan Goldstein, 167–186. Cambridge, Mass.: Blackwell, 1994.

Chebel, Malek. *Le corps en Islam.* Paris: Presses Universitaires de France, 1984.

Cheng, Chung-ying. "Confucius, Heidegger, and the Philosophy of the I-Ching: A Comparative Inquiry into the Truth of Human Being." *Philosophy East and West* 37 (1987): 51–70.

Chernus, Ira. *Mysticism in Rabbinic Judaism: Studies in the History of Midrash.* Berlin and New York: Walter de Gruyter, 1982.

Chevalier, Jacques M. *Scorpions and the Anatomy of Time*. Montreal and Kingston: McGill-Queen's University Press, 2002.

Chidester, David. *Word and Light: Seeing, Hearing, and Religious Discourse*. Urbana and Chicago: University of Illinois Press, 1992.

Chittick, William C. *Imaginal Worlds: Ibn al-ʿArabī and the Problem of Religious Diversity*. Albany: State University of New York Press, 1994.

———. "The Paradox of the Veil in Sufism." In *Rending the Veil: Concealment and Secrecy in the History of Religions*, edited by Elliot R. Wolfson, 59–85. New York and London: Seven Bridges Press, 1999.

———. "Rūmī and *waḥdat al-wujūd*." In *Poetry and Mysticism in Islam: The Heritage of Rūmī*, edited by Amin Banani, Richard Hovannisian and Georges Sabagh, 70–111. Cambridge: Cambridge University Press, 1994.

———. *The Self-Disclosure of God: Principles of Ibn al-ʿArabi's Cosmology*. Albany: State University of New York Press, 1998.

———. *The Sufi Path of Knowledge: Ibn al-ʿArabi's Metaphysics of Imagination*. Albany: State University of New York Press, 1989.

———. *The Sufi Path of Love: The Spiritual Teachings of Rumi*. Albany: State University of New York Press, 1983.

Choufrine, Arkodi. "On Eriguena's Appropriation of the Neoplatonic Concept of Self-Movement." *Journal of Neoplatonic Studies* 8 (1999): 19–58.

Christensen, F. M. *Space-Like Time: Consequences of, Alternatives to, and Arguments regarding the Theory That Time Is Like Space*. Toronto: University of Toronto, 1993.

Christian, William A. *An Interpretation of Whitehead's Metaphysics*. New Haven: Yale University Press, 1959.

Chung-yuan, Chang. *Tao: A New Way of Thinking, A Translation of the Tao Tē Ching with an Introduction and Commentaries*. New York: Harper & Row, 1975.

Cixous, Hélène. "Castration or Decapitation?" Translated by Annette Kuhn. *Signs: Journal of Women in Culture and Society* 7 (1981): 41–55.

———. *Portrait of Jacques Derrida as a Young Jewish Saint*. Translated by Beverley Bie Brahic. New York: Columbia University Press, 2004.

———. *Readings: The Poetics of Blanchot, Joyce, Kafka, Kleist, Lispector, and Tsvetayeva*. Translated by Verena Andermatt Conley. Minneapolis: University of Minnesota Press, 1991.

Clack, Beverley. "Virgins and Vessels: Feminist Reflections on Dominant Models of Spirituality." In *Religion and Sexuality*, edited by Michael A. Hayes, Wendy Porter, and David Tombs, 193–202. Sheffield: Sheffield Academic Press, 1998.

Clark, Elizabeth A. *Ascetic Piety and Women's Faith: Essays on Late Ancient Christianity*. Lewiston: E. Mellen Press, 1986.

———. *Jerome, Chrysostom, and Friends: Essays and Translations*. 2nd ed. New York: Edwin Mellen Press, 1982.

———. *The Origenist Controversy: The Cultural Construction of an Early Christian Debate*. Princeton: Princeton University Press, 1992.

———. *Reading Renunciation: Asceticism and Scripture in Early Christianity*. Princeton: Princeton University Press, 1999.

Clark, Gillian. "Women and Asceticism in Late Antiquity: The Refusal of Status and Gender." In *Asceticism*, edited by Vincent L. Wimbush and Richard Valantasis, 33–48. New York: Oxford University Press, 1995.

Clark, Maudemarie. *Nietzsche on Truth and Philosophy.* Cambridge: Cambridge University Press, 1990.

Cleary, Thomas, and Sarta Aziz. *Twilight Goddess: Spiritual Feminism and Feminine Spirituality.* Boston and London: Shambhala, 2000.

Clément, Catherine, and Julia Kristeva. *The Feminine and the Sacred.* Translated by Jane Marie Todd. New York: Columbia University Press, 2001.

Clement of Alexandria. *Stromateis: Books One to Three.* Translated by John Ferguson. Washington: Catholic University of America Press, 1991.

Cloke, Gillian. *This Female Man of God: Women and Spiritual Power in the Patristic Age, ad. 350–450.* London and New York: Routledge, 1995.

The Cloud of Unknowing. Edited with an introduction by James Walsh, preface by Simon Tugwell. New York: Paulist Press, 1981.

Cohen, Gerson D. *Studies in the Variety of Rabbinic Cultures.* Philadelphia: Jewish Publication Society, 1991.

Cohen, Martin S. *The Shiʿur Qomah: Liturgy and Theurgy in Pre-Kabbalistic Jewish Mysticism.* Lanham: University Press of America, 1983.

———. *The Shiʿur Qomah: Texts and Recensions.* Tübingen: Mohr, 1985.

Cohen-Alloro, Dorit. "Magic and Sorcery in the Zohar." Ph.D. dissertation, Hebrew University of Jerusalem, 1989 (Hebrew).

Cohn, Jacob. "Mystic Experience and Elijah-Revelation in Talmudic Times." In *Meyer Waxman Jubilee Volume on the Occasion of His Seventy-Fifth Birthday,* edited by Judah Rosenthal, Leonard C. Nishkin, and David S. Shapiro, 34–44 (English section). Jerusalem and Tel-Aviv: Mordecai Newman, 1966.

Colilli, Paul A. *The Idea of a Living Spirit: Poetic Logic as a Contemporary Theory.* Toronto: University of Toronto Press, 1997.

Collins, John J. *Between Athens and Jerusalem: Jewish Identity in the Hellenistic Diaspora.* 2nd ed. Grand Rapids: W. B. Eerdmans, 2000.

———. *Jewish Wisdom in the Hellenistic Age.* Edinburgh: T & T Clark, 1997.

Coltman, Rodney R. *The Language of Hermeneutics: Gadamer and Heidegger in Dialogue.* Albany: State University of New York Press, 1998.

Colville, Jim, trans. *Two Andalusian Philosophers: The Story of Hayy ibn Yaqzan by Abu Bakr Muhammad ibn Tufayl and The Definitive Statement by Abu'l Walid Muhammad ibn Rushd.* London and New York: Kegan Paul International, 1999.

Conkey, Margaret W., and Ruth E. Tringham. "Archaeology and the Goddess: Exploring the Contours of Feminist Archaeology." In *Feminisms in the Academy,* edited by Domna C. Stanton and Abigail J. Stewart, 199–247. Ann Arbor: University of Michigan Press, 1995.

Constas, Nicholas. *Proclus of Constantinople and the Cult of the Virgin in Late Antiquity: Homilies 1–5, Texts and Translations.* Leiden: Brill, 2003.

Cooey, Paula M. *Religious Imagination and the Body: A Feminist Analysis.* New York and Oxford: Oxford University Press, 1994.

Cooper, Catherine Fales. *The Virgin and the Bride: Idealized Womanhood in Late Antiquity.* Cambridge, Mass.: Harvard University Press, 1996.

Cooper, Jerold S. "Gendered Sexuality in Sumerian Love Poetry." In *Sumerian Gods and Their Representations,* edited by Irving L. Finkel and Markham J. Geller, 85–97. Groningen: Styx Publications, 1997.

The Coptic Gnostic Library: A Complete Edition of the Nag Hammadi Codices. 5 vols. Edited with English translation, introduction and notes. Leiden: E. J. Brill, 2000.

Corbin, Henry. *Avicenna and the Visionary Recital.* Translated by Willard R. Trask. New York: Bollingen Foundation, 1960.
———. *Creative Imagination in the Sūfism of Ibn ʿArabī.* Translated by Ralph Manheim. Princeton: Princeton University Press, 1969.
———. *Face de Dieu, Face de l'homme: Herméneutique et Soufisme.* Paris: Flannarion, 1983.
———. *History of Islamic Philosophy.* Translated by Liadain Sherrard with the assistance of Philip Sherrard. London and New York: Kegan Paul International, 1993.
———. *L'Iran et la Philosophie.* Paris: Librairie Arthème Fayard, 1990.
———. *The Man of Light in Iranian Sufism.* Translated by Nancy Pearson. New Lebanon: Omega Publications, 1994.
———. *Le paradoxe du monothéisme.* Paris: Éditions de l'Herne, 1981.
———. *Le Shīʿsme duodécimain.* Vol. 1 of *En Islam Iranien: Aspects spirituels et philosophiques.* Paris: Éditions Gallimard, 1971.
———. *Spiritual Body and Celestial Earth: From Mazdean Iran to Shiʿite Iran.* Translated by Nancy Pearson. Princeton: Princeton University Press, 1977.
———. *Temple and Contemplation.* Translated by Philip Sherrard with the assistance of Liadain Sherrard. London: KPI Limited, 1986.
———. *The Voyage and the Messenger: Iran and Philosophy.* Translated by Joseph Rowe. Berkeley: North Atlantic Books, 1998.
Cornford, Francis M. *Plato's Cosmology: The Timaeus of Plato Translated with a Running Commentary.* New York: Humanities Press, 1952.
Corradi Fiumara, Gemma. *The Other Side of Language: A Philosophy of Listening.* London and New York: Routledge, 1990.
Corrington, Gail Person. "The Defense of the Body and the Discourse of the Appetite: Continence and the Greco-Roman World." *Semeia* 57 (1992): 65–74.
Corrington, Robert S. *Ecstatic Naturalism: Signs of the World.* Bloomington and Indianapolis: Indiana University Press, 1994.
Coudert, Allison P. *Alchemy: The Philosopher's Stone.* London: Wildwood House, 1980.
———. *The Impact of the Kabbalah in the Seventeenth Century: The Life and Thought of Francis Mercury van Helmont (1614–1698).* Leiden: E. J. Brill, 1999.
Coulmas, Corinna. "Principes masculin et feminin dans le Zohar ou la rigueur d'une méthode." *Cahiers d'études juives* 1 (1986): 41–70.
Coulter, James A. *The Literary Microcosm: Theories of Interpretation of the Later Neoplatonists.* Leiden: E. J. Brill, 1976.
Courtine, Jean-François. *Extase de la raison: Essais sur Schelling.* Paris: Éditions Galilée, 1990.
Cousins, Ewert. "The Fourfold Sense of Scripture in Christian Mysticism." In *Mysticism and Sacred Scripture,* edited by Steven T. Katz, 118–137. Oxford and New York: Oxford University Press, 2000.
Cox Miller, Patricia. "'Pleasure of the Text, Text of Pleasure': Eros and Language in Origen's *Commentary on the Song of Songs.*" *Journal of the American Academy of Religion* 54 (1986): 241–253.
Cragg, Kenneth. *Jesus and the Muslim: An Exploration.* Oxford: Oneworld Publications, 1999.
Craig, William L. "Relativity and the 'Elimination' of Absolute Time." In *Time, Reality, and Transcendence in Rational Perspective,* edited by Peter Øhrstrøm, 91–127. Aalborg: Aalborg University Press, 2002.
———. *Time and the Metaphysics of Relativity.* Dordrecht: Kluwer Academic, 2001.
Cramer, John G. "The Plane of the Present and the New Transactional Paradigm of Time." In

Time and the Instant: Essays on the Physics and Philosophy of Time, edited by Robin Durie, 177–189. Manchester: Clinamen Press, 2000.

Crawford, Sidnie W. "Lady Wisdom and Dame Folly at Qumran." *Dead Sea Discoveries* 5 (1998): 355–366.

Crignon, Philippe. "Figuration: Emmanuel Levinas and the Image." *Yale French Studies* 104 (2004): 100–125.

Cristin, Renato. *Heidegger and Leibniz: Reason and the Path.* Translated by Gerald Parks with a Foreword by Hans Georg Gadamer. Dordrecht: Kluwer Academic, 1998.

Critchey, Simon. *The Ethics of Deconstruction: Derrida and Levinas.* 2nd ed. West Lafayette: Purdue University Press, 1999.

Cryer, Frederick H. "Magic in Ancient Syria-Palestine—and in the Old Testament." In *Witchcraft and Magic in Europe: Biblical and Pagan Societies*, edited by Bengt Ankarloo and Stuart Clark, 97–152. Philadelphia: University of Pennsylvania Press, 2001.

Cueille, Jean-Nöel. "La profondeur du négatif: Merleau-Ponty face à la dialectique de Hegel." In *Merleau-Ponty: De la nature à l'ontologie*, 301–335. Paris: Philosophique J. Vrin, 2000.

Culianu, Ioan P. "A Corpus for the Body." *Journal of Modern History* 63 (1991): 61–80.

———. *Psychanodia I: A Survey of the Evidence Concerning the Ascension of the Soul and Its Relevance.* Leiden: E. J. Brill, 1983.

Cupitt, Don. *Mysticism after Modernity.* Oxford: Blackwell, 1998.

Curtius, Ernst Robert. *European Literature and the Latin Middle Ages.* Translated by Willard R. Trask. Princeton: Princeton University Press, 1990.

Dainton, Barry. *Time and Space.* Montreal and Kingston: McGill-Queen's University Press, 2001.

Daley, Brian E. "The 'Closed Garden' and the 'Sealed Fountain': Song of Songs 4:12 in Late Medieval Iconography of Mary." In *Medieval Gardens*, edited by Elizabeth B. MacDougall, 255–278. Washington: Dumbarton Oaks, 1986.

Dallmayr, Fred. *The Other Heidegger.* Ithaca and London: Cornell University Press, 1993.

Daly, Mary. *Beyond God the Father: Towards a Philosophy of Women's Liberation.* Boston: Beacon Press, 1985.

———. *Pure Lust: Elemental Feminist Philosophy.* London: Women's Press, 1984.

Dan, Joseph. "Beyond the Kabbalistic Symbol." *Jerusalem Studies in Jewish Thought* 5 (1986): 363–385 (Hebrew).

Dange, Sadashiv Ambadas. *Sexual Symbolism from the Vedic Ritual.* Delhi: Ajanta Publications, 1979.

D'Angelo, Mary Rose. "Gender Refusers in the Early Christian Mission: Gal 3:28 as an Interpretation of Gen 1:27b." In *Reading in Christian Communities: Essays on Interpretation in the Early Church*, edited by Charles A. Bobertz and David Brakke, 149–173. Notre Dame: University of Notre Dame Press, 2002.

———. " 'Knowing How to Preside over His Own Household': Imperial Masculinity and Christian Asceticism in the Pastorals, *Hermas*, and Luke-Acts." In *New Testament Masculinities*, edited by Stephen D. Moore and Janice Capel Anderson, 265–295. Atlanta: Society of Biblical Literature, 2003.

———. "Transcribing Sexual Politics: Images of the Androgyne in Discourses of Antique Religion." In *Descrizioni e iscrizioni: politiche del discorso*, edited by Carla Locatelli and Giovanna Covi, 115–146. Trento: Editrice Università degli Studi di Trento, 1998.

———. "Veils, Virgins, and the Tongues of Men and Angels: Women's Heads and Early Christianity." In *Women, Gender, Religion: A Reader*, edited by Elizabeth A. Castelli with the assistance of Rosamond C. Rodman, 389–419. New York: Palgrave, 2001.

Daniel, Constantin. "Esséniens et Eunuques (Matthieu 19, 10–12)." *Revue de Qumran* 6 (1968): 353–390.

Dastur, Françoise. *Chair et langage: Essais sur Merleau-Ponty.* La Versanne: Encre Maine, 2001.

———. *Heidegger and the Question of Time.* Translated by François Raffoul and David Pettigrew. Atlantic Highlands: Humanities Press, 1998.

———. *Telling Time: Sketch of a Phenomenological Chrono-logy.* Translated by Edward Bullard. London: Athlone Press, 2000.

———. "World, Flesh, Vision." In *Chiasms: Merleau-Ponty's Notion of Flesh,* edited by Fred Evans and Leonard Lawlor, 23–49. Albany: State University of New York Press, 2000.

Dauenhauer, Bernard P. *Silence: The Phenomenon and Its Ontological Significance* Bloomington: Indiana University Press, 1980.

Davidson, Arnold I. "Ethics as Ascetics: Foucault, the History of Ethics, and Ancient Thought." In *Foucault and the Writing of History,* edited by Jan Goldstein, 63–80. Cambridge, Mass.: Blackwell, 1994.

Davidson, Ronald M. *Indian Esoteric Buddhism: A Social History of the Tantric Movement.* New York: Columbia University Press, 2002.

Davies, Paul. *About Time: Einstein's Unfinished Revolutions.* New York: Simon and Schuster, 1995.

Davies, Stevan L. *The Gospel of Thomas and Christian Wisdom.* Translated by Stevan L. Davies. Woodstock: Skylight Paths, 2002.

Davies, William D. *Christian Engagements with Judaism.* Harrisburg: Trinity Press International, 1999.

Davis, Duane H. "Reversible Subjectivity: The Problem of Transcendence and Language." In *Merleau-Ponty Vivant,* edited by Martin C. Dillon, 31–45. Albany: State University of New York Press, 1991.

Davis, Stephen J. "Crossed Texts, Crossed Sex: Intertextuality and Gender in Early Christian Legends of Holy Women Disguised as Men." *Journal of Early Christian Studies* 10 (2002): 1–36.

———. "A 'Pauline' Defense of Women's Right to Baptize? Intertextuality and Apostolic Authority in the Acts of Paul." *Journal of Early Christian Studies* 8 (2000): 453–459.

Davis, Thomas A. "The *Deinon* of Yielding at the End of Metaphysics." In *Crises in Continental Philosophy,* edited by Arleen B. Dallery and Charles E. Scott, 161–174. Albany: State University of New York Press, 1990.

Dawes, Gregory W. *The Body in Question: Metaphor and Meaning in the Interpretation of Ephesians 5:21–33.* Leiden: Brill, 1998.

Dawson, David. "Allegorical Reading and the Embodiment of the Soul in Origen." In *Christian Origins: Theology, Rhetoric and Community,* edited by Lewis Ayres and Gareth Jones, 26–43. London and New York: Routledge, 1998.

Dearman, J. Andrew. "Theophany, Anthropomorphism, and the *Imago Dei*: Some Observations about the Incarnation in the Light of the Old Testament." In *The Incarnation: An Interdisciplinary Symposium on the Incarnation of the Son of God,* edited by Stephen T. Davis, Daniel Kendall, and Gerald O'Collins, 31–46. Oxford and New York: Oxford University Press, 2002.

DeConick, April D. "The Great Mystery of Marriage: Sex and Conception in Ancient Valentinian Traditions." *Vigiliae Christianae* 57 (2003): 307–342.

———. *Seek to See Him: Ascent and Vision Mysticism in the Gospel of Thomas.* Leiden: E. J. Brill, 1996.

———. "The True Mysteries: Sacramentalism in the Gospel of Philip." *Vigiliae Christianae* 55 (2001): 225–261.

Deghaye, Pierre. "L'homme virginal selon Jakob Böhme." In *L'androgyne*, 155–196. Paris: Éditions Albin Michel, 1986.

Delcourt, Marie. *Hermaphrodite: Mythes et rites de la bisexualité dans l'Antiquité classique*. Paris: Presses Universitaires de France, 1958.

Deleuze, Gilles. *Nietzsche and Philosophy*. Translated by Hugh Tomlinson. New York: Columbia University Press, 1983.

———. *Pure Immanence: Essays on a Life*. Translated by Anne Boyman, introduction by John Rajchman. New York: Zone Books, 2001.

Depraz, Natalie. "Phénoménologie et docétisme: L'apparaître charnel." In *La gnose, une question philosophique: Pour une phénoménologie de l'invisible*, edited by Natalie Depraz and Jean-François Marquet, 87–105. Paris: Éditions du Cerf, 2000.

Derrida, Jacques. *Acts of Literature*. Edited by Derek Attridge. London and New York: Routledge, 1992.

———. *Acts of Religion*. Edited and with an introduction by Gil Anidjar. New York and London: Routledge, 2002.

———. *The Archeology of the Frivolous: Reading Condillac*. Translated and with an introduction by John P. Leavey, Jr. Lincoln and London: University of Nebraska Press, 1980.

———. *Archive Fever: A Freudian Impression*. Translated by Eric Prenowitz. Chicago and London: University of Chicago Press, 1996.

———. *Demeure: Fiction and Testimony*. Translated by Elizabeth Rottenberg. Stanford: Stanford University Press, 2000.

———. "Devant la loi." Translated by Avital Ronell. In *Kafka and the Contemporary Critical Performance: Centenary Readings*, edited by Alan Udoff, 128–149. Bloomington and Indianapolis: Indiana University Press, 1987.

———. *Dissemination*. Translated with an introduction and additional notes by Barbara Johnson. Chicago: University of Chicago Press, 1981.

———. *The Gift of Death*. Translated by David Wills. Chicago: University of Chicago Press, 1995.

———. *Given Time: I. Counterfeit Money*. Translated by Peggy Kamuf. Chicago: University of Chicago Press, 1992.

———. *Glas*. Translated by John P. Leavet and Richard Rand. Lincoln: University of Nebraska Press, 1986.

———. "How to Avoid Speaking: Denials." In *Languages of the Unsayable: The Play of Negativity in Literature and Literary Theory*, edited by Sanford Budick and Wolfgang Iser, 3–70. New York: Columbia University Press, 1989.

———. *The Instant of My Death / Maurice Blanchot. Demeure: Fiction and Testimony / Jacques Derrida*. Translated by Elizabeth Rottenberg. Stanford: Stanford University Press, 2000.

———. "Living On: Border Lines." Translated by James Hulbert. In *Deconstruction and Criticism*, edited by Harold Bloom, 75–176. New York: Seabury, 1979.

———. *Margins of Philosophy*. Translated with additional notes by Alan Bass. Chicago: University of Chicago Press, 1982.

———. "Of an Apocalyptic Tone Newly Adopted in Philosophy." In *Derrida and Negative Theology*, edited by Howard Coward and Toby Foshay, 25–71. Albany: State University of New York Press, 1992.

———. *On the Name*. Edited by Thomas Dutoit, translated by David Wood, John P. Leavey, Jr., and Ian McLeod. Stanford: Stanford University Press, 1995.

———. ". . . and Pomegranates." In *Violence, Identity, and Self-Determination*, edited by Hent de Vries and Samuel Weber, 326–344. Stanford: Stanford University Press, 1997.

———. "Sending: On Representation." In *Transforming the Hermeneutic Context: From Nietzsche to Nancy*, edited by Gayle L. Ormiston and Alan D. Schrift, 107–138. Albany: State University of New York Press, 1990.

———. "A Silkworm of One's Own: Points of View Stitched on the Other Veil." In *Veils*, Hélène Cixous and Jacques Derrida, 17–92. Stanford: Stanford University Press, 2001.

———. *Spurs: Nietzsche's Styles/Éperons, Les Styles de Nietzsche*. Translated by Barbara Harlow. Chicago and London: University of Chicago Press, 1979.

———. *Writing and Difference*. Translated with an introduction and additional notes by Alan Bass. Chicago and London: University of Chicago Press, 1978.

Derrida, Jacques, and Maurizio Ferraris. *A Taste for the Secret*. Translated by Giacomo Donis, edited by Giacomo Donis and David Webb. Cambridge: Polity Press, 2001.

Derrida, Jacques, Frank Kermode, Toril Moi, and Christopher Norris. *Life. After. Theory*. Edited by Michael Payne and John Schad. London and New York: Continuum, 2003.

De Ruk, L. M. "Causation and Participation in Proclus: The Pivotal Role of 'Scope Distinction' in His Metaphysics." In *Proclus and His Influence in Medieval Philosophy*, edited by Egbert P. Bos and P. A. Meijer, 1–34. Leiden: E. J. Brill, 1992.

Desmond, William. *Being and the Between*. Albany: State University of New York Press, 1995.

Deutsch, Eliot. "Truth and Mythology." In *Myths and Fictions*, edited by Shlomo Biderman and Ben-Ami Scharfstein, 41–50. Leiden: E. J. Brill, 1993.

Deutsch, Nathaniel. *The Maiden of Ludmir: A Jewish Holy Woman and Her World*. Foreword by Janusz Bardach. Berkeley: University of California Press, 2003.

Deutsch, Yaacov. "New Evidence of Early Versions of *Toldot Yeshu*." *Tarbiẓ* 69 (2000): 177–197 (Hebrew).

Deutscher, Penelope. *Yielding Gender: Feminism, Deconstruction and the History of Philosophy*. London and New York: Routledge, 1997.

Diamond, Eliezer. *Holy Men and Hunger Artists: Fasting and Asceticism in Rabbinic Culture*. Oxford: Oxford University Press, 2003.

Diamond, James A. *Maimonides and the Hermeneutics of Concealment: Deciphering Scripture and Midrash in the Guide of the Perplexed*. Albany: State University of New York Press, 2002.

DiCenso, James J. *The Other Freud: Religion, Culture, and Psychoanalysis*. London and New York: Routledge, 1999.

Dillon, Martin C. "Aletheia, Poiesis, and Eros: Truth and Untruth in the Poetic Construction of Love." In *Philosophy and Desire*, edited with an introduction by Hugh J. Silverman, 17–25. New York and London: Routledge, 2000.

———. *Merleau-Ponty's Ontology*. Bloomington and Indianapolis: Indiana University Press, 1988.

———. "Preface: Merleau-Ponty and Postmodernity." In *Merleau-Ponty Vivant*, edited by Martin C. Dillon, xviii–xix. Albany: State University of New York Press, 1991.

———. "The Unconscious: Language and World." In *Merleau-Ponty in Contemporary Perspectives*, edited by Patrick Burke and Jan van der Veken, 67–83. Dordrecht: Kluwer Academic, 1993.

Dilthey, Wilhelm. *Poetry and Experience*. Edited by Rudolf A. Makkreel and Frithjof Rodi. Princeton: Princeton University Press, 1985.

Dimant, Deborah. "Men as Angels: The Self-Image of the Qumran Community." In *Religion and Politics in the Ancient Near East*, edited by Adela Berlin, 93–103. Bethesda: University Press of Maryland, 1996.

Dionysius the Areopagite. *Corpus Dionysiacum I: Pseudo-Dionysius Areopagita, De Divinis Nominibus*. Edited by Beate Regina Suchla. Berlin and New York: Walter de Gruyter, 1990.

———. *Corpus Dionysiacum II: Pseudo-Dionysius Areopagita, De Coelesti Hierarchia, De Ecclesiastica Hierarchia, De Mystica Theologia, Epistulae.* Edited by Günter Heil and Adolf Martin Ritter. Berlin and New York: Walter de Gruyter, 1991.

———. *The Divine Names and Mystical Theology.* Translated from the Greek with an introductory study by John D. Jones. Milwaukee: Marquette University Press, 1980.

———. *Pseudo-Dionysius: The Complete Works.* Translation by Colm Luibheid, foreword, notes, and translation collaboration by Paul Rorem, preface by Rene Roques, introduction by Jaroslav Pelikan, Jean Leclercq, and Karlfried Froehlich. New York and Mahwah: Paulist Press, 1987.

Doane, Mary Ann. "Veiling over Desire: Close-ups of the Woman." In *Feminism and Psychoanalysis,* edited by Richard Feldstein and Judith Roof, 119–126. Ithaca: Cornell University Press, 1989.

Dobbs-Weinstein, Idrit. "Matter as Creature and Matter as the Source of Evil: Maimonides and Aquinas." In *Neoplatonism and Jewish Thought,* edited by Lenn E. Goodman, 217–235. Albany: State University of New York Press, 1992.

Dodd, Charles H. *The Interpretation of the Fourth Gospel.* Cambridge: Cambridge University Press, 1953.

Doherty, Joseph E. *Sein, Mensch und Symbol: Heidegger und die Auseinandersetzung mit dem Neukantianischen Symbolbegriff.* Bonn: Bouvier Verlag Herbert Grundmann, 1972.

Donoghue, Denis. *Adam's Curse: Reflections on Religion and Literature.* Notre Dame: University of Notre Dame Press, 2001.

Doran, Robert. *Birth of a Worldview: Early Christianity in Its Jewish and Pagan Context.* Boulder: Westview Press, 1995.

Dorje, Garab. *The Golden Letters: The Three Statements of Garab Dorje, the First Teacher of Dzogchen, Together with a Commentary by Dza Patrul Rinpoche Entitled "The Special Teaching of the Wise and Glorious King."* Translated by John Myrdhin Reynolds. Ithaca: Snow Lion Publications, 1996.

Dotan, Aron. "Saadia Gaon on the Origins of Language." *Tarbiẓ* 65 (1996): 237–249 (Hebrew).

Drob, Sanford L. *Kabbalistic Metaphors: Jewish Mystical Themes in Ancient and Modern Thought.* Northvale: Jason Aronson, 2000.

———. *Symbols of the Kabbalah: Philosophical and Psychological Perspectives.* Northvale: Jason Aronson, 2000.

DuBois, Page. *Sowing the Body: Psychoanalysis and Ancient Representations of Women.* Chicago and London: University of Chicago Press, 1988.

Dudley, Guilford, III. *Religion on Trial: Mircea Eliade and His Critics.* Philadelphia: Temple University Press, 1977.

Dufrenne, Mikel. *In the Presence of the Sensuous: Essays in Aesthetics.* Edited by Mark S. Roberts and David Gallagher. Atlantic Highlands: Humanities Press International, 1990.

Dünkelsbühler, Ulrike Oudée. *Reframing the Frame of Reason: "Trans-lation" in and beyond Kant and Derrida.* Translated by Max Statkiewicz, preface by Jacques Derrida. Amherst: Humanity Books, 2002.

Dunlap, Knight. *Mysticism, Freudianism and Scientific Psychology.* Saint Louis: C. V. Mosby, 1920.

Ebertshäuser, Caroline H., Herbert Haag, Joe H. Kirchberger, and Dorothee Sölle. *Mary: Art, Culture, and Religion through the Ages.* Translated by Peter Heinegg. New York: Crossroad, 1997.

Eckhart. *Meister Eckhart, Sermons and Treatises.* Translated by Maurice O'Connell Walshe. 3 vols. Rockport: Element Books, 1991.

———. *Wandering Joy: Meister Eckhart's Mystical Philosophy.* Translated and commentary by Reiner Schürmann, introduction by David Appelbaum. Great Barrington: Lindisfarne Books, 2001.

Eco, Umberto. *Experiences in Translation*. Translated by Alastair McEwen. Toronto: University of Toronto Press, 2001.

———. *The Search for the Perfect Language*. Oxford: Oxford University Press, 1995.

———. *Semiotics and the Philosophy of Language*. Bloomington: Indiana University Press, 1984.

Edie, James M. *Merleau-Ponty's Philosophy of Language: Structuralism and Dialectics*. Lanham: University Press of America, 1987.

Edwards, James C. *The Authority of Language: Heidegger, Wittgenstein, and the Threat of Philosophical Nihilism*. Tampa: University of South Florida Press, 1990.

Efros, Israel. *Studies in Medieval Jewish Philosophy*. New York and London: Columbia University Press, 1974.

Ehrlich, Uri. *The Non-Verbal Language of Jewish Prayer*. Jerusalem: Magnes Press, 1999 (Hebrew).

———. "The Place of the *Shekhina* in the Consciousness of the Worshipper." *Tarbiẓ* 65 (1995): 315–329 (Hebrew).

Eilberg-Schwartz, Howard. *God's Phallus and Other Problems for Men and Monotheism*. Boston: Beacon Press, 1994.

———. *The Savage in Judaism: An Anthropology of Israelite Religion and Ancient Judaism*. Bloomington and Indianapolis: Indiana University Press, 1990.

Elam, Diane. *Feminism and Deconstruction: Ms. en Abyme*. London and New York: Routledge, 1994.

Elder, Linda Bennett. "The Woman Question and Female Ascetics among Essenes." *Biblical Archaeologist* 54 (1994): 220–234.

Eldridge, Richard Thomas. *Beyond Representation: Philosophy and Poetic Imagination*. Cambridge: Cambridge University Press, 1996.

El Guindi, Fadwa. *Veil: Modesty, Privacy and Resistance*. Oxford and New York: Berg, 1999.

Eliade, Mircea. *The History of Religions: Retrospect and Prospect: A Collection of Original Essays*. Translated by Joseph Mitsuo Kitagawa. New York: Macmillan, 1985.

———. *A History of Religious Ideas*. Translated by Willard R. Trask. 3 vols. Chicago: University of Chicago Press, 1978.

———. *Images and Symbols: Studies in Religious Symbolism*. Translated by Philip Mairet. Princeton: Princeton University Press, 1991.

———. *Journal II, 1957–1969*. Translated from the French by Fred H. Johnson, Jr. Chicago and London: University of Chicago Press, 1989.

———. *Journal III, 1970–1978*. Translated from the French by Teresa Lavender Fagan. Chicago and London: University of Chicago Press, 1989.

———. *Myth and Reality*. Translated by Willard R. Trask. New York: Harper & Row, 1963.

———. *Myths, Dreams, and Mysteries: The Encounter between Contemporary Faiths and Archaic Realities*. New York: Harper & Row, 1960.

———. *Occultism, Witchcraft, and Cultural Fashions: Essays in Comparative Religions*. Chicago: University of Chicago Press, 1976.

———. *Patterns in Comparative Religion*. Translated by Rosemary Sheed, introduction by John C. Holt. Lincoln and London: University of Nebraska Press, 1996.

———. *The Quest: History and Meaning in Religion*. Chicago and London: University of Chicago Press, 1969.

———. *The Two and the One*. Translated by J. M. Cohen. Chicago: University of Chicago Press, 1965.

———. *Yoga: Immortality and Freedom*. Translated by Willard R. Trask. New York: Bollingen Foundation, 1958.

Elias, Jamal J., trans. *Death before Dying: The Sufi Poems of Sultan Bahu*. Berkeley: University of California Press, 1998.

Elior, Rachel. "Jewish Studies in Israel and the Limits of Pluralistic Orientations in Jewish Studies in the Post-Modern Age: Individual Readings and Scholarly Common Denominators." *Jewish Studies Quarterly* 4 (1997): 1–11.

———. "The Metaphorical Relation between God and Man and the Significance of the Visionary Reality in Lurianic Kabbalah." *Jerusalem Studies in Jewish Thought* 10 (1992): 47–57 (Hebrew).

Elizur, Shulamit. "On the Role of the *Yoẓer* in the Legacy of Eleazar bi-Rabbi Qillir: New Findings." *Tarbiẓ* 66 (1997): 351–394 (Hebrew).

Ellington, Donna Spivey. *From Sacred Body to Angelic Soul: Understanding Mary in Late Medieval and Early Modern Europe*. Washington: Catholic University Press of America, 2001.

Elliott, Dyan. *Fallen Bodies: Pollution, Sexuality, and Demonology in the Middle Ages*. Philadelphia: University of Pennsylvania Press, 1999.

———. *Spiritual Marriage: Sexual Abstinence in Medieval Wedlock*. Princeton: Princeton University Press, 1993.

Elliott, Mark W. *The Song of Songs and Christology in the Early Church, 381–451*. Tübingen: Mohr Siebeck, 2000.

Elm, Susanna. *Virgins of God: The Making of Asceticism in Late Antiquity*. Oxford: Clarendon Press, 1994.

Elqayam, Avraham. "Between Referentialism and Performativism: Two Approaches in Understanding the Kabbalistic Symbol." *Daʿat* 24 (1990): 5–40 (Hebrew).

———. "On the 'Knowledge of Messiah'—The Dialectic of the Erotic Peak in the Messianic Thought of Nathan of Gaza." *Tarbiẓ* 65 (1996): 637–670 (Hebrew).

Elwolde, John. "Human and Divine Sexuality: The Zohar on Genesis 5.2." In *Religion and Sexuality*, edited by Michael A. Hayes, Wendy Porter and David Tombs, 64–84. Sheffield: Sheffield Academic Press, 1998.

Emad, Parvis. "Thinking More Deeply into the Question of Translation: Essential Translation and the Unfolding of Language." In *Reading Heidegger: Commemorations*, edited by John Sallis, 323–340. Bloomington and Indianapolis: Indiana University Press, 1993.

Emmet, Dorothy. *Whitehead's Philosophy of Organism*. 2nd ed. New York: St. Martin's Press, 1966.

Empedocles. *Empedocles: The Extant Fragments*. Edited with an introduction, commentary, and concordance by M. R. Wright. New Haven and London: Yale University Press, 1981.

Endo, Masanobu. *Creation and Christology: A Study in the Johannine Prologue in the Light of Early Jewish Creation Accounts*. Tübingen: Mohr Siebeck, 2002.

Engammare, Max. *Qu'il me baise des baisiers de sa bouche. Le Cantique des Cantiques à la Renaissance: Étude et bibliographie*. Geneva: Librairie Droz S.A., 1993.

Epstein, Julia, and Kristina Straub, eds. *Body Guards: The Cultural Politics of Gender Ambiguity*. New York and London: Routledge, 1991.

Erickson, Stephen A. *Language and Being: An Analytic Phenomenology*. New Haven and London: Yale University Press, 1970.

Ernst, Carl W. "Mystical Language and the Teaching Context in the Early Lexicons of Sufism." In *Mysticism and Language*, edited by Steven T. Katz, 181–201. Oxford and New York: Oxford University 1992.

Escoubas, Eliane. "Ontology of Language and Ontology of Translation in Heidegger." In *Reading Heidegger: Commemorations*, edited by John Sallis, 341–347. Bloomington and Indianapolis: Indiana University Press, 1993.

Eskola, Timo. *Messiah and the Throne: Jewish Merkabah Mysticism and Christian Exaltation Discourse.* Tübingen: Mohr Siebeck, 2001.

Esmail, Aziz. *The Poetics of Religious Experience: The Islamic Context.* London and New York: I. B. Tauris, 1998.

Ess, Josef van. "Verbal Inspiration? Language and Revelation in Classical Islamic Theology." In *The Qur'an As Text,* edited by Stefan Wild, 177–194. Leiden: E. J. Brill, 1996.

Evans, D. "Can Philosophers Limit What Mystics Can Do? A Critique of Steven Katz." *Religious Studies* 25 (1989): 53–60.

Everson, William. *Dark God of Eros: A William Everson Reader.* Edited with an introduction by Albert Gelpi. Berkeley: Heyday Books, 2003.

———. *The Excesses of God: Robinson Jeffers as a Religious Figure.* Stanford: Stanford University Press, 1988.

———. *Prodigious Thrust.* Santa Rosa: Black Sparrow Press, 1996.

———. *River-Root: A Syzygy for the Bicentennial of These States.* Berkeley: Oyez Press, 1976.

———. *The Veritable Years: Poems, 1949–1966.* Santa Rosa: Black Sparrow Press, 1998.

Everson, William, and Albert Gelpi, eds. *Dark God of Eros: A William Everson Reader.* Berkeley: Heyday Books, 2003.

Evola, Julius. *Eros and the Mysteries of Love: The Metaphysics of Sex.* Rochester: Inner Traditions International, 1983.

Exum, J. Cheryl. *Fragmented Women: Feminist (Sub)versions of Biblical Narratives.* Sheffield: Sheffield Academic Press, 1993.

Faierstein, Morris M. "*Maggidim,* Spirits, and Women in Rabbi Hayyim Vital's *Book of Visions.*" In *Spirit Possession in Judaism: Cases and Contexts from the Middle Ages to the Present,* edited by Matt Goldish, with a foreword by Erika Bourguignon and an introduction by Joseph Dan, 186–196. Detroit: Wayne State University Press, 2003.

———. "Personal Redemption in Hasidism." In *Hasidism Reappraised,* edited by Ada Rapoport-Albert, 214–224. London: Litman Library of Jewish Civilization, 1996.

Fakhry, Majid. *A History of Islamic Philosophy.* 2nd ed. New York: Columbia University Press, 1983.

Falck, Colin. *Myth, Truth, and Literature: Towards a True Post-Modernism.* 2nd ed. Cambridge: Cambridge University Press, 1994.

Falk, Marcia. "Notes on Composing New Blessings." In *Weaving the Visions,* edited by Judith Plaskow and Carol Christ. New York: Harper Collins, 1989.

Falk, Ze'ev. *Jewish Matrimonial Law in the Middle Ages.* London: Oxford University Press, 1966.

Farber, Asi. "The Concept of the Merkabah in Thirteenth-Century Jewish Esotericism: Sod ha-Egoz and Its Development." Ph.D. dissertation, Hebrew University, 1986 (Hebrew).

———. "On the Sources of Rabbi Moses de Leon's Early Kabbalistic System." In *Studies in Philosophy, Mysticism, and Ethical Literature presented to Isaiah Tishby on his Seventy-fifth Birthday,* edited by Joseph Dan and Joseph Hacker, 67–96. Jerusalem: Magnes Press, 1986 (Hebrew).

———. "Traces of the *Zohar* in the Writings of R. Joseph Gikatilla." *Alei Sefer* 9 (1981): 70–83 (Hebrew).

Farber-Ginat, Asi. " 'The Shell Precedes the Fruit'—On the Question of the Origin of Metaphysical Evil in Early Kabbalistic Thought." In *Myth and Judaism,* edited by Ḥaviva Pedaya, 118–142. Jerusalem: Bialik Institute, 1996 (Hebrew).

Farías, Victor. *Heidegger and Nazism.* Edited, with a foreword, by Joseph Margolis and Tom Rockmore. Philadelphia: Temple University Press, 1989.

Farley, Wendy. *Eros for the Other: Retaining Truth in a Pluralistic World.* University Park: Pennsylvania State University Press, 1996.

Fatum, Lone. "Image of God and Glory of Man: Women in the Pauline Congregations." In *Image of God and Gender Models in Judaeo-Christian Tradition*, edited by Kari Elisabeth Børresen, 50–133. Oslo: Solum Forlag, 1991.

Faure, Bernard. *The Red Thread: Buddhist Approaches to Sexuality.* Princeton: Princeton University Press, 1998.

Fausto-Sterling, Anne. *Sexing the Body: Gender Politics and the Construction of Sexuality.* New York: Basic Books, 2000.

Fay, Thomas. "The Ontological Difference in Early Heidegger and Wittgenstein." *Kantstudien* 82 (1991): 319–328.

Faye, Jan. "When Time Gets Off Track." In *Time, Reality and Experience*, edited by Craig Callender, 1–17. Cambridge: Cambridge University Press, 2002.

Feder, Ellen K., and Emily Zakin. "Flirting with the Truth: Derrida's Discourse with 'Woman' and Wenches." In *Derrida and Feminism: Recasting the Question of Woman*, edited by Ellen K. Feder, Mary C. Rawlinson, and Emily Zakin, 1–6. New York and London: Routledge, 1997.

Feldman, Jonathan. "The Power of the Soul over the Body: Corporeal Transformation and Attitudes towards the Body in the Thought of Naḥmanides." Ph.D. dissertation, New York University, 1999.

Felski, Rita. *Doing Time: Feminist Theory and Postmodern Culture.* New York and London: New York University Press, 2000.

Felstiner, John. *Paul Celan: Poet, Survivor, Jew.* New Haven and London: Yale University Press, 1995.

Fenner, Peter. *The Ontology of the Middle Way.* Dordrecht: Kluwer Academic, 1990.

Fenton, Paul. "Daniel Ibn al-Māshiṭa's 'Taqwīm al-Adyān': New Light on the Oriental Phase of the Maimonidean Controversy." In *Genizah Research after Ninety Years: The Case of Judaeo-Arabic. Papers Read at the Third Congress of the Society for Judaeo-Arabic Studies*, edited by Joseph Blau and Stefan C. Reif, 74–81. Cambridge: Cambridge University Press, 1992.

———. "La 'Hitbodedut' chez les premiers Qabbalists en Orient et chez les Soufis." In *Prière, mystique et Judaïsme: Colloque de Strasbourg (10–12 septembre 1984)*, edited by Roland Goetschel, 133–157. Paris: Presses Universitaires de France, 1987.

———. "The Influences of Sufism on the Kabbalah in Safed." *Maḥanayyim* 6 (1993): 170–179 (Hebrew).

———. "A Mystical Commentary on the Song of Songs in the Hand of David Maimonides the Second." *Tarbiẓ* 69 (2000): 539–589 (Hebrew).

———. *The Treatise of the Pool: al-Maqala al-Hawdiyya.* London: Octagon Press, 1981.

Feuerstein, Georg. *Tantra: The Path of Ecstasy.* Boston and London: Shambhala, 1998.

Ficino, Marsilio. *Platonic Theology.* Vol. 3. Translated by Michael J. N. Allen with John Warden, Latin text edited by James Hankins with William Bowen. Cambridge, Mass., and London: Harvard University Press, 2003.

Fine, Lawrence. "The Contemplative Practice of Yiḥudim in Lurianic Kabbalah." In *Jewish Spirituality from the Sixteenth-Century Revival to the Present*, edited by Arthur Green, 64–98. New York: Crossroad, 1987.

———. "Maggidic Revelation in the Teachings of Isaac Luria." In *Mystics, Philosophers and Politicians*, edited by Jehuda Reinharz and Daniel Swetschinski, 141–157. Durham: Duke University Press, 1982.

———. *Physician of the Soul, Healer of the Cosmos: Isaac Luria and His Kabbalistic Fellowship.* Stanford: Stanford University Press, 2003.

———. "Purifying the Body in the Name of the Soul: The Problem of the Body in Sixteenth-Century Kabbalah." In *People of the Body: Jews and Judaism from an Embodied Perspective*, edited by Howard Eilberg-Schwartz, 117–142. Albany: State University of New York Press, 1992.

———. "Recitation of Mishnah as a Vehicle for Mystical Inspiration: A Contemplative Technique Taught by Ḥayyim Vital." *Revue des études juives* 141 (1982): 183–199.

Finkelberg, Margalit. "Plato's Language of Love and the Female." *Harvard Theological Review* 90 (1997): 231–261.

Finney, Paul C. *The Invisible God: The Earliest Christians on Art.* New York and Oxford: Oxford University Press, 1994.

Fiorenza, Elisabeth Schüssler. *In Memory of Her: A Feminist Theological Reconstruction of Christian Origins.* New York: Crossroad, 1983.

Fioretos, Aris. "Nothing: History and Materiality in Celan." In *Word Traces: Readings of Paul Celan*, edited by Aris Fioretos, 295–341. Baltimore and London: Johns Hopkins University Press, 1994.

Fischer, Steven R. *A History of Language.* London: Reaktion Books, 1999.

Fishbane, Eitan P. "Contemplative Practice and the Transmission of Kabbalah: A Study of Isaac of Acre's *Meʾirat ʿEinayim.*" Ph.D. dissertation, Brandeis University, 2003.

———. "Tears of Disclosure: The Role of Weeping in Zoharic Narrative." *Journal of Jewish Thought and Philosophy* 11 (2002): 25–47.

Fishbane, Michael A. *The Exegetical Imagination: On Jewish Thought and Theology.* Cambridge, Mass., and London: Harvard University Press, 1998.

———. *The Kiss of God: Spiritual and Mystical Death in Judaism.* Seattle: University of Washington Press, 1994.

———. "The Song of Songs and Ancient Jewish Religiosity: Between Eros and History." In *Von Enoch bis Kafka: Festschrift für Karl E. Grözinger zum 60. Geburtstag*, edited by Manfred Voigts, 69–81. Wiesbaden: Harrassowitz Verlag, 2002.

Fishbane, Simcha. "'Most Woman Engage in Sorcery': An Analysis of Sorceresses in the Babylonian Talmud." *Jewish History* 7 (1993): 27–42.

Fishman, Talya. "A Kabbalistic Perspective on Gender-Specific Comments: On the Interplay of Symbols and Society." *AJS Review* 17 (1992): 199–245.

Fitzmyer, Joseph A. *The Genesis Apocryphon of Qumran Cave 1: A Commentary.* 2nd ed., rev. ed. Rome: Biblical Institute Press, 1971.

Fiumara, Gemma Corradi. *The Other Side of Language: A Philosophy of Listening.* London and New York: Routledge, 1990.

Five Lost Classics: Tao, Huanglao, and Yin-Yang in Han Chin. Translated with an introduction and commentary by Robin D. S. Yates. New York: Ballantine Books, 1997.

Fletcher-Louis, Crispin H. T. "4Q374: A Discourse on the Sinai Tradition: The Deification of Moses and Early Christology." *Dead Sea Discoveries* 3 (1996): 236–252.

———. *All the Glory of Adam: Liturgical Anthropology in the Dead Sea Scrolls.* Leiden: Brill, 2002.

———. *Luke-Acts: Angels, Christology, and Soteriology.* Tübingen: Mohr Siebeck, 1997.

———. "Some Reflections on Angelomorphic Humanity Texts among the Dead Sea Scrolls." *Dead Sea Discoveries* 7 (2001): 292–312.

———. "The Worship of Divine Humanity as God's Image and the Worship of Jesus." In *The Jewish Roots of Christological Monotheism: Papers from the St. Andrews Conference on the Historical*

Origins of the Worship of Jesus, edited by Carey C. Newman, James R. Davila, and Gladys S. Lewis, 112–128. Leiden: Brill, 1999.

Flood, Gavin D. *Beyond Phenomenology: Rethinking the Study of Religion*. London and New York: Cassell, 1999.

Flusser, David. *Jesus*. In collaboration with R. Steven Notley. Jerusalem: Magnes Press, 1997.

Flynn, Bernard. "Merleau-Ponty et la position philosophique du scepticisme." In *Notes de cours sur L'origine de la géométrie de Husserl suivi de recherches sur la phénoménologie de Merleau-Ponty*, edited by Renaud Barbaras, 147–161. Paris: Presses Universitaires de France, 1998.

Flynn, St. John E. "The Saint of the Womanly Body: Raimon de Cornet's Fourteenth-Century Male Poetics." In *Sex and Gender in Medieval and Renaissance Texts: The Latin Tradition*, edited by Barbara K. Gold, Paul A. Miller, and Charles Platter, 91–109. Albany: State University of New York Press, 1997.

Folin, Alberto. "La figure du silence dans l'imaginaire moderne: Leopardi et Jabès." In *Écrire le livre: Autour d'Edmond Jabès: Colloque de Cerisy-la-Salle*, edited by Richard Stamelman and Mary Ann Caws, 147–156. Seyssel: Éditions Champ Vallon, 1989.

Fonrobert, Charlotte E. "The Beginnings of Rabbinic Textuality: Women's Bodies and Paternal Knowledge." In *Beginning/Again: Toward a Hermeneutics of Jewish Texts*, edited by Aryeh Cohen and Shaul Magid, 49–68. New York and London: Seven Bridges Press, 2002.

———. *Menstrual Purity: Rabbinic and Christian Reconstructions of Biblical Gender*. Stanford: Stanford University Press, 2000.

Ford, J. Massyngberde. *Revelation: Introduction, Translation and Commentary*. Garden City: Doubleday, 1975.

Forgie, J. William. "Hyper-Kantianism in Recent Discussions of Mystical Experience." *Religious Studies* 21 (1985): 205–218.

Forman, Robert K. C. *Meister Eckhart—The Mystic as Theologian: An Experiment in Methodology*. Rockport: Element, 1991.

———, ed. *The Problem of Pure Consciousness: Mysticism and Philosophy*. Oxford: Oxford University Press, 1990.

Foshay, Toby. "Introduction: Denegation and Resentment." In *Derrida and Negative Theology*, edited by Howard Coward and Toby Foshay, 1–24. Albany: State University of New York Press, 1992.

Fossum, Jarl E. *The Name of God and the Angel of the Lord: Samaritan and Jewish Concepts of Intermediation and the Origin of Gnosticism*. Tübingen: J. C. B. Mohr, 1985.

Fóti, Véronique. *Heidegger and the Poets: Poiesis, Sophia, Techne*. Atlantic Highlands: Humanities Press, 1992.

———. *Vision's Invisibles: Philosophical Explorations*. Albany: State University of New York Press, 2003.

Foucault, Michel. *The History of Sexuality*. 3 vols. Translated by Robert Hurley. New York: Vintage Books, 1988.

———. *Language, Counter-Memory, Practice: Selected Essays and Interviews*. Ithaca: Cornell University Press, 1977.

———. *Religion and Culture*. Selected and edited by Jeremey R. Carrette. New York: Routledge, 1999.

Fraade, Steven. "Ascetical Aspects of Ancient Judaism." In *Jewish Spirituality from the Bible to the Middle Ages*, edited by Arthur Green, 253–288. New York: Crossroad, 1986.

Franck, Adolphe. *Die Kabbala oder die Religions-Philosophie der Hebräer*. Translated by Adolf Jellinek. Leipzig: Heinrich Hunger, 1844.

Frank, Daniel. "Karaite Commentaries on the Song of Songs from Tenth-Century Jerusalem." In *With Reverence for the Word: Medieval Scriptural Exegesis in Judaism, Christianity, and Islam*, edited by Jane Dammen McAuliffe, Barry D. Walfish, and Joseph W. Goering, 51–69. Oxford: Oxford University Press, 2003.

———. "The *Shoshanim* of Tenth-Century Jerusalem: Karaite Exegesis, Prayer, and Communal Identity." In *The Jews of Medieval Islam: Community, Society, and Identity*, edited by Daniel Frank, 199–245. Leiden: E. J. Brill, 1995.

———. "'The Voice of the Turtledove Is Heard in Our Land': The Commentaries of the Karaites Salmon ben Jeroham and Japheth ben Eli on the Song of Songs." *International Rennert Guest Lecture Series* 7 (2001).

Freimark, Hans. *Okkultismus und Sexualität: Beiträge zur Kulturgeschichte der Vergangenheit und Gegenwart*. Sinzheim: Archiv für Altes Gedankengut und Wissen, 2003.

Freud, Sigmund. *Collected Papers*. Edited by James Strachey. London: Hogarth Press, 1953.

———. *The Complete Introductory Lectures on Psychoanalysis*. Translated by James Strachey. New York: W. W. Norton, 1966.

———. *Group Psychology and the Analysis of the Ego*. Translated by James Strachey. New York and London: W. W. Norton, 1959.

———. *Moses and Monotheism*. Translated by Katherine Jones. New York: Vintage Books, 1967.

———. *Totem and Taboo*. Translated by James Strachey. New York: W. W. Norton, 1989.

Freudenberger, Silja. "The Hermeneutic Conversation as Epistemological Model." In *Feminist Interpretations of Hans-Georg Gadamer*, edited by Lorraine Code, 259–283. University Park: Pennsylvania State University Press, 2003.

Frey, Hans-Jost. "Hölderlin's Marginalization of Language." In *The Solid Letter: Readings of Friedrich Hölderlin*, edited by Aris Fioretos, 356–374. Stanford: Stanford University Press, 1999.

Fricker, Miranda. "Knowledge as Construct: Theorizing the Role of Gender in Knowledge." In *Knowing the Difference: Feminist Perspectives in Epistemology*, edited by Kathleen Lennon and Margaret Whitford, 95–109. London and New York: Routledge, 1994.

Friedman, Mordecai A. "The Ethics of Medieval Jewish Marriage." In *Religion in a Religious Age*, edited by Shlomo D. Goitein, 83–101. Cambridge, Mass.: Association for Jewish Studies, 1974.

———. "Halacha as Evidence for the Study of Sexual Mores among Jews in Medieval Islamic Countries: Face Coverings and Mutʿah Marriages." In *View into the Lives of Women in Jewish Societies*, edited by Yael Azmon, 161–182. Jerusalem: Zalman Shazar Center for Jewish History, 1995.

Friedman, Shamma. "Graven Images." *Graven Images: A Journal of Culture, Law, and the Sacred* 1 (1994): 233–238.

Friedrich, Gerhard, ed. *Theological Dictionary of the New Testament*. Translated and edited by Geoffrey W. Bromiley. Grand Rapids: Wm. B. Eerdmans, 1972.

Friedrich-Silber, Ilana. *Virtuosity, Charisma, and Social Order: A Comparative Sociological Study of Monasticism in Theravada Buddhism and Medieval Catholicism*. Cambridge: Cambridge University Press, 1995.

Friesen, Ilse E. *The Female Crucifix: Images of St. Wilgefortis since the Middle Ages*. Waterloo: Wilfrid Laurier University Press, 2001.

Frisby, David. "Walter Benjamin's Prehistory of Modernity as Anticipation of Postmodernity? Some Methodological Reflections." In *"With the Sharpened Axe of Reason": Approaches to Walter Benjamin*, edited by Gerhard Fischer, 15–32. Oxford: Berg, 1996.

Froment-Meurice, Marc. *That Is To Say: Heidegger's Poetics*. Translated by Jan Plug. Stanford: Stanford University Press, 1998.

Frosh, Stephen. *Sexual Difference: Masculinity and Psychoanalysis.* London and New York: Routledge, 1994.

Frost, Kate Gartner. *Holy Delight: Typology, Numerology, and Autobiography in Donne's Devotions upon Emergent Occasions.* Princeton: Princeton University Press, 1990.

Frymer-Kensky, Tikva. *In the Wake of the Goddesses: Women, Culture, and the Biblical Transformation of Pagan Myth.* New York: Free Press, 1992.

———. *Reading the Women of the Bible: A New Interpretation of Their Stories.* New York: Schocken Books, 2002.

Fulton, Rachel. *From Judgment to Passion: Devotion to Christ and the Virgin Mary, 800–1200.* New York: Columbia University Press, 2002.

———. "The Virgin Mary and the Song of Songs in the High Middle Ages." Ph.D. dissertation, Columbia University, 1994.

Funke, Gerhard. "Phenomenology and History." In *Phenomenology and the Social Sciences,* edited by Maurice Natanson, 2:3–101. 2 vols. Evanston: Northwestern University Press, 1973.

Furuta, Hirokiyo. *Wittgenstein und Heidegger: "Sinn" und "Logik" in der Tradition der analytischen Philosophie.* Würzburg: Verlag Königshausen & Neumann GmbH, 1996.

Fuss, Diana. *Essentially Speaking: Feminism, Nature and Difference.* New York and London: Routledge, 1989.

———. "'Essentially Speaking': Luce Irigaray's Language of Essence." In *Revaluing French Feminism: Critical Essays on Difference, Agency, and Culture,* edited by Nancy Fraser and Sandra Lee Bartky, 94–112. Bloomington and Indianapolis: Indiana University Press, 1992.

Fynsk, Christopher. *Language and Relation . . . that there is language.* Stanford: Stanford University Press, 1996.

Gadamer, Hans-Georg. "Meaning and Concealment of Meaning in Paul Celan." In *Gadamer on Celan: "Who am I and Who are You? and Other Essays,* translated and edited by Richard Heinemann and Bruce Krajewski, 167–178. Albany: State University of New York Press, 1997.

———. *On Education, Poetry, and History: Applied Hermeneutics.* Edited by Dieter Misgeld and Graeme Nicholson, translated by Lawrence Schmidt and Monica Reuss. Albany: State University of New York Press, 1992.

———. "Text and Interpretation." In *Dialogue and Deconstruction: The Gadamer-Derrida Encounter,* edited by Diane P. Michelfelder and Richard E. Palmer, 21–51. Albany: State University of New York Press, 1989.

———. *Truth and Method.* New York: Crossroad, 1982.

Gager, John G. *Moses in Greco-Roman Paganism.* Nashville: Abingdon Press, 1972.

———. *Reinventing Paul.* Oxford and New York: Oxford University Press, 2000.

Gallagher, Shaun. "Disrupting Seriality: Merleau-Ponty, Lyotard, and Post-Husserlian Temporality." In *Rereading Merleau-Ponty: Essays Beyond the Continental-Analytic Divide,* edited by Lawrence Hass and Dorothea Olkowski, 97–119. Amherst: Humanity Books, 2000.

———. *The Inordinance of Time.* Evanston: Northwestern University Press, 1998.

———. "On the Pre-Noetic Reality of Time." In *Écart & Différance: Merleau-Ponty and Derrida on Seeing and Writing,* edited by Martin C. Dillon, 134–148. Atlantic Highlands: Humanities Press, 1997.

Galli, Barbara E. "Introduction: Translating Is a Mode of Holiness." In *Cultural Writings of Franz Rosenzweig,* edited and translated by Barbara E. Galli, with a foreword by Leora Batnitzky, 3–57. Syracuse: Syracuse University Press, 2000.

———. *Franz Rosenzweig and Jehuda Halevi: Translating, Translations, and Translators.* Montreal and Kingston: McGill-Queen's University Press, 1995.

Gallop, Jane. *The Daughter's Seduction: Feminism and Psychoanalysis.* Ithaca: Cornell University Press, 1982.

———. *Reading Lacan.* Ithaca: Cornell University Press, 1985.

Gamlieli, Deborah. "Stages of 'Becoming' in the Creation: Parallelism with Philosophical and Psychological Terminology." *Kabbalah: Journal for the Study of Jewish Mystical Texts* 12 (2004): 233–320 (Hebrew).

Ganeri, Jonardon. *Philosophy in Classical India: An Introduction and Analysis.* London and New York: Routledge, 2001.

Garb, Jonathan. "The Kabbalah of Rabbi Joseph Ibn Ṣayyaḥ as a Source for the Understanding of Safedian Kabbalah." *Kabbalah: Journal for the Study of Jewish Mystical Texts* 4 (1999): 255–313 (Hebrew).

———. "Power and Kavvanah in Kabbalah." Ph.D. dissertation, Hebrew University of Jerusalem, 2000 (Hebrew).

———. "Trance Techniques in the Kabbalistic Tradition of Jerusalem." *Peʿamim* 70 (1997): 47–67 (Hebrew).

García Düttmann, Alexander. *The Gift of Language: Memory and Promise in Adorno, Benjamin, Heidegger, and Rosenzweig.* Translated by Arline Lyons. Syracuse: Syracuse University Press, 2000.

Gardaz, Élisabeth. "Rhétorique et figures du silence dans l'œuvre de Jabès." In *Écrire le livre: Autour d'Edmond Jabès: Colloque de Cerisy-la-Salle,* edited by Richard Stamelman and Mary Ann Caws, 31–43. Seyssel: Éditions Champ Vallon, 1989.

Gardt, Andreas. *Sprachreflexion in Barock und Frühaufklärung: Entwürfe von Böhme bis Leibniz.* Berlin and New York: Walter de Gruyter, 1994.

Garfield, Jay L., and Graham Priest. "Nāgārjuna and the Limits of Thought." *Philosophy East and West* 53 (2003): 1–21.

Garver, Newton, and Seung-Chong Lee. *Derrida and Wittgenstein.* Philadelphia: Temple University Press, 1994.

Gasché, Rodolphe. *Of Minimal Things: Studies on the Notion of Relation.* Stanford: Stanford University Press, 1999.

———. "Saturnine Vision and the Question of Difference: Reflections on Walter Benjamin's Theory of Language." In *Benjamin's Ground: New Readings of Walter Benjamin,* edited by Rainer Nägele, 83–104. Detroit: Wayne State University Press, 1988.

Gaston, Lloyd. *Paul and the Torah.* Vancouver: University of British Columbia Press, 1987.

Gatens, Moira. *Feminism and Philosophy: Perspectives on Difference and Equality.* Bloomington and Indianapolis: Indiana University Press, 1991.

———. *Imaginary Bodies: Ethics, Power and Corporeality.* London and New York: Routledge, 1996.

Gauchet, Marcel. *The Disenchantment of the World: A Political History of Religion.* Translated by Oscar Burge. Princeton: Princeton University Press, 1997.

Gavin, William J. *William James and the Reinstatement of the Vague.* Philadelphia: Temple University Press, 1992.

Gay, Peter. *A Godless Jew: Freud, Atheism, and the Making of Psychoanalysis.* New Haven: Yale University Press, 1987.

Gellrich, Jesse M. *The Idea of the Book in the Middle Ages: Language Theory, Mythology, and Fiction.* Ithaca and London: Cornell University Press, 1985.

Gerhart, Mary. "The Word Image Opposition: The Apophatic-Cataphatic and the Iconic-Aniconic Tensions in Spirituality." In *Divine Representations: Postmodernism and Spirituality,* edited by Ann W. Astell, 63–79. New York and Mahwah: Paulist Press, 1994.

Gersh, Stephen. ΚΙΝΗΣΙΣ ΑΚΙΝΗΤΟΣ: *A Study of Spiritual Motion in the Philosophy of Proclus*. Leiden: E. J. Brill, 1973.

———. *Middle Platonism and Neoplatonism: The Latin Tradition*. 2 vols. Notre Dame: University of Notre Dame Press, 1986.

Ghazālī. *The Niche of Lights: A Parallel English-Arabic Text*. Translated by David Buchman. Provo: Brigham Young University Press, 1998.

Gianotti, Timothy J. *Al-Ghazali's Unspeakable Doctrine of the Soul: Unveiling the Esoteric Psychology and Eschatology of the Ihyaʿ*. Leiden: Brill, 2001.

Gibbons, B. J. *Spirituality and the Occult: From the Renaissance to the Modern Age*. London and New York: Routledge, 2001.

Gibbs, Robert. "Reading Heidegger: Destruction, Thinking, Return." In *Tainted Greatness: Antisemitism and Cultural Heroes*, edited by Nancy A. Harrowitz, 157–172. Philadelphia: Temple University Press, 1994.

Gibson, Joan. "Could Christ Have Been Born a Woman? A Medieval Debate." *Journal of Feminist Studies in Religion* 8 (1992): 65–82.

Gier, Nicholas F. *Wittgenstein and Phenomenology: A Comparative Study of the Later Wittgenstein, Husserl, Heidegger, and Merleau-Ponty*. Albany: State University of New York Press, 1981.

Gieschen, Charles A. *Angelomorphic Christology: Antecedents and Early Evidence*. Leiden: E. J. Brill, 1998.

Giffen, Lois Anita. *Theory of Profane Love among the Arabs: The Development of the Genre*. New York: New York University Press, 1971.

Gill, Jerry H. *Merleau-Ponty and Metaphor*. Atlantic Highlands: Humanities Press, 1991.

Giller, Pinchas. *Reading the Zohar: The Sacred Text of Kabbalah*. Oxford and New York: Oxford University Press, 2001.

Gilman, Sander L. *Freud, Race, and Gender*. Princeton: Princeton University Press, 1993.

Gilson, Étienne. *The Mystical Theology of Saint Bernard*. Translated by Alfred Howard Campbell Downes. Kalamazoo: Cistercian Publications, 1990.

Ginsburg, Elliot K. *The Sabbath in Classical Kabbalah*. Albany: State University of New York Press, 1989.

Ginzberg, Louis. *The Legends of the Jews*. 7 vols. Philadelphia: Jewish Publication Society of America, 1968.

Girard, René. *Violence and the Sacred*. Translated by Patrick Gregory. Baltimore: Johns Hopkins University Press, 1977.

Glendinning, Simon. *On Being with Others: Heidegger—Derrida—Wittgenstein*. London and New York: Routledge, 1998.

Glünz, Michael. "The Poet's Heart: A Polyfunctional Object in the Poetic System of the Ghazal." In *Intoxication Earthly and Heavenly: Seven Studies on the Poet Ḥafiz of Shiraz*, edited by Michael Glünz and J. Christoph Bürgel, 53–68. Bern: Peter Lang, 1991.

Goddard, Hugh. *Muslim Perceptions of Christianity*. London: Grey Seal, 1996.

Godelier, Maurice. *The Enigma of the Gift*. Translated by Nora Scott. Chicago: University of Chicago Press, 1999.

Goitein, Shlomo D. *A Mediterranean Society: The Jewish Community of the Arab World as Portrayed in the Documents of the Cairo Geniza*. 6 vols. Berkeley: University of California Press, 1967–1994.

———. "The Sexual Mores of the Common People." In *Society and the Sexes in Medieval Islam*, 43–61. Edited by Afaf Al-Sayyid-Marsot. Malibu: Undena Publications, 1979.

Gokak, Vinayak Krishna. *An Integral View of Poetry: An Indian Perspective*. New Delhi: Abhinav Publications, 1975.

Gold, Penny Schine. *The Lady and the Virgin: Image. Attitude, and Experience in Twelfth-Century France*. Chicago and London: University of Chicago Press, 1985.

Goldberg, Ben Zion. *The Sacred Fire: The Story of Sex in Religion*. New York: University Books, 1958.

Goldberg, Ellen. *The Lord Who Is Half Woman: Ardhanarisvara in Indian and Feminist Perspective*. Albany: State University of New York Press, 2002.

Goldberg, Joel. "Mystical Union, Individuality, and Individuation in Provençal and Catalonian Kabbalah." Ph.D. dissertation, New York University, 2001.

Goldman, Shalom. *The Wiles of Women/The Wiles of Men: Joseph and Potiphar's Wife in Ancient Near Eastern, Jewish, and Islamic Folklore*. Albany: State University Press of New York, 1995.

Goldziher, Ignaz. *Introduction to Islamic Theology and Law*. Translated by Andras and Ruth Hamori, with an introduction and additional notes by Bernard Lewis. Princeton: Princeton University Press, 1981.

Golitzin, Alexander. " 'Suddenly Christ': The Place of Negative Theology in the Mystagogy of Dionysius Areopagites." In *Mystics: Presence and Aporia*, edited by Michael Kessler and Christian Sheppard, 8–37. Chicago and London: University of Chicago Press, 2003.

Gondek, Hans-Dieter. "Das übersetzen Denken: *Über*setzen und über*setzen*." *Heidegger Studies* 12 (1996): 37–55.

González-Casanovas, Roberto J. "Male Bonding as Cultural Construction in Alfonso X, Ramon Llull, and Juan Manuel: Homosocial Friendship in Medieval Iberia." In *Queer Iberia: Sexualities, Cultures, and Crossings From the Middle Ages to the Renaissance*, edited by Josiah Blackmore and Gregory S. Hutcheson, 157–192. Durham and London: Duke University Press, 1999.

Goodenough, Erwin Ramsdell. *The Psychology of Religious Experiences*. New York: Basic Books, 1965.

Goodman, Lenn E. "Matter and Form as Attributes of God in Maimonides' Philosophy." In *A Straight Path Studies in Medieval Philosophy and Culture: Essays in Honor of Arthur Hyman*, edited by Jeremiah Hackett, Michael S. Hyman, R. James Long, and Charles H. Manekin, 86–97. Washington, D.C.: Catholic University of America Press, 1988.

Gordon, Peter E. "The Erotics of Negative Theology: Maimonides on Apprehension." *Jewish Studies Quarterly* 2 (1995): 1–38.

———. *Rosenzweig and Heidegger: Between Judaism and German Philosophy*. Berkeley: University of California Press, 2003.

Gordon, Pierre. *Sex and Religion*. New York: Social Sciences Publishers, 1949.

The Gospel of Thomas: Annotated and Explained. Translated and annotated by Stevan Davies, foreword by Andrew Harvey. Woodstock: Skylight Paths, 2002.

The Gospel of Thomas: The Hidden Sayings of Jesus. New translation, with introduction, critical edition of the Coptic text, and notes by Marvin Meyer, interpretation by Harold Bloom. New York: HarperCollins, 1992.

Gottfarstein, Joseph. *Le Bahir: Le livre de la clarté*. Paris: Éditions Verdier, 1983.

Gottlieb, Ephraim. *Studies in the Kabbala Literature*. Edited by Joseph Hacker. Tel-Aviv: Tel-Aviv University Press, 1976 (Hebrew).

Gottlieb, Isaac B. "The Jewish Allegory of Love: Change and Constancy." *Journal of Jewish Thought and Philosophy* 2 (1992): 1–18.

Goudriaan, Teun. "The Stages of Awakening in the Svacchanda-Tantra." In *Ritual and Speculation in Early Tantrism: Studies in Honor of André Padoux*, edited by Teun Goudriaan, 139–173. Albany: State University of New York Press, 1992.

Gould, Graham. "The Image of God and the Anthropomorphic Controversy in Fourth Century Monasticism." In *Origeniana Quinta*, edited by R. Daly, 549–557. Leuven: Leuven University Press, 1992.

Grace, George W. *The Linguistic Construction of Reality*. London: Croom Helm, 1987.

Graf, Fritz. *Magic in the Ancient World*. Translated by Franklin Philip. Cambridge and London: Harvard University Press, 1997.

Graham, William A. *Beyond the Written Word: Oral Aspects of Scripture in the History of Religion*. Cambridge: Cambridge University Press, 1987.

———. "Das Schriftprinzip in vergleichender Sicht." In *Gott ist schön und Er liebt die Schönheit: Festschrift für Annemarie Schimmel zum 7. April 1992*, edited by Alma Giese and J. Christoph Bürgel, 209–226. Bern: Peter Lang, 1994.

Granier, Jean. "Perspectivism and Interpretation." In *The New Nietzsche: Contemporary Styles of Interpretation*, edited and introduced by David B. Allison, 190–200. New York: Dell, 1977.

Grant, Robert "The Mystery of Marriage in the Gospel of Philip." *Vigiliae Christianae* 15 (1961): 129–140.

Green, Arthur. "Introduction." In *The Zohar: Pritzker Edition*, vol. 1, translation and commentary by Daniel C. Matt, xxxi–lxxxi. Stanford: Stanford University Press, 2004.

———. "Kabbalistic Re-Vision: A Review Article of Elliot Wolfson's *Through a Speculum That Shines*." *History of Religions* 36 (1997): 265–274.

———. *Keter: The Crown of God in Early Jewish Mysticism*. Princeton: Princeton University Press, 1997.

———. "Shekhinah, The Virgin Mary, and the Song of Songs: Reflections on a Kabbalistic Symbol in Historical Context." *AJS Review* 26 (2002): 1–52.

———. "The Song of Songs in Early Jewish Mysticism." *Orim* 2 (1987): 49–63.

———. *Tormented Master: A Life of Rabbi Nahman of Bratslav*. Tuscaloosa: University of Alabama Press, 1979.

Green, Monica H. "From 'Diseases of Women' to 'Secrets of Women': The Transformation of Gynecological Literature in the Later Middle Ages." *Journal of Medieval and Early Modern Studies* 30 (2000): 5–39.

Greenstein, David. "Aimless Pilgrimage: The Quotidian Utopia of the *Zohar*." Ph.D. dissertation, New York University, 2003.

Gregg, Joan Young. *Devils, Women, and Jews: Reflections of the Other in Medieval Sermon Stories*. Albany: State University of New York Press, 1997.

Gregory of Nyssa. *Commentary on the Song of Songs*. Translated by Casimir McCambly. Brookline, Mass.: Hellenic College Press, 1987.

———. *Contra Eunomium libri*. Edited by Werner Jaeger. Leiden: E. J. Brill, 1960.

———. *The Life of Moses*. Translated by Abraham J. Malherbe and Everett Ferguson. New York and Mahwah: Paulist Press, 1978.

———. *The Lord's Prayer, the Beatitudes*. Translated by Hilda C. Graef. New York: Paulist Press, 1954.

———. *La vie de Moïse; ou Traité de la perfection en matière de vertu*. Introduction, critical text, and translation by Jean Daniélou. 3rd ed. Paris: Éditions du Cerf, 1987.

Griffiths, Paul J. *On Being Mindless: Buddhist Meditation and the Mind-Body Problem*. La Salle: Open Court, 1986.

Grigg, Ray. *The Tao of Zen*. Edison: Alva Press, 1999.

Grimaldi, Nicolas. *Le désir et le temps*. 2nd ed. Paris: Librairie Philosophique J. Vrin, 1992.

Gritz, Sharon Hodgin. *Paul, Women Teachers, and the Mother Goddess at Ephesus: A Study of 1 Timothy 2:9–15 in Light of the Religious and Cultural Milieu of the First Century*. Lanham: University Press of America, 1991.

Gross, Abraham. *Iberian Jewry from Twilight to Dawn: The World of Rabbi Abraham Saba*. Leiden: E. J. Brill, 1995.

———. "Reasons for the Commandment of Circumcision—Historical Currents and Influences in the Middle Ages." *Daʿat* 21 (1988): 25–46 (Hebrew).

Gross, Rita M. *Buddhism after Patriarchy: A Feminist History, Analysis, and Reconstruction of Buddhism*. Albany: State University of New York Press, 1993.

———. *Feminism and Religion: An Introduction*. Boston: Beacon Press, 1996.

———. "Some Buddhist Perspectives on the Goddess." In *Women and Goddess Traditions in Antiquity and Today*, edited by Karen L. King, 406–425. Minneapolis: Fortress Press, 1997.

Grossman, Avraham. *Pious and Rebellious: Jewish Women in Europe in the Middle Ages*. Jerusalem: Zalman Shazar Center for Jewish History, 2001 (Hebrew).

Grosz, Elizabeth. "Histories of the Present and Future: Feminism, Power, Bodies." In *Thinking the Limits of the Body*, edited by Jeffrey J. Cohen and Gail Weiss, 13–23. Albany: State University of New York Press, 2003.

———. *Space, Time, and Perversion: Essays on the Politics of Bodies*. New York and London: Routledge, 1995.

———. *Volatile Bodies: Toward a Corporeal Feminism*. Bloomington and Indianapolis: Indiana University Press, 1994.

Grözinger, Karl E. "Tradition and Innovation in the Concept of Poetry in the Zohar." *Jerusalem Studies in Jewish Thought* 8 (1989): 347–355 (Hebrew).

Gruber, Mayer I. *The Motherhood of God and Other Studies*. Atlanta: Scholars Press, 1992.

Gruenwald, Ithamar. "Some Critical Notes on the First Part of *Sefer Yeẓira*." *Revue des études juives* 132 (1973): 475–512.

Guberman, Karen. "The Language of Love in Spanish Kabbalah: An Examination of the *Iggeret ha-Kodesh*." In *Approaches to Judaism in Medieval Times*, edited by David R. Blumenthal, 53–95. Chico: Scholars Press, 1984.

Gudorf, Christine E. *Body, Sex, and Pleasure: Reconstructing Christian Sexual Ethics*. Cleveland: Pilgrim Press, 1994.

Guenther, Herbert. *From Reductionism to Creativity: Rdzogs-Chen and the New Sciences of Mind*. Boston and Shaftesbury: Shambhala, 1989.

———. *Matrix of Mystery: Scientific and Humanistic Aspects of Rdzogs-Chen Thought*. Boulder and London: Shambhala, 1984.

———. *The Teachings of Padmasambhava*. Leiden: E. J. Brill, 1996.

Guest, Gérard. "La Phénoménologie de Wittgenstein." *Heidegger Studies* 7 (1991): 53–74.

Guetti, James. *Wittgenstein and the Grammar of Literary Experience*. Athens and London: University of Georgia Press, 1993.

Guilding, Aileen. *The Fourth Gospel and Jewish Worship: A Study of the Relation of St. John's Gospel to the Ancient Jewish Lectionary System*. Oxford: Oxford University Press, 1960.

Guillemin, Elaine. "Jesus/Holy Mother Wisdom (Mt. 23:37–39)." In *The Lost Coin: Parables of Women, Work and Wisdom*, edited by Mary Ann Beavis, 244–267. London and New York: Sheffield Academic Press, 2002.

Guindi, Fadwa El. *Veil: Modesty, Privacy, and Resistance*. Oxford and New York: Berg, 1999.

Gunn, Alan M. F. *The Mirror of Love: A Reinterpretation of "The Romance of the Rose."* Lubbock: Texas Tech Press, 1952.

Gupta, Bina, ed. *Sexual Archetypes, East and West.* New York: Paragon House, 1987.

Gutas, Dmitri. *Avicenna and the Aristotelian Tradition: Introduction to Reading Avicenna's Philosophical Works.* Leiden: E. J. Brill, 1988.

———. "Ibn Ṭufayl on Ibn Sīnā's Eastern Philosophy." *Oriens* 34 (1994): 222–241.

———. "Plato's *Symposion* in the Arabic Tradition." *Oriens* 31 (1988): 36–60.

Habermas, Jürgen. *The Liberating Power of Symbols: Philosophical Essays.* Translated by Peter Dews. Cambridge, Mass.: MIT Press, 2001.

Haddad, Yvonne Yazbeck, and John L. Esposito, eds. *Daughters of Abraham: Feminist Thought in Judaism, Christianity, and Islam.* Gainesville: University Press of Florida, 2001.

Hadley, Judith M. "From Goddess to Literary Construct: The Transformation of Asherah into Ḥokhmah." In *Feminist Companion to Reading the Bible: Approaches, Methods and Strategies*, edited by Athalya Brenner and Carole Fontaine, 360–399. London and Chicago: Fitzroy Dearborn, 1997.

Hadot, Pierre. *Plotinus, or, the Simplicity of Vision.* Chicago: University of Chicago Press, 1993.

Ḥāfiz. *Fifty Poems of Ḥāfiz.* Translated by Arthur J. Arberry. Cambridge: Cambridge University Press, 1962.

———. *The Gift: Poems by Ḥafiz the Great Sufi Master.* Translated by Daniel Ladinsky. New York: Penguin Compass, 1999.

———. *The Green Sea of Heaven: Fifty Ghazals from the Dīwān of Ḥāfiz.* Translated by Elizabeth T. Gray. Ashland: White Cloud Press, 1995.

Hagberg, Garry. *Art as Language: Wittgenstein, Meaning, and Aesthetic Theory.* Ithaca and London: Cornell University Press, 1995.

Hagemann, Ludwig, and Ernst Pulsfort. *Maria, die Mutter Jesu, in Bibel und Koran.* Würzburg: Echter, 1992.

Hale, Rosemary D. "'Taste and See, For God Is Sweet': Sensory Perception and Memory in Medieval Christian Mystical Experience." In *Vox Mystica: Essays on Medieval Mysticism in Honor of Professor Valerie M. Lagorio*, edited by Anne Clark Bartlett, with Thomas H. Bestul, Janet Goebel, and William F. Pollard, 3–14. Cambridge: D. S. Brewer, 1995.

Hales, Steven D., and Rex Welshon. *Nietzsche's Perspectivism.* Urbana and Chicago: University of Illinois Press, 2000.

Halivni, David Weiss. "On the Supposed Anti-Asceticism of Simon the Just." *Jewish Quarterly Review* 58 (1968): 243–252.

Halkin, Abraham S. "Ibn Aknin's Commentary on the Song of Songs." In *Alexander Marx Jubilee Volume*, edited by Saul Lieberman, 389–420. New York: Jewish Theological Seminary of America 1950.

Ḥallamish, Moshe. "The Place of Kabbalah in Ritual." In Daniel Sperber, *The Rituals of Israel: Sources and Developments*, vol. 3, 173–225. Jerusalem: Mosad ha-Rav Kook, 1994 (Hebrew).

———. "The Relation to the Nations of the World in the World of the Kabbalists." *Jerusalem Studies in Jewish Thought* 14 (1998): 289–311 (Hebrew).

Hallyn, Fernand. *The Poetic Structure of the World: Copernicus and Kepler.* Translated by Donald M. Leslie. New York: Zone Books, 1993.

Hambly, Gavin R. G. "Becoming Visible: Medieval Islamic Women in Historiography and History." In *Women in the Medieval Islamic World: Power, Patronage, and Piety*, edited by Gavin R. G. Hambly, 3–27. New York: St. Martin's Press, 1988.

Hamburger, Jeffrey F. *The Rothschild Canticles: Art and Mysticism in Flanders and the Rhineland Circa 1300.* New Haven and London: Yale University Press, 1990.

Hames, Hayyim. "Elijah and a Shepherd: The Authority of Revelation." *Studia Lulliana* 34 (1994): 93–102.
Hammad, Ahmad Z. M. *Mary, the Chosen Woman: The Mother of Jesus in the Quran: An Interlinear Commentary on Surat Maryam*. Bridgeview: Quranic Literary Institute, 2001.
Hancock, Curtis L. "Negative Theology in Gnosticism and Neoplatonism." In *Neoplatonism and Gnosticism*, edited by Richard T. Wallis and Jay Bregman, 167–186. Albany: State University of New York Press, 1992.
Handelman, Susan A. *Fragments of Redemption: Jewish Thought and Literary Theory in Benjamin, Scholem, and Levinas*. Bloomington and Indianapolis: Indiana University Press, 1991.
Hanegraaff, Wouter J. "From the Devil's Gateway to the Goddess Within: The Image of the Witch in Neopaganism." In *Female Stereotypes in Religious Traditions*, edited by Rita Kloppenborg and Wouter J. Hanegraaff, 213–242. Leiden: E. J. Brill, 1995.
———. *New Age Religion and Western Culture: Esotericism in the Mirror of Secular Thought*. Albany: State University of New York Press, 1998.
Hannah, Darrell D. *Michael and Christ: Michael Traditions and Angel Christology in Early Christianity*. Tübingen: Mohr Siebeck, 1999.
Hare-Mustin Rachel T., and Jeanne Mareck. "Beyond Difference." In *Making a Difference: Psychology and the Construction of Gender*, edited by Rachel T. Hare-Mustin and Jeanne Mareck, 184–201. New Haven and London: Yale University Press, 1990.
Harkness, Deborah E. *John Dee's Conversations with Angels: Cabala, Alchemy, and the End of Nature*. Cambridge: Cambridge University Press, 1999.
Harley, Timothy. *Moon Lore*. London: S. Sonnenschein, 1885.
Harpham, Geoffrey Galt. *The Ascetic Imperative in Culture and Criticism*. Chicago and London: University of Chicago Press, 1987.
Harr, Michael. *Nietzsche and Metaphysics*. Translated and edited by Michael Gendre. Albany: State University of New York Press, 1996.
Harries, Karsten. *Infinity and Perspective*. Cambridge, Mass.: MIT Press, 2001.
Harrington, Hannah K. "Holiness and Law in the Dead Sea Scrolls." *Dead Sea Discoveries* 8 (2001): 124–135.
———. *Holiness: Rabbinic Judaism and the Graeco-Roman World*. London and New York: Routledge, 2001.
Harris, Manford. "Marriage as Metaphysics: A Study of the *Iggereth ha-Kodesh*." *Hebrew Union College Annual* 33 (1962): 197–226.
Harris, William V. *Restraining Rage: The Ideology of Anger Control in Classical Antiquity*. Cambridge, Mass.: Harvard University Press, 2001.
Harrison, Nonna V. "Women, Human Identity, and the Image of God: Antiochene Interpretations." *Journal of Early Christian Studies* 9 (2001): 205–249.
Harrison, Verna. "Allegory and Eroticism in Gregory of Nyssa." *Semeia* 57 (1992): 113–130.
Hart, David Bentley "The Mirror of the infinite: Gregory of Nyssa on the *Vestigia Trinitatis*." In *Re-Thinking Gregory of Nyssa*, edited by Sarah Coakley, 111–131. Oxford: Blackwell, 2003.
Hart, Kevin. "The Experience of Nonexperience." In *Mystics: Presence and Aporia*, edited by Michael Kessler and Christian Sheppard, 188–206. Chicago and London: University of Chicago Press, 2003.
———. "The Experience of Poetry." *Boxkite: A Journal of Poetry and Poetics* 2 (1998): 285–304.
———. *The Trespass of the Sign: Deconstruction, Theology, and Philosophy*. Cambridge: Cambridge University Press, 1989; reprinted New York: Fordham University Press, 2000.

Harvey, Andrew. *The Return of the Mother.* Berkeley: Frog, 1995.

Harvey, Stephen. "The Meaning of Terms Designating Love in Judaeo-Arabic Thought and Some Remarks on the Judaeo-Arabic Interpretation of Maimonides." In *Judaeo-Arabic Studies: Proceedings of the Founding Conference of the Society for Judaeo-Arabic Studies*, edited by Norman Golb, 175–196. Amsterdam: Harwood Academic, 1997.

Hass, Lawrence. "Sense and Alterity: Rereading Merleau-Ponty's Reversibility Thesis." In *Merleau-Ponty, Interiority and Exteriority, Psychic Life and the World*, edited by Dorothea Olkowski and James Morley, 91–105. Albany: State University of New York Press, 1999.

Hassan, Riffat. "An Islamic Perspective." In *Sexuality: A Reader*, edited by Karen Lebacqz and David Sinacore-Guinn, 337–372. Cleveland: Pilgrim Press, 1999.

Hassoun, Jacques. *The Cruelty of Depression: On Melancholy.* Translated by David Jacobson. Reading: Addison-Wesley, 1997.

Hatley, James. "Grund and Abgrund: Questioning Poetic Foundations in Heidegger and Celan." In *Questioning Foundations: Truth/ Subjectivity/ Culture*, edited by Hugh J. Silverman, 196–212. New York and London: Routledge, 1993.

———. *Suffering Witness: The Quandary of Responsibility after the Irreparable.* Albany: State University of New York Press, 2000.

Hauptman, Judith. *Rereading the Rabbis: A Woman's Voice.* Boulder: Westview Press, 1998.

Hawkins, Beth. "Perpetuating the Death of God: Edmond Jabès's Post-Nietzschean Midrash." *Journal of Jewish Thought and Philosophy* 10 (2001): 289–372.

———. *Reluctant Theologians: Kafka, Celan, Jabès.* New York: Fordham University Press, 2003.

Hawley, John C. *Divine Aporia: Postmodern Conversations about the Other.* Lewisburg: Bucknell University Press, 2000.

Hawley, Richard. "The Problem of Women Philosophers in Ancient Greece." In *Women in Ancient Societies*, edited by Léonie J. Archer, Susan Fischler, and Maria Wyke, 70–87. New York: Macmillan, 1993.

Hawting, G. R. *The Ideal of Idolatry and the Emergence of Islam: From Polemic to History.* Cambridge: Cambridge University Press, 1999.

Hayes, Michael A., Wendy Porter, and David Tombs, eds. *Religion and Sexuality.* Sheffield: Sheffield Academic Press, 1998.

Hayman, A. Peter. "Monotheism—A Misused Word in Jewish Studies?" *Journal of Jewish Studies* 42 (1991): 1–15.

———. "The 'Original Text': A Scholarly Illusion?" In *Words Remembered, Texts Renewed: Essays in Honour of John F. A. Sawyer*, edited by Jon Davies, Graham Harvey, and Wilfred G. E. Watson, 434–449. Sheffield: Sheffield Academic Press, 1995.

Hayoun, Maurice-Ruben. *Le Zohar aux origins de la mystique juive.* Paris: Éditions Noêsis, 1999.

Healey, Richard. "Can Physics Coherently Deny the Reality of Time?" In *Time, Reality and Experience*, edited by Craig Callender, 293–316. Cambridge: Cambridge University Press, 2002.

Heath, Peter. *Allegory and Philosophy in Avicenna (Ibn Sīnā) With a Translation of the Book of the Prophet Muhammad's Ascent to Heaven.* Philadelphia: University of Pennsylvania Press, 1992.

Hecker, Joel. "Each Man Ate an Angel's Meal: Eating and Embodiment in the Zohar." Ph.D. dissertation, New York University, 1996.

———. "Eating Gestures and the Ritualized Body in Medieval Jewish Mysticism." *History of Religions* 40 (2000): 125–152.

Hedley, Douglas. "Schelling and Heidegger: The Mystical Legacy and Romantic Affinities." In *Heidegger, German Idealism, and Neo-Kantianism*, edited by Tom Rockmore, 141–155. Amherst: Humanity Books, 2000.

Hegel, Georg Wilhelm Friedrich. *Hegel's Logic: Being Part One of The Encyclopaedia of the Philosophical Sciences (1830).* Translated by William Wallace, with a foreword by J. N. Findlay. Oxford: Oxford University Press, 1975.

———. *Phenomenology of Spirit.* Translated by A. V. Miller with analysis of the text and foreword by J. N. Findlay. Oxford: Oxford University Press, 1977.

Heide, Albert van der. "Pardes: Methodological Reflections on the Theory of the Four Senses." *Journal of Jewish Studies* 34 (1983): 147–159.

Heidegger, Martin. *Basic Writings: From Being and Time (1927) to the Task of Thinking (1964).* Rev. and expanded ed. Edited by David Farrell Krell. San Francisco: HarperSanFrancisco, 1993.

———. *Being and Time: A Translation of Sein und Zeit.* Translated by Joan Stambaugh. Albany: State University of New York Press, 1996.

———. *Beiträge zur Philosophie (Vom Ereignis).* Frankfurt am Main: Vittotio Klostermann, 1989.

———. *The Concept of Time.* Translated by William McNeill. Oxford: Blackwell, 1992.

———. *Contributions to Philosophy (From Enowning).* Translated by Parvis Emad and Kenneth Maly. Bloomington and Indianapolis: Indiana University Press, 1999.

———. *Early Greek Thinking.* Translated by David Farrell Krell and Frank A. Capuzzi. New York: Harper & Row, 1975.

———. *Einführung in die Metaphysik.* Tübingen: Max Niemeyer, 1953.

———. *Elucidations of Hölderlin's Poetry.* Translated by Keith Hoeller. Amherst: Humanity Books, 2000.

———. *History of the Concept of Time: Prolegomena.* Translated by Theodore Kisiel. Bloomington and Indianapolis: Indiana University Press, 1992.

———. *Hölderlin's Hymn "The Ister."* Translated by William McNeill and Julia Davis. Bloomington and Indianapolis: Indiana University Press, 1996.

———. *Holzwege.* Frankfurt am Main: Vittorio Klostermann, 1950.

———. *Identity and Difference.* Translated and with an introduction by Joan Stambaugh. New York: Harper & Row, 1969.

———. *Introduction to Metaphysics.* Translated by Gregory Fried and Richard Polt. New Haven and London: Yale University Press, 2000.

———. *Kant and the Problem of Metaphysics.* Translated by Richard Taft. 4th ed., enlarged. Bloomington and Indianapolis: Indiana University Press, 1990.

———. "Das mythische Denken von Ernst Cassirer." *Deutsche Literaturzeitung* 21 (1928): 1000–1012.

———. *Nietzsche, Erster Band.* Stuttgart: Verlag Günther Neske, 1961.

———. *Nietzsche, Zweiter Band.* Stuttgart: Verlag Günther Neske, 1961.

———. *On the Way to Language.* Translated by Peter D. Hertz. San Francisco: Harper & Row, 1971.

———. *On Time and Being.* Translated by Joan Stambaugh. New York: Harper & Row, 1972.

———. *Parmenides.* Translated by André Schuwer and Richard Rojcewicz. Bloomington and Indianapolis: Indiana University Press, 1992.

———. *Pathways.* Edited by William McNeill. Cambridge: Cambridge University Press, 1998.

———. *The Piety of Thinking: Essays by Martin Heidegger.* Translation, notes, and commentary by James G. Hart and John C. Maraldo. Bloomington and London: Indiana University Press, 1976.

———. *Poetry, Language, Thought.* Translated by Albert Hofstadter. New York: Harper & Row, 1971.

———. *The Principle of Reason.* Translated by Reginald Lilly. Bloomington: Indiana University Press, 1991.

———. *Schelling's Treatise on the Essence of Human Freedom.* Translated by Joan Stambaugh. Athens: Ohio University Press, 1985.

———. *Sein und Zeit.* Tübingen: Max Niemeyer, 1993.

———. "Über das Prinzip 'Zu den Sachen selbst.'" *Heidegger Studies* 11 (1995): 5–8.

———. *Unterwegs zur Sprache.* Pfullingen: Neske, 1959.

———. *Vorträge und Aufsätze.* Stuttgart: Verlag Günther Neske, 1954.

———. *Vorträge und Aufsätze, II.* Pfullingen: Neske, 1967.

———. *What Is Called Thinking?* Translated by J. Glenn Gray. New York: Harper & Row, 1968.

———. *The Will to Power as Art.* Vol. 1 of *Nietzsche.* Translated with notes and an analysis by David Farrell Krell. New York: Harper & Row.

———. *The Will to Power as Knowledge and as Metaphysics.* Vol. 3 of *Nietzsche.* Translated by Joan Stambaugh, David Farrell Krell, and Frank A. Capuzzi. San Francisco: Harper & Row, 1987.

———. *Zollikon Seminars: Protocols—Conversations—Letters.* Edited by Medard Boss, translated from the German with notes and afterwords by Franz Mayr and Richard Askay. Evanston: Northwestern University Press, 2001.

Heidegger, Martin, and Eugen Fink. *Heraclitus Seminar 1966/67.* Translated by Charles Seibert. Tuscaloosa: University of Alabama Press, 1979.

Heiler, Friedrich. "Contemplation in Christian Mysticism." In *Spiritual Disciplines: Papers from the Eranos Yearbook,* edited by Joseph Campbell, 136–238. Princeton: Princeton University Press, 1985.

Heinämaa, Sara. *Toward a Phenomenology of Sexual Difference: Husserl, Merleau-Ponty, Beauvoir.* Lanham: Rowman & Littlefield, 2003.

Heine, Steven. *Existential and Ontological Dimensions of Time in Heidegger and Dōgen.* Albany: State University of New York Press, 1985.

Heinen, Anton M. *Islamic Cosmology: A Study of as-Suyūṭī's al-Hay'a as-sanīya fī l-hay'a as-sunnīya, with Critical Edition, Translation, and Commentary.* Wiesbaden: Franz Steiner, 1982.

Hekmat, Anwar. *Women and the Koran: The Status of Women in Islam.* Amherst: Prometheus Books, 1997.

Hellner-Eshed, Melila. "The Language of Mystical Experience in the Zohar: The Zohar Through Its Own Eyes." Ph.D. dissertation, Hebrew University, 2001 (Hebrew).

Helting, Holger. *Heidegger und Meister Eckehart: Vorbereitende Überlegungen zu ihrem Gottesdenken.* Berlin: Duncker & Humblot, 1997.

Hennecke, Edgar. *New Testament Apocrypha.* Edited by Wilhelm Schneemelcher, English translation edited by Robert McL. Wilson. 2 vols. Philadelphia: Westminster Press, 1963.

Henoch, Chayim. *Ramban: Philosopher and Kabbalist: On the Basis of His Exegesis to the Mitzvoth.* Northvale: Jason Aronson, 1998.

Henshaw, Richard A. *Female and Male, the Cultic Personnel: The Bible and the Rest of the Ancient Near East.* Allison Park: Pickwick, 1994.

Herdt, Gilbert. "Introduction: Third Sexes and Third Genders." In *Third Sex, Third Gender: Beyond Sexual Dimorphism in Culture and History,* edited by Gilbert Herdt, 21–81. New York: Zone Books, 1994.

Héritier, Françoise. "The Symbolics of Incest and Its Prohibition." In *Between Belief and Transgression: Structuralist Essays in Religion, History, and Myth,* edited by Michel Izard and Pierre Smith, translated by John Leavitt, with an introduction by James A. Boon, 152–179. Chicago and London: University of Chicago Press, 1982.

Herkert, Petra. *Das Chiasma: Zur Problematik von Sprache, Bewusstsein und Unbewusstem bei Maurice Merleau-Ponty.* Würzburg: Königshausen and Neumann, 1987.
Herman, A. L. "A Solution to the Paradox of Desire in Buddhism." *Philosophy East and West* 29 (1979): 91–94.
Heschel, Abraham Joshua. *The Earth Is the Lord's: The Inner World of the Jew in East Europe.* New York: Henry Schuman, 1950.
———. *Prophetic Inspiration after the Prophets: Maimonides and Other Medieval Authorities.* Edited by Morris M. Faierstein, preface by Moshe Idel. Hoboken: Ktav, 1996.
Heschel, Susannah. "Genre et historiographie juive." *Raisons politiques: Études de pensée politique* 7 (2002): 157–180.
Hildegard of Bingen. *Symphonia: A Critical Edition of the Symphonia armonie celestium revelationum* [*Symphony of the Harmony of Celestial Revelations*]. With introduction, translations, and commentary by Barbara Newman. 2nd ed. Ithaca and London: Cornell University Press, 1998.
Hillman, James. "On Paranoia." *Eranos Jahrbuch* 54 (1985): 269–324.
Hirshman, Marc G. *A Rivalry of Genius: Jewish and Christian Biblical Interpretation in Late Antiquity.* Albany: State University of New York Press, 1995.
Hitchcock, Peter. "The Eye and the Other: The Gaze and the Look in Egyptian Feminist Fiction." In *The Politics of (M)Othering: Womanhood, Identity, and Resistance in African Literature,* edited by Obioma Nnaemeka, 69–81. London and New York: Routledge, 1997.
Hobbes, Thomas. *Leviathan.* Edited with an introduction and notes by John C. A. Gaskin. Oxford: Oxford University Press, 1998.
Hobson, Marian. *Jacques Derrida: Opening Lines.* London and New York: Routledge, 1998.
Hoff, Johannes. *Spiritualität und Sprachverlust: Theologie nach Foucault und Derrida.* Paderborn: Ferdinand Schöningh, 1999.
Hoffman, Lawrence A. *Covenant of Blood: Circumcision and Gender in Rabbinic Judaism.* Chicago: University of Chicago Press, 1996.
Hoffmann, Susan-Judith. "Gadamer's Philosophical Hermeneutics and Feminist Projects." In *Feminist Interpretations of Hans-Georg Gadamer,* edited by Lorraine Code, 81–107. University Park: Pennsylvania State University Press, 2003.
Hoffman, Valerie J. "Muslim Sainthood, Women, and the Legend of Sayyida Nafia." In *Women Saints in World Religions,* edited by Arvind Sharma, 107–144. Albany: State University of New York Press, 2000.
Holdcroft, David. *Saussure: Signs, System, and Arbitrariness.* Cambridge: Cambridge University Press, 1991.
Hollywood, Amy M. *Sensible Ecstasy: Mysticism, Sexual Difference, and the Demands of History.* Chicago: University of Chicago Press, 2002.
———. *The Soul as Virgin Wife: Mechthild of Magdeburg, Marguerite Porete, and Meister Eckhart.* Notre Dame: University of Notre Dame Press, 1995.
Hoodfar, Homa. "The Veil in Their Minds and on Our Heads: Veiling Practices and Muslim Women." In *Women, Gender, Religion: A Reader,* edited by Elizabeth A. Castelli with the assistance of Rosamond C. Rodman, 420–446. New York: Palgrave, 2001.
Hopkins, Jasper. *A Concise Introduction to the Philosophy of Nicholas of Cusa.* Minneapolis: University of Minnesota Press, 1978.
———. *A Miscellany on Nicholas of Cusa.* Minneapolis: Arthur J. Banning Press, 1994.
———. *Nicholas of Cusa's Dialectical Mysticism: Text, Translation, and Interpretive Study of De Visione Dei.* Minneapolis: Arthur J. Banning Press, 1985.

———. *Nicholas of Cusa's Metaphysic of Contraction*. Minneapolis: Arthur J. Banning Press, 1983.
———. *Nicholas of Cusa on God as Not-Other: A Translation and an Appraisal of De Li Non Aliud*. Minneapolis: University of Minnesota Press, 1979.
———. *On Learned Ignorance: A Translation and an Appraisal of* De Docta Ignorantia. Minneapolis: Arthur J. Banning Press, 1990.
Hopkins, Jeffrey. *Emptiness in the Mind-Only School of Buddhism: Dynamic Responses to Dzong-ka-ba's* The Essence of Eloquence. Berkeley: University of California Press, 1999.
———. *Meditation on Emptiness*. London: Wisdom Publications, 1983.
Hori, Victor Sōgen. *Zen Sand: The Book of Capping Phrases for Kōan Practice*. Honolulu: University of Hawaii Press, 2003.
Horkheimer, Max. "Allgemeiner Teil." In *Studien über Autorität und Familie: Forschungsberichte aus dem Institut für Sozialforschung* edited by Max Horkheimer, 3–76. Paris: Libraire Félix Alcan, 1936.
Horosz, William. *Search without Idols*. Dordrecht: Kluwer, 1987.
Horowitz, Maryanne Cline. *Seeds of Virtue and Knowledge*. Princeton: Princeton University Press, 1998.
Horst, Pieter W. van der. "Images of Women in Ancient Judaism." In *Female Stereotypes in Religious Traditions*, edited by Rita Kloppenborg and Wouter J. Hanegraaff, 43–60. Leiden: E. J. Brill, 1995.
———. *Japheth in the Tents of Shem: Studies on Jewish Hellenism in Antiquity*. Leuven: Peeters, 2002.
Horstmanshoff, Manfred. "Who Is the True Eunuch?: Medical and Religious Ideas about Eunuchs and Castration in the Works of Clement of Alexandria." In *From Athens to Jerusalem: Medicine in Hellenized Jewish Lore and in Early Christian Literature*, edited by Samuel Kottek, Manfred Horstmanshoff, Gerhard Baader, and Gary Ferngren, 101–118. Rotterdam: Erasmus, 2000.
Hottois, Gilbert. *L'inflation du langage dans la philosophie contemporaine: Causes, formes et limites*. Preface by J. Ladrière. Brussels: Éditions de l'Université de Bruxelles, 1979.
Hough, Sheridan. *Nietzsche's Noontide Friend: The Self as Metaphoric Double*. University Park: Pennsylvania State University Press, 1997.
Howard, Don, and John J. Stachel. *Einstein: The Formative Years, 1879–1909*. Boston: Birkhäuser, 2000.
Howell, Kenneth J. *God's Two Books: Copernican Cosmology and Biblical Interpretation in Early Modern Science*. Notre Dame: University of Notre Dame Press, 2002.
Howells, Christina. *Derrida: Deconstruction from Phenomenology to Ethics*. Cambridge: Polity Press, 1999.
Hügel, Friedrich von. *The Mystical Element of Religion as Studied in Saint Catherine of Genoa and Her Friends*. 2nd ed. London: J. M. Dent, 1923.
Hughes, Aaron W. *The Texture of the Divine: Imagination in Medieval Islamic and Jewish Thought*. Bloomington and Indianapolis: Indiana University Press, 2004.
Hulin, Michel. "Nietzsche and the Suffering of the Indian Ascetic." In *Nietzsche and Asian Thought*, edited by Graham Parkes, 64–75. Chicago and London: University of Chicago Press, 1991.
Humbert, Paul. "La femme étrangère du livre des Proverbes." *Revue des études sémitiques* 6 (1937): 40–64.
Hundert, Gershon D. *Jews in Poland-Lithuania in the Eighteenth Century: A Genealogy of Modernity*. Berkeley: University of California Press, 2004.
Hunnings, Gordon. *The World and Language in Wittgenstein's Philosophy*. Albany: State University of New York Press, 1988.

Hunter, David G. "Clerical Celibacy and the Veiling of Virgins: New Boundaries in Late Ancient Christianity." In *The Limits of Ancient Christianity: Essays on Late Antique Thought and Culture in Honor of R. A. Markus*, edited by William E. Klingshirn and Mark Vessey, 139–152. Ann Arbor: University of Michigan Press, 1999.

———. "The Paradise of Patriarchy: Ambrosiaster on Woman as (Not) God's Image." *Journal of Theological Studies* 43 (1992): 447–469.

Huntington, C. W., Jr., with Geshé Namgyal Wangchen. *The Emptiness of Emptiness: An Introduction to Early Indian Madhyamika.* Honolulu: University of Hawaii Press, 1989.

Huot, Sylvia. *The Romance of the Rose and Its Medieval Readers: Interpretation, Reception, Manuscript Transmission.* Cambridge: Cambridge University Press, 1993.

Hurtado, Larry W. "The Binitarian Shape of Early Christian Worship." In *The Jewish Roots of Christological Monotheism: Papers from the St. Andrews Conference on the Historical Origins of the Worship of Jesus*, edited by Carey C. Newman, James R. Davila, and Gladys S. Lewis, 187–213. Leiden: E. J. Brill, 1999.

———. *Lord Jesus Christ: Devotion to Jesus in Earliest Christianity.* Grand Rapids: William B. Eerdmans, 2003.

———. *One God, One Lord: Early Christian and Ancient Jewish Monotheism.* 2nd ed. Edinburgh: T & T Clark, 1998.

Huss, Boaz. "The Appearance of *Sefer ha-Zohar.*" *Tarbiẓ* 70 (2001): 507–542 (Hebrew).

———. "*Genizat ha-Or* in Simeon Lavi's *Ketem Paz* and the Lurianic Doctrine of *Ẓimẓum.*" Jerusalem Studies in Jewish Thought 10 (1992): 341–362 (Hebrew).

———. "NiSAN—The Wife of the infinite: The Mystical Hermeneutics of Rabbi Isaac of Acre." *Kabbalah: Journal for the Study of Jewish Mystical Texts* 5 (2000): 155–181.

———. "*Sefer ha-Zohar* as a Canonical, Sacred and Holy Text: Changing Perspectives of the Book of Splendor between the Thirteenth and Eighteenth Centuries." *Journal of Jewish Thought and Philosophy* 7 (1998): 257–307.

———. *Sockets of Fine Gold: The Kabbalah of Rabbi Shimʿon Ibn Lavi.* Jerusalem: Magnes Press, 2000 (Hebrew).

Husserl, Edmund. *Logical Investigations.* Translated by J. N. Findlay. 2 vols. New York: Humanities Press, 1970.

Hutcheon, Linda. *A Poetics of Postmodernism: History, Theory, Fiction.* New York and London: Routledge, 1988.

Hyman, Arthur. "Rabbi Simlai's Saying and Belief Concerning God." In *Perspectives on Jewish Thought and Mysticism*, edited by Alfred L. Ivry, Elliot R. Wolfson, and Alan Arkush, 49–62. Amsterdam: Harwood Academic, 1998.

Iamblichus. *De mysteriis.* Translated by Emma C. Clarke, John M. Dillon, and Jackson P. Hershbell. Atlanta: Society of Biblical Literature, 2003.

Ian, Marcia. *Remembering the Phallic Mother: Psychoanalysis, Modernism, and the Fetish.* Ithaca and London: Cornell University Press, 1993.

Ibn al-ʿArabī, Muḥyīddīn. *The Bezels of Wisdom.* Translation and introduction by Ralph W. J. Austin, preface by Titus Burckhardt. New York: Paulist Press, 1980.

———. *Divine Governance of the Human Kingdom, At-Tadbīrāt al-ilāhiyyah fī iṣlāḥ al-mamlakat al-insāniyyah.* Translated by Shaykh Tosun Bayrak al-Jerrahi al-Halveti. Louisville: Fons Vitae, 1997.

———. *The Meccan Revelations: Ibn al ʿArabi.* Vol. 1. Edited by Michel Chodkiewicz, translated by William C. Chittick and James W. Morris. New York: Pir Press, 2002.

Ibn Rushd. *Averroes' Tahafut al-Tahafut (The Incoherence of the Incoherence)*. Translated with introduction and notes by Simon van den Bergh. 2 vols. London: E. J. W. Gibb Memorial Trust, 1954.
Idel, Moshe. "A. Abulafia, G. Scholem, and W. Benjamin on Language." In *Jüdisches Denken in einer Welt ohne Gott: Festschrift für Stéphane Mosès*, edited by Jens Mattern, Gabriel Motzkin, and Shimon Sandbank, 130–138. Berlin: Verlag Vorwerk 8, 2000.
———. *Absorbing Perfections: Kabbalah and Interpretation*. Foreword by Harold Bloom. New Haven and London: Yale University Press 2002.
———. "Abulafia's Secrets of the Guide: A Linguistic Turn." In *Perspectives on Jewish Thought and Mysticism*, edited by Alfred L. Ivry, Elliot R. Wolfson, and Alan Arkush, 289–329. Amsterdam: Harwood Academic, 1998.
———. "A la recherché de la langue originelle: Le témoignage du nourrisson." *Revue de l'Histoire des Religions* 214 (1996): 415–442.
———. "The Beloved and the Concubine: The Woman in Jewish Mysticism." In *Blessed That I Was Made a Woman?: The Woman in Judaism from the Bible to the Present*, edited by David Ariel, Maya Lebovitz, and Yoram Mazor, 141–157. Tel Aviv: Sifrei Ḥamad, 1999 (Hebrew).
———. "The Concept of Torah in Hekhalot Literature and Its Metamorphosis in Kabbalah." *Jerusalem Studies in Jewish Thought* 1 (1981): 23–84 (Hebrew).
———. "The Contribution of Abraham Abulafia's Kabbalah to the Understanding of Jewish Mysticism." In *Gershom Scholem's Major Trends in Jewish Mysticism 50 Years After*, edited by Joseph Dan and Peter Schäfer, 117–143. Tübingen: Mohr, 1993.
———. "Defining Kabbalah: The Kabbalah of the Divine Names." In *Mystics of the Book: Themes, Topics, and Typologies*, edited by Robert A. Herrera, 97–122. New York: Peter Lang, 1993.
———. "Eros in der Kabbala: Zwischen gegenwärtiger physischer Realität und idealen metaphysischen Konstrukten." In *Kulturen des Eros*, edited by Detlev Clemens and Tilo Schabert, 59–102. Munich: Wilhelm Fink, 2001.
———. "Female Beauty: A Chapter in the History of Jewish Mysticism." In *Within Hasidic Circles: Studies in Hasidism in Memory of Mordecai Wilensky*, edited by Immanuel Etkes, David Assaf, Israel Bartal, and Elchanan Reiner, 317–334. Jerusalem: Bialik Institute, 1999.
———. "Franz Rosenzweig and the Kabbalah." In *The Philosophy of Franz Rosenzweig*, edited by Paul Mendes-Flohr, 162–171. Hanover and London: University Press of New England, 1988.
———. *Golem: Jewish Magical and Mystical Traditions on the Artificial Anthropoid*. Albany: State University of New York Press, 1990.
———. "Hieroglyphs, Keys, Enigmas: On G. G. Scholem's Vision of Kabbalah: Between Franz Molitor and Franz Kafka." In *Arche Noah: Die Idee der "Kultur" im deutsch-jüdischen Diskurs*, edited by Bernhard Greiner and Christoph Schmidt, 226–248. Freiburg im Breisgau: Rombach, 2002.
———. "The Infant Experiment: The Search for the First Language." In *The Language of Adam: Die Sprache Adams*, edited by Allison P. Coudert, 57–79. Wiesbaden: Harrassowitz, 1999.
———. "Infinities of Torah in Kabbalah." In *Midrash and Literature*, edited by Geoffrey H. Hartman and Sanford Budick, 141–157. New Haven and London: Yale University Press, 1986.
———. "In the Light of Life: A Study of Kabbalistic Eschatology." In *Sanctity of Life and Martyrdom: Studies in Memory of Amir Yekutiel*, edited by Isaiah M. Gafni and Aviezer Ravitzky, 191–211. Jerusalem: Zalman Shazar Center for Jewish History, 1992 (Hebrew).
———. "Introduction to the Bison Book Edition." In Johann Reuchlin, *On the Art of the Kabbalah: De arte cabalistica*, v–xxix. Translation by Martin and Sarah Goodman, introduction by G. Lloyd Jones. Lincoln and London: University of Nebraska Press, 1993.

———. "Jerusalem in Thirteenth-Century Jewish Thought." In *The History of Jerusalem: Crusades and Ayyubids, 1099–1250*, edited by Joshua Prawer and Haggai Ben-Shammai, 264–286. Jerusalem: Ben Zvi Institute, 1991 (Hebrew).
———. "Kabbalah and Elites in Thirteenth-Century Spain." *Mediterranean Historical Review* 9 (1994): 5–19.
———. *Kabbalah: New Perspectives*. New Haven and London: Yale University Press, 1988.
———. "Kabbalah-Research: From Monochromatism to Polymorphism." *Studia Judaica* 8 (1999): 15–46.
———. "The Kabbalistic Interpretation of the Secret of *ʿArayot* in Early Kabbalah." *Kabbalah: Journal for the Study of Jewish Mystical Texts* 12 (2004): 89–199 (Hebrew).
———. "Kabbalistic Material from the School of R. David ben Judah he-Ḥasid." *Jerusalem Studies in Jewish Thought* 2 (1983): 169–207 (Hebrew).
———. *Language, Torah, and Hermeneutics in Abraham Abulafia*. Albany: State University of New York Press, 1989.
———. "Maimonides and Kabbalah." In *Studies in Maimonides*, edited by Isadore Twersky, 31–81. Cambridge, Mass.: Harvard University Press, 1990.
———. *Messianic Mystics*. New Haven and London: Yale University Press, 1998.
———. *The Mystical Experience in Abraham Abulafia*. Translated by Jonathan Chipman. Albany: State University of New York Press, 1988.
———. "Pardes: Some Reflections on Kabbalistic Hermeneutics." In *Death, Ecstasy, and Other Worldly Journeys*, edited by John J. Collins and Michael Fishbane, 249–268. Albany: State University of New York Press, 1995.
———. *Le Porte della Giustizia, Saʿare Ṣedeq*. Milan: Adelphi Edizioni, 2001.
———. "The Problem of the Sources of the *Bahir*." *Jerusalem Studies in Jewish Thought* 6:3–4 (1987): 55–72 (Hebrew).
———. "Rabbinism versus Kabbalism: On G. Scholem's Phenomenology of Judaism." *Modern Judaism* 11 (1991): 281–296.
———. "Radical Hermeneutics: From Ancient to Medieval, and Modern Hermeneutics." In *Convegno Internazionale sul tema ermeneutica e critica: Roma 7–8 Ottobre 1996*, 165–210. Rome: Accademia Nazionale dei Lincei, 1998.
———. "Reification of Language in Jewish Mysticism." *Mysticism and Language*, edited by Steven T. Katz, 42–79. Oxford and New York: Oxford University Press, 1992.
———. "The *Sefirot* above the *Sefirot*." *Tarbiẓ* 51 (1982): 239–280 (Hebrew).
———. "Sexual Metaphors and Praxis in the Kabbalah." In *The Jewish Family: Metaphor and Memory*, edited by David Kraemer, 197–224. New York and Oxford: Oxford University Press, 1989.
———. "Some Remarks on Ritual and Mysticism in Geronese Kabbalah." *Journal of Jewish Thought and Philosophy* 3 (1993): 111–130.
———. *Studies in Ecstatic Kabbalah*. Albany: State University of New York Press, 1988.
———. "Torah: Between Presence and Representation of the Divine in Jewish Mysticism." In *Representation in Religion: Studies in Honor of Moshe Barasch*, edited by Jan Assmann and Albert I. Baumgarten, 197–236. Leiden: E. J. Brill, 2001.
———. "Two Remarks on R. Yair ben Sabbatai's Sefer Ḥerev Piffiyot." *Qiryat Sefer* 53 (1979): 213–214 (Hebrew).
———. "The Writings of Abraham Abulafia and His Teaching." Ph.D. dissertation, Hebrew University, Jerusalem, 1976 (Hebrew).
———. "The Zohar as Exegesis." In *Mysticism and Sacred Scripture*, edited by Steven T. Katz, 89–91. Oxford and New York: Oxford University Press, 2000.

Idinopulos, Thomas A., and Edward A. Yonan, eds. *Religion and Reductionism: Essays on Eliade, Segal, and the Challenge of the Social Sciences for the Study of Religion.* Leiden: E. J. Brill, 1994.
Ihde, Don. *Sense and Significance.* Pittsburgh: Duquesne University Press, 1973.
Ilan, Tal. *Integrating Women into Second Temple History.* Tübingen: Mohr Siebeck, 1999.
———. *Jewish Women in Greco-Roman Palestine.* Tübingen: J. C. B. Mohr, 1995.
———. *Mine Are Yours Are Hers: Retrieving Women's History from Rabbinic Literature.* Leiden: E. J. Brill, 1997.
Inge, William Ralph. *Mysticism in Religion.* London: Hutchinson's University Library, 1947.
———. *The Philosophy of Plotinus.* 3rd ed. London and New York: Longmans, Green, 1948.
Irigaray, Luce. *Democracy Begins between Two.* Translated by Kirsten Anderson. New York: Routledge, 2001.
———. *An Ethics of Sexual Difference.* Translated by Carolyn Burke and Gillian C. Gill. Ithaca: Cornell University Press, 1993.
———. *Marine Lover of Friedrich Nietzsche.* Translated by Gillian C. Gill. New York: Columbia University Press, 1991.
———. "Questions to Emmanuel Levinas on the Divinity of Love." In *Re-Reading Levinas,* edited by Robert Bernasconi and Simon Critchley, 109–118. Bloomington and Indianapolis: Indiana University Press, 1991.
———. *Sexes and Genealogies.* Translated by Gillian C. Gill. New York: Columbia University Press, 1993.
———. *Speculum of the Other Woman.* Translated by Gilliam C. Gill. Ithaca: Cornell University Press, 1985.
———. *This Sex Which Is Not One.* Translated by Catherine Porter with Carolyn Burke. Ithaca: Cornell University Press, 1985.
———. *To Be Two.* Translated by Monique M. Rhodes and Marco F. Cocito-Monoc. New York: Routledge, 2001.
———. "What Other Are We Talking About?" *Yale French Studies* 104 (2004): 67–81.
———. *Why Different? A Culture of Two Subjects: Interviews with Luce Irigaray.* Edited by Luce Irigaray and Sylvère Lotringer, translated by Camile Collins. New York: Semiotext(e), 2000.
Irwin, Alexander C. *Eros toward the World: Paul Tillich and the Theology of the Erotic.* Minneapolis: Fortress Press, 1991.
Iser, Wolfgang. *The Range of Interpretation.* New York: Columbia University Press, 2000.
———. "Representation: A Performative Act." In *The Aims of Representation: Subject/ Text/History,* edited by Murray Krieger, 217–232. New York: Columbia University Press, 1987.
Ivry, Alfred L. "Neoplatonic Currents in Maimonides' Thought." In *Perspectives on Maimonides: Philosophical and Historical Studies,* edited by Joel L. Kraemer, 115–140. London: Litman Library of Jewish Civilization, 1996.
Izutsu, Toshihiko. "Between Image and No-Image." *Eranos Jahrbuch* 48 (1979): 427–461.
———. *The Concept and Reality of Existence.* Tokyo: Keio Institute of Cultural and Linguistic Studies, 1971.
———. *Creation and the Timeless Order of Things: Essays in Islamic Mystical Philosophy.* Foreword by William C. Chittick. Ashland: White Cloud Press, 1994.
———. *On Images: Far Eastern Ways of Thinking.* Dallas: Spring Publications, 1988.
Jacobi, Jolande. *Complex/ Archetype/ Symbol in the Psychology of C. G. Jung.* Translated by Ralph Manheim. New York: Pantheon Books, 1959.
Jacobs, Carol. *In the Language of Walter Benjamin.* Baltimore and London: Johns Hopkins University Press, 1999.

———. *Telling Time: Lévi-Strauss, Ford, Lessing, Benjamin, de Man, Wordsworth, Rilke*. Baltimore and London: Johns Hopkins University Press, 1993.

Jacobsen, Knut A. "The Female Pole of the Godhead in Tantrism and the Prakrti of Samkhya." *Numen* 43 (1996): 56–81.

Jacobson, Eric. *Metaphysics of the Profane: The Political Theology of Walter Benjamin and Gershom Scholem*. New York: Columbia University Press, 2003.

Jacobson, Yoram. "The Aspect of the Feminine in the Lurianic Kabbalah." In *Gershom Scholem's Major Trends in Jewish Mysticism 50 Years After*, edited by Joseph Dan and Peter Schäfer, 239–255. Tübingen: Mohr, 1993.

Jager, Eric. *The Book of the Heart*. Chicago and London: University of Chicago Press, 2000.

Jaggar, Alison M. "Human Biology in Feminist Theory: Sexual Equality Reconsidered." In *Knowing Women: Feminism and Knowledge*, edited by Helen Crowley and Susan Himmelweit, 78–89. Cambridge, Mass.: Polity Press, 1992.

———. "Sexual Difference and Sexual Equality." In *Living with Contradictions: Controversies in Feminist Social Ethics*, edited by Alison M. Jaggar, 18–28. Boulder: Westview Press, 1994.

Jakobson, Roman. *Language in Literature*. Edited by Krystyna Pomorska and Stephen Rudy. Cambridge, Mass., and London: Harvard University Press, 1987.

———. *Verbal Art, Verbal Sign, Verbal Time*. Edited by Krystyna Pomorska and Stephen Rudy, with the assistance of Brent Vine. Minneapolis: University of Minnesota Press, 1985.

Jameson, Frederic. *The Prison-House of Language: A Critical Account of Structuralism and Russian Formalism*. Princeton: Princeton University Press, 1972.

Jammer, Max. *Einstein and Religion: Physics and Theology*. Princeton: Princeton University Press, 1999.

Janicaud, Dominique. *The Shadow of That Thought: Heidegger and the Question of Politics*. Translated by Michael Gendre. Evanston: Northwestern University Press, 1996.

Jankélévitch, Vladimir. *Music and the Ineffable*. Translated by Carolyn Abbate. Princeton: Princeton University Press, 2003.

Janowitz, Naomi. *Magic in the Roman World: Pagans, Jews and Christians*. London and New York: Routledge, 2001.

Jantzen, Grace M. *Becoming Divine: Towards a Feminist Philosophy of Religion*. Bloomington and Indianapolis: Indiana University Press, 1999.

———. *Julian of Norwich: Mystic and Theologian*. New York: Paulist Press, 2000.

———. "Mysticism and Experience." *Religious Studies* 25 (1989): 295–315.

———. *Power, Gender and Christian Mysticism*. Cambridge and New York: Cambridge University Press, 1995.

Jaouën, Françoise, and Benjamin Semple. "Editors' Preface: The Body into Text." *Yale French Studies* 86 (1994): 1–4.

Jaspers, Karl. *Schelling: Grösse und Verhängnis*. Munich: R. Piper, 1955.

Jay, Martin. *Downcast Eyes: The Denigration of Vision in Twentieth-Century French Thought*. Berkeley: University of California Press, 1993.

Jeffrey, David Lyle. *People of the Book: Christian Identity and Literary Culture*. Grand Rapids: Eerdmans, 1996.

Jellinek, Adolph. *Philosophie und Kabbala. Erstes Heft*. Leipzig: Heinrich Hunger, 1854.

Jervell, Jacob. *Imago Dei. Gen. I:26f. im Spätjudentum, in der Gnosis und in den paulinischen Briefen*. Göttingen: Vandenhoeck & Ruprecht, 1960.

Jewett, Robert. *Paul's Anthropological Terms: A Study of Their Use in Conflict Settings*. Leiden: E. J. Brill, 1971.

Johnson, Barbara. "Taking Fidelity Philosophically." In *Difference in Translation*, edited with an introduction by Joseph F. Graham, 142–148. Ithaca and London: Cornell University Press, 1985.

Johnson, Christopher. *System and Writing in the Philosophy of Jacques Derrida*. Cambridge: Cambridge University Press, 1993.

Johnson, Galen A. "Desire and Invisibility in 'Eye and Mind': Some Remarks on Merleau-Ponty's Spirituality." In *Merleau-Ponty in Contemporary Perspectives*, edited by Patrick Burke and Jan van der Veken, 85–96. Dordrecht: Kluwer, 1993.

———. "Generosity and Forgetting in the History of Being: Merleau-Ponty and Nietzsche." In *Questioning Foundations: Truth/ Subjectivity/ Culture*, edited by Hugh J. Silverman, 196–212. New York and London: Routledge, 1993.

———. "Introduction: Alterity as a Reversibility." In *Ontology and Alterity in Merleau-Ponty*, edited by Galen A. Johnson and Michael B. Smith, xvii–xxxiv. Evanston: Northwestern University Press, 1990.

Johnson, Luke T. *The First and Second Letters to Timothy: A New Translation with Introduction and Commentary*. New York: Doubleday, 2002.

Johnson, Mark. *The Body in the Mind: The Bodily Basis of Meaning, Imagination, and Reason*. Chicago and London: University of Chicago Press, 1987.

Johnson, Penelope D. *Equal in Monastic Profession: Religious Women in Medieval France*. Chicago: University of Chicago Press, 1991.

Johnstone, Albert A. *Rationalized Epistemology: Taking Solipsism Seriously*. Albany: State University of New York Press, 1991.

Jōkin, Keizan, and Jiyu Kennett. *The Denkōroku, or the Record of the Transmission of the Light*. Translated by Hubert Nearman. 2nd ed. Mount Shasta: Shasta Abbey Press, 2001.

Jonas, Hans. *The Gnostic Religion: The Message of the Alien God and the Beginnings of Christianity*. Boston: Beacon Press, 1963.

Jones, Judith A. *Intensity: An Essay in Whiteheadian Ontology*. Nashville and London: Vanderbilt University Press, 1998.

Jonge, Marinus de. *Christology in Context: The Earliest Christian Response to Jesus*. Philadelphia: Westminster Press, 1988.

———. "Monotheism and Christology." In *Early Christian Thought in its Jewish Context*, edited by John Barclay and John Sweet, 225–237. Cambridge and New York: Cambridge University Press, 1996.

Jonte-Pace, Diane. "The Quest for the Religious Freud: Faith, Morality, and Gender in Psychoanalysis." *Annals of Scholarship* 6 (1989): 493–505.

Joós, Ernest. *Poetic Truth and Transvaluation in Nietzsche's Zarathustra: A Hermeneutic Study*. New York: Peter Lang, 1991.

Joris, Pierre. "Celan/Heidegger: Translation at the Mountain of Death." In *Poetik der Transformation: Paul Celan—Übersetzer und Übersetzt*, edited by Alfred Bodenheimer and Shimon Sandbank, 155–166. Tübingen: Max Niemeyer, 1999.

Josipovici, Gabriel. *The World and the Book: A Study of Modern Fiction*. Stanford: Stanford University Press, 1971.

Jospe, Raphael. "The Superiority of Oral over Written Communication: Judah Ha-Levi's Kuzari and Modern Jewish Thought." In *From Ancient Israel to Modern Judaism Intellect in Quest of Understanding: Essays in Honor of Marvin Fox*, edited by Jacob Neusner, Ernest S. Frerichs, and Nahum M. Sarna, vol. 3, 127–156. 4 vols. Atlanta: Scholars Press, 1989.

Joy, Morny. "Beyond Essence and Intuition: A Reconsideration of Understanding in Religious Studies." In *Secular Theories on Religion: Current Perspectives*, edited by Tim Jensen and Mikael Rothstein, 69–86. Copenhagen: Museum Tusculanum Press, 2000.

Julian of Norwich. *A Book of Showings to the Anchoress Julian of Norwich, Part Two: The Long Text, Appendix, Bibliography, Glossary, Index*. Edited by Edmund Colledge and James Walsh. Toronto: Pontifical Institute of Medieval Studies, 1978.

———. *Julian of Norwich's Showings*. Translated from the critical text with an introduction by Edmund Colledge and James Walsh, preface by Jean Leclercq. New York: Paulist Press, 1978.

Julien, Philippe. *Jacques Lacan's Return to Freud: The Real, the Symbolic, and the Imaginary*. Translated by Devra Beck Simiu. New York and London: New York University Press, 1994.

Jullien, François. *The Propensity of Things: Toward a History of Efficacy in China*. Translated by Janet Lloyd. New York: Zone Books, 1995.

Jung, Carl G. *Aion: Researches into the Phenomenology of the Self*. Translated by Richard F. C. Hull. 2nd ed. Princeton: Princeton University Press, 1968.

———. *Alchemical Studies*. Translated by Richard F. C. Hull. Princeton: Princeton University Press, 1967.

———. *The Archetypes and the Collective Unconscious*. Translated by Richard F. C. Hull. 2nd ed. Princeton: Princeton University Press, 1969.

———. *The Gnostic Jung*. Selected and introduced by Robert A. Segal. Princeton: Princeton University Press, 1992.

———. *Memories, Dreams, Reflections*. Edited by Aniela Jaffé, translated by Richard and Clara Winston. New York: Vintage Books, 1989.

———. *Mysterium Coniunctionis: An Inquiry into the Separation and Synthesis of Psychic Opposites in Alchemy*. Translated by Richard F. C. Hull. 2nd ed. Princeton: Princeton University Press, 1970.

———. *On the Nature of the Psyche*. Translated by Richard F. C. Hull. Princeton: Princeton University Press, 1960.

———. *The Practice of Psychotherapy: Essays on the Psychology of the Transference and Other Subjects*. Translated by Richard F. C. Hull. 2nd ed. Princeton: Princeton University Press, 1966.

———. *Psychology and Alchemy*. Translated by Richard F. C. Hull. 2nd ed. Princeton: Princeton University Press, 1968.

———. *The Spirit in Man, Art, and Literature*. Translated by Richard F. C. Hull. Princeton: Princeton University Press, 1966.

———. *The Symbolic Life: Miscellaneous Writings*. Translated by Richard F. C. Hull. Princeton: Princeton University Press, 1989.

———. *Symbols of Transformation: An Analysis of the Prelude to a Case of Schizophrenia*. Translated by Richard F. C. Hull. 2nd ed. Princeton: Princeton University Press, 1967.

Kahn, Charles H. *The Art and Thought of Heraclitus: An Edition of the Fragments with Translation and Commentary*. Cambridge: Cambridge University Press, 1979.

Kakar, Sudhir. *The Analyst and the Mystic: Psychoanalytic Reflections on Religion and Mysticism*. Chicago: University of Chicago Press, 1991.

Kalsched, Donald E. "The Limits of Desire and the Desire for Limits in Psychoanalytic Theory." In *The Fires of Desire: Erotic Energies and the Spiritual Quest*, edited by Redrica R. Halligan and John J. Shea, 66–93. New York: Crossroad, 1992.

Kalupahana, David J. *Nagarjuna: The Philosophy of the Middle Way*. Albany: State University of New York Press, 1986.

Kambala. *A Garland of Light: Kambala's Ālokamālā*. Translated by Christian Lindtner. Fremont: Asian Humanities Press, 2003.

Kamin, Sarah. *Jews and Christians Interpret the Bible*. Jerusalem: Magnes Press, 1991 (Hebrew).

Kamin, Sarah, and Avrom Saltman, eds. *Secundum Salomonem: A Thirteenth Century Latin Commentary on the Song of Solomon*. Ramat Gan: Bar-Ilan University Press, 1989.

Kanarfogel, Ephraim. *Peering through the Lattices: Mystical, Magical, and Pietistic Dimensions in the Tosafist Period*. Detroit: Wayne State University Press, 2000.

Kantorowicz, Ernst H. *The King's Two Bodies: A Study in Medieval Political Theology*. Princeton: Princeton University Press, 1957.

Kaplan, Aryeh. *Sefer Yetzirah: The Book of Creation in Theory and Practice*. York Beach: Weiser, 1990.

Katz, Claire Elise. *Levinas, Judaism, and the Feminine: The Silent Footsteps of Rebecca*. Bloomington and Indianapolis: Indiana University Press, 2003.

Katz, Jacob. *Exclusiveness and Tolerance: Studies in Jewish-Gentile Relations in Medieval and Modern Times*. London: Oxford University Press, 1961.

———. *Tradition and Crisis: Jewish Society at the End of the Middle Ages*. Translated and with an afterword by Bernard Dov Cooperman. New York: New York University Press, 1993.

Katz, Steven T. "The 'Conservative' Character of Mystical Experience." In *Mysticism and Religious Traditions*, edited by Steven T. Katz, 3–60. Oxford and New York: Oxford University Press, 1983.

———. "Mystical Speech and Mystical Meaning." In *Mysticism and Language*, edited by Steven T. Katz, 3–41. Oxford and NewYork: Oxford University 1992.

———. "Mysticism and the Interpretation of Sacred Scripture." In *Mysticism and Sacred Scripture*, edited by Steven T. Katz, 21–32. Oxford and New York: Oxford University Press, 2000.

———, ed. *Mysticism and Philosophical Analysis*. Oxford and New York: Oxford University Press, 1978.

———, ed. *Mysticism and Religious Traditions*. Oxford and New York: Oxford University Press, 1983.

———. ed., *Mysticism and Sacred Scripture*. Oxford and New York: Oxford University Press, 2000.

———. "Utterance and Ineffability in Jewish Neoplatonism." In *Neoplatonism and Jewish Thought*, edited by Lenn E. Goodman, 279–298. Albany: State University of New York Press, 1992.

Kaufmann, David. "Imageless Refuge for All Images: Scholem in the Wake of Philosophy." *Modern Judaism* 20 (2000): 147–158.

Kaufmann, Felix. "The Phenomenological Approach to History." *Philosophy and Phenomenological Research* 2 (1941–1942): 159–172.

Kavka, Martin. *Jewish Messianism and the History of Philosophy*. Cambridge: Cambridge University Press, 2004.

Kay, Sarah. "Women's Body of Knowledge: Epistemology and Misogyny in the *Romance of the Rose*." In *Framing Medieval Bodies*, edited by Sarah Kay and Miri Rubin, 211–235. Manchester and New York: Manchester University Press 1994.

Kazashi, Nobuo. "On the 'Horizon': Where James and Merleau-Ponty Meet." *Analecta Husserliana* 58 (1998): 49–64.

Kearney, Richard. "Paul Ricoeur and the Hermeneutic Imagination." In *The Narrative Path: The Later Works of Paul Ricoeur*, edited by T. Peter Kemp and David Rasmussen, 1–31. Cambridge, Mass.: MIT Press, 1989.

———. *Poetics of Modernity: Toward a Hermeneutic Imagination*. Amherst: Humanity Books, 1999.

———, moderator. "On the Gift between Jacques Derrida and Jean-Luc Marion." In *God, the*

Gift, and Postmodernism, edited by John D. Caputo and Michael J. Scanlon, 54–78. Bloomington and Indianapolis: Indiana University Press, 1999.

Keiser, Elizabeth B. *Courtly Desire and Medieval Homophobia: The Legitimation of Sexual Pleasure in Cleanness and Its Contexts*. New Haven: Yale University Press, 1997.

Keizan. *Transmission of Light: Zen in the Art of Enlightenment*. Translated by Thomas Cleary. Boston: Shambhala, 1990.

Keller, Mary. *The Hammer and the Flute: Women, Power and Spirit Possession*. Baltimore and London: Johns Hopkins University Press, 2002.

Kellner, Menachem. "Gersonides' Commentary on Song of Songs: For Whom Was It Written and Why?" In *Gersonide en son temps: Science et philosophie médiévales*, edited by Gerhard Dahan, 81–107. Louvain and Paris: E. Peeters, 1991.

———. "Gersonides on the Song of Songs and the Nature of Science." *Journal of Jewish Philosophy and Thought* 4 (1994): 1–22.

———. "Philosophical Misogyny in Medieval Jewish Philosophy—Gersonides vs. Maimonides." *Jerusalem Studies in Jewish Thought* 14 (1998): 113–128 (Hebrew).

Kemal, Salim. *The Philosophical Poetics of Alfarabi, Avicenna and Averroës: The Aristotelian Reception*. London and New York: RoutledgeCurzon, 2003.

———. *The Poetics of Alfarabi and Avicenna*. Leiden: E. J. Brill, 1991.

Kenney, John P. *Mystical Monotheism: A Study in Ancient Platonic Theology*. Hanover and London: University Press of New England, 1991.

Kerényi, Karl. *Eleusis: Archetypal Image of Mother and Daughter*. Princeton: Princeton University Press, 1967.

Kern, Stephen. "The Prehistory of Freud's Theory of Castration Anxiety." *Psychoanalytic Review* 62 (1975): 309–314.

Kerouac, Jack. *Poems All Sizes*. San Francisco: City Lights Books, 1992.

Kersten, Frederick. "Phenomenology, History and Myth." In *Phenomenology and Social Reality: Essays in Memory of Alfred Schultz*, edited by Maurice Natanson, 234–269. The Hague: Martinus Nijhoff, 1970.

Keshavarz, Fatemeh. *Reading Mystical Lyric: The Case of Jalal al-Din Rumi*. Columbia: University of South Carolina Press, 1998.

Kessler, Herbert L. *Spiritual Seeing: Picturing God's Invisibility in Medieval Art*. Philadelphia: University of Pennsylvania Press, 2000.

Keyes, Charles F. "Ambiguous Gender: Male Initiation in a Northern Thai Buddhist Society." In *Gender and Religion: On the Complexity of Symbols*, edited by Caroline Walker Bynum, Stevan Harrell, and Paula Richman, 66–96. Boston: Beacon Press, 1986.

Kieckhefer, Richard. *Magic in the Middle Ages*. Cambridge: Cambridge University Press, 1989.

Kiener, Ronald C. "Jewish Isma'ilism in Twelfth Century Yemen: R. Nethanel al-Fayyumi." *Jewish Quarterly Review* 74 (1984): 249–266.

Kierkegaard, Søren. *Concluding Unscientific Postscript*. Translated by David F. Swenson and Walter Lowrie. Princeton: Princeton University Press, 1941.

Kilcher, Andreas B. "Die Kabbala als Trope im ästhetischen Diskurs der Frühromantik." In *Kabbala und die Literatur der Romantik: Zwischen Magie und Trope*, edited by Eveline Goodman-Thau, Gert Mattenklott, and Christoph Schulte, 135–166. Tübingen: Max Niemeyer, 1999.

———. *Die Sprachtheorie der Kabbala als ästhetisches Paradigma: Die Konstruktion einer ästhetischen Kabbala seit der frühen Neuzeit*. Stuttgart and Weimar: Verlag J. B. Metzler, 1998.

Kimelman, Reuven. *The Mystical Meaning of Lekhah Dodi and Kabbalat Shabbat*. Jerusalem: Magnes Press, 2003 (Hebrew).

———. "Rabbi Yoḥanan and Origen on the Song of Songs: A Third-Century Jewish-Christian Disputation." *Harvard Theological Review* 73 (1980): 567–595.

King, Karen L. *The Gospel of Mary of Magdala: Jesus and the First Woman Apostle*. Santa Rosa: Polebridge Press, 2003.

———. *Revelation of the Unknowable God: With Text, Translation, and Notes to NHC XI, 3 Allogenes*. Santa Rosa: Polebridge Press, 1995.

———. "Why All the Controversy? Mary in the *Gospel of Mary*." In *Which Mary? The Marys of Early Christian Tradition*, edited by F. Stanley Jones, 53–74. Atlanta: Society of Biblical Literature, 2002.

King, Richard. *Orientalism and Religion: Post-Colonial Theory, India and "the Mystic East."* London and New York: Routledge, 1999.

Kingsley, Peter. *In the Dark Places of Wisdom*. Inverness: Golden Sufi Center, 1999.

Kirk, Geoffrey S., and John E. Raven. *The Presocratic Philosophers: A Critical History with a Selection of Texts*. Cambridge: Cambridge University Press, 1979.

Kirschner, Suzanne R. *The Religious and Romantic Origins of Psychoanalysis: Individuation and Integration in Post-Freudian Theory*. Cambridge: Cambridge University Press, 1996.

Kisāʾi, Muḥammad Ibn ʿAbd Allāh. *Tales of the Prophets (Qiṣaṣ al-anbiyāʾ)*. Translated by Wheeler M. Thackston. Chicago: Great Books of the Islamic World, 1997.

Klein, Anne C. *Meeting the Great Bliss Queen: Buddhists, Feminists, and the Art of the Self*. Boston: Beacon Press, 1995.

———. *Path to the Middle: Oral Mādhyamika Philosophy in Tibet*. Collected, translated, edited, annotated and introduced by Anne C. Klein. Albany: State University of New York Press, 1994.

Klein, Jacob. "The Phenomenological Concept of 'Horizon.'" In *Philosophical Essays in Memory of Edmund Husserl*, edited by Marvin Farber, 143–163. Cambridge, Mass.: Harvard University Press, 1940.

Klein-Braslavy, Sara. *Maimonides' Interpretation of the Adam Stories in Genesis: A Study in Maimonides Anthropology*. Jerusalem: Reuben Mass, 1986 (Hebrew).

Klijn, Albertus F. J. "The 'Single One' in the Gospel of Thomas." *Journal of Biblical Literature* 81 (1962): 271–278.

Kloppenborg, Ria. "Female Stereotypes in Early Buddhism: The Women of the Terigatha." In *Female Stereotypes in Religious Traditions*, edited by Ria Kloppenborg and Wouter J. Hanegraaff, 151–169. Leiden: E. J. Brill, 1995.

Knorr von Rosenroth, Christian. *Kabbala Denudata*. 2 vols. Sulzbach: Abrahami Lichtenthaleri, 1677–1684.

Knysh, Alexander D. *Islamic Mysticism: A Short History*. Leiden: E. J. Brill, 2000.

Kochan, Lionel. *Beyond the Graven Image: A Jewish View*. New York: New York University Press, 1997.

Kockelmans, Joseph J. "Language, Meaning, and Ek-sistence." In *On Heidegger and Language*, edited by Joseph J. Kockelmans, 3–32. Evanston: Northwestern University Press, 1972.

———. *On the Truth of Being: Reflections on Heidegger's Later Philosophy*. Bloomington and Indianapolis: Indiana University Press, 1984.

Koester, Helmut. *Ancient Christian Gospels: Their History and Development*. Philadelphia: Trinity Press, 1990.

———. "Gnostic Writings as Witnesses for the Development of the Sayings Tradition." In *The School of Valentinus*, edited by Bentley Layton, 238–261. Vol. 1 of *The Rediscovery of Gnosticism:*

Proceedings of the International Conference on Gnosticism at Yale, New Haven, Connecticut, March 28–31, 1978. Leiden: E. J. Brill, 1980.

Koester, Helmut, and Elaine Pagels. "Introduction." In *Nag Hammadi Codex III, 5: The Dialogue of the Savior*, translated and edited by Stephen Emmel, 1–17. Vol. 3 of *The Coptic Gnostic Library: A Complete Edition of the Nag Hammadi Codices*. Leiden: E. J. Brill, 2000.

———. "Report on the Dialogue of the Savior (CG III, 5)." In *Nag Hammadi and Gnosis: Papers Read at the First International Congress of Coptology, Cairo, December 1976*, edited by Robert McL. Wilson, 66–74. Leiden: E. J. Brill, 1978.

Kojève, Alexandre. *Le concept, le temps et le discours: Introduction au système du savoir*. Paris: Éditions Gallimard, 1990.

Kojima, Hiroshi. *Monad and Thou: Phenomenological Ontology of Human Being*. Athens: Ohio University Press, 2000.

Kolakowski, Leszek. *Husserl and the Search for Certitude*. New Haven: Yale University Press, 1975.

Koren, Sharon F. "Mystical Rationales for the Laws of *Niddah*." In *Women and Water: Menstruation in Jewish Life and Law*, edited by Rahel R. Wasserfall, 101–121. Hanover and London: University Press of New England, 1999.

———. " 'The Woman from Whom God Wanders': The Menstruant in Medieval Jewish Mysticism." Ph.D. dissertation, Yale University, 1999.

Kosolowski, Peter. *Philosophien der Offenbarung: Antiker Gnostizismus, Franz von Baader, Schelling*. Paderborn: Ferdinand Schöningh, 2001.

Köstenberger, Andreas J. *Studies on John and Gender: A Decade of Scholarship*. New York: Peter Lang, 2001.

Kotoh, Tetsuaki. "Language and Silence: Self-Inquiry in Heidegger and Zen." In *Heidegger and Asian Thought*, edited by Graham Parkes, 201–211. Honolulu: University of Hawaii Press, 1987.

Kovacs, George. "Being Truth, and the Political in Heidegger (1933–1934)." *Heidegger Studies* 19 (2003): 31–48.

Kraemer, Joel. "Women's Letters from the Cairo Geniza." In *View into the Lives of Women in Jewish Societies*, edited by Yael Azmon, 161–182. Jerusalem: Zalman Shazar Center for Jewish History, 1995 (Hebrew).

Krajewski, Bruce. *Traveling with Hermes: Hermeneutics and Rhetoric*. Amherst: University of Massachusetts Press, 1992.

Krassen, Miles. *Uniter of Heaven and Earth: Rabbi Meshullam Feibush Heller of Zbarazh and the Rise of Hasidism in Eastern Galicia*. Albany: State University of New York Press, 1998.

Krauss, Lawrence. *Quintessence: The Mystery of Missing Mass in the Universe*. New York: Basic Books, 2000.

Krauss, Samuel. *The Jewish-Christian Controversy: From the Earliest Times to 1789. Volume I: History*. Edited and revised by William Horbury. Tübingen: J. C. B. Mohr, 1995.

Kremer, Detlef. "Kabbalistische Signaturen: Sprachmagie als Brennpunkt romantischer Imagination bei E. T. A. Hoffmann und Achim von Arnim." In *Kabbala und die Literatur der Romantik: Zwischen Magie und Trope*, edited by Eveline Goodman-Thau, Gert Mattenklott, and Christoph Schulte, 197–221. Tübingen: Max Niemeyer, 1999.

Kreisel, Howard. "Asceticism in the Thought of Baḥya and Maimonides." *Daʿat* 21 (1988): 5–22.

Kress, Jill M. "Contesting Metaphors and the Discourse of Consciousness in William James." *Journal of the History of Ideas* 61 (2000): 263–283.

Kripal, Jeffrey J. *Kali's Child: The Mystical and the Erotic in the Life and Teachings of Ramakrishna*. Chicago and London: University of Chicago Press, 1995.

———. *Roads of Excess, Palaces of Wisdom: Eroticism and Reflexivity in the Study of Mysticism*. Chicago and London: University of Chicago Press, 2001.

Kristeva, Julia. *Desire in Language: A Semiotic Approach to Literature and Art*. Edited by Leon S. Roudiez. Translated by Thomas Gora, Alice Jardine, and Leon S. Roudiez. New York: Columbia University Press, 1980.

Kristeva, Julia. *In the Beginning Was Love: Psychoanalysis and Faith*. Translated by Arthur Goldhammer. New York: Columbia University Press, 1987.

———. *Language: The Unknown: An Initiation into Linguistics*. Translated by Anne M. Menke. New York: Columbia University Press, 1989.

———. *Revolution in Poetic Language*. Translated by Margaret Waller. New York: Columbia University Press, 1984.

———. *The Sense and Non-Sense of Revolt: The Powers and Limits of Psychoanalysis*. Translated by Jeanine Herman. New York: Columbia University Press, 2000.

———. *Tales of Love*. Translated by Leon S. Roudiez. New York: Columbia University Press, 1987.

———. "Women's Time." *Signs: Journal of Women in Culture and Society* 7 (1981): 13–35.

Kristeva, Julia, and Catherine Clément. *The Feminine and the Sacred*. Translated by Jane Marie Todd. New York: Columbia University Press, 2001.

Krois, John M. "Cassirer's Unpublished Critique of Heidegger." *Philosophy and Rhetoric* 16 (1983): 147–159.

Krombach, Hayo. "Husserl and the Phenomenology of History." In *Reason and History: Or Only a History of Reason?* edited by Philip Windsor, 89–112. Ann Arbor: University of Michigan Press, 1990.

Kudszus, W. G. *Poetic Process*. Lincoln and London: University of Nebraska Press, 1995.

Kuefler, Mathew. *The Manly Eunuch: Masculinity, Gender Ambiguity, and Christian Ideology in Late Antiquity*. Chicago and London: University of Chicago Press, 2001.

Kugel, James L. *In Potiphar's House: The Interpretive Life of Biblical Texts*. New York: HarperCollins, 1990.

Kumin, Seth Daniel. *The Logic of Incest: A Structuralist Analysis of Hebrew Mythology*. Sheffield: Sheffield Academic Press, 1995.

Kuntz, Marion Leathers. "The Original Language as a Paradigm for the *restitution omnium* in the Thought of Guillaume Postel." In *The Language of Adam, Die Sprache Adams*, edited by Allison Coudert, 123–149. Wiesbaden: Harrassowitz, 1999.

Kushnir-Oron, Michal. "The *Sefer ha-Peli'ah* and the *Sefer ha-Kanah*: Their Kabbalistic Principles, Social and Religious Criticism and Literary Composition." Ph.D. dissertation, Hebrew University of Jerusalem, 1980 (Hebrew).

Kutsko, John F. *Between Heaven and Earth: Divine Presence and Absence in the Book of Ezekiel*. Winona Lake: Eisenbrauns, 2000.

Kvaerne, Per. "On the Concept of Sahaja in Indian Buddhist Tantric Literature." *Temenos* 11 (1975): 88–135.

Kwant, Remigius C. *From Phenomenology to Metaphysics: An Inquiry into the Last Period of Merleau-Ponty's Philosophical Life*. Pittsburgh: Duquesne University Press, 1963.

———. *The Phenomenological Philosophy of Merleau-Ponty*. Pittsburgh: Duquesne University Press, 1963.

Labouvie-Vief, Gisela. *Psyche and Eros: Mind and Gender in the Life Course*. Cambridge: Cambridge University Press, 1994.

Lacan, Jacques. *Écrits: A Selection.* Translated by Jacques-Alain Miller. New York: W. W. Norton, 1977.

———. *Feminine Sexuality: Jacques Lacan and the École freudienne.* Edited by Juliet Mitchell and Jacqueline Rose, translated by Jacqueline Rose. New York: W. W. Norton, 1985.

———. "Les formations de l'inconscient." *Bulletin de Psychologie* 12 (1958): 152.

———. *The Language of the Self: The Function of Language in Psychoanalysis.* Translated by Anthony Wilden. Baltimore: Johns Hopkins University Press, 1968.

———. "Positions of the Unconscious." In *Reading Seminar XI: Lacan's Four Fundamental Concepts of Psychoanalysis*, translated by Bruce Fink, edited by Richard Feldstein, Bruce Fink, and Maire Jaanus. Albany: State University of New York Press, 1995.

———. *Reading Seminar XI: Lacan's Four Fundamental Concepts of Psychoanalysis.* Translated by Bruce Fink, edited by Richard Feldstein, Bruce Fink, and Maire Jaanus. Albany: State University of New York Press, 1995.

———. *The Seminar of Jacques Lacan. Book I: Freud's Papers on Technique 1953–1954.* Edited by Jacques-Alain Miller, translated with notes by John Forrester. New York and London: W. W. Norton, 1991.

———. *The Seminar of Jacques Lacan. Book VII: The Ethics of Psychoanalysis 1959–1960.* Edited by Jacques-Alain Miller, translated with notes by Dennis Porter. New York and London: W. W. Norton, 1992.

———. *The Seminar of Jacques Lacan. Book XI: The Four Fundamental Concepts of Psychoanalysis.* Edited by Jacques-Alain Miller, translated by Alan Sheridan. New York and London: W. W. Norton, 1981.

———. *The Seminar of Jacques Lacan. Book XX: Encore 1972–1973, On Feminine Sexuality: The Limits of Love and Knowledge.* Edited by Jacques-Alain Miller, translated with notes by Bruce Fink. New York and London: W. W. Norton, 1998.

Lacoste, Jean-Yves. "The Work and Complement of Appearing." In *Religious Experience and the End of Metaphysics*, edited by Jeffrey Bloechl, 68–93. Bloomington and Indianapolis: Indiana University Press, 2003.

Lacoue-Labarthe, Philippe. *Poetry as Experience.* Translated by Andrea Tarnowski. Stanford: Stanford University Press, 1999.

Ladner, Gerhart B. *The Idea of Reform: Its Impact on Christian Thought and Action in the Age of the Fathers.* New York: Harper & Row, 1967.

LaFargue, Michael. *Language and Gnosis: The Opening Scenes of the Acts of Thomas.* Philadelphia: Fortress Press, 1985.

Lafont, Cristina. *Heidegger, Language, and World-Disclosure.* Translated by Graham Harman. Cambridge: Cambridge University Press, 2001.

———. *The Linguistic Turn in Hermeneutic Philosophy.* Translated by José Medina. Cambridge, Mass., and London: MIT Press, 1999.

LaFountain, Marc J. "Bataille's Eroticism, Now: From Transgression to Insidious Sorcery." in *Philosophy and Desire*, edited with an introduction by Hugh J. Silverman, 26–41. New York and London: Routledge, 2000.

Lagerwey, John. "Écriture et corps divin en Chine." In *Corps des dieux*, edited by Charles Malamoud and Jean-Pierre Vernant, 383–398. Paris: Éditions Gallimard, 1986.

Laird, Martin. "Under Solomon's Tutelage: The Education of Desire in the *Homilies on the Song of Songs.*" In *Re-Thinking Gregory of Nyssa*, edited by Sarah Coakley, 77–95. Oxford: Blackwell, 2003.

Lambden, S. N. "From Fig Leaves to Fingernails: Some Notes on the Garments of Adam and Eve in the Hebrew Bible and Select Early Postbiblical Jewish Writings." In *A Walk in the Garden: Biblical, Iconographical, and Literary Images of Eden*, edited by Philip Morris and Deborah Sawyer, 74–90. Sheffield: JSOT Press, 1992.

Lamberth, David C. *William James and the Metaphysics of Experience*. Cambridge: Cambridge University Press, 1999.

Landgrebe, Ludwig. "Phenomenology as Transcendental Theory of History." In *Husserl: Expositions and Appraisals*, edited with introductions by Frederick Elliston and Peter McCormick, 101–113. Notre Dame: University of Notre Dame Press, 1977.

Lang, Berel. *Heidegger's Silence*. Ithaca and London: Cornell University Press, 1996.

Lang, Bernhard. *The Hebrew God: Portrait of an Ancient Deity*. New Haven and London: Yale University Press, 2002.

———. "Lady Wisdom: A Polytheistic and Psychological Interpretation of a Biblical Goddess." In *Feminist Companion to Reading the Bible: Approaches, Methods and Strategies*, edited by Athalya Brenner and Carole Fontaine, 400–423. London and Chicago: Fitzroy Dearborn, 1997.

Lang, Hermann. *Language and the Unconscious: Lacan's Hermeneutics of Psychoanalysis*. Translated by Thomas Brockelman. Atlantic Highlands: Humanities Press, 1997.

Lange, Armin. *Weisheit und Prädestination: Weisheitliche Urordnung und Prädestination in den Textfunden von Qumran*. Leiden: E. J. Brill, 1995.

———. "Wisdom and Predestination in the Dead Sea Scrolls." *Dead Sea Discoveries* 2 (1995): 340–354.

Langer, Georg. *Die Erotik der Kabbala*. Munich: Eugen Diederichs, 1989.

———. *Liebesmystik der Kabbala*. Munich: Otto Wilhelm Barth, 1956.

Langer, Susanne K. *Mind: An Essay on Human Feeling*. Vol. 2. Baltimore and London: Johns Hopkins University Press, 1972.

Laozi. *The Classic of the Way and Virtue: A New Translation of the Tao-te ching of Laozi as Interpreted by Wang Bi*. Translated by Richard John Lynn. New York: Columbia University Press, 1999.

———. *Dao de Jing: The Book of the Way*. Translation and commentary by Moss Roberts. Berkeley: University of California Press, 2001.

———. *Tao Te Ching: The Definitive Edition/Lao Tzu*. Translation and commentary by Jonathan Star. New York: Penguin Putnam, 2001.

Laqueur, Thomas Walter. *Solitary Sex: A Cultural History of Masturbation*. New York: Zone Books, 2003.

Layard, John. "The Incest Taboo and the Virgin Archetype." *Eranos-Jahrbuch* 12 (1945): 254–307.

Laycock, Steven William. *Mind as Mirror and the Mirroring of Mind: Buddhist Reflections on Western Phenomenology*. Albany: State University of New York Press, 1994.

Layton, Bentley. *The Gnostic Scriptures: A New Translation with Annotations and Introductions*. Garden City: Doubleday, 1987.

Lazeroff, Alan. "Baḥya's Asceticism against Its Rabbinic and Islamic Background." *Journal of Jewish Studies* 21 (1973): 11–38.

Lazreg, Marnia. "Women's Experience and Feminist Epistemology: A Critical Neo-Rationalist Approach." In *Knowing the Difference: Feminist Perspectives in Epistemology*, edited by Kathleen Lennon and Margaret Whitford, 45–62. London and New York: Routledge, 1994.

Leclaire, Serge. *Psychoanalyzing: On the Order of the Unconscious and the Practice of the Letter*. Translated by Peggy Kamuf. Stanford: Stanford University Press, 1998.

Leclerc, Diane. *Singleness of Heart: Gender, Sin, and Holiness in Historical Perspective*. Lanham and London: Scarecrow Press, 2001.

Leclerc, Ivor. *Whitehead's Metaphysics: An Introductory Exposition*. New York: Humanities Press, 1958.

Leclercq, Jean. *The Love of Learning and the Desire for God: A Study of Monastic Culture*. Translated by C. Misrahi. New York: Fordham University Press, 1961.

———. *Women and St Bernard of Clairvaux*. Translated by Marie-Bernard Saïd. Kalamazoo: Cistercian Publications, 1989.

Lee, Jung H. "Problems of Religious Pluralism: A Zen Critique of John Hick's Ontological Monomorphism." *Philosophy East and West* 48 (1998): 453–477.

Lefebvre, Henri. *Introduction to Modernity: Twelve Preludes September 1959–May 1961*. Translated by John Moore. London and New York: Verso, 1995.

———. *The Production of Space*. Translated by Donald Nicholson-Smith. Oxford and Cambridge, Mass.: Blackwell, 1991.

Lefort, Claude. "Flesh and Otherness." In *Ontology and Alterity in Merleau-Ponty*, edited by Galen A. Johnson and Michael B. Smith, 3–13. Evanston: Northwestern University Press, 1990.

Legendre, Pierre. *Dieu au miroir: Étude sur l'institution des images*. Paris: Fayard, 1994.

———. *Law and the Unconscious: A Legendre Reader*. Edited by Peter Goodrich. Translated by Peter Goodrich with Alain Pottage and Anton Schütz. New York: St. Martin's Press, 1997.

Le Goff, Jacques. *The Medieval Imagination*. Translated by Arthur Goldhammer. Chicago: University of Chicago Press, 1988.

Lehmann, O. H. "The Theology of the Mystical Book Bahir and Its Sources." *Studia Patristica* 1 (1957): 477–483.

Leicht, Reimund. "Gnostic Myth in Jewish Garb: Niriyah (Norea), Noah's Bride." *Journal of Jewish Studies* 51 (2000): 133–140.

Leirvik, Oddbjōrn. *Images of Jesus Christ in Islam: Introduction, Survey of Research, Issues of Dialogue*. Uppsala: Swedish Institute of Missionary Research, 1999.

———. *The Muslim Jesus: Sayings and Stories in Islamic Literature*. Translated by Tarif Khalidi. Cambridge, Mass.: Harvard University Press, 2001.

Leiter, Brian. "The Paradox of Fatalism and Self-Creation in Nietzsche." In *Willing and Nothingness: Schopenhauer as Nietzsche's Educator*, edited by Christopher Janaway, 217–255. Oxford: Oxford University Press, 1998. Reprinted in *Nietzsche*, edited by John Richardson and Brian Leiter, 281–321. Oxford: Oxford University Press, 2001.

Leland, Dorothy. "Lacanian Psychoanalysis and French Feminism: Toward an Adequate Political Psychology." In *Revaluing French Feminism: Critical Essays on Difference, Agency, and Culture*, edited by Nancy Fraser and Sandra Lee Bartky, 113–135. Bloomington and Indianapolis: Indiana University Press, 1992.

Lemaire, Anika. *Jacques Lacan*. Translated by David Macey. London: Routledge and Kegan Paul, 1977.

Lesses, Rebecca. "Exe(o)rcising Power: Women as Sorceresses, Exorcists, and Demonesses in Babylonian Jewish Society of Late Antiquity." *Journal of the American Academy of Religion* 69 (2001): 343–375.

———. *Ritual Practices to Gain Power: Angels, Incantations, and Revelation in Early Jewish Mysticism*. Harrisburg: Trinity Press International, 1998.

Leuze, Reinhard. *Christentum und Islam*. Tübingen: J. C. B. Mohr, 1994.

Levin, David M., ed. *Modernity and the Hegemony of Vision*. Berkeley: University of California Press, 1993.

———. *The Opening of Vision: Nihilism and the Postmodern Situation*. New York and London: Routledge, 1988.

———. *The Philosopher's Gaze: Modernity in the Shadows of Enlightenment*. Berkeley: University of California Press, 1999.

———. *Sites of Vision: The Discursive Construction of Sight in the History of Philosophy*. Cambridge, Mass.: MIT Press, 1997.

Levinas, Emmanuel. *Collected Philosophical Papers*. Translated by Alphonso Lingis. Dordrecht: Martinus Nijhoff, 1987.

———. *Otherwise Than Being or Beyond Essence*. Translated by Alphonso Lingis. Dordrecht: Kluwer Academic, 1991.

———. *Proper Names*. Translated by Michael B. Smith. Stanford: Stanford University Press, 1996.

Levine, Baruch A. " 'Seed' versus 'Womb': Expressions of Male Dominance in Biblical Israel." In *Sex and Gender in the Ancient Near East: Proceedings of the 47th Rencontre Assyriologique Internationale, Helsinki, July 2–6, 2001*, edited by Simo Parpola and Robert M. Whiting, 337–343. Helsinki: University of Helsinki, 2002.

———. "Silence, Sound, and the Phenomenology of Mourning in Biblical Israel." *Journal of the Ancient Near Eastern Society* 22 (1993): 89–106.

Levinson, Joshua. "Cultural Androgyny in Rabbinic Literature." In *From Athens to Jerusalem: Medicine in Hellenized Jewish Lore and in Early Christian Literature*, edited by Samuel Kottek, Manfred Horstmanshoff, Gerhard Baader, and Gary Ferngren, 119–140. Rotterdam: Erasmus, 2000.

Leyerle, Blake. *Theatrical Shows and Ascetic Lives: John Chrysostom's Attack on Spiritual Marriage*. Berkeley: University of California Press, 2001.

Lidke, Jeffrey S. "A Union of Fire and Water: Sexuality and Spirituality in Hinduism." In *Sexuality and the World's Religions*, edited by David W. Machacek and Melissa M. Wilkcox, 103–132. Santa Barbara: ABC-CLIO, 2003.

Lieberman, Saul. "Mishnath Shir ha-Shirim." In Gershom Scholem, *Jewish Gnosticism, Merkabah Mysticism, and Talmudic Tradition*, 118–121. New York: Jewish Theological Seminary of America, 1965.

Liébert, Georges. *Nietzsche and Music*. Translated by David Pellauer and Graham Parkes. Chicago and London: University of Chicago Press, 2004.

Liebes, Yehuda. *Ars Poetica in Sefer Yetsira*. Tel-Aviv: Schocken, 2000 (Hebrew).

———. "*Golem* in Numerology Is *Ḥokhmah*." Qiryat *Sefer* 63 (1991): 1305–1322 (Hebrew).

———. "How the Zohar Was Written." *Jerusalem Studies in Jewish Thought* 8 (1989): 1–71 (Hebrew).

———. "The Messiah of the Zohar." In *The Messianic Idea in Jewish Thought: A Study Conference in Honour of the Eightieth Birthday of Gershom Scholem*, 87–236. Jerusalem: Israel Academy of Sciences and Humanities, 1982 (Hebrew).

———. "Myth vs. Symbol in the Zohar and in Lurianic Kabbalah." In *Essential Papers on Kabbalah*, edited by Lawrence Fine, 212–242. New York: New York University Press, 1995.

———. "The Poems for the Meals of Sabbath Composed by the Holy Ari." *Molad* 4 (1972): 540–555 (Hebrew).

———. *Sections of the Zohar Lexicon*. Jerusalem: Akkadamon, 1976 (Hebrew).

———. *Studies in Jewish Myth and Jewish Messianism*. Translated by Batya Stein. Albany: State University of New York Press, 1993.

———. *Studies in the Zohar*. Translated by Arnold Schwartz, Stephanie Nakache, and Penina Peli. Albany: State University of New York Press, 1993.

———. " 'Tsaddiq Yesod Olam'—A Sabbatian Myth." *Da'at* 1 (1978): 73–120 (Hebrew).

———. "Zohar and Eros." *Alpayyim* 9 (1994): 67–115 (Hebrew).

Liesen, Jan. *Full of Praise: An Exegetical Study of Sir 39, 12–35*. Leiden: E. J. Brill, 1999.

Lingis, Alphonso. *Deathbound Subjectivity*. Bloomington and Indianapolis: Indiana University Press, 1989.

———. "Intentionality and Corporeity." *Analecta Husserliana* 1 (1971): 75–90.

———. "The Sensitive Flesh." In *The Collegium Phaenomeologicum: The First Ten Years*, edited by John C. Sallis, Giuseppina Moneta, and Jacques Taminiaux, 225–240. Dordrecht: Kluwer Academic, 1988.

Lipiner, Elias. *The Metaphysics of the Hebrew Alphabet*. Jerusalem: Magnes Press, 1989 (Hebrew).

Lipton, Sara. "'Tanquam effeminatum': Pedro II of Aragon and the Gendering of Heresy in the Albigensian Crusade." In *Queer Iberia: Sexualities, Cultures, and Crossings From the Middle Ages to the Renaissance*, edited by Josiah Blackmore and Gregory S. Hutcheson, 107–129. Durham and London: Duke University Press, 1999.

Liss, Hanna. *El'azar Ben Yehuda von Worms: Hilkhot ha-Kavod. Die Lehrsätze von der Herrlichkeit Gottes*. Tübingen: Mohr Siebeck, 1997.

Lisse, Michel. "Donner à lire." In *L'éthique du don. Jacques Derrida et la pensée du don: Colloque de Royaumont décembre 1990*, edited by Jean-Michel Rabaté and Michael Wetzel, 133–151. Paris: Métailié-Transition, 1992.

Liszka, James Jakób. *The Semiotic Myth: A Critical Study of the Symbol*. Bloomington and Indianapolis: Indiana University Press, 1989.

Ljamai, Abdelilah. *Ibn Ḥazm et la polémique Islamo-Chrétienne dans l'histoire de l'Islam*. Leiden: Brill, 2003.

Llewelyn, John. *The Hypocritical Imagination: Between Kant and Levinas*. London and New York: Routledge, 2000.

Lloyd, Anthony C. "The Principle That the Cause is Greater Than the Effect." *Phronesis* 21 (1976): 146–151.

Lloyd, Genevieve. *The Man of Reason: "Male" and "Female" in Western Philosophy*. 2nd ed. Minneapolis: University of Minnesota Press, 1993.

Lobel, Diana. *Between Mysticism and Philosophy: Sufi Language of Religious Experience in Judah ha-Levi's Kuzari*. Albany: State University of New York Press, 2000.

Loewe, Raphael. "Apologetic Motifs in the Targum to the Song of Songs." In *Biblical Motifs: Origins and Transformations*, edited by Alexander Altmann, 159–196. Cambridge, Mass.: Harvard University Press, 1966.

Lofts, Steve G. *Ernst Cassirer: A "Repetition" of Modernity*. Foreword by John M. Krois. Albany: State University of New York Press, 2000.

Lohse, Bernhard. *Askese und Mönchtum in der Antike und in der Alten Kirche*. Munich: R. Oldenbourg, 1969.

Longenecker, Richard N. *The Christology of Early Jewish Christianity*. London: SCM Press, 1970.

Longxi, Zhang. *The Tao and the Logos: Literary Hermeneutics, East and West*. Durham and London: Duke University Press, 1992.

Lopez, Donald S. *The Heart Sutra Explained: Indian and Tibetan Commentaries*. Albany: State University of New York Press, 1988.

Loraux, Nicole. *The Experiences of Tiresias: The Feminine and the Greek Man*. Translated by Paula Wissing. Princeton: Princeton University Press, 1995.

———. *Mothers in Mourning with the Essay of Amnesty and Its Opposite*. Translated by Corinne Pache. Ithaca and London: Cornell University Press, 1998.

———. *Tragic Ways of Killing a Woman*. Translated by Anthony Forster. Cambridge, Mass.: Harvard University Press, 1987.

The Lotus Sutra. Translated by Burton Watson. New York: Columbia University Press, 1993.

Low, Douglas. *Merleau-Ponty's Last Vision: A Proposal for the Completion of The Visible and the Invisible.* Evanston: Northwestern University Press, 2000.

Lowe, Donald M. "Intentionality and the Method of History." In *Phenomenology and the Social Sciences,* edited by Maurice Natanson, 2:103–130. 2 vols. Evanston: Northwestern University Press, 1973.

Lowe, Walter James. *Theology and Difference: The Wound of Reason.* Bloomington and Indianapolis: Indiana University Press, 1993.

Lowenthal, Naftali. "'Daughter/Wife of Hasid'—Or: 'Hasidic Woman'?" *Jewish Studies* 40 (2000): 21–28 (English section).

———. "Women and the Dialectic of Spirituality in Hasidism." In *Within Hasidic Circles: Studies in Hasidism in Memory of Mordecai Wilensky,* edited by Immanuel Etkes, David Assaf, Israel Bartal, and Elchanan Reiner, 7–65 (English section). Jerusalem: Bialik Institute, 1999.

Löwith, Karl. *Martin Heidegger and European Nihilism.* Edited by Richard Wolin, translated by Gary Steiner. New York: Columbia University Press, 1995.

Loy, David R. "Language against Its Own Mystifications: Deconstruction in Nagarjuna and Dōgen." *Philosophy East and West* 49 (1999): 245–260.

Lubac, Henri de. *Corpus mysticum: l'eucharistie et l'Église au Moyen âge.* 2nd rev. ed. Paris: Aubier, 1949.

Luedemann, Gerd. *Paul, Apostle to the Gentiles: Studies in Chronology.* Foreword by John Knox, translated by F. Stanley Jones. Philadelphia: Fortress Press, 1984.

Luepnitz, Deborah. "Beyond the Phallus: Lacan and Feminism." In *The Cambridge Companion to Lacan,* edited by Jean-Michel Rabaté, 221–237. Cambridge: Cambridge University Press, 2003.

Lusthaus, Dan. *Buddhist Phenomenology: A Philosophical Investigation of Yogācāra Buddhism and the Ch'eng Wei-shih lun.* London and New York: RoutledgeCurzon, 2002.

Lyotard, Jean-François. *Heidegger and "the jews."* Translation by Andreas Michel and Mark S. Roberts, foreword by David Carroll. Minneapolis and London: University of Minnesota Press, 1990.

———. *Phenomenology.* Translated by Brian Beakley. Albany: State University of New York Press, 1991.

MacDonald, Dennis R. "Corinthian Veils and Gnostic Androgynes." In *Images of the Feminine in Gnosticism,* edited by Karen L. King, 276–292. Philadelphia: Fortress Press, 1988.

———. *There Is No Male and Female: The Fate of a Dominical Saying in Paul and Gnosticism.* Philadelphia: Fortress Press, 1987.

Machacek, David W., and Melissa M. Wilkcox, eds. *Sexuality and the World's Religions.* Santa Barbara: ABC-CLIO, 2003.

Mack, Burton L. "The Christ and Jewish Wisdom." In *The Messiah: Developments in Earliest Judaism and Christianity,* edited by James H. Charlesworth, 192–221. Minneapolis: Fortress Press, 1992.

Mack, Michael. *German Idealism and the Jew: The Inner Anti-Semitism of Philosophy and German Jewish Responses.* Chicago and London: University of Chicago Press, 2003.

MacLeish, Archibald. *Poetry and Experience.* Boston: Houghton Mifflin, 1960.

Madigan, Daniel A. *The Qur'ān's Self Image: Writing and Authority in Islam's Scripture.* Princeton: Princeton University Press, 2001.

Madison, Gary B. *The Hermeneutics of Postmodernity: Figures and Themes.* Bloomington and Indianapolis: Indiana University Press, 1988.

———. *The Phenomenology of Merleau-Ponty.* Foreword by Paul Ricoeur. Athens: Ohio University Press, 1981.

Magee, Glenn Alexander. *Hegel and the Hermetic Tradition.* Ithaca and London: Cornell University Press, 2001.

Magid, Shaul. "Conjugal Union, Mourning and *Talmud Torah* in R. Isaac Luria's *Tikkun Ḥaẓot.*" *Da'at* 36 (1996): xvi–xlv.

———. "Gershom Scholem's Ambivalence toward Mystical Experience and His Critique of Martin Buber in Light of Hans Jonas and Martin Heidegger." *Journal of Jewish Thought and Philosophy* 4 (1995): 245–269.

Magness, Jodi. *The Archaeology of Qumran and the Dead Sea Scrolls.* Grand Rapids: William B. Eerdmans, 2002.

Mahon, Michael. *Foucault's Nietzschean Genealogy: Truth, Power, and the Subject.* Albany: State University of New York Press, 1992.

Malamud, Margaret. "Gender and Spiritual Self-Fashioning: The Master-Disciple Relationship in Classical Sufism." *Journal of the American Academy of Religion* 64 (1996): 89–117.

Maldiney, Henri. "Flesh and Verb in the Philosophy of Merleau-Ponty." In *Chiasms: Merleau-Ponty's Notion of Flesh,* edited by Fred Evans and Leonard Lawlor, 51–76. Albany: State University of New York Press, 2000.

Malin, Shimon. *Nature Loves to Hide: Quantum Physics and the Nature of Reality, a Western Perspective.* Oxford and New York: Oxford University Press, 2001.

Mallin, Samuel B. *Merleau-Ponty's Philosophy.* New Haven and London: Yale University Press, 1979.

Malul, Meir. *Knowledge, Control, and Sex: Studies in Biblical Thought, Culture, and Worldview.* Tel Aviv-Jaffa: Archaeological Center Publication, 2002.

Mamo, Plato. "Is Plotinian Mysticism Monistic?" In *The Significance of Neoplatonism,* edited by R. Baine Harris, 199–215. Norfolk: Old Dominion University, 1976.

Manchester, Peter. "The Noetic Triad in Plotinus, Marious Victorinus, and Augustine." In *Neoplatonism and Gnosticism,* edited by Richard T. Wallis and Jay Bregman, 207–222. Albany: State University of New York Press, 1992.

Mandel, Ross. "Heidegger and Wittgenstein: A Second Kantian Revolution." In *Heidegger and Modern Philosophy: Critical Essays,* edited by Michael Murray, 259–270. New Haven and London: Yale University Press, 1978.

Manetti, Giovanni. *Theories of the Sign in Classical Antiquity.* Translated by Christine Richardson. Bloomington and Indianapolis: Indiana University Press, 1993.

Mansfield, Victor. "Time and Impermanence in Middle Way Buddhism and Modern Physics." In *Buddhism and Science: Breaking New Ground,* edited by B. Alan Wallace, 305–321. New York: Columbia University Press, 2003.

———. "Time in Madhyamika Buddhism and Modern Physics." *Pacific World Journal of the Institute of Buddhist Studies* 11/12 (1995–1996): 10–27.

Maraldo, John C. "Rethinking God: Heidegger in the Light of Absolute Nothing, Nishida in the Shadow of Onto-theology." In *Religious Experience and the End of Metaphysics,* edited by Jeffrey Bloechl, 31–49. Bloomington and Indianapolis: Indiana University Press, 2003.

Marcovich, Miroslav. *Studies in Graeco-Roman Religions and Gnosticism.* Leiden: E. J. Brill, 1988.

Marcus, Ivan G. "The Song of Songs in German Hasidism and the School of Rashi: A Preliminary Comparison." *Jewish History* 6 (1992): 181–189.

Marcuse, Herbert. *Eros and Civilization: A Philosophical Inquiry into Freud.* Boston: Beacon Press, 1966.

Margolis, Joseph. "Philosophical Extravagance in Merleau-Ponty and Derrida." In *Écart & Différance,* edited by Martin C. Dillon, 112–132. Atlantic Highlands: Humanities Press, 1997.

Marion, Jean-Luc. *The Crossing of the Invisible.* Translated by James K. A. Smith. Stanford: Stanford University Press, 2004.

———. "The Event, the Phenomenon, and the Revealed." In *Transcendence in Philosophy and Religion,* edited by James E. Faulconer, 87–105. Bloomington and Indianapolis: Indiana University Press, 2003.

———. *God without Being: Hors-Texte.* Translated by Thomas A. Carlson, with a foreword by David Tracy. Chicago and London: University of Chicago Press, 1991.

———. *The Idol and Distance: Five Studies.* Translated with an introduction by Thomas A. Carlson. New York: Fordham University Press, 2001.

———. *In Excess: Studies of Saturated Phenomena.* Translated by Robyn Horner and Vincent Berraud. New York: Fordham University Press, 2002.

———. "In the Name: How to Avoid Speaking of 'Negative Theology.'" In *God, the Gift, and Postmodernism,* edited by John D. Caputo and Michael J. Scanlon, 20–53. Bloomington and Indianapolis: Indiana University Press, 1999.

———. "Introduction: What Do We Mean by 'Mystic'?" In *Mystics: Presence and Aporia,* edited by Michael Kessler and Christian Sheppard, 1–7. Chicago and London: University of Chicago Press, 2003.

———. *Le phénomène érotique: Six Méditations.* Paris: Bernard Grasset, 2003.

———. "The Saturated Phenomenon." In *Phenomenology and the "Theological Turn": The French Debate,* 176–216, edited by Dominique Janicaud, Jean-François Courtine, Jean-Louis Chrétien, Michel Henry, Jean-Luc Marion, and Paul Ricoeur. New York: Fordham University Press, 2000.

Marjanen, Antti. "Is *Thomas* a Gnostic Gospel?" In *Thomas at the Crossroads: Essays on the Gospel of Thomas,* edited by Risto Uro, 107–139. Edinburgh: T & T Clark, 1998.

———. "Women Disciples in the *Gospel of Thomas.*" In *Thomas At the Crossroads: Essays on the Gospel of Thomas,* edited by Risto Uro, 89–106. Edinburgh: T & T Clark, 1998.

Marks, Herbert. "On Prophetic Stammering." In *The Book and the Text: The Bible and Literary Theory,* edited by Regina M. Schwartz, 60–80. Cambridge: Basil Blackwell, 1990.

Marrati, Paola. "Le rêve et le danger: Où se perd la difference sexuelle?" In *L'éthique du don. Jacques Derrida et la pensée du don: Colloque de Royaumont décembre 1990,* edited by Jean-Michel Rabaté and Michael Wetzel, 194–211. Paris: Métailié-Transition, 1992.

Marrati-Guénoun, Paola. *La genèse et la trace: Derrida lecteur de Husserl et Heidegger.* Dordrecht: Kluwer Academic, 1998.

Marshall, David. "Christianity in the Qur'ān." In *Islamic Interpretations of Christianity,* edited by Lloyd Ridgeon, 3–29. New York: St. Martin's Press, 2001.

Martin, Glen T. *From Nietzsche to Wittgenstein: The Problem of Truth and Nihilism in the Modern World.* New York: Peter Lang, 1989.

Martinez, F. Garcia. "The Heavenly Tablets in the Book of Jubilees." In *Studies in the Book of Jubilees,* edited by Matthias Albni, Jörg Frey, and Armin Lange, 243–260. Tübingen: Mohr Siebeck, 1997.

Martinez, Roy, ed. *The Very Idea of Radical Hermeneutics.* Atlantic Highlands: Humanities Press, 1997.

Marx, Werner. *The Philosophy of F. W. J. Schelling: History, System, and Freedom.* Translated by Thomas Nenon. Bloomington: Indiana University Press, 1984.

———. *Reason and World: Between Tradition and Another Beginning.* The Hague: Martinus Nijhoff, 1971.

Massignon, Louis. *The Passion of al-Hallāj: Mystic and Martyr of Islam.* 4 vols. Translated by Herbert Mason. Princeton: Princeton University Press, 1982.

———. "Time in Islamic Thought." In *Man and Time: Papers from the Eranos Yearbooks*, edited by Joseph Campbell, 108–114. Princeton: Princeton University Press, 1957.

Masson, Jeffrey M. "Sex and Yoga: Psychoanalysis and the Indian Religious Experience." *Journal of Indian Philosophy* 2 (1974): 307–320. Reprinted in *Vishnu on Freud's Desk: A Reader in Psychoanalysis and Hinduism*, 235–249, edited by T. G. Vaidyanathan and Jeffrey J. Kripal. Delhi: Oxford University Press, 1999.

Matt, Daniel C. "Matnita Dilan: A Technique of Innovation in the Zohar." *Jerusalem Studies in Jewish Thought* 8 (1989): 123–145 (Hebrew).

———. "The Mystic and the *Miẓwot*." In *Jewish Spirituality from the Bible through the Middle Ages*, edited by Arthur Green, 367–404. New York: Crossroad, 1986.

Matter, E. Ann. *The Voice of My Beloved: The Song of Songs in Western Medieval Christianity.* Philadelphia: University of Pennsylvania Press, 1990.

May, Reinhard. *Heidegger's Hidden Sources: East Asian Influences on His Work.* Translated with a complementary essay by Graham Parkes. London and New York: Routledge, 1996.

May, Todd. *Reconsidering Difference: Nancy, Derrida, Levinas, and Deleuze.* University Park: Pennsylvania State University Press, 1997.

Mazis, Glen A. "Chaos Theory and Merleau-Ponty's Ontology." In *Merleau-Ponty, Interiority and Exteriority: Psychic Life and the World*, edited by Dorothea Olkowski and James Morley, 219–241. Albany: State University of New York Press, 1999.

———. "Merleau-Ponty and the 'Backward Flow' of Time: The Reversibility of Temporality and the Temporality of Reversibility." In *Merleau-Ponty: Hermeneutics and Postmodernism*, edited by Tom Busch and Shaun Gallagher, 53–68. Albany: State University of New York Press, 1992.

Mazzoni, Cristina. *Saint Hysteria: Neurosis, Mysticism, and Gender in European Culture.* Ithaca and London: Cornell University Press, 1996.

McArthur, Harvey K. "Celibacy in Judaism at the Time of Christian Beginnings." *Andrews University Seminary Studies* 25 (1987): 163–181.

McCall, Storrs. "Time Flow." In *The Importance of Time: Proceedings of the Philosophy of Time Society, 1995–2000*, edited by L. Nathan Oaklander, 143–151. Dordrecht: Kluwer Academic, 2001.

McCarthy, Thomas. *Ideals and Illusions: On Reconstruction and Deconstruction in Contemporary Critical Theory.* Cambridge, Mass.: MIT Press, 1991.

McCumber, John. "Essence and Subversion in Hegel and Heidegger." In *Writing the Politics of Difference*, edited by Hugh J. Silverman, 13–29. Albany: State University of New York Press, 1991.

McEvilley, Thomas. "The Spinal Serpent." In *The Roots of Tantra*, edited by Katherine A. Harper and Robert L. Brown, 93–113. Albany: State University of New York Press, 2002.

McGaha, Michael. "Naming the Nameless, Numbering the infinite: Some Common Threads in Spanish Sufism, Kabbalah, and Catholic Mysticism." *Yearbook of Comparative and General Literature* 45 (1997–1998): 37–52.

———. "The *Sefer ha-Bahir* and Andalusian Sufism." *Medieval Encounters* 3 (1997): 20–57.

McGhee, Michael. *Transformations of Mind: Philosophy as Spiritual Practice.* Cambridge: Cambridge University Press, 2000.

McGinn, Bernard. *The Foundations of Mysticism: Origins to the Fifth Century.* New York: Crossroad, 1991.

———. *The Growth of Mysticism: Gregory the Great through the 12th Century.* New York: Crossroad, 1994.

———. "The Language of Love in Christian and Jewish Mysticism." In *Mysticism and Language*, edited by Steven T. Katz, 202–235. New York and Oxford: Oxford University Press, 1992.

———. "*Maximum Contractum et Absolutum*: The Motive for the Incarnation in Nicholas of Cusanus and His Predecessors." In *Nicholas of Cusa and His Age: Intellect and Spirituality: Essays Dedicated to the Memory of F. Edward Cranz, Thomas P. McTighe and Charles Trinkaus*, edited by Thomas M. Izbicki and Christopher M. Bellitto, 151–175. Leiden: Brill, 2002.

———. *The Mystical Thought of Meister Eckhart: The Man from Whom God Hid Nothing*. New York: Crossroad, 2001.

———. "*Unitrinum Seu Triunum*: Nicholas of Cusa's Trinitarian Mysticism." In *Mystics: Presence and Aporia*, edited by Michael Kessler and Christian Sheppard, 90–117. Chicago and London: University of Chicago Press, 2003.

McGrady, Donald. "More on the Image of the 'Rose among Thorns' in Medieval Spanish Literature." *La corónocia* 17 (1988–89): 33–37.

McGuinness, Brian, ed. *Wittgenstein and the Vienna Circle: Conversations Recorded by Friedrich Waismann*. New York: Barnes & Noble Books, 1979.

McGuire, Anne. "Virginity and Subversion: Norea against the Powers in the Hypostasis of the Archons." In *Images of the Feminine in Gnosticism*, edited by Karen L. King, 241–225. Philadelphia: Fortress Press, 1988.

———. "Women, Gender, and Gnosis in Gnostic Texts and Traditions." In *Women & Christian Origins*, edited by Ross Shepard Kraemer and Mary Rose D'Angelo, 277–282. New York and Oxford: Oxford University Press, 1999.

McIntyre, Alex. *The Sovereignty of Joy: Nietzsche's Vision of Grand Politics*. Toronto: University of Toronto Press, 1997.

McLaren, Margaret A. *Feminism, Foucault, and Embodied Subjectivity*. Albany: State University of New York Press, 2002.

McNamara, Jo Ann. "The Rhetoric of Orthodoxy: Clerical Authority and Female Innovation in the Struggle with Heresy." In *Maps of Flesh and Light: The Religious Experience of Medieval Women Mystics*, edited by Ulrike Wiethaus, 9–27. Syracuse: Syracuse University Press, 1993.

McNamer, Sarah. "The Exploratory Image: God as Mother in Julian of Norwich's Revelations of Divine Love." *Mystics Quarterly* 15 (1989): 21–28.

McPartland, Thomas J. *Lonergan and the Philosophy of Historical Existence*. Columbia, Mo., and London: University of Missouri Press, 2001.

McSheffrey, Shannon. *Gender and Heresy: Women and Men in Lollard Communities, 1420–1530*. Philadelphia: University of Pennsylvania Press, 1995.

McWhorter, Ladelle. *Bodies and Pleasures: Foucault and the Politics of Sexual Normalization*. Bloomington and Indianapolis: Indiana University Press, 1999.

Meeks, Wayne. *The First Urban Christians: The Social World of the Apostle Paul*. New Haven and London: Yale University Press, 1983.

———. "The Image of the Androgyne: Some Uses of a Symbol in Earliest Christianity." *History of Religions* 13 (1973–74): 165–208.

Meged, Matti. "The Kabbalah as Poetry." In *Proceedings of the Xth Congress of the International Comparative Literature Association*, edited by Anna Balakian, 558–564. New York: Garland, 1985.

Meier, Fritz. *Essays on Islamic Piety and Mysticism*. Translated by John O'Kane. Leiden: E. J. Brill, 1999.

———. "The Problem of Nature in the Esoteric Monism of Islam." In *Spirit and Nature: Papers from the Eranos Yearbooks*, 149–203. New York: Pantheon Books, 1954.

Meijer, P. A. "Participation in Henads and Monads in Proclus' *Theologia Platonica* III, CHS. 1–6." In *Proclus and His Influence in Medieval Philosophy*, edited by Egbert P. Bos and P. A. Meijer, 65–87. Leiden: E. J. Brill, 1992.

Melamed, Abraham. "Maimonides on Women: Formless Matter or Potential Prophet?" In *Perspectives on Jewish Thought and Mysticism*, edited by Alfred L. Ivry, Elliot R. Wolfson, and Allan Arkush, 99–134. Amsterdam: Harwood Academic, 1998.

———. "Women as Philosopher: The Image of Sophia in Y. Abravanel's Dialoghi d'Amore." *Jewish Studies* 40 (2000): 113–130 (Hebrew).

Melchior-Bonnet, Sabine. *The Mirror: A History*. Translated by Katharine H. Jewett. New York and London: Routledge, 2001.

Meltzer, Françoise. "Re-embodying: Virginity Secularized." In *God, the Gift, and Postmodernism*, edited by John D. Caputo and Michael J. Scanlon, 260–281. Bloomington and Indianapolis: Indiana University Press, 1999.

Mendel, Arthur P. *Vision and Violence*. Ann Arbor: University of Michigan Press, 1999.

Mendelsohn, Ezra. "People of the Image." In *Studies in Contemporary Jewry: An Annual* 16 (2000): 305–312.

Mendes-Flohr, Paul R. *From Mysticism to Dialogue: Martin Buber's Transformation of German Social Thought*. Detroit: Wayne State University Press, 1989.

Menke-Eggers, Christoph. *The Sovereignty of Art: Aesthetic Negativity in Adorno and Derrida*. Translated by Neil Solomon. Cambridge, Mass.: MIT Press, 1998.

Merlan, Philip. *Monopsychism, Mysticism, Metaconsciousness: Problems of the Soul in the Neoaristotelian and Neoplatonic Tradition*. The Hague: Martinus Nijhoff, 1963.

Merleau-Ponty, Maurice. *Phénoménologie de la perception*. Paris: Librairie Gallimard, 1945.

———. *Phenomenology of Perception*. Translated by Colin Smith. New York: Humanities Press, 1962.

———. *La prose du monde*. Edited by Claude Lefort. Paris: Éditions Gallimard, 1969.

———. *The Prose of the World*. Edited by Claude Lefort. Translated by John O'Neill. Evanston: Northwestern University Press, 1973.

———. *Signes*. Paris: Éditions Gallimard, 1960.

———. *Signs*. Translated with an introduction by Richard C. McCleary. Evanston: Northwestern University Press, 1964.

———. *Le visible et l'invisible*. Paris: Librairie Gallimard, 1964.

———. *The Visible and the Invisible*. Edited by Claude Lefort, translated by Alphonso Lingis. Evanston: Northwestern University Press, 1968.

Mernissi, Fatima. *Beyond the Veil: Male-Female Dynamics in Modern Muslim Society*. Rev. ed. Bloomington and Indianapolis: Indiana University Press, 1987.

———. *The Veil and the Male Elite: A Feminist Interpretation of Women's Rights in Islam*. Translated by Mary Jo Lakeland. Reading: Addison-Wesley, 1991.

Meroz, Ronit. "A Bright Light in the East: On the Time and Place of Part of *Sefer ha-Bahir*." *Daʿat* 49 (2002): 137–180 (Hebrew).

———. "Early Lurianic Compositions." In *Massuʾot: Studies in Kabbalistic Literature and Jewish Philosophy in Memory of Prof. Ephraim Gottlieb*, edited by Michal Oron and Amos Goldreich, 311–338. Jerusalem: Bialik Institute, 1994 (Hebrew).

———. "Redemption in the Lurianic Teaching." Ph.D. dissertation, Hebrew University, Jerusalem, 1988 (Hebrew).

———. "Zoharic Narratives and Their Adaptations." *Hispania Judaica Bulletin* 3 (2000): 3–63.

Meskin, Jacob. "Textual Reasoning, Modernity, and the Limits of History." *Crosscurrents* 49 (1999–2000): 475–490.

Mews, Constant J. "Virginity, Theology, and Pedagogy in the *Speculum Virginum*." In *Listen, Daughter: The Speculum Virginum and the Formation of Religious Women in the Middle Ages*, edited by Constant J. Mews, 15–40. New York: Palgrave, 2001.

Meyer, Marvin W. "*Gospel of Thomas* Logion 114 Revisited." In *For the Children, Perfect Instruction: Studies in Honor of Hans-Martin Schenke on the Occasion of the Berliner Arbeitskreis für koptisch-gnostische Schriften's Thirtieth Year*, edited by Hans-Gebhard Bethge, Stephen Emmel, Karen L. King, and Imke Schletterer, 101–111. Leiden: Brill, 2002.

———. "Making Mary Male: The Categories 'Male' and 'Female' in the Gospel of Thomas." *New Testament Studies* 31 (1985): 554–570.

———. *Secret Gospels: Essays on Thomas and the Secret Gospel of Mark*. Harrisburg: Trinity Press International, 2003.

Michelson, Peter. *Speaking the Unspeakable: A Poetics of Obscenity*. Albany: State University of New York Press, 1993.

Milchman, Alan, and Alan Rosenberg, eds. *Martin Heidegger and the Holocaust*. Atlantic Highlands: Humanities Press, 1996.

Miles, Margaret. *Carnal Knowing: Female Nakedness and Religious Meaning in the Christian West*. Boston: Beacon Press, 1989.

———. *Plotinus on Body and Beauty: Society, Philosophy, and Religion in Third-Century Rome*. Oxford: Blackwell, 1999.

———. "Textual Harassment: Desire and the Female Body." In *The Good Body: Asceticism in Contemporary Culture*, edited by Mary G. Winkler and Letha B. Cole, 49–63. New Haven and London, Yale University Press, 1994.

Miller, Julie B. "Eroticized Violence in Medieval Women's Mystical Literature: A Call for a Feminist Critique." *Journal of Feminist Studies in Religion* 15 (1995): 25–49.

Miller, Nancy K. "The Text's Heroine: A Feminist Critic and Her Fictions." In *Conflicts in Feminism*, edited by Marianne Hirsch and Evelyn Fox Keller, 112–120. New York and London: Routledge, 1990.

Miller, Patricia Cox. "'Pleasure of the Text, Text of Pleasure': Eros and Language in Origen's *Commentary on the Song of Songs*." *Journal of the American Academy of Religion* 54 (1986): 241–253.

Minces, Juliette. *La femme voilée l'Islam au féminin*. Paris: Calmann-Lévy, 1990.

Mir, Mustansir. "Kabbalah and Sufism: A Comparative Look at Jewish and Islamic Mysticism." In *Jewish-Muslim Encounters: History, Philosophy and Culture*, edited by Charles Selengut, 165–179. St. Paul: Paragon House, 2001.

Misgeld, Dieter. "Poetry, Dialogue, and Negotiation: Liberal Culture and Conservative Politics in Hans-Georg Gadamer's Thought." In *Festivals of Interpretation: Essays on Hans-Georg Gadamer's Work*, edited by Kathleen Wright, 161–181. Albany: State University of New York Press, 1990.

Mitchell, W. J. Thomas. *Iconology: Image, Text, Ideology*. Chicago and London: University of Chicago Press, 1986.

Moezzi, Mohammad Ali Amir. *The Divine Guide in Early Shiʿism: The Sources of Esotericism in Islam*. Translated by David Streight. Albany: State University of New York Press, 1994.

Moi, Toril. *Sexual/Textual Politics: Feminist Literary Theory*. London: Methuen, 1985.

———. *What Is a Woman?* Oxford and New York: Oxford University Press, 1999.

Mole, Gary D. *Lévinas, Blanchot, Jabès: Figures of Estrangement*. Gainesville: University Press of Florida, 1997.

Mommaers, Paul. *The Riddle of Christian Mystical Experience: The Role of the Humanity of Jesus.* Leuven: Peeters Press, 2003.

Mookerjee, Satkari. *The Buddhist Philosophy of Universal Flux: An Exposition of the Philosophy of Critical Realism as Expounded by the School of Dignāga.* Calcutta: University of Calcutta, 1935.

Moore, Stephen. "The Song of Songs in the History of Sexuality." *Church History* 69 (2000): 328–349.

Mopsik, Charles. "The Body of Engenderment in the Hebrew Bible, the Rabbinic Tradition and the Kabbalah." In *Fragments for a History of the Human Body,* edited by Michel Feher with Ramona Naddaff and Nadia Tazi, 49–73. New York: Zone Books, 1989.

———. "Le corpus Zoharique ses titres et ses amplifications." In *La formation des canons scripturaires,* edited by Michel Tardieu, 75–105. Paris: Cerf, 1993.

———. "Genèse 1:26–27: L'image de Dieu, le couple humain et le statut de la femme chez les premiers cabalistes." In *Rigueur et passion: Mélanges offerts en hommage à Annie Kriegel,* edited by Stéphane Courtois, Marc Lazar, and Shmuel Trigano, 341–361. Paris: Éditions du Cerf, 1994.

———. *Les grands textes de la Cabale: Les rites qui font Dieu.* Paris: Éditions Verdier, 1993.

———. *Lettre sur la sainteté: Le secret de la relation entre l'homme et la femme dans la cabale.* Paris: Éditions Verdier, 1986.

———. "Moïse de León, le *Sheqel ha-Qodesh* et la rédaction du Zohar: Une réponse à Yehuda Liebes." *Kabbalah: Journal for the Study of Jewish Mystical Texts* 3 (1998): 117–218.

———. "Pensée, voix et parole dans le *Zohar.*" *Revue de l'Histoire des Religions* 213–4 (1996): 385–414.

———. "Recherches autour de la *Lettre sur la sainteté.* Sources, texte, influences. Tome I: La dualité masculin/feminin dans la cabale. Tome II: La secret de la relation entre l'homme et la femme." Ph.D. dissertation, Sorbonne, Paris, 1987.

———. *Le sexe des âmes: Aléas de la différence sexuelle dans la Cabale.* Paris: Éditions de l'éclat, 2003.

———. "Union and Unity in the Kabbala." In *Between Jerusalem and Benares: Comparative Studies in Judaism and Hinduism,* edited by Hananya Goodman, 223–242. Albany: State University of New York Press, 1994.

Moran, Dermot. *The Philosophy of John Scottus Eriugena: A Study of Idealism in the Middle Ages.* Cambridge: Cambridge University Press, 1989.

Morley, James. "Inspiration and Expiration: Yoga Practice through Merleau-Ponty's Phenomenology of the Body." *Philosophy East and West* 51 (2001): 73–82.

Morray-Jones, Christopher A. "Transformational Mysticism in the Apocalyptic-Merkabah Tradition." *Journal of Jewish Studies* 43 (1992): 1–31.

Mortley, Raoul. *Womanhood: The Feminine in Ancient Hellenism, Gnosticism, Christianity and Islam.* Sydney: Delacroix Press, 1981.

Mosès, Stéphane. *Der Engel der Geschichte: Franz Rosenzweig, Walter Benjamin, Gershom Scholem.* Frankfurt am Main: Jüdischer, 1994.

———. "Patterns of Negativity in Paul Celan's 'The Trumpet Place.'" In *Languages of the Unsayable: The Play of Negativity in Literature and Literary Theory,* edited by Sanford Budick and Wolfgang Iser, 209–224. New York: Columbia University Press, 1989.

———. "Rosenzweig et Lévinas: Au-delà de la guerre." In *Emmanuel Lévinas et l'histoire: Actes du Colloque international des facultés universitaires Notre-Dame de la Paix (20–21–22 mai 1997),* edited by Nathalie Frogneux and Françoise Mies, 137–155. Paris: Les Éditions du Cerf, 1998.

Muldoon, Mark S. "Silence Revisited: Taking the Sight out of Auditory Qualities." *Review of Metaphysics* 50 (1996): 275–298.

Mundkur, Balaji. *The Cult of the Serpent: An Interdisciplinary Survey of Its Manifestations and Origins.* Albany: State University of New York Press, 1983.

Muneto, Sonoda. "The Eloquent Silence of Zarathustra." In *Nietzsche and Asian Thought*, edited by Graham Parkes, 226–243. Chicago and London: University of Chicago Press, 1991.

Munro, Winsome. "Women Disciples: Light from Secret Mark." *Journal of Feminist Studies in Religion* 8 (1992): 47–64.

Murata, Sachiko. " 'Mysteries of Marriage': Notes on a Sufi Text." In *The Legacy of Mediæval Persian Sufism*, edited by Leonard Lewisohn, foreword by Dr. Javad Nurbakhsh, introduction by Seyyed H. Nasr, 343–351. London and New York: Khaniqahi Nimatullahi Publications, 1992.

———. *The Tao of Islam: A Sourcebook on Gender Relationships in Islamic Thought.* Foreword by Annemarie Schimmel. Albany: State University of New York Press, 1992.

———. "Witnessing the Rose: Yaʿaqūb Ṣarfi on the Vision of God in Women." In *Gott ist schön und Er liebt die Schönheit: Festschrift für Annemarie Schimmel zum 7. April 1992*, edited by Alma Giese and J. Christoph Bürgel, 349–361. Bern: Peter Lang, 1994.

Murcott, Susan. *The First Buddhist Women: Translations and Commentaries on the Therigatha.* Berkeley: Parallax Press, 1991.

Murray, Peter Durno. *Nietzsche's Affirmative Morality: A Revaluation Based in the Dionysian World-View.* Berlin and New York: Walter de Gruyter, 1999.

Murti, Tiruppattur Rameseshayyar Venkatachala. *Studies in Indian Thought: Collected Papers of Prof. T. R. V. Murti.* Edited by Harold G. Coward. Delhi: Motilal Banarsidass, 1983.

Myers, Jody. "The Midrashic Enterprise of Contemporary Jewish Women." *Studies in Contemporary Jewry: An Annual* 16 (2000): 119–141.

Nadeau, Robert L. *S/He Brain: Science, Sexual Politics, and the Myths of Feminism.* Westport and London: Praeger, 1996.

Nadler, Allan. *The Faith of the Mithnagdim: Rabbinic Responses to Hasidic Rapture.* Baltimore and London: Johns Hopkins University Press, 1997.

Naeh, Shlomo. "Freedom and Celibacy: A Talmudic Variation on Tales of Temptation and Fall in Genesis and Its Syrian Background." In *The Book of Genesis in Jewish and Oriental Christian Interpretation: A Collection of Essays*, edited by Judith Frishman and Lucas Van Rompay, 73–89. Leuven: Peeters, 1997.

Nag Hammadi Codex II, 2–7. 2 vols. Edited by Bentley Layton. Vol. 2 of *The Coptic Gnostic Library: A Complete Edition of the Nag Hammadi Codices.* Leiden: E. J. Brill, 1989.

Nag Hammadi Codex III, 5: The Dialogue of the Savior. Translated and edited by Stephen Emmel. Vol. 3 of *The Coptic Gnostic Library: A Complete Edition of the Nag Hammadi Codices.* Leiden: E. J. Brill, 2000.

Nag Hammadi Codices III, 3–4, and V, 1. Edited by Douglas M. Parrott. Leiden: E. J. Brill, 1991. Vol. 3 of *The Coptic Gnostic Library: A Complete Edition of the Nag Hammadi Codices.* Leiden: E. J. Brill, 2000.

Nagao, Gadjin M. *Mādhyamika and Yogācāra: A Study of Mahāyāna Philosophies.* Edited, collated, and translated by Leslie S. Kawamura. Albany: State University of New York Press, 1991.

Nāgārjuna. *Nāgārjuna's Twelve Gate Treatise.* Translated with introductory essays, comments, and notes by Hsueh-li Cheng. Dordrecht: D. Reidel, 1982.

Nagataki, Shōji. "Husserl and Merleau-Ponty: The Conception of the World." *Analecta Husserliana* 58 (1998): 29–45.

Nagatomo, Shigenori. *Attunement through the Body.* Albany: State University of New York Press, 1992.

Najman, Hindy. "Interpretation as Primordial Writing: Jubilees and Its Authority Conferring Strategies." *Journal for the Study of Judaism* 30 (1999): 379–410.

Nancy, Jean-Luc, and Philippe Lacoue-Labarthe. *The Title of the Letter: A Reading of Lacan.* Translated by François Raffoul and David Pettigrew. Albany: State University of New York Press, 1992.

Nasafī, ʿAzīz. *Persian Metaphysics and Mysticism: Selected Treatises of ʿAzīz Nasafī.* Translated by Lloyd V. J. Ridgeon. Richmond: Curzon, 2002.

Nash, Kathleen. "The Language of Mother Work in the Gospel of Thomas: Keeping Momma out of the Kingdom (*Gos. Thom.* 22)." In *The Lost Coin: Parables of Women, Work and Wisdom,* edited by Mary Ann Beavis, 174–195. London and New York: Sheffield Academic Press, 2002.

Nasio, Juan-David. *Five Lessons on the Psychoanalytic Theory of Jacques Lacan.* Translated by David Pettigrew and François Raffoul. Albany: State University of New York Press, 1998.

Nasr, Seyyed Hossein. *Sufi Essays.* Albany: State University of New York Press, 1973.

Natanson, Maurice. *Edmund Husserl: Philosopher of infinite Tasks.* Evanston: Northwestern University Press, 1973.

———. *Literature, Philosophy and the Social Sciences: Essays in Existentialism and Phenomenology.* The Hague: Martinus Nijhoff, 1962.

Nehamas, Alexander. "How One Becomes What One Is." *Philosophical Review* 92 (1983): 385–417. Reprinted in *Nietzsche,* edited by John Richardson and Brian Leiter, 255–280. Oxford: Oxford University Press, 2001.

Nettler, Ronald L. *Sufi Metaphysics and Qurʾānic Prophets: Ibn ʿArabī's Thought and Method in Fuṣūṣ al-Ḥikam.* Cambridge: Islamic Texts Society, 2003.

Neumann, Erich. *The Fear of the Feminine and Other Essays on Feminine Psychology.* Translated by Boris Matthews, Esther Doughty, Eugene Rolfe, and Michael Cullingworth. Princeton: Princeton University Press, 1994.

———. *The Fear of the Feminine and Other Essays on Feminine Psychology.* Translated by Boris Matthews, Esther Doughty, Eugene Rolfe, and Michael Cullingworth. Princeton: Princeton University Press, 1994.

———. *The Great Mother: An Analysis of the Archetype.* Translated by Ralph Manheim. Princeton: Princeton University Press, 1955.

———. *The Origins and History of Consciousness.* Translated by R. F. C. Hull, foreword by Carl G. Jung. Princeton: Princeton University Press, 1954.

Neumark, David. *History of Jewish Philosophy.* 2 vols. Jerusalem: Maqor, 1971 (Hebrew).

Neusner, Jacob. *The Midrash Compilations of the Sixth and Seventh Centuries: An Introduction to the Rhetorical, Logical, and Topical Program.* 4 vols. Atlanta: Scholars Press, 1989.

Neville, Robert C. *Eternity and Time's Flow.* Albany: State University of New York Press, 1993.

Newman, Barbara. *From Virile Woman to WomanChrist: Studies in Medieval Religion and Literature.* Philadelphia: University of Pennsylvania Press, 1995.

———. *God and the Goddesses: Vision, Poetry, and Belief in the Middle Ages.* Philadelphia: University of Pennsylvania Press, 2003.

———. "Poet: 'Where the Living Majesty Utters Mysteries.'" In *Voice of the Living Light: Hildegard of Bingen and Her World,* edited by Barbara Newman, 176–192. Berkeley: University of California Press, 1998.

———. *Sister of Wisdom: St. Hildegard's Theology of the Feminine.* With a new preface, bibliography, and discography. Berkeley: University of California Press, 1997.

Newsom, Carol A. *Songs of the Sabbath Sacrifice: A Critical Edition.* Atlanta: Scholars Press, 1985.

———. "Woman and the Discourse of Patriarchal Wisdom: A Study of Proverbs 1–9." In *Gender and Difference in Ancient Israel*, edited by Peggy L. Day, 142–160. Minneapolis: Fortress Press, 1989.

Nicholas of Cusa. *Complete Philosophical and Theological Treatises of Nicholas of Cusa*. Translated by Jasper Hopkins. Minneapolis: Arthur J. Banning Press, 2001.

Nicholson, Reynold A. *The Kashf al Mahjūb: The Oldest Persian Treatise on Sūfism*. London: Luzac, 1936.

———. *The Mystics of Islam: An Introduction to Sufism*. London: Routledge & Kegan Paul, 1963.

———. *Studies in Islamic Mysticism*. Cambridge: Cambridge University Press, 1921.

Niehoff, Maren. *The Figure of Joseph in Post-Biblical Jewish Literature*. Leiden: E. J. Brill, 1992.

Nieli, Russell. *Wittgenstein: From Mysticism to Ordinary Language: A Study of Viennese Positivism and the Thought of Ludwig Wittgenstein*. Albany: State University of New York Press, 1987.

Nietzsche, Friedrich. *Basic Writings of Nietzsche*. Translated and edited with commentaries by Walter Kaufmann. New York: Modern Library, 1968.

———. *Beyond Good and Evil: Prelude to a Philosophy of the Future*. Translated with commentary by Walter Kaufmann. New York: Vintage Books, 1966.

———. *The Gay Science with a Prelude in German Rhymes and an Appendix of Songs*. Edited by Bernard Williams, translated by Josefine Nauckhoff, poems translated by Adrian del Caro. Cambridge: Cambridge University Press, 2001.

———. *Philosophy and Truth: Selections from Nietzsche's Notebooks of the Early 1870's*. Translated by Daniel Breazeale. Amherst: Humanity Books, 1999.

———. *Philosophy in the Tragic Age of the Greeks*. Translated by Marianne Cowan. South Bend: Gateway Editions, 1962.

———. *The Pre-Platonic Philosophers*. Translated and edited with an introduction and commentary by Greg Whitlock. Urbana and Chicago: University of Illinois Press, 2001.

———. *Thus Spake Zarathustra: A Book for Everyone and No One*. Translated with an introduction by R. J. Hollingdale. New York: Penguin Books, 1969.

———. *Twilight of the Idols; and The Anti-Christ*. Translated with an introduction and commentary by R. J. Hollingdale. New York: Penguin Books, 1968.

———. *The Will to Power*. Translated by Walter Kaufmann and R. J. Hollingdale, edited with commentary by Walter Kaufmann. New York: Random House, 1967.

Nishitani, Keiji. "Reflections on Two Addresses by Martin Heidegger." In *Heidegger and Asian Thought*, edited by Graham Parkes, 145–153. Honolulu: University of Hawaii Press, 1987.

Nnaemeka, Obioma. "Introduction: Imag(in)ing Knowledge, Power, and Subversion in the Margins." In *The Politics of (M)Othering: Womanhood, Identity, and Resistance in African Literature*, edited by Obioma Nnaemeka, 1–25. London and New York: Routledge, 1997.

Norris, Kathleen. "A Word Made Flesh: Incarnational Language and the Writer." In *The Incarnation: An Interdisciplinary Symposium on the Incarnation of the Son of God*, edited by Stephen T. Davis, Daniel Kendall, and Gerald O'Collins, 303–312. Oxford and New York: Oxford University Press, 2002.

Norris, R. "The Soul Takes Flight: Gregory of Nyssa and the Song of Songs." *Anglican Theological Review* 80 (1998): 517–532.

Nota, John H. *Phenomenology and History*. Translated by Louis Grooten and the author. Chicago: Loyola University Press, 1967.

Novak, David. *Covenantal Rights: A Study in Jewish Political Theory*. Princeton: Princeton University Press, 2000.

———. *The Election of Israel: The Idea of the Chosen People*. Cambridge: Cambridge University Press, 1995.

Nuki, Shigeto. "Temporality and Historicity: Phenomenology of History beyond Narratology." In *The Many Faces of Time*, edited by John B. Brough and Lester Embree, 149–165. Dordrecht: Kluwer Academic, 2000.

Nurbakhsh, Javad. *Jesus in the Eyes of the Sufis*. Translated by Terry Graham, Leonard Lewisohn, and Hamid Mashkuri. London: Khaniqahi-Nimatullahi Publications, 1983.

Nussbaum, Martha. "Eros and the Wise: The Stoic Response to a Cultural Dilemma." In *The Emotions in Hellenistic Philosophy*, edited by Juha Sihvola and Troels Engberg-Pedersen, 271–304. Dordrecht: Kluwer Academic, 1998.

———. *Love's Knowledge: Essays on Philosophy and Literature*. New York and Oxford: Oxford University Press, 1990.

Nye, Andrea. *Philosophy and Feminism at the Border*. New York: Twayne, 1995.

———. "The Voice of the Serpent: French Feminism and Philosophy of Language." In *Women, Knowledge, and Reality: Explorations in Feminist Philosophy*, edited by Ann Garry and Marilyn Pearsall, 323–338. 2nd ed. New York and London: Routledge, 1996.

Nygren, Anders. *Agape and Eros*. Translated by Philip Saville Watson. London: SPCK, 1953.

Ochs, Peter. "An Introduction to Postcritical Scriptural Interpretation." In *The Return to Scripture in Judaism and Christianity: Essays in Postcritical Scriptural Interpretation*, 3–51. New York: Paulist Press, 1993.

———. *Peirce, Pragmatism and the Logic of Scripture*. Cambridge: Cambridge University Press, 1998.

O'Connor, Dennis T. "Reconstructive Time: Écart, Différance, Fundamental Obscurity." In *Écart & Différance: Merleau-Ponty and Derrida on Seeing and Writing*, edited by Martin C. Dillon, 149–166. Atlantic Highlands: Humanities Press, 1997.

Odeberg, Hugo, ed. *Enoch or The Hebrew Book of Enoch*. Cambridge: Cambridge University Press, 1928.

O'Flaherty, Wendy Doniger. *Asceticism and Eroticism in the Mythology of Siva*. London: Oxford University Press, 1973.

———. *Women, Androgynes, and Other Mythical Beasts*. Chicago and London: University of Chicago Press, 1980.

Ofrat, Gideon. *The Jewish Derrida*. Translated by Peretz Kidron. Syracuse: Syracuse University Press, 2001.

Ohly, Friedrich. *Hohelied-Studien: Grundzüge einer Geschichte der Hoheliedauslegung des Abendlandes bis um 1200*. Wiesbaden: Franz Steiner, 1958.

Økland, Jorunn. "Man is the Measure of all Things: Gender and Integration in Paul's Ekklesia." In *Gender and Religion: European Studies*, edited by Kari Elisabeth Børresen, Sara Cabibbi, and Edith Specht, 59–82. Rome: Carocci Editore, 2001.

The Old Testament Pseudepigrapha. 2 vols. Edited by James H. Charlesworth. New York: Doubleday, 1983.

Olkowski, Dorothea. "Merleau-Ponty and Bergson: The Character of the Phenomenal Field." In *Merleau-Ponty: Difference, Materiality, Painting*, edited by Véronique M. Fóti, 27–36. Atlantic Highlands: Humanities Press, 1996.

Olschner, Leonard. "Poetic Mutations of Silence: At the Nexus of Paul Celan and Osip Mandelstam." In *Word Traces: Readings of Paul Celan*, edited by Aris Fioretos, 369–385. Baltimore and London: Johns Hopkins University Press, 1994.

Olson, Alan M. *Hegel and the Spirit: Philosophy as Pneumatology*. Princeton: Princeton University Press, 1992.

Olson, Carl. "The Human Body as a Boundary Symbol: A Comparison of Merleau-Ponty and Dōgen." *Philosophy East and West* 36 (1986): 107–120.

———. "The Leap of Thinking: A Comparison of Heidegger and the Zen Master Dōgen." *Philosophy Today* 25 (1981): 55–62.

Olyan, Saul M. "'And with a Male You Shall Not Lie the Lying Down of a Woman': On the Meaning and Significance of Leviticus 18:22 and 20:13." *Journal of the History of Sexuality* 5 (1994): 179–206.

———. *Rites and Rank: Hierarchy in Biblical Representations of Cult.* Princeton: Princeton University Press, 2000.

O'Neill, John C. *Who Did Jesus Think He Was?* Leiden: E. J. Brill, 1995.

Oosthout, Henri. *Modes of Knowledge and the Transcendental: An Introduction to Plotinus Ennead 5.3 [49].* Amsterdam: B. R. Grüner, 1991.

Oppenheim, Michael. *Speaking/Writing of God: Jewish Philosophical Reflections on the Life with Others.* Albany: State University of New York Press, 1997.

O'Regan, Cyril. *Gnostic Apocalypse: Jacob Boehme's Haunted Narrative.* Albany: State University of New York Press, 2002.

———. "Hegel and Anti-Judaism: Narrative and the Inner Circulation of the Kabbalah." *Owl and Minerva* 28 (1997): 141–182.

Ormsby, Eric. *Poetry as Isotope: The Hidden Life of Words.* Montreal: Friends of the Library, McGill University, 1997.

Oron, Michal. "Introduction of *Sefer ha-Peliʾah.*" *Qoveṣ al Yad* 11 (1989): 273–295 (Hebrew).

———. "'Place Me as a Seal upon Your Heart': Reflections on the Poetics of the Author of the *Zohar* in the Section of *Sabba de-Mishpaṭim.*" In *Massuʾot: Studies in Kabbalistic Literature and Jewish Philosophy in Memory of Prof. Ephraim Gottlieb*, edited by Michal Oron and Amos Goldreich, 1–24. Jerusalem: Bialik Institute, 1994.

———. "Three Commentaries to the Story of Genesis and Their Significance for the Study of the *Zohar.*" *Daʿat* 50–52 (2003): 183–199 (Hebrew).

Orr, Leslie C. *Donors, Devotees, and Daughters of God: Temple Women in Medieval Tamilnadu.* New York and Oxford: Oxford University Press, 2000.

Ortner, Sherry B. "Is Female to Male as Nature Is to Culture?" In *Women, Culture, and Society*, edited by Michelle Zimbalist Rosaldo and Louise Lamphere, 67–87. Stanford: Stanford University Press, 1974.

Osborne, Catherine. *Eros Unveiled: Plato and the God of Love.* New York: Clarendon, 1994.

Osborne, Peter, ed. *A Critical Sense: Interviews with Intellectuals.* London and New York: Routledge, 1996.

Otten, Willemien. "The Parallelism of Nature and Scripture: Reflections on Eriugena's Incarnational Exegesis." In *Iohannes Scottus Eriugena: The Bible and Hermeneutics: Proceedings of the Ninth International Colloquium of the Society for the Promotion of Eriugenian Studies Held at Leuven and Louvain-la-Neuve June 7–10, 1995*, edited by Gerd Van Riel, Carlos Steel, and James McEvoy, 81–102. Leuven: University Press, 1996.

Ouaknin, Marc-Alain. *The Burnt Book: Reading the Talmud.* Translated by Llewellyn Brown. Princeton: Princeton University Press, 1995.

———. *Mysteries of the Kabbalah.* Translated by Josephine Bacon. New York: Abbeville Press, 2000.

Ozturk, Orphan M. "Ritual Circumcision and Castration Anxiety." *Psychiatry* 36 (1973): 49–60.

Pachter, Mordecai. "Circles and Straightness—A History of an Idea." *Daʿat* 18 (1987): 59–90 (Hebrew).

———. "The Concept of Devekut in the Homiletical Ethical Writings of 16th Century Safed." In *Studies in Medieval Jewish History and Literature, Volume 2*, edited by Isadore Twersky, 171–230. Cambridge, Mass.: Harvard University Press, 1984.

Pagels, Elaine. *Adam, Eve, and the Serpent*. New York: Random House, 1988.

———. *Beyond Belief: The Secret Gospel of Thomas*. New York: Random House, 2003.

———. "Exegesis of Genesis 1 in the Gospels of Thomas and John." *Journal of Biblical Literature* 118 (1999): 477–496.

———. "The 'Mystery of Marriage' in the Gospel of Philip." In *The Allure of Gnosticism: The Gnostic Experience in Jungian Psychology and Contemporary Culture*, edited by Robert A. Segal with June Singer and Murray Stein, 107–116. Chicago and La Salle: Open Court, 1995.

———. "Paul and Women: A Response to a Recent Discussion." *Journal of the American Academy of Religion* 42 (1974): 538–549.

Pai, Ashlynn K. "Varying Degrees of Light: Bonaventure and the Medieval Book of Nature." In *The Book and the Magic of Reading in the Middle Ages*, edited by Albrecht Classen, 3–19. New York and London: Garland, 1998.

Paige, Karen Ericksen, and Jeffrey M. Paige. *The Politics of Reproductive Ritual*. Berkeley: University of California Press, 1981.

Palumbo, Patrizia. "Gender Difference in the Franciscan Spirituality of Angela of Foligno and Iacopone of Todi." Ph.D. dissertation, Columbia University, 1996.

Panikkar, Raimon. *The Cosmotheandric Experience: Emerging Religious Consciousness*. Edited with introduction by Scott Eastham. Maryknoll: Orbis Books, 1993.

Papa-Grimaldi, Alba. *Time and Reality*. Aldershot: Ashgate, 1998.

Pardes, Ilana. *Countertraditions in the Bible: A Feminist Approach*. Cambridge, Mass.: Harvard University Press, 1992.

Park, David. *The Image of Eternity: Roots of Time in the Physical World*. Amherst: University of Massachusetts Press, 1980.

Parkes, Graham. "Thoughts on the Way: *Being and Time* via Lao-Chuang." In *Heidegger and Asian Thought*, edited by Graham Parkes, 105–144. Honolulu: University of Hawaii Press, 1987.

Parpola, Simo. *Assyrian Prophecies*. Helsinki: Helsinki University Press, 1997.

———. "The Assyrian Tree of Life: Tracing the Origins of Jewish Monotheism and Greek Philosophy." *Journal of Near Eastern Studies* 52 (1993): 161–208.

Parrinder, Geoffrey. *Jesus in the Qur'an*. London: Faber and Faber, 1965.

Parsons, Susan Frank. *The Ethics of Gender*. Oxford: Blackwell, 2002.

Parsons, William B. *The Enigma of the Oceanic Feeling: Revisioning the Psychoanalytic Theory of Mysticism*. New York and Oxford: Oxford University Press, 1999.

Patai, Raphael. *The Hebrew Goddess*. New York: Ktav, 1967.

———. *The Jewish Alchemists: A History and Source Book*. Princeton: Princeton University Press, 1994.

———. *The Jewish Mind*. New York: Scribners, 1977.

Patterson, Stephen J. *The Gospel of Thomas and Jesus*. Sonoma: Polebridge Press, 1993.

Paul, Diana Y. *Women in Buddhism: Images of the Feminine in Mahayana Tradition*. 2nd ed. Foreword by I. B. Horner, contributions by Frances Wilson. Berkeley: University of California Press, 1985.

Paul, Shalom. "Heavenly Tablets and the Book of Life." *Journal of the Ancient Near East Society of Columbia University* 5 (1973): 345–353.

Pavel, Thomas G. *The Spell of Language: Poststructuralism and Speculation*. English version by Linda Jordan and Thomas G. Pavel. Chicago and London: University of Chicago Press, 2001.

Payer, Pierre J. *The Bridling of Desire: Views of Sex in the Later Middle Ages.* Toronto: University of Toronto Press, 1993.

Peach, Lucinda Joy. "Social Responsibility, Sex Change, and Salvation: Gender Justice in the *Lotus Sūtra.*" *Philosophy East and West* 52 (2002): 50–74.

Pedaya, Ḥaviva. "'Flaw' and 'Correction' in the Concept of the Godhead in the Teachings of Rabbi Isaac the Blind." *Jerusalem Studies in Jewish Thought* 6, 3–4 (1987): 157–285 (Hebrew).

———. *Name and Sanctuary in the Teaching of R. Isaac the Blind: A Comparitive Study in the Writings of the Earliest Kabbalist.* Jerusalem: Magnes Press, 2001 (Hebrew).

———. "'Possessed by Speech': Towards an Understanding of the Prophetic-Ecstatic Patterns among Early Kabbalists." *Tarbiẓ* 65 (1996): 565–636 (Hebrew).

———. "The Provençal Stratum in the Redaction of *Sefer ha-Bahir.*" *Jerusalem Studies in Jewish Thought* 9, 2 (1990): 139–164 (Hebrew).

———. *Vision and Speech: Models of Revelatory Experience in Jewish Mysticism.* Los Angeles: Cherub Press, 2002 (Hebrew).

Peerbolte, L. J. Lietaert. "Man, Woman, and the Angels in 1 Cor 11:12–16." In *The Creation of Man and Woman: Interpretations of the Biblical Narratives in Jewish and Christian Traditions,* edited by Gerard P. Luttikhuizen, 76–92. Leiden: Brill, 2000.

Peperzak, Adriaan Theodoor. *Beyond: The Philosophy of Emmanuel Levinas.* Evanston: Northwestern University Press, 1997.

Pépin, Jean. "Theories of Procession in Plotinus and the Gnostics." In *Neoplatonism and Gnosticism,* edited by Richard T. Wallis and Jay Bregman, 297–335. Albany: State University of New York Press, 1992.

Perella, Nicolas J. *The Kiss Sacred and Profane: An Interpretative History of Kiss Symbolism and Related Religio-Erotic Themes.* Berkeley and Los Angeles: University of California Press, 1969.

Perniola, Mario. *Ritual Thinking: Sexuality, Death, World.* Foreword by Hugh J. Silverman, translated with an introduction by Massimo Verdicchio. Amherst: Humanity Books, 2001.

Perrett, Roy W. "Is Whatever Exists Knowable and Nameable?" *Philosophy East and West* 49 (1999): 401–414.

Perrinjaquet, Alain. "Some Remarks concerning the Circularity of Philosophy and the Evidence of Its First Principle in Jena Wissenschaftslehre." In *Fichte: Historical Contexts/Contemporary Controversies,* edited by Daniel Breazeale and Tom Rockmore, 71–95. Atlantic Highlands: Humanities Press, 1994.

Peskowitz, Miriam B. *Spinning Fantasies: Rabbis, Gender, and History.* Berkeley: University of California Press, 1997.

Peters, Edward. "Destruction of the Flesh—Salvation of the Spirit: The Paradoxes of Torture in Medieval Christian Society." In *The Devil, Heresy, and Witchcraft in the Middle Ages: Essays in Honor of Jeffrey B. Russell,* edited by Alberto Ferreiro, 131–148. Leiden: E. J. Brill, 1998.

Peterson, Daniel. "Hamīd al-Dīn al-Kirmānī on Creation." In *Perspectives arabes et médiévales sur la tradition scientifique et philosophique grecque: Actes du colloque de la Société internationale d'histoire des sciences et de la philosophie arabes et islamiques, Paris, 31 mars–3 avril 1993,* edited by Ahmad Hasnawi, Abdelali Elamrani-Jamal, and Maroun Aouad, preface by Roshdi Rashed, 555–567. Leuven: Peeters, 1997.

Pétrement, Simone. *A Separate God: The Christian Origins of Gnosticism.* San Francisco: HarperCollins, 1990.

Petroff, Elizabeth. *Body and Soul: Essays on Medieval Women and Mysticism.* Oxford and New York: Oxford University Press, 1994.

Pfeffer, Rose. *Nietzsche: Disciple of Dionysus.* Lewisburg: Bucknell University Press, 1972.

Philo. *Philo.* 10 vols. Loeb Classical Library. Cambridge, Mass.: Harvard University Press, 1953–1962.

———. *Supplement I: Questions and Answers on Genesis.* Translated by Ralph Marcus. Loeb Classical Library. Cambridge, Mass.: Harvard University Press, 1953.

———. *Supplement II: Questions and Answers on Exodus.* Translated by Ralph Marcus. Loeb Classical Library. Cambridge, Mass.: Harvard University Press, 1953.

Piekarz, Mendel. *The Beginning of Hasidism: Ideological Trends in Derush and Musar Literature.* Jerusalem: Bialik Institute, 1978 (Hebrew).

———. "Hasidism as a Socio-Religious Movement on the Evidence of *Devekut.*" In *Hasidism Reappraised,* edited by Ada Rapoport-Albert, 225–248. London: Litman Library of Jewish Civilization, 1996.

Pierson, Dominique. "Sur l'habitation poétique de l'homme." *Heidegger Studies* 6 (1990): 107–113.

Pines, Shlomo. "Naḥmanides on Adam in the Garden of Eden in the Context of Other Interpretations of Genesis, Chapters 2 and 3." In *Exile and Diaspora: Studies in the History of the Jewish People Presented to Professor Haim Beinart on the Occasion of His Seventieth Birthday,* edited by Aaron Mirsky, Avraham Grossman, and Yosef Kaplan, 159–164. Jerusalem: Magnes, 1988 (Hebrew).

———. "Nathanael ben al-Fayyumī et la théologie ismaëlienne." *Revue de l'histoire juive en Égypte* 1 (1947): 5–22.

———. "Points of Similarity between the Exposition of the Doctrine of the Sefirot in the Sefer Yeẓira and a Text of the Pseudo-Clementine Homilies." *Proceedings of the Israel Academy of Sciences and Humanities* 7 (1989): 63–142.

Plaskow, Judith. "Language, God, and Liturgy: A Feminist Perspective." *Response* 44 (1983): 3–14.

———. *Standing Again at Sinai: Judaism from a Feminist Perspective.* New York: Harper Collins, 1990.

Plato. *Plato and Parmenides; Parmenides' Way of Truth and Plato's Parmenides.* Translated with an introduction and running commentary by Francis Macdonald Cornford. Indianapolis: Bobbs-Merrill Education, 1977.

———. *Plato's Cosmology: The Timaeus of Plato Translated with a Running Commentary.* Translated by Francis Macdonald Cornford. New York: Humanities Press, 1952.

———. *Plato's Parmenides.* Translated with a commentary by Reginald E. Allen. Rev. ed. New Haven and London: Yale University Press, 1997.

———. *The Republic of Plato.* Translated with introduction and notes by Francis MacDonald Cornford. Oxford: Oxford University Press. 1941.

Plotinus. *Enneads.* 7 vols. Translated by Arthur Hilary Armstrong. Loeb Classical Library. Cambridge, Mass.: Harvard University Press, 1966–1988.

Plotnitsky, Arkady. *The Knowable and the Unknowable: Modern Science, Nonclassical Thought, and the "Two Cultures."* Ann Arbor: University of Michigan Press, 2002.

Poellner, Peter. "Perspectival Truth." In *Nietzsche,* edited by John Richardson and Brian Leiter, 85–117. Oxford: Oxford University Press, 2001.

Pöggeler, Otto. "West-East Dialogue: Heidegger and Lao-tzu." In *Heidegger and Asian Thought,* edited by Graham Parkes, 47–78. Honolulu: University of Hawaii Press, 1987.

Polen, Nehemia. "Miriam's Dance: Radical Egalitarianism in Hasidic Thought." *Modern Judaism* 12 (1992): 1–21.

Pomeroy, Sarah B. *Women in Hellenistic Egypt: From Alexander to Cleopatra.* New York: Schocken Books, 1984.

Pope, Marvin H. *Song of Songs: A New Translation with Introduction and Commentary*. New York: Doubleday, 1977.

Popov, S. "Wittgenstein's Analytic of the Mystical." Ph.D. dissertation, New School of Social Research, 1996.

Poppe, Susan O'Shaughnessy. "*Monde Vécu* and *Lebensform*: Merleau-Ponty and Wittgenstein on the Roots of Linguistic Meaning." Ph.D. dissertation, University of Notre Dame, 1995.

Porter, James I. *Nietzsche and the Philology of the Future*. Stanford: Stanford University Press, 2000.

Pottier, Bernard. *Dieu et le Christ selon Grégoire de Nysee: Etude systématique du "Contre Eunome" avec traduction inédite des extraits d'Eunome*. Preface by Mariette Canévet. Namur: Culture et Vérité, 1994.

Power, David N. *The Eucharistic Mystery: Revitalizing the Tradition*. New York: Crossroad, 1995.

Power, Kim. *Veiled Desire: Augustine on Women*. New York: Continuum, 1996.

Pranger, M. B. *Bernard of Clairvaux and the Shape of Monastic Thought: Broken Dreams*. Leiden: E. J. Brill, 1994.

Prickett, Stephen. *Words and The Word: Language, Poetics and Biblical Interpretation*. Cambridge: Cambridge University Press, 1986.

Priest, Stephen. *Merleau-Ponty*. London and New York: Routledge, 1998.

Proclus. *Commentaire sur le Timée*. 5 vols. Translation and notes by A. J. Festugiere. Paris: Librairie Philosophique J. Vrin, 1966–1968.

———. *The Commentaries of Proclus on the Timaeus of Plato, in Five Books*. 2 vols. Translated by Thomas Taylor, together with a concordance to the edition of Diehl and an appendix, "Proclus on the System of Theodorus of Asine," by Stephen Ronan. Reprint of 1820 ed. London: Chthonios Books, 1998.

———. *The Elements of Theology*. 2nd ed. Revised text with translation, introduction, and commentary by Eric R. Dodds. Oxford: Clarendon Press, 1963.

———. *In Platonis Timaeum Commentaria*. Edited by Ernest Diehl. Leipzig: B. G. Teubner, 1903.

———. *On the Existence of Evils*. Translated by Jan Opsomer and Carlos Steel. Ithaca: Cornell University Press, 2003.

———. *Proclus' Commentary on Plato's Parmenides*. Translated by Glenn R. Morrow and John M. Dillon, with introduction and notes by John M. Dillon. Princeton: Princeton University Press, 1987.

Proimos, Constantinos. "Martin Heidegger on *Mimesis* in Plato and Platonism." In *Neoplatonism and Western Aesthetics*, edited by Aphrodite Alexandrakis and Nicholas J. Moutafakis, 153–163. Albany: State University of New York Press, 2002.

Protevi, John. "The Stilling of the Aufhebung: Streit in 'The Origin of the Work of Art.'" *Heidegger Studies* 6 (1990): 67–83.

Proudfoot, Wayne. *Religious Experience*. Berkeley: University of California Press, 1985.

Pulcini, Theodore. *Exegesis as Polemical Discourse: Ibn Hazm on Jewish and Christian Scriptures*. Atlanta: Scholars Press, 1998.

Qimron, Elisha. "Celibacy in the Dead Sea Scrolls and the Two Kinds of Sectarians." In *The Madrid Qumran Congress: Proceedings of the International Congress on the Dead Sea Scrolls, Madrid, 18–21 March, 1991*, edited by Julio Trebolle Barrera and Luis Vegas Montaner, 287–294. Leiden: E. J. Brill, 1992.

———. "The Halacha of Damascus Covenant—An Interpretation of ʿAl Yitarev." *Proceedings of the Ninth World Congress of Jewish Studies: Division D, Vol. 1, Hebrew and Jewish Languages*, 9–15. Jerusalem: World Union of Jewish Studies, 1980 (Hebrew).

Quinn, Jerome D., and William C. Walker. *The First and Second Letters to Timothy: A New Translation with Notes and Commentary*. Grand Rapids: William B. Eerdmans, 2000.

Quispel, Gilles. "Gnosis and Alchemy: The Tabula Smaragdina." In *From Poimandres to Jacob Böhme: Gnosis, Hermetism and the Christian Tradition*, edited by Roelof van den Broek and Cis van Heertum, 304–333. Amsterdam: Bibliotheca Philosophica Hermetica, 2000.

———. "Qumran, John and Jewish Christianity." In *John and the Dead Sea Scrolls*, edited by James H. Charlesworth, 137–155. New York: Crossroad, 1990.

Qushayrī, ʿAbd al-Karim Ibn Hawazin. *Principles of Sufism*. Translated by Barbara R. Von Schlegell. Berkeley: Mizan Press, 1992.

Racevskis, Karlis. *Michel Foucault and the Subversion of Intellect*. Ithaca and London: Cornell University Press, 1983.

Ragland-Sullivan, Ellie. *Jacques Lacan and the Philosophy of Psychoanalysis*. Urbana and Chicago: University of Illinois Press, 1986.

Räisänen, Heikki. "The Portrait of Jesus in the Qurʾān: Reflections of a Biblical Scholar." *Muslim World* 70 (1980): 122–133.

Rajan, Tilottama. *Deconstruction and the Remainders of Phenomenology*. Stanford: Stanford University Press, 2002.

Rambuss, Richard. *Closet Devotions*. Durham and London: Duke University Press, 1998.

Rang, Bernhard. *Identität und Indifferenz: Eine Untersuchung zu Schellings Identitätsphilosophie*. Frankfurt am Main: Vittorio Klostermann, 2000.

Ranke-Heinemann, Uta. *Eunuchs for the Kingdom of Heaven: Women, Sexuality and the Catholic Church*. Translated by Peter Heinegg. New York: Doubleday, 1990.

Rapaport, Herman. "Time's Cinders." In *Modernity and the Hegemony of Vision*, edited by David M. Levin, 218–233. Berkeley: University of California Press, 1993.

Raphael, Melissa. "Goddess Religion, Postmodern Jewish Feminism, and the Complexity of Alternative Religious Identities." *Nova Religio: Journal of Alternative and Emergent Religions* 1 (1998): 198–215.

Rapoport-Albert, Ada. "On the Role of Women in Sabbatianism." *Jerusalem Studies in Jewish Thought* 16 (2001): 143–327 (Hebrew).

———. "On Women in Hasidism, S. A. Horodecky and the Maid of Ludmir Tradition." In *Jewish History: Essays in Honour of Chimen Abramsky*, edited by Ada Rapoport-Albert and Steven J. Zipperstein, 495–525. London: P. Halban, 1988.

Rapp, Beverlee Sian. "A Woman Speaks: Language and Self-Repesentation in Hildegard's Letters." In *Hildegard of Bingen: A Book of Essays*, edited by Maud Burnett McInerney, 3–24. New York and London: Garland, 1998.

Rappe, Sara. *Reading Neoplatonism: Non-discursive Thinking in the Texts of Plotinus, Proclus, and Damascius*. Cambridge: Cambridge University Press, 2000.

Raschke, Carl A. *Fire and Roses: Postmodernity and the Thought of the Body*. Albany: State University of New York Press, 1996.

Ravitsky, Y. "Immanuel of Rome—Commentary on Song of Songs, the Philosophical Section." M.A. thesis, Hebrew University, Jerusalem, 1970 (Hebrew).

Raw, Barbara Catherine. *Trinity and Incarnation in Anglo-Saxon Art and Thought*. Cambridge: Cambridge University Press, 1997.

Rawidowicz, Simon. *Studies in Jewish Thought*. Philadelphia: Jewish Publication Society of America, 1974.

Razavi, Mehdi Amin. *Suhrawardi and the School of Illumination*. Surrey: Curzon, 1997.

Read, John. *Prelude to Chemistry: An Outline of Alchemy, Its Literature and Relationships.* Cambridge, Mass.: MIT Press, 1966.

Regosin, Richard L. *Montaigne's Unruly Brood: Textual Engendering and the Challenge to Paternal Authority.* Berkeley: University of California Press, 1996.

Reif, Stefan C. "Abraham Ibn Ezra on Canticles." In *Abraham Ibn Ezra and His Age: Proceedings of the International Symposium*, edited by Fernando Díaz Esteban, 241–249. Madrid: Associación de Orientalistas, 1990.

Renard, John. *All the King's Falcons: Rumi on Prophets and Revelation.* Foreword by Annemarie Schimmel. Albany: State University of New York Press, 1994.

Rennie, Bryan S. *Reconstructing Eliade: Making Sense of Religion.* Albany: State University of New York Press, 1996.

Rentsch, Thomas. *Heidegger und Wittgenstein: Existential- und Sprachanalysen zu den Grundlagen philosophischer Anthropologie.* Stuttgart: Klett-Cotta, 1985.

Reuchlin, Johann. *On the Art of the Kabbalah: De Arte cabalistica.* Translation by Martin and Sarah Goodman, introduction by G. Lloyd Jones. New York: Abaris Books, 1983.

Rhodes, James M. *Eros, Wisdom, and Silence: Plato's Erotic Dialogues.* Columbia and London: University of Missouri Press, 2003.

Richardson, John. *Nietzsche's System.* Oxford: Oxford University Press, 1996.

Richardson, William J. *Heidegger through Phenomenology to Thought.* 3rd ed. The Hague: Martinus Nijhoff, 1974.

Richir, Marc. "Merleau-Ponty and the Question of Phenomenological Architectonics." In *Merleau-Ponty in Contemporary Perspectives*, edited by Patrick Burke and Jan van der Veken, 37–50. Dordrecht: Kluwer Academic, 1993.

Richlin, Amy. "Foucault's *History of Sexuality*: A Useful Theory for Women?" In *Rethinking Sexuality: Foucault and Classical Antiquity*, edited by David H. J. Larmour, Paul A. Miller, and Charles Platter, 138–170. Princeton: Princeton University Press, 1998.

Rickey, Christopher. *Revolutionary Saints: Heidegger, National Socialism, and Antinomian Politics.* University Park: Pennsylvania State University Press, 2002.

Ricks, Stephen D. "The Garment of Adam in Jewish, Muslim, and Christian Tradition." In *Judaism and Islam: Boundaries, Communication and Interaction: Essays in Honor of William M. Brinner*, edited by Benjamin H. Hary, John L. Hayes, and Fred Astren, 203–225. Leiden: Brill, 2000.

Ricoeur, Paul. *The Conflict of Interpretations.* Evanston: Northwestern University Press, 1974.

———. *Hermeneutics and the Human Sciences.* Edited and translated by John B. Thompson. Cambridge: Cambridge University Press, 1981.

———. "The History of Religions and the Phenomenology of Time Consciousness." In *The History of Religions: Retrospect and Prospect*, edited by Joseph M. Kitagawa, 13–30. New York: MacMillan, 1985.

———. *History and Truth.* Translated with an introduction by Charles A. Kelbley. Evanston: Northwestern University Press, 1965.

———. *Husserl: An Analysis of His Phenomenology.* Evanston: Northwestern University Press, 1967.

———. *The Symbolism of Evil.* Boston: Beacon Press, 1967.

———. *Time and Narrative.* 3 vols. Translated by Kathleen Blamey and David Pellauer. Chicago and London: University of Chicago Press, 1984–1988.

Ridgeon, Lloyd V. J. *Crescents on the Cross: Islamic Visions of Christianity.* Oxford and New York: Oxford University Press, 2001.

Riedel, Manfred. *Hören auf die Sprache: Die akroamatische Dimension der Hermeneutik*. Frankfurt am Main: Suhrkamp, 1990.

Rilke, Rainer Maria. *Sonnets to Orpheus*. Translation by Mary Dows Herter Norton. New York: W. W. Norton, 1962.

Ringrose, Kathryn M. "Living in the Shadows: Eunuchs and Gender in Byzantium." In *Third Sex, Third Gender: Beyond Sexual Dimorphism in Culture and History*, edited by Gilbert Herdt, 85–109. New York: Zone Books, 1994.

———. *The Perfect Servant: Eunuchs and the Social Construction of Gender in Byzantium*. Chicago and London: University of Chicago Press, 2003.

Risser, James. *Hermeneutics and the Voice of the Other: Re-reading Gadamer's Philosophical Hermeneutics*. Albany: State University of New York Press, 1997.

Rist, John M. "Back to the Mysticism of Plotinus: Some More Specifics." *Journal of the History of Philosophy* 27 (1989): 183–197.

———. *Eros and Psyche: Studies in Plato, Plotinus, and Origen*. Toronto: University of Toronto Press, 1964.

Ritter, Hellmut. *The Ocean of the Soul: Men, the World and God in the Stories of Farīd al-Dīn ʿAttār*. Translated by John O'Kane with editorial assistance of Bernd Radtke. Leiden: Brill, 2003.

Roberts, Alexander, and James Donaldson, eds. *The Ante-Nicene Fathers*. Grand Rapids: William B. Eerdmans, 1981.

Roberts, Gareth. *The Mirror of Alchemy: Alchemical Idea and Images in Manuscripts and Books from Antiquity to the Seventeenth Century*. Toronto and Buffalo: University of Toronto Press, 1994.

Roberts, Michael. *Poetry and the Cult of the Martyrs: The Liber Peristephanon of Prudentius*. Ann Arbor: University of Michigan Press, 1993.

Roberts, Tyler T. *Contesting Spirit: Nietzsche, Affirmation, Religion*. Princeton: Princeton University Press, 1998.

Robinet, Isabelle. *Taoism: Growth of a Religion*. Translated by Phyllis Brooks. Stanford: Stanford University Press, 1997.

———. *Taoist Meditation: The Mao-Shan Tradition of Great Purity*. Translated by Julian F. Pas and Norman J. Girardot. Albany: State University of New York Press, 1993.

Robinson, Gesine. "The Trimorphic Protennoia and the Prologue of the Fourth Gospel." In *Gnosticism and the Early Christian World In Honor of James M. Robinson*, edited by James E. Goehring, Charles W. Hedrick, and Jack T. Sanders, with Hans Dieter Betz, 37–50. Sonoma: Polebridge Press, 1990.

Robinson, James M., ed. *The Nag Hammadi Library in English*. 4th rev. ed. With an afterword by Richard Smith. Leiden: E. J. Brill, 1996.

Robinson, James T. "Samuel Ibn Tibbon's *Commentary on Ecclesiastes*." Ph.D. dissertation, Harvard University, 2002.

Robinson, Neal. *Christ in Islam and Christianity*. Albany: State University of New York Press, 1991.

———. "Jesus and Mary in the Qur'ān: Some Neglected Affinities." *Religion* 20 (1990): 161–175.

Robson, James. "Stories of Jesus and Mary." *Muslim World* 40 (1950): 236–243.

Rockmore, Tom. "Antifoundationalism, Circularity, and the Spirit of Fichte." In *Fichte: Historical Contexts/Contemporary Controversies*, edited by Daniel Breazeale and Tom Rockmore, 96–112. Atlantic Highlands: Humanities Press, 1994.

———. *On Heidegger's Nazism and Philosophy*. Berkeley: University of California Press, 1992.

Rockmore, Tom, and Joseph Margolis, eds. *The Heidegger Case: On Philosophy and Politics*. Philadelphia: Temple University Press, 1992.

Rogers, William Elford. *Interpreting Interpretation: Textual Hermeneutics as an Ascetic Discipline.* University Park: Pennsylvania State University Press, 1994.
Rojtman, Betty. *Black Fire on White Fire: An Essay on Jewish Hermeneutics, from Midrash to Kabbalah.* Berkeley: University of California Press, 1998.
Rorem, Paul. *Biblical and Liturgical Symbols within the Pseudo-Dionysian Synthesis.* Toronto: Pontifical Institute of Mediaeval Studies, 1984.
Rorty, Richard. *Contingency, Irony, and Solidarity.* Cambridge: Cambridge University Press, 1989.
———. "Wittgenstein, Heidegger, and the Reification of Language." In *The Cambridge Companion to Heidegger,* edited by Charles B. Guignon, 337–357. Cambridge: Cambridge University Press, 1993.
Rose, Gillian. *Mourning Becomes the Law: Philosophy and Representation.* Cambridge and New York: Cambridge University Press, 1996.
Rose, Paul L. *Bodin and the Great God of Nature: The Moral and Religious Universe of a Judaiser.* Geneva: Librairie Droz, 1980.
Rosen, Stanley. *Metaphysics in Ordinary Language.* New Haven and London: Yale University Press, 1999.
Rosen, Tova. *Unveiling Eve: Reading Gender in Medieval Hebrew Literature.* Philadelphia: University of Pennsylvania Press, 2003.
Rosenberg, Shalom. "Philosophical Hermeneutics on the Song of Songs: Introductory Remarks." *Tarbiẓ* 59 (1990): 133–151 (Hebrew).
Rosenblatt, Samuel. *The High Ways to Perfection of Abraham Maimonides.* New York: Columbia University Press, 1927.
Rosenthal, Franz. "Ibn ʿArabī between 'Philosophy' and 'Mysticism.'" *Oriens* 31 (1988): 1–35.
Rosenthal, Sandra B. *Time, Continuity, and Indeterminacy: A Pragmatic Engagement with Contemporary Perspectives.* Albany: State University of New York Press, 2000.
Rosenzweig, Franz. *Briefe.* Selected and edited by Edith Rosenzweig. Berlin: Schocken, 1935.
———. *Philosophical and Theological Writings.* Translated and edited with notes and commentary by Paul W. Franks and Michael L. Morgan. Indianapolis: Hackett, 2000.
———. *The Star of Redemption.* Translated by William W. Hallo. New York: Holt, Rinehart and Winston, 1970.
Rosman, Moshe. *Founder of Hasidism: A Quest for the Historical Baʿal Shem Tov.* Berkeley: University of California Press, 1996.
Rospatt, Alexander von. *The Buddhist Doctrine of Momentariness: A Survey of the Origins and Early Phase of This Doctrine up to Vasubandhu.* Stuttgart: F. Steiner, 1995.
Ross, Tamar. "Modern Orthodoxy and the Challenge of Feminism." *Studies in Contemporary Jewry: An Annual* 16 (2000): 3–38.
Rossi, Donatella. *The Philosophical View of the Great Perfection in the Tibetan Bon Religion.* Ithaca: Snow Lion, 1999.
Rotenberg, Mordechai. *The Yetzer: A Kabbalistic Psychology of Eroticism and Human Sexuality.* Northvale: Jason Aronson, 1997.
Roth, Michael. *The Poetics of Resistance: Heidegger's Line.* Evanston: Northwestern University Press, 1996.
Roudinesco, Elisabeth. *Jacques Lacan.* Translated by Barbara Bray. New York: Columbia University Press, 1997.
Rougemont, Denis de. *Love in the Western World.* Translated by Montgomery Belgion. Princeton: Princeton University Press, 1983.

Rousselle, Aline. *Porneia: On Desire and the Body in Antiquity.* Translated by Felicia Pheasant. Cambridge, Mass.: Harvard University Press, 1993.

Rubin, Milka. "The Language of Creation or the Primordial Language: A Case of Cultural Polemics in Antiquity." *Journal of Jewish Studies* 49 (1998): 306–333.

Rubin, Miri. *Corpus Christi: The Eucharist in Late Medieval Culture.* Cambridge: Cambridge University Press, 1991.

Rubin, Nissan, and Admiel Kosman. "The Clothing of the Primordial Adam as a Symbol of Apocalyptic Time in the Midrashic Sources." *Harvard Theological Review* 90 (1997): 155–174.

Rubin, Solomon. *Heidenthum und Kabbala: Die Kabbalistische Mystik ihrem Ursprung wie ihrem Wesen nach, gründlich aufgehellt und populär dargestellt.* Vienna: Commissions-Verlag von Bermann and Altmann, 1893.

Rubin, Uri. *Between Bible and Qur'ān: The Children of Israel and the Islamic Self-Image.* Princeton: Darwin Press, 1999.

———. "Traditions in Transformation: The Ark of the Covenant and the Golden Calf in Biblical and Islamic Historiography." *Oriens* 36 (2001): 196–214.

Rudavsky, Tamar M. "To Know What Is: Feminism, Metaphysics, and Epistemology." In *Women and Gender in Jewish Philosophy,* edited by Hava Tirosh-Samuelson, 179–203. Bloomington and Indianapolis: Indiana University Press, 2004.

Rudhart, Jean. "Coherence and Incoherence of Mythic Structure: Its Symbolic Function." *Diogenes* 77 (1972): 14–42.

Rudolph, Kurt. *Gnosis: The Nature and History of Gnosticism.* Translated by Robert McL. Wilson. San Francisco: Harper & Row, 1983.

———. *Historical Fundamentals and the Study of Religions.* New York: Macmillan, 1985.

Ruether, Rosemary R. "Misogynism and Virginal Feminism in the Fathers of the Church." In *Religion and Sexism: Images of Woman in the Jewish and Christian Tradition,* edited by Rosemary R. Ruether, 150–183. New York: Simon and Schuster, 1974.

———. "Mothers of the Church: Ascetic Women in the Late Patristic Age." In *Women of Spirit: Female Leadership in the Jewish and Christian Traditions,* edited by Rosemary R. Ruether and Eleanor McLaughlin, 71–98. New York: Simon and Schuster, 1979.

———. *Women and Redemption: A Theological History.* Minneapolis: Fortress Press, 1998.

Rūmī, Jalal al-Din. *Mystical Poems of Rumi.* Translated by A. J. Arberry. Chicago and London: University of Chicago Press, 1968.

———. *The Mathnawī of Jalālu'ddīn Rūmī.* Translated by Reynold A. Nicholson. London: Luzac, 1968.

———. *The Rumi Collection.* Edited by Kabir Helminski. Boston and London: Shambhala, 2000.

———. *Selected Poems from the Dīvāni Shamsi Tabrīz.* Edited and translated with an introduction, notes, and appendices by Reynold A. Nicholson. Cambridge: Cambridge University Press, 1889.

Russell, Jeffrey Burton. *A History of Heaven: The Singing Silence.* Princeton: Princeton University Press, 1997.

Russell, Paul S. "Ephraem the Syrian on the Utility of Language and the Place of Silence." *Journal of Early Christian Studies* 8 (2000): 21–37.

Rutherford, Donald. "Philosophy and Language in Leibniz." In *The Cambridge Companion to Leibniz,* edited by Nicholas Jolley, 224–269. Cambridge: Cambridge University Press, 1995.

Sack, Beracha. *The Kabbalah of Rabbi Moshe Cordovero.* Jerusalem: Bialik Institute, 1995 (Hebrew).

Safran, Bezalel. "Rabbi Azriel and Naḥmanides: Two Views of the Fall of Man." In *Rabbi Moses*

Naḥmanides (Ramban): Explorations in His Religious and Literary Virtuosity, edited by Isadore Twersky, 75–106. Cambridge, Mass.: Harvard University Press, 1983.

Safranski, Rüdiger. *Martin Heidegger: Between Good and Evil*. Translated by Eswald Osers. Cambridge, Mass., and London: Harvard University Press, 1998.

Salecl, Renata. *(Per)versions of Love and Hate*. London and New York: Verso, 2000.

Salih, Sarah. "When Is a Bosom Not a Bosom? Problems with 'Erotic Mysticism.'" In *Medieval Virginities*, edited by Anke Bernau, Ruth Evans, and Sarah Salih, 14–32. Toronto: University of Toronto Press, 2003.

Salisbury, Joyce E. *Church Fathers, Independent Virgins*. London and New York: Verso, 1991.

Sallis, John. *Delimitations: Phenomenology and the End of Metaphysics*. Bloomington and Indianapolis: Indiana University Press, 1986.

———. *Echoes: After Heidegger*. Bloomington and Indianapolis: Indiana University Press, 1990.

———. "The Identities of the Things Themselves." *Research in Phenomenology* 12 (1982): 113–126.

———. "Image and Phenomenon." *Research in Phenomenology* 5 (1975): 61–75.

———. "Interrupting Truth." In *Heidegger toward the Turn: Essays on the Work of the 1930s*, edited by James Risser, 19–30. Albany: State University of New York, 1999.

Saltman, Avrom. "Jewish Exegetical Material in Alexander Nequam's Commentary on the Song of Songs." In *The Bible in the Light of Its Interpreters: Sarah Kamin Memorial Volume*, edited by Sara Japhet, 421–452. Jerusalem: Magnes Press, 1994 (Hebrew).

Salvaggio, Ruth. *Enlightened Absence: Neoclassical Configurations of the Feminine*. Urbana and Chicago: University of Illinois Press, 1988.

Samuel, Geoffrey. "The Body in Buddhist and Hindu Tantra: Some Notes." *Religion* 19 (1989): 197–210.

Sandbothe, Mike. *The Temporalization of Time: Basic Tendencies in Modern Debate on Time in Philosophy and Science*. Translated by Andrew Inkpin. Lanham: Rowman & Littlefield, 2001.

Sanders, E. P. *The Historical Figure of Jesus*. London and New York: Penguin Press, 1993.

Sanders, Seth L. "Writing, Ritual, and Apocalypse: Studies in the Theme of Ascent to Heaven in Ancient Mesopotamia and Second Temple Judaism." Ph.D. dissertation, Johns Hopkins University, 1999.

Sandford, Stella. *The Metaphysics of Love: Gender and Transcendence in Levinas*. London: Athlone Press, 2000.

Sands, Kathleen M. "Uses of the Thea(o)logian: Sex and Theodicy in Religious Feminism." *Journal of Feminist Studies in Religion* 8 (1992): 7–33.

Sandywell, Barry. *Reflexivity and the Crisis of Western Reason: Logological Investigations*. 3 vols. London and New York: Routledge, 1996.

Saperstein, Marc. *"Your Voice Like a Ram's Horn": Themes and Texts in Traditional Jewish Preaching*. Cincinnati: Hebrew Union College Press, 1996.

Sarukkai, Sundar. "Inside/Outside: Merleau-Ponty/Yoga." *Philosophy East and West* 52 (2002): 459–478.

Satlow, Michael L. *Jewish Marriage in Antiquity*. Princeton: Princeton University Press, 2001.

———. "Shame and Sex in Late Antique Judaism." In *Asceticism*, edited by Vincent L. Wimbush and Richard Valantasis, 535–543. New York: Oxford University Press, 1995.

———. *Tasting the Dish: Rabbinic Rhetorics of Sexuality*. Atlanta: Scholars Press, 1995.

———. "'Texts of Terror': Rabbinic Texts, Speech Acts, and the Control of Mores." *AJS Review* 22 (1996): 273–297.

———. "'They Abused Him Like a Woman': Homoeroticism, Gender Blurring, and the Rabbis in Late Antiquity." *Journal of the History of Sexuality* 5 (1994): 1–25.
———. "'Try to Be a Man': The Rabbinic Construction of Masculinity." *Harvard Theological Review* 89 (1996): 19–40.
———. "'Wasted Seed,' The History of a Rabbinic Idea." *Hebrew Union College Annual* 65 (1994): 137–175.
Sato, Marito. "The Incarnation of Consciousness and the Carnalization of the World in Merleau-Ponty's Philosophy." *Analecta Husserliana* 58 (1998): 3–15.
Sawyer, Deborah F. *God, Gender and the Bible: Biblical Limits*. London and New York: Routledge, 2002.
Scaglione, Aldo D. *Nature and Love in the Late Middle Ages*. Berkeley and Los Angeles: University of California Press, 1963.
Scarborough, John. "The Pharmacology of Sacred Plants, Herbs, and Roots." In *Magika Hiera: Ancient Greek Magic and Religion*, edited by Christopher A. Faraone and Dirk Obbink, 138–174. New York and Oxford: Oxford University Press, 1991.
Scetis, Isaiah of. *Abba Isaiah of Scetis Ascetic Discourses*. Translated by John Chryssavgis and Pachomios Penkett. Kalamazoo: Cistercian Publications, 2002.
Schaeffer, Jean-Marie. *Art of the Modern Age: Philosophy of Art from Kant to Heidegger*. Translated by Steven Rendall with a foreword by Arthur C. Danto. Princeton: Princeton University Press, 2000.
Schäfer, Peter. "Daughter, Sister, Bride, and Mother: Images of the Femininity of God in the Early Kabbala." *Journal of the American Academy of Religion* 68 (2000): 221–242.
———. *Mirror of His Beauty: Feminine Images of God from the Bible to the Early Kabbalah*. Princeton: Princeton University Press, 2002.
———. "'Die Philologie der Kabbala ist nur eine Projektion auf eine Fläche': Gershom Scholem über die wahren Absichten seines Kabbalastudiums." *Jewish Studies Quarterly* 5 (1998): 1–25.
———, ed. *Synopse zur Hekhalot-Literatur*. Tübingen: J. C. B. Mohr, 1981.
Scharfenberg, Joachim. *Sigmund Freud and His Critique of Religion*. Translated by O. C. Dean, Jr. Philadelphia: Fortress Press, 1988.
Scheindlin, Raymond P. *The Gazelle: Medieval Hebrew Poems on God, Israel, and the Soul*. Philadelphia: Jewish Publication Society, 1991.
Schelling, Friedrich Wilhelm Joseph. *The Ages of the World, Third Version (c. 1815)*. Translated with an introduction by Joseph M. Wirth. Albany: State University of New York Press, 2000.
———. *Philosophical Investigations into the Essence of Human Freedom and Related Matters*. Translated by Priscilla Hayden-Roy. In *Philosophy of German Idealism*, edited by Ernst Behler, 217–284. New York: Continuum, 1987.
Schimanowski, Gottfried. *Die himmlische Liturgie in der Apokalypse des Johannes: Die frühjüdischen Traditionen in Offenbarung 4–5 unter Einschluss den Hekhalotliteratur*. Tübingen: Mohr Siebeck, 2002.
Schimmel, Annemarie. *As through a Veil: Mystical Poetry in Islam*. New York: Columbia University Press, 1982.
———. *Deciphering the Signs of God: A Phenomenological Approach to Islam*. Albany: State University of New York Press, 1994.
———. "Eros—Heavenly and Not So Heavenly—in Sufi Literature and Life." In *Society and the Sexes in Medieval Islam*, edited by Afaf Lutfi al-Sayyid-Marsot, 119–141. Malibu: Undena Publications, 1979.

———. "Jesus and Mary as Poetical Images in Rūmī's Verse." In *Christian-Muslim Encounters*, edited by Yvonne Y. Haddad and Wadi Z. Haddad, 143–157. Gainesville: University of Florida Press, 1995.

———. "Mawlānā Rūmī: Yesterday, Today, and Tomorrow." In *Poetry and Mysticism in Islam: The Heritage of Rūmī*, edited by Amin Banani, Richard Hovannisian, and Georges Sabagh, 5–27. Cambridge: Cambridge University Press, 1994.

———. *My Soul Is a Woman: The Feminine in Islam*. Translated by Susan H. Ray. New York: Continuum, 1999.

———. *Mystical Dimensions of Islam*. Chapel Hill: University of North Carolina Press, 1975.

Schleifer, Aliah. *Mary the Blessed Virgin of Islam*. Louisville: Fons Vitae, 1997.

Schmidt, Dennis J. "Black Milk and Blue: Celan and Heidegger on Pain and Language." In *Word Traces: Readings of Paul Celan*, edited by Aris Fioretos, 110–129. Baltimore and London: Johns Hopkins University Press, 1994.

———. "Poetry and the Political: Gadamer, Plato, and Heidegger on the Politics of Language." In *Festivals of Interpretation: Essays on Hans-Georg Gadamer's Work*, edited by Kathleen Wright, 209–228. Albany: State University of New York Press, 1990.

Schmidt-Biggemann, Wilhelm. "The Christian Kabbala: Joseph Gikatilla (1247–1305), Johannes Reuchlin (1455–1522), Paulus Ricius (d. 1541), and Jacob Böhme (1575–1624)." In *The Language of Adam, Die Sprache Adams*, edited by Allison Coudert, 81–121. Wiesbaden: Harrassowitz, 1999.

———. "Jakob Böhme und die Kabbala." In *Christliche Kabbala*, edited by Wilhelm Schmidt-Biggemann, 157–181. Ostfildern: Jan Thorbecke Verlag, 2003.

Schnell, Alexander. "Das Problem der Zeit bei Husserl. Eine Untersuchung über die husserlischen Zeitdiagramme." *Husserl Studies* 18 (2002): 89–122.

Scholem, Gershom. "The Beginnings of Christian Kabbalah." In *The Christian Kabbalah: Jewish Mystical Books and Their Christian Interpreters*, edited by Joseph Dan, 17–51. Cambridge, Mass.: Harvard College Library, 1997.

———. *Das Buch Bahir*. Darmstadt: Wissenschaftliche Buchgesellschaft, 1970.

———. "The Concept of Kavvanah in the Early Kabbalah." In *Studies in Jewish Thought: An Anthology of German Jewish Scholarship*, edited by Alfred Jospe, 165–180. Detroit: Wayne State University Press, 1981.

———. "Eine kabbalistische Erklärung der Prophetie als Selbstbegegnung." *Monatsschrift für Geschichte und Wissenschaft des Judentums* 74 (1930): 285–290.

———. "Eine unbekannte mystische Schrift des Mose de Leon." *Monatsschrift für Geschichte und Wissenschaft des Judentums* 71 (1927): 109–123.

———. *Explications and Implications: Writings on Jewish Heritage and Renaissance*. Vol. 2. Edited by Avraham Shapira. Tel Aviv: Am Oved, 1989 (Hebrew).

———. *The Fullness of Time: Poems*. Translated by Richard Sieburth, introduced and annotated by Steven M. Wasserstrom. Jerusalem: Ibis Editions, 2003.

———. *Gershom Scholem: A Life in Letters, 1914–1982*. Edited and translated by Anthony David Skinner. Cambridge, Mass., and London: Harvard University Press, 2002.

———. *Gershom Scholem's Annotated Zohar*. Jerusalem: Magnes Press, 1992.

———. *Jewish Gnosticism, Merkabah Mysticism, and Talmudic Tradition*. New York: Jewish Theological Seminary of America, 1965.

———. *Judaica 3: Studien zur jüdischen Mystik*. Frankfurt am Main: Suhrkamp, 1973.

———. *Kabbalah*. Jerusalem: Keter, 1974.

———. *The Kabbalah in Provence.* Edited by Rivka Schatz. Jerusalem: Akkadamon, 1970 (Hebrew).
———. *The Kabbalah of Sefer ha-Temunah and Abraham Abulafia.* Edited by Joseph Ben-Shlomo Jerusalem: Akkadamon, 1965 (Hebrew).
———. *Major Trends in Jewish Mysticism.* New York: Schocken Books, 1954.
———. *The Messianic Idea in Judaism and Other Essays on Jewish Spirituality.* New York: Schocken Books, 1971.
———. "The Name of God and the Linguistic Theory of the Kabbala." *Diogenes* 79 (1972): 59–80; 80 (1972): 164–194.
———. "A New Document for the History of the Beginning of Kabbalah." In *Sefer Bialik,* 141–162. Tel Aviv: Emunot, 1934 (Hebrew).
———. *On Jews and Judaism in Crisis: Selected Essays.* New York: Schocken Books, 1976.
———. *On the Kabbalah and Its Symbolism.* Translated by Ralph Manheim. New York: Schocken Books, 1969.
———. *On the Mystical Shape of the Godhead: Basic Concepts in the Kabbalah.* Translated by Joachim Neugroschel, edited and revised by Jonathan Chipman. New York: Schocken Books, 1991.
———. *On the Possibility of Jewish Mysticism in Our Time and Other Essays.* Edited with an introduction by Avraham Shapira, translated by Jonathan Chipman. Philadelphia, Pa., and Jerusalem: Jewish Publication Society of America, 1997.
———. *Origins of the Kabbalah.* Edited by R. J. Zwi Werblowsky, translated by Allan Arkush. Princeton: Princeton University Press, 1987.
———. "The Paradise Garb of Souls and the Origin of the Concept of Ḥaluqa de-Rabbanan." *Tarbiẓ* 24 (1955): 290–306 (Hebrew).
———. *Pirqei Yesod be-Havanat ha-Qabbalah u-Semaleha.* Translated by Joseph Ben-Shlomo. Jerusalem: Bialik Institute, 1977.
———. *Reshit ha-Qabbalah.* Jerusalem and Tel-Aviv: Schocken, 1948.
———. *Sabbatai Ṣevi: The Mystical Messiah,* translated by R. J. Zwi Werblowsky. Princeton: Princeton University Press, 1973.
———. *Studies in Kabbalah (I).* Edited by Joseph Ben-Shlomo and Moshe Idel. Tel-Aviv: Am Oved, 1998.
———. "Traces of Gabirol in the Kabbalah." In *Me'assef Sofrei Ereṣ Yisra'el,* 160–178. Jerusalem, 1940.
———. "The Traditions of R. Jacob and R. Isaac the Sons of R. Jacob ha-Kohen." *Madda'ei ha-Yahadut* 2 (1927): 165–293 (Hebrew).
———. *Von der mystischen Gestalt der Gottheit: Studien zu Grundbegriffen der Kabbala.* Zürich: Rhein, 1962.
———. *Walter Benjamin: Die Geshichte einer Freundschaft.* Frankfurt am Main: Suhrkamp, 1975.
———. *Walter Benjamin: The Story of a Friendship.* Philadelphia: Jewish Publication Society of America, 1981.
———. *Zur Kabbala und ihrer Symbolik.* Zürich: Rhein, 1960.
Scholes, Robert. *Semiotics and Interpretation.* New Haven and London: Yale University Press, 1982.
Schoneveld, Jacobus. "Torah in the Flesh: A New Reading of the Prologue of the Gospel of John as Contribution to a Christology without Anti-Judaism." *Immanuel* 24–25 (1990): 77–94.
Schott, Robin May. *Cognition and Eros: A Critique of the Kantian Paradigm.* Boston: Beacon Press, 1988.
Schottroff, Luise. "Itinerant Prophetesses: A Feminist Analysis of the Sayings Source Q." In *The*

Gospel behind the Gospels: Current Studies on Q, edited by Ronald A. Piper, 347–360. Leiden: E. J. Brill, 1995.

———. *Lydia's Impatient Sisters: A Feminist Social History of Early Christianity*. Translated by Barbara and Martin Rumscheidt. Louisville: Westminster John Knox Press, 1995.

Schroeder, Frederic M. Schroeder, "Plotinus and Language." In *The Cambridge Companion to Plotinus*, edited by Lloyd P. Gerson, 336–355. Cambridge: Cambridge University Press, 1996.

———. "The Vigil of the One and Plotinian Iconoclasm." In *Neoplatonism and Western Aesthetics*, edited by Aphrodite Alexandrakis and Nicholas J. Moutafakis, 61–74. Albany: State University of New York Press, 2002.

Schuback, Marcia Sá Cavalcante. "La perplexité de la presence—Notes sur la traduction de *Dasein*." *Études Philosophiques* 3 (2002): 257–279.

Schulitz, John. *Jakob Böhme und die Kabbalah: Eine vergleichende Werkanalyse*. New York: Peter Lang, 1993.

Schulenburg, Jane Tibbets. *Forgetful of Their Sex: Female Sanctity and Society ca. 500–1100*. Chicago and London: University of Chicago Press, 1998.

Schuller, Eileen. "Evidence for Women in the Community of the Dead Sea Scrolls." In *Methods of Investigation of the Dead Sea Scrolls and the Khirbet Qumran Site: Present Realities and Future Prospects*, edited by Michael O. Wise, Norman Golb, John J. Collins, and Daniel Pardee, 252–265. New York: New York Academy of Sciences, 1994.

Schulte, Christoph. "Kabbala in der deutschen Romantik. Zur Einleitung." In *Kabbala und Romantik*, edited by Eveline Goodman-Thau, Gert Mattenklott, and Christoph Schulte, 1–19. Tübingen: Max Niemeyer, 1994.

———. "Ẓimẓum in the Works of Schelling." *Iyyun* 41 (1992): 21–40. German version "Ẓimẓum bei Schelling." In *Kabbala und Romantik*, edited by Eveline Goodman-Thau, Gert Mattenklott, and Christoph Schulte, 97–118. Tübingen: Max Niemeyer, 1994.

Schulze, Wilhelm August. "Friedrich Christoph Oetinger und die Kabbala." *Judaica* 4 (1948): 268–274.

———. "Jacob Boehme und die Kabbala." *Judaica* 11 (1955): 12–29.

———. "Schelling und die Kabbala." *Judaica* 13 (1957): 65–99, 143–170, 210–232.

Schürmann, Reiner. *Heidegger on Being and Acting: From Principles to Anarchy*. Translated by Christine-Marie Gros. Bloomington: Indiana University Press, 1990.

———. "Trois penseurs du délaissement: Maître Eckhart, Heidegger, Suzuki." *Journal of the History of Philosophy* 13 (1975): 56–60.

———. "Trois penseurs du délaissement." In *Wandering Joy: Meister Eckhart's Mystical Philosophy*, translated and commentary by Reiner Schürmann, introduction by David Appelbaum, 217–222. Great Barrington: Lindisfarne Books, 2001.

Schüssler Fiorenza, Elisabeth. *In Memory of Her: A Feminist Theological Reconstruction of Christian Origins*. New York: Crossroad, 1983.

Schwartz, Dov. "Avicenna and Maimonides on Immortality: A Comparative Study." In *Medieval and Modern Perspectives on Muslim-Jewish Relations*, edited by Ronald L. Nettler, 185–197. Luxembourg: Harwood Academic, 1995.

Schwartz, Regina M. "From Ritual to Poetry: Herbert's Mystical Eucharist." In *Mystics: Presence and Aporia*, edited by Michael Kessler and Christian Sheppard, 138–160. Chicago and London: University of Chicago Press, 2003.

Schwarz, Arthuro. *Kabbalah and Alchemy: An Essay on Common Archetypes*. Northvale: Jason Aronson, 2000.

Schweid, Eliezer. *Judaism and Mysticism according to Gershom Scholem: A Critical Analysis and Programmatic Discussion.* Translated with an introduction by David Avraham Weiner. Atlanta: Scholars Press, 1985.

Scott, Charles E. "The Mask of Nietzsche's Self-Overcoming." In *Nietzsche as Postmodernist: Essays Pro and Contra,* edited and with an introduction by Clayton Koelb, 217–229. Albany: State University of New York, 1990.

———. *The Time of Memory.* Albany: State University of New York Press, 1999.

Scott, George Ryley. *Phallic Worship: A History of Sex and Sex Rites in Relation to the Religions of All Races from Antiquity to the Present Day.* London: Luxor Press, 1966.

Scott, Joan Wallach. "Deconstructing Equality—Versus—Difference: On the Uses of Poststructuralist Theory for Feminism." In *Conflicts in Feminism,* edited by Marianne Hirsch and Evelyn Fox Keller, 134–148. New York and London: Routledge, 1990.

———. *Gender and the Politics of History.* New York: Columbia University Press, 1988.

Scroggs, Robin. "Paul and the Eschatological Woman." *Journal of American Academy of Religion* 40 (1972): 283–303.

———. "Paul and the Eschatological Woman Revisited." *Journal of the American Academy of Religion* 42 (1974): 532–537.

The Secret of the Golden Flower: A Chinese Book of Life. Translated and explained by Richard Wilhelm, with a commentary by Carl G. Jung. New York: Harcourt Brace Jovanovich, 1965.

Sed-Rajna, Gabrielle. *Commentaire sur la liturgie quotidienne, introduction, traduction annotée et glossaire des termes techniques.* Leiden: E. J. Brill, 1974.

Segal, Alan. "The Incarnation: The Jewish Milieu." In *The Incarnation: An Interdisciplinary Symposium on the Incarnation of the Son of God,* edited by Stephen T. Davis, Daniel Kendall, and Gerald O'Collins, 116–139. Oxford and New York: Oxford University Press, 2002.

———. *Paul the Convert: The Apostolate and Apostasy of Saul the Pharisee.* New Haven and London: Yale University Press, 1990.

———. "Paul's '*Soma Pneumatikon*' and the Worship of Jesus." In *The Jewish Roots of Christological Monotheism: Papers from the St. Andrews Conference on the Historical Origins of the Worship of Jesus,* edited by Carey C. Newman, James R. Davila, and Gladys S. Lewis, 258–276. Leiden: E. J. Brill, 1999.

———. *Two Powers in Heaven: Early Rabbinic Reports about Christianity and Gnosticism.* Leiden: E. J. Brill, 1977.

Segal, Robert. "In Defense of Reductionism." *Journal of the American Academy of Religion* 51 (1983): 97–124.

———. *The Poimandres as Myth: Scholarly Theory and Gnostic Meaning.* Berlin: Walter de Gruyter, 1986.

Sells, Michael. *Approaching the Qur'an: The Early Revelations.* Ashland: White Cloud Press, 1999.

———. *Early Islamic Mysticism: Sufi, Qur'an, Miraj, Poetic and Theological Writings.* New York: Paulist Press, 1996.

———. *Mystical Languages of Unsaying.* Chicago and London: University of Chicago Press, 1994.

Semple, Benjamin. "The Male Psyche and the Female Sacred Body in Marie de France and Christine de Pizan." *Yale French Studies* 86 (1994): 164–186.

Sendor, Mark B. "The Emergence of Provençal Kabbalah: Rabbi Isaac the Blind's *Commentary on Sefer Yeẓirah.*" 2 vols. Ph.D. dissertation, Harvard University, 1994.

Sevrin, J.-M. "Les noces spiritueles dans l'Évangile selon Philippe." *Le Muséon* 87 (1974): 143–193.

Shāntideva. *The Way of the Bodhisattva: A Translation of the Bodhicharyāvatāra.* Translated from the Tibetan by the Padmakara Group, foreword by the Dalai Lama. Boston and London: Shambhala, 1997.

Shapiro, Gary. "Translating, Repeating, Naming: Foucault, Derrida, and *The Genealogy of Morals.*" In *Nietzsche as Postmodernist: Essays Pro and Contra,* edited and with an introduction by Clayton Koelb, 39–55. Albany: State University of New York, 1990.

Shapiro, Susan E. "A Matter of Discipline: Reading for Gender in Jewish Philosophy." In *Judaism since Gender,* edited by Miriam Peskowitz and Laura Levitt, 158–173. New York: Routledge, 1997.

———. "Toward a Postmodern Judaism: A Response." In Steven Kepnes, Peter Ochs, and Robert Gibbs, *Reasoning after Revelation: Dialogues in Postmodern Jewish Philosophy,* 77–92. Boulder: Westview Press, 1998.

Sharf, Robert H. "Buddhist Modernism and the Rhetoric of Meditative Experience." *Numen* 42 (1995): 228–283.

Shaw, Miranda. *Passionate Enlightenment: Women in Tantric Buddhism.* Princeton: Princeton University Press, 1994.

Shaw, Teresa M. *The Burden of the Flesh: Fasting and Sexuality in Early Christianity.* Minneapolis: Fortress Press, 1998.

Shayegan, Daryush. "The Visionary Typography of Ḥāfiẓ." In *The Green Sea of Heaven: Fifty Ghazals from the Dīwān of Ḥāfiẓ,* translated by Elizabeth T. Gray, 15–34. Ashland: White Cloud Press, 1995.

Sheres, Ita, and Anne Kohn Blau. *The Truth about the Virgin: Sex and Ritual and the Dead Sea Scrolls.* New York: Continuum, 1995.

Shillony, Helena. "Métaphores de la négation." In *Écrire le livre: Autour d'Edmond Jabès: Colloque de Cerisy-la-Salle,* edited by Richard Stamelman and Mary Ann Caws, 23–30. Seyssel: Éditions Champ Vallon, 1989.

Shmueli, Ephraim. *Seven Jewish Cultures: A Reinterpretation of Jewish History and Thought.* Translated by Gila Shmueli. Cambridge: Cambridge University Press, 1990.

Shoham, Shlomo Giora. *The Bridge to Nothingness: Gnosis, Kabala, Existentialism, and the Transcendental Predicament of Man.* Rutherford: Fairleigh Dickinson Press, 1994.

Shokek, Shimon. *Jewish Ethics and Jewish Mysticism in Sefer ha-Yashar.* Lewiston: E. Mellen Press, 1991.

———. *Kabbalah and the Art of Being: The Smithsonian Lectures.* London and New York: Routledge, 2001.

Shumway, David R. "Genealogies of Knowledge." In *Critical Essays on Foucault,* edited by Karlis Racevskis, 82–98. New York: G. K. Hall, 1999.

Signer, Michael. "Thirteenth Century Christian Hebraism: The *Expositio on Canticles* in Ms. Vat. lat. 1053." In *Approaches to Judaism in Medieval Times,* vol. 3, edited by David R. Blumenthal, 89–100. Atlanta: Scholars' Press, 1988.

Sikka, Sonya. *Forms of Transcendence: Heidegger and Medieval Mystical Theology.* Albany: State University of New York Press, 1997.

Siklós, Bulcsu. *The Vajrabhairava Tantras: Tibetan and Mongolian Versions, English Translation and Annotations.* Tring: Institute of Buddhist Studies, 1996.

Silman, Yochanan. *Philosopher and Prophet: Judah Halevi, the Kuzari, and the Evolution of His Thought.* Translated by Lenn J. Schramm. Albany: State University of New York Press, 1995.

Silverman, Hugh J. *Questioning Foundations: Truth/Subjectivity/Culture.* New York: Routledge, 1993.

Simmer-Brown, Judith. *Dakini's Warm Breath: The Female Principle in Tibetan Buddhism*. Boston and London: Shambhala, 2001.

Simon, Uriel. *Four Approaches to the Book of Psalms: From Saadiah Gaon to Abraham Ibn Ezra*. Translated by Lenn J. Schramm. Albany: State University of New York Press, 1991.

Sinclair-Brull, Wendy. *Female Ascetics: Hierarchy and Purity in an Indian Religious Movement*. Richmond: Curzon, 1997.

Singer, June. *Androgyny: The Opposites Within*. 2nd ed. Boston: Sigo Press, 1989.

Siorvanes, Lucas. *Proclus: Neo-Platonic Philosophy and Science*. New Haven and London: Yale University Press, 1996.

Skehan, Patrick W. *The Wisdom of Ben Sira*. New translation with notes, introduction and commentary by Alexander A. Di Lella. New York: Doubleday, 1987.

Sklar, Lawrence. *Space, Time, and Spacetime*. Berkeley: University of California, 1974.

Smalley, Beryl. *The Study of the Bible in the Middle Ages*. Notre Dame: University of Notre Dame Press, 1964.

Smart, Ninian. *Dimensions of the Sacred: An Anatomy of the World's Beliefs*. Berkeley: University of California Press, 1996.

Smelik, Willem F. "On Mystical Transformation of the Righteous into Light in Judaism." *Journal for the Study of Judaism* 26 (1995): 122–144.

Smith, J. C., and Carla Ferstman. *The Castration of Oedipus: Feminism, Psychoanalysis, and the Will to Power*. New York and London: New York University Press, 1996.

Smith, Jane I., and Yvonne Y. Haddad. "The Virgin Mary in Islamic Tradition and Commentary." *Muslim World* 79 (1989): 161–187.

Smith, Jonathan Z. *Imagining Religion: From Babylon to Jonestown*. Chicago and London: University of Chicago Press, 1982.

Smith, Margaret. *Rābiʿa the Mystic and Her Fellow-Saints in Islam*. Cambridge: Cambridge University Press, 1928.

Smith, Mark S. *The Origins of Biblical Monotheism: Israel's Polytheistic Background and the Ugaritic Texts*. Oxford: Oxford University Press, 2001.

Smith, Robert. *Derrida and Autobiography*. Cambridge: Cambridge University Press, 1995.

Snyder, Jane McIntosh. *The Woman and the Lyre: Women Writers in Classical Greece and Rome*. Carbondale: Southern Illinois University Press, 1989.

Sōhō, Takuan. *The Unfettered Mind: Writings of the Zen Master to the Sword Master*. Translated by William Scott Wilson. Tokyo: Kodansha International, 1986.

Sokol, Moshe Z. "Attitudes toward Pleasure in Jewish Thought: A Typological Proposal." In *Reverence, Righteousness, and Raḥamanut: Essays in Memory of Rabbi Dr. Leo Jung*, edited by Jacob J. Schachter, 293–314. Northvale: Jason Aronson, 1992.

Sokolowski, Robert. *Husserlian Meditations: How Words Present Things*. Evanston: Northwestern University Press, 1974.

———. *Presence and Absence: A Philosophical Investigation of Language and Being*. Bloomington: Indiana University Press, 1978.

———. "Truth within Phenomenological Speech." In *Phenomenological Perspectives: Historical and Systematic Essays in Honor of Herbert Spiegelberg*, 188–217. The Hague: Martinus Nijhoff, 1975.

Soloveitchik, Joseph B. "A Halakhic Approach to Suffering." *The Torah u-Madda Journal* 8 (1998–1999): 3–24. Reprinted in *Out of the Whirlwind: Essays on Mourning, Suffering and the Human Condition*, edited by David Shatz, Joel B. Wolowelsky, and Reuven Ziegler, 86–115. Jersey City: Ktav, 2003.

Sommer, Benjamin D. "Revelation at Sinai in the Hebrew Bible and in Jewish Theology." *Journal of Religion* 79 (1999): 422–451.

Songe-Møller, Vigdis. *Philosophy without Women: The Birth of Sexism in Western Thought.* Translated by Peter Cripps. London and New York: Continuum, 2002.

Sontag, Frederick. *Wittgenstein and the Mystical: Philosophy as an Ascetic Practice.* Atlanta: Scholars' Press, 1995.

Sosnowski, Saúl. *Borges y la Cabala: La búsqueda del verbo.* Buenos Aires: Pardés Ediciones, 1986.

Spanos, William V. *Heidegger and Criticism: Retrieving the Cultural Politics of Destruction.* Foreword by Donald E. Pease. Minneapolis and London: University of Minnesota Press, 1993.

Spiro, Melford E. *Gender Ideology and Psychological Reality: An Essay on Cultural Reproduction.* New Haven and London: Yale University Press, 1997.

Spisani, Franco. *Significato e struttura del tempo: The Meaning and Structure of Time.* Bologna: Azzoguidi, 1972.

Spivak, Gayatri Chakravorty. "Displacement and the Discourse of Woman." In *Feminist Interpretations of Jacques Derrida,* edited by Nancy J. Holland, 43–71. University Park: Pennsylvania State University Press, 1997.

Sponberg, Alan. "Atttitudes toward Women and the Feminine in Early Buddhism." In *Buddhism, Sexuality, and Gender,* edited by José Ignacio Cabezón, 3–36. Albany: State University of New York Press, 1992.

Srinivasan, Thaiyar M. "Polar Principles in Yoga and Tantra." In *Sexual Archetypes, East and West,* edited by Bina Gupta, 106–115. New York: Paragon, 1987.

Stace, William T. *Mysticism and Philosophy.* London: Macmillan, 1960.

Stambaugh, Joan. "Heidegger, Taoism, and the Question of Metaphysics." In *Heidegger and Asian Thought,* edited by Graham Parkes, 79–91. Honolulu: University of Hawaii Press, 1987.

———. *Impermanence Is Buddha-nature: Dōgen's Understanding of Temporality.* Honolulu: University of Hawaii Press, 1990.

———. *The Other Nietzsche.* Albany: State University of New York Press, 1994.

Stamelman, Richard. "Le dialogue de l'absence." In *Écrire le livre: Autour d'Edmond Jabés: Colloque de Cerisy-la-Salle,* edited by Richard Stamelman and Mary Ann Caws, 201–217. Seyssel: Éditions Champ Vallon, 1989.

Standish, Paul. *Beyond the Self: Wittgenstein, Heidegger, and the Limits of Language.* Aldershot: Avebury, 1992.

Stankiewicz, Edward. "Poetics and Verbal Art." In *A Perfusion of Signs,* edited by Thomas A. Sebeok, 54–76. Bloomington and London: Indiana University Press, 1977.

Starobinski, Jean. *Largesse.* Translated by Jane Marie Todd. Chicago and London: University of Chicago Press, 1997.

Staten, Henry. *Wittgenstein and Derrida.* Lincoln and London: University of Nebraska Press, 1984.

Steenburg, David. "Chaos at the Marriage of Heaven and Hell." *Harvard Theological Review* 84 (1991): 447–466.

Steffney, John. "Man and Being in Heidegger and Zen Buddhism." *Philosophy Today* 25 (1981): 46–54.

———. "Transmetaphysical Thinking in Heidegger and Zen Buddhism." *Philosophy East and West* 27 (1977): 323–336.

Stegemann, Hartmut. *The Library of Qumran: On the Essenes, Qumran, John the Baptist, and Jesus.* Leiden: E. J. Brill, 1998.

Stein, Dina. "A Maidservant and Her Master's Voice: Discourse, Identity, and Eros in Rabbinic Texts." *Journal of the History of Sexuality* 10 (2001): 375–397.

Steinbock, Anthony J. "Merleau-Ponty, Husserl, and Saturated Intentionality." In *Re-Reading Merleau-Ponty: Essays beyond the Continental-Analytic Divide*, edited by Lawrence Hass and Dorothea Olkowski, 53–74. Amherst: Humanity Books, 2000.

Steiner, George. *After Babel: Aspects of Language and Translation*. 3rd ed. Oxford and New York: Oxford University Press, 1997.

———. *Real Presences*. Chicago and London: University of Chicago Press, 1991.

Stendahl, Krister. *The Bible and the Role of Women: A Case Study in Hermeneutics*. Translated by E. Sander. Philadelphia: Fortress Press, 1966.

Stephens, Walter. *Demon Lovers: Witchcraft, Sex, and the Crisis of Belief*. Chicago and London: University of Chicago Press, 2002.

Stern, David. "Jesus' Parables from the Perspective of Rabbinic Literature: The Example of the Wicked Husbandmen." In *Parable and Story in Judaism and Christianity*, edited by Clemens Thoma and Michael Wyschogrod, 42–80. New York: Paulist Press, 1989.

———. *Parables in Midrash: Narrative and Exegesis in Rabbinic Literature*. Cambridge, Mass.: Harvard University Press, 1991.

Stern, David G. "Heidegger and Wittgenstein on the Subject of Kantian Philosophy." In *Figuring the Self: Subject, Absolute, and Others in Classical German Philosophy*, edited by David E. Klemm and Günter Zöller, 245–259. Albany: State University of New York Press, 1997.

Stern, Sacha. *Jewish Identity in Early Rabbinic Writings*. Leiden: E. J. Brill, 1994.

Stern, Samuel M. "'The First in Thought Is the Last in Action': The History of a Saying Attributed to Aristotle." *Journal of Semitic Studies* 7 (1962): 234–252.

Stevens, Richard. *James and Husserl: The Foundations of Meaning*. The Hague: Martinus Nijhoff, 1974.

Stevenson, Walter. "The Rise of Eunuchs in Greco-Roman Antiquity." *Journal of the History of Sexuality* 5 (1995): 495–511.

Stewart, Columbia. "Imageless Prayer and the Theological Vision of Evagrius Ponticus." *Journal of Early Christian Studies* 9 (2001): 173–204.

Stillman, Yedida K. "'Cover Her Face': Jewish Women and Veiling in Islamic Civilisation." In *Israel and Ishmael: Studies in Muslim-Jewish Relations*, edited by Tudor Parfitt, 13–31. New York: St. Martin's Press, 2000.

Stokhof, Martin. *World and Life as One: Ethics and Ontology in Wittgenstein's Early Thought*. Stanford: Stanford University Press, 2002.

Stokstad, Marilyn. "The Garden as Art." In *Medieval Gardens*, edited by Elizabeth B. MacDougall, 177–185. Washington: Dumbarton Oaks, 1986.

Stordalen, Terje. *Echoes of Eden: Genesis 2–3 and Symbolism of the Eden Garden in Biblical Hebrew Literature*. Leuven: Peeters, 2000.

Stoudt, John Joseph. *Jacob Boehme: His Life and Thought*. Foreword by Paul Tillich. New York: Seabury Press, 1968.

Streete, Gail Corrington. "Women as Sources of Redemption and Knowledge in Early Christian Traditions." In *Women & Christian Origins*, edited by Ross Shepard Kraemer and Mary Rose D'Angelo, 347–350. New York and Oxford: Oxford University Press, 1999.

Strong, Tracy B. *Friedrich Nietzsche and the Politics of Transfiguration*. Berkeley: University of California Press, 1975.

Stroumsa, Gedaliahu A. G. *Another Seed: Studies in Gnostic Mythology*. Leiden: E. J. Brill, 1984.

———. "Jewish and Gnostic Traditions among the Audians." In *Sharing the Sacred: Religious Contacts and Conflicts in the Holy Land*, edited by Arieh Kofsky and Guy G. Stroumsa, 97–108. Jerusalem: Yad Izhak Ben Zvi, 1998.

Strozier, Robert M. *Foucault, Subjectivity, and Identity: Historical Construction of Subject and Self.* Detroit: Wayne State University Press, 2002.

Stuckrad, Kocku von. "Relative, Contigent, Determined: The Category 'History" Its Methodological Dilemma." *Journal of the American Academy of Religion* 71 (2003): 906.

Sugarman, Richard Ira. *Rancor against Time: The Phenomenology of "Ressentiment."* Hamburg: Felix Meiner, 1980.

Suhrawardī, Shihābuddīn Yaḥya. *The Book of Radiance: A Parallel English-Persian Text.* Edited and translated with an introduction by Hossein Ziai. Costa Mesa: Mazda, 1998.

———. *The Philosophical Allegories and Mystical Treatises.* Translated by Wheeler M. Thackston. Costa Mesa: Mazda, 1999.

———. *The Philosophy of Illumination: A New Critical Edition of the Text of Ḥikmat al-ishrāq with English Translation, Notes, Commentary, and Introduction by John Walbridge and Hossein Ziai.* Provo: Brigham Young University Press, 2000.

———. *The Shape of Light: Hayakal al-Nur.* Interpreted by Shaykh Tosun Bayrak al-Jerrahi al-Halveti. Louisville: Fons Vitae, 1998.

Sultan, Bahu. *Death before Dying: The Sufi Poems of Sultan Bahu.* Translated by Jamal J. Elias. Berkeley: University of California Press, 1998.

Sutrop, Margit. "Imagination and the Act of Fiction-Making." *Australian Journal of Philosophy* 80 (2002): 332–344.

Sutter, Georg. *Mystik und Erotik: Ein Beitrag zur Philosophie der Liebe das Mannes zum Weib auf werttheoretischer Grundlage.* Heidelberg: C. Winter, 1929.

Suzuki, Daisetz T. *Mysticism: Christian and Buddhist.* New York: Harper, 1957.

Sviri, Sara. *The Taste of Hidden Things: Images on the Sufi Path.* Inverness: Golden Sufi Center, 1997.

Swanson, Paul L. "The Spirituality of Emptiness in Early Chinese Buddhism." In *Buddhist Spirituality: Indian, Southeast Asian, Tibetan, Early Chinese,* edited by Takeuchi Yoshinori in association with Jan Van Bragt, James W. Heisig, Joseph S. O'Leary, and Paul L. Swanson, 373–396. New York: Crossroad, 1993.

Swartz, Merlin L., ed. *A Medieval Critique of Anthropomorphism: Ibn Al-Jawzī's Kitāb Akhbār as-Sifāt: A Critical Edition of the Arabic Text with Translation, Introduction and Notes.* Leiden: Brill, 2002.

Swartz, Michael D. *Scholastic Magic: Ritual and Revelation in Early Jewish Mysticism.* Princeton: Princeton University Press, 1996.

Swietlicki, Catherine. *Spanish Christian Cabala: The Works of Luis De León, Santa Teresa De Jesús, and San Juan De La Cruz.* Columbia: University of Missouri Press, 1986.

Taft, Robert F. "Byzantine Communion Rites I. The Early Ritual of Clergy Communion." *Orientalia Christiana Periodica* 65 (1999): 307–345.

Talbot, Alice-Marry M. "A Comparison of the Monastic Experience of Byzantine Men and Women." *Greek Orthodox Theological Review* 30 (1985): 1–20.

Talmage, Frank. "Apples of Gold: The Inner Meaning of Sacred Texts in Medieval Judaism." In *Jewish Spirituality from the Bible through the Middle Ages,* edited by Arthur Green, 313–355. New York: Crossroad, 1986.

Talmon, Shemaryahu. "The Community of the Renewed Covenant: Between Judaism and Christianity." In *The Community of the Renewed Covenant: The Notre Dame Symposium on the Dead Sea Scrolls,* edited by Eugene Ulrich and James Vanderkam, 3–24. Notre Dame: University of Notre Dame Press, 1994.

Tamburello, Dennis E. *Union with Christ: John Calvin and the Mysticism of St. Bernard.* Louisville: Westminster John Knox Press, 1994.

Taminiaux, Jacques. *Poetics, Speculation, and Judgment: The Shadow of the Work of Art from Kant to Phenomenology.* Translated and edited by Michael Gendre. Albany: State University of New York Press, 1993.

———. *The Thracian Maid and the Professional Thinker: Arendt and Heidegger.* Translated by Michael Gendre. Albany: State University of New York Press, 1997.

Tarrant, Harold. *Thrasyllan Platonism.* Ithaca and London: Cornell University Press, 1993.

Taubes, Susan A. "The Gnostic Foundations of Heidegger's Nihilism." *Journal of Religion* 34 (1954): 155–172.

Taves, Ann. *Fits, Trances, & Visions: Experiencing Religion and Explaining Experience from Wesley to James.* Princeton: Princeton University Press, 1999.

Taylor, Eugene. *William James on Consciousness Beyond the Margin.* Princeton: Princeton University Press, 1996.

Taylor, Mark C., ed. *Critical Terms for Religious Studies.* Chicago and London: University of Chicago Press, 1998.

———. "Introduction: System . . . Structure . . . Difference . . . Other." In *Postmodernism: Critical Concepts, Volume III: Disciplinary Texts: Humanities and Social Sciences,* edited by Victor E. Taylor and Charles E. Winquist, 373–404. London and New York: Routledge, 1998.

———. *Tears.* Albany: State University of New York Press, 1990.

Teugels, Lieve. "The Creation of the Human in Rabbinic Interpretation." In *The Creation of Man and Woman: Interpretations of the Biblical Narratives in Jewish and Christian Traditions,* edited by Gerard P. Luttikhuizen, 107–127. Leiden: Brill, 2000.

Thiede, Carsten Peter. *The Dead Sea Scrolls and the Jewish Origins of Christianity.* New York: Palgrave, 2001.

Thōng, Huynh Sanh. *The Golden Serpent: How Humans Learned to Speak and Invent Culture.* Hamden: Mekong Printing, 1999.

Thornton, Bruce S. *Eros: The Myth of Ancient Greek Sexuality.* Boulder: Westview Press, 1997.

Tillich, Paul. *Mysticism and Guilt-Consciousness in Schelling's Philosophical Development.* Translated with an introduction and notes by Victor Nuovo. Lewisburg: Bucknell University Press, 1974.

Tirosh-Rothschild, Hava. "Continuity and Revision in the Study of Kabbalah." *AJS Review* 16 (1991): 161–192.

Tishby, Isaiah. *Mishnat ha-Zohar.* 2 vols. Jerusalem: Bialik Insitute, 1975.

———. *The Wisdom of the Zohar.* Translated by David Goldstein. Oxford: Oxford University Press, 1989.

Toorn, Karel van der. "Torn between Vice and Virtue: Stereotypes of the Widow in Israel and Mesopotamia." In *Female Stereotypes in Religious Traditions,* edited by Rita Kloppenborg and Wouter J. Hanegraaff, 1–13. Leiden: E. J. Brill, 1995.

Tougher, Shaun F. "Byzantine Eunuchs: An Overview, with Special Reference to Their Creation and Origin." In *Women, Men and Eunuchs: Gender in Byzantium,* edited by Liz James, 168–184. London and New York: Routledge, 1997.

———. "Images of Effeminate Men: The Case of Byzantine Eunuchs." In *Masculinity in Medieval Europe,* edited by Dawn M. Hadley, 89–100. London and New York: Longman, 1999.

Trachtenberg, Joshua. *Jewish Magic and Superstition: A Study in Folk Religion.* New York: Behrman, 1939.

Trakatellis, Demetrios. *The Transcendent God of Eugnostos: An Exegetical Contribution to the Study of the Gnostic Texts of Nag Hammadi with a Retroversion of the Lost Original Greek Text of Eugnostos the Blessed.* Translated by Charles Sarelis. Brookline: Holy Cross Orthodox Press, 1991.

Travis, Yakov M. "Kabbalistic Foundations of Jewish Spiritual Practice: Rabbi Ezra of Gerona on the Kabbalistic Meaning of the Mizvot." Ph.D. dissertation, Brandeis University, 2002.

Tréguier, Jean-Marie. *Le corps selon la chair: Phénoménologie et ontologie chez Merleau-Ponty*. Paris: Éditions Kimé, 1996.

Trevett, Christine. "Spiritual Authority and the 'Heretical' Woman: Firmilian's Word to the Church in Carthage." In *Portraits of Spiritual Authority: Religious Power in Early Christianity, Byzantium and the Christian Orient*, edited by Jan Willem Drijvers and John W. Watt, 45–62. Leiden: E. J. Brill, 1999.

Trías, Eugenio. "Thinking Religion: the Symbol and the Sacred." In *Religion*, edited by Jacques Derrida and Gianni Vattimo, 95–110. Stanford: Stanford University Press, 1998.

Troup, Calvin L. *Temporality, Eternity, and Wisdom: The Rhetoric of Augustine's Confessions*. Columbia: University of South Carolina Press, 1999.

Troy, Lana. "Engendering Creation in Ancient Egypt: Still and Flowing Waters." In *A Feminist Companion to Reading the Bible: Approaches, Methods and Strategies*, edited by Athalya Brenner and Carole Fontaine, 238–268. London and Chicago: Fitzroy Dearborn, 1997.

Tuana, Nancy. "Re-Fusing Nature/Nurture." In *Hypatia Reborn: Essays in Feminist Philosophy*, edited by Azizah Y. Al-Hibri and Margaret A. Simons, 70–89. Bloomington and Indianapolis: Indiana University Press, 1990.

Tugendhat, Ernst. "Heidegger's Idea of Truth." In *Hermeneutics and Truth*, edited by Brice R. Wachterhauser, 83–97. Evanston: Northwestern University Press, 1994.

Turner, Denys. *The Darkness of God: Negativity in Christian Mysticism*. Cambridge: Cambridge University Press, 1995.

———. *Eros and Allegory: Medieval Exegesis of the Song of Songs*. Kalamazoo: Cistercian, 1995.

Turner, John D. *Sethian Gnosticism and the Platonic Tradition*. Leuven and Paris: Éditions Peeters, 2001.

———. "Time and History in Sethian Gnosticism." In *For the Children, Perfect Instruction: Studies in Honor of Hans-Martin Schenke on the Occasion of the Berliner Arbeitskreis für koptisch-gnostische Schriften's Thirtieth Year*, edited by Hans-Gebhard Bethge, Stephen Emmel, Karen L. King, and Imke Schletterer, 203–214. Leiden: Brill, 2002.

Turner, Jonathan H. *On the Origins of Human Emotions: A Sociological Inquiry into the Evolution of Human Affect*. Stanford: Stanford University Press, 2000.

Twersky, Isadore. *Rabad of Posquières: A Twelfth-Century Talmudist*. Cambridge, Mass.: Harvard University Press, 1962.

Tzu, Chuang. *The Complete Works of Chuang Tzu*. Translated by Burton Watson. New York: Columbia University Press, 1968.

Ueki, Masatoshi. *Gender Equality in Buddhism*. New York: Peter Lang, 2001.

Underhill, Evelyn. *Mysticism: A Study in the Nature and Development of Man's Spiritual Consciousness*. London: Methuen, 1911.

Urbach, Ephraim E. "Askesis and Suffering in Talmudic and Midrashic Sources." In *Yitzhak F. Baer Jubilee Volume*, edited by Salo W. Baron, 48–68. Jerusalem: Historical Society of Israel, 1960 (Hebrew).

———. "The Homiletical Interpretations of the Sages and the Expositions of Origen and the Jewish-Christian Disputation." *Scripta Hierosolymitana* 22 (1971): 247–275.

———. *The Sages: Their Concepts and Beliefs*. Translated by Israel Abrahams. Jerusalem: Magnes Press, 1975.

Uro, Risto. "Is *Thomas* an Encratite Gospel?" In *Thomas at the Crossroads: Essays on the Gospel of Thomas*, edited by Risto Uro, 140–162. Edinburgh: T & T Clark, 1998.

ur-Raḥim, Muḥammad ʿAta. *Jesus: Prophet of Islam.* Elmhurst: Tahrike Tarsile Qur'an, 1991.
Vaidyanathan, T. G., and Jeffrey J. Kripal, eds. *Vishnu on Freud's Desk: A Reader in Psychoanalysis and Hinduism.* Delhi: Oxford University Press, 1999.
Vail, Loy M. *Heidegger and Ontological Difference.* University Park and London: Pennsylvania State University Press, 1972.
Vajda, Georges. *L'amour de Dieu dans la théologie juive du moyen âge.* Paris: J. Vrin, 1957.
———. *Le commentaire d'Ezra de Gérone sur le Cantique des Cantiques.* Paris: Aubier-Montaigne, 1969.
———. *La théologie ascétique de Baḥya Ibn Paquda.* Paris: Imprimerie Nationale, 1947.
Valantasis, Richard. "Constructions of Power in Asceticism." *Journal of the American Academy of Religion* 63 (1995): 775–821.
———. *The Gospel of Thomas.* London and New York: Routledge, 1997.
Vallega, Alejandro. " 'Beyng-Historical Thinking' in Heidegger's *Contributions to Philosophy.*" In *Companion to Heidegger's Contributions to Philosophy,* edited by Charles E. Scott, Susan M. Schoenbohm, Daniela Vallega-Neu, and Alejandro Vallega, 48–65. Bloomington and Indianapolis: Indiana University Press, 2001.
Vallega-Neu, Daniela. "Poietic Saying." In *Companion to Heidegger's Contributions to Philosophy,* edited by Charles E. Scott, Susan M. Schoenbohm, Daniela Vallega-Neu, and Alejandro Vallega, 66–80. Bloomington and Indianapolis: Indiana University Press, 2001.
Valler, Shulamit. *Women and Womanhood in the Stories of the Babylonian Talmud.* Tel-Aviv: Hakibbutz Hameuchad, 1993 (Hebrew).
VanderKam, James C. *The Book of Jubilees: A Critical Text.* 2 vols. Leuven: Éditions Peeters, 1989.
Varela, Francisco J. "Pour une phénoménologie de la *Sunyata* (I)." In *La gnose, une question philosophique: Pour une phénoménologie de l'invisible,* edited by Natalie Depraz and Jean-François Marquet, 121–148. Paris: Éditions du Cerf, 2000.
Vater, Michael G. "Schelling's Neoplatonic System-Notion: 'Ineinsbildung' and Temporal Unfolding." In *The Significance of Neoplatonism,* edited by R. Baine Harris, 275–299. Norfolk: Old Dominion University, 1976.
Vattimo, Gianni. *The Adventure of Difference: Philosophy after Nietzsche and Heidegger.* Baltimore: Johns Hopkins University Press, 1993.
———. *Beyond Interpretation: The Meaning of Hermeneutics for Philosophy.* Translated by David Webb. Stanford: Stanford University Press, 1994.
Veenker, Ronald A. "Forbidden Fruit: Ancient Near Eastern Sexual Metaphors." *Hebrew Union College Annual* 70–71 (1999–2000): 57–73.
Velkley, Richard L. "Realizing Nature in the Self: Schelling on Art and Intellectual Intuition in the System of Transcendental Idealism." In *Figuring the Self: Subject, Absolute, and Others in Classical German Philosophy,* edited by David E. Klemm and Günter Zöller, 149–168. Albany: State University of New York Press, 1997.
Verma, Ram S. *The Genome.* New York: VCH, 1990.
Verman, Mark. *The Books of Contemplation: Medieval Jewish Mystical Sources.* Albany: State University of New York Press, 1992.
———. "The Evolution of the Circle of Contemplation." In *Gershom Scholem's Major Trends in Jewish Mysticism 50 Years After: Proceedings of the Sixth International Conference on the History of Jewish Mysticism,* edited by Peter Schäfer and Joseph Dan, 163–177. Tübingen: J. C. B. Mohr, 1993.
———. "Kabbalah Refracted: Review Essay." *Shofar* 14 (1996): 123–130.

Veyne, Paul. *Did the Greeks Believe in Their Myths? An Essay on the Constitutive Imagination*. Translated by Paula Wissing. Chicago and London: University of Chicago Press, 1988.

Viller, Marcel. "Le martyre et l'ascèse." *Revue d'Ascèse et de Mystique* 6 (1925): 105–142.

———. "Martyre et perfection." *Revue d'Ascèse et de Mystique* 6 (1925): 3–25.

Vimalakīrti. *The Holy Teaching of Vimalakīrti: A Mahāyāna Scripture*. Translated by Robert A. F. Thurman. University Park: Pennsylvania State University Press, 1976.

———. *The Vimalakirti Sutra*. Translated by Burton Watson. New York: Columbia University Press, 1997.

Visker, Rudi. *Michel Foucault: Genealogy as Critique*. Translated by Chris Turner. London and New York: Verso, 1995.

Visotzky, Burton L. "The Conversation of Palm Trees." In *Tracing the Threads: Studies in the Vitality of Jewish Pseudepigrapha*, edited by John C. Reeves, 205–214. Atlanta: Scholars Press, 1994.

Visvader, John. "The Use of Paradox in Uroboric Philosophies." *Philosophy East and West* 28 (1978): 455–467.

Vitz, Paul C. *Sigmund Freud's Christian Unconscious*. New York: Guilford Press, 1988.

Vogt, Kari. "'Becoming Male': A Gnostic and Early Christian Metaphor." In *Image of God and Gender Models in Judaeo-Christian Tradition*, edited by Kari Elisabeth Børresen, 172–187. Oslo: Solum Forlag, 1991.

Vries, Hent de. *Philosophy and the Turn to Religion*. Baltimore and London: Johns Hopkins University Press, 1999.

Vulliaud, Paul. *Le Cantique des Cantiques d'aprés la tradition juive*. Paris: Éditions d'aujourd'hui, 1975.

Wabel, Thomas. "Die Hineinnahme der Sprachgrenzen in das Nachdenken über die Grenzen der Sprache in Theologie und Sprachphilosophie." In *Die Grenzen der Sprache: Sprachimmanenz—Sprachtranszendenz*, edited by Christoph Asmuth, Friedich Glauner, Burkhard Mojsisch, 85–106. Amsterdam and Philadelphia: B. R. Grüner, 1998.

Wachterhauser, Brice R. "Gadamer's Realism: The 'Belongingness' of World and Reality." In *Hermeneutics and Truth*, edited by Brice R. Wachterhauser, 148–171. Evanston: Northwestern University Press, 1994.

Waelhens, Alphonse de. *Une philosophie de l'ambiguïté: L'existentialisme de Maurice Merleau-Ponty*. 4th ed. Leuven: Éditions Nauwelaerts, 1970.

Wafer, Jim. "Vision and Passion: The Symbolism of Male Love in Islamic Mystical Literature." In *Islamic Homosexualities: Culture, History, and Literature*, edited by Stephen O. Murray and Will Roscoe, 107–131. New York and London: New York University Press, 1997.

Waghorne, Joanne Punzo. "A Body for God: An Interpretation of the Nature of Myth beyond Structuralism." *History of Religions* 21 (1981): 20–47.

Waite, Arthur E. *The Holy Kabbalah: A Study of the Secret Tradition in Israel*. Introduction by Kenneth Rexroth. Secaucus: University Books, 1960.

Walbridge, John. *The Leaven of the Ancients: Suhrawardī and the Heritage of the Greeks*. Albany: State University of New York Press, 2000.

Waldenfels, Bernard. "The Paradox of Expression." In *Chiasms: Merleau-Ponty's Notion of Flesh*, edited by Fred Evans and Leonard Lawlor, 89–102. Albany: State University of New York Press, 2000.

Waldstein, Michael. "Hans Jonas' Construct 'Gnosticism': Analysis and Critique." *Journal of Early Christian Studies* 8 (2000): 341–372.

———. "The Primal Triad in the Apocryphon of John." In *The Nag Hammadi Library after Fifty*

Years: Proceedings of the 1995 Society of Biblical Literature Commemoration, edited by John D. Turner and Anne McQuire, 154–187. Leiden: E. J. Brill, 1997.

Waley, Arthur. *The Way and Its Power: A Study of the Tao Tē Ching and Its Place in Chinese Thought.* New York: Grove Press, 1958.

Walfish, Barry D. "An Annotated Bibliography of Medieval Jewish Commentaries on the Song of Songs." In *The Bible in the Light of Its Interpreters: Sarah Kamin Memorial Volume*, edited by Sara Japhet, 518–571. Jerusalem: Magnes Press, 1994 (Hebrew).

Walker, Paul E. *The Wellsprings of Wisdom: A Study of Abū Yaʿqūb al-Sijistānī's Kitāb al-Yanābīʿ*. Salt Lake City: University of Utah Press, 1994.

Walker, William P., Jr. "Corinthians 11:2–16 and Paul's Views regarding Women." *Journal of Biblical Literature* 94 (1975): 94–110.

Wallace, Carolyn M. "The Priesthood and Motherhood in the Church of Jesus Christ of Latter-day Saints." In *Gender and Religion: On the Complexity of Symbols*, edited by Caroline Walker Bynum, Stevan Harrell, and Paula Richman, 117–140. Boston: Beacon Press, 1986.

Wallis, Richard T. "ΝΟΥΣ as Experience." In *The Significance of Neoplatonism*, 121–153. Edited by R. Baine Harris. Norfolk: Old Dominion University, 1976.

Wallulis, Jerald. *The Hermeneutics of Life History: Personal Achievement and History in Gadamer, Habermas, and Erikson*. Evanston: Northwestern University Press, 1990.

Walsh, Carey Ellen. *Exquisite Desire: Religion, the Erotic, and the Song of Songs*. Minneapolis: Fortress Press, 2000.

Walsh, David. *The Mysticism of Innerworldly Fulfillment: A Study of Jacob Boehme*. Gainesville: University Press of Florida, 1983.

Walsh, James, ed. *The Cloud of Unknowing*. New York: Paulist Press, 1981.

Walter, Guy. "La spiritualité du silence après la Choah dans le livre des questions." In *Écrire le livre: Autour d'Edmond Jabés: Colloque de Cerisy-la-Salle*, edited by Richard Stamelman and Mary Ann Caws, 71–88. Seyssel: Éditions Champ Vallon, 1989.

Walton, Roberto J. "World-experience, World-representation, and the World as an Idea." *Husserl Studies* 14 (1997): 1–20.

Ward, Graham. "Allegoria: Reading as a Spiritual Exercise." *Modern Theology* 5 (1999): 271–295.

Ward, John O. "Women, Witchcraft and Social Patterning in Later Roman Lawcodes." *Prudentia* 13 (1981): 99–118.

Warner, Marina. *Alone of All Her Sex: The Myth and the Cult of the Virgin Mary*. New York: Knopf, 1976.

Warraq, Ibn. *Why I Am Not a Muslim*. Amherst, NY: Prometheus Books, 1995.

Warren, Mary Anne. "Is Androgyny the Answer to Sexual Stereotyping?" In *"Femininity," "Masculinity," and "Androgyny": A Modern Philosophical Discussion*, edited by Mary Vetterling-Braggin, 170–196. Totowa: Littlefield, Adams, 1982.

Washington, Harold C. "The Strange Woman (*ishshah zarah / ishshah nokhriyyah*) of Proverbs 1–9 and Post-Exilic Judaean Society." *A Feminist Companion to Wisdom Literature*, edited by Athalya Brenner, 157–185. Sheffield: Sheffield Academic Press, 1995.

Wasserstrom, Steven M. "Further Thoughts on the Origins of *Sefer Yeṣirah*." *Aleph* 2 (2002): 201–221.

———. "Jewish Pseudepigrapha in Muslim Literature: A Bibliographical and Methodological Sketch." In *Tracing the Threads: Studies in the Vitality of Jewish Pseudepigrapha*, edited by John C. Reeves, 87–114. Atlanta: Scholars Press, 1994.

———. *Religion after Religion: Gershom Scholem, Mircea Eliade, and Henry Corbin at Eranos*. Princeton: Princeton University Press, 1999.

———. "*Sefer Yeṣira* and Early Islam: A Reappraisal." *Journal of Jewish Thought and Philosophy* 3 (1993): 1–30.

Waugh, Linda R. "The Poetic Function and the Nature of Language." *Poetics Today* 2 (1980): 57–82.

Webb, R., and Michael Sells. "Lacan and Bion: Psychoanalysis and the Mystical Language of Unsaying." *Theory and Psychology* 5 (1995): 195–215.

Weber, Alison. *Teresa of Avila and the Rhetoric of Femininity*. Princeton: Princeton University Press, 1990.

Wechsler, Judith Glatzer. "A Change in the Iconography of the Song of Songs in Twelfth- and Thirteenth-Century Latin Bibles." In *Texts and Responses: Studies Presented to Nahum N. Glatzer on the Occasion of his 70th Birthday by His Friends*, edited by Michael A. Fishbane and Paul R. Flohr, 73–93. Leiden: E. J. Brill 1975.

———. "Eli Lissitzky's 'Interchange Stations': The Letter and the Spirit." In *The Jew in the Text: Modernity and the Construction of Identity*, edited by Linda Nochlin and Tamar Garb, 187–200. London: Thames and Hudson, 1995.

Weeks, Andrew. *Boehme: An Intellectual Biography of the Seventeenth-Century Philosopher and Mystic*. Albany: State University of New York Press, 1991.

———. *German Mysticism from Hildegard of Bingen to Ludwig Wittgenstein: A Literary and Intellectual History*. Albany: State University of New York Press, 1993.

Wefelmeyer, Fritz. "Raphael's *Sistine Madonna*: An Icon of the German Imagination from Herder to Heidegger." In *Text into Image: Image into Text—Proceedings of the Interdisciplinary Bicentenary Conference held at St. Patrick's College Maynooth (The National University of Ireland) in September 1995*, edited by Jeff Morrison and Florian Krobb, 105–118. Amsterdam: Rodopi, 1997.

Wegner, Judith. *Chattel or Person? The Status of Women in the Mishnah*. New York and Oxford: Oxford University Press, 1988.

Weigel, Sigrid. *Body- and Image-Space: Re-Reading Walter Benjamin*. Translated by G. Paul, R. McNicholl, and J. Gaines. London and New York: Routledge, 1996.

———. *Entstellte Ähnlichkeit: Walter Benjamins theoretische Schreibweise*. Frankfurt am Main: Fischer Taschenbuch, 1997.

———. "Scholems Gedichte und seine Dichtungstheorie: Klage, Adressierung, Gabe und das Problem einer biblischen Sprache in unserer Zeit." In *Gershom Scholem: Literatur und Rhetorik*, edited by Stéphane Mosès and Sigrid Weigel, 16–47. Cologne: Böhlau, 2000.

Weihe, Edwin. "Merleau-Ponty's Doubt: The Wild of Nothing." In *Merleau-Ponty in Contemporary Perspectives*, edited by Patrick Burke and Jan van der Veken, 99–107. Dordrecht: Kluwer Academic, 1993.

Weil, Kari. *Androgyny and the Denial of Difference*. Charlottesville and London: University of Virginia Press, 1992.

Weiler, Moses C. "Kabbalistic Doctrine of R. Joseph Gikatilla in His Works, *Ginnat Egoz* and *Shaʿarei Orah*." In *Temirin*, edited by Israel Weinstock, 1:157–186. Jerusalem: Mosad ha-Rav Kook, 1972 (Hebrew).

———. "Studies in the Kabbalistic Terminology of R. Joseph Gikatilla and His Relationship to Maimonides." *Hebrew Union College Annual* 37 (1966): 13–44 (Hebrew section).

Weinfeld, Moshe. "Feminine Elements in the Descriptions of the Israelite Divinity—The Sacred Union and the Holy Tree." *Beit Miqra* 143 (1995): 348–358 (Hebrew).

Weinryb, Bernard D. *The Jews of Poland: A Social and Economic History of the Jewish Community in Poland from 1100 to 1800*. Philadelphia: Jewish Publication Society of America, 1976.

Weinstein, Sara. *Piety and Fanaticism: Rabbinic Criticism of Religious Stringency.* Northvale: Jason Aronson, 1997.
Weinstock, Israel. *Studies in Jewish Philosophy and Mysticism.* Jerusalem: Mosad ha-Rav Kook, 1969 (Hebrew).
Weissler, Chava. *Voices of the Matriarchs: Listening to the Prayers of Early Modern Jewish Women.* Boston: Beacon Press, 1998.
Wensinck, Arent J. *La pensée de Ghazali.* Paris: Adrien-Maisonneuve, 1940.
Werblowsky, R. J. Zwi. *Joseph Karo: Lawyer and Mystic.* Philadelphia: Jewish Publication Society of America, 1977.
Weston, Kath. *Gender in Real Time: Power and Transience in a Visual Age.* New York and London: Routledge, 2002.
Westreich, Elimelech. *Transitions in the Legal Status of the Wife in Jewish Law: A Journey among Traditions.* Jerusalem: Magnes Press, 2002 (Hebrew).
Weyl, Hermann. *The Continuum: A Critical Examination of the Foundation of Analysis.* Translated by Stephen Pollard and Thomas Bole. New York: Dover Publications, 1994.
———. *The Open World: Three Lectures on the Metaphysical Implications of Science.* New Haven: Yale University Press, 1932.
———. *Space—Time—Matter.* Translated by Henry L. Brose. New York: Dover, 1952.
Wheeler, Brannon M. *Moses in the Quran and Islamic Exegesis.* London: RoutledgeCurzon, 2002.
Wheeler, Samuel C., III. *Deconstruction as Analytic Philosophy.* Stanford: Stanford University Press, 2000.
White, David A. *Heidegger and the Language of Poetry.* Lincoln and London: University of Nebraska Press, 1978.
White, David G. *The Alchemical Body: Siddha Traditions in Medieval India.* Chicago: University of Chicago Press, 1996.
———. *Kiss of the Yoginī: "Tantric Sex" in Its South Asian Contexts.* Chicago and London: University of Chicago Press, 2003.
———. "Tantric Sects and Tantric Sex: The Flow of Secret Tantric Gnosis." In *Rending the Veil: Concealment and Secrecy in the History of Religions,* edited by Elliot R. Wolfson, 249–270. New York and London: Seven Bridges Press, 1999.
Whitehead, Alfred North. *Adventures of Ideas.* New York: Macmillan, 1933.
———. *Process and Reality: An Essay in Cosmology.* Corrected ed. Edited by David R. Griffin and Donald W. Sherburne. New York: Free Press, 1978.
Whitman, Walt. *Leaves of Grass.* New York: Modern Library, 1921.
Wieseltier, Leon. *Kaddish.* New York: Vintage Books, 1998.
Wiethaus, Ulrike. "Introduction." In *Maps of Flesh and Light: The Religious Experience of Medieval Women Mystics,* edited by Ulrike Wiethaus, 1–8. Syracuse: Syracuse University Press, 1993.
Wijnhoven, Jochanan. "The Mysticism of Solomon Ibn Gabirol." *Journal of Religion* 45 (1965): 137–152.
Wilcox, Donald J. *The Measures of Times Past: Pre-Newtonian Chronologies and the Rhetoric of Relative Time.* Chicago and London: University of Chicago Press, 1987.
Wild, Stefan. " 'We Have Sent Down to Thee the Book with the Truth . . .': Spatial and Temporal Implications of the Qur'anic Concepts of Nuzūl, Tanzīl, and 'Inzāl." In *The Qur'an as Text,* edited by Stefan Wild, 137–153. Leiden: E. J. Brill, 1996.
Wilensky, Sara O. Heller "Isaac Ibn Laṭif—Philosopher or Kabbalist?" In *Jewish Medieval and Renaissance Studies,* edited by Alexander Altmann, 185–223. Cambridge, Mass.: Harvard University Press, 1967.

Williams, Craig A. *Roman Homosexuality: Ideologies of Masculinity in Classical Antiquity.* Oxford and New York: Oxford University Press, 1999.

Williams, Michael A. *The Immovable Race: A Gnostic Designation and the Theme of Stability in Late Antiquity.* Leiden: E. J. Brill, 1985.

———. "Uses of Gender Imagery in Ancient Gnostic Texts." In *Gender and Religion: On the Complexity of Symbols*, edited by Caroline Walker Bynum, Stevan Harrell, and Paula Richman, 196–227. Boston: Beacon Press, 1986.

Williams, Rowan. "Troubled Breasts: The Holy Body in Hagiography." In *Portraits of Spiritual Authority: Religious Power in Early Christianity, Byzantium and the Christian Orient*, edited by Jan Willem Drijvers and John W. Watt, 63–78. Leiden: Brill, 1999.

Wilson, Liz. "Buddhist Views on Gender and Desire." In *Sexuality and the World's Religions*, edited by Machacek, David W. and Melissa M. Wilkcox, 135–175. Santa Barbara: ABC-CLIO, 2003.

———. *Charming Cadavers: Horrific Figurations of the Feminine in Indian Buddhist Hagiographic Literature.* Chicago and London: University of Chicago Press, 1996.

Wilson, Robert Mcl. "Old Testament Exegesis in the Gnostic Exegesis on the Soul." In *Essays on the Nag Hammadi Texts in Honour of Pahor Labib*, edited by Martin Krause, 217–224. Leiden: E. J. Brill, 1975.

Wimsatt, James I. "St. Bernard, the Canticle of Canticles, and Mystical Poetry." In *An Introduction to the Medieval Mystics of Europe*, edited by Paul Szarmach, 77–95. Albany: State University of New York Press, 1984.

Wimsatt, Jr., William K. *The Verbal Icon: Studies in the Meaning of Poetry.* Lexington: University of Kentucky Press, 1954.

Winkler, John J. "The Constraints of Eros." In *Magika Hiera: Ancient Greek Magic and Religion*, edited by Christopher A. Faraone and Dirk Obbink, 214–243. New York and Oxford: Oxford University Press, 1991.

Winston-Allen, Anne. *Stories of the Rose: The Making of the Rosary in the Middle Ages.* University Park: Pennsylvania State University Press, 1997.

Wire, Antoinette Clark. *The Corinthian Women Prophets: A Reconstruction through Paul's Rhetoric.* Minneapolis: Fortress Press, 1990.

Wiskind-Elper, Ora. *Tradition and Fantasy in the Tales of Reb Nahman of Bratslav.* Albany: State University of New York Press, 1998.

Wismer, Don. *The Islamic Jesus: An Annotated Bibliography of Sources in English and French.* New York: Garland, 1977.

Wisse, Frederik. "Flee Femininity: Antifemininity in Gnostic Texts and the Question of Social Milieu." In *Images of the Feminine in Gnosticism*, edited by Karen L. King, 297–307. Philadelphia: Fortress Press, 1988.

Witherspoon, Edward. "Logic and the Inexpressible in Frege and Heidegger." *Journal of the History of Philosophy* 40 (2002): 89–113.

Wittgenstein, Ludwig. *Culture and Value.* Edited by G. H. Von Wright in collaboration with Heikki Nyman, translated by Peter Wince. Chicago: University of Chicago Press, 1984.

———. *Philosophical Grammar.* Edited by Rush Rhees and translated by Anthony Kenny. Berkeley and Los Angeles: University of California Press, 1978.

———. *Philosophical Investigations.* 2nd ed. Translated by G. E. M. Anscombe. Oxford: Blackwell, 1958.

———. *Philosophical Remarks.* Edited by Rush Rhees and translated by Raymond Hargreaves and Roger White. Oxford: Blackwell, 1975.

———. *Tractatus Logico-Philosophicus.* German text with an English translation by C. K. Ogden, introduction by Bertrand Russell. London: Routledge & Kegan Paul, 1922.

———. *Tractatus Logico-Philosophicus.* Translated by D. F. Pears and B. F. McGuinness, with introduction by Bertrand Russell. London: Routledge & Kegan Paul, 1961.

Wogan-Browne, Jocelyn. "Chaste Bodies: Frames and Experiences." In *Framing Medieval Bodies,* edited by Sarah Kay and Miri Rubin, 24–42. Manchester and New York: Manchester University Press, 1994.

Wolfson, Elliot R. *Abraham Abulafia—Kabbalist and Prophet: Hermeneutics, Theosophy, and Theurgy.* Los Angeles: Cherub Press, 2000.

———. *Alef, Mem, Tau: Kabbalistic Musings on Time, Truth, Death.* Berkeley: University of California Press, 2005.

———. *Along the Path: Studies in Kabbalistic Myth, Symbolism, and Hermeneutics.* Albany: State University of New York Press, 1995.

———. "Anthropomorphic Imagery and Letter Symbolism in the Zohar." *Jerusalem Studies in Jewish Thought* 8 (1989): 147–181 (Hebrew).

———. "Assaulting the Border: Kabbalistic Traces in the Margins of Derrida." *Journal of the American Academy of Religion* 70 (2002): 475–514.

———. "Beautiful Maiden without Eyes: *Peshaṭ* and *Sod* in Zoharic Hermeneutics." In *The Midrashic Imagination: Jewish Exegesis, Thought, and History,* edited by Michael Fishbane, 155–203. Albany: State University of New York Press, 1993.

———. "Before Alef/Where Beginnings End." In *Beginning/Again: Towards a Hermeneutics of Jewish Texts,* edited by Aryeh Cohen and Shaul Magid, 135–161. New York and London: Seven Bridges Press, 2002.

———. "Beneath the Wings of the Great Eagle: Maimonides and Thirteenth-Century Kabbalah." In *Moses Maimonides (1138–1204)—His Religious, Scientific, and Philosophical Wirkungsgeschichte in Different Cultural Contexts,* edited by Görge K. Hasselhoff and Otfried Fraisse, 209–237. Würzburg: Ergon, 2004.

———. "Beyond Good and Evil: Hypernomianism, Transmorality, and Kabbalistic Ethics." In *Crossing Boundaries: Essays on the Ethical Status of Mysticism,* edited by G. William Barnard and Jeffrey J. Kripal, 103–156. New York and London: Seven Bridges Press, 2001.

———. "Beyond the Spoken Word: Oral Tradition and Written Transmission in Medieval Jewish Mysticism." In *Transmitting Jewish Traditions: Orality, Textuality and Cultural Diffusion,* edited by Yaakov Elman and Israel Gershoni, 166–224. New Haven and London: Yale University Press, 2000.

———. "'By Way of Truth': Aspects of Naḥmanides' Kabbalistic Hermeneutic." *AJS Review* 14 (1989): 103–178.

———. *Circle in the Square: Studies in the Use of Gender in Kabbalistic Symbolism.* Albany: State University of New York Press, 1995.

———. "Circumcision and the Divine Name: A Study in the Transmission of Esoteric Doctrine." *Jewish Quarterly Review* 78 (1987): 77–112.

———. "Circumcision, Vision of God, and Textual Interpretation: From Midrashic Trope to Mystical Symbol." *History of Religions* 27 (1987): 189–215.

———. "Constructions of the *Shekhinah* in the Messianic Theosophy of Abraham Cardoso, with an Annotated Edition of *Derush ha-Shekhinah.*" *Kabbalah: Journal for the Study of Jewish Mystical Texts* 3 (1998): 11–143.

———. "Coronation of the Sabbath Bride: Kabbalistic Myth and the Ritual of Androgynisation." *Journal of Jewish Thought and Philosophy* 6 (1997): 301–344.

———. "The Cut That Binds: Time, Memory, and the Ascetic Impulse." In *God's Voice From the Void: Old and New Studies in Bratslav Hasidism*, edited by Shaul Magid, 103–154. Albany: State University of New York Press, 2002.

———. "Divine Suffering and the Hermeneutics of Reading: Philosophical Reflections on Lurianic Mythology." In *Suffering Religion*, edited by Robert Gibbs and Elliot R. Wolfson, 101–162. New York and London: Routledge, 2002.

———. "The Engenderment of Messianic Politics: Symbolic Significance of Sabbatai Ṣevi's Coronation." In *Toward the Millennium: Messianic Expectations from the Bible to Waco*, edited by Peter Schäfer and Mark R. Cohen, 203–258. Leiden: E. J. Brill, 1998.

———. "Eunuchs Who Keep the Sabbath: Becoming Male and the Ascetic Ideal in Thirteenth-Century Jewish Mysticism." In *Becoming Male in the Middle Ages*, edited by Jeffrey J. Cohen and Bonnie Wheeler, 151–185. New York: Garland, 1997.

———. "The Face of Jacob in the Moon: Mystical Transformations of an Aggadic Myth." In *The Seductiveness of Jewish Myth: Challenge or Response?* edited by S. Daniel Breslauer, 235–270. Albany: State University of New York Press, 1997.

———. "Facing the Effaced: Mystical Eschatology and the Idealistic Orientation in the Thought of Franz Rosenzweig." *Journal for the History of Modern Theology* 4 (1997): 39–81.

———. "Fore/giveness on the Way: Nesting in the Womb of Response." *Graven Images: Studies in Culture, Law and the Sacred* 4 (1998): 153–169.

———. "Forms of Visionary Ascent as Ecstatic Experience in the Zoharic Literature." In *Gershom Scholem's Major Trends in Jewish Mysticism 50 Years After: Proceedings of the Sixth International Conference on the History of Jewish Mysticism*, edited by Peter Schäfer and Joseph Dan, 209–235. Tübingen: J. C. B. Mohr, 1993.

———. "From Sealed Book to Open Text: Time, Memory, and Narrativity in Kabbalistic Hermeneutics." In *Interpreting Judaism in a Postmodern Age*, edited by Steven Kepnes, 145–178. New York: New York University Press, 1995.

———. "Gender and Heresy in the Study of Kabbalah." *Kabbalah: Journal for the Study of Jewish Mystical Texts* 6 (2001): 231–262 (Hebrew).

———. "Hebraic and Hellenic Conceptions of Wisdom in *Sefer ha-Bahir*." *Poetics Today* 19 (1998): 151–156.

———. "Iconicity of the Text: Reification of Torah and the Idolatrous Impulse of Zoharic Kabbalah." *Jewish Studies Quarterly* 11 (2004): 215–242.

———. "Iconic Visualization and the Imaginal Body of God: The Role of Intention in the Rabbinic Conception of Prayer." *Modern Theology* 12 (1996): 137–162.

———. "The Image of Jacob Engraved upon the Throne: Further Speculation on the Esoteric Doctrine of the German Pietism." In *Massu'ot Studies in Kabbalistic Literature and Jewish Philosophy in Memory of Prof. Ephraim Gottlieb*, edited by M. Oron and A. Goldreich, 131–185. Jerusalem: Bialik Institute, 1994 (Hebrew). English translation in Elliot R. Wolfson, *Along the Path: Studies in Kabbalistic Myth, Symbolism, and Hermeneutics*, 1–62. Albany: State University of New York Press, 1995.

———. "Images of God's Feet: Some Observations on the Divine Body in Judaism." In *People of the Body: Jews and Judaism from An Embodied Perspective*, edited by Howard Eilberg-Schwartz, 143–181. Albany: State University of New York Press, 1992.

———. "Imaging the Imageless: Iconic Representations of the Divine in Kabbalah." Paper delivered at the conference on "Iconotropism" held at Bar-Ilan University, Ramat Gan, Israel, March 1998.

———. "Judaism and Incarnation: The Imaginal Body of God." In *Christianity in Jewish Terms*, edited by Tikva Frymer-Kensky, David Novak, Peter Ochs, David Fox Sandmel, and Michael A. Signer, 239–254. Boulder: Westview Press, 2000.

———. "Language, Secrecy, and the Mysteries of Law: Theurgy and the Christian Kabbalah of Johannes Reuchlin." *Kabbalah: Journal for the Study of Jewish Mystical Texts* 13 (2005).

———. "Left Contained in the Right: A Study in Zoharic Hermeneutics." *Association for Jewish Studies Review* 11 (1986): 27–52.

———. "Letter Symbolism and Merkavah Imagery in the Zohar." In *Alei Shefer: Studies in the Literature of Jewish Thought Presented to Rabbi Dr. Alexandre Safran*, edited by Moshe Ḥallamish, 195–236 (English section). Ramat Gan: Bar-Ilan Press, 1990.

———. "Light through Darkness: The Ideal of Human Perfection in the Zohar." *Harvard Theological Review* 81 (1988): 89–91.

———. *Luminal Darkness: Imaginal Gleanings from Zoharic Literature*. Madison: University of Wisconsin Press, 2005.

———. "Lying on the Path: Translation and the Transport of Sacred Texts." In *The Unknown, Remembered Gate: Religious Experience and Hermeneutical Reflection in the Study of Religion*, edited by Elliot R. Wolfson and Jeffrey J. Kripal, 17–42. New York and London: Seven Bridges Press, 2005.

———. "Martyrdom, Eroticism, and Asceticism in Twelfth-Century Ashkenazi Piety." In *Jews and Christians in Twelfth-Century Europe*, edited by John Van Engen and Michael Signer, 171–220. Notre Dame: University Press of Notre Dame, 2001.

———. "Metatron and Shiʿur Qomah in the Writings of Ḥaside Ashkenaz." In *Mysticism, Magic, and Kabbalah in Ashkenazi Judaism: International Symposium Held in Frankfurt am Main, 1991*, edited by Karl Grözinger and Joseph Dan, 60–92. Berlin: Walter de Gruyter, 1995.

———. "Mirror of Nature Reflected in the Symbolism of Medieval Kabbalah." In *Judaism and Ecology: Created World and Revealed Word*, edited by Hava Tirosh-Samuelson, 305–331. Cambridge, Mass.: Harvard University Press, 2002.

———. "Mystical Rationalization of the Commandments in *Sefer ha-Rimmon*." *Hebrew Union College Annual* 59 (1988): 217–251.

———. "The Mystical Significance of Torah-Study in German Pietism." *Jewish Quarterly Review* 84 (1993): 43–78.

———. "Negative Theology and Positive Assertion in the Early Kabbalah." *Daʿat* 32–33 (1994): v–xxii.

———. "Occultation of the Feminine and the Body of Secrecy in Medieval Kabbalah." In *Rending the Veil: Concealment and Secrecy in the History of Religions*, edited by Elliot R. Wolfson, 113–154. New York and London: Seven Bridges Press, 1999.

———. "Ontology, Alterity, and Ethics in Kabbalistic Anthropology." *Exemplaria* 12 (2000): 129–155.

———. "The Problem of Unity in the Thought of Martin Buber." *Journal of the History of Philosophy* 27 (1989): 423–444.

———. "Re/membering the Covenant: Memory, Forgetfulness, and the Construction of History in the Zohar." In *Jewish History and Jewish Memory: Yerushalmi Festschrift*, edited by Elisheva Carlebach, John Efron, and David S. Myers, 214–246. Hanover and London: University of New England Press, 1998.

———. "Sacred Space and Mental Iconography: Imago Templi and Contemplation in Rhineland Jewish Pietism." In *Ki Baruch Hu: Ancient Near Eastern, Biblical, and Judaic Studies in Honor of*

Baruch A. Levine, edited by Robert Chazan, William W. Halo, and Lawrence H. Schiffman, 593–634. Winona Lake: Eisenbrauns, 1999.

———. "The Secret of the Garment in Naḥmanides." *Daʿat* 24 (1990): xxv–lxix (English section).

———. "Seven Mysteries of Knowledge: Qumran E/Sotericism Recovered." In *The Idea of Biblical Interpretation: Essays in Honor of James L. Kugel*, edited by Hindy Najman and Judith H. Newman, 177–213. Leiden: Brill, 2004.

———. "Text, Context, and Pretext: Review Essay of Yehuda Liebes's *Ars Poetica* in *Sefer Yetsira*," *Studia Philonica Annual* 17 (2004).

———. "The Theosophy of Shabbetai Donnolo, with Special Emphasis on the Doctrine of *Sefirot* in His *Sefer Ḥakhmoni*." *Jewish History* 6 (1992): 281–316.

———. *Through a Speculum That Shines: Vision and Imagination in Medieval Jewish Mysticism*. Princeton: Princeton University Press, 1994.

———. "*Tiqqun ha-Shekhinah*: Redemption and the Overcoming of Gender Dimorphism in the Messianic Kabbalah of Moses Ḥayyim Luzzatto." *History of Religions* 36 (1997): 289–332.

———. *Venturing Beyond—Law and Morality in Kabbalistic Mysticism*. Oxford: Oxford University Press, 2005.

———. "Walking as a Sacred Duty: Theological Transformation of Social Reality in Early Hasidism." In *Hasidism Reconsidered*, edited by Ada Rapoport-Albert, 180–207. London: Litman Library of Jewish Civilization, 1996. Reprinted in Elliot R. Wolfson, *Along the Path: Studies in Kabbalistic Myth, Symbolism, and Hermeneutics*, 89–109. Albany: State University of New York Press, 1995.

———. "Weeping, Death, and Spiritual Ascent in Sixteenth-Century Jewish Mysticism." In *Death, Ecstasy, and Other Worldly Journeys*, edited by John J. Collins and Michael Fishbane, 209–247. Albany: State University of New York Press, 1995.

———. "Woman—The Feminine as Other in Theosophic Kabbalah: Some Philosophical Observations on the Divine Androgyne." In *The Other in Jewish Thought and History: Constructions of Jewish Culture and Identity*, edited by Laurence Silberstein and Robert Cohn, 166–204. New York: New York University Press, 1994.

———. "*Yeridah la-Merkavah*: Typology of Ecstasy and Enthronement in Early Jewish Mysticism." In *Mystics of the Book: Themes, Topics, and Typologies*, edited by Robert A. Herrera, 13–44. New York: Peter Lang, 1993.

Wolfson, Harry A. *Philo: Foundations of Religious Philosophy in Judaism, Christianity, and Islam*. 2 vols. Cambridge, Mass.: Harvard University Press, 1947.

———. *The Philosophy of the Kalam*. Cambridge, Mass: Harvard University Press, 1976.

———. *Studies in the History of Philosophy and Religion*. 2 vols. Edited by Isadore Twersky and George H. Williams. Cambridge, Mass.: Harvard University Press, 1973–1977.

Wolin, Richard. *Walter Benjamin: An Aesthetic of Redemption*. New York: Columbia University Press, 1982.

Wolosky, Shira. *Language Mysticism: The Negative Way of Language in Eliot, Beckett, and Celan*. Stanford: Stanford University Press, 1995.

———. "Mystical Language and Mystical Silence in Paul Celan's 'Dein Hinubersein.'" In *Argumentum e Silentio. Paul Celan International Symposium*, edited by Ami Colin, 364–375. Berlin and New York: Walter de Gruyter, 1987.

Wood, David. *The Deconstruction of Time*. Atlantic Highlands: Humanities Press International, 1989.

———, ed. *Philosophers' Poets*. London and New York: Routledge, 1990.

Wood, David, and Robert Bernasconi, eds. *Derrida and Différance*. Evanston: Northwestern University Press, 1988.

Woods, Gregory. *Articulate Flesh: Male Homo-Eroticism and Modern Poetry*. New Haven: Yale University Press, 1987.

Wright, C. S. "The Influence of the Exegetical Tradition of the 'Song of Songs' on the Secular and Religious Love Lyrics in Ms. Harley 2253." Ph.D. dissertation, University of California, Berkeley, 1966.

Wright, T. R. "Midrash and Intertexuality: Ancient Rabbinic Exegesis and Postmodern Reading of the Bible." In *Divine Aporia: Postmodern Conversations about the Other*, edited by John C. Hawley, 97–119. Lewisburg: Bucknell University Press, 2000.

Wurzer, Wilhelm S. ". . . wild being/*écart*/capital." In *Écart & Différance: Merleau-Ponty and Derrida on Seeing and Writing*, edited by Martin C. Dillon, 234–244. Atlantic Highlands: Humanities Press, 1997.

Wyschogrod, Edith. "Texts in Transit: From the Academy to Religious Experience and Back." In *The Unknown, Remembered Gate: Religious Experience and Hermeneutical Reflection in the Study of Religion*, edited by Elliot R. Wolfson and Jeffrey J. Kripal, 43–54. New and York and London: Seven Bridges Press, 2005.

Yahalom, Joseph. "Angels Do Not Understand Aramaic: On the Literary Use of Jewish Palestinian Aramaic in Late Antiquity." *Journal of Jewish Studies* 47 (1996): 33–44.

Yao, Xinzhong. "Harmony of Yin and Yang: Cosmology and Sexuality in Daoism." In *Sexuality and the World's Religions*, edited by David W. Machacek and Melissa M. Wilkcox, 67–99. Santa Barbara: ABC-CLIO, 2003.

Yates, Francis. *The Occult Philosophy in the Elizabethan Age*. London: Routledge & Kegan Paul, 1979.

Yee, Gale A. "I Have Perfumed My Bed with Myrrh: The Foreign Woman (*'issā zarā*) in Proverbs 1–9." In *A Feminist Companion to Wisdom Literature*, edited by Athalya Brenner, 110–126. Sheffield: Sheffield Academic Press, 1995.

Yourgrau, Palle. *The Disappearance of Time: Kurt Gödel and the Idealistic Tradition in Philosophy*. Cambridge and New York: Cambridge University Press, 1991.

Zaehner, Robert C. *Mysticism, Sacred and Profane: An Inquiry into Some Varieties of Praeter-Natural Experience*. Oxford: Oxford University Press, 1957.

Zarader, Marlène. *La dette impensée: Heidegger et l'héritage hébraïque*. Paris: Éditions du Seuil, 1990.

———. *Heidegger et les paroles de l'origine*. Preface by Emmanuel Lévinas. Paris: Librairie Philosophique J. Vrin, 1986.

———. "Phenomenality and Transcendence." In *Transcendence in Philosophy and Religion*, edited by James E. Faulconer, 106–119. Bloomington and Indianapolis: Indiana University Press, 2003.

Zebiri, Kate. "Contemporary Muslim Understanding of the Miracle of Jesus." *The Muslim World* 90 (2000): 71–90.

Zeitlin, Froma I. *Playing the Other: Gender and Society in Classical Greek Literature*. Chicago and London: University of Chicago Press, 1996.

Zhang, Longxi. *The Tao and the Logos: Literary Hermeneutics, East and West, Post-Contemporary Interventions*. Durham: Duke University Press, 1992.

Zhang, Shi-Ying. "Heidegger and Taoism." In *Reading Heidegger: Commemorations*, edited by John Sallis, 307–320. Bloomington and Indianapolis: Indiana University Press, 1993.

Ziai, Hossein. "Ḥāfeẓ, Lisān al-Ghayb of Persian Poetic Wisdom." In *Gott ist schön und Er liebt die*

Schönheit: Festschrift für Annemarie Schimmel zum 7. April 1992, edited by Alma Giese and J. Christoph Bürgel, 449–469. Bern: Peter Lang, 1994.

———. *Knowledge and Illumination.* Atlanta: Scholars Press, 1990.

Ziarek, Krzysztof. *The Historicity of Experience: Modernity, the Avant-Garde, and the Event.* Evanston: Northwestern University Press, 2001.

———. *Inflected Language: Toward a Hermeneutics of Nearness: Heidegger, Levinas, Stevens, Celan.* Albany: State University of New York Press, 1994.

Zias, Joseph E. "The Cemeteries of Qumran and Celibacy: Confusion Laid to Rest?" *Dead Sea Discoveries* 7 (2000): 220–253.

Zimmer, Heinrich. "On the Significance of the Indian Tantric Yoga." In *Spiritual Disciplines: Papers from the Eranos Yearbook*, edited by Joseph Campbell, 3–58. Princeton: Princeton University Press, 1985.

Žižek, Slavoj. *For They Know Not What They Do: Enjoyment as a Political Factor.* 2nd ed. London and New York: Verso, 2002.

———. *The Puppet and the Dwarf: The Perverse Core of Christianity.* Cambridge, Mass.: MIT Press, 2003.

———. *Tarrying with the Negative: Kant, Hegel, and the Critique of Ideology.* Durham: Duke University Press, 1993.

Zupancic, Alenka. *The Shortest Shadow: Nietzsche's Philosophy of the Two.* Cambridge, Mass.: MIT Press, 2003.

Index of Names and Book Titles

Aaron: lifting of his hands, 152, 177, 232, 377; sister of, 530n247; sons of, 266, 548n34
Abel, 80, 459n250, 505n195
Abihu, 266, 267, 548n38; death of atones for the sins of Israel, 548n36
Abraham, 37, 69, 433n367, 457n236; and the attempted sacrifice of Isaac, 160; covenant of, 243; and the covenant of circumcision, 139, 488nn210–11; change in his visionary status, 135; daughter given to, 494n53, 497n84; epiphany of three angels in the form of men, 252; first to be circumcised and to abolish the left, 486n184; Hebrew spoken by, 203; letters of transposed into *meha-ever,* 139; merited seeing the incarnation of the Trinity, 485n180; rendered perfect by circumcision, 82; *Sefer Yesirah* attributed to, 509n244; visionary status of after the circumcision, 135
Abraham bar Ḥiyya, 565n98
Abraham ben David of Posquiéres, 167–68, 170–71, 280, 505n198, 518n92
Abraham ben Isaac, 529n237
Abulafia, Abraham, 27, 88, 120, 139–40, 203, 204, 234, 236–42, 317, 348, 400n11, 403n288, 406n78, 423n257, 424n292, 487nn208–209, 488nn210–12, 494–495n29, 504n184, 505n196, 518n94, 518n99, 519n112, 520n123, 522n136, 534n309, 535nn314–16, nn318–19, n321; 536nn323, n325, nn327–28, n335, nn337–38; 536–37n344, 537nn347, n348, n351; 547n29; 554n142; 555n151; 569n168; 576n25; 583n123; 586n150; disciples of, 120, 345; and Yoga, 535n310
Abulafia, Todros ben Joseph Abulafia, 145, 283–84, 490n20
Acts of Thomas, 498n98, 499n102
Adam, 9, 11, 35, 36, 51, 61, 80, 109, 148, 248, 258, 356; adopted celibacy after the sin in the Garden of Eden, 561n35; androgynous nature of, 169, 170, 171, 173, 175, 177, 260, 376, 471n435, 490n19, 493n44, n45; angelic body of, 248; bestowed names on all living creatures, 197; came into being from two virgins, 503n172; cast down from heaven to earth, 51; comprises male and female, 146, 149, 151, 180, 259, 310; configured as the name YHWH, 128; constructed by means of the letters, 208; copulation after the sin of, 185; correlated with Israel, 258; corresponds to *Ze'eir Anpin,* 185; created before Eve, 53; created by means of the Written and Oral Torah, 257; created by the mystery of faith, 146; created from the virgin earth, 491n36; created in the image of God, 121, 147, 168, 169, 176, 209; created in the image of seven forms, 164; created initially as male, 171; created two-faced, 62, 145–46, 151, 168, 176; death arises as a consequence of the separation of Eve from, 165, 491n36; designation applies only to a man who is married, 506n206; endowed with image of God, 35; enlarged the crown, 369; and Eve engaged with intelligible matters, 315; Eve separated from, 166, 470–71n431, 594n40; Eve's desire to be equal to, 61; female created from, 159, 356, 373, 376, 493n45, 504n172, 508n244; form of completed the ten *sefirot,* 169; garbed angelically, 248; Jesus on a par with, 226; Hebrew spoken by, 203, 519n102; language, 197; limbs of correspond to the commandments, 539n376; made in the image of the name, 208; mystery of, 259; original embodiment of, 253; original unity of, 376; pos-

sessed a spiritualized body, 569n152; primal/primordial, 9, 35, 61, 62, 109, 128, 175, 176, 208, 369, 439n35, 471n435, 544n450, 548n29; primordial sin, 369, 439n39; prior to having eaten the forbidden fruit completely spiritual, 248; reparation of by restoring the female to the male, 375; represents the perfect man, 432n367; secret of, 547n29; sexual intimacy with Eve troped as a form of knowledge, 270, 528n228, 549n58; *Shekhinah* in the image of, 384; sin of consisted of expanding the crown of *Ze*ʿ*eir Anpin*, 369; supernal, 180; symbolized by Christ, 52, 491n36; transgression of, 80, 459n251, 511n263; transgression of rectified by the messiah, 183, 369; twelve signs of, 384; women excluded from the category of, 59

Adir ba-Marom, 452n187, 453n196, 459n252, 591n11

Agrippa von Nettesheim, Heinrich Cornelius, 594n40

Aḥer (Elisha ben Abuyah), 369; and the heresy of two powers, 174

Air and Dreams, 476n55

Alkabets, Solomon, 506n207

Allah, 574n2; all things created by will of, 205; beyond male and female, 563n76; covered by a veil, 232; designated as unseen (*ghayb*), 228; envisioned as father, 207; face of abiding, 228; Folk of, 528n230; light of reflected in the mirror of the soul, 475n46; liturgical glorification of, 205; prayer directed exclusively to, 205

Allogenes, 157, 303

Altmann, Alexander, 244

Ambrose, 335

Ami, Rabbi, 521n135

Amora, Rabbi, 164, 277

Amrani, Azariah Ḥai, 484n153

al-Āmulī, Abu ʾl-ʿAbbās, 227

al-Fayyūmī, Nathanel Ibn, 517–18n89

Anatoli, Jacob, 566n109

Anaxagoras, 212

An Essay on Man, 6

Antigonus, 247

Apocryphon of John, 157, 303

Aqiva, Rabbi, 253, 335, 348, 359, 369, 370, 580n75

Aripul, Samuel, 576n28

Aristotle, xix, 32, 108, 268, 303

Asclepius, 572n204

Asher ben David, 172, 428n324, 445n98, 492n38, 496n76, 503n158, 505nn190, n197, 521n131, 543n436, 545n452

Asherah, 143

Ashkenazi, Joseph ben Shalom, 64, 178, 179, 203, 518n92

Astarte, 143

ʿAṭṭār, Farīduddīn, 225, 305

Aṭeret Shalom, 589n217

Augustine, 205, 339, 430n354, 519n109, 545n458, 561n41

Avina, Rabbi, 237

Averroës (Ibn Rushd), 27–28, 541n400

Avicenna, 27, 239, 346

Avodat ha-Qodesh, 431n365

Avot de-Rabbi Natan, 517n88, 538n356, 541n388, 550n76

Azulai, Abraham, 443n81, 457n231, 587n165

Azriel of Gerona, 29, 96–99, 178, 198, 199, 200, 208, 208–209, 249, 250, 281, 283, 288, 293–294, 425n294, 425n300, 458n240, 466nn333, n335, n337, nn342–44, n348, 467nn351, n353, n354, n356, n357, 468n492, 515nn61–62, 520n120, 528n224, 529n237, 539n374, 540n384, 542nn403, n404, n406, n408, n409, 546n12, 552nn110, n118, n119, 555nn153, n154, 556n184, 569n156

Baʿalei ha-Nefesh, 170, 505n198

Bachelard, Gaston, 476n55

Bachrach, Naftali, 372, 431n357, 590n1

Baddei ha-Aron u-Migdal Ḥananel, 198, 282, 502n143, 515n55, 553nn121–123, nn125–n126, n129, 566n107

Baḥya ben Asher, 32, 425n296, 594n176, 506n213, 548n29, 568n140, 569n152, 570n176, 582n105

Barbelo, 303, 304

Barnabas, 50

Barthes, Roland, 113

Basil of Ancyra, 302

Bataille, Georges, 297

Baudelaire, Charles, 41–42

Beauvoir, Simone de, 302

Beit Moʿed, 535n322

Beiträge zur Philosophie (Vom Ereignis), 13

Ben Azzai, 369

Benjamin, Walter, 9, 11, 12, 26, 119, 123; affinities with Wittgenstein, 406n85; and Heidegger, 407n89, 416n189; impact on Scholem's understanding of mystical language, 405n74; relationship of his theory of language to the kabbalah, 405–406n78

Ben Zoma, 161, 264, 369

Berachiah, Rabbi, 308
Bergson, Henri, xvi, xxvii
Bernard of Clairvaux, 338–44, 577nn35, 36, 578nn38, n39, n40, n42, n43, n44, n46, n47, n48, n49, n50, n51, n53, n54, 579nn55, n56, n57, n59, n60, n62, n63, n64, n65, n66, n69
Betti, Emilo, 114
Be'ur al ha-Torah (Baḥya), 548n29, 569n152, 570n176
Be'ur al ha-Torah (Recanati), 568n147, 569n152, 571n190
Bezalel, and Moses, 458n239
Bhaskararaya, 559n17
Bisṭāmī, Abū Yazīd al-, 227
Blake, William, 212, 297
Blanchot, Maurice, 113, 287, 288–89, 292
Bloom, Harold, 42, 45
Boethius, 547n28
Böhme, Jacob, xvi, 8, 103, 197, 402n49, 423n259, 514n45; affinity with Jewish esotericism, 392n1, 393n2, 421n241; affirms a nexus between circumcision of the flesh and revelatory experience of divine embodiment, 485–86n180; conception of the androgynous Adam affirmed by, 471n435; influenced by Christian kabbalah, 468n392
Book of Mirrors, 425n302, 450n157, 492n38, 507nn232, n237, 508nn238, n242
Book of the Covenant, 566n109
Book of the Pomegranate, 426nn305, n308, n309, 427nn320, n323, 428n327, 431n358, 445n98, 450n164, 457n236, 458n246, 505n195, 511n264, 573n217, n223, 594n43. *See also* Sefer ha-Rimmon
Borges, Jorge Luis, 114, 473n15, 539–40n380
Bourdieu, Pierre, 79
Brenner, Althalya, 187
Buddha, 56–57, 441n66, 442n72; maternal images attributed to, 456n231
Burrus, Virginia, 299
Bustan al-ʿuqul, 517n89
Bynum, Caroline Walker, 81, 344

Cacciari, Massimo, 116–17
Cain, 80; associated with the attribute of the feminine that comes forth from the power of judgment, 459n250; identified symbolically as the Tree of Knowledge on the leftm 505n195; progeny of Samael and Eve, 444n86; root of, 548n38, 590n2
Cassianus, Julius, 52
Cassirer, Ernst, 6, 7
Celan, Paul, 418n206, 431–32n362
Chevalier, Jacques, 89
Christ: androgynous nature of, 491n36; aura encircles body of, 543n436; baptized in, 49, 50; beyond being, 422n248; born from a virgin, 503n172; bride of, 301, 302, 344, 563n67, 569n173, 571n196; and the Church, 166, 334, 335, 337, 344, 500n127, 574n7; circumcision a sign to receive, 486n180; communion with, 343; depicted as a Lamb, 89; divinity of from a Muslim perspective, 531n249; elevation of the body in the glorified spirit of, 343; Eucharistic presence of, 190; glorified flesh of, 513n2; head of man, 51 icon of the image of God, 478n75; image of God embodied in, 217; incarnate body of, 216, 256, 340; Jesus transfigured into, 504n172; joins male and female in the bridal chamber, 166; kiss of, 338, 339, 340; 577n32; love of the body of, 342; meeting of divine and human in, 334; men passive in the presence of, 301; name of poured like oil, 340; one in the body of, 301; overcoming of sexual difference in body of, 51, 438n22, 439n35, n44; perfect Adam symbolized by, 52; portrayed as the Lamb, 89; production of woman from the side of, 491n36; putting on, 50; radiance of in body of Scripture, 342; soul's ascetic yearning to unite with, 334; spiritual love of, 525n182, 573n224; symbol of mother ascribed to, 456–57n231; task of to repair union of male and female, 166; unified body of, 50; union with, 341, 344; virgins of, 299; wisdom of, 341; worship of, 299. *See also* Jesus
Chrysostom, John, 301
Cixous, Hélène, 87
Clement of Alexandria, 52–53, 215, 498n98
Cohen, Abraham Herrera de, 154, 402n50, 508–509n244
"Commentary on *Idra Rabba*," 512n278
Commentary on Talmudic Aggadoth, 425n300, 458n240, 466n343, 467n356, 520n120, 528n224, 529n237, 540n384, 542n403, n406, n409, 546n12, 552n110, n111, n118, n119, 555n154, 569n156
Corbin, Henry, xii, xviii, 28, 29, 30, 39, 49, 221, 239
Cordovero, Moses, 179–80, 374, 402n50, 443n81, 445n98, 447n118, 451n179, 484n164, 508n243, n244, 569–70n174; 572n206
Corrington, Robert, 205
Cozbi the Midianite, 267
Critchey, Simon, 86

Cusanus, Nicholas, xix, 30–31, 96, 100, 424nn279–84, 426–27n310, 429n336

Dainton, Barry, xviii
Daly, Mary, 136
David, 221, 377; conjoined to the three patriarchs, 353, 367; conjoined to *Yesod*, 138; praise of, 275, 278; song of, 356; symbolic of *Shekhinah*, 84, 138, 353, 458–59n250; throne of, 377, 378
David ben Ḥayyim, 576n26
David ben Yehudah he-Ḥasid, 178; 425n302, 450n157, 492n38, 507n232, 507–508n234, 508n238, 508n242
De apice theoriae as posse ipsum, 96
de Certeau, Michael, 42
de León, Moses, 33, 34, 35, 36, 37, 38, 48, 71–72, 75, 82, 84, 177, 183, 204, 222, 381–382, 425n299, 426n305, n308, n309, 425n299, 426n305, n308, n309, 427n320, n321, n323, 428n326, n327, n328, 429n342, 431n358, 450n164, 451n166, 451 n184, 457n236, 458n243, n246, n248, 459n252, 497n83, 505n195, 511n265, 527–28n219, 545n452, 557n192, 570n176, 573n217, n223, 588n183, 592–93n27, 593n33, 594n43, n44
De docta ignorantia, 30
De interpretatione, 32
Derekh ha-Qodesh, 589n226
Derrida, Jacques, xxviii, 3, 90–93, 113, 116, 158–60
Descartes, René, 194
De semine, 303
Desmond, William, 268
De vita Moysis, 216
Der Wille zur Macht, 44
Dialogue of the Savior, 54
Die fröhliche Wissenschaft, 44
Die Philosophie der Symbolischen Formen, 6
Die Weltalter, 102
Dilthey, Wilhelm, 4, 5
Divine Names, 217–18, 558n12
Dionysius the Areopagite, 10, 97, 122, 124, 213, 217–18, 271–72, 403n61, 422n248, 466n346, 479n87, 524n164, 550n67, 558n12
Donnolo, Sabbatai, 274, 275, 550n81
Dorje, Garab, 537n352
Dzogchen, 537n352

Eckhart, Meister, 42, 298, 418–19n211, 426n310, 429n336, 457n232, 472n6, 475n44, 524n162, 558–59n13
Eco, Umberto, 37, 205
Edom, 258; feminization of Jacob in relation to, 560n32; kings of, 180, 309–310, 311, 385, 386, 387, 567n117, n121, n122, 596n59; land of, 311, 386; power of from the hands, 265; symbolic of Roman Christianity, 386
Ehrenburg, Rudolf, 88
Einführung in die Metaphysik, 13
Einstein, Albert, xvii, xxx
Eleazar, Rabbi, 257, 258, 266, 354, 379, 587n179
Eleazar of Worms, 144, 276, 557n189
Eliade, Mircea, xviii, 49, 261, 263
Eliezer ben Abraham ha-Levi, 475n46
Eliezer ben Hyrcanus, 580n75
Elijah, 248, 251, 358, 587–88n179
Elijan ben Solomon (Vilna Gaon), 510n249
Elimah Rabbati, 447n118, 508n243
Emerald Tablet, 7, 61
Emerson, Ralph Waldo, 114
Empedocles, 33, 40, 212
Encyklopädie der philosophischen Wissenschaften im Grundrisse, 101
Enoch, xii, 80, 248, 251, 459n250
Enneads, 423n254, 467n362, 523n150, n153, n154, n156, n157, 524n163, n166, n168, 525n170, n172, n173, n174, n175, n176, n178, n179, 541n400
Ephraim, 132, 273; identified as the female of the arrayments of *Shekhinah*, 459n250
Epstein, Qalonymous Qalman ha-Levi, 508n242
Eriugena, John Scotus, 395n34, 466n345, 524n165, 544n436
Eṣ Ḥayyim (Ḥayyim ha-Kohen of Sativa), 422n245
Eṣ Ḥayyim (Ḥayyim Vital), 483n153, 502n143, 508n241, 510n254, n257, 511n208, 512n274, n281, n286, 549n62, 566n116, 569n169, 590n243, n244, n245, 596n63, n64, n65, n67, n68
Esau, 258; hands of, 265
Esmail, Aziz, 127
Esther, 72, 187; name of *Shekhinah*, 484n164
Eudorus, 7
Eugnostos the Blessed, 157
Eve, 53, 80, 248, 270, 302, 459n250, 493n45; and Adam created androgynous, 173; and Adam engaged in contemplation of intelligible matters, 315; contained within Adam, 165; corresponds to matter, 547–48n29; corresponds to *Nuqba* in the divine realm, 185; created from the virgin Adam, 492n36; daughters of, 554n140; desired to be equal in stature to Adam, 61; emerged from Adam, 470n431, 594n40; garments of, 248; Hebrew spoken by, 203; inseminated by the ser-

pent, 58, 59, 444n86; Mary rectifies the transgression of, 595n53; replaces the Virgin, 471n435; responsible for original sin, 53; seductive nature of, 302; separated from Adam, 166, 511n263; superiority to Adam, 594n40; weakened position of, 62
Even ha-Shoham, 447n118
Everson, William, 285, 553–54n140
Exodus Rabbah, 501n137, 502n141, 551n96, 557n188
Expository Treatise on the Soul, 155–57, 166
Ezekiel, xiii; chariot vision of, 73, 382
Ezra, identified as son of God, 531n249
Ezra ben Solomon of Gerona, 33, 34, 95, 96, 169, 246–48, 250, 263, 264, 280, 281, 288, 346, 349–50, 351, 352, 376, 389, 427n314, 498n332, n333, 505n191, 522n137, 529n237, 540n381, n382, n384, n385, 541 n387, n395, n396, 534n436, 546n12, n14, 16, 552n110, n120, 572n207, 584n131, n132, n133, 585n137

Fano, Menaḥem Azariah of, 186–87, 512n285, n287
Fausto-Sterling, Anne, 80
Ferstman, Carla J., 306
Foucault, Michel, 3, 80, 85, 300
Freud, Sigmund, 119, 126, 129, 298
Fuṣūṣ al-ḥikam, 229
Futūḥāt al-makkiyya, 232

Gabriel, 226, 231; identified as the Active Intellect, 534n302
Gadamer, Hans-Georg, 10, 12, 112, 113
Galante, Abraham, 446n115, 553n137
Galen, 107–108, 269, 303, 353
Galya Raza, 353–54
Garlands of Light, 558n10
Gate of Heaven (*Puerta del Cielo*), 508–509n244
Genesis Apocryphon, 444n91
Genesis Rabbah, 274, 445n104, 451n173, 457n236, 458n243, 458n244, 490n19, 501n139, 505n139, 507n226, 510n252, 516n79, 529n237, 535n312, 541n401, 547n25, 550n77, 551n96, 566–67n117, 594n50, 596n65
George, Stefan, 16, 20
Gerad, René, 160
German Pietists, 144, 348. *See also* Rhineland Jewish Pietists
Gerondi, Jonah, 199, 586n151
Ghazālī, Abū Ḥāmid al-, 27–28, 230, 533n285, n286, n287, 541n400
Gikatilla, Joseph, 63, 137–40, 149, 203, 207–208, 256, 331, 332, 348, 351, 358–59, 371, 427n320, 445n98, 447n120, n122, 448n124, n125, 487n201, n205, n207, 488n213, 493n46, 520n114, 533n278, 538n354, 548n29, 553n113,565n93, 570n176, 565n93, 570n176, 573n221, 574n243, n246, 583n124, n125, 586n156, 588n185, n187, n191, 590n249
Ginnat Egoz, 348, 427n320, 583n126
Goethe, J. W., 8
Gold, Penny, 77
Gold, Thomas, xviii
Gospel according to the Egyptians, 52, 304
Gospel of Mary, 54
Gospel of Philip, 165–66
Gospel of Thomas, 50, 53–54, 55, 165, 304, 373
Gospel of Truth, 272
Green, Monica, 134
Gregory of Nyssa, 53, 215–18
Gross, Rita, 56, 58
Grosz, Elizabeth, 87, 146
Guide of the Perplexed, 88, 220, 239, 346, 443n83, 486n184, 526n210, 527n219, 535n317, 546n15, 547n29, 568n151, 569n159, 582n102, n107, 585n150
Gulshan-e Rāz, 29

Hadar: corresponds symbolically to *Yesod*, 311; eighth of the Edomite kings, 310, 387; identified as the attribute of Hesed, 567n122; only Edomite king whose wife is mentioned, 311
Ḥāfiẓ, Muḥammad Shamsuddīn, 233
Halevi, David ben Samuel, 580n75
Halevi, Judah, 203, 204, 469n396, 486n184, 517n84, n85, n86, n87, n88, n89, 518n92, 519n101, n102, 564n85, 583n98
Hamnuna Sava, 38, 361
Harpham, Geoffrey, 115
Ḥaver, Yiṣḥaq Isaac, 465n322
Ḥayyat, Judah, 121, 484n160
Ḥayy ibn Yaqẓān, 346
Ḥayyei ha-Nefesh, 537n347
Ḥayyei Olam ha-Ba, 237–38, 240, 408n210, 536n325, n327, n335, n357, 536n344, 547n29
Hegel, G. W. F., 101–102, 104, 129; and the idea of system, 89; and the identity of identity and non-identity, 26; and the logic of identity of difference, 101
Hegyon ha-Nephesch ha-Atzuvah, 565n98
Heidegger, Martin, xiv, xvi, xxix, xxx, 3, 6, 10, 12–23, 25, 32, 98, 103, 111–12, 191, 195; and Benjamin, 407n89, 416n189; and Nazism,

420–21n241; and the rabbinic mode of midrashic hermeneutics, 415–16n184; and Wittgenstein, 410nn127–29, 413n173, 419n211
Heidenthum und Kabbala, 3
Heikhalot Rabbati, 143
Hélios, 66
Ḥemdat Yamim, 564n89
Heracleon, 498n98
Heraclitus, 114, 410n130, 414n178, 434n386
Hermès, 66
Ḥesed le-Avraham, 457n231, 587n164
Hezeqiah, 48, 49
Ḥikmat al-ishrāq, 532n268
Hildegard of Bingen, 344, 456n230, 457n231, 595n53
Hilkhot ha-Kavod, 276
Hillman, James, 126
Hippocrates, 353
Hippolytus, 304, 498–99n102
Ḥisda, Rabbi, 284
Ḥiyya, Rabbi, 257
Hölderlin, F., xiv, 16
Hollywood, Amy, 343
Ḥovot ha-Levavot, 346, 582n94
Horkheimer, Max, 125
Horowitz, Isaiah ben Abraham, 564n88
Horowitz, Maryanne Cline, 317
Ḥoter ben Shelomo, 583n120
House of Divinity (*Casa de la Divinida*), 508–509n244
Howells, Christina, 91
al-Hujwīrī, ʿAlī al-Jullābī, 227–28
Husserl, Edmund, xxiv, xxvi, xxviii, xxix, xxx, 6, 7, 11, 90, 91, 192

Ibn Adret, Solomon, 121, 198
Ibn al-ʿArabī, Muḥyīddīn, 28, 206, 207, 221, 222, 229, 231–32, 239, 391n3, n5; 423n266, 454n211, 493n40, 505n197, 530n239, 532n276, 533n282, n295, n296, 564n81, 585n145
Ibn Aqnin, Joseph ben Judah, 347, 350, 351, 536n332, 583n108, n109, n110
Ibn Ezra, Abraham, 346, 452n190, 486n184, 517n87, 519n102, 534n309, 584n130
Ibn Gabbai, Meir, 41, 431n356, 586n161
Ibn Gaon, Shem Tov, 198, 282, 502n143, 515n55, 566n107
Ibn Latif, Isaac, 535n314
Ibn Malka, Judah ben Nissim, 294
Ibn Paquda, Baḥya, 346, 582n94
Ibn Sahula, Isaac, 350, 351, 352, 576n21, 585n138, n139, n140, n149
Ibn Ṣayyaḥ, Joseph, 447n118
Ibn Ṭabul, Joseph, 184
Ibn Tibbon, Judah, 507n232
Ibn Tibbon, Moses, 347, 582n107, 583n111, n112, n113, n114, n115
Ibn Tibbon, Samuel, 526n211, 582–83n108, 584n134
Idel, Moshe, 81, 204, 346
Idra Rabba, 76, 179, 180–81, 183, 316, 402n55, 424n290, 428n334, 429n339, 507n218, 567n122
Idra Zuṭa, 8–9, 402n53, 507n220, 590n233, 594n40
Iggeret ha-Qodesh, 314–16, 565n93, 569n152, n154, n159
Iggeret Ḥay ben Meqiṣ, 346
Iggeret le-Burgos, 556n184
Iggeret Sod ha-Geʾullah, 475n46
Ihde, Don, 6
Imrei Shefer, 203, 487n209, 488n211, 494–95n59, 504n184, 505n196, 518n95
Irenaeus, 110, 498n98
Irigaray, Luce, 80, 86, 87, 134
Isaac, 37, 69, 83, 265; attempted sacrifice of, 160
Isaac, Rabbi, 59, 257, 310, 313, 328, 355
Isaac ben Ḥayyim ha-Kohen, 422n245
Isaac ben Todros, 198
Isaac ha-Kohen, 497n83
Isaac of Acre, 61–62, 124–25, 133, 291
Isaac the Blind, 33, 120, 168, 199–200, 208, 210–11, 218–19, 220, 249, 263, 264, 280, 285, 291, 308, 309, 451n176, 453n197, 503n158, 515n65, 519n102, 521n136, 523n145, 529n237, 543n436, 596n60
Ishmael, Rabbi, xii, 253, 255; school of, 236
Israel ben Eliezer, Baʿal Shem Tov, 388
Isserles, Moses, 580n75
Izutsu, Toshihiko, 29–30

Jabès, Edmond, 418n206, 432n362
Jacob, 8, 33, 37, 38, 123, 124, 132, 258; and the attribute of mercy, 37, 505n195; and the attribute of truth, 33, 534n306; blessings of bestowed on Ephraim and Menasseh, 132; contest with the angel, 536n332; designation of *Malkhut*, 537n344; did not die, 251; feminization of in relation to Edom, 560n32; granddaughter of, 597n83; and the holy spirit, 69; icon of engraved on the throne, 143, 144, 145, 426n306, 489–90nn17–18; identity of blurred with the throne, 145; and the image of the sun, 360; Joseph saved by seeing the image of, 567n117; journey from Beersheba to

Ḥaran, 123, 124; metamorphosis of into Israel, 33; mystery of, 505n195; mystical hermeneut in emulation of, 534n306; and the name YHWH, 581n92; never separated from the supernal light, 316; perennial struggle with Esau, 258; Rebekah kissed by, 586n162; relationship with Rebekah, 581n91; secondary divine/angelic power depicted as the bride-throne, 143; stone lifted by, 377; vision of contrasted with Moses, 38; voice of, 124, 265
Jacob ben Asher, 568n145
Jacob ben Sheshet, 33, 39–40, 60, 99, 154, 197, 220, 264, 280–81, 285, 313, 314, 425n301, 430n351, 451n176, 458n240, 467n360, n361, 496n76, 504n186, 505n190, 515n51, 526n211, 546n18, 552n113, n114, n116, n117, n119, 554n143, 568n141, 569n155
Jaʿfar al-Ṣādiq, 228
Jakobson, Roman, 4, 6, 89
James, William, 398n116, 418n207
Jantzen, Grace, 338, 341, 343, 344
Japeth ben Eli, 345
Jerome, Saint, 301, 335
Jesse, 362
Jesus, 55, 207, 302, 304; admonition to shun marriage, 471n435; androgyny of, 491n36; angelic form of, 430n354; attribution of spirit to, 531n253; born by the womb of Mary, 55, 491n36; breaking the bread, 342; characterization of in the Qu'rān, 531n249; circumcised penis of, 305; contrasted with Adam, 503–504n172; death of, 486n180; depicted as *ben niddah*, 538n248; depicted as generative mother, 82, 456–57n231; depicted as male lover in relation to the soul, 350, 573n224, 574n248; dicta of, 200; embodiment of the *coincidentia oppositorum*, 424n279; emphasis on humility of, 579n69; emptying himself, 340–41; emulation of, 341; erasure of sexual difference in the unity of, 301; female disciples of, 438n27; feminine images of, 457n232; firstborn of God, 156; gaze of, 424n282; husband of Margery Kempe, 571n196; ideal of ascetic practice in Sufism, 531n252; identified as glory of God and divine name, 430n354; icon of the invisible God, 478n75; identified as wisdom, 430n354, 457n231; in the Qu'rān, 531n249; incarnation of the Word in the person of, 191, 243, 260, 305, 342; issued from womb of a virgin, 167; kiss of, 339, 340; love of, 341–42; maternal representations of, 456–57n231; mother of, 305; mystery embedded within, 422n248; offspring of an adulterous act, 531 n. 248; on a par with Adam, 226; portrayed as feminine, 51; provides an androgynous model of personhood, 457n231; relation to the Church depicted figuratively in the Song, 334, 337; representation of in female images, 438n28; response to the Sadducees, 302; response to Salome, 52; response to Simon Peter, 53–54, 165; self-deprecation of, 341; son of God, 498n97; suffering of, 300; uncreated Word of God, 519n108; union of female with, 344; unites with virgin in the bridal chamber, 498n98; unity of all baptized in, 49–50, 301; virginal conception of, 444n86, 530n248; word incarnate, 31, 40, 424n279; worship of, 531n250; zoharic fraternity compared to the circle of, 259
Jewel Brocade, 56
John, 342
John of Salisbury, 10
Jose, Rabbi, 256, 379, 427n315
Joseph, 132, 453n367; blessing bestowed upon, 132; designated the righteous one, 132, 380, 459n250, 512n280; drops of his semen and the ten martyrs of the kingdom, 310, 387, 567n117, 596n66; embodies the phallic potency, 459n250; emission of semen in vain, 566n116, female spouse of, 593n30; marked of the masculine, 459n250; occluded nature of, 132; placed in a coffin, 593n37; saw the icon of Jacob, 567n117; sold into slavery, 310; sons of, 132; wife of, 530n247; withstood the temptation of the wife of Potiphar, 566–67n117
Joseph, Rabbi, 59, 436n8
Joseph of Hamadan, 72–73, 178, 243–45, 256, 349, 352, 383–84, 447n122, 448n125, 451n171, n172, n175, n176, n177, 484n164, 528n223, 539n363, n365, n366, n367, n372, 586n150, n154, 587n165, 588n198, 589n207, 594n48, n49, n51, 594–95n52
Joshua, 252
Joshua ben Levi, 273, 274, 384, 594n41
Judah, Rabbi, 257, 258, 377, 378
Judas, 54–55
Julian of Norwich, 82, 457n231
Junayd, Abū l-Qāsim al-, 227
Jung, Carl G., 49, 67; description of poetry as the conflation of the visual and verbal, 411n134; on the nexus of asceticism and eroticism, 558n6; on the role of quaternity in Western alchemy, 154

Kabbala Denudata, 103, 154
Kad ha-Qemaḥ, 582n105

Kafka, Franz, 92, 93
Kant, Immanuel, xxx, 67, 195
Karo, Joseph, 580n75
Kashf al-maḥjūb, 227
Keizan, 423n255
Kempe, Margery, 571n196
Kerouac, Jack, 432n366
Ketem Paz, 176–77, 465n321, 507n227
Kierkegaard, Søren, 160, 432n366
Kimhi, Joseph, 566n109
Kitāb al-aḥadiyah, 232
Kitāb al-mawāqif, 225
Kumin, Seth Daniel, 48

Lacan, Jacques, 128–32, 135–36, 148, 269, 278, 279; explicit reference to kabbalah made by, 482n119
Lao-tzu, 107
Laozi, 107
Lavi, Simeon, 94, 176, 284, 465n321, 507n227
Leah, 270
Lekhah Dodi, 506n307
Lemaire, Anika, 129
Levinas, Emmanuel, 113, 287, 403n60, 432n362
Leviticus Rabbah, 490n19, 492n39, 495n63, 538n356, 548n34, 551n96, 575n16, 590n248
Liebes, Yehuda, 36–38, 48
Lilith, 59, 568n144; and Mary, 68, 137; and Samael, 137; and *Shekhinah*, 60, 444n95
Liqquṭei Eṣot, 570n181
Liqquṭei Halakhot, 469n411
Liqquṭei MoHaRaN, 106, 469n409
Liqquṭei Raza de-Malka Qaddisha, 511n267
Liqquṭei Shikheḥah u-Fe'ah, 403n61, 452n192, 541n391, n396
Liqquṭei Torah, 458n247, 465n325, 566n116, 590n240, n241
Lotus Sutra, 441n66, 442n71
Lovejoy, Arthur, 221
Luke, 342
Luria, Isaac, 76, 77, 79, 80, 95, 105, 118, 120, 181, 182, 270, 310, 368, 386, 388, 392n2, 412n155, 454n212, 458n241, 476n59, 511n264, 512n280, 586n149, 589n217, 590n2
Lusthaus, Dan, xvi
Luzzatto, Moses Ḥayyim, 75–77, 95, 105, 375, 388, 392, 452n187, n188, 453n196, n199, 459n252, 466n330, n331, 591n10, n11

Ma'amar al ha-Aṣilut ha-Semo'lit, 497n83
Ma'amar Yiqqawu ha-Mayim, 526n211
Ma'amar al Penimiyyut ha-Torah, 351
Ma'arekhet ha-Elohut, 121, 172, 477n61, n64, 506n207, n209
Mahakasyapa, 56
Maimonides (Moses ben Maimon), 88, 198, 203, 220, 236, 237, 238, 240, 252, 264, 307, 346, 348, 352, 425n297, 443n83, 486n184, 519n102, 526nn209–211, 527–28n219, 535n317, 546n15, 547–48n29, 560n25, 564n85, 568n139, n145, n151, 569n159, 581n90, 582n101, n105, n106, n107, 583n124, 585–86n149
Major Trends in Jewish Mysticism, 47, 388
Malmad ha-Talmidim, 566n109
Ma'or wa-Shemesh, 508n242
Maria the Prophetess, 154
Marion, Jean-Luc, 9
Marsanes, 304
Martyrdom of Peter, 50
Mary, 55, 68, 81; and the body of the Church, 302; Christological symbol of, 157; devotional imagery, 259; iconographic depictions of, 77–78; identification with Eve, 595n53; occlusion of behind the curtain, 226; portrayed as a sealed garden, 485n166; rectifies transgression of Eve, 595n53; and representations of *Shekhinah*, 435n2, 455–56n224, 545n454; virginity of emulated by brides of Christ, 344; virgin status in the Qur'ān, 226
Maryam, 225; included in the ranks of men at the time of the resurrection, 305
Mary Magdalene, 53–55; transformed into a male, 165
Mathnawī, 228
Matthew, 54
Mavo She'arim, 512n286, 596n 63, 70
McGinn, Bernard, 333
McGuire, Anne, 110
Mehetabel, 311
Meir, Rabbi, 561n35
Meir ben Simeon of Narbonne, 255
Me'irat Einayim, 125, 479n92, 484n162, 505n200, 569n154, 574n240
Mekhilta de-Rabbi Ishmael, 551n91
Menaḥem Mendel, 589n218
Menaḥem Mendel of Shklov, 589n226
Menasseh, 132
Merleau-Ponty, Maurice, xxi–xxx, 24, 25, 190, 191–96; and Eastern philosophy, 396n69, 420n229, 513n9; and Wittgenstein on language and embodiment, 419n227
Metaphysics, 107

Metatron, xii, 354, 487n209; assumes the firgure of Torah, 241; anthropomorphic personification of the Active Intellect, 240; depicted as an infant, 555n137; desire of Moses to behold, 487n209; identified as the angel of the presence, 240; identified as Moses, 240, 487n209; opposites cohere in, 536–37n344; represented symbolically as the high priest, 239; and the Tree of Knowledge, 537n344; visualized either as young or old, 537n344
Midrash ha-Neʿelam, 427n316, 444n85, 487n209, 549n43, 568n140, n144, n146, 570n176, n177, 579–80n75, 585n149, 588n188
Midrash Mishle, 567n118
Midrash Tanḥuma, 501n137
Midrash Tehillim, 389, 467n354, 550n76, 596n79
Miles, Margaret, 136
Miller, Patricia Cox, 335
Minḥat Yehudah, 484n160
Mishkāt al-anwār, 230
Mishnah, 299; masters of, 365; secret of, 146, 266
Mishneh Torah, 220, 346, 425n297, 526n209, 535n314, 568n145, n151, 571n180, 582n100
Moi, Toril, 79
Molitor, Franz Joseph, 406n78
Mopsik, Charles, 148, 312
Moses, 38, 39, 41, 50, 173, 354; alludes figuratively to Metatron, 240; beheld the ineffable and mysterious illumination, 216; and Bezalel, 458n239; body of materialized and sustained through the splendor of the presence, 254, 255; celibacy of, 313, 321; comprises the souls of all the Israelites, 431n357; and the covenant of the tongue, 139; denied comprehension of the fiftieth gate of understanding, 188; denied vision of God's face, 228; desire of to behold Metatron, 487n209; divested himself of the body, 216; entered into a dark cloud, 217; inability to gaze upon the face of, 385; inaugural vision of, 353; interminable exodus initiated by, 116; letters of transposed into *ha-shem*, 139; name *ehyeh asher ehyeh* revealed to, 196; plunged into the darkness of unknowing, 218; removed sandals from his feet, 216; saw the glory through the speculum that shines, 228; sees the divine without any screen, 228; separated from his wife, 313, 321; song of, 356, 362; staff of, 590n244; Torah of, 200; united with *Shekhinah*, 313, 321, 389. *See also* mosheh
Moses and Monotheism, 119
mosheh, decoded as *meṭaṭron sar ha-panim*, 240
Muḥammad, 224, 228, 231, 517n84, 586n151
Mysterium Magnum, 485–86n180.
Mystical Theology, 218, 403n61, 466n346

Nadab, 266, 267; death of atones for the sins of Israel, 548n36
Nāgārjuna, 403n61, 404n62, 422n249, 441n67
Naḥman of Bratslav, 106, 469n409; 570n181
Naḥmanides (Moses ben Naḥman, Ramban), 121, 198, 199, 249, 250, 251, 252, 253, 254, 255, 282, 452n192, 494n53, 539n362, 542nn411–18, 543nn420–24, 426, 428–430, 433, 569n159
Narcissus, myth of, 272
Nasafī, ʿAziz ibn-Muhammad-I, 29
Nathan of Gaza, 511n267
Nathan of Nemirov, 106
Neumann, Erich, 67, 105, 126–27, 141, 272
Nietzsche, Friedrich, xxiii, xxviii, 14, 15, 32, 42–45, 114, 297
al-Niffarī, Muhammad ibn ʿAbd al-Jabbār, 225, 231
Noah, 377, 380, 382
Norea, 302
Numbers Rabbah, 466n347, 487n180, 501n137, 538n356

Oetinger, Friedrich Christoph, 103
Olat Tamid, 477n69
"On Language as Such and On the Language of Man," 11
Or ha-Sekhel, 236–37, 535n318, n319, 536n323, 537n344
Origen, 215, 334, 335, 341
Orr, Leslie, 79
Or Zaruʿa, 427n320
Oṣar Eden Ganuz, 139–40, 236, 241–42, 487n208, 488n210, n212, 518n95, n99, 520n123, 535n315, 537n344, n351, 554n142, 569n168, 576n25, 583n123
Oṣar Ḥayyim, 124
Oṣerot Ramḥal, 591n10

Pardes Rimmonim, 447n118
Parmenides, 65, 66, 221
Parmenides, goddess of, 413n173
Pascal, 195
Patocka, Jan, 159
Pattai, Raphael, 72, 142
Paul, 49–51, 126, 165, 166, 301
Peach, Lucinda Joy, 57–58
Peirce, Charles Sanders, 115
Perella, Nicholas, 337

Peratae, 498–99n102
Perush Eser Sefirot (Azriel of Gerona), 467n351, 515n64
Perush ha-Merkavah, 557n189
Perush ha-Tefillah (Azriel of Gerona), 466n337, n348, 467n354, 542n406, n409, 552n119
Perush ha-Tefillot (Ibn Malka), 556nn185–86
Perush Ma'aseh Bere'shit, 505n190
Perush Shir ha-Shirim (Ezra of Gerona), 466n332, 505n191, 529n237, 540n382, 546n14, n16, 591n12
Perush Sifra di-Ṣeni'uta, 79, 182, 454n212, 465n329, 512n280, 549n60
Perushei ha-Torah (Ibn Ezra), 452n190
Perushei ha-Torah (Naḥmanides), 452n192, 539n362, 542n412, n414, n415, n416, n418, 543n420, n422, n426, n428
Pesiqta de-Rav Kahana, 501n137
Pesiqta Rabbati, 521n134
Peter, 50; crucified in inverted position, 51
Phaedo, 65
Phänomenologie des Geistes, 101
Phénoménologie de la perception, xxii, xxv, xxix
Philo, 8, 200, 217, 334, 440–41n57
Philosophische Untersuchungen, 100
Phineḥas, 266; emblematic of the androgynous phallus, 267; Nadab and Abihu reincarnated in the person of, 266–67, 548n38; upholds the covenant by uniting male and female, 267; zealous with respect to the covenant, 379, 549n41
Pirani, Alix, 86
Pistis Sophia, 157
Pitḥei She'arim, 465n322
Plaskow, Judith, 85
Plato, xvii, 11, 65, 66, 126, 212, 221, 268, 302, 334, 344
Plotinus, 100, 212–15, 218, 221. *See also* Enneads
Poimandres, 573n233
Porphyry, 212
Porta Coelorum, 154
Power, Kim, 301
Prajna, 47
Proclus, 34, 65–66
Protevangelium of James, 444n86
Pythagoras, 107

Qatina, 64
Qillir, Eleazar bi-R., 576n.
Qol Bokhim, 553n137
Quispel, Gilles, 7
Qushayrī, 'Abd al-Karīm al-, 226, 227, 531n258

Ra'aya Meheimna, 48, 426n308, 458n239, 548n38, n40, 567n133, 572n207, 589n220, n225, 593n35
Rabba, Menaḥem ben Moses, 535n322
Rābi'a of Basra, 225–26, 305; celibate renunciation of, 225; deputy of Maryam, 225–226; veiled in the veil of sincerity, 225; the second, spotless Mary, 226
Rachel, 38, 325; weeping over her children, 376
Ragland-Sullivan, Ellie, 129
Raphael, Melissa, 85
Rav, 254, 490n21
Rava, 521n135
Rebekah, 325, 581n92
Recanati, Menaḥem, 251, 256, 426n305, 568n147, 569n152, 571n190
Reḥumai, Rabbi, 308
Republic, 66
Re'shit Ḥokhmah, 557n192, 571n194
Reuchlin, Johannes, 1, 404n69, 431n361, 467n351
Rhineland Jewish Pietists, 120, 144, 276, 489n17, 495n62, 581n86
Ricoeur, Paul, 17, 112
Rilke, Rainer Maria, 43
River-Root, 553–54n140
Risāla al-Qushayriyya, 226
Rogers, William Elford, 115
Roman de la Rose, 547n28, 560n30
Rosen, Tova, 78
Rosenroth, Christian Knorr von, 103
Rosenzweig, Franz, 10, 88–89, 113, 202–203, 336; affinity with kabbalistic gnosis, 202; his notion of system dependent on the later philosophy of Schelling, 463; and the new thinking, 113
Rubin, Solomon, 3, 4
Rūmī, Jalal al-Din, 228, 432–33n367
Ruth the Moabite, 438n23
Ryōkai, Tōzan, 533n297

Sabbath Songs of Sacrifice, 295
Sadducees, 302
Sa'id Ibn Da'ud, 583n121
Salome, 52
Samuel, 60, 534n306; archon of Edom, 258; Cain the progeny of Eve and, 444n86; and Lilith, 137; portrayed as the castrated male, 309; progenitor of idolatry, 258. *See also* Satan
Sarah, 83, 325
Sarug, Israel, 508n244

Satan, 258, 309
Saussure, Ferdinand de, xxi, 5, 89
Schelling, Friedrich W. J., xvi, 6, 43, 100–104, 105, 119; affinity to kabbalah, 100, 392–93n2, 407n90, 421n241, 469n369, 475n49, 551n99; Rosenzweig's notion of system and the later philosophy of, 463
Schimmel, Annemarie, 117, 206
Scholem, Gershom, xi, 1, 2, 4, 8, 12, 26, 35, 36, 47, 48, 59, 60, 68, 71, 74, 75, 81, 82, 94, 104, 123, 286, 287, 307–308, 388
Schopenhauer, Arthur, 42
Scott, George Ryley, 127, 261
Scott, Joan, 85
Second Epistle of Clement to the Corinthians, 50
Second Treatise of the Great Seth, 304
Seder Avodah le-Yom ha-Kippurim, 274
Sefer Gerushin, 374
Sefer ha-Bahir, 139, 146–67, 169, 188, 197, 257, 269, 271, 276–79, 282, 283, 308, 377, 428n333, 443n79, 458n239, 467n358, 470n422, 481n117, 487n194, 490n26, 491n30, n31, n33, n34, n35, 492n37, 493n47, 494n48, n51, n57, 495n60, n61, n64, n67, n68, n72, n73, 496n81, n82, 497n83, n84, n85, n86, 498n87, 501n132, n133, n134, n135, n136, n138, 502n140, n141, n145, n146, n150, n151, n153, n155, 503n159, n160, n162, 504n176, n177, n178, 512n290, 515n47, 545n454, 546n13, 547n19, 549n57, 551n97, 565n101, 566n103, n104, 592n21
Sefer ha-Derushim, 454n212, 465n329, 505n195, 510n260, 512n280, 549n60, 590n240, n241
Sefer ha-Emunah we-ha-Biṭṭaḥon, 60, 451n176, 467n360, 505n190, 515n51, 546n18, 552n113, n116, 554n143, 568n141, 569n155
Sefer ha-Gilgulim, 455n219, 459n250
Sefer ha-Ḥezyonot, 446n115
Sefer ha-Kelalim, 591n11
Sefer ha-Kuzari, 203, 469n396, 486n184, 517n85, n87, n89, 519n101, n102
Sefer ha-Mishkal / Mishqal, 36, 425n299, 426n305, n309, 428n328, 527n217, 528n219, 570n176, 595n27; symbolic meaning of the title, 527–28n219
Sefer ha-Qanah, 354, 444n87, 586n159
Sefer ha-Peli'ah, 107, 108–109, 586n159
Sefer ha-Rimmon, 36. *See also* Book of the Pomegranate
Sefer ha-Temunah, 256
Sefer ha-Yiḥud, 256, 539n371
Sefer ha-Yiḥud (Asher ben David), 445n98, 492n38, 496n76, 503n158, 506n205, 521n131
Sefer ha-Zohar, 8, 9, 31, 34, 37, 38, 47–48, 58, 59, 69, 70, 71, 82, 83, 104–105, 118, 123–24, 132, 134, 145–46, 147, 169, 171–72, 173, 176, 188, 204, 221, 233, 243, 245, 256, 257, 284, 291, 292, 294–95, 307, 313, 314, 320, 320–21, 325, 326, 328, 329, 330, 354–62, 376, 379–82, 385, 402n52, n53, n55, 424n290, n291, 426n305, n308, 427n315, n316, n317, n319, 428n332, 429n337, n339, n353, 431n 355, n357, n358, 436n8, 443n79, n84, 444n85, 445n97, n98, n102, n111, 450n156, n157, n159, n161, n162, n163, 451n183, 453n195, n197, 457n236, n237, n238, 458n239, n245, n246, 458–59n250, 459n252, n253, n254, 465n328, 469n402, 479n86, 484n154, n155, 485n167, n168, n177, 490n22, n23, 494n54, 497n83, 500n127, 502n154, 505n195, n199, 506n204, n210, n215, n216, 507n218, n220, n222, n225, n234, 508n240, n242, 510n248,n251, 511n264, n268, 512n277, n291, 513n294, 517n86, n88, 519n100, 527n215, n217, n219, 528n220, n224, n225, 534n306, 539n369, n373, 544n437, n438, n440, n441, n448, n450, 545n452, n456, 548n32, n35, n36, n39, n40, 549n41, n43, n53, 550n65, 553n127, 554n147, 556n172, n173, n174, n188, 557n190, n192, 566n113, n114, 567n122, n126 n130, n131, n132, n133, n137, 568n138, n142, n144, n146, n148, 569n161, n163, 570n175, n176, n177, n178, 571n186, n187, n189, n190, n193, n195, 572n207, n208, 573n217, n218, n220, n221, n223, n224, n228, n230, n232, n235, n236, n238, 574n240, 580n75, 582n104, 585n146, n147, n149, 586n150, n156, n162, 587n165, n169, n170, n174, n178, 588n182, n186, n188, n190, n192, n193, n195, n201, 589n209, n214, n215, n216, n220, n225, 590n231, n232, n233, n235, n237, n238, 591n5, n6, n13, n14, n15, 592n17, n19, n26, 592–93n27, 593n28, n30, n32, n33, n34, n35, n36, n37, n38, n39, 594n40, n46, 596n58, n60, n61, n73, 597n83
Sefer Meshiv Devarim Nekhoḥim, 425n301, 450n351, 451n176, 458n240, 467n360, 515n51, 526n211
Sefer Sar Shalom, 576n28
Sefer Tashak / Tashaq, 73, 244, 451n171, n172, n175, n176, n177, 484n164, 528n223, 539n365, n366, n367, 584n128, 586n150, n152, 587n164, 588n197, 589n207, 594n48, n51, 595n52.
Sefer Yeṣirah, 3, 64, 98, 99, 120, 139, 140, 144, 151,

152, 161, 178, 179, 197, 198, 201, 203, 204, 207, 208, 210, 218, 220, 241, 242, 250, 271, 274, 276, 281, 282, 283, 294, 309, 326, 352, 367, 400n12, 425n292, 425n294, 427n313, 427n320, 448n128, 448n130, 466n336, 489n10, 492n38, 496n76, 499n102, 501n131, 507n233, 508n236, n239, 515n49, n66, 518n89, n92, n95, 520n116, 523n144, 536n339, 537n344, 542n411, 550n66, 553n124

Sein und Zeit, xxix, 6

Ṣemaḥ, Jacob, 137

Ṣevi, Sabbatai, 62

Shaʿar ha-Gemul, 252, 254

Shaʿar ha-Gilgulim, 457n231, 459n250, 476n59, 510n254, 548n38, 566n116, 590n2

Shaʿar ha-Haqdamot, 511n271, n272, 512n276, 596n69

Shaʿar ha-Kawwanot, 484n161, 549n58

Shaʿar ha-Niqqud, 207

Shaʿar ha-Pesuqim, 512n282, 549n58, n59, n61

Shaʿar ha-Shamayim (Ibn Latif), 535n314

Shaʿar ha-Shamayim (Jacob ben Sheshet), 467n361, 496n76

Shaʿar Maʾamerei Rashbi, 454n212, 465n329, 512n280, 549n60

Shaʿar Ruaḥ ha-Qodesh, 477n69

Shaʿarei Ṣedeq, 234–35, 424–25n292, 534n308, n309, 544n450, 553n126, 581n91

Shaʿarei Ṣedeq (Gikatilla), 447n122

Shaʿarei Qedushshah, 120, 121, 476n57, 477n60, n63, n65, n66, n67, n70

Shabastarī, Maḥmūd, 29, 30

Shaddai, 240

Shakti, 47

Shariputra, 442n72

Sheʾelot u-Teshuvot, 426n305, 428n326, 429n342, 458n243, 497n83, 511n265

Sheila, Rabbi, 540n384

Shelomo ha-Bavli, 275

Shemen ha-Sullam, 484n153

Shenei Luḥot ha-Berit, 564n88

Sheqel ha-Qodesh, 426n305, 451n166, 459n252, 528n219, 545n452, 557n192; symbolic meaning of the title, 528n219

Sheshet the Blind, Rabbi, 556n188

Shirah le-Dawid, 576n26

Shir ha-Shirim Rabbah, 336, 501n137, 551n96, 575n19, 576n19, 576n25, 582n104

Shir ha-Shirim Zuṭa, 335

Shiʿur Qomah, 121, 122, 144

Shiʿur Qomah (Cordovero), 447n118

Shoshan Sodot, 535n312, 570n180

Shulamit, 346

Shushan Edut, 34, 84, 426n305, 427n321, n323, 452n184, 458n248, 511n264, 588n183, 592n27, 593n33, 594n44

Sifra de-vei Rav, 538n356

Sifra di-Ṣeniʿuta, 180, 309, 386, 453n197

Silesius, Anegelus, 417n200, 482n119

Simeon ben Yoḥai, 37, 70, 146, 222, 266, 291, 326, 330, 364, 384, 388, 445n104, 570n176, 587n179, 597n83; fraternity of based on Jesus and his disciples, 259

Simlai, Rabbi, 539

Simon Peter, 53, 165

Simon, Rabbi, 202

Siphre ad Numeros, 466n347, 556n188

Sisera, 590n2

Sitrei Torah (Abulafia), 88, 238, 240–41, 423n257, 463n288, 487n209, 518n94, 536n328, n338

Sitrei Torah (*Zohar*), 123–24, 445n97, 479n86, 497n83, 549n43, 568n142

Smith, J. C., 306

Smith, Margaret, 305

Socrates, 65

Sod Eṣ ha-Daʿat, 248

Sod ha-Ḥashmal, 149

Sōhō, Takuan, 297

Solomon, 63, 153, 313, 347; all of his wisdom equal to the Torah, 335; bears the name God, 163, 335; bestowing of wisdom upon, 155; bestows the bread of the Song, 342; built the Temple, 356; by means of the holy spirit uttered the Song, 360; coronation of, 366; elevated to wisdom, 357; establishes his rule, 378; holy chariot for, 367; the king to whom peace belongs, 163, 367; made handles for theTorah, 336; personified as the son in the divine triad, 155; seated upon the throne of David, 377, 378; song of, 356; wearing the crown given to him by his mother, 162, 366, 389

Solomon ben Isaac (Rashi), 345; 426n305, 495n63, 510n263, 521n135, 580n86

Solomon ben Jeroḥam, 345

Song of Songs, 333–71; allegorical application to God's relationship to Israel, 334; allegorical depiction of the relationship of soul to God in medieval Jewish philosophy, 345–48; ascends to the world of the masculine, 362; ascetic renunciation prerequisite for study of, 339; begins with *shin* to signify the mystery of the chariot, 588n181; celebrates the great Sabbath beyond the division of night and day, 367; contemplative interpretation in medieval monastic culture, 336–45; custom to chant on Friday evening, 587n164; depicted as the book of experience, 342; dialogue refers to the relationship of God to the soul or Jesus to the Church, 334, 337; embodies the convergence of language, eros, being, 334; epitomizes the mystery of the Word made flesh, 342; equivalent to the Torah in its entirety, 335–36, 359, 361; erotic yearning of depicts the exile, 354; esoteric meaning relates to the gender transformation of *Shekhinah* and her elevation to *Binah*, 357–58; expresses poetically the desire of mind to be conjoined to the intelligible world of incorporeal light, 349; heterosexual imagery transposed into a male homoeroticism, 337–38; identified as the holy of holies, 335, 359; identified symbolically as the supenal phallus, 589n207; figurative depiction of the soul's ascetic yearning to unite with Christ, 334; identified as the Tetragrammaton, 361, 588n197; messianic significance of lies in the gender transposition of *Shekhinah* occassioned by her restitution to *Binah*, 359, 360; and the mystery of revelation, 335; paradigm of paradigms, 336; principle of: account of creation, coronation of the name, exile of Egypt, expulsions of Israel and their redemption, resurrection of the dead, the Torah, 360; recitation of on the day of the dedication of the Jerusalem Temple, 355, 360; related to the supernal chariot constituted by four names that correspond to *Shekhinah*, *Yesod*, *Tif'eret*, and *Binah*, 360; theosophic and ecstatic elements in the zoharic interpretation, 351–56; theosophic interpretation based on the sacred union between the male and female, 349, 362; utterance of attributed to Elijah, 358; utterance of located at Sinai, 336; weeping and the utterance of, 580n75

Sophia, 68, 157, 502n152; demiurgical potency, 494n102; double doctrine of in Valentinian Gnosticism, 155, 506n201; myth of the fallen, 153; and *Shekhinah*, 455n218

Sophist, 66

Speculum Virginum, 561n37

Spinoza, 8, 96

Sprache und Mythos, 6

Steiner, George, 117, 118

Suhrawardī, 239, 392n11, 401n18, 424n272, 475n46, 522n136, 532n268, 534n302

Sullam ha-Aliyyah, 477n62

Sūtra of Sagara, the Naga King, 56

Sūtra on Changing the Female Sex, 57

Tabula Smaragdina, 7

Tahāfut al-Falāsifa, 27

Tahāfut al-Tahāfut, 27

Talbot, Alice-Marry M., 301

Tamakh, Abraham ben Isaac ha-Levi, 581n86

Tao-te Ching, 107, 108

Targum, 334

The Ascetic Imperative in Culture and Criticism, 115

"The Nature of Language," 20

Tiqqunei Zohar, 133, 310, 365, 366, 383, 384, 402n50, 445n97, 484n157, 497n83, 512n284, 549n58, 553n127, 566n115, 570n177, n178, 587n179, 589n221, n223, n225, 592n26, 594n47, 595n54, n56, 596n66

Tolaʿat Yaʿaqov, 586n161

Toledot Adam, 507n230

Torat ha-Adam, 252

Torat ha-Nefesh, 346

Tractatus Logico-Philosophicus, 289–91, 409n85, 555nn162–63, 556n165, n167–70

Trauerspiel, 11

Trimegistus, Hermes, 7

Trimorphic Protennoia, 157

Ṭurei Zahav, 580n75

Turner, Denys, 343–44

Vidas, Elijah de, 321, 571n194

Vimalakirti Sutra, 442n72

Vital, Ḥayyim, 80, 94, 120–22, 132–33, 137, 179, 181–85, 270–71, 310, 317–18, 368–70, 386–87, 446n115, 454n212, 455n219, 457n231, 458n247, 459n251, 465n325, n329, 476n56, n57, n58, 476–77n59, 483n153, 484n161, 502n143, 505n195, 508n241, 510n253, n254, n255, n257, n260, 511n268, n271, n272, 512n274, n276, n281, n282, n283, 548n38, 549n58, n59, n60, n61, n62, 566n116, 569n169, 590n240, n241, n243, n244, n245, 590n2, 596n63, n64, n67, n68, n69, n70; fivefold path enunciated by, 120

Weyl, Hermann, xvii

Whitehead, Alfred North, xviii

Whitman, Walt, 127, 481n108, 595–96n57

Wittgenstein, Ludwig, 15, 16, 289–91; affinities with Benjamin, 406n85; compared with Derrida, 406–407n85; and Heidegger, 410n127–29, 413n173, 419n211; and Merleau-Ponty, 419n227; mystical dimensions of his thought, 555–56n163

Woods, Gregory, 118
Wu-wen kuan, 534n305

Xeno, xxv

Yael, 590n2
Yannai, 275–76
Yesod Mora, 486n184
Yinnon, 165, 166
Yonat Elem, 512n287
Yoni, 126
Yose ben Yose, 274
Yose, Rabbi, 328

Zaehner, Robert C., 298–99
Zekharya ha-Rofe, 583n120
Zevi Hirsch of Zidachov, 317–18
Zimmer, Heinrich, 235
Zimri, 267
Zizek, Slavoj, 130, 279, 297
Zohar Ḥadash, 426n308, 429n339, 444n85, 484n169, 487n209, 528n228, 538n355, 549n43, 555n151, 567n133, 568n144, 570n176, 571n187, 580n75, 585n147, n148, 587n167, n171, n175, n177, 587–88n180, n182, n186, n187, n191, n196, 589n203, n205, n207, n208, n214, n225, 592n24
Zohar ha-Raqiʿa, 590n2
Zosimus the Panopolitan, 154
Zostrianos, 55, 303
Zupancic, Alenka, 297
Zwelling, Jeremy, 244

Index of Subjects and Terms

Abba, 181
Abba, four facets of consciousness: *Ḥokhmah*, *Binah*, *Ḥesed*, and *Gevurah*, 369
abgrund, 23, 102, 123
absence, present, 243; visible, 196
abstention, form of symbolic castration, 302–303; and the obliteration of the autonomy of the feminine, 301–302
abstinence, facilitates reintegration of the feminine into the masculine, 327, 365
abyss, of formlessness, 123
abyssal thinking, 42
Active Intellect, 554n142; angelic presence of, 241, 535n322; anthropomorphic personification of, 240, 536n332; associated with the image of the mother, 581n91; assumes the shape of an anthropos in the imaginative faculty, 238; configured in the imagination as an angel, 238; conjunction with, 241, 581n91; and the cup of Jamshīd, 534n302; designated "Assembly of Israel," 240; desire of soul to become one with, 347; encounter of prophet with, 241; engendered as masculine in relation to the soul, 345, 348; figurative account of the conjunction of the human with, 536n332; and the Holy Spirit, 239, 534n302; identified as Gabriel, 534n302; identified as Metatron, 240, 487n209; identified as Torah, 237, 239, 240, 241, 535n314; identified with one of the *sefirot*, 476n52; interpretation of the Song as a dialogue between the soul and, 350; imaginal form of, 239; linguistic nature of, 241; matrix of providence, 241; mother of governance, 240; Moses the personification, 487n209; and the name Israel, 581n92; and the symbol of *malbush*, 535n314. *See also* sekhel ha-poʿel
Adam Qadmon, 35, 154, 508–509n244
Adonai, 69, 71
afisat ha-maḥshavah, 389
agnosia, 214, 218
aḥadiyyat al-aḥad, 29, 230
aḥadiyyat al-kathra, 29, 230
aḥdut ha-shaweh, 99
ʿālam al-mithāl (*mundus imaginalis*), xviii, 189, 391n3, 538n353. *See also* imaginal world
alchemy, 47, 108
alef, broken orthographically into *yod*, *waw*, and *yod*, 282–83, 365; comprises all the *sefirot*, 553nn126–27; demarcates the supernal world of masculinity, 354; denotes the primary *sefirah*, 196; in the word *anokhi*, 99; name hidden within, 283; semiotic encoding of the triune unity, 283; symbolic of the father, 279; *yod* in the head of, 282, 283
aletheia, 19; and the concealment of concealing, 413n173; contrasted with correspondence theory of truth, 408n93; philologically registers the belonging-together of untruth and truth, 413n173
al-lawḥ al-maḥfūẓ, 206
allegory, 40; eroticization of, 334–36
alma be-hippukha, 31–32
alma de-nuqba, 82, 83. *See also* world of the feminine
alma di-dekhura, 82, 187. *See also* world of the masculine
alterity, and the Levinasian *l'autre*, 287, 507n221; linked to the emergence and constitution of the feminine, 285; ontological problem of, 500n111
amen, liturgical response of greater than uttering the blessing, 281, 284; signifies the unity of everything, 284; unites wisdom at the beginning with

wisdom at the end, 284; utterance of augments the source of blessing, 281
amr ilāhī (*inyan elohi*), 203
analogical discourse, 220, 221
analogical exemplarism, 224
androcentrism, 47, 55, 56, 57, 58, 61, 78, 81, 109, 110, 186, 304, 306, 373; and phallic aggression, 307
androgyne, 3, 55, 145; created in one body, 176; female, 68, 450n153; male, 68, 94, 110, 146, 148, 149, 155, 165, 173, 180, 183, 267, 323, 366, 373, 375, 376, 387, 441n57; 447–48n122; 449n137, n150; 465n327, 471n435, 510n261; mystery of, 73, 145, 388; realized in the mystical bonding of the male fraternity, 388; severance of, 356; status of the soul, 156. *See also* du-parṣufim
androgynous male, 162, 184, 374, 592n16; splintering of into male and female, 109, 162
androgynous phallus, 131, 135, 146, 151, 169, 388, 567n123, 592n16; embodied in the figure of Phinehas, 267; ritually embodied in the circumcised penis, 311; reconstituted in the eschaton, 384, 388
androgyny, 49, 64, 67, 144, 146; androcentric character of, 139; applied to the Great Mother, 68, 456n231; characteristic of each of the *sefirot*, 63; implies the containment of each gender in the other, 362; locus of in the phallus, 169; and the metaphysical principles of bestowal and receptivity, 145; masculine nature of, 171, 176; of the divine signified by the complete name, 169, 180; of Jesus, 491n36; ontic status of Adam, 168; phallomorphic nature of, 140, 146; predicated on the containment of the female in the male, 55, 139; reconfiguration of the primordial state of, 166; reconstitution of, 165; represented by the straight *nun*, 166; spiritual nature of, 52
angel, 38; androgynous nature of, 69; bread eaten by, 253; correspond to Israel below, 221; emblematic of transfigured masculinity beyond sexual desire, 302; garbed in the garment of this world, 221; good, 247; imaginal form of the Active Intellect, 238, 239; individuates itself, 239; masculine nature of, 55, 302; ministering, 540n384; mystic transformed into, 240; of death, 247; of God, 240; of the presence, 239; ontically composed of the Hebrew letters, 241; personification of *Shekhinah*, 69; redeeming, 69; serves as a guide on the way of gnosis, 239. *See also* mal'akh; mal'akh ha-elohim; mal'akh ha-go'el; mal'akh ha-panim; mal'akhei ha-sharet
angelification, consequent to renunciation of the carnal body, 299–300; of the mystic, 121, 240; and the incorporation into Torah, 241
angelophany, the form of every theophany, 239
angelus interpres, imaginal form of, 239
annihilation, and abiding, 227, 228
anointed one (*meshiaḥ yhwh*), mystic transformed into, 240, 241
anthropomorphism; 39, 40; and letter symbolism, 118; in kabbalistic interpretation, 246
anthropos, conduit connecting divine and mundane, 209; divine and human, 173, 209; form imagined in the prophetic vision, 239; identified as the circumcised male Jew, 209; lower and upper, 121; of the divine configured in the quaternity of father, mother, son, and daughter, 312; prophetic, 238, 239; *sefirot* configured in the imagination as the form of the primal, 200, 209
apophasis, and kataphasis, 219, 343; and mystical envisioning, 215; not-speaking by speaking rather than speaking by not-speaking, 220
apophatic, 195; interplay of with the kataphatic, 119, 291; juxtaposed with the kataphatic, 215, 217
apophaticism, xxvii, 289; interweaving of anagogy and, 217
aqedah, 160
arafel, 217
Aramaic, the mundane language in contrast to the holy language of Hebrew, 203; semantic kinship to Arabic and Hebrew, 203
archetype, 67
Arikh Anpin, 76, 316; aspect of *Malkhut* within, 184; messianic state marked by the reign of, 368; homoertoic conjunction of *Ze'eir Anpin* and, 368; realm of complete mercy, 368; right side is masculine and left side feminine, 183; single eye set in the forehead of, 181, 375; unites with *Ze'eir Anpin* on the day of Sabbath, 368; without a female counterpart, 181, 183, 184. *See also* Atiq Yomin
asarah harugei malkhut/melukhah, 310, 387, 596n66
asceticism, 42–43; and the angelmorphic transformation of the carnal body, 299–300; anticipates the condition of the eschaton, 364; and construction of gender, 299; and the contemplative ideal, 308; and cleaving to the divine phallus, 327; counters passions with a surplus of pure passion, 297; cultivated by kabbalists in Provence, 308; dialectically related to phallomorphism, 135; and eroticism, 136, 296–99, 319, 322, 363, 558n6, 559n17,

569n173; escape from the femaleness of somatic desire, 441n62; expression of a primal narcissistic impulse, 135; encratic nature of, 52, 55; erotic nature of, 86, 118; escape from femaleness of somatic desire, 441n62; and fasting, 247, 299, 300, 479n59, 559n24, 560n26; a form of mimetic participation in the incarnational kenosis, 341; form of veiling the female, 302; homoerotic underpinnings of, 328; in ancient throne mysticism, 306; in the classical rabbinic corpus, 307; in Christianity attacked by Jews, 309; in Jewish Sufism, 307; in medieval Jewish pietisic treatises, 307; and kabbalistic piety, 246, 255, 307, 363, 477n59; lustful, 136; masculinization of the feminine, 55, 306; and martyrdom, 300, 560n34, 561n41; on the part of women and an internalized misogyny, 344; purification of the imagination by means of, 235; on the part of women in early Christianity and rabbinic Judaism contrasted, 299–300; and redemption, 364; and Sabbatian eschatology, 564n89; and social disengagement, 559n21; and spiritual marriage, 299; subjugation of the body, 120–21; and textual interpretation, 115

aṣilut, 33; configurations of, 509n244; world of, 270, 508–509n244

astral body, xiv

Aṭarah, 61; designation of *Shekhinah*, 254, 452–53n192; elevation to *Keter*, 263; symbolic of the emanation of the blessing and surplus from the spirit of the living God, 389; symbolized by the second *he* of YHWH, 125

aṭeret baʿlah, 72, 80, 185, 186, 376

aṭeret berit, 73, 186, 453n199; designation of the clitoris, 77; elevation of and transformation into *keter malkhut*, 271; female assimilated into, 389; object of vision, 137

aṭeret ṣevi, 254

aṭeret tifʾeret, 72, 365

aṭeret yesod, 75, 76, 77, 133, 184, 453n199

Atiqa, characterized by one eye, 179; entirely right without any left, 179

Atiqa de-atiqin, 76

Atiqa Qaddisha, 221, 509n244, 511n267; banquet of, 368; illumines *Zeʿeir Anpin*, 368

Atiq Yomin, 368; above the five configurations, 184; spirit awakened by, 316; transcends gender differentiation, 183. *See also* Arikh Anpin

Aufhebung, 129

autoaffection, 284

autoeroticism, and the construction of the other, 511n267; homoeroticism as aspect of, 329; and the initial arousal of the Godhead, 182, 271, 283, 285, 510n261, 551n100, 573n234

autogenesis, 26, 77; of divine wisdom and the texture of temporality, 281

avodah zarah, 243, 258

axis mundi, identified as the linga, 323

Ayin, 97, 314; bestowing and receiving unified in the depths of, 176; brings forth beginning and end, 105; distinguished from Ein Sof, 104; knows and does not know Ein Sof, 105, 368; identified as the name of *Keter*, 179, 368; threshold to the place that is no place, 233–34, 375. *See also* Keter

baptism, 49–50; and becoming male, 55; erasure of gender difference, 51

baqāʾ, 227, 228, 232, 234; and the annihilation of *nafs*, 227

bat ayin, 383

beginning, 13; characterized by division, 277; concealment within Thought, 105; distinguished from origin, 196; doubling of, 102; end in the, 99; locus of memory yet to be remembered, 279; made possible by the phallic impulse to bestow, 285; marked by the obsessional drive of the male to reiterate, 279; of salvation, 156; of thought, 173; of the work, 113; origin of, 187; paradox and duplicity of, 91; perfect symmetry between end and, 388; second that is first, 196; signified by the letter *beit*, 277, 383; and the splintering of the androgynous male, 109; supernal point, 105; textual nature of, 90; thought of the, 187; unity characteristic of, 104

being, chain of, 210; fleshliness of, 195; fragment of, 194; grammar of, 194; indistinguishable from not-being, 100; language and, 193, 197; and nothing, 27

beit, comprised of three sides, 257, 258, 294; denotes the beginning, 196, 277; embodies the totality of Torah in three knots of faith, 257; and the feminine, 353, 354; first letter of Torah, 257, 354, 587n179; marks the mystery of the threefold unity, 258; opened on one side and closed on three sides, 257; signifies the beginning, 277, 383; signifies the dual Torah, 257; symbolic of the daughter, 279; symbolic of the fullness of divine blessing, 277; symbolic of *Ḥokhmah*, 383; three sides of allude symbolically to three holy, supernal lights bound as one, 257, 258; and the word *bayit*, 294

bilddenken, 119
Binah, 69, 72, 74, 81, 83, 138, 178, 197, 258, 270; corresponds to the tongue, 173; covenant of, 138; demarcated as the faint silent voice (*qol demamah daqqah*), 294–95; depicted as king, 84, 358; divested of all images and garments, 294–95; emblematic of the mother, 196; fifty gates of, 188; identified as *tohu*, 294; name of Solomon ascribed to, 358; place of the hidden wine, 360; secret of the jubilee, 371; supernal Sabbath that transcends the division of Sabbath into day and night, 360, 371; and the symbol of: the great Sabbath, 367, 371; the mother, 154, 358; Yom Kippur, 364, 371; *teshuvah*, the place of return, 367, 368; transposition from vessel that contains to spring that overflows, 83; united with *Malkhut* on Yom Kippur, 364, 371; upper mother, 83; upper world, 292; womb of being, 70, 83; womb that bears the seed-thought of *Ḥokhmah*, 196, 286; womb of all-that-is-to-come, 367; world of the masculine, 82, 367; world that is coming, 367; world-to-come, 292, 358, 360, 367, 371
binyan elohi, 248
binyan ha-nuqba, 285
blessing, before the blessing, 265; bestowed only in place where masculine and feminineare united, 266; rests only on the man who is married, 312
blindness, true insight, 217; vision of the incomprehensible, 96, 230; vision of the invisible, 556n179
bodhicitta, 322
body, aligned with the feminine, 51; as lived presence in contrast to physical mass, 245–46; consciousness of, 24; constructed from the letters, 241; correlated with the book, 191; dual role as stigma of the fall and instrument of redemption, 190; ecstatic and enstatic, 197; garbing the soul, 248; ethereal, 191; image of Christ's humanity, 51; intertext of world and, 194; like the existence of the soul, 253; linguistic nature of, 118, 201, 248, 250; linked to the demonic potency, 246; literal, 191; locus of evil, 247; luminous, 191, 248; natural as opposed to angelic, 251, 255; negative view of adopted by kabbalists, 246, 307; of engenderment, 148, 312; of the text, 223, 241, 335; openness of, 192; phenomenology of, 191; purification of, 121; reflexivity of, 193; restored to the first matter, 241; ritualized, 250; sexualized nature of, 81; socially constructed, 81; spiritual, 248; spiritualization rather than abrogation of, 251; text of the, 335; textual nature of, 118, 191, 246, 248, 259, 285, 330
book, correlated with the body, 191; idolatry of, 206; mother of the, 206; of concealment, 95; of the heart, 191; of nature, 8, 202, 206; speculum of nature, 202; three books by which world was created: *sefar*, *sippur*, and *sefer*, 204; weighed on the balance, 95; world compared to, 206
boṣina de-qardinita, 137, 321
brahmarandhra, 323
brain, of consciousness, 270; ontic root of mercy and judgment contained therein, 270; semen originates in, 269, 271; site of the phallic potency, 270
bride, nakedness of, 181; of Christ, 301, 302, 344
bridal chamber, identified as the womb of the Virgin Mary, 503–504n172; king alone with the bride within, 229; male and female joined within, 166; and the restoration of the androgynous image, 437n15; spiritual marriage of son and daughter within, 156
Buddhism, 42, 47, 56; status of women in, 437n15, 441n66, 441–42n71, 456n231
burning bush, epiphany at, 216; foreshadowing of the mystery of the incarnation, 216
burnt offering, 82

castration, child's fear of linked to the phallus the mother lacks, 131; combined with fertility, 67; contrasted with circumcision, 134; and the cutting of desire at the root, 562n52; and enlightenment, 570n185; fostered model of manliness in unmanliness, 303; and heterosexual lovemaking, 131; mystical, 302; of penis to erect the phallus, 136; of Samuel contrasted with the circumcised male Jew, 309; phallus covered by, 129; resistance to writing, 485 n. 173; sexual renunciation viewed as a symbolic form of, 306, 319; symbolic substitute for circumcision, 485n173
catharsis, 26, 387
Cause of Causes (*causa causarum, illat ha-illot*), 178, 179, 403n61
celibacy, 52; ambivalence toward in rabbinic and kabbalistic texts, 309; at Qumran, 560–61n35; form of emasculinization, 386; kabbalistic polemic against the Christian monastic ideal of, 312, 385; on the part of kabbalists depicted symbolically by the image of the righteous wearing crowns on their heads, 366; and the role of martyr in formative Christianity, 300; of Moses, 313, 321; on the part of women, 300
chain, four links on: marked, hewn, engraved, and measured, 211; holy and pure, 245; of being, 210, 221, 229; of tradition, 236

chariot, xii, xiii; androgynous nature of, 63; four legs of, 84; and the image of the nut, 144; made by Solomon, 63
chastity, 134
cherubim, 63–64; *Shekhinah* rests upon, 69–70
chiasm, 25
childbearing, antidote to the punishment of death, 53; commandment of incumbent on Jewish men, 59
Christian kabbalah, 1, 256
Christian Platonism, 42
Christianity, associated with the image of masculine impotence, 311, 385–86; attitude of zoharic kabbalists towards, 258–59; and the seduction of magic and sexual temptation, 259; viewed as idolatry, 243, 258
Christos Angelos, 536n330
circle, begins and ends with wisdom, 280; circulation of, 158; considered in conjunction with the line, 38; contained within the square, 188; everlasting, 272; feminine identified as the nucleus of, 382; hermeneutical, 10–11, 112, 472n2, 549n64; infinite, 100; Iyyun, 99; noetic, 214; of concepts, 268; of contemplation, 269; of divine thought, 283; of divine unity, 453n199; of economy, 158; of exchange, 499n108; of expression and of being-expressed, 17; of kabbalists in Gerona, 8; of Luria, 586n149; of mastery, 42; of mystics, 388; of the Special Cherub, 489n17; of thought thinking itself, 271; of transcendence, 268; oneness and infinity coincide within, 429n336; squaring of, 512n291; unity of beginning and end within, 284, 550n66; of wisdom, 283; quadrant of, xvi; zoharic, 63, 72, 137, 266, 317, 318, 321, 324, 364, 366, 565n96
circumcision, 46, 82, 435n4; abrogation of sexual desire, 135; affirmation of phallic desire through its negation, 141; androgynous nature of, 140; baptismal overcoming of, 50; and the bearing of the divine seal on the flesh, 276; and castration, 134, 434n391; and contemplative envisioning, 135; covenant of, 133,139, 331; and the dissimilitude of esotericism, 134, 135; eight days of, 147; embodies the dialectic of concealment and disclosure, 141; and the enigmatic, 135; and feminization of the male body, 436n4; induces seeing the unseen, 382; mark of, 380; mark of the simulacrum, 434n391; marker of ethnic identity, 135; midpoint of, 373, 382; the mystery revealed to Israel, 135; and the name, 128, 137; of Abraham, 82, 135; paradigm for an esoteric hermeneutic, 135; and the paradox of visualizing the hidden in hiding the visual, 382; point enclosed in the center of, 382; and redemption in inverse relationship, 382; ritual embodiment of androgynous phallus, 311; secret of and the four beasts, 140; and sexual renunciation, 486n184; sign of phallic empowerment, 486n188; and the study of Torah, 137, 144; two parts of: *milah* and *peri῾ah*, 140
citron, symbolic of the feminine, 150; corresponds to the heart, 151. *See also* etrog
coincidence, xxiv, xxv, 192; distinguished from indifference, 467n351; in contrast to coherence, 536n344; of being and nothing, 27; of coincidence, 193; of concealment and disclosure, 595n53; of darkness and light, 422n245; of language and embodiment, 42; of opposites, xx, 27, 29, 98, 106, 261, 262, 422n245, 447n118, 456n231, 469n396, 531n99; of opposition, 100; of the optic and verbal, 10; of planes of vision, 233; opposition of, 100; without transcendence, xxiv
coincidentia oppositorum, xix, 30, 97, 467n351; and the character of truth, 403n58; dialectic logic of, 96; in Eliade, 262, 545–46n5; and *Keter*, 97; of the absolute and contracted maximum, 424n279; of the hidden and manifest, xii; of the limited and unlimited, 30; of unity and multiplicity, 29; and the overcoming of gender dimorphism, 174; and time's other, xix
coitus, androcentric explanation of, 148; considered a form of *imitatio dei*, 312; intention of the kabbalist in the act of, 319; means to participate in the sacred marriage that anticipates the redemption, 308; sanctifying oneself in the act of, 267; symbolic depiction by the image of the crown, 389
conjunctio oppositorum, 373
commandments, configured as the holy and pure body, 248; constitute the mystery of Adam, 259; equated with light, 247; identified as the attributes, 248; identified as the glory, 249; means by which soul separates from body, 247; reward of, 247; tissue of the body and fiber of the soul, 250; yoke of, 309
complex infinity, envisioned from infinite complexity, 211
concealment, confluence of disclosure and, 384; demarcated as the invisible of the visible, 195; letter of, 237; lower world revealed in the conceal-

ment of the upper world, 292; and unconcealment, 17, 18, 19, 26, 27; within the mystery of mysteries, 292. *See also* Verborgenheit
confluence, of the visual and verbal, 293, 411n134
conjunction, 32, 35, 120; incorporation into the body of the text, 241; incorporation into the name, 237; mystical intent of prayer and study, 209; and negative theology, 218; of secret to secret, 593 n. 37; of the soul, 122, 209, 251; of thought, 209, 549–50n64; and prophecy, 209; patriarchs in constant state of, 316; sublation of fleshy passion, 267; to nothing, 264; union with Torah, 237; with the Active Intellect, 241; with the *Shekhinah*, 251. *See also* devequt
consciousness, xxii, 5, 12, 24, 30, 68, 79, 112, 279, 532n266; ascending and descending, 315; and being coincide, xxix; between wakefulness and sleep, 226; *bodhi*, 57; brain of, 270; circularity of, 550n64; compounded with body, xxvi; datum of, xxx; confluence of speech and perception in, 404n70; contemplating self as other, 279; embodied state of, 25, 190, 192, 193; entangled with language, 418n207; erotic, 261; facets of, 369; fount of, 270; gaze of, 24; imaginal configuration of God in, 127; immanent and transcendent, xxvi; immanent of, xxx; impressional, xxv; intentional structure of, 6; internal, 6; internal time, xvi, xxviii, 404n65; linguistic, 518n90; loss of, 535n312; matriarchal, 68; messianic, 316; mirror of, 121, 141; modules of, 126; mystical, xix, 122, 287; mystified, 79; mythological, 141; Neumann's analytical notion of, 127; noematic presence within, 235; of body, 24; of eros, 261; of the Father, 370; of God, 477–78n72; of the masculine, 184; of the oneness of all being, 305; of the presence of God, 478n72; of thought, 349; of women, 460n260; phenomena, 420n230; philosophy of, 546n11; pure, 192, 215, 343; of the present, xxv, 5; orgasmic in nature, 271; prereflective, 420n229; protentional nodes of, xxi; reflexivity of, 269; self, 11, 278; silence of, 24; and symbolic making, 401n34; time, xxiv, xxvii; time, being, and, 396n69; transcendental, xxviii; two forms of, 270; unitary, 141; and world, xxi, 25
consecrated host, 255
conservation, and innovation, 88
contemplation, by way of allusion, 219; correspondence between contemplative ecstasy and seminal emission, 316; culminates in vision, 214; depicted in apophatic terms,123, 216; erotics of, 268; ladder of, 123; of one thing from another, 210; path of, 214; phallic nature of, 138; poetic envisioning wherein words are seen as images and images heard as words, 293; predicated on ascetic renunciation of sensual desire, 308; process of purification and emptying the mind, 214; progression to what cannot be contemplated, 217; self-enclosed circle of, 269; that has no substance, 210; way of, 212. *See also* hitbonenut
contemplative envisioning, xii, 118, 119, 133, 263, 268, 294, 322, 366, 399n11; coincidence of optic and verbal, 210; nexusbetween circumcision and, 135; occasioned by the iconoclastic breaking of all form, 213; and the phallic potency, 481n117; spiritual eros of, 269
contemplative prayer, 209
conversion, a crossing of ontic boundaries, 223, 243; mystery of, 222, 223, 438n23; and the overcoming if difference embodied in the messianic figure, 438n23
copulation, after the sin of Adam, 185; between *Shekhinah* and *Yesod*, 362, 512n280; copula and, 118; first, 182, 271; and the material world, 509n244; means to join left and right, 95; of male and female waters, 95; of the mind, 270, 322; of the soul in relation to the divine, 298; referred to as knowledge, 549n58; sanctity of, 370; secret of, 270, 553n137; and the secret doctrine of kabbalah, 585n145; seminal drop of, 270, 549n58; and *shaʿashuʿa*, 553n137; spiritual, 267; source of, 317; supernal, 270, 549n58; and the truth of duplicity, 196. *See also* ziwwug; ziwwug ruḥani
coronation, of Solomon, 366; and the overcoming of gender dimorphism, 74; reciprocal nature of in relation to the *Shekhinah* and kabbalists, 366; understood symbolically as cleaving to the corona of the male organ, 388; symbolic of coitus, 389
corporeal intentionality, 24
corporeality, linguistic conception of, 208, 285
corpus astrale, 251
corpus glorificationis, 255
cosmic semiotics, 201
cosmos, constituted by the multiple veils through which God is manifest, 231
covenant, identified as the Community of Israel, 381; of *Binah*, 138; of circumcision, 139, 140; of the foreskin, 139, 144, 208; God's remembering the, 380, 381; of the lips, 139; of the living God, 139; of the master, 139; of the mouth, 139, 144;

of oneness, 144; of peace, 139; of the rainbow, 139; of Sabbath, 139; of the sacred language, 140; of the tongue, 139, 144; of Torah, 139; of unity, 64; sign of, 137; three kinds of, 138–39; symbolically identified with Torah, 138; uplifting of, 381; and the letter *yod*, 379
creation, account of, 168; balance of judgment and mercy, 270; identical withredemption, 94; identified as emanation, 33; process with the divine, 94; versus eternity, 88
crown, feminine assuming the posture of, 365; of royalty, 271; on the head of the righteous, 365; on the Torah scroll, 365; premature elongation of, 369; transformed from a vessel, 94
cutting the shoots, 199

daʿat elyon, 253; in the pattern of the phallus, 270
day, side of light on the right, 175
death, 52, 53, 264; angel of, 247; before one dies, 213, 352, 523–24n162, 586n152; caused by the separation of Eve from Adam, 165; by the kiss of *Shekhinah*, 582n106; ecstatic experience of conjunction compared to, 346; ensues from union with *Shekhinah*, 571n185; eros of, 353; erotic undertones of, 352; and the feminine, 106, 354; kiss of, 346, 582n104, 586n149; linked to the supplication prayer, 571n185; nexus of love and, 352, 586n154; of the body, 587n162; of the body of Moses, 431n357; of the Edomite kings, 311, 386, 387; of eros, 353; of Jesus, 486n180; of language, 481n114; of the martyrs of Caesarea, 310; of Nadab and Abihu, 266–67; of the righteous a means of atonement, 548n36; personification of, 534n306; and the philosophical life, 213; simulated, 121, 240, 571n185; vision of the divine presence occurs at the moment of, 352, 586n150; wisdom of, 498n88; world of, 354
deconstruction, 90, 93; as *clōtural* reading, 86
dehiscence, 196
demonic, 60; impurity associated with nations of the world, 223
demut, xii, 109; secret of the forms in *Malkhut*, 149
dénégation, 160 archaic
derekh ha-shemot, 234
desire, abolition of in the eschatological Sabbath, 371; abrogation of, 52, 296, 314, 350, 364; advent of, 129; and asceticism, 558n1; and the ascetic ideal of the artist, 42–43; axis of, 131; Buddhaland divested of, 57; beyond desire, 267, 313; castration and the cutting off of, 562n52; chain of, 325; circumcision and the abrogation of, 135; consummation of, 359; contrasted with love, 582n105; culmination of the vision of God, 352; death of Jesus and the overcoming of, 486n486; dependent on the construction of a feminine to receive, 285, 376, 381; and the depiction of *Shekhinah* as bride, 376; detachment from, 119; distinguished from will, 166; domestication of in Gregory of Nyssa's intepretation of the Song, 525n182; economy of, 449n137; empty of, 121; for intellect as the efficient cause in the universe, 554n144; for invisibility, 192; for the kiss, 585n149; for lost unity, 288–89; for the other as other, 129, 130, 269, 287, 288; for the other as self, 324; for self-representation, 284; for system, 92; for transcendence, 289; harnessing of, 42; hermeneutics of, 442n71; and homoerotic bonding, 327; imaginary object of, 131; increased by delight and joy, 182; intelligible in contrast to sensible, 351; and the interior experience of poetry, 292; in the Garden of Eden, 569n152; lacking in Ein Sof, 368; and light, 317; linked to the female, 52, 53, 55, 304; manliness attained by the ascetic renunciation of, 306; and mental activity, 278; not to be understood, 91; not to desire, 136, 232, 269, 297, 298, 558 n10; ocular, 135; of angels to push away Aqiva, 369; of ape to be like man, 203; of Christian men to become brides of Christ, 301; of Eve to be equal to Adam, 61; of the father for the daughter, 497n83, 586–87n163; of the female for the male aroused by supernal waters, 353; of the feminine to receive, 188, 386; of the four spirits, 361; of the glory to ascend, 349; of God for the phallic potency, 378; of God for the righteous, 328; of God for *Shekhinah*, 329, 330; of the male to copulate, 182, 271; of the male to ejaculate without female, 310, 386, 387; of the male to project, 77, 183, 378; of the male to restore what has been taken from him, 148, 323, 376, 493n40; of the man to arouse the woman, 314; of the man to be contained, 381; of the masculine above aroused by *Shekhinah*, 324; of the masculine to amass power, 49, 173; of the masculine to overcome duality and separation, 323; of the mind to be conjoined to the intelligible world, 349; of Moses to behold Metatron, 487n209; of the rational soul for God, 346; of renunciation, 297; of the *Shekhinah* for the righteous man, 325; of the soul for the divine, 298; of the soul to become one with the Active Intel-

lect, 347; of woman directed to man, 61, 171; of *Yesod*, 362; originating in the imagination, 347; overcoming of, 302; overcoming of as a prerequisite to attain esoteric wisdom, 566n107; paradox of, 288, 298; personified as temptress, 300; phallic nature of, 136, 141, 378, 553–54n140; and the poetic gesture, 432n362; primordial, 14; procreation the rectification of, 267; psychic landscape of, 458n241; rational, 269; and rectification, 311; reflective nature of, 297; renunciation of, 297; renunciation of and the contemplative ideal, 269, 308, 318, 364; resonating in the Song of Songs, 336, 337, 343, 355, 361; resurrected body and the celibate conquest of, 471n435; righteous void themselves of, 70; ritual as escape from, 560n25; root of the ascetic impulse, 296; satiation of, 297; scopic nature of and the veil, 529n235; sensible and intelligible, 351; severed from its metaphysical basis, 315; signifier of, 128, 129; space of, 132; surplus of, 130; and temporality, 396n67; and thought, 551n100; to consummate union, 336, 343; to contain, 95; to desire or not to desire, 297; to envision the invisible and to utter the ineffable, 293; to know the wisdom of holy unity, 326; to participate in the Good, 524n163; to see God, 229; to surrender the phallus, 306; virility the conquering of, 264; without an other, 269; and the yearning to transcend otherness, 389

devarim ruḥaniyyim, 247, 248

devequt, 32, 35, 39, 122, 237, 267, 288, 477n71, 569n159; consequent to love of God, 583n125; David's longing for, 377; ecstatic separation of soul from body, 477n67; erotic dynamic of, 354, 581n90, 582n105; of male and female, 591n5; of the soul, 264, 347, 349, 350; of spirit with spirit, 361; of thought, 209; to nothing, 264; and sexual cohabitation, 315; and the theurgical task of *tiqqun*, 565n96; with the Presence, 389; and worship of the heart, 234; and visualization, 377. *See also* hitdabbequt

devequt ba-ayin, 264

devequt ha-neshamah, 350

dharma, neither male nor female, 56

dhikr, 226

différance, 3, 86; hermeneutical condition of, 160; indifference of, 102; writing as, 87

difference, identical, 374

dimyonot, 203, 242

Din, 64, 68, 181

disclosure, concealment of, 160; paradoxically identified as occlusion/concealment, 17, 31

discourse, extending beyond language, 197–98

dissemination, 91

dissimulation, of the secret, 160

diyoqna, 9, 38

donkey driver, discourse of, 222

dugma, 33, 35, 36, 37, 38, 336, 426n305

du-parṣufim, 145, 167, 176, 505n196

duplicity, and the beginning, 91; feminine, 59; hermeneutical, 133; of meaning, 336; of revealing and concealing, 224; of secrecy, 2, 160, 262; truth of, 196

dyad, 196

ecstasy, experience of, 261; of contemplative envisioning, 268; of mystical union, 299, 322; and textual engagement, 322; and theurgy, 209

Edomite kings, 180, 385; archetypal representation of the emasculated power of Christian celibate priests, 309–310, 386; come forth from the aspect of *malkhut*, 311; death of signifies the purification of judgment and the production of *Malkhut*, 311, 386; engendered as female, 311; female waters without a masculine counterpart, 311; forces of impurity in the Godhead, 386; identified as the female points, 596n59; lack of balance between male and female, 386; and masturbation, 386; no correlation between the impulse to bestow and the desire to receive, 386; nullification of due to the fact that Adam was not arrayed as a unity of male and female, 310, 387; swayed to ejaculate with no female vessel to receive the seminal discharge, 385; unbalanced forces of judgment, 180, 311. *See also* primordial kings

efes, designation of the Infinite, 96; space betwixt matter and form, 97

egoity, the will to overflow, 102

Egypt, symbolic of the carnal realm, 156

Ein Sof, 27, 29, 64, 67, 68; beyond all names, 124; cannot be known, 105; cleaving to, 288; collapse of polarity within, 97; delineated as divested of all garments, 404n69; demarcated as the place that is no place, 233; depicted as formless, 123, 200; described as the world of masculinity, 187; distinguished from *Ayin*, 104, 179; does not produce end or beginning, 105; equanimous nature of, 104; the head-that-is-no-head, 269; the hyperessence of the inessential, 269; and the image of the abyss, 431n361; indifference of, 105; initiating gesture mirrors transgression of Adam, 182; light that is above *Keter*, 181; musing that comes from, 199; nondifferentiated oneness of, 95, 99; ontically inseparable from *Keter*, 179; otherwise-than-being, 125; possibility of being absorbed in, 269; prayer situated within, 281; pure mercy with no admixture of judgment, 105, 181; resolution of opposites in, 104; root of indifference, 98; sefirotic edifice unites with and ascends to, 389; soul cleaving to, 125; source of all being, 198; trace of the light of, 186; transcends all enumeration and demarcation, 179; and the uroboric union of father and mother, 105

Elohim, the aspect of the male, 180; the attribute of judgment, 95; conjoined to YHWH, 170

emanation, progression from silence to thought, voice, and speech, 286

emasculation, characteristic of the primordial kings of Edom, 310; mark of the demonic, 266

embodiment, 24, 46; conscious, 192; cultural and biological aspects of, 80; erotic nature of, 119; and language in the poetic symbol, 42; and the image of the garment, 248; linguistic comportment of, 246, 259; of language, 194; of the splendor of *Shekhinah*, 255; semiotic nature of, 136, 201; taxonomy of, 201; textual, 191, 211, 240, 246, 260, 263

engenderment, bodily, 302; body of, 148, 312; chain of, 53, 356; human sexuality, 363; line of, 106, 188; of the human body, 267; symbols of, 80

enthronement, of the celestial king, xii; portrayed as sacred union, 143, 356, 378; and worship, 391n5

epoché, 6, 91

ereignis, 18

erlebnis, 4

eros, ascetic transformation of, 318; articulation of the flesh, 118; awakening from the left, 285; beyond the psychosexual, 126; carnal an image of the true, 271; closed circle of thought thinking itself, 271; convergence of erotic and noetic, 269; death of, 353; eschatological transmutation from bisexual to monosexual, 324; and the fantasy of the male to attain psychosomatic wholeness, 373; and gnosis, 269; identified as the phallic potency, 287; and the image of the rose, 63; intellectual, 267, 286; and language, 118; and the libidinal drive, 118, 126; linked to man's desire to be contained by the woman, 381; merging of body and word, 45; metaphorical nature of, 336; mysterious nature of, 63; mystery of, 261; and noesis, 268, 286, 316, 328; noetic quality of, 271; of consciousness, 261; of the impossible, 289; of the kiss, 362; of mystery, 261; of mystical experience dependent on the renunciation of carnal eros, 298; of perplexity, 268; of *sha'ashu'a*, 281; ontology of, 117; personified as female, 53; phallus the focalpoint of, 373; pitched in the human body, 118; Platonic, 288; play of, 269; of self-contemplation, 182; poetic nature of, 46; reversal of, 367; spiritualization of, 318; and the striving of all being for ontic unity, 118; subjugated to the rule of logos, 306; suffering of, 374; texture of shaped by the sexual desires and anxieties of men, 373; and thanatos, 352, 571n185; totality of and the striving for self-actualization, 269; worldly and spiritual, 128

eroticism, and asceticism, 86, 136, 296–99, 319, 322, 352, 363; and esotericism, 269, 399n6; and martyrdom, 318; of knowledge, 269; of language, 118; of the Song expressive of the movement betwixt the pull of attraction and the push of deferment, 355; sacred nature of, 297; spiritual, 333, 363; subsumed under the body of the text rather than the text of the body, 335; and the texture of mystical experience, 308

eschaton, angelmorphic state of, 300–301; ascetic renunciation of carnal sexuality anticipates the spiritual eros of, 364, 367; marked by the overcoming of gender dimorphism in the repairing of the male androgyne, 366, 390; ontic restoration of all divine grades, 389; retrieval of the primordial beginning, 364; signifies the reintegration of the feminine as part of the masculine, 387

eshet ḥayyil, 80

esotericism, 143, 197; dialectic of, 17; dissimilitude of, 134; and eroticism, 261, 399n6, 474n33, 489n13; hermeneutical dilemma of, 222; and hermeneutics, 399n6; Islamic, 30, 225, 422n247, 529n231, 536n330, 577n33; of kabbalah and the symbol of the veil in Sufism, 224; origins of in Ancient Greece, 469n414; phallomorphic nature of, 46, 75, 128, 144, 146; philosophical, 410n131; popularization of, 446n116; structure of exhibited by the veil, 233; veritable deception of, 16; wisdom of encoded in rabbinic dicta, 59

etrog, 150, 151; 494n47

eshet ḥayyil, 80, 185, 186, 459n250, 495n71, 591n11

eternal recurrence, 44

ethereal body, 38, 251

Eucharist, 190, 513n2; and the breaking of the bread,

342; ecstatic ingestion of, 569n173; mystery of, 543n433; sacrament of, 342
eunuch/s, 67, 136; demarcates the members of the zoharic fraternity, 319; designation of a third kind of gender that is neither male nor female, 303; erotic and phallic nature of, 320; ideal of the manly, 302; for the sake of the kingdom of heaven, 302; an emasculated male, 303; priests of the Mother Goddess, 570–71n185; signifies the state of an implied phallic potency, 265; symbol of masculine fecundity, 321; who keep the Sabbath, 318–19
evil inclination, 59; corresponds to the lower *Shekhinah*, 595n195; creation of and the arousal of, 443n84; filth of, 121; harnessed together with the good inclination, 169; purpose of ritual to subdue, 247; symbolized by the serpent, 548n29
exile, characterized by sexual dimorphism, 373; conjugal mating of male and female rectifies the ontological separation of, 381; fragmentation of, 165; marked by the seeing of what should be concealed, 382; overcome by sexual union, 367; and the nature of commentary, 117; and prophetic envisioning, 383; of *Shekhinah*, 308, 319, 355, 374, 593n35; *Shekhinah* compared to a bride entering the nuptial chamber when she comes out of, 376; and the separation of masculine and feminine aspects of the divine, 354, 380; vision indicative of, 382
eye, apple of, 383; evil, 132; fashion eyes in place of an, 50; gaze of, 593n33; of the intellect, 176, 384; of a fish, 375; of the Lord, 181; of the mind/heart, 196, 212, 214, 523n150; of spiritual vision, 529n231; on the right not complemented by eye on the left, 179–82; open, 179, 375; single, 375, 508n242; spiritual, 194; symbol for female genitalia, 508n242; that sees is the eye that is seen, 214; that sees with blindness, 42; third, 508n242; and the upper phallus, 508n242, 572n200; what is perceptible to, 32

face, disclosed as veil, 224; euphemism for the phallus, 136; of God beheld by means of *Shekhinah*, 377; of *Shekhinah*, 137; to-face, 108, 175, 177, 185, 223, 224, 228, 313, 352, 355, 376, 386, 528n228, 529n233, 555n151, 591n14; unmasking the, 223; unveiling of, 225
faith, harmonized with thought, 263; mysteries of, 64; mystery of, 146, 324, 361; mystical import of and the paradoxical identity of beginning and end, 284; the opening created by the three closed sides of *beit*, 258; secret abode of, 258; self-enclosed circle of wisdom, 283; technical designation of *Shekhinah*, 318, 319; three festive meals of, 368; three knots of, 257, 258
fanā, 30, 227, 228; *al-fanā*, 227, 232, 234; effacement of the distinction between perceiver and perceived in the supreme mystical state of, 230
fear, 109
fearful asymmetry, 177
female, adorned like a bride entering the nuptial chamber, 376; assimilated into the corona of the phallus, 389; assumes the form of the encircling line that crowns the point, 180; assumes the posture of the crown on the head of the righteous, 365, 387; and the attribute of judgment, 69, 80, 95, 181, 379; becoming male, 301, 437n15, 440–41n57; comprises the thirty-two paths of masculine wisdom, 161; conceived as the vessel that delimits the limitlessly overflowing potency of the male, 385; contained in the male, 105, 156, 164, 174, 175, 176, 188, 376; constituted by the phallic energies of the masculine, 161; crown of the male, 389; and the demiurgical role of creation, 150; demonic character of portrayed as rageful warrior and alluring Gentile woman sexually baiting the male, 374; demonization of expressed in the image of the effeminate male, 385; depicted as wife who is the crown of her husband, 387; depicted as a vessel to receive the seminal discharge, 376; derivation from the male, 52, 72, 75, 150; derives from the brain of the male, 94; duplicitous nature of, 60, 154; encircling crown on head of male, 110; encompassing the male, 187; eschatological restoration to the male, 85, 110, 365, 376; exclusive worship of, 171; and the image of the fringe, 385; impotent male has the same status as, 385; inferior status to the male, 66, 164; life-bestowing qualities phallically transforms, 151; masculinized in the moment of sexual union, 389; memorialization of, 374; the not-all that sets the limit to the all, 130; ontic root of in the corona of the phallus, 180, 375; ontically restored to the *membrum virile*, 381, 382; ontological locus in the male, 311; primal garment, 108; reification of as an autonomous force considered to be idolatrous, 385; sexed rather than gendered, 187; sexual instability associated with, 53; surrounding the male, 376; transposed into the corona of the phallus, 311,

323, 365; two aspects of, 75; who provides space to enclose the male becomes thereby the encircling part of the male, 381; womb and ground of being, 150
female/feminine waters (*mayyin nuqvin*), 76, 77, 182, 183; and the corona of the phallus, 184; Edomite kings arose in the secret of, 310–11; incite male waters to overflow, 311
femaleness, bondage of, 55, 303
feminine, adulation of, 49, 72; aligned with the left, 58, 59, 64, 76, 95, 104, 105, 107, 108, 169, 171, 175, 177–78, 179, 180, 181, 183, 285, 353, 354, 375, 443n84, 447n118, 470n419, 493n40, 511–12n272; alleged autonomy of obliterated, 301–302; ancillary position of, 62; arrayment of, 376, 587n178; associated with nature, 150; associated with the world of death, 354; attached to yet separate from the masculine, 152; and the attribute of speech, 362; attribution of excess and justice to, 60; beginning of its existence in the corona, 76, 184, 186; body and sensuality aligned with, 51, 54, 299, 304, 363, 595n53; capacity to receive, 104, 169, 183, 277, 279, 284; capacity to withhold, 95; characterization of the lower glory vis-à-vis the upper masculine glory, 145; characterized as darkness, 353; characterized as receptive, 75; comprised in the male, 174; constitution of, 285; contained in the male, 176, 188; and constriction, 83, 108; crowning part of the male, 187; demarcated as the dwelling place of the phallic potency, 373; and the demonic, 81, 302; and the demiurgical role of creation, 150; depicted as the nucleus in the infinite circle, 382; depicted as a single point, 375; depicted at the beginning as the point occluded within the ether, 383; desire to receive, 188; and disclosure, 132; duplicitous nature of, 154; Edomite kings characterized as, 310, 311; elevated to the masculine, 301; encompasses the male, 187; enfolded in the masculine, 105, 176; eschatological restoration to the masculine, 85, 365–66; and the figure of Wisdom, 143, 163, 277; force of gestation, 189; garment that reveals the light it conceals, 384; gender transformation of, 186, 365; glory of the masculine, 150; and the heart, 151, 161, 495n62; idolatry identified as the exclusive worship of, 154, 172; and the image of the mirror, 595n53; and the image of the veil, 224; in the position of the crown on the head of the male in the beginning and in the end, 365–66; incorporated in the masculine, 183; inferior or weakened male, 164; inscripted on the corona of the phallus, 311; integration of in the masculine, 152; integration of in the phallus, 324; and interiority, 134; Jewish collectivity portrayed as, 300; and *jouissance*, 130, 279; and judgment, 64, 66, 80, 95, 105, 106, 168, 172, 173, 311, 325, 353; light of diminished, 62; liminal status of, 153; linked epistemically to the feminine, 385; male who ejaculates without a female transvalued as, 310, 387; masculinization of, 55, 167, 327; and materiality, 265, 326; mirror that veils the unveiling of the veil, 384; and negative commandments, 266; ontic root of in the male androgyne, 180, 366; ontically derived from masculine, xiv, 174; ontically inferior status of, 170; ontologically containment of in the masculine, 149, 164, 165; ontologically contextualized as the corona of the phallus, 151, 366; and the Oral Torah, 133, 139, 257; phallicization of, 324; point hidden in the ether, 383; portrayal of Jesus as, 51; reabsorbed into the masculine, 105; reintegrated into the masculine, 175, 323, 327; restitution to the phallus, 324; restoration to the masculine, 107, 110, 311, 324, 325, 387; restored to the corona, 324; ring that envelops the glory it exposes, 384; root of in the primordial kings who died, 386; and the second *he* of the Tetragrammaton, 154, 172, 326; saintly, 302; *Shekhinah* imaginally configured in the language of, 46; shelter that reveals the masculine potency concealed therein, 385; sheltered in her boundaries like a point enclosed in the center of the circle, 382; signified by the letter *beit*, 353; site of impurity, 353; subordination of, 49; subservience of, 265; subsidiary to the masculine, 86; surrounds the male in the image of the corona, 76; symbolic of the resistance to symbolic identification, 130; symbolically depicted as the citron, 150, 151; and the textual artifact, 304–305; textual body of consituted by male community of kabbalists, 330; throne characterized as, xii, 143; three images of: sister, daughter, mother, 161; Torah portrayed in images of, 143, 274; transformed into an aspect of the masculine, 71, 323; transposition of male mystic in relation to God, 350; two aspects of, 75–76; union of masculine and, 312, 319, 325; and the vital soul, 306; vilification and veneration of, 59; world of, 82; yearns to be the space to contain the phallic potency, 355
femininity, and the aspect of disclosure, 132, 133;

capacity to withhold, 95; correlated with body/sexuality, 54, 57, 304; and the demonic, 59, 81; fleeing from, 303; and the figure of Cain, 80; and interiority, 134; liminal status of, 153; linked to matter, 265; related to division, 76; represented as the membrane of the ether of the supernal wisdom, 76–77; subordination to the masculine, 49; and the symbolic state of poverty, 164; symbolized by the lily, 67; and the textual artifact, 304–305
field, connected to yet separate from the garden, 164; symbolic of the feminine, 154, 161
first copulation (*ziwwug ri'shon*), autoerotic arousal of the male, 182
First Principle, 66
fish, eye of, 375
flesh, 25; adhering to place and time, 194; articulated by language, 118, coiling over of visible and tangible, 194; enfolding of, 193; incarnation of the word into, 191, 194, 216; midway between object and subject, 194; of the visible, 193, 194; ontology of, 191; semiotic, 262; textual nature of, 262; thorny, 216; transfiguration of into word, 191, 194; word made, 194
food, symbolic of the divine overflow, 330
foot/feet, of Moses, 216; sandals removed from, 216; symbolic of the phallic potency, 257
footstool, 39
foreskin, 137; removal of diminishes the sex drive, 486n184
forgetfulness, 17
forgiveness, 367
four, levels of meaning in Scripture, 221, 223; mystery of the, 360
fourfold, 35, 36; born from the union of the spirit/breath of the male and the spirit/breath of the female, 362; expressed in the word *shabbat*, 84; in Heidegger's thought, 20, 21, 416n188, 417n195
fraternity, 37, 41, 132, 222, 314, 319; ascetic lifestyle of, 570n176; bonding of comprises mystery of the androgyne, 388; constitute the face of *Shekhinah*, 573n237; engaged in Torah study and sustained by spiritual food of the angels, 527n219; homoerotic nature of, 388, 572n214; male members constitute the feminine *Shekhinah*, 329, 355; members of constitute the male body of God, 327; of male mystics rise at midnight, 330; mystical bonding of, 388; of Simeon ben Yoḥai, 259, 364; prolepsis of eschatological transformation anticipated by, 324; and the redemptive hermeneutic of walking, 374; *Zohar* produced by, 48, 207, 334; zoharic, 82, 133, 243, 257, 320, 528n224. *See also* ḥavrayya

Garden of Eden, 61, 73, 74; Adam adopted celibacy after the sin in, 561n35; at midnight God enters into, 320, 570n178; condition of Adam and Eve prior to the sin in, 315; fruits of, 248; God takes delight in the souls of the righteous in, 328, 329; righteous sit in, 73, 74, 320; sexual desire in, 569n152; sin of Adam and Eve in, 166, 369, 548n29
garment, 8, 9, 10, 37; body compared to, 222; exoteric meaning of text, 221, 222; God's donning symbolic of the emanation of wisdom, 529n237; hides and reveals the name, 208; image of in kabbalistic literature, 225, 234; incarnation of the glory in anthropomorphic form of an angel, 254; in which the dead are attired, 54; medium that reveals by concealing and conceals by revealing, 225; the mirror that overcomes the inside/outside dichotomy, 234; mystery of, 200, 234; the name that reveals the nameless it conceals, 219; of light, 248; of males, 597 n. 83; of skin, 248; of Torah, 221; putting Christ on as, 50; rabbinic, 251; second, 251; secret seen through, 222, 223. *See also* levush / levushin, levusha, and malbush
gaze, xii, xxii, 141; center of, 293; contemplative, 198; eroticism of, 274; face to face, 175, 528n228; fixed on Noah's rainbow, 382; no longer focused on *Shekhinah* as an autonomous female persona but as the diadem that encircles the head of the male, 375; of consciousness, 24; of imagination, 145; of Jesus, 341, 424 n. 282; of God, 329, 379; of God upon the rainbow to remember the sign of the covenant, 378; of the male, 560n33; on the diadem, 377; on King Solomon, 162, 366; on the rainbow prohibited, 593 n. 33; phallic, 133, 135, 137; phallocentric nature of, 136; phallomorphic, 378; transforms the feminine, 378; upon a candle, 326; upon the face of Moses forbidden, 385; upon the iconic manifestation of God, 244
Gelassenheit / Gelāzenheit, 42, 432n364, 472n6
Genealogy, 2–3
gender, dynamic nature of, 94; dimorphism, 56, 360; correlative nature of, 177; eschatological overcoming of, 49, 58, 74, 84, 94, 174, 332, 360, 366, 390; function of difference, 177; not a function of correlation but of self-actualized singularity, 178; transformation of, 49; transposition of, 107

Gevurah, 37, 178, 367; corresponds to the left arm, 174; on the left, 181
gift, 21, 23, 33, 155; and absence of reciprocity, 158; bestowed by father upon his daughter, 586–87n162; daughter given to the son as, 157–61; defies the limits of temporal possibility, 159; denotes an intentional transgression of a sexual norm, 161; Derridean explanation of, 158–60; and the impossible, 158; of love, 339; of the perfect, 65; opens the circle of economy, 158; and secrecy, 159; and the temporalization of language, 158; time of in the present, 159
gimmel, symbolic of the son, 279
ghayb, 228, 230
glory, xiii, 34, 39, 73; angelic nature of, 430–31n354; appears in the likeness of a human form, 209; assumes tangible shape, 253; commandments identified as, 249; crowning vision of, 353; desires and yearns to ascend to the supernal light, 349; face of envisioned through mask of Jacob's visage, 145; feminine status of, 153, 172; male virginal, 303; masculine nature of, 143; phallic connotation of, 163; receive image of, 55; rendered most conspicuous in the occlusion of its sign, 383; upper and lower: masculine and feminine, 145. *See also* kavod
Gnosticism, 110, 389–90
God, absent from the text in which he is present, 257; bemuses himself with Torah, 273, 278; composed of negative and affirmative forces, 104; conceals esoteric matters in Scripture, 243; contemplates intelligible world, 220; diadem of made from the prayers of Israel, 389; elevated as a heave offering by the spiritual elite of Israel, 308; face of beheld through *Shekhinah*, 377; feminization of male mystic in relation to, 350; homoerotic bonding of with kabbalists, 329–32, 350; hides secrets in garments of Torah, 223; and his name, 249; identical with Torah, 247; identified with Israel and Torah, 245; imaginal body of, 119, 246; infinity of, 138; linguistic evolution of, 284; looked into Torah and created the world, 274, 285; male body of constituted by kabbalistic fraternity, 327; mystical body of, 243; relation to circumcised Jewish males, 276; seven holy forms attributed to, 147, 149, 164, 491n29, n33; sons of, 302; takes counsel with angelic retinue, 220; textual body of, 249; threefold unity of, 245, 283; took delight with Torah two thousand years prior to creation, 277, 281; vision of, 331; visits the souls of the righteous in the Garden of Eden at midnight, 320, 328; and world identical in their difference, 230
good inclination, corresponds to the upper *Shekhinah*, 595n195; harnessed together with the evil inclination, 169; 247
governance, 250
Great Mother, 67; androgynous nature of, 68; and ritual copulation, 126
gufei torah, 243, 249

halakhah, 58
hanhagah, 250
harmony, 104
hashwa'ah, 98, 99, 104
hashwa'at ha-aḥdut, 104
hatha yoga, 322
ḥavrayya, 37, 314
hawwayot, 285
heart, book of, 191; contemplation of, 362; directed toward heaven, 314; focus of, 291; identified as the woman, 327; permutation of letters contemplated in the, 238; pledging of to be removed from the world, 308–309; polishing of, 433n367; rendered metaphoriocally as the cup of cosmic vision, 233; reveals the veil, 233; righteous direct the will to the supernal king, 327; rumination of, 199; screen/veil through which the internal is externalized and the external internalized, 235; site of spiritual vision, 226, 233; symbolic of the feminine, 161; tablet of, 566n107; and the throne, 234, 534n307; wise of the, 223. *See also* qalb
heavenly tablets, 202
Hebrew, the Adamic language to which all other languages may be traced, 197; angels composed of, 241; body composed of, 240, 251; comprises all other languages, 204; constituitive element of all that exists, 209, 285; contained in the *yod*, 282; derives from the Holy Spirit, 518n92; divine language that God taught to Adam, 203; first language created by Adam, 519n102; form and name of divinity, 244; the holy language, 203, 518n92; hylomorphic substance of Torah, 240; images of divinity, 244; instrument of creation and revelation, 202; language spoken by God and the angels, 203, 517n88; letters of comprise seed-thought of *Ḥokhmah*, 196, 285, 286, 321; material by which the human body, Adam, the tabernacle, and the Torah is constituted, 259; material of the astral body, 251; matrix language of creation, xiii,

5, 118, 197, 200, 204, 294; most perfect of all languages, 203; natural as opposed to conventional, 203, 207, 518–19n99; permutation of the letters of, 235; prime matter by which Torah is composed, 241; revealed and concealed through the veil of matter, 201; semantic kinship to Arabic and Aramaic, 203; seventy languages contained within, 203; twenty-two letters comprised in the Tetragrammaton, 10, 128, 139–40, 196, 197, 207, 208, 240, 244; twenty-two letters comprised in the *yod*, 282. *See also* leshon ha-qodesh
Heikhalot literature, 292
henosis, 218
heresy, 172; linked to the female, 505–506n201
hermeneutic, circle, 112, 114; duplicity, 133; reflexivity, 262; unendingness, 117
hermeneutical, inseparable from the ontological, 223
hermeneutics, ascetic discipline, 115; nihilistic vocation, 114; of secrecy exemplified by the veil, 232; radical, 116–17
Ḥesed, 37, 41, 61, 64, 181, 367; corresponds to the right arm, 174
hierogamy, 165, 175
hieros gamos, and the endogamous tendency, 160; occurs with the spatial confines of the holy of holies, 355; of enthronement, 356; of the King and Matrona, 357
hierophany, 262
hieroglyphs, 214
high priest, 238
ḥijāb, 27, 226, 227, 228, 532n262
ḥikmat al-ishrāq, 239
Hinduism, 47
hitbodedut, 120, 121, 346, 475n46
hitbonenut, 210
hitdabbequt, 120
Hod, 61, 64, 178; corresponds to the left foot, 174
Ḥokhmah, 63, 69, 178, 197, 258, 270, 286, 365; beginning of the lower nine *sefirot*, 105; bridge that connects *Keter* and *Binah*, 197; corresponds to the brain and palate, 173; emblematic of the father, 196; and the image of the father, 154, 358; seed-thought of, 196; seminal fluid of, 83; supernal point, 105; signified by the *beit*, 383; signified by the *yod*, 125; upper and lower: symbolic of father and daughter, 282
ḥokhmat ha-ṣeruf, 240
holiness, priestly ideal of, 250
holy One, blessed be he, 34, 70; crowned from above and below, 70; in the future will be a crown on the head of the righteous, 73
holy spirit, 50, 69; by means of Solomon uttered the Song, 360; comprehension of, 120; enlightened kabbalist gains knowledge of the letters by means of, 282; identified as *Shekhinah*, 528n224; illuminates the soul by virtue of the song, 350–351; in Shīʿite belief, 239; gift of, 340; vision of, 545n452. *See also* ruaḥ ha-qodesh; rūḥ alquds; ruaḥ qudsha
holy unity (*yiḥuda qaddisha*), 169
homoeroticism, 312, 322; between father and son in the divine, 368, 370; and the bonding of the righteous man below and the phallic gradation above, 593n37; carnality of celibate renunciation, 324, 367; climaxes in the highest manifestation of the divine, 368; framed in heterosexual language, 331–32, 366–67, 388; heterosexual eros gives way to, 324, 327; heterosexual imagery of the Song transposed into, 337–38, 350; and mystical ecstatsy, 388; of the mystical experience distinguished from homosexuality, 367; realized in the mystical bonding of the male fraterniy, 388; and the texture of messianic unification, 370; underpinnings of the heteroerotic symbolism, 370
homoousios, 40
Horizonthaftigkeit, 195
humility, the means by which the soul participates in the mystery of incarnation, 342
hyperousios, 10, 289

icon, of the invisible God, 122; of Jacob, 143, 144
identity, and indifference, 102, 104; difference of, 98, 104, 284, 373; differentiating by identifying difference, 117; indifferent, 374; of difference, 64, 66, 98, 101, 104, 270–71, 284, 373; of opposites, 27; of opposition versus opposition of, 98; realized through difference, 232
idolatry, and the desire to see God, 229; impulse for, 122; of the book, 206; worship of the female as autonomous, 154, 172, 374
illicit sexuality, mystery of, 159; secret of, 299. *See also* sitrei/sod arayot
image, comprises male and female, 146, 312; configured in the imagination, 119; and thecorrespondence of human and divine limbs, 147; lacking in the holy of holies, 292; of an anthropos, 121; of God, 35, 36, 50, 55, 121, 122, 164, 312; of Jacob, 144, 145; of negation, 219; of the One, 214; and sound, 210; symbolic representation of the invisible and inaudible, 127; and word converge, 287, 293
imagelessness, refuge of all images, 123

imaginal body, 35, 39, 42; of God, 119, 122, 125, 246, 249; incarnate form of YHWH, 128, 240; and the supernal Torah, 41, 219
imaginary, feminine and masculine, 86; and the real, 279
imagination, xii, 4–7, 10, 18, 25, 29, 32, 39; carnal desire originates in, 347; cleansed by ascetic control of body, 119, 121; configuration of time and space in, 38; depicted as the flame of the encircling sword, 235; divine element of the soul, 120; draws a veil between this world and the world-to-come, 476n55; endows the formless with form, 384; exegetical nature of, 88; gaze of, 145; hermeneutical function of, 120; human cognition intractably dependent on, 236; image of the *sefirot* conjured within, 124, 200; and the imaging of the imageless, 120; linked to the feminine, 384, 595n53; locus of in the heart, 120, 122, 125; mirror of, 178, 235; and poetic fabrication, 44; and the role of deformation, 476n55; site of temporality, 23; spiritual entities assume corporeal form within, 122; symbols located within, 120; throne upon which *Shekhinah* dwells, 122; vehicle by which soul merges with Torah, 239; word-become-image configured therein, 40
imago terrae, and the Sophianic potency, 153
imitatio Christi, 300
Imma, 181, 369
immanence, 31
incarnation, 30; convergence of semiotic and somatic, 40; and the image of the bread that is broken, 342; and the identification of God and Torah, 243; kenotic intepretation of, 340–41; and the mystical intent of the kiss of Christ, 340; of the divine form in the revealed text, 205; of the flesh in the word, 191, 260; of the name in the body of Torah, 255; of the Word in Jesus, 243, 257, 260, 305, 340; of the Word in the flesh, 191, 260; poetic, 191, 197, 211, 246, 260; understood docetically, 243
incest, 48, 183; attributed mythopoeically to God, 160; between father and daughter, 162; figurative depiction of divine unity, 160
incomprehensible, measured in the comprehension of the immeasurable, 219
indifference, 98, 99; in Schelling's thought, 100; metalogic of, 99–100; ontological, 196; rendered indifferent, 377
ineffability, mystical claims of, 219; of language, 420n240; of the name preserved by the epithet, 291; paradox of uttering a statement of, 343
infinite, beyond predication and negation, 98; beyond temporal emplacement, 105; circular nature of, 100; coincidence of opposites within, 98; non-differentiatedness of, 99; originary arousal and the phallic yearning to become other, 270; semiosis, 205; shapeless abyss, 123; speaking, 197; will to create and sexual autoexcitation, 182; word in the, 218
intellect, image of the One, 214
intentionality, corporeal, 197; essence of corporeity, 192; required of Jewish male at the time of intercourse, 313. *See also* kawwanah
intercorporeality, 25, 192
intercourse, means by which female is restored to male, 148, 175, 267; midnight the propitious time to engage in, 320; mimetic rite that facilitates conjunction in the Godhead, 308; rectification of the male androgyne, 149, 175, 267; sanctity of, 317; spiritual as opposed to physical, 321
interflesh, 193
interpretation, 111–12; arises from the confrontation of text and reader, 115; play of, 91; translation a mode of, 112, 223
intertext, of body and world, 194
inverted world, 31
invisible, chasm between subject and object, 196; contrasted with non-isible, 195; presence, 196
invisibility, at the heart of all that is visible, 420n240; depth of the visible, 414n181; renders visible the invisible, 195–96; visibility of the medium consists of its, 233
ʿishq, 346, 568n151, 582n103
ish zar, 243
Israel, 33, 258; Aaron blessed people of, 152; and the Active Intellect, 581n91; aligned with the holy right side of mercy, 243; angelic status of, 203, 205, 210; angel of God sent before, 241; and angels balanced on one scale, 221; Assembly of, 240, 241; banishment of Jews from the land of, 374; bearers of the sign of the covenant, 275, 305; blood of covenant binds God and, 334; body politic of, 327; bride of, 587n164; capacity to contemplate to the infinite from the measure visualized in the heart, 211; children of, 41; Christian triumphalist claims regarding God's rejection of, 354; cleave to God, 273, 275, 551n87; collectivity of, 575n15; community of, 60, 82, 145, 320, 321, 326, 329, 330, 348, 349, 352, 353, 355, 381, 445n104, 575n17, 576n28, 584–85n135, 586n156, 591n5; condition below

reflects status of divine above, 354; configured as one supernal pattern, 245; conjoined to *Shekhinah*, 326; constitute the limbs of the chariot, 245; contemplate wisdom, 497n83; correspond to the angels above, 221; correlated with divine purity, 223; corronation of God by the prayers of, 453n199; covenantal bond of, 334; crown of God made from the prayers of, 389; depicted by the image of the lily, 593n35; designated by the term *naʿarah*, 327; designated the firstborn of God, 156, 200; desolation of the land of, 376; distinction between nations and, 58; distinguished from the nations, 58; distinguished linguistically, 204; elders of, 257; enlightened of, 211, 309, 566n103; ensouled with a higher body on Yom Kippur, 364; erotic relationship between God and, 275, 276; exile of, 323, 335, 360, 374, 376, 378, 435n2; expulsions of, 360; faithful household in, 265; form of the primal anthropos, 200, 238, 243; future of, 257; glorious form seated upon the throne, 145; God appears before, 331; and God circumscribed in monopsychic unity, 210; God of, 75, 95, 142, 305, 484n160; God's love for, 162, 496n81; go out from exile, 378; guardians of the cosmic language, 205; homolgy between Torah and, 41; house of, 275; ideal politic of, 41; identity of God, Torah, and, 245; land of, 153, 276, 374, 376, 501n136, 519n102; lift God through their prayers, 308; linguistic distinction of, 204; love between God and, 336, 345, 587n165; mercy of *Shekhinah* in relation to, 455n224; metamorphosis of Jacob into, 33; miracles performed to save, 356; monotheistic ideal of, 142; Moses placed Torah before the sons of, 58; mystery of circumcision revealed to, 135; name of *Keter*, 537n344; name of the living creature, 451n14, 489n17; people of, 291; power of derived from the voice, 265; prayers of ascend heavenward, 263; prophets of, 557n193; prophets reveal secret to, 518n95; received the Torah, 257; response to Moses, 535n322; referred to as the people of the book, 229; request to know the name, 263; righteous and pious of, 308, 332; root of the souls of, 431n357; sacred history of, 334, 588n164; *Shekhinah* ascends by means of the benevolent acts of, 592n24; sinners oppress *Shekhinah* and, 593n35; sojourn of in the desert, 291; sons of God, 328; special status of, 551n88; spiritual elite of, 308, 332; splendor of, 41; supreme state of perfection associated with, 565n98; symbolic identification of God, Torah, and, 245; symbolic import of the land of, 153; Tabernacle constructed by, 507–508n234; Tetragrammaton united with, 332; title *adam* applies exclusively to, 245, 258; Torah revealed to, 336;; Torah transmitted to, 41; transformed from masculine to feminine, 327; transformed into the Active Intellect, 535n322; two houses of, 505n195; united with *Shekhinah*, 326; utter doxology, 143, 145; virgin of, 589n225; wisdom mediates between God and, 496n81

ishshah perushah, 299

iterability, xxviii, 90, 92; and the gesture of naming, 92

Iyyun circle, 99

jouissance, ascetic response to displeasure, 297; contemplative ideal of, 550n72; ecstatic state of orgasmic unity, 278; feminine supplementary to the phallus, 130, 279; of submission, 306; phallic nature of, 131, 132, 135, 279, 359; renunciation of beyond phallic desire, 136, 269, 306, 482n119; and *shaʿashʿua*, 278; spiritual eros in kabbalistic lore, 273; and the supplement of mystical ejaculation, 130

judgment, acts in consort with mercy, 168; amelioration of by mercy, 382; capacity to receive, 65, 104; changes into and contained within mercy, 60, 169, 173; characteristic of the female, 95, 104, 106, 168, 379; containment of in mercy, 170; depicted as a pregnant woman, 69; destructive consequences of, 69; the final *he* that completes the Tetragrammaton, 172; joined together with mercy, 173; kabbalists identified as masters of, 327; and the name Elohim, 168; and nothingness, 96; of the male in contrast to the female, 180; shells come forth from, 80; side of magic, 59; sweetened by mercy, 95; symbolized by gold, 162; transformed into mercy, 373; women cleave to, 58

Kabbalah, androcentrism of, xiv, 47, 108; chain of, 86, convergence of theogony and cosmogony, 35; ecstatic, 3, 204; evolved in highly literate circles, 78; genealogy of, 2; and hermeneutic dissembling, 27; imparts meaning to suffering, 42; influence upon Schelling, 43; and the language of poetry, 421n242; Lurianic, 26, 76; monolithic nature of gender symbolism promoted by, xiv; morphology of, 2, 36; phallomorphic dimensions of, 46, 47, 87; phenomenological resemblance of

Christianity and, 256; poetic nature of, xi, 45; polymorphous nature of, 263; prophetic, 88, 120; proximity of Christian faith and the gnosis promulgated by, 257; pure mercy with no admixture of judgment, 105; reified androcentric hegemony, 79; repository of feminist images, 85; resonance of with Spinoza; 96; secret gnosis of, 103; secret side of the feminine, 46–47; site for feminine imaginary, 80; speculative theosophy, xiii; symbol and metaphor in, 36; symbolic orientation of, xiv, 9, 25; tendency to radicalize sexual difference, 58; theosophic, 3, 120, 204; threefold chord enfolded within, 2; typological distinction between theosophic and ecstatic, 399n11; zoharic form of, 48

kamakaladhyana, 559n17

kashf, 226

Karaites, 345. *See also* Mourners of Zion

kavod, phallic connotation of, 163

kawwanah, 95, 120, 122, 209. *See also* intentionality

kelal, formal principle of inclusion and expansion, 284

keli, material principle of exclusion and constriction, 284

kenesset yisra'el, 60, 61, 221, 240

kenosis, and the impulse to empty oneself of impulse, 368; of the image, 556n179; and the mystery of incarnation, 340–41

Keter, 29, 63, 186, 197; above gender differentiation, 64, 178; absolute simplicity of, 64; cannot be comprehended, 179; characterized by one eye, 180, 182; concealed of the concealed, 360, 368; coterminous with infinity, 196; corresponds to the head, 173; demarcated as *efes*, 97; depicted as the place that is no place, 233–34, 375; displays no potentiality for duality, 178; distinguished from the Cause of Causes, 179; entirely right, 180, 447n118; exclusively male, 178, 448n125; fullness of being beyond being and nonbeing, 97; identified as *ayin*, 179, 368; has no feminine other, 184; identified as ether, 383; included in the enumeration of the *sefirot*, 179; indistinguishable from Ein Sof, 63–64, 178; initially a single point comprised of ten, 181; luminous dark of, 180; and the name *ehyeh*, 196; a pure and refined vessel, 181; supernal will, 368; symbolized by the tip of the *yod*, 125, 447n121; the will that empties itself of will, 368; the will that expands infinitely, 97, 314, 368; the will of wills, 368

keter malkhut, 76, 271, 375

keter elyon, 152, 173, 178, 179

kiss, conjunction of spirit and spirit, 361; denotes union of *Binah* and *Malkhut*, 359; eros of, 362; from the mouth of Christ, 338; gift of the Holy Spirit, 340; in Christian mystical interpretation of the Song, 337; identified as Jesus, 339–40; of death, 346, 352, 582n105; of love divides into four spirits, 361; of the mouth distinguished from kiss of the feet and kiss of the hand, 339; possibility of soul receiving dependent on the humbling of self, 340; signifies the mystery of the incarnation of the Word in the flesh, 340, 341, 343; symbol for the joy of the conjunction of the soul in the source of life, 349–50; symbolic of the comprehension that arises from the soul's passionate love for God, 346; symbolic of the conjunction of the human soul and the Separate Intellect, 347; symbolic of the soul's pleasure as it cleaves to the name, 264; symbolic of the union that is holy and chaste, 339, 350; theosophic and ecstatic explanations of, 350, 351; union of spirit to spirit, 352

Kol Nidrei, rectification of the covenant of the tongue, 589n217

knowledge, about sexual difference, 85; archaeology of, 2; by presence, 225; carnal, 549n56; constitutive understanding of, 141; contextualist approach to, 343; and copulation, 549n58; discursive, 212, 213; eternal light of, 303; erotic nature of, 269; gods of, 295; esoteric, 327; experiential, 337; inferential, 521 n. 135; ladder of self-, 213; locus of in phallic potency, 370; mediated nature of, 5; mystical, 1, 575n15; mystical illumination cannot be reified as an object of, 212; of the divine names, 124, 583n126; of faith, 30; of God, 227, 282; of God, self, and cosmos, 32; of the Last Things, 260; of the name, 140, 234, 263, 264, 521n128, 542n406; of the real, 279; of secrets, 399n3; of secrets of Torah, 477n59; of self, 213; of truth, 211; of *Ze'eir Anpin*, 370, 590n245; and the phallus, 270; relativization of, xx; replaced by sight, 96; rupturing of, 270; salvific, 55; scientific, 395n31; and the secret of copulation, 260; seeds of, 317; and the Son, 537n352; spring of, 270; stripping mind of, 218; supernal, 253, 270; and supernal copulation, 270; and theophanic experience, 525n176; Torah imparts cosmological and anthropological forms of, 202; Tree of, 248, 505n195, 537n344; triad of wisdom, understanding, and, 527n219; and unknowing, 218; and the veil not unveiled, 231;

visionary, 391n3; women deficient in, 549n55. *See also* yediʿah
Kopulation, 195
kulayāga, 323
kuṇḍalinī, 322, 572n205

ladder, of contemplation, 124; of self-knowledge, 213; Tetragrammaton depicted as, 125, 291
language, 10, 11, 12, 14, 25; and being, 13, 14–17, 21, 24, 193, 197, displays the interplay of oral and graphic, 287; distinguished from speech, 25, 194; embodied, 194; embodiment in the poetic symbol, 42; emerges at the intersecting point between oral speech and written text, 286; eroticism of, 118; expresses the impulse to overflow, 284; natural versus conventional, 203; silence the source of, 410n132; simultaneity of oral and written, 287; temporalization of, 158; and thought, 289
Lebensformen, 16
left, contained in the right, 177
leshon ha-qodesh, 201, 203, 222, 294, 516n78
letter/letters, body composed of, 208, 241; branches stemming from the tree inscribed with YHWH, 208; combination of, 234, 240, 274; comprise the seed whence the sefirotic emanations come to be, 321; constitute the bodies of Torah, 243; of concealment, 237; of the veil, 260; permutation of, 238; veil of, 260; vestments through which the ineffable name is woven, 200; signposts that lead from the revealed to the concealed, 198
levirate marriage, secret of, 493n40
levush / levushin, 9, 225, 251, 379, 529n237, 535n314
levusha, 9, 222, 597n83
libido, associated with Platonic eros, 126
Lichtung, 18, 19
light, appears as Immortal Androgynous Man, 157; beyond light, 122; commandment identified as, 247; constitutes the texture of desire, 317; crowned by, 256; efficient cause of the sense of sight, 317; encompassed from within (*or penimi*), 284; encompasses from without (*or maqif*), 284; ineffable, 157; intellectual, 218; magnet for the soul, 247; of life, 247; return of to be hidden, 177; ways of, 247
Lilith, malevolence of, 568n144; and Mary, 68; and Samael, 137; and *Shekhinah*, 59, 60, 444n95
limb, strengthens limb, 246
limit-experience, 289
linear circularity, 38; 428–29n336
linga, androgynous nature of, 323, 572n213
lingam, 126, 480n102
lisān al-ghayb, 233
logocentrism, 305
Logos, 17; and the penis, 306
logos spermatikos, 317
luminous darkness, 217

maʾamarot, 147
maʿaseh bereʾshit, 168. *See also* creation, account of
macroanthropos, imaginal body of, 219
Mādhyamika (middle way), 403n61, 404n62
magic, act of reflection and the secret of, 204; spiritual enticement of Christianity in the guise of, 259
maḥshavah ha-deveqah, 264, 292
maḥshevet ha-remez, 219
malʾakh, 38, 69, 70, 238, 253
malʾakh ha-elohim, 240, 241, 450n156, 452n192
malʾakh ha-goʾel, 69, 450n156, 452n192
malʾakh ha-panim, 239
malʾakhei ha-sharet, 540n384
malbush, 225, 234, 235, 252, 535n314
male, assumes the nature of the female, 301; and the attribute of mercy, 379; carrier of memory, 187; contains the female, 178; crowned by the female, 389; effeminate, 264; engendered as the veiled face in contrast to the female who is the exposed back, 385; and female one and the same, 50; characteristic of mercy, 95, 104, 105; contained in the female, 188; surrounded by female, 376; virginal glory, 303; without a complementary female, 179
male androgyne, 68, 94, 110, 146, 148, 149, 155, 165, 173, 180, 183, 267, 323, 366, 373, 375, 376, 387, 441n57; 447–48n122; 449n137, n150; 465n327, 471n435, 510n261
male/masculine waters (*mayyin dukhrin*), 75, 76, 77, 95, 182, 183; drop of, 185
maleness, salvation of, 303
male virgin, 303, 304; androgynous nature of, 304; designation of Barbelo, 304
Malkhut, 72, 178, 258, 267, 286, 322, 351; ascent of to *Keter*, 375, 376; ascent of to the rank of *aṭeret baʿlah*, 376; assuming the posture of the female surrounding the male, 376; the celestial daughter of Zion, 174; the celestial Jerusalem, 174; configured in the countenance of David, 84; craftsman of the lower world, 84; designated by the term *kol*, 174; elevation to the rank of crown, 72,

109; final point of the *sefirot*, 105; fourth leg of the chariot, 84; the glorious house, 174; identified as the house of God, 174; kingly mother, 84; lower mother, 83; masculine nature of, 84; ontic root of in the corona of the phallus, 185, 187; portrayed as the heart, 174; providential nature of, 84; praise of God revealed through her, 375; referred to as the soul, 174; rendered holy when she receives from the father, 365; root of darkness and evil, 375; *sof davar*, 105; stretches from the upper to the lower point of emanation, 365; united with *Binah* on Yom Kippur, 364; the will by which the supernal will is manifest, 174; world of the feminine, 82

man, androgynous, 157; born from woman, 51; comprised of all the spiritual matters, 247, 248; yearns to cohabit space of woman, 148

mandorla, 543n436

manna, 253; identified as wisdom or Torah, 342

marginalia, 116

maʿrifa, 28, 225

marriage, precondition for one to be bound to *Shekhinah*, 312; symbolic realization of the union of God and *Shekhinah*, 307

masculinity, and the ascetic sublimation of the erotic, 321; and the aspect of secrecy, 132, 133; and the attribute of mercy, 69, 95, 105; and the attribute of the voice, 362; before the division into female and male, 179, 304; blessing linked to, 354; correlated with mind/spirit, 54, 57, 265, 304; demarcated by *alef*, 354; linked to form, 265; phallocratic order, 87; and the potency to overflow, 95, 104; proportionate to impulse control and Torah study, 264; and the world of life, 354

mashal, 346; interplay of inner and outer, 336; and *peshaṭ* converge, 336. *See also* metaphor

maskil / maskilim, 95, 133, 137, 138, 238, 263, 282, 317, 353, 520n123, 534n306, 535n312, 535n322, 552n120, 566n103, 566n107, 595n55

maskilei yisraʾel, 211, 309

masturbation, 183, 386; and the Edomite kings, 386–87; expressive of phallic enjoyment, 279, 483n140; first copulation in the Godhead rendered symbolically as, 271; identified as the primal transgression, 386; pietistic works dedicated to the rectification of, 511n264; symbolically feminizes the male, 387; and the transvulation of male as female, 310

matqela, 95, 176, 222, 510n249, 596n60

Matrona, 72, 73, 153; adornment of, 356; beauty of, 357; cleaves to the King, 176; encompasses and covers the righteous, 73; holy covenant pours fine oil upon, 73; illumination of the face of, 357; image of *Shekhinah*, 375, 501n134; intercourse with, 319; in the king's chamber, 153; and the mystery of the androgyne, 73; phallic joy of, 106; revealed in garments of royalty, 379; sits with the King, 175; situated underneath the bridal canopy, 356; united with the King, 72, 318, 319, 357, 359, 370

meaning, four levels of: *remiza*, *derasha*, *hiddah*, and *razin setimin*, 223

meditation, 120; stripping away of all things corporeal, 121. *See also* hitbodedut

mem, open and closed, 166–67

membrum virile, focal point of contemplative visualization, 128; ontic source of masculinity and femininity, 184

menstruation, 60

mercy, acts in consort with judgment, 168; aligned with matter, 97; changes into and contained with judgment, 60, 169; designation of the penis, 181; joined together with judgment, 173; judgment transformed into, 373, 379; and the male, 379; on the right, 181; potency to bestow, 65, 69; symbolized by silver, 162; and the Tetragrammaton, 168, 172

merkavah, xii

Messiah, androgynous aspect of, 167; coming of, 360; feet of, 378; of David and Ruth the Moabite, 438n23; proper name of, 165; transgression of Adam not rectified until the arrival of, 183, 369; virgin birth of, 545n454

messianic enlightenment, characterized by a tension between seeing and unseeing, 382

messianicity, 92

metaphor, 36, 127; disclosure of truth through the apperance of image, 336; duplicity of meaning, 336; erotic nature of, 336; and literal coincide, 223; material sphere of, 150. *See also* mashal

metaphysical idolatry, 39

metempsychosis, 222

middah, 210

middat ha-emet, 33

mind, ascent of, 213; beyond mind, 217; expansion of, 211

mirror, xiii, 6, 9, 24, 25, 30, 32, 33, 35, 43, 119, 204; depicted as a garment, 234, 242; God compared to, 426 n. 310; heart purged of images compared to, 229, 235; the image of creative redoubling,

425n293; mind compared to, 538n352; and mirrored in causal reciprocity, 74; mirroring the mirror, 213, 283; nature identified as, 427n310; of appearance, 336; of consciousness, 121; of the feminine, 150, 595n53; of God's beauty, 595n53; of imagination, 178, 235; of the infinite, 217, 229; of the invisible world, 233; of the mirror, 90; of mirroring, 224; of the text, 246, 262; reflecting the mind that mirrors, 235; soul compared to, 122, 432n367; thought compared to, 213; translucent, 234, 235; the veil through which the face is seen as veil and the veil as face, 232; veils the unveiling of the veil, 384

misogyny, 53, 54, 56, 57, 81, 134

modesty, 133, 135

moment, abides in its passing and passes in its abiding, 227; novelty of, 89, 111; singularity of, 92. *See also* waqt

Monad, assumes the likeness of Father, Mother, and Son, 303

monasticism, and masculinity, 303; depicted as a *vita militaris* to strengthen male virility, 303; in Catholic clergy and Cathar *perfecti*, 309; in Christianity portrayed demonically by kabbalists, 309

monosophism, 283

monopsychic union, 309

monopsychism, 283

moon, desired to shine with same brilliance as the sun, 61; face of turned to the face of the sun, 177; feminine nature of, 151, 168; illumination by light of the sun, 356, 360; light of diminished, 168, 177; liturgical blessing of, 168; shining from one's own bosom, 228; and sun made use of one crown, 177; world of, 358

morphology, as opposed to typology, 209

mother, and daughter reunion, 358; images of applied to Buddha and Jesus, 456–57n231; king loves princess as, 161–62; of governance, 240

motherhood, phallic nature of, 82–84, 456n231; symbol of in Tibetan Buddhism, 458n249

Mourners of Zion, 345

mundus imaginalis, xviii, 189

mystery, disclosed to the humble, 135; erotic nature of, 63; of Adam: male and female, 259; of Adonai, 450n163; of the amelioration of judgment by mercy, 173; of the androgyne, 73, 171; of *beit*, 196; of Christ and the Church, 166; of circumcision, 135; of conversion of the Gentile, 223; of the covenant, 528n224; of the crown, 74; of the divine anthropos, 260; of eros, 261; of faith, 146, 171, 324, 361; of the four names of the four splendors, 360; of the garbing of angels as men, 252; of the garment, 200; of illicit sexual relations, 159; of the incarnation, 216; of one body, 259; of the patriarchs, 360; of providence, 250; of reflection, 145; of reincarnation and impregnation, 457n231; of Sabbath, 74; of sex within God, 307; of *Shekhinah*, 358; of spiritual marriage, 344; of the supernal chariot, 588n180; of the tabernacle, 259, 450n163; of transubstantiation, 190; of the Trinity, 100; of the two kings sharing one crown, 168; of unity, 259; of wisdom, 69, 243; of the wisdom of the supernal, inscribed name, 361; of the world of unity, 176; of worship, 377; unfolds in its enfolding, 262; world of, 166

mystical agnosticism, 218

mystical nihilism, 123

mysticism, expressed in the threefold path: purgation, illumination, and union, 218; in Christianity, 122

myth/mythic, and the conception of wisdom, 163–64, 277, 282, 497n83; and the construction of gender, 78; construction of in the guise of the imaginal symbol, 141; cosmogonic, 77, 182; cultural forms of, 67; defined as a semiological system, 404n70; engendering, 156, 167, 169, 279, 387, 553n140, 592n16; import of Yom Kippur, 367; incarnational, 245; kabbalistic, 145, 146; logic of, 143, 183; of the androgyne, 146, 176, 283, 390, 441n57, 448n122, 469n413, 471n435, 493n45; of the androgynous phallus, 131, 387; of the ascent of the crown, 453n199; of catharsis, 26; of cosmic reversal, xvii; of creation, 147; of creation as a paradigm for ethical praxis, 481n105; of the creation of woman out of man, 149, 170, 304; of the descent of personified wisdom, 516n74; of divine unity, 388; of the division of the androgynous male, 162; of the Edomite kings, 310, 386, 567n121, 596n59; of the engenderment of the ineffable name, 294; of the fallen Sophia, 153; of the female Torah, 274; of God bemusing himself, 273; of God engaged in contemplative activity of an erotic nature, 276; of God taking delight with righteous souls in the Garden of Eden, 328; of the heavenly tablets, 202; of the image of Jacob engraved upon the throne, 489n17; of the incarnation of the Word, 257; of the narcissistic nature of divine eros, 279; of Narcissus, 272; of reciprocal coronation, 366; and the secret of illicit sexual relations, 365; of

the self-enclosed circle of wisdom, 283; of *shaʿashuʿa*, 279; of the uroboros, 271, 279, 283; of the virgin birth of messiah, 545n454; of the zoharic fraternity, 364; rabbinic, 278; and representation of God, 58; ritual and, 86, 313; Scholem's reversal of in study of Judaism, 480n105; semiotic understanding of, 404n70; somatic imagery of, 107; structure of theosophic, 135; and symbol, 7, 37–39, 188; and the symbolic triad, 155, 157, 499n102; theogonic, 182, 285, 288, 532n266; Torah understood in light of, 256
mythos, logic of, 157; and logos, 60

name, cleaving to, 241; conjoined to, 240; equated with the divine body, 257; expressive of the inexpressible, 220; identification of Torah as, 257; incorporation into, 237; knowledge of, 234, 308; garment by which the nameless is revealed, 219; mystical essence of Torah, 250; seventy-two-letter, 240, 244, 536n344; shibboleth of, 243; that is spoken, 240; vocalization of, 236
nameless, ascent to through the name, 291; concealed in the garment of the name by which it is revealed, 219; name of embodied in Scripture, 205
namelessness, 197
narcissism, 129, 193; and anthropomorphic representationalism, 461n264; and autoeroticism, 182, 279; characteristic of the bond between God and the righteous, 329; and the divine eros, 279; Freud's account of mystical experience as an illustration of, 550n72; and God's wisdom, 284; and the image of uroborus, 279; marriage as a domestication of, 471n432; and metaphysical monism, 288; phallic nature of, 135, 272, 367
nations of the world, aligned with the unholy left side of judgment, 243; correlated with demonic impurity, 223
nature, book of, 8, 202, 206; primordial beginnings of, 102; semantic character of, 202; speculum of the book, 202
Natursprache, 197
necessary of existence, 231
neʿelemet, 210
negation, of images, 219
negative theology, xxvii
Neoplatonism, 22, 33, 35, 122, 255, 268, 307
nervure, 194
Neṣaḥ, 61, 64, 178; corresponds to the right foot, 174
night, side of darkness on the left, 175
noesis, erotic quality of, 271, 328
noesis noeseos, 268
nogah, 73
nothing, the force of overflowing and the force of receiving unified in the depths of, 94, 284; superessentiality of everything that is, 97; uppermost *sefirot* replication of, 197
nothingness, difference between identicals, 196
nun, bent and straight, 165
Nuqba, 75, 80, 181, 185, 375; on Sabbath eve couples with *Zeʿeir Anpin*, 367; emanated from the crown of strength, 185
nut, characterized as hermaphrodite, 144; secret of, 144

omniscience, 220
One, transcendent to and immanent in all things, 221
ontological chain, 198
ontological horizon, 23; monomorphism, 49
ontology, inseparable from language, 118
ontotheology, 103, 221
Oral Torah, 252; depicted as lower waters, 133; and the *Shekhinah*, 528n223, 588n187, 589n226; symbolic of the feminine, 139, 140, 141, 257
Oriental philosophy, 239
origin, 13, 20; distinguished from beginning, 196; nondual state prior to the beginning, 94
original sin, 53

Paḥad, 61
palaces, 291–92
palm branch (*lulav*), symbolic of the masculine, 150, 151
palm tree (*tamar*), comprises male and female, 151, 169
panenhenic / panenhenism, 30, 35, 424n289, 428n325
panentheism / panentheistic, 402n50, 425n299
pansemioticism, 37
pantheism / pantheistic, 402n50, 424n289, 428n325, 428n302
parable, history transmuted into, 394n24; and the hermeneutics of secrecy, 499n111; in *Bahir*: 149, 150, 158, 159, 160, 162, 164, 276–77, 278, 494n47, 497n84, 499–500n111, 501nn134–35, n38, 502n141, n52, 504n178; in Islamic esotericism, 529n231; in *Zohar*: 223, 379, 527n19; of the beautiful maiden without eyes, 223–24; and the Song of Songs, 346, 348, 576n25; speaking

through, 529n231; twofold structure of, 336, 527n219
paradise, attainment of union in, 535n312; depiction of women in, 447n199, 456n227, 597n83; return to facilitated by ascetic renunciation, 300
paradox, of newness and repetition, 92
Pardes, 348, 369, 370
participation, 66
patriarchs, crowned by *Shekhinah*, 85, 379; represent the three central *sefirot*: mercy judgment, and compassion, 379; symbolized by *shin*, 84
patriarchy, Greco-Roman image of, 265; and rabbinic culture, 87
peace, name of God, 163; phallic connotation of, 370; renders opposites equal, 98
pelag gufa, 175, 266, 312
penis, comprises virility of the whole body, 128; distinguished from phallus, 128–29; extension of, 181; and the logos, 306; measure of the mouth of, 180; necessity to conceal, 135; of God, 144
peridat ha-nefesh, 240, 241
perishut, 250
peshaṭ, 223
peshaṭei di-qera, 223
phallic monism, 130
phallocentrism, 74, 109, 146; and the activity of writing, 78; narcissistic character of, 129–30; and sexual symbolism in kabbalistic sources, 125, 127; and the visionary gaze, 136
phallomorphism, 47, 144; and the covenant of Torah, 140; dialectically related to ascetic denial of sensual pleasure, 135
phallus, absent presence of, 141; androgynous, 131, 133, 146, 151, 169, 267, 311, 384, 388, 567n123, 592n6; attributed to God, 127; body of, 147; called "covenant" when manifest as mercy and "rainbow" when manifest as judgment, 384; cloaked, 134; concealed nature of, 132; consecration of, 196; corona of, 75–76, 133, 137, 180, 184, 185; correlated with the tongue, 64, 139, 140; differential mark of sexual identification, 129; distinguished from the penis, 128–29; focus of divine unity, 144; forbidden to gaze upon, 135; gender construed therefrom, 68; and the identity of sexual difference, 130; imaginary signifier, 136; imaginary symbol, 128; impulse to bestow, 285; insignia that appears when all the veils are lifted, 129; invisibility of, 131; and *jouissance*, 131; locus of androgyny, 169; locus of secrecy, 132, 133, 593n37; marker of absence present in presence of its absence, 132; mediates alterity, 129; object of visionary contemplation, 129, 134, 138; of the supernal pure and holy form, 383; ontic source of androgyny and sexual difference, 311; ontological root of masculinity and femininity, 146; the place that must be hidden, 380; potency of in the brain, 77; presence of determined by its absence, 131; prohibited from looking at, 382, 383; rectification of, 589n217; representation of the nonrepresentational, 131; represented by the minus sign, 132; river that comes forth from Eden to irrigate the garden, 75; semiotic inscription, 128; sign that embodies the law that forces renunciation, 132; signification of the feminine lacking signifier, 131; signifier of castration, 132; signifier of desire, 128, 129; signifier that cannot be specularized, 131–32; signifier without a signified, 128, 483n144; supernal, 137; site of androgyny, 140; and the symbol of the window, 162; symbolic organ defined by negation, 131; tool of writing, 79; ultimate mark of signification, 128; veiled disclosure of, 141; veiled object of mystical vision, 128; veiling of, 129; withholding the ejaculation of the, 316; and the womb, 83, 188, 359
Pharisee, 50
philology, 111
philosophers, contrasted with kabbalists, 40
philosophy, double bind of, 93
Platonic idealism, 200
pleasure, intellectual, 347; noetic, 267; of no pleasure, 136; of the body contrasted with pleasure of the soul, 264
plentitude, and negativity, 403n57
pleroma, depicted in the image of four nodules, 286; triadic structure of, 157
poetic, dwelling, 271, 411n135; envisioning, 32, 293; incarnation, 191, 197, 211, 246, 260, 263; metaphor, 233; nature of Torah, 336; orientation, 25–26; sensibility and the paradoxical identification of opposites, 422n245; thinking, 17, 46, 416n188
poetry, 4, 14, 16, 18, 19, 21, 22; assault on language through language, 421n244; communication of the ineffable, 421n244; disclosure of what must be concealed, 418n206; experience of, 292–93; and kabbalah, 45, 421n242; and lovemaking, 131; and the mystery of incarnation, 411n139, 513n7; revolt against language, 293; and thinking, 98
poiesis, xiv, 10, 42, 47; as construction of narrative form, 39; erotic nature of, 46; makingimages in time, 43; noetic, 262; originary word of, 128

pornography, and religion in dialectical conjunction, 306, 486n191
prayer, and the annihilation of womanhood, 55; cast in visionary terms, 377; elevation of word to silence, 97; extending the measure to the immeasurable, 97; and the iconic representation of the divine in the imagination, 229, 579n65; and the imagination, 391n5; imageless, 123; mystical intentionality of, 95; and seeking God's face, 229; situated in Ein Sof, 281
presence, and absence, 16, 18, 23, 131, 133, 135, 337, 403n57; absent, 195, 243; metaphysics of, 141; of the world, 192
primordial kings, 310, 386, 387. *See also* Edomite kings
procreation, actualizes the continuous self-becoming of God, 312; ascetic understanding of, 266; failure to fulfill necessitates reincarnation, 266; rectification for sexual desire, 267; spiritual nature of which engendered as male, 55
prophecy, 120; breath of, 362; cant of, 205; cast in terms of the wisdom of kabbalah, 211; conjunction of rational soul and Active Intellect, 348; conjunction with the intelligible world of incorporeal light, 348; and the contemplative ideal of conjunction, 209, 234; expansion of mind, 211; and imaginative representation of the divine as an anthropos, 121; intellective and imaginal component of, 209; of all prophets but Moses through a speculum that does not shine, 228; and the poetic sensibility to image what has no image, 122; progression from image to speech to intellect, 241–42; role of the imaginative faculty, 237
prostration, and the ascetic debasing of the body, 309
protention, xxviii, xxix
providence, 250
psychology, and religion, 125–26
pūjā, Hindu form of Yoga, 235

qalb, 226
qelippot, 80
qeshet, 380. *See also* rainbow
qol gadol, 196
quaternity, encoded semiotically in the Tetragrammaton, 154, 258; feminine completes the, 326; imaginal anthropos configured as, 312–13; superior to the Christian trinity, 286
Queen of Heaven, 143
Qumran, 200, 295
Qur'ān, 205; book of envisioned as the son, 207; depiction of Jesus in, 226; hypostatic personification of, 207; identified as the mother of the book, 206; identified as the well-preserved tablet, 206; images of Mary in, 226; inscripted text of revelation, 206; the fore/script that comprises the forms of all that exists, 206; virginal conception affirmed in, 226

Raḥamim, 37, 367
rainbow, adorned in colors of the bride when Israel goes out from exile, 378, 379, 381; androgynous nature of, 593n34; attired in the garment of the patriarchs, 379; and the attribute of judgment, 384; covenant of, 139, 383; demarcates transition from exile to redemption, 380; disclosure of and exposure of the corona, 487n196; elevation to the position of the crown, 380; exposed corona compared to, 137, 487n196; female aspect of the phallus, 384; gender transformation of, 381–82; God's gazing upon, 378, 381; liminal symbol, 380; material body transferred into lights of, 538n352; memory engendered by God's looking upon, 381–82; messianic secret of, 377, 378; necessity to conceal, 383; of Noah, 382; not seen in the days of R. Joshua ben Levi, 384; phallic transposition of, 382, 593n32; physical expression of *Shekhinah*, 379; prohibition to look at, 380, 382, 593n353; and the radiance that surrounds the glory, 382; revealed when there is no righteous man, 379; secret of the holy covenant, 380, 382; seen in glorious garments of royalty, 379; seen in luminous colors at the time of prayer, 592n24; *Shekhinah* appears in the guise of, 382, 383; sign of redemption, 382
raza di-meheimanuta, 171, 361, 505n195
raza di–verit, 389, 502, 528
reading, erotic nature of, 114; and the flow of temporality, 113; interpretative nature of, 113; as (re)writing, 113
reason, aligned with the masculine, 51; erotic nature of, 268
redemption, 55; accomplished through the power of *Arikh Anpin*, 375; all the feminine forces united in the aspect of *keter malkhut* in the time of, 375; and asceticism, 364; anticipated in the sacred marriage, 308; and the assimilation of the other to the same, 373; brought about through unification of masculine and feminine, 165, 172, 354, 380; characterized by the paradox that the glory is rendered most conspicuous in the occlusion of

the sign, 383; correlated with *Shekhinah*, 281; heterosexual eros characteristic of the first phase of, 311, 376, 381, 389; holy union on Sabbath an anticipation of, 319; in inverse relation to circumcision, 382; intial phase entails envisioning *Shekhinah* as female other but final goal is integration of female into male, 376; marked by the union of the lower and upper worlds, 359; and the occlusion the glory that was exposed, 382; and the overcoming of sexual dimorphism, 374; reconfiguration of the male androgyne,165, 323; and the reconstitution of the androgynous male, 374; restoration of the feminine to the masculine, 110, 165, 311, 390; restoration of the spiritual order and the obliteration of the feminine as an autonomous power, 301–302; re/turn of daughter to mother, 359; and the securing of the feminine as the nucleus in the infinite circle, 382; and the sheltering of the feminine like the point enclosed in the circle, 382; and the task of making the female male, 54, 57, 165, 373; transformation of the female into the male, 55, 165; transposition of *Shekhinah* from feminine other to the sign of the covenant, 311; unseeing the seen, 382

reflective redoubling, 194

reincarnation, 266

remembrance, 17, 20, 21

remez ha-mahshavah, 199, 219

remiza, 223

renunciation, and belonging, 117; an emulation of incarnation, 342; means to restore primal androgyne, 55; and the masculinization of the female, 301; phallic empowerment of, 70; pneumatic integration facilitated by, 364; of carnal eros and the mystical experience of eros, 298; of physical pleasure and sensual gratification, 252; of sexuality and pornographic lasciviousness, 307; and participating in the suffering of Jesus, 300; and the prohibition to images, 119

repentance, 156; associated with *Binah*, 367, 368

representation, 11, 12

resurrection, 156, 251, 252, 360; eradication of all individuality and difference at the time of, 305; in the thought of al-Ghazālī, 541n400; sons of, 302

retention, xxviii, xxix

revelation, and creation, 202

Rhineland Jewish Pietists, 120, 144, 581n86

right, contained in the left, 177

righteous, ascetic renunciation of, 366; bound homoerotically to God, 328; cause the divine phallus to be erect, 324; crowned by a diadem, 73; crowned by the letter *zayin*, 73; depicted as the covenant to uphold the covenant, 369; designated "Israel," 328; garbed in the supernal light, 328; impoverished in the ways of the world, 70; light hidden for, 73; sitting in the Garden of Eden with crowns on their heads, 74, 254, 365, 366; sons of God, 328; souls of ascend at midnight to the Garden of Eden, 328; stands between two females, 324; wings of, 595n52

ritual, 49, 59; androgynization, 165; ascetic understanding of, 250; copulation, 126; endowed with magical efficacy, 308; means by which the corporeal body is textualized and the textual body corporealized, 248; and mystical transfiguration, 246–55; theurgical implications of, 245–46

rose, and the demonic potency, 445n97; and the nature of eros, 63; red and white, 60; sexual intent of, 445n97; symbolic of *Shekhinah*, 60, 63

ruaḥ ha-qodesh, 222, 264, 349, 492n38; designation of the *sekhel ha-poʿel*, 240; identified as the mother, 499n102

rūḥ al-quds, 239

ruaḥ qudsha, 69, 545n452

Sabbath, 61, 175; covenant of, 73, 139; crown and diadem of the days of creation, 73; decoded into *shin* and *bat* representing the three patriarchs and *Shekhinah*, 367, 379; eunuchs who keep, 318–19; fourfold unity of, 84–85; liturgical rhythm moves from sacrality of sexual union to ascetic denial of sexual gratification, 367, 370; mate of the community of Israel, 445n104; mystery of, 74; mystical significance of the third meal of, 368; of Sabbaths, 367; and the phallic gradation, 61; proper time to engage in intercourse, 314, 315, 319, 320, 321, 332; secret of and circumcision, 140; *Shekhinah* liberated on, 319; supernal, 359, 360; time of the afternoon service called the propitious time of the supernal coupling on the eve of, 314, 367; union of *Arikh Anpin* and *Zeʿeir Anpin* occurs on the day of, 368; union of King and Queen occurs on, 108, 367; the world-to-come, 360; and *zayin*, 73–74

sacrifice, of the self, 300

ṣaddi, decomposed into *yod* on top of *nun*, 151

ṣaddiq, 71; attribute of, 73, 74, 151; corresponds to the divine phallus, 388

sahasrāra, 323
sakti, 323, 572n205
salvation, beginning of, 156; marked by the restoration of female materiality to male spirituality, 304; moment of demarcated by seeing the sign secreted in the restoration of the female to the male and the androgynous phallus reconstituted, 384
sar ha-panim, 240, 487n209, 536n344
scale, 35; meaphor for the process of symbolization, 427n322, 527–28n219; supernal and lower worlds balanced on, 221, 222; symbolic of the male-female binary, 176
secrecy, 2, 27; double arc of projecting and withholding, 224; double bind of, 2, 160; and exposure, 195; and the gift, 159; hermeneutic of, 196, 232; and the male organ, 128, 133; and the role of the symbolic, 399n5; of secrecy, 261; play of, 262; and sexuality, 46; and *Yesod*, 132
secret, 9, 27, 38; beyond spatial demarcation, 210; cannot be revealed, 159; communicated by means of a whisper, 521n135; denial of, 160; disclosed in the literal meaning, 223; doubling of, 261; duplicity of, 160; and erotic imagery, 399n6; esoteric method of transmitting, 294; exposed only to one willing to receive it, 272; and female genitalia, 134; hermeneutic bridge that binds text and interpretation, 133; and the hermeneutical condition of *différance*, 160; hidden beneath the veil, 336; ineffability of, 159; of Adonai, 140; negation that negates itself, 160; of the androgyne, 145; of the bridegroom and bride, 108; of the cherubim, 63–64, 349; of communion and the perfect intention, 120; of circumcision, 135; of conjunction, 120; of the covenant, 380, 502; of the covenant of circumcision, 139; of the covenant of the tongue, 139; of denial, 160; of the drops of Joseph's semen, 310; of El Ḥai, 140; of the equilibrium, 180; of equanimity, 120; of faith, 264; of the female waters, 311–12; of the feminine, 137; of the feminine encompassing the male, 187; of the high priest, 238; of the holy covenant, 379; of illicit sexuality, 288; of incarnation of the glory, 252; of judgment, 95; of levirate marriage, 493n40; of magic, 204; of mercy, 76, 95; of meditation, 120; of the Mishnah, 146, 266; of the mysteries of Torah, 384; of the nut, 144, 581n87; of permutation of the alphabet, 207; of poetic incarnation, 260; of prophecy, 241; of the property of all letters, 207; of the rotation of all entities, 207; of ruddiness, 311; of *shamor*, 140; of the supernal will that is entirely masculine, 182; of the supplement, 375; of textual embodiment, 211; of the Tree of Knowledge, 248; of Torah, 139; of the wine that gladdens, 182; of worship, 169; of *zakhor*, 140; persists as secret, 159; preserved by speaking what cannot be spoken, 160; revealed in the concealment of its revelation and concealed in the revelation of its concealment, 233; seen through the garment of the text, 222; symbolized by fingers of the hand and toes of the feet, 250; wisdom of kabbalah, 211
ṣedeq, 71, 377
sefirot, 3, 4, 8, 9, 10, 26, 32, 34, 68, 84, 140, 161, 359; *amen* denotes the unity of, 28; androgynous nature of, 63, 67, 178, 311, 447n122; anthropomorphic form of, 64, 107, 121, 122, 173–174, 198, 209; ascend to *Keter*, 180; boundary that emanates from Ein Sof, 199; bowing down before God's word, 309; by which heaven and earth were sealed, 152; characterized by terms derived from sense experience, 326; circumscribed within the circle that begins and ends with wisdom, 280; completed by the creation of Adam, 169; comprise the unity of the name and its epithet, 280; concealed in the disclosure of their concealment, 220; configured as a spiritual body, 200; contained within YHWH, 124, 138, 154; correspond to the ten fingers, 144, 152; correspond to the first ten letters of the alphabet, 282; correspond to the ten upper potencies, 218; correspondence between ten divine utterances and the, 256; demarcated as spiritual matters, 247; depicted as depths, 98; designated by the term *devarim*, 208; disclosure of the hidden wisdom of the Primordial Torah, 220; divided into four quarters: natural, sensible, intelligible, and concealed, 198; efflux of compared to oil, 74; emanation of depicted as proliferation of wisdom, 284; finite power that is unlimited, 199, 288; gender hybridity, 60; identified as the separate intellects, 476n52; imaginal forms, 39; in *Sefer ha-Bahir*, 152; inclusion of in the letter *alef*, 553nn126–27; inner vitality of, 187; the intelligible realities contemplated by Adam and Eve in the Garden of Eden, 315; limited in comparison to the limitless commandment, 220; mandate to investigate, 120; manifest visibility of the invisible Ein Sof, 67; measure of ten that are infinite, 285; mixed from *alef, mem, shin*, 64; paradox of the tenfold unicity,

200; principle for everything bounded, 199; understood as a projection of the unconscious archetype of Self, 479n96; unification of, 326; unified in Ein Sof, 95, 125; unified in the root of unity, 180; unified like a flame bound to the coal, 263, 352; union of the sixth and tenth, 169; unity of, 99, 280; uroboric depiction of, 271, 281; vision of, 210
sekhel ha-poʿel, identified as: angel of the Lord, 535n322; holy spirit, 240; name of Israel, 581n91; Torah, 237n240. *See also* Active Intellect
ṣelem, 109; secret of the forms in *Yesod*, 149
ṣelem elohim, 147, 169
selfhood, the propensity to withdraw, 102
semen, ascetic practice of retaining the discharge of, 271, 316, 322; constituted by the Hebrew letters, 285; corresponds to light-seed of the brain, 316, 322; elevating back to the brain, 316, 322; originates in the brain, 269, 271, 316, 322
semiotics, 115; convergence of with the somatic, 40; and the encoding of the erotic impulse, 118; inseparable from cosmology, 5; and neuroscience, 89
serpent, 53; inseminated Eve, 58–59; seductive snare of, 303
Sethian gnosticism, 303–304
setima de-khol setimin, 360
seʿudatei di-meheimanuta, 368
sexual difference, erasure of, 301
sexuality, abnegation of, 370; abrogation of, 366; allegorical depiction of spiritual union, 344, 345; androcentric and gynocentric perspectives on, 299; and asceticism, 307–318, 344; ascetic renunciation of, 299, 364; as a cultural marking, 81; associated with the woman, 54; confluence of the theosophic and ecstatic, 565n97; detached from spiritual intention, 315; dialectically related to the ascetic impulse, 313, 363; displaced by spiritual eroticism, 363; encratic rejection of, 52, 341, 344; and the engenderment of the divine image, 312, 363; and the eroticism of the Song of Songs, 333, 344; and the feminine body, 299, 344; genital nature of, 126; holiness of proportionate to eradication of carnal gratification, 317; illicit form of, 288; images of in ancient Egyptian mythology, 126; in rabbinic Judaism and the kabbalistic tradition, 309; and the inversion of the imaginary and real, 279; Jewish women's renunciation of, 300; kabbalistic approach to distinguished from medieval Christian mystics, 313, 363; kabbalists' abstaining from, 135, 319–20, 324; and knowledge, 269; and the love of God, 297; of ancient Christian ascetic women, 299; of the male in Lurianic kabbalah, 310, 387; positive value accorded to, 312; and procreation, 265, 332; and religion, 117, 261; sacrality of, 307; sacralization of and the ascetic impulse, 313; sacrament that celebrates union of male and female in the divine, 312; and the sacred, 298; and secrecy, 46; and the semantic, 118; and speech, 118; and spirituality, 261–62; theurgical significance accorded to, 109, 312, 313; transformed into a spiritual act, 313
shaʿashuʿa, 182, 257, 273–285; and the act of writing, 278; autoerotic arousal of the male, 285; denotes mental activity and sexual desire, 278; division within the indivisible, 285; incessant compulsion to repeat anew, 279; and the Lacanian *jouissance*, 278; and the primal dialectic of bestowing and receiving, 277; and temporality, 278
shem ha-nikhbad, 251
shalom, designation of the phallus, 163
shame, 156, 297; associated with the sensual, 297; caused to *Shekhinah*, 380, 382; integument of identified as the body, 52; of Adam and Eve brought about by the sin, 315
Shekhinah, 38, 39, 46, 47, 48, 49, 83, 108, 352; above and below, 164; accompanies Israel in exile, 374; androgynous angel, 72–74; androgynous nature of, 67, 69, 73, 74; ark of the covenant, 71; ascent of, 292, 367; associated symbolically with the heave offering, 565–66n102; assumes the demiurgical characteristics of *Binah*, 357–58; assumes the name *malkhut* when the king is enthroned, 378; and the attribute of *ṣedeq*, 377; body of, 251; bride comprised of the All, 108; called the "crown of splendor" when she receives from *Keter*, 365; compared to a bride entering the nuptial chamber when she exits from exile, 376; compared to the moon illumined by the sun, 360; composed ontically by male kabbalists, 329; correlated with redemption, 281; crown of her husband, 72, 375; crown on the Torah scroll, 365; demarcated as the glorious name, 251; demiurgical character of, 84, 155; denoted by *zoʾt*, 377; depicted as the blue–black flame, 326; depicted as daughter fallen into captivity and as mother weeping over her children, 374; depicted as a house, 384; depicted in male symbols, 69; designated Community of Israel, 82, 352, 355, 381; diminished status of, 62; doubling of, 154; dons

the demiurgical cloak of *Binah*, 84; dual prism of, 61; dwells upon the heart, 122; earth that yields the living creature, 75; effluent state signified by the letter *he*, 70; elevation to crown the patriarchs, 85, 365, 367, 379; embodied as the angel of the presence, 239; entrusted with divine providence, 71; envelops the righteous like a crown, 74, 365; eschatological restitution to *Binah*, 358, 359; eschatological transformation into *aṭeret baʿlah*, 375; exile of, 308, 319, 355, 374; face of, 137, 329; face of constituted by members of the mystical fraternity, 573n237; and the figure of David, 84, 138; and the figure of Esther, 72, 484n164; fluctuation and ambivalence of, 60; footstool of throne elevated to crown on head of king, 373; forbidden woman whose feet go down to death, 374; foundation stone rejected by the fathers, 377; gateway through which the worshipper enters to reach God, 377; gender transformation of, 382; glorious crown, 72; hidden and revealed, 484n164; house of judgment below, 132; identified as the angel of God, 450n156, 452n192; identified as the seventh palace, 292; image of Adam, 384; imaginal representation through which the invisible God is visually apprehended, 385; immanent in the physical universe, 153; indwelling of, 312; investiture of in the attribute of *malkhut*, 379; and Ishtar, 455n218; kabbalists mimic the indigenous virginal state of, 366; kabbalists referred to as those who receive the, 389; liberated on Sabbath, 319; lifted from the dust, 381; light that does not shine, 84; light that emanates from first light, 164; impoverished state signified by the *dalet*, 70; in relation to Eve, 62; in the garb of an angel, 38; and Lilith, 59, 60, 444n95; lower wisdom, 71; and Marian imagery, 435n2, 455–56n224, 545n454; masculinization of, 359, 373; masculinized as a consequence of the erotic encounter with the righteous, 354; mirrors the activity of *Binah*, 358; mounting of in the form of the ascending throne, 357; mystery of, 358; object of conjunction, 239, 251; ontological assimilation of male mystics into, 330–31; ontological elevation of, 356; phallic potency of, 222; phallic transmutation of, 71–72; portrayed as daughter, 84, 155, 258, 367; portrayed as goddess, 72; positioned as midpoint of the circle, 373; positioned between two righteous males, 324, 325; prism through which all prophetic forms are manifest, 384–85; redeeming angel, 69, 450n156, 452n192; rests only on the married man, 312; righteous souls constitute an abode for, 252; rooted in and displaced from the pleroma, 153; the single dark point, 357; signified by the second *he* of the Tetragrammaton, 258, 326, 357, 358; speculum that does not shine, 61, 71; splendor of, 253, 254; suffering of, 376; suffering of portrayed in the image of Rachel weeping over her children, 376; supernal light of, 253; symbolically linked to Rachel, 38; symbolized by the *dalet*, 164, 326; symbolized by the dove, 329; symbolized by the fiery ever-turning sword, 450n157; symbolized by the red and white rose, 60; two-faced character of, 63; transposed from cistern to well, 70; transformation from passive receptacle to active force that overflows, 358; transposition from female to male, 70; transposition from feminine other to the sign of the covenant, 311, 373; unseeing of in the guise of an autonomous feminine imaginary, 374; upper and lower, 71, 154; uroboric nature of, 68; virginity of depicted in images of the locked garden and sealed spring, 366; voice of, 329; wedded to, 389; and wisdom, 155; woman in the pattern of, 109; woman of valor, 72; women located in the mystery of, 48–49

shem ha-eṣem, 238

shem ha-toʾar, 238, 239

sight, 194; light the cause of, 317

signa data, 205

signa naturalia, 205

signifier, discloses nature of signified, 221

silence, 14, 21, 22, 23, 25, 42, 97; absence of word, 196; bears speech as flesh, 194; clamor of, 294; fecund negative of, 196; fount of speech, 414n181; horizon of sound in human discourse, 418n211; the margin that demarcates the center of language, 289; of not-speaking contrasted with unsaying, 215; realized in unsaying as opposed to not-speaking, 219; speech comes to and as, 196; tissue of speech woven from the thread of, 414n181

ṣimṣum, 26; and Heidegger's notion of *Lichtung*, 412n155.

sitrei / sod arayot, 159, 365. *See also* illicit sexuality

siva, 323

snake, circular nature of, 67; feminine vital energy configured in the form of, 322; symbolic of the male, 67

sod, contained in the *peshaṭ*, 223

sod ha-egoz, 144, 581n86
soul, ascent of, 292; compared to a clear and bright mirror, 122; enclothed in the body, 248; eternality of attained in being annihilated in the divine, 353; feminization of, 298–99; five aspects of: *nefesh, ruaḥ, neshamah, ḥayyah, yeḥidah*, 80, 181; fruit of, 248; infinite expansion of, 211; of the Jew entrapped in the body of a Gentile, 243; of the righteous ascend at midnight to the Garden of Eden, 328; portrayed as feminine in relation to the divine, 337, 350, 352; separated from the body, 121–22, 240, 241, 247; stripped of its fleshly encasement, 251; transmigration of, 266; united with supernal knowledge, 253
space, apophatic, 525n182; between dark and light, 376; character of cylindrical, xvii; configured in human imagination, 38; contraction of the infinite to create, 26; correlated with the femininity, 83, 355, 357, 374, 381, 482 n. 125; devoid of all content, 500n116; dissolving into, 538n52; fantasy, 279, 552n105; fissures in, 43; for the feminine imaginary, 80; four-dimensional, 395n37; from which Ein Sof vacated its light, 186; hollowing of, 278; imaginal, 124; intergalactic, xxviii; into which to project, 188; measurable, 150; of desire, 132; of the horizon, 23; of inescapable difference, 115; of temporal emplacement, 20; of the relations of words, 292; of time, 393n5; of transcendence, 90; of a woman, 148; only a married priest can enter sacred, 266; opened by translation, 461n270; phallus marks the signification of empty, 152; phallic desire to project into, 378; primal narcissistic impulse to expand phallically into, 135; primordial, 275, 511n267; sacred, 266, 335; suspended betwixt matter and form, 97; that differentiates, 292; three-dimensional, 287; topological, 195; women provides, 83
spacetime, xxviii; continuum, 201; gravitational arrangement of, 201
speculum: that does not shine, 61, 71, 228; that shines, 71, 124, 138, 247
speech, distinguished from language, 25, 194; leads to unsaying as opposed to silence, 289; and the unspoken, 26, 42, 287, 418n208
spermatogenesis, 284, 321
spirit, materialization of, 211
spiritual, discerned through the physical, 222
spiritual marriage, 339, 481n106, 559n19; and ascetic behavior, 299; and the denial of carnality, 344; mystery of, 344; of the kabbalist and the divine, 318, 321; of son and daughter, 156; reconstitution of original androgynous state, 166; restoration of the female to the male, 157; with Christ, 341, 344
sprachdenken, 113
Sprachspiele, 16
square, contained within the circle, 188
Stoics, 317
structure, and heterogeneity, 93
suffering, 44; emulation of the mystery of incarnation, 341; of God, 2; of *Shekhinah* in exile, 376
Sufism, affinity with medieval Jewish mystical piety, 229; attitude to Arabic analogous to kabbalistic approach to Hebrew, 206; and the cultivation of the ideal of the female becoming male, 305–306; and the eradication of the feminine through the ascetic denial of the body, 306; eschatological conception of the moment embraced by, 225; exclusively male nature of, 305; Jewish, 307; influence on: Ibn Paquda, 346, Halevi, 203, kabbalists, 477n71; masters of, 222; and the status of the feminine, 436–37n12, 493n40, 563n76; unitive vision affirmed by, 229, 305
summum bonum, 301
sun, face of turned to the moon, 177; and moon made use of one crown, 177; personified as male in relation to the moon, 168; *sunyātā* (emptiness), 57; eyes of, 56; 403n61
supernal will, entirely masculine, 271
symbol, 6, 7, 12, 31, 36, 67, 119; as bridge, 37; communication of the incommunicable, 26; and conceptual indeterminacy, 145; and the construction of myth, 141, 402n42; diaphonous nature of, 39; distinguished from icon, 34; embodied nature of, 127; fusion of opposite equals, 127; iconic nature of, 122; imaginal realm of, 150; Jungian theory of, 67; the means by which the form of divine embodiment inheres in the imagination, 127; of the paradigm, 220; paradigmatic, 220; polychromatic nature of, 402n57; referential and performative aspect of, 248; reveals and conceals concurrently, 127; uroboric and pleromatic nature of, 67; verbal prism, 188
symbolic, form, 141; images, 119; and magical, 36; and mythical, 36–37, 39
synesthesia, 10, 210, 400–401n18, 522n136, 555n151
system, interruption of order by chaos, 88; novelty of interpretation, 88; and unpredictability, 93
syzygy, 145, 156,164

tabernacle, arrayment of, 259; the body in which God's will becomes tangible, 244; built by means

of the letters, 259; constructed in the shape of an anthropos, 259, 260; in the pattern of what is above, 259; mystery of, 259; of the gods of knowledge, 295; of the pact, 291; textualization of, 260
Tabernacles, 150
tamar, 151. *See also* palm tree
tanzīh, 229, 527n213
Taoism, 108
Tantrism, 261–62, 271; affinity to kabbalah, 316, 322–24; and the nexus of asceticism and eroticism, 559n17; Sahajiya school of, 263
tashbīh, 229, 527n213
tawḥīd, 28
ṭemira di-ṭemirin, 76
temporal bend, 197
temporality, and desire, 396n67; and language, 158; and the eternal, 37; and the hermeneutic circle, 112; texture of and the autogenesis of divine wisdom, 281
ten martys of Caesarea, correspond to the seminal drop cast in vain by Joseph, 310; sacrificial substitutes for the ten brothers who sold Joseph into slavery, 310. *See also* asarah harugei malkhut
Tent of Meeting, 250
terumah, 171, 244, 245, 565–66n102
teshuvah, the second *sefirah* symbolized by the he, 125
Tetragrammaton, xiii, 10, 34, 70, 71; configured as human form, 40, 122, 124; depicted as a ladder, 125, 291; and the encoding of the sefirotic quaternity: father, mother, son, and daughter, 154; identified as Torah, 40, 124, 128, 138, 219, 242; and the inherently symbolic nature of language to express the inexpressible, 402n57; model to convey the paradoxical confluence of the hidden and revealed, 291; and the mystery of the Song, 361, 588n197; not pronounced as written, 237; numerical value of forty-five, 183; numerical value of fifty-two, 183; originary word of poiesis, 128; root-word, 128; symbolic significance of, 172; ten *sefirot* contained within, 154; trunk of the sefirotic tree, 138; ultimate datum of mystical experience, 555n151; ultimate signifier, 219; world-to-come and this world created by the first two letters of, 207. *See also* YHWH
text, as body, 259; as homeland, 117; boundary of, 117; compared to a changing river, 114; encountered by reader face-to-face, 223; internal heterogeneity of, 93; literal embodiment of, 223; mirror of, 246; pleasure of, 113
textuality, ascetic discipline, 115; bodily nature of, 246; in the thought of Derrida, 90, 158; open-ended nature of, 87
theogony, and cosmogony, 35
theomonism, 28, 221
theomorphism, 39
theophanism, 239
theophany, 29, 31; at Sinai depicted in matrimonial language, 336; in the form of an angelophany, 239
theosis, 218
theurgy, and ecstasy, 209; ecstasy, and theosophy: intertwined branches on one tree, 308; and human sexuality, 312; and the kabbalistic understanding of ritual, 246
thinking, conceptual versus symbolic, 119
thought, allusion of, 199, 219; as unthought, 269; circle of, 549–50n64; concretization of, 211; constituted as seeds of light, 317; dysfunction of, 92; expansion of, 566n106; extending of to that which thought cannot comprehend, 309; foetus will be in accord with, 313; leads to the unthought as opposed to the unthinkable, 289; nothingness of, 389; of allusion, 219; of the unthinkable, 288; of what cannot be thought, 123, 288; pathway of, 116; subtle essence in which there are ten *sefirot*, 219; that thinks more than itself, 287; thinking itself, 268–69, 283; thinking that which will not let itself be thought, 289; unthinkable, 288; unthought of, 195
throne, 235, 275, 533n284; ascent of, 357; borne by four beasts, 489n17; blurring of the difference between glory and, 489n17; celestial beast that sits upon, 489n17; chamber of, 234; consisting of light, 550n77; depicted as a bride, 143; feminine character of, xii, 70, 72, 143, 145, 488n6, 491n13, 497n83; four legs of, 84; icon of Jacob engraved upon, 143, 144, 145, 489n17, 489n18; and the image of the nut, 144; and the imagination, 122; and the heart, 534n307; land of Israel corresponds to, 276; liturgical worship directed to, 557n194; lower anthropos, 121; of David, 377, 378; of glory, 84, 238, 239, 326, 356; and the open *mem*, 504n178; prophets identified as, 238; rising to be crown, 373; *sefirot* bow down before, 210; song uttered before, 562n50; symbolic of *Tif'eret*, 39; throne to the, 502n143; to be conjoined to, 39
Tibetan Buddhism, Nyingmapa school, 537n352
Tif'eret, 39, 41, 60, 64, 69, 109, 258, 267, 286, 322, 351, 352, 369; and the image of the son, 154, 358;

corresponds to the extension of the body, 173; depicted as the white flame, 326; positioned between *Binah* and *Malkhut*, 83, 324; speculum that shines, 124, 138; symbolized by the *waw* of YHWH, 125; voice of Jacob, 124
tif'eret adam, 385
Tif'eret Yisra'el, 221
time, xv–xxxi, 20, 21, 23; abolition of in the thought of Eliade and Corbin, 394n25; and the characteristic of looping back, 201; and the coming to be of the beginning of emanation, 285; asymmetries of, 394n28; at once circular and linear, 372; circularity of, 159; curve of, 197; curve of and the symbolic imagination, 394n23; four modes of in zoharic narrative, 37–38; and hermeneutics, 396n65; hierophanic, 394n23; instant of novel reiteration, 88; and interpretative activity, 393n4; and language, 44; linked to the beginning, 277; reversibility of, xxi–xxv, 49, 306, 294n25; singularity of each moment, 92; trajectory of, 372
time-space, 23, 37, 419n220
tiqqun, 148; only in the place of *qilqul*, 372; phallomorphic texture of, 370
tiqqun ha-berit, 511n264
tiqqun ha-nuqba, 376
tiqqun haṣot, 376, 591–92n16
tiqqun ha-yesod, 589n218
Torah, xiii, 26; Adam made in the image of, 208, 260; androgynous nature of, 139, 260; begins with *beit*, 257, 354, 587n178; bodies of, 243, 249; body of intermediate between matter and form, senses and reason, 241; composed entirely of the names of God, 252; conceals in the charade of revealing, 222; configured imaginally as the ideal anthropos or Israel, 243; crowns of, 258; delighted in the lap of God for two thousand years, 277; demarcated as a divine structure hewn from the name, 248; depicted as a garment, 235, 242; depicted as the spring of living water, 277; the divine form that assumes the shape of an anthropos, 244; embodiment of the divine glory, 244; envisioned in the heart of the kabbalist as the imaginal body, 219; equated with the essences of divine wisdom, 220; equated with Song of Songs, 335–36; erotic relationship between the wise of heart and the, 223; exposes herself to her lover, 223; given exclusively to men, 59; given to Moses, 252; garbed in the garment of this world, 221; God looked into before creating the world, 220; iconic manifestation of God, 244; identical with God, 247; identified as the book of nature, 202; identified as the name, 40, 124, 128, 137, 138, 208, 219, 237, 242, 243, 244, 245, 246, 248, 249, 250, 256, 257, 258; identified as wisdom, 155, 277; inherent parabolic nature of, 336; imaginal form through which the formless is envisioned, 236; incarnate in the Active Intellect, 237, 241; infinity of, 138; inscripted as black fire upon white fire, 252, 543n420; instructs about the pattern of God, 244; in the pattern of the holy and pure chain, 245; locus of imaginary forms in and through which the imageless God is made accessible, 242; materialization of in the body of the name, 255, 260; medium through spirit is embodied and the embodied spiritualized, 242; mystical intent of the study of, 209; mystical understanding of, 223; and the name YHWA, 239; nocturnal study of, 328–30; object of divine musing, 143, 257; Oral and Written, 133, 139, 140–41, 257; pattern of the supernal form, 244, 245; poetic nature of, 336; portrayed as God's feminine playmate, 143; primordial, 220, 252, 274, 277, 281, 282, 543n420; prototype of all books, 202; rested in the bosom of God, 277; generations prior to the creation of the world, 550n76; secret of, 139; the shadow of God, 244; sitting in the lap of God, 143; Song of Songs equated with, 335–36; speaks in the language of man, 236; strapped on the arm of God like a phylactery, 143; study of limited to circumcised Jewish male, 137, 144; symbolic identification of and the covenant, 138; textual body of, 252; threefold unity of God, Israel, and, 245; totality of, 257, 258; written black fire on white fire, 252, 550n76; world created by means of, 200; woven from the names of God, 138
touch, 194
Tower of Babel, 12
tradition, in Judaism, 116; writing of continuous displacements, 116
transgression, 93; and the hypertrophy of the feminine, 82; primordial nature of and the spilling of seed in vain, 385–86; separation of the masculine and feminine, 154
transcendence, 31, 90; accessible through a web of symbolic deflections, 127; desire for, 289; dualism of corporeality and, 200; experience of elicited by the symbol at the limit of the temporal horizon, 127; noetic, 304
translation, an act of interpretation, 223

transubstantiation, 255; noetic, 269
Tree of Life, 41
tremendum mysterion, 262
trinity, 207
truth, 19, 23, 25, 114; and appearance, 200; attribute of, 33; beyond language, 219; comes forth as unveiling the unveiling of the veil, 231; conflated with untruth, 19, 26, 413n173, 414n175; contrasted with that which is born of woman, 54; depicted as a coincidence of opposites, 262, 403n57; directly mirrored in the mirror of appearance, 336; dissimulating nature of and the image of a woman, 434n391; meaning that appears through questioning the text, 114; novel and erstwhile, 88; of the veil seen in the veil of the truth, 230; polysemous and dissimulating nature of, 224; uncovered in enfolding of noetic poiesis unfolding poetic noesis, 262; unmasking of and the simulacrum of the woman, 44; uttered by a woman, 54

umm al-kitāb, 206; envisioned as mother, 207
Umwelt, 195
Unendlichkeit, 195
Ungrund, 100; Böhme's depiction of, 103; indifference of, 100–101
unio mystica, 209
union, beyond mind, 218; occasioned by psychic transport, 209; with the intellectual light, 218
unity, of three: father, daughter, and son, 279, 365
unknowing, 217; darkness of, 218; God most truly known through, 218
unnameable, 197
unrepresentability, conditioned by representational forms, 129
unsaid, 20, 22, 25
unsaying, heard in the infinite speaking, 197; mystical language of, 219; of the mystical utterance distinguished from the silence of not-speaking, 215
unspoken, and the concealed, 294; everything spoken stems from, 20; intersection of language and, 20; and mystical silence, 291; persists in the saying of the poet, 19, 26, 293, 480n97; speech originates from, 287; speech that is, 286, 414n178; spoken in speaking the unspoken, 481n208; subverts all forms of language, 411n132; and the influence of Taoist philosophy in Heidegger, 415n182
unveiling, denotes mystical awakening of the heart, 227; erotic implications of, 229; of the beloved, 225; of the truth manifest in the heart, 226; of the veil in veiling the unveiled, 374; state of consciousness between wakefulness and sleep, 226; the veil before the face, 230; and the veil equal, 231; to be veiled from the, 231. *See also* kashf
uroboros, 67, 271; in zoharic literature, 550n65
Ursprache, 9
Ursprung, 13

vagina, depicted figuratively as the holy of holies, 134; and the nucleus of the date, 151
veil, 9, 10, 13, 17, 27, 30, 133, 262; abolished in the passing away of passing away, 232; ascetic self-annihilation a form of veiling the, 302; conceals the face it reveals by revealing the face it conceals, 229, 291; conveys both the incomparability and similarity of the face and its image, 229; disposing of, 231; exhibits the structure of the esoteric hermeneutic, 224, 233; face beyond the, 206, 222; and face identical in their difference, 224, 232; function of to disclose by hiding, and to hide by disclosing, 206; goal of the path to rend, 229; letter of, 260; lifting of to uncover truth, 224; manifests qualities engendered as feminine, 224, 302; of absence, 135; of clouding, 532n262; of covering, 532n262; of the letter, 260; of matter, 201; of the other, 287; of otherness, 206; of presuming there is an unveiling, 242; of Rābʿia, 225, 305; of selfhood, 534n300; of sincerity, 225; of the text, 113, 242; of thinking there is no veil, 232; of the truth, 230; paradoxical mystery of, 231; renders the face spectacular, 222; renders the invisible visible and the visible invisible, 205; revelation implies the possibility of a, 227; and scopic desire, 529 n. 235; secret hidden beneath, 336; seventy veils of light and dark, 29, 230, 231; seventy veils of light between Allah and Gabriel, 231; site of disclosure and concealment, 225; symbol of in Sufism, 27–29, 224–33, 484n153; text of, 242; to see the face behind, 231; truth of, 230; unveils the veiling of the veil, 263; vision of God through, 232; worn by Arab men as a sign of being desert warriors, 224; worn by women as mark of modesty and subservience, 51, 224, 225. *See also* ḥijāb
Verborgenheit, 195
via negativa, 238, 403n61
virginal spirit, male untainted by female otherness, 303; to become an emasculated bridegroom through, 304

virginity, 53; combined with fertility, 67; image of used on the part of rabbis to describe the ascetic male, 300; in early Christianity, 299; marked by putting on the veil, 302; masculine nature of, 303–304; *Shekhinah* described in the image of, 366; signifies the pneumatic overcoming of physical appetite, 304
visio intellectualis, 339
vision, ambivalence with respect to, 382; double, 192; identified as blindness, 230; indicative of exile, 382; liberation of through vision, 242; of God, 339; of the invisible, 214; of unseeing, 217; persists as the impossibility of not seeing, 293; sustained by blindness, 293; three levels of: cosmological, anthropological, and theophanic, 216
vita angelica, 301
void, 24

waḥdat al-wujūd, 28, 206, 221, 225
waqt, 225, 227, 530n239
wheel, of be/coming, 367; self-rolling, 182; within wheel, 194, 262
will, coeternal with Ein Sof, 104; concealed of all concealed, 105; of wills, 105; opposites unified within, 99; supernal, 105
wisdom, androgynous form of, 155; at the head and at the end, 283; bestowed upon Solomon, 155; circle of, 283; compared to a daughter the father bestows upon the son, 158, 365; depth of, 218; and the divine glory, 153; emanation from undifferentiated unity to unified differentiation, 285; envisioned as garden and spring, 277; essences of, 285; feminine and masculine manifestation, 277; feminine figure of, 59, 143; first of God's creations, 200; flux of, 282; gifting of, 158; God's female playmate, 202; human thought united with, 288; idealized as woman of valor, 200; identified as Torah, 155, 200–201, 277; mystery of, 69, 243; of the holy unity, 326; of illumination, 239; personified as father and daughter, 155; primordial, 200; splintering of into principles of bestowing and receiving, 279; textualization of, 202; thirty-two paths of, 151, 161, 243; upper and lower, 164
woman, ascetic, 299, 300; and the aspect of death, 106; as truncated man, 130; concealed from the phallic gaze, 133; constructed as sexual object, 300; created from man, 51, 62, 108, 109, 147, 151, 304, 373; defined as negativity or lack, 130; depicted metaphorically as a house, 83, 134; derives from left side, 58; excluded from kabbalistic fraternities, 78; exempt from commandments, 58; idealized versus degrading, 200; in the pattern of *Shekhinah*, 109; in the service of Christ called a man, 301; and melancholy, 106; mirror of God's beauty, 595n53; occlusion of, 134; of valor, 80, 185, 186; personified as the temptress, 300; portrayed as hidden, 133; serpentine nature of, 59; phallic definition of as taxonomic exception, 131; and sorcery, 58–59; speculum to reflect the male glory, 61; subservient to man, 170; vessel to receive seminal discharge, 61
womb, designated by the term *yesod*, 77; of *Binah*, 138; of the body contrasted with womb of the soul, 156; of the soul compared to male genitals, 156; of the virgin symbolized by the closed *mem*, 167; phallic nature of, 83, 167, 188; and the point of Zion, 270; return to denotes overcoming of heterosexual eros, 365; sterile, 167; virginal nature of, 55
word, and image converge, 26, 287
world, that is concealed, 363; that is exposed, 363; of chaos, 596n59; of death, 354; of the feminine, 354, 357, 359, 363; of life, 354; of the masculine, 357, 359, 360, 362, 363; of the moon, 358; of separation / differentiation (*olam ha-perud; alma di-peruda*), 198, 358; of unity (*olam ha-yiḥud; alma di-yeḥuda*), 198, 358
world-to-come, 139, 221, 251, 292, 358, 360; characterized rabbinically as a state beyond sensual joy, 364; the great Sabbath not measured by alternating nocturnal and diurnal rhythms, 367; a plane of being beyond gender bifurcation, 367
worship, 251, 264; asceticism and sexuality, 344; conjunction the true mystical intent of, 209, 263; directed exclusively to Allah, 205; essence of, 263; false nature of, 243, 258; iconic form of, xiii; and the iconoclastic ban on images, 120; ideal of intellectual, 346, 348, 521n131, 568n151; in ancient Israelite mythology and the image of enthronement, 391n5; in Hindu Yoga, 235; mystery of, 377; mystical form of, 123; of Christ, 299; of a female counterpart to Yahweh, 143; of the female and idolatry, 154, 171–72, 374, 505n200; of goddesses, 142; of the golden calf, 229, 532n276; of the heart, 234, 568n151; of Jesus, 430–31n354, 531n250; of Mary, 437n13, 531n250; phallic nature of, 127; and poetic composition, 557n194; quest for reunion with God, 584n130; ritual, 39; and the restoration of every-

thing to nothingness, 97; secret of, 169; spiritual act of, 55; Sufi nature of, 564n81; task of to unite thought and faith, 263; theurgical and mystical significance of, 145; and the vision of God, 228
writing, as *différance*, 87; in the margin, 116; phallocentric nature of, 78
Written Torah, depicted as the upper waters, 133; the masculine potency, 139, 140, 257; secret of, 41; symbolic of *Tif'eret*, 588n187

yanuqa, 38, 69, 132
yedi'ah, connotes both cognition and conjugal intimacy, 315
yedi'at ha-shem, 234
yeḥidah, gradation of soul that corresponds to *Arikh Anpin*, 181
Yesod, 41, 61, 64, 82, 137; composed of male and female, 133; corresponds to the phallus, 174; David conjoined to, 138; designated: *el ḥai*, 138, *zohar ḥai*, 362; disclosed as the locus of concealment, 133; hidden and concealed place, 132; and knowledge, 270; locus of secrecy, 132; mystery of Torah, 133; place whence all blessings disseminate, 132; speculum that shines, 71; window through which King and Queen are united, 108
YHWH, 8, 26, 41, 63, 69; and the name *adam*, 384, 385; attribute of mercy, 95; comprises all the letters of the Hebrew alphabet, 208; configured as an anthropos, 124, 128, 137, 246; conjoined to Elohim, 170; conjoined to the letters of, 264; four chariots of, 555n151; inscribed on the trunk of the Tree, 208; letters of correspond to the four faces of Ezekiel's chariot vision, 384; letters of correspond to the four letters of the word *ahavah*, 361; mystical essence of Torah, 128, 137, 138, 208, 246; perfection of all aspects, 124; root word and origin of all language, 208; symbolic of the aspect of the male, 180; transmitted only to one who is circumcised, 139. *See also* Tetragrammaton
yin and *yang*, 107–108
yod, comprises two as one, 266; contained in the final *mem*, 188; corona of the phallus, 73; four worlds contained therein, 186; inclusion of everything, 282; *Keter* demarcated by the jot on top of, 447n121; placed in the head of *alef*, 282, 283; of the covenant that emerges from the supernal *yod*, 379; the point that comprises the ten *sefirot*, 282, 283; primary point of wisdom, 284; sealed with primary wisdom, 282; sign of the covenant, 137, 186, 267, 365, 379; tip of, 63, 282; two sides of: *Keter* and *Hokhmah*, 282; twenty-two Hebrew letters contained within, 282
yoga, erotic nature of, 262
Yom Kippur, 134; and the abrogation of physical pleasure, 364; and affliction of the soul, 364; bonding of mother and daughter, 364; designated the Sabbath of Sabbaths, 367; Jewish souls absorbed into *Shekhinah*, 364; on this day the moon receives illumination of the ten *sefirot* in the form of one hundred lights, 364; and sexual purity, 589n218; and the *Shekhinah*, 364; symbolically linked to *Binah*, 364; theosophic explanation for prohibition of sexual intercourse on, 364–65; time of return to the womb, 367; union of *Binah* and *Malkhut*, 364

zayin, broken into *yod* atop *waw*, 74, 589n225; symbolic of Sabbath, 73
Ze'eir Anpin, 181, 185; comprises mercy and judgment, 179, 368; coupling on Sabbath eve between *Nuqba* and, 367; emanated from the crown of mercy, 185; head of, 270; mind of, 369; six crowns of, 316; twenty-two letters of, 354; two eyes ascribed to, 180; union with *Arikh Anpin* on the day of Sabbath, 368; unites with Leah, 270
Zion, 34; point of, 270
ziw ha-shekhinah, 253, 254
ziwwug, 95, 148, 182, 267, 270, 271, 313, 314, 317, 320, 321, 549n58; 553n137
ziwwug ruḥani, 267
Zoroastrianism, 103